W9-BAX-797

The Oxford Companion to American History

THOMAS H. JOHNSON

in consultation with
HARVEY WISH

The Oxford Companion to American History

New York
OXFORD UNIVERSITY PRESS
1966

Library of Congress Catalogue Card Number: 66-22263

Second printing, 1966

Printed in the United States of America

Preface

THIS Companion attempts to serve as a one-volume reference book on American history. Most of the articles in it are summaries of lives, events, and places significant in the founding and growth of the nation. It gives attention to social, political, and labor movements, the observations of travelers, both foreign and domestic, and includes the fields of art, science, commerce, literature, education, and law. There are also articles dealing with sports and entertainment.

The matter of proportion has been an especially acute problem. The longest articles on persons, those for example on Washington, Franklin, Jefferson, and Lincoln, do not exceed 2000 words. Such events as the War of Independence, the Civil War, and both World Wars are of similar proportion. Cross references, indicated in the articles by small capitals, give the reader quick access to all information on closely related themes, and make possible the relative brevity of most articles. The longer articles are concluded with reference to the most recent authoritative bibliographical sources. In general, living persons are briefly treated. Tables provide quick reference to the names and dates of persons who have held high office, such as cabinet members and Justices of the Supreme Court. The texts of the Constitution and its Amendments are given at the end of the book.

Since this compilation is in fact a sister volume to *The Oxford Companion to American Literature,* it is intended to supplement that work by emphasizing the historical rather than the literary importance of writers. Thus William Cullen Bryant is chiefly viewed as an influential newspaper editor, and William James is given far more space as a pioneer in psychology than is his equally influential novelist brother, Henry James.

Preface

Although my lifelong concern with American studies has given me a limited knowledge of the nation's past, particularly in the areas of colonial, literary, and cultural history, I undertook this assignment ten years ago with the full realization that one person, indeed, even a team of experts, can never record the history of a nation in absolutely reliable terms. History is not static, and historians do not agree in their conclusions even after time has given them opportunity to sort the evidence. This Companion therefore attempts to be a dictionary adhering to two main sources: the most recently available published factual data, and current expert judgment about persons and affairs.

When Samuel Johnson brought out his dictionary of the English language in 1755 he was sometimes wrong in his definitions because he had little professional assistance in a pioneer undertaking. My errors will also be discovered, but I will not be able to say, as he did in his letter to the Earl of Chesterfield, when his dictionary was on the verge of publication: 'Is not a patron, my Lord, one who looks with unconcern on a man struggling for life in the water, and, when he has reached ground, encumbers him with help?' I have received vigorous and expert help in a multitude of ways from the beginning.

Lawrenceville, New Jersey T.H.J.
May 1966

The Oxford Companion to American History

Note

Both historical and mythological persons are entered under their surnames, the former in bold capitals, the latter in ordinary bold type (e.g. William James under '**JAMES,** WILLIAM' and Paul Bunyan under '**Bunyan,** PAUL') unless the two names are considered an indissoluble whole (e.g. '**John Henry**').

Persons who used pseudonyms are entered under their proper names (e.g. '**CLEMENS,** SAMUEL' rather than '**Mark Twain**' and '**CODY,** WILLIAM' rather than '**Buffalo Bill**'). In all cases the pseudonym is entered with a cross reference to the proper name. When the real name is little known or forgotten, the entry is under the pseudonym (e.g. '**Billy the Kid**' rather than '**BONNEY,** WILLIAM,' and '**BLACKBEARD**').

Full names are given; those not ordinarily used are enclosed in brackets (e.g. '**JAMES,** JESSE [WOODSON]'). Where initials are customarily used for the given names the full given names are enclosed in brackets (e.g. '**MENCKEN,** H. L. [HENRY LOUIS]').

When an entire family is famous, there is an entry for that family as well as a separate entry for each of its most celebrated members (e.g. '**Adams Family**' and '**ADAMS,** JOHN'). If several members of a family are equally well known, they are discussed under the family entry (e.g. 'JOHN BARRYMORE' under '**Barrymore Family**').

Treaties, wars, documents, Supreme Court cases, etc., are entered under the names by which they are best known rather than under their official titles (e.g. '**Pinckney's Treaty**' rather than '**Treaty of San Lorenzo**').

The texts of the Constitution of the United States and the Amendments thereto are given in full on pages 889–906. The **Constitution** is discussed in a separate entry, and there is a general entry on **Amendments.** The specific entry on the first ten Amendments is under '**Bill of Rights**'; Amendments other than the first ten are entered under their numbers (e.g. '**Fourteenth Amendment**').

Cross references within entries are in SMALL CAPITALS; when the entry itself is a cross reference, the cross reference is in *italics.*

Abbreviations

b. = born.	e.g. = *exempli gratia,* for example.
c. = *circa,* about.	*fl.* = *floruit,* flourished.
d. = died.	i.e. = *id est,* that is.

A

AAA, see *Agricultural Adjustment Act.*

Aachen, Treaty of, see *Aix-la-Chapelle.*

ABBE, CLEVELAND (1838–1916), New York-born meteorologist, while director of the Cincinnati Observatory (1868–73), inaugurated daily weather reports using the telegraph to obtain data. Abbe was a pioneer meteorologist in the U.S. Signal Service (1871–91), and director of the U.S. Weather Bureau (est. 1891). 'Old Probs' also taught meteorology at George Washington University (1886–1905) and at Johns Hopkins (1896–1914). His *Report on Standard Time* (1879) started the agitation that resulted in the adoption of standard hour meridians from Greenwich, England.

ABBOT, CHARLES GREELEY (1872–), New Hampshire-born astrophysicist, as director of the astrophysical observatory of the Smithsonian Institution (1907–44) and as its secretary (1928–44), studied the variation of the sun's radiation and its effects on climatic conditions. He also designed machines that use the sun's energy. His writings include *The Sun* (1911), and *The Earth and the Stars* (1925; rev. ed., 1946).

ABBOTT, JACOB (1803–79), born in Hallowell, Maine, graduated from Bowdoin (1820) and studied at Andover Seminary before entering the Congregational ministry. He founded three schools: one in Boston, for girls, the Mt. Vernon School (1828), and two in New York, one for boys (also called the Mt. Vernon School) and one for girls, the Abbott Institute. Of his more than 180 story books, designed to educate and to give moral instruction, the *Rollo* series (begun in 1835) became notable for an entire generation. Little Rollo, inquisitive, intelligent, but not a prig, was the first genuine child character in American literature.

ABBOTT, LYMAN (1835–1922), son of JACOB ABBOTT, was born in Roxbury, Massachusetts, graduated from New York University (1853), and practiced law briefly before entering the Congregational ministry. He succeeded Henry Ward Beecher as minister of the Plymouth Church in Brooklyn (1888–99) and edited the *Christian Union,* which became (1893) the *Outlook,* a journal of wide circulation. He was a leader in the cause of CHRISTIAN SOCIALISM and urged evolutionary doctrines in his modernist theology. His interest in the church's role in social issues, reflected in the pages of the *Outlook,* assisted the Progressive movement.

A.B.C. Powers, so called (Argentina, Brazil, Chile) offered to act as mediators between the U.S. and the warring Mexican factions of Venustiano Carranza and General Huerta, after the U.S. had violated Mexican territory in the VERA CRUZ INCIDENT (1914). Through the conference they set up (May 1914) the A.B.C. Powers helped avert war between the U.S. and Mexico, although their attempt, with the co-operation of the U.S., to mediate a truce between Carranza and Huerta was unsuccessful. This mediation conference was the first in the history of Latin America.

ABEL, JOHN JACOB (1857–1938), Cleveland-born physiological chemist, was a professor of pharmacology at Johns Hopkins (1893–1932) and after 1932 director of the university's laboratory for endocrine research. His basic work led to the discovery (1901) of adrenaline by the Japanese chemist Jokichi Takamine. He isolated amino acids in the blood, thereby making possible important investigations in protein metabolism. He was co-founder with Dr. Christian A. Herter (1905–9) of the *Journal of Biological Chemistry* and founder and editor (1909–32) of the *Journal of Pharmacology and Experimental Therapeutics.*

ABERCROMBY, JAMES (1706–81), replaced JOHN CAMPBELL, Earl of Loudoun, as commander in chief of British forces in America during the FRENCH AND INDIAN WAR (1758). He assembled 12,000 troops at Lake George and marched on Fort Ticonderoga, garrisoned by 3000 troops commanded by the French general, Montcalm. In a frontal attack

Abercromby's forces were routed by withering fire, and the British suffered 1500 casualties in one of the bloodiest engagements of that era. Abercromby was replaced by JEFFREY AMHERST.

Ableman* v. *Booth (1859), was a U.S. Supreme Court case that had been appealed from the Wisconsin Supreme Court. It followed the passage of a number of state PERSONAL LIBERTY LAWS directed against the enforcement of the FUGITIVE SLAVE LAWS. The Wisconsin decision had freed an abolitionist editor, one Booth, who had been convicted of violating one of the fugitive slave laws. The U.S. Supreme Court on appeal denied the right of a state judiciary to interfere in Federal cases, thereby affirming Federal supremacy. Chief Justice Taney delivered the opinion. The federal government rearrested and imprisoned Booth. The ruling led the Wisconsin legislature to defend state sovereignty by adopting resolutions similar in spirit to the KENTUCKY AND VIRGINIA RESOLVES (1798). Thus by 1859 the slavery issue had set off threats of nullification in the North as well as in the South.

Abnaki Indians, a loose confederation of Algonquian tribes, at one time occupied all Maine, the valley of the St. John's river, and ranged northwest to the St. Lawrence. (Early settlers called them Tarrateens.) Component tribes, the Penobscot, Passamaquoddy, and Malecite, were allies of the French, and conducted raids on northern English settlements during KING WILLIAM'S WAR (1689–97). The Jesuit missionary Sébastian Rasle (1657–1724) lived with them after 1689 and compiled a dictionary of their language (published in 1833). Their term for house (*wigwam*) came into general use in English to designate an Indian dwelling. (The TEPEE was a dwelling used by Plains Indians.) Remnants of the Abnaki in Maine number some 1500.

Abolition Movement was the militant phase of the general effort to do away with slavery, as opposed to the gradualist phase, of which Lincoln and the Republicans or the FREE-SOILERS were representative.

Slavery was generally abolished in the North during or soon after the Revolution, partly for humanitarian or moral reasons, but chiefly because it was an economic liability. Abolition laws were enacted first in Rhode Island (1774), then in Vermont (1777), Massachusetts (1781), New Hampshire (1783), and Connecticut (1784). Pennsylvania abolished slavery in 1780, New York in 1799, and New Jersey in 1804, with gradual emancipation provisions. By 1846 slavery was illegal throughout the North, while in the South the institution flourished and slaves were valuable property, in part due to the invention of the cotton gin (1793).

During the first two decades of the 19th century the abolitionists generally took individual action, though small groups, often impelled by religious principle, began to form locally. Between 1824 and 1833 abolitionism became a prominent force in the antislavery movement, sparked by a resurgence of revivalism that began in New York in 1824, and stimulated by the success of the English antislavery leaders in abolishing slavery in the British Empire (1833).

After 1833, abolition propaganda began to flood the country. When abolitionist tracts poured into the South during the 1830's, Jackson's Postmaster General in effect denied the abolitionists the use of the mails by tolerating the tactics of proslavery men who prevented the distribution of the propaganda. Abolitionism was urged by publications of the ANTISLAVERY SOCIETIES, by newspapers, sermons, novels, and addresses, and by the revealing narratives of escaped slaves. Most effective, despite a rather small list of subscribers, was *The Liberator,* edited by WILLIAM LLOYD GARRISON, who renounced the gradualism of his former Quaker associate, BENJAMIN LUNDY, to urge the British slogan of 'immediate emancipation.' John Greenleaf Whittier's *Ichabod* stung the moderates who were ready to follow Daniel Webster in his support of the Compromise of 1850, and Harriet Beecher Stowe's *Uncle Tom's Cabin* had an enormous impact — about 1,500,000 copies were sold in the first year of publication (1852). Activities of the UNDERGROUND RAILROAD certainly inflamed public opinion at the time, both in the North and in the South.

Among the influential abolitionist

organizers was THEODORE WELD, who trained the noted 'seventy' abolitionist agents to use revivalist techniques in advancing the cause of the American Anti-Slavery Society. Boston Brahmin WENDELL PHILLIPS, using lyceum platforms, swayed middle-class audiences by his denunciation of any union with slaveholders, and Negro abolitionists like the ex-slave FREDERICK DOUGLASS persuaded thousands through lectures and newspaper articles. HENRY WARD BEECHER and W. E. CHANNING, distinguished clergymen, also carried their congregations into the antislavery crusade. There were dedicated and militant antislavery leaders in the Congress as well, notably JOSHUA GIDDINGS and CHARLES SUMNER. Bitterness in the South mounted against expatriate Southerners who attacked the 'peculiar institution,' like JAMES G. BIRNEY and the Grimké sisters, as well as against Northerners like ELIJAH LOVEJOY, who became the martyr to the cause. Lovejoy, a St. Louis editor, was killed when a mob attacked his press (1837) after he had refused to stop publishing abolitionist opinions. His murder gave the abolitionists the opportunity to accuse the proslavery men of violating the constitutional guarantee of freedom of the press. Antislavery militants also drew support from leaders of other reform causes — women's rights, temperance, pacifism, and free schools — as well as from the Quakers.

The issue of abolition dominated politics after 1840. Abolitionists as well as gradualists won seats in northern state legislatures and in Congress. So many antislavery petitions were presented to Congress that southern members passed a 'GAG RULE' to table them (1836). The rule was later repealed (1844), but it gave the abolitionists more constitutional ammunition, as it was a denial of the right to petition. Abolitionists and gradualists quarreled with the proslavery men over the various issues that grew out of the annexation of Texas (1845), the War with Mexico (1846), and the WILMOT PROVISO (never passed), which sought to bar slavery from the territories won from Mexico. Abolitionists and gradualists alike first tried to defeat, then boycotted, the stringent FUGITIVE SLAVE ACT (1850), which required among other things the co-operation of bystanders in capturing escaping slaves.

When the NAT TURNER INSURRECTION (1831) resulted in the death of more than 50 whites, many Southerners believed that the abolitionists led by Garrison were responsible, although there is no evidence at all that this was so. By the 1850's most Southerners were convinced that abolitionism aimed at a race war, and when JOHN BROWN, in an alleged attempt to stir up a slave insurrection and establish a free state, raided HARPERS FERRY (1859), the South felt their case was proved. Although many abolitionists in fact wanted emancipation without violence, the Civil War ended any such hope. Freedom came with Lincoln's EMANCIPATION PROCLAMATION (1863), a war measure to free slaves within enemy lines, and the THIRTEENTH AMENDMENT (1865), which formally abolished slavery throughout the U.S.

See G. H. Barnes, *Antislavery Impulse* (1933) and a recent corrective, Louis Filler, *The Crusade Against Slavery, 1830–1860* (1960).

Abraham, Plains of, see *Plains of Abraham.*

Absentee voting was first established during the Civil War to allow Union soldiers in service to vote. Nearly all states now permit any qualified voter who expects to be unable to get to his precinct on election day to cast his ballot *in absentia,* if he makes a written application for such a ballot prior to a specified time before the date of election day. Vermont was the first state to allow general absentee voting (1896).

Academies (the term derives from Plato's famous school), as types of secondary schools in the U.S., displaced the LATIN GRAMMAR SCHOOLS during the 18th century, and were in turn largely supplanted after the Civil War by public HIGH SCHOOLS. They stressed the classics, but also taught English, mathematics, and practical science. Franklin's Academy of Philadelphia (later the University of Pennsylvania) adopted a broad nonsectarian curriculum, but most academies were local centers of orthodoxy with a wide range of quality. They existed then as they do now through the elementary to the high school level. Tuition fees were flexible.

Variously known as academies, seminaries, and collegiate institutes, many were co-educational, and most were private and controlled by self-perpetuating boards of trustees. Since academies stimulated interest in the training of teachers, they were the forerunners of NORMAL SCHOOLS. During the 1850's they numbered some 6000. Today the independent, nonsectarian private schools (corresponding to the public schools in England) flourish in large numbers throughout the U.S. Among the oldest are PHILLIPS ACADEMY at Andover (1778), PHILLIPS EXETER ACADEMY (1783), and THE LAWRENCEVILLE SCHOOL (1810).

Acadia National Park (est. 1919), on Mount Desert Island in Maine, is an area of 30,000 acres, attractive for its mountain and rocky coast scenery. The region has been a resort area since the mid-19th century.

Acadians, the French inhabitants of Nova Scotia, refused to accept British rule at the outbreak of the French and Indian War (1755), and some 6000 were dispersed to other English colonies further south. About 2000 Acadians ultimately found their way to Louisiana, where in the region of the Teche and Lafourche rivers they developed and still preserve a French culture and dialect characteristically their own. Their exile is the subject of Longfellow's *Evangeline*. Many later returned to Nova Scotia, where their descendants may be found today. See also *Cajuns* and *Creoles*.

ACHESON, DEAN GOODERHAM (1893–), after graduation from Yale (1915) and Harvard Law School (1918) joined a New York law firm and built up a practice that he left to enter government service. He was Assistant Secretary of State (1941–45) during World War II. While Under Secretary of State (1945–47) he helped formulate the ACHESON-LILIENTHAL PLAN (1946) for control of atomic energy. An architect of the United Nations, he entered President Truman's cabinet as Secretary of State (1949–53). His policies during the Korean War and his stand against Russian aggression in the Berlin crisis were supported by the President. Acheson was under repeated attack in Congress. He was blamed for encouraging Red aggression in Korea by stating that Korea was outside America's Far Eastern 'defense perimeter'; however, this was actually a misreading of his speech.

Acheson-Lilienthal Plan (1946) recommended the creation of an International Atomic Development Authority, with exclusive control over fissionable material, and the production and custody of atomic weapons. It was first formulated by a committee headed by Dean Acheson, Under Secretary of State, and David Lilienthal, chairman of the Tennessee Valley Authority. The BARUCH PLAN incorporated its principal features.

Act of Havana (1940) extended the protection of the American republics to the Caribbean and South American dependencies of all European powers. Designed to prevent Nazi encroachments, it made the Monroe Doctrine multilateral by providing that the American republics, in the interest of common defense, might take over (collectively or individually) any New World possession endangered by aggression. Historically the Monroe Doctrine had been the exclusive policy of the United States.

Acts of Trade and Navigation, see *Navigation Acts*.

ADAIR, JAMES (*c.* 1709–*c.* 1783), born in Ireland, traded with the Indians of the South for 30 years. He wrote *The History of the American Indians* (1775; repr., 1930). In spite of his fanciful theory that the Indians were descended from the lost tribes of Israel, his study is a good source of ethnological data about the southern Mississippi valley, and the first important book written from a frontiersman's point of view.

ADAMIC, LOUIS (1899–1951), came to the U.S. from Slovenia (now part of Yugoslavia) in 1913 and made a career of writing, especially about the Americanization of immigrants. *Dynamite* (1931; rev. ed., 1934) is a study of class violence in the U.S. *Laughing in the Jungle* (1832) is a personal record. Two studies of minorities under the New

Deal are *From Many Lands* (1940) and *A Nation of Nations* (1945). *The Native's Return* (1934) is his report of a visit to his homeland.

Adams Family, distinguished in American history, first became prominent in the decade before the Revolution, when JOHN ADAMS emerged as a leader of the Massachusetts Whigs. Adams and his wife Abigail established a family line that has extended into the present century. Their son, JOHN QUINCY ADAMS, was the father of CHARLES FRANCIS ADAMS (1807–86), of whose many children the best known are BROOKS ADAMS, CHARLES FRANCIS ADAMS (1835–1915), and HENRY ADAMS. The Adams family papers (some 300,000 pages of material covering the years 1630–1920), now in the possession of the Massachusetts Historical Society, are in process of publication.

ADAMS, ANDY (1859–1935), in his youth moved from Indiana to Texas, became a cowboy, and went to Colorado during the mining boom. His picture of life on the range, *The Log of a Cowboy* (1903), is the first of his well-written and authentic reconstructions. Later a Texas cattle baron, Adams wrote such semi-autobiographical accounts of 'the Old Trail days' as *The Outlet* (1905) and *Cattle Brands* (1906).

ADAMS, BROOKS (1848–1927), son of CHARLES FRANCIS ADAMS (1807–86), was born in Quincy, Massachusetts, and like his brother Henry was a historian. A proponent of the cyclical interpretation of history, which he saw as the rise and fall of civilizations analogous to the concentration and dispersion of energy, he carried forward his unrewarded search for a mechanistic theory in *The Law of Civilization and Decay* (1895). A constant speculator in theories, in *America's Economic Supremacy* (1900; repr., 1947) he concluded that China would offer the great problem of the future and that Russia and the U.S. would be the two great antagonists for power. Although his ideas often do not cohere logically, they prompted Justice Holmes to acknowledge their vitality by saying of *Civilization and Decay* that it was 'about the most (immediately) interesting history I ever read.'

ADAMS, CHARLES FRANCIS (1807–86), Boston-born son of JOHN QUINCY ADAMS, like his father chose politics as a career. After graduation from Harvard (1825) he practiced law in Boston, served in the state legislature (1841–45), and as a 'Conscience Whig' helped form the FREE-SOIL PARTY (1848), which nominated him for Vice President on the unsuccessful ticket with Martin Van Buren. He entered Congress as a Republican (1859), and at the insistence of Secretary of State Seward he was appointed by Lincoln minister to England (1861), a post he occupied for eight years.

Adams conducted his difficult Civil War mission, in the face of British sympathy for the Confederacy, with skill, tact, and a firm energy that won respect both at home and in England. His famous note to Lord Russell on the armored rams built in England for the Confederates ('It would be superfluous in me to point out to your lordship that this is war'), though intended as an ultimatum, actually was written two days after Russell had decided to detain the ships.

In 1871–72 Adams headed the U.S. commission that settled the explosive ALABAMA CLAIMS dispute, a triumph that raised the prestige of arbitration as a major instrument of world peace. He edited the *Works of John Adams* (10 vols., 1850–56), and the *Memoirs of John Quincy Adams* (12 vols., 1874–77). He was the father of CHARLES FRANCIS ADAMS (1835–1915), BROOKS ADAMS, and HENRY ADAMS.

ADAMS, CHARLES FRANCIS (1835–1915), economist and historian, was a son of CHARLES FRANCIS ADAMS (1807–86). He graduated from Harvard (1856), and after serving in the Civil War as a brigadier general of volunteers, became a railroad expert. He exposed the corrupt financing of the Erie Railroad in *Chapters of Erie* (1871), and later set forth his practical knowledge of transportation in *Railroads: Their Origin and Problems* (1878), a study which led to his selection as chairman of the government directors of the Union Pacific (1878) and later (1884–90) as president of the railroad. In addition to historical studies dealing chiefly with New England, he wrote a life of Richard Henry Dana (1890), a biography of his father

(1900), and his own autobiography (ed. by W. C. Ford, 1916).

ADAMS, Charles Kendall (1835–1902), Vermont-born university teacher and administrator, received his graduate training in Europe. As professor of history at the University of Michigan (1867–85), he introduced the seminar method of teaching at about the same time that the method was being instituted by Herbert Baxter Adams at Johns Hopkins and Henry Adams at Harvard. He was later president of Cornell (1885–92) and of Wisconsin (1892–1901). Under his leadership those institutions expanded their facilities for graduate study.

ADAMS, Henry [Brooks] (1838–1918), historian and man of letters, was fourth of the seven children of CHARLES FRANCIS ADAMS (1807–86). After graduation from Harvard (1858) and desultory study in Germany, he became European correspondent for the Boston *Courier*. He served as secretary to his father while the latter was minister to England (1861–68). After his return he joined the history department at Harvard (1870–77), where he introduced the seminar method, and edited the *North American Review* (1870–76). Since he wished to write about history rather than teach it, he settled in Washington to be near the sources of the documents he would use. *Documents Relating to New England Federalism, 1800–1815* (1877) was followed by the *Writings* (3 vols.) and *The Life and Writings of Albert Gallatin* (1879), which is still recognized as one of the great political biographies.

While engaged in these historical studies, he began and completed a novel, *Democracy* (1880), so transparent a satire of current politics that he published it anonymously. In the next three years he wrote another biography, *John Randolph* (1882), and another novel, *Esther* (1884). While doing so, he was planning his most ambitious work, the *History of the U.S. during the Administrations of Jefferson and Madison* (9 vols., 1889–91), a major creative accomplishment that has been superseded on very few points. It is detached and mildly ironic.

In 1895 Adams began his study of the great cathedrals of France, from which grew the sensitive and scholarly *Mont-Saint-Michel and Chartres* (1904), 'a study in thirteenth-century unity.' In the autobiographical *Education of Henry Adams* (1907), 'a study of twentieth-century multiplicity,' the 'dynamo' replaces the 'Virgin' in his theory of history. He postulates that human thought by passing through phases determined by attraction, acceleration, and decay, is subject to the same laws of disintegration as the universe itself. In later years, as his pessimism increased, he tried to make history a natural science in the image of the Second Law of Thermodynamics. The skepticism in the account of his self-termed failure makes the *Education* a study of ideas rather than a portrait. Yet though more is hidden than revealed, it remains a most remarkable 'confession.' Ever brooding about the destiny of man, Adams takes rank as the most intensely searching American historian.

Biographies include those by Ernest Samuels (2 vols., 1948–58), and Elizabeth Stevenson (1955).

ADAMS, Herbert Baxter (1850–1901), Massachusetts-born historian, immediately after receiving his doctorate at Heidelberg (1876), joined the original faculty at Johns Hopkins. During the 1880's he established a department modeled on German seminars and attracted to the institution the most gifted history faculty in any American graduate school. Such talented students as Frederick Jackson Turner worked under Adams there. Chiefly remembered as an organizer and an inspiring teacher, he founded the *Johns Hopkins Studies in Historical and Political Science* (1882), and led in establishing the American Historical Association (1884).

ADAMS, John (1735–1826), 2nd President of the U.S. (1797–1801), was born in Quincy, Massachusetts, the son of a fourth-generation Bay Colony farmer. After graduation from Harvard (1755) Adams took up the practice of law. In 1764 he married Abigail Smith of Weymouth, a woman of perception, charm, and ability.

Adams became a leader of the Massachusetts Whigs during the agitation caused by the Stamp Act (1765), which he opposed in four notable articles published anonymously in the *Boston Gazette,* and later brought out in London under his name as *A Dissertation on the Canon and Feudal Law* (1768). As a member of the Continental Congress (1774–78), he seconded Washington's nomination to military command in the War of Independence, and with Jefferson, Franklin, Livingston, and Sherman served on the committee appointed (1776) to draft the Declaration of Independence, of which instrument, as Jefferson noted, Adams was 'the pillar of support' in the debate on its adoption. A commissioner to France (1777–79) and a negotiator in Holland (1780–82), Adams was a logical selection to act with Franklin and Jay on the commission that signed the TREATY OF PARIS of 1783, ending the Revolution. He went as first envoy to Great Britain (1785–88).

On his return from the Court of St. James's, Adams was chosen as the nation's first Vice President (1789–97), although his inept suggestion that governing representatives of the people should be 'the rich, the well-born, and the able' nearly cost him the election. He thus began his eight years in that office in an atmosphere of grievance and suspicion. Even though he chafed under the limitations of the vice presidency, as president of the Senate Adams was instrumental in developing Senate procedures, and he cast the deciding vote in a number of critical cases in which the Senate was tied.

In the presidential campaign of 1796, the first to be contested by political parties, the Federalists backed Adams and the Democratic-Republicans backed Jefferson. Under the rule then in effect whoever got the second largest number of electoral votes became the Vice President; Adams secured 71 votes and Jefferson 68.

Because political parties of that period were indeed 'factions,' Adams was faced with the difficult problem of leading the nation in both domestic and foreign affairs while dealing with an active opposition party led by his Vice President. The situation was complicated by France's reaction to JAY'S TREATY, which she believed to be pro-British. France, already at war with England, engaged the U.S. in an undeclared naval war, attacking the U.S. merchant fleet, with some encouragement from the Republicans. Adams sent envoys to France in an attempt to negotiate, but the envoy's report of the XYZ AFFAIR swayed American opinion, particularly Federalist opinion, to the brink of war. The stature of Adams as President rests primarily on his successful resistance to his own party's demand for changing a limited conflict with France into an all-out war. Although the breach between the U.S. and France was ultimately negotiated, it did result in the creation of a separate Navy Department and passage of the ALIEN AND SEDITION ACTS.

Adams lost his bid for re-election in the so-called 'revolution of 1800,' and Jefferson and Burr took office. In an effort to preserve some Federalist strength in the face of a solid Republican Congress, Adams used his appointive power on the eve of his retirement to place Federalists in the judiciary. Among his 'MIDNIGHT JUDGES' he selected Jefferson's political foe, John Marshall, as chief justice of the Supreme Court. Adams then retired to private life in Quincy, and in later years he and Jefferson became fast friends and sparkling correspondents.

Although testy, contentious, and vain, Adams was a political philosopher of great influence, who lived by the ideal of a government of law rather than men, and he was implicitly trusted as a man of unflinching moral courage. Throughout his life he influenced the course of events by the respect accorded him as a constitutional lawyer as well as by virtue of his character.

A definitive edition of his diary and correspondence is in progress (1961–). See the biography by Page Smith (2 vols., 1962).

ADAMS, JOHN QUINCY (1767–1848), 6th President of the U.S. (1825–29), was the eldest son of JOHN ADAMS. He accompanied his father to Europe (1778–80) and began his higher education at the age of eleven in Paris. He was attending the University of Leiden when he began his famous diary (1780). After graduating from Harvard (1787) he practiced law in Boston, and began a series of political essays on the strength of which Washington appointed him minister to the Netherlands (1794). Selected by his father as minister to Prussia (1797), he resigned when Jefferson took office (1801), and two years later was elected Federalist senator from Massachusetts. Never a strict party man, he shifted to Jeffersonian Republicanism in 1807, and failed to be re-elected.

Meanwhile Adams had been appointed the first Boylston professor of rhetoric and oratory at Harvard, a chair he left to become Madison's envoy to Russia (1809–15), chief of the peace commission to negotiate the TREATY OF GHENT (1814), and minister to England (1815–17). He entered Monroe's cabinet as Secretary of State (1817–24), and, during that eight-year 'era of good feelings,' he skillfully negotiated the FLORIDA TREATY with Spain, postponed the OREGON BOUNDARY DISPUTE, secured the recognition of the independence of the Latin American republics, and drafted the MONROE DOCTRINE. In the presidential campaign of 1824 no candidate received a majority of the electoral votes, and thus the election was decided by the House of Representatives. Adams won the election over his nearest rival, Andrew Jackson, when Henry Clay, a clearly defeated candidate, threw his support to Adams. Charges of 'corrupt bargain' followed Adams's appointment of Clay as Secretary of State, and the feud thus created between Adams and Jackson made the period of Adams's presidency virtually a do-nothing term, since Jacksonians bitterly opposed his program of extending federal powers. When Jackson won the election of 1828 with an overwhelming electoral vote, Adams retired to Quincy.

Although Adams's political career appeared to be over, actually the most noteworthy years lay ahead, for he was elected to the House of Representatives (1831) and served there until his death. He opposed extension of slavery and the Mexican War. His fight to repeal the 'GAG RULE' ended in victory and enhanced the reputation of 'old man eloquent' as a peerless parliamentary debater.

His state papers and occasional publications are numerous, and include the celebrated *Report on Weights and Measures* (1821), and the absorbing *Memoirs* (12 vols., 1874–77), diary comments on a half-century of political activity. Reserved and austere, at times irascible and harsh, he took to heart the rancor of an opposition in public life which his sturdy independence aroused. Yet in the light of history his qualities of principle, of courage, and of action have given him stature as perhaps the greatest of all in that family which for four generations devoted its considerable talents to the public good.

See the biography by S. F. Bemis (2 vols., 1949–56).

ADAMS, MAUDE (1872–1953), born Maude Kiskadden in Salt Lake City, adopted her mother's stage name after leaving home to begin her own acting career at sixteen. She became John Drew's supporting lady (1892–97), and in 1897 made her appearance in Barrie's *Little Minister,* the first of his plays (including *Peter Pan*) in which she starred. Honored as a leading actress, she retired in 1918, and after 1937 served as professor of drama at Stephens College.

ADAMS, SAMUEL (1722–1803), a cousin of JOHN ADAMS, graduated from Harvard (1740), and, although he repeatedly failed in business, won election to various town offices in his native Boston. Politics became his absorbing interest and after 1764 his sole occupation. He was a member of the Massachusetts House of Representatives (1765–74), and as clerk of the assembly (1766–74) wrote a large number of its radical protests. He was one of the first political leaders to advocate separation from Great Britain, and to that end he wrote voluminously.

As chief organizer of opposition to the Stamp Act in Massachusetts, Sam Adams managed the BOSTON TEA PARTY (1773). Adept as a politician and a master of propaganda, he achieved his ends by the tactics of a born revolutionary. He was a delegate to the Continental Congress (1774–81), signed the Declaration of Independence, and opposed any concession to the crown. In 1779 he helped frame the Massachusetts constitution and was author of its bill of rights. Although he served his state as lieutenant governor (1789–94) and as governor (1794–97), his constructive work had ended in the decade of the 1770's, for his skill as an agitator and polemicist had little scope in situations requiring adjustment and consolidation.

Adams-Onís Treaty (1819), signed at Washington by Secretary of State J. Q. Adams and the Spanish minister Luis de Onís, followed the seizures of Spanish property by Andrew Jackson in East Florida (1818). By its terms Spain renounced all claims to West Florida and ceded East Florida to the U.S.; the U.S. gave up its claim to Texas; and our western boundary was defined as running from the mouth of the Sabine river, on the Louisiana-Texas border, northwesterly along the Red and Arkansas rivers to the 42nd parallel, and thence due west to the Pacific. The U.S. assumed the claims of its citizens against Spain to a total of $5,000,000 and the nonconflicting articles of PINCKNEY'S TREATY (1795) remained in force. In effect, Spanish claims to the Pacific Northwest were surrendered to the U.S.

Adamson Act (1916), forced through Congress by the railway unions, established an eight-hour day on all interstate railroads. Although designed to prevent a threatened strike during the period of defense preparation before the U.S. entered World War I, it in fact established a fundamental trade union standard of work hours per day.

ADDAMS, JANE (1860–1935), social worker, was born in Cedarville, Illinois, and graduated from Rockford College (1881). In 1889 she and Ellen Gates Starr opened Hull-House in Chicago, one of the earliest SOCIAL SETTLEMENTS in the U.S., devoted to the improvement of community and civic life in the slums. She furthered the settlement movement by sponsoring child labor laws, adult education for the foreign-born, and major welfare research projects. She told the story of her life work in *Twenty Years at Hull-House* (1910), following that classic with *The Second Twenty Years at Hull-House* (1930). In 1931 she shared with Nicholas Murray Butler the Nobel Peace prize, which she earned by valiant efforts to find moral substitutes for war.

Addyston Pipe and Steel Company* v. *U.S. (1899) was a case resulting in a unanimous U.S. Supreme Court decision that declared a market-allocation scheme unlawful, as a conspiracy to interfere with the flow of interstate commerce and as an infringement of the SHERMAN ANTITRUST ACT (1890). The ruling restored a measure of effectiveness to the Act, which had been impaired by the ruling in U.S. *v.* E. C. KNIGHT (1895).

Adirondack Mountains, in northeast New York, extend from the Canadian border to the Mohawk valley. (They are not part of the Appalachians.) Geologically among the oldest rock formations in the world, they are granitic uplifts that have been eroded since pre-Cambrian times. Mount Marcy (5344 ft.) is the highest elevation. Much of the region has been set aside as a national forest.

Adjusted Compensation, see *Bonus*.

Adkins* v. *Children's Hospital (1923) was a case that resulted in a U.S. Supreme Court ruling (5–3) invalidating an act of Congress that had authorized a wage board for the District of Columbia to fix minimum wages for women. The conservative majority held that such legislative action violated the principle of freedom of contract guaranteed by the Fifth Amendment. A setback for the legislative 'police power' to correct conditions leading to ill health and immorality, the ruling was reversed in WEST COAST HOTEL COMPANY *v.* PARRISH (1937).

ADLER, FELIX (1851–1933), German-born social welfare leader, six years after graduation from Columbia (1870) started the ETHICAL CULTURE MOVEMENT and established the first free kindergarten in New York City. He later founded the first child study society in the U.S. (1883), and after 1902 was professor of political and social ethics at Columbia. His writings include *An Ethical Philosophy of Life* (1918), and *The Reconstruction of the Spiritual Ideal* (1923).

Administration of Justice Act (1774), third of the COERCIVE ACTS, was intended to assure crown officials in Massachusetts that they might safely execute unpopular laws, by providing that judges, soldiers, and revenue officers indicted for a murder or other serious crime committed in the execution of their official duty could be returned to England to be tried, thus avoiding trial before a colonial, and therefore hostile, jury. This so-called 'Murder Act' suggested to an aroused populace that Great Britain was seeking in effect to establish a military despotism.

Admirals, naval officers of highest rank, were not so titled in the U.S. until DAVID FARRAGUT was successively named rear admiral (1862), vice admiral (1864), and admiral (1866). Until 1862 the ranking naval commander was a captain, who by courtesy was titled commodore if he was in charge of a squadron. (The rank of commodore was created in 1862 and abolished in 1899. It was re-established during World War II, but fell into disuse at the end of the war, although the rank still exists.) DAVID D. PORTER was made a vice admiral in 1866, and admiral in 1870, after the death of Farragut. By law the two highest ranks ceased to exist on the death of their incumbents: Vice Admiral S. C. Rowan (1890), and Admiral Porter (1891). In 1899 the title of admiral of the fleet was conferred upon Rear Admiral GEORGE DEWEY. When the navy was expanded in 1915, Congress re-established the ranks of admiral and vice admiral. In 1944 the rank of fleet admiral of the navy was created.

Admiralty courts are tribunals with jurisdiction over all maritime cases within the three-mile limit, whether of a civil or criminal nature. They were first specifically established in America by the Constitutional Convention (1787), which vested admiralty powers exclusively in the Federal courts. Previously such jurisdiction had been exercised by common law courts or by courts of vice admiralty commissioned by colonial governors or by royal patents. Admiralty jurisdiction is vested in the district courts of the U.S., subject to revision by the Circuit Court of Appeals and the Supreme Court. The authority of admiralty courts extends to shipping on the Great Lakes and on navigable rivers.

Adult Education in the U.S., as a movement, dates from the establishment of Benjamin Franklin's JUNTO CLUB (1727), organized for the 'mutual improvement' of artisans. The rise of mechanics' institutes early in the 19th century, patterned on their British counterparts, was succeeded by the LYCEUM MOVEMENT in the 1830's, the CHAUTAUQUA MOVEMENT (1874), and the subsequent development of free public lectures.

The term 'adult education' came into general use in the U.S. when the Carnegie Corporation of New York began studies (1924) leading to the establishment of the American Association for Adult Education. A wide variety of programs and activities was soon developed through university extension services, planned reading clubs, correspondence schools, open forums, vocational training classes, and educational television.

Adventists are members of various sects whose dogma affirms the second coming of Christ. Also known as Millerites, they are followers of William Miller (1782–1849), a New York farmer who declared that the world would end in 1843, then 1844. In 1845 Millerites stated that they believed in the millennium, but placed the date in the indefinite future.

The Advent Christian Church was organized in 1854. Seventh-Day Adventists (1863) adopted Saturday as the Sabbath. In 1965 Adventist bodies in the U.S. reported some 408,000 members, chiefly the Seventh-Day group.

Adventurers, as the term was applied in the 16th and 17th century, were those merchants or business associations that 'adventured' (invested) their money in commercial enterprises. Most of the attempts at colonization in the New World were financed by such means. Planters were those who 'planted' homes. The word 'plantation' did not connote spacious acres for growing tobacco or rice; it meant any agricultural undertaking, however unpromising. Absentee 'adventurers' were induced to underwrite 'planters' (who presumably could return a profit to the investors) through advertising literature, such as that published by John Smith.

A.E.F., see *American Expeditionary Force.*

A.F. of L., see *American Federation of Labor.*

AGASSIZ, ALEXANDER (1835–1910), Swiss-born son of LOUIS AGASSIZ, came to the U.S. in 1849. After graduation from Harvard (1855) he became a member of the U.S. Coast Survey and an authority on ocean fish. His success in exploiting an extraordinarily productive copper mine in Michigan, located by his father's geological survey, gave him the means to endow the Harvard Museum of Comparative Zoology, which he served as curator (1874–85). His *Contribution to American Thalassography* (2 vols., 1888) is a classic account of three oceanographic explorations that enabled him to substantiate his theory that many coral atolls and barrier reefs are formed by the natural growth of coral on banks carved by prevailing currents. He was a restless spirit with a far-ranging mind, and his posthumously issued *Letters and Recollections* (1913) is source material for the intellectual history of his day.

AGASSIZ, [Jean] Louis [Rodolphe] (1807–73), Swiss-born zoologist and geologist, began his paleontological studies in Paris, where he received encouragement from Cuvier, and did important work in the classification of fossil fish. In 1836, while serving as professor of natural history at Neuchâtel, he began his investigation of glaciers. His *Etudes sur les glaciers* (1840) ushered in the Ice Age concept by showing that the geological formations he had been studying were the result of glacial flow and deposit from an earlier epoch. Two years after coming to the U.S. (1846), he was appointed professor of zoology and geology at Harvard, where he founded the museum of comparative zoology (1859). He became nationally known as teacher and lecturer, and headed two world-wide natural history expeditions.

In his summary of his scientific views, *Contributions to the Natural History of the U.S.* (4 vols., 1857–62), he gave his support to the theories of his friends Cuvier and Humboldt, by accepting their belief that a succession of vast cataclysms interrupted the continuity of the geological record (catastrophism), and he firmly rejected the Darwinian idea of natural selection. Indeed, his high scientific prestige was a factor in retarding the acceptance of evolutionism.

In 1850, after the death of his first wife, he married Elizabeth Cabot Cary (1822–1907), the first president of Radcliffe College (1879–1903).

See Edward Lurie, *Louis Agassiz: A Life of Science* (1960).

Age of Reform, see *Progressive Era.*

Agrarian Ideal, the concept that supplanted the economic doctrine of MERCANTILISM toward the end of the 18th century, held that the American farmer, not the merchant, was the backbone of the expanding nation. Crèvecœur, Franklin, John Taylor of Caroline, and thousands more envisaged America as a land of almost limitless expanse, capable of supporting millions. Self-contained and centering on the Mississippi valley, the land and its vast natural resources should be molded, the theory held, to create a new society whose members would live in independence and dignity under simple laws.

The agrarian ideal determined Jefferson's policies of state. For 30 years (1821–51) Thomas Hart Benton (1782–1857) was its chief proponent, giving his congressional support to Federal aid to western exploration and expansion. At the outbreak of the Civil War the major political parties were still in part aligned on the issue of whether the mercantile control of the East and North or the physical geography of the South and West would determine the nation's destiny.

Chief among the new forces that shattered the ideal was the technological revolution wrought by steam in the decade following the Civil War. Communications and rail transport improved, and the growth of industry assured the continuing prosperity of commercial agriculture. Thus the increased accumulation of capital in the interior of the continent, and the consequent growth of such metropolitan cities as St. Louis, Chicago, and Cleveland, effected an Agricultural Revolution, and brought an end to the agrarian ideal.

Agrarian Revolt, so called, was the effort of farmers after the Civil War to solve their social and economic difficulties resulting from overproduction, the collapse of farm prices, and the policies of the railroads, grain warehouses, and farm suppliers. Most important was the

GRANGER MOVEMENT (1867–80), which began with a social program but quickly shifted to radical experiments. The Grangers captured Middle West legislatures, and Granger lobbyists joined such antimonopolist groups as the GREENBACK and the POPULIST parties, which urged inflationary ideas, railroad legislation, and the easing of credit to prevent foreclosures. Within this agrarian revolt were the CO-OPERATIVE SOCIETIES, organized for the purchase and sale of farm commodities, which worked to effect various farm credit expedients. From the revolt developed a significant literature of social protest.

Agrarians, Southern, were the writers in the 1920's and 1930's who championed an obsolete Jeffersonian agrarian economy for the South, in the belief that, as people adapt themselves to the geography, economy, and culture of a region, their intellectual patterns reflect its indigenous qualities. Supporters of this form of Regionalism included Robert Penn Warren, John Gould Fletcher, John Crowe Ransom, Donald Davidson, and Allen Tate.

Agricultural Adjustment Act (AAA) (1933), part of the New Deal legislation, created an agency designed to raise commodity prices, reduce overproduction of farm crops, and give the farmer a purchasing power comparable to his position in 1909–14. In the first year more than 40,000,000 acres of land were taken out of production, farmers received several hundred millions of dollars in benefit payments, and by 1935 the national farm income had nearly doubled (a rise in part accounted for by dollar devaluation). In 1936 the Supreme Court in *U.S.* v. *Butler* declared the Act invalid, largely on the grounds that the tax on the processing of the products, by which the government subsidized farmers, was an invasion of states' rights. Congress then passed a second AAA (1938) authorizing a system of federal crop insurance and of PARITY PAYMENTS to assure an 'ever normal granary,' as well as stricter types of marketing quotas and acreage allotments. By 1939 some 3000 county associations were administering the program.

Agricultural Marketing Act, see *Farm Legislation.*

Agriculture, particularly in the Middle Colonies and the South, almost from the beginning tended toward commercial farming rather than mere subsistence. In the South, the small diversified farm remained the norm, even when the plantation system began, with its labor gangs, strong management, and the planters' social, economic, and political organization. English mercantilists, interested in agricultural exports, encouraged the production of timber and tar for the navy, indigo, and above all, tobacco for the world market. New England afforded opportunities in commerce rather than food-raising, because of its stony soil. Thus, the Middle Colonies, which had exceptionally fertile soil, became the bread basket of the colonies.

By the 1790's, southern planters, particularly in the tobacco lands, had exhausted some of their land, though there was always new land for them to use. This situation was not corrected until the 1850's, when marl and guano were used as fertilizers. The vast cotton export trade, which accounted for most American exports in the early 19th century, was created by Britain's Industrial Revolution of the 18th century, which had transformed the traditional household textile manufacture into a machine process. Just when slavery seemed on the way out, the invention of the cotton gin made cultivation of short-staple upland cotton profitable, thereby making the Deep South a land of cotton nabobs. The plantations of the COTTON KINGDOM raised much of their own food, but they also provided a market for the wheat, corn, hogs, and mules of the expanding West. They also bought similar products from the innumerable small farms of the south.

Farm prosperity in the northern and middle states owed much to progress in transportation, such as the macadam roads and the later development of the canal and railroad systems. The European wars of the French Revolutionary era insured large markets for American farmers. The Agricultural Revolution began in the late 1700's, and has continued into the present. It brought seed drills and row planting, the use of fertilizers, crop rotation, and superior breeds of animals, such as the merino sheep. Agricultural societies were influential in both the North and South. They investigated European methods, sponsored farm exhibitions, and published farm journals such as *The American Farmer* (Baltimore, 1819), which inspired many imitators.

The penetration of the Middle West, during the first half of the 19th century, followed along the rich bottom lands of the Ohio. Thus, Indiana, Illinois, and Missouri gained statehood by 1821. The Prairie Revolution came in the 1840's, when farmers learned to cultivate the tougher soils of the interior of the Old Northwest. Consequently, Michigan, Iowa, and Wisconsin were admitted to the Union before 1850. At that time 90 per cent of Americans were engaged, directly or indirectly, in farming. Cyrus Hall McCormick, a Virginian, invented the reaper in 1831, and after 1847 the new city of Chicago became a distributing center for farm machinery.

After the Civil War, farmers settled the Great Plains, even though the land was relatively arid. Deep plowing and pumps powered by windmills helped solve the water problem, and barbed wire replaced timber for fencing. The federal government aided the farmer through the conservation movement, 'cow colleges' (beginning with the Morrill College Land Grant Act of 1862), Federal roads, and assistance from the Department of Agriculture. The post-Civil War era of the cattle range, though celebrated, scarcely lasted a generation, for it vanished with the passing of the open range. The sheep ranchers hastened the end of the cattle era, but it was the homesteader and his barbed wire that destroyed the power of both the cattle barons and the great sheep-owners. By 1900 the Trans-Mississippi West rested economically to a very large extent on the output of the farmer.

By the 1880's the Agricultural Revolution had produced a technology that drove countless marginal farmers to the cities or into an AGRARIAN REVOLT. This technology was marked by the use of expensive farm machinery, the rapid growth of commercial farms into large-scale enterprises, a fast-growing domestic market, particularly in the cities, and new agricultural sciences, such as the new soil chemistry introduced from Germany by Liebig. By 1900 the American farms were so productive that their shrunken population (only 37 per cent) could easily feed the nation and many other countries as well. This was to be true of an even smaller percentage of farmers during two World Wars.

But long before 1900 the farmer had been in trouble. The Civil War, by overturning the plantation system in the South, had created new forms of labor, the SHARECROPPERS and TENANT FARMERS, who seldom were able to free themselves from a state of economic bondage. In the West, abundance itself was a problem; glutted markets dropped the price of staple products and began to dislocate the nation's economy. This was one of the causes of the recurrent depressions of 1893, 1921, and 1929. The closing of the frontier also was a hardship for the small farmer; before it ended, he had been able to buy government land with little capital, if he would homestead on it. By the late 1800's farmers had begun to fight for their interests by forming FARMERS' ASSOCIATIONS and urging passage of GRANGER LAWS. But as the decades passed the economic and political position of the farmers grew worse.

Out of the struggle of discontented staple farmers during the 1920's came many of the New Deal farm ideas, particularly the theories of price parity based on crop restriction and outright subsidies. The New Deal farm advisers of the 1930's looked back upon the prosperous era of 1909–14 as a time when the farmers' share of the national income had reached a highly desirable ratio, an explicit ideal expressed in the AGRICULTURAL ADJUSTMENT ACT (1933). The New Deal also tried to arrest the rising tide of farm foreclosures, which had been worsened by the Depression. Between 1932 and 1935 nearly a quarter of the nation's farms were lost by foreclosure, and the annual net income of farm workers at that time was $200 a year (for sharecroppers, $122). Farm incomes, which had totaled sixteen billion dollars in 1919, had shrunk by two-thirds a decade later. In 1933 Congress passed the Farm Credit Act and other measures designed to strengthen the farmers' position. The regional plan of the Tennessee Valley Authority was in part a New Deal attempt to rehabilitate the agriculture of the South. Although these measures were generally effective, in the mid-1930's a severe drought struck the western Great Plains, and the arid conditions, combined with overgrazing and deep plowing of land best suited for pasture, created a Dust Bowl. Thousands of farms were devastated. To combat the Dust Bowl, Congress passed legislation restricting the use of public lands and providing for the creation of windbreaks, reforestation, and the use of a number of other conservationist techniques. These, plus the return of the rains, gradually restored the region, though it is still subject to periodic drought.

World War II produced an unprecedented demand for farm products, and agriculture boomed. But the postwar readjustment, especially after 1953, compelled the government to continue the New Deal expedients; price supports seemed a political necessity. Federal marketing relieved the gluts through Kennedy's 'Food for Peace' and sales of wheat to Russia, and Johnson's Congress emphasized an attack on rural slums and encouraged recreational use of surplus farm land. But the problem of overproduction, which is unique in the history of the world, cannot dim the tremendous achievements of American agriculture in providing the highest level of nourishment ever known, and at the same time feeding starving nations.

Agriculture, U.S. Department of, was created by Congress in 1862 under the direction of a commissioner. In 1889 the commissioner was renamed Secretary of Agriculture and given cabinet status. The department includes some 30 administrative heads, and its 100,000 employees do the work of a score of agencies. Its annual appropriation in 1965 approached $8,000,000,000. Together with state departments of agriculture and the colleges they help foster, it maintains experimental stations, issues reports and bulletins in a variety of fields, and deals with problems of marketing and long-range planning. Secretaries of Agriculture and the Presidents under whom they served are as follows.

CLEVELAND
Norman J. Colman (Mo.) 1889

B. HARRISON
Jeremiah M. Rusk (Wis.) 1889

CLEVELAND
J. Sterling Morton (Neb.) 1893

MC KINLEY
James Wilson (Iowa) 1897

T. ROOSEVELT
James Wilson (Iowa) 1901

TAFT
James Wilson (Iowa) 1909

WILSON
David F. Houston (Mo.) 1913
Edward T. Meredith (Iowa) 1920

HARDING
Henry C. Wallace (Iowa) 1921

COOLIDGE
Howard M. Gore (W. Va.) 1924
William M. Jardine (Kan.) 1925

HOOVER
Arthur M. Hyde (Mo.) 1929

F. D. ROOSEVELT
Henry A. Wallace (Iowa) 1933
Claude R. Wickard (Ind.) 1940

TRUMAN
Clinton P. Anderson (N.M.) 1945
Charles F. Brannan (Colo.) 1948

EISENHOWER
Ezra Taft Benson (Utah) 1953

KENNEDY
Orville L. Freeman (Minn.) 1961

L. B. JOHNSON
Orville L. Freeman (Minn.) 1963

AGUINALDO, EMILIO (1869–1964), was the first of the great Filipino revolutionaries. He led a rebellion against Spain in 1896 which failed, and he was exiled to Hong Kong. Admiral Dewey encouraged his return after the battle of MANILA BAY, and, with his Filipino *insurrectos,* Aguinaldo assisted in the capture of Manila (August 1898). He could not control his 'Visayan Republic' on Luzon, and the ensuing insurrection against the United States (1899) was stamped out by methods deemed throughout the U.S. as discreditably imperialistic. In 1935 he ran for the presidency of the newly established Commonwealth of the Philippines, but was defeated by Manuel Quezon. When American forces reoccupied the islands during World War II he was accused of having aided the Japanese, and was imprisoned (1945). He was released at the war's end and retired to private life.

Air-conditioning was first incorporated in a system designed (1902) by the Buffalo mechanical engineer Willis H. Carrier (1876–1950). Refrigerating equipment, expensive to install and mechanically inefficient, was at first used chiefly to control industrial processes. A few theaters, office buildings, and hotels were partially air-conditioned before 1920.

After Carrier invented a centrifugal refrigerating machine (1921), air-conditioning could provide constant temperatures, automatically controlled. The Milam Building in San Antonio, completed in 1929, was the first office structure to be entirely air-conditioned. Refinements during the 1930's paved the way for small, economical units for the home. By 1950 factory-assembled, year-round air-conditioners had become standard equipment for any type of enclosed area.

Aircraft Industry, see *Aviation.*

Air Force, U.S., organized while experiments in AVIATION were in their elementary stage, began as the Aeronautical Division of the Signal Corps (1907), and consisted of one officer and two enlisted men. In 1916 the Army used planes for scouting during the MEXICAN BORDER CAMPAIGN. The U.S. entered World War I with 55 planes, increased to 500 at war's end. In May 1918, partly to advertise air force development, the Army and the Post Office departments together set up an experimental airmail line.

Although commercial air transport developed rapidly during the 1920's, military and naval authorities differed over the role of the airplane in warfare. In 1921 Colonel WILLIAM MITCHELL conducted significant bombing tests against surface ships to demonstrate their vulnerability to air attack. The War and Navy departments came to no conclusions about Mitchell's demonstration, and for his public statements in 1925 of 'treasonable negligence' he was court-martialed and suspended from the service (though he was posthumously elevated to the rank of major general). In 1926 the air branch became the U.S. Army Air Corps, its official designation until 1941.

During the 1930's Major General H. H. ARNOLD worked to build the Air Corps into an effective striking power. At the outbreak of World War II the Corps was enlarged into the Army Air Force. The Air Force trained 30,000 pilots a year, and industry annually produced 95,000 planes, flown and maintained by a personnel of nearly 2,500,000, providing the answer to Hermann Goering's quip that 'Americans can't build planes; only electric iceboxes and razor blades.' This great air arm was a decisive factor in winning the BATTLE OF THE ATLANTIC and the BURMA CAMPAIGN.

After the war the Armed Services Unification Act (1947) removed the Air Force from the Department of the Army and created the Department of the Air Force as a separate executive branch of the Department of Defense. In 1954 the U.S. Air Force Academy was established at Denver; it was moved to its permanent campus near Colorado Springs four years later.

Air Mail, see *Aviation; Postal system.*

Aix-la-Chapelle, Treaty of (1748), ended KING GEORGE'S WAR. It returned LOUISBOURG to France. To mollify the New Englanders, who had done most of the fighting, the crown assumed all expenses for the expedition that had forced the surrender of that Nova Scotia fortress. For North America the treaty proved to be only a truce. The FRENCH AND INDIAN WARS were resumed seven years later.

Alabama, probably named after a Creek tribe, was first explored by the Spanish, perhaps by NARVÁEZ (1528), certainly by DE SOTO (1539). The territory of the present state was included in the province of Carolina, granted by Charles II to members of his court in the charters of 1663 and 1665. Despite English claims, the French settled on the Mobile river in 1702 and erected Fort Louis. By the TREATY OF PARIS of 1763 England took undisputed possession of much of the area. The present boundaries were fixed when WEST FLORIDA was eliminated (1819).

The region became subject to U.S. jurisdiction after the War of 1812. Then slave plantations were established by settlers from the adjoining states, and they began growing cotton on a large scale. Alabama was organized as a territory in 1817, and two years later it was admitted to the Union as the 22nd state, with Montgomery as its capital. By the Treaty of Fort Jackson (1814), the CREEK ceded their claims, and the CHEROKEE, CHOCTAW, and CHICKASAW did so soon after. By 1832 Indian 'problems' had been solved in Alabama.

The state seceded from the Union in January 1861 and supplied troops for the Confederacy throughout the Civil War. Its legislature ratified the THIRTEENTH AMENDMENT in December 1865, and the state was readmitted to the Union in 1868.

A high percentage of the state's population is Negro, and it has had race problems for many years. In 1955 a successful Negro boycott of the Montgomery bus system began the 'Negro Revolution,' which encouraged non-violent resistance and led to civil rights successes in Birmingham and tense demonstrations in Selma by the followers of Dr. MARTIN LUTHER KING.

Although Alabama is predominantly a farming state, it is also a leading industrial area in the South, using the hydroelectric systems of the TENNESSEE VALLEY AUTHORITY. In the decade 1950–60 the total population declined somewhat, but that of Birmingham, an iron and steel center, rose from 326,000 to 341,000; of Mobile, a shipping terminus on the Gulf, from 120,000 to 203,000; and of Montgomery, a produce market, from 106,000 to 134,000.

The University of Alabama (Tuscaloosa, est. 1831) is the leading institute of higher learning. Tuskegee Normal and Industrial Institute (est. 1881), organized by BOOKER T. WASHINGTON, is outstanding among Negro vocational schools. In 1965 the University, with a faculty of 1320, enrolled 14,900 students; the Institute had a faculty of 309 and enrolled 2530.

***Alabama* Claims,** settled in 1872, were preferred by the U.S against Great Britain for the depredations caused during the Civil War by warships, particularly C.S.S. *Alabama* and *Florida,* built in Great Britain for the Confederate government. In 1869 the Senate, led by Charles Sumner, overwhelmingly rejected the first attempt at settlement, the JOHNSON-CLARENDON CONVENTION. Sumner demanded collateral damages of $2,125,000,000. In 1871 Secretary of State Hamilton Fish negotiated the TREATY OF WASHINGTON, which set up an international arbitral tribunal (Italy, Brazil, Switzerland, and the interested parties). Charles Francis Adams (1807–86) led the commission that represented the U.S. when the tribunal met at Geneva (1871–72). The arbitrators awarded the U.S. $15,500,000; indirect claims were denied.

Alamance, Battle of, see *Regulators.*

Alamo, in San Antonio, Texas, was originally a heavy-walled mission, later converted into a fort. Manned during the Texas Revolution by fewer than 200 Texans, it was besieged on 24 February 1836 by 3000 troops led by Santa Anna. Colonel JAMES BOWIE and his co-commander, William B. Travis (1811–36), gave a 'victory or death' order, and the Texans held out against repeated assaults until 6 March. When the walls were finally breached, the Texans continued the fight in hand-to-hand combat until the last few defenders were taken and slaughtered. Both commanders were killed in the encounter, as was David Crockett. The report of the massacre stiffened Texan resistance, and under the rallying cry, 'Remember the Alamo,' the Texans defeated the Mexican army and captured Santa Anna at SAN JACINTO on 21 April.

Alaska, in area the largest political division of the U.S. (more than twice the size of Texas) and in population the smallest (226,000 in 1960), was admitted to the Union in 1959 as the 49th state. Arctic Alaska is a barren tundra. Central Alaska is an area of valleys and mountains; from its plateaus rises the 20,320-ft. peak of Mt. McKinley, the highest point on the continent and a national park since 1917. The Yukon river flows through this central region to the Bering Sea. The 4700-mile coast line is more temperate in climate than the inland regions; along it there are numerous islands, mountains, fjords, glaciers, and a vast area of volcanoes (Katmai National Monument).

In 1725 the Russian government engaged the Danish navigator Vitus Bering to explore the waters off northeast Asia, and his discovery of the Aleutian Islands (1741) opened the region to fur trading. Later explorations by the Spanish led to the NOOTKA SOUND SEIZURES (1789). Rival claims between Spain and England were settled by the Nootka Convention (1790). Russian trading monopolies at Kodiak and Sitka were ended by a Russian treaty with England (1825) by which boundaries were fixed. During the administration of President Andrew Johnson, Secretary of State Seward purchased Alaska ('Seward's icebox') from Russia for $7,200,000. Surveys confirmed its resources in furs, timber, and metals. An Alaska-Canadian boundary dispute, precipitated by the discovery of gold in the KLONDIKE, was settled (1903) in favor of U.S. claims.

Alaska was organized as a civil and judicial district in 1884, and was granted status as a territory in 1912. Juneau has been its capital since 1906. The population of Anchorage, the largest city, jumped from 11,000 to 44,000 in the decade 1950–60; that of Fairbanks, the largest in the interior, from 5000 to 13,000. This growth is reflected in the marked increase in enrollment at the University of Alaska (Fairbanks, est. 1922) from 870 in 1962 to 3590 in 1965.

Alaska's major industries are fishing and lumber; its chief minerals, petroleum and coal, are under development.

Albany, New York, on the west side of the Hudson river near its confluence with the Mohawk, was first settled as Fort Orange (1624), a fur-trading post of the Dutch West India Company. The English took it over in 1664 and renamed it. It was chartered as a city in 1686. Three years later it was the site of the first intercolonial convention, a meeting with representatives of the IROQUOIS CONFEDERACY to plan a system of defense against the French. In the 18th century, during the French and Indian Wars, Albany, as the gateway to the Iroquois country, was the starting point for expeditions against Canada and the Lake Champlain country. The strategic importance of the city was also recognized during the War of Independence; it was the object of Burgoyne's campaign south from Canada in 1777. In 1797 Albany became the state capital. The city's commercial growth began with the completion of the ERIE CANAL (1825), which though mainly superseded by the St. Lawrence Seaway, is still in use. In 1960 Albany had a population of 130,000.

Albany Plan of Union (1754) was a proposal that the colonies federate for their greater security. On the recommendation of the London Board of Trade a congress of delegates from the assemblies of New Hampshire, Massachusetts, Connecticut, Rhode Island, New York, Pennsylvania, and Maryland met at Albany, New York. Aware of the imminence of war with France, the congress sought to work out a closer league of friendship with the Iroquois, and to arrange a permanent union of the colonies. Drafted by Benjamin Franklin, the plan provided for a representative governing body, or Grand Council, to be chosen triennially by the colonial legislatures. It would impose taxes, nominate civil executives, regulate Indian affairs, and take general charge of military concerns. A President-General, with veto power, would preside, and the acts of the Council would be valid throughout the colonies unless vetoed by the crown.

After a debate led by Franklin, Thomas Hutchinson, and Stephen Hopkins, the congress approved the plan. But the colonies, unwilling to surrender so much power, refused to ratify and since the plan was not ratified, it was never submitted to Parliament. The meeting nevertheless set a precedent for later congresses, and the plan itself was a forerunner of the Articles of Confederation and of the Constitution.

Albany Regency was the derogatory term applied by THURLOW WEED to the New York Democratic political machine organized about 1820 by MARTIN VAN BUREN and WILLIAM L. MARCY. For more than a generation it dominated the politics of the state. Operating through the 'spoils system,' it controlled party patronage and influenced national, state, and local affairs. When Van Buren's power declined (about 1848), so did the Regency.

Albemarle Settlements, see *North Carolina.*

Alcaldes, in colonies governed by Spanish law, were the mayors. Their judicial powers were similar to those of a justice of the peace. Until California was admitted to the Union in 1850, the alcalde was recognized by military governors as the civil executive authority.

ALCOTT, AMOS BRONSON (1799–1888), born in Connecticut and largely self-educated, in early life earned his living as a peddler and schoolteacher. His advanced educational views attracted notice (often unfavorable) when he conducted his Temple School in Boston (1834–39) with the assistance of ELIZABETH PEABODY. He encouraged self-instruction by way of self-analysis, and introduced the honor system. In 1840 he moved his family to Concord, and after a visit to England (1842), where an Alcott House had been established to experiment with his educational ideas, he returned to start the short-lived communistic venture FRUITLANDS. When he became superintendent of Concord schools (1859), he introduced singing, dancing, reading aloud, and physiology.

His mystical transcendentalism, expounded in 'conversations' (informal talks on a great range of subjects), bewildered many and irritated some, but he was always held in high regard by his Concord neighbors Emerson and Thoreau. His greatest influence developed through the CONCORD SCHOOL OF PHILOSOPHY, of which he was a guiding spirit. His writings do not reflect the lucid, even brilliant, aspects of his thought, felt strongly by those who shared his conversations.

See Odell Shepard, *Pedlar's Progress* (1937).

ALCOTT, LOUISA MAY (1832–88), daughter of BRONSON ALCOTT, drew upon her family life for characters and events in her most popular book, *Little Women* (2 vols., 1868–69), a work which enjoyed a phenomenal sale. She thereafter continued writing books for children, and by her success relieved the chronic poverty of her father.

ALDEN, JOHN (*c.* 1599–1687), *Mayflower* Pilgrim and signer of the Mayflower Compact, was an original settler of Duxbury, Massachusetts, and a neighbor and friend of Miles Standish. The story of his marriage to Priscilla Mullins (or Molines), told in Longfellow's poem *The Courtship of Miles Standish,* follows a legend current in the 19th century and has no historical foundation.

ALDRICH, NELSON WILMARTH (1841–1915), Republican senator from Rhode Island (1881–1911), was a lifelong spokesman for eastern manufacturing interests. As an Old Guard policy maker for the Taft administration, he was able to block the Progressive program started under Theodore Roosevelt. His conservative views were incorporated in such legislation as the GOLD-STANDARD ACT (1900), the ALDRICH-VREELAND ACT (1908), and the PAYNE-ALDRICH TARIFF ACT (1909). He was so bitterly excoriated by such insurgents among his Senate colleagues as George Norris and Robert La Follette that he did not stand for re-election. The 'Aldrich plan' (1911) for sound currency legislation was not passed by the Senate, but it was used by the Democrats in setting up the FEDERAL RESERVE SYSTEM (1913).

ALDRICH, RICHARD (1863–1937), after graduation from Harvard (1885) and further musical study in Germany, joined the music staff of the New York *Tribune* (1891–1902). Aldrich left the *Tribune* to become the chief music critic of *The New York Times* (1902–23). The musical taste of his day is recorded in *Concert Life in New York,* a collection of his essays published posthumously (1941).

Aldrich-Vreeland Act (1908), an emergency measure to ease the credit supply following the PANIC OF 1907, permitted national banks to issue notes on securities other than Federal bonds. Though it was in itself a stop-gap measure, it led to the creation of the NATIONAL MONETARY COMMISSION.

ALEXANDERSON, ERNST FREDERIK WERNER (1878–), Swedish-born electrical engineer and inventor, came to the U.S. in 1901, and in 1902 joined the General Electric Company at Schenectady, New York, where he pioneered in radio and television electronics. Among his more than 300 inventions, many of which revolutionized the field of radio communications, are the Alexanderson high frequency alternator, which made world-wide wireless possible; the multiple-tuned antenna; the tuned radio frequency receiver; and the vacuum tube radio telephone transmitter.

Algeciras Conference (1906) was called jointly by France, Great Britain, Germany, and Spain, through the instrumentality of President Theodore Roosevelt, to settle the Moroccan crisis of 1905–6. Germany, late in the race for empire, had challenged the French hegemony in Morocco, a confrontation that might easily have resulted in a world war. The settlement, drawn up at Algeciras, Spain, affirmed Moroccan independence, although the actual result was increased authority of the French in Morocco. The U.S. was represented, and the Senate ratified the treaty, with the proviso that such approval was not to be construed as a departure from the traditional U.S. policy of noninvolvement in purely European affairs.

ALGER, HORATIO (1832–99), Massachusetts-born writer of boys' stories, graduated from Harvard Divinity School (1860) and for a time lived a Bohemian life in Paris. He was ordained a Unitarian minister in 1864, but two years later left his New England pulpit, settled in New York, and began his literary career. All his books stress the idea that moral earnestness and persistent endeavor (and luck) lead to fame and fortune. The 'rags to riches' theme, repeated in three separate series, enjoyed an enormous vogue in its day, and the sale of the 130 Alger novels has been estimated to have exceeded 20,000,000 copies. He gave away most of his large income to the street boys he befriended. He himself died in poverty.

Algonquian Family of Indians was one of the most widely distributed linguistic stocks on the North American continent. Unlike the UTO-AZTECAN group, which occupied definite areas, the Algonquian tribes inhabited territories from Newfoundland to Vancouver. Among them were the FLATHEADS on the Pacific coast; the BLACKFOOT, CHEYENNE, and ARAPAHO in the Plains region; the CREE, KICKAPOO, MIAMI, OJIBWA, OTTAWA, SAUK AND FOX, POTAWATOMI, and SHAWNEE in the Middle West; and the ABNAKI, DELAWARE, MAHICAN, MASSACHUSET, NARRAGANSETT, PEQUOT, and WAMPANOAG along the Atlantic slope.

All tribes had definite hunting and fishing areas, and moved only when game was scarce. Agricultural produce was their secondary supply, but from them the first white settlers learned to cultivate such native resources as maple sugar, tobacco, corn, tomatoes, squash, and pumpkins. Allies of the French in Canada, they took part in fighting the English, who were allied with their bitter enemies the IROQUOIS. Among their great leaders were KING PHILIP, TAMMANY, MASSASOIT, KEOKUK, PONTIAC, TECUMSEH, and POWHATAN. Place names of American states, counties, cities, lakes, rivers, and even local organizations testify to the great impress of the Algonquian inheritance.

Alien and Sedition Acts (1798), were legislated by a Federalist-dominated Congress in a spirit of partisan bigotry. Because of the popular reaction against the Acts, they opened the way for Jefferson's election to the presidency, and thus advanced the very ends that the Federalists sought to prevent. The country was expecting war with France, the XYZ AFFAIR had fanned chauvinism to the point where all alien Frenchmen were suspect, and the Republican press was deemed libelous in its defamation of the government.

This alleged crisis was met by the passage of four laws. The Naturalization Act (repealed in 1802) extended the period of residence necessary for aliens to achieve citizenship from five to fourteen years. The Alien Enemies Act gave the President executive power to expel foreigners whom he judged dangerous in time of war (a law that was never invoked, though it hastened the departure of many Frenchmen from the U.S.). The Alien Act and the Sedition Act, which were to expire in two years, dealt with sedition. They forbade treasonable conspiracies and any published utterance 'with the intent to defame' (i.e. criticize) the President or the government. The penalty, a fine and a term of imprisonment, was invoked in about 25 cases. Ten of the convictions involved Republicans, tried by Federalist judges and juries. Republicans held the Sedition Act to be unconstitutional, but among Federalist leaders only John Marshall openly opposed it.

Republicans were quick to point out that the Sedition Act was being used to convict Republican journalists of slandering President Adams, while no less scurrilous abuse by Federalists of Vice President Jefferson went unrebuked. A noteworthy case was the imprisonment of THOMAS COOPER, the English-born scientist whose sympathies with republicanism had led to his migration to the U.S. The fact that men like Cooper were effective anti-Federalist agitators was sufficient reason to create bias against them, a bias that led Federalist judges to so untenable an interpretation of 'sedition' as to make popular heroes of the victims.

Unable to think of the Republicans as a 'loyal opposition,' the Federalists took an extreme position of Federal sovereignty against which many states protested, notably in the KENTUCKY AND VIRGINIA RESOLVES. No further peacetime antisedition legislation was enacted until the ALIEN REGISTRATION ACT of 1940.

Alien Registration Act (1940), also known as the Smith Act, strengthened existing laws governing the admission and deportation of aliens, and contained the first peacetime antisedition provisions since the Alien and Sedition Acts of 1798. Designed primarily to check subversive activities, it made the advocacy of violent overthrow of government unlawful. Many liberals objected to the fact that it embraced the doctrines of guilt by intent and guilt by association, but in DENNIS *v.* U.S. the Supreme Court upheld its constitutionality (1951).

Allegheny Mountains are a western section of the Appalachian system, with a mean elevation of 3000 ft. They extend through Pennsylvania, Maryland, West Virginia, and Virginia. The steep eastern escarpment (the Allegheny Front), with few passes, was an impediment to westward migration until roads were constructed early in the 19th century. The Alleghenies extend into the CUMBERLAND PLATEAU on the south.

ALLEN, ETHAN (1738–89), Connecticut-born leader of the Vermont GREEN MOUNTAIN BOYS, refused to recognize the jurisdiction of New York in the area between the Connecticut and Hudson rivers. In the 1760's, together with his brothers, Ira and Levi Allen, he had acquired and settled on large property holdings in the area then known as the New Hampshire Grants (present state of Vermont), the ownership of which New York disputed. (The operation of Vermont tax laws ultimately dispossessed the Allens of their holdings.)

During the Revolution, in a surprise attack, Ethan Allen and Benedict Arnold captured Fort Ticonderoga on 10 May 1775, calling upon the garrison commander (according to Allen's unsubstantiated report) to surrender 'in the name of the great Jehovah and the Continental Congress.' In September of that year Allen led an expedition against Canada, was captured, and was exchanged three years later. Although he had been made a brevet colonel by Congress, he returned to Vermont, where he was made major general of the Vermont militia, and resumed opposition to New York, acting with his brothers to assure Vermont's independence even if, to win his cause and protect his holdings, Vermont became a British province. He did correspond with Governor Haldimand of Canada, possibly — though his motives are unclear — to that end.

Allen typified the blustering frontiersman whose self-confidence gave him stature. He was a prolific if polemical writer and a homespun deist. His best-known book, *Reason the Only Oracle of Man* (1784), is largely the product of his friend, the free-thinker Dr. Thomas Young (1732–77).

Alliance for Progress, a concept of hemisphere-wide effort for economic and social development, was announced by President Kennedy in March 1961. It grew out of a reaction to Fidel Castro's effort to make Cuba not only a communist country but also a vigorous exporter of revolution to the other nations of the New World. Its purpose was to strengthen Latin American countries in such ways that they themselves would be able to resist communism. The Alliance was formally adopted in a treaty signed five months later by twenty American republics (all except Cuba). By 1965 this twenty-billion-dollar program had shown results in low cost housing, rural resettlement, financial projects, mass education, and plans for population control.

Alliances, see *Treaties.*

Allied Council for Japan, see *Japan, Occupation of.*

Allied High Commission, see *Germany, Occupation of.*

ALLOUEZ, CLAUDE JEAN (1622–89), French Jesuit missionary in North America, was appointed vicar general (1663) for all fur traders and natives of the Northwest. His visits along the shores of Lakes Superior and Nipigon (1665–67) gave him the opportunity to map the region. His reports, published in the JESUIT RELATIONS, were significant in attracting attention to the Great Lakes.

ALLSTON, WASHINGTON (1779–1843), born in South Carolina, after graduation from Harvard (1800) studied painting under Benjamin West in London. During his European sojourn of seventeen years he published a volume of poems (1813), spent four years in Italy, and became intimate with such leaders of the romantic movement as Coleridge, who pronounced Allston the one American who in painting could express 'the life of nature.' Allston's *Moonlit Landscape* (Boston Museum) in fact attempts to communicate in oil the sense of mystery which pervades Coleridge's *The Rime of the Ancient Mariner.* His paintings of supernatural happenings from the Old Testament, such as his *Witch of Endor* (Gardiner Museum, Boston), won him prizes in London and made him one of the famous artists of the period.

Well on his way to becoming an important and highly original artist, in 1818 he returned to Boston with his almost completed *Belshazzar's Feast* (Boston Athenaeum), already so extravagantly admired that Boston citizens raised a $10,000 subscription for its purchase. But a nervous disorder had set in, and the more Allston labored to finish the work, the more confused it became. Allston came to symbolize the art that withered in the 'cruel air' of America. Thereafter in the New England countryside he painted Italian hills and Spanish scenes. In his day Allston was regarded as an artist above the crudities of a raw nation, and he was acclaimed by some as the only great American painter.

Almanacs, calendars of days, weeks, and months, have for centuries supplied astronomical and statistical data especially useful to farmers and fishermen. With the exception of a broadside, the first work printed in the British colonies was *An Almanack of New England for the Year 1639.* Almanacs were the most widely distributed publications during the colonial period and provided much of the reading material later absorbed into newspapers. In America as in England they were compendiums of popular science, remarkable events, proverbs, jests, practical information, and miscellaneous data. The best almanacs satirized superstitions and explained the new Copernican and Newtonian ideas.

Benjamin Franklin's *Poor Richard* almanacs (1728–58) are probably the best known. Franklin shrewdly issued them in three annual editions, with contents varying to feature local information for New England, the Middle Colonies, and the South. The CROCKETT ALMANACS, a popular 19th-century series, specialized in tall tales of the frontier. *Farmer's Almanack* (1793–current) is one of the oldest periodicals in the U.S. It later was titled *Old Farmer's Almanac* to distinguish it from imitators. Founded by Robert Bailey Thomas (1766–1846) of Sterling, Massachusetts, it still bears his name as editor.

Since almanacs were the most popular 'books' of their day, they were a profitable publishing venture. Later they were a medium through which religious groups or reform organizations advanced their causes, or the means by which entrepreneurs (often patent medicine agents) advertised their products. Out of this ancestry grew the modern newspaper-sponsored almanac, now used as a convenient reference book.

Alphabet Agencies, so called (especially by the conservative opposition), were the numerous offices established by Congress during the period of the New Deal to administer relief and recovery measures. Such were the CCC (Civilian Conservation Corps) and the WPA (Works Progress Administration).

Alta California, see *California.*

ALTGELD, JOHN PETER (1847–1902), German-born lawyer and reformer, who was reared in Ohio, settled in Chicago where he wrote an attack on *Our Penal Machinery and Its Victims* (1884), declaring that the poor had difficulty in obtaining justice. In some measure he was able to implement his views while serving as judge of the Cook county court (1886–91). As governor of Illinois (1893–97) he improved penal and charitable institutions and, in co-operation with Jane Addams's circle at Hull-House, he sponsored laws to regulate child labor.

He first came into national prominence (1893) when he pardoned the three surviving 'anarchists' convicted for their alleged part in the HAYMARKET RIOT. Because of his action in that affair, and his demand for the withdrawal of Federal troops ordered to Chicago by President Cleveland during the PULLMAN STRIKE in 1894, Altgeld was subjected to a vilification seldom equaled in American public life, and he was defeated for re-election. The consensus after emotions cooled was that Altgeld was one of the most enlightened public servants of his time and a pioneer in social and political reform.

ALVORD, CLARENCE WALWORTH (1868–1928), Massachusetts-born historian, while teaching history at Illinois (1901–20) and Minnesota (1920–23), was influential in transforming historical societies into effective instruments of scholarship. He founded (1914) the *Mississippi Valley Historical Review* (recently renamed *The Journal of American History*), and was highly regarded among his colleagues as a pioneer in directing attention to the importance of regional studies. His chief work, *The Mississippi Valley in British Politics* (1917), stresses the Imperial Perspective as the key to decisions affecting the transmontane West acquired from France in 1763. He influenced historiography by publishing the *Kaskaskia Records* (1909) and numerous other documentary collections.

Amana Society originated in Germany as a Pietist religious sect during the 18th century. In 1842 some 600 members came to the U.S. and settled near Buffalo, New York, under the leadership of Christian Metz (1794–1867). Best known among their simple prophet leaders was the revered Barbara Heinemann. In 1855 the Society purchased some 20,000 acres near Davenport, Iowa, where it set up a Christian communistic type of community and developed a successful co-operative organization of small shops, mills, and farms. In 1932 it reorganized as a joint stock company and ended religious rule in temporal affairs. There were 755 Amanists in 1965.

Ambassadors are the highest ranking members of the diplomatic service. They represent the person of the President of the U.S., and therefore have direct access to rulers of state. The U.S. contented itself with ministers for more than a century. The first ambassador was Thomas F. Bayard (1828–98), Cleveland's Secretary of State (1885–89), appointed by Cleveland during his second administration as ambassador to Great Britain (1893–97). (Sir Julian Pauncefote was immediately presented to President Cleveland as Great Britain's first ambassador to the U.S.) Thereafter ambassadors were appointed to and received by the principal European and Western Hemisphere powers. At present ambassadors represent the President in almost all the nations of the world.

Amendments to the U.S. Constitution are the alterations made in that instrument by changes or additions. The first ten amendments constitute the BILL OF RIGHTS and were ratified in 1791. The ELEVENTH (1798) limited the extent of the Federal judiciary, and the TWELFTH (1804) provided that electors shall cast separate ballots for President and Vice President. The next three are the so-called Civil War amendments: the THIRTEENTH (1865) abolished slavery; the FOURTEENTH (1868) set forth individual privileges and immunities, limited state action, and recognized racial equality; and the FIFTEENTH (1870) enfranchised the Negro. The SIXTEENTH (1913) empowered Congress to levy an income tax, and the SEVENTEENTH (1913) provided for the popular election of U.S. Senators. After World War I the EIGHTEENTH (1919) ushered in the prohibition era, and the NINETEENTH (1920) gave the vote to women. The TWENTIETH (1933) ended the 'lame duck' session of Congress, the TWENTY-FIRST (1933) repealed the Eighteenth, the TWENTY-SECOND (1951) limited the number of terms a President may serve, the TWENTY-THIRD (1961) granted the franchise to resident citizens of Washington, D.C., the TWENTY-FOURTH (1964) banned the poll tax as a voting requirement in Federal elections, and the TWENTY-FIFTH (1966) established presidential succession.

Constitutions that can be altered by the same processes that establish ordinary laws are called 'flexible.' The Federal Constitution (by provision of Article V) is 'rigid,' in that it can be amended only by ratification of three-fourths of the states. Although some 2500 resolutions proposing constitutional changes have been introduced in Congress over the years, Congress has adopted and submitted to the states only 30, five of which were never ratified. (Two of the five were part of the original Bill of Rights.) The three later unratified proposals were those (1) forbidding the acceptance of titles of nobility (1810), (2) prohibiting interference with slavery (1861), and (3) authorizing Federal child labor legislation (1924).

So cumbrous is the machinery of formal amendment that proposals have frequently been made suggesting an easier process. But the consensus at present holds that for a document as fundamental as the Constitution, any method of amendment less deliberate is undesirable, since the instrument itself is limited to enduring principles and therefore open to new interpretations. Chief Justice Earl Warren summarized that view: 'Any serious effort to amend the Constitution should provide the occasion for a great national debate.'

America, discovery of. America was first 'discovered' by migratory bands of Siberian Mongoloids, who entered the Western World toward the end of the last Ice Age by way of Bering Strait. (The recent radiocarbon dating of artifacts suggests that Man first penetrated the continent at least 25,000, perhaps 35,000, years ago.) In the course of millennia these people developed linguistic families, traversed both continents, and became the tribes which Columbus, seeking India, by misapprehension named INDIANS.

The earliest penetration in historical times was made about the year 1000, when LEIF ERICSSON or his kinsman THORFINN KARLSEFNI established a community on 'Vinland,' a place identified in 1963 (by radiocarbon dating of charcoal among Viking artifacts) at L'Anse aux Meadows on the northern tip of Newfoundland. But these voyages of Norsemen were of scant interest to Europeans just emerging from the Dark Ages.

The first effective discovery was that of CHRISTOPHER COLUMBUS, who sighted the Bahamas on 12 October 1492. By his four voyages he gave Europe its first news of the New World (both North and South America) and its Caribbean Islands. Other navigators, also seeking sea routes to the Orient, soon began their voyages. JOHN CABOT embarked on a northern venture in 1497. Vasco da Gama's southern route in 1498 took him to Brazil. On one such enterprise along the west coast of South America in 1501, AMERIGO VESPUCCI concluded that the land mass was not a part of Asia, and his name was given to the entire Western Hemisphere, although in Spain and Portugal for two centuries North America continued to be the 'New World' or 'Indies' or 'West Indies.'

The face of the globe then changed rapidly. The Spanish outpost island of Hispaniola served as a base for further discoveries, including those of BALBOA. The great viceroyalty of NEW SPAIN was created (1535), and from Mexico City the CONQUISTADORS began their penetration of the SOUTHWEST, and dispatched from the SPANISH MAIN their treasure fleets, which were subject to repeated raids by such privateers as FRANCIS DRAKE and JOHN HAWKINS. 'There has been no other conquest like this in the annals of the human race,' says the historian S. E. Morison. 'In one generation the Spaniards acquired more new territory than Rome conquered in five centuries.'

Meanwhile France had sent VERRAZANO (1524) and CARTIER (1534) to follow up Cabot's survey of the northern Atlantic coast of America, and if possible to find a NORTHWEST PASSAGE to the Orient. The English geographer RICHARD HAKLUYT compiled his great travel collection (1589) to supply his countrymen with first-hand accounts of the latest discoveries, hoping thereby to stir them to fresh commercial rivalries with Spain and France. His work bore fruit. At the turn of the 17th century the overseas ventures of such men as WALTER RALEIGH, BARTHOLOMEW GOSNOLD, and HUMPHREY GILBERT opened the eyes of Englishmen to the possibilities of trade and colonization. JOHN SMITH undertook to map and describe in promotion tracts the whole region of 'Virginia,' an area then extending north to New England.

HENRY HUDSON in 1609 gave the Dutch a foothold in territory soon to become NEW NETHERLAND (which later absorbed the short-lived NEW SWEDEN). But the most extensive colonial venture of the 17th century was that inaugurated by CHAMPLAIN in establishing NEW FRANCE (1608), an empire which at its full extent embraced nearly a quarter of the North American continent. With the establishment of colonial settlements, the period of discovery ended, and that of EXPLORATIONS began.

American Academy in Rome (1894) was established as a school of architecture under the presidency of C. F. MCKIM, and chartered in 1905 by act of Congress. It now comprises schools of fine arts and classical studies. Fellowships (for U.S. citizens) are awarded in architecture, painting, music, sculpture, and landscape architecture.

American Academy of Arts and Letters (1904) is the honorary circle of 50 elected members chosen from the National Institute of Arts and Letters (1898). The Institute, with 250 members, is modeled upon the French Academy. 'The actual work of the Academy is to promote American literature and art by giving the stamp of its approval to the best that both the past and the present have to offer.'

American Academy of Arts and Sciences (1780), the second oldest learned society in the U.S., was chartered at Boston with JAMES BOWDOIN as first president. It supports intellectual endeavors in many fields, with emphasis on pure science. Its publications include *Memoirs* (since 1785) and *Proceedings* (since 1846). The latter was superseded (1955) by the quarterly *Daedalus,* notable in the field of behavorial sciences.

American Antiquarian Society (1812), founded by ISAIAH THOMAS at Worcester, Massachusetts, has assembled some 600,000 manuscripts and an immense collection of early American imprints. Its file of American state, county, and local histories, and American newspapers printed before 1820, is unrivaled. Its *Proceedings* (begun in 1843) have been important as the medium for publication of rare items of Americana.

American Bible Society (1816), organized by ELIAS BOUDINOT, distributes translations of the Scripture throughout the world. The entire Bible has been issued in 235 languages, and portions of it in some 1000 other languages and dialects. The Society distributes millions of copies.

American Civil Liberties Union (1920), a privately financed organization, donates its services in cases involving civil rights. It first became nationally known when its director, ARTHUR GARFIELD HAYS, was prominently associated with such legal struggles as the SCOPES TRIAL (1925); the Sweet case (1925), which involved Negro segregation; and the SACCO-VANZETTI CASE (1927).

American Colonization Society (1817–1912) was established with the purpose of removing free Negroes from the U.S. to Liberia. It purchased a tract of land in Africa, and in 1827 sought a congressional appropriation. The northernmost slave states (Virginia, Maryland, and Kentucky) favored the resolution, but it was blocked by the cotton states on the ground that extension of slavery was essential to their welfare.

By 1831 the Society had sent a token number of 1400 Negroes to Africa. Some 15,000 Negroes had been colonized by 1860, after which time the Society functioned chiefly as trustee for the settlement it had helped to create. The number of descendants of Americo-Liberians is estimated today at 20,000.

American Equal Rights Association, see *Woman suffrage movement.*

American Expeditionary Force (A.E.F.), commanded by General JOHN J. PERSHING, served in Europe during World War I. The first troops arrived in France on 26 June 1917, and at the time of the armistice (11 November 1918) some 2,000,000 troops and 4,400,000 tons of cargo had been transported across the Atlantic. The A.E.F. was concentrated in eastern France, in the area east of Verdun that formed the Toul sector. Pershing established his general headquarters at Chaumont.

The American success at CANTIGNY was quickly followed by thrusts at CHATEAU-THIERRY and BELLEAU WOOD (May–June 1918). Some 275,000 American troops were engaged in the second battle of the MARNE (July). The American engagement at ST. MIHIEL (September) preceded the final Allied push, the MEUSE-ARGONNE OFFENSIVE (26 September–11 November), involving 1,200,000 American troops. A.E.F. casualties exceeded 300,000. The last division embarked from France in August 1919, and Pershing and his staff returned to the U.S. in September.

American Federation of Labor (1886) was founded by SAMUEL GOMPERS as a national organization of trade unions. By promoting independent and autonomous trade groups (a reorganization of the Federation of Organized Trade and Labor Unions of the U.S. and Canada formed in 1881) it sought to vie with the centrally controlled unionism of the KNIGHTS OF LABOR. In its efforts to improve the economic status of wage earners the A.F. of L. used strikes and boycotts to force COLLECTIVE BARGAINING.

Gompers was succeeded as president (1924–52) by WILLIAM GREEN, who built up the largest labor federation in the U.S. (7,500,000 members). During the 1930's those favoring an organization based on industrial unionism were led by JOHN L. LEWIS to form the Congress of Industrial Organizations. Green's successor, GEORGE MEANY, arranged for a merger (1955) of the A.F. of L.–C.I.O., which then became the world's largest labor federation, with WALTER REUTHER (then president of C.I.O.) as vice-president in charge of a new industrial union department. The 15,000,000 members of this group are expected to exercise their 'right and duty' to work for increasingly favorable labor legislation. Their state and Federal lobbies are politically potent.

American Fur Company (1808) was chartered by JOHN JACOB ASTOR as a rival to the two Canadian companies, Hudson's Bay Company and the North West Company. After the post at ASTORIA was absorbed by British interests (1812), the company moved out of the Pacific Northwest and took over trade in the Great Lakes region (with headquarters at Mackinac), expanding into the Missouri river basin and the Rocky Mountains. One of the first powerful monopolies, it opened frontier commerce on the Great Lakes and on the chief rivers of the West, greatly affecting Indian policies, land speculation, and settlement. Astor withdrew in 1834 and the company was disbanded during the 1840's.

American Geographical Society (1852), founded in New York, is the oldest geographical society in the U.S. It is primarily a research institution designed to encourage the advancement of geographical knowledge. Its collections of books, periodicals, maps, atlases, and photographs make it the leading American organization for scientific study in its field. It publishes *Geographical Review,* first issued as a *Journal* (1859–1900), and continued until 1916 as a *Bulletin.*

American Historical Association (1884), with headquarters in Washington, D.C., carries on scholarly activities through standing committees and through its quarterly *American Historical Review,* a medium for articles and documents. Since 1932 its Pacific coast branch (est. 1903) has issued the *Pacific Historical Review.*

American language was first informally promoted as a subject deserving study by the New York Philological Society (*fl.* 1788–89), of which NOAH WEBSTER was a member. Two early linguistic scientists who specialized in native elements of American speechways were JOHN PICKERING, whose *Vocabulary* (1816) dealt with Americanisms; and PETER DU PONCEAU, who published (1838) a study of American Indian language systems. The *Dictionary of Americanisms* (1848), compiled by JOHN R. BARTLETT, was a vigorous defense of American speech. His point of view was supported in the 1850's by the philological studies of GEORGE PERKINS MARSH.

In 1889 FRANCIS JAMES CHILD established the American Dialect Society, whose project for a dictionary resulted in Richard H. Thornton's *An American Glossary* (2 vols., 1912; vol. 3, 1939). By the mid 20th century American English had been very fully treated in special DICTIONARIES. The study by H. L. MENCKEN, *The American Language* (1919), has been revised, twice supplemented (1936–48), and abridged (1963).

Generally regarded as the two founders of modern American linguistics are EDWARD SAPIR and LEONARD BLOOMFIELD.

Regional speech and localisms, and the changes wrought by immigrant groups, have been studied by specialists. The most comprehensive journal is *American Speech* (1925–current), issued quarterly, with a bibliography in each issue to serve as a guide to the increasing number of books and articles in the field of speech and linguistics.

American League, see *Baseball.*

American Legion, a national association of the veterans of both World Wars, was founded in Paris and incorporated by act of Congress in 1919. With a membership in 1965 of 2,000,000, it continues, in the words of its preamble, to 'perpetuate one hundred per cent Americanism.' During the 1920's, like the G.A.R. in the 1880's, by the sheer weight of its voting power it intimidated congressmen and held a threat over Presidents who vetoed its repeated demands for increased veterans' bonuses. It sponsors welfare programs, unemployment relief, and Americanization contests.

American Liberty League (1934–40), a conservative organization whose principles were directed against the NEW DEAL, dissolved shortly before World War II. Formally nonpartisan, it embraced an impressive array of dissidents. Leaders among them included such ex-Wilsonians as John W. Davis and Bainbridge Colby, such critics of New Deal financial policies as Alfred E. Smith and the du Ponts, and such southern states' rights proponents as Governor Talmadge of Georgia. In the contest between Roosevelt and Landon they failed to stem President Roosevelt's landslide re-election by a unique electoral margin of 523 to 8.

American Museum of Natural History (1869) in New York City was founded to promote the study of the natural sciences in related fields. It is one of the world's largest institutions devoted to natural history exhibits. It engages in exploration and research, and its publications and facilities for study are extensive. Outstanding collections include exhibits of mammals, fishes, insects, gems and minerals, and especially birds and fossil vertebrates. Its Department of Astronomy is incorporated in the American Museum–Hayden Planetarium (opened in 1935).

American National Red Cross (1881) was founded as a humanitarian society by CLARA BARTON. Since 1905 it has operated under congressional charter, with the President of the U.S. as honorary chairman. (He appoints eight of its 50-member board of governors.) In wartime it functions principally through its medical and nursing services. In peacetime it provides relief on a world-wide scale. Its national disaster relief organization and extensive community services include a blood program serving both civilian and Federal hospitals; the training of millions in first aid, water safety, and home nursing; and the successful utilization of junior and senior high school Red Cross members for local and even international activities. It was supported in 1965 by well over 47,000,000 members, senior and junior.

American Party, see *Know-Nothing Party.*

American Peace Society (1828), founded by WILLIAM LADD, in its early years formally condemned all wars, though it supported the Union in the Civil War and the U.S. Government during both World Wars. Its headquarters were in Washington, and it issued a periodical, *World Affairs*. After the formation of the United Nations (1945), the Society was dissolved.

American Philosophical Society (1743), first scientific organization in America, was established in Philadelphia, with the lawyer Thomas Hopkinson (1709–51) as its first president and Benjamin Franklin as secretary. An outgrowth of the JUNTO, a 'mutual improvement' club, it met irregularly until it was re-organized in 1769 with Franklin as president. Franklin's immediate successors were David Rittenhouse (1791–96) and Thomas Jefferson (1797–1815). From the beginning its membership, which is still limited, has included leaders in science, statecraft, and letters. Its chief publications are *Transactions* (since 1771), *Proceedings* (since 1838), and *Memoirs* (since 1900). Its library, one of the oldest in the country, holds significant collections dealing with the history of science in America and with the American Revolution. From a large endowment the Society makes grants-in-aid for research in a broad field of subjects.

American Samoa, comprising the seven eastern islands of the Samoa group, is a coral atoll 2300 miles southwest of Hawaii. (The western group, originally a New Zealand mandate, has been an independent nation since 1962.) American Samoa became a possession of the U.S. by virtue of a convention with Great Britain and Germany in 1899. It is administered by the Department of the Interior. Some 70 per cent of the land is forest, and its chief exports are fish products and copra. It is racially predominantly Polynesian, with a population in 1960 of about 20,000.

American system, a term coined by Henry Clay in his tariff speech of 30–31 March 1824, was intended to protect American business at a time when tariffs favored foreign markets. Clay urged that a protective tariff be combined with a national system of 'internal improvements' (public works at Federal expense), which would expand the domestic market and lessen U.S. dependence upon overseas sources. With John C. Calhoun, Clay was a nationalist leader who feared the growing particularism of the sections, and his device, intended as a binding force whose strength lay in self-interest, won general support in an era of expanding nationalism. In fact, the 'American system' became an article of faith for the Whig party after its founding in the 1830's.

The phrase 'American system' has also been used to describe the system of interchangeable machinery parts (devised by ELI WHITNEY), which paved the way for mass production.

American Telephone and Telegraph Company (1877) was organized as a joint-stock concern by THEODORE N. VAIL and assumed its present name in 1900. It is the world's largest corporation, controlling some 30 billions of dollars in assets. In 1965 it reported a net income of nearly $2,000,000,000, the second largest in the nation.

AMES, FISHER (1758–1808), son of NATHANIEL AMES, after graduation from Harvard (1774) practiced law and served for eight years in Congress as a Federalist (1789–97). He was influential in putting through Hamilton's financial program and his defense of JAY'S TREATY swayed Congress in its favor. The archetype of the New England conservative, Ames regarded Jeffersonian Republicanism as the road to anarchy and chaos. After retirement his essays and correspondence made him an oracle of the Federalist party.

AMES, JAMES BARR (1846–1910), as professor in Harvard Law School (1877), and later as dean (1895), exerted great influence on the thinking of lawyers, jurists, and teachers of law for two generations. As a disciple of his predecessor in the deanship, CHRISTOPHER C. LANGDELL, he carried forward the case method of study. As writer and teacher he was especially able in defining the meaning and application of COMMON LAW.

AMES, NATHANIEL (1708–64), a physician of Dedham, Massachusetts, compiled one of the most widely circulated almanacs in the colonies (1725–95), which was continued after 1764 by Nathaniel Ames, Jr. It served as a model for Benjamin Franklin's *Poor Richard's*

Almanack, and for others. Ames's almanacs are source material on the intellectual interests of rural communities, especially of those in New England.

AMHERST, JEFFREY, BARON (1717–97), was given the rank of major general and was sent (1758) by William Pitt to command a British expedition against the French in North America. After the British success at Louisbourg, where WILLIAM PEPPERRELL captured the French fortress on Nova Scotia, Amherst replaced JAMES ABERCROMBY as supreme commander in America. He captured Crown Point and Ticonderoga (1759), and Montreal (1760). Appointed governor-general of British North America (1761–63), Amherst conducted the unsuccessful operations against the Indians led by Pontiac, a defeat which brought about his recall. He refused to lead British troops in America during the War of Independence, but served as chief adviser at headquarters. He was later created a peer and made field marshal. The Massachusetts town (and college) of Amherst was named for him.

Amherst College (1821), in Amherst, Massachusetts, is a nonsectarian liberal arts college for men. Chartered in 1825 by Congregationalists, at the start, like similar educational ventures, it fostered a missionary spirit and a classical ideal of education. The Folger Shakespeare Library, in Washington, D.C., was established under its trusteeship. In 1965, with an endowment of $47,700,000 and a faculty of 130, it enrolled over 1000 students.

Amish, see *Mennonites.*

***Amistad* Case** (1841) involved the most famous U.S. Supreme Court decision about slavery before that rendered in the DRED SCOTT CASE. The 54 slaves on the Spanish schooner *Amistad* mutinied near Cuba (1839), murdered part of the crew, and forced the remainder to sail north. Captured by a U.S. warship off Long Island, the mutineers were taken to Connecticut, where a decision of a lower Federal court that the Negroes be surrendered was appealed to the Supreme Court. In the background had been southern demands that the slaves be surrendered to Spain or tried for murder and piracy, while abolitionists, then becoming a vocal political force, insisted upon freedom and provided the legal defense. So persuasive were the arguments of John Quincy Adams (himself not an abolitionist) that the Court ordered the Negroes set free, and they were returned to Africa.

Amnesty Act (1872), see *Civil War Amnesty.*

Anabaptists (not to be confused with BAPTISTS) were members of a Central European religious sect formed after Luther's revolt from Rome. Among the most radical of reform bodies, they were constantly harried, partly for their contention that true religious reform involves social melioration, a view which appealed especially to the oppressed and the disinherited. Absolute pacifists, they condemned oaths, held no public offices, and refused to obey laws in conflict with their consciences. A community of Anabaptists, persecuted in Russia, settled in South Dakota (1874), but it did not long survive as a denomination.

Anarchism, a mass ideology with emotional and religious overtones, may be defined as an attempt to establish equality (justice) by eliminating the state. It opposes capitalism, free enterprise, majority rule, and such co-ordinated groups as trade unions. A description of the historical development of anarchism is difficult since by its nature anarchism can never be an organized movement. Anarchists regard any organizing force as an 'instrument of tyranny.' In the U.S. the HAYMARKET RIOT (1886) and the assassination of President McKinley (1901) by an anarchist led to the enactment of laws forbidding the entry of anarchists from abroad. The names of a few theorists, such as EMMA GOLDMAN, NICOLA SACCO, and BARTOLOMEO VANZETTI, are still remembered.

ANDERSON, CARL DAVID (1905–), professor of physics at the California Institute of Technology (since 1939), has done extensive research in the field of gamma rays and cosmic radiation. With V. F. Hess of Austria he shared the 1936 Nobel Prize in physics for his discovery (1932) of the positron (positively charged electron), thus experimentally confirming postulations about the structure of the universe. In 1937 with Seth Neddermeyer he discovered the heavy electron, or meson, which has a mass some 200 times that of an electron.

ANDERSON, MARIAN (1907–), Negro contralto, won her first successes in Europe, where she began her concert career in 1924. She returned in 1935 to the U.S., where her artistry and rich voice brought her acclaim. In 1939 she became the center of a *cause célèbre* when she was denied the concert facilities of Constitution Hall in Washington (belonging to the D.A.R.), presumably because she was a Negro. The subsequent liberal outcry led to a widespread consideration of current race policies.

Andersonville Prison, largest and most notorious of Confederate stockades for captured Union soldiers, was hastily constructed in Georgia toward the end of the Civil War (February 1864), when the South was working desperately to conserve its dwindling resources of food, clothing, and medical supplies. The bare log enclosure, covering a mere 26 acres and occupied in mid-summer by 32,000 prisoners, became a site of horror. Lack of drugs and doctors, bad sanitation, and overcrowding led to the spread of diseases from which nearly half the prisoners died. Northerners believed that the Confederates had deliberately murdered the captives. In the summer of 1865 the commander, Captain Henry Wirz, was charged with murder, convicted, and hanged. Later investigation revealed that Wirz was faced with conditions that were probably beyond his power to control.

ANDRÉ, JOHN (1751–80), a major serving as adjutant general of the British army during the Revolution, was selected by Sir Henry Clinton to carry on secret negotiations with the American traitor, General BENEDICT ARNOLD, then in command of West Point. In civilian clothes, André began his return on horseback to Clinton's headquarters in New York, having concluded arrangements with Arnold for the betrayal of the fortress of West Point (21 September 1780). André was apprehended and searched, and incriminating documents were found on him. Arnold, informed of André's capture, fled aboard the British sloop of war *Vulture,* which had brought André to the meeting place. Clinton sought André's release on the ground that the negotiation had taken place under a flag of truce, but he did so in vain, for, as André informed his chief, 'The event of coming within an Enemy's posts and of changing my dress, which led to my present Situation, were contrary to my own Inclination as they were to your orders.' He was tried by a military board on 29 September, convicted, and hanged three days later.

ANDREWS, CHARLES MCLEAN (1863–1943), Connecticut-born historian, trained at Johns Hopkins and taught there and at Bryn Mawr before accepting a chair in American history at Yale (1910–31). He devoted his principal studies to the influence of British imperial policies in shaping the settlements along the eastern seaboard. His chief labor, *The Colonial Period of American History* (4 vols., 1934–38), deals with English origins. He saw the Revolution as a conflict between the colonial tendency toward increasing self-government and England's imperial aims.

ANDROS, SIR EDMUND (1637–1714), was appointed governor of New York (1674–81) by the Duke of York (who became James II in 1685). When the Northern Colonies were consolidated as the DOMINION OF NEW ENGLAND, James bestowed the vice-regency upon Andros (1686–89), who administered the reforms necessary to meet the growing power of New France to the north. With a view toward creating a neat administration with a centralized control (like that effected by France), James extended the authority of Andros over New York and the Jerseys (1688).

Although Andros took pains not to interfere with the churches, schools, and the college of the Puritan commonwealth, his exercise of the newly created authority made him unpopular. When he sought to alter existing charters, colonists were aroused to the point of hiding the Connecticut instrument under CHARTER OAK. When the colonists learned in April 1689 that William of Orange had succeeded James, they deposed and arrested Andros in a local 'glorious revolution.'

The failure of the dominion gave warning to the crown that the provinces were best governed by their local assemblies, each colony managing its affairs under the loosest supervision. Internal dissension was too great a risk so long as the French and Spanish threat persisted. Former charters were therefore restored, and Andros was returned to England, ostensibly for trial. He was immediately released without charges being pressed. He later served as governor of Virginia (1692–97), but was recalled as a result of charges preferred by the influential Virginia clergyman JAMES BLAIR, whose irascibility outmatched the imperiousness of Andros.

ANGHIERA, PIETRO MARTIRE, see *Martyr, Peter.*

Anglican Church, see *Protestant Episcopal Church.*

ANGLIN, MARGARET MARY (1876–1958), Canadian-born actress, made her New York debut in 1894 in Bronson Howard's *Shenandoah*. She won fame in such plays as *Cyrano de Bergerac* and *Camille,* and especially in her later performances of *Antigone, Electra,* and *Medea.*

Annapolis, see *Naval Academy, U.S.*

Annapolis Convention (September 1786), called by the Virginia legislature at the instigation of James Madison, met in the State House at Annapolis, Maryland. Disputes had arisen over navigation of the Potomac, and delegates from New York, New Jersey, Pennsylvania, Delaware, and Virginia assembled to work out a system of interstate commerce. Alexander Hamilton proposed, in view of the complexity of issues bound up with the question under discussion, that all the states should convene in order to 'render the constitution of the Federal government adequate to the exigencies of the Union.' Madison and Hamilton used this Annapolis meeting as a way by which the Articles of Confederation might be revised. In February 1787 the Annapolis congress invited all states to a convention, for the sole purpose of such revision, to be held at Philadelphia in May. Thus did those two statesmen adroitly guide the states into the FEDERAL CONSTITUTIONAL CONVENTION.

ANTHONY, SUSAN BROWNELL (1820–1906), was born in Adams, Massachusetts, the daughter of a Quaker manufacturer. In the decade preceding the Civil War she made antislavery, feminism, and temperance her causes. In the national election of 1872 she deliberately courted arrest by attempting to cast a vote. Vigorously militant, she ignored frequent insults, greatly advanced her cause, and won international acclaim. With ELIZABETH CADY STANTON and others she collaborated in writing the first three volumes of the *History of Woman Suffrage* (1881–86), still authoritative.

Anthracite Strike (1902), called by 150,000 members of the UNITED MINE WORKERS under the leadership of John Mitchell, was a bid for higher wages, shorter hours, and union recognition. It lasted four months and paralyzed the industry. George F. Baer, president of the Morgan Company–controlled Reading Railroad and a key figure in the railroad-and-coal 'empire,' as spokesman for the operators unintentionally roused sympathy for the miners by his grotesque observation that 'The rights and interests of the laboring man will be protected and cared for, not by the agitators, but by the Christian men to whom God in his infinite wisdom has given the control of the property interests of the country.'

The first attempt of President Theodore Roosevelt to offer Federal mediation was rejected. But when the President threatened to take over the mines, the operators were persuaded to accept a committee of arbitration. The strike ended in a signal victory for the miners and a triumph for the cause of arbitration.

Anthropology, see *Ethnology.*

Antietam, Battle of (17 September 1862), took place in Maryland, near the Virginia border. After his victory of Second Bull Run (Manassas) on 30 August, Lee crossed the Potomac to invade Maryland. McClellan learned of Lee's maneuver, and with a Union force of 70,000 moved south toward Frederick Town where Lee's 30,000 men were concentrated. (Lee had sent Jackson's corps south and Longstreet's west, expecting that McClellan would need some time to reorganize after his defeat at Bull Run.) At Sharpsburg, on Antietam Creek, Lee took up his battle position. McClellan's unco-ordinated attacks mauled Lee's army but did not rout it. Lee's entire force had been engaged before darkness ended the battle. McClellan still had 20,000 men in reserve, yet on the 18th he did not renew the attack, and that night Lee was able to recross the Potomac into Virginia.

The Union dead numbered some 12,000, and the Confederate losses were proportionally as many. This nearly decisive battle, which could have ended the war had McClellan pressed his advantage, placed the Confederate armies thenceforward entirely on the defensive. Politically it gave advantage to the North, and five days later Lincoln issued his Emancipation Proclamation.

Anti-Federalists were the political group led by such able statesmen as Patrick Henry (Virginia), George Clinton (New York), and Elbridge Gerry (Massachusetts). They opposed ratification of the Constitution on the ground that it relinquished too much state sovereignty and did not spell out a bill of individual rights. Not yet a political party, the group became one during Washington's second administration, in an alignment broadly shaped by mercantile versus agrarian principles. From the split developed the FEDERALIST and the DEMOCRATIC-REPUBLICAN parties.

Anti-Imperialism, following the Spanish-American War (1898), was a reform movement that opposed colonial expansion. It cut across party lines and enlisted the support of such political spokesmen as George F. Hoar, George F. Edmunds, John Sherman, and Thomas B. Reed. Leaders in the ranks of labor, education, and social service, of the press and pulpit joined in denouncing IMPERIALISM. Samuel Gompers, Charles W. Eliot, Jane Addams, E. L. Godkin, and Henry Van Dyke spoke with one voice against the annexation of the Philippines. They were supported by such leaders in business as Andrew Carnegie, and such men of letters as Mark Twain and William Vaughn Moody. William Jennings Bryan made anti-imperialism the principal presidential campaign issue in 1900, and although he lost the election, he substantially influenced later campaigns.

Anti-Inflation Act, see *Economic Stabilization Act.*

Anti-Masonic Party (1826), first of the THIRD PARTY MOVEMENTS, was a one-idea formation similar in social significance to such later groups as the FREE-SOIL, KNOW-NOTHING, and PROHIBITION parties. Although FREEMASONS are members of a fraternal order of which fifteen Presidents have been members, during the period 1826–38 Freemasonry aroused such attacks that states legislated against it.

The Anti-Masonic party was formed in consequence of the disappearance of one Morgan, a western New York bricklayer alleged to have betrayed his oath by divulging lodge secrets in a book. The Morgan case created a political issue involving the question how many oaths of allegiance a man may give. Politicians saw vote-catching possibilities in the reaction to the event and made capital of hysteria. A corpse dredged from the Niagara river elicited the comment that it was 'good enough Morgan until after election.'

Anti-Masonry spread from New York to neighboring states and influenced many local and state elections. The Baltimore national Anti-Masonic convention of 1831 nominated William Wirt for President, and in 1832 he won seven electoral votes. Some 100 Anti-Masonic newspapers sprang up in New York and Pennsylvania, and in the 1832 election the party drew enough Whig support away from Clay to help sweep Jackson into office. But the issues had no lasting attraction, and the party faded away.

Anti-Monopoly Parties, independent reform groups, were organized during the 1870's by Western farmers. The party platforms made issues chiefly over tax reductions and the elimination of railroad abuses. The parties were of brief duration, for they either disappeared or merged with other organizations such as the GREENBACK PARTY. In 1884 an Anti-Monopoly party was formed at Chicago, with a program designed to assist farmers. It subsequently fused with the Greenback Labor party to become part of the POPULIST PARTY (1891).

ANTIN, MARY (Mary Antin Grabau) (1881–1949), emigrated with her family from Poland (1894), and attended public schools in Boston. She studied at Columbia and Barnard (1901–4), but before receiving a degree became a settlement worker at Hale House in Boston. In her autobiography *The Promised Land* (1912) she described the hardships and aspirations of European Jews, and extoled America as a land of opportunity for the persecuted immigrant child from the ghetto.

Antinomian Controversy was a theological dispute brought about in Boston (1636) by ANNE HUTCHINSON. Antinomianism holds that the elect, saved by their belief in Christ and justified by their faith, are freed from the moral law as set forth in the Old Testament by the new dispensation of grace as set forth in the gospels. Believers are thus directly infused with the holy spirit, and therefore are prompted by an inner light, an explicit revelation, in matters of conduct.

Such an extreme interpretation has been known to lead to fanaticism, although it never has among the Quakers, nor did it in the instance of Anne Hutchinson or of Roger Williams. Mistress Hutchinson preached to small gatherings, and among her converts were her brother-in-law, the Rev. JOHN WHEELWRIGHT, and the governor of the Massachusetts Bay Colony, HENRY VANE. The issue thus became political. Quite clearly the authority of such orthodox Puritan leaders as John Cotton and John Winthrop was directly challenged. Anne Hutchinson was banished and Vane returned to England.

Antioch College (est. 1853) was founded at Yellow Springs, Ohio, as a coeducational institution by HORACE MANN, who served as its first president. It fosters a co-operative program whereby its students alternate periods of study with periods of full work, taking paid jobs in communities across the country to learn how people live and work. In 1965, with a faculty of 125, it enrolled 1800 students.

Anti-Rent War (1839–46), an agitation by landholders in New York along the Hudson river, reached a climax after the death (1839) of STEPHEN VAN RENSSELAER. Farmers had long resented the feudal system by which the wealthy PATROONS from colonial times had exercised their manorial rights. The so-called 'Helderberg War' broke out when Van Rensselaer heirs tried to collect some $400,000 in back rent, due in produce, labor, or money. Governor Seward quelled this uprising of farmers with the militia, but similar disturbances ensued in neighboring areas, and Anti-Rent Associations brought political pressure to bear. In 1846 the state legislature abolished the old tenure laws, which by their nature exacted homage, and old leases were converted into fee simple ownership. Cooper's trilogy *Littlepage Manuscripts* (1845–46) traces the history of this agrarian anachronism.

Anti-Saloon League, see *Temperance movement*.

Antislavery societies were humanitarian organizations that condemned the institution of SLAVERY on the ground that personal freedom is an inalienable right. Antislavery sentiment, expressed by religious groups from the earliest colonial days, was first formally recorded when a group of Germantown Quakers drew up (1688) a memorial protesting slavery. In 1701 a similar resolution was registered in a Boston town meeting, and during the 18th century the right of the Negro to be free was defended by such statesmen as James Oglethorpe, Thomas Jefferson, and Benjamin Franklin.

The earliest antislavery society was founded at Philadelphia (1775), with Franklin and Dr. Benjamin Rush among its first presidents. Ten years later a similar organization was headed in New York by John Jay, and thereafter the number multiplied. During the 1830's the ABOLITION MOVEMENT became militant. After formation of the New England Anti-Slavery Society (1832) and (in New York) the American Anti-Slavery Society (1833), groups sprang up in such numbers that by 1840 there were some 2000 such organizations with a total membership of 200,000. Their abolition propaganda helped create an insurgent bloc in Congress, leading to the formation of the LIBERTY PARTY (1840), the FREE-SOIL PARTY (1847–48), and divisions that coalesced during the 1850's to form the REPUBLICAN PARTY.

Antitrust laws are regulations enacted to control unfair business practices, or business combinations which are adjudged conspiracies in RESTRAINT OF TRADE. The practice of LAISSEZ FAIRE in American enterprise has been traditionally upheld in court rulings, but during the 1880's the public awoke to the need for regulation of large-scale corporate practices then being developed. The problem was complex because states, not the federal government (except in a limited area), charter corporations. By law, corporations are 'persons,' and thus are protected from state legislation if the court decides that they have been deprived of property without 'due process of law.'

The issue of monopolistic practice was forced into politics by labor spokesmen and independent producers, wholesalers, and other middlemen, and by so vocal a citizenry that both major parties in 1888 built their platforms on the pledge of opposition to trusts and monopolies. The first formal result was the SHERMAN ANTITRUST ACT (1890). That statute was soon rendered ineffective by Supreme Court decisions. In 1914 it was amended by the CLAYTON ANTITRUST ACT and by the creation of the FEDERAL TRADE COMMISSION, both of which still substantially control the issues of fair practice in trade.

ANZA, JUAN BAUTISTA DE (1735–88), one of the most notable Spanish frontiersmen, was sent by the viceroy of New Spain to occupy Alta (Upper) California. Accompanied by Father GARCÉS, in 1774 he led a large party to the Gila river, across the desert to San Gabriel, north of Los Angeles. A year later he guided colonists to Monterey and moved on to found San Francisco, where a presidio was dedicated (1776) and a mission established. He was later governor of New Mexico (1777–88). Journals and diaries are incorporated in *Anza's California Expeditions* (ed. by H. E. Bolton, 5 vols., 1930), and *Forgotten Frontiers* (ed. by A. B. Thomas, 1932). They are important source material for the history of the early West.

Anzio landings were made by British and American troops north of the German lines at Anzio, Italy, early in 1944. Their purpose was to cut German communications with Rome and to force the evacuation of Kesselring's command of the hilltop (monastery abbey) town of Cassino. Both sides suffered heavy casualties, and the bold Allied sortie achieved no immediate results.

Anzus Council (1952) was established at Honolulu by Australia, New Zealand, and the U.S. as a mutual security organization. It is one of several treaty agreements into which the U.S. entered during the 1950's.

Apache Indians, of Athapascan stock, were groups of unsettled tribes in the Southwest. Linguistically related to the NAVAHO, they were expert horsemen, notoriously predatory, and they constantly terrorized PUEBLOS and whites with their guerrilla warfare. All the Apache tribes practiced some agriculture, but they subsisted principally on game and wild plants. They did not weave cloth or make pottery to any extent, but their baskets are prized by collectors. After the death of COCHISE and the capture of GERONIMO (1886), most were settled on reservations in Arizona.

Apostle of the Indies, see *Las Casas.*

Apostle to the Indians, see *Eliot, John.*

Appalachia is the term applied to the region extending from Pittsburgh, Pennsylvania, to Birmingham, Alabama, comprising about 165,000 square miles. Despite the wealth of some of its cities, which are pockets of plenty in the midst of poverty, during the 1950's it had become the nation's biggest economic problem and the largest and most stubborn rural slum. It is chronically depressed; although it has rich and largely untapped resources, it is inadequately developed. Congress in 1964 attempted an anti-poverty drive, aimed at improving the economy of the area.

Appalachian Mountains form the vast belt extending from Newfoundland to central Alabama. Geologically they were formed by the folding of sedimentary rocks, and are much older than the Rocky Mountains and the Coast Ranges. The system has no dominating altitudes and no perpetually snow-capped summits. The highest peak is Mount Mitchell (6,684 ft.) in the Black Mountains. The central sections were long a barrier against westward migration, for the eastern escarpment is steep, with few passes. For a description of individual ranges, see WHITE MOUNTAINS, GREEN MOUNTAINS, CATSKILL MOUNTAINS, ALLEGHENY MOUNTAINS, BLUE RIDGE, BLACK MOUNTAINS, GREAT SMOKY MOUNTAINS, CUMBERLAND PLATEAU. (The ADIRONDACK MOUNTAINS are not part of the system.)

APPLEGATE, JESSE (1811–88), born in Kentucky, in 1843 emigrated to Oregon. There he helped organize the Provisional Government (1845) and the legislative body that formed the Oregon Territory (1849). As surveyor general he carried out exploration which opened the Applegate Trail, a wagon route to California. *A Day with the Cow Column in 1843* (ed. by Joseph Schafer, 1934) is his account of the 'great migration' along the OREGON TRAIL.

APPLESEED, JOHNNY, see *Chapman, John.*

Appomattox, a village in Virginia, was the scene of the surrender of the Confederate Army of Northern Virginia to the Union Army of the Potomac, 9 April 1865. On the night of 2 April, Lee had been forced to evacuate Petersburg and Richmond. He attempted further resistance by pushing toward Lynchburg, but at Appomattox Courthouse, surrounded on three sides by Federal troops, he ordered a white flag to be displayed. About 1:00 Lee rode into the village. At the house of Major Wilmer McLean, Lee, in new full-dress uniform, faced Grant, dressed in an unbuttoned private's blouse.

After formal greetings and brief small talk, Grant wrote out the generous terms of surrender. Officers would retain their side arms, and surrendered troops would be paroled. 'Let all men who claim to own a horse or mule take the animals home with them to work their little farms.' On 12 April the Confederate troops marched into an open field, laid down their weapons, and the Union guard presented arms. Grant peremptorily stopped the cheer that broke out: 'The war is over; the rebels are our countrymen again.'

Arabella (*Arbella*), flagship of the fleet of seventeen sail chartered by the Massachusetts Bay Company, entered Salem harbor on 12 June 1630. The fleet bore 900 to 1000 men and women, founders of the Bay Colony.

Arapaho Indians, a numerous Plains tribe of Algonquian stock, ranged from Arkansas to Wyoming. They resisted the encroachments of frontiersmen, and under the leadership of the CHEYENNE they were often a hazard to traders along the SANTA FE TRAIL. Their annual SUN DANCE was a major tribal event. Remnants of the tribe were settled on reservations in Oklahoma and Wyoming.

Arbitration, industrial, is the final resort in COLLECTIVE BARGAINING. Employers and unions agree upon a state or Federal arbitrating agency, whose decision in the dispute is final and enforceable in the courts. The most important mediation agency is the Conciliation Service of the U.S. Department of Labor, established in 1913. A number of laws have dealt with the settlement of labor disputes, such as the many RAILROAD MEDIATION ACTS (1898 and after), the TAFT-HARTLEY ACT (1947), and the LABOR-MANAGEMENT REPORTING AND DISCLOSURE ACT (1959).

Arbitration, international, occurs when two or more nations, unable to settle a dispute by direct negotiation, submit the controversy to a disinterested tribunal. JAY'S TREATY (1794) established a precedent for such arbitration by setting up mixed commissions to examine problems rising from the terms of the TREATY OF PARIS of 1783. The successful arbitration of the U.S. and Britain in the matter of the ALABAMA CLAIMS and the BERING SEA CONTROVERSY led other nations to recognize the possibility of peaceful settlement of disputes, and paved the way for the PERMANENT COURT OF ARBITRATION (the Hague Tribunal) in 1899.

At the close of World War I the U.S. helped formulate the Covenant of the League of Nations, Article XIII of which provided for arbitration. The BUENOS AIRES CONFERENCE (1936) called for submission to arbitration of questions of a juridical nature by inter-American nations. With the creation of the United Nations (1945), new machinery for peaceful settlement of differences was introduced by the establishment of its International Court of Justice, which gives advisory opinions and renders judgments that are final. The U.S. has settled some 100 disputes with 25 nations or more through the process of arbitration.

Arbor Day, tree-planting day, was first observed in Nebraska (April 1872). It is now observed throughout the U.S. and Canada, usually in late April or early May, and in some states it is a legal holiday.

Arbuthnot and Ambrister Affair was an incident that occurred at the time of the annexation of Florida (1818). After his attack on the Seminole Indians, who had been making war on American settlers, General Andrew Jackson captured and hanged Alexander Arbuthnot, a Scots trader who had warned the Indians of the impending raid, and court-martialed and shot an English trader, Robert Ambrister, who had stirred up an Indian uprising. The British press and public denounced the 'ruffian' who had 'murdered' two subjects of the crown, demanding an apology and reparation. The British government ignored the incident. Secretary of War Calhoun wished to arrest and try Jackson for his high-handed course, but Secretary of State Adams vigorously defended the general, and President Monroe took no action.

The episode took on further implications. At the international level England chose as a matter of policy not to interfere in American affairs. On the domestic level the affair was revived in 1831 by W. H. CRAWFORD, who, wishing to ruin Calhoun politically, revealed to Jackson (then President) what had taken place thirteen years before in the cabinet meeting. The breach in relations between President Jackson and Vice President Calhoun was thereby further widened.

Archaeology, closely associated in the U.S. with ETHNOLOGY, had its beginnings in the 19th century with investigations of the life and culture of aboriginal groups. The work of ALBERT GALLATIN, JOHN L. STEPHENS, E. G. SQUIER, DANIEL BRINTON, and A. F. A. BANDELIER was carried into the 20th century by such authorities in the American field as CLARK WISSLER. Studies of the BASKET MAKERS, CLIFF DWELLERS, MOUND BUILDERS, and the FOLSOM CULTURE have shed light on early North American civilizations. Field investigations are conducted by major universities and such organizations as the METROPOLITAN MUSEUM OF ART, the AMERICAN MUSEUM OF NATURAL HISTORY, and the SMITHSONIAN INSTITUTION.

Archangel and Siberian Interventions (1918–20) were ordered by President Wilson in July 1918 in response to repeated appeals toward the close of World War I by the British and French, who judged such action essential to the defeat of Germany. The whole affair was a misadventure which, in the words of Secretary of War Baker, 'will always illustrate the eccentricities of a remote and irrational emanation from the central madness of a warring world.'

Wilson rejected intervention against the Soviets but agreed to send a token force to guard military stores and to encourage the formation of new Russian forces in remote Siberia. He promised aid to a Czech legion stranded at Vladivostok, erroneously believing that the Czechs were endangered by armed German and Austrian prisoners. He disregarded all pressure to participate in direct military intervention.

In September 1918 an American expeditionary force of 5000 arrived in Archangel, having been shifted from Murmansk and placed under British command. They consequently became involved in skirmishes rising out of Soviet raids upon their positions. When the war ended in November, Wilson insisted that they return as soon as feasible. Nothing had been accomplished and their objectives were construed by the Soviets as counterrevolutionary.

Meanwhile a second contingent of 9000 men under General William S. Graves had arrived in Vladivostok at a time when the Czechs, who held much of eastern Siberia, had allied themselves with Russian underground elements and were battling the new Red Army of that area. The Japanese had gone far beyond the earlier Allied agreement for joint action by sending a force, not of 7000 but of 72,000, to hold northern Siberia. Graves stoutly resisted every pressure to depart from his instructions of avoiding military intervention against the Reds, but the situation got out of hand. American policy makers wished to wait for the final decisions of the peace conference at Paris, and refused to leave the field to Japan. Though American troops were not used in the ill-starred Kolchak counterrevolution, they did engage in two skirmishes with the Reds. Seemingly the U.S. had joined in the attempt to destroy Bolshevism. As Graves was ruefully aware, he was fighting the wrong war, at the wrong time, in the wrong place, and against the wrong enemy. The troops were withdrawn by April 1920. In 1933, after Litvinov, Soviet ambassador to Washington, had been shown confidential U.S. documents on the Siberian episode, he publicly withdrew all Soviet claims arising from U.S. intervention in Siberia.

See George F. Kennan, *Russia and the West under Lenin and Stalin* (1960).

Architecture in America began in the 17th and 18th centuries with reproduction of styles brought from Europe but modified by the exigencies of climate and the use of native materials. The chief models were Spanish in Florida, the Southwest, and California; French in the Mississippi valley; Dutch in New York; and predominantly English elsewhere. Log cabins, unknown in England, were introduced by the Swedes (or Finns) along the Delaware and became the prevailing Scotch-Irish frontier dwellings. The structures of 17th-century New England, a few of which are still preserved in Salem, Massachusetts, were built of timber frame, tightly sheathed against the weather, with leaded windows and a massive and supporting central fireplace. After 1700 such houses were generally replaced by others built in the English baroque style (itself provincial), derived largely from illustrations representing houses designed by Sir Christopher Wren and his followers. Though the most elaborate, like Stratford and Westover, were built in the South, those of New England became more typical of later American practice (symmetrical, with double hung windows, dormers, and sometimes with chimneys at either end). Naved and steepled churches, in the manner of Wren and Gibbs, began to replace the square meetinghouses. The buildings designed by PETER HARRISON, the foremost American architect of the mid-18th century, carried forward the Wren tradition.

The European reaction against baroque, which had set in by 1750, was reflected in America by a CLASSIC REVIVAL, and Roman forms, imitated by Adam in England, toward the end of the century characterized the work of the professional architect CHARLES BULFINCH and such carpenter builders as SAMUEL MCINTIRE and ASHER BENJAMIN. Coinciding with the post-Revolutionary period, their architecture is known as 'Federal.' The freest use of antique forms was that begun by THOMAS JEFFERSON, who directly imitated a Roman temple for the state capitol at Richmond (1785), because he believed that such forms best embodied the ideals of the new Republic. He lent support to L'ENFANT, who planned the city of Washington, and he consulted LATROBE in designing the University of Virginia. The gleaming Greek temples set into the American landscape (in the South until the Civil War) attest the vitality of this particular impulse.

But the neo-classical forms were too fixed to satisfy the American need for mobility. The European 'picturesque' movement found its champions after 1840 in such landscape architects as A. J. DOWNING, CALVERT VAUX, and FREDERICK LAW OLMSTED. Asymmetrical, nature-evoking suburbs, like Riverside, Illinois (1859), spread throughout the U.S.

The monumental masonry building of the era, whether 'Second Empire' (Philadelphia City Hall) or 'Gothic Revival' (Smithsonian Institution), had the quality of 'masculinity,' as it was termed. RICHARD UPJOHN and JAMES RENWICK were leading exponents of this new phase of Gothic revival. The full flower of such exuberance, in wood, masonry, and iron and glass alike, blossomed in the CENTENNIAL EXPOSITION (1876). At its worst the exuberance expressed itself in such useless and ostentatious decoration as filigree scrolls carved by jigsaw.

The organization and professionalization of architecture in the U.S. began with the founding of the American Institute of Architects (1857) by Richard Upjohn. Schools of architecture began to emerge: the first, at Massachusetts Institute of Technology (1866), was followed by similar departments at Yale (1869), Illinois (1870), and Cornell (1871). But until the turn of the century the most promising students of architecture usually received their training abroad.

Yet at the Centennial itself a reaction was perceptible. The reproductions of colonial houses were related to new work already being done by H. H. RICHARDSON. Whether built of heavy stone or of wood clad with shingles, Richardson's buildings created a new image of permanence and solidarity, and as a designer he laid a more lasting groundwork than any other architect of his time, either in the U.S. or in Europe. The shingled houses built during the 1880's by scores of talented architects working under his influence directly shaped the concepts of FRANK LLOYD WRIGHT, who outlived the later 19th- and early 20th-century academic and eclectic traditions, best represented by the firm of MC KIM, MEAD, AND WHITE, and by BERTRAM GOODHUE, RALPH ADAMS CRAM, CASS GILBERT, and CHARLES PLATT. It was Wright's teacher LOUIS SULLIVAN who developed the SKYSCRAPER, which together with the complex of highway interchanges, has created an architectural image that is uniquely American.

Wright's early work crucially affected modern architecture in Europe. The arrival in the U.S. of such Europeans as WALTER GROPIUS and LUDWIG MIES VAN DER ROHE heralded what became in the 1930's a truly INTERNATIONAL STYLE. Wright, however, did not approve of the impersonality which often characterized that style.

American architecture, significantly influenced by Sullivan and Wright, after 1950 was represented in the structures designed by such younger professionals as PHILIP JOHNSON, LOUIS KAHN, PAUL RUDOLPH, and EERO SAARINEN. The combination of functional interiors, decorative exteriors, and landscaping (in part absorbed from a study of Japanese modes) has been increasingly applied to designs for airports, schools, and shopping centers. Today architects in the U.S. are especially known for the corporate organization of their firms. Such, for example, is the Architects Collaborative (TAC), first headed by Gropius, and so named to 'typify a concept,' thus expressing a faith in teamwork.

Archives, see *Historical Sources and Archives, Historical Records Survey, National Archives.*

ARGALL, SIR SAMUEL (1572–1626), English navigator and adventurer, first went to Virginia in 1609 to discover a short route across the ocean. In the following year he conducted Lord Delaware to Jamestown, returning to England with him in 1611, after supplying the struggling colony with grain, seed, and livestock. On later voyages to Virginia and New England he aided English colonists against the French, but his service as deputy governor of Virginia (1617–19) was cut short because of his questionable official practices. He managed to justify his conduct and subsequently (1625) became an admiral, capturing rich prizes, and serving as a member of the New England Royal Council.

Argonne Offensive, see *Meuse-Argonne.*

Arikara Indians, of Caddoan stock, related to the PAWNEE, had long been inhabitants of North and South Dakota, and of the Platte valley in Nebraska, when white men encountered them. They built substantial houses in stockaded villages, hunted bison, and cultivated garden produce, especially maize. The French traded with them as early as 1700, and Lewis and Clark found them friendly in 1804, but encroachments on their hunting grounds led to conflicts with white settlers, which were resolved by a treaty in 1825. Warfare, particularly with the Sioux, and disease decimated them. In the late 19th century the remnants were settled on a reservation in North Dakota.

Arizona (the name derives from Puma Indian, 'little spring place') was admitted to the Union (1912) as the 48th state. The area was first explored in 1540 by CORONADO, who was searching in the SOUTHWEST for the rumored 'Seven Cities of Cíbola.' During the 17th century Franciscan missionaries labored among the Hopi, as did the Jesuit EUSEBIO KINO, who after 1700 founded missions, the sole centers of European influence until the beginning of Mexican rule (1821). Apache raids limited white settlements. The treaty of GUADALUPE HIDALGO (1848) and the GADSDEN PURCHASE (1853) made Arizona a part of the U.S. It was designated a territory in 1863.

Arizona is a plateau of the Rocky Mountains, crossed by the Colorado river. A region of deserts and mountains, it retained its frontier character until the 1920's. It is the site of one national monument, Painted Desert, and of two national parks, Grand Canyon (1919) and Petrified Forest (1962). The state ranks thirteenth in the value of its mineral production, chiefly copper. Although it has built much of its economy around the tourist trade, it is rapidly becoming a manufacturing state, with power supplied by massive dams (Coolidge, Hoover, Glen Canyon) on the Colorado. These changes are reflected in a phenomenal growth in population, which nearly doubled in the decade 1950–60. The population of Phoenix, the capital and commercial center, jumped from 106,000 to 439,000, and that of Tucson, a winter and health resort, from 45,000 to 213,000. Extensive tracts are set aside as Indian reservations, where the population (Hopi, Navaho, Apache) exceeds 66,000. The leading institution of higher learning, the University of Arizona (Tucson, est. 1885), in 1965 enrolled 18,700 students.

Arkansas, in the SOUTHEAST region of the U.S., was a part of the Louisiana Purchase (1803), organized as a territory in 1819, and admitted to the Union in 1836 as the 25th state. (The present spelling and pronunciation [*Ark'-an-saw*] was adopted by legislative action in 1881; the word is a French variant of Kansas, and is spelled *Akansas* on a map of 1718.) It was first explored by DE SOTO (1541), later by MARQUETTE and JOLLIET (1673), and most significantly by LA SALLE and TONTI (1682), who took possession of the Mississippi valley in the name of France. Tonti established a Catholic mission (1689) on the Arkansas river and developed an extensive trade with the English in Carolina. Most of the early settlers were tied into the cotton-growing southern economy, and at the outbreak of the Civil War the state joined the Confederacy. It was readmitted to the Union in 1868.

During the depression of the 1930's dispossessed sharecropping 'Arkies,' both Negroes and whites, migrated (like the 'Okies' in neighboring Oklahoma) to California. Recent efforts to diversify industry and farming have given new vigor to the state's economy, centered on lumbering, cotton growing, and bauxite mining. Little Rock, the capital, with a population (in 1960) of 108,000, is the commercial center. The mineral baths of Hot Springs were set aside in 1921 as a national park. Best known among the institutions of higher learning is the University of Arkansas (Fayetteville, est. 1872).

Arlington National Cemetery, located at Fort Myer, Virginia, directly across the Potomac from Washington, D.C., is on property originally part of the estate of George Washington and later of Robert E. Lee. Administered by the Department of the Army, it was established (1864) to pay tribute to the memory of those who have honored their nation, whether in peace or war. It is the site of the TOMB OF THE UNKNOWNS.

Arminianism is a doctrine promoted by followers of Jacobus Arminius (1560–1609), Dutch theologian and founder of the anti-Calvinist Remonstrant school in the Reformed church. In an age of enforced uniformity his position appealed to those of liberal temper. Arminians held that God's sovereignty is exercised in compatibility with the freedom of man, that all believers (not merely the elect) may be assured of salvation, that a regenerated man is free to will and perform the right, and that such believers are able to live without sin. This point of view was later shared by Unitarians and Methodists. The doctrines led Jonathan Edwards to react by attacking the writings of the Boston ministers CHARLES CHAUNCY and JONATHAN MAYHEW, and to defend Calvinism in *Freedom of Will.* The appeal of Arminianism was especially strong on the frontier, where doctrinal theology was uncongenial. It also attracted those who argued for a larger tolerance in matters of human duties, and who stressed the equality of all men in the sight of God.

Armistice Day, see *Veterans' Day.*

Armory Show (1913) was an exhibit of art held in New York City at the Armory of the 69th Regiment by the Association of American Painters and Sculptors under its president, ARTHUR DAVIES. Aided by the modernist group called THE EIGHT, the exhibit introduced contemporary European art to an unprepared, shocked, but curious America. Examples of distortion and vivid colors used to evoke emotion created an interest in POSTIMPRESSIONISM and gave impetus to the collecting of such modern painters as Matisse, Derain, and Braque. The Armory Show became a symbol of America's artistic coming of age.

ARMOUR, PHILIP DANFORTH (1832–1901), laid the foundation of his fortune by selling provisions in California during the gold rush (1852–56). After heading a wholesale grocery and commission business in Milwaukee (1863), he established a meat-packing plant (Armour and Co.) in Chicago (1868). Following the method inaugurated by GUSTAVUS SWIFT, he created a nation-wide distributing system, using refrigerated railroad cars and warehouses. After he gained control of stockyards, he began to develop a wide variety of by-products. The stockyards were investigated by the federal government during the Spanish-American War, and when Upton Sinclair's exposé of the loathsome conditions there was published in *The Jungle* (1906) an aroused public demanded Federal action. This culminated in the Meat Inspection Act and the PURE FOOD AND DRUG ACT.

Armour's bequest of $100,000 for the establishment of a mission for poor Chicago youngsters was a start toward the technical institution bearing the family name.

Arms Embargo, see *Neutrality Acts.*

ARMSTRONG, EDWIN HOWARD (1890–1954), professor of electrical engineering at Columbia after 1936, was associated with M. I. PUPIN in electrical research. Important among his inventions are the super-heterodyne circuit (1918), basic to radio receivers; the super-regenerative circuit, used in two-way radio systems; and the method of eliminating static in radio by means of frequency modulation (1939).

ARMSTRONG, JOHN (1758–1843), aide-de-camp to Horatio Gates during the War of Independence, in 1783 drew up the abortive NEWBURGH ADDRESSES. He later served as U.S. Senator from New York (1800–1804) and as Jefferson's minister to France (1804–10). He was briefly Madison's Secretary of War (1813–14), but the disasters of the War of 1812, notably the burning of Washington, forced his resignation, and he retired from public life.

ARMSTRONG, LOUIS ['Satchmo'] (1900–), Negro trumpeter and jazz orchestra leader, began his professional career as cornetist in Kid Ory's band in New Orleans (1917). Eight years later he formed his own band in Chicago, and developed his solo trumpet style. His popular U.S. and European tours during the 1930's were later followed by tours of the Middle East (1956) and of Africa (1960), sometimes as part of the Federal cultural exchange program. Many of his recordings are now collectors' items.

Army, Department of the, formerly the independent DEPARTMENT OF WAR, in 1947 was given its present name and merged with the Department of the Navy and the newly created Department of the Air Force into the DEPARTMENT OF DEFENSE. It is charged with organizing, equipping, and training all land forces in the U.S. It also administers affairs in the Panama Canal Zone, flood control projects, and river and harbor installations.

Army of the Potomac, see *Potomac, Army of the.*

Army, U.S., differs from other armies in origin, organization, and employment.

At the outbreak of the War of Independence the king's troops suddenly became enemies, and the colonies were entirely dependent upon their own MILITIA. When Washington was given central command, he was dealing with forces that had no permanency, and Congress therefore created the CONTINENTAL ARMY. After the war the troops were discharged, but frontier problems on occasion required Federal control and thus created the tradition continuing to the present. A small Regular Army is backed when necessary by state National Guards, which pass under Federal control in times of war. In 1789 Congress created the Department of War with a Secretary of cabinet rank, and in 1802 established the U.S. MILITARY ACADEMY.

The procedure of raising state troops for muster into Federal service was used during the Civil War, and the method was also used in both World Wars. After World War I and the dispersion of the National Army (a term that officially existed for only sixteen months during 1917–18), Congress restudied the whole army structure. A corps of reserve officers and enlisted men insures the prompt mobilization of a new army, in which a heavy detail of regular army officers forms a nucleus. Command and staff officers receive their training at Fort Leavenworth. The ARMY WAR COLLEGE trains general officers. The RESERVE OFFICERS' TRAINING CORPS (ROTC) gives instruction in schools and colleges to prospective officers. Since 1958 the U.S. Army has maintained an average of some 800,000 personnel on active duty.

See O. L. Spaulding, *The U.S. Army in War and Peace* (1937); and W. A. Ganoe, *The History of the U.S. Army* (1942).

Army War College, in Washington, D.C., organized by Secretary of War Root in 1901, is the final graduate school of the U.S. Army. A selected number of officers receive instruction there in the political and economic problems with which high command and general staff officers are expected to deal.

ARNOLD, BENEDICT (1741–1801), fourth-generation New Englander to bear the name, began service in the War of Independence by aiding Ethan Allen in the capture of Fort Ticonderoga (1775). His gallant services soon thereafter during the invasion of Canada won him the respect of Washington, and after his vigorous attack on the British at Ridgefield, Connecticut (April 1777), he was commissioned a major general. Under Horatio Gates he took a leading part in the decisive SARATOGA CAMPAIGN (during which he was seriously wounded in the leg), and in June 1778 Washington placed him in command of Philadelphia, then being evacuated by the British. From that appointment can be dated the events leading to Arnold's treachery.

Since boyhood Arnold had been restive under restraint and particularly sensitive to admonition. He had been irritated in 1777 when Congress promoted five generals over his head. In his opinion the Congress did not recognize his full merits. His exasperation was then compounded by a clash with Pennsylvania civil authorities, leading to charges against him which Congress referred to a court-martial. Thus incited by bitterness, Arnold initiated treasonable correspondence with Sir Henry Clinton, with a view to shifting his allegiance. In 1780 he asked Washington for command of West Point (key to the Hudson river valley), a post which Washington conferred, and began secret negotiations with Clinton to surrender the fort. He set his price for betrayal at £20,000. Forewarned when Clinton's emissary, Major JOHN ANDRÉ, was captured, Arnold fled to New York. He later assisted the British in devastating raids in Virginia and in his native Connecticut. In 1781 he removed to England, where his final years were humiliating. The monument erected honoring his valor on the field of battle at Saratoga does not bear his name. It depicts a booted leg with a bullet hole.

ARNOLD, HENRY HARLEY (1886–1950), Pennsylvania-born graduate of the U.S. Military Academy (1907), contributed notably to the development of the Air Corps of the U.S. Army during the 1930's. As chief of the Army Air Force during World War II, 'Hap' Arnold built that branch into a tremendously effective striking power. He was a vital member of the Joint Chiefs of Staff throughout the war. In 1944 he was appointed general of the army.

Aroostook War (February–May 1839) was the undeclared and bloodless 'war' which took place in northern Maine along the Aroostook river. The boundary between Maine and Canada was still unsettled, and Maine lumberjacks, camped along the river, had a merry time trying to oust rival 'trespassing' Canadians. Both state and provincial militias were called out. President Van Buren, sensing potential trouble, since the CAROLINA AFFAIR was then coming to a head, sent General Winfield Scott to negotiate a truce with the New Brunswick authorities until the boundary committee, then in session, could render its report. The dispute was settled and the boundary fixed by the WEBSTER-ASHBURTON TREATY (1842).

ARP, BILL, pseudonym of C. H. SMITH.

ARROWSMITH, AARON (1750–1823), London cartographer, founded a mapmaking and publishing business of distinction. The Hudson's Bay Company and the North West Company provided information for his *Map Exhibiting All the Discoveries in the Interior of North America* (1795, reissued repeatedly with additions and corrections). One important source of his information, never acknowledged, derived from the manuscript maps of the great surveyor DAVID THOMPSON.

'Arsenal of Democracy,' see *Lend-Lease Act*.

ARTHUR, CHESTER ALAN (1830–86), 21st President of the U.S. (1881–85), was born in Fairfield, Vermont. Upon graduation from Union College (1848) he practiced law in New York City. His active support of the Republican party was rewarded by President Grant, at the nod of Senator ROSCOE CONKLING, with an appointment as collector of customs for the port of New York. The customhouse was long conspicuous for flagrant abuses of the spoils system, but Arthur turned it into a political machine of such disreputable character that President Hayes demanded his resignation. Conkling espoused Arthur's case successfully until the Senate recessed (July 1878); then Hayes removed him from his post. Later the Senate approved Hayes' action.

The Republicans in 1880 selected as presidential nominee James A. Garfield, a 'dark horse' from Ohio, but to placate the 'stalwart' Republicans, the party accepted Conkling's henchman Arthur as Garfield's running mate. The ticket won the election, and upon the death of Garfield (19 September 1881), Arthur took oath as his successor.

To the surprise of all, Arthur became something of a reformer. On the whole his appointments were unexceptionable. He showed little favor to spoilsmen, vigorously prosecuted the STAR ROUTE FRAUDS in the Post Office Department, and vetoed the CHINESE EXCLUSION ACT as well as a pork barrel $18,000,000 river and harbor bill. Most significantly, his administration pushed through the PENDLETON ACT (1883), the first important civil service reform measure. Although Arthur sought the nomination in 1884, the Republicans chose James G. Blaine, who lost the election to Grover Cleveland. Upon retirement Arthur returned to New York City.

See G. F. Howe, *Chester A. Arthur* (1934).

ARTHUR, TIMOTHY SHAY (1809–85), while editor of *Arthur's Home Magazine* (1853–85), poured out a stream of moralistic tracts and novels in the cause of temperance. His novel *Ten Nights in a Barroom and What I Saw There* (1854) rivaled *Uncle Tom's Cabin* in popularity. It satisfied the public taste for the sensational, won the endorsement of Sunday schools, and long continued in dramatic form on theater circuits.

Articles of Confederation were the law of the land for eight years (March 1781–March 1789). After the outbreak of the War of Independence the Continental Congress appointed a committee (one member from each state) to frame an instrument of confederacy. In July 1776 the committee reported its 'Articles of Confederation and Perpetual Union.' Congress debated them intermittently for over a year, and in November 1777 adopted a draft which it submitted to the states as the only proposal that might afford 'any tolerable prospect of a general ratification.' Most of the states had adopted the Articles by early 1779, but Maryland delayed for nearly three years, pending settlement of the issue concerning WESTERN LANDS.

Although recognized at the time as inadequate, this 'firm league of friendship' among the states was acknowledged as sound in principle and a means, as John Marshall later pointed out, of preserving union until a longer experience could guide the planning of a more efficient system. The states retained all rights (including the control of taxes and regulation of commerce) not expressly ceded to the Federal agency. States might annually appoint two to seven delegates to Congress, each state limited to a single vote. Amendments must be unanimously approved. Congress would manage foreign and Indian affairs, regulate coinage, establish a postal system, borrow money, and settle disputes between states.

One great weakness lay in the fact that Congress was powerless to enforce its measures. Some states ignored their contractual obligations, or trespassed on rights they had specifically relinquished. The absence of a Federal executive and judiciary was soon recognized as a defect. So was the delegation of authority in matters relative to commerce and taxation. By 1786 the Articles were in discredit. Yet they had admirably served their purpose as a stepping-stone to the CONSTITUTION, to which they gave way in 1789. They had outlined a Federal system, and without them confederation after Yorktown might have been impossible to secure.

Arts, see *Architecture, Music, Painting,* and *Sculpture.*

As goes Maine, so goes the Union was a phrase originated by the Whigs in the presidential election of 1840. While Maine's election of a Republican governor was frequently followed by election of a Republican President in November, this had no predictive value; the nation was normally Republican and the margin for victory for state and national elections showed no correlation.

ASBURY, FRANCIS (1745–1816), at the age of twenty-six was sent (1771) by the Wesleyan conference in London as a missionary to America, where he ordained many of the lay CIRCUIT RIDERS. Indefatigable until his death, he traveled on horseback from New Hampshire to the Mississippi Territory. (In advanced age he drove a battered sulky.) In 1784 he established himself as the first bishop of the Methodist Episcopal Church in America. The growth of the denomination from a handful of adherents to nearly a quarter of a million and into one of the three dominant religious groups in the South in his lifetime is testimony to his administrative skill. His *Journals* (3 vols., 1852) are valuable social history, especially of frontier life during the early years of the Republic.

ASCH, SHOLEM (1880–1957), Polish-born novelist and playwright, settled in the U.S. in 1914. Writing in Hebrew, Yiddish, and German, he dealt with Jewish themes, especially the problems of Jews, as in *The Mother* (1930) and *East River* (1946), which depict Jewish life in New York City. His best-selling and substantial trilogy on the life of Jesus, *The Nazarene, The Apostle,* and *Mary* (1939–49), sought a synthesis of Judaism and Christianity.

Ashburton Treaty, see *Webster-Ashburton Treaty.*

Ashley Expeditions (1822–26) were fur-trading ventures up the Missouri river into the Rocky Mountains, organized at St. Louis by William Henry Ashley (1778–1838), lieutenant governor of Missouri. In 1822 he created the association which later became the Rocky Mountain Fur Company, a powerful rival of such groups as the HUDSON'S BAY COMPANY. The first expeditions (1822–23) were badly mauled by the Blackfoot and Arikara, but in 1824, with reinforcements, Ashley assembled his third expedition, which he put in charge of the intrepid twenty-six-year-old JEDEDIAH SMITH. This undertaking penetrated to Great Salt Lake, and discovered the wealthiest fur sections of the West.

In 1824, during August, when Ashley reached the Green river valley in Wyoming (near the crossing of the Oregon Trail), he held the first of the annual mountain trappers' 'rendezvous,' a meeting where the trappers could sell furs and purchase supplies. His abandonment of the trading fort and introduction of the rendezvous and the brigade system for dispatching furs to St. Louis revolutionized the fur trade industry. In 1826 he retired from control of the company, having made a fortune in furs.

The importance of the expeditions lies in the fact that Ashley's exploration of the vast expanse of the Northwest gave the U.S. a firm hold on disputed areas. Much credit for that accomplishment goes to the noted guides among the MOUNTAIN MEN.

Assiniboin Indians, of Siouan stock, were a northern Plains tribe. After 1800 they began migrating from the upper Missouri north to the Saskatchewan and Assiniboine rivers. A southern branch was almost constantly at war with the Dakota Indians until the 1870's, when it was settled on a Montana reservation.

Assistants, those men who comprised the governing bodies of the early New England colonies, were provided for in the charters. The Massachusetts Bay Company charter (1629) set the number of assistants at eighteen. They were to be annually elected by the stockholders (freemen). The Court of Assistants, the governor and any six assistants, constituted a quorum. Its functions were executive, legislative, and judicial. The assistants also constituted a standing committee of advisers to the governor. As soon as the Company became a Commonwealth, the assistants became the magistrates, the upper chamber of a bicameral legislature or GENERAL COURT. The Connecticut charter (1662) provided a similar governing body, but limited the number to twelve.

Associated Press, newsgathering agency, was an outgrowth of a combination (1827) known as the New York Associated Press. This early agency sent reporters in rowboats to offshore vessels to get reports from Europe to the city by semaphore or carrier pigeons before the ships docked. When the telegraph came into use (1844), telegraph companies opened their own services, but by 1860 the Associated Press (as it was then called) had absorbed most rivals, and its facilities extended into Canada. Attacked in Congress as a monopoly, in 1900 it was reorganized. Its chief rival today is UNITED PRESS INTERNATIONAL.

'Association, The,' formed after passage of the BOSTON PORT ACT, was a plan adopted by the First Continental Congress (1774), whereby members pledged themselves not to import, export, or consume British goods if grievances continued unredressed. It was inaugurated by pressure-group tactics and developed through vigilance committees. It was a major factor in dividing 'loyalists' from 'patriots,' and was used as a device for recruiting troops.

Assumption (Funding) Act (1790), pushed by Hamilton over the objections of Jefferson, was adopted by Congress and signed by Washington. Ten days after Hamilton took office as Secretary of the Treasury (September 1789), at the request of Congress he began his report of a plan for 'adequate support of public credit.' This he laid before the House in January 1790. To establish the credit of the national government, he proposed to pay both foreign and domestic creditors at par. Speculators favored the idea, since securities were available at the time for a quarter of their face value.

In addition, Hamilton wished to assume the debts incurred by the several states during the Revolution, as a means of strengthening their federation, even though the assumption would raise the national debt by one-third (from $56,000,000 to more than $74,000,000). He therefore proposed a sinking fund, and a Bank of the U.S. All his proposals were eventually carried, but the feeling aroused by them for a time was acrimonious. Some states had already paid more of their debts than others. The North, with its larger taxable population, was in a better financial condition than the South. Central in the issue was the fact that farmers, wage earners, shopkeepers, and discharged soldiers (a large segment of the nation) had suffered heavily from the discount of their government securities.

Yet as Washington and other leading Southerners clearly saw, the national credit was at stake. Jefferson therefore adroitly linked the Assumption bill with the issue of whether the national capital should be located in the North (perhaps in New Jersey) or in the South (perhaps on the Potomac). At an informal dinner to which Jefferson invited Hamilton, each statesman gave the other his support. Hamilton secured his Assumption Act, and Jefferson was able to lay plans for the new Federal city of Washington on the Potomac.

ASTOR, JOHN JACOB (1763–1848), after emigrating from Germany (1784), set himself up in the fur business. So astute was his management that by 1800, with chartered ships plying the Atlantic and Pacific, he had established the beginnings of a commercial empire. His AMERICAN FUR COMPANY (1808) in less than ten years became the dominant fur trading organization of the western plains and mountains, with headquarters for a time at ASTORIA, where the Columbia river flows into the Pacific.

Astor's investments in Manhattan real estate, together with profits made in helping to finance the War of 1812, created the first of the great American FORTUNES. He sold his control of the fur trade in 1834, and occupied his later years in managing his real estate holdings. His $400,000 bequest set up the Astor Library, since 1895 incorporated as a part of the New York Public Library.

See K. W. Porter, *John Jacob Astor, Business Man* (2 vols., 1931).

Astor Place Riot, occurring 10 May 1849, at the Astor Place Opera in New York, resulted from the intense jealousy that EDWIN FORREST entertained for his English rival William Macready. Both were billed for performances that evening, and both had ardent partisans, Forrest's inclined to class hatred and anglophobia. A mob led by one Judson, perhaps with the connivance of Forrest, gathered outside the Opera, where Macready was playing *Macbeth*. Unable to disperse it, the police called upon the militia. Meanwhile the mob had gutted the building with a violence which caused injury or death to more than 50 persons. Judson was sentenced to a year in prison.

Astoria, at the mouth of the Columbia river in Oregon, was briefly (1811–12) the seat of the AMERICAN FUR COMPANY, established by JOHN JACOB ASTOR, who was compelled to move his headquarters at the outbreak of the War of 1812. Though Astoria was restored to the U.S. in 1818, it continued to be a factor in the OREGON BOUNDARY DISPUTE. Irving's *Astoria* (1836, rev., 1849) is the classic account of this enterprise, in which rivals neither asked nor gave quarter in securing trade monopolies.

Astronomy was taught as part of the Harvard curriculum as early as 1642. The Copernican system was presented there before 1659. JOHN WINTHROP (1606–76), the first systematic observer in the colonies of celestial phenomena, was making astronomical observations in 1660 with a 10-ft. telescope, and in 1672 presented the college with a 3-ft. refractor, through which THOMAS BRATTLE made observations helpful to Newton in writing his *Principia* (1687). The study of comets made by INCREASE MATHER in *Kometographia* (1683) is a classic of early American science. During the 18th century THOMAS ROBIE and Professor JOHN WINTHROP (1714–79) were elected members of the Royal Society for their scientific contributions (which included astronomical observations), and DAVID RITTENHOUSE was acclaimed by enthusiastic Americans as the leading astronomer of his day.

In 1840 Harvard erected the first college observatory under the direction of W. C. BOND, and in the same decade MARIA MITCHELL was cited abroad for her discovery of a comet. Notable American astronomers whose work continued into the 20th century include S. P. LANGLEY, SIMON NEWCOMB, PERCIVAL LOWELL, J. E. KEELER, W. H. PICKERING, and G. E. HALE. Their pioneer work laid the base for recent advances in cosmology made by H. N. RUSSELL, HARLOW SHAPLEY, E. P. HUBBLE, and F. L. WHIPPLE, leaders among a large number of productive scholars, including such distinguished women astronomers as ANNIE CANNON and HENRIETTA LEAVITT. (Astronomy has been a field in which American women over a long period have won high distinction.)

One of the great scientific innovations of the 20th century was the introduction of radio astronomy (1931) by KARL JANSKY, who established the interstellar origin of certain radio interference noises. The recently installed steerable

300-ft. radio dish at Green Bank, West Virginia, scans the universe for radio waves. Such equipment, in this country and elsewhere, is expected to enable man to penetrate and chart a universe of infinite vastness.

Athapascan Family of North American Indians was a widely distributed linguistic group with diverse cultures, varying from the nomadic hunters of the Yukon to the predatory tribes of the Southwest. In the U.S. the best known members of the stock are the APACHE and the NAVAHO.

Atlanta, capital of Georgia since 1868, is the cultural and commercial center of the state and a port of entry. It was founded (1837) as Terminus, the end of a railroad line. The name Atlanta was adopted in 1845 and the town was incorporated as a city two years later when it began developing its marketing and industrial potential. It was an important focus for Confederate communications and supplies during the Civil War. Its near annihilation in the ATLANTA CAMPAIGN (1864) is vividly reconstructed in Margaret Mitchell's novel *Gone With the Wind* (1936). The *Atlanta Constitution* (founded in 1868) is a leading newspaper, first nationally known during the editorship of H. W. GRADY. The population growth of Atlanta during the decade 1950–60 from 331,000 to 487,000 corresponds to its industrial expansion. It is the site of many institutions of higher learning, including Emory (est. 1836), Georgia Institute of Technology (est. 1885), and the Atlanta University System (est. 1929), comprising four Negro colleges.

Atlanta Campaign (May–September 1864) began when Sherman advanced on Atlanta (5 May) simultaneously with Grant's attack on Richmond, a strategy intended to totally destroy the Confederacy (as it did) in the Civil War. Sherman's army of 110,000, twice the size of Johnston's defending force, maneuvered Johnston from point to point. Johnston wisely withdrew to fortified positions, but he was relieved of his command because he 'failed to arrest the advance of the enemy.' His successor, J. B. Hood, began violent attacks which were repulsed with heavy losses. The inevitable was delayed until 1 September, when Hood evacuated the city. All persons remaining in Atlanta were deported and the city was destroyed. Sherman then began his triumphal march of destruction to the sea.

Atlantic, Battle of the (1941–44), took place throughout the Atlantic Ocean, where the British and Germans had been engaged since the outbreak of World War II. It began for the U.S. in late summer of 1941, when a U-boat attack on a U.S. destroyer off Iceland drew from President Roosevelt the order to 'shoot on sight' any Axis vessels approaching the Western Hemisphere. After the U.S. entered the war in December the Battle of the Atlantic was grimly pursued. The German submarine commander, Admiral Doenitz, sent out 'wolf packs,' which wreaked appalling destruction on American coastal shipping as well as that along all major seaways. By April 1942 half a million tons had been sunk, a toll that was more than doubled by June. The casualties among merchant and naval seamen were enormous.

Yet Allied shipyards actually were able to live up to their slogan, 'sixty vessels in sixty days'; engineers performed the impossible in building strategic airfields; and, most ominously for the Germans, the number of submarine-attacking planes more than quadrupled. Early in 1944 U-boat losses were so formidable that Doenitz ceased using them to attack Atlantic convoys. Of the 198 U-boats built during the last half of 1944, Germany lost 186. The battle was won by the lethal use of air power, without which the war itself could have been lost.

Atlantic cable was first successfully laid in the summer of 1858. In February 1857, assisted by vessels loaned by the governments of Great Britain and the U.S., CYRUS W. FIELD began laying a transatlantic submarine telegraph cable between Valentia Bay, Ireland, and Trinity Bay, Newfoundland, but the cable parted after 300 miles of it had been laid. A second attempt in June 1858 was likewise frustrated. The third venture succeeded, and on 17 August President Buchanan and Queen Victoria exchanged the first cabled message: 'Europe and America are united by telegraph. Glory to God in the highest. On earth peace and good-will toward men.' Later difficulties temporarily discredited the venture, but Field persisted, and in 1866 an improved arrangement assured a permanent transatlantic link.

Atlantic Charter (August 1941) was a joint declaration of principles drawn up (at sea off Newfoundland) and signed by President Roosevelt and Prime Minister Churchill at a time when American public and political opinion was strongly isolationist. The two nations agreed not to make territorial claims or to recognize territorial changes except in accord with the peoples concerned. They affirmed the right of self-government everywhere, and the restoration of such rights to those under duress. Economic security, access to trade, and improved standards of labor were pledged as national policy.

The freedoms to be reaffirmed or inaugurated dealt first with freedom of the seas, then with freedom from want, from fear, and from aggression. The purpose of the Charter was to restate, at a moment of chaos, what Wilson had envisioned in his FOURTEEN POINTS during World War I. The aims of the Atlantic Charter are embodied in the Charter of the United Nations.

Atlantic Monthly (1857–current) was founded in Boston as a magazine of literature, politics, and the arts. Its 19th-century editors included James Russell Lowell, James T. Fields, William Dean Howells, and T. B. Aldrich. Among its early contributors were Emerson, Holmes, Longfellow, Motley, Parkman, and H. B. Stowe. In the 20th century the heritage of interest in letters and politics has been preserved.

Atlantic Pact, see *North Atlantic Treaty*.

Atlantic States, see *Eastern States*.

Atomic energy, see *Nuclear energy*.

Atomic Energy Commission, U.S. (AEC), established by Congress in 1946, is a five-man civilian body appointed by the President. It controls a vast industrial and engineering complex. It is granted sole authority over all fissionable material, including rights of patents, ownership, operation, and dissemination of technical information in the field of nuclear energy. Its industrial and research facilities extend into every state of the Union and embrace all areas of usefulness, whether for peace or for war.

In 1956 it authorized construction of the first two large-scale private atomic power plants. Its plans include the release of materials to foreign countries and the establishment of graduate schools in atomic studies. In 1964 its full-time complement of some 7000 employees was steadily increasing, and it was operating with a $2,500,000,000 budget. Enormous plants for the creation of atomic energy, first established at Hanford, Washington, are in process of construction throughout the country. Research laboratories are located at Hanford, Los Alamos (N.M.), Argonne (Ill.), Oak Ridge (Tenn.), Brookhaven (N.Y.), and elsewhere. Especially distinguished among its awards is the Enrico Fermi Award (a gold medal, a citation, and $50,000), bestowed annually for contributions to nuclear physics.

The following have served as chairmen of the Commission:

David E. Lilienthal (1946–50)
Gordon E. Dean (1950–55)
Lewis L. Strauss (1953–58)
John A. McCone (1958–61)
Glenn T. Seaborg (1961–)

Attainder, Bill of, see *Bill of Attainder*.

Attorney General, the chief law officer of the federal government, occupies an office established in 1789 but not raised to cabinet rank until 1814. For many years after the adoption of the Constitution the duties of the Attorney General were very light. He advised the President on legal matters, argued government cases before the Supreme Court, and had time for private practice. Official responsibilities gradually increased, although he had no control over U.S. attorneys and marshals until 1861, and he was given full control only after he was designated head of the JUSTICE DEPARTMENT, created in 1870. Attorneys General and the Presidents under whom they served are as follows.

Washington
Edmund Randolph (Va.) 1789
William Bradford (Pa.) 1794
Charles Lee (Va.) 1795

John Adams
Charles Lee (Va.) 1797
Theophilus Parsons (Mass.) 1801

Jefferson
Levi Lincoln (Mass.) 1801
Robert Smith (Md.) 1805
John Breckenridge (Ky.) 1805
Caesar A. Rodney (Del.) 1807

Madison
Caesar A. Rodney (Del.) 1809
William Pinkney (Md.) 1811
Richard Rush (Pa.) 1814

Monroe
Richard Rush (Pa.) 1817
William Wirt (Va.) 1817

J. Q. Adams
William Wirt (Va.) 1825

Jackson
John McP. Berrien (Ga.) 1829
Roger B. Taney (Md.) 1831
Benjamin F. Butler (N.Y.) 1833

Van Buren
Benjamin F. Butler (N.Y.) 1837
Felix Grundy (Tenn.) 1838
Henry D. Gilpin (Pa.) 1840

W. H. Harrison
John J. Crittenden (Ky.) 1841

Tyler
John J. Crittenden (Ky.) 1841
Hugh S. Legaré (S.C.) 1841
John Nelson (Md.) 1843

Polk
John Y. Mason (Va.) 1845
Nathan Clifford (Me.) 1846
Isaac Toucey (Conn.) 1848

Taylor
Reverdy Johnson (Md.) 1849

Fillmore
John J. Crittenden (Ky.) 1850

Pierce
Caleb Cushing (Mass.) 1853

Buchanan
Jeremiah S. Black (Pa.) 1857
Edwin M. Stanton (Ohio) 1860

Lincoln
Edward Bates (Mo.) 1861
Titian J. Coffey (Pa.) 1863
James Speed (Ky.) 1864

Attorney General

Johnson
James Speed (Ky.) 1865
Henry Stanbery (Ohio) 1866
William M. Evarts (N.Y.) 1868

Grant
Ebenezer R. Hoar (Mass.) 1869
Amos T. Akerman (Ga.) 1870
George H. Williams (Ore.) 1871
Edwards Pierrepont (N.Y.) 1875
Alphonso Taft (Ohio) 1876

Hayes
Charles Devens (Mass.) 1877

Garfield
Wayne MacVeagh (Pa.) 1881

Arthur
Benjamin H. Brewster (Pa.) 1881

Cleveland
Augustus Garland (Ark.) 1885

B. Harrison
William H. H. Miller (Ind.) 1889

Cleveland
Richard Olney (Mass.) 1893
Judson Harmon (Ohio) 1895

Mc Kinley
Joseph McKenna (Cal.) 1897
John W. Griggs (N.J.) 1898
Philander C. Knox (Pa.) 1901

T. Roosevelt
Philander C. Knox (Pa.) 1901
William H. Moody (Mass.) 1904
Charles J. Bonaparte (Md.) 1906

Taft
George W. Wickersham (N.Y.) 1909

Wilson
James C. McReynolds (Tenn.) 1913
Thomas W. Gregory (Tex.) 1914
A. Mitchell Palmer (Pa.) 1919

Harding
Harry M. Daugherty (Ohio) 1921

Coolidge
Harry M. Daugherty (Ohio) 1923
Harlan F. Stone (N.Y.) 1924
John S. Sargent (Vt.) 1925

Hoover
William D. Mitchell (Minn.) 1929

F. D. Roosevelt
Homer S. Cummings (Conn.) 1933
Frank Murphy (Mich.) 1939
Robert H. Jackson (N.Y.) 1940
Francis Biddle (Pa.) 1941

TRUMAN
Tom C. Clark (Tex.) 1945
J. Howard McGrath (R.I.) 1949
J. P. McGranery (Pa.) 1952

EISENHOWER
Herbert Brownell, Jr. (N.Y.) 1953
William P. Rogers (N.Y.) 1957

KENNEDY
Robert F. Kennedy (Va.) 1961

L. B. JOHNSON
Robert F. Kennedy (Va.) 1963
Nicholas deB. Katzenbach (Pa.) 1964

Attu, 30-mile-long island, is the westernmost of the Aleutian Islands off the Alaska coast. Extremely rugged, it rises more than 4000 ft. In World War II it was occupied by the Japanese (1942), who removed the inhabitants to Japan. U.S. forces recaptured it in 1943 and established an air base. In 1945 the natives were repatriated.

ATWATER, WILBUR OLIN (1844–1907), professor of chemistry at Wesleyan (after 1873), founded there the first state agricultural experiment station (1875–77). In 1888 he became the first director of the Office of Experiment Stations in the U.S. Department of Agriculture under the HATCH ACT (1887), which had been passed largely at his instigation. With his famous Atwater-Rosa calorimeter he demonstrated the validity of the law of conservation of energy for human beings, as in the process of food oxidation. He prepared tables giving the calorific value of various foods and introduced experiments in nutrition that were influential here and abroad.

AUDUBON, JOHN JAMES (1785–1851), born in Haiti, after study in Paris under the painter David, settled briefly (1804) on his father's farm near Philadelphia. There his two chief interests, nature and sketching, led him to ventures as diverse as portrait painting and taxidermy. He eventually decided to prepare a volume of colored plates that should include every known American bird, and to that end he spent several years in travel. In 1826 he took his drawings to England, obtained subscribers, and published in elephant folio *The Birds of America* (1827–38), with superb colored plates engraved by Robert Havell, Jr. The accompanying text, *Ornithological Biography* (5 vols., 1831–39), includes Audubon's impressionistic but first-hand descriptions of his frontier adventures.

Although ornithologists can point to errors in Audubon's depiction of bird life, he combined artistry with skilled observation to a degree that makes his work one of the great achievements in American intellectual history. Cuvier called the drawings 'the most magnificent monument yet raised by art to science.' On his return Audubon lived near the Hudson river on northern Manhattan, and with the naturalist JOHN BACHMAN began *The Viviparous Quadrupeds of North America* (2 vols., 1842–45), the text for which (3 vols., 1846–54) Bachman was largely responsible. Extracts from Audubon's frontier observations have been collected in *Delineations of American Scenery and Character* (1926) and *Audubon's America* (1940). Further source material on the frontier is in his *Journal* (1929) and *Letters* (1930).

Biographies include those by F. H. Herrick (2 vols., 1917), Constance Rourke (1936), and G. C. Fisher (1949).

AUER, LEOPOLD (1845–1930), Hungarian-born violinist, and one of the notable artists of his time, taught for 50 years (1868–1917) at the St. Petersburg Conservatory. He came to the U.S. in 1918, and taught at the Institute of Musical Art (New York), and the Curtis Institute (Philadelphia). In 1926 he became a U.S. citizen. He was held in great esteem by such pupils as Mischa Elman, Jascha Heifetz, and Efrem Zimbalist.

Aurora, The (1794–1835), was founded in Philadelphia as the *General Advertiser* (1790–4). With Benjamin Franklin Bache (1769–98) as editor it became the voice of Jeffersonian Republicanism. Its violent Anti-Federalist stand led it to scurrilous abuse of President Washington, whom it attempted to discredit by the publication of forged letters. Its office was wrecked (1797) by enraged Federalist supporters, and the ALIEN AND SEDITION ACTS (1798) were framed in part to suppress it and journals like it. After Bache died the newspaper continued its advocacy of Republican principles. It was suspended in 1822.

Aurora Community, see *Bethel Community.*

AUSTIN, STEPHEN FULLER (1793–1836), a New Englander by ancestry, was born in Virginia and raised in Kentucky. He settled in Missouri, and upon the death of his father (1821) fell heir to a grant of 66,000 acres of land in Texas which had been given as a standing offer from the Mexican government on the condition that whoever took it would encourage 200 families to emigrate to this fertile region. With the aid of the relatively few he could attract, he established (1822–23) the trading center named for him (now the state capital). He governed the settlement expertly for six years. Although he officially opposed independence, in Mexico City he represented those colonizers who desired it, and he was imprisoned for a year for proposing separate Texas statehood. On his return (1835) he took part in the Texas Revolution. He lost his campaign for the presidency of the Lone Star Republic to Sam Houston, who appointed him Secretary of State, a post Austin held until his death.

Australian ballot, first used in South Australia in the 1880's, was introduced into the U.S. in 1888, and is the ballot in general use today. It requires that the names of all candidates for office be listed on the same sheet of paper, that the ballot be printed at government expense on white paper, and that the marking and polling be carried out in secret. Originally opposed by PARTY MACHINES, the method is now accepted as an essential part of the democratic process of voting.

Austria, Treaty of Peace with, see *Vienna, Treaty of* (1921).

Automation, an industrial technique brought about during the 1950's by the development of self-regulating machines, has put large parts of the industrial system under automatic control, which not only saves labor but in many instances improves on human operations. Electronic computers, working at enormous speeds (in excess of microseconds), can count, memorize, and correct the operations they control through feedback devices. These computers have been developed to a point where, in the words of the physicist EDWARD TELLER, they can 'become teachable, acquire experience, form judgments, develop emotions, and take initiative.' The mathematician NORBERT WIENER said that the assumption that machines cannot possess any degree of originality 'should be rejected in its entirety.' Automation is thus much more than an accelerated stage of the Industrial Revolution.

Automation has created many problems as well as obvious benefits of abundance. It has decreased the need for labor in certain processes in a period of sharply increasing population. Unskilled workmen, Negroes particularly, have been adversely affected, although most have been reabsorbed into the labor force through retraining and employment in service industries. The working day, week, and year have in some industries been shortened, the demand for higher wages has increased, and the problem of leisure has become acute. Solutions in part have been found by building obsolescence into products themselves, creating new consumer wants, shipping surplus commodities and goods to needy countries, and diverting a larger part of the economy to government spending for public purposes.

Automobile racing, developed as a sport in France (1894), was introduced to the U.S. in 1895 and is now estimated to attract more spectators than any other sport. Best known (since 1911) is the Indianapolis Speedway meet. Among the 150 races held annually in the U.S., those at Daytona Beach, and Sebring, Florida, and the Grand Prix of the U.S. at Watkins Glen, New York, draw large followings. The official world speed record of 536.71 m.p.h. was set by Art Arfons at Bonneville, Utah, in 1964. Because the racer used in these trials resembles a jet fighter, the U.S. Auto Club records this new class as 'Jet-Powered Vehicles.'

Automobiles are not the invention of any one person. They began evolving in the late 19th century from experiments with internal-combustion engines. German and French inventiveness made possible the first gasoline-powered automobile, built by the German engineer Karl Benz in 1885. Among pioneers in the U.S. were ELWOOD HAYES, CHARLES AND FRANK DURYEA, and HENRY FORD, all of whom had constructed automobiles before 1895.

Until World War I automobiles were regarded as a luxury. They were usually custom built, and were subject to frequent mechanical collapse. Transportation facilities along roadways in 1910 were not appreciably different from those a century earlier. Roadbeds were seldom surfaced and they followed the contours of the landscape. By 1915 a revolution in transportation had begun that within a generation altered the social and industrial structure of the nation. C. F. KETTERING had perfected the electric self-starter. Ford's mass-production technique was bringing the cost of a 'Model T' within the range of almost any American pocketbook. Some 70 companies were manufacturing 200,000 automobiles annually. Local and national clubs were sponsoring speed contests. Most significantly, state legislatures were outlining road-building programs, enacting regulatory laws, and establishing motor vehicle departments.

By 1920 some 9,000,000 automobiles were in use, and by 1930 the number had tripled. The impact of this transportation upheaval was felt both in the tremendous industrial upswing and in the pattern of daily living for nearly every family in the country. Automobiles were now viewed as a necessity. They brought village dwellers within easy reach of larger towns and cities, thereby greatly expanding business, educational, and cultural facilities. Automobiles could satisfy the restless urge to go somewhere, but they also created new problems of urban traffic congestion, of crime, and especially of danger to human life. In spite of billions of dollars spent by federal, state, and municipal governments, merging their facilities to construct express throughways and to improve the million miles of automobile highways, accidents continue to exact a high annual toll of fatalities; in 1960 the number exceeded 37,000, and fatalities have increased some 1000 each year since.

In addition to the recreational facilities that have been opened by the automobile, business opportunities have expanded enormously. Great industrial plants, formerly located in urban centers, have been moving into undeveloped areas, where maintenance costs are reduced, access to raw material is simplified, and parking facilities are easily provided for the thousands of employees arriving by motor transport. In 1965 some 90,000,000 motor vehicles were registered in the U.S.

Aviation by means of lighter-than-air craft, steered and driven by engine, was first achieved in Europe by dirigibles during the 19th century. In the U.S. from 1887 until 1903, S. P. LANGLEY endeavored to solve the problem of the power-driven air glider or airplane. Langley died in 1906, unrecognized as the inventor (1896) of a power-driven heavier-than-air machine, later acknowledged as the pioneer airplane. WILBUR and ORVILLE WRIGHT put into flight (1903) the first such machine, a biplane, and in 1909 the U.S. Army adopted their model. They then began to manufacture airplanes, as did GLENN H. CURTISS, who flew from Albany to New York in 1910 at an average speed of 49 miles an hour. In 1911 Galbraith P. Rogers flew from New York to California in 68 days, with an elapsed time of 49 days.

Although used in World War I, airplanes were still too undeveloped to be a decisive weapon, as they were in World War II, but after 1920 aviation made giant strides. A U.S. Navy NC-4 crossed the Atlantic by way of the Azores in 1919. Airmail, first carried in 1918, soon became an integral branch of the postal service. In 1923 a plane crossed the continent non-stop in less than 27 hours, and in 1924 two army planes circled the globe in 15 days elapsed time, though they took 175 days to complete the trip. A milestone in aviation history, which encouraged a flow of investment, was the solo 3600-mile non-stop flight of CHARLES A. LINDBERGH from New York to Paris in 1927. By 1933 Wiley Post was able to complete a round-the-world trip in fewer than 8 days, a record broken 5 years later by Howard R. Hughes, who accomplished the feat in 3 days, 19 hours.

By this time types and sizes of planes

were multiplying, and commercial air routes had been put on regular schedules across continents and oceans. During World War II, land, sea, and amphibious planes were a major factor in offensive and defensive strategy. Indeed, the AIR FORCE spelled the difference between Allied victory and defeat.

Achievement of supersonic speed by jet-propelled military aircraft (1947) marked a new era in aviation history. Subsonic JET PROPULSION was commercially inaugurated in 1958. In 1962 scheduled airlines carried more than 60,000,000 passengers in the U.S. A course record from Los Angeles to New York was established that year by a military jet with an elapsed time of 2 hours (1214 m.p.h.).

All altitude, time, and distance records, however, are subject to continuous revision upward. U.S. aerial reconnaissance, for instance, is intensive, continuous, and widespread, and is performed by many different types of aircraft. In 1964 President Johnson announced that the A-11 was in operation, a supersonic, high-altitude plane with a speed of 2000 miles per hour and a range of 3500 miles at an altitude of more than 100,000 ft.

AVILÉS, PEDRO DE MENÉNDEZ, see *Menéndez de Avilés.*

Awakening, the Great, see *Great Awakening.*

Axis Powers, the term first applied to the coalition of Germany and Italy when Italy invaded Ethiopia (1935), became an effective alliance when Italy withdrew from the League of Nations (1937). Japan became an Axis member by an alliance with Germany and Italy (the Berlin Pact) in September 1940, though she did not become an active belligerent in World War II until December 1941.

B

BABBITT, Irving (1865–1933), after graduation from Harvard (1889) and study abroad, returned to Harvard, where he taught French literature (1894–1933). As a leader of the critical new humanism movement, he was a foe of realism on the one hand and romanticism on the other. Only literature that embodies both a moral and a historical awareness, he argued, can convey the sense of permanence which gives meaning to experience. Insistently partisan, throughout his life he led onslaughts in defense of moderation and restraint. The singular quality of his polemical writing is the clarity with which he defines the poles of an argument. His doctrines are set forth in several volumes of essays, including *The New Laokoön* (1910), *Rousseau and Romanticism* (1919), and *Democracy and Leadership* (1924).

BACHE, Alexander Dallas (1806–67), left his post as professor of natural history and chemistry at Pennsylvania (1828–36) to become the first president (1836–42) of Girard College, where he established (1839) the first magnetic observatory in North America. His visit abroad at the time resulted in a *Report on Education in Europe* (1839), influential in developing a system of free education in the U.S. As superintendent (1843–67) of the U.S. Coast Survey, Bache was charged with mapping the entire Atlantic seaboard, and under his direction the Coast and Geodetic Service carried out exploration in the northeast and the antarctic. He was a founder and first president (1863–67) of the national academy of sciences.

BACHMAN, John (1790–1874), Lutheran pastor at Charleston, South Carolina, was a lifelong student of fauna in the South. He collaborated with his friend J. J. audubon on *The Viviparous Quadrupeds of North America* (plates, 30 parts, 1842–45). Bachman wrote a large portion of the text (3 vols., 1846–54), and edited the entire work.

BACKUS, Isaac (1724–1806), a Baptist preacher in Massachusetts, became the New England spokesman in the cause of religious freedom and the independency of church organization. He was a founder of Brown University (1764), and his *History of New England, with Particular Reference to the . . . Baptists* (3 vols., 1777–96), although frankly partisan and awkwardly written, is source material of great value, characterized by George Bancroft as a work of 'clear discernment, and determined accuracy.'

Bacon's Rebellion (1676) was in a measure the result of stricter enforcement of the navigation acts after 1660, which narrowed the margin of profit for planters of all classes and bore down especially on the small landholders, who found themselves constantly in debt. Its causes, still obscure, were not clear even to contemporaries. In part it gained momentum because Virginia settlers inland, with few political privileges, could not rouse Governor Berkeley to stop the Indian massacres.

Nathaniel Bacon (1647–76) was a wealthy young planter with property at Curle's Neck on the James river and a seat on the Council. He first took up arms in an effort to avenge the death of an overseer slain by Indians. Then, without waiting for a commission, he led a force against the natives. His move was approved not only by frontiersmen but by the substantial traders and planters who likewise had suffered from Indian depredations.

With Bacon as leader, Berkeley's enemies were soon demanding sweeping changes. A new House of Burgesses was elected and Virginia was split into warring factions. Berkeley fled to the Eastern Shore, and Bacon captured and burned Jamestown lest it fall into Berkeley's hands when he returned with his militia. At the moment when Bacon was prepared to carry through tax and franchise reforms, he was stricken with a fever and died (18 October). Without a leader his 'army' melted away. Bitter and humiliated, Berkeley engaged in an orgy of executions, until Charles II recalled his aging deputy with the comment: 'That old fool has hanged more men in that naked country than I have done for the murder of my father.' The

Rebellion served notice that the ruling gentry must take care lest they deny the rights that Englishmen are guaranteed under the common law.

See T. J. Wertenbaker, *Torchbearer of the Revolution* (1940), and a recent corrective, Wilcomb Washburn's *The Governor and the Rebel.*

BADGER, JOSEPH (1708–65), Massachusetts-born glazier and house painter, turned to portraiture and became Boston's most popular artist. His work is noted for distinctive mannerisms, including both charm and stiff archaic style. Typical of his later portraits are those of Jonathan Edwards (Yale) and John Adams (Detroit Institute of Art).

Badlands are regions of barren, severely eroded beds of soft rock. In the U.S. the Badlands area is the arid plateau in southwestern South Dakota east of the Black Hills. Volcanic ash from prehistoric eruptions in the cordilleran range covers several hundred miles of the region to a depth of 300 ft. Herds of mammoths, elephants, camels, horses, and other creatures were engulfed by the ash, and the fossil remains are a rich source for palaeontological study. Since 1939 a part of the region has been set aside as a National Monument.

BAEKELAND, LEO HENDRIK (1863–1944), Belgian-born chemist, emigrated to the U.S. (1889) to serve as consultant for a photographic firm. In 1899 he sold his invention of a photographic paper (velox) to Eastman Kodak Company for $1,000,000. His invention of the synthetic resin bakelite (1909) founded the modern plastics industry and gave a new turn to organic chemistry, inducing chemists to focus on 'big' molecules, the background for the invention of synthetics.

BAFFIN, WILLIAM (*c.* 1584–1622), English navigator, was pilot on two expeditions (1615–16) commanded by Robert Bylot, who was sent out to search for the NORTHWEST PASSAGE to the Orient. The first expedition sought a channel through Hudson Bay, and the second, through Davis Strait, led to exploration of Baffin Bay. Baffin's conviction that no transit was possible was long accepted as true, although ironically in the 19th century Baffin Bay proved to be the entrance to the only natural waterway across the continent.

BAGBY, GEORGE WILLIAM (1828–83), Virginia journalist, while editor of the *Southern Literary Messenger* (1860–64) wrote humorous, local-color sketches intended to effect 'the unkind but complete destruction' of sentimental romancing about the Old Dominion. The repeated success of his lecture 'Bacon and Greens,' a panegyric on life in rural ante-bellum Virginia, led him to create other idealized portraits, among which 'The Old Virginia Gentleman' (1877) is representative.

BAILEY, LIBERTY HYDE (1858–1954), professor of horticulture at Cornell (1888–1903), and director and dean (1903–13) of its College of Agriculture, made basic contributions to the study of botany and horticulture. He edited *The Standard Cyclopedia of Horticulture* (6 vols., 1914–17, and later eds.), and *Cyclopedia of American Agriculture* (4 vols., 1907–9). With E. Z. Bailey he compiled *Hortus* (1930; rev. ed., 1935), and *Hortus Second* (1941). In 1909 President Theodore Roosevelt appointed him to head the Country Life Commission, from which grew Federal-state grants for agricultural and industrial education.

Bailey* v. *Drexel Furniture Company (1922) involved the second Child Labor Act (1919), which levied prohibitive taxes upon the products of child labor in interstate commerce. Chief Justice Taft, for the majority, declared the law invalid on much the same grounds as the decision in HAMMER *v.* DAGENHART (1918): that it was a regulation of local labor conditions rather than of commerce and hence violated the reserved powers of the states under the Tenth Amendment.

BAIRD, SPENCER FULLERTON (1823–87), after graduation from Dickinson College (1840) taught natural history there (1846–50) until he began his long association with the Smithsonian Institution as assistant secretary (1850–78), and as secretary (1878–87). While serving as the first U.S. Commissioner of Fish and Fisheries (1871–87), he established the marine biological laboratory at Woods

Hole, Massachusetts. His scientific papers (over 1000 titles) cover a broad range, including ichthyology, geology, mineralogy, botany, and, most importantly, ornithology, the field in which his influence was greater than that of any American of his day. His major studies include *Catalogue of North American Mammals* (1857) and (with Brewer and Ridgway) the *History of North American Birds* (5 vols., 1875–84). His books on birds inaugurated the 'Baird school' of accurate ornithological description.

BAKER, George Fisher (1840–1931), having learned banking in the New York state banking department (1858–63), joined three others in founding the First National Bank of New York (1863), which, under his presidency (after 1877), became one of the strongest financial institutions in the U.S. During the 1880's he helped James J. Hill build his railroad empire, and soon became a commanding figure in railroads, insurance, and utilities, as well as in the steel and rubber industries. Among his large philanthropies (Baker Field at Columbia, Baker Memorial Library at Dartmouth) was his gift to Harvard in 1924 to provide the buildings for its graduate school of business administration (est. 1908).

BAKER, George Pierce (1866–1935), after graduation from Harvard (1887) taught in the English department there (1888–1924), instituting in 1905 the 47 Workshop, the first college drama laboratory in which problems of play construction were experimentally studied. Students trained by Baker include EUGENE O'NEILL and ROBERT EDMOND JONES. Baker became professor of drama and director of the university theater at Yale in 1925, and there continued his teaching of theater techniques until his retirement (1933).

BAKER, Newton Diehl (1871–1937), was born in Martinsburg, West Virginia, the son of an antiracist Confederate physician. After graduation from Johns Hopkins (1892), he practiced law in Cleveland, Ohio. An ardent admirer of the municipal reformer TOM LOFTIN JOHNSON, Baker served as city solicitor (1902–12) and mayor (1912–16). President Wilson chose Baker, a fervent internationalist, as Secretary of War (1916–21), and Baker's organizing genius during World War I is attested by the fact that within eighteen months he created an effective army of 4,000,000 men, more than half of which was transported to France.

He later served as a member of the Permanent Court of Arbitration at The Hague (1928). Although Baker had been a reform Democrat in the Progressive era, he became increasingly conservative. A close contender for the 1932 Democratic presidential nomination, he later challenged the constitutionality of the Tennessee Valley Authority and other New Deal measures.

BAKER, Ray Stannard (1870–1946), after joining the staff of *McClure's Magazine* (1897), made substantial contributions to the MUCKRAKING movement in his attacks on railroad and financial abuses. A close friend of Woodrow Wilson, whose *Life and Letters* he wrote (8 vols., 1927–39), he directed the press bureau at the Versailles Conference in 1919. (Under the pen name of David Grayson he produced several volumes of informal essays.) He set forth his autobiography in *Native American* (1941) and *American Chronicle* (1945).

Baker* v. *Carr (1962) was a case resulting in a ruling by the U.S. Supreme Court which held that Federal courts have the power and duty to pass on the validity of distribution of state legislative seats. In this historic turnabout the Court departed from its traditional reluctance to decide questions of the fairness of legislative districting. In 1964 the Court went even further in substituting its own judgment in such matters by ruling in WESTBERRY *v.* SANDERS that congressional districts within each state should be substantially equal in population.

Balance of power, see *Interventionist movements.*

Balance of trade, see *Commerce.*

BALANCHINE, George (1904–), Russian-born choreographer, came to the U.S. in 1933, after having established a reputation throughout Europe as a dancer and organizer of ballet theaters. In 1934 he helped found the School of American Ballet in New York. Called by many ballet authorities the world's greatest choreographer in modern times, he has exerted a constantly widening influence on choreographic practices throughout the Western World. He worked intimately with the composer IGOR STRAVINSKY, and the Stravinsky-Balanchine team has produced some of the greatest ballets of the century, including *Apollo, Agon,* and *Movements for Piano and Orchestra.*

BALBOA, VASCO NÚÑEZ DE (1475–1517), Spanish conquistador, in 1510 sailed from Hispaniola (Haiti) to Panama as a stowaway to escape creditors. On reaching the Isthmus he was chosen civil administrator (alcalde) and then appointed governor (1512). On numerous expeditions he learned from Indians of a great 'South Sea' to the west, and of a country far southward rich in gold. Determined to discover both, he made his epic 25-day march across the Isthmus and from the summit of the range he crossed, 'a peak in Darien,' he gazed upon the Pacific Ocean (29 September 1513). Entering its waters, he claimed it, and all its shores, in the name of the kings of Castile. For this discovery Ferdinand named him admiral of the Pacific. This aroused the jealousy of Pedrias, the new governor of the Darien colony, who seized Balboa at the moment he was embarking for Peru. Charges of treason were sustained and Balboa was publicly beheaded.

BALCH, EMILY GREENE (1867–1961), a leader among PACIFISTS, was in the first graduating class of Bryn Mawr (1889). Beginning her career in social service as a settlement-house worker in Boston, she was professor of economic and social science at Wellesley (1913–18) until her antiwar activities led the trustees to ask for her resignation (an action for which the college later sought to atone). She founded the Women's League for Peace and Freedom (1919), and continued her world-wide efforts in the cause of better understanding among nations. In 1946 she shared with J. R. MOTT the Nobel Peace prize.

BALDWIN, ABRAHAM (1754–1807), Connecticut-born statesman, after graduation from Yale (1772) served as a chaplain in the Revolution, studied law, and took up practice (1784) in Georgia. He was a member of the Continental Congress (1785–88), and his change of vote (resulting in a tie in his committee) led to the framing of the compromise system of representation, by states in the Senate and by population in the House. He was a Representative from Georgia in Congress (1790–99), and as Senator (1799–1807) staunchly supported Jefferson's policies.

BALDWIN, JAMES MARK (1861–1934), a graduate of Princeton (1884), taught philosophy at Toronto (1889–93), where he established the first psychological laboratory in the British Empire. As professor of psychology at Princeton (1893–1903), Johns Hopkins (1903–9), and the National University of Mexico (1909–13), he became internationally known for his studies in child and social psychology. He founded and edited the *Psychological Review* (1894–1909).

BALL, THOMAS (1819–1911), Massachusetts-born sculptor, was known for his portrait busts and equestrian statues, inspired chiefly by American themes, even during his long residence in Florence (1865–97). His work is well represented by his mounted figure of Washington in the Boston Public Gardens; his statue of Daniel Webster in Central Park, New York; and by his *Emancipation* group in Washington, D.C.

Ball-Burton-Hatch-Hill Resolution, see *Connally Resolution.*

Ballet in the U.S. did not become a native art form until the second quarter of the 20th century. The Austrian ballet dancer Fanny Elssler (1810–83) had made a triumphal tour of the U.S. in 1841, but only after two great Russian dancers introduced the *ballet russe* did theater-goers in the U.S. begin to appreciate ballet as a performing art. Anna Pavlova (1882–1931) made her American debut (1910) at the Metropolitan Opera House in New York. The founder of modern ballet, Michel Fokine (1880–1942), who had created *The Dying Swan* for Pavlova, in 1932 became a citizen of the U.S., where he formed companies and conducted a ballet school.

As an art form, the ballet was given a new dimension by ISADORA DUNCAN, who insisted upon a natural pose. As a medium for expression of complex emotions and abstract ideas, the ballet has been developed in America by such imaginative artists and choreographers as RUTH ST. DENIS, TED SHAWN, MARTHA GRAHAM, AGNES DE MILLE, JEROME ROBBINS, and GEORGE BALANCHINE. The best known organization is the (New York) School of American Ballet (est. 1934), which has developed talent well displayed at the New York City Center Ballet. (Both are directed by Balanchine and the ballet promoter Lincoln Kirstein.) Other companies have been established in San Francisco, Washington, Philadelphia, Salt Lake City, Houston, and Boston. The fact that ballet is increasingly attracting the attention of Americans everywhere was dramatically illustrated in 1963, when the Ford Foundation made grants totaling more than $7,700,000 to further the development of professional ballet in the U.S. This is the largest sum any foundation has ever allotted at one time to a single art field.

Ballinger-Pinchot controversy (1909–11) grew out of differences of opinion in matters of forest conservation. President Theodore Roosevelt dramatized the need for conservation of soil, water, and forests by appointing an Inland Waterways Commission and calling a conference at the White House, to which were invited all the governors as well as notables in many fields. Out of this grew the National Conservation Commission (1908). Taft's effort to support Roosevelt's conservation policies did not work out well. His Secretary of the Interior, Richard A. Ballinger (1858–1922), was publicly accused by GIFFORD PINCHOT, chief of the Division of Forestry, a close friend of Roosevelt and an ardent conservationist, of refusing to protect water power sites and of blocking investigation of certain coal lands obtained by private interests in Alaska. A joint congressional investigating committee exonerated Ballinger, and Pinchot was dismissed. But Ballinger soon resigned (1911), unable to regain public confidence. The controversy widened the growing breach between Taft and Roosevelt, which indirectly culminated (1912) in the formation of the PROGRESSIVE PARTY.

Ballot, originally a little ball used in secret voting, has come to mean a printed or written paper, or 'ticket,' used in secret voting. The scandals growing out of fraudulent elections, in which openly written ballots were altered, led to the use of the AUSTRALIAN BALLOT. Automatic voting machines are now replacing the paper ballot in many states.

BALLOU, ADIN and HOSEA, see *Hopedale Community.*

Baltimore, on the Patapsco river near Chesapeake Bay, was incorporated in 1792 and is now the largest city in Maryland. It was not laid out as a town until 1729. In 1752 it was a settlement of only 25 houses and 200 inhabitants. By 1775 its population had grown to 6800, however, and five years later it became a port of entry. By that time its excellent harbor facilities came to match New England in the West Indies trade in grain and flour, and good roads made it a leading market for Virginia tobacco and a trading center for Pennsylvania farmers. It was a seat of Congress while the British occupied Philadelphia (1777–78). In 1790 JOHN CARROLL was consecrated bishop of Baltimore, the first Roman Catholic see in America and a diocese that embraced the entire country until 1808. The first cathedral built in the U.S. was erected in Baltimore (1805–18). It was designed by the architect B. H. LATROBE.

By 1800 the city was approaching Boston in population and was famous for its clipper ships. Culturally it was a center of musical interests, and its traditions, predominantly southern, were reflected in the dash and charm of its social life. (White marble doorsteps, especially associated with Baltimore houses, are still a feature of the city's architecture.)

Competing with New York and Philadelphia for western trade, in 1830 the city became the eastern terminal for the first major railroad, the Baltimore and Ohio. The city thereafter was often the meetingplace of national political conventions. At the opening of the Civil War, because mobs attacked a Union regiment passing through Baltimore, the city was placed under military rule and so remained throughout the war. The state sided with the Union, but Baltimore was an especially divided city.

During both World Wars Baltimore was important as a shipbuilding and supply-shipping center. In 1960, with a population approaching 1,000,000, it continued to be a leading cultural center of the Middle Atlantic area. It is widely known for many educational institutions, including the Maryland Academy of Sciences (est. 1797), Peabody Institute (est. 1859), and Johns Hopkins University (est. 1876).

Baltimore and Ohio Railroad (1827) was the first passenger railroad in the U.S. When the ERIE CANAL began to divert trans-Allegheny traffic from Baltimore in 1825, business leaders were given a franchise to construct a rail system, the first fourteen-mile division of which was opened in 1830. It reached Wheeling, West Virginia, in 1853. By 1857 it had direct connections to St. Louis. It was an important factor in opening the Ohio valley, and an invaluable means of transportation during the Civil War. In the 1870's it was extended to Chicago and New York.

Baltimore Lords, see *Maryland*.

BANCROFT, EDWARD (1744–1821), born in Massachusetts, studied medicine in London, where he settled to pursue scientific and literary interests. There he met Franklin, and during the War of Independence became the trusted friend (and spy) of Franklin, Arthur Lee, and Silas Deane when the three commissioners were negotiating the alliance with France (1776–78). Meanwhile Dr. Bancroft was appointed also an agent for the British government at an annual fee of £500, and a life pension. A most accomplished double agent, Bancroft at the end of the war was still in the good graces of the American Peace Commission. The discovery of the breadth of his services was not made for nearly a century. It required another 50 years for scholars to prove that after 1780 Deane himself had been tarnished by Bancroft's nimble manipulations.

BANCROFT, GEORGE (1800–1891), Massachusetts-born historian, after graduation from Harvard (1817) pursued graduate study in Greek and natural sciences in Berlin and at Göttingen (1820). During travel on the continent he was received by the great men of his day, including Goethe, Humboldt, Hegel, Cousin, and Mazzini. On his return he taught briefly at Harvard, founded and taught for eight years in the Round Hill School at Northampton, where he introduced novel progressive theories of education, and then made a career of politics and writing. As collector of the port of Boston, he controlled patronage, and he became the Democratic boss of Massachusetts. In 1845 President Polk invited him into the cabinet as Secretary of the Navy, during which term Bancroft established the U.S. Naval Academy. Greatly respected as a political adviser, Bancroft later served as minister to England (1846–49) and minister to Germany (1867–74), where he particularly distinguished himself.

Throughout these years Bancroft was creating his enduring monument, *A History of the U.S.* (to 1782) (10 vols., 1834–74, with later revisions that extended the text to 1789). Enthusiastically received in its day and widely translated, it was a best seller throughout most of the 19th century. At that time Bancroft was regarded as the dean of American historians. Although his great reputation survived him by only a few years, the *History* is regarded as an unjustly neglected classic. Bancroft died at the very time a more objective pragmatic school of American historiography was replacing the rhetorical, nationalistic approach which he epitomized. To Bancroft the ideas of freedom and democracy were providentially Anglo-American and Protestant, and his writing (like his statecraft) espoused the cause of 'manifest destiny.' He was so representative a spokesman for his day that President Harrison ordered the flags of official Washington flown at half-staff when Bancroft died, a tribute bestowed on no other American historian before or since.

See the biographies by M. A. De

Wolfe Howe (2 vols., 1908), and Russel B. Nye (1944).

BANCROFT, HUBERT HOWE (1832–1918), established (1852) at San Francisco what soon became the leading bookstore and publishing house west of Chicago. An interest in western American history led him to begin his collection of regional source materials: manuscripts, books, newspapers, pamphlets, maps, official documents, and dictated narratives, an impressive assemblage of 60,000 items, since enlarged and now the Bancroft Library in the University of California at Berkeley. Bancroft drew on this collection for his historical compilations, and he still remains the chief historian of the West Coast. Under his supervision a staff of specialists compiled *History of the Pacific States* (34 vols., 1882–90), published under his name. The first basic synthesis of researches into Indian life is *The Native Races of the Pacific States* (5 vols., 1874–76), to which Bancroft was the leading contributor.

Band music, as it is known today, originated for military bands, and marching or concert bands in the U.S. have long been an integral part of community life, and school and college functions. Many communities still draw the public to summer evening amateur bandstand concerts. The U.S. Marine Band (est. 1798), the first important marching ensemble, is still outstanding. The concert band, first developed in the U.S. by PATRICK S. GILMORE (1859), was made immensely popular by JOHN PHILIP SOUSA. In 1918 EDWIN F. GOLDMAN organized the Goldman Band, which for many years has performed summer concerts in New York City.

BANDELIER, ADOLPH FRANCIS ALPHONSE (1840–1914), Swiss-born archaeologist, was brought to the US. in 1848, and spent 40 years acquiring first-hand knowledge of the archaeology and ethnology of Peru, Bolivia, Mexico, and the American Southwest. His classic papers on the Aztecs, their conduct of war, land tenure and distribution, and social organization, were published in reports of the Peabody Museum (1877–79). His conclusion, which also had been reached by L. H. MORGAN, that the Aztec chieftains were heads of families or clans, not 'kings,' still has not entirely supplanted the romantic notion that Montezuma was a member of royalty in the European pattern. His numerous studies of the Southwest remain authoritative. Still the best reconstruction of Pueblo life before the coming of the white man is *The Delight Makers* (1890).

BANISTER, JOHN (1650–92), after emigrating to Virginia, kept in touch with his naturalist friends in England, to whom he sent descriptions and specimens of American insects. He contributed a paper (1693) to the Royal Society on American molluscs, and his catalog of the plants of Virginia, published in John Ray's *Historia Plantarum* (3 vols., 1686–1704), is the first systematic study of American botanical specimens.

Bank of Augusta* v. *Earle (1839) was a case resulting in an important decision in which the U.S. Supreme Court recognized the general right, as a courtesy, of a corporation chartered in one state to do business under interstate comity in other states. But in stating the Court's opinion, Chief Justice Taney made it clear that state legislatures had the right to regulate 'foreign' corporations.

Bank of North America, the first private commercial bank in the U.S. and the first government-incorporated bank, was chartered by Congress (December 1781), and under ROBERT MORRIS as Superintendent of Finance it opened (January 1782) in Philadelphia with a capital of $400,000. Original stockholders and depositors included Franklin, Jefferson, Hamilton, Monroe, and Jay. It fed and clothed Washington's army in the closing years of the Revolution, and supplied vital financial aid to the government. By the confidence it instilled abroad it was a major factor in getting the financial assistance from France and Holland that turned the tide of war in favor of the Americans.

Bank of the U.S., First (1791–1811), proposed by Hamilton and approved by Washington over the objections of Jefferson, was incorporated with a twenty-year charter. Anti-Federalists argued that the Constitution did not grant the government power to establish a central bank. Located in Philadelphia, it was governed by a 25-member board of directors, and through its main office and eight branches served as fiscal agent for the Government, its principal stockholder and customer. When its charter expired, it ceased business. Although it returned a profit on each share, Jeffersonian Democrats had steadily challenged its constitutionality.

The **Second Bank of the U.S.** (1816–36), modeled on the first, was incorporated five years after the demise of the first, and its constitutionality was upheld in MC CULLOCH *v.* MARYLAND. It suffered during the PANIC OF 1819, but under the capable management of NICHOLAS BIDDLE (1823–36) its prestige was re-established, although Biddle's political ineptness spelled its doom. (Urged by Henry Clay, Biddle had allowed the rechartering of the bank to become a political issue in the election campaign of 1832.) President Jackson, who disliked banks in general and feared eastern commercial monopoly in particular, did not wait for expiration of the charter of this 'hydra of corruption.' In 1833 he removed the Federal accounts from its books to various 'pet' state banks. When the charter expired in 1836 Biddle obtained a charter from Pennsylvania. As a leading American investment and commercial house, it continued to be of first importance in the American economy until it was forced into liquidation in 1841.

Bankhead-Jones Farm Tenant Act, see *Farm Security Administration.*

Banking during the colonial period was limited to agencies lending money secured by real estate. The first bank in the modern sense was the BANK OF NORTH AMERICA (1781), founded by Robert Morris. Ten years later (1791) the First BANK OF THE U.S. (succeeded by the Second, 1816–36) officially conducted the business of the government and carried out central banking functions by providing inexpensive commercial credit and a sound currency. The powerful rivals of national banks were STATE BANKS, where during most of the 19th century surplus capital was concentrated. A banking mania in the second decade (1811–15) increased the number of banks from 88 to 208, many of which collapsed because the value of specie could not support the credit that the banks created. After President Jackson vetoed the re-charter of the Second Bank of the U.S., for several years the government, with no Federal regulatory system, made its deposits in state banks (Jackson's PET BANKS), and loose banking practices created financial chaos.

Overspeculation in western lands and some corrupt gambling with public money led to the defaulting of several 'pet banks,' and to the PANIC OF 1837. Van Buren then introduced his INDEPENDENT TREASURY bill by which was enacted (1840) a system to provide depositories for Federal funds. Though temporarily abolished (1841–46), the Act (amended by the NATIONAL BANK ACT of 1863) created the basic Federal currency system until the FEDERAL RESERVE SYSTEM (1913) instituted a central banking organization.

The COINAGE ACT OF 1792 had established a standard of BIMETALLISM by which the U.S. dollar was declared legal tender, though from 1861 until 1879 the nation's currency was the authorized paper GREENBACKS. The BLAND-ALLISON ACT (1878) and the SHERMAN SILVER PURCHASE ACT (1890) were efforts to restore a bimetallic standard, but the need for a thorough overhauling of the banking and currency system was evident. (U.S. legal tender circulated in the form of gold notes, depreciated silver certificates, greenbacks, national bank notes, and a variety of coins.) Such stop-gap legislation as the GOLD STANDARD ACT (1900) gave some relief, and the Federal Reserve Act of 1913 added immeasurably to the nation's financial stability, but the PANIC OF 1929 (the most severe in the nation's history) made it clear that even the Federal Reserve System was inadequate and required revision.

The RECONSTRUCTION FINANCE CORPORATION (1932) eased conditions somewhat by buying preferred stock in distressed banks, but not until creation of the FEDERAL DEPOSIT INSURANCE CORPORATION (1933) was the financial structure stabilized. In a single year (1934) Congress passed the GOLD RESERVE ACT, the SILVER PURCHASE ACT, the SECURITIES AND EXCHANGE ACT, and chartered the EXPORT-IMPORT BANK. Today the regulatory power of Federal agencies is accepted as a way of gaining protection from repeated financial disasters.

See also the growth of and differences between INVESTMENT BANKING and COMMERCIAL BANKING, treated in separate entries.

The classic study is David R. Dewey, *Financial History of the U.S.* (12th ed., 1934), a standard work since 1903. See also W. J. Schultz and M. B. Caine, *Financial Development of the U.S.* (1937); and Paul Studenski and H. E. Krooss, *Financial History of the U.S.* (1952).

BANKS, NATHANIEL PRENTISS (1816–94), Massachusetts politician, entered Congress first as a Democrat (1853), then briefly as a Know-Nothing (1854), and next as a Republican (1855–57). In 1856 he won the speakership of the House in the bitterest contest for that office in history, a struggle that lasted two months and was aggravated by his uncompromising attack on the extension of slavery. (This has been called the first national victory of the Republican party.) He resigned his post to serve his state as governor for three terms (1858–60). With no military experience, but for reasons of community pride, at the outbreak of the Civil War he was appointed a major general of volunteers in the Union army. Always outmaneuvered by Jackson in the Shenandoah campaign (1861–62), he gave some assistance to Grant in the West (1863–64). He was later returned to Congress (1865–73, 1875–77, 1889–91).

Baptists, the most numerous Protestant denomination in the U.S., follow the religious doctrine that the sacrament of baptism should be received only by believers. The General Baptist Church (1611) was organized in London by members of scattered Independent groups. Baptist tenets stress separation of church and state, independence of congregations, a faith derived from an understanding of the Scriptures, and immersion as the Scriptural form of baptism.

Rhode Island became the center of the Baptist faith in America shortly after ROGER WILLIAMS established the Providence Plantation (1636). During most of the 17th century Baptists outside Rhode Island were persecuted in New England, but they flourished in the Middle Colonies. The Baptist Association was formed at Philadelphia (1707) and later adopted (1742) a Calvinistic Confession of Faith. This group of Particular Baptists held that atonement is individual, and differed from General Baptists, who followed the Arminians in asserting that salvation is possible to all, not merely to the elect. Since then, most American Baptists have been followers of Calvin in their theology. Rhode Island College (Brown University) was the first institution of higher learning founded under Baptist sponsorship (1764).

Schisms occurred as a result of the GREAT AWAKENING (*c.* 1740–50) throughout the colonies. The Separatist (or Revivalistic) Baptists organized churches in Virginia and North Carolina. Led by uneducated farmer-preachers, this form of evangelism was especially popular on the frontier, where (after 1818) opposition to foreign missions led to a further schism. These anti-mission Baptists were known as 'Hard-Shells.' The slavery issue tended to separate northern and southern Baptists, and prompted the formation (1845) of a Southern Baptist Convention.

Various Baptist State Conventions, organized to counter the anti-intellectualism and enthusiasm of frontier churches, promoted the cause of education. By the mid 19th century nearly every state had its Baptist-supported college. In 1965 the denomination (strongest in the South) had a total membership of more than 23,600,000.

BARA, THEDA (1890–1955), stage name of Theodosia Goodman, in 1915 established sex as a dominant motive in motion pictures with her performance in *A Fool There Was*. Within three years she appeared in 40 pictures under the direction of William Fox, all following the same pattern. The vamp, 'fascinating and unfathomable,' sets her trap for a man but is vanquished. Her vogue waned after World War I.

Barataria, see *Lafitte, Jean.*

Barbados, easternmost island in the British West Indies, 166 square miles in area, was colonized by the English two decades after Captain John Powell established possession in 1605. Its association with the mainland of North America took place chiefly during the colonial period, when trade with New England, New York, and Virginia was brisk (and not always legitimate) in sugar, cotton, molasses, and ginger. Charleston, South Carolina, was founded (1670) by several hundred Barbadian settlers.

Barbary Coast, popular name for the section of San Francisco that was notorious for its gambling resorts, dance halls, and brothels, is often mentioned in fiction. It was largely destroyed by the disastrous earthquake and fire of 1906.

Barbary Wars, see *Tripolitan War.*

Barbed wire, in its influence on the development of the Great Plains, was comparable to that of the cotton gin on the development of the South. Without absolute control of his land and stock, no rancher could afford extensive improvements. 'Slick' wire would not hold range stock, and plank fences were too expensive. In 1874 J. F. GLIDDEN put barbed wire on the market, and by 1890 most of the range land under private ownership had been fenced.

BARBER, SAMUEL (1910–), Pennsylvania-born composer, graduated from the Curtis Institute of Music (1932). His concertos, symphonies, chamber music, and stage works reveal an independent style of expression, neither ultraconservative nor ultramodern. His distinct lyrical gifts have full range in such vocal works as *Dover Beach* (1931), *Knoxville: Summer of 1915* (1948), *Melodies Passagères* (1951), and his elaborate *Prayers of Kierkegaard* (1954). His opera *Vanessa,* with libretto by Gian Carlo Menotti, was performed by the Metropolitan Opera Company (1958–59), and won the 1958 Pulitzer Prize in music.

BARD, SAMUEL (1742–1821), was the son of John Bard (1716–99), the first president of the Medical Society of the State of New York. Samuel Bard took his medical degree at Edinburgh (1765), founded the medical school of King's College (Columbia) in 1767, and later served as its dean (1792–1807). In 1813 the school was absorbed into the College of Physicians and Surgeons, of which Bard was president (1811–21). He wrote a standard text on 'midwifery' (1807), and influential papers on medical education.

BARKLEY, ALBEN WILLIAM (1877–1956), a graduate of Virginia Law School (1902), practiced law in Kentucky, where he entered politics. A lifelong Democrat, he served in the U.S. House of Representatives (1913–27) and in the Senate (1927–49). During his years as majority leader (1937–46) he gave firm support to Roosevelt's New Deal legislation. He was Truman's running mate in 1948, and served one term as Vice President (1949–53).

BARLOW, JOEL (1754–1812), Connecticut-born writer and diplomat, graduated from Yale (1778), served as chaplain in the Continental army (1780–83), and was admitted to the bar in Hartford (1786). He early became a member of the CONNECTICUT WITS, and his ambitious epic, *The Vision of Columbus* (1787), was judged at the time to be a literary masterpiece.

Abroad in 1788, he acted as the European agent in France for the Scioto (land) Company, whose failure shook him severely. As an ardent republican he moved in the liberal circles of William Godwin, Joseph Priestley, and Lafayette. When Thomas Paine suffered imprisonment in France during the French Revolution, Barlow arranged for the publication of *The Age of Reason.* His own liberal political essays won him honorary French citizenship. During 1795–1805, as consul to Algiers, he arranged treaties with the Barbary states, freed American prisoners, and aided Robert Fulton's inventions financially. Jefferson and Madison looked upon him as a confidential friend and adviser. In 1811 Madison sent him as minister to France, charged with negotiating a commercial treaty with Napoleon, but Barlow died near Cracow without seeing the Emperor.

BARNARD, FREDERICK AUGUSTUS PORTER (1809–89), after graduation from Yale (1828), taught in several southern institutions before serving as president of the University of Mississippi (1856–61), and of Columbia University (1864–89). At Columbia he extended the elective system, and increased and enriched the curriculum, particularly in the sciences. A prolific writer in the fields of mathematics, economics, and education, he challenged Darwinism as inconsistent with God's existence and the soul's immortality. His wish to see educational advantages extended to women was immediately realized after his death by the establishment on Morningside Heights of the college that bears his name.

BARNARD, George Grey (1863–1938), Chicago sculptor, laid the foundation of his reputation in France, with such works as *Brotherly Love* (Langesund, Norway), and the allegorical *Two Natures* (Metropolitan Museum). Later works, commissioned for public buildings and parks, include the colossal *Hewer* (1902), at Cairo, Illinois; the decorations flanking the entrance of the Pennsylvania state capitol; and the heroic rough-hewn *Lincoln* (1917), in Manchester, England (replica in Cincinnati). His collection of medieval art is now part of The CLOISTERS. Though tending to moralize, his work is substantial and vigorous.

BARNARD, Henry (1811–1900), after graduation from Yale (1830) devoted himself to the cause of education. While serving in the Connecticut legislature (1837–39), he introduced reforms similar to those being carried through by Horace Mann in Massachusetts, leading to the establishment of state school systems and the professional training of teachers. As school commissioner of Rhode Island (1843–49), and as superintendent of schools in Connecticut (1850–54), he gave those states, according to Mann, one of the best systems of education in the world.

While chancellor of the University of Wisconsin (1858–60), Barnard devoted himself to similar stimulating plans. As the first U.S. Commissioner of Education (1867–70), he prepared extensive reports on school legislation and on educational problems in the U.S. and Europe. For many years (1855–82) he edited the *American Journal of Education,* enormously important in the history of pedagogy. His translations of hitherto unavailable European educational classics, first published in the *Journal,* were issued in his 'Library of Education' (52 vols.). They transmitted to American educators the new Swiss and Prussian ideas of progressive education. With the exception of Mann, no other 19th-century American educator contributed so much to the cause of school reforms.

Barnard College (est. 1889), an undergraduate liberal arts college for women, is an independent corporation forming (since 1900) part of COLUMBIA UNIVERSITY. In 1965, with an endowment of $12,480,000 and a faculty of 170, it enrolled 1550 students.

Barnburners, the radical and progressive wing of the Democrats in New York state (1843–48), in national politics opposed extension of slavery and favored the WILMOT PROVISO (1846). Their agitation against machine control was so strong that, like the Dutchman who burned his barn to rid it of rats, they bolted the party to escape its abuses. By coalition with the Conscience (antislavery) Whigs of New England, and the abolitionist LIBERTY PARTY (1840), they formed the FREE-SOIL PARTY (1847–48) to take revenge on Lewis Cass, who 'stole' the Democratic nomination from Van Buren. Their ticket of Van Buren and C. F. Adams lost the election, and since the three elements comprising the party were basically incompatible, most of the Barnburners returned to the Democratic fold after the COMPROMISE OF 1850. Those with strong antislavery sentiment later joined the REPUBLICAN PARTY.

BARNES, Harry Elmer (1889–), historian and sociologist, was associated at various times with Columbia, Smith, and the New School for Social Research. His concern with the development of Western thought and historiography is reflected in such influential studies as *New History and the Social Studies* (1925), *History of Western Civilization* (2 vols., 1935), and *Social Institutions* (1942). An authority on penology, with N. K. Teeters he published *New Horizons in Criminology* (1943; 2nd ed., 1951). An energetic historical revisionist, he made Russia the chief war criminal in *The Genesis of the World War* (1926) and continued his revisionist position during the Pearl Harbor controversy.

BARNEY, Joshua (1759–1818). Maryland-born naval hero, while still in his teens commanded transatlantic merchant vessels. During the Revolution he engaged in large-scale privateering with such skill that his exploits inspired the men under his command. His capture of the British vessel *General Monk* in Delaware Bay (1782) was a notable achievement. For a time, after the Continental navy was dismantled, he served in the French navy (1796–1802). In the War of 1812 he commanded a flotilla at the battle of BLADENSBURG, but he was unable to prevent the British from entering Washington. Wounded and captured during the engagement, he was later released. His name became a symbol of gallantry in the early years of American naval history.

BARNUM, Phineas Taylor (1810–91), Connecticut-born prince of hoax and humbug, in his day was America's best known showman. He began his career as an entrepreneur in New York (1835) by exhibiting the blind and toothless Negro woman, Joyce Heth, representing her as the 161-year-old nurse of George Washington. In 1841 Barnum purchased the 'American Museum,' and by his exhibits of curiosities built a $4,000,000 fortune. He toured England with his midget, 'General Tom Thumb,' and in 1850 brought Jenny Lind from Sweden to sing in 150 engagements at $1000 a performance. In 1855 he retired to his fantastic home, 'Iranistan,' a tourist attraction outside Bridgeport, Connecticut, erected in Indo-Persian style. There he published his *Life* (1855), a best seller which he frequently revised. He returned to showmanship in 1871, and ten years later combined with a rival to form Barnum and Bailey's Circus, 'the greatest show on earth.'

BARR, Alfred Hamilton, Jr. (1902–), Michigan-born art historian, after graduation from Princeton (1922), taught fine arts in various colleges. As the first director of the Museum of Modern Art (1929–43), and as a counselor to departments of art in several institutions, he has been a shaping force in the development of contemporary American art. His writings include *Cubism and Abstract Art* (1936), and *What Is Modern Painting?* (1943).

BARRETT, Lawrence (1838–91), born in New Jersey of Irish parents named Brannigan, made his New York debut as an actor (1856) in *The Hunchback*. Excelling in tragic-romantic roles, he toured England and America with notable success. He is remembered especially for his association with Edwin Booth in Shakespearean plays.

Barron* v. *Baltimore (1833), the last case decided by the U.S. Supreme Court while John Marshall was on the bench, dealt with the issue of whether the Bill of Rights, and in particular the 'just compensation' clause of the Fifth Amendment, limited state as well as Federal action. The ruling, changed only since the 1950's, held that the prohibitions in the first eight amendments were protection against Federal, not state, infringements. A generation later, Senator John Bingham (Ohio) of the Committee of Fifteen on Reconstruction cited the decision to explain why he restricted state action depriving 'any person of life, liberty, or property,' and thus applied the new Fourteenth Amendment to the protection of corporations as well as Negroes.

BARRY, John (1745–1803), Irish-born naval officer, as the commander of the brig *Lexington* during the War of Independence was the first to capture a British ship of war (1776), the tender *Edward*. His later services were important and accomplished with gallantry. He commanded the frigate *Alliance* (after 1779) when she captured the privateers *Alert, Mars,* and *Minerva,* and forced two British brigs to strike. In March 1783 *Alliance* defeated the British ship *Sybil* in the last naval action of the war. After John Paul Jones, Barry ranks as the foremost naval hero of the Revolution.

Barrymore Family of actors had its beginning with Maurice Barrymore (1847–1905), born Herbert Blythe in India of British parents. He graduated from Cambridge, was admitted to the bar, but gave up law for the stage. He came to the U.S. in 1875, joined the stock company of Augustin Daly, and married (1876) Georgiana, daughter of the actor JOHN DREW (1827–62). The couple, both prominent actors, reared their three children, Lionel, Ethel, and John, in the tradition of the stage and thus established the 'royal family' of the American theater.

LIONEL BARRYMORE (1878–1954), after playing in the company headed by his uncle, JOHN DREW (1853–1927), starred in Barrie's *Pantaloon* (1905) and other romantic dramas. He was among the earliest actors of distinction to appear in motion pictures, starring in such films as *Grand Hotel* and *Dinner at Eight.* In later years he drew a nation-wide radio audience for his representation of Scrooge in Dickens's *Christmas Carol.*

ETHEL BARRYMORE (1879–1959) first appeared under the management of Charles Frohman. She gained top rank for her performance in such plays as Ibsen's *A Doll's House* and Galsworthy's *The Silver Box.* She was distinguished for the range, depth, and dignity of her acting, and in later years appeared with success in motion pictures.

JOHN BARRYMORE (1882–1942) had his first success in *The Fortune Hunter* (1909). After appearances in problem and romantic plays, he was acclaimed for his performances in the role of Hamlet (1924–25). Like his brother and sister, he appeared in motion pictures, and in *Rasputin and the Empress* (1933) all three co-starred.

BARTLETT, PAUL WAYLAND (1865–1925), Connecticut-born sculptor, was son of the art critic and sculptor Truman H. Bartlett. At the age of fifteen he began study in Paris at the Beaux-Arts under Cavelier. His *Bohemian Bear-Tamer* (Metropolitan Museum) won a gold medal at the Salon in 1888. His principal works include the equestrian *Lafayette* in the square of the Louvre (a gift to France from the school children of the U.S.), and his *Columbus* and *Michelangelo* in the rotunda of the Library of Congress. The virile strength of his representations extends to the bronze patinas of fish, reptiles, and insects, which are distinguished for their craftsmanship.

BARTOK, BELA (1881–1945), Hungarian-born composer and pianist, in 1905 began a collection of Magyar, Slovakian, and Romanian folk tunes, the rhythms and melodies of which influenced his subsequent compositions. In 1940 he settled in New York City, and the works of his 'American period' (1940–45) included his *Concerto for Orchestra* (1943), *Sonata for Solo Violin* (1944), and *Piano Concerto No. 3* (1945). Bartok's important secondary work in musicology was his transcription (in collaboration with Albert Lord) of the large collection of Serbo-Croatian folk tunes at Columbia.

As a pianist, Bartok played frequently in the U.S. He held academic posts at Columbia (research associate) and Harvard (Lamb lecturer), but he consistently refused to teach composition. In reduced circumstances, during the last year of his life he was supported anonymously by a grant from ASCAP (American Society of Composers, Authors, and Publishers).

BARTON, CLARA (1821–1912), founder of the AMERICAN NATIONAL RED CROSS, was a clerk in the U.S. Patent Office (1854–61) when she organized a volunteer service to aid sick and wounded Civil War soldiers on the field and in hospitals. Lincoln made her officially responsible (1865) for handling correspondence about missing soldiers and identifying unmarked graves. She went to Geneva (1869) as a member of the International Red Cross, and at the outbreak of the Franco-Prussian War (1870) she represented the German Red Cross group at the front. After a long campaign she won U.S. membership in the international group, and became the first president of the American group (1882–1904). At her instigation the American branch extended its activities to include relief on a wide scale for disasters of any nature.

BARTRAM, JOHN (1699–1777), self-taught pioneer American botanist, bought a farm near Philadelphia on which he established (1728) a botanical garden that attracted international interest. (It still exists as part of the Philadelphia park system.) To gather specimens he journeyed, mostly on foot, from the Catskills to Florida, and from Pennsylvania to Ontario. He corresponded with leading European scientists, and welcomed to his home and gardens the distinguished men of the day, who were eager to see the collections of the man that Linnaeus called 'the greatest natural botanist in the world.'

By exchanging seeds and bulbs, and by some attempt at cross fertilizing, he introduced many new plants. His *Observations* (1751), the best known of his published journals, is an account of a scientific expedition to western New York and Lake Ontario. Crèvecœur idealized Bartram as the archetype of the American farmer and democrat.

See Ernest Earnest, *John and William Bartram* (1940).

BARTRAM, WILLIAM (1739–1823), like his father JOHN BARTRAM, whom he accompanied on exploring trips, devoted his life to botany. His *Travels* (1791), vividly describing his botanizing in the Carolinas, Georgia, and Florida, not only attracted the attention of naturalists, but appealed to the sensibilities of European creative artists. It remains an essential document in the history of American romanticism. Coleridge drew upon the *Travels* for the landscape of *Kubla Khan* through which meanders, in Bartram's words, an 'inchanting and amazing chrystal fountain.' Bartram was also a pioneer ornithologist; his list of 215 native birds was the most complete until, at his insistence, ALEXANDER WILSON undertook his own scientific investigations.

BARUCH, BERNARD MANNES (1870–1965), after graduation from the College of the City of New York (1889), entered the brokerage business, in which his successful stock speculations made him wealthy before he was thirty. An adviser to government officials on problems of national defense at the outbreak of World War I, he was virtually economic dictator of the country as director (1918) of the WAR INDUSTRIES BOARD. His function as economic adviser continued into the 1920's and was renewed during World War II on matters relating to mobilization. As U.S. representative to the United Nations Atomic Energy Commission (1946) he submitted the BARUCH PLAN for international atomic energy control. His advice was frequently sought by Presidents and other highly placed public servants.

Baruch Plan, proposed (1946) by Bernard Baruch while he was serving as U.S. representative on the United Nations Atomic Energy Commission, incorporated the principal features of the ACHESON-LILIENTHAL PLAN, and added a provision for international inspection of atomic developments. The Soviet Union rejected it on the grounds that inspection was an invasion of sovereignty, and that suspension of the veto power in the Security Council (which the plan envisioned) would destroy the basic structure of the Council. The Commission therefore reached no conclusions.

Baseball is generally regarded as the national pastime of the U.S. Its bat-and-ball origins are probably as old as history, but certainly the English game of rounders figures in its ancestry. The myth that it was 'invented' by ABNER DOUBLEDAY at Cooperstown, New York, in 1839 is enduring folklore. It took its present character in 1845, when the New York Knickerbocker Club adopted a code of rules which basically remains in effect. At first a game played by gentleman amateurs, during the 1850's it became more widely popular. In that decade the National Association of Base Ball Players organized some 50 clubs, which scheduled games to attract admission-paying spectators. During the Civil War it was a popular recreation among the troops, and returning soldiers made its popularity nationwide: 'the leading feature in the outdoor sports of the U.S.,' a sports writer called it in 1866. Indeed, its combination of team play and individual virtuosity, its possibilities for quickly turning the predictable into the unexpected, give it endless fascination to participants and spectators alike.

Baseball thereafter became a business enterprise. In 1869 the Cincinnati Red Stockings, as the first professional team, toured the nation. Other professional teams were formed. The bribing of players and operation of illegal pools soon followed, and brought the game into disrepute until it was effectively stabilized by formation of the National League (1876). In 1901 the American League was organized as a permanent and powerful rival. The World Series, a series of games played between the champion teams of the two leagues, has been an annual affair of first importance in the sports world since 1903.

After 1920 both the profession and business of baseball were profoundly affected by the playing skill of BABE RUTH, who almost singlehandedly changed the game into an offensive contest, and the rulings imposed by KENESAW MOUNTAIN LANDIS, who as baseball commissioner enforced strict discipline upon players and management. Other famous baseball names include A. G. SPALDING, TY COBB, HANS WAGNER, CARL HUBBELL, WALTER JOHNSON, CONNIE MACK, JOHN MC GRAW, CHRISTY MATHEWSON, LOU GEHRIG, JOE DI MAGGIO, and JACKIE ROBINSON.

See R. M. Smith, *Baseball: A Historical Narrative of the Game* (1947), and Harold Seymour, *Baseball* (1960).

Bases Transfer Agreement, see *Destroyer Transfer Agreement.*

Basketball, one of the most popular amateur sports in the U.S., is unique among games in that it was originated by an American, James A. Naismith (1861–1939). While director of athletics at the Springfield (Mass.) YMCA, Naismith invented it (1891) as an indoor sport to be played on inclement days. Although it is played professionally, it is chiefly a sport in schools and colleges.

Basket Makers, so called, were the predecessors of the PUEBLO INDIANS in the Southwest who made fireproof vessels by covering baskets with clay and baking them. Their culture is believed to extend back to 1500 B.C., and is designated as Basket Maker I (hunters), Basket Maker II (farmers), Basket Maker III (town or CLIFF DWELLERS).

BASS, SAM (1851–78), Indiana-born desperado, after working in Texas as a cowboy and serving as a deputy sheriff, 'went bad' and joined cattle rustlers. He then became a train and bank robber until he was ambushed and shot by Texas Rangers. His career and death were the subject of frontier ballads.

Bastogne, Defense of (20–26 December 1944), was part of the battle of the BULGE in the last months of World War II in Europe. It became one of the epic engagements in American military history, and led to the decisive defeat of the German armies. Rundstedt's massive penetration of the Allied lines (16–26 December) pushed the center 50 miles in 11 days, with the Germans nearing the Meuse and the Channel coast. The success of the advance was frustrated only at the Belgian town of Bastogne, a strategic network of crossroads and the headquarters of the American VIII Corps. To von Rundstedt its capture was essential.

Fully realizing the situation and with the odds heavily against him, General Troy Middleton decided to defend the town whatever the cost. He evacuated the headquarters personnel and ordered the 101st Airborne Division into action. After two days of continuous bombardment from ground and air, the plight of the beleaguered town had seemingly become so hopeless (22 December) that the Germans formally demanded surrender, drawing from General Anthony McAuliffe the classic response, 'Nuts.' Clearing weather on the 23d permitted a five-hour air drop of supplies, and with the Third Army's valiant circling movement the besieged garrison was relieved. On 26 December the 4th Armored Division loosened the German pincers and reached the town.

Bataan, Defense of, began in January 1942. Vainly hoping to preserve Manila from destruction, General Douglas MacArthur evacuated the city late in December 1941, and made the island of CORREGIDOR off the Bataan Peninsula his headquarters. The tight Japanese blockade denied the defenders all supplies. Ordered to Australia, MacArthur left the besieged armies under the command of Lieutenant General Jonathan M. Wainwright (1883–1953). On Bataan itself, where all the troops were at the point of starvation, Major General Edward P. King (1884–1958) surrendered his forces, some 12,500 Americans and 60,000 Filipinos, whose numbers were decimated by the infamous 'death march' to prison camps. Bataan was liberated at the end of the PHILIPPINES CAMPAIGN (1945).

BATES, SANFORD (1884–), after heading the Massachusetts Department of Correction (1919–29), became the first chief of the new Federal Bureau of

Prisons (1930, 1933–37). He then joined the faculty of the New York School of Social Work, and became an adviser to or member of numerous crime prevention organizations. In *Prisons and Beyond* (1936) he argued that an adequate system must be built around the concept that 'prisoners must be returned to society,' and that society is protected only when prisoners are rehabilitated.

Battery, The, southwestern tip of MANHATTAN, is so called because the Dutch fortifications of New Amsterdam (New York City) were constructed there (1639) with a battery of cannon. In the 18th century it became a fashionable promenade. Castle Clinton (1807), was converted into Castle Garden, an amusement hall and opera house. For many years (1896–1941) the Battery was the site of the municipal aquarium.

Battle Hymn of the Republic, see *Howe, Julia Ward.*

Bay Psalm Book, so called, was the approved hymnal in the Massachusetts Bay Colony, compiled by Richard Mather, Thomas Weld, and John Eliot, the chief compiler. Issued at Cambridge by Thomas Day as *The Whole Book of Psalmes Faithfully Translated into English Metre* (1640), it is the earliest surviving book printed in British North America. It follows its stated intent to preserve accuracy at the sacrifice of grace of diction, but in its accuracy it exemplifies editorial scholarship of a high order.

For a century it remained the most widely used volume of hymns in the colonies, adopted as far south as Philadelphia. It went through 18 editions in England, 22 in Scotland, and possibly 70 in America, the last in 1773. The early edition printed the hymns only, but the ninth edition (1698) included thirteen tunes, and is the first book of music printed in America. Eleven rare and extremely valuable copies are known to survive of the original edition of about 1700 books.

BEACH, AMY MARCY (Cheney) (1867–1944), began her musical career at sixteen as a piano virtuoso, but after 1885 devoted herself chiefly to composition. She was the first American composer to write a symphony of importance, the *Gaelic Symphony* (1896). It was performed by the Boston Symphony Orchestra. Today she is best known for her songs and chamber music.

Bear Flag Republic (1846) existed briefly when a band of American squatters in the Sacramento valley of California, under the leadership of William B. Ide (and with the blessing of John C. Frémont) 'captured' the village of Sonoma, headquarters of the Mexican commandant. Hoisting their flag, which bore a grizzly bear facing a red star, the attackers proclaimed the Republic of California (the 'Bear Flag' state). The achievement had little importance. Three weeks later, on 7 July, Commodore JOHN SLOAT raised the American flag at Monterey upon the outbreak of the Mexican War, declaring California a part of the U.S.

BEARD, CHARLES AUSTIN (1874–1948), while teaching politics at Columbia (1904–17), with James Harvey Robinson wrote *The Development of Modern Europe* (2 vols., 1907), a pioneer text of economic, political, and cultural history. Beard resigned his post on an issue of academic freedom. His *Economic Interpretation of the Constitution* (1913) and *Economic Origins of Jeffersonian Democracy* (1915), attributing the work of the founders of the Republic to self-interest, affected a generation of left-wing historians. In *The Rise of American Civilization* (4 vols., 1927–43) written with his wife, Mary Ritter Beard, he carried forward his belief that history must regard the development of ideas as well as social and economic forces. His violently expressed isolationist sentiment in *President Roosevelt and the Coming of the War* (1948) lost him much of the esteem in which he had been held. Even his famous classic on the economic interpretation of the Constitution has been riddled by recent historians on the score of both facts and logic. But he greatly stimulated professional interest in historiography.

BEARD, D. C., see *Boy Scouts.*

'Beat' generation, see *'Lost' generation.*

BEAUMONT, WILLIAM (1785–1853), Connecticut-born army surgeon, pioneered in gastric physiology. He initiated his famous contribution to medical history while stationed on the frontier post of Fort Mackinac (1822). An accidental gunshot wound in the stomach of a nineteen-year-old soldier did not close (gastric fistula), and for ten years Beaumont continued at intervals to study the perforation. His exhaustive report, *Experiments and Observations on the Gastric Juice and the Physiology of Digestion* (1833; facsimile ed., 1929), remains a classic in its field. It revolutionized theories of the physiology of the stomach and the chemistry of gastric digestion.

BEAUREGARD, PIERRE GUSTAVE TOUTANT (1818–93), Louisiana-born graduate of the U.S. Military Academy (1838), served as an engineer on General Scott's staff in the Mexican War. Appointed superintendent of the Military Academy (1860), he resigned almost immediately to join the Confederacy as a brigadier general in charge of the Charleston district, and under his direction the first gun of the Civil War was fired against Fort Sumter. Second in command at the first battle of BULL RUN (July 1861), he was soon promoted to full general and sent to the West, where after SHILOH (1862) he commanded the Army of Tennessee, even though he feuded continually with Jefferson Davis. Ill health temporarily removed him from the field. He later returned to the front, and with J. E. Johnston surrendered his forces to Sherman at war's end. He later became a railroad president, and as a highly-paid director of the Louisiana Lottery he grew wealthy. He is regarded as an excellent engineer and a good combat soldier, whose strategic plans were sometimes more dashing than successful.

Beaver, TONY, 'a sort of relative' of the mythical Paul Bunyan, was the giant hero of tall tales told by lumberjacks of the Southern mountains. His exploits 'up Eel River' included such inventions as that of peanut brittle, created by damming the river with peanuts and molasses to prevent a flood.

BECKER, CARL LOTUS (1873–1945), professor of history at Cornell (1917–41) gained wide respect for his analysis of institutions. His views are embodied in *The Eve of the Revolution* (1918); *The Declaration of Independence* (1922); and the broader study, *The Heavenly City of the Eighteenth-Century Philosophers* (1932). The originality of his thought was matched by his ability to consider the writing of history as a literary endeavor.

BECKWOURTH, JAMES P. (1798–*c.* 1867), Virginia-born frontiersman, in 1823 joined the second of the ASHLEY EXPEDITIONS into the Rocky Mountains. His exploits as trapper and guide and his egotistic bombast made him a legendary figure among the MOUNTAIN MEN. His *Life and Adventures* (1856) is the authentic if exaggerated account of a mountaineer and scout whose aid was indispensable to explorers in the Far West.

BEEBE, [CHARLES] WILLIAM (1877–1962), naturalist and explorer, upon graduation from Columbia (1898) and further study there became curator of ornithology (1899) of the New York Zoological Society. He remained in lifelong association with that organization, later serving as director of its Department of Tropical Research. A thorough scholar, he was also able to popularize his subject by describing his numerous expeditions to many parts of the world in such books as *Jungle Days* (1925); *Half Mile Down* (1934), an undersea investigation of ocean fauna in a bathysphere; and *Unseen Life of New York* (1953).

BEECHER, CATHARINE ESTHER (1800–1878), daughter of LYMAN BEECHER, became an indefatigable propagandist as a writer and lecturer in behalf of household arts and education of the young. In 1827, at Hartford, Connecticut, she opened the Hartford Female Seminary, which flourished until she moved with her family in 1832 to Cincinnati, where she established the Western Female Institute. She encouraged better primary schools and emphasized teacher training for women. Hundreds of her pupils found posts in the South and West.

She opposed woman suffrage, but labored tirelessly for 'woman's profession' in the domestic sphere. Her books include *Treatise on Domestic Economy*

(1841), a classic in the teaching of domestic science; *Domestic Receipt Book* (1842), long in enormous demand; and (with her sister, Harriet Beecher Stowe) *The American Woman's Home* (1869), issued in a special school edition, a work well in advance of its time in matters of domestic planning and arrangement.

BEECHER, HENRY WARD (1813–87), son of LYMAN BEECHER, after graduation from Amherst (1834), began preaching in Indiana. Called to the Plymouth (Congregational) Church in Brooklyn, which he served for 40 years (1847–87), he drew weekly audiences that came to average 2500, and his sermons, issued in pamphlet form, were widely circulated. A man of easy congeniality, Beecher addressed himself to political and social, as well as religious themes with emotional directness, and his moral crusades had a lyric attraction that made him the foremost pulpit orator of his century.

Fervid in his denunciation of slavery, in the name of his church he subscribed a token number of rifles ('Beecher's Bibles') to the antislavery forces during the Kansas-Nebraska dispute (1856). As a modernist, he later supported Darwinism and the current reforms of the day. His defense in the adultery suit (1847) brought against him by Theodore Tilton (1835–1907), New York journalist and popular lecturer, was upheld, but by a divided jury, and thus the shadow of scandal was never quite dispelled.

BEECHER, LYMAN (1775–1863), a graduate of Yale (1797), became one of the leading revivalists in the West. Widely known in his day for his enthusiastic pulpit oratory, he was especially vigorous in denouncing intemperance and Catholicism. In fact, his fiery anti-Catholic lectures of 1831 were held responsible for a Boston mob's attack on the Ursuline Convent at Charlestown.

While president (1832–50) of the newly founded Lane Theological Seminary in Cincinnati, he faced charges of heresy for being a 'moderate Calvinist,' but was acquitted. His remarkable family of eleven children, including Henry, Catharine, and Harriet Beecher (Stowe) was regarded as a race apart: 'saints, sinners, and Beechers'; and gave him the reputation of being the father of more brains than any other man in America. His *Autobiography and Correspondence* (2 vols., 1863–64; repr., 1961) was gathered by his children and is a storehouse of vivid reminiscences by one of the notable American evangelists.

BEER, GEORGE LOUIS (1872–1920), historian, writer, and statesman, on retiring from the tobacco business (1903) devoted himself to economic aspects of British colonial policy, represented by *The Old Colonial System, 1660–1754* (2 vols., 1912). He is classified as one of the 'Imperial School,' which rejected the responsibility of George III for the Revolution. As a member of the American Peace Delegation (1919), he headed the Mandate Division, and was author of the mandate principle as then applied to forfeited German colonies.

BEERS, CLIFFORD WHITTINGHAM (1876–1943), Connecticut-born founder of the mental hygiene movement, soon after graduation from the Yale Sheffield Scientific School (1897) suffered mental disorders that led to institutional confinement. After his recovery, the publication of his reflections on the abuses he had suffered, in *A Mind That Found Itself* (1908), heralded the beginning of a new era in the management of the mentally ill by encouraging the foundation of psychiatric clinics.

Behaviorism, in psychology, is the doctrine that animal and human behavior can be explained by physiological response to stimuli. Whether such behavior is entirely mechanistic, as the term implied early in the 20th century, is now a study undergoing careful scrutiny. Mechanistic concepts, stemming from Hobbes and earlier philosophers, were first subjected to laboratory techniques during the 1890's by Pavlov and others, who made studies of conditioned reflexes. In the U.S. after 1900 E. L. THORNDIKE made systematic experiments in animal psychology, and J. B. WATSON pioneered in the 'behavioristic' approach to psychological issues. The work has been carried forward in the field of comparative psychology and psychobiology. Such men as R. M. YERKES, K. S. LASHLEY, and B. F. SKINNER have influenced the direction of psychology as an empirical science by demonstrating the essential similarity between human and infrahuman learning.

BEISSEL, JOHANN CONRAD (1690–1768), emigrated from Germany to Pennsylvania in 1720, and some ten years later founded at Lancaster the Ephrata Cloister, a semimonastic branch of DUNKARDS, famed for its music. He compiled the first Pennsylvania German hymnal, *Göttliche Liebes und Lobes Gethöne* (1730), printed by Benjamin Franklin. Author of more than 400 printed hymns (he is credited with over 1000), Beissel evolved a primitive system of metrical harmony, explained in his *Dissertation on Harmony* and embodied in the central collection of Ephrata hymns, *The Turtle Dove* (1747), comprising some 700 selections. He was one of the first composers in the colonies whose musical works were published.

BELASCO, DAVID (1853–1931), dramatist and producer, came to New York (1882) from his native San Francisco, where from his youth he had been associated with the theater as actor and manager. As playwright he created or adapted almost every type of dramatic device then flourishing. He was sensitive to popular taste and wrote smash hits no longer performed (with the exception of his adaptation of J. L. Long's *Madame Butterfly,* reworked by Long and Belasco, and set to music in opera by Puccini in 1904). As a producer his contribution to stagecraft, setting, costume, and (especially) lighting was influential. As a manager he discovered and developed some of the best actors of his time, including MRS. LESLIE CARTER, DAVID WARFIELD, and INA CLAIRE. As a showman he was unequaled in his ability to give plausibility to the implausible.

BELKNAP, JEREMY (1744–98), upon graduation from Harvard (1762) entered the ministry, but established his reputation as a historian. His *History of New Hampshire* (3 vols., 1784–92) is still respected for its objective scholarship and literary merit. His nationalism and interest in scholarship led him to compile sketches of early worthies, generally known as *American Biography* (2 vols., 1794–98), and to take the lead in founding the MASSACHUSETTS HISTORICAL SOCIETY, the first organization of its kind in the U.S.

BELL, ALEXANDER GRAHAM (1847–1922), Scottish-born scientist, came to the U.S. in 1871. As a professor of vocal physiology at Boston University (1873–77), he applied the method of his father, the distinguished phoneticist Alexander Melville Bell (1819–1905), to the education of the deaf. By means of 'visible speech,' or graphic diagrams of letters as uttered in talking, he taught the deaf to speak. His transmission of sound by electric waves led to the invention (1876) of the first telephone. His later inventions helped Edison to perfect the phonograph, and aided S. P. Langley in problems involving balance in aeronautics. He founded the journal *Science* (1883), and was one of the early presidents of the National Geographic Society (1896–1904).

BELL, JOHN (1797–1869), after practicing law in Nashville, Tennessee, served in the House of Representatives (1827–41), where he was distinguished as a debater. Estranged from Jackson, he became a leader of the Whig party in the South after 1835. For six months in 1841 he was Harrison's Secretary of War, but the death of Harrison and the rupture between the Whigs and President Tyler ended his cabinet service. As a member of the Senate (1847–59), he was one of the two Southerners in the chamber to vote against the KANSAS-NEBRASKA bill (1854). In fact, hoping to swing the border states to the cause of the Union, on the eve of the Civil War he accepted the candidacy for President on the ticket of the CONSTITUTIONAL UNION PARTY. Campaigning solely for the preservation of the Union, he won the electoral votes of Tennessee, Kentucky, and Virginia. Unable to prevent the secession of his own state, he silently accepted its verdict. He took no active part in politics after 1860.

BELLAMY, EDWARD (1850–98), after travel in Europe (1868) and admission to the bar (1871) engaged in journalism, first in his native state as an editor of the Springfield (Massachusetts) *Union,* then as a writer for the New York *Evening Post.* His first three novels went unnoticed, but *Looking Backward: 2000–1887* (1888) became a moral force. Ostensibly a utopian romance, it was soon recognized as a statement of social aims for a new co-operative order. Private enterprise, shown as a system fostering waste, inequality, and poverty, is made to give way to the collective organization of the State, an evolution that advances opportunity for all in an environment offering each man a chance to develop his own talents. The book was translated into several foreign languages and won such popularity that it led to the formation in the U.S. of a chain of Nationalist Clubs.

The power of Bellamy's ideas was impressive. They were partly embodied in the platform of the POPULIST PARTY, whose presidential candidate in 1892 polled over a million votes. Meanwhile Bellamy was lecturing widely, and had founded two journals, the *Nationalist* (1889–91), and the *New Nation* (1891–94). His early death ended a meteoric career of social reform, but he had initiated a debate about state capitalism and the co-operative commonwealth that affected economic thinking throughout the world.

Belleau Wood, Battle of (6–21 June 1918), the first sizable U.S. action in World War I, was an offensive engagement fought by the 2nd Division (Major General Omar Bundy, 1861–1940) and the 4th Marine Brigade (James G. Harbord, 1866–1947, temporarily disengaged as chief of staff) to preserve Allied gains made at CHÂTEAU-THIERRY. These forces withstood violent counterattacks, and by thrusting the German lines three miles back, cleared the wood.

BELLOWS, GEORGE WESLEY (1882–1925), after nearly completing undergraduate courses at Ohio State University, studied painting in New York with Robert Henri. Having achieved success with his realistic depictions, notably such prizefight canvases as *Stag at Sharkey's* (1907), he turned to lithography and produced prints now regarded as important as his paintings. He thus revived the art of illustration in the U.S.

Fascinated by strength and movement, Bellows made dramatic use of light and dark, and his varied portraits communicate directly through the medium of line, mass, and color. His larger canvases include *The Return of the Useless* (1918), picturing a trainload of French peasants returned by Germany as unfit for work, and *The Pic-nic* (1924), a domestic gathering.

BELMONT, AUGUST (1816–90), German-born New York financier, came to the U.S. in 1837 as a representative of the banking house of Rothschild and later founded his own bank. He served as minister to the Netherlands (1853–58), but his greatest public service lay in his energetic support of the Union during the Civil War. The influence which he exerted upon merchants and financiers in England and France helped prevent recognition of the Confederacy by those countries. He was an influential pro-Union Democrat, a princely art collector, and as the president of the American Jockey Club represented the elite of the Four Hundred.

Bemis, Heights of, see *Freeman's Farm.*

BENEDICT, RUTH FULTON (1887–1948), after graduation from Vassar (1909) became a student of anthropology under Franz Boas at Columbia, where she taught after 1924. She enlarged the scope of field studies in cultural anthropology to embrace the role of culture in personality formation. Her major contributions include *Patterns of Culture* (1934), *Race: Science and Politics* (rev. ed., 1943), and *The Chrysanthemum and the Sword: Patterns of Japanese Culture* (1946), a distinguished application of anthropological techniques to the study of an advanced modern society.

BENÉT, STEPHEN VINCENT (1898–1943), before graduation from Yale (1919) had published two volumes of poetry. His interest in American themes became evident in *A Ballad of William Sycamore* (1923), and his full maturity was recognized in *John Brown's Body* (1928), a verse narrative of the Civil War written with keen historical insights. His posthumous *Western Star* (1943), the first section of a projected epic of American history, describes the Jamestown and Plymouth settlements.

Collections of short stories are *Thirteen O'Clock* (1937), and *Tales Before Midnight* (1939). *The Headless Horseman* (1937) and *The Devil and Daniel Webster* (1939) are two one-act operas for which Douglas Moore wrote the music.

BENEZET, ANTHONY (1713–84), French-born philanthropist and teacher, settled (1731) in Philadelphia, where he helped organize the first antislavery group in America and founded and endowed a Negro school. He wrote several pamphlets against the slave trade (1762–71) and on behalf of the Indians.

BENJAMIN, ASHER (1773–1845), Massachusetts architect, built churches and houses throughout New England, but his influence spread principally through his *Country Builder's Assistant* (1797), and *The American Builder's Companion* (with Daniel Reynard, 1806), both of which went through a number of editions. The many plates in those volumes helped popularize the Adam or (in America) Federal style.

BENJAMIN, JUDAH PHILIP (1811–84), Louisiana planter and lawyer-statesman, was born in the West Indies. Spectacularly successful in his profession, he entered politics and served in the U.S. Senate, at first as a Whig (1853–56), then as a Democrat (1856–61). In the Confederate government he held successively three cabinet posts under Jefferson Davis, serving as Attorney General, Secretary of War, and Secretary of State. With a more realistic view of the desperate plight of the South than most of his compatriots, in the later months of the Civil War as an emergency measure he urged the arming of slaves, with the promise of emancipation. Angry southern planters defeated his proposal, though the Confederate Congress provided for slave soldiers. By this time, however, the war was coming to a close. After Appomattox, Benjamin eluded capture and as an exile eventually reached England (1866). There he was soon admitted to the bar, resumed his law practice, and as a queen's counsel made an impressive record.

BENNETT, FLOYD (1890–1928), an aviator, accompanied DONALD MAC MILLAN on his Greenland expedition (1925). For piloting RICHARD BYRD on his flight over the North Pole (1926) Bennett was awarded the Medal of Honor. His early death from pneumonia, contracted during a rescue operation, occurred just as he was to have accompanied Byrd to the antarctic as second in command. The U.S. Navy airport in Brooklyn, Floyd Bennett Field, is named for him.

BENNETT, JAMES GORDON (1795–1872), Scottish-born newspaper proprietor, came to the U.S. in 1819. After establishing a reputation as a news correspondent, he launched his four-page New York *Herald* (1835). By his energetic handling of news gathering he soon built up the largest newspaper circulation in New York City and made the *Herald* the best-known American paper in the world, with a circulation of 100,000 by 1864. He introduced YELLOW JOURNALISM in the U.S. by admitting sensational accounts of political maneuvers, illicit love affairs, sports, and violent crime as news. He was the first to employ foreign correspondents, and the first to use the telegraph as a news-gathering device. His innovations were far-reaching, for he sought to present news free from partisan bias, and his effort to give full news presentation was revolutionary.

His son, JAMES GORDON BENNETT (1841–1918), took over the editorship soon after the Civil War, and elaborated the established pattern of the paper by including feature items, at their best written by such observers as Mark Twain and Richard Harding Davis. He also sponsored newsworthy expeditions, beginning with that of HENRY STANLEY into Africa (1870–71) to find the explorer David Livingstone.

Bennington, Battle of (August 1777), was an engagement during the War of Independence fought near Bennington, Vermont, in which General JOHN STARK defeated German mercenaries sent on a raiding expedition by General Burgoyne. Attacked front and rear by some 1600 Green Mountain Boys, Lieutenant Colonel Friedrich Baum's 1200 dragoons, afoot in heavy boots, were all but annihilated. Although a minor encounter, it encouraged the American militia to take the field in similar frays, thus leading in a matter of weeks to the decisive blow at SARATOGA.

BENT, WILLIAM (1809–69), frontier trader, was the first permanent white settler in Colorado, and one of the best known men in the West. He erected Bent's Fort (*c.* 1832) on the bank of the Arkansas river, near Rocky Ford. The fort became the leading trading post of the Southwest, both for mountain fur business and overland Santa Fe commerce.

BENTON, THOMAS HART (1782–1858), was instrumental in building the territory of Missouri into a state, and as its most distinguished citizen served in the U.S. Senate for 30 years (1820–50). As an ardent champion of President Jackson (despite the fact that in an armed fracas Benton had once shot Jackson in the leg), he did creditable service to the nation as legislative leader of the Democrats. He was a rigid hard-money man, and as 'Old Bullion' Benton he led the administration forces in their successful war on the Bank of the U.S., and drew up Jackson's famous SPECIE CIRCULAR (1836).

An equally zealous supporter of western interests, Benton advocated government support of frontier explorations, with which he kept in close touch through the expeditions of his son-in-law JOHN C. FRÉMONT. Benton's staunch adherence to the Union cause cost him his Senate seat and virtually ended his political career. He then began his autobiography, *Thirty Years' View* (2 vols., 1854–56), and his *Abridgment of the Debates in Congress from 1789 to 1856* (15 vols., 1857–61), both invaluable as source material on political activities in his lifetime. Benton was free from self-interest, and his uncompromised principles were fully as creditable as those of his colleagues Webster and Clay. He remains one of the most colorful figures in American political history.

Two biographies are those by W. N. Chambers (1956) and E. B. Smith (1958).

BENTON, THOMAS HART (1889–), Missouri artist and grandnephew of Senator Benton, became known for his realistic portraits and murals of life in the Midwest and the South, represented by *Cotton Pickers, Homestead,* and *June Hay.* A graphic dramatizer of American types and themes, often truculent and chauvinistic, Benton shares with J. S. CURRY and GRANT WOOD leadership in the Regionalist movement, which demanded that artists paint the everyday world that they know.

Berea College, in Berea, Kentucky, was opened as a school in 1855. Nonsectarian and co-educational, it became a college in 1869. Berea's policy after the Civil War of admitting Negroes inspired Kentucky's law forbidding mixed schools. (The act was upheld in 1908 by the U.S. Supreme Court, although Justice Harlan, himself a Kentuckian, dissented vigorously.) The college owns and the students operate the town utilities. Crafts are taught and the products sold. The campus includes extensive farm and forest lands, and extension services are offered to the mountain people of eastern Kentucky. Berea charges no tuition. In 1965, with an endowment of $34,500,000 and a faculty of 112, it enrolled 1270 students.

BERENSON, BERNARD (1865–1959), Lithuanian-born art critic and historian, after graduation from Harvard (1887) took up residence in Italy. He made his lifework the study of Italian painting, especially of the Renaissance, on which he became an authority. In addition to many books specifically on the field, such as *Venetian Painters of the Renaissance* (1894), he later wrote more generally on the philosophy of art in such studies as *Aesthetics, Ethics, and History* (1948). He bequeathed his Florentine villa, *'I Tatti,'* to Harvard as a center for the study of Italian Renaissance culture.

BERGER, VICTOR LOUIS (1860–1929), Austrian-born political leader and émigré of 1878, with EUGENE V. DEBS founded the Socialist party (1901) and edited the *Social Democratic Herald* (1901–11). As the editor (after 1911) of the influential Milwaukee *Leader,* he opposed the non-socialist labor policies of the American Federation of Labor under SAMUEL GOMPERS. With Socialists in control of Milwaukee, he was the first member of his party to win election to Congress (1911–13). Twice re-elected (1918, 1919), he was both times excluded from the House on grounds of sedition, and sentenced to a twenty-year prison term under the wartime ESPIONAGE ACT of 1917. (His newspaper had branded the war a capitalist conspiracy.) The Supreme Court reversed the decision in 1921, the government withdrew all other cases against him in 1922, and in 1923 he was seated. His constituency returned him to Congress repeatedly after 1925.

BERING, VITUS JONASSEN (1681–1741), Danish navigator, at the request of Peter the Great commanded a Russian expedition across Siberia to determine whether Asia and North America were separate continents. Bering left St. Petersburg on this long journey in 1725 and arrived in Kamchatka three years later. The indefinite results of his mission seemed unconvincing to those who studied his data upon his return. Bering headed a second expedition in 1741, reached the coast of Alaska, and thus opened the region to Russian fur traders. During this undertaking Bering died on Bering Island in the sea that now bears his name. The accuracy with which he mapped coastlines was not fully recognized until Captain JAMES COOK proved their value by his discoveries along the northern coast of North America.

BERKELEY, GEORGE (1685–1753), Irish-born bishop of the Church of England, was one of the earliest and most important among the idealistic philosophers. He wrote *Principles of Human Knowledge* (1710) to refute Locke's belief in external, material reality. Appointed dean of Derry (1724), Berkeley shortly obtained a patent allowing him to found a college in Bermuda, and he expressed his vision in the opening line of a poem which anticipates his voyage: 'Westward the course of empire takes its way.' He wished his institution, which would educate Negroes, to inaugurate a system of such schools throughout America. Having won what he believed was the government's promise of £20,000, he sailed for America (1728), settling in Rhode Island while his plans matured. There he founded a Literary and Philosophical Society, and wrote *Alciphron* (1732), a set of Socratic dialogues refuting deism. Meanwhile certain gentlemen, including the Virginia planter WILLIAM BYRD (formerly the colonial agent in London), persuaded the authorities of defects in Berkeley's project, which was never realized. Berkeley returned home late in 1731.

In 1754 King's College (Columbia) was founded as an episcopal institution under the presidency of SAMUEL JOHNSON, the leading exponent in America of Berkeleian IDEALISM. Berkeley's name is honored at Yale in Berkeley College, and in the name of the city which is the site of the University of California.

BERKELEY, SIR WILLIAM (1606–77), one of the CAROLINA PROPRIETORS, was appointed royal governor of Virginia, and during his first term (1642–52) enjoyed considerable popularity with the colonists because of the improvements he instituted. An Anglican and a Royalist who denied toleration to nonconformists, during the interregnum he was forced from office and retired to his plantation. With the monarchy restored (1660), Charles II renewed Berkeley's commission, and Berkeley remained in office until his natural arrogance, hardened into audacity, manifested itself in tyrannical procedures during BACON'S REBELLION (1676) and led to his recall.

Berkshire Symphonic Festival was established (1934) as a summer music season near Stockbridge, Massachusetts, with Henry Hadley conducting 65 members of the New York Philharmonic Orchestra. In 1936 the festival was taken over by Serge Koussevitzky and the Boston Symphony Orchestra at Tanglewood, in nearby Lenox. Since 1940 the Berkshire Music Center has conducted a summer school in conjunction with the festival.

BERLIN, IRVING (Israel Baline) (1888–), Russian-born song writer, was brought to the U.S. in 1893. He has composed more than 1000 songs, many of which have been notable hits, beginning with 'Alexander's Ragtime Band' (1911) and 'Oh, How I Hate to Get Up in the Morning,' written during World War I. Lacking formal musical training, he played tunes in the key of F sharp on a piano adapted to change key mechanically. His *Watch Your Step* (1914) was the first of many successful musical comedies, which included the lavish *Music Box Revue* (1921). His earliest film musical, *Top Hat* (1935), was followed by *Easter Parade*. More recent stage hits are *Annie Get Your Gun* (1946) and *Call Me Madam* (1950).

Berlin airlift (April 1948–September 1949) was a concerted and successful effort of British and U.S. air forces to fly supplies into Berlin when the Soviet Military Government set up a land blockade of the city. The Allied Control Council had failed to guarantee the Western Allies access to their sectors of Berlin. The American commander, General LUCIUS CLAY, countered with a massive airlift, during which period British, French and American planes delivered to the city of Berlin nearly 2,250,000 tons of supplies, including food and coal. The blockade was lifted when it proved futile.

Berlin Decree (1806), issued by Napoleon in answer to the British blockade, declared that such a blockade of purely commercial ports was contrary to international law, and in retaliation forbade neutral ships to enter or leave British ports. The Decree initiated the CONTINENTAL SYSTEM.

Berlin, Treaty of (1921), formally established peace between the U.S. and Germany after World War I. It accepted many of the provisions of the Treaty of VERSAILLES (which the Senate had rejected two years earlier), including the provisions respecting disarmament, responsibility for the war and the war debts, and colonies. It rejected the features respecting the League of Nations, boundaries, and the International Labor Organization.

Berlin wall, a barrier lying along the borders of the Soviet controlled sector of the city and the French, British, and American sectors, was erected by the Soviet authorities in 1961 to interfere with the peaceful commerce between the sectors, which had been guaranteed to the citizens of Berlin by the original Four-Power agreements. At the beginning of the Allied occupation, travel between the sectors was generally free, and it remained so, except for a short interval of about 30 days in the mid-1950's, when the Soviets set up a minor blockade of crossing points and cut the telephone lines between their sector and the other three. On 13 August 1961 the Soviet authorities set up barbed wire blockades in the subways and elevated lines, cutting all mass transportation to and from their sector of the city. Within a matter of weeks the 'wall' had been set up, dividing the city from one end to the other, and blocking all but a few crossing points. About half of this 'wall' is a high, concrete structure, topped with barbed wire; the rest consists of barbed wire fences, with obstacles to prevent vehicles from crashing through it, and a few houses that have been blocked up or are being used by East German police.

BERLINER, EMILE (1851–1929), German-born inventor, came to the U.S. in 1870. Shortly after Alexander Graham Bell invented the telephone, Berliner devised the microphone (1877). In 1887 he invented the 'gramaphone,' a flat recording disc for reproducing sound. The device helped establish the Victor Talking Machine Company.

BERNARD, SIR FRANCIS (1712–79), after service as royal governor of New Jersey (1758–60) was transferred to Massachusetts (1760–69). He was an able administrator, but he had the duty of enforcing such unpopular laws as the STAMP ACT (1765) and the TOWNSHEND ACTS (1767). After publication of the MASSACHUSETTS CIRCULAR LETTER (1768) Bernard dissolved the Massachusetts assembly, and a year later he was recalled. An amateur architect, he designed Harvard Hall (1764) at the request of the College.

BERNSTEIN, LEONARD (1918–), after graduation from Harvard (1939) and the Curtis Institute of Music (1941), began his career as pianist, composer, and conductor. He directed the New York City Symphony (1945–48), and appeared frequently elsewhere as guest conductor before becoming director of the Berkshire Music Center (1951) and the New York Philharmonic (1958). In his frequent television appearances he has discussed subjects as varied as 'The Bach Mass in B Minor' and 'The Anatomy of Jazz.'

BETHE, HANS ALBRECHT (1906–), born in Alsace-Lorraine, was a professor of physics at Cornell after 1937, and directed the theoretical physics division at the Los Alamos Science Laboratory (1943–46), where the atom bomb was developed during World War II. His writings, devoted chiefly to nuclear theory, include *Mesons and Fields* (1955).

Bethel Community (1844–79), a communistic, agricultural experiment, was established by William Keil (1812–77), a German immigrant, on some 4000 acres in Missouri. His followers, mostly Germans and Pennsylvania Dutch from Ohio and regions near Pittsburgh, lived under a loosely governed but sternly moral patriarchy, subscribing to no religious tenet. Property and labor were shared, and the group prospered and was self-sufficient. The Aurora Community, in Aurora, Oregon (1855–81), was founded by Keil with similar purpose. Both organizations disbanded after Keil's death.

BEVERIDGE, ALBERT JEREMIAH (1862–1927), Republican senator from Indiana (1899–1911), was a pro-Roosevelt foe of trusts. At the same time he tried to liberalize his party, especially in the matter of child labor laws. His bitter 'insurgent' opposition to the upward revision of the PAYNE-ALDRICH TARIFF ACT was the cause of his defeat in the election of 1910. He then helped organize the PROGRESSIVE PARTY, and delivered the keynote speech nominating Theodore Roosevelt in 1912. In foreign policy he displayed jingoism, imperialism, and hostility toward the League of Nations. Unable to regain office, he devoted himself to writing history, and his *Life of John Marshall* (4 vols., 1916–19), though partisan, is a substantial and lively account of the struggle for ratification of the Constitution. It discusses the leading Supreme Court cases and is a major biographical study of a great jurist. Beveridge began his *Life of Abraham Lincoln* in 1922, but he lived only long enough to complete two rather critical volumes, covering the years to 1858.

BEVERLEY, ROBERT (1673–1722), Virginia planter, wrote an important and neglected account of *The History and Present State of Virginia* (1705, enlarged in 1722). Set forth with acerb humor, the narrative is shrewd in its comments on the southern gentry (in whose favor it is obviously biased), and on earlier chroniclers and foreign critics. Purporting to replace older works, it draws heavily upon them, but it is rich in Beverley's own observations of the life and the events he had experienced.

Evidence points to Beverley as author of the anonymous pamphlet *An Essay upon the Government of the English Plantations on the Continent of America* (1701; repr. with introd. by Louis B. Wright, 1945). An original paper of great political interest, the tract offers a plan of union among the colonies for mutual aid and defense, and has been termed 'one of the earliest and best reasoned contributions to the discussion of colonial government published by an American.'

Bible societies, Protestant organizations formed to distribute Bibles, were founded on a national scale in the U.S. by the establishment (1816) of the American Bible Society. The Gideon International (est. 1899) places Bibles in hotel rooms throughout the U.S. and in foreign lands. The United Bible Societies, with headquarters in both London and Geneva, was established in 1946 as an association of more than a score of such bodies.

Bicycling, after major improvements had introduced light, hollow-steel frames, ball bearings, and pneumatic rubber tires (1888), became a fad of major proportions in the U.S. Bicycle clubs already had been formed, and both men and women participated in what became one of the most popular sports. Such organizations as the League of American Wheelmen (1880) contributed importantly through their agitation for good roads. By 1893 more than 1,000,000 bicycles were in use. In the U.S. bicycling declined with the coming of the automobile.

BIDDLE, NICHOLAS (1786–1844), Philadelphia man of letters and financier, graduated with high honors at fifteen from the College of New Jersey (Princeton) in 1801. After serving abroad (1804–7) as secretary first to John Armstrong, minister to France, then to James Monroe, minister to Great Britain, he returned home and became associate editor of Joseph Dennie's *Port Folio,* and later its editor (1812). His literary discrimination appears best in his editing of the notes and journals used in compiling the *History of the Expedition under the Command of Captains Lewis and Clark* (2 vols., 1814), one of the great travel accounts. Biddle sensed the grandeur of the compact narrative, and presented the manuscripts as he found them, with a minimum of editorial tidying.

Biddle also proved himself one of the most competent of all American bankers. As president of the Second BANK OF THE U.S. (1823–36), he used his ample financial and administrative talents to provide sound currency and inexpensive commercial credit. However, his firm management brought on him the enmity of local bankers and businessmen, especially in the South and West, an opposition on which President Jackson was able to capitalize. Biddle was politically inept in handling the bank's recharter, permitting it to become a political issue in the election campaign of 1832. After the Federal charter expired (1836), Biddle obtained a new one from the state of Pennsylvania. But he had turned from able direction of central banking to hazardous business ventures about which he made serious misjudgments. He retired from the presidency in 1839 and two years later the bank was forced into liquidation. Biddle lost his fortune. He was tried on criminal charges, released on a technicality, and died a broken man.

BIENVILLE, JEAN BAPTISTE LE MOYNE, Sieur de (1680–1768), son of the Sieur de LONGUEUIL and brother of the Sieur d'IBERVILLE, after exploring with his brother in the Hudson Bay region (1697), accompanied him to the lower Mississippi. Bienville founded Mobile (1710) and New Orleans (1718), and was chiefly responsible for creating the French colony of Louisiana.

BIERSTADT, ALBERT (1830–1902), German-born painter of the HUDSON RIVER SCHOOL, won popularity for his topographically correct canvases, executing such Rocky Mountain vistas as *Estes Park, Colorado,* and *The Valley of Yosemite.* His flamboyant landscapes in oil satisfied the American love of size and convinced his wealthy patrons that they were getting their money's worth. Critics disliked the monotony of these large canvases, but recent admirers cite the freshness and charm of his earlier small-scale landscapes.

Big Bend National Park (1944), 698,000 acres of deep canyons, desert plains, and mountains in western Texas, offers sharp contrasts in wilderness scenery. A huge triangle, on two sides it is bordered by the Rio Grande.

Big business is a popular term first used in the latter part of the 19th century to describe large corporate enterprises that controlled production, patents, markets, prices, and labor forces in many different American industries and businesses. See ABSENTEE OWNERSHIP, BUSINESS CONSOLIDATION, CORPORATIONS, HOLDING COMPANIES, INTERLOCKING DIRECTORATE, MERGER, MONOPOLY, POOLS, and TRUSTS.

Big Five was the term applied to executive heads of state at the VERSAILLES PEACE CONFERENCE (1919): Wilson (U.S.), Lloyd George (Great Britain), Clemenceau (France), Orlando (Italy), and Saionji (Japan). In World War II it designated the U.S. (or Roosevelt), Great Britain (or Churchill), the U.S.S.R. (or Stalin), China (or Chiang Kai-shek), and France (or de Gaulle).

At the Versailles Conference, Wilson, Lloyd George, Clemenceau, and Orlando constituted the BIG FOUR, a designation which in World War II applied to Roosevelt, Churchill, Stalin, and Chiang Kai-shek.

The BIG THREE at Versailles were Wilson, Lloyd George, and Clemenceau. In World War II the term designated Roosevelt, Churchill, and Stalin.

Big stick is a phrase popularized by President Theodore Roosevelt in one of his early speeches requesting a large naval appropriation: 'There is an old adage that says, "Speak softly, and carry a big stick, and you will go far."' He did not use the words to incite war, but it fired the imagination of editors and cartoonists, both friendly and unfriendly, who saw the implication that recalcitrant nations or business organizations might be brought to heel by a show of power.

BIGELOW, Jacob (1786–1879), professor of materia medica at Harvard (1815–55), collected and systemized New England flora, and his *American Medical Botany* (3 vols., 1817–20) long remained the most important work of its kind. Bigelow believed that the healing process in some diseases is aided by withholding medical treatment. His *Discourse on Self-limited Diseases* (1835), a protest against excessive bloodletting and drugs, was characterized in 1879 by Dr. Oliver Wendell Holmes as having exerted more influence on medical practice in America than any other publication.

BIGELOW, John (1817–1911), author and diplomat, graduated from Union College (1835) and in 1838 was admitted to the New York bar. For some years (1848–61) he shared with William Cullen Bryant the ownership and editing of the New York *Evening Post,* stressing a strong antislavery policy. Thereafter he served as consul at Paris (1861–64), and minister to France (1864–67), during which period his diplomatic labors were crucial in preventing French recognition of the Confederacy.

His principal literary achievements were his annotated editions of the autobiographical writings of Franklin (3 vols., 1874) and his edition of Franklin's works (10 vols., 1887–89). His biography of Bryant (1890) was written from intimate acquaintance. As president of the board of trustees of the New York Public Library and executor and trustee of the estate of SAMUEL J. TILDEN (1886), he was largely responsible for setting up the great reference collections in the library by amalgamating the Astor, Lenox, and Tilden foundations (1895). His autobiography, *Retrospections of an Active Life* (5 vols., 1909–13), sets forth the reflections of an able public servant and observant commentator.

Biglow Papers, The, began as nine satirical 'letters' in verse, written (1846–48) in Yankee dialect by James Russell Lowell to express his resentment against slavery and the Mexican War. They were widely circulated in newspapers, collected in book form (1848), and immediately recognized as the high point of Yankee humor. A second series, supporting the North during the Civil War, was published in the *Atlantic Monthly* and collected in 1867.

Bill of Attainder is a legislative act declaring a person attainted — that is, without civil right — without judicial trial. It was originally used in England (1459) to destroy political opponents. It fell into discredit in the late 18th century. The U.S. Constitution specifically denies Congress and the states the right to pass such a bill (Art. I, sects. 9 and 10).

Bill of Rights, the first ten amendments to the Constitution of the U.S., was proposed by Congress (1789), chiefly at the instigation of James Madison, and soon ratified by the states (1791). Like many of the state bills, it is closely modeled on the Virginia Declaration of Rights (1776), the work of GEORGE MASON, and it spells out the protections usually assumed under a common-law form of government, in which individual rights are assumed to exist as inalienable. The First Amendment sets up prohibitions against legislative action, giving citizens freedom of religion, assembly, speech and press, and the right of petition. The next seven secure the rights of property and guarantee the rights of persons accused of crime (defendants' rights). The Ninth protects rights held concurrently by the people and the federal government. The Tenth assures the reserved rights of the states.

In 1788, when the Constitution was adopted, two schools of thought contested the issue of adopting such a bill. Although the state constitutions had some form of declaration of rights, many of the framers of the Federal Constitution believed that an enumeration of individual rights was unnecessary and perhaps unwise, since the rights already were presumed to exist, and a statement of them might imply the extension of government into spheres where it did not operate. 'The truth is,' said Hamilton in the *Federalist,* that 'the Constitution is itself, in every rational sense, and to every useful purpose, a bill of rights.'

On the other hand, both in and out of Congress, there was a feeling that a definite statement of rights would be a restraining influence on the gradual encroachments toward which governments naturally are prone, and could be a specific guide to the judiciary in reaching decisions to protect individual rights. Many states therefore, when they ratified the new Constitution, did so with the recommendation that explicit rights be written immediately into the instrument. Thus the first Congress prepared and submitted to the states twelve amendments, all but two of which were adopted. (The rejected items, quite out of place in so basic a document, apportioned Representatives and established salaries for members of Congress.)

Although various provisions of the Bill of Rights have been questioned from time to time, in general their validity is so strongly entrenched that infringements on them continue to rouse a moral and political protest so formidable that alterations in any foreseeable future are quite unlikely. Similar bills in the state constitutions in all instances emphasize the same rights as those protected in the Federal Constitution.

See Irving Brant, *The Bill of Rights: Its Origin and Meaning* (1965).

BILLINGS, John Shaw (1839–1913), a graduate of Miami University (1857), received his medical training at the Medical College of Ohio, and served as a surgeon in the Civil War. Later as medical inspector of the Army of the Potomac he organized the Surgeon General's Library, which he built into one of the great institutions of its kind. His *Index Catalogue of the Library of the Surgeon-General's Office* (16 vols., 1880–94) made history in the field of medical bibliography. When the New York Public Library was consolidated, he assumed its direction (1896–1913), creating the form that similar great public libraries in the U.S. have emulated. Billings was Daniel Gilman's principal adviser in laying the foundations for the Johns Hopkins Hospital and Medical School.

BILLINGS, William (1746–1800), born in Boston, where he died in abject poverty, was the first professional American musician. Though unschooled in music, he wrote hymns and sacred choruses of great vitality. Published in a series of collections from *The New England Psalm Singer* (1770) to *The Continental Harmony* (1794), they include 'fuguing tunes' (a rugged counterpoint), compelling in style and often deliberately iconoclastic. His patriotic anthems written during the Revolution include the belligerent 'Chester,' and paraphrases of the Psalms invoking God's mercy for the patriot cause. An innovator in the use of the pitch pipe, he favored the double-bass or cello in church services, and campaigned for vigorous congregational singing. He founded the Stoughton (Mass.) Musical Society (1786), the oldest singing group in the U.S. still in existence.

Bills of Credit, promissory notes or FIAT CURRENCY, were first issued in the colonies by Massachusetts (1690) as a device to pay soldiers in anticipation of tax collection, and proved so successful that they were adopted and used as a regular practice by all the colonies before 1760. But they were issued in excess, and in 1764 Parliament forbade the circulation of paper currency. To finance the Revolution, Congress issued CONTINENTAL CURRENCY. Under emergency conditions Congress issued TREASURY NOTES in 1812, 1837, 1846, 1857, and during the Civil War made GREENBACKS legal tender. The RESUMPTION ACT (1875) provided for the redemption of such notes in gold, and thereafter, with approval of the Supreme Court in the last of the LEGAL TENDER CASES (1884), they became a part of the currency in permanent circulation.

Billy the Kid, nickname of William H. Bonney (1859–81), who was a desperado of the Southwest. His exploits as a wholesale cattle thief made his name legendary even in his lifetime. He is reputed to have committed more than twenty murders before a sheriff finally shot him.

BIMELER, Joseph Michael, see *Zoar Society*.

Bimetallism, legalized by the COINAGE ACT of 1792, fixed the value of silver and gold at a ratio of 15 to 1, but in the domestic market silver slightly outvalued gold for several decades. The Coinage Act of 1853 in practice allowed the operation of a GOLD STANDARD, since gold could more profitably be used for large transactions. Both gold and silver disappeared from circulation during the Civil War with the issuance of GREENBACKS, and the COINAGE ACT of 1873 ended legal bimetallism and established the gold standard, which then by law (and later *de facto*) has continued to the present.

BINGHAM, GEORGE CALEB (1811–79), was born in Virginia but spent most of his life in Missouri. He began his study of painting in Philadelphia and continued it abroad (1856–59). He returned to Missouri, where he painted portraits for a living but made his reputation with genre studies, everyday subjects that won contemporary popularity. *The Jolly Flatboatmen* (1844) was the first of his 'river life' series. In 1851 he began his political series with *County Election* and *Canvassing for a Vote*.

BINGHAM, HIRAM (1875–1956), professor of Latin American history at Yale (1907–25), headed many expeditions into South America. His best studies culminated in *Machu Picchu* (1930), and *Lost City of the Incas* (1948). Active in Republican politics, he served Connecticut as governor (1924–25) and U.S. Senator (1925–33). He headed U.S. military aviation schools during World War I, and then and later helped advance the cause of aeronautics.

BINNEY, HORACE (1780–1875), after graduation from Harvard (1797) practiced law in Philadelphia, and for half a century was a distinguished leader of the U.S. bar. As a Whig member of the House of Representatives (1833–35), he ably defended the Bank of the U.S. against the onslaught of President Jackson, and helped NICHOLAS BIDDLE temporarily re-establish its prestige. His arguments in the case involving the fortune of STEPHEN GERARD, in which he successfully opposed Daniel Webster, influenced the interpretation of the law on charitable bequests.

Biography, in colonial America, appealed especially because it reflected the lives of men who shaped institutions. Thus the biographical studies written by Plutarch, Suetonius, and the English antiquarian Thomas Fuller were staple items in early libraries. The earliest American biographer of importance was COTTON MATHER. Although his *Magnalia* (1702) is pietistic, it is a notable collection of sketches of New England worthies, and does not embellish legends. Benjamin Franklin's *Autobiography* is a classic. The forerunner of the more extensive 'lives' is John Marshall's *Life* of Washington (5 vols., 1804–7), partisan and somewhat plagiaristic, but the major effort of a young man of action to record events of consequence while his memory of them was still green.

Washington Irving's *Columbus* (4 vols., 1827–28), superbly written, represents the beginning of independent research into archives, and has the respect of contemporary scholars. JARED SPARKS, working from manuscript resources, edited the *Library of American Biography* (25 vols., 1834–47). It filled a glaring gap and still continues to be useful. JAMES PARTON established his literary reputation with a life of Horace Greeley (1855), and his vivid portraits of Burr, Jackson, Franklin, and Astor are still respected.

After the Civil War biography attracted the able talents of J. L. Motley and Henry James. Henry Adams's *Life* of Gallatin (1879) applied the methods of historical research and criticism to a notable degree. The 10-volume *Abraham Lincoln: A History* (1890), by Nicolay and Hay is in fact more history than biography, but it spurred later monumental studies of individuals. GAMALIEL BRADFORD created portraits in miniature (after 1912) by analysis of characteristics of his subjects.

Fictionalized biography attempts to invent the thoughts and conversations of its characters. Examples are Gertrude Atherton's portrayal of Alexander Hamilton as *The Conqueror* (1902) and Catherine Bowen's representation of Justice Holmes in *Yankee from Olympus* (1944). The 20th-century psychologies of Freud and others were reflected in biographies as in criticism, and a school of 'debunkers' flourished briefly during the 1920's. The increasing attention of biographers to men and women in nonpolitical spheres has given a balance previously lacking.

Landmarks in American biographical writing include Carl Sandburg's *Lincoln* (6 vols., 1926–39), Douglas Freeman's *Lee* (4 vols., 1934–35), and Dumas Malone's *Jefferson* (5 vols., 1948–). Significant also are the delineations of Wilson by Arthur Link and of F. D. Roosevelt by Frank Freidel. The most important biographical encyclopedia is Allen Johnson and Dumas Malone, eds., *Dictionary of American Biography* (22 vols., 1928–44, with supplements).

Biology, see *Botany; Zoology.*

Birch Society, a radical rightist organization, was formed in 1958 by Robert H. W. Welch of Massachusetts to honor the memory of John Birch, a Fundamentalist Baptist missionary (whom Welch never knew) killed by Chinese communists shortly after V-J Day (1945). Its cells of 'Americanists' dedicate themselves to exposing the 'communist conspiracy,' which allegedly is infiltrating the highest Federal offices. In 1961 Welch offered $2300 in prizes to college students for the best essays pleading for the impeachment of Chief Justice Earl Warren on the ground that Warren's actions and legal decisions were communist inspired. The Society, according to its critics, shares the tradition of such nativist elements as the KU KLUX KLAN and MC CARTHYISM.

Bird Woman, see *Sacajawea.*

BIRNEY, JAMES GILLESPIE (1792–1857), although son of a Kentucky slaveholder, believed in emancipation. After graduation from the College of New Jersey at Princeton (1810) he practiced law before moving to Alabama, where he briefly entered politics and mismanaged a slave plantation. He returned to Kentucky, freed his slaves, and after 1833 abandoned the Whig party to devote himself wholly to the abolitionist cause, thus becoming an outstanding example of the few wealthy abolitionist patricians who accepted the ostracism which their principles made inevitable.

After removing to Ohio to aid the UNDERGROUND RAILROAD, he founded the *Philanthropist* (1836–37), an antislavery weekly that was influential in the area. Wholehearted in his support of the Union, he sharply differed from the uncompromising position of William Lloyd Garrison, and sought to end slavery by political action. Moderate abolitionists formed the LIBERTY PARTY with Birney as presidential nominee (1840), and his electoral vote in 1844 was sufficient to divert New York from Clay and thus place Polk in the White House. Birney's importance in U.S. history is greater than his public record would indicate.

Birth control movement, the effort to limit the size of families as a step in social progress, made no headway in the U.S. until the public-health nurse Margaret Sanger (1883–1966) gained support for establishment of the first permanent birth control clinic (New York, 1923), allowing physicians to give advice for 'the cure and prevention of disease.' In 1936 the Federal law prohibiting the mailing of 'obscene' contraceptive information was modified. Thereafter 'planned parenthood' became a widely used phrase. After World War II the 'population explosion' made birth control an issue of debate on a world-wide scale. In 1965 two impressive actions in the field of birth control were taken, one judicial and one legislative. The U.S. Supreme Court in a landmark decision struck down a Connecticut birth control ban, thereby establishing a new constitutional guarantee of right of privacy, and the New York Assembly repealed an 84-year-old ban on the dissemination of birth control devices and information.

Bismarck Sea, Battle of (2–3 March 1943), was a major air-sea engagement in World War II, fought by an American fleet under Admiral William F. Halsey against Admiral Yamamoto's Japanese fleet, which was approaching New Guinea. By skip-bombing, General George C. Kenney's Army Air Force sank 22 Japanese ships, including the entire Japanese troop convoy. Admiral Yamamoto was killed in the action.

Bison, see *Buffalo.*

Bituminous Coal Act (1935), the Guffey-Snyder Act, known as the 'little NRA,' sought to administer production quotas, price fixing, and labor relations on the NRA code. The Supreme Court invalidated it in *Carter* v. *Carter Coal Co.* (1936). Congress re-established its chief provisions in the Guffey-Vinson Act (1937), which omitted the wages-and-hours clause.

BLACK, GREENE VARDIMAN (1836–1915), Illinois-born dentist, after graduation from Missouri Dental College (1877), became a professor at the Chicago College of Dental Surgery (1884–89). As the dean of the Northwestern University Dental School (after 1897), he taught operative dentistry, pathology, and bacteriology. His contributions to dentistry as a teacher, author, and originator of methods and instruments give him unique importance in his field. His writings include *Dental Anatomy* (1891), and *Operative Dentistry* (2 vols., 1908).

BLACK, HUGO LA FAYETTE (1886–), first won prominence as a lawyer in Birmingham, Alabama. He served in the U.S. Senate (1927–37), where he fought big-business combinations, introduced the controversial 30-hour-week bill to assist labor, and led the move resulting in passage of the FAIR LABOR STANDARDS ACT. Appointed an Associate Justice of the U.S. Supreme Court (1937) by President Roosevelt, Black continued to uphold strong welfare and civil liberties legislation. He helped to apply the restrictions in the Bill of Rights to the states as well as the federal government. This offset the revelation at the time of appointment that he had once been a member of the Ku Klux Klan; he explained publicly that he had held a membership card briefly under mitigating circumstances.

BLACKBEARD was the name given to the English pirate Edward Teach (also Thack, Thatch, *d.* 1718), whose fancily braided coal-black whiskers gave him the appearance of 'a frightful meteor.' He was originally a privateer during the War of the Spanish Succession (1701–14). He later preyed on shipping in the West Indies and the Virginia-North Carolina coast. He was protected by the governor of North Carolina, Charles Eden, but the governor of Virginia, Alexander Spotswood, sent out a twenty-gun sloop which ended the pirate's career. Blackbeard's exploits became legendary, as did stories of his oft-sought buried treasures.

Black Belt, a crescent-shaped area of nearly 5000 square miles, mainly in Alabama, is a region of black soil which contrasts with the red clay to the north and south. From 1830 to 1860 it was especially productive of cotton. Because of its large slave population, the expression has often been used to denote Negroes in general throughout the Deep South.

Black Codes, see *Reconstruction.*

Blackfoot Indians, so-called because of the color of their moccasins, comprised a group of bison-hunting Plains tribes of Algonquian stock. They ranged from the Yellowstone river northward to Saskatchewan and westward to the Rockies. During the early years of the 19th century they were among the strongest Indian confederacies, in frequent conflict with the Crows, and often hostile to the whites.

Black Friday (24 September 1869) was the climactic day during the months in which the stock gamblers JAY GOULD and JAMES FISK tried to corner the U.S. ready gold supply. Greenbacks at the time were not legal tender for all purposes, and the question rose whether the government intended to redeem them in gold, which had become a speculative commodity on the New York stock exchange. A lobbyist who was a brother-in-law of President Grant (A. R. Corbin) was induced to exert pressure to prevent the government from selling gold. The President was then entertained on Fisk's steamboat, where he discussed high finance.

Grant's understanding of stock market operations was elementary and his responses were noncommittal, but Fisk and Gould spread the rumor that the President opposed such government sales, and they began purchasing gold on a large scale. On Grant's instruction Secretary of the Treasury GEORGE BOUTWELL placed four million gold dollars on the market, and the gold price plunged from 162 to 135, to the ruin of many speculators. The nation was aroused, and Grant was branded as incompetent for permitting himself to be enmeshed in the scandal.

BLACK HAWK (1767–1838), chief of the SAUK AND FOX INDIANS, was leader in the BLACK HAWK WAR (1832), in which he was captured. After temporary imprisonment he was taken by the government on a tour of eastern cities, and presented at the White House to President Jackson. Released in 1837, he spent his final year on the Sauk and Fox reservation on the Des Moines river. In defense of his action as a war leader he wrote his *Autobiography* (1833; reissued 1955), a classic statement of the Indian view of white encroachments.

Black Hawk War (1832) was a conflict between the SAUK AND FOX INDIANS, led by Chief BLACK HAWK, and U.S. militia and regulars commanded by General Henry Atkinson (1782–1842). In the 30 years following the Louisiana Purchase (1803), well over 100 treaties had been more or less forcibly concluded with western tribes. By a final treaty (1830) with the Sauk and Fox, title to all lands east of the Mississippi river was presumably ceded, and white settlers began staking claims in Wisconsin and Illinois. In 1831 the encroachment of squatters in the Illinois country led Black Hawk to reprisal after he had witnessed the plowing of his ancestors' graves. The militia drove him into Missouri territory, but, threatened by famine and hostile Sioux, he recrossed the river into Illinois with several hundred tribesmen, hoping to plant corn. When Atkinson ordered him back to Iowa, he refused to comply, and the war was on. (Among the militia officers who pursued Black Hawk into the Wisconsin wilderness was young Captain Abraham Lincoln.) The starving warriors were finally cornered during the summer of 1832 and, together with women and children, were massacred.

Black Hills, comprising an area of 6000 square miles, skirt Wyoming but are chiefly located in South Dakota. Rising from the semiarid plains, they are an upthrust reaching 7242 ft. at Harney Peak. Mineral resources abound in great variety. On the side of Mount Rushmore GUTZON BORGLUM sculptured the colossal faces of four American Presidents.

Blacklists, in labor relations, were lists of men known to belong to unions. They were used by anti-union business firms to prevent the employment of union members. They were outlawed by the WAGNER-CONNERY ACT (1935).

Black Mountains, part of the Appalachian system, are in western North Carolina. They rise to 6684 ft. at Mt. Mitchell, the highest elevation east of the Rockies.

'Black Reconstruction,' see *Reconstruction.*

Black Republicans, so called by their antagonists, were the Northerners who, aroused by the KANSAS-NEBRASKA ACT (1854), first met on the local and state level in 1854 and 1855, and in national convention in 1856 to establish the REPUBLICAN PARTY. The term was later contemptuously applied by Southerners during the Reconstruction period to Northerners who made the problems of the Negro freedmen their special concern.

***Black Warrior* Affair** occurred when the coastwise trading vessel *Black Warrior,* touching at Havana in February 1854, was seized by Spanish authorities after the ship's master refused to produce a cargo manifest. Secretary of War Davis urged President Pierce to make an issue of the case in order to provoke Spain into a war, the result of which, Davis believed, could be the annexation of Cuba. Secretary of State Marcy, however, handled the case tactfully. Spain apologized, remitted the fine, and later paid $53,000 indemnity. A farcical anticlimactic link was the OSTEND MANIFESTO.

BLACKWELL, ELIZABETH (1821–1910), born in England, was the first woman in the U.S. to receive a medical degree, granted her (1849) by Geneva (N.Y.) Medical College. Encouraged by the New York Quakers and by Florence Nightingale, she and her sister, Dr. Emily Blackwell, founded the New York Infirmary for Women and Children (1854) where she gave clinical experience to women aspiring to be doctors. During the Civil War she made Bellevue Hospital an intensive short-course training center for women nurses entering military hospitals, thus replacing the system of male nurses. In 1867 at Bellevue she established the Woman's Medical College, with the first school for nurses in the U.S. Two years later she returned to England to teach gynecology in a school she founded in London, and became a professor at the new London School of Medicine for Women (1875–1907). Welfare Island off New York City, known before 1921 as Blackwell's Island, was once named for her.

Bladensburg, Battle of (24 August 1814), was fought during the War of 1812 by untrained American militia against British regulars at Bladensburg, Maryland. Under the command of Major General Robert Ross, 4500 British troops were making their way along the banks of the Patuxent river toward Washington. Some 7000 militia, led by the inept General William Winder, took up a position to await the encounter. (President Madison and most of his cabinet had left Washington and were nearby to witness the fray.)

The raw recruits checked the British for a while and sustained a few casualties, but their battle line disintegrated. Commodore JOSHUA BARNEY and his boat squadron put up gallant resistance until their ammunition was exhausted. Winder ordered a retreat, and Ross entered Washington and burned the public buildings, including the Capitol and the White House. Congress whitewashed the affair, but public criticism of the national disgrace forced the resignation of Secretary of War Armstrong.

BLAINE, JAMES GILLESPIE (1830–93), Pennsylvania-born politician, after graduation from Washington College (now Washington and Jefferson) in 1847 studied law and settled in Maine. There he edited an influential newspaper, helped found the Republican party in that state, and made politics his career. While in Congress (1863–76), for six years as Speaker (1869–75), he became a leading presidential possibility. But shortly before the Republican convention of 1876 a house investigating committee, on the testimony of James Mulligan, charged him with using his political influence to aid railroads in which he had an interest. The 'Mulligan letters,' written by Blaine to a Boston businessman, were in Mulligan's possession until Blaine, the 'plumed knight' of the convention, procured and refused to surrender them. The episode was a factor in swinging the nomination from Blaine to Hayes, but Blaine nevertheless won election to the Senate (1876–81). He sought his party's nomination for the presidency again in 1880, but he had alienated the reform wing (MUGWUMPS) and had made enemies of the party STALWARTS. This time he lost to Garfield, who won the election and appointed Blaine his Secretary of State. Upon the President's assassination, Blaine resigned. In 1884 he campaigned for the presidency a third time and won the Republican nomination.

Spectacular campaign mud-slinging was invited by the fact that Cleveland, the choice of the Democrats, publicly acknowledged his illegitimate child, and that Blaine had never been able to explain the postscript 'Burn this letter' in the Mulligan affair. The *coup de grâce* was administered by the hapless remark of a clerical supporter, who denounced the Democrats before an Irish-Catholic audience in New York City as the party of 'Rum, Romanism, and Rebellion.' The insult to the race and faith of his New York friends cost Blaine the state's electoral vote, and the presidency.

Blaine nevertheless continued to be the leader of his party, shaping its platforms and guiding its slate of candidates, and with the return of the Republicans to office (1889), Benjamin Harrison chose Blaine as his Secretary of State (1889–92), in which post Blaine strengthened Latin-American ties and gave evidence of his unquestioned intellectual grasp of statesmanship. A magnificent orator with great personal charm, he was idolized by many, and his autobiography, *Twenty Years of Congress* (2 vols., 1884–86), was widely read. He was loathed by others as a cynical party politician willing to make corrupt alliances with big business. His adeptness at playing the political game severely handicapped him as a moral force, and kept him from the eminence to which he aspired.

See David A. Muzzey, *James G. Blaine: A Political Idol of Other Days* (1934).

BLAIR, FRANCIS PRESTON (1791–1876), was the brilliant, Virginia-born founder of one of the most influential families in 19th-century American politics. He was raised in Kentucky, and studied law at Transylvania. He graduated in 1811, and in that year helped his father, the state's attorney general, prepare the arguments for the right of a state to tax the U.S. Bank. His early effectiveness as an editorial writer for the Frankfort *Argus* brought him President Jackson's invitation to found the Washington *Globe* (1830–45) as the Democratic administration organ. For many years he wielded influence as the editor of the *Congressional Globe* (1837–72), a record of the debates and acts of Congress, and predecessor of the present *Congressional Record*. As a leading member of Jackson's KITCHEN CABINET he influenced major state policies. He joined Van Buren and the Free-Soilers in 1848, broke completely with the Democrats over the Kansas-Nebraska Act (1854), and presided over the Republican Convention that nominated (1856) his presidential choice, John C. Frémont. Four years later he gave strong support to Lincoln's nomination. He played a dramatic role in promoting the HAMPTON ROADS CONFERENCE (1865); in this affair he conferred privately with President Jefferson Davis, suggesting an armistice during which troops could be sent to oust the French puppet Maximilian from Mexico. After the war, like his sons, Blair broke with the party over radical Reconstruction, and returned to the Democratic fold.

His Kentucky-born son, MONTGOMERY BLAIR (1813–83), after graduation from the U.S. Military Academy (1835), also studied law at Transylvania. In 1837 he settled in St. Louis, where he practiced law and held several public offices as the protégé of Senator Thomas Hart Benton before moving to Washington, D.C. (1855). Like all the Blairs, he left the Democrats for the new Republican party. He won national prestige in the antislavery cause as counsel for Dred Scott and John Brown. He played a key role in Lincoln's cabinet as Postmaster General, not only as an unusually effective innovator in that department, but as the persistent advocate of reinforcing the southern forts, particularly Fort Sumter. His bitter feud with the radicals over their desire to punish the South led to his resignation from the cabinet in 1864 and his return to the Democratic party. In 1876 he established a paper to strengthen Samuel Tilden's claim to the presidency and acted as his counsel before the Electoral Commission on the disputed votes.

A younger son, FRANCIS PRESTON BLAIR (1821–75), also born in Kentucky, was educated for politics as a contributor to his father's *Globe*. After graduation from Princeton (1841), like his brother he practiced law in St. Louis, where he supported Henry Clay. Although he was a slaveholder, he took an increasingly advanced antislavery position in Missouri politics, published a Free-Soil paper, the *Barnburner*, organized a Free-Soil party in the state, and like the other Blairs rejected the Kansas-Nebraska Act as proslavery. He was twice elected to Congress (1856–58, 1860–62), where his remarkable oratory and organizing ability helped him create a Unionist party at home. He directed organization of the armed 'Wide Awakes' of St. Louis to stop a secessionist effort of the Missouri militia that was supported by the governor, and to save the Federal arsenal on the eve of the war. In Congress he stood for the Jefferson-Clay policy of emancipation coupled with colonization, and warned the South that slavery was moribund. He ruined himself financially during the Civil War by financing troops for the campaign that led to Vicksburg, and he served as a major general in Sherman's march to the sea. Again, following family policy after the war, he broke with the radicals and revived the Democratic party in Missouri. After the defeat (1868) of the Democrats, who had nominated him as a running mate of Horatio Seymour, he became a liberal Republican and helped Horace Greeley secure the presidential nomination in 1872. He was selected to serve in the Senate by the Missouri legislature in 1871, but he failed to be reelected two years later.

See William E. Smith, *The Francis Preston Blair Family in Politics* (2 vols., 1933).

BLAIR, JAMES (1655–1743), Scottish-born clergyman, was sent (1685) as Episcopal missionary and personal representative of the Bishop of London to reform the church in Virginia. The founder and first president (1693–1743) of the College of William and Mary, he labored unceasingly to make the institution a training center for Anglican clergymen, and his influence on the intellectual life of the colony was unrivaled. He helped prepare (1697) for the

London Board of Trade *The Present State of Virginia and the College* (published in 1727), and withstood the opposition of Governor Andros, for whose recall in 1697 this irascible Scot was largely responsible. For one year (1740–41) he served as governor of the colony.

BLAKELOCK, RALPH ALBERT (1847–1919), son of a New York physician and graduate of the College of the City of New York (1867), abandoned the study of medicine to make a career of painting. Largely self-taught, he was fascinated by landscapes, which he reproduced with a markedly original if imperfect technique. In the fantasy of his haunting forms and dark harmonies he bears kinship to ALBERT RYDER. Poverty and mental strain ended his creativeness in 1899, when he was committed to an asylum until 1916. His principal works include *Brook by Moonlight* (Toledo Museum), and *Moonrise* (National Museum).

BLALOCK, ALFRED (1899–1964), Georgia-born surgeon-in-chief of the Johns Hopkins Hospital after 1941, made notable contributions in the fields of surgical shock and of hypertension and heart disease. Blalock was the first to perform the Blalock-Taussig operation, based on studies by the Hopkins pediatrician, Helen Taussig. This operation, by making possible normal circulation and oxygenation of the blood, remedies the condition of 'blue babies.'

BLAND, JAMES A. (1854–1911), Negro composer born in Flushing, N.Y., was educated at Howard University, and as a member of a minstrel troupe toured the U.S. and England. A prolific song writer, he is best remembered for *Carry Me Back to Old Virginny, Oh, Dem Golden Slippers,* and *In the Evening by the Moonlight.*

BLAND, RICHARD (1710–76), was a member of the Virginia House of Burgesses (1745–74) and delegate to the Continental Congress (1774–75). He was the author of the earliest published defense of the colonies in their stand on taxation, *Inquiry into the Rights of the British Colonies* (1766), which argues that since the colonies owe their existence solely to the crown, they are in no way obligated to Parliament.

Bland-Allison Silver Act (1878), the first of several government subsidies to silver producers and farmers who wished to re-establish BIMETALLISM, was pushed through Congress over the veto of President Hayes. The RESUMPTION ACT (1875), by causing an appreciation of GREENBACKS, had been condemned by those for whom a sound money program worked hardship, chiefly debtors and western farmers. The Bland-Allison Act provided for the monthly purchase of $2,000,000 to $4,000,000 worth of silver bullion to be coined into standard silver dollars at the legal ratio with gold. The object was to increase the per capita circulation of money and thus raise commodity prices. It never appreciably added to the currency, partly because successive secretaries of the treasury continued a policy of purchasing the minimum amount of silver, and thus the price of silver steadily declined in the world market. The silver agitation continued, and in 1890 Congress passed the SHERMAN SILVER PURCHASE ACT.

BLATCH, HARRIOT STANTON, see *Stanton, Elizabeth Cady.*

BLAVATSKY, HELENA PETROVNA (1831–91), after a turbulent childhood in Russia and extensive wanderings in the Far East, came to New York (1873), where she took the lead in founding the first Theosophical Society (1875) to investigate the 'hidden mysteries of nature' and psychic phenomena. (She later formed similar societies in England and India.) To disciples her *Isis Unveiled* (1877) was an inspired text, proclaiming that man's soul is 'Deific Absolute Essence, infinite and unconditioned . . . from which all starts, and into which everything returns,' meanwhile inhabiting many different bodies in various incarnations. Theosophic 'lodges' continue to be active.

Bleeding Kansas was the phrase applied to the five-year Border War (1854–59) following passage of the KANSAS-NEBRASKA ACT, when the territory was racked by a civil strife which stirred the entire nation to partisan bitterness. The law gave those who settled the territory the right to determine whether it would be slave or free, but even before the government could open its first land office (1854), many Free-Soilers from the Midwest (those opposing the extension of slavery) had scrambled to stake their claims. Thus in the absence of any legal means for registering and protecting land claims, disputes resulted. Such 'squatter sovereignty' blocked the entry of eastern Free-Soilers into Kansas. BORDER RUFFIANS began crossing into the territory to vote illegally. Brawls then ensued with northern 'Jay Hawks.' Both sides engaged in horse stealing, arson, pillage, lynching, and pitched battles. The New England EMIGRANT AID SOCIETY, at the instigation of such fervid abolitionists as the preacher Henry Ward Beecher, sent in precision rifles ('Beecher's Bibles'). When the border ruffians sacked Lawrence, John Brown retaliated by staging the 'Pottawatomie massacre' (May 1856), a brief reign of terror.

In the same month Senator Charles Sumner delivered his intemperate speech on 'The Crime against Kansas,' for which three days later a southern extremist caned him into insensibility. The Republicans then used the phrase 'bleeding Kansas' (attributed to Horace Greeley) as a campaign slogan, implying that the violence in Kansas stemmed solely from the disagreement over Douglas's 'squatter sovereignty.' In 1857 the Kansas LECOMPTON CONSTITUTION not only failed to be adopted but was a major cause of the North-South split in the Democratic party. Thus the preliminary skirmishes of the Civil War were fought in Kansas.

BLISS, TASKER HOWARD (1853–1930), a graduate of the U.S. Military Academy (1875), having held several administrative posts in the U.S. Army, was appointed chief of staff in 1917, shortly after the U.S. entered World War I. He was a delegate to the VERSAILLES PEACE CONFERENCE (1919) and supported Wilson's plea for U.S. entry into the League of Nations.

BLISS, WILLIAM DWIGHT PORTER (1856–1926), sociologist, was born of missionary parents in Constantinople, and entered the Congregational ministry after graduation from Amherst (1878). In 1889 he founded the first society in the CHRISTIAN SOCIALISM movement and edited its organ *Dawn* (1889–96). He lectured in the U.S., Canada, and England on problems of labor and social reform, and with EDWARD BELLAMY and H. D. LLOYD published the monthly *American Fabian* (1895–1900). He is chiefly remembered as editor of *Encyclopedia of Social Reform* (1897; rev. ed., 1907), with articles contributed by scholars. It was a pioneer attempt to gather primary social data focused upon the aspirations of the Social Gospel.

BLITZSTEIN, MARC (1905–1964), after study at the Curtis Institute and in Berlin, composed the operas *The Cradle Will Rock* (1937), *No for an Answer* (1941), and *Reuben, Reuben* (1951). A successful writer of symphonies and song plays for radio and television, he has attempted to give social significance to themes comprehensible to the unsophisticated.

Bloc, as the term is used in the U.S., is a combination of groups within different political parties acting together for a common purpose. Such co-operation has always occurred in legislative assemblies, but deliberately organized blocs are recent innovations, beginning with the farm bloc (1921). Since the 1920's such organizations as the bonus bloc, the farm tariff bloc, or the far western bloc have become common in America.

BLOCH, ERNEST (1880–1959), Swiss-born composer, directed the Cleveland Institute of Music (1920–25), the San Francisco Conservatory (1925–30), and after a nine-year interlude in Switzerland settled permanently in the U.S. as professor of music at the University of California at Berkeley. His desire to express his religious background has led him often to choose Jewish themes, as in the symphony *Israel.* Mentor and teacher of many distinguished American composers, he is represented in his later works by *Rhapsodie Hebraique* (1951), *Concerto Grosso, No. 2* (1953), and *Proclamation* (1955). He is recognized as a master of contemporary music, and his works, written in a variety of forms, gain steadily in reputation.

Blockade, the effective denial of egress

from or ingress to a port, has been an important military and diplomatic factor in U.S. history. The Treaty Plan (1784) of the Continental Congress maintained that a blockade to be 'legal' must be effective against neutrals, and during the Napoleonic wars President Madison protested to Great Britain and other powers the 'pretended blockades' used after British vessels sailed under ORDERS IN COUNCIL. His proclamation (1814) against the 'paper' British blockade, which he asserted was being used as a pretext for plundering American commerce, claimed that because it was ineffective it was therefore unlawful.

At the outbreak of the Mexican War (1846) naval commanders were ordered to blockade as many Mexican ports as possible on the Gulf and Pacific coasts. The most effective and extensive blockade ever attempted was that ordered by Lincoln, clamped on the ports of the Confederate states by the Union navy. During the Spanish-American War the U.S. Navy blockaded all ports of Cuba and Puerto Rico. It similarly blockaded German ports during both World Wars.

Blockade-running, Confederate, at the start of the Civil War, was a lucrative trade, since the risk of capture was only one in ten for the 800 southern vessels evading the Union blockade. Putting in at the Bahamas, runners exported over 1,250,000 bales of cotton, and smuggled back to Confederate ports goods valued at some $200,000,000, including food, clothing, munitions, and hospital supplies. But the traffic drained off gold, and thereby depreciated Confederate currency. The Union blockade constantly tightened (in 1864 only one in three runners got through), and became a major factor in winning the war.

Bloody Angle, the climax of the first phase of the WILDERNESS CAMPAIGN, was a section of the battlefield at Spotsylvania, Virginia, where (12 May 1864) the armies of Grant and Lee fought one of the most sanguinary battles of the Civil War.

Bloody Shirt, in the expression 'to wave the bloody shirt,' was a vote-getting stratagem relying upon sectional rivalries, used by Republicans during the elections of 1872 and 1876 especially, to offset Democratic charges of corruption during the administrations of President Grant. One explanation for the origin of the phrase goes back to the Scottish massacre at Glencoe (1692), when widows of the slain are said to have waved the bloody shirts of their husbands to arouse action for vengeance.

BLOOMER, AMELIA JENKS (1818–94), proposed 'the emancipation of woman from intemperance, injustice, prejudice and bigotry,' according to the masthead of her periodical *The Lily* (1848–54), devoted to woman's uplift. Her advocacy of Turkish trousers in place of the fashionable hoop skirt met enough response to give the name 'bloomers' to such revolutionary dress, and drew audiences to Bloomer minstrels, Bloomer parades, and a farce of the 1850's titled *The Bloomers, or Pets in Pants.* As recently as 1944 she was the subject of a musical comedy, *Bloomer Girl.*

BLOOMFIELD, LEONARD (1887–1949), was professor of Germanic philology at Chicago (1927–40), and of linguistics at Yale thereafter as successor to EDWARD SAPIR. His classic study, *Language* (1933), greatly influenced later work in the field by establishing the principle that language must work from the spoken rather than the written symbols; that grammar definitions depend upon the forms, not the meanings, of words; and that the history of a form cannot reveal its meaning, since language develops as a system of sounds and forms independent of the past.

Blue Eagle was the insignia displayed by merchants on posters and other publicity material to testify compliance with the provisions of the NATIONAL INDUSTRIAL RECOVERY ACT (1933). The emblem was an American eagle with spread wings, printed in blue.

Blue laws is the term applied to legislation of a restrictive character meant to dictate standards of morality. Scholars dispute the origin of the term. Some say the laws got their name because 17th-century Puritans adopted blue as their emblem; others suggest that such laws were bound in blue or printed on blue paper. Such laws have been enacted from early times in many countries. After the Reformation, Parliament passed a succession of strict Sunday observance laws which generally were transplanted to the American colonies. The first law compelling church attendance was passed in Virginia (1624), and Massachusetts enacted a similar ordinance ten years later. Sumptuary laws, prescribing wearing apparel, were designed as aids in distinguishing the status of social groups. In New England the Puritan sumptuary laws were modeled on those which Parliament had enacted from time to time, and followed Puritan practice in avoidance of ostentation, but the act of 1651, which itemized materials or ornaments prohibited to persons with estates under £200, was patently a class measure. Laws forbidding work, sports, and travel on Sunday were common throughout the colonies well into the 18th century.

The term was popularized by the Reverend Samuel Peters's anti-Puritan book, *General History of Connecticut* (1781), which contained many imaginary 'blue laws,' such as those forbidding women to kiss their children on the Sabbath or to dance or play cards.

After the War of Independence few such laws were enforced, although many long remained on the statute books, and to a limited degree some are still felt in various states. Anti-tobacco legislation, beginning in the earliest colonial period, has had the longest history. Even in the 20th century national prohibition attests to the resurgence from time to time of the blue law spirit.

Today every state in the union except Alaska has some ban on Sunday activities. The laws range from the prohibition of a single activity (boxing in California, barbering in Oregon) to broad bans on industry and commerce. They are riddled with erratic contradictions. In Pennsylvania bicycles may be sold on Sundays, but not tricycles. In Massachusetts it is legal to dig for clams, but not to dredge for oysters. The situation has proved so confusing that even the U.S. Supreme Court gets lost in the tangle.

Blue Ridge, a range of the Appalachian mountain system, extends from northwestern Maryland through Virginia, West Virginia, and North Carolina into Georgia. Its southern reaches are the highest, with an altitude of 5000 ft. The section in northern Virginia forms Shenandoah National Park (est. 1935).

Blues are a type of song written in a characteristic major key, with bittersweet mood and syncopated rhythms. Entirely American in form, they were introduced by Negroes in the Deep South during the 19th century. The length and proportion of the songs derive from European harmonies, but the inner form is the African call-and-response pattern of Negro work song ballads. The difference between the blues and religious music was never sharp, and some blues form as a shouting spiritual. Since the melody, harmony, and rhythm allow infinite complication, the blues require expert musicianship to maneuver. The *Memphis Blues* (1911), composed by W. C. HANDY, was the earliest dance-band exploitation of the idiom. When JACK TEAGARDEN arrived in New York City (1927), he was the only known white trombonist and singer who could render the blues in an 'authentic' manner. Not until the 1930's, with such performances as those of BESSIE SMITH and CHARLIE PARKER, were recordings accurately labeled 'The Blues.' The twelve-bar blues are at the core of modern JAZZ.

BLUME, PETER (1906–), Russian-born painter, was brought to the U.S. in 1911 and became a citizen ten years later. Trained at the Art Students League and at the Beaux-Arts, he became a leading exponent of SURREALISM. He is characteristically represented by *South of Scranton* (Metropolitan Museum), and *Parade* (Museum of Modern Art), works which combine the incongruous with sharp focus to produce the intensity and illogical quality of a dream.

BLY, NELLIE, see *Seaman, Elizabeth C.*

Board of Trade and Plantations, appointed by the king, was virtually the colonial office of the English government from 1696 until the eve of the War of Independence. (It supplanted a committee of the Privy Council known as Lords of Trade and Plantations.) As a paid board of eight members, on which the chiefs of state served *ex officio,* it was the group through which most colonial matters were routed. Its powers were advisory only, but it was central in the political system and its members were subject to party shifts. Functioning under the Secretary of State for Foreign Affairs, it regulated foreign commerce, enforced trade and navigation acts, supervised colonial administration, and negotiated commercial treaties. Although it had no authority to make decisions, it shaped the policies by which Great Britain met her IMPERIAL PROBLEMS.

The position of the president of the Board of Trade became especially important under the energetic direction of Lord HALIFAX, who took office in 1748 and was admitted to the cabinet in 1756. Others who served significantly as president of the Board include CHARLES TOWNSHEND, Lord SHELBURNE, and Lord HILLSBOROUGH.

BOAS, FRANZ (1858–1942), German-born professor of anthropology at Columbia (1899–1937), was an authority on the ethnology and folklore of American Indians. His training of many distinguished students for objective field studies replaced (or supplemented) library research. His *Tsimshian Mythology* (1916) is a monumental work dealing with tribal myths of the Northwest Coast Indians, and a model for later studies. He also pioneered in applying statistical methods to biometric studies.

Determined to make anthropology a practical weapon against bigotry, he did much to destroy the racist assumptions underlying the Immigration Act of 1924, with its National Origins Clause which favored Nordics over 'inferior peoples.' Influential among his numerous writings are the cultural theories presented in *The Mind of Primitive Man* (1911), *Anthropology and Modern Life* (1928), and *Race, Language, and Culture* (1940).

Boat racing in the U.S. began to flourish in the 1830's with the formation of amateur racing and rowing clubs. With the establishment of yacht clubs, such as the New York Yacht Club (1844), YACHTING as a competitive sport grew in popularity. Professional crews and single scullers emerged in the 1850's. Harvard and Yale first held crew races in 1852, and have done so annually since 1876.

Boat racing as an organized sport for canoes, motorboats, and iceboats developed late in the 19th century. Prominent racing contests are: for sailing canoes, the International Challenge Cup race; for iceboats, the Stuart International Cup race; for power boats, the British International (Harmsworth) Trophy (first won for the U.S. by Gar Wood's *Miss America* in 1920), the Gold Cup race, and the Silver Cup race; for yachts, the *America*'s Cup race, the Newport-Bermuda race, and the Los Angeles-Honolulu race.

Bobsledding, an offspring of tobogganing, developed in Switzerland in the late 19th century, and has been included as a sport in the Olympic Games since 1928. The most notable course in North America is the Mt. Van Hoevenberg run at Lake Placid, New York.

BODMER, CARL (1809–93), Swiss artist and illustrator, in 1832 accompanied ALEXANDER PHILIP MAXIMILIAN, German prince of Wied, as artist-reporter on a two-year expedition up the Missouri river into the Montana region. Bodmer's 81 'elaborately colored plates' form the great attraction of Maximilian's *Travels in the Interior of North America* (2 vols., 1839–41). These bold watercolors of Blackfoot and Hidatsa Indians, with meticulous notation of clothing and decorations, expressions and personalities, are unsurpassed as a graphic record of the American West in the era of trappers and hunters. Since 1962 the Joslyn Art Museum of Omaha, Nebraska, has displayed 427 of Bodmer's original sketches and paintings, recently acquired from the archives of the Wied-Neuwied Rhineland palace. They have revived the fame of this skilled draftsman after more than a century of almost total eclipse.

Body of Liberties, see *Massachusetts Body of Liberties.*

BOLDEN, BUDDY (Charles Bolden) (1878–1931), Negro cornetist, organized in New Orleans the first authentic jazz band (*c.* 1900), and was the first jazzman to win the title 'King' by popular acclaim. His specialty was the BLUES and tradition ranks him as an extraordinary trumpeter.

BOLTON, HERBERT EUGENE (1870–1953), left Stanford's faculty in 1911 to become professor of Latin American history at the University of California at Berkeley, and curator of the Bancroft Library, which has notable Far Western collections. He greatly modified F. J. Turner's exclusively Anglo-American synthesis of American history by emphasizing the unities and common history of all the Americas with their Anglo-French, Anglo-Spanish, and varied European influences. His works include *The Spanish Borderlands* (1921), *Outpost of Empire* (1931), and *New Spain and the Anglo-American West* (1933). When he became president of the American Historical Association in 1932 (the first scholar so honored west of the Mississippi), he chose as a fitting subject 'The Epic of Greater America.'

BOND, THOMAS (1712–84), Maryland-born physician, after studying medicine in Paris, returned to America, and, with the support of Benjamin Franklin, founded the Pennsylvania Hospital in Philadelphia (1752), the oldest institution in the U.S. intended solely for the care of the sick, injured, and insane. There Bond inaugurated (1766) the earliest course of clinical lectures to be offered in America. Bond was one of the founders of the American Philosophical Society (1768), and a leader in the intellectual life of the city.

BOND, WILLIAM CRANCH (1789–1859), self-taught astronomer, was made director of the newly founded Harvard Observatory (1839), supervised its construction, and through its 15-inch telescope, installed in 1847, made elaborate studies of sunspots and other solar phenomena. He pioneered in the use of the chronometer and telegraph to determine longitude. His son, GEORGE PHILLIPS BOND (1825–65), after graduation from Harvard (1845) assisted his father, whom he succeeded (1859) as director of the observatory. The younger Bond was a pioneer in the use of photography for sky mapping, determining stellar parallax, and measuring double stars.

Bonded Servants, see *Indentured Servants.*

Bonds, Government, see *Debt, Public.*

Bonhomme Richard, see *Jones, J. P.*

BONNEVILLE, BENJAMIN LOUIS EULALIE DE (1796–1878), Paris-born U.S. army officer, was given a two-year leave of absence (1832–34) to head a party of 110 trappers and traders into the Rocky Mountains, and in 1832 took the first wagons over SOUTH PASS. His maps were expertly drawn, and furnished the first reliable geographic knowledge of the Far West. Washington Irving's *Adventures of Captain Bonneville* (1837) was based upon conversations with him.

Bonneville Dam (1937) is one of the large Federal hydroelectric power plants, and part of the Columbia River Project. It is located at the head of the tidewater on the lower Columbia, and its power is marketed by the Bonneville Power Administration (in the Department of the Interior). The BPA serves as the agency for power generated at some twenty Federal multipurpose projects, including GRAND COULEE.

BONNEY, WILLIAM, see *Billy the Kid.*

Bonus Army, so called, was an assemblage of some 17,000 unemployed World War I veterans from all sections of the U.S., who marched or hitchhiked to Washington late in May 1932, at the depths of the Depression, to present Congress its 'petition on boots,' urging immediate and full payment of the veterans' BONUS. Camping in jerry-built shacks within sight of the Capitol, the 'army' for the most part was persuaded to disband after Congress in June voted down their request. But when in July the remaining 2000 campers refused to leave, President Hoover ordered the army to remove them forcibly. Public sentiment, even though it was not sympathetic to the marchers, was cool to such military measures, which at best were inept.

Bonus Bill Veto (1817) followed Calhoun's effort to subsidize INTERNAL

IMPROVEMENTS (public works at Federal expense) by creating a permanent fund. The bill proposed setting aside the $1,500,000 bonus paid by the Bank of the U.S. for its charter and all future dividends from Bank stock held by the government. Congress passed the bill but President Madison vetoed it on the ground that the constitution did not authorize the federal government to subsidize internal improvements. Thus the Hamiltonian doctrine of implied powers in the 'general welfare' clause was rejected. The issue was raised again (1822) when Congress sought to collect tolls on the CUMBERLAND ROAD, and was finally settled by Jackson's MAYSVILLE ROAD VETO (1830).

Bonus, Veterans', is not a pension, but a benefit paid in a lump sum to ex-servicemen, whether disabled or not. In a modest way such BOUNTIES were appropriated by the Continental Congress in 1778: commissioned officers received five years' full pay, and all others a cash bounty of about $80. Veterans of the War of 1812, the Mexican War, and various Indian wars received small bonuses; those of the Spanish-American War none at all. Civil War veterans were given small bonuses adjusted to length of service, but the attempt of Congress in 1875 to 'equalize the bounty' was vetoed by President Grant, and for many years thereafter bounty payments did not become a political issue.

After World War I the American Legion lobbied for 'adjusted compensation,' a bill which Congress passed and President Harding vetoed. It passed again a year later (1923), only to meet a second veto from President Coolidge. It became law, however, in 1924 because its proponents mustered enough support to override the President's veto. It provided some $3,500,000,000 in the form of Adjusted Compensation Certificates, with an average value of $1000. The depression years brought further demands, and in 1931 Congress provided a larger cash outlay, this time over the veto of President Hoover. To spur congressional reconsideration, the so-called BONUS ARMY descended on Washington in 1932, but a close vote in Congress rejected their demands. Nevertheless, the issue was kept alive, and in 1936 a bill providing for immediate cash payment of the Certificates was passed over the veto of President Roosevelt. Thus after seventeen years of agitation, veterans received payment of a special bonus, and the issue was removed from politics after it had culminated in a large-scale treasury raid and elicited the vetoes of four successive Presidents.

Following World War II, the problem of veterans' readjustment compensation was intelligently handled by passage of the so-called G.I. BILL OF RIGHTS.

Boogie woogie, a form of jazz which was developed by honky-tonk pianists in the 1920's and early 1930's, is a loud, rhythmical use of Negro field-holler and ring-shout to create a percussive effect. It makes use of a 'walking' bass, a repeated pattern in the left hand.

Book clubs offer their members current book publications at retail or discount prices, with dividends from time to time of extra books. The Book-of-the-Month Club (1926) and The Literary Guild (1927) set the pattern, and within twenty years some 50 different clubs (many of them specialized) were distributing 75,000,000 books annually, one-sixth of all the U.S. book sales. Such mail-order distribution has probably increased reading throughout the country. Title selections are usually made by boards of judges.

Book publishing in America began when STEPHEN DAY issued the *Bay Psalm Book* (1640) from his press at Cambridge, Massachusetts. Since printing was under state control in colonial times, few presses were set up. Bookselling was seldom an independent vocation before 1850, and was developed first in the Boston area.

WILLIAM BRADFORD (1663–1752) came to America with William Penn, set up the first press in Philadelphia (1685), and in nearby Roxboro established the earliest paper mill in British America (1690). In 1693 he moved to New York, where for 30 years he was the sole printer. His monopoly later extended to New Jersey (1703–33). His son, Andrew Bradford (1686–1743), and his grandson, William Bradford (1722–91), were Philadelphia printers, the latter establishing (1742) a printery that continued for 80 years as one of the leading publishing houses of its day. Benjamin Franklin opened his Philadelphia shop in 1728. As towns developed throughout the colonies, printing offices with weekly newspapers were established, and books were occasionally issued from their presses.

The most notable printer of his day was ISAIAH THOMAS (1749–1831) of Worcester, Massachusetts, where he was also active as a bookseller. Thomas had branch bookshops elsewhere as well. MATHEW CAREY organized (1801) the American Company of Booksellers to foster fairs and stimulate American authorship. In 1822 he established at Philadelphia the firm of Carey and Lea, which for twenty years was the largest and best-known publishing house in America. James Harper (1795–1869) and his brothers founded a printing establishment in New York (1817), which they built into a major publishing firm.

For many decades an author commonly followed the practice of paying for the manufacturing of his books, letting booksellers handle them on commission. The royalty method of payment seems to have originated with George Palmer Putnam (1814–72) of New York, the first of the great publishers in America in the modern sense; in 1845 he was offering 10 per cent to authors. Also in New York, soon to become the book publishing center in the U.S., Charles Scribner (1821–71) founded (1846) the publishing house which in 1878 became Charles Scribner's Sons. Harper, Putnam, and Scribner all published notable MAGAZINES. So extensive had the book industry become after the Civil War (with leading houses also in Boston and Philadelphia) that the trade journal, *Publishers' Weekly,* directed to retail booksellers, was issued (1872–current).

In the period 1860–1900 DIME NOVELS had a sensational vogue; and juvenile literature, first conspicuously successful in the works of LOUISA MAY ALCOTT, came increasingly to command the attention of publishers. New literary and distribution trends were encouraged by the rise of such publishing houses as Alfred A. Knopf (est. 1915), with emphasis on books by distinguished European authors, and Boni and Liveright (est. 1917), with its moderate-priced Modern Library series. In this period the establishment of American university presses opened the field to scholarly and scientific works.

Two major distribution trends after World War I were the establishment of BOOK CLUBS and the advent of inexpensive paperbound books with their appeal to the mass market. Inaugurated in 1939 by Pocket Books, the paperback industry after World War II had in fact revolutionized American publishing. Paperbacks began as reprints of popular fiction, but they spread into all fields, including reprints of classics and authoritative studies in science and the humanities. The rash of publishing house mergers in 1960 was largely prompted by a desire to capture the rapidly expanding textbook market.

Boondoggling is a term which, used derogatorily, means to be engaged in useless or frivolous occupations. It was thus specifically applied during the 1930's by critics of the New Deal to ridicule the so-called unproductive or make-work projects of various relief programs.

BOONE, DANIEL (1734–1820), as a youth moved with his family from Pennsylvania to the North Carolina frontier. In 1755 he was a wagoner and blacksmith in Braddock's disastrous campaign, and for the next twenty years he roamed and trapped, chiefly in the wilds of Kentucky. In 1775, under the authority of the TRANSYLVANIA COMPANY, he led a group of settlers along the Wilderness Road to establish Boonesborough. In 1778 he was captured by the Shawnees, but escaped after five months, and returned to Boonesborough. In September of that year the settlement was attacked by the Indians. The attack and its repulse gave currency to the popular image of Boone. Improperly registered land tracts deprived him of his holdings, and after various removes he settled in Missouri, where he died.

Boone was a resourceful hunter, trapper, and Indian fighter, and he became the prototype of frontiersmen who blaze trails, yet resent the encroachment of civilization. Byron apostrophized him in *Don Juan,* and Cooper had him in mind in the character of Leatherstocking. The concept was embodied in the allegorical sculpture of Boone by Horatio Greenough in the rotunda of the National Capitol, where Boone the civilizer grapples with a barbarous Indian warrior. The Boone legend does not alter the fact that Boone the frontiersman won his fame by fortitude and endurance, and the ability to 'think Indian.'

BOOTH, EDWIN THOMAS (1833–93), was a son of the British actor Junius Brutus Booth (1796–1852), who emigrated to the U.S. in 1821, and despite intemperance and attacks of insanity, sustained a reputation as tragedian rivaled only by Edmund Kean. Edwin Booth, likewise best known for his Shakespearean roles, was acclaimed on both sides of the Atlantic as the leading Hamlet of his day, and is generally regarded as the foremost American actor of his century. He reached the peak of his career in the years 1869–74 in performances given in Booth's Theater, which he built in New York City. He was founder (1888) and first president of the Players' Club, to which he gave its present building on Gramercy Park, New York City.

His brother, JOHN WILKES BOOTH (1838–65), possessed the family talent and the father's instability. He fatally shot President Lincoln (14 April 1865) in Ford's Theatre, Washington, shouting as he jumped from Lincoln's box to the stage, 'Sic semper tyrannis! The South is avenged.' Two weeks later he was shot and killed when forces surrounded and burned the barn in which he was hiding at Bowling Green, Virginia.

BOOTH, EVANGELINE CORY (1865–1950), English-born daughter of William Booth, founder of the SALVATION ARMY, began her evangelical preaching at seventeen. Commander of the army in Canada for nine years (1895–1904), she spent most of her life as commander in the U.S. (1904–34), during which period the Salvation Army enhanced its reputation.

Bootlegging, in American slang, was a term widely used during the PROHIBITION ERA of the 1920's to designate the illicit traffic in liquor, and probably derived from the custom of early Indian traders, who concealed liquor in the upper part of a boot. After passage of the VOLSTEAD ACT (1919) gangsters and racketeers organized bootlegging into an illegal industry that annually grossed millions of dollars. Elaborate NIGHT CLUBS, which served liquor openly, if illicitly, were then part of the restaurant world, and such 'speakeasies' were constantly subject to police raids. Fortunes in bootlegging were made by such gangsters as AL CAPONE. The repeal of the Eighteenth Amendment in 1933 ended bootlegging as a profitable industry.

Bop was a revolutionary style of jazz created in the Harlem section of New York City just before World War II. Weird modulations, improvised most noticeably by trumpeters, attracted a sophisticated audience of 'hipsters,' who were mesmerized by 'zombie' music. The dominant characteristic of bop was ninths augmented by flatted fifths (tritones). CHARLIE PARKER was the most prominent bop musician.

BORAH, WILLIAM EDGAR (1865–1940), after practicing law at Lyons, Kansas (1890–91), settled in Boise, Idaho, where he entered politics and served his state as a Republican senator from 1907 until his death. A perfervid nationalist, he led the 'irreconcilables' in their fight against American participation in the League of Nations and the World Court. He was for a quarter-century the powerful spokesman for the isolationists, and served as chairman of the Senate Committee on Foreign Relations from 1924 to 1933. He was an erratic member of the progressive faction in the Senate, with no consistent political program. As a courageous individualist following his conscience, he commanded extravagant respect.

Border ruffians, so called, were citizens of Missouri who attempted to establish slavery in Kansas. The term, first derogatorily applied (1855) in the New York *Tribune* to Governor A. H. Reeder (never a 'border ruffian'), was adopted by Missourians as a badge of honor. Some, like Senator D. R. Atchison, were respected leaders. But many were hooligans who formed themselves into bands ('Blue Lodges,' 'Doniphan

Tigers,' and 'Kickapoo Rangers') that illegally interfered in Kansas elections, baited abolitionists, and raided the settlements of Northerners. The pitched battles over a period of years with antislavery 'Jay Hawks' gave rise to the phrase BLEEDING KANSAS.

Border states, so called, were the slave states bordering on the North: Delaware, Maryland, Virginia, Kentucky, and Missouri. Though southern by tradition, they were divided on the slavery issue, and their economic ties were with the North. When the Civil War broke out, none seceded except Virginia, from which West Virginia then seceded. Kentucky for a few months in 1861 tried to remain neutral, but all save Delaware furnished troops in considerable numbers to the Confederacy. The border states alone actively supported the CRITTENDEN COMPROMISE in the peace conference summoned by the Virginia legislature (February 1861).

Border war, see *Bleeding Kansas.*

BORGLUM, [JOHN] GUTZON DE LA MOTHE (1871–1941), Idaho-born sculptor and painter, studied in Paris at the Académie Julian and at the Beaux-Arts. He is best known for his two colossal groups: the Mount Rushmore Memorial portraits of Washington, Jefferson, Lincoln, and Theodore Roosevelt, carved out of the Black Hills in South Dakota; and those on the side of Stone Mountain, Georgia, memorializing leaders of the Confederacy. His naturalistic designs may be seen in the Sheridan Monument in Washington, the statue of Lincoln in the rotunda of the national Capitol, and the figures of the Apostles in the Cathedral of St. John the Divine, New York City.

Boston, capital of Massachusetts and the cultural, industrial, and maritime center of New England, is situated at the head of Massachusetts Bay. With a population (in 1960) of 697,000, it is the hub of some 80 surrounding towns and cities in a metropolitan area of 2,600,000.

The site was chosen (1630) by members of the MASSACHUSETTS BAY COMPANY as the most suitable for defense and for commerce, and in 1632 it became capital of the colony. Two years later a public reservation of 48 rolling acres, the Boston Common, was set aside for pasture and parade ground, and here the oldest military organization in the country, the Ancient and Honorable Artillery Company, began drilling in 1638. Meantime the Boston Latin School (1635) and Harvard College (1636) had been founded. The center of American PURITANISM throughout the 17th century, Boston early became known for its vigorous intellectual life.

In 1704 the first permanent newspaper in America, the *Boston News-Letter,* was established. A growing prosperity during the 18th century made Boston, a town of some 15,000 in 1760, the most flourishing community in New England. Almost every important landmark today is associated with the intellectual and political ferment of the period, notably OLD NORTH CHURCH (1723), OLD SOUTH CHURCH (1729), and FANEUIL HALL (1763). The Old State House (1748) was the seat of the royal government and later of the commonwealth, until the present State House (designed by Charles Bulfinch) was erected in 1795. King's Chapel (1688, rebuilt 1749) became the first Episcopal church in New England (1689); a century later (1785) its congregation removed trinitarian doctrine from the liturgy, thus introducing UNITARIANISM in America.

Following the battle of BUNKER HILL (1775), the first large-scale engagement of the Revolution, Boston witnessed the departure of 1100 Tory refugees, thereby losing many distinguished families. Under siege until the British withdrew in 1776, the town thereafter remained undisturbed. A stronghold of Federalism, Boston opposed the EMBARGO ACT (1807) which crippled its maritime development. Thenceforth the town became increasingly industrial. When Boston received its city charter in 1822, it had a population of 44,000 (fourth after New York, Philadelphia, and Baltimore), and was taking rank as a center of cultural pursuits and liberal causes. Before the Civil War the publishing firm of Ticknor and Fields (1832) was well established, the LOWELL INSTITUTE (1839) was offering free public lectures, and the Public Library had been chartered (1852). Its institutions of higher learning include Boston College (1863), New England Conservatory of Music (1867), Boston University (1869), and Northeastern (1898).

The era of the clipper trade (1830–60) made Boston known around the world, and industrial prosperity supplied the means and the leisure to enjoy the fruits of an intellectual flowering unique in its day. After the Civil War Boston became the center of the import trade in cotton, wool, and leather, and the influx of Italian and Irish gradually gave the city a new municipal character. But the financial traditions of State Street and the Brahmin social hegemony of Beacon Hill have altered very little over the years.

Boston Athenaeum (1805), an outgrowth of the ANTHOLOGY CLUB, was incorporated in 1807 as a private association of literary men, modeled on the Liverpool Athenaeum. Open to scholars, it is strong in the entire field of Americana, especially in 19th-century American periodicals, fiction, and poetry. It has the bulk of George Washington's private library, and a remarkable collection of Confederate imprints.

Boston Massacre, so called, occurred on 5 March 1770, when a mob of some 60 hecklers, expressing the community's resentment at the quartering of British troops in the town of Boston, began to snowball a squad of redcoats. A fracas developed, during which, without orders, some soldiers opened fire on the mob, killing three and wounding eight, two of whom later died. Radical patriots like Sam Adams and Joseph Warren deliberately characterized the brawl as a 'massacre' for propaganda purposes, and Paul Revere engraved a stirring but entirely fanciful picture of the event. Captain Preston and the British soldiers, tried for manslaughter, were acquitted, though two were branded on the hand. Governor Hutchinson was forced to remove the soldiers to Castle William, and thus the radicals had won a strategic advantage. This melee, in which the Americans were partly at fault, was so maneuvered as to create strong anti-British feeling and an outspoken demand for American independence.

Boston police strike (September 1919) occurred when the police commissioner refused to allow the Boston police to unionize. Mayor Andrew J. Peters, by calling out the Boston companies of militia, restored order after rioting occurred, and broke the strike. Acting tardily and unwisely, Governor CALVIN COOLIDGE ordered the police commissioner to take charge, and called out the entire militia. Coolidge declared afterwards (to the labor leader Samuel Gompers), 'There is no right to strike against the public safety by anybody, anywhere, any time.' The remark gave Coolidge unmerited political prestige as a courageous defender of law and order, and led to his nomination (and election) as Vice President in 1920.

Boston Port Act (1774) was the first of the COERCIVE ACTS, enjoined as a punitive measure directed against the Boston colonists in reprisal for the BOSTON TEA PARTY. The port of Boston would be closed until the East India Company had been paid for the tea that had been dumped in the harbor, and the king given satisfaction that future import duties would be met. The ADMINISTRATION OF JUSTICE ACT followed.

Boston Tea Party, which led to the punitive BOSTON PORT ACT, occurred on the night of 16 December 1773. It stemmed from passage earlier in the year of the TEA ACT, which gave the East India Company a monopoly on all tea exported to the colonies. In effect this act gave a monopoly the power to raise taxes, but only in Boston, the largest maritime trading center, was there active resistance at first. (Elsewhere amid similar 'parties' the tea was either impounded or returned to England, for consignments were boycotted everywhere.) The opportunity afforded the SONS OF LIBERTY was expertly gauged. Dressed as Mohawk Indians, they boarded the ships in Boston harbor in the presence of a large assemblage gathered to watch the merriment, broke open 342 chests of tea, and heaved them into the water. The fact that the episode aroused sympathy for Massachusetts in England as well as in the colonies stiffened the COERCIVE ACTS which immediately followed.

Boston University (est. 1839) was chartered in Boston as a Methodist theological seminary and developed as a co-educational, nonsectarian institution, comprising (in 1965) ten undergraduate and five graduate schools and colleges. Its principal campus was located in 1939 near the Charles river. In 1965, with an endowment of $16,000,000 and a faculty of 2550, it enrolled 19,500 students.

Botany has been associated with medicine from prehistoric times, because herbs have been universally employed to preserve health. Opportunities to discover native cures in the New World were exploited from the first, and the accounts of early naturalists found ready publishers in Europe. JOHN LAWSON reported on the flora of Carolina (1709), COTTON MATHER (1716) and PAUL DUDLEY (1724) described wind pollination (Mather's account being the first known in print), and JAMES LOGAN undertook the earliest American horticultural experiments.

Botany in America, as a separate branch of natural history, was first systematically studied by JOHN BANISTER and professionally developed by JOHN BARTRAM, who established (1728) a botanical garden in Philadelphia that attracted international interest. Through correspondence with Linnaeus and others, JOHN CLAYTON, JOHN MITCHELL, and CADWALLADER COLDEN introduced the accepted classification of plants. JARED ELIOT, a pioneer in scientific agriculture, and ALEXANDER GARDEN wakened a general interest in botany. The College of Philadelphia, as part of its medical studies, offered the first course in botany (1768).

The early 19th-century botanical observations of JACOB BIGELOW and JOHN TORREY are still important, and the expeditions of THOMAS NUTTALL across the continent before 1818 are recorded in significant reports. The eminent botanist ASA GRAY furthered both the scholarly and popular study of the subject. In the 20th century the horticultural studies of L. H. BAILEY have been basic; and the agricultural researches of E. M. EAST, G. H. SHULL, and D. F. JONES have been important in the development of the hybrid-corn industry, the foundations of which were laid by HENRY A. WALLACE. G. W. CARVER helped promote diversified farming in the South, and the hybridization experiments of LUTHER BURBANK received wide publicity.

BOTTA, CARLO GIUSEPPE GUGLIELMO (1766–1837), Italian surgeon and historian, was exiled from Italy because of his strongly expressed republican sympathies. His *History of the War of Independence of the United States of America* (1809, transl., 3 vols., 1820–21), which was inspired by his admiration for Washington and the American cause, is historically important as testimony of the world-wide significance of the Revolution. It remained the best study of the subject until Bancroft began his *History* in 1834.

BOUCHER, JONATHAN (1738–1804), English-born Virginia planter, took holy orders in 1762 and served as Anglican rector in Virginia and Maryland. He gave influential support to the loyalist belief in a natural aristocracy and a divinely ordained government. He was so firm a Tory that he returned to England in 1775, where he later published *A View of the Causes and Consequences of the American Revolution* (1797), a militant and comprehensive presentation, which he dedicated to his former neighbor George Washington. His vivid *Reminiscences of an American Loyalist* did not appear in print until 1925.

BOUDINOT, ELIAS (1740–1821), New Jersey lawyer and statesman, as president of the Continental Congress (1782–83) directed negotiations leading to the TREATY OF PARIS of 1783. A founder and first president of the AMERICAN BIBLE SOCIETY (1816), throughout his life he was interested in philanthropic causes. His adopted son of the same name (*c.* 1803–39), a Cherokee Indian, edited the *Cherokee Phoenix* (1828–35), a bilingual Georgia weekly.

BOULANGER, NADIA (1887–), French conductor and teacher of composition, first came to the U.S. in 1924 to lecture, and returned frequently thereafter to conduct and to guide advanced music pupils. One of the notable teachers of her day, she greatly influenced contemporary American music through her work with such composers as Walter Piston, Aaron Copland, Virgil

Thomson, Roy Harris, and Marc Blitzstein. In 1945 she became director of the Paris Conservatory.

Boulder Dam, see *Hoover Dam.*

Boundaries of the U.S. were established by purchase of territory from France, Spain, Mexico, and Russia; and by treaties with Great Britain, Spain, and Mexico; but they were not finally adjusted until the 20th century. After the War of Independence, by the TREATY OF PARIS of 1783, Great Britain recognized the center of the Great Lakes, throughout their extent, as the northern boundary, and the Mississippi river as the western. The first southern boundary was created by PINCKNEY'S TREATY (1795). The LOUISIANA PURCHASE (1803), negotiated with Napoleon, added an immense continental tract from upper Canada to the Gulf, and raised questions about the northern boundary west of the Great Lakes, which the TREATY OF GHENT (1814) met by setting up arbitration commissions. The terms of the ADAMS-ONÍS TREATY (1819) defined the western boundary of Louisiana from the mouth of the Sabine river, along the Red and Arkansas rivers to the 42nd parallel, and thence due west to the Pacific. The RUSH-BAGOT AGREEMENT (1817), followed by the CONVENTION OF 1818, fixed the Canadian boundary west of the Great Lakes along the 49th parallel to the crest of the Rocky Mountains, and created the longest and best-respected unfortified international boundary line on the globe.

By the WEBSTER-ASHBURTON TREATY (1842) the long-disputed Maine-Canada line was established, and four years later the even more vexed OREGON BOUNDARY DISPUTE was settled, extending the Canadian boundary to the Pacific. After the annexation of Texas (1845), the unsuccessful SLIDELL MISSION to Mexico left the Mexican boundary in dispute, but at the conclusion of the Mexican War the TREATY OF GUADALUPE HIDALGO (1848) recognized the annexation of Texas, ceded all territory west of Texas and south of the Oregon country to the U.S., and established the Rio Grande as the definitive boundary, completed by the GADSDEN PURCHASE (1853).

Alaska was purchased from Russia in 1867, and when mining in the Klondike drew attention to disputed areas in the Alaska panhandle, clarification of the wording in the treaty with Russia became necessary to settle the Alaska-Canadian dispute. This was accomplished by an international tribunal of British and American jurists who met and sustained the claims of the U.S. (1903). Thus the settlement of all continental U.S. boundaries was completed.

Bounties, as subsidies paid by federal or state governments to stimulate enterprise, whether by increasing (or decreasing) production, building utilities, or exterminating predatory animals, have been a constant factor in American economic development. Parliament sought to discourage colonial trade with foreign nations by paying bounties for the tillage of such items as hemp and flax. Colonial governments themselves encouraged manufacture by subsidies. After the Revolution the loss of British bounties in rice, indigo, and naval stores ended flourishing enterprises in the South.

Land bounties were granted by Congress and the states as a bonus to veterans of the Indian wars and the Mexican War. In more recent times the MC KINLEY TARIFF ACT (1890) helped create the sugar beet industry of the Far West, and during the 1930's the Department of Agriculture was empowered to rent land to take it out of production.

Military bounties in land and cash helped recruit troops from colonial times through the Civil War. To fill quotas and avoid resorting to the draft during the Civil War both the states and the federal government paid a total of $600,000,000 in bounties. The baleful practice of bounty-jumping was inherent in the system, which made it possible for a man to get a steady income by enlisting, deserting, and re-enlisting. The SELECTIVE SERVICE ACT (1917) ended the practice.

BOURGET, PAUL CHARLES JOSEPH (1852–1935), French journalist and novelist, while sojourning in the U.S. during the year of the Chicago World's Fair (1893), traveled in the South and West, and recorded his impressions in *Outre-Mer: Impressions of America* (1895). A penetrating discussion of American society and education, it stresses the individualism upon which American democracy was founded, and remains in closer touch with its subject than most of its many successors written by foreign observers.

BOURKE, John Gregory (1846–96), upon graduating from the U.S. Military Academy (1869) served with the cavalry in the Southwest. His intimate knowledge of Indian tribes resulted in *The Snake Dance of the Moquis of Arizona* (1884), which was a pioneer study of the Hopi; *The Medicine Men of the Apache* (1892); and other significant ethnological papers. Important as personal reminiscence is his record *On the Border with Crook* (1891).

BOURNE, Randolph Silliman (1886–1918), before and after his graduation from Columbia (1913) made a career of radical assessments of American social and literary values. He was spokesman for a generation vigorous in its attack on hypocrisy and cant, and is best remembered for two posthumous collections of essays: *Untimely Papers* (1919), a statement of his pacifist convictions; and *The History of a Literary Radical* (1920), a summary of his philosophic and critical views. He seemed headed for one of the most brilliant careers in American intellectual life when he died of influenza.

BOUTWELL, George Sewall (1818–1905), Massachusetts politician, served his state as governor (1851–52) and helped organize the Republican party there (1855). As a member of Congress (1863–69) he was prominent among the radical republicans, and became a leader in the movement to impeach President Johnson. Although Boutwell knew little about finance, President Grant selected him as Secretary of the Treasury (1869–73), in which office Boutwell broke an attempted corner in gold in the black friday scandal. Thereafter he served in the Senate (1873–77), practiced law, and compiled his *Reminiscences* (1902), a review of his 60 years in public office.

BOWDITCH, Henry Ingersoll (1808–92), son of nathaniel bowditch, after graduation from Harvard (1832) and study abroad, became professor of clinical medicine at Harvard (1859–67). A specialist in diseases of the chest, he took the lead in advocating open-air treatment for tuberculosis. During the Civil War he introduced an ambulance service. He served as a member of the Massachusetts state board of health (1869–79), and as author of *Public Hygiene in America* (1877) he stimulated the public health movement.

BOWDITCH, Henry Pickering (1840–1911), grandson of nathaniel bowditch, after graduation from Harvard (1861) and study abroad, joined the faculty of the Harvard Medical School, where he established the first physiological laboratory in the country, and carried out important research on functional nerve blockage and on anthropometry. As dean of the medical faculty (1883–93), he radically modified the curriculum. His most important discovery was that in heart muscle a stimulus is either strong enough to excite the heart completely, or not at all. He thus established the 'all-or-nothing' principle, basic to heart physiology.

BOWDITCH, Nathaniel (1773–1838), self-educated navigator and mathematician, was born and lived in Salem, Massachusetts. On five long voyages after 1795 he made studies in navigation that allowed him to correct and substantially rewrite and enlarge Moore's *Practical Navigator* (1799). The revised manual he published under his own name as *The New American Practical Navigator* (1802). This immediately became the seaman's bible, known simply as *Bowditch*. Since 1868 it has been published by the U.S. Hydrographic Office (H.O. No. 9). Regularly revised, it remains the basic reference book for navigation. Bowditch translated and edited Laplace's *Mécanique Céleste* in four volumes with a 4000-page commentary (1829 and later), the most considerable mathematical work yet to have appeared in America. He was then offered, but declined, a chair in mathematics and astronomy at Harvard. For his accomplishments Bowditch was widely honored in his lifetime at home and abroad. When he died, ships of all nations flew their flags at half-mast.

BOWDOIN, James (1726–90), Boston merchant and Revolutionary War statesman, inherited his business from his father, reputedly the wealthiest merchant in New England. He graduated from Harvard in 1745 and began his political career in 1753, when he was elected to the General Court. In 1757 he was chosen a member of the Council, the governor's advisory body, and for twenty years continued so to serve. He presided at the state constitutional convention (1779), and as governor (1785–87) suppressed SHAYS'S REBELLION. He was a founder and first president of the American Academy of Arts and Sciences (1780–90), to which he bequeathed his library. Two years before his death he was elected to the Royal Society. BOWDOIN COLLEGE (1794) was founded by an endowment of a large part of his considerable estate.

Bowdoin College, at Brunswick, Maine, was established (1794) by a bequest from the Boston merchant JAMES BOWDOIN. It opened in 1802 as a liberal arts college for men, which it remains. In 1965, with an endowment of $23,-800,000 and a faculty of 100, it enrolled 832 students.

Bowery (Dutch *bouwerie:* farm) is that section of lower Manhattan in New York City, between Chatham Square and Astor Place, east of Broadway. The street which gives the area its name was once the road to the farm of Governor Stuyvesant. Bowery Lane in the 18th century was a fashionable residential district. By 1860 it was known for its theaters and dance halls. It later became, and still is, a skid row for derelicts.

BOWIE, JAMES (1799–1836), Georgia-born frontiersman, after moving to Texas (1828) became a leader among the American settlers who opposed Mexican rule. With William B. Travis (1811–36) he shared command of the garrison that resisted the attack on the ALAMO, where he died.

Bowie knife, before the invention of the six-shooter, was part of the equipment of all soldiers and frontiersmen from Florida to California. Devised by JAMES BOWIE (or his brother Rezin Bowie), it was an all-purpose one-edged blade with guarded hilt, and so nicely balanced that it could be thrown with deadly effect.

BOWLES, SAMUEL (1826–78), succeeded his father, SAMUEL BOWLES (1779–1851), as editor of the weekly Springfield (Massachusetts) *Republican.* The son made the paper a daily and controlled it (1851–78) during the critical years of the Civil War and Reconstruction, when it became the most powerful small-town newspaper in the country. (Its weekly edition carried Bowles's opinions into the Ohio and Mississippi valleys.) It supported Lincoln, fought corruption under Grant, denounced Tammany, and by its liberal independence justified Horace Greeley's belief that it was 'the ablest country journal ever published on this continent.' A man of wide interests and inexhaustible energy, Bowles traveled extensively. His incisive travel letters, reprinted from the newspaper as *Our New West* (1869), are an important historical source dealing with the expanding nation. A son, SAMUEL BOWLES (1851–1915), succeeded his father as editor.

BOWMAN, ISAIAH (1879–1950), while teaching geography at Yale (1905–15), was called to the directorship of the American Geographical Society (1915–35), then to the presidency of Johns Hopkins (1935–48). An authority on both physical and political geography, he led important expeditions to the central Andes. He served as chief territorial specialist at the peace conference following World War I, and thereafter was an adviser to the Department of State in matters involving territorial settlement. His writings include *Forest Physiography* (1911), and *The Pioneer Fringe* (1931).

Boxer Rebellion (1900), nationalist uprising in China, was directed against the reactionary Dowager Empress and the foreign nations that had established spheres of influence. Beginning in May, it led to the murder of some 250 extraterritorials and Chinese Christians. The siege of the legations in Peking in June was raised in August by a concerted military expedition of 5000 troops from Great Britain, Russia, Germany, France, Japan, and the U.S. The indemnity of $25,000,000 levied by the U.S. against the Chinese government was in large part subsequently returned, and the remainder set aside as a fund to be used for educating Chinese students in American institutions.

Boxing, popularized as a sport in England in the 18th century, spread to America, but at first without popular following. Prize fights, attended by 'the fancy,' were bare-knuckle affairs conducted secretly, since they were illegal in every state. The code of rules introduced (1865) by the Marquess of Queensberry transformed pugilism into boxing, which first achieved nation-wide popularity in 1882, when the world bare-knuckle champion JOHN L. SULLIVAN toured the U.S., putting on boxing exhibitions with gloves. By 1889 the National Boxing Association was formed, and the Queensberry rules generally became standard, although the sport still was illegal in most states. In 1892 Sullivan lost the championship to JAMES J. CORBETT.

The boom days of prize fighting thereafter set in, with such champions as JAMES J. JEFFRIES (1899–1910), JACK JOHNSON (1910–15), and JESS WILLARD (1915–19). In 1920 boxing was fully legalized in New York state, and legalization of the sport soon followed elsewhere. The showmanship of the sports promoter Tex Rickard for a time made prize fighting one of the country's most popular spectator sports. The JACK DEMPSEY–Georges Carpentier championship bout in 1921 grossed $1,600,000, a figure nearly doubled when Dempsey lost the championship (1926) to GENE TUNNEY. With Tunney's retirement in 1928, prize fighting markedly declined, though the rise of JOE LOUIS in 1937 somewhat revived interest in the sport, which, as a professional spectacle, was falling into disrepute through gambling and corrupt manipulation.

See N. S. Fleischer, *The Heavyweight Championship* (1949), a survey from 1719 to 1949.

Boycott, the concerted refusal to purchase services or commodities from those who are deemed unfair in their LABOR RELATIONS, is chiefly used as a means of securing better terms of employment. In international trade the boycott is the refusal of one nation to purchase from another. The Stamp Act Congress of 1765 and the Continental Congresses in effect voted boycotts against Great Britain.

In the U.S., legal definition has established a 'primary' boycott as one that involves employees directly concerned in a dispute, and a 'secondary' boycott as one that attempts to coerce third parties into the practice. In 1908 the Supreme Court held in the DANBURY HATTERS' CASE that the secondary boycott constitutes a conspiracy in RESTRAINT OF TRADE. The CLAYTON ANTITRUST ACT (1914) did not anticipate secondary boycotts, which were declared illegal 33 years later by the TAFT-HARTLEY ACT (1947).

Boycotts have been used as a weapon to force social change. The U.S. Supreme Court decided in BROWN *v.* BOARD OF EDUCATION (1954) that segregation of white and Negro children in public schools, solely on the grounds of race or color, was unconstitutional, and soon extended the ruling to apply to all public gathering places. Negro boycotts of schools and businesses, stemming from those rulings, have created issues still to be resolved.

BOYD, BELLE (1843–1900), Confederate spy (1861–63), supplied information to the Army of Northern Virginia. Twice arrested, she escaped to England (1864), where she began her stage career and published her memoirs, *Belle Boyd in Camp and Prison* (1865). She subsequently toured widely in the U.S.

BOYLSTON, ZABDIEL (1679–1766), born in Brookline, Massachusetts, after private education in medicine took up practice in Boston. In the smallpox epidemic of 1721 Cotton Mather persuaded him to inoculate, and against the bitter opposition of colleagues Boylston introduced the practice in America. The uproar was so great after Boylston had administered the pustule to members of his family and to nine or ten other persons that the lives of Boylston and Mather were endangered by mob violence. By February 1722 Boylston had inoculated some 245 persons, of whom but six died. During a visit to England in 1724–26 Boylston was elected a fellow of the Royal Society, and published *An Historical Account of the Small-pox*

Inoculated in New England (1726), a masterly presentation, and the first clinical document written by an American.

Boy Scouts of America, incorporated in 1910 and granted a Federal charter in 1916, was founded by Daniel C. Beard (1850–1941), an illustrator of books on woodcraft and animal life. The organization, modeled on that founded in England (1908) by the British soldier Sir Robert Baden-Powell, provides constructive programs of leisure-time activities for boys over twelve years old, including training in citizenship and sports. In 1965 its membership was reported at some 5,585,000.

Bozeman Trail, also known as the 'Powder River Road,' was charted (1863–65) by John M. Bozeman (1835–67) as the easiest and shortest emigrant route to the Montana gold fields at Virginia City. It started as a branch of the OREGON TRAIL, leaving the North Platte west of Fort Laramie in Colorado, running east and then north of the Big Horn Mountains. The establishment of army forts to make the trail a military route led to a major fight with the Sioux under RED CLOUD and to its temporary abandonment in 1868. After 1877 it was re-established as a cattle route from Texas, north through Colorado and Wyoming.

BRACKENRIDGE, HENRY MARIE (1786–1871), son of HUGH HENRY BRACKENRIDGE, grew up in Pittsburgh, practiced law in St. Louis, and later helped frame the judiciary system of Louisiana. The journal of his travels with fur traders, *Views of Louisiana* (1814; enlarged, 1816), is a perceptive commentary on the French cultural legacy in the Mississippi valley, and a shrewd analysis of the role the West would soon come to play. As secretary to the first governmental commission to study conditions in the southern hemisphere, he described the exploration in *Voyage to South America* (1819). His *Recollections of Persons and Places in the West, 1800–1821* (1834; rev., 1868) is source material dealing with the Ohio valley.

BRACKENRIDGE, HUGH HENRY (1748–1816), Scottish-born jurist and author, after graduation from the College of New Jersey at Princeton (1771) taught school, wrote poetry and plays, and served as a chaplain during the Revolution. He gave up the ministry to practice law in the frontier village of Pittsburgh. Brackenridge was a leading supporter of the Constitution, and he later became a justice of the Pennsylvania supreme court (1799–1816). His creative literary interests stemmed from his college days and his friendship with Philip Freneau. His literary reputation rests on his long picaresque novel *Modern Chivalry* (1792–1815), the basic intent of which was to satirize the chicanery and ineptness of government as he had witnessed it during his years as a lawyer in western Pennsylvania, and to criticize attacks on the judiciary and hostility to learning.

BRADDOCK, EDWARD (1695–1755), after service with the Prince of Orange, was appointed (1754) commander of all the British forces in America. The last of the French and Indian Wars was imminent. After arriving in Virginia (April 1755), Braddock began his campaign by leading 1400 British regulars and 450 colonials under Lieutenant Colonel George Washington against Fort Duquesne (Pittsburgh), the gateway to the West (April 1755). Crossing the Monongahela near the fort, he was met by a mixed force of 900 French and Indians, flanked on both sides, and routed at the Battle of the Wilderness (9 July). Braddock was mortally wounded, and Washington led the remnant back to Fort Cumberland, Maryland. (WILLIAM SHIRLEY succeeded as commander of the British forces.)

The most recent historical analysis of the defeat concludes from fresh evidence that the traditional story of Braddock's incompetence is correct. Arrogant and opinionated, Braddock had failed to employ the best tactics of European warfare, and those he did use were not adapted to wilderness conditions. As a result of the British defeat the frontier of Virginia and adjacent regions were exposed to hostile Indians, contemptuous of British weakness.

BRADFORD, GAMALIEL (1863–1932), Massachusetts-born author, began his impressive series of literary portraits with *Lee, the American* (1912). He applied a subjective technique, which he called 'psychography,' to his sketches, with the analysis focused upon characteristic features in the lives of his subjects. A representative collection is *Damaged Souls* (1923), dealing with such Americans as Tom Paine, John Randolph, and Aaron Burr. Others are *Confederate Portraits* (1914) and *Union Portraits* (1916).

BRADFORD, WILLIAM (1590–1657), British-born member of the Separatist congregation that had settled in Leyden, sailed from Plymouth, England, on the *Mayflower* (1620), was elected governor of the Plymouth Colony (1621), and served as such almost continually throughout his life. Probably the ablest and best educated leader of the group, Bradford preserved isolated Plymouth from famine, Indians, and internal schisms. He maintained the integrity of his colony against encroachments of the Massachusetts Bay Colony, and by astute negotiation he won control from the merchant investors in England who had financed this wilderness undertaking.

His firm guidance in legislative matters was matched by his tact in dealing with the Indians. His *History of Plymouth Plantation,* covering the years 1630–46, is one of the major documents in the record of events that led to the founding of the nation. It was used in manuscript by early historians, and first published in 1856. It has been informatively edited in modern English by S. E. Morison (1952).

See Bradford Smith, *Bradford of Plymouth* (1952).

BRADFORD, WILLIAM (1663–1752), after learning the printer's trade in London, emigrated with William Penn and set up the first press in Philadelphia (1685). Five years later in nearby Roxboro he established the first paper mill in British America. Removing to New York (1693), he became official printer for that colony (1693–1742) and later for New Jersey (1703–33). His New York *Gazette* (1725–44) was the colony's first newspaper.

His son, ANDREW BRADFORD (1686–1742), established the first newspaper in the Middle Colonies, at Philadelphia, the *American Weekly Mercury* (1719–46), a journal widely read in both North and South. The principles of freedom of the press that he expressed provided the lawyer ANDREW HAMILTON with many of the arguments in the famous trial of JOHN PETER ZENGER.

The son of Andrew Bradford, WILLIAM BRADFORD (1722–91), gained the name 'patriot-printer of 1776.' He was official printer for the First Continental Congress, and his *Weekly Advertiser* (1743–97) had wide appeal. The printery he established (1742) continued for 80 years as one of the leading publishing houses of America.

BRADLEY, JOSEPH P. (1813–92), a graduate of Rutgers (1836) and a Republican member of the New Jersey bar, was nominated by President Grant to the U.S. Supreme Court at the same time (February 1870) that Grant appointed William Strong, also a Republican. The appointments provoked charges that Grant had packed the Court to reverse the decision on the LEGAL TENDER Acts. Bradley's appointment to the famous ELECTORAL COMMISSION (1877), which settled the Hayes-Tilden dispute over the presidential election, gave him the unique power to elect a President, because his vote was the margin of victory for 'Old 8-to-7' Hayes.

BRADLEY, OMAR NELSON (1893–), after graduation from the U.S. Military Academy (1915), made the Army his career. As commanding general of the American II Corps (1943) in World War II, he led his troops through Tunis and Sicily to open the way for the invasion of Italy. Selected to head the American land contingent during the NORMANDY CAMPAIGN (1944–45), he took a signal part in concluding the war in the European theater. He was the first permanent chairman of the U.S. joint chiefs of staff (1948–53), and in 1950 became a General of the Army.

BRADSTREET, ANNE DUDLEY (1613–72), daughter of THOMAS DUDLEY and wife of SIMON BRADSTREET, came with her husband to the Massachusetts Bay Colony in 1630. She was the first American poetess, extravagantly praised for *The Tenth Muse Lately Sprung Up in*

America (London, 1650). The verses are discourses which, in the Puritan tradition, subordinate sensuousness to instruction. Today she is more highly regarded for her later poems, included in a second edition and posthumously issued as *Several Poems* (1678). Less imitative and moralistic, they reflect the homely scenes of the New England world that she knew.

BRADSTREET, SIMON (1603–97), attended Emmanuel College, Cambridge, before emigrating to the Massachusetts Bay Colony (1630). From his arrival until 1692 he was almost continuously in public service, as ASSISTANT, Secretary of the colony, Deputy Governor, and finally Governor (1679–86, 1689–92). The arrival of a new charter during his last year in office forced him into premature retirement at the age of eighty-nine. For 33 years he served as a commissioner to the NEW ENGLAND CONFEDERACY, which he had helped organize (1643). His first wife was the poet ANNE BRADSTREET. He became a large landowner through gifts bestowed for his services, and was a member of a company that developed frontier trading.

BRADY, JAMES BUCHANAN (1856–1917), known as 'Diamond Jim' because of his ostentatious display of jewelry, was born and lived in New York. As a successful promoter of railroad equipment in later years, he dispensed his considerable fortune on Broadway productions, lavish entertainment, and horse races. In 1912 Brady gave the funds to establish the James Buchanan Brady Urological Institute at Johns Hopkins, and in his will he left a bequest to New York Hospital to establish the Department of Urology, James Buchanan Brady Foundation.

BRADY, MATHEW B. (*c.* 1823–96), who had studied painting with S. F. B. Morse, established a photographic portrait studio in New York early in the 1840's. His daguerreotypes, which were immensely popular, won the first gold medal awarded in an exhibit (1849). The publication of his *Gallery of Illustrious Americans* (1850) established him as the leading American photographer. He is best remembered for his 3500 photographs of persons, places, battles, and camp scenes taken during the Civil War.

BRAGG, BRAXTON (1817–76), a graduate of the U.S. Military Academy (1837) who had resigned from the regular army (1856) and retired to his Louisiana plantation, took up service in the Confederate army at the outbreak of the Civil War. In 1862 he succeeded Beauregard in command of the Army of Tennessee, and after facing Rosecrans at the indecisive battle of MURFREESBORO (1863), crushed him three months later at CHICKAMAUGA. Grant concentrated enormous forces against him, and the CHATTANOOGA CAMPAIGN ended in a Confederate rout. Although Bragg was relieved of command, Jefferson Davis kept him in service as military adviser (1864–65). Though he was a skilled soldier, Bragg was also a martinet, and the friction he created with his officers unfavorably affected the conduct of his operations.

Brahmins are Hindus of the highest, or priestly, caste. The phrase 'Boston brahmins' is satirically applied to the social or intellectual elite of Massachusetts, who have perpetuated what Oliver Wendell Holmes described as their 'untitled aristocracy.'

Brain Trust, so called, was the group of advisers to F. D. Roosevelt, formed (1932) while he was governor of New York. It included such specialists in law, economics, and social welfare as Samuel Rosenman, Rexford G. Tugwell, Raymond Moley, A. A. Berle, Jr., Robert M. Lovett, and FRANCES PERKINS, and it helped to develop the social and economic principles of the NEW DEAL.

BRANDEIS, LOUIS DEMBITZ (1856–1941), born in Louisville, Kentucky, after graduation from Harvard Law School (1877) became a successful Boston lawyer (1879–1916). He first established his reputation as the 'people's attorney' by defending, without fee, Boston clients who sought the regulation of local public utilities. Deeply concerned with problems of social justice, Brandeis argued the rights of individuals in cases involving life insurance, wages and hours, and railroad monopolies. His book, *Other People's Money* (1914), so impressed President Wilson that he appointed Brandeis to the U.S. Supreme Court (1916). Brandeis remained an Associate Justice until his retirement in 1939.

Brandeis's essays and legal decisions opposed uneconomic types of bigness in business, and championed collective bargaining, the right of free speech, and the value of experimentation by the states in social and economic legislation. He influenced President Wilson's adoption of the 'New Freedom,' which stressed the prevention of monopoly rather than trust-busting and introduced the Federal Trade Commission. Through his testimony in the Eastern Rate hearings, Brandeis helped to create enthusiasm for INDUSTRIAL MANAGEMENT, by pointing out in detail how rational planning could insure profits without raising rates or prices. Brandeis made legal history by introducing the 'Brandeis Brief' (the use of social facts instead of mere precedent and general argument) in MULLER *v.* OREGON (1908). In his later years he became a leader of the American wing of the Zionist movement.

Brandeis University (1948), at Waltham, Massachusetts, is a co-educational liberal arts college and graduate school, and the first Jewish-sponsored nonsectarian institution of higher learning in the U.S. In 1965, with an endowment of $16,600,000 and a faculty of 418, it enrolled 1490 students.

Brandywine, Battle of (11 September 1777), was fought near Brandywine Creek, between Philadelphia and Wilmington, just inside the Pennsylvania border. General Howe commanded a force of 18,000 British and Hessian regulars. Washington's army of 11,000 Americans, largely militia, gallantly met the attacking force, but was compelled to retreat. Howe followed up his victory, and on 27 September he entered Philadelphia.

BRANT, JOSEPH (1742–1807), Mohawk chief, during the FRENCH AND INDIAN WAR (1755–63) was commissioned a colonel by Sir WILLIAM JOHNSON, and later fought with the Loyalists during the Revolution. In his youth he had attracted the attention of Johnson, who sent him to Eleazar Wheelock's Indian school at Lebanon, Connecticut. Brant commanded the attack on American settlers in the CHERRY VALLEY MASSACRE (1778), and engaged in other frontier raids, but after the war he aided U.S. commissioners in securing peace treaties with Indian tribes.

Brant became a devout Anglican (to the despair of the Seneca chief RED JACKET), engaged in missionary work, translated parts of the Bible into the Mohawk tongue, and was lionized in England (1786), where he raised funds for the first Episcopal church in Upper Canada. Soon thereafter the British government settled him on an estate on the banks of Lake Ontario. No other Indian warrior so combined the qualities of a fearless leader, dedicated missionary, and skilled diplomat. The town of Brantford, Ontario, named for him, erected a monument to him in 1886.

BRATTLE, THOMAS (1658–1713), after graduation from Harvard (1676) and brief travel abroad, in 1693 became lifelong treasurer of Harvard. Through the college telescope he observed the Great Comet of 1680, and by communicating his information to the Royal Astronomer at Greenwich supplied a check, which Newton acknowledged, upon Newton's theory of cometary orbits. By confusing Thomas Brattle with his brother William Brattle (1662–1717), also a Harvard administrator, the Royal Society elected William to membership in 1714, the year after the death of Thomas. Though William declined the honor, he donated his brother's scientific papers to the Society. King's Chapel, the Anglican church in Boston, acquired an organ in 1713, the first in New England, with money bequeathed by Thomas Brattle.

BRAY, THOMAS (1656–1730), English clergyman, was the 'Great Small man' commissioned by the bishop of London to invigorate the Anglican church in Maryland, where he founded parochial libraries for each of the 30 parishes (1699–1700). In 1701 he organized the Society of the Propagation of the Gospel in Foreign Parts (SPG), which engaged in missionary activities, especially in the Carolinas. A philanthropist, he set up libraries elsewhere for Anglican communities, from Boston to Charleston, and founded a number of layman's libraries as well. These were the most important semi-public libraries in the colonies after those at Harvard and William and Mary.

BREASTED, James Henry (1865–1935), professor of Egyptology and Oriental history at the University of Chicago (1905–33), became widely known for archaeological discoveries in Egypt and Asia Minor. He organized and led many expeditions, and his chronological system for ancient Egypt is generally accepted. His works include *A History of Egypt* (1905), and *The Conquest of Civilization* (1926). His textbook, *Ancient Times* (1916), has had an unusual vogue, and scholars prize his translation of *Ancient Records of Egypt* (5 vols., 1906–7).

BRÉBEUF, Jean de (1593–1649), called 'the Ajax of the mission,' was a French Jesuit missionary among the Huron Indians in Ontario (1625–29, 1633–49), who sent home important observations that were published in the JESUIT RELATIONS. Brébeuf and his colleague GABRIEL LALEMANT were tortured to death when the Iroquois captured the Huron village (near the present site of Midland, Ontario) where he was living. In 1930 he was canonized as one of the Martyrs of North America.

BRECKINRIDGE, John Cabell (1821–75), after practicing law in Lexington, Kentucky, served as a Democratic member of the House of Representatives (1851–55). A leader of his party in Kentucky, in 1856 he was elected Vice President on the Buchanan ticket. Though strongly in favor of slavery and states' rights, he presided over the Senate with scrupulous impartiality under trying circumstances. In 1860, nominated for the presidency by the proslavery men who had seceded from the Democratic national convention, he polled 72 electoral votes. During the Civil War he served with distinction as a major general in the Confederate army, and in January 1865 Davis appointed him secretary of war. He later resumed the practice of law in Lexington.

Breed's Hill, Battle of, see *Bunker Hill, Battle of.*

BREMER, Fredrika (1801–65), Swedish novelist and inveterate traveler, was at the height of her international fame when she visited the U.S. in 1849. *The Homes of the New World: Impressions of America* (2 vols., 1853), an account of her two-year sojourn, was immediately popular. Hawthorne so enjoyed her leisurely, intimate observations of home life in the U.S. that he thought her 'worthy of being the maiden aunt of the whole human race.' Further travel-letters are gathered in *America of the Fifties* (1924).

Bretton Woods Conference (1944), the United Nations Monetary and Financial Conference, met at Bretton Woods, New Hampshire, with 28 nations participating. It set up two agencies to stabilize currencies and establish credit for international trade, the INTERNATIONAL MONETARY FUND and the INTERNATIONAL BANK FOR RECONSTRUCTION AND DEVELOPMENT (the World Bank).

BREWSTER, William (1567–1644), a well-to-do Cambridge-trained layman, after helping to organize the SEPARATISTS in England, removed with them to Leyden (1608). There he set up a little publishing house and turned out English Calvinist tracts for export. He emigrated to America on the *Mayflower* in 1620, and until his death he continued to act as a ruling elder in Plymouth, preaching 'both powerfully and profitably to the great contentment of the hearers and their comfortable edification.' He held no public office, but his influence matched that of his good friend WILLIAM BRADFORD.

Bricker Amendment, so called, was a proposed isolationist amendment to the Constitution sponsored in 1953 by Senator John Bricker of Ohio. It in effect required congressional approval of international agreements that the U.S. might make, and imposed controls on the power of the President to conduct foreign relations. President Eisenhower disregarded his party's 1952 endorsement of the Bricker idea to declare himself 'unalterably opposed' to it. Both he and Secretary of State Dulles feared it would endanger treaties needed for mutual defense. It was supported by isolationists in both parties. After extended debate the Senate rejected the proposal by a vote of 60 to 31, one vote short of the two-thirds majority required to submit it to the states.

Bridge, a card game derived from whist, first became widely popular in the U.S. around 1920, shortly after auction bridge was introduced (1907) from England. The sportsman Harold S. Vanderbilt in 1925 developed contract bridge, which, owing largely to the activities of ELY CULBERTSON, became a national craze.

BRIDGER, JAMES (1804–81), Virginia-born trapper and frontier guide, was probably the most famous of the MOUNTAIN MEN. He accompanied the fur trading expeditions of William Ashley (1822) and Jedediah Smith (1823) into the Far West, and discovered Great Salt Lake (1824). His ability to deal with Indians whose languages he spoke (though he was illiterate) was an invaluable asset in guiding the Bonneville explorations (1832–34), surveying the Bozeman Trail (1835), and similar undertakings. He was responsible for building Fort Bridger (1843), and he established the route through Bridger's Pass (1856), west of the North Platte in southern Wyoming. No tall tales of the Rocky Mountains, particularly those dealing with Yellowstone Park, have been more widely circulated than those Jim Bridger told or those that were told about him. Very few persons who have lived so adventurously have lived so long as this 'Old Man of the Mountains.'

Bridges as first constructed in America were all of wood, supported by wooden piles or cribs of logs, or by stone piers. Late in the 17th century builders began using stone arches with short spans. Bridges were open to the sky until about 1800, when COVERED BRIDGES were devised. Toll bridges antedate toll roads by nearly a century, and throughout the 18th century they were operated by private corporations at a profit. During the 19th century the duplication of highway routes reduced the profit of toll bridges, and by 1850 most roads and bridges had become free and public.

Wooden bridges continued to be used by railroads late into the 19th century, and viaducts across deep gorges sometimes contained thousands of heavy timbers. Iron bridges came into use after 1800, but the earliest engineering feats of bridge building were those performed by JOHN A. ROEBLING, who erected the railroad span at Niagara Falls (1855), and by JAMES B. EADS, who spanned the Mississippi at St. Louis (1874). Roebling's Brooklyn Bridge, completed in 1883, was at the time the longest of all suspension bridges; today the Verrazano Narrows Bridge is the world's longest and heaviest.

Notable large bridges in the U.S. include the following:

Suspension

Verrazano Narrows (1964) 4260 ft.
New York Harbor

Golden Gate (1937) 4200
San Francisco Bay

Mackinac (1958) 3888
Straits of Mackinac

George Washington (1931) 3500
Hudson River

Cantilever

New Orleans-Algiers (1958) 1575
Mississippi River

Transbay (1936) 1400
San Francisco Bay

Tappan Zee (1955) 1212
Hudson River

Steel Arch

Bayonne (1931) 1652
New York–New Jersey

Glen Canyon (1959) 1028
Colorado River

Continuous Truss

Mackinac (1957) 2082
Straits of Mackinac

See H. G. Tyrrell, *History of Bridge Engineering* (1911).

BRIDGMAN, LAURA (1829–89), born in New Hampshire, at the age of two through illness lost all her senses but that of touch. Six years later, under the guidance of Dr. SAMUEL HOWE, director of the Perkins Institution in Boston, she began the training that taught her to read and write. She became so expert at sewing that she remained at Perkins as a teacher of needlework throughout her life. She was the first blind deaf-mute to be successfully educated, and thus came to symbolize the hope that could be held out to others so handicapped.

BRIDGMAN, Percy Williams (1882–1961), professor of physics at Harvard (1926–54), made extensive researches in high pressure, set forth in such authoritative studies as *The Physics of High Pressure* (1931), and *The Nature of Thermodynamics* (1941). His discoveries proved immensely useful in determining the effects of high pressure on hitherto unexplained phenomena, and in 1946 he was awarded the Nobel Prize in physics. Bridgman formulated the concept of OPERATIONALISM, one of the most influential American philosophies of science, and set it forth in *The Logic of Modern Physics* (1927).

BRIGGS, Le Baron Russell (1855–1934), after graduation from Harvard (1875), taught English there (1883–1925), and was dean of the college (1891–1902) and of the faculty (1903–25). For twenty years he served as president of Radcliffe (1903–23). He modernized the teaching of freshman English composition and won note for his advanced creative writing course, which influenced many major writers. As an administrator he fought commercialism in college athletics, and his theories influenced teaching practices throughout the country.

BRINTON, Daniel Garrison (1837–99), internationally recognized in his day as the leading American anthropologist, taught American linguistics and archaeology at the University of Pennsylvania (1886–99), and made significant contributions to the knowledge of Indian culture. He was the first to correlate such studies in *The Myths of the New World* (1868), an analysis of Indian lore which, though modified by later investigations, was an important pioneer inquiry. His systematic classification of Indian racial groups, *The American Race* (1891), broke ground for later investigations, even though he avoided field work and clung to racial errors. He edited a *Library of Aboriginal American Literature* (8 vols., 1882–90), presenting almost everything still known from early records.

BRISBANE, Albert (1809–90), born in Batavia, New York, became a disciple of the French social theorist Fourier after extensive travel in Europe and the Near East. He first set forth his communitarian ideas in *Social Destiny of Man* (1840). He felt that society could best realize itself if organized into phalanxes, each large enough for all industrial and social requirements, and grouped according to occupation, capabilities, and attractions. Horace Greeley gave Brisbane a column in the New York *Tribune* (1842–44), to expound the cause of SOCIAL UTOPIANISM, and Brisbane was instrumental in the formation of more than 40 socialized communities in the U.S., the most successful of which was the NORTH AMERICAN PHALANX. Sometimes called the first American socialist, Brisbane, a wealthy man, gave capitalism a share in the co-operative economy, and later stated his principles in *General Introduction to Social Science* (1876).

His son, Arthur Brisbane (1864–1936), was editor (1897–1921) of the New York *Evening Journal* and of other Hearst newspapers.

BRISTOW, Benjamin Helm (1832–96), Kentucky-born lawyer, served as a Union officer in the Civil War and was the first U.S. Solicitor General (1870–72). As Grant's Secretary of the Treasury (1874–76) he was especially zealous in attempting to weed out corruption. Grant dismissed him when Bristow's courageousness in prosecuting the WHISKY RING became embarrassing to the President. In 1878 Bristow moved to New York, where he won distinction as an attorney.

British Commanders in Chief in America. The dynastic wars conducted by European monarchs are known in their American phases as King William's War (1689–97), Queen Anne's War (1702–13), the War of Jenkins' Ear (1739), King George's War (1744–48), and the French and Indian War (1755–63). These wars are known generically as the FRENCH AND INDIAN WARS. Until 1755 there was no unified British command. In 1754 George II sent EDWARD BRADDOCK with authority of commander in chief. After the British rout in 1755 at Fort Duquesne (Pittsburgh), Braddock, who had died of wounds received in the battle, was succeeded by Governor WILLIAM SHIRLEY of Massachusetts for a few months. Shirley's unsuccessful attack on Fort Niagara did not increase English prestige with the Indians.

JOHN CAMPBELL, Earl of Loudoun, served briefly (1756–57), won no victories, and was replaced by JAMES ABERCROMBY, whose inept attack on Fort Ticonderoga (1758) led to his immediate recall. William Pitt, the newly appointed secretary of state for war, now began to shake the incompetents out of command. He gave JEFFREY AMHERST the supreme post (1758–63) and placed directly under him the thirty-year-old JAMES WOLFE. Wolfe's victorious expedition against Quebec proved decisive in ending French hegemony in North America.

THOMAS GAGE succeeded Amherst as commander in chief (1763–75) and was serving in that capacity at the outbreak of the War of Independence. His recall followed differences that arose after the engagement at Bunker Hill, and he was replaced by the general who had commanded the British forces in that battle, Sir WILLIAM HOWE. For nearly three years Howe was in supreme command, but, unable to win decisive conclusions, in 1778 he was replaced by Sir HENRY CLINTON. After the defeat of Cornwallis at Yorktown (1781), which virtually ended the war, Clinton returned to England, and was succeeded in 1782 by Sir GUY CARLETON, who administered the evacuation of British troops after the war (1783).

British Empire in America, see *Imperial Problems.*

Broadway, originally a residential street in New York City, by mid-19th century had become the main business artery. The longest street in the world, it extends 150 miles, from Bowling Green, near the southern tip of Manhattan, to Albany. Today its best-known section is the THEATER district near Times Square, popularly known from its brilliant illumination as the Great White Way.

BROCKWAY, ZEBULON REED (1827–1920), as superintendent of the House of Correction at Detroit (1861–75), in 1869 sought to introduce the indeterminate sentence for first offenders as an incentive to self-improvement, and although the state of Michigan enacted such a law, the courts nullified it. As first superintendent of the New York state reformatory at Elmira (1876–1900), Brockway gave direction to that state's penal legislation and introduced a system of physical training, education, and trade instruction in prisons.

BRODIE, STEVE (*fl.* 1886), well known as a New York saloon-keeper during the latter part of the 19th century, gained notoriety by jumping 140 ft. from Brooklyn Bridge into the East river, and surviving the fall.

Bronco, see *Mustang.*

Bronx, The, northernmost borough of the City of New York; was originally a district comprising several towns in Westchester county, an area settled by Jonas Bronck (a Dane) for the Dutch West India Company in 1641. Its 41 square miles include large areas of parks (Bronx, Cortlandt, and Pelham Bay). In 1960 its population exceeded 1,425,000.

Brook Farm, at West Roxbury, Massachusetts, was the best remembered of experiments in UTOPIAN SOCIALISM, and lasted for six years (1841–47). Largely directed by GEORGE RIPLEY, who after 1845 edited its weekly newspaper, *The Harbinger,* it trebled in size when ALBERT BRISBANE in 1845 transformed the simple 'Institute of Agriculture and Education' (milch cows in the barn and Latin in the classroom) into a center of Fourierist propaganda. Hawthorne briefly joined the venture and recorded his experience in *The Blithedale Romance* (1852).

Notable more for its intellectual ferment and its ties with transcendentalism than for its solution to labor problems, it was described by Emerson, who lent it support, as 'a perpetual picnic, a French Revolution in small, an age of reason in a patty-pan.' Its associates included such intellectual leaders as C. A. DANA, J. S. DWIGHT, G. W. CURTIS, ORESTES BROWNSON, and THEODORE PARKER. It came to an abrupt end when fire destroyed a nearly completed central 'phalanstery.'

Brooklyn, on the southwestern tip of Long Island, was settled about 1637 by Dutch farmers, who named it for Breukelen, Holland. Brooklyn Heights was the scene of the battle of LONG ISLAND (1776). In 1816, with a population of 4500, it was incorporated as a village, and in 1834, when its population had grown to 24,000, it was chartered as a city. By 1855 it had become one of the few large cities in the U.S., with a population of nearly 280,000. Long Island was first connected to Manhattan by the Brooklyn Bridge (1883). In 1898 the city gave up its independent municipal organization, and has since become the largest borough of the City of New York, with a population (1960) of more than 2,700,000.

BROOKS, PHILLIPS (1835–93), born in Boston, after graduation from Harvard (1855) and ordination in the Episcopal ministry, for ten years (1859–69) occupied pulpits in Philadelphia. Called to the rectory of Trinity Church in Boston, he became widely known for his eloquence. He defined preaching as 'the bringing of truth through personality,' and the statue of him at Trinity, designed by Saint-Gaudens, bears witness to Brooks's influence upon his times. He was consecrated bishop of Massachusetts in 1891. Best remembered is his carol, 'O Little Town of Bethlehem,' written for his Sunday School and sung at Christmas, 1868.

BROOKS, VAN WYCK (1886–1963), after graduation from Harvard (1908) began his long career as critic and literary historian. He is best represented by his five-volume *Makers and Finders: A History of the Writer in America* (1953). It covers the period 1800–1915, and comprises *The Flowering of New England, 1815–65* (1936), *New England: Indian Summer, 1865–1915* (1940), *The World of Washington Irving* (1944), *The Times of Melville and Whitman* (1947), and *The Confident Years: 1885–1915* (1952).

More literature than literary history, these studies reveal Brooks as an artist and a lover of the picturesque, with their frequent, discursive, and stimulating footnotes. He served as literary critic of the *Freeman* (1920–24) and wrote for other publications. Virtually all his adult life he remained at his craft, which exemplifies his belief that writers need a sense of belonging to a continuing tradition. As one of the most eminent American literary critics of his day, he did more than any other to define the cultural climate of the U.S.

Brother Jonathan, as a generic name for a shrewd Yankee, gained currency briefly after the Revolution. 'We must consult Brother Jonathan,' Washington is reputed to have said, referring to Governor JONATHAN TRUMBULL of Connecticut, on whose advice he often depended. The epithet is applied to the chief character in the subplot of Royall Tyler's play *The Contrast* (1787) to typify homespun sagacity.

BROUN, HEYWOOD [CAMPBELL] (1888–1939), after attending Harvard (1906–10) became a reporter and columnist for the New York *Tribune* (1912–21) and the New York *World* (1921–28). He later worked for other New York papers, to which his liberal and outspoken syndicated column, 'It Seems to Me,' was transferred. In 1933 he became the first president of the American Newspaper Guild. The best of his writing was posthumously issued in *A Collected Edition* (1941). Those who knew him as an Episcopalian, then as a militant freethinker, were startled in 1939 to learn that he had become a Catholic.

BROWDER, EARL RUSSELL (1891–   ), converted to Marxism as a boy, and imprisoned (1917–19) under the Espionage Act, became a member of the U.S. COMMUNIST PARTY at its founding (1919) and was twice its presidential candidate (1936, 1940). Convicted for passport fraud and again imprisoned (1940), he was pardoned by President F. D. Roosevelt. His opposition to party policies resulted in his expulsion from the party in 1946. His writings include *What Is Communism?* (1936) and *War and Peace with Russia* (1947).

BROWN, JACOB (1775–1828), at the outbreak of the War of 1812, as a brigadier general in the New York militia, was given command of troops along the frontier. Commissioned a brigadier in the regular army in 1813, he was soon raised to the rank of major general and succeeded the incompetent JAMES

WILKINSON in command of forces at Niagara. After occupying Fort Erie, he was in a position to fight the battle of LUNDY'S LANE, where he was twice wounded. He was commanding general of the U.S. Army from 1821 until his death. Admiral Mahan rated his operations at Lundy's Lane second in distinction only to the Battle of New Orleans during the War of 1812.

BROWN, JOHN (1800–1859), abolitionist leader, grew up in Ohio, where he unsuccessfully engaged in the tanning business, sheep-raising, and the wool trade. After various removes he settled on a small farm in North Elba, New York (1849), from which in 1854 five of his sons, bred to a hatred of slavery, moved to Kansas to participate in antislavery activities developing there. Debtridden, Brown followed them in the next year, leaving the rest of his numerous family at home.

Believing himself the Lord's chosen instrument to destroy those who favored slavery, Brown led a party of six, which, in the 'Pottawatomie massacre,' killed five innocent proslavery men. This was but one incident in the border warfare which was making a national issue of BLEEDING KANSAS. 'Brown of Osawatomie' became a rallying cry for Eastern abolitionists, who gave money to help him establish a stronghold in the mountains of western Virginia to assist fugitive slaves (as he envisioned his task). With about twenty men Brown seized the U.S. arsenal at Harpers Ferry (16 October 1859). Captured two days later, he rejected his counsel's plea of insanity, and after being convicted of treason and murder he was hanged.

Brown's bloody role in the crisis years from 1856 to 1859 gave rise to an extraordinary range of opinions. Southerners feared a slave insurrection. Many responsible Republican and Democratic newspapers in the North condemned his acts as criminal. The antislavery spokesmen of the North, particularly in the area of the Western Reserve, mourned him as a martyr. His statement from jail that he was about to die 'for God's eternal truth' led Emerson to call him 'That new saint who will make the gallows glorious like the cross.' Thus what Brown *said* about slavery had the power of an Old Testament prophet.

See O. G. Villard, *John Brown* (1943).

BROWN, JOHN CARTER (1797–1874), son of the Providence, Rhode Island, manufacturer and philanthropist Nicholas Brown (1769–1841), collected 7500 volumes of early Americana, many extremely rare, which became the nucleus of the John Carter Brown Library (Brown University). The endowments of subsequent members of the family have created the best collection in the U.S. of European books dealing with the discovery and exploration of the Western World.

Brown University (1764) was established as Rhode Island College, a Baptist institution, at Warren, Rhode Island. In 1770 it was transferred to Providence, where it served as a barracks and hospital during the War of Independence. In 1804 it was renamed to honor the benefactions of the merchant Nicholas Brown (1769–1841). It has a graduate school of arts and sciences, a division of engineering, and Pembroke College (est. 1891) for women. In 1965, with an endowment of $41,576,000 and a faculty of 911, it enrolled 4500 students.

Brown* v. *Board of Education of Topeka (May 1954) was a case resulting in a historic decision by the U.S. Supreme Court, which unanimously ruled that segregation of white and Negro children in public schools, solely on the ground of race and color, denied to Negro pupils the equal protection guaranteed by the FOURTEENTH AMENDMENT. It thus substantially altered the opinion handed down by Justice Field in 1885 that the terms of the Amendment had been met if they affected 'alike all persons similarly situated,' a ruling that in *Plessy* v. *Ferguson* (1896) had been interpreted to mean 'separate but equal' accommodations.

In May 1955 the Court issued another ruling, decreeing that state and local laws must honor the principle, and instructed Federal courts to require a start toward desegregation 'with all deliberate speed.' It soon extended the ruling to apply to public gathering places, common carriers, and to state-supported colleges and universities.

Although white resistance was strong and statewide in some areas with a large Negro population, the great violence at first predicted did not come to pass. But by 1964 Negro organizations complained of too much 'tokenism' in the progress toward desegregation.

BROWNE, JOHN ROSS (1821–75), Irish-born traveler and government servant, shipped out of New Bedford, Massachusetts, on a whaling vessel in 1842. His observations, *Etchings of a Whaling Cruise* (1846), influenced Melville in writing *Moby-Dick*. His shrewd and humorous *An American Family in Germany* (1886) is an early account of travel in central Europe. He left a record of his travel in the Near East and in the American Far West. For a brief time (1868) he served as minister to China, but was recalled when his publicly expressed opinions ran counter to the BURLINGAME TREATY.

Brownists, a term applied to English Separatist Puritans (*c.* 1580–1660), the group which broke away from the Church of England, derives from Robert Browne, whose *Treatise of Reformation without Tarrying for Anie* (1583) asserts the inalienable right of churches to effect reforms by selecting their own officers without civil interference. This essentially Congregationalist polity was carried by the Pilgrims to Plymouth. Although the settlers of Massachusetts Bay insisted that they had never 'separated' from the Anglican church, they soon adopted the Congregational way.

BROWNLOW, WILLIAM GANNAWAY (1805–77), after serving as an itinerant preacher in his native Tennessee (1826–36) became a journalist and entered politics. His Knoxville *Whig* (1849–61), the most influential paper in the state, was suppressed because of its defiant Union sympathies. In 1862 his lecture tour through the North attracted large and distinguished audiences, and his *Sketches of the Rise, Progress, and Decline of Secession* (1862) stirred sympathy for him.

Sections of Tennessee had been strongly Unionist throughout the war, and at its conclusion 'Parson' Brownlow gained control of state politics and as governor (1865–69) was uncompromising in enforcing Republican policies. Thereafter, as a member of the U.S. Senate (1869–75), he was a consistent Radical Republican.

BROWNSON, ORESTES AUGUSTUS (1803–76), Vermont-born preacher and liberal writer, for varying periods between 1822 and 1844 became successively a Presbyterian, Universalist, independent, and Unitarian. While editing the *Democratic Review* (1842–44), chiefly a journal of his own opinions, his interest in transcendentalism led him to support the experiments in utopian socialism at BROOK FARM. Converted to Catholicism in 1844, he remained in that faith. His philosophic bent made him at first a somewhat independent follower of the idealistic social aims of Comte and Cousin. As a humanitarian reformer he was chiefly stirred by Robert Owen, until he accepted Catholicism, after which time the question of his orthodoxy, as he expounded his ideas in such books as *The Convert* (1857), occasionally gave concern to the Roman see.

Brownson's advocacy of his varied and changing concepts was always guided by an overruling purpose, whether in support of the Workingman's Party (1828), abolition, or the 'despotism' of the Church. He is best remembered as editor of *Brownson's Quarterly Review* (1844–64, 1873–75). His *Works* (20 vols.) were posthumously collected by his son.

BRULÉ, ÉTIENNE (*fl.* 1592–1632), French explorer in North America, was sent inland (1610) by Samuel de Champlain to investigate the Great Lakes region, and he later guided Champlain to Lake Huron. In 1615 Brulé traveled down the Susquehanna to Chesapeake Bay, returning about 1620 to explore in the Lake Superior region. He lived intimately among Huron tribes until a quarrel led to his death. He was reputed to have outdone the Indians in savagery.

BRUSH, CHARLES FRANCIS (1849–1929), after graduation from Michigan (1869), returned to Cleveland as a consulting chemist for the city. His invention of the Brush electric arc light (1878), with his subsequent inventions relating to electroplating and improvement of the dynamo, revolutionized the lighting systems of buildings and city streets.

BRY, THEODOR DE (1528–98), German publisher and engraver, with the assistance of the geographer RICHARD HAKLUYT began his monumental *Collectiones Peregrinationum in Indiam Orientalem et Indiam Occidentalem* (1590–1634), which was completed by his sons and issued in many parts, copied, translated, and variously titled. These finely illustrated accounts of explorations, assembled with imagination and scholarly integrity, gave Europeans their first view of many parts of the globe.

The first issue (1590) combined the eye-witness account of Virginia made by THOMAS HARIOT in 1585 with engravings of watercolors made at the same time by the artist JOHN WHITE. The second issue (1591) contained the narrative and drawings of Jacques Le Moyne, who had accompanied RENÉ LAUDONNIÈRE to Florida in the 1560's. Bry's skill as an engraver has never been surpassed.

BRYAN, WILLIAM JENNINGS (1860–1925), political leader and orator, was born in Salem, Illinois. After graduation from Illinois College (1881) and from Union College of Law, Chicago (1883), he settled in Lincoln, Nebraska (1887), where he practiced law and became active in Democratic politics. Elected to Congress, he served two terms (1891–95), and his speeches against the protective tariff (1892) and against repeal of the silver purchase clause in the Sherman Act (1893) made him the leader of the FREE SILVER movement. His celebrated free silver speech in the Democratic national convention of 1896 against the GOLD STANDARD concluded: 'You shall not press down upon the brow of labor this crown of thorns, you shall not crucify mankind upon a cross of gold.' The ringing words of the 'Boy Orator of the Platte' made him the idol of the silver forces, and won him the presidential nomination of the party.

The campaign that followed made clear-cut issues of Democratic (western) radical agrarianism and Republican (eastern) conservative mercantilism, and was the most hotly contested event at the polls since the election of Jackson in 1828. Bryan in his swing through 27 states captured large audiences, but William McKinley was swept into office by an emphatic electoral vote.

Still the unchallenged leader of his party, in 1900 Bryan made the charge of imperialism the primary campaign issue, and in so doing drew to the support of the Democrats an impressive number of the country's intellectual leaders, who deplored the chauvinistic spirit of the times. But wages were up, the price of agricultural commodities was rising, the Republicans had guided affairs during the era when the U.S. was becoming a world power, and so McKinley was returned to office by a large plurality. Bryan then founded the *Commoner* (1901), a weekly journal by which his political views gained currency, but in 1904 his party, less concerned with reform, selected for their candidate Alton B. Parker, chief justice of the Court of Appeals in New York. The decisive defeat of Parker at the polls gave party control back to Bryan, who in 1908 was for a third time the unsuccessful Democratic nominee for President. But Bryan still had enormous political prestige. In the Democratic convention at Baltimore in 1912, intent upon disowning Tammany Hall and the New York bosses, he was able to lead delegates away from Champ Clark, the favored candidate, and helped to secure the nomination of Woodrow Wilson, who upon election appointed Bryan Secretary of State.

As much an idealist as his chief, Bryan had less understanding of the realities of international affairs. Although Bryan contributed to good relations in Latin America, and formulated weak conciliation treaties to reduce friction among nations, he refused to sign Wilson's note of protest (9 June 1915) to the German government after the sinking of the *Lusitania,* and resigned his post.

Bryan spent his last days crusading for Fundamentalism, as prosecuting attorney for the state of Tennessee in the spectacle of the SCOPES TRIAL (1925), during which he was subjected to the withering examination of the defense attorney CLARENCE DARROW. Bryan died at Dayton, Tennessee, five days after the trial ended.

A man of extraordinary political influence, during the three decades of his political career Bryan served in public office only on two relatively brief occasions. Passionate in his convictions, of unquestioned integrity, audacious in tactics, genuinely fond of plain people in whose wisdom he sincerely believed and whose affection he never lost, Bryan won his title 'the Great Commoner.'

See M. R. Werner, *Bryan* (1929).

BRYANT, William Cullen (1794–1878), born in western Massachusetts, after scant formal education (less than a year at Williams College) by private study gained admittance to the bar (1815). His 'Thanatopsis,' published in the *North American Review* (1817), was soon followed by other nature poems, and the appearance of his collected *Poems* (1821) brought him recognition as the foremost American poet of his day. At thirty he abandoned the practice of law in his native Berkshires to become editor and part owner of the New York *Evening Post* (1829–78). Firmly established as New York's leading citizen by 1850, Bryant achieved eminence as an editor not through innovations but by the quality of his writing, the soundness of his judgment, his unwavering courage, and his adherence to the principle that no race or nation should be kept in bondage.

A lifelong opponent of slavery, Bryant coined the phrase 'Truth, crushed to earth, shall rise again,' in his poem 'The Battlefield' (1839). He recorded his affection for the prewar South in *Letters of a Traveller* (1850), which he wrote after taking a journey instigated by his friend William Gilmore Simms. He was a founder of the Republican party (1854), and, except for a conservative policy on Reconstruction, remained a vigorous defender of liberal causes. As poet and discriminating critic, he helped raise the standard of taste, and as an observer of nature, both in prose and verse, he wrote with dignity and charm.

See the biography by H. H. Peckham, *Gotham Yankee* (1950).

BRYCE, James (1838–1922), British historian and diplomat, after holding a Regius chair in civil law at Oxford, and serving in Parliament and in the Cabinet, came as British ambassador to the U.S. (1907–13). His analysis of American political institutions, *The American Commonwealth* (1888), still highly respected, is based on wide study and written with distinction. It pointed out frankly the dangers of local corruption like that of the Tweed Ring, but stressed the promise of America's democracy because of classlessness, the general diffusion of property, and the absence of chronic pauperism. So great was his prestige in the U.S. that the controversial Bryce Report of 1915 on German atrocities in Belgium converted many to the Allied cause.

Bryce Canyon National Park (est. 1928), 36,000 acres in southwestern Utah, is a box canyon with pastel-hued sandstone walls, within which innumerable pinnacles are shaped by erosion into fantastic forms. Southwest of it is Zion National Park.

Bryn Mawr College (est. 1885), founded at Bryn Mawr, Pennsylvania, by Quakers, is a liberal arts college for women. Its curriculum plan was modeled on that of Johns Hopkins, and it opened with a pioneer graduate school for women. In 1965, with an endowment of $22,200,000 and a faculty of 184, it enrolled 1000 students.

Buccaneers, or freebooters, piratical ruffians of many nationalities, established themselves on Tortuga Island, off northern Haiti in the Caribbean, during the 1620's. They preyed on the neighboring Spanish colonies until, driven out by the French in 1640, they operated elsewhere. They were for the most part suppressed in 1697, after the treaty of RYSWICK. HENRY MORGAN and BLACKBEARD were among their picturesque leaders.

BUCHANAN, James (1791–1868), 15th President of the U.S. (1857–61), after graduation from Dickinson College (1809), began the practice of law in his native Pennsylvania, entered politics, and was elected to Congress (1821–31). A converted Democrat, he ardently supported Jackson, who rewarded him with a post as minister to Russia (1832–33). He was serving in the Senate (1835–45) when Polk brought him into the cabinet as Secretary of State (1845–49), where he was a principal in the annexation of

Texas, the Mexican War, and the settlement of the Oregon Boundary Dispute. As President Pierce's minister to England (1853–56), Buchanan was in the fortunate position during the 1856 election of having no record of commitments in the partisan issues then shaking the nation. Northern Democrats were cool to both Stephen A. Douglas, who drafted the KANSAS-NEBRASKA ACT, and to Pierce, who would be obliged to enforce the measure. Buchanan had won the good will of Southerners for his part in drawing up the OSTEND MANIFESTO, and thus as a compromise candidate he was nominated and won the presidential election with 174 electoral votes. (The Republican candidate, John C. Frémont, received 114, and the 'Know-Nothing' candidate, Ex-President Fillmore, trailed with eight.)

Buchanan's troubles began when three southern members of his cabinet took measure of his pusillanimity and played upon his partisan hatred of Republicans and his legalistic cast of mind to gain his support in 1857 for the proslavery Kansas LECOMPTON CONSTITUTION. After acrid debates Congress refused to sanction the instrument, but Buchanan had lost the last good chance to crush secessionist tendencies.

The four-month interval between Lincoln's election and inauguration (November 1860–March 1861) was particularly awkward for a President who lacked convictions. South Carolina seceded in December, the Confederate government was formed in February, and the President's Attorney General advised him that secession was illegal but that the chief executive had no power of coercion. Trying vainly to compose a settlement, Buchanan supported both the CRITTENDEN COMPROMISE, which the Republicans rejected, and the Peace Conference (February 1861) summoned by Virginia, for which the southern states by then had no stomach. Thus his term in office expired in an atmosphere of futility and gloom, and he retired to his home in Lancaster, Pennsylvania.

Buchanan was industrious, capable, and tactful, but he was vacillating to the point where he denied his own authority to act in a crisis.

See Allan Nevins, *The Emergence of Lincoln* (2 vols., 1950).

BUCK, PEARL [SYDENSTRICKER] (1892–), novelist reared by missionary parents in China, graduated from Randolph-Macon College in 1914. She made China the setting for many of her stories, of which the best known is *The Good Earth* (1931). For her novels, translations, and nonfictional writings, which contributed to Western understanding of Oriental customs and problems, she received the 1938 Nobel Prize in literature.

BUCKINGHAM, JAMES SILK (1786–1855), British lecturer and member of Parliament, was a founder of the literary weekly *Athenaeum* (1828). He set forth an account of his four-year tour of the U.S. (1837–40) in *America: Historical, Statistic, and Descriptive* (2 vols., 1841), *The Eastern and Western States of America* (3 vols., 1842), and *The Slave States of America* (2 vols., 1842). Buckingham was the most indefatigable and encyclopedic of the 19th-century English travelers, and deliberately gave his series the quality of impartial guide books in order to offset the usual emphasis on American manners.

Buckshot War (1838), so called, occurred when both Whigs and Democrats claimed a majority in the contest of the Pennsylvania House of Representatives, in which two speakers were elected. A mob then assembled in Harrisburg. The governor called out the militia, equipped with rounds of buckshot. A few Whigs altered their votes, and the 'war' was over.

Budget, Bureau of the, was created by Congress (1921) to centralize the process of evaluating budget estimates, which at that time were made by nine separate congressional committees. It functions under a Director, appointed by the President for an indefinite term. Its general accounting office is headed by a COMPTROLLER GENERAL. Originally within the Treasury Department, in 1939 the Bureau was transferred to the Executive Department, where the Director, as personal agent of the President, is responsible to the President alone. The Bureau annually receives estimates of funds needed for the ensuing fiscal year (1 July to 30 June) from all branches of the government. In consultation with the President, the Director prepares the President's budget message, which is submitted to Congress each January. The Bureau supervises executive agencies and examines and revises budgets. No Federal expenditure is made without the approval of the Comptroller General.

BUELL, Abel (1742–1822), Connecticut printer and typefounder, in 1769 cast the first font of native-made American type. In 1784, using all available surveys, he produced the earliest large-scale map of the U.S. He invented machinery for cutting and polishing gems, and for a time produced copper coins for the state.

BUELL, Don Carlos (1818–98), after graduation from the U.S. Military Academy (1841), took part in the Seminole War and the Mexican War. During the Civil War he was an efficient organizer of Union forces, and was breveted a major general (March 1862), in command of the Army of the Ohio. At odds with the administration after he fought Bragg in the indecisive battle of PERRYVILLE (October 1862), he was replaced by Rosecrans. The results of a subsequent investigation were not published, but a year later Buell was relieved of command. He thereupon resigned his commission (1864) and withdrew from the service.

Buena Vista, Battle of (22–23 February 1847), occurred during the Mexican War, when Zachary Taylor with an army of 4700 defeated Santa Anna and a Mexican force three times that size. This 'splendid picture-book battle' of ready batteries, deep columns of infantry, and ranks of eager lancers was fought on a sun-baked plain. At Taylor's command to 'Double-shot your guns and give 'em hell,' the artillerymen directed a fire that routed the enemy. The victory enhanced Taylor's growing popularity and led to his election as President in 1848.

Buenos Aires Conference, see *Pan-American Conferences.*

Buffalo (*Bison bison*), when explorers penetrated the New World, ranged from Mexico to Canada and from the Atlantic to the Pacific. Until about 1870 herds of prodigious size still roamed the High Plains region east of the Rocky Mountains, and for native tribes they continued to be a source of food, clothing, shelter, and weapons. Their decimation began with the building of the Union Pacific Railroad, completed in 1869. In the first decade of transcontinental rail travel a train might be held up for hours while a herd estimated as a million head was migrating either north or south. During the 1870's the price of hides, which were worth $1 to $3, encouraged hunters to engage in a systematic and wholesale slaughter. Statistics compiled in 1883 indicate that some 13,000,000 buffalo had been killed, but the actual number is thought to be far greater. By 1900 the buffaloes in the U.S. were nearly extinct, and the few that remain today are chiefly in zoos or on reservations.

BUFFALO BILL, see *Cody, W. F.*

BULFINCH, Charles (1763–1844), the first professional architect in New England, after graduation from Harvard (1781) and study abroad, returned to his native Boston. He designed the earliest playhouse in New England, the Federal Street Theater (1794); the State House (1799), whose dome still commands the view from Beacon Hill; University Hall at Harvard (1815); and the Massachusetts General Hospital (1820). He succeeded BENJAMIN LATROBE as architect of the National Capitol, and saw it through to completion. His grouping of houses in a unified curved row on Franklin Crescent in Boston (1793) became known as the 'Bulfinch front.' Simply planned, his works follow the proportion of the Greek orders, and they exerted a strong influence on the taste of his period.

Bulge, Battle of the (16–26 December 1944), in the final months of World War II, was the last great counteroffensive against the Allied invasion of Germany. It was staged by Field Marshal von Rundstedt in the Ardennes along an eighty-mile front. This surprise assault mauled the inadequate number of U.S. troops, and, concentrating on the center of the front, the Germans penetrated fifty miles, almost within striking distance of the Channel coast. The defense of the surrounded town of BASTOGNE stemmed the drive. The battle resulted in a total of 41,315 U.S. casualties, but the battered German armies were never able to recover offensive strength. The original line was restored by the end of January 1945, and four months later Germany surrendered.

Bull Moose Party, popular name given to the PROGRESSIVE PARTY in 1912, was a tribute to Theodore Roosevelt, who had used the term on the occasion of his nomination for Vice President, in writing to Mark Hanna in 1900: 'I am as strong as a bull moose and you can use me to the limit.'

Bull Run, First Battle of (First Manassas), the earliest major engagement in the Civil War (21 July 1861), was fought by some 13,000 Federals under General Irwin McDowell, and 11,000 Confederates under Generals Joseph E. Johnston and Pierre Beauregard. The Union volunteers had been sent to Manassas Junction, Virginia, 30 miles southwest of Washington, expecting to besiege Richmond. Beauregard's army was athwart the main highways and occupied a line along Bull Run, a creek. Residents of Washington, newspapermen, and members of Congress swarmed out to witness the impending fray. Shortly after dawn McDowell's forces attacked, and thus commenced 'the best planned and worst fought' battle of the war.

The troops of both armies were inexperienced and ill-trained. Orders miscarried, the variety of flags and uniforms proved confusing, and for several hours the melee raged from Bull Run to the Henry House plateau whither the Confederates were driven, and where General Jackson stationed his brigade 'like a stone wall.' The arrival of fresh brigades of Johnston's army tipped the balance. The Federal retreat became a rout and troops streamed back to Washington in panic flight. The Confederates did not recognize their victory in time to follow up their success.

The Federals suffered 2700 casualties, the Confederates about 2000. The humiliation of the defeat spurred the North to earnest preparation for a long war. The jubilation of the South, which vainly believed that the victory would procure them foreign recognition, lulled them into a period of false security.

Bull Run, Second Battle of (Second Manassas), fought 29–31 August 1862, was a shattering Union defeat. On 24 August General Lee put into execution a daring plan by sending Jackson with 23,000 troops to cut the lines of communication of Major General John Pope's newly organized Army of Virginia (of equivalent strength) impregnably placed athwart the upper reaches of the Rappahannock river in northern Virginia. Jackson raided Pope's base at Manassas on the 26th, then moved five miles northward to form for the impending attack.

According to plan, Lee arrived on the 29th with 32,000 fresh troops, and the opposing armies met in battle. Although similarly reinforced by a large part of the Army of the Potomac, Pope was outmaneuvered. His men retreated to their Washington defenses. The bold strategy of Lee, brilliantly executed by Jackson, had thus canceled all the gains made by the Union armies in the Virginia theater of war during an entire year of fighting. Pope was relieved of field command. The Union losses (some 15,000) were nearly twice the Confederate casualties.

BULLOCK, WILLIAM A. (1813–67), expert New York mechanic, by his invention of the Bullock press (1865) revolutionized the printing industry by giving high-speed production of newsprint its start. He devised a press which was fed from a continuous roll of paper, and printed both sides of the sheet, which was then cut at intervals.

BUNCHE, RALPH JOHNSON (1904–), after graduation from the University of California at Los Angeles (1927), and advanced study at Harvard and the London School of Economics, taught political science at Howard University (1928–50) and served as chief aid to Dr. Gunnar Myrdal in his monumental study of the American Negro. Having served as research analyst in the Office of Strategic Services, he became a department chief in the Department of State. His chief contribution was made as Acting Mediator in Palestine following the assassination of Count Folke Bernadotte in September 1948. He skillfully negotiated a cease-fire order and a *de facto* peace between warring Arabs and Jews. While director of the Trusteeship Division of the United Nations (1948–54), he received the Nobel Peace prize (1950). In 1958 he became that organization's undersecretary for special political affairs. He was one of the first Negroes to serve in high Federal office.

Buncombe, a term used to describe empty talk (*bunkum* or *bunk*), derives from the name of a county in North Carolina. In 1820 a U.S. Congressman representing the district explained to a bored House during the Missouri Compromise debate that he was only 'talking for Buncombe.'

Bundling, or 'tarrying,' was a colonial custom (inherited from Europe) of courtship in cold weather. The couple reclined fully clothed on a bed or couch wrapped by heavy blankets sewed together on three sides and down through the middle. Confined largely to provincial areas, the custom had died out by the late 18th century.

Bunker Hill, Battle of (17 June 1775), took place in the early months of the Revolution when General WILLIAM HOWE, with an assault force of 2400 British regulars, sought to dislodge 1600 Americans from the redoubt they had constructed on the height above Charleston peninsula (actually Breed's Hill, nearer Boston than Bunker Hill). Twice Howe's troops were turned back by the murderous fire of the New Englanders, commanded by Colonel William Prescott (1726–95), but Prescott's supply of powder gave out, and in their third assault the British seized the hill. The British sustained more than 1000 casualties (including 92 officers), and the Americans lost some 400. Though Bunker Hill plunged American participants into deep gloom, the raw militiamen had gained the respect of such British commanders as General Burgoyne, who said: 'The retreat was no flight; it was even covered with bravery and military skill.' The battle in effect served as a rallying cry to unite the colonists.

BUNTLINE, NED, see *Judson, E. Z. C.*

Bunyan, PAUL, the legendary hero of lumberjacks from Michigan to the Pacific Northwest, was created as a native myth. Inventor, orator, and entrepreneur, Bunyan was a giant boss logger who scooped out the Grand Canyon, dredged Puget Sound, invented the double-bitted ax, and fashioned a pancake griddle so huge that it was greased by skaters with sides of bacon on their boots. His logging crews knew the Winter of the Big Snow, so cold that cuss words, frozen, thawed with a bang on the Fourth of July. His companion, Babe the Blue Ox, measured '42 ax handles and a plug of chewing tobacco' between the eyes. In southern lumber camps he was known as Tony Beaver, and sometimes as John Henry.

BURBANK, LUTHER (1849–1926), Massachusetts-born plant breeder, after 1875 lived at Santa Rosa, California, where his experiments in cross-breeding thousands of plants led to new types and improved varieties, including the Shasta daisy and the Burbank potato. Concerned only with concrete results — and many of them were impressive — he did not formulate original genetic theories, nor did he become wealthy from his experimentation. He published descriptive catalogs, and outlined his methods in the extensive work, *How Plants Are Trained to Work for Man* (8 vols., 1921).

BURCHFIELD, CHARLES (1893–), first became known as a painter of somber relics of the Middle Western landscape, such as *False Front* (Metropolitan Museum) and *Freight Cars under a Bridge* (Detroit Institute), subjects treated with semirealism and slight irony. In later watercolors, represented by *Autumn Fantasy* (1945), Burchfield drew upon memories of his Ohio boyhood to create a dreamlike atmosphere. Most important, his realistic depiction of decayed rural houses influenced the socially conscious regionalists of the 1930's, particularly Thomas Hart Benton.

Bureaucracy is the system of conducting the business of federal, state, or local government by means of bureaus or departments, each headed by a chief. The first Federal bureaucracy was created (1789) when Congress established the departments of State, Treasury, and War. Once traditions and precedents are established, bureaucracies tend to be unresponsive in matters of administrative detail, and to innovations and changes in procedures. To counter such a tendency, the principle of ROTATION IN OFFICE was established soon after the Republic was founded, but the practice soon led to the SPOILS SYSTEM, by which the government was administered through PARTY MACHINES.

Civil service reforms, especially after passage of the PENDLETON ACT (1883), greatly reduced 'amateurism' in government, and helped reduce the number of appointments made on the basis of patronage. After World War II the number of agencies, boards, and commissions created for special purposes had proliferated to such an extent that in 1947 Congress established the HOOVER COMMISSION to suggest ways whereby clear lines of control in the hierarchies of government could be effected.

BURGESS, JOHN WILLIAM (1844–1931), political scientist, was son of a pro-Union Tennessee slaveholder. After graduation from Amherst (1867) and study abroad he taught at Amherst (1873–76) before embarking upon a distinguished career at Columbia (1876–1912), where he organized graduate work in history and politics. In *The Middle Period, 1817–1858* (1898) he attacked the liberal natural rights philosophy and stigmatized abolitionism as 'the literal interpretation of the Declaration of Independence.' More influential was *Reconstruction and the Constitution* (1905), a 'revisionist' condemnation of Radical Reconstruction for racist or white supremacist reasons.

BURGOYNE, JOHN (1722–92), English soldier, politician, and playwright, had acquitted himself so well as a brigade commander in Portugal (1762) that before the outbreak of the War of Independence he had become a major general. In 1775 he interrupted his parliamentary duties to accept a command in America, and arrived in Boston with reinforcements for the beleaguered General Gage, after the initial encounter at LEXINGTON. Believing the colonial problem demanded more than garrison occupation, Burgoyne returned to England and helped persuade the North ministry that the issue was one of reconquest.

He was sent back to America in the spring of 1776 as commander in chief of a northern army to effect an invasion from Canada. After he recaptured Ticonderoga he was promoted to the rank of lieutenant general, but through a series of blunders (for which the British war office was initially heavily at fault) Burgoyne was compelled to surrender his entire army at SARATOGA (October 1777). 'Gentleman Johnny' then returned to England in disgrace and was deprived of his rank. His demand for a trial was refused. Later when his political friends came into office he was restored to rank as a colonel. He then retired to private life and occupied himself principally with literary and dramatic work.

BURKE, EDMUND (1729–97), British statesman, though he never held a responsible position in government, was regarded by his peers and is esteemed today as one of the great political philosophers of his time and an orator of universal rank. His speech in Parliament *On American Taxation* (1774) urged repeal of the TEA ACT, not because he doubted the right of that body to legislate on its IMPERIAL PROBLEMS, but because he was informed and realistic: 'The question with me is not whether you have the right to render your people miserable, but whether it is not your interest to make them happy.' His speech *On Conciliation with the American Colonies* (1775) pressed the same points and met similar indifference. His *Letter to the Sheriffs of Bristol* (1777), defending his position, was evoked by the fact that members of his Whig party were confused by the revolutionary turn of events in America, and were refusing to deal further with the Americans except by military measures. After the defeat of Cornwallis in 1781, Burke could truly assert: 'I do not say I saved my country; I am sure I did my country important service.'

Burke Act (1906), which supplemented the DAWES ACT of 1887, provided that

Indians be granted citizenship only at the expiration of the 25-year probationary period. The purpose was to guarantee to the Indians the unrestricted ownership of property, which that period required for citizenship, thus safeguarding their patents against exploitation. The provisions were further amended in 1934 by the WHEELER-HOWARD ACT.

Burke-Wadsworth Act, see *Selective Service and Training Act.*

Burlesque, as a form of stage entertainment featuring low comedy, obscene humor, and lewd dancing, became successful in the U.S. with *The Black Crook* (1866–67), an extravaganza of the British Blondes and the first appearance of women in tights. In the latter part of the 19th century attendance at burlesque shows was often surreptitious and somewhat adventurous, since the performances were under constant threat of police raids. They lost ground rapidly after 1930 in part through competition with musical comedy and motion pictures, but chiefly because of legal restrictions. In New York City burlesque theaters were refused a renewal of their licenses in 1937, and thus were permanently closed.

Burlingame Treaty (1868), between the U.S. and China, established free immigration between the countries; pledged the right of travel, residence, and education to nationals of either country on a 'most favored nation' basis; and guaranteed, on the part of the U.S., noninterference in Chinese domestic affairs. Anson Burlingame (1820–70), who had recently been minister to China (1861–67), served as head of mission for China; Secretary Seward signed for the U.S. The immigration clause was later modified by the CHINESE EXCLUSION ACTS.

Burma Campaign (1942–45), one of the most complex undertakings in World War II, had as its objective the reopening of a land route to China, whose southwest defenses needed to be secured. The Japanese had blocked the BURMA ROAD and overrun Burma and Thailand. China was thereby sealed off from her Anglo-American allies except for the 'Hump,' the perilous airlift from India over the eastern Himalaya range. This airlift was operated with amazing efficiency by such air groups as General Frank Merrill's famous Marauders, and General Orde Wingate's Raiders. Its severely limited monthly supply in 1942 of 2000 tons was steadily increased to 49,000 tons by 1945, enough to mount an offensive. But the mere trickle in 1943 persuaded Roosevelt, Churchill, and Chiang Kai-shek at the CAIRO CONFERENCE that the three allies should attempt to open surface communications with China by driving the Japanese from northern Burma, and thus regain access to the Burma Road.

In March 1944 General Joseph Stilwell began what General George Marshall described as the 'most difficult campaign of World War II.' Air power was effectively used to meet every obstacle, under conditions in which weather, geography, and logistics offered handicaps of unparalleled severity. In April the Japanese launched an attack which overran most of the important airdromes in China from which General Claire Chennault's superb XIV Army Air Force operated to supply the bases for the Burma offensive. Stilwell's plea for command of all Chinese ground forces met Chiang's refusal. Stilwell was recalled, and the Chinese front disintegrated, thus temporarily halting the Burma campaign.

The political turn of events had already made it clear that defeat of Japan could not be based upon using China as an ally. In July General MacArthur flew to Pearl Harbor for a meeting with President Roosevelt and Admiral Nimitz, and there plans were laid for the great PHILIPPINE CAMPAIGN. The reopening of the Burma Road by Chinese Nationalists in January 1945 again established Chinese-American co-operation. With the defeat of Germany imminent in the spring of 1945, a new Burma offensive was undertaken as a naval operation. The capture of Rangoon and Mandalay led to the evacuation of Japanese forces, and the end of the Burma campaign.

Burma Road, from Lashio, Burma, to Kunming, China, was constructed (1936–38) as the principal Anglo-American supply route to China. It was blocked when the Japanese captured

Rangoon in February 1942. General Lewis A. Pick and his corps of engineers built a new Ledo Road (1943–44) from Assam, India, to link with the Burma Road, which the Chinese opened in January 1945. After the BURMA CAMPAIGN it was renamed the Stilwell Road by Generalissimo Chiang Kai-shek, in honor of General Joseph W. Stilwell.

BURNHAM, DANIEL HUDSON (1846–1912), trained as an architect in Chicago, there established a partnership, with J. R. ROOT, which became internationally famous after they were assigned the planning of the WORLD'S COLUMBIAN EXHIBITION (1893). According to LOUIS SULLIVAN (the father of modern American architecture), however, Burnham spread the 'virus of the World's Fair' for a 'bogus antique' (the Classical Revival), thus delaying the advent of functionalism.

A pioneer in the development of steel-frame buildings, Burnham was widely consulted as a city planner, serving as chairman of the committee appointed (1900) to beautify Washington, D.C. His works include the Flatiron Building and the Wanamaker store in New York City, Filene's store in Boston, Selfridge's in London, and Union Station in Washington.

BURNSIDE, AMBROSE EVERETT (1824–81), a graduate of the U.S. Military Academy (1847), commanded a Union brigade in the first battle of BULL RUN, and in the early months of the Civil War headed successful naval-military expeditions along the northeastern seacoast. Promoted major general, he commanded McClellan's left wing at ANTIETAM, and upon McClellan's removal (November 1862) Lincoln appointed Burnside commanding general of the Army of the Potomac. The incompetence that Burnside exhibited at FREDERICKSBURG (December 1862) was so costly that he was transferred to Ohio. In 1864 he led a corps under Grant in the Wilderness and the Petersburg campaigns, in which latter undertaking his failure to win the battle of the Crater ('the Burnside mine') brought about his resignation. He later served as governor of Rhode Island (1866–69) and as U.S. Senator (1875–81). From his flowing side-whiskers originated the name *burnsides,* or *sideburns.*

Burnt-Over District, see *Revivals.*

BURR, AARON (1756–1836), son of the Reverend Aaron Burr (1715–57), second president of the College of New Jersey (Princeton), and grandson of Jonathan Edwards, graduated from the College (1772), and served with distinction as a field officer for four years during the War of Independence. He practiced law in New York City, entered politics, and served as U.S. Senator (1791–97). When national parties formed, he allied himself with the Democratic-Republicans, and constructed the political machine which gave Tammany Hall its early power. His organization gained a majority in the state legislature of 1800, and in the presidential contest of that year Burr won the same number of votes as Jefferson (73), a tie broken in the House of Representatives after thirty-five ballots by the election of Jefferson. Hamilton's influence decided the issue.

Burr therefore became Vice President, and presided over the Senate with dignity. But Burr and Hamilton had long been political rivals in New York politics, and some weeks after Burr had failed to win nomination for the New York governorship (1804), defeated again mainly by Hamilton's influence, Burr challenged Hamilton to a duel provoked by published aspersions. They met at Weehawken, New Jersey (11 July), where Burr shot to kill and Hamilton died the next day. The Vice President, an exile from New York (where, as in New Jersey, he had been indicted for murder), served out his term in office and then became a political adventurer.

The traditional view that he planned a separation of the West from the Union, for a time discredited, today receives the support of some historians. Burr seems to have envisioned the creation of a new political unit west of the Alleghenies, with New Orleans as capital. He presented to those who would listen to his scheme only such portions of it as might have individual appeal. Before leaving Washington, and while still in office, Burr gave the British minister reason to believe that for the sum of $500,000 England could win the loyalty of the western states. Minister Merry favored the idea, but the British government rejected it. Burr then went West, allegedly to conquer Mexico. His persuasive arguments attracted the support of a diverse company: the Catholic bishop of New Orleans; Andrew Jackson, then on the bench of the Tennessee Supreme Court; James Wilkinson, the ranking general of the U.S. Army and a master at double-dealing; and the fanciful Irish exile Harman Blennerhassett, mesmerized by Burr's promise to make him a grand potentate after Burr had become emperor of Mexico.

Again in Washington, Burr persuaded the Spanish minister to give him $10,000, ostensibly to defend Spanish America. With 60 followers and a bizarre flotilla of five or six flatboats, Burr reached the lower Mississippi in the summer of 1806. Burr's meager facilities could have done little except take up a large land claim he had purchased in western Louisiana. The devious Wilkinson informed President Jefferson of 'a deep, dark, wicked, and widespread conspiracy' to seize Spanish-American territory. The presumption was that Burr was seeking to promote the secession of Louisiana Territory, of which he expected to become president. Arrested and indicted for treason, Burr was tried before Chief Justice Marshall, whose interpretation of the constitutional definition of 'levying war' resulted in Burr's acquittal (1807). Thus ended the most serious threat of dismemberment of the Union prior to 1860.

The years 1808–12 Burr spent abroad, where his filibustering schemes (to overthrow Jefferson, to unite France and Britain against the U.S., to return Canada to France) were repeatedly snubbed. Returning to New York, he resumed the practice of law, and at 77 married his second wife, the wealthy widow Eliza Jumel (1775–1865), who soon divorced him after he had squandered much of her fortune. Endowed with uncommon natural gifts, and with a charm of manner acknowledged even by those who despised him, Burr is believed by many to have been a pliant and corrupt politician, whose unscrupulousness tainted all his relationships, both public and private; however, this has been the dominant, but not exclusive, interpretation.

See Nathan Schachner, *Aaron Burr* (1937) and T. P. Abernethy, *The Burr Conspiracy* (1954).

BURRITT, Elihu (1810–70), educated himself while working at his New Britain, Connecticut, forge. In his thirties this 'learned blacksmith' could read nearly 50 tongues, an erudition he displayed for amusement by translating several Longfellow poems into Sanskrit. Profoundly idealistic, to further the cause of world peace Burritt conducted the *Christian Citizen* (1844–51), wrote voluminously, organized the League of Universal Brotherhood (1846), and was the leading spirit at the second Universal Peace Congress in Brussels (1848). He helped to avert war with England over Oregon in 1846 through the 'friendly address' movement in the press of both countries, and in 1850 he urged workmen 'to unite and refuse to fight.' His widely read books include *Sparks from an Anvil* (1846), and *Ten Minute Talks* (1873), excerpts from lectures delivered in the U.S. and Europe in behalf of philanthropic causes.

BURROUGHS, John (1837–1921), first set down his observations of the trees, birds, and rural scenes of his native Catskill Mountains in *Wake-Robin* (1871). His popular essays on nature studies not only led readers to make pilgrimages to his home, 'Slabsides,' but to record their own nature observations in their letters to him. His later works include *Signs and Seasons* (1886) and *Ways of Nature* (1905). He was a friend of Walt Whitman, and one of the first to recognize the poet's qualities of mystic and seer in *Notes on Walt Whitman* (1867).

BUSH, Vannevar (1890–   ), professor and dean of engineering at Massachusetts Institute of Technology (1923–38), served as president of the Carnegie Institution after 1939. As director (1941–46) of the Office of Scientific Research and Development, he organized the Manhattan Project, which sponsored the construction of the first atomic bomb.

BUSHNELL, Horace (1802–76), after graduation from Yale (1827) was ordained pastor of the North (Congregational) Church in Hartford, Connecticut (1833–59). As an influential leader of the liberal wing of his denomination, he supported those who sought in religion an intuitive experience. *Christian Nurture* (1847) sets forth his doctrine of the natural goodness of man, and illustrates the moral and intellectual dilemmas of those who were strongly influenced by the humanitarian currents of the time, yet were bound by their traditional Calvinism. He was keenly aware of sociological changes, and made central in his pronouncements the teaching of Christ as set forth in the Gospels.

Business consolidation is the elimination of industrial competition, and seeks to exploit the national market by lowering unit costs through consolidated high-volume production and marketing by way of MERGERS, POOLS, and HOLDING COMPANIES. Consolidations during the 1880's led to passage of the SHERMAN ANTITRUST ACT (1890), which as a weapon against trusts proved ineffective. The great era of consolidation for manufacturing and mining companies occurred about 1900; that for public utilities and financial companies was during the 1920's and 1930's. Since World War II, consolidations have taken place in all areas, and government antitrust policy has turned against price conspiracy rather than bigness that is justified economically.

Business cycles are periodic fluctuations or recurring phases of depression, revival, prosperity, and recession in business. They have been studied most systematically by WESLEY C. MITCHELL and his associates. Although the order of the phases in modern times has usually been constant, the intensity or duration of a phase may vary markedly from cycle to cycle. The first major depression in America, largely the result of a currency famine and inadequate banking controls after the Revolution, resulted in the PANIC OF 1785. The period of prosperity following the passage of the PUBLIC LAND ACT (1800) lasted through the War of 1812, after which a severe depression culminated in the PANIC OF 1819. Similar cyclic periods of depression resulted in the PANICS OF 1837, 1857, 1873, 1883, 1893, 1907, 1920, and 1929. Although business recessions have occurred in the past three decades, severe crises have been averted by more adequate banking and other government controls than had previously been in force.

BUTLER, BENJAMIN FRANKLIN (1818–93), after graduation from Waterville College (Colby) in 1838, practiced law first in Lowell, Massachusetts, and later in Boston. He entered politics, went as a delegate to four Democratic national conventions (1848–60), and as a politically appointed major general served in the Union army. He was military governor of New Orleans (May–December 1862) until his highhanded rule brought about his recall. Thereafter he led the Army of the James, repeatedly suffering defeat, and in 1864 he was relieved of field command.

Butler served in Congress as a Republican (1867–75, 1877–79), and as a leader among the radicals opened the impeachment proceedings against President Andrew Johnson in 1868. He exercised a considerable influence over President Grant, and was able to push through the FORCE ACTS (1870–75) and similar legislation designed to compel the South to accept the radical Republican platform. He later served as governor of Massachusetts (1882–84), and in 1884 he received the nominations of the Greenback and Anti-Monopoly parties for President. A brilliant lawyer, Butler was an erratic soldier and administrator, and a controversial politician.

BUTLER, NICHOLAS MURRAY (1862–1947), after graduation from Columbia (1882) taught philosophy there (1885–1902) and for more than 40 years served the institution as president (1902–45). He had been one of the founders of Teachers College (1888), and during his long administration instituted other changes that gave the university international renown. For many years (1925–45) he was president of the Carnegie Endowment for International Peace, and in 1931 he shared with JANE ADDAMS the Nobel Peace prize.

Butler's Rangers (1777–84) was a loyalist regiment recruited by John Butler (1728–96). It undertook marauding expeditions throughout Pennsylvania and New York during the War of Independence, particularly in the Mohawk Valley, to spread terror among patriots. With Mohawk Indians they carried out the WYOMING MASSACRE, the most wantonly savage episode of the war. The regiment was disbanded thereafter.

BYRD, RICHARD EVELYN (1888–1957), a graduate of the U.S. Military Academy (1912), entered the Aviation Service in 1917. For his flight over the North Pole (May 1926) he and his pilot FLOYD BENNETT were awarded the Medal of Honor. On his first expedition to the Antarctic (1928–30) Byrd established LITTLE AMERICA. He was promoted to the rank of rear admiral, and made a second expedition to Antarctica (1933–35), recorded in his books *Discovery* (1935), and *Alone* (1938). He undertook important geographical surveys of the South Pole region in two later expeditions (1939–40, 1946–47).

BYRD, WILLIAM (1674–1744), son of a wealthy Virginia aristocrat, studied law at the Middle Temple in London, and as a friend of the dramatists Wycherley and Congreve developed an interest in *belles lettres* which was sound and abiding. He returned to Virginia as master of the baronial estate at Westover (1704), and became an active farmer and trader, and a lifelong member of the Council of State. He was elected (1696) a corresponding member of the Royal Society of London, and at his death his library of 4000 volumes, in all branches of learning, was reputedly the largest in the colonies.

Although Byrd spent several years as colonial agent in England (1697–1705, 1715–26), he devoted his time chiefly to multiplying his land holdings, which he increased from 26,000 acres to 180,000. He kept up correspondence with both his learned and urbane friends in England, and as an avocation recorded (in shorthand) diary accounts of episodes and daily events while he participated in surveying the division between North Carolina and Virginia (1728). Some of his observations, humorous, shrewd, and caustic, were first published (1841) in *History of the Dividing Line,* and relate the lives of poor whites in 'Lubberland.' Similar diaries (for the years 1709–12, 1717–21, 1739–41) have recently been decoded and published (1941–42, 1958).

BYRNES, JAMES FRANCIS (1879–), born in Charleston, South Carolina, was admitted to the bar (1903), served in Congress (1911–25), and engaged in the practice of law at Spartanburg, South Carolina (1925–31). While serving in the U.S. Senate (1931–41), Byrnes, then considered a consistent liberal, was appointed to the U.S. Supreme Court (1941). He resigned a year later to accept appointment as director of economic stabilization (1942–43), a post he left when he became director of war mobilization (1943–45). President Truman called Byrnes into the cabinet as Secretary of State (1945–47), in which office Byrnes sought to meet the challenge of the Cold War. He later served (1951–55) as governor of South Carolina, in which post he was a conservative, especially on racial issues.

C

CABET, ÉTIENNE (1788–1856), French reformer, developed his scheme for a Utopian society in *Voyage en Icarie* (1840), an immensely popular romance describing a community in which an elected government controls all economic activity and supervises social affairs, the family alone remaining an independent unit. With some 500 Icarians, Cabet established a co-operative settlement in Fannin county, Texas (1848), where freedom of speech and religion prevailed, and soon after established other communities in Nauvoo, Illinois, and elsewhere. Dissensions arose, and, a week before his death, Cabet and 180 followers withdrew to St. Louis. None of his communitarian ventures survived.

CABEZA de VACA, ÁLVAR NÚÑEZ (*fl.* 1490–1550), as a veteran soldier accompanied NARVAÉZ on the disastrous expedition wrecked in Florida (1528). After aimless wanderings through Florida swamps, the 250 survivors built five small boats and followed the shore line to the west. The storms they encountered sank some of the boats and separated the rest. Cabeza and two other white men and a Moorish Negro slave reached shore near Galveston, Texas. While living as captives of roving Indian tribes, they inspired enough confidence through their ingenuity as traders and medicine men that they were able to escape. They survived a six-year 3000-mile trek across Texas and northern Mexico to the Pacific Ocean.

They arrived at Mexico City in 1536, and Cabeza returned to Spain the following year. The story of his incredible venture is set forth in his *Relación,* a basically reliable source book, the earliest of the INDIAN CAPTIVITIES, and the first narrative of travel through the present U.S. Cabeza was probably the first white man to see 'hunchback cows,' the buffalo. The significant expeditions of FRAY MARCOS (1539) and CORONADO (1540–42) relied upon his reports of the Narváez explorations.

Cabinet, the, of the President of the U.S. differs in origin, size, function, and political status from the British Cabinet, with which it has few points of similarity except in name. It was not created by statutory or constitutional law. The Federal Constitutional Convention of 1787 discussed the matter of providing the President with a privy council, but finally wrote into the Constitution the provision (Art. II, sec. 2) that the President 'may require' the advice of such heads of departments as Congress might create. Unwilling to make vital decisions without consultation, Washington chose as his 'official family' an executive council of four: the secretaries of State, Treasury, and War, and the Attorney General. This conference was generally accepted as a cabinet when Washington began his second term as President, but not until 1907 did statute law officially recognize it by name. Thus the establishment of the President's council originated in custom, which likewise has made the selection of members a personal prerogative of the President, whose choices, although subject to Senate approval, are almost always promptly confirmed.

To consolidate party support, the President usually gives consideration to political and geographical factors in his appointments. Department heads serve at the pleasure and discretion of the Chief Executive, and by custom submit their resignations after a four-year term in office, or in the event that the President dies in office. Unlike the British Cabinet, which constitutes the Ministry, the President's cabinet merely advises its chief, and its members are responsible only to him. Each department has one or more 'undersecretaries' or 'assistant secretaries,' who may on invitation attend cabinet meetings. In recent years some Presidents have invited the Vice President to attend such meetings regularly, a custom now evidently well established.

On occasion Presidents have been less influenced by official advisers than by unofficial ones. Such was the so-called KITCHEN CABINET of Jackson, and the BRAIN TRUST of F. D. Roosevelt. In 1954 Eisenhower approved a cabinet system never before adopted. He called regular meetings to act on a fixed agenda, for which position papers had been circulated by a cabinet secretariat. But the system has no permanence by law, nor does it establish a precedent, for each President is free to arrange the meetings of his official family as he sees fit.

At present the cabinet consists of eleven members: secretaries of STATE, TREASURY, DEFENSE, the ATTORNEY GENERAL, the POSTMASTER GENERAL, secretaries of the INTERIOR, AGRICULTURE, COMMERCE, LABOR, of HEALTH, EDUCATION AND WELFARE, and of HOUSING AND URBAN DEVELOPMENT. The U.S. ambassador to the United Nations is accorded cabinet rank at the pleasure of the President, not by statutory right.

CABLE, GEORGE WASHINGTON (1844–1925), New Orleans author, after serving with the Confederate cavalry (1863–65), became a reporter for the New Orleans *Picayune* (1865–70). Soon, as a free-lance writer, he began publishing stories of Louisiana life, especially of the Creoles. His later essays, castigating the rising tendency to treat the Negro as a perpetual alien through the newly legalized Jim Crow system, aroused the resentment of Southerners, and after 1885 Cable lived in Northampton, Massachusetts. These essays were gathered and published as *The Silent South* (1885), *Strange True Stories of Louisiana* (1889), and *The Negro Question* (1890).

Cable, see *Atlantic Cable.*

CABOT, GEORGE (1752–1823), Boston shipping merchant and a strong Federalist supporter of Hamilton, during his term in the U.S. Senate (1791–96), carried authority as an adviser on economic and commercial matters. He was appointed (1793) a director of the Bank of the U.S., and president of its Boston branch after 1803. In 1798 President Adams named him the first Secretary of the Navy, a post confirmed by the Senate, but Cabot performed no duties and was soon replaced. Cabot's espousal (1802) of the ESSEX JUNTO led to his selection in 1814 as president of the HARTFORD CONVENTION, where he successfully resisted the secessionist radicals. He was an effective moderator but not a statesman.

CABOT, JOHN (1450–98), born in Genoa, became a naturalized citizen of Venice in 1476. After establishing himself as a merchant in Bristol, England, he was granted a patent (1496) by Henry VII similar to that which the Spanish sovereigns had furnished Columbus. In May 1497 with a crew of eighteen he sailed due west, thus initiating a search for the NORTHWEST PASSAGE to the Orient which was destined to continue for nearly four centuries. In late June he anchored off Cape Breton or Newfoundland long enough to discover the cod-fishing grounds off the Grand Bank, and returned to Bristol in August, never doubting that he had reached northeast Asia.

Supplied with a fleet of five ships manned by 300 adventurous crewmen, he set out on his second voyage (1498) to reach Japan and the Spice Islands by following the American shore line south. Presumably he approached Chesapeake Bay, but the records are conflicting. Some ships returned to England. The evidence suggests that his own ship foundered off Newfoundland. Yet his importance in the age of discovery is immense, for the English claim to North America was based on the voyages of John Cabot.

His son, SEBASTIAN CABOT (*c.* 1485–1556), probably accompanied his father on these two voyages. Later, searching again for the Northwest Passage, Sebastian Cabot may have entered Hudson Strait and seen Hudson Bay (1508), but historians still have not reached agreement on this little-known and long-disputed venture.

CABRILLO, JUAN RODRÍGUEZ (d. 1543), Portuguese captain in the employ of Spain, sailed up the west coast of Mexico, hoping to open a direct route to the East Indies through Spanish waters. He landed at the present location of San Diego (September 1542), and explored the coastal areas nearby, thus discovering California. Cabrillo National Monument, a 50-acre tract in the vicinity, is named for him.

Caddoan Family of North American Indians are a linguistic stock that moved north from Louisiana and Mississippi through the Plains region to the Dakotas. Best known among tribes of this family are the PAWNEE (Kansas and Nebraska) and the ARIKARA (to the north).

CADILLAC, ANTOINE DE LA MOTHE *(c.* 1658–1730), French colonial administrator, came to New France in 1683, and later, as the head of a fur trade monopoly, established a military post at Mackinac (1694). In 1701 he founded Detroit, where he was given trading privileges. He was for a time governor of the vast territory of Louisiana (1713–16), but his contentiousness led to his recall.

CAHAN, ABRAHAM (1860–1951), Russian-born journalist, came to New York in 1882. In 1897 he established the influential Jewish newspaper *Daily Forward,* the chief literary outlet and source of support for Yiddish writers. He helped found the SOCIAL DEMOCRATIC PARTY (1898), and after 1901 he was a leader of the SOCIALIST PARTY, becoming later a supporter of the New Deal. His novel (in English) *The Rise of David Levinsky* (1917) is a realistic story of a Russian Jew who emigrated to America in 1885. His autobiography (in Yiddish, 5 vols., 1916–36) is primary source material on the Jewish community in New York during the 50 years it covers.

Cairo Conference (22–26 November 1943), a meeting of President F. D. Roosevelt, Prime Minister Churchill, and Premier Chiang Kai-shek, was called for the purpose of formulating a postwar Far Eastern policy. Its Declaration (1 December) affirmed that war against Japan would be prosecuted until Japan had surrendered unconditionally, and outlined territorial settlements that included the independence of Korea and the restoration to China of Manchuria and the Pescadores. At a second Cairo conference (4–6 December 1943) Roosevelt and Churchill met with President Ismet Inönü of Turkey to affirm ties of amity. Military decisions reached at this meeting conferred the command of the invasion of western Europe on General Dwight D. Eisenhower.

Cajuns, a term of relatively recent origin, is used to designate those persons on the Alabama and Mississippi gulf coast who are of mixed white, Indian, and Negro blood. Locally the term differentiates the group from the French-descended CREOLES. Cajuns should not be confused with the Teche Louisiana ACADIANS.

Calamity Jane, the nickname of Martha Jane Canary (1852–1903), seems to have been derived from her threat that 'calamity' would overtake those who viewed her pistols lightly. An expert horsewoman, she dressed as a man, was a practiced shot, and became a frontier figure in mining towns, principally in Deadwood, South Dakota, where she lived most of her life.

CALDER, ALEXANDER (1898–), Philadelphia-born sculptor, and son of the sculptor Alexander S. Calder (1870–1945), was educated as an engineer. His ingenious experimental abstractions, which he termed 'mobiles' (fashioned of wire and twisted metals) pioneered in mobile sculpture, a form that usually hangs from the ceiling and is engineered to shift its long arms and decorative appendages. After 1938 he worked also in stationary sheet metals to create 'stabiles.'

CALEF, ROBERT (1648–1719), Boston merchant, answered Cotton Mather's *The Wonders of the Invisible World* (1693), an apologia for the Salem witchcraft trials, with his abusive *More Wonders of the Invisible World* (1700), chiefly an attack on Mather. Sometimes referred to as an intellectual liberal, Calef nowhere denies the existence of witches, a notion which at the time would have rendered any man suspect. But he did see that some innocent blood had been shed.

Calendar, the, in use before the Gregorian (New Style or N.S.) was the Julian (Old Style or O.S.). The error of reckoning, which had accumulated ten days since the time of Julius Caesar, was corrected by a decree of Pope Gregory in 1582; the ten days between 4 and 15 October were stricken from the calendar for that year. But Great Britain and her colonies did not officially adopt the N.S. until 14 September (3 September, O.S.) in 1752. N.S. years begin on 1 January and O.S. years on 25 March. Since both styles were used concurrently, a double-dating (e.g. 1628/29) between 1 January and 25 March became necessary on English documents from 1582 to 1752.

CALHOUN, JOHN CALDWELL (1782–1850), statesman and political philosopher, was born of Scots-Irish parents on the South Carolina frontier. After graduating with distinction from Yale (1804) he practiced law, entered politics, and through marriage to his cousin Floride Bouneau (1811) acquired a large plantation in Abbeville, South Carolina. Financially independent, he made politics his career. In Congress as a Democrat (1811–17), with the strong support of Speaker Henry Clay he was soon made chairman of the committee on foreign affairs. As a spokesman for the southern 'WAR HAWKS,' who favored annexation of Florida and Texas, he was instrumental in committing the U.S. to the War of 1812.

After serving Monroe as Secretary of War (1817–25), Calhoun won election as Vice President, and for eight years presided over the Senate (1825–32). After passage of the high protective Tariff of 1828, which to South Carolinians was a 'tariff of abominations,' he issued the 'South Carolina Exposition' to justify the state's nullification of federal laws and secured adoption in his state of the ORDINANCE OF NULLIFICATION (1832) to resist the collection of customs duties. President Jackson then steered passage of a Force Bill to override the South Carolina law. At odds with Jackson, Calhoun resigned the vice presidency late in 1832 after being elected to the Senate (1832–44), where he became the leading proponent of states' rights. He sponsored the COMPROMISE TARIFF of 1833 in an effort to resolve the nullification crisis, but the larger issue of states' rights persisted.

Calhoun as southern leader had come to believe that the North-South cleavage was permanent, and that the southern minority must either direct government policies as they affected sectional interests or undergo a social and economic upheaval. At this point, as Calhoun saw it, northern abolitionists created new tensions, for their uncompromising attacks on the institution of slavery destroyed the possibility of a moderate Democratic wing in the South. No enemy of the Union, Calhoun came to embody the idea that the South's minority status must be guaranteed against the 'tyranny of the majority.' If secession came, it should be the last resort, but so steadfast was Calhoun in his opposition to the prevailing trend in the Democratic party that he usually voted with the Whigs.

Declining to be a candidate for President in 1844, a post he had earlier coveted, he entered Tyler's cabinet in its final year (1844–45) as Secretary of State. While holding this office he devoted his energies to the acquisition of Texas, hoping thereby to balance power against the steadily growing North. In his final years he again served his state in the Senate (1845–50), where he sought to deny Congress the power to prohibit slavery in the territories. His 'Fourth of March Speech' (1850), attacking Clay's COMPROMISE OF 1850, was answered by Webster's 'Seventh of March Speech,' defending it, and he died while the issue was still being debated. His posthumously published *Disquisition on Government* (1851), and *Discourse on the Constitution* (1851) set forth the main lines of his political thought.

Lacking Clay's magnetism, Webster's versatile brilliance, and without their clear vision of an indivisible union, Calhoun surpassed them both in tenacity and boldness. Of unquestioned integrity in private and public life, he nevertheless uncompromisingly forced the sectional issues that were sundering the nation.

Biographies include those by W. M. Meigs (2 vols., 1917), and C. M. Wiltse (3 vols., 1944–51).

California, third in size and first in population among the states, was admitted to the Union in 1850 as the 31st state. The name was applied before 1540 to the unknown American northwest, and derives from that of an imaginary island in a romance by Ordoñez de Montalvo (1510). Cortés knew of the existence of the peninsula of Baja (Lower) California in 1533. Cabrillo made his way to the site of San Diego in 1542, and Drake touched along the northern coast in 1579. Permanent settlements began in 1769, when the first of a score of Spanish presidios and Franciscan seminaries were established from San Diego to San Francisco. The missions declined when Spanish rule ended in 1822, and Alta (Upper) California became a Mexican province.

Overland immigration to California began with the arrival (1826) of JEDEDIAH SMITH, who was followed in the next two decades by numerous small groups of hunters and trappers. The attempt to set up an independent BEAR FLAG REPUBLIC (1846) shortly preceded the Mexican War, after which Mexico ceded California to the U.S. (1848). Rapid settlement began with the CALIFORNIA GOLD RUSH (1849). Admission to the Union was accomplished by the COMPROMISE OF 1850, with Sacramento as capital (after 1854), and political parties formed themselves on the slavery issue. The northern commercial interests of the state were dominant in 1860, and the state's electoral vote went to Lincoln. In the same period communication with the East was established by the OVERLAND MAIL (1857) and the PONY EXPRESS (1860). A new era began when the CENTRAL PACIFIC and the UNION PACIFIC railroads were joined in 1869.

Geographically California embraces the vast wastes of the south, notably the Mojave Desert and Death Valley; the long alluvial valleys of the central portion; and, further north, the Sierra Nevada range, in which lie eighteen national forests (one-fifth of the state), and three national parks: YOSEMITE, SEQUOIA, and KING'S CANYON. The state's principal river, the SACRAMENTO, empties into San Francisco Bay.

Productive fruit and truck growing (the most extensive in the country) benefit from vast irrigation systems. In 1960 the state ranked third in the production of petroleum. Its diversified manufacturing is especially distinguished by its defense and aerospace industry, developed from the aircraft industry of World War II. The 100-odd institutions of higher learning include the UNIVERSITY OF CALIFORNIA, with numerous campuses; STANFORD; CALIFORNIA INSTITUTE OF TECHNOLOGY; and the UNIVERSITY OF SOUTHERN CALIFORNIA.

California gold rush began after a workman discovered gold in the Sacramento valley (January 1848) in the millrace of JOHN A. SUTTER. When President Polk reported the sensational news in his farewell message to Congress in December, a mania developed. By February 1849 several score vessels of every description were on their way round the Horn from all ports on the eastern seaboard. Ships were diverted from regular service to accommodate all classes of adventurers, some from as far away as the Marquesas Islands. Soldiers deserted, sailors jumped ship, husbands deserted their families and mortgaged their homes.

Within a year some 80,000 persons arrived, needing but a pick, a shovel, and a tin pan to create the greatest pandemonium since *Paradise Lost.* The village of San Francisco became a city of 20,000 in a matter of months. Such necessities as whisky could be bought with gold dust, and such luxuries as eggs were sold by the unit. Fortunes made by day were lost at night in the faro palaces. The pattern had been established by the first wave of 'Forty-niners,' who became squatters on Sutter's estate, scoured his land, arrogated his cattle, and left Sutter bankrupt. The military government being impotent, the frenzy which possessed a rootless society led to the creation of vigilance committees, lynch law, and popular courts. Order was restored, but very few who survived the venture managed to avoid economic prostration.

California Institute of Technology, at Pasadena, was chartered (1891) as Throop Polytechnic Institute, later Throop College of Technology (1913–20). It emphasizes research, and offers highly skilled training at the undergraduate and graduate level in the humanities as well as in science. In 1965, with an endowment of $80,200,000 and a faculty of 534, it enrolled 1300 students.

California Trail was an emigrant route (1841–46) from Independence, Missouri, to Sutter's Fort in the lower Sacramento valley. The route varied in its eastern portions, but in its western sector it mainly followed the Humboldt river in Nevada and thence to the Sierra range in the vicinity of Reno or Carson City. It was the route of the ill-fated DONNER PARTY. By 1859 the well-proved sections had become a road.

California, University of (est. 1868), is located on widely separated campuses throughout the state. It is one of the largest and most liberally supported institutions of higher learning in the U.S. In 1965 some 26,400 of its 68,700 students were enrolled at Berkeley (1868), and more than 23,000 at Los Angeles (1919). Other campuses are at San Francisco (1873), Davis (1906), Riverside (1907), San Diego (at La Jolla) (1912), and Santa Barbara (1944). San Diego until recently was limited to graduate instruction and research in oceanography. Lick Observatory (1888), directed by the University, is on Mount Hamilton, just east of San Jose in the Coast Range.

CALVERT, GEORGE, 1st Lord Baltimore (1580–1632), while serving as Privy Councillor (1619–25) became a Catholic. Though he was thus compelled to resign his office, the king created him Baron. In 1632 Charles I granted him the region in America that was chartered as Maryland. Calvert died before the charter was sealed, and it was issued to his son Cecilius, 2d Baron Baltimore (1604–75), who hoped to make Maryland a refuge for Catholics. He never visited the colony, but in 1634 he sent his brother, Leonard Calvert (1606–47), as the first governor.

Calvinism, the body of theological concepts formulated by the French Protestant reformer John Calvin (1509–64), fundamentally rests upon the idea of God as absolute sovereign. Totally depraved through Adam's fall, man is by nature unable to exercise free will. God elects to salvation those whom He chooses, and man can neither win salvation by good works nor profitably speculate about God's method of predestination. Calvinism differs theologically from Roman Catholicism in its treatment of grace, accepting only the sacraments of baptism and communion. It differs from Lutheranism chiefly in stressing the doctrine of predestination. Calvinism became the accepted doctrine of the churches called Reformed (Huguenot, Presbyterian, and Puritan), and through the Reformed churches Calvinist systems passed to America.

Early PURITANISM in Massachusetts, a COVENANT THEOLOGY, placed more emphasis on God's grace than on His predestination, and the trend was continued by CONGREGATIONALISTS, who further modified Calvinism in the late 17th century by introducing the concept of the HALF-WAY COVENANT. Not until JONATHAN EDWARDS reasserted the principle of predestination during the 1740's did strict Calvinism gain adherents in America. PRESBYTERIANS had always remained more strictly predestinarian, and their influence spread coincidentally with that of Edwards.

Edwards's theology, and that of many Presbyterian divines influenced by it, found a place in the legalistic Calvinist system by adding a personal and emotional element that made Calvinism effective for REVIVAL MEETINGS. At the same time, Edwards's pupil SAMUEL HOPKINS developed 'Hopkinsianism' into a theological system, and TIMOTHY DWIGHT as president of Yale (1795–1817) made this New England theology a bulwark against such 'infidelities' of the time as DEISM. The most flourishing 'New School Calvinism' in the West during mid-19th century was the 'Oberlin theology,' strongly revivalistic, and given respectability by Oberlin's president CHARLES G. FINNEY. The reaction against Edwardsean Calvinism by this time was well advanced and moving especially in two channels: the Unitarianism of WILLIAM E. CHANNING, and the antirevivalism of HORACE BUSHNELL.

Cambridge, Massachusetts, situated on the Charles river opposite Boston, was originally settled (1631) as Newtown by members of the Massachusetts Bay Company, who soon abandoned their intent to make it the seat of government. Three years after Harvard College was founded (1636), the village was renamed in honor of the English university town.

An intellectual center from the first, Cambridge was the home of the earliest printing press in British America, established (1639) by STEPHEN DAY. It was the gathering place for colonial troops on the eve of the War of Independence, and here Washington took command of the Continental army, 3 July 1775. Radcliffe College and Massachusetts Institute of Technology are located in Cambridge. The city is also a manufacturing center. It was incorporated as a city in 1846, and in 1960 had a population of 107,000.

Cambridge Platform (1648), drawn up by a synod of Massachusetts and Connecticut ministers at the request of the Massachusetts General Court, was drafted by RICHARD MATHER and printed as *A Platform of Church-Discipline* (1649). It was intended as a formal statement upholding the existing Congregational polity, and was aimed against the activities of those who wished to impose a Presbyterian discipline on New England. In effect it conferred upon the churches which it represented a quasi-establishment, or STANDING ORDER, which was not legally abolished in Massachusetts until 1833.

Camden, Battle of (16 August 1780), fought in South Carolina during the CAROLINA CAMPAIGN of the War of Independence, was a stinging defeat for the Americans. It was fought by the patriot General Horatio Gates and his army of 3500 regulars and militia against Cornwallis and his 2400 veterans. Exhausted from marching, Gates's 2000 inexperienced militiamen fled after the first encounter, and his remaining regulars were all but annihilated. Gates was replaced by NATHANAEL GREENE. Two months later the patriot forces took revenge on their loyalist foes at the battle of KING'S MOUNTAIN.

Camels were imported, chiefly from Egypt but some from Asia by way of Siberia, by the U.S. government after the Mexican War as a carefully planned means of mail and express transportation across the arid stretches of the Southwest. In 1855 Congress appropriated $30,000 to purchase the animals, and some 100 were brought to Texas and California. Edward F. Beale, superintendent of Indian affairs in California and later surveyor general of the state, attempted to use them as draft animals in 1857 to build a Federal wagon road, but the experiment did not succeed, probably because the camels were too much of an innovation for the army mules. The camels did not escape or run wild, as has been popularly supposed. Some were finally taken away to army forts, where they were kept for many years, and others remained on west Texas ranches. Unless a few descendants survive by breed in circuses or zoological parks, all are now extinct.

CAMERON, SIMON (1799–1889), after accumulating a considerable fortune in banking and railroad enterprises in Pennsylvania, entered politics and established the Republican party machine in his state (1854), over which he exerted undisputed control all his life. At various times between 1845 and 1877 he served in the U.S. Senate. Lincoln appointed him Secretary of War (1861), but Cameron's method of placing army contracts forced Lincoln to request his resignation and subsequently drew a vote of censure from the House of Representatives. Meanwhile Lincoln sent him as minister to Russia (January–November 1862). One of the ablest party organizers in American history, Cameron exemplified 'boss rule.' The Cameron machine controlled the Pennsylvania legislature and, in a period when public morals were notoriously at an ebb, auctioned off legislation to the highest bidder. Cameron defined the honest politician as a man 'who when he is bought will stay bought.'

His son, JAMES DONALD CAMERON (1833–1918), a graduate of Princeton (1852), was trained in the political school of his father. Grant took Don Cameron into his cabinet as Secretary of War (1876–77), a post he held until he entered the U.S. Senate (1877–97). In the Republican national convention of 1876 he effectively blocked the nomination of JAMES G. BLAINE, and later directed the Republican strategy by which the ELECTORAL COMMISSION (1877) seated Hayes as President.

CAMP, WALTER CHAUNCEY (1859–1925), after graduation from Yale (1880), became football coach (1888) and athletic director there, taking a leading part in developing football and writing its rules. In 1889 he originated the practice of selecting All-American football teams (the mythical squad of eleven players, annually chosen as best in their positions). In World War I he introduced into training camps the calisthenics known as the 'daily dozen.'

Campaign of 1789 and of 1792 were not political contests. The state legislatures appointed (or elected) electors. In the first Washington received the entire 69 votes cast by the 10 states voting. As second choice John Adams received 34 votes. Another 35 were scattered among 10 other candidates. Adams therefore became Vice President. In 1792 Washington was again elected without opposition by 132 votes by electors from 15 states. Adams, in second place, defeated the Anti-Federalist George Clinton (N.Y.) by 77 to 50 votes.

Campaign of 1796 was the first national election in U.S. history to be contested by political parties. The Federalists informally chose John Adams to succeed Washington, who probably would again have been unanimously elected had he been willing to serve. Thomas Pinckney (S.C.) had second place. The Democratic-Republicans (hereafter until 1832 referred to as Republicans) chose Thomas Jefferson (Va.) and Aaron Burr (N.Y.). Of the total electoral votes from 16 states, Adams secured 71, Jefferson 68, Pinckney 59, and Burr 30. Under the constitutional ruling then in effect, Adams and Jefferson took office as President and Vice President, respectively.

Campaign of 1800, as the first national election in which PARTY MACHINES were an essential element, was a turning point in American political history. Presidential candidates were selected by party caucuses in Congress, and the Republicans threw their support to Jefferson (Va.) and Burr (N.Y.). The Federalists renominated John Adams (Mass.) and Charles Pinckney (S.C.). Electioneering was done through newspapers, pamphlets, and partisan rallies. Whispering campaigns were as important as real issues. The Federalists were convinced that the Republicans aimed to destroy property and religion. The Republicans charged that the Federalists would subject the nation to a northern plutocracy. They hailed the Kentucky and Virginia Resolutions of 1798, formulated by Madison and Jefferson to discredit Adams's ALIEN AND SEDITION ACTS, which the Republicans held to be a partisan device for punishing democratic critics. A majority of Republican electors were chosen, and Jefferson and Burr tied for first place with 73 votes each, as against 65 for Adams and 64 for Pinckney. After 35 ballots (and with the deciding assistance of Alexander Hamilton) the House of Representatives broke the tie and gave the presidency to Jefferson and the vice presidency to Burr.

Campaign of 1804 was the first to be conducted under the Twelfth Amendment (1804), which required separate electoral ballots for President and Vice President. It had been adopted to prevent such accidental ties as had occurred in the previous election. Jefferson was overwhelmingly re-elected (162 electoral votes) with George Clinton (N.Y.) as Vice President. The Federalist candidate, Charles Pinckney (S.C.), received 14 votes.

Campaign of 1808 was conducted when Jefferson's embargo produced a schism in the Republican party. James Madison (Va.), supported by Jefferson (who, like Washington, had refused a third term), was nominated for the presidential succession by a congressional caucus. Virginia 'pure Republicans' nominated James Monroe, and the New York legislature nominated George Clinton as an antiembargo Republican. Federalist opposition was led by Charles Pinckney (S.C.) and Rufus King (N.Y.). Madison won with an electoral vote of 122 out of 176. Clinton was re-elected Vice President.

Campaign of 1812 ended with the re-election of Madison (128 electoral votes). Elbridge Gerry (Mass.) was chosen Vice President. The Federalist presidential candidate, De Witt Clinton (N.Y.), aided by antiwar factions, won 89 votes, mostly in New England and the Middle States. The results doubled the Federalist vote in Congress, thus handicapping the war effort.

Campaign of 1816 was scarcely a party contest, since the Federalists were in eclipse after the HARTFORD CONVENTION (1814–15), in which extremists had urged New England's secession from the Union. Madison's choice, James Monroe (Va.), with Governor Daniel C. Tompkins (N.Y.) as running mate, won the election with 183 votes. The Federalist Rufus King (N.Y.) received 34.

Campaign of 1820 offered no party rivalry whatsoever. James Monroe (Va.) was re-elected (231) with but one dissenting electoral vote thrown by a Republican to John Quincy Adams (Mass.). Tompkins was likewise re-elected Vice President.

Campaign of 1824 was a free-for-all, with voter alignments breaking into factions. All five presidential candidates were nationally prominent representatives of emerging sectional interests. All were Republicans and nationalists. Secretary of the Treasury William H. Crawford was heir apparent of the Virginia dynasty. Secretary of State John Quincy Adams (Mass.) had the support of the industrial East. Secretary of War John C. Calhoun (S.C.) was the favorite son of the lower South. Speaker of the House Henry Clay (Ky.) had the interests of the West at heart. General Andrew Jackson (Tenn.) as a popular military figure drew support from all quarters, but especially from the West.

Illness virtually eliminated Crawford. Clay's support was weak. Calhoun withdrew to become the candidate for Vice President on both the Adams and Jackson tickets. No candidate received a majority electoral vote: Jackson received 99, Adams 84, Crawford 41, and Clay 37. (Jackson was likewise ahead by popular vote, 155,000 to Adams's 105,000.) The election therefore, by provision of the Twelfth Amendment to the Constitution, was decided by the House of Representatives. After a series of personal conferences, the members on their first ballot elected Adams by a majority of one state. After Adams selected Clay as Secretary of State, Jacksonians made the charge 'corrupt bargain' successful propaganda for the campaign of 1828. Party labels also changed. Adams's men became National Republicans, and Jackson's followers became Democratic Republicans.

Campaign of 1828, a contest between President J. Q. Adams and General Andrew Jackson of Tennessee, the frontier war hero, was the first in which the candidates were the victims of mudslinging and baseless innuendoes. It was not waged on any clear-cut political issues, although Jackson's supporters used the 'Tariff of Abominations' cry to discredit Adams's appeal to industrialists. Standing for re-election as a National Republican, Adams polled 509,000 popular and 83 electoral votes. Jackson, a Democrat, won the election with 647,000 popular and 178 electoral votes. He carried Pennsylvania, most of New York, and the South and West. Voting in this campaign was essentially along class rather than sectional lines, for Jackson won support mainly among those who regarded him as the champion of the common man. Calhoun was re-elected Vice President.

Campaign of 1832 saw the emergence of the first of the 'third parties,' the ANTI-MASONIC PARTY, which placed former Attorney General William Wirt (Md.) in nomination. Anti-Jacksonians, newly named Whigs, supported Senator Henry Clay (Ky.). Wirt drew enough Whig support away from Clay to sweep Andrew Jackson back into office. This campaign was the first in which presidential candidates were chosen at national conventions. The tally of popular and electoral votes stood, for Jackson, 687,000 and 219; for Clay, 530,000 and 49. Wirt carried only Vermont (7 electoral votes). Martin Van Buren (N.Y.), a Jackson supporter, was elected Vice President. A major factor in this victory was Jackson's ability to unite the foes of the conservative policies of the Second Bank of the U.S. by vetoing the recharter bill and then campaigning against the 'Monster' as monopolistic, privilege seeking, and unconstitutional.

Campaign of 1836 was a contest chiefly between Jackson's choice, the Democrat Martin Van Buren (N.Y.), and the Whig William Henry Harrison (Ohio), veteran campaigner of the War of 1812. Van Buren won by 762,000 popular and 170 electoral votes. Harrison received 548,000 and 73. No candidate for Vice President had a majority of the electoral vote, so the Senate in February 1837 chose the Democratic contender for that office, Congressman Richard M. Johnson (Ky.).

Campaign of 1840 gave the Whig party its first national victory, and was unique for an emotional appeal whipped up by the Whigs to sway the electorate. The Whigs offered as their ticket William Henry Harrison for President (for the second time) and John Tyler (Va.) for Vice President. The Democrats renominated President Van Buren. (For details of this rollicking 'Log Cabin and Hard Cider' campaign, see the entry on Harrison.) Harrison was elected by 1,275,000 popular and 234 electoral votes. Van Buren received 1,128,000 and 60.

Campaign of 1844 was contested by the Democratic candidate James K. Polk (Tenn.), the first 'dark horse' in a presidential campaign (with his running mate George M. Dallas of Pennsylvania), against the Whig choice, Henry Clay. Polk won by 1,337,000 popular and 170 electoral votes to Clay's 1,300,000 and 105.

Polk had taken the Democratic nomination from Jackson's protégé Van Buren, who had antagonized Old Hickory by publicly rejecting the immediate annexation of Texas. On the other hand, Clay, who had made a similar statement, fatally reversed himself during the campaign, thus angering antislavery men. He lost New York (and the election) by a margin of 5000 when James Birney, the Liberty party (antislavery) candidate, received 15,800 votes from the antislavery Whigs of the western New York counties.

Campaign of 1848 resulted in the victory of the Whig nominee, General Zachary Taylor (Ky.) over the Democrat Lewis Cass (Mich.). The new Free-Soil party, headed by Martin Van Buren, contributed to Taylor's success by splitting the Democratic vote in New York. Taylor received 1,360,000 popular and 163 electoral votes. Cass received 1,220,000 and 127. Van Buren drew 291,000 votes. The prominent New York Whig Millard Fillmore was elected Vice President.

Campaign of 1852 was conducted at a time when the Whig party was so moribund that a Democratic victory was a practical certainty. The leading Democratic contenders, Lewis Cass, James Buchanan, and Stephen A. Douglas, were eliminated when none could secure the necessary two-thirds vote for nomination. The convention settled on the 'dark horse' Franklin Pierce (N.H.), with Senator William R. King (Ala.) as his running mate, on a platform condemning congressional agitation of slavery. The Whigs chose General Winfield Scott, and the Free-Soilers named Senator John P. Hale (N.H.). Pierce won with 1,601,000 popular and 254 electoral votes. Scott received 1,386,000 popular and 42 electoral votes. Hale's vote totaled 155,000.

Campaign of 1856 took place after the organization of the Republican party, which nominated John C. Frémont (Cal.). The American (Know-Nothing) party ran ex-President Fillmore. The Democratic ticket paired James Buchanan (Pa.) with ex-Congressman John C. Breckinridge (Ky.). The Republicans blamed the Democrats for the events of 'Bleeding Kansas,' while the Democrats condemned the sectionalism of the 'Black Republicans.' Buchanan won with 1,928,000 popular and 174 electoral votes to Frémont's 1,391,000 and 114. Fillmore received 874,000 popular and 8 electoral votes.

Campaign of 1860 was a contest bitterly fought on the slavery issue. When the Democratic national convention met in April at Charleston, southern delegates withdrew because northern delegates refused to adopt a black code for all territories. The northern delegates assembled a rump convention at Baltimore in June and chose Senator Stephen A. Douglas (Ill.), with the Georgia Unionist leader Herschel V. Johnson as his running mate. The southern delegates nominated Vice President John C. Breckinridge for President and adopted an extreme proslavery platform. Meanwhile old Whigs and moderates of both North and South convened the Constitutional Union party, ignored sectional issues, and presented a ticket of Senator John Bell (Tenn.) and Edward Everett (Mass.).

The Republican party, guided by seasoned politicians in its Chicago convention, pledged nonextension of slavery but no interference with slavery in the states. Neither William H. Seward (N.Y.) nor Salmon P. Chase (Ohio) won sufficient delegate support, and on the third ballot the convention chose Abraham Lincoln (Ill.) Senator Hannibal Hamlin (Me.) was named in second place.

The Republicans appealed not only to antislavery people, but to businessmen desiring internal improvements, transcontinental railroads, and tariffs, and to those attracted by the promise of free homesteads ('Vote Yourself a Farm'). The split in the Democratic party made possible the election of Lincoln, who received 180 electoral votes, to 72 for Breckinridge, 39 for Bell, and 12 for Douglas. But the popular vote was closest between Lincoln and Douglas: Lincoln received 1,866,000, Douglas 1,375,000, Breckinridge 845,000, and Bell 589,000.

Campaign of 1864 was dominated by a Union National Convention, so designated to appeal to Union sentiment. Lincoln was unanimously renominated, with a leading Democratic Unionist, Andrew Johnson (Tenn.), as running mate. (Radical Republicans, angry at Lincoln's veto of the Wade-Davis bill for radical reconstruction of the South, demanded a new convention and a new candidate.) The Democrats, with a platform advocating cessation of Civil War hostilities, which were going against the Union that summer, put up General George B. McClellan and Congressman George H. Pendleton. Sherman's victories in Georgia before election time gave Lincoln support at the polls. He was returned to office by 2,216,000 popular and 212 electoral votes to McClellan's 1,808,000 and 21.

Campaign of 1868 made southern reconstruction the issue. The Democrats pledged payment of war bonds in greenbacks, and nominated Horatio Seymour (N.Y.) for President and Francis Blair (Mo.) for Vice President. The Republicans picked the war hero General Ulysses S. Grant, with Schuyler Colfax (Ind.) as his running mate, and pledged the party to continue radical reconstruction. The campaign was bitterly fought. Grant won by 3,015,000 popular and 214 electoral votes to 2,709,000 and 80. Since Grant's victory was decided by over 700,000 Negro votes, the radicals ensured Negro suffrage by hurrying through the Fifteenth Amendment (1870).

Campaign of 1872 saw the emergence of the LIBERAL REPUBLICAN PARTY as a protest movement against the Grant administration. It nominated Horace Greeley, with B. Gratz Brown (Mo.) as his running mate. The Democrats accepted the nominees of the Liberal party and its platform demanding civil service reform and specie payment. Grant was renominated by the Republicans, with Senator Henry Wilson (Mass.), a leading radical Republican, as running mate. Grant won the election with 3,597,000 popular and 292 electoral votes to 2,834,000 and 66.

Campaign of 1876, resulting in a disputed election, was one of the most significant in U.S. history, for it marked the resurgence of the Democrats and the political re-entry of the South into the Union. The bankruptcy of the Grant administration led the Republicans to nominate the respectable Ohio governor, Rutherford B. Hayes, although the leading candidate until the final ballot was James G. Blaine, who was discredited by the exposure of a railroad bond scandal. The Democrats named the dynamic reform governor of New York, Samuel J. Tilden. (The newly organized Greenback party ran the eighty-five-year-old philanthropist Peter Cooper, who polled 81,000 votes.)

The election gave Tilden a margin of 250,000 popular votes. The electoral vote in some southern states was disputed and the Republicans claimed that Tilden was one vote short of the necessary majority, 184 to Hayes's 185. This involved and precarious situation was resolved by an ELECTORAL COMMISSION, which declared Hayes elected. Congressman William A. Wheeler (N.Y.), Hayes's running mate, took office as Vice President. Southern Democrats apparently supported the Electoral Commission as a result of Republican promises to withdraw Federal troops from the South and to aid southern internal improvements.

Campaign of 1880 was largely a contest of personalities. The Republicans, split by two factions headed by James G. Blaine and Roscoe Conkling, nominated a 'dark horse' from Ohio, General James A. Garfield. To placate Conkling and the New York 'stalwarts' who had supported Grant, the convention named Conkling's henchman Chester A. Arthur for second place. The Democrats chose Winfield Scott Hancock (Pa.), a nonpolitical Civil War general. The Greenback party put up another Civil War veteran, General James B. Weaver (Iowa). Garfield won by a close popular decision over Hancock, 4,449,000 to 4,442,000 (electoral vote, 214 to 155). Weaver polled a popular vote of 307,000.

Campaign of 1884 was waged primarily between the Republican party leader James G. Blaine (Me.) and the incumbent Democratic governor of New York, Grover Cleveland. Party issues were virtually nonexistent and personalities were luridly highlighted. A large body of Republicans who could not stomach Blaine became Cleveland Democrats (MUGWUMPS). (For details of this vituperative contest, see the entry on Blaine.) Cleveland won by 4,911,000 popular and 219 electoral votes over Blaine's 4,848,000 and 182. Cleveland's running mate, the Indiana political leader Thomas A. Hendricks, was elected Vice President.

Campaign of 1888 was decided by the tariff issue. Senator Benjamin Harrison (Ind.) as Republican standard bearer stood for high tariff demands. President Cleveland, renominated by the Democrats, pledged the party to tariff reform. Cleveland's popular vote (5,540,000) exceeded that of Harrison (5,444,000), but the Republicans by carrying New York gave Harrison the electoral margin (233 to 168). Harrison's running mate was the New York banker and politician Levi P. Morton. The Republicans won also because they promised generous pensions to Civil War veterans and used the 'MURCHISON LETTER' to give the impression that Britain was behind Cleveland's low tariff policy.

Campaign of 1892, again a contest between Cleveland and Harrison, resulted in a victory for Cleveland, with popular and electoral votes of 5,554,000 and 277 to 5,190,000 and 145. Cleveland's former First Assistant Postmaster General, Adlai E. Stevenson (Ill.) was elected Vice President. This campaign differed from the previous one in that great strength was mustered by the POPULIST PARTY, whose candidate, James B. Weaver, polled 22 electoral votes and a popular vote of over a million. Most of this defection came from old Republican strongholds in the Middle West. Republicans also suffered from public reaction to the violent HOMESTEAD STRIKE (1892), one of the most bitterly fought industrial disputes in U.S. labor history.

Campaign of 1896 followed the Panic of 1893 and ushered in a sixteen-year period of Republican domination. The Democratic party seemed on the verge of disintegration. Silver Democrats everywhere were effecting fusion with Populists, and neither Cleveland nor other Democratic supporters of the gold standard could stem the tide. At the party convention silver delegates gained control after William Jennings Bryan made his ringing 'Cross of Gold' speech, and Bryan won the nomination. The Republican campaign was managed by the Ohio industrialist Mark Hanna, uniquely successful in his lifetime as a national political 'boss.' He secured the nomination of his choice, Governor William McKinley of Ohio, on the first ballot. The convention committed itself to the gold standard. Garret A. Hobart, prominent in New Jersey politics, was selected as McKinley's running mate.

Not since the election of Jackson in 1828 had a campaign been so hotly contested. The issues were clear-cut between Democratic (western) radical agrarianism and Republican (eastern) conservative mercantilism. Bryan in his swing through 27 states captured audiences in unprecedented numbers with his forensic ardor. Hanna managed McKinley's campaign with adroitness, choosing to have the candidate remain in his home city, Canton, to be visited by and to address a succession of Republican delegations. The election was close but McKinley won by popular and electoral votes of 7,035,000 and 271 to 6,467,000 and 176 for Bryan. Despite defeat on the transitory silver issue, the Democrats emerged as a liberalized party through their populistic campaign against trusts, high tariffs, labor injunctions, and conservative court decisions.

Campaign of 1900 for the most part presented the same issues and candidates as in 1896. The Republicans renominated President McKinley, with Governor Theodore Roosevelt of New York as his running mate. They courted the labor vote with the 'Full Dinner Pail' slogan. The Democrats again named Bryan, who campaigned against imperialism as well as against the gold standard. McKinley was re-elected with 7,219,000 popular and 292 electoral votes to Bryan's 6,358,000 and 155. This was the first campaign in which the Socialist Eugene V. Debs ran; he polled 96,000 votes.

Campaign of 1904 followed Theodore Roosevelt's succession to the presidency after the death of McKinley. The Republicans nominated Roosevelt by acclamation and with him paired Senator Charles W. Fairbanks (Ind.) for Vice President. The Democrats jettisoned Bryan and selected a conservative New York judge, Alton B. Parker. Roosevelt swept the country by 7,628,000 popular and 336 electoral votes and carried large Republican majorities into Congress. Parker received 5,084,000 and 140. Joseph Pulitzer's New York *World* and Judge Parker publicly interpreted the heavy corporate gifts to the Republicans as blackmail to suspend antitrust prosecutions, an allegation which Roosevelt termed 'a wicked falsehood.' This victory led him to the rash promise never to be 'a candidate for or accept another nomination.' In this campaign the Socialists were considerably stronger; Eugene V. Debs ran again, and received 402,000 votes.

Campaign of 1908 was contested chiefly between the Republican, Roosevelt's protégé and Secretary of War, William Howard Taft, and the veteran Democratic candidate William Jennings Bryan. Taft urged a businesslike budget and accounting system (which became law only in 1921), defended labor injunctions, and demanded outlawry of the labor boycott and the closed shop (not unlike his son's Taft-Hartley law). Bryan rejected this labor philosophy and proposed Federal insurance of bank deposits to halt the current bank failures, an idea denounced by Taft as socialistic and dangerous. Taft was elected by 7,679,000 popular and 321 electoral votes. Bryan received 6,409,000 and 162. Congressman James S. Sherman (N.Y.) won the vice presidency on the Taft ticket. Again the Socialist candidate Eugene V. Debs made a substantial showing, this time with 420,000 votes.

Campaign of 1912 brought into existence the PROGRESSIVE PARTY OF 1912 and returned the Democrats to power after sixteen years of Republican rule. The battle between the progressive and conservative wings of the Republican party resulted in a split. The Progressives nominated Theodore Roosevelt after Robert La Follette failed to secure support. The Republicans renominated President Taft, who had helped to eliminate Roosevelt as a nominee of the party despite the primaries favoring Teddy. At the Democratic convention Speaker of the House Champ Clark had the support of a majority of the delegates but failed to secure the necessary two-thirds. When Bryan transferred his support to the second leading contender, Governor Woodrow Wilson of New Jersey, a shift began that gave Wilson the nomination.

The Republican split insured a sweeping Democratic victory; Wilson won and the Democrats gained control of both houses of Congress. Popular and electoral votes for Wilson totaled 6,286,000 and 435; for Roosevelt, 4,126,000 and 88; for Taft, 3,483,000 and 8. Wilson's running mate was Governor Thomas R. Marshall of Indiana.

In this campaign Roosevelt's New Nationalism accepted trusts as a necessary evil to be sternly regulated by government. Wilson's New Freedom stressed preventive methods of preserving competition. Many non-Socialist protest voters deserted both parties for the Socialist candidate Eugene V. Debs, who polled 897,000 votes.

Campaign of 1916 was carried on during the months when President Wilson, turning toward a program of military preparedness, sought re-election under the slogan (which he himself did not aver) 'He kept us out of war.' The Progressive party was moribund. The Republican party, pro-Ally in leadership, selected U.S. Supreme Court Justice Charles Evans Hughes as nominee. Hughes attacked Wilson for surrendering to the powerful railway unions in demanding that Congress enact the Adamson Eight Hour Law. Thereafter Progressives swung to Wilson. Early returns seemed to indicate that Hughes had won, but the final count showed that hundreds of thousands of Socialists had voted for the man who had 'kept the nation out of war.' Wilson was re-elected by 9,129,000 popular and 277 electoral votes. Hughes received 8,538,-000 and 254. Marshall was returned as Vice President. California, where the Republican schism hurt Hughes, became the narrow margin of success for Wilson.

Campaign of 1920 was determined in large part by the debate over whether the U.S. should join the League of Nations, but inflation and unemployment affected many votes. Wilson's call for a 'solemn referendum' on the League issue was the chief plank in the Democratic platform and doomed the party to defeat. Wilson was not standing for re-election and none of the possible Democratic candidates, including William G. McAdoo, Alfred E. Smith, and John W. Davis, commanded a large following. On the 44th ballot the Ohio political leader, Governor James M. Cox, was nominated. The Republicans, after Governor Frank O. Lowden (Ill.) had deadlocked with General Leonard Wood, chose Senator Warren G. Harding (Ohio) with Governor Calvin Coolidge (Mass.) as his running mate. While Cox and the internationalist Republican Committee of Thirty One strongly endorsed the League, Harding soon switched to isolationist platitudes.

The Republican candidates were swept into office by large popular and electoral majorities: 16,152,000 and 404 votes for Harding to 9,147,000 and 127 votes for Cox. The strength of all the third parties (five in number) totaled less than 5 per cent. The Socialist candidate, Eugene V. Debs, in prison for violating provisions of the Espionage Act of 1917, received 920,000 votes.

Campaign of 1924 was waged chiefly by three contenders. President Coolidge, who had succeeded to office on the death of Harding, received the Republican nomination with the international Chicago banker Charles G. Dawes as his running mate. After Alfred E. Smith and William G. McAdoo had become deadlocked by efforts of the urban-immigrant 'wets' to denounce the powerful Ku Klux Klan by name (against the resistance of rural, fundamentalist southern delegates), the Democrats, after 102 ballots, finally picked the liberal Wilsonian corporation lawyer John W. Davis. A coalition of Independents, Progressives, and Socialists ran the liberal Senator from Wisconsin, Robert M. La Follette, as the Progressive party's candidate. Coolidge won by a wide margin. The popular and electoral votes of the three totaled, for Coolidge, 15,725,-000 and 382; for Davis, 8,385,000 and 136; and for La Follette, 4,822,000 and 13. (La Follette received only Wisconsin's electoral vote.)

Campaign of 1928, more exciting than any since 1896, was a contest of rival personalities. After President Coolidge announced that he did not 'choose to run' for re-election, the Republicans turned to his logical successor, Herbert Hoover, the able administrator of the Commerce Department. The Democratic nominee (on the first ballot) was Alfred E. Smith, whose brilliant pro-labor and civil rights record as governor of New York especially enlisted the support of liberals. On the prohibition issue, then agitating American politics, he was an avowed 'wet.'

Both parties raised enormous campaign funds (the Republicans spent more than $10,000,000), and, by radio, the candidates entered the living rooms of the nation. As a Tammany Catholic, Smith had small appeal to the rural South and West. Hoover, hailed as a great humanitarian and apostle of scientific management, won decisively by 21,392,000 popular and 444 electoral votes to Smith's 15,016,000 and 87. Yet Smith did far better in popular votes than Davis and La Follette combined in 1924, and almost as well as Coolidge himself that year. Hoover's running mate was Senator Charles Curtis of Kansas.

Campaign of 1932 was conducted three years after the severest stock market and financial crash in American history. The Republican renomination of Hoover was not contested and the Republican platform (somewhat ambiguous) promised a balanced budget, a higher tariff, and immigration reduction. Governor Franklin D. Roosevelt of New York was by far the most prominent of several aspirants for the Democratic nomination, which he won on the fourth ballot.

His Commonwealth Club address in San Francisco pointed out that the frontier safety valve had gone, that the nation's industrial plant had been built, and that the welfare of all distressed classes (the 'forgotten man') required a New Deal to plan the equitable use of national resources.

In the election Roosevelt carried all but six states and the Democrats gained control of both houses of Congress. No President or party had ever received a clearer mandate to inaugurate new policies. His popular and electoral vote was 22,821,000 and 472 to Hoover's 15,761,000 and 59. His running mate was Speaker of the House John N. Garner (Texas), who had been a formidable rival for the Democratic nomination.

Campaign of 1936 was waged chiefly by Republicans determined to defeat the NEW DEAL against jubilant Democrats, who renominated Roosevelt by acclamation and abolished the two-thirds rule for nomination in their convention. The Republicans on their first ballot named Governor Alfred M. Landon of Kansas. Alfred E. Smith, an outspoken foe of New Deal monetary policies, defected to the conservative Liberty League, followed by several old-line Wilsonians. Southern Liberty Leaguers backed Governor Eugene Talmadge of Georgia, who ran on a 'White Supremacy' ticket. A formidable anti-New Deal coalition died with the assassination in 1935 of Senator Huey P. Long of Louisiana, leader of the radical Share-Our-Wealth movement.

There remained the radical anti-New Dealer, Representative William Lemke of North Dakota, inflationist, isolationist, and foe of 'international bankers,' who headed the new Union party. He received the support of Father Charles Coughlin, popular radio priest, and his National Union for Social Justice. But Lemke, despite extravagant claims, polled only 891,858 votes and shortly thereafter disappeared from the national scene.

Most newspapers and almost all business supported Landon, and the *Literary Digest* poll predicted his victory, yet Roosevelt, aided by labor votes and contributions, was returned to office in the greatest landslide in American political history. (The Democratic victory in state and congressional elections was equally smashing.) Landon carried but two states, Vermont and Maine. Roosevelt's popular and electoral vote was 27,751,000 and 523 to Landon's 16,681,000 and 8. Garner was again elected Vice President.

Campaign of 1940 lacked real issues, although with Europe at war it was dominated by foreign affairs. Three leading Republican contenders, Senator Robert A. Taft (Ohio), Senator Arthur Vandenberg (Mich.), and District Attorney Thomas E. Dewey (N.Y.), were outmaneuvered by political amateurs. The convention on the sixth ballot chose Wendell Willkie, a Wall Street lawyer and business executive with no political experience. He gained his strength from the fact that, unlike the others, he was an avowed internationalist and a lifelong progressive. The Democrats renominated Roosevelt on the first ballot, thus breaking the two-term tradition. Roosevelt won by 27,243,000 popular and 449 electoral votes to Willkie's 22,304,000 and 82. This time Roosevelt's running mate was his Secretary of Agriculture, Henry A. Wallace (Iowa).

Campaign of 1944 was conducted during World War II and issues were few. The Republicans selected Governor Thomas E. Dewey of New York and the Democrats renominated Roosevelt. Both were chosen on the first ballot and favored some form of postwar league as well as the major New Deal laws. Roosevelt carried 36 states with popular and electoral votes of 25,602,000 and 432 to Dewey's 22,006,000 and 99. The second place on the Democratic ticket this time went to Senator Harry S Truman of Missouri. One outcome of the election was the wholesale defeat of numerous isolationist Congressmen and Senators.

Campaign of 1948, conducted two years after the Republicans had gained control of Congress, gave that party confidence of winning the election. Thus for the first time in its history it renominated a defeated candidate (Thomas E. Dewey). The Democratic party was disintegrating by a split both to the left and the right. Henry Wallace had organized a Progressive party, and southern Democrats formed a States Rights party with Governor Strom Thurmond of South Carolina as their candidate. Almost everyone believed that the Democratic nominee, President Truman, was doomed, but his aggressive campaign defied the Gallup poll predictions and won him election. The popular and electoral votes stood thus: Truman, 24,045,000 and 304; Dewey, 21,896,000 and 189; Thurmond, 1,168,000 and 38; Wallace, 1,137,000 and no electoral votes. The Democrats recaptured control of both houses of Congress. Truman's running mate was Senate majority leader Alben Barkley (Ky.). The President's election owed much not only to the unions but also to the staple farmers whom he promised high price supports in his strenuous 'whistle stop' train tour of doubtful farm states.

Campaign of 1952 gave Republicans their first victory in twenty years. At the Republican convention General Dwight D. Eisenhower was named on the first ballot despite the initial strength of Senator Robert A. Taft. Second place went to Senator Richard Nixon of California. The Democrats nominated Governor Adlai Stevenson of Illinois after Truman ruled himself out. For the first time television played an important part in a presidential campaign. The great popularity of General Eisenhower was the determining factor. He won with 33,936,000 popular votes to Stevenson's 27,314,000 and carried 39 states with 442 electoral votes. Stevenson carried 9 states with 89 electoral votes. Republicans controlled the House by a narrow margin, and tied the Democrats in the Senate.

Campaign of 1956 was again a contest between Eisenhower and Stevenson. Eisenhower was renominated by acclamation and named Vice President Nixon as his running mate. Eisenhower won with 35,590,000 popular and 457 electoral votes to Stevenson's 26,022,000 and 73. In spite of the President's personal popularity (almost unprecedented), the Democrats carried both houses of Congress.

Campaign of 1960 followed passage of the Twenty-second Amendment which made a renomination of Eisenhower impossible. Eisenhower placed the mantle on Vice President Nixon. The Republican convention nominated Nixon on the first ballot. Young Senator John F. Kennedy (Mass.) challenged the older Democratic politicians, entered the primaries in seven widely separated states, and won them all. He campaigned with a powerful organization and ample funds, and won the nomination on the first ballot. He persuaded his chief rival, Senator Lyndon B. Johnson (Texas), to accept second place on the ticket. The election, reflecting the Catholic issue and racial factors, was the closest since that of 1916, and Kennedy won by a popular majority of only 118,000 out of 68,000,000 votes. His popular and electoral vote was 34,221,000 and 303 to Nixon's 34,108,000 and 219.

Campaign of 1964 took place in the year following the assassination of President Kennedy, who had been succeeded in office by Vice President Lyndon B. Johnson. The Democratic convention nominated Johnson by acclamation and chose Senator Hubert H. Humphrey (Minn.) as his running mate. The leading Republican candidates for nomination were Governor Nelson Rockefeller (N.Y.), Governor William Scranton (Pa.), Governor George Romney (Mich.), and Senator Barry M. Goldwater (Ariz.). After a split developed which gave control of the party to the extreme right, the convention nominated Goldwater, with Representative William E. Miller (N.Y.) in second place.

Seldom has a presidential campaign aroused less interest, for the electorate seemed already to have determined its preference. The candidates traveled widely, and for the most part sidestepped issues. The returns were electrifying. Goldwater carried but five states, chiefly in the Deep South, where he won the support of segregationists. Johnson's electoral margin of 486 to 52 votes was the greatest of any since the campaign of 1936. But his landslide popular margin of 61 per cent of the record 70,000,000 votes cast was the most emphatic vote of preference ever given to a national candidate. The amount of ticket splitting, however, was exceptional, and many Republican governors and congressmen won election even though their state's electoral vote went to Johnson.

Campaigns, see *Presidential campaigns.*

CAMPBELL, JOHN, 4th Earl of Loudoun (1705–82), served as commander in chief of British forces in America (1756–57). He won no victories in the French and Indian War, and was recalled after his plans to take the French fortress of Louisbourg in Nova Scotia came to naught. He was replaced by JAMES ABERCROMBY.

Camp meetings, outdoor religious assemblies for prayer and exhortation, were a prominent part of evangelical revivalism, especially in the trans-Allegheny West, from 1800 to 1840. The practice of holding such gatherings, sometimes attended by many hundreds of men, women, and children, and lasting the better part of a week, originated with the preaching of JAMES MC GREADY of Kentucky, under Presbyterian auspices during the Great Revival of 1800. After 1805 Methodist CIRCUIT RIDERS were almost the only preachers still using the camp meeting technique, and under Methodist discipline the emotional excesses of the early years were restrained. Such meetings were important social institutions by which frontier groups could enjoy 'the most mammoth picnic possible.' After 1840 the institution died out, as churches and auditoriums were built.

Campbellites, see *Disciples of Christ.*

Canada, Invasion of (1775–76), was undertaken because the Continental Congress sought to deprive Britain of a base of attack upon the northern colonies. In October 1774 Congress wrote inviting the Canadians to join with the colonies, but received no answer. Having learned in June 1775 that the British commander in Canada, SIR GUY CARLETON, was planning an invasion of New York, Congress authorized a counterthrust by General PHILIP SCHUYLER. With 1000 men Schuyler began an advance late in August up Lake Champlain, and laid siege to St. John's, near Montreal. Schuyler fell ill, and the command was given to General RICHARD MONTGOMERY, to whom the garrison capitulated on 12 November. Carleton escaped to Quebec, and the Americans occupied Montreal ten days later.

Meanwhile, in September, Benedict Arnold, with Washington's best hopes, had set out for Quebec from Cambridge, Massachusetts, with 1100 men. He moved up the Kennebec into the Maine wilderness, crossed a snow-covered mountain, and after surmounting the difficulties of an unknown terrain, arrived with his equipment and 600 survivors on the east bank of the St. Lawrence opposite Quebec (25 October). He later crossed the river and in early December was joined by Montgomery with 300 men from Montreal. The two commanders wished to delay an assault until January, but they were forced to consider that by the terms of enlistment the expeditionary contingent would be dissolved at the year's end. They therefore launched a disastrous attack in a blinding snowstorm on the night of 31 December. Montgomery was killed, Arnold wounded, and nearly half their men were casualties. In the spring Arnold retreated. The arrival in May of 10,000 regulars from England insured British success in Canada. The invasion as a campaign had failed, but its diversion of British troops into Canada promoted the decisive American victory at SARATOGA.

Canada, Invasion of (1812–14), see *War of 1812.*

Canals, together with turnpikes, were the transportation facilities which first united the West with the East. A few canals had been dug before 1800 around the falls of rivers flowing into the Atlantic. The great era of canal building was initiated (1825) when the ERIE CANAL opened the Great Lakes area to eastern markets, and made New York City the gateway to the West. In 1826 Philadelphia began a route to Pittsburgh, and two years later Maryland and Ohio financed construction of the Chesapeake and Ohio Canal. By 1834 the Great Lakes had been linked with the Mississippi, and within a decade 3000 miles of canals had been constructed. Cleveland and Toledo were important lake ports by mid-19th century, and Congress allotted some 4,000,000 acres of public lands in the Midwest for canal construction. The growth of railroads after the Civil War made most canals unprofitable.

Canning industry in the U.S. began in the decade after the French inventor Nicholas Appert originated a method (1806) of preserving food in air-tight glass containers by immersing them for a short time in boiling water. The tin can was introduced soon thereafter. The Civil War produced a canning industry that multiplied the annual national pack sixfold, to 30,000,000 cans. Radical improvements in techniques and scientific knowledge early in the 20th century led to refinements in packing and in growing and harvesting crops for canning. The sanitary 'open top' can became standard, and research laboratories developed by the industry analyzed and increased the nutritive values of products. Canning today is a billion-dollar industry.

CANNON, ANNIE JUMP (1863–1941), a graduate of Wellesley (1884), became a member of the staff of Harvard Observatory in 1897, and astronomer and curator of their photographs (1911–38). She discovered 300 variable stars herself, and compiled a bibliography of 200,000 variables. She also completed the HENRY DRAPER Catalogue, which she extended to include some 300,000 stellar spectra.

CANNON, JOSEPH GURNEY (1836–1926), after practicing law in Illinois, was elected to Congress (1872), where he served almost continuously for 50 years (1873–91, 1893–1913, 1915–23). As leader of the 'Old Guard' Republicans and as a resourceful if ruthless parliamentary strategist, 'Uncle Joe' exerted more power as Speaker of the House (1901–11) than any of his predecessors. He was stripped of his appointive control in the 'Revolution of 1910' by a combination of Democrats and insurgent Republicans, who gained passage of a resolution by which the Speaker was deprived of membership on the powerful Committee on Rules. The office thenceforth became elective. Thus 'Cannonism,' the virtual dictatorship inherent in the office of Speaker, disappeared.

CANONICUS (*c.* 1567–1647), powerful Narragansett Indian chief from whom Roger Williams purchased much of Rhode Island, remained a staunch friend to the English. Williams regarded him with veneration, and the old chieftain treated Williams as a son.

CANONCHET, see *King Philip.*

Cantigny, Battle of (28 May 1918), took place in World War I when the American 1st Division captured and held the town of Cantigny, some 80 miles north of Paris, where the Germans had set up an observation post. This first U.S. success, under French command, led to the decision that permitted General Pershing to establish a separate army.

Canuck, in the U.S. is slang often used for any Canadian; in Canada, for a French Canadian.

Capital of the U.S. (locations before 1800). Before the city of Washington became the permanent national capital in 1800, the seat of government was located for a time at Philadelphia. There the first Continental Congress met in September 1774, and the second assembled in the following May. Driven from the city by the British in 1776, Congress met for several weeks at Baltimore. In 1777 it assembled for one day (27 September) at Lancaster, Pennsylvania, before moving to nearby York (30 September 1777 to 27 June 1778). It then returned to Philadelphia, where it sat for five years. During 1783–84 it moved thrice: to Princeton, New Jersey (30 June to 4 November 1783), to Annapolis, Maryland (20 November 1783 to 3 June 1784), and to Trenton, New Jersey (November 1784). In 1785 it was situated in New York and there remained during Washington's inauguration. By the Jefferson-Hamilton deal of 1790 over the Federal assumption of state debts, sectional votes were won by transferring the capital from New York to Philadelphia for ten years; thereafter, in deference to Southerners, it was established in the new city of Washington.

Capital punishment in the colonial period, though less common than in England, was meted out for various felonies, and executions were public spectacles. In 1788 Ohio effected a substantial reform by limiting the death penalty to murder. New York abolished public hangings in 1835, and most other states soon followed suit. Michigan abolished the death penalty in 1847. Those jurisdictions that have no death penalty today are Alaska, Delaware, Hawaii, Maine, Michigan, Minnesota, North Dakota, Rhode Island, Wisconsin, Puerto Rico, and the Virgin Islands. In many states imprisonment for life may be imposed instead of death, if the jury decides or recommends the sentence.

Capitol, The, at Washington, D.C., on the site chosen by Pierre L'Enfant, was originally planned (1793) by Dr. William Thornton. President Washington laid its cornerstone (September 1793) with Masonic rites. The completed northern wing, executed by James Hoban and others, housed Congress and the Federal courts in 1800. Burned by the British in 1814, the Capitol was rebuilt (1815–17) by B. H. Latrobe, reoccupied in 1819, and completed (1827) by Charles Bulfinch. The wings were added (1857–59) by T. U. Walter. A major task of rebuilding, completed in 1961, extended the central portion of the East Front forward 32 ft., but did not alter Walter's design.

The bronze statue of *Freedom* (1863), surmounting the dome, was modeled by Thomas Crawford, and the terraces were landscaped by Frederick Law Olmsted. Early colonial paintings and murals include the work of John Trumbull, John Vanderlyn, and Emanuel Leutze.

CAPONE, AL [ALPHONSE] (1899–1947), Italian-born gangster, was associated with organized crime in New York City before moving to Chicago (1920), where his crime syndicate terrorized the city. Through his control of gambling, vice, and BOOTLEGGING, 'Scarface' Al is conservatively estimated to have netted $105,000,000 in 1927 alone. He was indicted by a Federal grand jury for evasion of income-tax payment in 1931, sent to jail, and released eight years later.

Capper-Volstead Act (1922), designed to aid farmers, exempts agricultural cooperatives from the application of antitrust laws, but empowers the Secretary of Agriculture to prevent such associations from becoming monopolies.

Capuchins, a mendicant order of FRANCISCAN friars, were first assigned missions in America by Richelieu, in New England (1630) and Acadia (1632). For a time they held ecclesiastical jurisdiction over Louisiana, where they established the first churches and schools (1722). Although they are inactive in Louisiana today, they continue their work elsewhere in the U.S.

CARDOZO, BENJAMIN NATHAN (1870–1938), after graduation from Columbia (1889) practiced law in New York City until elected on a Fusion ticket to the New York supreme court (1913). He was appointed a member of the state's court of appeals in 1917, and was elected its chief judge ten years later. President Hoover elevated him to the U.S. Supreme Court (1932), where Cardozo became a vigorous supporter of liberal views on social and economic issues. His classic study of *The Nature of the Judicial Process* (1921) is a philosophic commentary on the interrelations of law, history, tradition, and sociology, and the role of the judge in blending them. *The Growth of the Law* (1924), and *The Paradoxes of Legal Science* (1928) amplify his views that sociological jurisprudence should relax precedent in the light of changing times.

CAREY, HENRY CHARLES (1793–1879), son of MATHEW CAREY, retired from his Philadelphia publishing house (1835) to devote himself to economic studies. His *Essay on the Rate of Wages* (1835) accepted the doctrine of laissez-faire on the ground that natural laws tend to produce a universal harmony of interests. In *Principles of Political Economy* (3 vols., 1837–40) he defined rent as a special kind of interest, since he equated land values with their invested capital. He thus denied the Ricardo theory that rent must constantly increase in a growing community, since labor and capital themselves increase. His disagreement with Malthus stemmed from his belief that man's power over nature was such that only ineptitude leads to failure in farming. His advocacy of tariff protection in *The Past, the Present, and the Future* (1848), and similar studies, influenced the MORRILL TARIFF ACT (1861). He was always a champion of an agrarian economy. His influence abroad is witnessed by the translation of his principal writings into nine languages.

CAREY, MATHEW (1760–1839), Irish-born publisher and economist, removed to Philadelphia (1784) after conviction for libelous criticism of the British government in his defense of Irish Catholics. His firm of Carey and Lea became the leading publishing house of its day. In 1819 he retired from business to organize the Philadelphia Society for the Promotion of National Industry, before which his many addresses gave him national standing as an effective advocate of the 'AMERICAN SYSTEM,' which was championed by Henry Clay as a way to promote domestic industry. His effort to resolve factional differences during the War of 1812 is set forth in *The Olive Branch* (1814). *The New Olive Branch* (1820) was a strong plea for protective tariffs. His later tracts dealt with banking reform and such public questions as immigration and labor. His points of view and his vigorous interest in economics were shared by his son H. C. CAREY.

Carey Land Act (1894) authorized the President to grant to each state 1,000,000 acres of PUBLIC LANDS in desert areas of the West, to be sold by the states to private interests for purposes of irrigation, reclamation, and occupancy. Work lagged until the NEWLANDS RECLAMATION ACT (1902) provided the funds from public land sales for irrigation, which in the next 30 years opened up nearly 20,000,000 acres for profitable ventures.

Caribbean policy, the special interest of the U.S. in the political affairs of Caribbean countries, was initially formulated in the MONROE DOCTRINE (1823). This executive statement proclaimed, after Spain's Latin American colonies had successfully revolted, that the U.S. would not tolerate renewed European colonial expansion or foreign intervention in the affairs of the Western Hemisphere. In the CLAYTON-BULWER TREATY (1850) the U.S. and Britain agreed to avoid exclusive control or fortifications in the event that an isthmian canal should be constructed. Later Great Britain ceded her Central American protectorates to Honduras and Nicaragua (1859–60), thus renouncing any balance of power in the Caribbean. The suggestion made in the OSTEND MANIFESTO (1854) that the U.S. should purchase or seize Cuba was immediately disavowed by President Pierce, but American prestige had thereby been lowered in Central America as well as in Europe, since the idea revealed a latent wish for territorial expansion.

By the Treaty of Paris of 1898, which terminated the Spanish-American War, the U.S. acquired Puerto Rico for strategic reasons (it was granted self-government in 1917), and though Cuba's independence was guaranteed by the PLATT AMENDMENT (1902), the U.S. reserved the right to intervene in Cuba's domestic affairs. The Amendment was abrogated in 1934. In his desire to complete the building of the Panama Canal, Theodore Roosevelt encouraged a scheduled revolution in Panama (1903). The U.S. immediately recognized the Republic proclaimed by the insurgents. Roosevelt's method of applying the 'big stick' was extended in 1904 by his pronouncement of the 'Roosevelt corollary' to the Monroe Doctrine, by which the U.S. assumed the right to police Caribbean areas. To encourage European and American investors in the strategic canal area, the State Department placed an American receiver-general in control of the revenues of Santo Domingo, an act which, even though it brought stability to the Dominican economy and averted intervention by foreign creditors, gave rise to the charge of Yankee imperialism. Taft's use of bankers to stabilize Caribbean finances and his effort to make treaties with Nicaragua and Honduras were denounced by the Senate as 'dollar diplomacy.' As a result of intervention in the domestic affairs of Cuba (1906–17, 1961), Nicaragua (1909–33), Haiti (1915–34), and Santo Domingo (1916–24, 1965), in order to protect American property, supervise elections, restore financial integrity, avert civil war, or to insure national safety, as in the Cuban missile crisis of 1962, U.S. naval forces were occasionally accused of turning the Caribbean into an 'American lake.'

The Hoover administration adopted a clear policy of nonintervention, and F. D. Roosevelt continued this orientation by declaring the 'good neighbor policy' at the Seventh Pan-American Conference in 1933. The Eighth Pan-American Conference (1938) ushered in a new era of hemispheric solidarity by affirming the principle of the equal sovereignty of States, enacting reciprocal trade agreements, and setting up an effective exchange of cultural facilities. The U.S. as a member of the 21-nation ORGANIZATION OF AMERICAN STATES (O.A.S.) has continued to follow these policies of co-operation and mutual consultations among the hemispheric nations on matters of common concern in the Caribbean.

See Dana G. Munro, *The U.S. and the Caribbean Area* (1933); Chester Lloyd Jones, *The Caribbean Since 1900* (1936); and Dexter Perkins, *Hands Off: A History of the Monroe Doctrine* (1941; new ed., 1955).

CARLETON, SIR GUY (1724–1808), after the capture of Quebec (1756), in which engagement he distinguished himself, was promoted to the rank of brigadier general. In 1766 he was appointed governor of Quebec and commander of British forces in Canada. The rumor that he was planning an invasion of New York state precipitated as a counterthrust the unsuccessful INVASION OF CANADA at the outbreak of the War of Independence (1775–76). In 1777 JOHN BURGOYNE replaced him as commander of military forces. In 1782 Carleton replaced SIR HENRY CLINTON as commander in chief of British forces in America, remaining in that post until November 1783, when British troops evacuated New York City.

His tact and skill in protecting the Loyalists while withdrawing the British forces from the frontiers in New York and Vermont won the admiration of both Loyalists and Patriots. Created 1st Baron Dorchester, he was sent to Canada (1786–96) as governor general and commander of forces. He is recognized as one of the ablest administrators and generals of his day.

CARLISLE, JOHN GRIFFIN (1835–1910), served for many years (1877–91) as a Kentucky Democrat in the U.S. House of Representatives, where he was one of its notable Speakers (1883–89). He served briefly in the U.S. Senate (1890–93), but resigned to enter Cleveland's cabinet as Secretary of the Treasury (1893–97). As a 'gold Democrat' he supported Cleveland's fiscal policies during the PANIC OF 1893. In the 1896 campaign he persisted in making 'sound money' speeches despite the threats of free silverites. Like Cleveland, he was an economic conservative, a low tariff man, and an anti-imperialist. He later practiced law in New York City.

Carlisle Indian School (1879–1918), a co-educational (Methodist Episcopal) institution of higher learning was established at Carlisle, Pennsylvania, by Captain R. H. Pratt (1840–1924), for the education of Indian children whose parents had been moved to reservations. Maintained by the U.S. government and housed in an army barracks, it offered practical and domestic courses, and included an 'Outing System,' by which students spent a year on farms or in neighboring homes or industries. Under the direction of its founder it expanded in 25 years to accommodate 1000 students, but its decline set in when Pratt retired (1904).

Carlsbad Caverns National Park (est. 1930), 45,000 acres in southeastern New Mexico, is an area of limestone caves, discovered in 1901, with stalactite and stalagmite formations within tremendous chambers, some of them more than 1000 ft. below the surface. The caverns, which are inhabited by millions of bats, are still only partially explored.

Carmelites, a Roman Catholic monastic order, in the early days of French settlements were sent to Louisiana, where they were briefly (1722) given charge of religious and educational training until their administration was absorbed by the CAPUCHINS. Since 1790, when Bishop JOHN CARROLL sponsored a convent of Carmelite nuns in Maryland, the order has been established in several dioceses.

CARNEGIE, ANDREW (1835–1919), Scottish-born industrialist, began his business career (1853) as private secretary to Thomas A. Scott of the Pennsylvania Railroad, and became superintendent of its Pittsburgh division. In the early months of the Civil War he reorganized the Union telegraph system with conspicuous success. In 1868 he established iron mills at Pittsburgh, and in 1873 he built the J. Edgar Thomson Steel Works, the largest mill in the country. Concentrating on the manufacture of steel, the Carnegie Steel Company well before 1900 had become an immense industry, which Carnegie sold in 1901 to the U.S. Steel Corporation for the unprecedented sum of $447,000,000.

Believing that the rich should act as trustees for the public benefit, he advanced his thesis in his famous essay, 'The Gospel of Wealth,' which first appeared in the *North American Review* for June 1889. Thereafter he devoted himself to philanthropy, setting up trusts and foundations for libraries and educational institutions. Notable among them are the CARNEGIE INSTITUTION (1902), to further research; the CARNEGIE FOUNDATION for the Advancement of Teaching (1905); and the CARNEGIE CORPORATION (1911), to support programs in science and the humanities.

Carnegie Corporation of New York (1911), first of the great endowed FOUNDATIONS, was established by Andrew Carnegie with a gift of $135,000,000. It was the chief depository of his wealth and remains a pioneering force in the distribution of private funds for public purposes, especially in the field of higher education and international affairs. Its grants have built more than 2500 libraries in the U.S. and other English-speaking countries. The Corporation was the first foundation to establish area study programs at many colleges (such as the Russian Research Center at Harvard), and to finance major research surveys. In 1965 it disbursed $13,695,000 from assets of $333,667,000.

Carnegie Endowment for International Peace, established (1910) by a gift of $10,000,000 from Andrew Carnegie, finances publications, research, and conferences on peace, especially through the United Nations. In 1965, from assets of $41,900,000, it disbursed $1,272,000 to organizations working for human welfare on a global scale.

Carnegie Foundation for the Advancement of Teaching (1905) was established by a gift from Andrew Carnegie of $10,000,000, which was later increased. It chiefly provides retirement benefits for teachers of higher learning in Canada and the U.S. In 1965, from its assets of $23,199,000, it disbursed $978,000.

Carnegie Institute of Technology (1905), at Pittsburgh, was founded by Andrew Carnegie as a co-educational institution in the sciences and humanities, with research laboratories specializing in coal and metals. It pioneered in social relations courses for engineers, and in 1914 opened the first collegiate department in drama. In 1965, with an endowment of $80,250,000 and a faculty of 500, it enrolled 5000 students.

Carnegie Institution of Washington (1902), endowed by Andrew Carnegie, is supported by the CARNEGIE CORPORATION. An administrative body under the direction of eminent scholars, it provides opportunities for research in science and the humanities at units located in Boston; Cold Spring Harbor, New York; Baltimore; and Stanford University.

Carolina Campaign (1780–81) during the War of Independence began after Sir Henry Clinton successfully besieged Charleston, forcing its surrender (May 1780). In the ensuing months South Carolina was overrun by the British. Nathanael Greene, who replaced Horatio Gates after the latter's defeat in August in the battle of CAMDEN, was in command of the American forces. His excellent strategy in the battle of KING'S MOUNTAIN (October) forced Cornwallis to move south. At the battle of COWPENS (January 1781) the brilliant victory of General Daniel Morgan gave Morgan and Greene the opportunity to join forces against Cornwallis in March at GUILFORD COURTHOUSE. Cornwallis won that engagement but with such losses that he had to wait for reinforcements by sea. Their arrival in August opened the YORKTOWN CAMPAIGN.

Carolina Proprietors, a group of eight promoters and politicians, obtained from Charles II a proprietary patent in 1663 to all North America between the 31st and 36th parallels, under the name Carolina. This was soon enlarged to embrace all territory between the Virginia-North Carolina line and Florida. Prime movers were the wealthy

Barbadian planter Sir John Colleton and the Chancellor of the Exchequer, Sir Anthony Ashley Cooper (later Earl of Shaftesbury). The other venturers were Edward Hyde, Earl of Clarendon; George Monk, Duke of Albemarle; William, Lord Craven; John, Lord Berkeley; SIR GEORGE CARTERET; and SIR WILLIAM BERKELEY. To attract settlers the proprietors drew up the CONCESSIONS AND AGREEMENTS (1665), which set forth the rights of resident landowners.

They went even further. At Cooper's direction the philosopher John Locke drew up the 'Fundamental Constitutions of Carolina' (1669), an elaborate scheme of government, grafting advanced concepts onto a romanticized feudalism. A Grand Council of executive and judicial authority was to function with a provincial assembly, comprising the Governor, hereditary nobles, and deputies. The apex of society were to be landgraves (counts with baronies), caciques (chiefs), and lords of manors, separated from serfs and slaves by freeholders. The eight proprietors were to be the Palatine Court. Land and rank were to be synonymous; the loss of one would mean the loss of the other. This pretentious system never went into effect, but Charleston, founded in 1670 by several hundred Barbadians, did become the center of a landed aristocracy.

Since the enterprise returned no profit, the proprietors became indifferent to the needs of the colony, which was threatened in the first decades of the 18th century by pirates, and ravaged during the TUSCARORA and YAMASSEE wars. The resulting revolution in South Carolina (1719) gave the crown the opportunity to take it over. Ten years later North Carolina was likewise purchased from the proprietors.

***Caroline* Affair** (1837), an incident that strained Anglo-American relations more severely than any other between the War of 1812 and the Civil War, was precipitated by a Canadian border dispute. A group of Canadian malcontents, organized into a secret society of Hunters' Lodges and fired with a somewhat belated 'Spirit of '76,' pledged themselves to drive British dominion from North America. For more than a year one William Mackenzie, with the active support of border residents in New York and Vermont, had recruited smugglers and refugees from Canadian justice to make looting forays into Canada from American bases. An island in the Niagara river served as headquarters for the 300 or so 'liberators,' who were supplied from the American shore by the steamer *Caroline*.

In December 1837 a body of Canadian volunteers set the vessel afire and one American was killed. Soldiers under General Winfield Scott were rushed to the scene to prevent American violence, and tempers cooled. International complications arose after a drunken Canadian (McLeod) was indicted for murder after boasting in a New York barroom that he had killed the American in the *Caroline* affair. Thereupon British Foreign Minister Palmerston, fearful of a border war, admitted that he had ordered the *Caroline* destroyed to check 'pirates' and demanded McLeod's release. Fortunately, McLeod was freed at his trial. But the border problems created by the *Caroline* Affair and the AROOSTOOK WAR (1839) kept relations with Great Britain tense until differences were resolved by the WEBSTER-ASHBURTON TREATY (1842).

CAROTHERS, WALLACE HUME (1896–1937), theoretical organic chemist, after completing his graduate studies at Illinois (1924), and teaching briefly at Harvard, became a research chemist at the E. I. du Pont de Nemours Experiment Station in Wilmington, Delaware. His pioneer investigations of polymerization processes culminated in his invention (1934) of nylon, the first truly 'synthetic' fiber.

Carpetbaggers, Northerners who went south after the Civil War presumably to exploit unsettled conditions, were contemptuously so named because they allegedly could transport their entire assets in a satchel. They swarmed through the South in the decade following the RECONSTRUCTION ACTS of 1867, which brought the states of the former Confederacy under radical control. In alliance with southern white 'Scalawags,' they often adventured after financial and political profit. Some were sent as agents of the FREEDMEN'S BUREAU, and others were impelled by missionary zeal.

Many of these were exemplary individuals, genuinely interested in the Negro, who identified themselves with their adopted southern communities, and several were elected to Congress by the newly reconstructed states. But often they were venal.

Of the seven governors in states restored to the Union in 1868, four were carpetbaggers, and the resulting administrations, executive, legislative, and judiciary, were sometimes extravagant and sordidly corrupt. Their misrule (as well as legitimate postwar costs) trebled and even quadrupled the debts of southern states. Governor Warmoth of Louisiana, typical of the mischievous spoilsmen, though more successful than most, in four years built a personal fortune of half a million dollars by looting the state treasury. After the rule of the radical Republicans had ended, and Hayes had succeeded to the presidency (1877), white home rule in the South was restored, and the carpetbaggers as a class disappeared.

CARREL, Alexis (1873–1944), French-born surgeon and experimental biologist, after joining the staff of the Rockefeller Institute in 1906, served as a member until 1939, when he returned to France. In 1912 he received the Nobel Prize in physiology and medicine for his work on vascular suture and the transplantation of blood vessels and organs. During World War I, with the research chemist H. D. Dakin, he developed a method of irrigating wounds with a solution of sodium hypochlorite. In 1936, with the help of C. A. LINDBERGH, he originated the perfusion pump, called an artificial heart, by means of which tissues and organs can be kept alive during surgery while the individual's heart is being repaired. His writings include *Man, the Unknown* (1935).

CARROLL, Charles (1737–1832), Revolutionary patriot, was educated abroad in French Jesuit colleges. After studying law in Paris and London, he returned to Maryland, settling as a landed proprietor at Carrollton Manor, his estate in Frederick county. He entered politics, served in the Continental Congress (1776–78) and signed the Declaration of Independence. At the request of Congress, with Benjamin Franklin, Samuel Chase, and his cousin, Father JOHN CARROLL, he undertook the fruitless mission to Montreal in 1776 to persuade the French Canadians to join in the revolt of the colonies. As a staunch Federalist in the U.S. Senate (1789–92) he supported Hamilton's policies. Reputed to be the wealthiest American of his time, in his later years Carroll pioneered in transportation, backing the Potomac Company's plan for a water route to the West and presiding over the first board of directors of the Baltimore and Ohio Railroad (1828).

CARROLL, John (1735–1815), a cousin of CHARLES CARROLL of Carrollton, after study in Jesuit colleges abroad was ordained a priest (1769). He served briefly as professor of philosophy and theology at Liège before returning to Maryland in 1774. Active in the patriot cause, he went with Benjamin Franklin, Samuel Chase and Charles Carroll to Montreal (1776) in the attempt to win French Canadians to the American cause.

Consecrated the first Roman Catholic bishop in America (1790), he founded the hierarchy of the Church in the U.S., established Georgetown University (1791), and became the first archbishop of Baltimore (1811). During a formative period he sought greater autonomy for the maturing American Catholic Church, free from competing French, Irish, and English influences. His accomplishments to that end have brought him recognition as perhaps the greatest figure in the Roman Catholic Church of the U.S.

CARSON, Kit [Christopher] (1809–68), Kentucky-born frontiersman and scout, in 1826 began his career as professional hunter and guide at Taos, New Mexico, which became his headquarters and lifelong home. One of the ablest of MOUNTAIN MEN, he guided John C. Frémont in mapping trips along the Oregon Trail and into California (1842–46). He took a prominent part in the seizure of California (1847) during the Mexican War, and led emigrant convoys to the Pacific coast during the gold rush (1849).

He was a U.S. Indian agent in the Southwest (1853–60, 1865–68), and during the Civil War, with the rank of brigadier general, he served with distinction, organizing Union scouts in the West. The legends that gathered about his name place it with those of Daniel Boone and David Crockett among frontier heroes. The capital of Nevada, Carson City, is named for him.

Cartagena Expedition, see *Jenkins' Ear, War of.*

CARTER, SAMUEL POWHATAN (1819–91), a graduate of the U.S. Naval Academy (1846), was serving in the navy when, at the outbreak of the Civil War, he was transferred to the War Department to organize regiments in his native (eastern) Tennessee. He successfully participated in important cavalry encounters with Confederate raiders. After the war he returned to the navy. He is unique in the history of the American armed services in having been both a major general and a rear admiral.

Carter* v. *Carter Coal Company, see *Guffey-Snyder Coal Act.*

CARTERET, SIR GEORGE (c. 1610–80), ardent Royalist during the English Civil War, was descended from a family long prominent as landowners on the island of Jersey. One of the eight CAROLINA PROPRIETORS, he obtained a further grant when the Duke of York (later James II) in 1664 ceded the lands between the Hudson and Delaware rivers to Lord John Berkeley and Carteret as the 'Province of Nova Caeseria or New Jersey.' Upon the death of Sir George, his widow sold to William Penn and a group of proprietors all her New Jersey holdings at auction, for the nominal sum of £3400.

CARTERET, PHILIP (1639–82), first colonial governor of New Jersey, was appointed in 1665 to office by his cousin Sir George Carteret, and presided over the first legislative assembly in 1668. When the province was divided in 1676, he became the governor of East New Jersey only. A quarrel with the governor of New York, SIR EDMUND ANDROS, over the collection of custom duties at New York ports, led to his capture (1680), trial, and acquittal, and contributed to the censure and recall of Andros.

CARTIER, JACQUES (1491–1557), discoverer of the St. Lawrence river and, after Columbus, the most resolute explorer of North America, was granted 6000 livres by Francis I to search for the NORTHWEST PASSAGE to Asia. Cartier reached Newfoundland in May 1534 with two ships and 61 men, entered the strait of Belle Isle, explored the long shore lines and the islands of the gulf of the St. Lawrence in early summer, and sailed home in September. He returned with three vessels in May 1535, anchored in Pillage Bay and gave it the name St. Lawrence, which in a short time was extended to the gulf and the river.

Guided by Huron-Iroquois Indians, he discovered Quebec, reached the site which he named Mont Real, and proceeded to the nearby rapids. These he named La Chine, since presumably they led to China, and he wintered at Quebec, regaled by the Indians with tall tales of the 'kingdom of Saguenay,' as opulent as Cathay. Returning to France in 1537, he so impressed Francis that the king equipped him for a third voyage with a fleet of five vessels in 1541, a convoy that the Spanish government refrained from attacking in the hope that Cartier's venture would be more of a hazard to France than to Spain.

In 1542 this intrepid seaman presented his king with gold and diamonds which unhappily were assayed as iron pyrites and quartz crystals, but the voyages had determined the shape of history by establishing the claim of France to the St. Lawrence valley, and making clear that the Atlantic seaboard of North America was unbroken. Cartier not only contributed enormously to geographic knowledge, but gave the first extensive accounts of the Iroquois and Algonquin Indians.

See the biographies by J. P. Baxter (1906) and C. G. M. B. de La Roncière (1931).

CARTWRIGHT, PETER (1785–1872), most famous of the CIRCUIT RIDERS, was raised in Kentucky and licensed at seventeen as a Methodist itinerant preacher. He was ordained a deacon at twenty, and two years later this 'Kentucky boy' was made a presiding elder. For 50 years Cartwright rode the frontier circuits in the Middle West, drawing large semi-literate audiences to his revival meetings by his hell-fire preaching and racy style. In 1846, running for Congress as the Democratic candidate from Illinois, he lost by a small majority to his Whig opponent Abraham Lincoln. Colorful pictures of frontier life along the Ohio are in his *Autobiography* (1856), and *Fifty Years as a Presiding Elder* (1871).

CARUSO, ENRICO (1873–1921), Italian operatic tenor, made his debut in New York (1903) with the Metropolitan Opera Company, and thenceforth remained the leading male singer of the company. He possessed a voice of such power, range, and resonance that it was judged by critics and public alike to be one of the memorable voices of the century. He was among the first opera singers to make recordings (1902), reaping a large personal income ($150,000 annually) from that source alone.

CARVER, GEORGE WASHINGTON (*c.* 1864–1943), botanist, was born into slavery. After graduation from Iowa State College (1894) he became the director of agricultural research at Tuskegee Institute (1896), where he taught for the rest of his life. His outstanding achievements in developing many products from soy beans, sweet potatoes, and peanuts were an important influence on the shift of the southern agricultural economy from dependence on a single crop to diversified farming.

CARVER, JOHN (*c.* 1576–1621), wealthy merchant and deacon of the Leyden church of which the Separatist John Robinson was pastor, was instrumental in chartering the *Mayflower,* in which the Pilgrims emigrated to America (1620). He was largely responsible for securing the grant from the VIRGINIA COMPANY, and was the first governor of the PLYMOUTH COLONY.

CARVER, JONATHAN (1710–80), born in Connecticut, was the first English-speaking traveler to leave a record of explorations west of the Mississippi. Probably under secret orders from Major ROBERT ROGERS to make investigations in the interest of fur trading, he journeyed west to Lake Superior (1766–68). His account of the trip, *Three Years Travels through the Interior Parts of North America* (London, 1778), was widely translated and went through more than 30 editions. It was the most widely known book of American authorship written in the 18th century, but much of its discourse on Indians, for which it was acclaimed, was drawn from the French accounts (later translated) of LAHONTAN and CHARLEVOIX.

CARVER, THOMAS NIXON (1865–1961), professor of economics at Harvard (1902–32), won note for such studies as *The Distribution of Wealth* (1904) and *The Present Economic Revolution in the U.S.* (1925). The depression of the 1930's discredited his overoptimistic equilibrium theories, which envisioned an imminent 'equality of prosperity,' the disappearance of classes, and the unlikelihood of more great depressions.

Casablanca Conference (14–24 January 1943), held in French Morocco soon after the invasion of North Africa (November 1942), was the occasion on which President Roosevelt and Prime Minister Churchill declared that World War II would be fought to secure the 'unconditional surrender' of the enemy. Plans were outlined for the invasion of Sicily and Italy, and General Eisenhower was given command of the Allied forces in the theater.

Cascade Range, the northern continuation of the SIERRA NEVADA, extends from northern California through Oregon and Washington into British Columbia. It is 100 miles inland and parallel to the COAST RANGES. It is volcanic in origin; all of its high summits are snow-covered, extinct volcanic cones, from which slope glacier fields. Its forests are an important source of lumber. The best-known peaks are Mount Shasta (14,162 ft.) in California, Mount Hood (11,245 ft.) in Oregon, and Mount Rainier (14,410 ft.) in Washington. Three rivers cut through the range to the Pacific: the Klamath, Fraser, and Columbia. Large areas are set aside as national parks: MOUNT RAINIER, CRATER LAKE, and LASSEN VOLCANIC.

'Cash and carry,' see *Neutrality Acts.*

CASS, LEWIS (1782–1866), New Hampshire-born soldier and statesman, moved West in 1801 and in the following year was admitted to the Ohio bar. He served as a major general in the War of 1812 and was appointed governor of Michigan Territory, a post he filled for nineteen years (1813–31). The expedition he conducted in 1820 along the shores of Lake Superior to the headwaters of the Mississippi was highly successful in uncovering the resources of the region.

As Jackson's Secretary of War (1831–36), Cass supported the President through the South Carolina NULLIFICATION crisis and settled the BLACK HAWK uprising. He served both Jackson and Van Buren as minister to France (1836–42), where his anti-British maneuvering made him popular at home. Failing to secure the Democratic presidential nomination in 1844, he entered the Senate (1845–48), where he led opposition to British interest in the Oregon country, and championed the Mexican War. His famous 'Nicholson letter,' written to the prominent Tennessee politician Alfred Nicholson in 1848 to explain his position on the WILMOT PROVISO, was the earliest enunciation of the doctrine of POPULAR SOVEREIGNTY, the theory that people of a territory have the right to decide for themselves whether or not they should have slavery. His stand on that issue brought him the 1848 Democratic presidential nomination, but the defection of the antislavery wing to Van Buren and the Free-Soil party drew off sufficient votes to elect the Whig candidate, Zachary Taylor.

Cass was returned to the Senate (1849–57), but he failed to be re-elected in 1857 because of the increasing opposition to slavery in his state. Buchanan selected him as Secretary of State (1857–60), a post Cass resigned in protest against Buchanan's decision not to reinforce Fort Sumter. He was a man of principle, and foremost among spokesmen for a conservative nationalism.

See Frank B. Woodford, *Lewis Cass, the Last Jeffersonian* (1950).

CASSATT, MARY (1845–1926), Pittsburgh-born artist, after study in Europe (1868–74) continued to live abroad. Strongly influenced by Degas, she came to be popularly associated with the French Impressionists. Her *Mother and Child* (Metropolitan Museum) and her double portrait *The Loge* (National Gallery) are representative in theme, color harmonies, and linear design of the style for which she is distinguished.

Of great importance was the advice she gave to such collectors as Mrs. Potter Palmer of Chicago and Mr. and Mrs. Horace Havemeyer of New York, who through her guidance brought to the U.S. paintings by Renoir, Monet, and Pissarro even before such artists had come to be fully recognized as masters.

CASTLE, VERNON (1887–1918), stage name of the English-born dancer Vernon Castle Blythe, who, with his wife IRENE, won fame for originating the 'Castle walk,' the one-step, and the 'hesitation' waltz. Irene Castle introduced bobbed hair and the boyish figure to the ballroom and the world of fashion. Vernon Castle died while serving as a pilot during World War I.

Castle Garden, see *Battery*.

CATESBY, MARK (1679–1749), English botanist, twice came to America expressly to make natural history studies. After nearly ten years of travel (1710–19) he prepared his classic *Natural History of Carolina, Florida, and the Bahama Islands* (1731–42) with some 200 illustrations, a work which still may be read with profit and enjoyment. On his second trip he lived briefly in the South. His posthumously issued *Hortus Britanno-Americanus* (1763–67) encouraged the exchange of trees and shrubs between England and America.

CATHER, WILLA [SIBERT] (1873–1947), born in Virginia, grew up in Nebraska among the immigrants whom she portrays with restrained sensitivity in her novels. After graduation from the University of Nebraska (1895), and a brief period of teaching, she joined the staff of *McClure's* (1906–12), leaving it to devote herself to creative writing. Her best novels include *O Pioneers* (1913), *My Ántonia* (1918), *A Lost Lady* (1923), and her masterpiece, *Death Comes for the Archbishop* (1927). Her writing, distinguished for its purity of style, is concerned with the conflict between the good life and worldly ambition.

Catholic University of America (1889) founded at Washington, D.C., by JAMES CARDINAL GIBBONS, is administered by the Catholic hierarchy and is the only U.S. pontifical university. In 1965, with a faculty of 739, it enrolled 5690 students.

Catholicism, see *Roman Catholic Church.*

CATLIN, GEORGE (1796–1872), educated for the law, practiced but two years in Philadelphia before establishing himself as a self-taught portrait painter in New York. In 1830, resolving to preserve Indian types, he began his eight-year journey into the trans-Mississippi wilderness, where he sketched and painted some 600 portraits, landscapes, hunting and domestic scenes, depicted with fine detail and sweeping rhythmic mastery. He covered thousands of miles, mostly by boat or canoe, and came to know 48 Indian tribes. He also traveled in South America, where he braved the Amazon and crossed the Andes into Peru, and he visited Alaska and the Aleutians.

His splendid ethnological series (1832–33) of the Mandans was followed by sketches of other Siouan tribes along the upper Missouri and Mississippi rivers, especially the Hidatsa and Assiniboin. In Texas he portrayed the Comanche. He exhibited his work to great acclaim in London and Paris, but the U.S. Congress would not buy his large collection. After his death the paintings were given principally to the Smithsonian Institution in Washington, D.C. They are the chief source material for all later knowledge of early Indian life.

Catskill Mountains, a range of the Appalachian system in southeast New York just west of the Hudson river, cover an area of 1000 square miles. The wooded region of gorges and waterfalls, with summits generally about 3000 ft. high (Slide Mountain reaches 4204 ft.), is a watershed for the Hudson and Delaware rivers. Long a scenic resort area, the Catskills inspired the HUDSON RIVER SCHOOL of artists and writers, and are the setting of the Rip Van Winkle legend.

CATT, CARRIE CHAPMAN (1859–1947), born in Ripon, Wisconsin, after studying at Iowa State College served as a principal and superintendent of schools. As president of the National American Woman Suffrage Association (1900–1904, 1915–47), she was a leader in the movement which helped bring about passage of the Nineteenth Amendment (1920), guaranteeing the right of women to vote. In 1920 she organized the LEAGUE OF WOMEN VOTERS.

CATTELL, JAMES MCKEEN (1860–1944), professor of psychology at Pennsylvania (1888–91), and at Columbia (1891–1917), conducted research in psychological measurements and was a pioneer in developing 'mental' tests. He edited the *Psychological Review* (1894–1904), *Scientific Monthly* (1900–1944), *School and Society* (1915–39), and other journals of psychology and education.

Cattle drives, long-distance driving of herds to market, originated with the Spanish ranching industry in Mexico (1540). Spanish settlers in Texas during the 18th century drove horses and cattle to Louisiana markets. Davy Crockett as a boy began his career as a cattle driver (1790) from Tennessee to Virginia, and by 1800 Ohio farmers were profitably driving herds of cattle and swine to Philadelphia. The 'beef trail' from Texas to New Orleans was well established by 1840, when it was extended northward, principally to St. Louis.

The boom period of the drives began in 1867 with the opening of the CHISHOLM TRAIL from Texas to Kansas. Roundups took place in July or August, and then began the 'long drive' north, moving some twelve or fifteen miles a day, for a period of six weeks or more, to such rail points as Abilene. The barbed wire of homesteaders rapidly encroached on the open ranges, and by 1895 railroad expansion had made trail-driving uneconomical. But the preceding quarter-century had given America the romantic tradition of the 'cattle kingdom' and the COWBOY.

Cattle industry, important in the economy of America from colonial times, developed on a gigantic scale as soon as railroads had been extended into the High Plains after the Civil War. The halt of Indian migrations and the mass extermination of the BUFFALO, both results of white penetration, made large tracts available to grazers, and led to the establishment of great stockyards and packing centers, such as those in Chicago, Kansas City, and Fort Worth. The invention of refrigeration cars, in use by 1875, opened commerce in dressed beef to foreign markets, which by 1885 were buying some 17,000,000 pounds annually. In the same decade 5,500,000 steers, bred for the market, were annually forming the great CATTLE DRIVES.

The 'cattle kingdom,' of which Texas was the capital, was a vast range stretching from Mexico to Canada and from the edge of the eastern forests to the Rockies, an area embracing nearly one-fourth of the U.S. Here beef cattle fed on the lush grasses of the unoccupied lands, which were opened up after 1865 as a public domain. Throughout the Southwest, especially in Texas, such land was sold on liberal terms, and purchased by enterprising 'cattle barons' in gigantic tracts. After 1890, when settlers had begun to occupy so much of the range area that the geographic frontier no longer existed, the vast ranches were broken up, although many large ones still remain. Application of scientific methods to livestock farming made possible the slaughter of cattle at a relatively early age, and the industry thus mechanized at the production source brought an end to the picturesque world of the cattle baron and the COWBOY.

See E. E. Dale, *The Range Cattle Industry* (1930); Louis Pelzer, *The Cattlemen's Frontier* (1936); and E. S. Osgood, *The Day of the Cattleman* (1929).

Cattle rustlers, or thieves, in the days when cattle roamed the open range, before laws had been enacted, or were hard to enforce, either appropriated cattle by stealth or seized them in pitched battles. Branded identifications and rigidly enforced penalties gradually made rustling a relatively unprofitable means of livelihood. Occasionally 'dogies,' motherless calves, still disappear.

Caucus, the meeting of party leaders to decide on candidates or policies, was used early in the 18th century, especially in Boston, where 'caucus clubs' endorsed candidates in local elections. These primary caucuses, entirely unregulated before 1866, were gradually eliminated by law, and preliminary elections now universally use the DIRECT PRIMARY. The first congressional caucus was employed when Washington announced his retirement from the presidency in 1796. Federalist members of Congress, meeting in secret conference, selected Adams and Pinckney for President and Vice President; Republicans similarly chose Jefferson and Burr. In 1800 the respective parties again met, selected candidates and formulated programs, but the public increasingly felt that congressional selection of the two highest elective offices by caucus was contrary to the spirit of the Constitution, and in 1824 friends of Andrew Jackson held meetings throughout the country to denounce 'King Caucus.'

The caucus was subsequently replaced by the NATIONAL CONVENTION for choice of presidential candidates, but the practice continues to be an effective way, in Congress and at state and local levels, to nominate candidates for party offices and committees and to promote party action in matters of legislative organization and procedure.

Cavaliers were Royalists in the reign of Charles I, and a few of them fled to Virginia (1647–49) after the overthrow of the king. The term originally had political significance only, but it later was applied to the planter oligarchy that set the social tone in the South. In the eyes of many Northerners, every owner of a dozen slaves was a 'cavalier,' a gay, gracious idler, who broke his routine of riding to hounds with an occasional duel. This notion fitted into the romantic tradition of 'southern chivalry,' and flourished most vigorously during the second quarter of the 19th century.

Cayuga Indians, see *Iroquois Confederacy*.

Cayuse, see *Mustang*.

Cedar Creek, Battle of (October 1864), occurred late in the Civil War, when Jubal Early launched a surprise attack on the Union army of Philip Sheridan at dawn along Cedar Creek near Strasburg in northern Virginia, throwing the Federal corps into panic, but then halting his own advance. Sheridan, returning from Washington, had spent the previous night at Winchester, fifteen miles away. Wakened by the sound of artillery, he reached the front in midmorning, rallied his men, and turned the Confederate 'victory' into a rout.

Census, official enumeration of the population, is required every ten years by the U.S. Constitution as a means of apportioning Representatives from the several states 'according to their respective numbers.' The U.S. was the first nation to provide for a census by law. The first two censuses (1790 and 1800) gathered population data. For apportionment, Indians were not counted and a slave was always reckoned as three-fifths of a white person. In 1810, manufactures were added; in 1820, occupations. Gradually new data were tabulated, yet prior to 1880 figures were only approximately reliable since the statistics were assembled by politically appointed U.S. marshals, who hired their own enumerators.

The census of 1880 was carried out under a new Federal law providing for a Superintendent of the Census. In 1902 Congress set up a permanent Census Office, and the tabulation categories were increased. The Census Office was transferred in 1913 from the Interior Department to the newly created Department of Commerce. In 1940 the Census Bureau became a permanent agency, with a field organization. A census clock, in the lobby of the Bureau, now gives a daily estimate of the population changes.

Centennial Exposition (1876), held in Philadelphia to celebrate a century of American independence, was the first world's fair in the U.S. Some 450 acres were set aside in Fairmount Park, and after ten years of planning the fair opened in 167 buildings, housing 30,000 exhibits from 50 nations. The Machine Age had arrived. Intense public interest was aroused by impressive displays of working models and processes in the field of science and invention. The exhibit of Alexander Graham Bell's telephone was a particular attraction. Confused architectural styles, ornate and grandiose, drew attention to the taste of the 'Gilded Age,' but the exhibits of foreign craftsmen provided an immense stimulus to the aesthetic consciousness of the nation. Significant changes were reflected two decades later in the WORLD'S COLUMBIAN EXPOSITION at Chicago.

Central Intelligence Agency (C.I.A.), established by Congress in 1947, was the first permanent, all-embracing intelligence bureau in the U.S. Responsible solely to the President through the National Security Council, whose chairman is the C.I.A. director, it is charged with co-ordinating all other Federal intelligence agencies. It collects and evaluates data and supervises the organization of all foreign intelligence functions, employing agents abroad. As an undercover agency, its annual budget (estimated to be $1,000,000,000) is not subject to congressional scrutiny. Its personnel is presumed to be some 30,000. In 1961 Congress created a new post of director of national intelligence to serve immediately under the President, leaving operational responsibility with C.I.A.

Central Pacific Railway, built eastward from Sacramento, California, to meet the UNION PACIFIC, had to surmount the almost insuperable obstacles of winding gorges, difficult grades, mountain blizzards, and desert heat. Labor gangs of thousands of men laid rails along vast expanses of uninhabited country. To link the East with the Far West required aid from federal, state, and local governments, and such help was given generously in the form of land grants, loans, subsidies, and tariff remissions, secured by COLLIS P. HUNTINGTON and LELAND STANFORD. The historic race (1867–69) between the companies to complete the link was spurred by a Federal guarantee of a larger subsidy to the company building the most track, and from owners to migratory day laborers, each group bent to the task of winning the bounty.

The Central Pacific pushed its way over the Sierras, along the Humboldt river through Nevada, into a desert spot north of Ogden, Utah, where at Promontory Point (10 May 1869) it joined the Union Pacific. The ceremony was marked by the driving of a golden spike. The Union Pacific was the technical winner, but the Central Pacific had realized enough from sales of its millions of acres of land grants (and the purchased good will of the California legislature) to pay the total cost of construction: $90,000,000.

Central Powers, the coalition which opposed the ALLIED POWERS in World War I, comprised Germany, Austria-Hungary, Turkey, and Bulgaria.

Central States, see *Middle West.*

Central Treaty Organization (CENTO), formed in 1959, is a Middle Eastern alliance of Iran, Turkey, Pakistan, and Great Britain. Although the U.S. signed 'bilateral agreements of co-operation,' it did not enter the alliance. However, it has participated in meetings of CENTO's ministerial council, and has committed several millions of dollars to regional projects (such as transportation and communication systems), thus carrying forward the mutual security objectives of the Baghdad Pact (1955).

Certiorari, in law, is a writ issuing from a superior court to call up the record of a proceeding in an inferior court or judicial body, so that it may be reviewed (or tried) in the superior court. The writ of certiorari has loomed large in U.S. Supreme Court practice, since it is a discretionary writ under which the Court chooses the cases which it wishes to hear.

Chaco War (1932–35), between Bolivia and Paraguay, was precipitated by the discovery of oil in the Gran Chaco, a barren region divided among Bolivia, Paraguay, and Argentina. The war ended only after a million lives were lost and both sides were exhausted. Six mediating nations, including the U.S., proposed a treaty, which the contestants signed in 1938.

Chain stores are organizations defined by the Bureau of the Census as four or more stores in the same general business, operating under one central management, which utilizes mass buying and warehousing. Few chain stores existed before 1900. The largest chain in the U.S., The Great Atlantic and Pacific Tea Company, began (1859) as a single store. F. W. WOOLWORTH inaugurated the variety chains when he opened his '5-and-10-cent' store in Utica, New York (1879). The United Cigar Stores date from 1892. Chain stores pioneered in improved retail methods, including fresher stocks of merchandise, rapid turnover, and low-cost operation. Their great increase in number after World War I culminated in the SUPERMARKETS.

CHAMBERS, WHITTAKER, see *Hiss, Alger.*

CHAMPLAIN, SAMUEL DE (1567–1635), began his expeditions to the New World with a trip to the West Indies and Mexico (1599–1601). On the first of his eleven voyages to Canada (1603), he explored the St. Lawrence to the rapids above Montreal, and on his return published his valuable *Des Sauvages* (1604), which helped him win aid in attempting to establish a trade route that might lead to China. With that end in view he returned (1604–6), charting the 1000-mile coast line south to Cape Cod. On his third voyage (1608–9) he planted the white standard of St. Louis (July 1608) on the rock which he named Quebec, thus establishing the first permanent French colony in America.

In the spring of 1609 Algonquians and Hurons led Champlain to the lake that bears his name. Near the present Ticonderoga he assisted his Indian allies in their war with the Iroquois, who in turn enlisted the Dutch and English in their cause. Unwittingly Champlain had inaugurated the series of conflicts with the Five Nations that would bear, in Parkman's words, 'havoc and flame to generations yet unborn.' Soon made lieutenant governor of New France, he penetrated up the Ottawa river to lakes Ontario and Huron.

In 1629, unable to withstand the English siege, Champlain surrendered Quebec, and for three years he remained a prisoner in England, where he prepared the final edition of his *Voyages* (1632). With the restoration of Canada to France, he returned to his post. Tenacious and farseeing, Champlain was an idealist who devoted his life to founding an empire that should be ruled 'with justice and mercy, by

France, but for God.' He set forth in vivid and authentic detail the record of his extensive travels. His *Works* (6 vols., 1922–27) are among the great reports of discovery and conquest, and take their place with Caesar's *Commentaries*.

See Morris Bishop, *Champlain: The Life of Fortitude* (1948).

Champlain, Lake, extending some 110 miles from Whitehall, New York, to St. Johns, Quebec, forms the northern Vermont–New York border. Discovered (1609) by the explorer for whom it is named, it was the scene of clashes between the French and English throughout the long period of French and Indian Wars (1689–1763), and between the British and Americans during the Revolution, when CROWN POINT and TICONDEROGA were strategic command points. In the War of 1812 Thomas Macdonough won the battle of PLATTSBURG on Champlain. Today the lake is an important link in the waterway between the Hudson and St. Lawrence valleys.

Chancellorsville, Battle of (2–4 May 1863), was a major engagement in the Civil War, fought between General Hooker, with a Union army of 130,000 men, and General Lee, with fewer than 60,000 Confederates. After the battle of FREDERICKSBURG, Lee clung to strong positions below the Rappahannock. Hooker crossed the river and advanced to attack. Lee decided upon the same daring tactics that he had used at the second battle of BULL RUN. He split his forces, sending Jackson with 30,000 men to hit the Union's right flank, and held the front and left himself. Hooker was dazed when Jackson launched his furious attack, and reeled back, demoralized to such a degree that only superb staff work prevented a Union catastrophe. Lee carried the day, but Chancellorsville was the South's costliest victory. Not only had Lee sacrificed 11,000 men, but Stonewall Jackson, Lee's 'right arm,' was mortally wounded. Hooker suffered a like number of casualties.

CHANDLER, ZACHARIAH (1813–79), wealthy Detroit merchant, was long the Republican party boss of Michigan. As U.S. Senator (1857–75), he was a leader of the RADICAL REPUBLICANS. He opposed Lincoln's war policies, and with B. F. WADE and THADDEUS STEVENS spearheaded the move to impeach President Johnson. When 'Old Zack' lost his seat in the Democratic landslide of 1874, Grant appointed him Secretary of the Interior, a post in which Chandler continued to exert his influence as party spoilsman. He was chairman of the Republican National Committee in the disputed Hayes-Tilden election (1876), and maneuvered the campaign that swung the electoral votes in doubtful states to Hayes.

CHANNING, EDWARD (1856–1931), son of the poet William Ellery Channing (1818–1901) and long a teacher of history at Harvard (1883–1929), distilled his years of study in *A History of the U.S.* (6 vols., 1905–25), an outstanding interpretation of the period it covers (1000–1865). Critics liked his vigorous personal and frequently ironic style and his industrious research, but deplored his indifference to the West, his Anglo-Saxon and New England bias, and his tendency to minimize social evaluations.

CHANNING, WILLIAM ELLERY (1780–1842), after graduation from Harvard (1798), became a lifelong pastor of the Federal Street Church in Boston (1803–42). In his *Baltimore Sermon* (1819), preached at the ordination of JARED SPARKS, he created an issue with Trinitarianism, and his discourse on *The Moral Argument against Calvinism* (1820) made him the leading spokesman for UNITARIANS. He rejected dogma and coercion, and by his 'unremitting appeals to the reason and conscience' paved the way for TRANSCENDENTALISM. Believing in man's perfectibility, he steadily wrote pamphlets on pacifism, prison reform, education, and child labor, gathered in his *Works* (6 vols., 1841–43), and the ferment that he created on such issues spread much more widely than he lived to see.

His younger brother EDWARD TYRELL CHANNING (1790–1856) was a founder and editor of the *North American Review* (1818–19), and, as a distinguished teacher of rhetoric and oratory at Harvard (1826–50), he was warmly remembered by such pupils as Emerson and Thoreau.

His nephews WILLIAM HENRY CHAN-

NING (1810–84) and [WILLIAM] ELLERY CHANNING (1818–1901) were important in the Transcendental movement and in the world of letters of their day.

Chapbooks, so called because they were sold by chapmen, or peddlers, bore the same relation to public taste in the first half of the 19th century, in size, quality, and distribution, that comic books do today. Crudely illustrated, they included marvels, jests, riddles, and songs; tales of heroes and rascals, shipwrecks, Indian captivities, and practical advice. Like almanacs, they were 'throwaway' literature. Purchased by the tens of thousands, they could augment the salary of an itinerant parson, like MASON WEEMS, or be a sideline for an enterprising publisher, like ISAIAH THOMAS.

CHAPLIN, CHARLES SPENCER [CHARLIE CHAPLIN] (1889–   ), English-born motion picture comedian, made his screen debut in 1914. He soon established his reputation as a brilliant mime in early Keystone films, in the character of the wistful tramp. In 1918 he entered independent production, starring and directing productions of his own creation. His burlesque sharpened into fantasies in a playful or ironic mood, and into satire. Notable in their genre are *The Kid* (1921), *The Gold Rush* (1925), *City Lights* (1931), and *Modern Times* (1936). In such later films as *The Great Dictator* (1940), *Monsieur Verdoux* (1947), and *Limelight* (1952) he introduced dialogue, deepened the satire, and tended toward greater seriousness. No actor in the history of motion pictures has matched the universality of his appeal. In 1962 Oxford University awarded him an honorary doctorate in humane letters.

CHAPMAN, JOHN (1774–1847), Massachusetts-born orchardist, is popularly known in legends and tall tales as 'Johnny Appleseed.' From his nursery near Pittsburgh Landing, Pennsylvania, he distributed apple saplings and seeds to settlers moving into the Ohio valley. He himself later followed, planting apple seeds, and later pruning and tending the mature trees.

Chapultepec, Act of (1945), signed by representatives of twenty American republics in Mexico City, called for joint action in repelling any aggression against an American state. Significantly, this includes aggression by an American as well as a non-American state.

Chapultepec, Battle of (13 September 1847), was the final engagement in the Mexican War. General Winfield Scott launched his attack against the 200-ft. rocky eminence commanding the approach to Mexico City. Americans scaled the walls with ladders, and the immediate surrender of the Mexicans led to the treaty of GUADALUPE HIDALGO in February 1848.

Charity schools, or pauper schools, in colonial days and later provided free education for orphans or children of indigent parents. They were supported by private gifts or other benevolence. Such schools, modeled on their English counterparts, offered a curriculum at a most elementary level, and attached to the idea of free education a stigma that persisted well into the 19th century.

Charles River Bridge* v. *Warren Bridge (1837) was a case that arose when a corporation chartered by Massachusetts in 1785 to build and operate a toll bridge leading out of Boston sought by implication to secure a monopoly of crossing the waters of the Charles river by asking the courts to invalidate a state law that authorized the charter of a proposed free bridge. The case was carried to the U.S. Supreme Court, where Chief Justice Taney ruled that no implied rights could be claimed beyond the specific terms of a grant. This substantial modification of John Marshall's earlier rulings defending the sanctity of contract, notably in the DARTMOUTH COLLEGE CASE (1816), was the first Supreme Court pronouncement asserting the modern doctrine of the social responsibility of private property. Legislative grants were to be construed strictly in favor of the public.

Charleston, 25 miles up the Ashley river in South Carolina, was first settled at the confluence with Cooper river in 1670 by a small number of colonists from England and several hundred Barbadians. The present site, on the best harbor between Chesapeake Bay and the Gulf of Mexico, was chosen ten years later. When Charleston was incorporated as a city in 1783, it had become the wealthiest and largest community in the South, with a population of 16,000. An important base in the War of Independence, it was captured by Clinton in 1780 and remained under British rule for two years. It was capital of the colony and the state until 1790, and during the first half of the 19th century it developed a vigorous literary tradition.

Charleston became the spearhead of NULLIFICATION, and the firing on FORT SUMTER (1861) in its harbor opened the Civil War. Described as 'acres of pitiful and voiceless barrenness' at the war's end, it later (1886) suffered one of the most devastating earthquakes in U.S. history. Today it is a center of cotton trade, with a population (1960) of 76,000, nearly half of which is Negro. The College of Charleston (est. 1790) was the first municipal institution of higher learning in the U.S. The Citadel (est. 1842) is a well-known military academy.

Charleston, an American popular dance in 4-4 time, was introduced about 1922. Characteristic of the JAZZ AGE, it was highly popular with both professional entertainers and the general public. Its distinguishing feature is an exuberant side kick.

CHARLEVOIX, PIERRE FRANÇOIS XAVIER DE (1682–1761), was sent by the French authorities to discover an interior route through North America to the Western Sea. Ostensibly making a tour to inspect Jesuit missions, Charlevoix in 1720–22 went around the Great Lakes, entered Illinois, and voyaged down the Mississippi to New Orleans and Biloxi, interviewing Indians and traders along the way. His *Journal Historique* (1744) is one of the most detailed 18th-century travel accounts of the North American frontier.

Charter Colonies were first established by TRADING COMPANIES under charters from the crown, but they very early changed their status. In 1624 Virginia became a royal colony, the first in English history; and Massachusetts did so seven years after its charter was revoked (1684). Connecticut and Rhode Island were founded as squatter colonies by dissenting Puritans from Massachusetts, but they later received charters of incorporation. The failure of the VIRGINIA COMPANY and the moribund state of the COUNCIL FOR NEW ENGLAND by 1630 persuaded the king to set up PROPRIETARY COLONIES, and the next royal grant (1632), that of Maryland to Lord Baltimore, was of the feudal type, as were all succeeding grants.

When the government of Charles II (after 1660) sought to build a colonial policy, it found charters an obstacle, and with a view to consolidation it established the DOMINION OF NEW ENGLAND under a royal governor (1686–89). Though the failure of that attempt created some reaction in favor of charter colonies, in general the people preferred to be governed as ROYAL COLONIES, and by 1776 there remained only two proprietary colonies (Maryland and Pennsylvania) and two incorporated colonies (Connecticut and Rhode Island).

Charter Oak, a tree near Hartford, Connecticut, according to tradition was the hiding place of the Connecticut charter of 1662, when Sir Edmund Andros, seeking to alter existing charters in 1686 in an effort to consolidate the DOMINION OF NEW ENGLAND, demanded the return of that instrument in the name of James II. Although Andros failed to secure the charter, he dissolved the existing government. After William of Orange succeeded James in the Glorious Revolution of 1688, the charter government was resumed and crown lawyers decided that the charter had never been invalidated. The much-venerated widespreading oak fell in 1856.

Charters, see *Colonial charters; College charters.*

CHASE, SALMON PORTLAND (1808–73), New Hampshire-born statesman and jurist, after graduation from Dartmouth (1826), practiced law in Cincinnati, where after 1836 he identified himself with the antislavery movement as a leader of those who opposed Garrison and the extreme abolitionists. Conspicuous as a counsel for fugitive slaves, he abandoned the Whig party (1841), first to support Birney and the Liberty party, and later (1848) Van Buren and the Free-Soilers. He was sent by Free-Soilers and Democrats to the U.S. Senate (1849–55), where he vigorously opposed both the Compromise of 1850 and the Kansas-Nebraska bill (1854). His 'Appeal of the Independent Democrats,' published in *The New York Times* (24 January 1854), was the earliest draft of the Republican party creed, and led to his election as Republican governor of Ohio (1855–59). He lost the party's presidential nomination in 1860 to Lincoln, who made Chase Secretary of the Treasury (1861–64). He offered to resign the post in 1862 after a cabinet dispute with Secretary of State Seward, but Lincoln refused his resignation.

An able politician rather than a financier, Chase mildly resisted passage of the LEGAL TENDER ACT of 1862, and secured passage of the NATIONAL BANK ACT (1863). In 1864 Senator Samuel Pomeroy of Kansas, a radical Republican, opposed Lincoln's re-election, and when the confidential 'Pomeroy Circular,' favoring the candidacy of Chase, was made public, Chase again offered his resignation. Again Lincoln refused to accept it, but later in the year, when Lincoln and Chase differed in the matter of an appointment, Lincoln accepted Chase's resignation.

Chase coveted the presidential nomination, but after the movement to revive his candidacy fell through, he campaigned for Lincoln, who, six months later (December 1864), appointed Chase Chief Justice of the U.S. Supreme Court (1864–73). Ambitious and opinionated, Chase was nevertheless a man of probity and moral courage, and his insistence upon strict legal procedures in the impeachment trial of President Andrew Johnson (1868) was a large factor in Johnson's acquittal.

CHASE, SAMUEL (1741–1811), Maryland-born jurist, while serving in the Continental Congress was appointed (1776) with Benjamin Franklin, Charles Carroll, and John Carroll to engage in the unsuccessful mission to win Canada to the Revolution. At Washington's request, Chase resigned as chief judge of Maryland (1791–96) to accept an appointment to the U.S. Supreme Court. A radical Federalist, he was particularly obnoxious to Republicans, and his overbearing manner and abusive tongue, while presiding at trials rising out of the ALIEN AND SEDITION ACTS, led to action for his impeachment in 1804. The charges of malfeasance were not sustained, and Chase resumed his place on the bench (1805), although his powers thereafter declined. The case demonstrated the impracticality of attempting impeachment proceedings to curb the power of the Federal court for purely political ends. No such steps have ever been taken since to remove a member of the Supreme Court.

CHASE, STUART (1888–), after graduation from Harvard (1910) and service with the Federal Trade Commission (1917–22), began his economic and sociological analyses, including *The Tragedy of Waste* (1925), *The Economy of Abundance* (1934), and *Rich Land, Poor Land* (1936). His later writings continued to break down conventional assumptions, defining anew such concepts as well-being, freedom, and democracy.

CHASTELLUX, FRANÇOIS-JEAN DE BEAUVOIR, Chevalier (later Marquis) de (1734–88), although a lifelong soldier was also a familiar figure during his thirties in literary salons and was elected to the French Academy. He served as a major general under Rochambeau in the War of Independence, and travelled extensively from Virginia to New Hampshire (1780–82). His observant *Voyages* (1786) describe both the gay society of wartime Philadelphia and the crude accommodations of backwoods lodgings with equally sympathetic interest. Washington trusted him and Jefferson gave him unstinted respect. The *Voyages* were immediately translated (1787) as *Travels in North America* by an 'English gentleman' (George Grieve), who appended valuable notes.

Long unprocurable, the work now is issued in a revised translation, edited by Howard Rice, Jr. (2 vols., 1963).

CHATEAUBRIAND, FRANÇOIS RENÉ, Vicomte de (1768–1848), French writer and statesman, spent six months in the U.S. (July–December 1791), traveling from Baltimore to Niagara Falls. His celebration of primitivism in *Atala* (1801), which was translated into almost all the languages of Europe, impressed the romantic image of the American wilderness on the readers of his day. His American settings in *René* (1802) and *Les Natchez* (1826) likewise provided 'abundant aliment for day-dreams.' His account of those American travels was largely fictitious, derived chiefly from earlier travel journals. But the captivating effect of his earliest tale is commemorated in the names of Attala county, Mississippi, and the town of Attalla, Alabama.

Chateaugay, Battle of (25 October 1813), was a minor skirmish in the War of 1812, in which Major General WADE HAMPTON, with 4000 troops, allowed 800 British to bar his advance into Canada. Hampton lacked water transport, and had been instructed by Secretary of War Armstrong that he and his army were shortly to go into winter quarters. He therefore undoubtedly realized that his threat to Montreal was illusory.

Château-Thierry, Battle of (3–4 June 1918), blocked the German advance on Paris in World War I by stopping Hindenburg at the Marne. Assisted by French forces, American troops launched a counterattack after the enemy had entered the town of Château-Thierry. The Allied gains were preserved by the battle of BELLEAU WOOD.

Chatham, see *Pitt, William.*

Chattanooga Campaign (September–November 1863), launched to put a wedge between northern and western Confederate armies, was a major engagement in the Civil War. Confederate forces were led throughout by Braxton Bragg, in whom President Davis stubbornly placed his faith. The Union armies at first were commanded by two inept generals, Burnside and Rosecrans. The first battle of the campaign, at CHICKAMAUGA (19–20 September), ended in a Union defeat which was prevented from becoming a rout only by the brilliant tactics of General GEORGE H. THOMAS, but Rosecrans was penned up in Chattanooga. Lincoln gave General Grant, who in July had successfully concluded the VICKSBURG CAMPAIGN, supreme command of the western Federal armies (16 October), and Grant placed Thomas in command of the Army of the Cumberland, with the order to hold Chattanooga 'at all hazard.' The battle of LOOKOUT MOUNTAIN drove the Confederates from the steep ridges above the city, and made possible the great battle of MISSIONARY RIDGE. The Union success thus attained opened the way for Sherman's drive eastward to the sea.

CHAUNCEY, ISAAC (1772–1840), as commodore of U.S. naval forces on Lakes Erie and Ontario during the War of 1812, assisted in the capture of York (Toronto) in April 1813. During the summer he pursued the British flotilla here and there, but always from a distance. When the cruising season was over, he returned to Sackett's Harbor, where he remained for the duration of the war. His failure to co-operate with General Jacob Brown on the Niagara frontier in 1814 was a decisive factor in the subsequent U.S. retreat from the Canadian side of the region, and he was relieved of his command. In later years he served as president of the board of naval commissioners (1833–40).

CHAUNCY, CHARLES (1705–87), a graduate of Harvard (1721), became a lifelong pastor of the First Church in Boston (1727–87). As a leading exponent of ARMINIANISM, Chauncy vigorously opposed Jonathan Edwards and the revivalists of the GREAT AWAKENING in such works as his sermon *Enthusiasm Described* (1742), and his ponderous *Seasonable Thoughts* (1743). His *Compleat View of Episcopacy* (1771), arguing against the institution of bishops, was long regarded as the classic statement of the Congregational position. Late in life he drifted into Universalism, expounded in *The Mystery Hid from Ages* (1784).

The Arminian controversy roused great interest in Europe, and Chauncy became better known abroad than any other 18th-century American divine except Edwards. Chauncy, who was dull as a preacher, was admired in his day for his great learning.

Chautauqua Movement, akin to the LYCEUM MOVEMENT, was a development in adult education. In 1874, at Chautauqua, New York, Bishop John H. Vincent (1832–1920) helped establish the Chautauqua Assembly. Thus what had been a summer Sunday-school institute for Methodist Episcopalians expanded into a program offering courses in science and the humanities. In 1878, under the educational direction of WILLIAM RAINEY HARPER (later president of the University of Chicago), a home reading program was instituted, and thereafter the summer Assembly began to attract lecturers of note.

After 1900 traveling 'chautauquas' were promoted by lecture bureaus. Such groups moved from town to town during the summer season, and under large tents (until about 1925) presented popular lectures, and offered musical and dramatic entertainment.

Checkoff, made legal under the TAFT-HARTLEY ACT (1947), is the system under which employers, by agreement with unions, withhold union dues of employees, and turn the dues over directly to the unions.

Checks and Balances is the term used to describe the separation, or balance, of the powers of the executive, legislative, and judicial branches of the U.S. government. The political philosophy of Montesquieu, who strongly influenced the arrangement, was adopted in large part because of the American colonial experience with an executive (the colonial governor) and a legislature (the colonial assembly) so closely interrelated that neither branch was free to act independently. Madison argued in *Federalist Paper* 51 (February 1788) that power is 'an encroachment of nature' which requires an interior structure of government so contrived 'that its several constituent parts may, by their mutual relations, be the means of keeping each other in their proper places.' Incorporated into the Constitution, the device separates the branches of government from each other, thereby legally protecting the judicial, legislative, and executive branches from each other and yet permitting each to exercise restraints upon the others.

Chemistry was put to industrial use in America as early as 1608, when the first Virginia colonists manufactured potash, tar, and glass on a small scale. Salt, leather, and iron were also being produced by 1620. JOHN WINTHROP, JR. (1606–76), easily first in scientific interest among colonists during the 17th century, built an ironworks in 1644, thus initiating industrial chemistry as a commercial venture. As a separate discipline, chemistry was stimulated by the work of JOSEPH PRIESTLEY, THOMAS COOPER, and especially by S. L. MITCHILL, who introduced the discoveries of Lavoisier and Davy. The first chair of chemistry was established at Pennsylvania (1769), with BENJAMIN RUSH as its incumbent.

The greatest advance in the early 19th century was made at Yale by BENJAMIN SILLIMAN. Later strides were effected by J. P. COOKE at Harvard, F. A. GENTH at Pennsylvania, WILLARD GIBBS at Yale, and IRA REMSEN at Johns Hopkins, where U.S. graduate research in chemistry began (1876). A pioneer in soil chemistry was EDMUND RUFFIN of Virginia, predecessor of such agricultural experimenters as W. O. ATWATER and G. W. CARVER.

The researches carried out by L. H. BAEKELAND, and those organized by W. R. WHITNEY in the General Electric laboratories, have revolutionized 20th-century techniques. The pioneer work of G. N. LEWIS in the field of atomic structure was followed up by W. D. HARKINS. More recently significant discoveries have been made by W. H. CAROTHERS, R. B. WOODWARD, and E. J. COHN. The work of such biochemists as E. V. MC COLLUM and E. C. KENDALL has given a new dimension to the field of medicine.

The Nobel Prize in chemistry has been awarded to the following Americans:

1914 Theodore W. Richards (Harvard). Exact determinations of atomic weights of many elements.

1932 IRVING LANGMUIR. Investigations and discoveries in surface chemistry.

1934 HAROLD C. UREY. Research leading to the industrial production of heavy water.

1946 James B. Sumner (Cornell), Wendell M. Stanley (Rockefeller Institute), and John H. Northrop

(Rockefeller Institute). Pioneer research in enzymes and viruses.

1949 William F. Giauque (University of California at Berkeley). Discoveries concerning the behavior of substances at extremely low temperatures.

1951 EDWIN M. MC MILLAN and GLENN T. SEABORG. Research leading to discoveries of transuranic elements.

1954 LINUS C. PAULING. Research concerning the forces binding proteins and molecules.

1955 Vincent du Vigneaud (Cornell). Synthesis of hormones produced by the pituitary gland that aid in childbirth.

1960 Willard F. Libby (University of California at Los Angeles). Discovery of radiocarbon dating.

1961 Melvin Calvin (University of California at Berkeley). Establishing the sequence of chemical reactions involved when a plant assimilates carbon dioxide.

1965 Robert B. Woodward (Harvard). Effecting the complete synthesis of chlorophyll.

Cherokee Indians, an Iroquoian stock which De Soto encountered in 1540, were long the most important tribe in the Southeast. By 1700 they occupied the large region south of the Ohio river to Alabama. They were allies of the British during the French and Indian Wars and in the War of Independence. Later reduced to a small fragment, by treaties with the U.S. they set up their own Cherokee Nation (1827) in the uplands of northwestern Georgia, erected frame houses, built roads, and maintained their customs. For a time they published books in an alphabet devised by SEQUOYAH, and enjoyed their own newspaper, the *Cherokee Phoenix* (1828–35), edited by their tribesman ELIAS BOUDINOT.

In defiance of treaty rights the state of Georgia claimed the Cherokee as subjects, thus creating a Federal-state issue which Chief Justice John Marshall decided (1832) in favor of the Cherokee (*Worcester* v. *Georgia*) on the ground that Georgia had no jurisdiction in the territory of the Cherokee Nation. The state ignored the decision, encouraged by the comment of President Jackson, who disliked both Marshall and the Cherokee: 'John Marshall has made his decision; now let him enforce it.' As a compromise a 'perpetual outlet, West' (known as the 'Cherokee Strip') was officially guaranteed to encourage migration to Oklahoma. In 1838 President Van Buren ordered the removal of the Cherokee to the Indian Territory. The U.S. purchased the 'Strip' in 1891; in 1906 the Cherokee gave up their tribal allegiance and became U.S. citizens.

Cherry Valley Massacre (11 November 1778) was a raid during the War of Independence on the outpost settlement of Cherry valley, in central New York, executed by BUTLER'S RANGERS, a Tory regiment whose Indian allies were led by JOSEPH BRANT. All buildings were razed, and some 40 survivors were massacred after they had surrendered. This and the WYOMING MASSACRE led Washington to organize a campaign in which General John Sullivan soundly defeated the Rangers in 1779.

***Chesapeake-Leopard* Incident,** an impressment issue in 1807, brought Great Britain and the U.S. to the verge of war. In June the American frigate *Chesapeake* was hailed off Norfolk Roads by the British frigate *Leopard*. When Commodore James Barron refused to permit a search of his vessel for four alleged British deserters, the *Leopard* fired three full broadsides in reply. Barron struck his flag, the *Chesapeake* was boarded and three Americans were removed. Barron was suspended from the Navy for negligence, but the insult united Americans in anti-British feeling. Jefferson's proclamation ordering British warships from American territorial waters was followed by a British proclamation ordering a more vigorous search of American vessels for British subjects. Congress then passed the EMBARGO ACT.

CHEVALIER, MICHEL (1806–79), an economist at the Collège de France, was sent to the U.S. (1833–35) by the French government to report on the revolution in transport and communications then taking place. His *Lettres sur l'Amérique du Nord* (1836) is a uniquely perceptive analysis of the transforming effect of industry when canals and railroads were making possible both physical expansion and industrial consolidation. Like TOCQUEVILLE he foresaw the emergence of the U.S. and Russia as world powers. His study, translated as *Society, Manners, and Politics in the U.S.* (1839) has been edited (1961) by J. W. Ward.

Cheyenne Indians, of Algonquian stock, during the 17th century began moving southwestward from Minnesota to the Missouri river. By 1800 they had become true Plains Indians and buffalo hunters. They later divided into northern and southern bands. Encroachments by whites on the Cheyenne hunting grounds led to retaliation in the form of raids. After Custer annihilated a large contingent in southern Oklahoma (1868), their resistance was broken. Remnants are settled on reservations in Oklahoma and Montana.

Chicago, second city of the U.S. in population (3,550,000 in 1960), commerce, and manufactures, is situated on the Chicago river at the foot of Lake Michigan in northeastern Illinois. The site was an early portage route, first visited by French explorers in the 1670's. Its importance as a center controlling the region from the Great Lakes to the Mississippi led to the establishment there (1804) of Fort Dearborn, occupied off and on by the army until 1836. In the following year, with a population of 4000, Chicago was incorporated as a city, and was the western terminus of a military highway (completed in 1833).

The giant growth of lake trade and rail connections with the East during the 1850's in one generation transformed a sprawling grain and livestock center into a metropolis, with a population in 1870 of 300,000. Today Chicago is the nation's greatest rail center, and its Board of Trade the major grain exchange.

After the holocaust of the CHICAGO FIRE (1871), industrial expansion began to fan out from THE LOOP, creating fortunes for such business men as ARMOUR, GARY, and PULLMAN. Social unrest and labor disputes culminated in the HAYMARKET RIOT (1886) and the PULLMAN STRIKE (1894). The WORLD'S COLUMBIAN EXPOSITION (1893) was an event of national importance. The civic and social reforms led by JANE ADDAMS before 1900 also became national in scale. When the St. Lawrence Seaway opened in 1959, Chicago became the major port for transatlantic shipping in the Midwest. The city is a major cultural center, with such noted institutions of higher learning as Northwestern University (est. 1851), and the University of Chicago (est. 1890).

Chicago Fire, one of the worst in modern history, was the conflagration of 8–9 October 1871, which, starting in the lumber district and spread by high winds, engulfed an area of three and a half square miles, including the business center of the city. Some 17,000 structures were destroyed and 80,000 persons rendered homeless. Loss of life is estimated at 250, and property damage at $200,000,000. A vast system of relief, much from abroad, helped rehabilitation, and within three years the city was rebuilt of far more durable structures.

Chicago School, see *Skyscraper.*

Chicago Tribune, established in 1847, became a major influence in the Midwest under the highly personal editorship (1855–99) of JOSEPH MEDILL, and to the present the paper has maintained its conservative Republican tone. After Medill's death (1899), the *Tribune* was controlled by an editorial board whose chief representatives (until 1914) were ROBERT W. PATTERSON and JOSEPH MEDILL PATTERSON. In 1914 ROBERT R. MC CORMICK, an economic conservative and isolationist, assumed control. The *Tribune* continues to have the widest circulation in the area (reported in 1965 as 845,000 daily, 1,190,000 Sunday).

Chicago, University of (est. 1891), was founded as a private, co-educational institution by a gift from John D. Rockefeller. Its first president, WILLIAM RAINEY HARPER, gathered a distinguished faculty even before there were students to teach, and made it the leading educational center west of the Alleghenies before he died (1906). The University was the first to hold regular summer sessions.

President ROBERT M. HUTCHINS in 1942 revised the curriculum to admit students at the end of their tenth-grade year, removed rigid barriers between departments, and substituted comprehensive examinations for course examinations, creating thereby a controversial but stimulating and influential program. Its research branches include Yerkes Observatory at Williams Bay, Wisconsin. Its 'Great Books' program, a feature in its adult education system, reaches thousands of homes throughout the U.S. In 1965, with an endowment of $163,000,000 and a faculty of 923, it enrolled 8100 students.

Chicago World's Fair, see *World's Columbian Exposition.*

Chickamauga, Battle of (19–20 September 1863), was the opening engagement of the CHATTANOOGA CAMPAIGN during the Civil War. In early September the Union General William S. Rosecrans and his Army of the Cumberland had maneuvered the unresourceful Braxton Bragg out of Chattanooga, gateway to the East. Jefferson Davis rushed Longstreet with 11,000 Confederate troops to reinforce Bragg. The 58,000 Federals engaged 66,000 Confederates at Chickamauga, northeast of the rail center. Bragg's poorly co-ordinated attacks on the first day were matched by Rosecrans's blunders on the second. Only the brilliant tactics of General George H. Thomas, the 'Rock of Chickamauga,' who held his corps against repeated Confederate assaults, prevented a Union rout. The engagement cost the Union some 16,000 casualties, the Confederates about 18,000. The Union forces withdrew into Chattanooga. Lincoln presently replaced Rosecrans with Grant.

Chickasaw Indians, of Muskhogean stock, and formerly inhabitants of northern Mississippi, were an important tribe related in customs and language to their neighbors the Choctaws and Creeks, with whom they were often at war. They were especially hostile to encroachments on their hunting grounds of white settlers. In 1832 by treaty with the U.S. government they emigrated west to Indian Territory, where they established themselves as one of the FIVE CIVILIZED TRIBES.

CHILD, LYDIA MARIA (1802–80), a New England author of patriotic romances, in 1826 established the *Juvenile Miscellany,* the first American monthly magazine for children. She later identified herself with various reforms, especially with the ABOLITION MOVEMENT, and her argument in *An Appeal in Favor of that Class of Americans Called Africans* (1833) won important support to the antislavery cause. She edited the influential *National Anti-Slavery Standard,* a New York weekly newspaper (1841–49); attracted considerable reaction for a pamphlet (1860) of her correspondence with the governor of Virginia and one Mrs. Mason, championing John Brown and abolition; and took the most advanced position regarding the intellectual potentialities of the Negro.

CHILD, ROBERT (1613–54), led a movement to extend suffrage and toleration in the Massachusetts Bay Colony. Though himself a Puritan and a respected gentleman of learning, he placed his name first on a Remonstrance (1646) deploring civil and religious discrimination against non-Puritans, and opposed that part of the MASSACHUSETTS BODY OF LIBERTIES which based its code on the Pentateuch rather than the laws of England. The magistrates were nettled by the truculence of the document, and frightened by Child's intent to take the matter to Parliament. The General Court declared: 'Our allegiance binds us not to the laws of England any longer than while we live in England.' In 1647 Child was tried for sedition, heavily fined, and allowed to return to England, the magistrates meanwhile having learned from the Lords Commissioners of Plantations that the colony's body of laws created no problem for the mother country.

Child labor is a term referring both to an economic practice and its attendant evil. The factory system in the U.S. dates from the establishment (1790) of a cotton mill by SAMUEL SLATER, who employed boys and girls ranging in age from seven to twelve. During the next 40 years mills and factories commonly employed children for an average working day of twelve hours. In the 1840's Massachusetts, Connecticut, and Pennsylvania attempted to limit the working hours of children, but the regulations were not enforced. The census report of 1870, showing an industrial employment of 750,000 children under fifteen, led to campaigns for regulatory legislation which many states enacted.

In 1904 a National Labor Committee was formed that successfully spearheaded a move to interest state legislatures in enforcement laws. The Committee was chartered by Congress in 1907. The Keating-Owen Act (1916) was an endeavor of Congress to regulate child labor, but two years later the Supreme Court declared it unconstitutional (HAMMER *v.* DAGENHART). A second child labor law (1919) was likewise invalidated (BAILEY *v.* DREXEL FURNITURE CO.). In 1924 Congress approved a Child Labor Amendment which it submitted to the states. The amendment was never ratified, largely because it sought to regulate the labor, not the 'employment,' of persons up to eighteen years of age. The FAIR LABOR STANDARDS ACT (1938), by controlling factory hire of children under sixteen, effectively restrains exploitation in industries producing goods for interstate commerce. However, the employment of children under sixteen in street selling, industrial homework, commercial agriculture, and in areas not subject to effective regulation has left the problem of exploitation solved only in part.

Child welfare, growing out of a recognition of the conditions created by slums and sweatshops, was given impetus in the U.S. when the social reformer Charles Loring Brace (1826–90) established the Children's Aid Society of New York (1854), a pioneer organization in the application of modern methods in child-welfare practice. The White House Conference of 1909, which dealt with the care of dependent children, led to remedial legislation on an extensive scale, both locally and nationally. The Children's Bureau, first established as a branch of the U.S. Department of Labor (1912), since 1935 has functioned within the SOCIAL SECURITY ADMINISTRATION. It makes grants to state public welfare agencies for the protection and care of homeless and dependent children, and children in danger of becoming delinquent. JUVENILE COURTS became part of the state judicial systems in the U.S. early in the 20th century.

Children's Courts, see *Juvenile Courts.*

China trade began in the years following the War of Independence, when excise taxes were imposed on American merchants who previously had profited from an untaxed WEST INDIAN TRADE. By 1789, from Salem to Philadelphia, scores of enterprising shipmasters were following the route around the Cape of Good Hope and crossing the Indian Ocean by way of the Dutch West Indies to Canton, the only port open to foreign markets. In exchange for silver dollars, cargoes of ginseng from the Hudson valley, seal and sea-otter pelts, and machinery and farm products, American skippers bought silk, tea, china, nankeen, and spices, as well as sandalwood and other items of trade obtained from Pacific islands.

The voyages were long and hazardous, but the profits were enormous, amounting at the height of the China trade (1820) to $20,000,000 per annum. Diplomatic relations lagged far behind the merchant exchanges. Commodore Lawrence Kearny was despatched to the Far East to protect American interests at the close of the Opium War (1840–42) between Great Britain and China, and to ask for MOST-FAVORED-NATIONS rights. Such rights were secured in 1844 with a treaty negotiated for the U.S. by CALEB CUSHING, whereby four additional 'treaty ports' were opened to American trade.

Chinese Exclusion Acts, the first of which was passed in 1882, were pushed through Congress after anti-Chinese sentiment on the Pacific coast had resulted in violence, leading to a demand for modification of the BURLINGAME TREATY (1868). The first Exclusion Act, prohibiting the entry into the U.S. of Chinese laborers for a period of ten years, was extended in 1892 for a similar period, and in 1902 was indefinitely extended. As a result, the Chinese population of the country declined from 107,000 in 1890 to 75,000 in 1930, thus bringing anti-Chinese agitation virtually to an end. The laws were repealed in 1943, at which time Chinese immigrants were admitted into the U.S. under the QUOTA ACT of 1921.

Chinook Indians, a Penutian linguistic stock at one time inhabiting the coastal region of North America from California to Alaska, were numerically few when white men reached the Indian settlements. The so-called Chinook jargon is a combination of such Indian, French, and English words as would allow mid-19th century traders and missionaries to communicate with tribal members.

Chippewa, Battle of (5 July 1814), was a brief engagement near the Niagara river during the War of 1812. General Jacob Brown's subordinate, Winfield Scott, with his 1300 American regulars, was belatedly celebrating the Fourth of July, when their parade was broken up by 1500 British regulars under General Sir Phineas Riall. The British retired after 30 minutes, but the encounter decided no issue of war.

Chippewa Indians, see *Ojibwa Indians.*

Chisholm Trail, the most famous route of the CATTLE DRIVES, ran from the Nueces river in east Texas to the Red river crossing, then north through the Indian Territory and Kansas. Established after the Civil War by a half-breed Cherokee trader and guide, Jesse Chisholm, to freight supplies north, it was ideally suited to an expanding commerce. The boom period of the drives followed the development of a stockyard and rail depot at Abilene (1867). When the trunk rail lines were extended south into Texas during the 1880's trail driving came virtually to an end.

Chisholm* v. *Georgia (1793) was a case resulting in a U.S. Supreme Court decision rendered in favor of two South Carolina citizens who had sued the state of Georgia for recovery of confiscated property. Georgia denied the Court's jurisdiction and refused to appear, even though the Constitution (Art. III, sec. 2) gave the Federal courts explicit jurisdiction over issues 'between a State and Citizens of another State.' Justice Iredell, dissenting, held that under common law no constitutional sanction supersedes the right of a sovereignty to be sued except with its consent. This minority opinion was confirmed by passage of the Eleventh Amendment (1798), adopted to protect the states against suits by individuals.

CHITTENDEN, HIRAM MARTIN (1858–1917), a graduate of the U.S. Military Academy (1884), was placed in charge of government engineering projects on several western rivers. He wrote such authoritative studies as *The American Fur Trade of the Far West* (3 vols., 1902) and *History of Early Steamboat Navigation on the Missouri* (2 vols., 1903). His report on irrigation, *Reservoirs in Arid Regions,* served as a basis for the National Reclamation Act (1902).

CHOATE, JOSEPH HODGES (1832–1917), nephew of RUFUS CHOATE, after graduation from Harvard (1852) was admitted to the New York bar and became one of the notable trial lawyers of his time. As a member of the Committee of Seventy (1871), he was instrumental in breaking up the TWEED RING. He succeeded John Hay as ambassador to Great Britain (1899–1905) and represented the U.S. at the second Peace Congress at The Hague (1907).

CHOATE, RUFUS (1799–1859), after graduation from Dartmouth (1819) practiced law in Salem until he settled in Boston (1834). He entered politics briefly, serving first as Whig congressman from Massachusetts (1830–34), and later filling out the unexpired term of Daniel Webster in the Senate (1841–45).

Although Choate continued his interest in public affairs, no amount of urging could persuade him to abandon the practice of law. In an age of notable orators he was pre-eminent, for he could be witty or weighty, plain or grand, as the occasion demanded. No one surpassed him in his day as a courtroom advocate.

Choctaw Indians, of Muskhogean stock and one of the FIVE CIVILIZED TRIBES, were originally an agricultural people inhabiting Alabama and Mississippi. They were usually allied with the French during the French and Indian Wars. By the Treaty of Dancing Rabbit Creek (1830) they ceded their lands to the U.S. (some 7,800,000 acres), and moved to Oklahoma.

Chouteau Family, originating in New Orleans, were instrumental in founding St. Louis and developing the trans-Mississippi fur trade. RENÉ AUGUSTE

CHOUTEAU (1749–1829) at fourteen accompanied a trading venture into the Illinois country. In 1764 he was left to establish a trading post below the confluence of the Mississippi and Missouri rivers; that post developed into the city of St. Louis. He later succeeded to the management of the family business (1778), and when St. Louis was incorporated (1809), he was chairman of its board of trustees.

JEAN PIERRE CHOUTEAU (1758–1849), a brother of René, became a partner and in 1802 established a post at the site of the present Salina, Oklahoma, where he traded chiefly with the Osage Indians. In 1809 he helped form the St. Louis Missouri Fur Company. His eldest son, AUGUSTE PIERRE CHOUTEAU (1786–1838), after graduation from the U.S. Military Academy (1806) entered his father's business, with headquarters at Salina. Washington Irving described his liberal hospitality in *A Tour on the Prairies* (1835).

The most spectacular success was achieved by Jean Pierre's younger son, PIERRE CHOUTEAU (1789–1865). After acting as agent for Astor's American Fur Company, in 1838 he organized Pierre Chouteau, Jr., and Company, and carried on a tremendous business from the Mississippi to the Rocky Mountains. He was the leading western financier of his day, with extensive commercial interests. In later years he made New York his headquarters.

Christian Endeavor, International Society of, is an organization founded at Portland, Maine, in 1881 as a fellowship to promote Christian service and teaching among the youthful members of Protestant churches. It numbers some 4,000,000 members in 80,000 societies throughout the world.

Christian Science, organized as the Church of Christ, Scientist, at Lynn, Massachusetts, in 1879 by MARY BAKER EDDY, stemmed from a fusion of mental therapeutics with the belief that 'man is not material; he is spiritual.' The term 'Christian science' was first used by Dr. Phineas P. Quimby (1802–66), a mesmerist and mental healer of Portland, Maine. As an enthusiastic patient of Quimby, Mrs. Eddy assisted the doctor in systematizing his ideas, and continued to develop them after his death. For ten years (1870–80) she taught her science to pupils at Lynn, and brought out her textbook, *Science and Health* (1875), to which she added a *Key to the Scriptures.* In 1882 she removed her church to Boston, where since 1892 it has been known as the Mother Church. From her newly organized Massachusetts Metaphysical College she graduated practitioners, authorized to teach spiritual healing. The College closed in 1889, but the impetus given to Christian Science by the success of the practitioners soon carried the movement across the continent and to Europe.

Science and Health was improved and enlarged, and in its fiftieth printing (1891) it was given essentially its present form. The theology of Christian Science denies the reality of both matter and 'mortal' mind. God, the perfect Good, alone is real, and through Christ's atonement as set forth in *Science and Health,* God's perfect love is manifest, together with His power to overcome error and the illusion of disease and death. The churches, which are self-governing, do not have pastors. Services are conducted by two readers, one citing from Scripture, the other from *Science and Health.*

The vigorous Christian Science Publishing Society issues numerous publications, including the *Christian Science Monitor* (1908–current), an international daily newspaper noted for its careful reporting. The denomination in 1965 comprised the Mother Church and more than 3200 branches in 48 countries. (It does not publish membership data.)

Christian Socialism developed in the last quarter of the 19th century as an attempt, principally within evangelical Protestant churches, to apply the teachings of Jesus to social and industrial problems created by the rapid growth of large-scale business. The orthodox emphasis on the supernatural elements of religion was subordinated to the 'social gospel': a search for remedies to the inequalities that bred city slums and tensions between employers and laborers.

A pioneer document in the 'social gospel' movement is *Our Country* (1885), by the Congregational minister

JOSIAH STRONG, who invoked the theory of organic evolution to support his belief that industry itself would inevitably become more democratically organized. Other influential clergymen who viewed the problems of natural man as environmental rather than individual were GEORGE D. HERRON, OCTAVIUS B. FROTHINGHAM, and WALTER RAUSCHENBUSCH, who preached the importance of a social consciousness, and proclaimed in the words of Herron that 'the Sermon on the Mount is the science of society.'

In 1889 a group led by such prominent ministers as W. D. P. BLISS and WASHINGTON GLADDEN and such political economists as RICHARD T. ELY met in Boston to organize the Society of Christian Socialists, stating their belief that socialism was the logical development of Christianity, and that the accumulation of wealth was contrary to the teachings of Christ. Since the movement had much in common with the aims of such working organizations as the KNIGHTS OF LABOR and such political groups as the POPULIST PARTY, it became national in scope, enlisted the aid of reformers, and gave rise to a vast body of writing, both imaginative and expository.

The sociological interest of the Reverend LYMAN ABBOTT was reflected in his *Outlook,* a journal of wide circulation, which invited the contributions of Ely, Jacob Riis, and Theodore Roosevelt, and emphasized the principle that 'tool-users' should be 'tool-owners.' Henry George and Edward Bellamy worked to the same end, and their influence in the cause of social betterment became worldwide.

Within Protestant churches in the U.S. the struggle between traditional orthodoxy and scientific inquiry had produced by the end of World War I a somewhat vague pattern, at first called 'modernism.' But the trend toward a social consciousness, which Christian Socialism strongly assisted, had begun to affect industrial relationships, and was reflected sharply during the 1930's by laws passed by Congress and thereafter by decisions rendered in the U.S. Supreme Court.

Studies of the movement include C. H. Hopkins, *The Rise of the Social Gospel in American Protestantism, 1865–1915* (1940), and James Dombrowski, *The Early Days of Christian Socialism* (1936).

CHRISTY, EDWIN P. (1815–62), established (*c.* 1842) the most popular of the early MINSTREL SHOWS in Buffalo, New York. For more than a decade his troupe toured the U.S. and England, receiving wide acclaim and establishing a routine that became standard. STEPHEN C. FOSTER sold first-performance rights for his songs to Christy, whose singing helped Foster's music gain its tremendous popularity.

Chrysler's Farm, Battle of (November 1813), was a minor engagement in the War of 1812. General JAMES WILKINSON, on his way from Sackets Harbor down the St. Lawrence to capture Montreal, directed General John P. Boyd to take the offensive against an enemy force that might hinder his advance. Boyd ineptly allowed 800 British to rout his own force of 2000 regulars. The rendezvous that Wilkinson had expected to make with General Wade Hampton became impossible, and Wilkinson had to go into winter quarters.

CHURCH, BENJAMIN (1639–1718), founder of Little Compton, Rhode Island, and a matchless guerrilla leader, was the most famous Indian fighter of his day. As captain (later colonel) of militia, he won special renown in 1676 for bringing an end to the main phase of KING PHILIP'S WAR by surrounding the camp of the Indian warrior, who was shot. In 1705, aged sixty-six, he led a regiment against the French on the Nova Scotia front during QUEEN ANNE'S WAR. Shortly before his death he dictated his memoirs to his son, Thomas Church, who organized his father's notes and published them as *Entertaining Passages Relating to Philip's War* (1716), a vivid account, widely read in its day, of Church's many hazardous expeditions.

CHURCH, BENJAMIN (1734–76), grandson of the redoubtable Indian fighter BENJAMIN CHURCH, after graduation from Harvard (1754) studied medicine in London, and established a lucrative practice in Boston. He was a member of the patriot Committee of Correspondence, served in the first Continental Congress, and in 1775 was appointed surgeon general of the Continental army. Previously suspected of disloyalty, he entered into treasonable correspondence with General Gage, and in October was court-martialed, tried, and sentenced to life imprisonment. On the plea of ill health he was paroled, and in the following year he sailed for the West Indies and perished in a vessel that foundered. His family was pensioned by George III.

CHURCH, Frederick Edwin (1826–1900), Connecticut-born landscape painter of the HUDSON RIVER SCHOOL, after study with Thomas Cole traveled from the north polar regions to South America, observing the picturesque. To gain a scientifically accurate eye, Church studied geology, meteorology, and optics. Excelling in panoramic scenes, he is characteristically represented by *The Heart of the Andes* (Metropolitan Museum), a huge canvas combining melodrama with literal detail. Church carried his romantic exuberance into designing *Olana,* the home he erected on the banks of the Hudson in Persian style. Its minarets, domes, and spires were embellished by a roof of red, black, and green.

Church and State were not separated in nine of the thirteen American colonies. The Congregational church was established by law in Massachusetts, Connecticut, and New Hampshire; the Anglican church in Maryland, Virginia, both Carolinas, and Georgia (and in New York City and three neighboring counties). After the Declaration of Independence (1776) and the formation of new state governments, separation of church and state came about as a matter of course where establishment had been more a theory than a fact. Among the Anglican groups only Virginia put up a fight to retain the establishment. There, after six years of bitter debate, James Madison took the lead in securing passage (1785) of Jefferson's 'Bill for Establishing Religious Freedom.' In New England disestablishment was much longer delayed. Nonconforming bodies, united with a growing liberal element in Congregationalism, at last brought about separation, first in Connecticut (1818) and New Hampshire (1819), and finally in Massachusetts (1833).

The First Amendment to the Federal Constitution states that 'Congress shall make no law respecting an establishment of religion, or prohibiting the free exercise thereof.' Some confusion and inconsistency has been made evident by interpretations of the Fourteenth Amendment, which has led the Supreme Court to enjoin the guarantees of the First upon the states. On the one hand, by such a decision (1954) schoolchildren may swear allegiance to one nation 'under God,' but by another (1962) they may not be compelled to hear Bible readings or be led in prayer. (The phrase *In God We Trust,* an inscription first used on U.S. coins during the Civil War, was designated by Congress in 1956 as the national motto.) The trend of Court decisions, however, has been toward the strict separation of church and state that Jefferson and Madison so vigorously championed.

Church of England, see *Protestant Episcopal Church.*

CHURCHILL, Winston Leonard Spencer (1874–1965), British statesman and historian, was son of Lord Randolph Churchill, onetime chancellor of the exchequer (1886) and leader in the House of Commons, and grandson of John Churchill, 7th Duke of Marlborough. His mother was the American Jennie Jerome. Educated at Harrow and Sandhurst, Churchill campaigned in the Sudan (1898) and in the South African War (1899). He entered Parliament in 1900 and thereafter was repeatedly a power in the British government. He was first lord of the admiralty (1911–15) at the outbreak of World War I, and later served as chancellor of the exchequer (1924–29). At the beginning of World War II (1939) he was again in the cabinet as first lord of the admiralty when he succeeded Neville Chamberlain as prime minister, a post he retained throughout the war (1940–45).

He met President Roosevelt at sea to sign the ATLANTIC CHARTER (1941) and twice addressed the U.S. Congress (December 1941, May 1942). He again visited the U.S. in 1946, and in a notable speech at Fulton, Missouri, he described the 'iron curtain' behind which Russia was creating satellite states. No British statesman in modern times has been so closely tied to the destiny of the U.S. In 1963 Congress bestowed American citizenship on Churchill, the only foreigner ever so honored by that body. At the time of Churchill's death, President Johnson ordered American flags to be flown at half staff, likewise a unique honor.

Cíbola, see *Coronado.*

Cimarron (Sp. *wild*), now the panhandle of Oklahoma, was the region settled during the 1880's by squatters and cattlemen. It was an unorganized territory, known as the Public Land Strip, or No Man's Land. The proposal in Congress (1887) to create the Territory of Cimarron failed, and in 1890 the region was incorporated into the Territory of Oklahoma.

Cincinnati, founded (1788) in southwestern Ohio, was incorporated as a village in 1802, and chartered as a city in 1819. Harriet Beecher Stowe lived in Cincinnati from 1832 to 1850, and there gathered much of her material for *Uncle Tom's Cabin* (1852). The city was an important station on the UNDERGROUND RAILROAD by which slaves escaped North, and was deeply sympathetic to the Union cause during the Civil War.

By 1840, Cincinnati was the 'Porkopolis of the West,' famous for its numerous slaughterhouses and cattle trail termini until succeeded by Chicago as the 'Hog Butcher for the World.'

Well located on the Ohio river to command western and southern markets, Cincinnati had become a manufacturing center by 1860, with a cosmopolitan population of 100,000 inhabitants, many of them German-born. The opening of trunk-line railroads in the 1870's, by reducing the importance of river trade, temporarily impeded the city's growth, but by expanding its land transportation facilities it regained its commercial prominence. With a population (1960) of 502,000 it is the second largest city in the state and the cultural center for an extensive area. Its city-manager government (since 1924) has been conspicuously successful. Hebrew Union College (est. 1875) is a major institution of Reform Judaism. The University of Cincinnati (est. 1873) is a municipal establishment; in 1965, with an endowment of $26,600,000 and a faculty of 1850, it enrolled 19,000 students.

Cincinnati, Society of the (est. 1783), was formed at the suggestion of General Henry Knox as a fraternal organization of Continental army officers. Washington served as its first president. It was attacked as an aristocratic military order with strong Federalist leanings, and thereby indirectly it encouraged the organization of democratic Tammany societies. It is perpetuated by a hereditary membership.

Cinema, see *Motion Pictures.*

C.I.O., see *Congress of Industrial Organizations.*

Circuit riders were preachers, usually Methodists, who needed but a horse and a saddlebag to carry the gospel to widely scattered settlements along the frontier. The system was extended after FRANCIS ASBURY came to America (1771) as a Wesleyan missionary, and it flourished especially during the first half of the 19th century. PETER CARTWRIGHT was a well-known circuit rider.

Circuits, Judicial, were established when the Federal judiciary system was created (1789). Two Supreme Court justices were assigned to each of three circuits (Eastern, Middle, Southern), and they were required to hold the courts twice a year, sitting with district judges. Since the Supreme Court had very little business to transact in the first few years, the justices found employment in riding the circuits. These tours were onerous; they extended from Georgia to New Hampshire, and roads and accommodations were often unpleasant. Some relief was granted in 1793 when but one judge was required to ride a circuit, which each did in turn without fixed assignment. With the development of the West, other circuits were added. In 1869 the system was altered by the appointment of Federal circuit judges. In the states, circuit courts existed from the outset, and in the early decades the judges of state courts were accompanied on their circuit rides by lawyers, who thus gained useful experience.

Circuses, as exhibitions of acrobats, clowns, freaks, menageries, began in the

U.S. as modest feats of horsemanship, and by 1800 became nomadic 'rolling shows.' By mid-19th century the traveling tent shows were visiting Europe. The showmanship of the circus impresario P. T. BARNUM was unmatched in his day, and the fame of his three-ring 'greatest show on earth,' founded in 1871, became world-wide. About 1890 WILLIAM F. CODY dramatized the horsemanship of the Great Plains in 'Buffalo Bill's Wild West Show,' since continued in exhibition roundups or RODEOS. By mid-20th century transportation costs and the growth of such entertainment media as television virtually ended the traveling circus, or confined it to spectacles presented in large arenas.

Cities during the colonial period were few and their growth relatively slow. In 1790 only five U.S. communities had more than 10,000 inhabitants (New York, 33,000; Boston, 18,000; Philadelphia, 16,000; Charleston, 16,000; Baltimore, 13,000). By 1820 the number of large cities had doubled, and New York had become a metropolis of 124,000. During the next 30 years expansion into the West created a substantial urban industry for the East, and thus while the population of the country in 1850 had risen 36 per cent, that of urban centers had jumped 90 per cent. Such concentration gave a more immediate and lasting character to America than westward migration.

In the 20th century urbanizing forces have become compelling. Mechanization has attracted labor into cities or 'megalopolis' enclaves, such as that now stretching from Nashua, New Hampshire, to Richmond, Virginia. The building of great hydroelectric plants in the Tennessee valley, the Missouri basin, on the Columbia in the Pacific Northwest and on the Colorado in the Southwest has introduced large industries in those areas, and is rapidly urbanizing sections which until recently had been rural or largely uninhabited. Despite the pressure of the Negro Revolution for desegregation and equal opportunity, many older industrial cities are to a rapidly increasing extent Negro, surrounded by a large ring of white suburbs, except for certain mixed urban renewal areas in the city proper, which attract middle-class whites.

In 1965 the total population of the U.S. was more than 194,000,000, and its cities of 25,000 or more had increased in the decade 1950–60 from 483 to 673, with the largest metropolitan areas surrounding New York (11,000,000), Los Angeles (7,000,000), Chicago (6,100,000), Philadelphia (4,300,000) and Detroit (3,700,000).

See *Albany, Atlanta, Baltimore, Boston, Cambridge, Charleston, Chicago, Cincinnati, Cleveland, Denver, Detroit, Houston, Kansas City, Los Angeles, New Orleans, New York, Philadelphia, Pittsburgh, Richmond, St. Louis, Salem, San Francisco, Seattle, Washington.*

Citizenship is the status of a freeman owing allegiance to and entitled to certain rights and privileges of a nation. When the American republic was established, the word connoted little either in law or practice. By terms of the Constitution, Americans became citizens of the U.S. and, strictly speaking, residents or inhabitants of their states. Yet the opinion of Justice Story that 'every citizen of a State is *ipso facto* a citizen of the U.S.' reflected the view, commonly held in the early years of the Republic, that claims of the states antecede those of the federal government, a view incorporated in the celebrated DRED SCOTT decision (1857). The Fourteenth Amendment (1868), enacted to settle the status of the Negro, reversed the order of precedence by establishing the principle that a member of any race, born in any place subject to the jurisdiction of the U.S., is an American citizen. The terms of the Amendment were not applied to the American Indian, since he lived tribally, but in 1924 Congress extended citizenship to all Indians. The Cable Act of 1922 protected women who married foreigners from losing their citizenship by that step.

Citizenship by naturalization is subject to the laws of Congress, and may be conferred either individually or collectively. For instance, the inhabitants of the Louisiana Territory were declared U.S. citizens by terms of the transfer of that territory from France to the U.S.

There have been but two honorary citizens of the U.S. In 1784 the Maryland General Assembly conferred citizenship on the Marquis de Lafayette and his male descendants in perpetuity.

In 1963 Congress bestowed American citizenship on Sir Winston Churchill.

City government, in the U.S., is established by state legislatures, and such governments have no sovereign power. Within the last few decades, in an effort to bring about MUNICIPAL REFORM, the development of the home rule principle has provided a degree of autonomy, the home rule charters being subject to review and revision by state legislatures. The three prevailing forms of city government are the mayor-council organization, the oldest and most universally adopted (an elected mayor as chief executive and the elected council as legislative body); the COMMISSION PLAN; and the CITY-MANAGER PLAN.

City-manager plan is a form of municipal government adopted by several hundred cities in the U.S. It was first developed by Staunton, Virginia, in 1908. A small council, chosen on a nonpartisan ballot, hires an administrative officer, or city manager, who appoints city officials and exercises full executive authority. To secure competent and disinterested administration, the council often chooses its manager from the outside. Generally regarded as the best form of municipal government, the plan has spread to county governments, and operates successfully wherever the managerial office remains outside of politics.

City planning began in America when William Penn in 1692 devised a plan for the eventual city of Philadelphia. He envisioned a tract of two square miles laid out with arterial highways and intersecting streets, reserving several open spaces for parks and public buildings. When PIERRE L'ENFANT planned the nation's capital on the Potomac in 1791, he superimposed on the checkerboard arrangement a number of radial avenues. In 1807 the upper portion of Manhattan (starting near the point where the streets begin to be numbered) was cut up into 2000 rectangular blocks, each 200 ft. wide. The monotonous symmetry of New York became the prevailing pattern for other cities.

The first city planning commission in the U.S. was that created in 1907 for Hartford, Connecticut. Three years later the National City Planning Association was founded. Since then, planning commissions, guided by trained engineers and architects, have been authorized in most large cities to enact ordinances which take into account transportation facilities, location of public buildings, recreation facilities, and zoning. (The first law empowering the authorities to divide the areas under their jurisdiction into zones for specified purposes was enacted in 1916 in New York City.) Thus the growth of cities is beginning to be more imaginatively planned. A major problem is still that of guiding the steadily increasing automobile traffic into and around cities, and arranging adequate garage accommodations.

See Lewis Mumford, *The City in History: Its Origins, Its Transformations, and Its Prospects* (1961), and John W. Reps, *The Making of Urban America* (1965).

Civil Aeronautics Authority (1938) was created by the Lea-McCarran Act as a five-member agency, appointed by the President. It is responsible for all matters affecting civilian air transportation. Under the governance of CAA is a five-member Board (CAB), also appointed by the President, which regulates the rules of flight, company agreements and finances, and passenger, freight and mail rates. Since 1940 CAA has operated within the Department of Commerce. In 1958 the Board's safety regulatory function was transferred to the newly created Federal Aviation Agency. The CAB investigates accidents for the FAA.

Civil Defense Administration, see *Federal Civil Defense Administration.*

Civil liberties is a term expressing the rights, privileges, and immunities of citizens in general, and extends to concepts by which citizens are protected by law from undue government interference. The idea of liberty formulated in Magna Carta (1215), carried to America by colonial charters, is specifically embodied in the national and state constitutions' Bills of Rights. The Fourteenth and Fifteenth Amendments extended civil liberties to Negroes.

On various occasions, in response to popular clamor, Congress has enacted laws to curb freedom of speech and of the press, notably in the ALIEN AND

SEDITION ACTS of 1798, the SEDITION ACT of 1918, and the SMITH ACT of 1940.

Important examples of Supreme Court interpretation of civil liberties are the SLAUGHTER HOUSE CASES (1873), the CIVIL RIGHTS CASES (1883), and BROWN *v.* BOARD OF EDUCATION (1954). The ESPIONAGE ACT of 1917, passed during World War I, went far beyond the needs of national safety and was not duplicated in World War II. Organizations such as the American Civil Liberties Union extend legal and financial aid to persons in need of support whenever they believe that their cases may in fact come within the purview of constitutional protection.

Historical studies of civil liberties include Zechariah Chafee, Jr., *Free Speech in the U.S.* (1941), and M. R. Konvitz, *The Constitution and Civil Rights* (1947).

Civil Rights Acts have been legislated in the U.S. from time to time since the Civil War, chiefly as efforts to enfranchise the Negro. The first (1866) bestowed citizenship upon the Negro and canceled the doctrine enunciated in the DRED SCOTT DECISION by granting citizenship to all persons born in the U.S. (except Indians, who were living tribally). Congress granted civil rights to Indians in 1924. In 1883 the Supreme Court, dealing with a series of CIVIL RIGHTS CASES, held the 1866 Act unconstitutional on the ground that it unwarrantably invaded states' rights. Similar invalidation of the Civil Rights Act of 1875 virtually ended Federal attempts to protect the Negro against discrimination by private persons for more than half a century.

The Civil Rights Act of 1957, empowering the Justice Department to sue on behalf of Negro voting rights in the South, was extended in the Civil Rights Act of 1960, which plugged some loopholes. But it was not until passage of the Civil Rights Act of 1964, complemented by the Voting Rights Act of 1965, that Congress granted power to Federal law enforcement agencies to insure the voting rights of Negroes which the Fifteenth Amendment had extended to them in 1870. Together those acts outlaw all racial discrimination in voting, employment, and public accommodations.

Civil Rights Cases (1883), a series of five, arose from suits brought in an attempt to implement one of the FORCE ACTS, which gave Negroes social equality in privately owned gathering places. They were invalidated by the U.S. Supreme Court on the ground that the Fourteenth Amendment was addressed only to deprivations of rights by the states and did not encompass private acts of discrimination. (Ironically, the only dissenting Justice was JOHN M. HARLAN, a Kentuckian and a former slaveholder.) The majority ruling in effect exiled Negroes to a state half slave and half free, since it ended Federal attempts to protect the Negro against discrimination by private persons unless the states themselves erected legal barriers. Not until the late 1950's, following the historic decision in BROWN *v.* BOARD OF EDUCATION (1954), was Harlan's reasoning adopted by rulings which reversed the 1883 concept of states' rights in matters of discrimination.

Civil Service includes all branches of the public service apart from the legislative, judicial, and armed services. The Federal Civil Service, created by Congress in 1789, is the largest body of employees within a single U.S. agency, some 3,500,000 persons by mid-20th century. The figure is more than doubled if state and municipal civil servants are included.

In 1853 Congress enacted laws requiring simple 'pass examinations' as a qualifying certificate for the service. The first effective reform was the creation of a CIVIL SERVICE COMMISSION (1883) to administer rules under a merit system. Similar reforms have been adopted by states and municipalities.

Through presidential direction, the merit system has been greatly expanded. President F. D. Roosevelt's Committee on Administrative Management (1936) led to a further extension and overhaul of the system. The Hatch Acts of 1939 protect Federal civil servants, and state employees paid by Federal funds, from intimidation by officeholders, and forbid employees to engage in 'pernicious political activities.'

Civil Service Commission, created by the Pendleton Act (1883), was the first of the FEDERAL REGULATORY COMMISSIONS. It was empowered to administer a new set of rules requiring many Federal appointments to be made according to a merit system, and by open competitive examinations. Such reform legislation, long sought and long overdue, had been blocked by powerful spoilsmen, but passage of the bill was assured by the death of President Garfield, who was assassinated by a disappointed office seeker. The Pendleton Act further prohibited assessment on officeholders for political purposes, and empowered the President to apply the rules to positions in the service not specified in the law. Since the Act immediately affected only about 10 per cent of the employees then at the disposal of Federal PATRONAGE, it was conspicuously ineffective. But in 1903 President Theodore Roosevelt promulgated a major set of Civil Service Rules and Orders, and later amendments broadened the merit classifications. The merit system was extended to first-, second-, and third-class postmasters in 1938, and in 1940 the President was empowered to bring into the competitive service a large number of positions previously exempt from classification.

Civil War, officially called the War of the Rebellion, and known in the South as the War Between the States, was a sectional struggle with roots in such a complex of political, economic, and social differences that no single basic cause can be specified. While historians may not agree as to the chief cause of the war, they do recognize that only a minority of Southerners owned any slaves. Some blame fanaticism and irresponsible politicians for the war, while others stress the factor of race, implying that the Southerners wished for a stringent white supremacy system, especially in the heavily Negro Deep South. Still others think that southern nationalists had increasingly come to believe that only by independence could the South free itself from northern domination.

Southern economy was founded on agriculture and the plantation system, and its social order was dependent upon SLAVERY. The North, a free society with small farms and rapidly expanding industry, had no need for the 'peculiar institution,' and was increasingly in disagreement with the South on slavery issues created by territorial expansion. The MISSOURI COMPROMISE (1820) was an attempt to ease the North-South tensions, but it failed as a long-term solution. During the 1830's the ABOLITION MOVEMENT deepened sectional bitterness, and the irritations were exacerbated when Texas, enormous in area, was admitted to the Union (1845) as a slave state, thus rousing both those who feared the political dominance of the South and those who disapproved the extension of slave territory.

The COMPROMISE OF 1850 ended the era of mutual concession. Daniel Webster and Henry Clay were succeeded by such intransigent sectionalists as Charles Sumner and S. P. Chase in the North and Jefferson Davis and Robert Toombs in the South. Passions became inflamed by the KANSAS-NEBRASKA ACT (1854) and by the Supreme Court decision in the DRED SCOTT CASE (1857), which invalidated the Missouri Compromise. The angry challenge of the abolitionist John Brown was matched in the South by the intemperate proslavery acts and utterances of 'fire-eaters.' The 'irrepressible conflict' was clearly foreshadowed when several states in the Deep South openly asserted during the presidential campaign of 1860 that the election of a 'Black Republican' would be a just reason for dissolving the Union, and backed their threat of secession by legislative appropriations to raise military forces. Though states further north believed that grievances could be remedied within the Union, South Carolina precipitated a crisis by calling a state convention after Lincoln's election and unanimously voting (20 December 1860) to secede from the Union, an action followed in the next two months by all the CONFEDERATE STATES except Virginia, Arkansas, Tennessee, and North Carolina. The war became inevitable when, in February 1861, the MONTGOMERY CONVENTION drafted the Confederate Constitution and elected Jefferson Davis provisional president. The bombardment of Fort SUMTER (12 April 1861) opened hostilities, and drove the remaining four slave states to the side of the Confederacy.

No struggle in world history, until the two recent World Wars, has matched the Civil War in scope. Its operations were spread over thousands of miles, and some 1,600,000 Federals were pitted against nearly 1,000,000 Confederates. Both sides fought with relentless determination, and the battles and skirmishes (of which 2400 are named) were among the bloodiest of any engagements in modern times. The invading Union armies sustained more than 600,000 casualties; the Confederate armies nearly half that number. The audacity of the South would seem to have preordained its defeat. It was a loose confederation of 9,000,000 persons, one-third of whom were slaves who might become an immense liability if the slavery issue could be effectively exploited. With an inadequate railroad system, few good harbors, and an agrarian economy, it was challenging a federated union of 22,000,000 to mortal combat. The North had military and naval superiority, better transportation facilities, and overwhelming financial and industrial reserves. The North was stirred by an equal determination, which the South underestimated, to resolve the issue by war. Senator James M. Mason of Virginia accurately defined the tragic necessity on the eve of its commencement as 'a war of sentiment and opinion by one form of society against another form of society.'

Yet unavailing as the effort proved, the Southerners believed they had taken excellently calculated risks. It was an empire nearly the size of Europe, with interior lines of communication, however inadequate, and its enormous stretches of coastal areas would make effective blockades extremely difficult. An immensely important exporter of cotton, it had good reason to count on foreign assistance. It could afford to lose battles, and indeed campaigns, for even if it were forced to sue for a negotiated peace, the North would have lost the war. Indeed, the best informed Europeans, who had witnessed many recent and successful revolutions won against greater odds, believed that the South would triumph. But Europeans, like Southerners, did not fathom the depth of the North's devotion to the idea of Union, the unique imponderable which gave the North moral determination to push through to final victory in spite of repeated tactical defeats.

General Winfield Scott advised Lincoln that 300,000 men and at least two years would be required to begin the conquest of the South. But the President followed the advice of Secretary of War Stanton, and on 15 April 1861 called for 75,000 volunteers for a 90-day enlistment, to supplement an army of 16,000 regulars. Three weeks later Lincoln sought to double the number, and the War Department followed the traditional method of creating an army by state quotas. In July Congress gave the President authority to recruit 500,000 men for the duration of the war. The failure of sufficient numbers to answer the President's call led to the passage in March 1863 of the first national CONSCRIPTION Act, a complex and inequitable system of recruiting which shortly led to the tragic DRAFT RIOTS. The CONFEDERATE ARMY, similarly recruited, was created by a mass levy on southern manhood.

In fighting capacity no two armies in history have been more closely matched. The North had far less effective numerical superiority than the figures suggest, since it was fighting offensive warfare and had to maintain long lines of communication. The theaters of war, determined by Confederate geography, were the nearly equal eastern, western, and trans-Mississippi areas. The eastern region embraced the Appalachian-Susquehanna-Chesapeake Bay theater, in which the spectacular campaigns took place, and where were located the two capitals, Washington and Richmond. Operations beyond the Mississippi were of small consequence, but the fate of the Confederacy was sealed when, in the territory west of the Appalachians, the Mississippi was blocked by Grant at VICKSBURG in 1863, allowing Sherman to swing eastward through Georgia to the sea.

Since the capture of the capitals had enormous propaganda value when war was engaged, the rallying cry 'On to Richmond' led to the first major encounter, the battle of BULL RUN (July 1861), a humiliating rout for the Federals, which gave the North reason for sober assessment of the nature and duration of the conflict, and stiffened the Southerners' determination to accept rigorous discipline lest invasion destroy their homes and way of life. In November General George B. McClellan was appointed to succeed the aging Scott, and began training his Army of the POTOMAC for the purpose of seizing Richmond.

Meanwhile a joint military and naval operation had been undertaken to blockade the southern coasts and prevent privateering. The CONFEDERATE NAVY, as such, did not possess mobility, but during the first year of the war some 800 southern vessels, with Nassau in the Bahamas as the major supply port, evaded the Union blockade, with chances of capture reckoned at one in ten (raised in the last year of the war to one in three). Between August and May 1861–62 the major bases between Cape Hatteras and New Orleans were rendered inactive by the Union blockade, although Wilmington, North Carolina, remained a hole during most of the war. In March 1862 occurred the battle of HAMPTON ROADS, the historic engagement of ironclads. The brilliant campaign of Commodore David Farragut in the Gulf sealed the mouth of the Mississippi.

In April 1862 Lincoln gave McClellan the opportunity to conduct his PENINSULAR CAMPAIGN, an attempt to capture Richmond. But General Lee compelled McClellan to withdraw, and by inflicting a second defeat at Bull Run during the summer opened the way for a Confederate invasion of Maryland. The Union success in September at ANTIETAM gave Lincoln the propitious moment to utter the EMANCIPATION PROCLAMATION, which ended all danger of foreign recognition of the Confederacy because it brought Lincoln the support of the liberal opinion throughout the world. But McClellan's failure to pursue Lee after Antietam, and thereby win the war, led to the appointment of Ambrose Burnside as McClellan's successor. The year closed with the shattering defeat of Burnside at FREDERICKSBURG, and his replacement by Joseph Hooker.

From the beginning the problem for the North on the diplomatic front had been to insure the neutrality of European countries, particularly the maritime nations, England and France. British opinion at first had been divided. All Englishmen viewed slavery as an anachronism, but commercial interests looked for free-trade markets in the South, and manufacturers could benefit from the defeat of northern competitors. As months passed, British dependence on northern wheat (which they could get) outweighed their dependence on southern cotton (increasingly difficult to import), and England remained officially neutral. Lincoln took proper action in the TRENT AFFAIR, British shipyards stopped outfitting Confederate warships, and after the war England indemnified the U.S. by settlement of the ALABAMA CLAIMS. Though Napoleon III took advantage of the war to intervene in Mexican affairs, and tacitly allowed French shipyards to build Confederate sloops, France officially took no side. Furthermore, public opinion, newly emerging throughout Europe, was unsympathetic to slavery.

The Confederacy was being entirely financed by issues of paper money, and the production of cotton, its sole export, rapidly began to drop. The Union, though financed by paper money issues and loans, was further supported by a small tax on incomes and by levies on sales and manufacturing. Wool production in the North became a venture industry, and iron mills and agricultural commodities were profitable. Its labor needs were met by steady immigration, encouraged by the CONTRACT LABOR ACT of 1864; some 800,000 Europeans emigrated to northern ports during the war, and half of them served in the Union army.

During 1862 General Grant achieved the first major Union victory of the war, by securing the surrender of Forts HENRY and DONELSON in the western theater, and after the bloody battle of SHILOH the Federals commanded the Mississippi down to Vicksburg. The encounter of D. C. Buell and his Ohioans with Braxton Bragg in October at PERRYVILLE, though indecisive, led to the engagement at MURFREESBORO, which ended Bragg's invasion of Kentucky.

The eastern campaigns in 1863 turned on the two great battles of CHANCELLORSVILLE and GETTYSBURG. At Gettysburg, after three days of memorable fighting, General George G. Meade won the decisive battle of the war (3 July 1863). Grant's capture of VICKSBURG on the following day gave Union forces command of the entire Mississippi, cut the Confederacy in two, and opened the way for the CHATTANOOGA CAMPAIGN. Thenceforth the South was on the defensive, and the struggle was a test of endurance. In an attempt to capture Richmond during the summer of 1864, Grant embarked on the bitter WILDERNESS CAMPAIGN, during which the fighting settled down to a war of attrition. Meanwhile General W. T. Sherman moved east from Tennessee to begin his invasion of Georgia. The success of his ATLANTA CAMPAIGN, ending with his devastating march to the sea, lifted Union morale and contributed to the Republican victory in the presidential campaign.

The shrunken Army of Northern Virginia under Lee and the Army of Tennessee under J. E. Johnston, caught between Grant's Army of the Potomac and Sherman's Army of the Tennessee, could not withstand the pressure. When on 1 April 1865 General P. H. Sheridan won the last important battle of the war at FIVE FORKS, Petersburg fell and Richmond was captured. On 9 April, Lee surrendered to Grant at APPOMATTOX, and the war was effectively ended. Lincoln, whose policies might have made a constructive reunion possible, died of an assassin's bullet on 15 April, and the 'tragic era' of RECONSTRUCTION began. The South was economically and physically prostrate, and while slavery was abolished the social problems it had raised remained unsolved.

See Allan Nevins, *The War for the Union* (2 vols., 1960).

Civil War Amendments to the U.S. Constitution, intended primarily to deal with the status of the Negro, are the THIRTEENTH (1865), which abolished slavery; the FOURTEENTH (1868), which established Negro citizenship; and the FIFTEENTH (1870), conferring suffrage. In a series of cases arising after their adoption, notably U.S. *v.* CRUIKSHANK (1876), U.S. *v.* HARRIS (1883), and the CIVIL RIGHTS CASES (1883), the Supreme Court held that the Amendments did not authorize the federal government to protect citizens from each other, that state legislation was valid so long as it was not discriminatory, and that 'discrimination' applied to civil, not social, rights. The Court's interpretation of discrimination underwent major revision in the decision rendered in BROWN *v.* BOARD OF EDUCATION (1954).

Civil War Amnesty was granted first as an aid to Reconstruction. President Andrew Johnson in May 1865 carried forward the measures outlined by Lincoln in his proclamation (December 1863) that, with some exceptions, persons who would swear to support the Constitution and the Union would receive pardon. The purpose was to give southern state governments a basis for re-establishing themselves. The Amnesty Act of 1872 restored to full political privilege almost all southern whites. In 1898 Congress restored the franchise to all ex-Confederates.

Civil Works Administration (CWA) was established (1933) as an emergency unemployment relief program to put 4,000,000 jobless persons to work on Federal, state, and local make-work projects. Administered by Harry L. Hopkins, it was absorbed in 1934 by the FEDERAL EMERGENCY RELIEF ADMINISTRATION.

Civilian Conservation Corps (1933) was established by Congress as a relief measure during the depression. Jobless young men, under the direction of army officers, were enrolled in work camps where they engaged in projects to preserve, restore, and increase the natural resources of the U.S. Some 2,000,000 persons were employed during the decade. In 1943 the CCC was absorbed into the FEDERAL WORKS AGENCY.

CLAIBORNE, WILLIAM (*c.* 1587–*c.* 1677), the lord of Kent Island in Chesapeake Bay, arrived in Virginia in 1621, and at various times served the colony as secretary of state and as a member of the council. He built his plantation into a small trading empire by playing off Virginians against Marylanders, Parliamentarians against Royalists, and settlers against Indians. However, in 1638 he lost his petty war with the proprietor, Lord Baltimore, to retain control over the Isle of Kent. In 1644–46 he exploited the anti-Catholic feeling in Maryland by inciting an insurrection which drove the governor out. Claiborne controlled the province, though he failed to regain Kent Island. Shrewd and calculating, he was the most enterprising merchant among early Virginians.

CLARK, Champ [James Beauchamp] (1850–1921), after practicing law in Missouri, served for many years in the U.S. House of Representatives (1893–95, 1897–1921). He led the 'congressional revolution' of 1910 to strip the excessive powers of the speakership held by the ultraconservative JOSEPH CANNON. Clark was Speaker (1911–19) when the Democrats came to power. During the sharp debate over the pending reciprocity agreement with Canada, he angered Canadian nationalists by saying that he supported the measure because he hoped to see the day 'when the American flag will float on every square foot of the British North American possessions clear to the North Pole.' This tactless jingoism helped to defeat reciprocity. At the Democratic National Convention in 1912 he had the support of a majority of the delegates, but failing to capture the necessary two-thirds, he lost the presidential nomination to Woodrow Wilson. Upon America's entrance into World War I, Speaker Clark reflected the views of many of his Missouri constituents (especially in St. Louis) when he fought the draft, declaring that 'there is precious little difference between a conscript and a convict.'

CLARK, George Rogers (1752–1818), born in Virginia, made his first journey into the Old Northwest (1772) as surveyor for the Ohio Company. In 1777, when he was commissioned a lieutenant colonel of Virginia militia, with 175 men he undertook an expedition against the British on the Illinois frontier, capturing Kaskaskia and Vincennes (1778) in the only successful campaign that American forces conducted in that year. Although Vincennes was lost in a British counterattack after Clark had left, he recaptured it in 1779, and forced the surrender of the British commander. He held much of the territory for the duration of the war. Although claims have been advanced that Clark's successes put the U.S. in a position to demand cession of the Northwest in the definitive TREATY OF PARIS of 1783, there is no evidence that the peace negotiators were concerned with Clark's exploits, which were actually impressive and historically significant.

His later years were unhappy. As a speculator in western lands, with dubious claims to portions still held by Spain, he accepted a commission from Citizen Genêt in a French *Armée du Mississippi* for the conquest of Louisiana. When the U.S. forced the recall of Genêt, the scheme collapsed, and Clark was in financial straits. Disappointed at what he regarded as his country's ingratitude, after 1798 he lived in comparative isolation, an embittered alcoholic.

See John E. Bakeless, *Background to Glory: The Life of George Rogers Clark* (1957).

CLARK, Mark Wayne (1896–), a graduate of the U.S. Military Academy (1917), commanded (1943–44) the U.S. Fifth Army in North Africa and Italy, and as a full general served as head of the U.S. army of occupation in Austria (1945–47). In 1952–53 he was supreme commander of United Nations forces in Korea. After 1954 he served as president of The Citadel Military College of South Carolina.

CLARK, William (1770–1838), a younger brother of GEORGE ROGERS CLARK, entered the U.S. Army as a lieutenant of infantry in 1792. With Meriwether Lewis he commanded the famous LEWIS AND CLARK EXPEDITION (1803–6) across the continent, and later headed surveys, notably into the Yellowstone. After serving as territorial governor of Missouri (1813–21), he was for the rest of his life Superintendent of Indian Affairs.

Clark University, at Worcester, Massachusetts, opened in 1889 under the leadership of G. STANLEY HALL as a pioneer graduate school specializing in psychology and education. Clark College for undergraduates was added in 1902. The University later established a graduate school of geography (1920), and a women's college (1941). In 1965, with an endowment of $13,000,000 and a faculty of 150, it enrolled 2300 students.

CLARKE, James Freeman (1810–88), after graduation from Harvard (1829) and Harvard Divinity School, became pastor (1833–40) of the Unitarian church at Louisville, Kentucky, where for three years (1836–39) he edited the *Western Messenger,* the most distinguished Western journal of its day, and one to which such Easterners as Emerson and William E. Channing contributed. He returned to Boston in 1841 to help found the (Unitarian) Church of the Disciples, which he served as pastor until his death. He had carried TRANSCENDENTALISM into the West, and he was an active liberal reformer. His popular *Ten Great Religions* (2 vols., 1871–83) typifies the 'free and catholic' spirit which he sought to foster, and drew attention to comparative religions at a time when orthodoxies were also being challenged by DARWINISM.

CLARKE, JOHN (1609–76), emigrated from Suffolk, England, to Boston in 1637. His sympathy with Anne Hutchinson in the ANTINOMIAN CONTROVERSY led him to move in 1639 to Rhode Island, where he helped found Newport, and where he served as Baptist minister and physician. With his friend Roger Williams he returned to England in 1651 to plead the cause of Rhode Island liberties, and there he remained until 1664, acting as colonial agent. His *Ill Newes from New England* (1652), arraigning the orthodoxy of the Boston leaders, helped secure the liberal charter of 1663 from Charles II. On his return to Rhode Island he served the colony in the general assembly (1664–69), and thereafter was thrice elected deputy governor.

Clarke-McNary Act, see *National Forests.*

Classic revival became a dominating influence in architecture before 1800, stimulated throughout Europe and the U.S. by archaeological discoveries in Greece and Italy during the mid-18th century. The Roman revival, chiefly 1785–1820, was quickened in America largely by the analogy between the ancient and the new republic. Thomas Jefferson modeled the Virginia state capitol (1789) on the Maison Carrée, the Roman temple at Nîmes. The Greek revival, principally spanning the years 1820–60, was introduced by BENJAMIN LATROBE, whose design for the Bank of Pennsylvania (1799) was modeled after a Greek Ionic temple.

The two styles eventually allied themselves in a Greco-Roman form. In no country was the Greek fashion in such vogue as in the U.S., where classic colonnades were appended alike to state capitols, county courthouses, and modest farm houses.

CLAY, HENRY (1777–1852), Virginia-born statesman, after three years of formal schooling, studied law, was admitted to the bar (1797), and soon built up a lucrative practice at Lexington, Kentucky, where he began a political career which lasted for half a century. After twice serving brief unfilled terms in the U.S. Senate he was sent to Congress, where he was immediately chosen Speaker (1811) by the 'WAR HAWKS.' He returned to his seat after serving on the commission which negotiated the Treaty of GHENT, and again presided as Speaker (1815–20, 1823–25), gaining the sobriquet 'Great Pacificator' for his eloquent defense of the MISSOURI COMPROMISE (1820). He won support for his 'AMERICAN SYSTEM' by securing (against strong opposition) an upward revision (1824) of the protective TARIFF OF 1816.

In the presidential campaign of 1824, Clay, who took fourth place in an election that produced no majority, was compelled by virtue of his office to cast the deciding ballot. An intense dislike for Andrew Jackson led him to vote for J. Q. Adams, despite instructions from Kentucky to the contrary, and notwithstanding the fact that, like Jackson, he had western interests at heart. When Adams gave Clay the State portfolio, John Randolph raised the cry of 'corrupt bargain,' and the consequent duel (though bloodless) hampered Clay's future political fortunes.

Embittered by Jackson's victory in 1828, Clay threatened to retire from politics, but loyal constituents elected him to the Senate (1831), and for the next twenty years, whether in or out of office, he dictated Whig policies. Again presidential candidate in 1832, Clay was overwhelmingly defeated by Jackson, whose principal issue had been his war on the BANK OF THE U.S. Clay's vexation this time was absorbed by the nullification crisis, during which Clay presented the COMPROMISE TARIFF OF 1833, adopted in an effort to mend the break in the Democratic party. He declined the Presidential nomination in 1836. No friend of slavery, he made clear that he was also an enemy of ABOLITION, and when told that his public utterances on the issue would injure him politically, he replied with the oft-quoted remark that he 'had rather be right than be President.' Clay declined to enter Harrison's cabinet as Secretary of State (1841), hoping to lead the Senate forces by which he might re-establish the Bank of the U.S., but the sudden death of Harrison brought into office John Tyler, who vetoed all of Clay's bank measures, thereby throwing Clay into such a rage that he resigned from the Senate (1842).

Openly opposed to the annexation of Texas, Clay became the party nominee (1844) for the third time. He campaigned against the Democratic expansionist James K. Polk, who so crushingly defeated Clay that the Whig party withheld from Clay the 1848 nomination. Returned to the Senate in 1849, Clay, as the representative of a divided border state, opposed extremists, and his magnificent oratory favoring the COMPROMISE OF 1850 earned him a second sobriquet as 'The Great Compromiser.'

A man of fine intelligence and unquestioned integrity, Clay was persuasive by eloquence and charm, although his imperious combativeness on occasion put him as well as his party at a disadvantage. Of the great triumvirate (Clay, Webster, and Calhoun), Clay is rememered for his personal magnetism, and, like Webster, for his unswerving devotion to a Union which he ceaselessly labored to preserve.

A classic biography is that by Carl Schurz (2 vols., 1887). More recent studies are those by Bernard Mayo [to 1812] (1937), G. G. Van Deusen (1937), and Clement Eaton (1957).

CLAY, LUCIUS [DUBIGNON] (1897–), a graduate of the U.S. Military Academy (1918), served as an engineering officer in many administrative posts. After World War II he was appointed commander in chief (1947–49) of U.S. forces in Europe, and military governor of the U.S. Zone in Germany, where he countered the Russian blockade of Berlin with a massive airlift. Retired in 1949 as a full general, in 1961 he served again in Germany, this time as special envoy to advise on the East-West crisis in the divided city of Berlin.

CLAYTON, JOHN (*c.* 1685–1773), English-born clerk of Gloucester county, Virginia, gathered the large number of plant specimens used by the Dutch botanist J. F. Gronovius for his *Flora Virginica* (1739–43), the leading colonial treatise on American botany. A collector and not a systematizer, Clayton, like JOHN BARTRAM, corresponded with Linnaeus, who drew extensively on Clayton's discoveries.

Clayton Antitrust Act (1914), leveled at the evils of BUSINESS CONSOLIDATION, filled gaps not covered by the SHERMAN ANTITRUST ACT (1890). It forbade practices which 'substantially tended' to lessen competition by outlawing price fixing, interlocking directorates, and acquisition of stock in competing companies. Provision of the act exempting labor unions from its terms (because a human being is not a commodity) led Samuel Gompers to hail it as 'labor's charter of freedom.' Although it banned restraining orders or injunctions in labor disputes, except in special instances, it did not anticipate SECONDARY BOYCOTTS or 'YELLOW DOG CONTRACTS.' In fact, the first Supreme Court decision (1921) based on the labor provisions of the act in the DUPLEX PRINTING PRESS case upheld the validity of secondary boycotts, which were not declared illegal until passage of the TAFT-HARTLEY ACT (1947).

Clayton-Bulwer Treaty (1850), negotiated by Secretary of State John M. Clayton and the British emissary Sir Henry Bulwer, was an agreement between the U.S. and Britain that their respective governments would jointly guarantee the neutrality of a canal, presumably to be built soon through Nicaragua. The terms specified that neither government would seek control of the isthmus, erect fortifications there, or acquire Central American colonies. Though the Senate was at once condemned for ratifying a self-denying ordinance, the fact remains that Britain had acquired interests in Central America during the 1840's without protest from the U.S., and the treaty was a reasonable compromise, since at the time the U.S. was seeking to build an isthmian waterway. The treaty was never popular, because it violated the spirit of the Monroe Doctrine. In 1901 it was superseded by the HAY-PAUNCEFOTE TREATY.

CLEMENS, SAMUEL LANGHORNE (1835–1910), grew up in Hannibal, Missouri, where he enjoyed the adventurous boyhood which he later immortalized. His pseudonym, Mark Twain (meaning 'two fathoms deep'), he derived from his experiences as a Mississippi riverboat pilot. Growing success as newspaper reporter after the Civil War launched him on a lifetime career as lecturer. Clemens at his best has no peer in his ability to write with humor and realism of the frontier he knew, recreated in the three classics *Tom Sawyer* (1876), *Life on the Mississippi* (1883), and *Huckleberry Finn* (1884).

Clements Library (The William L. Clements Library of American History) was the gift (1923) to the University of Michigan by the Michigan industrialist W. L. Clements (1861–1934). One of the leading research institutions in the U.S. specializing in Americana, it has a noteworthy collection of maps printed before 1800. Its manuscript gatherings relating to the War of Independence are unexcelled.

Clermont, see *Fulton, Robert.*

CLEVELAND, [STEPHEN] GROVER (1837–1908), 22nd and 24th President of the U.S. (1885–89, 1893–97), was born in Caldwell, New Jersey. His father, a Presbyterian minister, died in Clinton, New York, when Grover was only fifteen. He apprenticed himself to a law office, was admitted to the bar (1859), and made a name for himself as the 'veto mayor' of Buffalo, New York (1881), because of his administrative reforms. Elected Democratic governor of New York (1882), Cleveland vigorously opposed the corrupt machine politics of TAMMANY, and as a 'clean government' candidate for President won the 1884 election against James G. Blaine in a campaign notable for its close contest.

As President, Cleveland emphasized civil service reform, vetoed the disgraceful Civil War pension bills, and opposed the spoilsmen of his own party who tried to push through 'pork barrel' legislation. As his party's standard bearer in 1888, he supported lower tariffs, and although he won popular support at the polls on the issue, he lost the electoral vote to Benjamin Harrison.

In 1892 Cleveland again won election, chiefly by the support of those who were irritated by the high McKinley Tariff Act of 1890. The panic of 1893, the passage of the Wilson-Gorman Tariff Act of 1894 without Cleveland's signature, and Cleveland's effort to preserve the gold standard against insurgent party opposition created a gulf between the President and the radical Democrats, which was never bridged. The rift was widened when Cleveland used Federal troops in the Pullman strike (1894), and thereby alienated labor. In foreign affairs the Cleveland administration enlarged the scope of the Monroe Doctrine by its stand in the VENEZUELA BOUNDARY DISPUTE. By 1896 the 'silver Democrats,' under the control of Bryan, dominated the party.

Cleveland's stature derives chiefly from his stubborn championship of tariff reform and of honesty and efficiency in the civil service. His strength of character made him the most distinguished President between Lincoln and Theodore Roosevelt, and his counsel continued to be in demand after his retirement.

See Allan Nevins, *Grover Cleveland: A Study in Courage* (1932).

Cleveland, on Lake Erie, was laid out in 1796, when the Connecticut lawyer Moses Cleaveland (1754–1806), acting for the Connecticut Land Company, led a group into the WESTERN RESERVE region of Ohio to develop the chief settlement. Its growth followed the completion of the Ohio and Erie Canal (1832), and it was granted a city charter in 1836. One of the great ore ports in the country, it is also a center of iron and steel production. John D. Rockefeller established his oil holdings in Cleveland, and Mark Hanna made it the center of his venture in steel. The reforms inaugurated in its municipal government by Mayor Tom L. Johnson helped create civic consciousness throughout the nation. With a population (1960) of 876,000, Cleveland is one of the largest cities in the U.S. Its leading institution of higher learning is WESTERN RESERVE UNIVERSITY.

Cleveland Museum of Art (est. 1913) is supported by a large endowment and performs important educational functions. Its holdings include distinctive oriental acquisitions, the Guelph Treasure of the House of Brunswick, the Holden collection of European paintings, and the Wade collection of decorative art.

Cliff Dwellers, ancestors of the present PUEBLO INDIANS, flourished *c.* A.D. 900–1300. They built elaborate and highly defensible dwellings on the ledges of canyons and on top of the flat mesas of the Southwest. They developed a closely knit communal farming society, with expertly irrigated fields. Their culture evolved from the BASKET MAKERS and was ended presumably by a severe drought (1275–99) and invasion by the Navaho and the Apache from the north. Best known survivals of their villages are the 300 dwellings located in Mesa Verde National Park in Colorado.

CLINTON, DE WITT (1769–1828), son of General James Clinton (1733–1812), who served with distinction throughout the War of Independence, after graduation from Columbia (1786) was admitted to the New York bar. With the political support of his uncle GEORGE CLINTON, he served in the state legislature and was elected to the U.S. Senate (1802–3), where he introduced the Twelfth Amendment. While serving as mayor of New York City (1803–15) he also held state offices, finally as lieutenant governor (1811–13).

With support of the Federalists, Clinton won the fusion nomination for President in 1812, but lost the election to Madison. Thereafter he devoted himself to the cultural and industrial growth of his state, which twice made him governor (1817–21, 1825–28). He energetically sponsored the Erie and the Champlain-Hudson canals, and his active opposition to Tammany and the ALBANY REGENCY and his support of the public school movement and legal reform distinguish him as a public servant. He helped found the New York Historical Society (1804), and became its president in the first year of his governorship.

CLINTON, GEORGE (1739–1812), after studying law in New York City practiced in Ulster county, and was elected to the New York assembly, where he became a leader of the patriot party (1768). He served as a delegate to the Second Continental Congress (1775–76). While commanding as a brigadier general in the Revolution (1777), he lost Forts Clinton and Montgomery on the Hudson to SIR HENRY CLINTON. He was a framer of the New York constitution and the state's first governor (1777–95, 1801–4). An outspoken leader of the Anti-Federalists, he opposed the Federal Constitution, unwilling to surrender either his own power or any significant part of state sovereignty.

With Robert Livingston and Aaron Burr he helped Jefferson to organize the Democratic-Republican party, and served as Vice President (1805–12) during Jefferson's second administration and Madison's first. Clinton's deciding vote (1811), as president of the Senate, killed the bill to recharter the Bank of the U.S., and registered his old animosity against Hamilton and his contempt for Madison. He died in office.

CLINTON, SIR HENRY (*c.* 1738–95), son of Admiral George Clinton, governor of Newfoundland and subsequently of New York (1743–53), as a young officer served in the French and Indian War. His historic career began when he arrived in Boston (1775) with reinforcements of British troops, took part in the battles of BUNKER HILL and LONG ISLAND (1776), after which he was made a lieutenant general. Knighted in 1777, he succeeded to full command of British forces in America (1778), when Howe was recalled after the British defeat at SARATOGA.

At once concentrating his forces in New York, he substituted foraging expeditions for regular campaigns after defeating Washington in the battle of MONMOUTH, and was personally in charge during the siege of Charleston (1780). He returned to New York, where his fear of an attack by Washington in 1781 led him to withhold troops from Cornwallis, whose surrender at Yorktown ended the war. Superseded by SIR GUY CARLETON, Clinton returned to England and engaged in an acrimonious paper war with Cornwallis on the issue of losing the fighting one. Clinton was thought to have come off second best and he rapidly passed into oblivion, but students of history are inclined to revalue the situation to Clinton's credit.

Clipper ships, long, narrow wooden vessels with high masts and enormous sail area, were developed in the second quarter of the 19th century. Built principally at Baltimore and in New England (*c.* 1830–60), they were devised almost solely for the New York–China tea trade and for travel to the California gold mines. No sailing vessels of their day matched their speed and beauty. In 1850 *Sea Witch* cut the sailing time from New York to San Francisco round Cape Horn from 159 days to 97. The record of 89 days for the same trip was set by *Flying Cloud,* built by DONALD MC KAY in 1851, and has never been surpassed by a sailing vessel. The *Oriental* of New York was greeted at the West India docks in London, 97 days from Hong Kong, by crowds, and by a leader in the *Times* challenging British shipbuilders to match Yankee ingenuity.

In 1852 *Sovereign of the Seas,* the largest clipper built, made a day's run of 411 nautical miles. The record of 436 nautical miles, made by *Lightning,* another product of McKay's shipyard, was never equaled by a sailing ship. The advent of steam doomed the clippers, but the name was given appropriate extension; it was applied to the first great airships flying the ocean routes.

Cloisters, The, museum of medieval art in Fort Tryon Park, New York City, is a branch of the Metropolitan Museum of Art (and the gift of John D. Rockefeller, Jr.). Opened in 1938, the buildings include four French cloisters, a Romanesque chapel, and a 12th-century chapter house. To its objects of art, gathered in France by the sculptor George Grey Barnard, have been added further examples of stained glass, sculpture, painting, metalwork, furniture, and tapestries.

Closed shop, as distinguished from OPEN SHOP, is an establishment in which union membership is a condition of employment. Early TRADE UNIONS in the U.S. set up closed shops. Public opinion throughout the 19th century was hostile toward labor unions, and the closed shop was denounced as 'un-American.' So strong was the effort to destroy the power of the unions that in the 1920's, when unions often lost their strikes, union membership declined from 5,000,000 to 3,600,000. Conditions were sharply altered by the creation in 1935 of the NATIONAL LABOR RELATIONS BOARD, which functions to define and remedy UNFAIR LABOR PRACTICES and determine the rules for COLLECTIVE BARGAINING.

Closure, in parliamentary practice, applies to rules for limiting or stopping debate. In Congress, by bringing the matter to a vote, the House of Representatives may resort to the five-minute rule, whereby speeches may be curtailed, though members retain the right to publish their full addresses in the *Congressional Record.* In 1917 the Senate ruled that a one-hour limit on speeches might be invoked by an affirmative two-thirds vote of those present and voting after petition by at least sixteen Senators. Although repeatedly challenged on the ground that filibusters are thereby encouraged, the Senate rule continues in force. In all its history, the Senate has approved closure only seven times, most recently in 1965.

Clothing industry, see *Textile industry.*

Coal mining became a major industry after the Civil War, when a tremendous industrial and urban growth followed railroad construction, using coal as the chief source of energy. Coal is mined in 29 states; and coal areas, 13 percent of the U.S. land mass, contain more than one-half the world's supply. The chief coal-producing region is in the Appalachian mountain system; Pennsylvania and West Virginia mine half the nation's output.

By 1800 anthracite was an important industrial and domestic-heating fuel; in the next 40 years production rose annually from 215,000 tons to 1,000,000, and at the time of the Civil War had increased to 10,000,000. Bituminous (soft coal) production, largely used in iron, steel, and other heavy industry, had far outstripped anthracite production by 1900, and by 1950 anthracite, chiefly used for domestic heating, was marketed at the relatively small annual rate of 50,000,000 tons compared with the 600,000,000-ton rate of bituminous coal, a $2,000,000,000 business.

Coal mining presents the constant hazards of cave-ins or explosions, and such disasters as those in 1907 at

Monongah, West Virginia (361 fatalities), and at Jacobs Cave, Pennsylvania (239 fatalities) led to enactment of stringent safety laws. Strikes for higher wages followed the organization of the UNITED MINE WORKERS (1890), and the ANTHRACITE STRIKE of 1902 led to better management-labor relations.

Coal is the principal mineral in order of value in Alabama, Indiana, Kentucky, Ohio, Pennsylvania, Virginia, and West Virginia, and the second in Alaska and Illinois.

Coast and Geodetic Survey, U.S., was established by Congress (1807) within the Treasury Department under supervision of the geodesist F. R. HASSLER. Few operations were conducted until 1832, when the military value of coastal defense was recognized. Hassler was succeeded by A. D. BACHE, under whose direction (1843–67) extensive geodetic, topographical, and hydrographic surveys were undertaken. By 1871 geodetic mappings had been established throughout all the coastal areas of the nation. The survey became an agency within the newly created Department of Commerce and Labor (1903), and after 1913 it became a bureau within the Department of Commerce.

Coast Guard, U.S., established by law in 1915, replaced the Revenue Cutter Service, created for customs collection in 1790, and the Life Saving Service (est. 1871). In 1939 the Lighthouse Service of the Department of Commerce was transferred to the Coast Guard. It is administered by a Commandant with the rank of Vice Admiral, and is at all times a branch of the U.S. armed forces, operating through the Treasury Department except in wartime, when it functions as a branch of the Navy. Training facilities for its 25,000 personnel include various specialist schools and the Coast Guard Academy (est. 1876) at New London, Connecticut.

Coast Ranges, along the Pacific coast of North America, extend from Alaska to Mexico. In the U.S. they include the OLYMPIC MOUNTAINS in Washington, the Coast Range in Oregon, and several ranges in California, including the Diablo, the Santa Lucia, the San Rafael, and the Santa Monica. Geologically they are young, granitic formations. They are mostly well wooded.

COBB, HOWELL (1815–68), after graduation from the University of Georgia (1834) practiced law, served as a Democrat in Congress (1843–51, 1855–57), as governor of Georgia (1851–53), and as Buchanan's Secretary of the Treasury (1857–60). He united with the Whigs to win approval by supporting the Compromise of 1850, and stood firmly with his colleagues ALEXANDER H. STEPHENS and ROBERT TOOMBS for the cause of Union until the election of Lincoln, when he resigned from Buchanan's cabinet to organize secession in Georgia. He was chairman of the MONTGOMERY CONVENTION, and in the Civil War served as a major general in the Confederate army.

COBB, TY [Tyrus Raymond] (1886–1961), probably the greatest all-round star in baseball history, during his 24 years in the American League (1905–28) had a .367 lifetime batting average, made 4191 major-league hits, and stole 892 bases. The 'Georgia Peach,' noted for his daring base-stealing and for his skill at bat, for 9 years made more than 200 hits a season.

COBBETT, WILLIAM (*c.* 1763–1835), all his life a supporter of reforms, in his youth resigned from the British army to expose abuses, but fled to France to escape a suit based on unsubstantiated evidence. From France he came to America (1792), where his British patriotism expressed itself in witty but often vituperative pamphlets attacking the Republican friends of France. From his Philadelphia bookstore he issued *Porcupine's Gazette* (1797–99), but when the physician Benjamin Rush won a verdict of $5000 for Cobbett's allegation that Washington had died because Rush had treated Washington improperly, Cobbett returned to England. Again in the U.S. (1818–19), Cobbett took up farming on Long Island, wrote his graphic *Journal of a Year's Residence in the U.S.* (3 vols., 1818–19) and thereafter settled in England, where after the passage of the Reform Bill (1832) he was elected to Parliament.

COCHISE (*c.* 1815–74), Apache Indian chief noted for his courage and military skill, in 1860 promised not to molest the U.S. mail riders passing through his Arizona territory, and despite great provocation kept his word. The peace treaty he made in 1872 was kept while he lived, and he was later honored by having both a county and a mountain in Arizona named for him.

CODDINGTON, WILLIAM (1601–78), an official of the Massachusetts Bay Company, supported Anne Hutchinson in the ANTINOMIAN CONTROVERSY. With John Clarke and other religious liberals he emigrated to Rhode Island (1638), where he received assistance from Roger Williams, with Clarke founded Newport, and became its first governor (1640). Coddington built up a small fortune shipping horses and tobacco to the West Indies, and in later years was thrice elected governor of the Providence Plantations (1674–78).

Codes of Fair Competition, see *National Industrial Recovery Act.*

CODY, WILLIAM FREDERICK (1846–1917), became a frontier army scout during the Civil War. He was a buffalo hunter for railroad construction camps on the Great Plains, and in 1869 he was nicknamed Buffalo Bill by his friend NED BUNTLINE, who made him the hero of a series of dime novels and persuaded him to appear on the stage. In 1883 Buffalo Bill organized his 'Wild West' show, the prototype of many later ones, and toured with it in the U.S. and Europe. The exploits attributed to him in the novels of Buntline and PRENTISS INGRAHAM are only slightly more imaginative than those revealed in his autobiography (1904).

Coercive Acts (1774), or Restraining Acts (called by Americans the Intolerable Acts), were a series of laws passed by Parliament at the king's personal wish. They were designed to punish Boston for the Tea Party and to show other colonies that Parliament was the wellspring of imperial order by reducing Massachusetts to the status of a crown colony. The BOSTON PORT ACT closed the port of Boston, and the MASSACHUSETTS GOVERNMENT ACT abrogated the colony's charter. The ADMINISTRATION OF JUSTICE ACT gave officials the right to send accused persons to England for trial, and the QUARTERING ACT allowed the government to billet troops at will in the colonies. A fifth act, not intended as a punitive measure, the QUEBEC ACT, was lumped by Americans with the Coercive Acts because it seemed to point in the same direction of violating basic rights.

Instead of isolating Massachusetts, as Lord North confidently expected, the Acts united moderates everywhere, in England as well as America, because issues of sovereignty, not welfare, were raised. North had thought in terms of a local blockade. He had not expected that his strangulation of the leading American seaport would be interpreted as the 'massacre of American liberty.' Virginia rallied all other twelve colonies to 'consult upon the present unhappy state' of affairs. Thus the Coercive Acts led directly to the assembly (5 September 1774) of the First Continental Congress.

COFFIN, LEVI (1789–1877), North Carolina Quaker, after moving to Fountain City, Ohio (1826) made his home the meeting place of 'lines' of the UNDERGROUND RAILROAD, by which escaped slaves were guided North. In 1847 he moved to Cincinnati, where as a 'president' of the road he directed its organization. His *Reminiscences* (1876) are source material of the abolition movement.

COHAN, GEORGE MICHAEL (1878–1942), playwright, producer, and actor, appeared originally as one of 'The Four Cohans.' His first play, *The Governor's Son* (1901), which set new standards in musical comedy for speed and pacing, was followed by several others written before World War I, during which he composed words and music to the now classic song, 'Over There.' One of his last appearances was as President F. D. Roosevelt in *I'd Rather Be Right* (1937).

COHEN, MORRIS RAPHAEL (1880–1947), Russian-born philosopher, was brought to the U.S. in 1892. He graduated from the College of the City of New York (1900), and was a professor of philosophy there (1912–38), and at Chicago (1938–42). Although he rejected ethical absolutism, he believed that the formulation of ethical principles is a necessity in the ordering of human conduct. His writings on the logic of jurisprudence and of natural and social sciences, widely influential, include *Reason and Nature* (1931; 2nd ed., 1953), and *Law and the Social Order* (1933). His study of *The Meaning of Human History* (1947) is a distinguished contribution to the philosophy of history.

Cohens* v. *Virginia (1821), a case resulting in a decision of the U.S. Supreme Court, written by Chief Justice Marshall, vigorously reasserted the principle set forth in MARTIN *v.* HUNTER'S LESSEE (1816) upholding the constitutionality of section 25 of the Judiciary Act of 1789, which gave the Court the power to review decisions of state courts. It went further by construing judicial power, as set forth in the Eleventh Amendment, to mean that appellate courts might accept suits against a state, provided that the state had instituted the suit.

Coinage, see *Currency*.

Coinage Act of 1792, the first currency legislation in the U.S., was the response of Congress to Hamilton's recommendation that the government establish bimetallism as a monetary standard (with a ratio between silver and gold of 15 to 1). The new American gold dollar was fixed at 24.75 grains, the silver dollar at 371.25 grains, and lesser coins were of proportionate weight, adopted as legal tender and freely circulated without limit of number.

Coinage Act of 1873, also called the Demonetization of Silver Act, was for about two decades bitterly referred to by western miners and farmers as the 'Crime of 1873.' Since it legally ended BIMETALLISM in the U.S., the advocates of FREE SILVER charged that it was a conspiracy to establish the GOLD STANDARD. Actually it faced the fact that for many years silver had not been in circulation. Feeling at the time was so keen that until 1900 silver was a major issue in national politics.

COLBY, BAINBRIDGE (1869–1950), a graduate of Williams (1890), practiced law in New York City, helped found the Progressive party (1912), and became a leading supporter of Theodore Roosevelt. In 1916 he swung to the support of Woodrow Wilson, who appointed him Commissioner of the U.S. Shipping Board (1917–19), and Secretary of State (1920–21). Thereafter Colby resumed the practice of law.

Cold Harbor, Battle of (1–3 June 1864), was an attempt by Grant, following the battle of SPOTSYLVANIA, to drive his Army of the Potomac through Lee's center, cross the James river, and capture Richmond, ten miles to the southwest. It was the last engagement in the bloody WILDERNESS CAMPAIGN, and the costliest and most futile of all Civil War battles (on the last day alone Grant lost 12,000 men). It completely failed to dislodge Lee's strongly entrenched forces. Grant then withdrew and moved against PETERSBURG.

Cold war is the popular term applied after 1946 to the deterioration of U.S.-Soviet relations during an era when nuclear weapons prohibited a 'hot war.' The effort to stem the spread of communism became a principle of U.S. foreign policy, enunciated in 1947 in the TRUMAN DOCTRINE and the MARSHALL PLAN, and carried out by the BERLIN AIRLIFT (1948), the NORTH ATLANTIC TREATY (1949), the MUTUAL SECURITY ACT (1951), and by U.S. intervention (1950–52) in the KOREAN WAR.

The fundamental tensions dividing the U.S. and Soviet Russia were reflected on the domestic level by the passage of the Communist Control Act of 1954, outlawing the Communist party in the U.S. The Supreme Court upheld its provisions even when constitutional guarantees of the exercise of individual freedom seemed to be overridden. On the international level the cold war was global, fought especially to win commitments from such emergent colonial areas as Ghana and Guinea. The 'uncommitted' areas therefore have tended to hold the balance of power.

COLDEN, CADWALLADER (1688–1776), Scottish-born physician and public servant, five years after graduation from the University of Edinburgh (1705) emigrated to Philadelphia, where he practiced medicine. He removed to New York in 1718 at the behest of Governor Hunter, and as a conservative aristocrat he thereafter held public office as surveyor-general, member of the governor's council, and for many years lieutenant-governor. Thus he was supported at public expense while he devoted himself to the scientific pursuits by which he sought immortality.

He introduced the Linnaean botanical system into America, and his account of the Iroquois tribes, *The History of the Five Indian Nations* (1727), is the earliest substantiated treatise on the great confederacy. *A Treatise on Wounds and Fevers* (1765) is the most important of his medical works, widely known in their day. His *Enquiry into the Principles of Vital Motion* (1766) is typical of his interest in, and confusion about, speculative matters.

COLE, THOMAS (1801–48), English-born painter, came with his family to the U.S. in 1819, and in 1825 settled in Catskill, New York. Virtually self-taught, he was a founder of the HUDSON RIVER SCHOOL of painting, and first became known for romanticized delineations of New England and New York landscapes that enjoyed considerable vogue. *Last of the Mohicans* (1827), *In the Catskills* (1833), and *Oxbow of the Connecticut* (1836), picturing nature in her wildness, are representative.

Cole returned from a trip abroad (1829–32) with a taste for allegorical subjects, most ambitiously depicted (1836) in a series of five dramatic paintings, *The Course of Empire* (N.Y. Historical Society), in which man is viewed as moving from the savage state through civilization to destruction.

Colgate University, at Hamilton, New York, is a nonsectarian liberal arts college for men. Founded by Baptists as Hamilton Literary and Theological Seminary (1819), it was later called Madison University (1846), and renamed in 1890 for the soap manufacturer William Colgate (1783–1857), who liberally endowed it. In 1965, with an endowment of $12,000,000 and a faculty of 147, it enrolled 1500 students.

Collective bargaining, in labor relations, is the procedure by which union representatives negotiate with an employer to discuss the terms and relationship of employment. Almost until the mid-19th century such bargaining, under common-law doctrine, was judged an illegal conspiracy against the public welfare. The memorable decision in COMMONWEALTH *v.* HUNT (1842) first recognized a trade union as a lawful organization. The founding of the National Typographical Union (1850) was soon followed by the establishment of other national TRADE UNIONS. By the terms of the WAGNER-CONNERY ACT (1935), refusal of employers to bargain collectively is judged an unfair labor practice. The same restraint was imposed on labor unions by the TAFT-HARTLEY ACT (1947).

College Aid Act (1963) provides Federal grants and loans of $1,200,000,000 for the construction of college class rooms, laboratories, and libraries. It has been called the most significant educational enactment in American history, and is the first broad assistance program for colleges since passage of the MORRILL LAND GRANT ACT (1862). To maintain the lines of separation between church and state, no funds may be spent on chapels or divinity schools. The law moved the federal government's participation in education into a new phase.

College charters granted during the colonial period had dubious standing, for no colonial agency had the *explicit* right to grant charters. The point is still debatable, though the eminent jurist Roscoe Pound was of the opinion that colonizing corporations had a right to exercise quasi-sovereign powers that would have been clearly illegal if exercised in England. And in fact the law officers of the crown never challenged the Massachusetts General Court's exercise of sovereign power in creating the corporation of Harvard College (1650), or that of Connecticut in doing the same for Yale (1745).

In England *colleges* were numerous, self-governing units set up for instruction, but only the *universities* of Oxford and Cambridge possessed a legal degree-granting monopoly by royal charter. Thus when President Henry Dunster of Harvard granted the first college degree in 1642, he was appropriating a royal prerogative even before the institution had been incorporated, and the charter of 1650 avoids mention of degrees, presumably because the legislature was uncertain about its own authority. The legal foundation of Harvard and later colonial degree-granting institutions, and the question (in a legal sense) whether they were 'colleges' or 'universities,' may still be discussed, though the issues today are largely antiquarian. The College of William and Mary (1693) was established by royal charter and named for their Majesties, but its power to grant degrees was extralegal.

Yale came into existence (1701) as a 'collegiate school,' fearing that the legality of the Connecticut charter might be challenged if the institution took the name 'college,' and indeed its formal incorporation was delayed for nearly half a century, though it had been granting degrees from the first. Before the outbreak of the Revolution all nine of the surviving colonial colleges were granting degrees by 'prescription,' that is, by doing so without having their incorporation or their degree-granting power successfully challenged. Thus in America there never grew up an educational monopoly or a legal distinction between a college and a university. A far-reaching decision in the matter of college charters was that of the U.S. Supreme Court in the celebrated DARTMOUTH COLLEGE CASE (1816).

College of The City of New York, see *New York, City University of.*

Colleges, see *Education.*

Colonial administration, as it centrally functioned for the American plantations, under James I (1603–25) operated within the Privy Council, which exercised control over trade. Within that body Charles I first set up (1625) a Commission of Trade, and later (1634) created the Commission for Foreign Plantations, known as the 'Laud Commission,' since its chairman was Archbishop William Laud. In 1643 a Parliamentary Commission for Plantations assumed the functions of the Privy Council in colonial affairs, and after sixteen years it in turn was succeeded (1659) by the Council of State, with a standing committee to handle trade and plantations. After the Restoration (1660) Charles II appointed a Committee for Trade and Plantations (Lords of Trade and Plantations) within the Privy Council, which again became the governing body. Finally William III commissioned the BOARD OF TRADE AND PLANTATIONS (1696–1782), which governed colonial affairs in America until the outbreak of the Revolution.

Colonial agents were deputies sent to England by the American colonies to represent particular interests of a colony. Thus Rhode Island was represented for twelve years (1651–63) by JOHN CLARKE, and Pennsylvania for sixteen years (1757–62, 1764–74) by BENJAMIN FRANKLIN, who also served as agent for Georgia (1768–74), New Jersey (1769–74), and Massachusetts (1770–74). Agents attended hearings, presented petitions, and supplied information on which decisions could be based in such matters as boundary disputes, land grants, and Indian affairs. Although never officials of the government, they were invaluable in facilitating colonial administration.

Colonial assemblies were introduced when the first legislative body in America, the House of Burgesses, convened (30 July 1619) at Old Church in Jamestown, Virginia. The Plymouth colony (1620) set up a popular assembly, as did the Massachusetts Bay Colony (1632). The FUNDAMENTAL ORDERS of Connecticut (1639) was the first written constitution in North America, and written constitutions were subsequently adopted in all the colonies. Legislation was subject to review by the Privy Council, which functioned after 1696 through its BOARD OF TRADE AND PLANTATIONS.

The colonial assemblies were given the right to work out financial procedures, levy taxes, determine the nature of local governments, and exercise authority in military affairs; but judged by modern principles they were never wholly representative, since only property owners were enfranchised, and apportionment favored established communities against the frontier. (Eastern legislators feared a tax levy for frontier defense.) At the same time, proceedings were open to scrutiny and debate.

Assemblies tended to encroach on executive power because the governor, as an agent of the crown, was not officially representative of the constituency. Their greatest power derived from the fact that COLONIAL GOVERNORS were dependent upon them for salary and could usually be worn down by attrition when assemblies chose to make an issue. At the outbreak of the War of Independence the assemblies were well prepared to assume direction of the struggle.

Colonial charters for English settlements in America were authorizations from the crown giving private enterprises the right to colonize. At the outset they were chiefly issued to two types of promoters: to TRADING COMPANIES primarily interested in commercial ventures, and to PROPRIETARY COLONIES whose lords proprietors sought to develop land as a source of profit. The power to govern under trading company charters was vested in the company at home. Lords proprietors could themselves determine the form of government in their colonies, subject to the advice and consent of the freemen.

Toward the end of the 17th century the king found the charters an obstacle to direct control, and for the most part converted the corporation and proprietary governments into ROYAL COLONIES. By 1776 only two corporation colonies (Connecticut and Rhode Island) and only two proprietary colonies (Maryland and Pennsylvania) remained. Massachusetts was operating under a charter, but it was governed as a royal province. The right of the colonies to grant COLLEGE CHARTERS was never legally determined.

Colonial councils, acting in all the colonies as the upper legislative bodies, were appointed (in the royal provinces) by the crown or (in the proprietary provinces) by the proprietors. They varied in size (10 members in Rhode Island, 28 in Massachusetts), and with the governors were the supreme courts of appeal in civil affairs. Their duties were specified by law, and with the governors they formed the executive and administrative body of a colony.

Colonial currency was chiefly supplied by barter, because Great Britain forbade the export of specie, and the currency was as various as the local produce. At one time or another wampum, beaver skins, corn, rice, lumber, and tobacco were all legal tender. For the most part the coins in circulation were foreign: Dutch ducats, French crowns, Portuguese moidores, and Spanish doubloons and silver pesos (pieces of eight or Spanish dollars).

Each colony set its own arbitrary legal tender values on foreign coins, which therefore had fluctuating values. In defiance of English law, Massachusetts, the only colony to circulate local coinage, established a mint (1652), managed by JOHN HULL, who struck oak-, willow-, and pine-tree shillings for 30 years. When the governor of Nova Scotia, Sir Thomas Temple, called the attention of Charles II to the fact by producing a shilling, with the comment that the colony stamped the coin with a royal oak as a token of loyalty, the king pronounced the New Englanders 'a parcel of honest dogs,' and allowed the Boston mint to continue operations.

In 1690 Massachusetts became the first colony to issue BILLS OF CREDIT, and in 1740 the first to operate LAND BANKS, which were declared illegal by Parliament in the following year. Generally the colonies sought to attract currency by competitive depreciation, a practice which from time to time necessitated revaluation.

The War of Independence was largely financed by the credit money known as CONTINENTAL CURRENCY. In the period of confederation (1773–89) the new states made abortive efforts to establish mints. (Massachusetts succeeded in minting a few copper pieces, one one-hundredth of the Spanish dollar, the first decimal coinage in history.) Congress in 1789 ended coinage by the states, and adopted the system of BIMETALLISM.

Colonial governors, the chief civil magistrates of the American colonies, in the ROYAL PROVINCES were appointed by the crown; in the PROPRIETARY PROVINCES they were nominated by the proprietors and approved by the king; in the CHARTER COLONIES they were elected by the constituency. The duties of crown officials were explicit and detailed, and included the collection of customs levies and enforcement of the NAVIGATION ACTS.

Though royal governors were treated

with viceregal deference, they had scant incentive to seek office. Except in Virginia, the COLONIAL ASSEMBLIES controlled their salaries, which were kept small and often were irregularly paid. Perquisites and patronage were trivial. Given responsibility with scant power, and constantly thwarted by stubborn and provincial-minded assemblies, the royal or proprietary governors (usually honest and able men) were handicapped by problems beyond their control.

Colonial wars, see *Bacon's Rebellion, Pequot War, King Philip's War, Tuscarora War, King William's War, Queen Anne's War, King George's War, Jenkins' Ear, French and Indian Wars, Regulators.*

Colorado, admitted to the Union in 1876 as the 38th state, is in the heart of the ROCKY MOUNTAINS. Its name derives from the Colorado river (Sp. *red* or *colored*). The dispute for its possession by France and Spain was settled by the TREATY OF PARIS of 1763 in favor of France, although both French and Spanish traders had penetrated the region during the 18th century. The eastern part was transferred to the U.S. in the Louisiana Purchase (1803), and a southern segment came into American possession in 1845 as part of the state of Texas. The region west of the Continental Divide was included in the Mexican cession of 1848. In 1861, with boundaries fixed, the whole area was given territorial status.

ZEBULON PIKE had led the first official U.S. expedition into Colorado (1806), followed by STEPHEN LONG (1820), and JOHN C. FRÉMONT (1842–46). The trading post set up by WILLIAM BENT in 1832 opened an overland route along the Santa Fe Trail, and the gold rush during the 1860's disclosed immense ore reserves (including the now valuable uranium), augmented by fields of oil and coal. Today cattle and sheep raising are extensive, and crops are harvested on some 2,200,000 acres of irrigated land.

A state of great natural beauty, Colorado has a mean elevation of 6800 ft., with 50 mountains (including PIKES PEAK) rising above 14,000. It has two national parks: MESA VERDE (1906) and ROCKY MOUNTAIN (1915). DENVER, the capital, is the chief business and cultural center between Chicago and San Francisco. Pueblo is an industrial city whose population in the decade 1950–60 increased from 63,000 to 91,000. The resort city of Colorado Springs, with a growth in the same period of 45,000 to 70,000, is headquarters of the Continental Air Defense Command. Best known of the state's institutions of higher learning are the Colorado School of Mines (Golden, est. 1874), and the University of Colorado (Boulder, est. 1877).

Colorado river, 1360 miles long, rises in Colorado at the Continental Divide, and flows southwest to enter the Gulf of California. The great river of the Southwest, it drains seven states, 8 per cent of the area of the U.S. Hernando de Alarcón explored its lower reaches in 1540, and its spectacular canyons have long challenged explorers and scientists. In 1922 the Colorado River Compact was negotiated by Arizona, California, Colorado, Nevada, New Mexico, Utah, and Wyoming. It established a program for the development of water resources and the control of erosion and floods, which led to similar programs for the Columbia and Missouri rivers, and anticipated the TENNESSEE VALLEY AUTHORITY. Immense dams built since 1930 on the Colorado and its tributaries (including Hoover Dam, Parker Dam, and Glen Canyon Dam) have transformed vast arid regions into fertile land, and encouraged the industrial growth of the Southwest by creating practically limitless hydroelectric power.

'Colossus of the North,' see *Caribbean Policy.*

COLT, SAMUEL (1814–62), Connecticut inventor, in 1836 patented a revolving-breech pistol which the U.S. Army adopted in 1847. In 1848 he established his firearms factory at Hartford. As the first firearm which could be effectively used by a man on horseback, the 'six-shooter' was early associated with the Plains and Southwest frontier, and made the name Colt synonymous with revolver.

Columbia river, 1214 miles long, rises in British Columbia and flows principally south through the state of Washington. It is joined by its great tributary, the SNAKE RIVER, and becomes a boundary between Washington and Oregon on its way westward to the Pacific. The Columbia was discovered in 1792 by ROBERT GRAY, who named it after his vessel. Long known to Indians for its salmon runs, it was first explored overland by the LEWIS AND CLARK EXPEDITION.

It generates the greatest hydroelectric power of any river in the U.S. The vast Columbia River Project is designed to irrigate large tracts, establish flood controls, and produce hydroelectric power for homes and industries throughout the PACIFIC NORTHWEST. Among its twenty multipurpose dams are BONNEVILLE and GRAND COULEE.

Columbia University, in New York City. was chartered (1754) as King's College by a grant from George II. Under its first president, SAMUEL JOHNSON, it was established at Park Place in lower Manhattan. The Loyalist MYLES COOPER succeeded Johnson in 1763, but Cooper returned to England in 1775, and the college was closed in 1776, soon after the Revolution began. On reopening (1784), it was renamed Columbia College. In 1857 it was moved to Madison Avenue and 49 Street, where during the administration of F. A. P. BARNARD (1864–89) it added professional and graduate schools. Under SETH LOW it became Columbia University (1896), and in 1897 it was moved to its present site on Morningside Heights. During the long administration (1902–45) of NICHOLAS MURRAY BUTLER it changed from a small residential institution to one of the world's largest universities and became a center for graduate research.

Columbia College remains the undergraduate school. The oldest special school is that of medicine (1767). Other schools include those of law (1858), engineering (1864), architecture (1896), journalism (1912), business (1916), library service (1926), international affairs (1946), dramatic art (1948), and painting and sculpture (1948). Affiliated institutions are the College of Pharmacy (1829), Teachers College (1888), BARNARD COLLEGE (1889), and the New York School of Social Work (1940). In 1965, with an endowment of $201,000,000 and a faculty of 3430, it enrolled 16,700 students. (Teachers College, with a faculty of 337, enrolled 5300 students.)

Columbian Exposition, see *World's Columbian Exposition.*

Columbian Order, see *Tammany Societies.*

COLUMBUS, CHRISTOPHER (1451–1506), born at Genoa, Italy, was son of a woolen weaver. He went to sea in his youth, married the daughter of a Portuguese navigator when he was about twenty-seven years old, and settled in Lisbon. Portugal was then the home of the most advanced geographers. Portuguese mariners, the most dauntless in Europe, had discovered and colonized the Azores, and were feeling their way along new stretches of the African coast, where they created an enviable trade in gold and ivory. They also developed a new type of sailing vessel, the caravel, whose broad bows, high poop, and lateen sails made sea voyages faster and far less dangerous than before.

Columbus envisioned a sea route to 'the Indies' (the Far East) by westward passage, but the idea was rejected by learned men and mathematicians as impractical. Columbus's brother Bartholomew, an expert chart maker, supported him, and by charm and persistence Columbus won the Spanish monarchs, Ferdinand and Isabella, to risk the 'Enterprise of the Indies.' By the Capitulations of 17 April and the Title of 30 April 1492 Columbus was appointed Admiral of the Ocean Sea, Viceroy, and governor of whatever territory he might discover.

He manned a fleet of three small caravels with 90 picked Spanish seamen, and on 3 August 1492 embarked from Palos on the most important voyage in history. He left the Canary Islands on 9 September, and for 30 days, with Columbus in the lead in the *Santa María* and the *Niña* and *Pinta* following, the ships continued due west. He quelled a mutiny on 10 October by asking for three days of grace before turning home. At 2 a.m. on 12 October the lookout on the *Pinta* made landfall of the low, sandy Bahama island which Columbus named San Salvador (now Watlings), and possessed in the name of Spain, believing himself off the China mainland.

He explored the coast of Cuba, crossed the Windward Passage to Hispaniola (Haiti), and kept notes on the Indians and the unknown flora and fauna. The *Santa María* was wrecked off Haiti on Christmas Eve, and Columbus built a fort of her timbers (La Navidad). He returned to Spain on *Niña,* which, with *Pinta,* dropped anchor at Palos on 15 March 1493. He described the voyage in his famous 'Letter,' published at Barcelona in April, the first effective historical record of the New World. Columbus was given a hero's welcome, all his honors and privileges were confirmed to him, and he was served and saluted as a grandee of Spain.

For his second voyage Columbus was fitted out with a fleet of seventeen ships. In September 1493 with some 1200 men he sailed from Cádiz, reaching the Leeward Islands early in November. Moving through St. Kitts, the Virgin Islands, and Puerto Rico (which he assumed to be islands 'in the Indian Sea'), late in the month he returned to Hispaniola, where he found that his garrison had been wiped out. In January 1494 he began building the trading station of Isabella on the north coast, and here his troubles started. The Spanish 'colonizers' had come solely for gold, and resented the governor's orders to plant a colony and tend crops. While Columbus continued to survey the Caribbean Archipelago, malcontents seized vessels to return to Spain to complain of him and declare 'the Indies' a fraud. The food was inedible, the climate atrocious, the gold a delusion. Columbus left his brother Bartholomew in charge and reached Spain in June 1496. The immense enthusiasm of his first return had evaporated. After a year of lobbying he won grudging royal consent to continue his search for the mainland of 'Asia.'

On his third voyage (1498) he went further south, made landfall on Trinidad, and discovered the mouth of the Orinoco. When the Spanish monarchs in 1500 learned of the wretched conditions of colonization in Haiti, they dispatched a judge who assumed enough power to return the Columbus brothers in chains. Although immediately released, Columbus no longer enjoyed royal patronage. The great navigators Magellan and da Gama had reached the Orient which Columbus had been seeking, and former officers of earlier Columbus voyages, including VESPUCCI, were opening up the continent of South America.

In 1502 Columbus gathered four poorly equipped vessels, and hoping to reach Japan, struck the coast of Honduras and reached the Gulf of Darien in Panama. Two years later he returned to Spain, ill, discredited, and with curtailed privileges. Although he was financially well off, and by earlier royal favor had been able to found a noble line, he died in relative obscurity, uncertain of the size of the globe but aware that he had 'placed under their Highnesses' sovereignty more land than there is in Africa and Europe.'

A poor administrator, Columbus had a genius for exploration, and among great discoverers only Magellan and da Gama compare with him in skill, courage, and persistence. His earth-changing voyage in 1492 deserves the reverence in which the New World holds him. No other great venturer was so ill rewarded in his lifetime.

The authoritative biography is S. E. Morison, *Admiral of the Ocean Sea* (2 vols., 1942).

Columbus Day commemorates the discovery, 12 October 1492, of the New World. It is observed throughout most of the U.S., in Puerto Rico, in several of the Latin American republics, and in some cities in Spain and Italy.

Comanche Indians, members of the Shoshonean (Uto-Aztecan linguistic) group, were nomadic people ranging from the Platte river to the Texas border. Superb horsemen and fiercely warlike, from the days of Spanish settlements (about 1700) they effectively prevented white men from taking easy possession of the southern plains. In loose confederation with the Kiowa, Cheyenne, and Arapaho, they asserted their superiority by making their tongue the trading language. Never a large tribe, they numbered some 1500 members when they were gathered on their Oklahoma reservation in 1875.

Combinations, Business, see *Trusts.*

Comic strips, cartoons with dialog and a continuing character, developed during the 1890's as circulation builders for newspapers. They originated with a highly popular bad-boy character, 'The Yellow Kid' (1896), by Felton Outcault, in Pulitzer's New York *World.* They became a nationwide phenomenon in the U.S. after 1915, when they were syndicated as a newspaper feature. A few have secured a place in the history of American humor. Such include George Herriman's 'Krazy Kat,' Walt Kelly's 'Pogo,' Milt Gross's 'Nize Baby,' and George Baker's 'The Sad Sack.' Translators now prepare strips for distribution abroad, for the element of folk tale which many of them embody has universal appeal.

COMMAGER, HENRY STEELE (1902–), professor of history at New York University (1931–38), at Columbia since 1939, and at Amherst as well since 1957, is widely known as an interpreter of the American character. His extensive writings include *Theodore Parker* (1936), *America in Perspective* (1947), *The American Mind* (1951), and *Freedom, Loyalty, Dissent* (1954).

Commerce, during the early Stuart period, was not regulated by Parliament, which left colonial economic development to the crown. During the interregnum and thereafter (1650–1767) commerce was regulated by a series of NAVIGATION ACTS, designed to subordinate colonial interests to those of the mother country, and a principal function of colonial governors was the task of enforcing mercantile regulations. Restrictive measures enjoined from time to time include the WOOLENS ACT (1699), HAT ACT (1732), MOLASSES ACT (1733), IRON ACT (1750), and SUGAR ACT (1764). Overseas trade also had to meet the physical obstacles of piracy and of PRIVATEERING, as well as financial problems rising from lack of money and credit facilities.

Since Great Britain forbade the exportation of coins, early colonists were dependent upon barter, commodity money (such as tobacco and rice crop notes), local coinage, foreign coins, bills of exchange, paper money, and LAND BANKS. The 'TRIANGULAR TRADE' gave Northern Colonies, whose goods had no demand in England, the means to pay English merchants for imports. Tobacco and rice gave the South valuable export commodities, and other colonial exports included indigo, wheat, iron, furs, skins, and whale products. As late as 1769 Boston led in the coastal trade, with New York, Philadelphia, and Charleston as close rivals. But the chronic shortage of currency kept the colonies from a favorable trade balance, and during the War of Independence export industries lost not only their British outlets but much of their WEST INDIA TRADE, which had been a major outlet for the Northern colonies. The New England states soon inaugurated the CHINA TRADE to replace their European markets.

The rapid population growth in the Ohio and Mississippi valleys before 1830, with the consequent use of interior river systems, made Cincinnati and Louisville important shipping points. The completion of the Erie Canal in 1825 provided a means of moving western farm products to the East, and the establishment of east-west railroad lines in the early 1850's made Chicago a grain center. By 1860 the leading export cities were New Orleans (cotton), and New York (wheat).

The merchant marine grew steadily after New York merchants established a regular line of transatlantic PACKET SHIPS in 1818. Internationally famous CLIPPER SHIPS, trading with the Orient in the 1840's and 1850's, set speed records. By 1850 steamboats, first used in ocean trade in 1838, were in competition with packets on Atlantic runs. Blockades strangled southern commerce during the Civil War, but northern foreign trade was continuous, and tonnage moving through the Erie Canal increased.

Between 1866 and 1900 the value of exports grew from $434,000,000 to $1,500,000,000, chiefly from cotton, meat, grain, petroleum, and machinery. The expansion of railway networks and the growth of Great Lakes shipping ushered in the present era of U.S. commerce. In 1903 Congress established a Department of Commerce and Labor. During World War I American exports in munitions and wheat were enormous, and the U.S. emerged from the war as a creditor nation. Before and during World War II the annual excess of U.S. exports ($20,000,000,000) over imports

($8,000,000,000) was the greatest in U.S. history, and created a shortage of dollars held by foreigners (a dollar gap) remedied by such arrangements as Lend-Lease and the Marshall Plan. The growth of great DEPARTMENT STORES, MAIL-ORDER HOUSES, CHAIN STORES, and SUPERMARKETS now sets the national retail pattern. By mid-20th century, ranking exports included cotton, grain, and finished products; important imports included coffee, sugar, paper, rubber, and nonferrous metal.

See Clive Day, *A History of Commerce in the U.S.* (1925); J. H. Frederick, *The Development of American Commerce* (1932); and L. C. Hunter, *Steamboats on the Western Rivers* (1949).

Commerce, U.S. Department of, created in 1913, was a reorganization of the Department of Commerce and Labor, established by Congress in 1903. Its Secretary is a member of the President's cabinet. Its major divisions include Standards (for weights and measures), Census, International Commerce, Federal Highways, Coast and Geodetic Survey, Patent Office, and Weather Bureau. Secretaries of Commerce and Labor held office under two Presidents:

T. ROOSEVELT

George B. Cortelyou (N.Y.) 1903
Victor H. Metcalf (Calif.) 1904
Oscar S. Straus (N.Y.) 1906

TAFT

Charles Nagel (Mo.) 1909

Secretaries of Commerce and the Presidents under whom they served are as follows:

WILSON

William C. Redfield (N.Y.) 1913
Joshua W. Alexander (Mo.) 1919

HARDING

Herbert C. Hoover (Calif.) 1921

COOLIDGE

Herbert C. Hoover (Calif.) 1923
William F. Whiting (Mass.) 1928

HOOVER

Robert P. Lamont (Ill.) 1929
Roy D. Chapman (Mich.) 1932

F. D. ROOSEVELT

Daniel C. Roper (S.C.) 1933
Harry L. Hopkins (Iowa) 1939
Jesse Jones (Tex.) 1940
Henry A. Wallace (Iowa) 1945

TRUMAN

Henry A. Wallace (Iowa) 1945
W. Averell Harriman (N.Y.) 1946
Charles Sawyer (Ohio) 1948

EISENHOWER

Sinclair Weeks (Mass.) 1953
Lewis L. Strauss (N.Y.) 1958
Frederick H. Mueller (Mich.) 1959

KENNEDY

Luther H. Hodges (N.C.) 1961

L. B. JOHNSON

Luther H. Hodges (N.C.) 1963
John T. Connor (N.J.) 1965

Commercial banking places emphasis on loanable funds to create a working capital for trade expansion. Commercial banks make currency available for use by issuing notes on the deposits they have collected. INVESTMENT BANKING houses concentrate on the raising of capital for business ventures by marketing their securities. Many investment firms carried on commercial banking functions until the practice was forbidden by the GLASS-STEAGALL BANKING ACT of 1933.

Commission plan, as a system of municipal government, was first adopted at Galveston, Texas, as an emergency measure following the tidal flood of 1900. Its political effectiveness encouraged some 500 cities to adopt it by 1917. Under the plan, all executive and legislative power is vested in a small elective board, usually composed of five members. The plan simplifies city government, but the lack of unified and responsible executive authority has led many cities to abandon it in favor of the CITY-MANAGER PLAN.

Committee on Public Information, the 'Creel Committee,' established (1917) by act of Congress, functioned under the chairmanship of the publicist George Creel (1876–1953), with the Secretaries of State, War, and the Navy as members. It was designed to unite American public opinion in fighting World War I. An experienced and imaginative journalist, given ample public funds, Creel carried out his work at home and abroad with films, posters, some 100,000,000 pamphlets, 75,000 volunteer 'four minute men,' who spoke during theater intermissions, and daily news releases. From this barrage of propaganda emerged the image of Germans as 'barbaric Huns.'

Committees of correspondence were extralegal groups formed on the eve of the War of Independence to promote the patriot cause. Samuel Adams organized the first group at Boston in November 1772, and within three months 80 such committees had been formed locally in Massachusetts. In March 1773 Virginia organized legislative standing committees for intercolonial correspondence. The committee system spread through the colonies, and was the channel for directing public opinion. In 1775 the Continental Congress appointed a five-man Committee of Correspondence with wide discretionary powers to get in contact with 'our friends' abroad.

Committees of safety extended the work of committees of correspondence. The first was an eleven-man board appointed (October 1774) by the Massachusetts legislature, with John Hancock as chairman. It was empowered to mobilize the militia and seize military stores. Soon other colonies established similar committees in response to Parliament's COERCIVE ACTS.

In July 1775 the Second Continental Congress, recognizing the breakdown of constitutional modes of government, sanctioned such committees as the best way to control local affairs during a revolutionary period. The committees supplied the Continental army with men and equipment, apprehended Loyalists, and guided executive, legislative, and judicial procedures. They were officially discontinued for the most part as soon as the states adopted their constitutions.

Commodity Credit Corporation (1933) was authorized by Congress under the Agricultural Adjustment Act as an agency to buy, sell, or lend agricultural commodities with the object of supporting farm prices. Since 1939 it has functioned within the Department of Agriculture.

Common law originated in England out of usage and custom, and became the law 'common' to all by judicial interpretation, not by statutory enactment. It usually protected individuals against oppressive acts of government and private conspiratorial combinations. The Declaration of Independence and the Bill of Rights in the Federal and state constitutions embody the common-law principle that certain rights are inalienable. Jefferson and his followers fought the common law as too British, as hostile to unions and strikes (as conspiracies), and as too costly for the common man because of its technicalities requiring lawyers. Statute law was to borrow common-law principles forbidding combinations in restraint of trade, the protection of civil rights procedures, and common-law conceptions of liberty.

Common Market, see *European Economic Community*.

COMMONS, JOHN ROGERS (1862–1944), professor of economics at Wisconsin (1904–32), served on various government commissions that influenced social legislation. His noted *Legal Foundations of Capitalism* (1924) and *Institutional Economics* (1934) broadened the field of economics by considering it with other social sciences. Other works that stress a reformist point of view include *Principles of Labor Legislation* (with J. B. Andrews, 1916; 4th ed., 1936), and *Industrial Government* (1921). His section of the *History of Labor in the United States* (1918–35), a series, is usually regarded as the best in the field.

Commonwealth Fund (1918), established by Mrs. Stephen V. Harkness, is largely devoted to medical education and research. It annually offers fellowships to graduate students and civil servants from the British Commonwealth for medical education in the U.S. In 1965 its assets exceeded $154,000,000.

Commonwealth* v. *Hunt (1842), a case resulting in a ruling made by the Massachusetts Supreme Court, was the first recognition in the U.S. that the common law concerning conspiracy is inapplicable to LABOR UNIONS and that strikes for a CLOSED SHOP are legal. The opinion was stated by Chief Justice

Lemuel Shaw. Soon thereafter the courts of other states handed down similar rulings, thus increasing the prestige of labor organizations.

Communal societies, usually short-lived ventures in community living, existed from the early colonial period, but were most numerous during the second quarter of the 19th century. Some socio-religious groups, including the MENNONITES, AMANA, DUNKER, SHAKER, and MORMON communities, still continue. The LABADIST, HARMONY, ZOAR, HOPEDALE, and ONEIDA associations have disintegrated.

The nonreligious communitarian experiments, such as NASHOBA, NEW HARMONY, and the ICARIAN colonies, adopted various forms of UTOPIAN SOCIALISM. FOURIERISM was especially popular among the TRANSCENDENTALISTS. Best remembered among some 40 Fourierite 'phalanxes' were BROOK FARM near Boston and the NORTH AMERICAN PHALANX in New Jersey.

Communist party in the U.S., following the teachings of Marx and Lenin, was formally organized in 1919 by dissident groups of the SOCIALIST PARTY. Driven underground by the anti-Red hysteria of the early 1920's, various factions organized as the Workers' party, which in 1924 polled 33,000 votes and in 1928 48,000 votes for WILLIAM Z. FOSTER as presidential candidate. It became the leading revolutionary organization in the U.S. Allied with the Comintern, it avowed as its object the overthrow of capitalism and the establishment of an American proletarian dictatorship. Reorganized with a Stalinist ideology in 1932, the Communist party supported Foster at the polls with 102,000 votes.

At first the party had advocated 'boring from within.' After 1928 Communist-organized industrial strikes led to the founding of rival or dual unions, and cooperating idealistic liberals came to be known as 'fellow travelers.' In 1936 EARL BROWDER polled 80,000 presidential votes, but only 46,000 in 1940. When top Communist leaders were convicted on charges of conspiracy to overthrow the government (1949), PHILIP MURRAY was able to expel most Communist-dominated unions from the C.I.O. The frenetic character of Communist witch hunts was given the name MC CARTHYISM, from the nature of investigations conducted (1951–54) by Senator Joseph R. McCarthy. Congress ordered the party to register with the Department of Justice under the Subversive Control Act of 1950 as an organization directed from Moscow. However, in 1965 the Supreme Court unanimously ruled that individuals may refuse to register with the government as members of the Communist party by invoking their constitutional privilege against self-incrimination, thus essentially nullifying the registration rule. Thereafter, party spokesmen announced plans for a Communist convention, their own slate of candidates, and a specific platform.

Compact theory, involving the idea that the basis of government is in the consent of the governed, is implicit in the MAYFLOWER COMPACT, and in the writings of such ecclesiastical leaders as THOMAS HOOKER and JOHN WISE. As a political philosophy it is taken for granted in the Declaration of Independence. As a theory defending states' rights it is expounded in the various documents advocating NULLIFICATION.

Company unions were labor organizations dominated by employers, who exercised control (open or concealed) through financial aid to the union and the donation of materials or services for union work. They were declared illegal by the WAGNER-CONNERY ACT (1935) and by various state labor relations laws.

Compromise of 1850, proposed by Henry Clay, was an effort to stem the growing breach between North and South on issues of states' rights and the extension of slavery. The resolutions provided for the admission of California to the Union as a free state, the organization of New Mexico and Utah territories without restriction on slavery, adjustment of the Texas–New Mexico boundary, settlement of the Texas debt, abolition of the slave trade in the District of Columbia, and more stringent FUGITIVE SLAVE LAWS. Stephen A. Douglas drafted the bills and played a vital role in their passage.

The Senate debates that followed the introduction of this 'Omnibus Bill' were the most famous in U.S. history. Henry Clay argued (5–6 February) that secession would not remedy southern grievances. John C. Calhoun (4 March) opposed the compromise, declaring that territories on winning statehood must be free to decide slavery issues. Daniel Webster (7 March) supported Clay, contending that the issues would be solved by geography and climate. This crisis was the dramatic culmination of political developments that had absorbed national attention for years. The measures were enacted into law in September, and were hailed by North and South as a solution to the menace of national division, but when the issue of popular sovereignty was again raised four years later by passage of the KANSAS-NEBRASKA ACT (and northern crowds blocked the return of fugitive slaves), all effectiveness of the Compromise was canceled.

Compromise Tariff of 1833, sponsored by Henry Clay to end the crisis produced by the South Carolina ORDINANCE OF NULLIFICATION (1832), voided earlier tariff acts. It provided systematic tariff reductions for ten years in an effort to re-establish approximately the 20 per cent rate of 1816. South Carolina repealed the Ordinance, but the simultaneous passage of the FORCE BILL was symptomatic of the deep cleavage within the Democratic party.

COMPTON, ARTHUR HOLLY (1892–1962), professor of physics at Chicago (1923–45), and chancellor of Washington University at St. Louis (1945–53), did notable research in cosmic radiation. The change in wave length of scattered X-rays, which he discovered, is known as the 'Compton effect.' These experiments, for which he shared the 1927 Nobel Prize in physics with the English physicist C. T. R. Wilson, led to verification of Einstein's photon theory of light. Other contributions include his discovery of the electrical nature of cosmic rays. He was a major figure in building the atomic bomb.

COMPTON, KARL TAYLOR (1887–1954), as professor of physics at Princeton (1919–30), and as president of Massachusetts Institute of Technology (1930–48), did research in photoelectricity, radar, ionization of gases, and ultraviolet spectroscopy. In 1948–49 he was chairman of the research and development board of the National Military Establishment.

Comptroller General of the U.S., head of the General Accounting Office in the Bureau of the BUDGET, is appointed by the President for a fifteen-year term. Removable only by Congress, to whom he is responsible, he is charged with auditing and reviewing the financial transactions of Federal officers and agencies. During the New Deal, his independent powers to determine the reasonableness and validity of Federal expenditures before payment is made aroused a great controversy between the Executive and the conservative Comptroller General. Ultimately, new checks were introduced.

COMSTOCK, ANTHONY (1844–1915), as lifelong secretary of the New York Society for Suppression of Vice (1873), was author of the so-called Comstock law (1873), which excluded from the mails all matter 'designed to incite lust.' He took the lead in founding the Watch and Ward Society in Boston, and as 'the Roundsman of the Lord' was responsible for the arrest of more than 3000 persons and the destruction of 160 tons of allegedly objectionable books and pictures. A zealot of conventional morals, to many liberals, especially H. L. Mencken, Comstock seemed the symbol of licensed bigotry.

Comstock Lode, the greatest single deposit of silver ever discovered in the U.S., was located on Mount Davidson near Virginia City, Nevada. News of the discovery was made public (1859) by the trapper and prospector Henry Comstock, who soon sold his mining rights for $11,000. During the next twenty years the mine yielded more than $300,000,000, and thus laid the foundation of the mineral wealth of Nevada. The Consolidated Virginia Silver Mine, organized from a number of smaller claims in the 1870's, gave control of the 'Big Bonanza' to John W. Mackay, James G. Fair, James C. Flood, and others. From the Comstock came money that built San Francisco mansions and established many of that city's business enterprises. The mine was drained by the SUTRO TUNNEL, one of the greatest engineering feats of the century.

CONANCHET (or Canonchet), see *King Philip*.

CONANT, James Bryant (1893–), after graduation from Harvard (1913) taught chemistry there (1916–33) before serving the institution as president (1933–53). He was chairman (1941–46) of the National Defense Research Committee when it was enlarged (1942) into the vital office of SCIENTIFIC RESEARCH AND DEVELOPMENT. He resigned his university post to become high commissioner for Germany (1953–55), and ambassador to the West German Republic (1955–58).

His scientific writings include *The Chemistry of Organic Compounds* (1933; rev. ed., 1952), and *Growth of the Experimental Sciences* (1949). His later studies have centered on the education of children in the U.S., especially at the high school level. *The Child, the Parent, and the State* (1959) recommends increased emphasis on mathematics and foreign languages. *Slums and Suburbs* (1961) warns against two school systems, one for the poor and one for the privileged. *The Education of American Teachers* (1963) is a plea for more subject courses in teacher training programs.

CONANT, Roger (1593–1679), a London salter, accompanied a group of Separatists to Plymouth in 1623. He was serving as leader of the DORCHESTER COMPANY when remnants of that body left Cape Ann (Gloucester) in 1626 to set up a trading post at Naumkeag (Salem). He is thus credited with founding that Massachusetts settlement.

Conciliation, see *Mediation*.

Concord, Massachusetts, a village twenty miles northwest of Boston, was settled in 1635. It was the site of the first provincial congress (1774–75), and the objective of the British expedition (1775) that opened the War of Independence with the battle of LEXINGTON AND CONCORD. For some 25 years in the mid-19th century the quiet village was an intellectual center. The Old Manse, a public shrine since 1939, was the home of Emerson in the 1830's, and of Hawthorne during his Concord residence (1842–45), when he wrote *Mosses from an Old Manse* (1846). Concord was the lifelong home of Thoreau and the Alcotts, and to it was attracted the younger W. E. Channing, who made the village a center of TRANSCENDENTALISM.

Concord School of Philosophy (1880–88), founded at Concord, Massachusetts, by BRONSON ALCOTT with the support of W. T. HARRIS, was a highly successful forerunner of the American University summer session. Here the lingering transcendentalists and younger philosophical minds informally discussed Plato and Dante, Milton and Goethe, Kant and Hegel. The group sought to counteract the materialistic tendencies of the current scientific speculation; among the speakers were such leaders of thought as William James and John Fiske, James McCosh of Princeton, and Noah Porter of Yale.

Concurrent Resolutions, see *Resolutions, Legislative*.

Conestoga wagon, see *Covered wagon*.

Coney Island, an Atlantic Ocean sand bar on Long Island at the southern end of Brooklyn, is a seaside resort popular since the early 19th century. After 1875 its hotels and amusement centers, located along its six miles of beaches, began attracting throngs that can number over 1,000,000 persons on holiday weekends.

Confederate army, officially the Army of the Confederate States of America, was established 6 March 1861 by the Confederate Provisional Congress, which empowered President Davis to call for volunteers. The limited supply of arms was augmented late in the year by the arrival of 50,000 rifles, purchased in England. Conscription of able-bodied whites from eighteen to thirty-five began in April 1862; by 1864 the age range was seventeen to fifty. Some 900,000 Southerners were under arms during the course of the Civil War, but losses so crippled the Confederate army that the total number available to surrender in the closing months did not exceed 175,000.

Confederate navy, established in February 1861, never possessed an effective fleet, and the increasing tightening of the Union blockade deprived the Confederacy of necessary port facilities. Several vessels, however, such as the *Alabama* and the *Florida,* which were procured in England, were outfitted as cruisers, and took heavy toll of Federal shipping during the Civil War. The engagement of the *Monitor* and the *Merrimac* in the battle of HAMPTON ROADS revolutionized naval warfare by introducing ironclads.

Confederate States of America came into existence on 8 February 1861, when delegates from the seceding states of South Carolina, Georgia, Florida, Alabama, Mississippi, and Louisiana met in congress at Montgomery, Alabama, and adopted a 'Constitution for the Provisional Government of the Confederate States of America.' On the following day they unanimously elected Jefferson Davis (Miss.) as president, and Alexander Stephens (Ga.) as vice president.

Davis formed a cabinet of six members. On 11 March the Congress adopted a permanent constitution modeled upon that of the U.S., but with special STATES' RIGHTS provisions. The seceded states, which by then included Texas, soon ratified it. After the bombardment of Fort Sumter (12 April) the Confederacy was joined by the border states of Virginia, North Carolina, Tennessee, and Arkansas. When the Confederacy collapsed at the end of the war, it was compelled to repudiate its public debt of some $2,000,000,000, since by the terms of the Fourteenth Amendment all debts of the Confederate states were declared 'illegal and void.'

Confederation, see *Articles of Confederation.*

Congregationalists, adherents of the system of church government based upon the autonomy of the individual congregation, were the heirs of PURITANISM, and the most influential religious body in colonial America. Their tenets stressed the right and duty to organize for Christian worship, and the duty of the churches to co-operate with one another. Calvinist in doctrine, they were midway between episcopal and presbyterian government. The denomination, introduced by the radical Plymouth SEPARATISTS, guided the ecclesiastical practice in the Massachusetts Bay colony for two generations, although it had no direct legislative authority. Its tenets were explicitly set forth in the CAMBRIDGE PLATFORM of 1648, which made the colony a 'Bible Commonwealth' but never a THEOCRACY.

Since the differences between Congregationalists and Presbyterians were not doctrinal, by the 18th century those moving into new areas generally accepted the local forms of church government. The New England Congregationalist Jonathan Edwards, for example, accepted the invitation to become president of the Presbyterian College of New Jersey, in Princeton.

Congregational principles dominated the founding of several colleges, including Harvard, Yale, Williams, Amherst, and Oberlin. The church was established by law in Massachusetts, Connecticut, and New Hampshire, and in those areas constituted a STANDING ORDER which delayed the separation of CHURCH AND STATE longer than anywhere else in the U.S.

The United Church of Christ was formed in 1957 through union of the Congregational churches with the Evangelical and Reformed Church. This was the first joining in the U.S. of churches with differing forms of governments and different historical background. In 1965 its membership exceeded 2,000,000.

Congress of Industrial Organizations (C.I.O.) began to take form in 1938, after JOHN L. LEWIS had led eight unions within the AMERICAN FEDERATION OF LABOR in setting up a Committee for Industrial Organization (1935). The Committee's drive to unionize mass-production industries on an industrial (vertical) basis was opposed by the craft (horizontal) unions in the A.F. of L. Aggressive unionization drives in such great industries as steel, textile, automobile, and coal resulted in their expulsion (1937) from the A.F. of L. and the formation of the C.I.O., in which semiskilled and unskilled workers were also unionized. Under the presidency of Lewis the C.I.O. became a powerful rival of the A.F. of L. Lewis was succeeded as president by PHILIP MURRAY (1940). In 1955 the two great unions were merged as A.F.L.–C.I.O.

Congress of the U.S., provided for in Article I of the Constitution as the legislative branch of the federal government, functions in two component parts, the SENATE and the HOUSE OF REPRESENTATIVES. Its powers are those enumerated, specifically delegated, implied, and granted as 'necessary and proper' (Art. I, sec. 8). They include the power to collect taxes and duties; to provide for the common defense and general welfare of the U.S.; to regulate commerce, patents, and copyrights; to declare war, raise armies, and maintain a navy; to coin money; and to establish post offices and lower courts.

Powers specifically denied Congress are set forth in the Bill of Rights and elsewhere in the Constitution. For instance, Congress may not pass ex post facto laws or tax articles exported from the states (Art. I, sec. 9). The First Amendment denies Congress the right to make laws respecting an establishment of religion, or abridge the freedom of speech or of the press, or the right of the people peaceably to assemble. The Tenth Amendment reserves the powers not delegated to the U.S. to the states, and proponents of STATES' RIGHTS have always relied upon that amendment to curb the encroachment of Federal authority in the area of IMPLIED POWERS.

The First Congress under the Constitution met in New York on 4 March 1789, and since then, by constitutional requirement, in regular annual assembly, which now convenes (Twentieth Amendment, 1933) on 3 January.

The framers of the Constitution placed the larger part of governmental powers in the hands of Congress because they expected that the dominant department should be that which most intimately voices the will of the people. Over the course of years the President, as national party leader, has become the 'prime minister' of the people, and congressional supremacy, which had swung to its maximum power during the Reconstruction period following the Civil War, has waxed or waned in response to the different crises and needs of the time, or in proportion as the people have felt confidence in the leadership of their Chief Executive. Congress cannot compete with the President as a focus of attention, but congressional committee hearings have made clear Congress's very wide power of investigation. The committee system is immensely useful in exposing situations in need of legislative overhaul.

The directing machinery by which Congress works includes the party CAUCUS, whose meetings are irregular and whose powers are informal. The actual management is chiefly focused in the chairmen of standing committees, always chosen on the basis of seniority in office. Each important committee is dominated by a majority representing the party in power. The nature of such management is outlined in the separate articles on the SENATE and the HOUSE OF REPRESENTATIVES.

Congressional Medal of Honor, see *Medal of Honor.*

Congressional Record, published daily during sessions of Congress since the journal was established in 1873, is a verbatim (though unofficial) report of all speeches and statements made on the floor of Congress, or prepared but not delivered, and any further material a congressman may wish to have inserted. It was preceded by *Annals of Congress* (1789–1824), *Register of Debates* (1825–37), and the overlapping *Congressional Globe* (1834–73), all privately issued and sometimes inaccurate. The *Journals* of the Continental Congress have been collected (34 vols., 1904–37). The official record of the proceedings has been the *Journal* of the Senate and the House, published annually since 1789.

CONKLING, ROSCOE (1829–88), son of a New York congressman and Federal judge, on admission to the bar (1850) was immediately appointed district attorney of Albany. As U.S. Representative (1859–63, 1865–67) and Senator (1867–81), he came to be the undisputed Republican leader in his state. During the Grant administration (1869–77) he controlled Federal patronage. A dispute with President Garfield over appointments that Conkling believed he should be allowed to control led him to resign his Senate seat and retire from politics. A powerful spoilsman who opposed civil service reform, Conkling summed up his political philosophy in the remark: 'When Dr. Johnson defined patriotism as the last refuge of a scoundrel, he ignored the enormous possibilities of the word *reform.*'

Connally Resolution (November 1943), sponsored by Senator Tom C. Connally of Texas, urged U.S. leadership in world organization. It specified that the U.S. government must work to such an end only through constitutional procedures and must preserve its sovereign power. The Resolution was adopted by the Senate in place of the Ball-Burton-Hatch-Hill Resolution, which had been rejected on the ground that it relinquished too much sovereignty. The Connally Resolution was the basis for U.S. participation in the SAN FRANCISCO CONFERENCE (1945), which drafted the charter of the United Nations.

Connecticut, southernmost of the New England states and one of the Thirteen Colonies, derives its name from Algonquian words meaning 'long river place.' The Dutch discovered the Connecticut river in 1614, and later built a small fort (1633) on the site of Hartford, a town and area taken over by the British in 1654. EDWARD WINSLOW visited Connecticut in 1632, and soon thereafter the younger JOHN WINTHROP assumed governorship of the new plantation. The compact statement of government set forth in the FUNDAMENTAL ORDERS of 1639, largely written by THOMAS HOOKER and JOHN HAYNES, helped the framers of state constitutions after 1776.

When the NEW HAVEN COLONY, founded as a commercial settlement (1638), joined with the Connecticut colony to form the NEW ENGLAND CONFEDERACY (1643), Winthrop was in a position to secure the Connecticut charter from Charles II in 1662, and that charter remained in force until Connecticut became a state. The unsuccessful attempt of Governor Andros to seize the charter in 1687 made a legend of CHARTER OAK, where the instrument was hidden.

Boundaries of the present state were approximately fixed in 1665, although conflicts over the western boundary, 'to the sea,' continued for another century. They were settled finally in 1786 when the state ceded to the U.S. all its western territories except the WESTERN RESERVE. Because it had remained one of the CHARTER COLONIES, and therefore was privileged to elect its governor, in 1776 it was able to re-elect its patriot governor, JONATHAN TRUMBULL, the only chief executive so appointed after the outbreak of the War of Independence.

By 1800 Connecticut had become an important manufacturing state, whose industries today absorb half the employed population, principally clustered in four cities. Hartford, the largest (with a population in 1960 of 162,000), has been the capital since 1701, jointly until 1875 with New Haven (152,000). During the first half of the 19th century New Haven, still a port of entry, was an important whaling center. Bridgeport (157,000), on Long Island Sound and the leading industrial city, is likewise a port of entry. The brass industry of Waterbury (107,000) dates from the mid-18th century. Agriculture is most profitable for dairy farmers and tobacco growers. Chief among the state's many institutions of higher learning are Yale (New Haven, est. 1701), Trinity (Hartford, est. 1823), Wesleyan (Middletown, est. 1831), and the University of Connecticut (Storrs, est. 1881). The latter institution, with a faculty of 1670, in 1965 enrolled 13,600 students.

Connecticut Compromise, which solved the vexatious problem of state representation, was submitted to the Federal Constitutional Convention (1787) to break the deadlock created by the rejection of both the RANDOLPH PLAN and the PATERSON PLAN. By the terms of the compromise, advanced by Oliver Ellsworth and Roger Sherman, the legislature would be bicameral, one chamber to have equal representation from each state, the other to be based on 'Federal ratio,' or proportional representation. The plan was adopted (16 July) and the work of the convention moved forward.

Connecticut river, 407 miles long, rises in northern New Hampshire lakes, forms the boundary between Vermont and New Hampshire in much of its course, and flows through Massachusetts and Connecticut to enter Long Island Sound. It is a tidal stream to Hartford, and thus was an important artery for 17th-century traders and settlers. It remained a major thoroughfare into New England until the advent of railroads.

Connecticut Wits, or Hartford Wits, were a literary group formed during the late 18th century to celebrate American literary independence. Among its members were JOHN TRUMBULL, TIMOTHY DWIGHT, and JOEL BARLOW.

Conquistadors were the leaders of the Spanish conquest of the New World in the 16th century. They included besides Pizarro (Peru) and CORTES (Mexico), the searchers for gold through Florida and the Southwest: MENÉNDEZ DE AVILÉS, PONCE DE LEÓN, NARVÁEZ, DE SOTO, CABEZA DE VACA, CORONADO, and OÑATE. Daring and intrepid, they and the culture they brought left an indelible stamp on the continental U.S. from the Mississippi to the Far West. Their diaries and reports are important records of aboriginal America.

Conscience Whigs, see *Free-Soil party.*

Conscientious objectors are those who object to warfare, or to military service especially in time of war, on religious or moral grounds. During both World Wars such persons for the most part were allowed to serve in noncombatant branches of the military forces.

Conscription as a compulsory military service was introduced in the U.S. when President Lincoln's call for volunteers at the beginning of the Civil War proved inadequate. The Conscription Act of 1863 was inequitable since it allowed a person of means to escape conscription by hiring a substitute, and it resulted in the tragic DRAFT RIOTS in New York City.

Compulsory service was next invoked by the Selective Service Act (1917), prudently supervised by regional civilian boards. Congress passed a series of SELECTIVE SERVICE AND TRAINING ACTS in 1940 and in subsequent years during World War II. Under present laws individuals are inducted into the armed services through UNIVERSAL MILITARY TRAINING.

Conservation movement in the U.S. was long delayed because neither the public nor the government could be stirred to awareness that seemingly inexhaustible natural resources would ever be depleted. The spectacular rise in farm land values in the early 1900's first alerted the public to the necessity for conservation. As early as 1873 the American Association for the Advancement of Science had called attention to the reckless destruction of forest resources, and both GEORGE PERKINS MARSH and JOHN WESLEY POWELL had pointed out the vital need for a reclamation service. But western congressmen blocked government action because they were unwilling to revise the system which allowed the sale of public land to private interests. When economists at last came to count the cost of exploitive agriculture, they found that 100,000,000 acres of land had been irreparably destroyed by erosion, and twice that amount rendered almost useless. The Great Plains were turning into deserts and, as Powell had predicted, recurrent floods and droughts had become the inevitable consequence of a laissez-faire government conservation policy.

Congress finally passed the FOREST RESERVE ACT (1891) and the CAREY LAND ACT (1894). But reclamation lagged because the official attitude was sluggish, and railroads, lumber companies, and ranchers had the opportunity to perpetuate gigantic frauds. President Theodore Roosevelt, who knew and loved the West, began his uphill battle for conservation as soon as he came into office, and the most important achievement of his administration was the provision it made to conserve the natural resources of the nation.

The NEWLANDS RECLAMATION ACT (1902) created the Bureau of Reclamation and made provision for the purchase of western lands. Roosevelt transferred the NATIONAL FORESTS to the Department of Agriculture, whose Forest Service bureau, under the farsighted GIFFORD PINCHOT, administered them on scientific principles. In 1907 Roosevelt set aside further vast forest reserves and appointed an Inland Waterways Commission, which emphasized the connection between forests, water supply, and stream flow. Out of the recommendations of this Commission grew the plan for a national conservation conference, held at the White House (1908) and attended by state governors, cabinet members, justices of the Supreme Court, and notables in the fields of politics, science, and education. This was one of the most distinguished gatherings in American history.

From the meeting immediately stemmed the National Conservation Commission, which set about making the first inventory of the country's natural resources, a labor supplemented by the work of conservation bodies in 41 states. When Congress, still dominated by powerful anticonservation lobbies, hampered the work of the Commission by refusing to appropriate funds for its activities, Roosevelt persuaded the staffs of several Departments to volunteer their services, and ignored an amendment to the civil service bill forbidding Federal personnel to do outside work in such instances. Roosevelt made an issue of the problem, won popular support, and the Supreme Court upheld the constitutionality of his procedure.

The National Park Service was created in 1916. In 1920 the development of water power on navigable streams was placed under the control of the FEDERAL POWER COMMISSION, and in 1928 construction was begun on HOOVER DAM. But not until F. D. Roosevelt took office did another President see the problem of conservation as a unit or fully comprehend its relationship to national (indeed hemispheric) welfare. Nowhere did the New Deal, like the earlier Roosevelt's 'Square Deal,' institute more far-reaching changes than in the realm of power regulation and the conservation and utilization of natural resources. The first step, directed both to emergency relief and to permanent reform, was the creation of the CIVILIAN CONSERVATION CORPS (1933), which in the few years of its existence made enormous strides in preserving, restoring, and increasing the natural resources of the nation.

The purposes of creating the TENNESSEE VALLEY AUTHORITY (1933) and constructing mammoth dams on the Colorado and Columbia rivers and in the Missouri river basin were several, but principally the work has assured FLOOD CONTROL and has created vast sources of water for irrigation and hydroelectric power. By 1960 the agencies set up within the Departments of the Interior, Agriculture, and Commerce had been enabled, under professional direction and by congressional appropriations, to slow and perhaps to halt the exhaustion of the nation's natural resources. Presidents Kennedy and Johnson made conservation a major crusade, stressing a variety of measures to curb water pollution as well as to develop a saline water conversion program. One impressive project was the vast Pacific Southwest Water Plan of 1964, intended to benefit the five states of the Colorado river basin at a cost of $3.1 billion. In the following year, the federal government announced a regional plan for the Lake Erie region, aimed primarily at water pollution.

See C. R. Hise, *The Conservation of Natural Resources in the U.S.* (1924); L. H. Gulick, *American Forest Policy* (1951); Arthur Maass, *Muddy Waters* (1951); President's Materials Policy Commission, *Resources for Freedom* (5 vols., 1952).

Conspiracy laws, in the U.S. as in England, for a long time were directed against TRADE UNIONS, and the concerted stoppage of work by a group of employees in a strike could be judged criminal RESTRAINT OF TRADE. In 1805 a strike of Philadelphia shoemakers occasioned the first labor conspiracy case in American judicial annals; the defendants were found guilty, fined, and the strike was broken. The decision in COMMONWEALTH *v.* HUNT (1842) that members of a trade union were not collectively liable for the illegal acts of individuals later became a principle in American law. The SHERMAN ANTITRUST ACT (1890) and the CLAYTON ANTITRUST ACT (1914) were interpreted as applying to trade union combinations, but since the NORRIS-LA-GUARDIA ANTI-INJUNCTION ACT (1932), the subjection of unions to conspiracy charges has virtually ended.

Constitution of the U.S., the document embodying the basic law of the land, is the world's oldest written constitution. It was adopted 17 September 1787 by the FEDERAL CONSTITUTIONAL CONVENTION, and immediately sent by the Continental Congress to the states for ratification. The states took affirmative action as follows:

Delaware	7	Dec.	1787	unanimous
Penn.	12	Dec.	1787	46 – 23
New Jersey	18	Dec.	1787	unanimous
Georgia	2	Jan.	1788	unanimous
Conn.	9	Jan.	1788	128 – 40
Mass.	6	Feb.	1788	187 – 168
Maryland	28	April	1788	63 – 11
S. Carolina	23	May	1788	149 – 73
New Hamp.	21	June	1788	57 – 47
Virginia	26	June	1788	89 – 79
New York	26	July	1788	30 – 27
N. Carolina	21	Nov.	1789	194 – 77
Rhode Island	29	May	1790	34 – 32

With the ratification of the ninth state (New Hampshire) the instrument became effective, superseding the ARTICLES OF CONFEDERATION. On the day that Washington was inaugurated President (30 April 1789) Congress first met in session, and the Constitution was declared in effect.

The Constitution is primarily a document in federalism, and the political philosophy it embodies was expounded in the FEDERALIST PAPERS (1787–88), written by Alexander Hamilton, James Madison, and John Jay. That extraordinary treatise won support for the kind of federalism which the Constitution voices. It lays down rules for a central control which also recognizes the role of state governments. It is 'rigid' in the sense that it is superior to ordinary statutes, and it is alterable only by a gradual process of AMENDMENTS. Among its important features are provisions for separation of the legislative, executive, and judicial branches of government; a system of CHECKS AND BALANCES which legally protects the autonomy of those branches; and vital assurances of liberty to citizens, specified in its BILL OF RIGHTS in the form of limitations imposed upon the national and state governments. Its brevity and general statements of principle have given opportunity for statutory elaboration by Congress, and judicial construction by the Supreme Court. It creates its own sanctions, enforced by its own courts and officials. State officers are 'bound by oath or affirmation' to support it, and Congress is given the power to call state militias under the President's command 'to execute the laws of the Union.'

Yet the Constitution does not function alone, for the supremacy of Federal laws is limited to those made 'in pursuance of the Constitution,' and in no legal sense are states subordinate entities. Indeed, amendment ratifications themselves are dependent upon the consent of three-fourths of the state legislatures or conventions. The framers of the Constitution attempted to solve the problem of distribution of power among governments, to provide means for enforcing the terms of the distribution and at the same time protect the liberty of individuals. The Civil War decided the issue of states' rights in favor of the advocates of a strong national union. Since then, Federal power has gradually increased.

See H. C. Hockett, *The Constitutional History of the U.S.* (2 vols., 1939); C. B. Swisher, *American Constitutional Development* (1943); and A. H. Kelly and W. A. Harbison, *The American Constitution* (1948).

Constitution, 44-gun frigate, the most famous vessel in the history of the U.S. navy, was launched at Boston in 1797. She served in the undeclared naval war with FRANCE, and in the TRIPOLITAN WAR. While flagship of ISAAC HULL in the War of 1812, she defeated the British frigate *Guerrière,* thus bolstering a sagging national morale, and soon after, when she destroyed the *Java* in a duel off the coast of Brazil (under the command of William Bainbridge), the performance earned for her the sobriquet 'Old Ironsides.' Oliver Wendell Holmes's poem of that name roused popular sentiment to prevent her being dismantled in 1830, and she later served as a training ship. Since 1925, rebuilt by popular subscription, she has been berthed as a historic relic at Boston. She is the oldest vessel in the U.S. Navy still in commission.

Constitutional Amendments, see *Amendments.*

Constitutional Convention, see *Federal Constitutional Convention.*

Constitutional Union party, composed of former Whigs, 'Know-Nothings,' and southern Unionists, on the eve of the Civil War organized without a platform in a mood of desperation, with 'no political principle other than the Constitution of the country, the union of the states, and the enforcement of the laws.' Delegates from twenty states assembled at Baltimore (May 1860), and nominated JOHN BELL of Tennessee and EDWARD EVERETT of Massachusetts as candidates. Derisively known as the 'Do-Nothing' party, because it made no statements on the vital issues of slavery, it carried only the border states of Virginia, Kentucky, and Tennessee, and polled 39 electoral votes.

Consular Service, see *Foreign Service.*

Continental army, as distinct from militia and guerrilla companies, was created by Congress (June 1775) to fight the War of Independence. George Washington was unanimously chosen commander in chief and served without a salary. Congress voted the issue of CONTINENTAL CURRENCY, with the colonies pledged to share the burden of redemption in proportion to population. A general organizational plan was adopted, with the appointment of four major generals: ARTEMAS WARD (Massachusetts), CHARLES LEE (Virginia), PHILIP SCHUYLER (New York), and ISRAEL PUTNAM (Connecticut).

Washington's first task was to train officers and men in the rudiments of military discipline. Men often elected their own officers, and in the early months of the war practically no distinction was drawn between officers and enlisted men. Congress therefore sent Silas Deane to France (1776) to secure FOREIGN OFFICERS for service in America. Two of the most distinguished foreign officers of the Revolution reached Philadelphia in July 1777 and were commissioned major generals: LAFAYETTE and de KALB. Foremost among others were KOSCIUSKO (colonel of engineers, October 1776) and von STEUBEN (inspector general, May 1778).

No accurate figures are available as to the number of men who served. The rolls indicate that altogether there were some 231,000 in the Continental army, and 164,000 in the militia. Washington never commanded more than 26,000 at one time, and usually much fewer. Other generals seldom had more than 6000 under their command. Desertions were common, and in the Continental army the enlistment terms were for a year. (In the militia the terms were even briefer.) The fact that Washington not only kept the army from disintegration but won the war is evidence of his masterly conduct of affairs.

Continental Congress, assembled first as an advisory council for the colonies, eventually became the central government, however fragmentary its powers. Called simply 'The Congress,' the First Continental Congress sat at Philadelphia (5 September–26 October 1774) to consider action for recovery of rights forfeited under Parliament's repressive COERCIVE ACTS. These grievances not being redressed, the Second Continental Congress met in the same place on 10 May 1775, after hostilities had commenced at Lexington and Concord. It created the CONTINENTAL ARMY, and for nearly six years directed the War of Independence. Although it voiced the will of the several states in commonly shared activities, it was not a legislature. Actually it was a gathering of ambassadors from the colonies with authority derived only from general public approval.

Since peaceful arbitration of differences between Great Britain and the colonies was clearly impossible after the outbreak of hostilities, Congress voted to discuss (2 July 1776) a resolution 'that these United Colonies are, and of right ought to be, free and independent States.' Two days later it formally adopted The Declaration of Independence. Aware that an instrument of union, however imperfect, was a necessity, in November 1777 Congress agreed upon a framework of government, the ARTICLES OF CONFEDERATION. By 1781, when final ratification of the Articles was a fact, the theory of a league of independent states had largely become a fiction. The passage from the Articles to the Federal Constitution was stormy, but when the Continental Congress was superseded by the permanent Congress in 1789, it could give to the new government the benefits of tested experience, as well as an acceptable body of substantive law.

Continental currency was issued as bills of credit by the Continental Congress and by the states to finance the War of Independence. In June 1775 Congress authorized $2,000,000; by 1779 Congress had permitted issues of more than

$241,000,000, and the states an additional $200,000,000. Depreciation of so large an amount was inevitable, and by 1781 the currency was 'not worth a continental.' Under the ASSUMPTION ACT of 1790 it was accepted in subscription of U.S. bonds at the rate of 100 to 1.

Continental Divide, the 'backbone' of a continent, in North America is the great ridge of the ROCKY MOUNTAINS, separating watercourses that flow west to the Pacific Ocean, and east either into Hudson Bay or south into the Gulf of Mexico. It is sometimes called the Great Divide, a name especially used to designate the high, almost impenetrable ranges of the southern section. Within the Continental Divide are Glacier, Yellowstone, and Rocky Mountain national parks.

Continental navy originated when Congress appointed a Naval Committee (October 1775) which purchased four vessels and appointed ESEK HOPKINS commander in chief. During the War of Independence naval vessels were chiefly used to seize British supply ships and merchantmen, transport munitions from France, and carry agents and dispatches to and from Europe. The raids made by JOHN PAUL JONES pinned down British units that might have injured America, and as propaganda in France for the patriot cause they were especially important. The deployment of naval forces on Lake Champlain contributed to the American success at SARATOGA (1777), which persuaded France to enter into the war officially. Thereafter Congress gradually dismantled the Continental navy. During the war the navy employed 260 naval officers, 124 marine officers, and 73 vessels of all descriptions.

Continental System, the scheme of action adopted by Napoleon in his economic warfare with England, was initiated by the BERLIN DECREE (1806) and extended by others, especially by the MILAN DECREE (1807), which forbade any nation to trade with Great Britain. England retaliated by ORDERS IN COUNCIL, forbidding nearly all trade between nations obeying the Berlin Decree. Since England controlled the seas, the Continental System was doomed from the start. Large-scale smuggling throve everywhere, with the U.S. taking a major part in the illicit commerce, thereby aggravating Anglo-American relations already exacerbated by British IMPRESSMENT of American seamen.

Contract Labor Acts, affecting immigrant laborers, have twice been voted by Congress. The Contract Labor Act of 1864 sought to induce foreign workers to emigrate to America at a time of labor scarcity incident to the Civil War. Pressure from labor unions led Congress to repeal the Act in 1868.

In 1885 a new Contract Labor Act forbade the importation of foreign labor (except for professional, skilled, and domestic labor), and in the General Immigration Act of 1917 the scope of such protection to resident labor was greatly widened. Since World War II *braceros,* temporary Mexican farm hands, have been legally admitted.

Convention of 1787, see *Federal Constitutional Convention.*

Convention of 1818, signed at London by Richard Rush, minister to Great Britain, and Albert Gallatin, minister to France, fixed the northwest boundary between the U.S. and British North America along the 49th parallel from the Lake of the Woods to the crest of the Rocky Mountains. It also affirmed American rights to the fisheries off Newfoundland and Labrador. The disputed Oregon region was left open to a ten-year joint occupation, later renewed until final settlement of the OREGON BOUNDARY DISPUTE in 1846.

Conway Cabal, so called, was in fact an effort of a New England coterie (1777–78) to gain political control of the army by replacing Washington as commander in chief (recently defeated at Brandywine and Germantown) with General Horatio Gates, the victor at Saratoga. An indiscreet letter written by Major Thomas Conway to Gates became known in an offensive and garbled form to Washington, who made Gates aware of his knowledge. The maneuver to give Massachusetts control of affairs, rather than the Continental Congress, was inept.

Public opinion overwhelmingly supported Washington when some details leaked out. The conspirators, to effect a smoke screen, stigmatized Conway by fastening his name to the affair, with which Gates denied any connection. Subsequently, Congress quickly accepted Conway's resignation. The duel he fought with one of Washington's friends nearly proved fatal to him. That incident was followed by his apology to Washington, and the incident was closed.

CONWELL, Russell Herman (1843–1925), Philadelphia Baptist minister, was first president (1884) of Temple University. His lecture 'Acres of Diamonds,' first delivered in 1861, and repeated some 6000 times to audiences eager to hear that 'opportunity is in your own back yard,' stressed the responsibility of wealth, and reconciled Christianity with the spirit of capitalism.

COOK, Frederick Albert (1865–1940), New York physician, accompanied Robert E. Peary as surgeon on Peary's 1891–92 arctic expedition, and later participated in expeditions to Greenland, Alaska, and other remote places. Upon his return from an arctic expedition in 1909, his claims that he had discovered the North Pole in 1908 were challenged by Peary. The bitter controversy which followed was resolved by scientific evidence in Peary's favor.

COOK, James (1728–79), English naval captain and explorer, after circumnavigating the globe and exploring the Antarctic, in 1776 began a search for a passage from the Pacific Ocean to the Atlantic along the northern coast of North America. His sojourn at Nootka later precipitated the Anglo-Spanish NOOTKA SOUND CONTROVERSY (1789), settled in favor of Great Britain. Most importantly, it gave promise to English and American shipowners that a lucrative trade could be established by purchasing furs from the coastal Indians and selling them in China.

Satisfied that no passage was possible, he sailed south, effectively discovering (1778) Hawaii. (The Islands had been charted by the Spanish navigator Gaetano in 1555, but their existence had been forgotten.) There he was killed by a native. The scale of Captain Cook's survey work was such as to place him first among British maritime discoverers. His voyages touched the imaginations of men everywhere, not least in America, for Americans had been made aware of the world stretching westward of the American continent.

COOKE, Jay (1821–1905), Ohio-born financier, in 1861 founded Jay Cooke and Company, which became a leading banking house of Philadelphia. As the Treasury's fiscal agent during the Civil War, Cooke planned and carried out a masterful advertising campaign to sell bonds in small issues directly to the people, the first campaign of its type and a model for comparable fund drives in later wars. In 1870 Cooke sought to raise $100,000,000 for the Northern Pacific Railroad, and the spectacular failure of his company, through overexpansion and other errors, precipitated the PANIC OF 1873. He later repaid his creditors and through an investment in a silver mine again became wealthy.

The Tycoon, as his partners called him, was the first American investment banker to operate on a large scale, and though he himself failed, his general strategy was sound, and was successfully used by later bankers.

COOKE, John Esten (1830–86), Virginia author, for a time practiced law in Richmond, while devoting himself chiefly to writing. The publication of his novel of colonial life in Williamsburg, *The Virginia Comedians* (1854), gave him a nation-wide reputation. Cooke served in the Confederate army throughout the Civil War, which furnished him with material for two volumes of essays and a series of romances, including *Surrey of Eagle's Nest* (1866). He later chronicled Virginia history in works which idealized the past, and as entertainment such volumes as *Stories of the Old Dominion* (1879) are still absorbing.

COOLEY, Charles Horton (1864–1929), son of T. M. COOLEY, was a professor of sociology at Michigan, from which institution he graduated (1887), and where he taught throughout his life. He was a pioneer in the widely adopted concept of society known as the 'primary group,' composed of people who habitually (and often informally) deal with each other face-to-face; the group which, according to Cooley, forms the true reality of social existence. His writings include *Human Nature and the Social Order* (1902; rev. ed., 1922), *Social Organization* (1909), and *Social Process* (1918).

COOLEY, THOMAS MCINTYRE (1824–98) professor of American law (1859–84) and of American history (1884–98) at Michigan, was a justice of the state supreme court (1864–85), and first chairman of the Interstate Commerce Commission (1887–91). His arguments on the constitutional issue whether states can impair the obligations of contract are set forth in his *Treatise on the Constitutional Limitations . . .* (1868; 8th ed., 1927), which infers the freedom of the judiciary from legislative interference, and remains the great apologia for LAISSEZ-FAIRE economics in American constitutional law. His other writings include *The Law of Taxation* (1876), and *General Principles of Constitutional Law in the United States* (1880). With Joseph Story he ranks as the most influential commentator on the Federal Constitution.

COOLIDGE, [JOHN] CALVIN (1872–1933), 30th President of the U.S. (1923–29), was born at Plymouth, Vermont. He graduated from Amherst (1895), practiced law at Northampton, Massachusetts, and entered state politics, serving two terms as governor (1919–20). His use of militia to suppress the BOSTON POLICE STRIKE in 1919 and his wire to Gompers on that occasion ('There is no right to strike against the public safety by anybody, anywhere, any time') brought him into national prominence and won him the Republican nomination for Vice President in 1920. The ticket of Harding and Coolidge won the election.

Respected for his probity, Coolidge was untouched by the scandals of the Harding administration. Upon Harding's death, Coolidge succeeded to the presidency (3 August 1923), and he was elected President in 1924. His advocacy of tax cuts, economy in government, and his strong laissez-faire policy toward business coincided with an era of general prosperity, and gave the taciturn New Englander a strong popular backing. In 1928 he did not 'choose' to run for the nomination, which he probably could have won. Instead, he backed his secretary of commerce, Herbert Hoover, who was elected President. Cautious in domestic affairs and virtually an isolationist in relation to Europe, Coolidge typified the Republican philosophy of conservatism endorsed by an overwhelming majority of Americans during the era of the 1920's.

See W. A. White, *A Puritan in Babylon* (1938).

COOPER, JAMES FENIMORE (1789–1851), was reared in the Cooperstown, New York, frontier village which his father had settled. He entered Yale at thirteen, but was expelled two years later for some obscure disciplinary reason. He took to sea for five years, serving as midshipman in the U.S. navy, and after his marriage (1811) eventually moved to his manorial Cooperstown estate. A man of action accidentally turned novelist (on a dare from his wife), by 1825 Cooper had become, next to Scott, the most popular romancer in the language. At his death he left to posterity some 30 novels, several volumes of indispensable social criticism, and a name known throughout the world.

The *Leatherstocking Tales* depict the life of the American frontier, and the sea stories reflect a nautical knowledge which he used with scholarly precision in his *History of the Navy of the U.S.* (1839). Cooper's truculent criticism of his countrymen, inspired by an aristocratic ideal and a deep patriotism, was expressed in such writings as *The American Democrat* (1838). His *Gleanings in Europe* (3 vols., 1837–38), gathered during an eight-year sojourn abroad, are also trenchant and biting opinions of social and political aspirations as he observed them in France, England, and Italy.

COOPER, MYLES (1735–85), English-born Anglican clergyman, became professor of moral philosophy (1762) at King's College (Columbia) in New York, and a year later succeeded SAMUEL JOHNSON as president (1763–75). Among other promising teachers, he attracted SAMUEL BARD, who founded the medical school (1767), later the College of

Physicians and Surgeons. Cooper's intellectual standards increased the prestige of the institution, but on the eve of the War of Independence his outspoken loyalist pamphlets were deeply resented. In 1775 he returned to England.

COOPER, PETER (1791–1883), New York industrialist, at his ironworks in Baltimore constructed (1830) for the Baltimore and Ohio Railroad the first efficient steam locomotive built in the U.S. (*Tom Thumb*). His diversified holdings came to include rolling mills, from which he rolled the first structural iron for fireproof buildings (1854), foundries, and telegraph companies. He was the chief financial backer of the Atlantic cable laid by Cyrus Field. A civic-minded philanthropist, he organized improvements in New York municipal departments, the public school system, and founded COOPER UNION. As presidential candidate for the Greenback party in 1876, he polled 81,000 votes. For 40 years he was a partner in business, education, and philanthropy with his son-in-law ABRAM HEWITT.

COOPER, THOMAS (1759–1839), educated at Oxford, emigrated from England (1794) when he was threatened with persecution because of his strong sympathies for the French Revolution. He took up the practice of law in Pennsylvania. For his newspaper attacks (1799) on President Adams in the matter of the ALIEN AND SEDITION ACTS, Cooper (termed by Adams a 'learned, ingenious, scientific, and talented madcap') was fined and imprisoned. Like his friend Joseph Priestley, with whom he collaborated in scientific research, Cooper was highly esteemed by Thomas Jefferson, who procured Cooper's appointment (1811) as first professor of natural science and law in the University of Virginia. Cooper immediately resigned the post because his Unitarian views were denounced by the Virginia clergy.

After teaching briefly at Dickinson College and at the University of Pennsylvania, Cooper accepted a chair in chemistry at South Carolina College (1819). Elected president of the institution in 1820, he taught chemistry and political science. His *Lectures on the Elements of Political Economy* (1826) was a pioneer textbook on the subject. Although he was distinguished for his enlightened views of education, his vehement anticlericalism led to a 'trial' for atheism, and to his resignation (1834).

As a champion of free trade, state sovereignty, and the institution of slavery, Cooper prepared the way for the 'South Carolina movement.' His advocacy of nullification anticipated Calhoun's, and influenced the thinking of many southern statesmen.

See Dumas Malone, *The Public Life of Thomas Cooper* (1926).

Cooper Union, founded (1859) in New York City by PETER COOPER, pioneered in art and engineering schools and offers free courses in practical subjects to working people of all races and creeds. It charges no tuition. In 1965, with an endowment of $16,600,000 and a faculty of 146, it enrolled 1200 students.

Co-operative Marketing Act (1929), see *Federal Farm Board.*

Co-operative societies may be of two kinds. The more common and important are the consumers' co-operative associations for the purchase and sale of goods and commodities, developed in England by the Rochdale Pioneers (1844), influenced by the theories of ROBERT OWEN. Producers' co-operatives, on the other hand, were started by groups of workers in an effort to achieve freedom from wage labor, and, unlike consumers' co-operatives, generally failed.

The earliest co-operative in the U.S. was an industrial union established at Boston in 1844. During the 19th century consumers' co-operatives found their strongest support among farmers, and were fostered by the GRANGER MOVEMENT, and by such organizations as the NATIONAL LABOR UNION and the KNIGHTS OF LABOR. At present nearly 10,000 co-operative societies function, chartered and supervised by the Bureau of Federal Credit Unions under the Social Security Administration.

COPE, EDWARD DRINKER (1840–97), after study at the Philadelphia Academy of Natural Sciences and travel abroad, became curator of the Academy, and in 1889 professor of geology and paleontology at the University of Pennsylvania. He accompanied F. V. HAYDEN on Hayden's noted western surveys, and discovered many new species of extinct animals. Cope's work prepared the way for classification of North American reptiles, amphibians, and fish. He was a principal founder of 'Neo-Lamarckianism' (the theory of the inheritance of acquired characteristics), an issue which brought him into bitter controversy with the Yale paleontologist O. C. MARSH.

COPLAND, AARON (1900–), New York composer, studied under Goldmark and Boulanger. He vigorously advanced the cause of American music as a founder of the Yaddo Center (1932), the American Composers Alliance (1937), the Copland-Sessions concerts (1928–31), and as author of *Our New Music* (1941), a contemporary survey. Assistant director of the Berkshire Music Center since its beginning, he has exercised a powerful influence on the musical scene since 1927. His music ranges from the astringent style of his piano *Variations* (1930), *Sextet* (1937), *Quartet* (1950), and *Fantasy* (1957) to the deliberately popular *El Salón México* (1936), *Billy the Kid* (1938), and *A Lincoln Portrait* (1942). His ballet *Appalachian Spring* won the 1945 Pulitzer Prize in music. Representative of his dramatic works are *The Second Hurricane* (1937) for high schools, and *The Tender Land* (1954), a full-scale opera. Distinguished by craftsmanship, rhythmic vitality, and brilliant scoring, his music perhaps has been more widely performed in concert halls, in motion pictures and on the radio, than that of any other living American composer. His *Music and Imagination* (1952) sets forth his aesthetic principles.

COPLEY, JOHN SINGLETON (1738–1815), Boston-born painter, as a boy studied with the engraver and painter Peter Pelham (1695–1751), whose daughter he later married. At eighteen Copley became a professional portraitist, and a painting he sent for exhibition in London (1766) caught the eye of BENJAMIN WEST, who urged the young artist to come to London. Copley enjoyed patronage in New York and Philadelphia as well as Boston, but his loyalist sympathies determined his willingness to leave the country (1774) and settle in England, where he was elected to the Royal Academy (1783).

His later paintings, influenced by such fashionable portrait masters as Reynolds, Romney, and Gainsborough, never rivaled the severe simplicity, directness, and insight into character in his American work. Although he rejected his birthright, he is best in depicting what he knew it to be, and he is recognized as the first great American painter. He is well represented by such canvases as *Paul Revere* (Boston Museum); *John Hancock* (City of Boston); and *The Copley Family* (National Gallery), the most important group portrait by an American artist.

Copper mining became commercially profitable late in the 19th century, after the dynamo had been perfected, thereby supplying the large quantities of cheap electricity needed to refine the ore. Early settlers had located copper on the Atlantic coast, especially in Connecticut and New Jersey. The mines reported by Lewis Cass in his 1830 exploration of Michigan were valuable at the time because they yielded pure copper, which did not require reduction. Today the U.S. is the greatest source of copper (one-third of the world's supply). It is the principal mineral in order of value in Arizona, Nevada, and Utah, and the second in Montana.

Copperheads, during the Civil War, was the derogatory term applied to those Northerners (mostly Democrats) who, like the snake that strikes without warning, turned against their compatriots to support the South. The secret order of KNIGHTS OF THE GOLDEN CIRCLE was largely composed of such 'peace' Democrats, the most prominent of whom was CLEMENT L. VALLANDIGHAM. Flourishing chiefly in Ohio, Indiana, and Illinois, Copperheads influenced the Democratic party platform in 1864, and though discredited at the war's end, they handicapped the Democratic party for some years.

Copyright, as a protection of rights of literary property, was enacted into law by most of the states in the period immediately following the War of Independence. The earliest Federal copyright act was passed by the first Congress in 1790, pursuant to the constitutional guarantee that authors for a limited time may have exclusive rights to their work. Then followed a long struggle to gain protection against piracy abroad, and to cover such items as photographs, engraving, architectural designs, musical composition, and play productions. Not until passage of the so-called International Copyright Act (1891) were foreign writers given a measure of protection. The statute in force today was enacted in 1909, and applies to all published (and certain unpublished) works in the domain of literature, music, and art. It provides protection for a term of 28 years with a possible renewal for 28 years more.

Coral Sea, Battle of (7–8 May 1942), fought entirely by carrier-based planes, was the first naval engagement in history in which no surface vessels met in combat. The battle was a major U.S. victory, for at the start of World War II it prevented Japan from cutting the lifeline to Australia. The U.S. carrier *Lexington* was lost in the engagement.

CORBETT, JAMES JOHN (1866–1933), California-born pugilist, won the first heavyweight boxing title under the Marquis of Queensberry rules by knocking out JOHN L. SULLIVAN in the twenty-first round at New Orleans in 1892. One of the most popular champion prizefighters ever known in the U.S., in 1897 'Gentleman Jim' lost the title in a fourteen-round bout to the English boxer Bob Fitzsimmons (1862–1917) at Carson City, Nevada.

CORBIN, MARGARET (1751–1800), on the death of her husband in the attack on Fort Washington (in Manhattan) in 1776, commanded her husband's cannon until she was severely wounded. She was the first woman to be pensioned by the government, and a monument was erected in her honor at West Point (1916), where she is now buried.

Corn (Indian corn or maize) is a cereal native to the Western Hemisphere, where it had been domesticated and cultivated long before white men arrived in the New World. Now the leading grain crop in the U.S., it is used as food for man and fodder for animals. In the 1830's, Kentucky, Tennessee, and Virginia were the chief corn producers, but by 1860 the Middle West, from Ohio to Kansas and Nebraska, had come to be known as the Corn Belt. Hogs fattened on corn were driven to packing houses (chiefly in Cincinnati and Chicago), then shipped to retail markets throughout the country.

The ensiling process was developed in the 1880's, and in the dairy regions the corn silo is an essential adjunct of the American milk industry. Starch, sugar, and a variety of commercial products are made from corn. Most recently its husks and stalks have been the basis of new synthetic chemical industries. The importance of corn in the national economy was recognized by the establishment (1935) of a corn research institute at the Iowa agricultural station.

Cornell University, co-educational, land-grant institution located principally at Ithaca, New York, was chartered in 1865 and opened three years later. Founded by the industrialist Ezra Cornell (1807–74) as a nonsectarian college, under its first president, ANDREW D. WHITE, it gained national recognition as a liberal arts foundation specializing in the humanities, natural science, and engineering. Its school of medicine is in New York City, and its aeronautical laboratory in Buffalo. It is especially known for its experimental agricultural activities. In 1965, with an endowment of $145,590,000 and a faculty of 2288, it enrolled 13,000.

CORNPLANTER (*c.* 1740–1836), half-breed son of a Dutch trader, was a famous chief of the Seneca Indians. He led war parties for the British during the Revolution, but later became a powerful advocate for peace, and many Indian treaties (after 1784) bear his name. The state of Pennsylvania granted him land on the Allegheny river, where he lived to an advanced age, highly respected both by his Indian and white contemporaries.

CORNWALLIS, CHARLES (1738–1805), 1st Marquis, British general during the War of Independence, having served under Sir William Howe at the battle of Long Island, in the New Jersey campaigns, and at Brandywine, in 1778 became second in command when Sir Henry Clinton replaced Howe as commander in chief of British forces in America. His defeat of Gates in South Carolina at the battle of Camden (1780) opened the way for an invasion of North Carolina, and ultimately to his decision to establish a base at Yorktown in Virginia (1781), from which he could maintain communication with Clinton's forces in New York. This he did without Clinton's approval. Hemmed in by American and French attacks by land and sea, he surrendered his entire army to Washington, thus effectively bringing the war to a close. In the bitter Clinton-Cornwallis wrangle that ensued, Cornwallis was fully exonerated. But the fact remains that by selecting Yorktown as the site for a decisive engagement, Cornwallis gave Washington an ideal opportunity to inflict overwhelming defeat.

CORONADO, FRANCISCO VÁSQUEZ DE (*c.* 1510–54), governor of Nueva Galicia in Mexico, in 1540 set out to locate the fabulous wealth reported about the Seven Cities of Cíbola. He crossed southeastern Arizona into the Zuñi country of New Mexico, where he found only humble Indian pueblos. Still hopeful, in 1541 he undertook a journey to the promised land of Quivira. This second expedition, which took him east across the Texas Panhandle into Oklahoma and Kansas, proved as futile as the first. Disillusioned, he ingloriously returned to Nueva Galicia and, deprived of his governorship, lived thereafter in peaceful eclipse. Historically the expeditions were important, for they opened the Southwest to Spanish colonization.

Corporations, as bodies of persons associated to venture an enterprise, were the means by which the English settled America. Such were the great JOINT-STOCK COMPANIES of the early 17th century. Almost equivalent to royal monopolies, those corporate franchises came to be distrusted in the later colonial period, and thus the power of incorporation was vested with the individual states. After the Revolution corporations organized banks and insurance companies, built turnpikes, canals, and railroads; and soon expanded to areas of manufacture and trade.

General incorporation laws developed in the first part of the 19th century. The coming of the mass market created by the building of railroads led to large-scale output through the combining of factories (or marketing facilities), thus creating such giant corporations as the AMERICAN TELEPHONE AND TELEGRAPH COMPANY, GENERAL MOTORS CORPORATION, and the U.S. STEEL CORPORATION.

Corporate power was greatly strengthened by the Fourteenth Amendment (1868), which gave 'persons' (a word which legally includes corporations) the protection of the Federal courts from unfriendly state legislation. Furthermore, certain large corporations tended to incorporate in states with lenient incorporation laws, such as New Jersey, Delaware, and Maryland.

Corregidor, fortress island off Bataan peninsula at the entrance to Manila Bay, during the early phase of World War II was the last Allied stronghold in the Philippines. After the fall of BATAAN (April 1942) the men holding Corregidor under Lieutenant General Jonathan M. Wainwright (1883–1953) fought valiantly until Wainwright was compelled to surrender 'the Rock' on 6 May. It was recaptured from the Japanese in February 1945.

Corrupt Practices Acts are state and Federal laws passed to safeguard the honesty of political campaigns and elections. The first enactment, to eliminate bribery, illegal registration, and padded voting, was passed by New York (1890). Other states began erecting similar safeguards, and by 1952 all states had adopted such laws. In 1925 Congress regulated campaign spending for election to either house of Congress, prohibited banks or corporations from spending in behalf of candidates, and required identification of those who made large donations.

CORTES, HERNANDO (1485–1547), Spanish conquistador, having made voyages to Hispaniola (1504) and Cuba (1511), in February 1519 led an expedition to conquer Mexico. He arrived on the American mainland with 550 soldiers at a time when the Mexican natives were smarting under Aztec rule. Aided by coastal Indians, Cortes began his famous march from Vera Cruz to the great plateau capital of Tenochtitlán. He arrived in November and was received by Montezuma as a god, a descendant of the fabled Quetzalcoatl. At an opportune moment Cortes made the emperor a hostage, and set up a puppet government. Cortes then returned to the coast to face his rival NARVÁEZ, whom he defeated.

Meanwhile the Spanish deputy in charge of Montezuma had instigated a massacre of Aztecs. Soon after the return of Cortes the Aztecs attacked the Spanish; Montezuma was killed, and with heavy losses the Spaniards fought their way out of the city (June 1520). The next year on the plains of Teotihuacan, Cortes besieged the capital, which fell on 13 August 1521, and with it the Aztec empire.

Cortes then extended his conquest over most of Mexico and into Central America, thereby amassing spectacular treasure, and creating a New World empire for Spain. For years the Gulf of Mexico was known as the Sea of Cortes. When his power was usurped by others, he returned to Spain (1528–30) to seek redress, which in part Charles V granted. For the next ten years Cortes sponsored exploration of the west coast of New Spain, and his work in Baja (Lower) California was a major activity of the 1530's. But in the end Cortes was bested by his rival Mendoza. In 1540 he again sought a hearing in Spain, where, neglected by the court, he died in obscurity. His conquest of Mexico nevertheless takes rank as one of the prodigious feats in military annals.

See Henry R. Wagner, *The Rise of Hernando Cortes* (1944).

CORWIN, EDWARD SAMUEL (1878–1963), professor of politics (1911–18) and of jurisprudence (1918–46) at Princeton, was a leading authority on American political history and law. His many books include *The Doctrine of Judicial Review* (1914), *The Constitution and What It Means Today* (12th ed., 1958), and *The President, Office and Powers* (4th ed., 1958). One of his major public services was the preparation, under government aegis, of *The Constitution Annotated: Analysis and Interpretation,* Senate Document 170, 82nd Congress, 2nd Session (1953).

CORYELL, J. R., see *Dime novels.*

COTTON, JOHN (1584–1652), won fame as preacher and theologian at Emmanuel College, Cambridge, of which he was dean. He became vicar of the influential parish of St. Botolph's in Boston, England, where his Puritan innovations so disturbed the Anglican establishment that he resigned. In 1633 he emigrated to Boston in the Massachusetts Bay Colony and became one of the earliest exponents of Congregationalism, notably in his *Way of the Churches* (1645). In *Milk for Babes* (1646) he provided a standard catechism for Puritan orthodoxy that served children for several generations.

Like his friends THOMAS HOOKER and JOHN DAVENPORT, Cotton was a molder of the early church government in New England. At the request of the Massachusetts General Court, Cotton drew up the earliest compilation of New England laws (1636), the so-called MOSAIC CODE. The General Court rejected it in favor of a less stringent code, but many of its clauses were written in the laws of the NEW HAVEN COLONY. In the Antinomian controversy (1638) he befriended ANNE HUTCHINSON until the charges of numerous heresies presaged her banishment, and led him into a hasty retreat and greater theological inflexibility.

In his noted controversy with ROGER WILLIAMS, Cotton insisted upon the authority of the magistrate to control religious as well as secular questions, and he published these views in *The Keyes of the Kingdom of Heaven* (1643). The ideas expressed by Williams in defense of religious freedom and government by consent were anathema to Cotton. Democracy, he declared, was not 'a fitt government either for church or commonwealth.'

Cotton Kingdom, so called, by 1820 stretched from South Carolina to the Mississippi. Its economy was chiefly built upon a plantation system which produced cotton on a large scale by means of an abundant supply of slave labor. When plantation proprietors, during the period 1830–50, began extending their slave system into territories beyond the Mississippi, their expansionist spirit led to charges of 'agrarian imperialism.' By 1845 the Cotton Kingdom, then including Texas, controlled the Democratic party and shaped national policy, until the Kingdom was destroyed by the Civil War. (The term was popularized in 1861 by Frederick Law Olmsted's two-volume survey of the slave system, *The Cotton Kingdom.*)

During the 20th century the Cotton Belt was extended westward to New Mexico, Arizona, and southern California. Three-fourths of the nation's cotton is now grown west of the Mississippi.

Cotton gin, see *Whitney, Eli.*

Cotton industry, made possible by the textile and industrial revolution in England, increased enormously in the U.S. after ELI WHITNEY invented the cotton gin (1793). After 1815 cotton was the most valuable export from the ports of New Orleans, Baltimore, and New York. Hundreds of mills in the U.S., England, France, Germany, and Russia were eager for supplies. Thus prices rose and thousands of planters, at first chiefly in Virginia, Georgia, and the Carolinas, concentrated on harvesting this crop alone. The callous and forcible transfer of Indians (the Five Civilized Tribes) from Georgia and the Gulf states across the Mississippi during the 1830's opened the fertile black belt of Alabama and Mississippi. Before the Civil War an annual crop of some 4,500,000 bales, one-half of all American exports, was supplied by the COTTON KINGDOM, which extended from South Carolina to Texas and Arkansas. The cotton industry thus securely tied slavery into the southern economy. It not only dominated the life of the South but also influenced the economy of the nation. Union blockades during the Civil War reduced the great flow of commerce to a trickle. Following the war, the South's textile revolution 'brought the cotton mills to the cotton,' and by 1915 it had overtaken New England's textile leadership. Today the cotton belt, chiefly west of the Mississippi to southern California, produces one-half of all cotton fiber grown. In 1962 cotton was a factor in 50 per cent of all household textiles, 27 per cent of all industrial textiles, and 60 per cent of all wearing apparel in the country. Since the 1930's cotton raising has been revolutionized by the invention and improvement of the mechanical cotton picker, which has largely displaced Negro hand labor.

COUGHLIN, CHARLES EDWARD (1891–), Canadian-born Roman Catholic priest, while pastor of the Shrine of the Little Flower near Detroit, Michigan, began his disputatious radio addresses (1930) which in the next decade brought him national attention. His early anti-Wall Street and 'social justice' emphasis, which led to the creation of the Union party in 1936, gave way to anti-Semitic and pro-Fascist utterances. His magazine *Social Justice,* barred from the mails (1942) for violating the Espionage Act, likewise dogmatically expressed his political and economic views: 'It is Fascism or Communism . . . I take the road of Fascism.' He was silenced by his superiors.

Council for New England (1620), a closed corporation of 40 members chartered as a reorganized branch of the PLYMOUTH COMPANY (1606), was a group of nobles and landed gentry chiefly interested in developing manors rather than trade. They obtained the 'New England' area between latitudes 40° and 48° (roughly from southern Pennsylvania to northern Maine), which they planned to grant as fiefs. The leading spirit in the enterprise, SIR FERDINANDO GORGES, procured the title of governor general for his son, who went to New England in 1623 but had no luck in making settlements and soon returned. Though the attempts of the Council generally failed, its small grants to two non-member groups proved unexpectedly successful: PLYMOUTH COLONY survived, and the MASSACHUSETTS BAY COMPANY attracted Puritans in large numbers. The king gave the prospective colonizers royal charters, thus eliminating the Council for New England as intermediary.

Council of Foreign Ministers, informal organization of the foreign ministers of the U.S., Great Britain, France, Soviet Russia, and China, in accordance with agreements reached at the POTSDAM CONFERENCE (1945), met twice unsuccessfully in that year to draft peace settlements with the defeated Axis powers. Late in 1946 they agreed upon treaties for Finland, Italy, Hungary, Romania, and Bulgaria. In 1954 a meeting of the Council (without China) resulted in the GENEVA CONFERENCE, and the ensuing 'summit conference' of 1955. In that year Austrian sovereignty was restored, and though no accord was reached on the unification of Germany, negotiations have continued to drag on.

Council of National Defense, established in 1916, was organized under the chairmanship of Secretary of War Baker as an advisory body of six cabinet members. Charged with co-ordinating industry and resources for national security, it functioned through civilian experts. In 1940 President Roosevelt created a similar agency, which was soon absorbed into the Office of Production Management.

Councils, Colonial, see *Colonial councils.*

Councils of safety, see *Committees of safety.*

Counties, like shires in England, after which counties were modeled, are units of territorially demarcated local government within the states. (In Louisiana such local governments are called parishes; in Alaska, boroughs.) Counties organize the courts, and elect sheriffs, coroners, and prosecuting attorneys, but state governments for reasons of efficiency have gradually increased their control in such areas as welfare and relief. Counties are usually governed by elected boards, whose members are variously termed managers, commissioners, supervisors, or freeholders.

COUNTS, GEORGE SYLVESTER (1889–), professor of education at Teachers College, Columbia (1927–56), won a large following, especially during the depression years of the 1930's, for his theory that the school should build a new social order through frank indoctrination of noncommunist collectivism. Most educators suspected that the theory was mere propaganda. However, his efforts to persuade school boards to include representatives of nonpropertied groups was effective in broadening the membership of such bodies. His writings include *Education and American Civilization* (1952), and *The Challenge of Soviet Education* (1957).

Coureurs de bois were the unlicensed fur traders and trappers in New France during the latter half of the 17th century. Picturesque, adventurous, and defiant of authority, they left the early French settlements in considerable numbers, took to the wilderness, and played an important part in early trading and exploration. Some were given government support. Notable leaders among them include GROSEILLIERS, RADISSON, DULUTH, and PERROT. They are not to be confused with the later *voyageurs.*

'Courtpacking Plan,' see *Supreme Court.*

Courts in the U.S. are organized in two distinct systems, Federal and state, each supreme in its own jurisdiction, though in overlapping matters the Federal courts have decisive power. The Federal courts consist of District Courts, Courts of Appeal, and the Supreme Court, with such additional specialized courts as the Court of Claims and the Court of Tax Appeals. In addition to the law courts there are such Federal tribunals as the INTERSTATE COMMERCE COMMISSION and the courts-martial for administering MILITARY LAW. The judicial systems of the states vary, but under the Constitution they are established by state constitutions or state legislatures. Each state has its high court of appeals, a level of district or county courts of original jurisdiction, and a bottom tier of municipal, magistrate, and justice-of-the-peace courts for minor civil and criminal cases. All states have varying specialized courts for the administration of estates, domestic relations, and juvenile problems. Some states have an intermediate or appellate division above the district courts.

Courts-martial, see *Military law.*

Covenant theology (or federal theology), basic in the Puritanism of New

England, elaborated a doctrine of Calvin that had been developed in the writings of the English Puritans William Perkins and William Ames, and most fully expounded in New England by SAMUEL WILLARD. It postulated an agreement between God and Adam, the federal head of the race. As a Covenant of Works, it required of man an active obedience; God freely promised Adam and his posterity eternal happiness on condition that Adam obey the moral law, the instinct in man to do his duty. Adam broke the compact, and thus all mankind forfeited salvation. Even so, God instituted a new agreement, a Covenant of Grace, promising salvation provided that men have faith that Christ, by his resurrection, had 'satisfied' the Covenant of Works and thereby earned man's salvation. Although God is free to elect souls according to His pleasure, the presumption is that a very great number may be chosen. By the new Covenant punishment is not for an inherent sin, but for rejection of faith that Christ is intercessor. The later Calvinism of Jonathan Edwards put less stress upon the covenant theory and more upon the inherently corrupt nature of man.

Covered bridges were first devised about 1800, and continued to be built for about 70 years. The covering kept rain water and ice out of the joints, and rain and snow off the roadway. Such bridges also prevented horses from being frightened if the bridge was high above the stream. Some covered truss spans extended 250 ft. A common sight earlier in the 20th century, covered bridges now have all but disappeared.

Covered wagon, known also as a 'conestoga wagon,' because it was first manufactured at Conestoga, Pennsylvania, was a broad-wheeled vehicle used to freight goods over soft soil. Drawn by teams of horses, mules, or oxen, the covered wagon came into general use late in the 18th century to carry settlers across the Cumberlands. Later it was the vehicle in which families crossed the prairies to reach Utah and the Pacific Northwest. Essentially a wagon box, it was covered with a framework of hoop-shaped slats over which was stretched a canvas tent. West of the Missouri families organized into 'trains,' and moved westward. At night the wagons, guarded by sentinels, formed a circle for defense, which was also used as a corral for the animals. The trek to the Far West could be completed in such a wagon in four or five months. The covered wagons were also called 'prairie schooners.'

Cowboys, during the War of Independence, were lawless Tory marauders who roamed and pillaged the neutral ground of Westchester county, New York. (Their patriot counterparts were 'Skinners.')

Since then the word has been applied to mounted cattle herders in the Southwest. Before the vast ranches were fenced, they drove cattle to pasture, branded them at roundups, protected them from rustlers and predatory animals, and convoyed the CATTLE DRIVE to shipping points. Fearless and expert horsemen, they were celebrated for their skill with lasso and gun. Though they patterned their dress and certain traditions after the Mexican *vaquero,* their folk music and customs were distinctively American. Yet the considerable Spanish-Mexican influence is suggested by the terms ranch (*rancho*), lariat (*la reata*), bronco, rodeo, and even 'hoosegow' (*juzado*). The era of the 'cattle kingdom,' beginning after the Civil War, ended in the 1890's, when railroad expansion outmoded trail-driving, and made the cowboy an anachronism for large-scale undertakings. He survives today chiefly in ballads, tall tales, and in the movies.

Cowpens, Battle of (January 1781), one of the brilliant American victories in the War of Independence and a military classic, was part of the CAROLINA CAMPAIGN. After the American success at KING'S MOUNTAIN in the previous October, General DANIEL MORGAN selected a position near Cowpens, South Carolina, disposed his 940 militiamen with great care, and met Colonel Banastre Tarleton's assault of 1150 British regulars. Morgan suffered fewer than 75 casualties, inflicted more than 300, and captured twice that number. Cornwallis then pursued Morgan into North Carolina, where Morgan and General Nathanael Greene joined forces at GUILFORD COURTHOUSE.

The tactic that Dan Morgan had used (retiring the line of skirmish after three volleys at close range, and bringing it back after the enemy had thrown in its last reserves), though later outdated by improvements in cannon and small arms, was the tactical showpiece of the War of Independence. It was later used decisively at Sacketts Harbor in the War of 1812.

COX, GEORGE BARNSDALE (1853–1916), Republican boss of Cincinnati, began as a bootblack, became a saloonkeeper, and turned to politics after selling his Mecca Saloon in 1881. With brief interruptions he controlled city elections for a quarter-century (1886–1911), during which period his machine for collecting graft and kickbacks became a model of efficiency. He did not live to see the result of the reform movement, which destroyed his painstaking labor by establishing (1924) a city-manager plan.

COXE, TENCH (1755–1824), Philadelphia-born political economist, served in the Continental Congress (1788). His *Enquiry into the Principles on Which a Commercial Economic System for the U.S. Should Be Founded* (1787) supported the Hamiltonian proposals for an economy balanced between manufacturing and agriculture. As a Federalist he held the office of assistant secretary of the Treasury (1790–92) under Hamilton, and was appointed commissioner of the revenue (1792–98). Later he became a Republican, and he accepted Jefferson's appointment as purveyor of public supplies (1803–12). His knowledge of American economic conditions was unexcelled, and his *View of the U.S. of America* (1794) is a mine of dependable information for the economic historian. His digest of the 1810 census, *A Statement of the Arts and Manufactures of the U.S.* (1814), was compiled with skill and competence.

Coxey's army, symptomatic of the economic unrest following the PANIC OF 1893, was an 'army' of some 500 unemployed who were led from Ohio to Washington, D.C., in 1894 by James S. Coxey (1854–1951), a wealthy quarry owner, to demand relief measures from Congress. At the time, Coxey's petition for non-interest-bearing bonds and appropriations for road building excited only amused contempt, but the program he envisioned was very similar to that carried out by the Public Works Administration during the 1930's. In later years Coxey served as mayor of Massillon, Ohio (1931–33), and he was twice chosen as the Farmer-Labor candidate for President (1932, 1936).

Coyote, the small prairie wolf of the trans-Mississippi West, easily recognized by its yelping, doglike cry, is the subject of a body of native folk tales, trapper natural history, fiction, and verse. Though valuable as scavenger and destroyer of rodents, it is the bane of ranchers because it is a killer of small domestic animals.

Crackers, sometimes referred to as 'piney woods people,' 'rednecks,' or 'clay-eaters,' are the poor white inhabitants of the infertile pine barrens of the South, principally in Georgia and northern Florida. The origin of the term, recorded as early as 1784, is uncertain, although a principal article of their diet was cracked corn.

Cradle of Liberty, see *Faneuil Hall.*

Craig* v. *Missouri (1830) confronted the U.S. Supreme Court with the issue of whether a state law authorizing the issuance of loan certificates was a justifiable application of the state's borrowing power or was contrary to the constitutional clause (Art. I, sec. 10) prohibiting states from emitting bills of credit. Chief Justice Marshall, speaking for the majority in a 4 to 3 decision, ruled that the Missouri law was null and void. This opinion, termed a narrow interpretation of the constitutional clause, aroused deep resentment against the Court in expanding frontier states then seeking ways to find easy-money panaceas.

CRAM, RALPH ADAMS (1863–1942), New Hampshire-born architect, was an ardent advocate of Gothic architecture. For many years (1891–1914) he was an associate of B. G. GOODHUE. Cram designed several ecclesiastical and university edifices, notably the Cathedral of St. John the Divine in New York City, buildings for the U.S. Military Academy at West Point, and the Graduate College at Princeton. Cram fought Modernism (functionalism), although he believed that Gothic itself had been a dynamic evolving form until arrested by pagan Renaissance styles. His many writings include *Church Buildings* (1901), *The Gothic Quest* (1907), and *The Substance of Gothic* (1917).

CRANE, [Harold] Hart (1899–1932), Ohio-born poet, a disciple of Walt Whitman and the French symbolists, combined mystical perception with concrete imagery of the American scene in poems which were recognized as the best American verse of his era. The promise of *White Buildings* (1926) was fulfilled in *The Bridge* (1930), symbolizing America in transition. Believing that his undisciplined personal existence had led to the dissipation of his creativeness, he committed suicide. His poems were collected in 1933.

Crater Lake National Park (est. 1902), 160,000 acres in southwestern Oregon, includes the six-mile-wide Crater Lake, in the cone of an extinct volcano. The lake is noted for its shade of deepest blue. It lies at an elevation of 6000 ft., and is surrounded by cliffs rising from 500 to 2000 ft.

CRAWFORD, Thomas (1813–57), born in New York City and apprenticed to a wood carver, became one of the most productive early American sculptors. In 1835 he went to Italy to study under Thorvaldsen, and thereafter spent most of his life in Rome. His *Armed Freedom,* cast after his death in the foundry of clark mills (1860), crowns the dome of the National Capitol. More important historically than aesthetically, he executed such poetic sculptures as *Babes in the Wood, Flora,* and *Hebe and Ganymede.* His pediments in the Senate wing of the Capitol symbolize the progress of civilization in America. His representational works include the equestrian statue of Washington at Richmond, Virginia, and the bust of Josiah Quincy in the Boston Athenaeum. He was father of the novelist F. Marion Crawford.

CRAWFORD, William Harris (1772–1834), Virginia-born statesman, served as U.S. Senator from Georgia (1807–13), became Madison's minister to France (1813–15), and Secretary of War (1815–16) and of the Treasury (1816–17), in which latter post he continued to serve Monroe (1817–25). As heir-apparent of the Virginia dynasty, he was a leading contender for the 1824 presidential election, but during the campaign he was crippled by a paralytic stroke and finished a poor third after Jackson and J. Q. Adams. Crawford was a skillful organizer and a man of inflexible probity, but he never won general popularity, and by his tactlessness (such as his revelation to Jackson of Calhoun's part in the arbuthnot and ambrister affair) he lost the friendship of most of his peers.

CRAZY HORSE d. (1877), brave and skillful chief of the Oglala (Dakota) Sioux Indians, led several raids against other tribes and against the whites. He joined sitting bull in the annihilation of Custer's forces at Little Bighorn (1876), the most famous of all Indian victories. Suspected of instigating a revolt when his tribe was placed on a reservation, he was shot, ostensibly while resisting imprisonment.

Crédit Mobilier, a construction company created by leaders of the union pacific railroad in 1867, was exposed five years later as one of the major financial scandals in American history. Congressman Oakes Ames of Massachusetts, as head of the company, manipulated finances in such a way that when the road was finished (1869) the promoters had managed to divert some $20,000,000 to their own pockets. With the purpose of forestalling a congressional investigation, Ames assigned large blocks of Crédit Mobilier shares 'where they would do most good.'

The New York *Sun* was able to publish the names of the manipulators during the presidential campaign of 1872, thus initiating Senate investigations. Among those disgraced were Vice President Schuyler Colfax, Senator James W. Patterson of New Hampshire (recommended for expulsion), Representative James Brooks of New York, and Ames himself. Brooks and Ames were both formally censured by the House. Representative James A. Garfield of Ohio never satisfactorily explained his connection with the affair. In an era of gross political venality, censure was deemed punishment enough, and no one was prosecuted.

Cree Indians, of Algonquian stock, were a powerful tribe of hunters in the late 18th century, principally inhabiting Manitoba. One branch, the Plains Cree, moved south into buffalo territory and became allies of the Siouan Assiniboins.

Creek Indians (Natchez-Muskhogean stock) were a settled agricultural people, living mostly in Georgia and Florida. De Soto admired them, but in the colonial period they were allies of the English against the Spanish. Andrew Jackson gained his reputation as an Indian fighter by defeating them in the battle of HORSESHOE BEND (1814). They later ceded their lands and moved to Indian Territory (Oklahoma) as one of the FIVE CIVILIZED TRIBES. Since 1906 they have been American citizens.

'Creel Committee,' see *Committee on Public Information.*

Creoles, a term first applied in Latin America, designated the offspring of French and Spanish conquerors, to distinguish them from later immigrants of European blood (often local officials) and from Indians or Negroes. In Louisiana creoles were the descendants of the original French settlers, and later the French-speaking native portion of the white population were so called. Never precisely used, and sometimes applied to mulattoes, in Louisiana the term still is meant to distinguish the descendants of the original French settlers (many of them ACADIANS) from the CAJUNS. The colorful creole life is depicted in the writings of GEORGE W. CABLE, GRACE KING, and LAFCADIO HEARN.

CRÈVECŒUR, J. HECTOR ST. JOHN DE (1735–1813), born in France (and christened Michel-Guillaume Jean), served under Montcalm in Canada. In the decade after the fall of Quebec (1759) he explored the Great Lakes region and the Ohio valley, and traveled extensively in Pennsylvania and New York. In 1769 he settled on a farm in Orange county, New York, where he wrote *Letters from an American Farmer* (1782). Together with other letters found in 1922 and published as *Sketches of Eighteenth Century America* (1925), they give a vivid and realistic picture of the life of people living on the soil in the North.

The American environment, as Crèvecœur saw it, was transforming the European peasant into a freeholder. The American was an amalgam of all nations, and Americans had developed traits of character that drew them together in pursuit of common goals. His picture of the life of the American farmer carried his name all over Europe, and, at the suggestion of Ethan Allen, the town of St. Johnsbury, Vermont, was named for him (1786).

While serving as French consul in New York (1783–90), Crèvecœur introduced the system of cover crops and the culture of new crops, including alfalfa. He aided the American pioneers who were establishing botanical gardens, and returned to France when his official tour of duty was ended.

'Crime Against Kansas,' see *Sumner, Charles.*

'Crime of 1873,' see *Coinage Act of 1873.*

Crittenden Compromise was introduced (December 1860) by the Kentucky Senator John J. Crittenden (1787–1863), at that time the foremost champion of the Union in the South, as a desperate last-minute effort to prevent the Civil War. It offered a constitutional amendment in substance proposing recognition of slavery in territories south of latitude 36° 30′ (the line of the MISSOURI COMPROMISE), noninterference by Congress with slavery where it existed, and compensation to owners of fugitive slaves. President-elect Lincoln opposed 'as with a chain of steel' any sort of slavery extension, although he was willing to accept the noninterference and compensation clauses. He was solidly supported by the Republicans, and the measure was killed in committee.

Croatoan (Croatan), see *Roanoke Island.*

CROCKETT, DAVID (1786–1836), having fought the Creek Indians under Andrew Jackson and served (1821) in the Tennessee legislature, in 1823 moved into the western frontier of the state. From that new constituency he was sent as a Jackson Democrat for three terms to Congress (1827–31, 1833–35). The lusty backwoods humor and tall tales of Davy Crockett, the 'coonskin Congressman,' became proverbial. His picturesque exaggerations were seized upon by Whig journalists, who turned him into a professional frontiersman in such books as *Sketches and Eccentricities of Col. David Crockett* (1833). His naïve defection to the Whigs cost him re-election, and in pique he moved to Tennessee, then to Texas, where he took up the cause of Texas independence and died in the defense of the ALAMO. *A Narrative of the Life of David Crockett* (1834), purportedly an autobiography, is notable as one of the earliest books to use the American dialect with racy distinction.

Studies of Crockett include those of Constance Rourke (1934), M. M. Null (1954), and J. A. Shackford (1956).

Crockett almanacs, issued irregularly in various cities between 1835 and 1856, capitalized on the adventurous exploits of Davy Crockett, Daniel Boone, Mike Fink, Kit Carson, and other frontiersmen noted for their tall tales. Quite possibly at the start Crockett lent his name to the enterprise.

CROKER, RICHARD (1841–1922), Irish-born leader of Tammany Hall (1886–1902), inherited the New York City political machine from 'Honest John' Kelly. The Lexow Committee (1894), appointed by the New York Senate, gathered and spread before the public detailed evidence of the corruption of the police department, whose dishonest officials had grown fat on graft. Nevertheless Croker for a time was able to control 'the system,' somewhat disguised. With the election (1901) of SETH LOW as reform mayor, Croker left the U.S. and lived thereafter on his estate in Ireland.

CROLY, HERBERT [DAVID] (1869–1930), editor and reformer, was son of the New York newspaper writer David Goodman Croly (1829–89) and Jane Cunningham Croly (1829–1901), who specialized in women's feature articles. He studied intermittently at Harvard during the 1890's (receiving his A.B. degree in 1910), and for a time edited the *Architectural Record* (1900–1906). His *Promise of American Life* (1909), advocating a positive program of government regulation for social goals, was an influence in shaping Theodore Roosevelt's New Nationalism, which sought to regulate monopoly rather than break up trusts. In 1914 Croly founded the *New Republic,* a weekly journal of liberal opinion, which he edited until his death. He attracted to it one of the most brilliant editorial staffs in the history of American journalism, and during his editorship it took a commanding position in liberalizing political, social, and economic thought.

Cross of Gold Speech, see *Bryan, W. J.*

Crosser-Dill Act (1934), or Railway Labor Act, amended the WATSON-PARKER ACT of 1926 by creating a smaller Mediation Board and setting up a 36-member Adjustment Board, with members jointly chosen from management and labor, to handle individual grievances in matters of contracts. It gave employees the right to organize and bargain collectively by representatives of their own choosing. Valid labor organizations were safeguarded by clauses which placed COMPANY UNIONS in a difficult position, and 'YELLOW DOG' CONTRACTS were outlawed.

Crow Indians, of Siouan stock, were warlike nomadic hunters, living chiefly in Wyoming and Montana. Closely akin to the HIDATSA (Gros Ventres), they were at first regarded as rascals and thieves by the whites, whom later they helped fight the Sioux and Blackfoot.

Crown Point, on the west shore of Lake Champlain in northern New York, was the site of a French fort (1731) which Lord Amherst captured in 1759 during the French and Indian War. Its small English garrison surrendered to Colonel Seth Warner and his Green Mountain Boys in 1775, and thereafter it served chiefly as an advance post of Fort TICONDEROGA. In 1910 it became a state park.

Cuba, largest and westernmost island of the West Indies, from its strategic position in the Caribbean Sea has been important in the history of the Western Hemisphere ever since it was discovered by Columbus (1492) and settled by the Spanish (1515). Captured by the British in 1762, in the next year 'the pearl of the Antilles' was returned to Spain by the TREATY OF PARIS of 1763. Until the 1840's U.S. policy strongly favored Spanish retention of the island lest it become a pawn of France or England. In 1854 the imperialist aim of the OSTEND MANIFESTO, though quickly disavowed by the U.S. State Department, was symptomatic of expansionist sentiment in the period of 'MANIFEST DESTINY.' At the conclusion of the Spanish-American War (1898) Cuba was formally placed under military government. In 1902 Cuba became a republic, though it accepted the terms of the PLATT AMENDMENT, which allowed U.S. intervention. In two periods of political turbulence (1906–9, 1917–23) terms of the agreement were invoked, but in 1934 the Amendment was abrogated.

After 1960, under the Castro regime, Cuba's increasing political and economic alignment with Soviet Russia led to a break in U.S.–Cuba diplomatic relations. When Castro confiscated over $1 billion in U.S. properties, President Eisenhower cut off most exports to Cuba and drastically cut its sugar quota. President Kennedy gave partial aid to the unsuccessful 'Bay of Pigs' invasion attempted by Cuban exiles (17–19 April 1961), but avoided direct intervention by our military forces. When an emboldened Castro allowed the Soviets to set up secret missile bases, armed with nuclear missiles capable of hitting most Western Hemisphere cities, Kennedy set up a naval blockade against Soviet military shipments to Cuba, reinforced the U.S. base at Guantanamo, and compelled the Russians to dismantle their Cuban bases. Castro continued his attempts to subvert Latin America, which Kennedy and Johnson countered by strengthening their military co-operation with the ORGANIZATION OF AMERICAN STATES.

CULLOM, SHELBY MOORE (1829–1914), Illinois lawyer, served his state as governor (1876–83) and U.S. Senator (1883–1913). He was chairman of the committee that drew up the bill establishing the Interstate Commerce Commission (1887). On the eve of the Spanish-American War (1898) he gave simple expression to the political imperialism of the day by saying: 'It is time that someone woke up and realized the necessity of annexing some property.' After 1901 he was chairman of the Committee on Foreign Relations.

Cumberland Plateau, the southwest part of the Appalachian system, extends from West Virginia through eastern Kentucky and Tennessee into northern Alabama. Through the Cumberland Gap, a natural passage near the point where Virginia, Kentucky, and Tennessee meet, Daniel Boone in 1775 carved the WILDERNESS ROAD, for 50 years the principal route of westward migration. Throughout the Civil War the Gap was a strategic point, alternately held by Confederate and Union forces. It is now a National Historic Park.

Cumberland Road (the Old National Road) was the first of the INTERNAL IMPROVEMENTS provided by Congress (1806), and a chief artery for Western colonization in the development of the Ohio and upper Mississippi valleys. Construction of a surfaced highway linking Cumberland, Maryland, with the Ohio river traffic began in 1811. By 1818 the U.S. mail could be transported over the road to Wheeling, West Virginia. In 1822 Congress sought to authorize the collection of toll, but President Monroe vetoed the Cumberland Road bill on the same constitutional grounds that had prompted his BONUS BILL VETO (1817). (He believed that toll collecting was grounded in state, not Federal, authority.)

Subsequent extensions took the road to Columbus, Ohio, and across Indiana to Vandalia, Illinois, in 1838, but it never reached St. Louis to join the Oregon and Santa Fe trails. Railroads reduced its importance. For a time automobiles followed its general route along U.S. Highway 40, until the Pennsylvania Turnpike supplanted both (in the 1940's) as the chief automotive link between the same regions.

CUMMINS, ALBERT BAIRD (1850–1926), Iowa lawyer, while governor of his state (1902–8) won prominence by shattering the control of railroad interests in state politics and effecting strict government supervision of rail lines. While serving in the U.S. Senate (1908–26), he co-sponsored the ESCH-CUMMINS TRANSPORTATION ACT of 1920.

CURLEY, JAMES MICHAEL (1874–1958), made a lifelong profession of politics, at the local, state, and national levels. A power in the Democratic party of Boston, he resigned from the City Council to serve in Congress (1911–14). He was thrice elected to four-year terms as mayor of Boston (between 1914 and 1934) before becoming governor of Massachusetts (1935–37) and again entering Congress (1943–46). Once more elected mayor of Boston (1946–50), he was convicted of mail fraud and for five months in 1947 governed the city from jail until President Truman commuted his sentence. After Curley was defeated for re-election in 1949, the President, evidently feeling that the cause of justice had been served, gave Curley a full pardon. A colorful personality, Curley was one of the shrewdest machine politicians of his day.

Currency, see *Banking, Bills of credit, Bimetallism, Coinage acts, Colonial currency, Commerce, Continental currency, Free Silver, Gold standard, Greenbacks, Land banks, Paper money.*

CURRIER & IVES, New York lithographers, became immensely popular for their colored prints of contemporary political, social, and sporting scenes. Nathaniel Currier (1813–88) founded the business in 1835, fifteen years later took James Merritt Ives (1824–95) into partnership, and in 1857 the name of the firm first appeared on the prints. Though lacking artistic value, sentimental and journalistic, the lithographs took on value as collectors' items early in the 20th century. Single rare productions have sold at auction for some $3000.

CURTI, MERLE [EUGENE] (1897–), Nebraska-born educator, has been a professor of history at several universities, occupying a chair at Wisconsin after 1947. Best known among his studies of intellectual history are *The Social Ideas of American Educators* (1934), *The Growth of American Thought* (1943), and *The Roots of American Loyalty* (1946). Other studies include useful analyses of pacifism, philanthropy, and problems of historiography.

CURTIS, CYRUS HERMANN KOTZSCHMAR (1850–1937), Philadelphia publisher, in 1883 developed the *Ladies' Home Journal.* He founded the Curtis Publishing Company (1890), and in 1897 purchased the *Saturday Evening Post,* which, under the editorship of George Horace Lorimer (1899–1937), became the most prosperous magazine in America, with the largest weekly circulation (over 3,000,000). In 1913 Curtis purchased the Philadelphia daily *Public Ledger.* His philanthropies, chiefly devoted to colleges and hospitals, were extensive.

CURTIS, GEORGE TICKNOR (1812–94), after graduation from Harvard (1832), practiced law in Boston and (after 1862) in New York, where he became a distinguished patent attorney. He was a close associate of Daniel Webster and James Buchanan, whose biographies he wrote. His most notable work was *The Constitutional History of the U.S. . . . to the Close of the Civil War* (2 vols., 1889–96), the classic Federalist interpretation.

CURTIS, GEORGE WILLIAM (1824–92), publicist and reformer, in his day was one of the most influential of American writers. After traveling in the Near East as correspondent for the New York *Tribune,* he recorded his impressions in such popular books as *Nile Notes of a Howadji* (1851). In 1854 he began to write for the 'Easy Chair' in *Harper's Magazine,* and the collection *From the Easy Chair* (3 vols., 1892–94) is a picture of American political and social issues of the time. As lyceum lecturer and political editor of *Harper's Weekly* (after 1863), he was known as a champion of clean politics. President Grant made him head of the Civil Service Commission (1871), but Curtis resigned four years later, blocked in his efforts at reform by spoilsmen in high office. Independent, versatile, and scholarly, Curtis came to occupy something of the position formerly held by Horace Greeley. In his last years (1890–92) he served as chancellor of the University of the State of New York.

Curtis Institute of Music, in Philadelphia, was founded (1924) by Mary Louise Curtis Bok (later Mrs. Efrem Zimbalist), and named for her father, Cyrus Curtis. The Institute, which is coeducational, admits solely on scholarship, and recruits its faculty from distinguished concert artists. Its directors have been Josef Hofmann (1926–38), Randall Thompson (1939–41), and Efrem Zimbalist (1941–).

CURTISS, GLENN HAMMOND (1878–1930), pioneer in aviation, while owner of a New York motorcycle factory became a member of A. G. Bell's Aerial Experiment Association (1907–9), and established (1909) the first flying school in the U.S. At the earliest aviation meet, held at Los Angeles in 1910, he set new speed records, and in the same year made his spectacular flight from Albany to New York City, thereby winning the $10,000 New York *World* prize. Having developed his hydroplane or 'flying boat' (1912), he set about organizing his airplane company (1916), and thereafter introduced many radical improvements in plane manufacture. One of his Wasp NC (Navy-Curtiss) seaplanes achieved the first Atlantic crossing (1919).

CUSHING, CALEB (1800–1879), Massachusetts-born statesman, after graduation from Harvard (1817), practiced law and entered politics. He served in the Massachusetts legislature many times between 1825 and 1863, and was twice elected by the Whigs to the U.S. House of Representatives (1835–43). In 1843 President Tyler sent Cushing, an erudite scholar and one of the most eminent lawyers of his day, as commissioner to China. There Cushing negotiated the first commercial treaties between China and the U.S. He later shifted his party loyalty, became a power in Democratic politics, and was instrumental in securing the nomination of Franklin Pierce at the 1852 Democratic convention. Pierce brought him into the cabinet as Attorney General (1853–57), where he was an outspoken advocate of 'Manifest Destiny' expansionist policies. After the outbreak of the Civil War he joined the Republicans, and in later years received various diplomatic posts, notably as minister to Spain (1873–77).

CUSHING, FRANK HAMILTON (1857–1900), associated after 1879 with the U.S. Bureau of American Ethnology, was an authority on the Zuñi Pueblo Indians, with whom he lived for three years and who adopted him into their tribe. His best studies are incorporated in his translation of *Zuñi Creation Myths* (1896), and *Zuñi Folk Tales* (1901).

CUSHING, HARVEY WILLIAMS (1869–1939), after graduation from Yale (1891) was associated as a neurosurgeon with Johns Hopkins (1896–1912), Harvard (1912–32), and Yale (1933–37). His contributions to surgery of the brain received wide recognition. Among his writings are his classic treatise on the pituitary gland (1912), *Tumors of the Nervus Acusticus* (1917), and *The Life of Sir William Osler* (1925; Pulitzer Prize, 1926).

CUSHMAN, CHARLOTTE SAUNDERS (1816–76), became popular as an actress during the 1830's. After her triumphal tour of England (1845–49) she was acclaimed the leading actress of the American stage, and established herself in such regal Shakespearean roles as Lady Macbeth, Queen Katherine in *Henry the Eighth,* and in portrayals of Hamlet, Romeo, and Cardinal Wolsey. Her later years were devoted to dramatic readings and occasional 'farewell performances.'

CUSHMAN, PAULINE (1835–93), New Orleans-born Union spy during the Civil War, was captured (1863), court-martialed at General Bragg's headquarters in Tennessee, and sentenced to be hanged. Bragg's hasty retreat from Shelbyville gave her the opportunity to escape. An actress by profession, she later lectured in Federal uniform about her war experiences.

CUSTER, GEORGE ARMSTRONG (1839–76), two years after graduation from the U.S. Military Academy (1861) had been brevetted major general, and was one of the youngest general officers in the Union army. By war's end he had made a spectacular record as a leader of cavalry. In the postwar reorganization he was given the rank of lieutenant colonel, and thenceforth commanded expeditions into Indian territories. On

25 June 1876 Custer discovered a large Indian encampment at Little Bighorn, Montana. Despite the danger of ambush by the Sioux Indians, commanded by the wily and intrepid chiefs SITTING BULL and CRAZY HORSE, Custer detached two-thirds of his regiment and himself led a frontal attack in which he and his 250 men were annihilated.

By nature arrogant, and with a record that after 1867 required the intervention of General Sheridan to prevent a court-martial, Custer may have hoped to reap personal glory. On the other hand, his two subordinate commanders have been judged chiefly at fault by some historians. The battle he engaged in remains the most controversial episode in two and a half centuries of Indian warfare. The scene of Custer's 'Last Stand' is now a national monument. Custer's remains were reinterred at West Point. The most exhaustive study of the event is Edgar I. Stewart, *Custer's Luck* (1955).

CUTLER, MANASSEH (1742–1823), Connecticut-born clergyman, after graduation from Yale (1765) studied law, medicine, and divinity, and was ordained Congregational pastor (1771) at Hamilton, Massachusetts, his lifelong home. His botanical papers, the first systematic description and classification of New England flora, appeared in the *Proceedings* of the American Academy of Arts and Sciences, of which he was a member.

He was a shrewd organizer of the important OHIO COMPANY, which proposed the colonization of a huge tract along the Ohio river. When the Company secured 1,500,000 acres, Cutler successfully petitioned Congress to move quickly upon passage of the ORDINANCE OF 1787.

Cyclones, see *Tornadoes.*

D

DABLON, CLAUDE (1618–97), French Jesuit missionary, arrived in New France in 1655, and was appointed superior of the missions of the Upper Lakes in 1670. He directed the expansion of missionary work, and his reports of exploration in the Great Lakes region are set forth in the JESUIT RELATIONS.

Dairy industry in the U.S. developed rapidly after refrigeration made wide distribution possible. Important early factors were the invention of the centrifugal cream separator (1879), tuberculin testing of herds (1890), pasteurization (1893), and soon thereafter the development of automatic milking machinery and increasingly stringent sanitary regulations. Insulated tank trucks (1914) and tank cars (1924) made possible the unlimited distribution of dairy products. Milk and dairy foods have been made an integral part of health education programs. Today the 'dairy bar' is almost as common a sight on the American landscape as the gasoline filling station. American consumers spend an annual total of some $10 billion on dairy products.

Dakota Indians were the most powerful members of the SIOUAN FAMILY. The main body were the Teton (Western) Sioux, with a Plains culture (buffalo hunting and seasonal migration). Of their seven sub-tribes, the most prominent were the Oglala, numerous and skillful enough for many decades to outmaneuver their white opponents. Teton enemies also included their near relatives, the ASSINIBOIN, CROW, MANDAN, and OMAHA. The Teton under the leadership of such chiefs as SITTING BULL, CRAZY HORSE, and RAIN-IN-THE-FACE wiped out Custer at Little Bighorn in Montana (1876), and they were centrally involved in the GHOST DANCE uprising (1890), the last effective Indian outbreak in the U.S.

The Eastern Dakota Sioux, in Minnesota and South Dakota, had a woodland culture and were enemies of the ALGONQUIAN, particularly the OJIBWA tribe, with whom they were constantly at war until white settlements (after 1850) altered their tribal patterns.

The Dakota popularized the Indian dress now conventionally associated with all Indians. Illustrators still depict Pocahontas as a Dakota bride, and the Pilgrims as being welcomed by Dakota tribesmen. The Indian profile represented for a time on the U.S. five-cent piece was typical of theirs, and their costume was that adopted in Wild West shows. Composers seeking native American themes have found them in the music of the Dakota.

Dakota Territory, comprising the present states of North and South Dakota, and much of Wyoming and Montana, was established by Congress in 1861. The creation of Montana Territory (1864) and Wyoming Territory (1868) reduced Dakota Territory to the region that was divided in 1889 into the states of North Dakota and South Dakota.

DALI, SALVADOR (1904–), Spanish surrealist painter, resided in the U.S. for a short time after 1940, then returned to Spain. An expert draftsman, he created dream-world visions that consciously tend to irrationalism, strikingly represented by *Persistence of Memory,* with its limp watches. He designed costumes and scenery for operas performed by the Metropolitan Opera Company.

DALLAS, ALEXANDER JAMES (1759–1817), born in Jamaica, West Indies, settled in Philadelphia (1783), where he practiced law, became secretary to the state of Pennsylvania (1791–1801), and U.S. district attorney (1801–14). As Madison's Secretary of the Treasury (1814–16), Dallas restored confidence in U.S. credit after the War of 1812. With the aid of Calhoun in the Senate, he secured passage of a protective tariff, and established the second BANK OF THE U.S. (1816). His Treasury policies, similar to those of Albert Gallatin, redeemed the government from bankruptcy and established a financial system that endured for twenty years.

DALLAS, GEORGE MIFFLIN (1792–1864), son of A. J. DALLAS, after graduation from Princeton (1810), practiced law in Philadelphia. He served in the U.S. Senate (1831–33), and went as Van Buren's minister to Russia (1837–39). In 1844 he was elected Vice President on the Democratic ticket with Polk. Later President Pierce sent him as minister to Great Britain (1856–61), a post he held through Buchanan's administration. Dallas County, Texas, is named for him.

DALY, [JOHN] AUGUSTIN (1838–99), established himself in New York as a theatrical manager during the 1860's. In 1879 he opened Daly's Theatre on Broadway, and in 1893, Daly's Theatre in London. He was author or adapter of more than 100 dramatizations, but his reputation rests on his ability to select and train actors, some of the best of whom on the American stage owed their first successes to him. Among them were Ada Rehan, John Drew, Fanny Davenport, and Maude Adams. He was a master of theatrical technique, known especially for his meticulous concern with detail.

DALY, MARCUS (1841–1900), Irish-born copper magnate, during the 1880's bought property in and around Anaconda, Montana. The mines opened there yielded such fabulous returns that the name Anaconda came to symbolize bonanza ore pockets. To gain control of this wealth, Daly and other 'copper kings' bought legislatures and senatorships, fought each other ruthlessly, and corrupted the public life of Montana for a generation.

Dame schools were transplanted to the American colonies from England. They were so called because they were conducted by women in their homes for the beginning instruction of children. In New England such schools prepared children for the town schools, which would receive only those who could 'read words of two syllables and keep their places.'

DAMROSCH, LEOPOLD (1832–85), German-born composer and conductor, in 1871 came to New York, where he founded the Oratorio Society (1873) and the New York Symphony Society (1878). The seasons of Wagnerian opera began at the Metropolitan Opera House in 1884 under his baton.

His son, WALTER JOHANNES DAMROSCH (1862–1950), also a composer and conductor, organized the Damrosch Opera Company (1894), which on its tours introduced Wagnerian opera in many American cities. For many years he was director of the New York Symphony (1903–27). After 1927 he was musical adviser for the National Broadcasting Company, and made a contribution to radio broadcasting by introducing musical appreciation programs for children. Two of his operas, *Cyrano de Bergerac* (1913), and *The Man Without a Country* (1937), were first performed by the Metropolitan Opera Company.

Dams and reservoirs, constructed to develop power resources, impound water for irrigation, and control floods and erosion, were first built on a large scale in the U.S. during the 1930's along the COLORADO RIVER. Similar constructions in the past two decades along the COLUMBIA RIVER and in the MISSOURI RIVER BASIN have altered the agricultural and industrial character of vast regions. The TENNESSEE VALLEY AUTHORITY serves the Southeast. In California, dams along the SACRAMENTO and other rivers have reclaimed large areas.

Separate administrations within the Department of the Interior have been organized to market power in various regions. Among the four-score non-Federal hydroelectric plants, by far the largest (completed in 1963) is that at NIAGARA FALLS.

DANA, CHARLES ANDERSON (1819–97), after study at Harvard, and five years of residence at BROOK FARM, in 1847 began his fourteen-year association with HORACE GREELEY and the New York *Tribune* (1849–62). A brilliant editor, Dana resigned when Greeley and he disagreed on policy. After service as special investigating agent for the War Department (1862–64), during which he became, in Lincoln's words, the 'eyes of the administration,' he acted briefly (1864–65) as an Assistant Secretary of War.

In 1868 he became part owner and lifelong editor of the New York *Sun,* a journal which came to be known as the 'newspaperman's newspaper.' He followed no consistent editorial policy, but he achieved his aim of readability, and gathered around him a distinguished group of reporters, including RICHARD HARDING DAVIS, JACOB RIIS, and ALBERT BRISBANE. His *Recollections of the Civil War* (1898) is the personal record of an informed observer.

DANA, JAMES DWIGHT (1813–95), soon after graduation from Yale (1833) published his widely used *System of Mineralogy* (1837), a work that helped make him the accepted dean of American geologists and is still being revised and reprinted. After returning in 1842 from the globe-circling exploring expedition led by CHARLES WILKES, he published notable mineralogical and zoological data gathered during the four-year voyage. As successor to his father-in-law, BENJAMIN SILLIMAN, in the chair of natural history at Yale, and as editor of the *American Journal of Science,* he became internationally known. His *Manual of Geology* (1862), thrice revised, in its last edition somewhat reluctantly accepted the Darwinian concept of evolution. Daniel Coit Gilman wrote his biography (1899).

DANA, JOHN COTTON (1856–1929), after graduation from Dartmouth (1878) practiced law briefly before pioneering in library service. As director of the public library of Newark, New Jersey (1902–29), he established a children's library, a branch library for businessmen, and a library printing shop. In 1909 he founded the Newark Museum to display the work of native artists, and in it he assembled the first exhibition of industrial arts in the U.S.

DANA, RICHARD HENRY (1815–82), was son of the Boston poet and essayist Richard Henry Dana (1787–1879), a founder of the *North American Review* (1815). To regain his health young Dana interrupted his studies at Harvard and sailed to California (1834). After his return he published his journal of the 150-day trip as *Two Years before the Mast* (1840). It is a classic account of life at sea, and an important document in frontier history. Meanwhile he had returned home, studied law, and undertaken a lucrative practice in Boston. His treatise, *The Seaman's Friend* (1841), became a standard manual of maritime law for the common sailor. His edition of Wheaton's *Elements of International Law* (1866) supplied valuable commentary on such law, especially in its bearing on American diplomacy. Charles Francis Adams wrote his biography (2 vols., 1890–91).

Danbury Hatter's Case (*Loewe* v. *Lawler*) grew out of a nationwide boycott (1902) by the United Hatters of North America of the products of a nonunion Danbury (Connecticut) hat manufacturer, who then sued the union for combining to restrain trade in alleged violation of the SHERMAN ANTITRUST ACT. The U.S. Supreme Court unanimously ruled (1908) that a boycott by a labor union was a conspiracy in restraint of trade within the meaning of the act, and sent the case back for retrial. In 1912 the case was finally decided in favor of the company, and the costs of fines levied upon the workmen through attachments on homes and savings accounts threatened near-calamity to the city of Danbury. Thus individual union members were held liable for the actions of their officials.

Dancing Rabbit, Treaty of, see *Choctaw Indians.*

DANIELS, JOSEPHUS (1862–1948), North Carolina newspaper editor, was in charge of publicity for the Democratic party during the presidential campaigns of 1908 and 1912. He was rewarded by an invitation to serve as Wilson's Secretary of the Navy (1913–20), a post in which Daniels surprised many by proving himself an able administrator during World War I. For ten years he was Franklin Roosevelt's ambassador to Mexico (1933–42), where he enthusiastically implemented the Good Neighbor Policy. His writings include *The Wilson Era* (2 vols., 1944–46), and *Shirt-Sleeve Diplomat* (1947), both useful as personal records.

Danites, see *Mormons.*

DA PONTE, LORENZO (1749–1838), Italian-born poet, was serving as 'Poet to the Italian Theater' in Vienna when he wrote the librettos (1786–90) for three of Mozart's greatest operas, *The Marriage of Figaro, Don Giovanni,* and *Cosî fan tutte.* In 1805 he came to New

York, where he opened a bookshop, taught Italian, and built a small theater in his house to give his pupils opportunity to act in Italian comedies. In 1825 he was appointed to the chair of Italian language and literature at Columbia, where his library became the nucleus of the college's collection in the field. He promoted the building of the Italian Opera House in New York (1833), and was a pioneer in spreading Italian culture in the U.S.

DARE, VIRGINIA, see *Roanoke Island.*

'Dark and Bloody Ground,' see *Kentucky.*

Dark horse in U.S. politics is a candidate who is unexpectedly nominated by a party for high office, usually the presidency. Such persons are chosen when powerful rivals bring a national convention to a deadlock. James K. Polk may have been the first dark horse in presidential history (1840), although historians disagree over this designation for him. The term certainly applies to Franklin Pierce (1852), Warren G. Harding (1920), and Wendell Willkie (who lost the election in 1940 to F. D. Roosevelt).

DARROW, CLARENCE SEWARD (1857–1938), had built up a lucrative career as corporation lawyer in Chicago by the time he defended Eugene V. Debs for Debs's part in the PULLMAN STRIKE (1894). Thereafter he devoted himself to pleading causes for the 'underdog' with brilliant success. Over the years he exerted his skill in behalf of some 100 persons charged with murder, none of whom was sentenced to death. He defended William D. Haywood, charged with instigating the murder of the governor of Idaho (1906); defended the McNamara brothers, accused of dynamiting the Los Angeles *Times* building (1911); and defended the 'thrill' murderers Nathan Leopold and Richard Loeb (1924). An agnostic and a foe of fundamentalism, he conducted the defense during the SCOPES TRIAL (1925). As a staunch opponent of capital punishment, he wrote *Crime: Its Cause and Treatment* (1925).

Dartmouth College, at Hanover, New Hampshire, is a nonsectarian liberal arts college for men. Chartered in 1769 by authority of George III, it was an immediate outgrowth of Moor's Indian Charity School, opened (1755) at Lebanon, Connecticut, by the Congregationalist clergyman Eleazar Wheelock (1711–79). With a gift of £10,000 from the second Earl of Dartmouth, Wheelock moved to Hanover and made his establishment a college for whites and Indians. Primarily an undergraduate institution, it also includes three small graduate units: a school of medicine (1797), the Thayer school of engineering (1870), and the Tuck school of business administration (1900). In 1965, with an endowment of $82,900,000 and a faculty of 210, it enrolled 3436 students.

Dartmouth College Case arose in 1816, when the New Hampshire legislature, without the consent of the college trustees, amended the college charter of 1769 to bring the institution under state control as Dartmouth University. The trustees brought suit (*Dartmouth College* v. *Woodward*). Daniel Webster successfully defended his alma mater before the U.S. Supreme Court (1819), arguing that within the meaning of the Constitution such an amendment of the charter impaired the obligation of the contract originally made between the state and the college when the charter was granted.

Although the decision of the Court, which upheld Webster's argument, was of far-reaching importance, it created problems. While it protected private endowments from political interference and encouraged charitable gifts, it gave corporations an immunity from the judicial interference of state police power. In 1837 Chief Justice Taney limited Marshall's ruling (in CHARLES RIVER BRIDGE *v.* WARREN BRIDGE) by deciding that corporate charters are to be construed strictly in favor of the public.

Darwinism, as a concept of evolution, developed after the English naturalist Charles Darwin (1809–82) published *Origin of Species* (1859), a work which fundamentally influenced not only the natural sciences, but the social sciences, philosophy, and religion. Darwin's extensive observations led him to conclude that all life derives from a very small number of types, from which other types evolve, and that the struggle for survival (natural selection) is the means by which members of the same species, in different environments, undergo variations suitable to the new habitat. Modified by 20th-century knowledge of genetics, especially in matters of inherited and uninherited characteristics, Darwinism is now accepted as a scientific principle. But in the decades immediately following publication of his work, Darwin was violently opposed, since his hypothesis left no room for the age-old belief in special creation of each species. He had in effect demolished the 'argument from design,' the belief that the fitness of organisms to their function and environment is evidence of a great Designer. His concept started an intellectual revolution.

During the 1870's the leading American expounder and popularizer of Darwinism was the historian and philosopher JOHN FISKE. He wrote extensively on the subject and was enabled by President Eliot of Harvard to lecture under university aegis. The acknowledged interpreter of American scientific opinion was the botanist ASA GRAY, who immediately became a staunch supporter of the new theory. Later JAMES DWIGHT DANA, the dean of American geologists, swung over to it. LOUIS AGASSIZ (who died in 1873) alone among noted American naturalists never accepted Darwinism in any form.

The attempt to base religion on science was publicized in such books as *Scientific Theism* (1885), by Francis Ellingwood Abbot (1836–1903), founder of the Free Religious Association (1867); and Fiske's *Through Nature to God* (1899), works which suggested that science and religion may be different approaches to the same problem. Such leading clergymen as HENRY WARD BEECHER from the pulpit, JAMES MC COSH in the college classroom, and LYMAN ABBOTT in the editor's chair became the recognized spokesmen of those seeking to reconcile orthodox religion with Darwinism. CHRISTIAN SOCIALISM, the organized attempt to apply the teachings of Jesus to social problems, invoked the theory of evolution, often loosely made synonymous with 'progress,' to support the idea that industry itself must inevitably become more democratically organized.

The virulent hostility to the Darwinian hypothesis, manifest especially in the 1860's and 1870's, was expressed in such books as *What Is Darwinism?* (1874), by the Princeton theologian CHARLES HODGE. It was conveyed to large audiences throughout the country in the evangelism of DWIGHT L. MOODY, whose preaching exerted tremendous influence. At the other extreme, the espousal of Darwin's concept led to agnosticism and atheism in the writings and lectures of ROBERT INGERSOLL, immensely popular and fiercely denounced.

The person chiefly responsible for establishing the principles of Darwinism as a social philosophy was the English philosopher Herbert Spencer (1820–1903), who had in fact conceived the idea of natural selection six years before Darwin's study appeared. His vogue was enormous and his writings deeply influenced the founders of American SOCIOLOGY. He coined the phrase 'survival of the fittest,' opposed state interference, defended LAISSEZ FAIRE in business, and believed that the good life would be most fully realized by way of technological improvements, since human perfectibility, he reasoned, is inevitable. His staunchest American support in the business world came from the industrialist ANDREW CARNEGIE; in the classroom from the political economist WILLIAM GRAHAM SUMNER, who at Yale employed Spencer's *Study of Sociology* (1873) as a text, even though president Noah Porter at first forbade it as antitheistic.

By this time the concept of the evolution of species through natural selection dominated the outlook of American science. It was given support by ANDREW D. WHITE, the first president of Cornell (1867–85), and by DANIEL COIT GILMAN, under whose presidency (1876–1901) the first faculty at Johns Hopkins was assembled. Defended by the empiricist CHAUNCEY WRIGHT in his deeply influential *Philosophical Discussions* (1877), Darwinism entered the context of modern philosophy. Before 1900 the English language itself had begun to develop a new metaphor. 'Naturalism' became a literary method and Darwin's principles were incorporated into the thinking of intellectual leaders everywhere.

By the turn of the century the religious issues had been generally resolved in the U.S., although opposition to the teaching of evolutionary science is still a tenet of FUNDAMENTALISM. Significant contributions to evolutionary thought have recently been made by THEODOSIUS DOBZHANSKY, E. W. MAYR, and G. G. SIMPSON.

Daughters of the American Revolution, a society organized (1890) to perpetuate the spirit and memory of early patriots, has a membership of some 185,000 and a national headquarters at Constitution Hall in Washington, D.C. Assiduous in its devotion to the identification of historic places and the preservation of national relics, in its annual resolutions on such topics as foreign affairs, race problems, and civil liberties the society is dependably reactionary.

DAVENPORT, JOHN (1597–1670), a graduate of Oxford (1625), was an original stockholder of the Massachusetts Bay Company. He migrated to Boston in 1637, and in the following year, with THEOPHILUS EATON, led a group to Connecticut, where they founded the NEW HAVEN COLONY. There he was pastor of the church and a pillar of the colony until it was absorbed into the Connecticut jurisdiction (1664). He then returned to Boston as pastor of the First Church, where his ordination (1668) precipitated a quarrel leading to the formation of the Third (Old South) Church. He was author of numerous tracts on doctrine and church government, and sought to establish an oligarchy, to be governed by the orthodoxy that he prescribed.

DAVIDSON, JO (1883–1952), New York sculptor, studied at Art Students League and at the Beaux-Arts in Paris. He is best known for his vigorous portrait busts, including those of Anatole France and Woodrow Wilson in the Luxembourg Museum, Paris; and of Robert M. La Follette and F. D. Roosevelt in the national Capitol.

DAVIDSON, THOMAS (1840–1900), Scottish-born philosopher, after graduation from Aberdeen (1860), taught in Scotland and England before moving to Canada (1866), and then to the U.S. He developed his pluralistic idealism from his study of Rosmini-Serbati, and on a visit to London in 1883 he founded the Fellowship of the New Life, from which developed the Fabian Society. He later established a summer school at his home in the Adirondacks and elsewhere, as well as the 'Bread-Winner's College' of lecture classes for workers in New York City.

DAVIES, ARTHUR BOWEN (1862–1928), painter and lithographer, was largely responsible for the famous ARMORY SHOW (1913). A member of THE EIGHT, he was a romanticist whose rhythmic compositions are admired for their grace and subtle use of color. Characteristic are *The Dawning* (Brooklyn Museum), and *Crescendo* (Whitney Museum).

DAVIES, SAMUEL (1723–61), born in Delaware, in 1748 went to Hanover county, Virginia, where as a 'New Side' Presbyterian he became the center of the religious revival movement known as the GREAT AWAKENING. To further its aims he went to England to raise funds for support of the young College of New Jersey (Princeton) in 1753, and became its president (1759–61) shortly before his death.

DAVIS, ALEXANDER JACKSON (1803–92), the most prolific American architect of his day, was a successful practitioner of the Greek revival style, represented by such buildings as the Patent Office at Washington (1832), and the state capitols of Indiana (1835) and North Carolina (1837). He was a founder (1837) of the American Institute of Architects.

DAVIS, HENRY WINTER (1817–65), a Baltimore lawyer, as leader of the Maryland antisecessionists was largely responsible for keeping his state in the Union at the outbreak of the Civil War. He was sent to Congress (1863–65), and with Senator B. F. WADE formulated the WADE-DAVIS BILL (1864), a radical reconstruction program that was killed by Lincoln's pocket veto. Davis was a magnetic orator who practically dictated the actions of the RADICAL REPUBLICANS until he failed to be re-elected in 1864.

DAVIS, JEFFERSON (1808–89), born in Kentucky, moved as a boy with his parents to Mississippi, where the Davises became wealthy planters. For seven years after graduation from the U.S. Military Academy (1828) he served in the army. He resigned his commission in 1835, settled on a Mississippi plantation, and after service in the Mexican War (1847) was elected U.S. senator (1847–51). President Pierce appointed him Secretary of War (1853–57), and he then served again in the Senate (1857–61) until Mississippi withdrew from the Union and he resigned his seat. During this period he had urged Southern expansion to the Pacific through a railway, for which he secured the Gadsden Purchase (1854). As senator he had argued against Stephen Douglas's 'squatter sovereignty,' maintaining that neither Congress nor local law could interfere with slavery.

Chosen president of the Confederate provisional government, a year later (February 1862) he was inaugurated president of the Confederate States. His strong central rule, increasingly arbitrary as the Civil War progressed, was bitterly attacked by Southern political leaders, who believed that Davis was violating the very principles of states' rights for which the war was being fought.

Although his interference in military affairs constantly annoyed his generals, Lee himself said of Davis after the war: 'Few people could have done better. I know of none that could have done as well.' When Richmond fell, Davis and his cabinet fled, and Davis, captured in Georgia, was confined to Fortress Monroe for two years. He was indicted for treason, released on bail, and never brought to trial. After travel abroad he settled at Beauvoir, Mississippi, wrote his apologia, *The Rise and Fall of the Confederate Government* (1881), and was esteemed as a relic and symbol of the 'lost cause.'

Biographies include those by W. E. Dodd (1907), R. M. McElroy (2 vols., 1937), and Hudson Strode (2 vols., 1959–64).

DAVIS, JOHN (*c.* 1550–1605), English navigator, continued the work of Martin Frobisher in searching for the NORTHWEST PASSAGE to Asia. On his first voyage (1585) he discovered Cumberland sound off Baffin island, and on his third (1587) he sailed through Davis strait into Baffin bay. Although his attempts to find a passage failed, like all others until the 19th century, his efforts resulted in two of the most important early works on navigation: *The Seamans Secrets* (1594), and *The Worldes Hydrographical Description* (1595).

DAVIS, JOHN WILLIAM (1873–1955), New York corporation lawyer, was serving as a Democrat in Congress (1911–13) when he resigned to become Solicitor General of the U.S. (1913–18). Wilson sent him as ambassador to Great Britain (1918–21). As Democratic candidate for President in 1924, he polled 136 electoral votes to Coolidge's 382. In the election of 1936 he supported the anti-New Deal Liberty League.

DAVIS, RICHARD HARDING (1864–1916), son of the novelist Rebecca Harding Davis (1831–1910) at twenty-two became a reporter and was ultimately the leading correspondent of his day. A dashing and adventurous traveler and journalist, he covered wars on a global scale: Greco-Turkish, Spanish-American, Boer, Russo-Japanese, and (until his death) World War I. His many novels, vivid but without depth, are typified by *Soldiers of Fortune* (1897), a best seller.

DAVIS, STUART (1894–1964), Philadelphia-born painter and lithographer, studied under Henri, and at nineteen exhibited at the ARMORY SHOW. One of the major American artists, Davis was an abstractionist who used hard, dissonant colors. His best known murals probably are those in Rockefeller Center. His oil painting *New York under Gaslight* (1941), contrasting the era of the Gay Nineties with that of the skyscraper, is representative of his philosophy as artist: to be natively American while depicting a universal theme. By distorting and combining objects into an unnaturalistic design he sought to show a principle of order in a neon wilderness. His work is thought by some to have been a precursor of Pop art.

DAVIS, WILLIAM MORRIS (1850–1934), taught geography at Harvard (1878–1912), and as an authority on land forms greatly advanced the science of physiography. He was a prolific contributor to journals in his field, and many of his articles are collected in *Geographical Essays* (1909), which is global in range.

DAVISON, ARCHIBALD THOMPSON (1883–1961), a lifelong teacher of music and choral conductor at Harvard (1909–54) is credited with changing the whole course of American choral music by the results he obtained working with choral groups at Harvard and Radcliffe. His Concord series (with Thomas Surette) of simple scores for school and college singing and playing had wide influence in the U.S. His writings include *Music Education in America* (1926), and *Protestant Church Music in America* (1933).

DAWES, CHARLES GATES (1865–1951), after graduation from Marietta (1884) and law study, began practice in Lincoln, Nebraska. A leading figure in several Illinois banking institutions, he entered the U.S. army in 1917, and, while serving on General Pershing's administrative staff, 'Hell and Maria' Dawes became the general purchasing agent of the American Expeditionary Force. He was appointed the first director of the U.S. Bureau of the Budget (1921), and as head of the reparations committee (1923–24) after World War I, he formulated the DAWES PLAN, for which (jointly with Sir Austen Chamberlain) he was awarded the 1925 Nobel Peace prize. Elected Vice President (1924) as the running mate of Calvin Coolidge, he later served as ambassador to Great Britain (1929–32). He ended his public service as president of the Reconstruction Finance Corporation (1932).

Dawes (Severalty) Act (1887), sponsored by Senator Henry L. Dawes of Massachusetts, followed a government investigation and was intended to end the abuses described in Helen Hunt Jackson's *A Century of Dishonor* (1881), which alleged Federal violations of Indian treaties. The Act sought to assimilate the nomadic Indian by displacing his traditional tribal pattern with a settled farmer system. Family heads received 160-acre allotments inalienably, held in Federal trust for 25 years before title was given. Those Indians who renounced their tribal holdings became citizens. The Act, however, failed to integrate the Indian into American culture. In order to stabilize deteriorating Indian morale, the Collier Act of 1934 (the so-called New Deal for the Indian) stressed the preservation of the best values of Indian cultures.

Dawes Plan (1924) for collecting reparations from Germany after World War I was presented to the Reparations Commission of the Allies by the committee headed by the financier Charles G. Dawes. To avoid a clash with France (which demanded heavy reparations and had occupied the Ruhr to insure collections), the experts evaded the question of determining the grand total of reparations and scheduled annual payments instead. To stabilize German currency, the Reichsbank was reorganized under Allied supervision. The plan operated so successfully that in 1929 the YOUNG PLAN was formulated to liquidate reparations.

DAY (or **DAYE**), STEPHEN (*c.* 1594–1668), came to Boston in 1638 under contract to the Reverend Jose Glover, who was bringing the first printing press to the English colonies. Glover died on the voyage, however, and Day supervised establishment of the press in Cambridge, first issuing the broadside, *Oath of a Free-man* (1639). Of the twenty items that came from his press, the most famous was the BAY PSALM BOOK.

Daylight saving time is the advancing of the clock by one hour during the summer, usually from the last Sunday in April to the last Sunday in October. A daylight saving law was enacted in 1918, but so much opposition was voiced (chiefly by farmers) that Congress repealed the law over Wilson's veto in the next year. Thereafter DST, where in effect, was adopted either by state legislatures or by local option, until 1966, when Congress made DST uniform for all areas within a state (beginning 1967) unless the legislature voted to keep standard time.

D Day (6 June 1944) was the name applied to the date of the Allied invasion of Europe from England across the British Channel. It initiated the final campaigns of World War II in Europe. Germany surrendered eleven months later.

DEANE, Silas (1737–89), after graduation from Yale (1758), engaged in business and the practice of law at Wethersfield, Connecticut. As a delegate from the Continental Congress (1774–76) he went to France (1776) to negotiate for arms and supplies, and there enlisted the services of such officers as Lafayette, Pulaski, de Kalb, and von Steuben. Later in the year he was joined by Franklin and Arthur Lee to negotiate the FRANCO-AMERICAN ALLIANCE (1778). Accused by Lee of irregularities in his official accounts, he was called back for questioning by Congress.

When Deane returned to France in 1780 to adjust his affairs, he entered into what today would be called treasonable correspondence, through EDWARD BANCROFT, with a British agent. Letters of Deane advocating peace without independence were published in the New York press. He was denounced as a renegade and lived his final years in embittered exile. Congress in 1842 characterized Lee's charges as a 'gross injustice' and voted Deane's heirs $37,000 for expenses incurred by Deane in carrying out his difficult mission.

DEARBORN, Henry (1751–1829), born in New Hampshire, saw action as a captain of militia at Bunker Hill, Quebec, Saratoga, and Monmouth, and served on Washington's staff at Yorktown. He entered politics as congressman from Maine (1793–97), and served Jefferson as Secretary of War (1801–9). During the War of 1812, as major general he assumed command of the northern frontier from Niagara to the Atlantic coast. His strategic leadership in the field was inept, and in 1813 he was recalled. Fort Dearborn, on the site of Chicago, was established and named for him in 1803.

Death Valley, an arid basin in southeastern California, 282 ft. below sea level, lies within the GREAT BASIN near the Nevada line. With almost no rainfall and summer temperatures ranging above 130° F., this forbidding 100-mile long desert of alkaline flats and briny pools was named by California gold seekers, who in 1849 attempted to cross it. It is principally known today for its production of borax. In 1933 it was set aside as a national monument.

DE BOW, James Dunwoody Brownson (1820–67), as a youthful editor (1844–46) of the *Southern Quarterly Review* attracted national attention by his extended article defending American claims in the OREGON BOUNDARY DISPUTE. He moved from Charleston to New Orleans and began publishing his monthly commercial journal (1846), which was variously titled, but chiefly known until its demise in 1880 as *De Bow's Review*. Under De Bow's editorship it presented statistics, news items, and essays (many written by De Bow) to encourage the economic development of the South and West. It defended slavery, advocated secession, and led the movement to revive the African slave trade. His *Industrial Resources of the Southern and Western States* (3 vols., 1852–53) is a collection of many of his articles.

DE BRY, Theodor, see *Bry*.

DEBS, Eugene Victor (1855–1926), Indiana-born labor leader, at sixteen became a railroad fireman. He worked so effectively for industrial unionism that at twenty-five he was made national secretary and treasurer of the Brotherhood of Locomotive Firemen, and in 1893 was elected president of the newly organized American Railway Union. When he ignored the injunction served on the Union during the famous PULLMAN STRIKE (1894), he was sentenced to six months in jail, and emerged from his imprisonment a convert to socialism. In 1897 he founded the Social Democratic party, on whose national ticket in 1900 he polled 95,000 votes as candidate for President. Thenceforth as the party's presidential nominee over a span of twenty years, Debs won an increasing number of followers: he received 402,000 votes in 1904, 420,000 in 1908, and 897,000 in 1912. His party refused to participate in the war effort during World War I, and Debs as its leader was sentenced to a ten-year imprisonment in 1918 for violating the sedition provisions of the ESPIONAGE ACT. In 1920, while in jail, he polled 920,000 votes for President. Released in 1921 by President Harding, Debs was widely revered as a martyr to his principles.

Debt Assumption, see *Assumption Act (1790)*.

Debt Funding Commission, see *War Debt Commission.*

DECATUR, STEPHEN (1779–1820), Maryland-born naval officer, won promotion to a captaincy in 1804 by his daring recapture and burning of the frigate *Philadelphia* during the TRIPOLITAN WAR. In 1808 he served as a member of the court-martial that suspended Commodore James Barron after the CHESAPEAKE-LEOPARD INCIDENT. His effective strategy in the War of 1812 forced the Dey of Algiers to sign the treaty that ended American tribute to the Barbary pirates (1815). Acclaimed as a hero on his return, he responded to a toast made at a dinner given in his honor: 'Our country! In her intercourse with foreign nations, may she always be in the right; but our country, right or wrong.' Later as a member of the Board of Navy Commissioners, he opposed the reinstatement of Commodore Barron, by whom he was killed in a duel.

Declaration of Independence, the formal proclamation announcing the separation of the thirteen American colonies from Great Britain, was adopted on 4 July 1776. The First Continental Congress had assembled at Philadelphia in October 1774 to consider action for recovery of rights forfeited under Parliament's repressive COERCIVE ACTS. The armed skirmishes at Lexington and Concord (19 April 1775) had developed into the War of Independence, and the Second Continental Congress met in the same Old State House on 10 May 1775. Already the North Carolina Convention had empowered (12 April) its delegates in Congress to vote for such a declaration. On 15 May Virginia gave similar authorization, and on 7 June Richard Henry Lee called for a resolution 'that these United Colonies are, and of right ought to be, free and independent States.' During the debate (7–10 June) some delegates shared the opinion of Pennsylvania's Joseph Galloway that 'Independency means ruin. If England refuses it, she will ruin us; if she grants it, we shall ruin ourselves.' Nevertheless on 11 June Congress appointed a committee to 'prepare a declaration' in support of the resolution, and the committee, consisting of Franklin, Jefferson, John Adams, Robert Livingston, and Roger Sherman, selected Jefferson to write the draft.

On 28 June the committee reported to Congress 'A Declaration by the Representatives of the United States of America, in general Congress Assembled.' It was entirely the work of Jefferson, who said that he 'turned to neither book nor pamphlet' in preparing the paper. Drawing upon the prevalent 'natural rights' political philosophy, he compiled a list of despotic 'abuses and usurpations.' In doing so he assumed that the British Empire was a confederation of free peoples and implied that certain acts of the king showed a design to subject the Americans to arbitrary control. He therefore asserted the right and the duty of the colonies to dissolve their tie with the Empire and declare themselves independent states, since no people have a right to govern any other people without the consent of the governed.

On 2 July Congress unanimously adopted Lee's resolution. (The New York delegation under instruction abstained from voting.) After two days of debating the form and content of the Declaration, which underwent many changes, on 4 July the amended instrument was approved without dissent, New York again abstaining. The final resolution affecting the document, adopted on 19 July, concludes: 'That the Declaration passed on the 4th be fairly engrossed on parchment with the title and stile of "The unanimous Declaration of the thirteen united States of America" and that the same when engrossed be signed by every member of Congress.' Such was done on and after 2 August, its 56 signatories mutually pledging to each other 'our Lives, our Fortunes and our sacred Honor.' This document today is enshrined in the National Archives Building.

The Declaration was severely criticized in England for expressing a theory of government which reasons that men are by nature free and equal, and may not, without their own consent, be governed by another people. In France, on the other hand, it was deemed a simple and sublime statement of sacred rights long violated. Throughout the 19th century it was regarded by liberal groups everywhere as a classic charter of freedom. It remains the most timeless and eloquent of all American historical papers. Without it the Union could not have survived the Civil War. John Adams expressed its import in a letter to his wife: 'I am well aware of the toil and blood and treasure that it will cost us to maintain this Declaration.'

Studies of the instrument include those by historians Carl Becker (1922), Julian Boyd (1945), Dumas Malone (1954), and David Hawke (1964), and jurist Edward Dumbauld (1950).

Declaration of Rights, the resolution embodying the views of the First Continental Congress in the matter of violation of the rights of the colonies, was adopted in October 1774 in an effort to secure repeal of Parliament's COERCIVE ACTS. The grievances were not redressed, and in the summer of 1776 Congress proclaimed the colonies' independence.

The phrase also has reference to basic rights that devolve on any citizen of a modern society, recognized in such instruments as the English Bill of Rights (1689), the French Constitution of 1791, and the first ten Amendments to the U.S. Constitution.

Declaratory Act (March 1766) was intended by Parliament as an assertion of its powers after repeal of the offensive STAMP ACT. With doctrinaire authority it asserted that the American colonies were subordinate to both the crown and Parliament, and that all votes, resolutions, and proceedings questioning such prerogative would be 'utterly null and void.' The assumption by Parliament of warrant to annul colonial legislation was a novel exercise of power, and when Parliament suspended the New York Assembly (1767) for resisting the QUARTERING ACT, the Declaratory Act was viewed as a standing threat to colonial self-government, a most intolerable cause of grievance. Edmund Burke recognized its implications when he commented that no people is going to be argued into slavery.

Decoration Day, see *Memorial Day*.

Deerfield Massacre occurred on 29 February 1704, when a force of 50 French soldiers from Canada, with 200 Indian allies, entered the stockaded Massachusetts frontier village of 300 inhabitants, killed 50 and took 111 prisoners. After prolonged negotiation some 60 captives were allowed to return.

Defense, U.S. Department of, was created (1947) as the National Military Establishment, to co-ordinate the programs of the U.S. armed forces. It was given its present name under the National Security Act of 1949. It consolidates the Departments of the Navy (est. 1789), Army (est. 1789), and Air Force (est. 1947). Its annual appropriation in 1965 of $46,900,000,000 represented almost half the total Federal budget receipts. Secretaries of Defense and the Presidents under whom they served are as follows.

TRUMAN

James V. Forrestal (N.Y.) 1947
Louis A. Johnson (W. Va.) 1949
George C. Marshall (Pa.) 1950
Robert A. Lovett (N.Y.) 1951

EISENHOWER

Charles E. Wilson (Mich.) 1953
Neil H. McElroy (Ohio) 1957
Thomas S. Gates, Jr. (Pa.) 1959

KENNEDY

Robert S. McNamara (Mich.) 1961

L. B. JOHNSON

Robert S. McNamara (Mich.) 1963

Defiance, Fort (1794) was built in Ohio by Anthony Wayne during his Western campaign. 'I defy the English, Indians, and all the devils in hell to take it,' Wayne reputedly said. To which remark General Charles Scott replied, 'Then call it Fort Defiance.'

Definitive Treaty of Peace, see *Paris, Treaty of (1783)*.

DE FOREST, JOHN WILLIAM (1826–1906), the first American realistic novelist, drew on the letters he had written during his three years' service with a Connecticut regiment to write *Miss Ravenel's Conversion from Secession to Loyalty* (1867), the best Civil War novel based on actual experience. *Kate Beaumont* (1872) characterizes Southern types as De Forest knew them from his experience as a district commander of the Freedmen's Bureau in

South Carolina. His later political novels, *Honest John Vane* (1875) and *Playing the Mischief* (1876), have their setting in Washington during the Grant administration. His personal reminiscences of the Civil War, published in the 1860's, have been collected as *A Volunteer's Adventure* (1946) and *A Union Officer in the Reconstruction* (1948).

DE FOREST, LEE (1873–1961), radio engineer and inventor, after graduation from Yale (1896) pioneered in the development of wireless communications. His audion amplifier (1905), in its improved form the three-electrode vacuum tube, paved the way for developments which earned him the sobriquet 'father of broadcasting.' He patented more than 300 inventions that contributed significantly to television, high-speed facsimile transmission, and radiotherapy.

Deism is the term applied to the 18th-century concept which held that God created the world, which He rules by rational laws, and that men are rational creatures, capable of guiding their lives by the light of reason. Deists rejected the claims of supernatural revelation and took no share in formal religious practices. To be sure, the rationalism of the period is evident in the writings of orthodox clergymen who were by no means deists. CHARLES CHAUNCY and JONATHAN MAYHEW were firm in their opposition to Calvinism, and COTTON MATHER went so far as to espouse the current idea of benevolent design in the universe, but none was a deist.

The concept of a natural universal religion, a more positive deism, is basic in the thinking of Franklin and Jefferson, who shared a hope for man's perfectibility. Extreme freethinking, a term nearly synonymous with deism, is expounded in such works as Thomas Paine's *The Age of Reason* (1794–95), an attack on the Bible which alienated moderate deists. Deism was later absorbed into 19th-century skeptical thought by such 'Free Enquirers' as the universalist clergyman ABNER KNEELAND, and into the liberal rationalism of such religious doctrines as UNITARIANISM.

DE KALB, BARON, see *Kalb, Johann.*

DE KOONING, WILLEM (1904–), Dutch-born abstract expressionist painter, came to the U.S. in 1926. By the mid-1940's his influence on younger painters was significant beyond that of any other contemporary artist. He has organized pictorial space with originality, whether in representations of human figures, landscapes, or a field of force.

DE LANCEY, JAMES (1703–60), son of the Huguenot exile and wealthy New York merchant, Stephen De Lancey (1663–1741), was educated in England and became one of the most influential figures in the history of colonial New York. A justice (1731–33) and chief justice (1733–60) of the provincial supreme court, he also wielded great political power in the executive branch of the government, especially against the factions of Governor George Clinton and the Livingstons. Several members of the De Lancey family were prominent during the colonial period, and most of them were Loyalists during the War of Independence.

Delaware, first of the thirteen colonies to ratify the Federal Constitution (7 December 1787), was discovered by HENRY HUDSON in 1609. Within a year the governor of Virginia, Thomas West, Baron de la Warr, gave his name to the entrance of the bay, a name soon extended to the local Indian tribe, the river, and the colony.

From the first the region was contested by the Dutch and English, and shortly by the Swedes who, led by PETER MINUIT (1638), established Fort Christiana on the site of the present Wilmington, and launched NEW SWEDEN. After 1664 Delaware was chiefly an English colony. In 1682 the Duke of York transferred his claim to William Penn, and Delaware became the Three Lower Counties (New Castle, Kent, Sussex) of Pennsylvania. Under the Penn charter they were granted a separate assembly in 1704. Political ties with Pennsylvania remained close until 1776, when Delaware became a sovereign state with Dover as capital. During the Revolution it was a vigorous adherent to the patriot cause. Although it forbade further importation of slaves in 1787, it continued to be a slave-holding state, but remained loyal to the Union during the Civil War.

Industries center on Wilmington, where the present large and diversified business interests had their beginning in 1802, when the DU PONT FAMILY established its manufactures. The state also depends on the sea for its income, and it maintains a large fishing fleet for its shellfish industry. The population of Wilmington in the decade 1950–60 dropped from 110,000 to 95,000, but that of the state rose from 318,000 to 446,000, chiefly in the small towns and cities, the largest of which, after Wilmington, is Newark (11,000), the site of the University of Delaware (est. 1833).

Delaware Indians, of Algonquian linguistic stock, called themselves Lenni-Lenape (*real men*). Their remarkable tribal chronicle, *Walum-Olum,* places their origin far to the northwest, but at the time of the early white settlements they occupied the basin of the Delaware river in the present states of Pennsylvania, New Jersey, and New York. After their treaty of friendship with William Penn (1682), they lived peaceably with the English. They were defeated by the Iroquois in 1720, and thereafter gradually relinquished their lands, moving westward into Ohio. They were allies of PONTIAC in his rebellion against the British in 1763, but sided with them in the War of Independence. When Anthony Wayne routed them in 1794, some fled to Canada, but most crossed the Mississippi into Kansas and Texas, and were finally incorporated with the Cherokee in Oklahoma.

Delaware river, 280 miles long, rises in the Catskills and flows southeast between New York and Pennsylvania, New Jersey and Pennsylvania, and Delaware and New Jersey, to enter Delaware bay. Significant in commerce from the early colonial period, it was the main shipping route to Wilmington, Philadelphia, and Trenton, and the avenue for settlements along its entire course. Canal networks built in the 1820's and 1830's connected the Delaware with other important waterways (notably the Hudson), and until the advent of the railroad they were the chief means of inland transportation over a large segment of the eastern U.S.

DE LA WARR, THOMAS WEST, Baron (1577–1618), was chosen by the Virginia Company as first governor of the Virginia colony (1609). He dispatched SIR THOMAS GATES as his deputy, arriving himself a year later. In 1611 he returned to London to report on the conditions of the colony, and remained in England until 1618. On his voyage back to Virginia he died at sea. The state of Delaware and the Delaware river were named for him.

Delegated powers, specifically conferred upon Congress in the Federal Constitution, are enumerated in Article I, section 8. All others, except the IMPLIED POWERS in the same section, are reserved to the states by the Tenth Amendment. Especially important among the eighteen delegated powers are the right of Congress to levy taxes, coin money, regulate foreign and interstate commerce, grant patents and copyrights, establish post offices, and declare war.

Delegation of power is the conferral of that power normally within the jurisdiction of the different governmental departments upon particular agencies. The U.S. Congress has created such boards, bureaus, and commissions sometimes to handle special problems (such as the administration of the District of Columbia) and sometimes to free specialists from bureaucratic interference—a type of delegation represented by the Securities Exchange Commission, the Interstate Commerce Commission, and the Federal Trade Commission. Quasi-executive, -legislative, and -judicial, such agencies have been called 'floating islands of independent power in a sea of governmental administration.' Nominations to these groups are made by the President, subject to congressional appointment. They are independent of the official executive departments, and the President may remove a member only for 'just cause' as determined by the charter of the particular board, not for political reasons.

DE LEON, DANIEL (1852–1914), born in Curaçao, took his law degree at Columbia (1878), where he taught Latin American diplomacy (1883–86). A brilliant and inflexible Marxian revolutionist, he was a leader in the SOCIAL-

IST LABOR PARTY, and for many years edited its English organ, *Weekly People* (after 1892), as well as *Daily People* (after 1900). He helped found the IWW (1905), wrote extensively on socialism, and because of his vivid temperament became a controversial figure in labor reform.

De Lôme letter, written by Enrique de Lôme, the Spanish minister to the U.S., as a private communication to a friend in Cuba, was stolen from the Havana post office and published (9 February 1898) in Hearst's New York *Journal.* It called President McKinley (among other things) 'weak, and a bidder for the admiration of the crowd.' Repercussions were instantaneous and violent. De Lôme immediately resigned his post, but the incident served as a propaganda weapon against Spain, as Hearst had intended, and it was a factor leading to the Spanish-American War.

DE MILLE, AGNES (*c.* 1908–), dance recitalist and choreographer, made her debut in 1928. Her work in such productions as *Rodeo* (1942), and *Fall River Legend* (1948) brought American folklore to ballet. Her choreography for *Oklahoma!* (1943), and *Carousel* (1945) helped give a new direction to musical comedy by making incidental dances express the central feeling of the performance.

DE MILLE, CECIL B. [BLOUNT] (1881–1959), carried his spectacular career as a motion picture director from *The Squaw Man* (1913, cost $15,000) through 70 films to the production of *The Ten Commandments* (1956, cost $13,000,000), a movie which grossed $45,000,000. Famous for his staging of lavish productions, which were termed 'audacious and glittering,' De Mille had a gift for showmanship that enthralled audiences not concerned with reality.

Democratic party, formed in 1828, developed from the Jackson-Calhoun faction that opposed the Adams-Clay factions, the National Republicans, soon called the WHIG PARTY. It had close affinities with the older DEMOCRATIC-REPUBLICAN PARTY. It won the support of farmers, mechanics, and small businessmen, attracted state politicians seeking national power, and brought Jackson into office. With the exception of two elections (W. H. Harrison, 1840; Taylor, 1848) it was the dominant political party until 1860. Its success stemmed from superior party organization, which was upset when repeal of the Missouri Compromise (1854) and the Dred Scott decision (1857) led to the nomination of two Democratic candidates in 1860.

During the Civil War most Democrats, as 'War Democrats,' gave ardent support to Lincoln; those publicly opposed to his policies were called COPPERHEADS, a term which implied treason. The alleged corrupt practices of Republicans during Reconstruction helped create a 'solid South,' the most dependable source of Democratic strength for several decades. The growing strength of the agrarian West, which consistently urged a lower tariff, and the economic unrest in urban centers, elected Cleveland (1892). A Republican split in 1912 cleared the way for the liberal idealist Wilson, and F. D. Roosevelt's landslide in 1932 followed the Great Depression. The party's united support of New Deal measures, together with the nation's unity during World War II, kept the presidency in Democratic hands until 1952. The party was able to control Congress throughout Eisenhower's presidency. In 1960 it elected Kennedy and continued to dominate Congress. Its presidential nominee in 1964, Lyndon B. Johnson, was carried into office by the most emphatic vote of preference ever given to a national candidate.

Democratic-Republican party, developing from the political cleavage of FEDERALISTS and ANTI-FEDERALISTS, took shape late in Washington's first administration when Washington, who had at first, with Jefferson, favored maintaining friendship with France, veered toward the Federalists by accepting Hamilton's advice in foreign affairs. Because of this Jefferson resigned as Secretary of State effective on the last day of 1793. The breach between Hamilton the Federalist and Jefferson the Republican was not personal, and the parties thus established were not projections of rival personalities. The interests which Jefferson represented as promulgator of JEFFERSONIAN DEMOCRACY were those of the

Southern planters and the Northern yeoman farmers. The Republicans contended for control of the federal government against the mercantile-shipping-financial interest of the Federalists. (The ideological differences, already of long standing, ultimately were debated in the Civil War.)

In the beginning the Republicans drew support from those who were sympathetic to the French Revolution, hostile to England, and strongly in favor of limiting Federal power. The victory of Jefferson in the 'revolution' of 1800 brought the party into power and gave it prestige. It shortly split into two factions: conservative merchants and planters, and radical frontiersmen, mechanics, and debtors. The Republicans controlled both houses of Congress through the administrations of Jefferson, Madison, and Monroe (1801–25). With the overwhelming victory of the radical wing under Jackson in 1828, the party name was fixed as DEMOCRATIC. This second bloodless 'revolution' ushered in the era of JACKSONIAN DEMOCRACY.

Demonetization of Silver Act, see *Coinage Act of 1873.*

DEMPSEY, JACK [William Harrison] (1895–), born at Manassa, Colorado, won the world heavyweight boxing championship in 1919 from JESS WILLARD by scoring a technical knockout after three rounds of a scheduled twelve-round bout at Toledo, Ohio. He lost it to GENE TUNNEY by a decision in a ten-round fight at Philadelphia in 1926. The 'Manassa Mauler' attracted more spectators to his bouts than any other fighter in the history of U.S. boxing.

DEMUTH, CHARLES (1883–1935), painter and illustrator, studied art in New York and Paris, and began a series of line-and-wash illustrations for the works of Poe, Zola, and Henry James. He is well known for his still-life studies, and was one of the first Americans to develop a partial abstraction of his subjects, characteristically represented by *Cyclamen* (Metropolitan Museum).

DENNIE, JOSEPH (1768–1812), Boston-born editor and essayist, after graduation from Harvard (1790) and a brief legal career, settled for a time in Walpole, New Hampshire, where he edited the *Farmer's Weekly Museum* (1796–98), to which he contributed his Addisonian 'Lay Preacher' essays. As 'Oliver Oldschool,' a precise champion of tradition, he founded and edited (1801–9) in Philadelphia the PORT-FOLIO, thereby creating a standard for native literature that led Timothy Dwight to hail him as 'the father of American belles lettres.' An opinionated critic rather than a creator, Dennie had sound judgments in matters not affected by his prejudices, and he helped broaden the outlook of his readers through his attacks on provincialism. His confirmed Federalist views led him in 1805 to assail Jefferson so violently that he was tried for seditious libel. He was acquitted.

Dennis* v. *U.S. (1951) was a case resulting in a ruling by the U.S. Supreme Court upholding the Smith Act (1946), which made it a criminal offense to advocate the forceful overthrow of the government. In the opinion of Justice Black, dissenting, this limitation of free speech was a revival of the 'bad tendency' test criticized earlier by Justice Holmes. Black called for a return to the 'clear and present danger' doctrine. Justice Douglas, also dissenting, differentiated between a 'conspiracy' and the teaching of Communist dogma.

Dentistry, in the U.S. began as a profession when CHAPIN A. HARRIS pioneered in establishing the world's first dental periodical, the *American Journal of Dental Science* (1839), and the first dental school, the Baltimore College of Dental Surgery (1840). These, and the founding of The American Society of Dental Surgeons (1840), marked the birth of professionalism in dentistry. Later the contributions of GREENE V. BLACK, an originator of novel dental instruments and author of significant dental publications, gave him unique importance in his field.

By 1900 dental schools were rapidly being established as departments of universities and medical institutions, and those in the U.S. were taking world leadership. Since the 1930's dental public health programs have been services provided for communities by Federal, state, and local agencies. After 1960 belief that fluoridation of water would reduce tooth decay gained strong medical support.

Denver, settled in 1858, became the territorial capital of Colorado in 1867. Rich mineral strikes created mining booms, and during the 1870's Denver was the home of 'bonanza kings.' By 1900 it had become the transportation and distributing center for the livestock, agricultural, and mining industries of the Rocky Mountain region. The population totaled 930,000 in 1960. It is the chief city between Chicago and San Francisco, located on the South Platte river, at an altitude of 5280 ft., and is called 'the mile-high city.' Its leading institution of higher learning is the University of Denver (est. 1864).

Department stores, large-scale general retail enterprises in which each line operates its own department, were developed by ALEXANDER T. STEWART in New York (1862), and in succeeding years by MARSHALL FIELD in Chicago (1865), by JOHN WANAMAKER in Philadelphia (1876), and by Gimbel Brothers in Philadelphia (1894) and New York (1910), with later branches in other cities. R. H. Macy, established in New York (1858), long continued as a general merchandise store. See also *Mail-order houses, Chain stores,* and ***Discount houses.***

Depressions, see *Business cycles, Panics.*

Desegregation, see *Brown* v. *Board of Education.*

Deseret, see *Utah.*

Desert Land Act (1877), authorized individuals to acquire 640-acre lots at $1.25 an acre from the federal government, providing the land be irrigated within three years. By 1890 over 3,500,000 acres had been reclaimed.

DE SMET, PIERRE JEAN (1801–73), Belgian-born Jesuit missionary to the Indians of the Northwest, came to the U.S. in 1821 and began (1838) his labors in Iowa. He established missions in Montana and Idaho, and during his long career in that region often served as mediator between Indians and white immigrants. He was chiefly responsible for the temporary peace arranged (1868) with the Sioux. His *Letters and Sketches* (1843) and *New Indian Sketches* (1863) are source material in Western history.

DE SOTO, HERNANDO (*c.* 1500–1542), Spanish conquistador, having served with Pedrarias in Central America, and Pizarro in Peru, was selected by Charles V in 1539 to conquer 'Florida,' which then denoted the North American mainland. He landed at Tampa Bay with 600 soldiers, and in search of a 'golden city' headed north in his long trek across the Blue Ridge Mountains, then southwest to the region of Mobile. In the spring of 1541 he became the first white man to see and cross the Mississippi, near Memphis. He continued westward through the Ozarks, wintered in eastern Oklahoma, and returned to the Mississippi, where he died of a fever. His body was sunk in the river he had discovered, and the 300 survivors of the expedition made their way down the coast to Veracruz.

Destroyer Transfer Agreement (1940) was a defense arrangement between President F. D. Roosevelt and Prime Minister Churchill whereby the U.S. transferred to Great Britain 50 obsolete American destroyers in exchange for 99-year leases on a series of British military bases, from British Guiana to Newfoundland. The President called the arrangement 'the most important action in the reinforcing of our national defense that has been taken since the Louisiana Purchase.' During the Battle of Britain these destroyers helped to avert the full impact of a concentrated submarine attack by Hitler.

Determinism is the doctrine that psychological responses, acts of will, and social changes result from determining causes. In ethics it opposes belief in freedom of the will. The apparently deterministic implications of DARWINISM troubled WILLIAM JAMES, who presented his reflections on the conflict between the doctrines of free will and determinism in his classic study, *The Varieties of Religious Experience* (1902). Determinists have attempted to explain social phenomena in terms of the categories of natural science. Thus HENRY ADAMS argued that 'dissipation of energy' was fundamental to the nature of man.

Other such monistic views include the innate tendency theory of E. L. THORNDIKE, and the instinct theory of WILLIAM MC DOUGALL. The Yale geographer Ellsworth Huntington (1876–1947) emphasized geographical determinism in such studies as *Civilization and Climate* (1924), and *Principles of Economic Geography* (1940). As in BEHAVIORISM, the problem of such theories is that of developing measurements to determine the relative weight of causal factors.

DE TOCQUEVILLE, see *Tocqueville.*

Detroit, county seat of Wayne county, was founded (1701) in Michigan as Fort Pontchartrain du Detroit at the straits of Lake Erie, as part of the French policy to control the interior of North America. The British captured it in 1760, and its importance as a fur trading and shipping center made it the goal of the northwestern campaign of GEORGE ROGERS CLARK (1778–79). Destroyed by fire in 1805, it was immediately rebuilt, and made the territorial capital. Later it was made the state capital (1805–47). Its rapid growth after 1830 stemmed from its excellent harbor and its location in the network of Great Lakes commerce. With a population (in 1960) of 1,700,000, it is a cultural center and one of the great industrial cities in the U.S., with automobile manufacture a prime venture. Among its leading institutions of higher learning are Wayne State University (est. 1868), and the University of Detroit (est. 1877), with enrollments respectively (in 1965) of 25,200 and 9600.

DE VOTO, BERNARD AUGUSTINE (1897–1955), Utah-born historian of the American West, taught English at Northwestern (1922–27) and Harvard (1929–36), and occupied the 'Easy Chair' of *Harper's* (1935–55). His trilogy on the 'continental experience' chronologically begins with *The Course of Empire* (1952), and continues with *Across the Wide Missouri* (1947), and *The Year of Decision: 1846* (1943). He wrote authoritatively on Mark Twain, and his studies of American ideas are presented in *Forays and Rebuttals* (1936).

DEWEY, GEORGE (1837–1917), Vermont-born admiral, after graduation from the U.S. Naval Academy (1858) saw active service upward through the ranks. At the outbreak of the Spanish-American War (1898), as a Commodore, he commanded the Asiatic squadron and won renown in the battle of MANILA BAY. In a noteworthy victory that demonstrated the strength of America's 'New Navy,' he destroyed eight Spanish ships at the cost of eight Americans wounded, and thus made the U.S. a major Pacific power. (His order 'You may fire when ready, Gridley' soon became a popular quotation.) He was immediately promoted to the rank of rear admiral, thanked by Congress, and on his return to the U.S. feted with almost hysterical enthusiasm. In 1899 he was made Admiral of the Navy.

DEWEY, JOHN (1859–1952), after graduation from the University of Vermont (1879) and further study at Johns Hopkins, taught philosophy, chiefly at Chicago (1894–1904) and Columbia (1904–30). He formulated the type of pragmatism called instrumentalism, a position which seeks to incorporate the individualism of William James with the social emphasis of Charles Peirce. Since the problems of men constantly alter, truth itself is always hypothetical, and the instruments for handling human problems, according to Dewey, must be individually constructed. Unsympathetic to abstract learning and authoritarian methods in the classroom, Dewey created an upheaval by writing *The School and Society* (1899; rev. ed., 1915), in which he emphasized 'learning by doing,' and urged his conviction that men shape their environment by developing their native capacities. His immensely influential contribution to PROGRESSIVE EDUCATION was most fully expressed in *Democracy and Education* (1916), which postulates the instrumental approach. Intelligence should be trained to alter environment; distinctions between cultural and vocational training are not valid; subject matter should be adjusted to the child, not the child to the subject.

Dewey's pragmatism became militant

in his *Reconstruction in Philosophy* (1920), which attacks metaphysics as the product of an outmoded aristocracy, a philosophy of escapism for a leisure class which does not face the ethical problems in a democratic society. His concern with social welfare and political reform was tied into his general principles, and was expressed in *Human Nature and Conduct* (1922), *The Quest for Certainty* (Gifford Lectures, 1929), *Freedom and Culture* (1939), and *Problems of Men* (1946). Dewey's break with tradition was so sharp and his influence in education so dominating that a reaction was inevitable; it was most effectively expressed in the 1930's by R. M. HUTCHINS.

DEWEY, MELVIL (1851–1931), a pioneer in library science, after graduation from Amherst (1874), evolved his 'Dewey decimal system' of book classification, which, with modifications, is now used internationally. He was a founder of the American Library Association (1876), and while librarian at Columbia (1883–88) established the first school of library training (1884). When Dewey became librarian of the New York State Library (1889–1906), the school was reestablished at Albany. Later it was absorbed into the Columbia School of Library Service (1926).

DEWEY, THOMAS EDMUND (1902–), a graduate of the University of Michigan (1923), practiced law in New York City, where, as District Attorney of New York county, he came into national prominence in the 1930's through his prosecution of racketeers. Thrice governor of New York (1942–54), he was the Republican candidate in the 1944 presidential campaign, polling a popular vote of 22,000,000, but losing to F. D. Roosevelt by an electoral margin of 99 to 432. Again the party's candidate in 1948, he polled substantially the same popular vote as in 1944, but lost to Truman in the electoral college by 189 to 304.

Diamond fraud (1872) was a fantastic swindle in which two adroit miners salted rough jewels over rocky acres in northern Utah to tempt avaricious investors. The San Francisco banker William C. Ralston organized a mining corporation after the precious stones (rejects, principally diamonds, rubies, and sapphires purchased in Amsterdam) had been pronounced genuine by the jeweler Charles Tiffany and the mining authority Henry Janin. The fraud was exposed by the geologist CLARENCE KING. Meanwhile the swindlers had collected some $300,000 by the sale of their 'diamond field.'

DICKENS, CHARLES (1812–70), though but thirty years old when he embarked on his first tour of the U.S. (1842), was already established as a celebrated author. His reception was an episode without parallel in English literary annals, and he was greeted everywhere with huge acclaim. But when his *American Notes* appeared (1842), in the words of Carlyle, 'all Yankee-doodledom blazed up like one universal soda bottle.' Dickens's frank description of slavery nettled the South, and his picture of New York as a low, flat, straggling city, without baths or plumbing and scavenged by pigs, seemed ungracious.

The collapse of the 'Cairo City & Canal Company,' in which he had invested, partly accounts for the edginess of his tone in describing his Western tour, woven into *Martin Chuzzlewit* (1843–44). His attack on American financial vagaries proved a strain on Anglo-American relations at the time. In 1867, when the animus was forgotten, Dickens returned for a second visit to the U.S. and gave a series of readings on the lyceum platform. He always contended that he was no less sparing in his portraiture of Englishmen than of Americans, and his American friendships were enduring.

DICKINSON, EMILY [ELIZABETH] (1830–86), was born in Amherst, Massachusetts, where she spent almost all of her secluded life. She first became known as a poet when a slender volume of her verses was posthumously published by her friends Thomas Wentworth Higginson and Mabel Loomis Todd in 1890. Her fame slowly mounted as subsequent collections of further poems revealed a lyric talent of such originality and vigor as to become a primary influence in 20th-century poetry. By the time her more than 1770 brief lyrics had been gathered in a three-volume variorum edition (1955), she was recognized as one of the classic American poets. She dealt with universals, asserting that reason cannot solve the paradoxes of existence, and that faith alone can reduce the tensions created by loneliness and anxiety.

DICKINSON, John (1732–1808), Philadelphia lawyer, early became a leader of the conservatives in the Pennsylvania legislature, where he opposed Franklin's effort to abolish proprietary government by supporting the Penn family in their claim to broad political powers in the colony. As a member of the STAMP ACT CONGRESS (1765), he was the chief draftsman of its Resolutions. Passage of the TOWNSHEND ACTS (1767) led him to publish in the *Pennsylvania Chronicle* his series of *Letters from a Farmer in Pennsylvania* (1767–68), notable as the accepted American position in resisting the British policy of taxation in the colonies. As a member of both Continental Congresses, he urged conciliation, and he refused to sign the Declaration of Independence. When war came he acquiesced, however, and volunteered to serve in the Continental army. In the Constitutional Convention he vigorously championed the rights of small states, firmly supported the new government, and drafted the Articles of Confederation.

DICKINSON, Jonathan (1688–1747), Presbyterian clergyman, was born in Hatfield, Massachusetts. After graduation from Yale (1706) he settled in Elizabethtown, New Jersey, where he became the leading preacher and ecclesiastical authority in the middle colonies. He was an exponent of 'New Side' Presbyterianism during the GREAT AWAKENING, and was instrumental in founding the College of New Jersey (Princeton, 1746) and served as its first president.

Dictionaries in America, as serious ventures in lexicography, began with the publication of a *Compendious Dictionary* (1806) by NOAH WEBSTER, who 22 years later brought out his monumental *American Dictionary of the English Language* (1828). Two years later JOSEPH E. WORCESTER, competing for the lucrative schoolroom trade, published a rival volume, conservative and British in standards of pronunciation and spelling. College faculties and the press soon began to wage the 'war of the dictionaries' on the issue of the authors' respective merits. Webster, drawing upon American as well as British authors for his definitions, prevailed everywhere except at Harvard and the University of Virginia; after 1864, when Webster was revised by a company of scholars, even those strongholds fell.

The scholarly edition of the *Century Dictionary* (6 vols., 1889–91, with later supplements), edited by WILLIAM DWIGHT WHITNEY, has not yet been superseded in matters of definition. At present the standard work is *Dictionary of American English on Historical Principles* (4 vols., 1938–44), edited by Sir William Craigie and J. R. Hurlbert. M. M. Mathews's *Dictionary of Americanisms* (1951) stresses the distinctive additions that Americans have made to the English language.

DIDRIKSON, Mildred Babe, see *Zaharias, Babe Didrikson.*

Digger Indians, see *Paiute Indians.*

Dighton rock, in the Taunton river in Massachusetts, marked with an intricate inscription, was first observed in 1680, and for nearly three centuries its cryptic markings have been a source of speculation. Some of the scribblings were certainly made by Indians. That some were made by the lost Portuguese explorer Miguel Cortereale, in 1511, may be possible. In 1955 the rock was deeded to the state, and the legislature appropriated funds to convert the surrounding area into a state park.

DILLON, John Forrest (1831–1914) gave up a medical practice to teach himself law. While serving as Iowa state judge (1858–68) and as U.S. circuit court judge (1869–79), he wrote *Municipal Corporations* (1872), one of the earliest systematic studies of the subject. He was a professor of law at Columbia (1879–82), and won a reputation as a great legal scholar through his writings. He later practiced railroad law in New York City.

DI MAGGIO, Joe [Joseph Paul] (1914–), began his professional baseball career with the Pacific Coast League. After 1935 he played center field with the New York Yankees (American League). He was homerun leader for his league in 1937 and 1948, and its champion batter in 1939 and 1940.

Dime novels took their name from the ten-cent paperback thrillers first issued by Erastus F. Beadle, who published the immensely popular *Malaeska: the Indian Wife of the White Hunter* (1860), by Ann S. Stephens. Following conventional moral patterns in the tales of such writers as E. Z. C. JUDSON and PRENTISS INGRAHAM, they emphasized democratic vigor and attempted to maintain continuous suspense. Edward L. Wheeler created 'Deadwood Dick' (1884), and in the same decade John R. Coryell invented the detective 'Nick Carter.' In 1896 William G. Patten (1866–1945) under the name Burt L. Standish created his youthful 'Frank Merriwell' in a series that eventually sold some 25,000,000 copies. By 1910 dime novels, which had made a fortune for Beadle and one or two other publishers, were being replaced by PULP MAGAZINES.

Dingley Tariff Act (1897), an upward revision of most categories, enacted the highest protective tariff imposed by Congress up to that time, an average of 57 per cent. (Big business had contributed heavily to the Republican campaign of 1896.) The act replaced the WILSON-GORMAN TARIFF ACT (1893), and remained in force until it was modified by the PAYNE-ALDRICH TARIFF ACT (1909).

Direct primary has become since the early 1900's the method by which almost all voters in the U.S. annually select nominees for political office. Petitions are circulated, and candidates receiving the required number of signatures gain the right to enter the contest. Open primaries are unlike closed primaries in that they impose no test of party affiliation. They have fallen off in popularity, for unless a nominee receives a majority of votes, a run-off must be conducted. The direct primary is chiefly used in state and local elections, and is required by law in all states except Connecticut, Rhode Island, and New Mexico. In seventeen states PRESIDENTIAL PRIMARIES precede the NATIONAL CONVENTIONS.

Disarmament conferences, see *Hague Conferences* (1899, 1907), *Washington Naval Conference* (1921), *Geneva Conferences* (1927 and later), and *London Naval Conference* (1930). See also *Security Council* (United Nations).

Disciples of Christ, or Campbellites, are a Protestant religious sect founded (1809) in southwestern Pennsylvania by Irish-born Thomas Campbell (1763–1854) and his son Alexander Campbell (1788–1866). At first nominally Baptist and Presbyterian, the Disciples became a separate congregation, holding the belief that the only basis of faith and conduct is the Bible, which each individual must interpret as his understanding allows. Alexander Campbell founded and became president of Bethany College (1840). The church developed rapidly after the Civil War, especially in the north central states. In 1931 one branch (the Christian Church) merged with Congregationalists. Officially the denomination is the International Convention of Christian Churches. In 1965 it reported a membership of some 1,900,000.

Discount houses, which sprang up in the U.S. after World War II, are department stores that operate at considerably lower overhead costs than most conventional retailers. Transactions are generally cash-and-carry and customers serve themselves. So fast has been their growth and so large their discount (10 to 30 per cent below prevailing prices) that some authorities on retailing believe that before 1970 they may capture 25 per cent of the general-merchandise, apparel, and house-goods market.

Discovery of America, see *America.*

Dismal Swamp, originally an area of some 750 square miles on the Virginia–North Carolina coast line, was once heavily forested and almost impenetrable. WILLIAM BYRD described it in 1728. It is often mentioned in literature as a refuge for fugitives. Much of it has been drained, and today its area is greatly decreased.

DISNEY, Walt [Walter] (1901–), after study at the Chicago Academy of Fine Arts, made original animated comic films in Hollywood in his 'Mickey Mouse' series (1928). These were followed by such animated color cartoons as *Three Little Pigs* (1933); *Snow White* (1938), the first animated feature cartoon; and *Pinocchio* (1940). In collaboration with Leopold Stokowski he produced *Fantasia* (1940), a film concert with musical classics accompanied by animation. Later productions have included *Alice in Wonderland* (1951), and such documentaries on nature as *The Vanishing Prairie* (1954), and *The African Lion* (1955).

Displaced Persons Act (1948), see *Immigration.*

District of Columbia, see *Washington, D.C.*

DIVINE, Father (*c.* 1882–1965), Negro leader of a religious cult, moved (1915) from Georgia to the North, altered his name (George Baker) to Major M. J. Divine, and gathered about him worshipful followers (some of them whites), many of whom believed him to be the personification of God. The cult was especially active in the depression years of the 1930's, stressed economic cooperation, and opened missions ('heavens') for regenerate 'angels.' It spread from the Harlem district of New York to other cities in the U.S. and Europe.

DIX, Dorothea Lynde (1802–87), reformer and pioneer in the movement for specialized treatment of the insane, began her crusades by writing the famous *Memorial to the Legislature of Massachusetts* (1843), a scathing indictment of public indifference to the mentally ill. She was one of the few northern reformers to meet with sympathy and a considerable measure of success in the South before the Civil War, during which she served as superintendent of women nurses. She succeeded in persuading many states to assume responsibility for the care of the mentally ill. She was as highly regarded abroad as she was in the U.S.

Dixie is a collective designation of the southern states that formed the Confederacy, but the origin of the name is uncertain. The song 'Dixie' (1859) was written by d. d. emmett.

'Dixiecrats,' see *States' Right Party.*

Dixieland style of jazz developed about 1900 in New Orleans. It blended European harmonies and African rhythms to create a new form of American popular music.

DOBZHANSKY, Theodosius (1900–), Russian-born geneticist, came to the U.S. in 1927, and taught chiefly at Columbia and at the Rockefeller Institute. His contributions to evolutionary thought include *Genetics and the Origin of Species* (3d ed., 1951), and *Mankind Evolving* (1962). The latter develops the thesis that human evolution is a continuing process, always the result of interaction between biological and cultural factors.

DODD, William Edward (1869–1940), professor of history at Chicago (1908–33), as a Jeffersonian Democrat influenced an entire school of historians in such studies as *The Cotton Kingdom* (1919), and *The Old South: Struggles for Democracy* (1937). While ambassador to Germany (1933–37), he was one of the few diplomats in the era of appeasement to estimate the aims of Hitlerism correctly.

DODGE, Grenville Mellen (1831–1916), Massachusetts-born railroad builder, served with distinction as a Union corps commander in the Civil War. His greatest achievement was his service as chief engineer in constructing the Union Pacific Railroad. He was later prominently associated with railroad building in the Southwest.

DOLE, Sanford Ballard (1844–1926), born in Honolulu of American missionary parents, was first president of the Republic of Hawaii (1894). In 1898 he headed a commission to recommend legislation to Congress for the islands after their annexation to the U.S. When the Territory of Hawaii was organized (1900), he was appointed its first governor. After 1903 he served as U.S. district judge of Hawaii.

'Dollar diplomacy' was the name applied during the Taft administration to the policy of supporting U.S. commercial enterprises abroad, in rivalry with other powers, especially in Latin America and the Far East, for strategic purposes. Taft's message to Congress in December 1912 set forth his aims: 'This policy has been characterized as substituting dollars for bullets.' Though the policy fell into disrepute, it has been renewed whenever the government has wished to make political loans to foreign governments.

Dominican Republic, with a population (1962) of 3,200,000, occupies the eastern two-thirds of the Caribbean island of Hispaniola, discovered by Columbus in 1492. The capital, Santo Domingo, was founded in 1496 and is the oldest city in the Western Hemisphere. The country has been governed throughout most of its history alternately by Spain and France, and from 1822 to 1844 by its neighbor Haiti. In 1844 it became a republic, but it has seldom achieved political stability. Hopelessly bankrupt at the turn of the 20th century, in 1905 it became a U.S. protectorate. It was occupied by U.S. military forces for eight years (1916–24), and U.S. intervention continued into 1933. The capital was called Ciudad Trujillo for 26 years (1936–62) to honor the general and politician Molina Trujillo (1891–1961), who dictated affairs for eighteen years (1930–38, 1942–52). In 1962 a President was installed following the first legal election in 38 years. Seven months later he was ousted and the constitution under which he had functioned was declared void. After 1963 the Republic was ostensibly governed by a three-man junta. In April 1965 civil war broke out between the junta forces and the supporters of the deposed President. The U.S. intervened, later informing the O.A.S. of the action. After attempts to bring the two sides together for discussions ended in failure, the O.A.S. formed an Inter-American Peace Force to take over from the U.S. forces which were separating the rebel and junta armies. In late August of that year the rival forces agreed to accept the peace formula worked out by the O.A.S., and a provisional government was formed, which proposed to hold a general election within nine months. The future of the Republic, like its past, is politically uncertain.

Dominion of New England (1686–89) was an organization by which the British hoped to consolidate all American colonies south to the Jerseys to face the Dominion of France to the north. All power was to have been centralized, and a single chain of command was to lead to the crown. It was established at first under the presidency of JOSEPH DUDLEY but was shortly placed under the governorship of SIR EDMUND ANDROS. Actually it was an imperial organization on paper only, for Andros had little military equipment and few funds under his control. Furthermore, since Andros was commanded by James II to rule without benefit of representative assemblies, the colonists thwarted his administration at every turn. When news arrived early in 1689 of the Glorious Revolution in England, Andros was deposed and the Dominion collapsed.

This futile attempt to streamline imperial authority remained a standing warning to royal authorities, who thereafter allowed the colonies to govern themselves with only the loosest supervision. A thriving economy was a more valuable asset in the struggle with France than was a smartly efficient administration.

Donelson, Fort, twenty miles west of Fort HENRY on the Cumberland river, was the last obstacle to a Union advance on Vicksburg during the Civil War. Grant captured it (15 February 1862) on the terms which first brought him to Lincoln's attention: 'unconditional and immediate surrender.'

DONIPHAN, ALEXANDER WILLIAM (1808–87), Missouri lawyer and soldier, during the Mexican war organized a regiment of volunteers as part of General Stephen Kearny's force. He subdued and conducted difficult peace negotiations with the Navahos in 1846, occupied El Paso (December 25), and after the battle of Sacramento (28 February 1847) entered Chihuahua. By May Doniphan reached Saltillo, thus assuring the success of the campaign in northern Mexico. The entire march, covering 3600 miles and conducted under adverse circumstances with negligible losses, was one of the best conducted military expeditions in U.S. history.

DONNELLY, IGNATIUS (1831–1901), Philadelphia-born politician and reformer, after studying law entered Minnesota politics. He served as lieutenant governor (1859–63), U.S. Representative (1863–69), and thereafter was almost continuously a member of the state legislature. He was a leader in liberal third party movements, edited the weekly *Anti-Monopolist* (1874–79), and took a major part in organizing the GRANGER MOVEMENT. His *Representative* (1894–1901) was an organ of the POPULIST PARTY, which he helped found, and of which he was candidate for President when he died.

His Utopian fiction includes *Atlantis* (1882; rev. ed., 1949), a best seller which went through 50 printings; and *Caesar's Column* (1891), a romance that rivaled Bellamy's *Looking Backward* in popularity. As the 'sage of Nininger' and promoter of lost causes, Donnelly in his day was styled a 'crank.' (He wrote two books to prove that Bacon wrote Shakespeare's plays.) But he was a vivid personality who took an important part in the reform movement, and he gave color to state and local politics.

Donner Party was a group of California-bound emigrants, numbering 87 persons, whose nucleus was the Donner and Reed families from Illinois. In late October 1846 the party was blocked by early winter snows when it reached what is today Donner Lake in the Sierra Nevada. Trapped, and soon without food, the group suffered indescribable hardships before rescuing parties from California early in 1847 brought out the 47 survivors, some of whom had escaped starvation by resorting to cannibalism.

'Don't give up the ship,' the dying words of the naval hero JAMES LAWRENCE, were inscribed on the battle flag of Commodore O. H. PERRY after his famous victory (1813) over the British on Lake Erie.

DOOLITTLE, JAMES HAROLD (1896–), U.S. Army Air Force general, in World War II commanded the B-25 bombers that raided Tokyo and other Japanese cities (April 1942). The squadron took off from the carrier *Hornet* (President Roosevelt humorously named it *Shangri-La* at the time), and most of the fliers bailed out over China. The raids did little damage but boosted American morale. Doolittle later headed the North African Strategic Air Forces and commanded the 8th Air Force.

Dorchester Company (1624–26) was a joint-stock group of Dorsetshire men who planted a colony of some 50 farmers and fishermen on Cape Ann (Gloucester) in Massachusetts. The site proved ill-chosen as a trading post, and at the end of the stipulated three-year trial period some 30 members under the leadership of ROGER CONANT removed to Naumkeag (Salem). The rest returned to England. From the experience, however, developed the short-lived NEW ENGLAND COMPANY and the important MASSACHUSETTS BAY COMPANY.

Dorr's Rebellion (1842) occurred as a popular movement in Rhode Island, where the constitution, dating from the charter (1663) granted by Charles II, restricted suffrage to freeholders and their eldest sons. In 1841 a group of the disfranchised called a convention to frame a 'People's Constitution,' and in 1842 elected as governor Thomas Wilson Dorr (1805–54), a wealthy Providence lawyer. The incumbent regime declared the Dorr party in a state of insurrection, imposed martial law, and called out the militia. Both sides appealed for aid to President Tyler, who supported law and order, but expressed hope that resolution of differences would be achieved by conciliation. Dorr's men attempted to seize the state arsenal, and Dorr was tried and sentenced (1844) to life imprisonment, though amnestied and released a year later. Meanwhile (1843) the state constitution had been reformed.

DOUBLEDAY, ABNER (1819–93), resident of Cooperstown, New York, graduated from the U.S. Military Academy (1842), served in the Mexican War, and as a Union general participated actively throughout the Civil War. The legend that he 'invented' the game of BASEBALL in 1839 became so enduring that in 1939 the National Baseball Hall of Fame was built at Cooperstown.

'Doughboy,' term used colloquially during World War I by U.S. infantrymen to designate themselves, was similar to the term 'GI' (general issue) used in World War II. 'Doughboy' is said to have been current in the 1850's, when soldiers cleaned their white belts with a 'dough' of clay.

DOUGHTY, THOMAS (1793–1856), Philadelphia-born painter of the HUDSON RIVER SCHOOL, was the first American artist to make a successful career of landscape painting. Self-taught, he won recognition at home and abroad for such scenes as *A View of the Schuylkill* (Edinburgh Museum), and *A River Glimpse* (Metropolitan Museum).

DOUGLAS, STEPHEN ARNOLD (1813–61), Vermont-born statesman, at the age of twenty settled in Illinois, where he was admitted to the bar (1834), and served in the state legislature (1836–37) and on the bench of the state's supreme court (1841–43). After 1847 he lived in Chicago. As a leading Democrat he was elected to Congress (1843–47), and then to the U.S. Senate, where he served until his death.

He drafted the bills for the COMPROMISE OF 1850, and introduced the KANSAS-NEBRASKA ACT (1854). Unable to gain the presidential nomination in 1856, he threw his support to Buchanan, who won, but Buchanan's advocacy of the proslavery LECOMPTON CONSTITUTION for Kansas led Douglas to deliver a courageous speech rebuking the administration's stand, and thus to his separation from the proslavery Democrats. The Illinois senatorial campaign of 1858 pitted the 'Little Giant' against the Republican candidate Abraham Lincoln, and was made memorable by the LINCOLN-DOUGLAS DEBATES. Douglas won reelection, but the proslavery Democrats were able to deprive him of the chairmanship of the Committee on Territories.

On Douglas's recommendation the Democratic national convention of 1860 at Charleston adopted a platform advocating nonintervention with slavery in the territories, and 'fire eating' Southern delegates withdrew. Although Douglas as party nominee for President led on all 57 ballots, he could not muster the necessary two-thirds majority, and the convention adjourned. It reassembled at Baltimore, where Douglas was chosen after more Southern delegates bolted and split the party with their own candidate, JOHN C. BRECKINRIDGE. Lincoln won the election (180 electoral votes to 12 for Douglas), but the popular vote of 1,375,000 was very close to Lincoln's 1,866,000.

Upon the outbreak of the Civil War Douglas gave loyal and vigorous support to Lincoln and to the Union. While on a speaking tour to rally the West to the crisis he was stricken with typhoid fever and died. Short and stocky in physique, brisk, confident and aggressive in action, Douglas was a compelling orator and a statesman of broad vision, honorable in his attempt to reconcile the differences which in a period of bitter national controversy doomed him to political failure.

Biographies include those by Allen Johnson (1908), and G. F. Milton (1934). See also Allan Nevins, *The Emergence of Lincoln* (2 vols., 1950).

DOUGLAS, WILLIAM ORVILLE (1898–), while professor of law at Yale (1928–34), was appointed (1934) to the Security and Exchange Commission where he began a vigorous policy of reform, which he continued as chairman (1937–39). President Roosevelt named him an Associate Justice of the U.S. Supreme Court (1939), and on the bench he has been a consistent liberal. His judicial views are set forth in such books as *We the Judges* (1955), and *The Right of the People* (1958).

DOUGLASS, FREDERICK (1817–95), who never knew his white father, was a Maryland-born mulatto. He escaped from slavery in 1838, and became an agent and lecturer for the Massachusetts Anti-Slavery Society in 1841. To earn money to purchase his freedom he lectured in England and Ireland, and on his return to the U.S. established, at Rochester, New York, the antislavery weekly *North Star* (1847–64). During the Civil War he helped organize two Negro regiments. He was later marshal of the District of Columbia (1877–81), and U.S. consul general to Haiti (1889–91). His classic autobiography, *Narrative of the Life of Frederick Douglass* (1845), appeared in a longer version in

1855 and was completed in 1892. An important commentary on life in America during the 19th century, it thereafter went through numerous editions in several languages.

DOUGLASS, William (1691–1752), Scottish-born physician, studied medicine at Edinburgh and settled in Boston (1716), where he was the only physician with a medical degree. He joined the attack on COTTON MATHER and ZABDIEL BOYLSTON when Boylston inoculated patients during the smallpox epidemic of 1721. (Douglass later altered his view.) Although he is credited with the first adequate clinical description of diphtheria, he confused diphtheria with scarlet fever in the scarlet fever epidemic of 1735–36.

He later wrote *A Summary . . . of the British Settlements in North America* (2 vols., 1749–52), caustic, partisan, and disorganized, but the first of a long line of speculations that saw Americans as a distinct people whose manners and customs had created new social forms. He died in the smallpox epidemic of 1752.

DOVE, Arthur (1881–1946), Connecticut painter, was said to be the first 'pure' abstractionist in the world. His work, exhibited in the Stieglitz gallery during the first decade of the 20th century, was generally ignored.

DOW, Neal (1804–97), a Quaker-trained businessman, in 1838 founded the Maine Temperance Union, committed to total abstinence and prohibitory legislation. While mayor of Portland, Dow achieved celebrity as a temperance reformer by securing state legislative passage of the famous 'Maine Law' (1851), later repealed but then reenacted, forbidding the sale or manufacture of liquor. He lectured in his fiery style on prohibition throughout the U.S. and in England, and in 1880 was the presidential candidate of the Prohibition party.

DOWNES, [Edwin] Olin (1886–1957), after study of music history, harmony, and analysis, devoted his career to criticism. As music critic for the Boston *Post* (1902–24) and *The New York Times* (1924–57) he was the most widely known and respected reviewer of musical performances in his day.

DOWNING, Andrew Jackson (1815–52), architect and landscape gardener, with CALVERT VAUX designed and constructed many of the country estates along the Hudson. He initiated the design for light wooden houses with overhanging roofs, asymmetrical masses, board and batten sheathing, and skeletally constructed porches: features related to such new American structural inventions as the balloon frame. He planned the grounds for the White House, the national Capitol, and the Smithsonian Institution. The impact of his ideas is manifest by the fact that his *Treatise on the Theory and Practice of Landscape Gardening* (1841) had passed through ten editions by 1921.

Draft, see *Conscription.*

Draft riots during the Civil War, in consequence of the Conscriptive Act (March 1863) passed by Congress, occurred as disturbances in a few localities. All basically protested the inequity of a law that allowed persons to escape conscription by paying the government $300 or by hiring a substitute. The distinction between 'rich men's money and poor men's blood' created major violence in New York City, at a cost of hundreds of lives, thousands of casualties, and $1,500,000 in property loss. On 13 July 1863 a mob, mostly of Irish-American laborers, stormed a draft headquarters. It increased in numbers, overpowered police and firemen, lynched Negroes, and pillaged and burned residences. The riot was quelled four days later by Federal troops detached from Meade's army. In a sense, therefore, it constituted a Confederate victory two weeks after the battle of Gettysburg, for Meade could stage no offensive at the time against Lee.

Drago Doctrine, reinforcing the MONROE DOCTRINE, was formulated (December 1902) by Luis M. Drago, foreign minister of Argentina, during the dispute over the collection of Venezuelan debts. It stipulated that armed force must not be employed by a European power to collect the international debt of Western Hemisphere nations. The Hague Tribunal accepted the doctrine.

DRAKE, Daniel (1785–1852), after taking his medical degree at Pennsylvania (1816), founded in 1819 the Medical College of Ohio, in Cincinnati, and soon thereafter a mental asylum (1821), an eye infirmary (1827), and a school for the blind (1837). His study of disease as related to geography, *Systematic Treatise . . . on the Principal Diseases of the Interior Valley of North America* (2 vols., 1850–54), is a medical classic.

DRAKE, Sir Francis (*c.* 1540–96), English navigator and admiral, was one of the great sea dogs of history, and most of his eventful voyages to the New World were marauding expeditions against the Spanish during the 1570's. In 1579, separated from the remaining contingent of three ships of the original five of his fleet, Drake sailed north from Lima, Peru, in his famous *Golden Hind,* searching for treasure and a passage to the Atlantic. He anchored either in San Francisco Bay or Drake's Bay to the north (the latter is favored by most scholars), claimed the land for England, named it New Albion, and before departing in July, nailed up a brass plate to commemorate the event. (A plaque that may be Drake's was discovered in 1936.) He crossed the Pacific and arrived at Plymouth, England, in September 1580, thus completing an epochal circumnavigation of the globe, the first in which the commander himself returned. (Magellan had anticipated him but had died on the voyage.) For this feat and for the immense treasure Drake brought home, Queen Elizabeth went aboard his ship and dubbed him knight, thus proclaiming to Spain and the world her approval of such ventures anywhere. In 1586 Drake plundered the Florida coast, including the settlement of St. Augustine, and he rescued Sir Walter Raleigh's Roanoke colony on the Carolina coast. He was a principal commander when the Spanish Armada was defeated in 1588. Drake died of a fever at Portobelo while attempting, with his kinsman Sir John Hawkins, to make Panama an outpost of empire.

DRAPER, John William (1811–82), English-born scientist and historian, became professor of chemistry at New York University (1838), where he helped organize its medical school, became its president (1850–73), and did important research in radiant energy and photochemistry. His improvement of Daguerre's process allowed him to take one of the first two satisfactory photographic portraits (1840), a result of his pioneer work on the spectra of incandescent substances. Translated into many languages, his *Human Physiology . . .* (1856) was for many years the leading text in its field, and displayed the first microphotographs in print. Urged to expand his lecture at Oxford on Darwin, he wrote his *History of the Intellectual Development of Europe* (1863), still ranked as a brilliant accomplishment; and he shortly brought out a *History of the American Civil War* (3 vols., 1867–70), a study which General Sherman helped assemble, and one which 20th-century historians respect. His rationalistic presentation of the *History of the Conflict between Religion and Science* (1874) was one of the influential books of the late 19th century. See Donald Fleming, *John William Draper and the Religion of Science* (1950).

His son, Henry Draper (1837–82), a professor of physiology at New York University (1870–82), pioneered in the field of astronomical photography and spectrum analysis. Henry Draper's widow endowed the Henry Draper Catalogue of stellar spectra at Harvard College Observatory, the landmark in the founding of modern stellar spectroscopy, first greatly advanced by the work of Annie J. Cannon.

DRAPER, Lyman Copeland (1815–91), historical collector and librarian, spent years traveling throughout the country, from his native New York to the Mississippi, gathering documentary material on frontier history. He deposited his extensive collection with the Wisconsin Historical Society, of which he was librarian (1854–86). His editing of the first ten volumes of the Society's *Collections* (after 1855) is a model of textual fidelity.

DRAPER, Ruth (1884–1956), New York–born monologist, began her professional career in 1911. During the next 30 years she won world acclaim for her skill in portraying the wide variety of characters she created in her 36 original monologues.

Dred Scott Case (1857), which led to one of the most fateful U.S. Supreme Court decisions, developed from the fact that Dred Scott, a Negro slave, was taken (1834) by his master from Missouri to locations where slavery was prohibited. In 1846 Scott sued for his liberty in the Missouri courts, alleging that his four-year stay on free soil had given him freedom. A lower court's favorable judgment was overruled (1852) by the state supreme court. The case was appealed to the U.S. Supreme Court, where the majority opinion, for which Chief Justice Taney is customarily cited, held (a) that Scott as a Negro (and therefore not a citizen) could not sue in a Federal court; (b) that as he was suing in Missouri the Illinois law was not material to his status; (c) that Scott's temporary residence in free territory had not made him free; and (d) that the Missouri Compromise was unconstitutional, since it deprived persons of their property without due process of law, and was thus contrary to the Fifth Amendment.

The last point went beyond the necessities of the immediate issue, but was intended to clarify a phrase in the Constitution. Delivered at the moment when sectional feeling was bitter, the Taney decision was a direct blow to popular sovereignty because it widened the sectional cleavage. Essential parts of the decision were nullified by the FOURTEENTH AMENDMENT, but Taney's interpretation of DUE PROCESS created endless litigation in a number of fields for the next 75 years.

DREISER, THEODORE [HERMAN ALBERT] (1871–1945), Indiana-born novelist, attended Indiana University (1889–90) and was a newspaper reporter in Chicago, St. Louis, and Pittsburgh (1892–94). From 1894 to 1910 he pursued a career in New York as free-lance writer and magazine editor. His social philosophy, drawn from his reading of Huxley, Spencer, and other determinists, is reflected in his first novel, *Sister Carrie* (1900), withdrawn by its publisher when its realism was attacked as immorally frank. He is most unsparing in his portrait of the fictional character Cowperwood, an unscrupulous American business magnate depicted in the trilogy *The Financier* (1912), *The Titan* (1914), and *The Stoic* (1947).

His naturalistic concept of American society is developed in such studies as *The Genius* (1915), and *An American Tragedy* (1925), the novel which reached Dreiser's widest audience. He later embraced socialism and expressed his belief in such works as *America Is Worth Saving* (1941).

DREW, DANIEL (1797–1879), began life as a cattle drover and horse trader. He expanded his interests, successfully engaged in competition with Cornelius Vanderbilt for control of the Hudson river steamboat business, and though illiterate, in 1844 entered the Wall Street banking firm of Drew, Robinson and Company. Later he became an independent operator, and with Jay Gould and James Fisk, by manipulating stock of the Erie Railroad, prevented Vanderbilt from gaining control. Together the three made millions and ruined the financial structure of the Erie. Unscrupulous in his ventures, 'Uncle Dan'l' Drew was financially bested by Gould and Fisk, and after the PANIC OF 1873 he went bankrupt. A pious Methodist, in 1867 Drew contributed generously to Madison (N.J.) Theological Seminary, which became Drew Theological Seminary (now Drew University).

DREW, JOHN (1827–62), Irish-born actor, established his stock company in the Arch Street Theater, Philadelphia, where, with his wife, LOUISA LANE DREW (1820–97) as co-star, he performed in high comedy. After his death his widow maintained the theater's standards, and kept up her own reputation in such character parts as Mrs. Malaprop.

Their eldest son, JOHN DREW (1853–1927), in 1875 joined the Daly Company in New York, where he co-starred with Ada Rehan. After 1892, as the first of Charles Frohman's stars, he performed in modern comedies with Maude Adams. He remained a leading actor on the American stage until his death, while on tour. His sister, GEORGIANA DREW, successful as a comedienne, married MAURICE BARRYMORE, and thus established the 'royal family' of American actors.

DREXEL, ANTHONY JOSEPH (1826–93), Philadelphia banker and philanthropist, in 1847 entered Drexel and Company, founded by his father. In 1871 Drexel merged with J. P. Morgan and the new firm of Drexel, Morgan and Company, with offices on Wall Street in New York, became the most powerful investment banking house in America. In 1891 he founded in Philadelphia the Drexel Institute of Technology, now specializing in business administration, engineering, home economics, and library science. In 1965, with a faculty of 631, it enrolled 9300 students.

Dual sovereignty, see *Federalism.*

DUANE, WILLIAM (1760–1835), born in New York state, learned journalism in Ireland, and worked in India, where his attacks on the English government led to his deportation and the confiscation of his property. In Philadelphia he made the *Aurora* (1794–1835), a liberal journal founded by Benjamin Franklin Bache, the leading Jeffersonian organ. Duane's courageous articles spurred the Federalists to pass the ALIEN AND SEDITION ACTS. Duane was arrested, but the charges were dismissed when the Republicans came into office (1801). In the War of 1812 he served as adjutant general.

DUBINSKY, DAVID (1892–   ), Polish-born labor leader, escaped to New York after banishment to Siberia (1909) for his activity in the underground labor movement. As a cloak cutter he joined the International Ladies Garment Workers Union (1911), of which he became president in 1932. In 1935 he joined forces with John L. Lewis and other leaders in organizing the Committee for Industrial Organization, convinced that the A.F. of L. had no real intention to bring about the mass organization of the unskilled as well as skilled. Under Dubinsky the powerful ILGWU developed bargaining techniques that replaced Marxist class conflict with a novel class collaborationism, by which workers co-operated in financing or planning shop operations.

DU BOIS, WILLIAM EDWARD BURGHARDT (1869–1963), Negro historian and sociologist, after taking his Ph.D. degree at Harvard (1895), taught economics and history (1897–1910) and sociology (1933–44) at Atlanta University. (He assailed the conservative Booker T. Washington for ignoring the higher education of the 'talented tenth' who provided leaders for the Negro race.) For some years (1910–32) he edited the *Crisis,* a magazine devoted to the cause of Negro betterment. A passionate fighter for civil rights, he helped found the National Association for the Advancement of Colored People (1909), but broke with that group in 1948 after he lost patience with what he thought was too timid an approach by their leaders in the civil rights battle for American Negroes. In 1962 (aged ninety-four) he became a citizen of the African republic of Ghana, having some time before written a bitter commentary on the lot of a sensitive American Negro intellectual.

His books include sketches, poetry, and such influential sociological studies as *The Souls of Black Folk* (1903). More recent are *The Gift of Black Folk* (1924), *Black Reconstruction* (1935), and *The World and Africa* (1947). Du Bois was the first Negro to be elected to the National Institute of Arts and Letters.

DUDLEY, JOSEPH (1647–1720), son of Governor THOMAS DUDLEY, graduated from Harvard (1665), took part in King Philip's War (1675–76), and served as a commissioner of the NEW ENGLAND CONFEDERATION (1677–81). In 1682 he was sent to England as an agent to protest the threatened loss of the Massachusetts charter, and until the appointment of Andros, served as president (1686) of the DOMINION OF NEW ENGLAND. With the collapse of the Andros regime (1689) he had to leave America. He became an Anglican and returned as Chief of the Council of New York (1690–92). Again in England, he held a succession of preferments, and was finally sent back as governor of Massachusetts (1702–15), where his autocratic direction of affairs made him unpopular. PAUL DUDLEY was his son.

DUDLEY, PAUL (1675–1751), son of the Massachusetts governor, JOSEPH DUDLEY, after graduation from Harvard (1690), studied law at the Inner Temple in

London, and returned to Boston to assume the post of attorney general. In spite of the unpopularity of his father, he became prominent in the affairs of the commonwealth, serving in later years as chief justice (1745–51). His wide-ranging intellectual interests extended to natural science, and his dozen contributions to the *Transactions* of the Royal Society won him election to that body (1721). In his most important essay, 'Observations on some of the plants in New England' (1724), he describes wind pollination and variety crosses in Indian corn. His fourteen-page essay on the 'Natural History of Whales' (1725) in its day was authoritative.

DUDLEY, THOMAS (1576–1653), one of the organizers of the 1630 migration to the Massachusetts Bay colony, accompanied John Winthrop as deputy-governor. He spent the rest of his life in public office, serving four terms as governor. Autocratic and irascible, to heretics Dudley was constantly 'a whip and maul.' He was a principal founder of Harvard College and the father of ANNE DUDLEY BRADSTREET and JOSEPH DUDLEY.

Due process clauses are provisions in the Fifth and the Fourteenth amendments to the Constitution of the U.S. that deny both the federal and state government the right to deprive persons 'of life, liberty, or property, without due process of law.' These clauses have created endless litigation because they set limits which the Supreme Court is still trying to define. The problems were increased after the Civil War by the growth of big business and the complexities of interstate commerce. The fixed rates of common carriers, for instance, were determined on the basis of a fair return on a fair value, but the courts were expected to decide what was 'fair.' The Supreme Court increasingly interpreted the doctrine of due process of law as 'reasonable law,' a substantive distinction from the original procedural concept of the term. It thus applied the philosophy of what 'ought to be' to affairs which were undergoing a change with the times.

The due process clause of the Fourteenth Amendment was long interpreted to assure civil rights for all people, including corporations, but drastic reinterpretations since the 1930's permit state legislatures to make economic regulations without regard to the question whether the businesses concerned are 'affected with a public interest.' At present the Supreme Court recognizes that corporations, with their great potential power and size, may reasonably be subject to severer restrictions than other business organizations. Similarly, regulatory commissions with their quasi-judicial powers are subject to curbs when the courts deem their procedures incompatible with due process.

Dueling, common in many sections of the U.S. until after the Civil War, was illegal in most of the states from the earliest years, but the statutes against it were more lax in some states than others. Both New Jersey and New York had strict laws, and after the Burr-Hamilton duel in Weehawken, New Jersey, in 1804, Burr found himself indicted for murder in both states.

The dueling field at Bladensburg, Maryland, five miles from Washington, was the favorite spot after 1808 for statesmen and military and naval officers to satisfy honor, and there Commodore James Barron killed Commodore Stephen Decatur in 1820. Other famous dueling grounds were the 'Duelling Oaks' in New Orleans, and Bloody Island, St. Louis. In the Andrew Jackson–Charles Dickinson duel (1806), several of Jackson's ribs were broken and Dickinson was killed. Neither man was harmed in the John Randolph–Henry Clay duel in 1826. Public opinion and ridicule finally ended such private fights.

DUER, WILLIAM (1747–99), British-born American patriot and capitalist, was educated at Eton. He began his career as aide-de-camp to Robert Clive in India before going briefly to the West Indies to manage his father's estates. In 1768 he came to New York, purchased a tract of timberland on the Hudson, erected mills, and built himself a mansion, where, like the wealthy gentlemen he had been brought up with, he served fifteen wines at dinner. He took a prominent part in provincial affairs, and as a delegate to the Continental Congress (1777–79) was a member of seven committees. Ranked with Robert Morris as a skillful financier, he was selected

(1789) as Alexander Hamilton's assistant secretary of the Treasury. By this time he had become a large-scale land promoter, notably of the Scioto Company, a venture stemming from the organization of the OHIO COMPANY. His operation in forming a blind pool to speculate in government bonds produced a financial scandal in New York (1792), acutely embarrassed Hamilton (himself blameless), and landed Duer in jail for most of his remaining years.

His son WILLIAM ALEXANDER DUER (1780–1858) was a judge of the New York Supreme Court (1822–29), which post he resigned to serve as president of Columbia (1829–42). He broadened and modernized the curriculum there.

DUKE, JAMES BUCHANAN (1856–1925), tobacco industrialist and leader in the hydroelectric power business, after the development of cigarette-making machines (1884) moved his headquarters from Durham, North Carolina, to New York, and set up a world-wide organization for the manufacture and distribution of cigarettes. In 1890 he combined with four other firms, thus obtaining control of the cigarette industry. The new American Tobacco Company then took over most of the companies making plug tobacco, pipe tobacco, and snuff, and by 1900 had a monopoly of all tobacco products except cigars. Capitalized at more than $500,000,000, and controlling 150 factories, it was dissolved (1911) by the U.S. Supreme Court.

In 1924 Duke established the Duke Endowment to promote the welfare of specified beneficiaries in North and South Carolina. It is today one of the largest endowed FOUNDATIONS, and in 1965 from assets of nearly $600,000,000 disbursed some $16,800,000. Best known of his large benefactions are those which created DUKE UNIVERSITY.

Duke University, nonsectarian and coeducational, was chartered in Randolph county, North Carolina (1841), as a Methodist college. It moved in 1892 to Durham as Trinity College, and took its present name (1925) after receiving large gifts from James B. Duke and his family. Its three undergraduate colleges share the same campus with graduate schools of arts and sciences, law, divinity, forestry, medicine, and nursing. In 1965, with an endowment of $55,600,000 and a faculty of 964, it enrolled 6500 students.

DULANY, DANIEL (1722–97), Maryland lawyer and politician, was the son of Daniel Dulany (1685–1753), for many years a leader in Maryland affairs. One of the ablest pamphleteers in the colonies, the younger Dulany exposed the fallacy of the English principle of 'virtual representation' in Parliament, a representation by classes and interest rather than by locality. He opposed the STAMP ACT in *Considerations on the Propriety of Imposing Taxes in the British Colonies* (1765) on the ground that Americans by their situation could not be represented in Parliament, and he denied the authority of Parliament to tax the colonies either externally or internally.

DULLES, JOHN FOSTER (1888–1959), after graduation from Princeton (1908) practiced law in New York City, where he became eminent in the international field. He served as counsel to the American Peace Commission (1918–19) and was a delegate to the San Francisco Conference (1945) and to the United Nations (1946–50). He was the chief architect of the Japanese Peace Treaty (1951). As President Eisenhower's Secretary of State (1953–59), he formulated the policy of insuring the collective security of the U.S. and its allies through foreign and domestic defense measures, and traveled some 500,000 miles on missions abroad to achieve that end. Believing that Truman's policy of 'containment' of Communism was inadequate, he urged 'massive retaliation' (1954) with nuclear weapons to deter Soviet aggression, a method which his critics termed 'brinkmanship.' He designed the Eisenhower Doctrine (1957) for preserving peace in the Middle East, and during his last year in office gave official assurance that the U.S. would not abandon its commitments to West Berlin.

DULUTH, [DU LHUT], DANIEL GREYSOLON, Sieur (1636–1710), French explorer, was sent by the Comte de Frontenac to establish forts and trading posts (1678) in the western part of the

Great Lakes region, and to search for the Western Sea. He made the upper reaches of the Mississippi river a part of the French empire by the friendships he established with Indian tribes. His explorations during the next decade opened up the shores of Lake Superior and portage routes in the interior. The Minnesota city bearing his name is the industrial and cultural center of the area chiefly associated with his ventures.

Dumbarton Oaks Conference (1944), held near Washington, D.C., and attended by representatives of China, Great Britain, the Soviet Union, and the U.S., drew up the blueprint that served as the basis for the charter of the UNITED NATIONS. Agreement on the veto issue could not be reached, since Russia refused to bar a member of the Security Council from voting on a question to which it was itself a party. This problem was carried over into the SAN FRANCISCO CONFERENCE.

DUMMER, JEREMIAH (1645–1718), silversmith and engraver, was apprenticed (1659) to the Boston mintmaster JOHN HULL before setting up his own shop in Boston. He engraved plates for currency, designed silver, and today is represented in leading museums for the fine quality of his work. He also took up painting, and his portraits qualify him as one of the first competent American-born artists.

His son JEREMIAH DUMMER (1681–1739), after graduation from Harvard (1699), studied theology at Leyden and Utrecht, where he was granted the degree of doctor of philosophy, the first to be conferred on an American. He was regarded as brilliant but his theology was suspect when he returned home. Harvard had no place for him as a teacher and local churches rejected him as a pastor. He settled in London, engaged in business, became intimate at court, and was appointed colonial agent for Massachusetts, New Hampshire, and Connecticut. He was instrumental in persuading Elihu Yale to assist (1718) the infant college that now bears his name. Dummer himself sent some 800 volumes to the institution. His well-reasoned *Defence of the New England Charters* (1721) frustrated efforts in Parliament to recall colonial charters and closed discussion of the matter for a generation. On the eve of the War of Independence James Otis and John Adams based their legal appeals on Dummer's arguments.

DUNBAR, WILLIAM (1749–1810), Scottish-born scientist and Mississippi planter, under Spanish authority ran the boundary line (1798) which made the district of Natchez a part of the U.S. His meteorological observations of the region soon thereafter led to correspondence with President Jefferson, who commissioned him to explore the old Southwest. His reports are significant. They were the first to record such data as the existence of mineral wells at Hot Springs, Arkansas. He set up his own astronomical observatory, explored the Mississippi delta, and published his studies of regional plants and animals in the *Transactions* of the American Philosophical Society, of which he was a member.

DUNCAN, ISADORA (1878–1927), born in San Francisco, won her first triumphs as a dancer in Budapest (1903) and Berlin (1904). She studied the postures of Greek dancers as represented by ancient pottery and statues, and created scenes in which she danced barefoot in flowing robes. A dynamic personality, by rejecting the conventional ballet style and introducing a technique of natural pose and gesture, she contributed to the forms of the modern dance. She toured extensively and founded schools in Berlin, Moscow, Paris, and London. A moment after exclaiming 'Je vais à la gloire,' she met instant death when her long scarf caught in the wheel of her car while she was motoring at Nice.

Dunkards, Dunkers, or Tunkers (dippers), a sect of German Baptists, evolved from the early 18th-century Pietist movement. Not accorded freedom of worship in Germany, they emigrated (1719) to Germantown, Pennsylvania, and spread westward into Ohio and Canada. Distinctive features of their religious practice are triple immersion, and such rituals of the apostolic church as footwashing and the love feast. Their ministry is ordained but usually unsalaried. Dunkards conscientiously object to law suits, war, and giving of oaths. One branch, under J. C. BEISSEL, became the Seventh Day Baptists (1728), noted for their hymns and choral singing. In 1965 the group of five denominations, officially designated German Baptist Brethren, numbered some 248,000 members.

DUNLAP, WILLIAM (1766–1839), New Jersey-born playwright, painter, and historian, began his versatile career at sixteen as a professional painter, and for three years studied in London under Benjamin West. Enjoying only moderate success after his return to New York, he abandoned the medium to try his hand at drama. His first play, *The Father* (1789), was so warmly received that Dunlap continued writing for the stage, and became the first American to make a career of the drama. In the course of his life he turned out some 65 plays, half original, half translated adaptations of popular French and German dramas. In 1796 he became part owner of a New York theater which he soon took over. But his venture as manager failed, and in 1805 he went into bankruptcy.

He then returned to painting, meanwhile writing a novel, a biography of the novelist Charles Brockden Brown (1815), and later a history of New Netherland (2 vols., 1839–40). His interest in the arts led him to help found the National Academy of Design (1826), and to write *A History . . . of the Arts of Design in the U.S.* (2 vols., 1834; new ed., 3 vols., 1918), the principal authority on early American painters. His *History of the American Theatre* (1832) is likewise a source book. His voluminous diary has been published in part (3 vols., 1930). Though Dunlap did not achieve eminence in any particular cultural discipline, he is deservedly honored today as the founder of the American theater.

DUNMORE, JOHN MURRAY, Earl of (1732–1809), as royal governor of Virginia (1772–75) led troops against the Indian confederations during 1774 in an effort to control the northwest. Known as 'Lord Dunmore's War,' it resulted in a treaty that opened hunting grounds to colonists in Kentucky, and granted unmolested transport on the Ohio. In 1775, as a firm supporter of the crown, Dunmore began to recruit a loyalist army, placed the colony under martial law, established a base at Norfolk, and removed himself and his powder store to a ship of war. Decisively beaten by patriot forces, Dunmore returned to England.

DUNNE, FINLEY PETER (1867–1936), while editor of the Chicago *Journal* (1897–1900) created the character of Martin Dooley, an Irish saloon keeper, whose trenchant monologues on the imperialism and political pretentiousness of the day, delivered with wit in a rich Irish brogue, made Dunne's columns popular for two decades. The first gathering of his comments, *Mr. Dooley in Peace and in War* (1898), was followed by several other collections, excerpted in *Mr. Dooley on Iverthing and Iverbody* (1963).

DUNSTER, HENRY (1609–59), a graduate of Magdalene College, Cambridge (1631), emigrated to America, and became the first effective president of Harvard (1640–54). One of the college's greatest administrators, he worked to advance learning in its broadest sense. He resigned because of his Baptist leanings, but he left a flourishing university college of the arts, governed under a charter by a body of fellows and officers whose duties were regulated by statute. Thereafter he served as minister in Scituate, Massachusetts.

Duplex Printing Press Company* v. *Deering (1921) was a case resulting in the U.S. Supreme Court interpretation of the labor provisions of the CLAYTON ANTITRUST ACT (1914). It upheld the validity of secondary boycotts, those which attempt to coerce third parties into the practice, by ruling that the Clayton Act did not protect labor organizations from injunction proceedings. Secondary boycotts were declared illegal 33 years later by the TAFT-HARTLEY ACT.

DUPONCEAU, PETER STEPHEN (1760–1844), French-born lawyer and ethnologist, accompanied Baron von Steuben to America (1777) as secretary and interpreter. He became a citizen of Pennsylvania (1781), where he was admitted to the bar in 1785. As a lawyer he won international eminence for his conduct of cases involving European trade and commerce and for his legal treatises within his field. He was a pioneer U.S. philologist, best known today for his linguistic studies. For his *Grammatical System of the Languages of Several Indian Nations of North America* (1838) he was awarded the Volney prize by the French Institute.

Du Pont Family, notable for 150 years in U.S. industrial history, was established by PIERRE SAMUEL DU PONT (1739–1817), French economist and statesman. He was financial adviser to Turgot and later president of the Constituent Assembly during the French Revolution. His conservative views made him unpopular with the radicals, and after release from imprisonment he emigrated with his family to the U.S. (1799). His economic theories influenced those of Jefferson, and thus to an extent he shaped the economic policy of the young Republic. After an extended sojourn in France (1802–15) he returned to America, where he died.

His son ELEUTHÈRE IRÉNÉE DU PONT (1771–1834) was taught chemistry by Lavoisier in the French royal powder factory, and shortly after arrival in the U.S. he constructed a powder mill (1802) on the Brandywine, near Wilmington, Delaware. There he and his lineal and collateral descendants, as E. I. du Pont de Nemours and Company, became the principal manufacturers of powder in the U.S. LAMMOT DU PONT (1831–84) by his invention of a superior blasting powder gave the company a competitive advantage over other manufacturers of explosives.

It was a brilliant team of brothers who transformed the powder firm into the world's largest and most diversified chemical producer. PIERRE SAMUEL DU PONT (1870–1954), while serving as president (1915–19) inaugurated the farsighted program in basic research. IRÉNÉE DU PONT (1876–1963), after succeeding as president (1919–26), set up the system of committee management. Under the presidency (1926–40) of LAMMOT DU PONT (1880–1952) expansion and diversification were carried forward on a vast scale.

Pierre had helped organize the General Motors Corporation, which for a time he served as president (1920–23). So interlocking had the interests of the companies become by the mid-20th century that in 1961 the U.S. Supreme Court required du Pont to relinquish its General Motors holdings. By 1963 the company was an organization of 93,000 employees (of whom 2200 were Ph.D.'s), helping du Pont develop some 80 new products a year, with sales passing $2,500,000,000.

Duquesne, Fort, see *Pittsburgh.*

DURAND, ASHER BROWN (1796–1886), born in New Jersey, after establishing a reputation as engraver and portrait painter turned to landscape painting, and was among the earliest of the HUDSON RIVER SCHOOL. Painting directly from nature, rather than following the usual practice of constructing in a studio from pencil notes, Durand rendered the scenery of the Hudson river and Catskill mountains with romantic serenity. *Kindred Spirits* (New York Public Library), depicting his friends Thomas Cole and William Cullen Bryant surveying a wild gorge, is representative of Durand's literalness as well as his love of native themes.

DURYEA, CHARLES EDGAR (1862–1938), Massachusetts bicycle designer and toolmaker, with his brother J. FRANK DURYEA (1869–) built one of the first practical gasoline-powered vehicles in the U.S. They formed the Duryea Motor Wagon Company (1895), and in the same year a Duryea car won the first U.S. automobile race at Chicago. Charles Duryea, credited with the invention of the spray carburetor (1892), manufactured automobiles until 1914. Frank Duryea was associated with the Stevens-Duryea Company, one of the pioneer automobile enterprises.

Dust Bowl, see *Plains region.*

Dutch Reformed Church, see *Reformed Church in America.*

Dutch West India Company was chartered (1621) by the States General of the Dutch Republic. Its principal objectives were war against the Spanish possessions in the New World, and trade.

So profitable and patriotic did the enterprise appear that by 1623 subscribers had invested more than 7,000,000 guilders in the company, which in 1624 began the settlement of NEW NETHERLAND.

DUTTON, CLARENCE EDWARD (1841–1912), Connecticut-born geologist, after graduation from Yale (1860) served with the Union forces throughout the Civil War and was active as an ordnance officer until his retirement in 1901. In 1875 he was assigned to the U.S. Geological Survey of the Rocky Mountain region conducted by J. W. POWELL. Dutton's vigorous descriptions were set forth in several reports, notably those on the geology of the high plateaus of Utah (1879–80) and the tertiary history of the Grand Canyon district (1882). A pioneer in the isostatic theory of earth movements, he introduced the term *isostasy*. His account of *Hawaiian Volcanoes* (1884), like his other monographs, was a contribution to both science and sensitive nature writing.

DUVEEN, JOSEPH (1869–1939), English art dealer, was a notable benefactor to London galleries and influential in helping to establish important American art collections. He was created a baron in 1933, and the New York branch of his firm continues to be a leading medium for the distribution of art objects.

DVOŘÁK, ANTON (1841–1904), Czech composer, contributed significantly to American music when, as the director of the National Conservatory of Music in New York (1892–95), he stressed the importance of indigenous material. He composed at that time his popular symphony *From the New World* (1893), with themes suggesting the folk idiom. After his return to Prague he headed its Conservatory and became a leader of the nationalist movement there.

DWIGHT, JOHN SULLIVAN (1813–93), music critic, after graduation from Harvard (1832) occupied a Unitarian pulpit before joining the Utopian venture at BROOK FARM (1841–47). Later in Boston he founded and edited *Dwight's Journal of Music* (1852–81), a pioneer magazine in the field of critical reviews and for 30 years the most important musical periodical in the U.S.

DWIGHT, TIMOTHY (1752–1817), a grandson of Jonathan Edwards, graduated from Yale (1769) and became a chaplain in the Continental army. He was one of the literary elite among the CONNECTICUT WITS, admired in his day for such poems as *The Conquest of Canaan* (1785), and *Greenfield Hill* (1794). As president of Yale from 1795 until his death, he gave vigorous support to Calvinistic orthodoxy and the cause of religious revivals. So energetic was his leadership that 'old Pope Dwight' became the most cordially disliked public figure in his state, although he was always respected by his students. He was a prolific author of books on current politics and science as well as theology. He is most deservedly remembered for his *Travels in New England and New York* [1796–1815] (4 vols., 1821–22), eclectic in taste and shrewd in perception.

E

EADS, James Buchanan (1820–87), one of the leading engineers of his day, invented (*c.* 1841) a diving bell and conducted salvage operations in the Mississippi. Early in the Civil War, Lincoln drew upon Eads's knowledge of the river by having him construct a small fleet of ironclad gunboats, which cleared the Mississippi down to Vicksburg. After the war he constructed (1868–74) at St. Louis a bridge of three steel arches, an achievement which brought him international recognition. His system of jetties, by which the Mississippi dredges its own channel, made New Orleans an ocean port. As Eads won worldwide recognition, he became a technical adviser on harbors for many cities, receiving England's coveted Albert Medal as well as American honors.

Eagle, American, was adopted (1776) as the emblem on the Great Seal of the U.S., and appears on most U.S. currency. From antiquity the eagle has been the emblem of military strength. The Secretary of the Continental Congress, Charles Thomson, specified that the symbol should be the American white-headed or bald eagle.

'Spread-eagle' oratory, as in Fourth of July addresses, was a compound of exaggeration and patriotic bombast. At the turn of the 20th century 'spread-eagleism' came to signify bellicose chauvinism.

EAKINS, Thomas (1844–1916), a lifelong resident of Philadelphia, studied painting and anatomy both at home and abroad before he began teaching at the Pennsylvania Academy of the Fine Arts (1876–86). He belonged to no school. Believing that a painter should employ the technical skill of an engineer, he laid out perspective with mechanical drawings, and his effort to discover how the human body behaves in action led him to become a pioneer experimenter with motion pictures. Few in his day appreciated the realist who painted without romantic gloss, although Walt Whitman characterized his work by saying: 'Eakins is not a painter, he is a force.'

As a teacher Eakins developed original methods of anatomical study, but the scandal caused by his insistence that female art students paint from nude models led to his dismissal. Lonely and bitter, he continued to paint scenes and persons exactly as he saw them. He sold few of his 500 canvases, but late in life he began to enjoy a little of the superlative reputation he now holds. Representative of his works are *The Gross Clinic* (Jefferson Medical College, Phila.), *Chess Players* (Metropolitan Museum), and *Biglen Brothers Turning the Stake Boat* (Cleveland Museum).

EARHART, Amelia (1898–1937), Kansas-born aviator and wife (1931) of the publisher George Palmer Putnam (1887–1950), was the first woman to cross the Atlantic in an airplane (1928) and the first to do so in solo flight (1932). She was also the first woman to fly from the U.S. mainland to Hawaii (1935), and was lost in the southwest Pacific while attempting to fly around the world. Her fate still remains a mystery.

EARL, Ralph (1751–1801), self-taught Massachusetts painter, in 1775 was an eyewitness of the battle of Lexington, of which he sketched four scenes. They were the originals for the popular engravings by Amos Doolittle. The sketches are probably the first historic paintings of a contemporary event by an American. After study in London (1783–85) with Benjamin West, he returned to Boston and established a reputation as a portrait painter. Today he is highly regarded for the sturdiness of his earlier work, represented by *Roger Sherman* (Yale).

EARLY, Jubal Anderson (1816–94), a graduate of the U.S. Military Academy (1837), left the practice of law at Rocky Mount, Virginia, to serve in the Confederate army. He fought in all the campaigns of the Army of Northern Virginia, serving as a division commander, and later, in the Wilderness campaign, he led the 2nd Corps. After his defeat by Sheridan at Cedar Creek (October 1864) and by Custer at Waynesboro (March 1865), public opinion forced Lee to relieve him of command. He returned to his law practice, and was fiercely bitter toward the North throughout his life, especially in his memoirs of 1866.

Earthquakes in the U.S. were first recorded in New England (1638), but damage was negligible. One of the greatest earthquakes in history centered on New Madrid, Missouri, in December 1811, where intense shocks were felt for many weeks. Extensive topographical changes altered a 30,000-square-mile area, lifting or sinking the surface of the Mississippi valley region from five to fifteen feet, and in places changing the bed of the Mississippi river. Because the basin at the time had few permanent buildings, the cataclysm is largely of scientific interest. Three later severe shocks were those at Charleston, South Carolina (August 1886), which rendered a large part of the city uninhabitable; at San Francisco (April 1906), which caused fires that virtually destroyed the city; and at Helena, Montana (October 1935), which caused great property damage. The destructive force of the earthquake in Alaska (March 1964) was so great that Congress enacted emergency legislation to help rebuild the shattered communities.

EAST, EDWARD MURRAY (1879–1938), was a professor of experimental plant morphology (1914–26) and of genetics (after 1926) at Harvard. As one of the discoverers of hybrid vigor, he contributed basic research on the genetics and breeding of plants, especially corn and tobacco. His books *Mankind at the Crossroads* (1923) and *Heredity and Human Affairs* (1927) reflect the Nordic racist ideas of the era that produced severely restrictive immigration laws.

East Florida was established as a British province by the PROCLAMATION OF 1763. It comprised the peninsula of Florida north to the St. Mary's river and west to the Apalachicola river along the 31st parallel. It was returned to Spain by Great Britain in the TREATY OF PARIS of 1783. After the U.S. purchased Florida (1822) the region was joined to WEST FLORIDA to form the Territory of Florida.

East India Company (1600–1858), one of the longest-lived and most affluent of English TRADING COMPANIES, exercised a pervasive influence on British colonial policy, since it derived immense profits from trade in India. It figured specifically in the destiny of America when, in an effort to unload a surplus of 17,000,000 pounds of tea, it secured passage of the TEA ACT (1773), thus setting in motion events that culminated in the War of Independence.

East Side (Lower), densely populated area of New York City, is roughly bounded by 14th Street on the north, Catherine Street on the south, and the Bowery and Third Avenue on the west. Its streets and tenements, crowded with immigrants from many nations, gave the city its reputation as a 'melting pot.' It was the 'ghetto' for the waves of Jews who fled European persecutions and for the colonies of immigrants from eastern and southern Europe. For many years its poverty and inadequate housing made it a breeding ground of ill health and crime. Push carts were the common retail stores until the city built enclosed markets at Essex Street. Although slum clearance projects, such as Baruch and Wald Houses, are meliorating its physical problems, it still retains its foreign character.

Eastern Orthodox churches are at one in faith and morals with the ROMAN CATHOLIC CHURCH, but they do not recognize the primacy of the Pope. In the U.S. a number of their autonomous churches have been formed, chiefly Greek, Russian, and Bulgarian, as immigrants from eastern Europe have arrived. In 1965 the total membership of such churches was some 3,166,000.

Eastern states, see *Northeast* and *Southeast.*

EASTMAN, GEORGE (1854–1932), having invented a dry-plate process for PHOTOGRAPHY, established a factory at Rochester, New York, for manufacturing the plates (1880). He devised a roll film and the Kodak camera (1888), thus making amateur photography feasible. By mass-producing his cameras and films, which he steadily improved, he capitalized on the immense popularity of photography as a hobby. In 1928 he introduced a process for color photography. Eastman disbursed his great wealth in philanthropies, principally to the University of Rochester (where he established the Eastman School of Music), the Massachusetts Institute of Technology, and dental clinics throughout Europe.

EASTMAN, Joseph Bartlett (1882–1944), a graduate of Amherst (1904), became widely known as an expert transportation administrator. For many years a member of the Interstate Commerce Commission (after 1919), he was Federal co-ordinator of transportation (1933–36) during the Depression, and served during World War II as director of the Office of Defense Transportation (1941–44).

Eastman School of Music, see *Rochester, University of.*

EATON, Amos (1776–1842), upon graduation from Williams (1799) settled as a lawyer in Catskill, New York, where in 1810 he gave the first popular course of lectures on botany in the U.S. After studying chemistry and geology (1815) under Benjamin Silliman at Yale, he published an *Index to the Geology of the Northern States* (1818), based on firsthand observations. He became director (1825) of Stephen Rensselaer's newly established technical school at Troy, New York (now Rensselaer Polytechnic Institute), the first to grant engineering degrees (1835).

EATON, Peggy [Margaret O'Neale Eaton] (1796–1879), wife of John Henry Eaton (1790–1856), U.S. Senator from Tennessee (1818–29) and President Jackson's Secretary of War (1829–31), unwittingly created a situation during Jackson's Administration that came to be known as the 'Eaton malaria.' Noted for her wit and beauty, at sixteen Peggy O'Neale, daughter of a Washington boarding-house keeper, married a clerk in the navy. Both were on friendly terms with Eaton, who for a decade had been the tavern's star boarder. When Peggy's husband died in 1828, Eaton married the gay widow, with Jackson's blessing. The gossip that had spread before their union then created political issues.

The President, recently a widower, cherished the memory of Rachel Jackson, and both had smarted under similar boarding-house gossip. The wife of Vice President Calhoun was the acknowledged social leader of Washington. She refused to receive Eaton's bride, and her example was followed by the wives of all cabinet members, senators and congressmen, and ladies of the diplomatic corps. Jackson made an issue of the matter in a cabinet meeting. The political break with Calhoun was thus precipitated, and led to a cabinet reorganization (1831).

EATON, Theophilus (1590–1658), wealthy London merchant, emigrated to Massachusetts Bay in 1637. In 1638 with JOHN DAVENPORT he led a group to found the NEW HAVEN COLONY, which he served as governor until his death. His hopes of establishing a mercantile center between Massachusetts and New Netherland were never realized, and six years after his death the New Haven colony was absorbed into the Connecticut colony.

Economic theory, see *American System, Antitrust Laws, Capitalism, Commerce, Labor Movement, Laissez Faire, Mercantilism, Navigation Acts, Restraint of Trade, Tariff.*

Influential theorists in the 19th century among Americans include H. C. CAREY, W. G. SUMNER, HENRY GEORGE, and EDWARD BELLAMY; in the 20th century, J. R. COMMONS, R. T. ELY, E. J. JAMES, T. N. CARVER, J. L. LAUGHLIN, E. R. A. SELIGMAN, F. W. TAUSSIG, SUMNER SLICHTER, J. K. GALBRAITH, and OSKAR MORGENSTERN.

EDDY, Mary Baker (1821–1910), New Hampshire-born religious teacher and organizer, at twenty-two married George W. Glover, who died a few months later. For eighteen years thereafter she suffered from recurrent hysteria. In 1853 she married Daniel Patterson, a dentist who, unable to make a living, deserted her in 1861. In an effort to regain her health, in 1862 she consulted Phineas P. Quimby (1802–66), a mental healer in Portland, Maine, whose exhibitions of mesmerism and mental healing had gained him a large following throughout New England. After brief treatment by 'Doctor' Quimby, Mrs. Patterson was restored to comparative health and began traveling in eastern Massachusetts trying to eke a living by practicing Quimby's art.

In 1866, as the result of a fall, she suffered a temporary relapse, and her rapid and miraculous recovery she attributed to her discovery at that time of the principles of CHRISTIAN SCIENCE. For ten years (1870–80) she taught her 'science' to pupils at Lynn, published her textbook *Science and Health* (1875), and formed the Christian Scientists' Association (1876), which in 1879 became The Church of Christ, Scientist. During the decade she obtained a divorce from the dentist Patterson, and married one of her students, Asa Gilbert Eddy (who died in 1883). In 1882 she founded at Boston the Massachusetts Metaphysical College. Rapidly gaining adherents, she was able to send out 'spiritual healers,' and the success of the practitioners carried the movement across the continent and to Europe.

With the help of the Boston editor James H. Wiggin she improved her textbook, which in its fiftieth printing (1891) took on essentially its present form. In 1889 she closed her 'college' after a schism developed in church government, and by 1892 she had gained autocratic control in Boston of affairs governing what since has been known as the Mother Church. Wealthy from the sales of her books, she then retired to Concord, New Hampshire, from whence, although she suffered periodically from nervous ailments, she administered church affairs with undisputed authority until near the end of her life.

Biographies of Mrs. Eddy are numerous and seldom unbiased. That by Sibyl Wilbur (1929 ed.) is official. The study by E. F. Dakin (rev. ed., 1930) is critical. L. P. Rowell (1930) is as nearly impartial as any.

EDDY, THOMAS (1758–1827), wealthy New York insurance and stock broker, devoted himself to large-scale philanthropies and civic reforms. He persuaded the state legislature to build and superintend penal institutions on modernized principles, and was a prime mover and liberal donor in the erection of free schools and an asylum for the treatment of the insane.

EDISON, THOMAS ALVA (1847–1931), Ohio-born inventor, after three months of formal schooling became a newsboy, and then a telegraph operator in various cities. He was with the Western Union Telegraph Company in Boston when he patented his first invention, an electrographic vote recorder (1869). His career as inventor began when he established himself in New Jersey, first at Newark (1876–87), then at Menlo Park (1887–1931). His invention of the phonograph (1877) was soon followed by his improvement of electric lighting. In 1879 he produced the commercially useful incandescent lamp, and shortly thereafter (1881–82) constructed in New York City the first central electric-light power plant ever assembled.

At this time he made his one significant discovery in pure science, the 'Edison effect.' He unwittingly constructed a light bulb that served as a 'rectifier,' a device converting alternating current into direct current. The English electrical engineer John Fleming perceived the applicability of the device to reception of telegraph signals, and converted an Edison-effect light bulb into the precursor of the vacuum tube in radio, made practicable by the improvements of Lee De Forest.

Edison's 1000 patents, mostly the fruit of collective effort in his research laboratories, include improvements in products as various as motion pictures, the storage battery, dictaphone, mimeograph, and compressing dies. Seldom concerned with abstract science, Edison had an ability to apply scientific principles to practical problems that has made him the symbol of inventive genius.

See the biography by Matthew Josephson (1959).

EDMUNDS, GEORGE FRANKLIN (1828–1919), Vermont lawyer, served his state for many years in the U.S. Senate (1866–91). He helped draft the Sherman Antitrust Act (1890), fought inflationist schemes, and as a member of the reform wing of the Republican party opposed its expansionist policy. He won a considerable reputation in 1895 when he convinced the Supreme Court in POLLOCK *v.* FARMERS' LOAN AND TRUST COMPANY that the income tax was unconstitutional. He is best remembered for the Edmunds Act (1882), which out-

Education

lawed polygamy in the territories. It was aimed chiefly at the Mormon theocracy in Utah.

Education in the U.S. was first provided in the colonies by way of the customs transferred from Europe. Apprentice training was offered as a matter of course and of necessity. In 1642 the Massachusetts General Court directed parents to teach their children to read and write, and in 1647 made mandatory the appointment, in towns with 50 householders or more, of a teacher of reading and writing, the first law in the English-speaking world to require communities to establish and maintain elementary schools. Towns of over 100 families were expected to offer grammar-school training.

In the Middle Colonies the elementary school was generally a church or private undertaking. As in Europe, the larger independent political units made higher educational facilities available as soon as competent faculties could be assembled. Where such ventures did not gain a foothold, notably in the South, students received their higher education abroad, often in the London law schools or in Edinburgh, the nearest medical center.

Harvard had been founded early in the history of the Massachusetts colony (1636) by legislative act to insure Puritans a trained ministry able to lead settlers in frontier communities. Indeed, early educational institutions were almost invariably denominational. William and Mary (1693) in Virginia was opened to train Anglican clergymen. In Connecticut Yale (1701) was established by Congregationalists who looked askance at Harvard's growing liberalism. The GREAT AWAKENING was responsible for the founding of three colleges. 'New Light' Presbyterians set up the College of New Jersey at Princeton (1746). ELEAZAR WHEELOCK, a graduate of Yale, founded Dartmouth (1769) to train Indian preachers. The Baptists, hitherto without an educated ministry, established the College of Rhode Island (Brown) at Providence (1764).

King's College (Columbia, 1754) in New York City was Anglican. Queen's College (Rutgers, 1766) in New Brunswick, New Jersey, was Dutch Reformed. The only nonsectarian colonial college was the Philadelphia Academy (University of Pennsylvania, 1740). Later several of these institutions fostered preparatory schools to assure standards for their freshman classes. In the second half of the 18th century most of these early establishments were able to offer graduate studies, especially in theology and medicine. Like those that followed in the first decade of the 19th century, they existed precariously in their formative years.

Immediately after the Revolution the concept of the separation of church and state began to take root. The Presbyterians sponsored Liberty Hall (Washington and Lee, 1782) and Hampden-Sydney (1783) in Virginia, Dickinson in Pennsylvania (1783), and Transylvania in Kentucky (1785). The Anglicans supported Washington College (1782) and St. John's (1784) in Maryland, and the College of Charleston (1785) in South Carolina. Lutherans and the Dutch Reformed bodies opened the German-speaking Franklin College (1787) at Lancaster, Pennsylvania. Bishop John Carroll of Maryland founded Georgetown (1791), the first Catholic institution in the U.S. During the same period the legislatures of Maryland, Georgia, and North Carolina took steps to provide STATE UNIVERSITIES. (For a summary of the legal differences between *colleges* and *universities,* see COLLEGE CHARTERS.)

In the early national period education was left largely to private initiative, although Federal aid was provided in the form of land grants such as the ORDINANCE OF 1785, which set aside one lot of every township in the Northwest Territory for the maintenance of public schools. By 1821 the WOMEN'S EDUCATIONAL MOVEMENT was under way.

Fundamental elementary education, however, was neglected. In an effort to keep the cost of elementary schooling at a dollar a year per pupil, such teaching devices as the monitorial system were used, whereby older students instructed the younger. Most northern states operated some kind of public elementary school system, but only New England had the tradition of supporting schools by taxation. In the Middle States CHARITY SCHOOLS were maintained for the poor, thereby attaching a stigma to free education. In many instances children remained unlettered because parents, too poor to pay fees, were too proud to accept charity. Labor unions resented the 'pauper schools' and fought for a tax-supported system. The opposition to taxation came from persons of property, who resented supporting institutions which they did not patronize. But enlightened industrialists joined the crusade for mass education. After New York City established public elementary schools (1832), the taint of 'charity' lessened, but the growth of schools lagged behind the increase of population. The Common School revival movement was spurred by the fact that in 1850 there were nearly 1,000,000 white adult illiterates in the U.S.

In the West, where Federal land grants were intended to aid common schools, most of the funds were mismanaged, all proved inadequate, and many frontier families were prejudiced against 'book-larnin.' But the MORRILL LAND GRANT ACT (1862) made provision for land grant colleges and proved to be the most important piece of education legislation up to that time. The influence of the famous report (1837) on European public schools made by CALVIN STOWE, the work of HENRY BARNARD as first U.S. Commissioner of Education (1867), and that of HORACE MANN in helping to establish normal schools (the present TEACHERS COLLEGES) were pervasive. Meanwhile THOMAS GALLAUDET and SAMUEL HOWE had pioneered in teaching the deaf and blind. After the Civil War the work begun by Barnard and Mann was carried forward by WILLIAM T. HARRIS and others who admired the progressive ideas of Swiss and German educators.

The importance of the DARTMOUTH COLLEGE CASE (1819) was the fact that a Supreme Court decision protected privately supported endowments from state interference, and thereafter an amazingly large number of small colleges sprang up, no fewer than 516 before 1860. These rural institutions, with 6 to 12 professors and 100 to 300 students, had a high mortality, for they were competing not only with older institutions but with the increasing number of state universities able to absorb tuition from public funds. Although their curriculum was inferior to that of any first-class secondary school today, and sneered at by visitors from abroad, these small colleges supplied an integrated education, and their importance in disciplining the American character and giving it a respect for learning is incalculable. The LYCEUM had become the nucleus of adult education and HIGH SCHOOLS were supplanting ACADEMIES.

During the final decades of the 19th century higher education was given international standing by such leaders as CHARLES ELIOT (Harvard), ANDREW D. WHITE (Cornell), DANIEL COIT GILMAN (Johns Hopkins), and WILLIAM RAINEY HARPER (Chicago). Shortly before the turn of the century NICHOLAS MURRAY BUTLER organized what was to become Teachers College, famous for its applications of the new pedagogy, developed there and elsewhere by such teachers as G. STANLEY HALL, JOHN DEWEY, WILLIAM JAMES, and EDWARD THORNDIKE in the field of philosophy and psychology. The first quarter of the 20th century became the era of PROGRESSIVE EDUCATION.

By mid-20th century public schools enrolled 28,000,000 pupils at an annual expenditure of $11,000,000,000. Some 1200 institutions of higher learning depended on capital greatly in excess of that figure. More than 50 foundations were allocating $250,000,000 annually to advance educational programs, directly or indirectly benefiting the 400,000 students who yearly received bachelor degrees.

The U.S. Office of Education (1867), never itself an administrator of educational systems, conducts research for and provides grants-in-aid to educational projects. In 1953 it was incorporated into the newly created Department of Health, Education, and Welfare, whose Secretary holds cabinet rank.

An accelerated technological emphasis in education came after the Russians launched the satellite *Sputnik* (October 1957), which seemed to demonstrate superior engineering knowledge. As a result of an avalanche of critical books and articles as well as of Federal action, schools required more mathematics, science, modern languages, and stiffer classroom standards. Unprecedented grants from the government and from foundations raised teachers' salaries, promoted research on a princely scale, and financed vast building programs. Despite quarrels over the possible violation of the principle of church-state separation, Congress passed the COLLEGE AID ACT (1963) to provide colleges with grants and loans of more than a billion dollars, an enactment which takes rank as one of the most significant in the history of American education. Except for the armed services, education in the U.S. maintains the most expensive plants, employs the largest personnel, and costs the taxpayer and parent more than any other item in his budget.

See E. P. Cubberley, *Public Education in the U.S.* (rev. ed., 1934); E. D. Ross, *Democracy's College* (1942); and E. W. Knight, *Education in the U.S.* (rev. ed., 1951).

EDWARDS, JONATHAN (1703–58), grandson of Richard Edwards, a well-to-do Hartford, Connecticut, merchant, was the son of Timothy Edwards (Harvard, 1691), pastor of a church in Windsor, Connecticut, and Esther Stoddard Edwards, daughter of the Reverend SOLOMON STODDARD of Northampton, Massachusetts. The account that he wrote from observation at eleven or twelve 'Of Insects' is presumably the earliest natural history essay on the subject of flying (or balloon) spiders, and those on 'The Rainbow' and 'Colours' show his sound understanding of Newton's *Optics* (1704). He entered Yale at twelve, and in his junior year wrote 'Notes on Natural Science' and 'The Mind,' responses to new courses in natural philosophy (physics) which were based on the writings of Newton and Locke.

After graduation (1720) and further study Edwards joined his grandfather as colleague, and after Stoddard's death (1729) he became sole pastor of the church which Stoddard had made the most important inland parish in New England. In 1737 he published his classic *Faithful Narrative* describing the religious revival at Northampton. The account was reprinted abroad, translated into Dutch and German, and under its inspiration John Wesley founded the Methodist church. During the 1740's the GREAT AWAKENING spread through the colonies and gave warrant for Edwards' *Treatise Concerning Religious Affections* (1746), a notable study in the psychology of religion.

Since Edwards had then come firmly to believe that regeneration takes place only when some inner transformation occurs, he decided to reject the so-called HALF-WAY COVENANT, which his grandfather had extended to allow all who wished to become church members. His congregation resented the change, and in 1750 they dismissed him. He then became pastor to a small group of frontier settlers in Stockbridge, Massachusetts, and missionary to the local Indians. Here during the remaining seven years of his life he wrote his greatest treatises. His *Freedom of the Will* amplifies his position against ARMINIANISM. He believed that true liberty is circumscribed, and forever 'caused' by situations beyond man's power of choice. His defense of *Original Sin* (1758) postulates that men partake of sin as a 'necessity,' since man's propensity to error is natural. The *Two Dissertations* (1765) on the nature of virtue and God's purpose discuss the quality of excellence and the need of man for something better than himself. The Calvinism that Edwards reasserted (he was the first American to do so) sought to combat the 'liberalism' which proclaims that tensions and anxieties can be overcome by ignoring or denying the unpleasant, and he insisted on an ethic which postulates that reality is never a man-created affair. Not until the 20th century did students of intellectual history come to realize that Edwards was a philosopher-theologian of the first rank.

In January 1758 Edwards accepted a call to the presidency of the College of New Jersey at Princeton. He died two months later from the effects of a smallpox inoculation.

Ola E. Winslow's narrative biography (1940) is supplemented by the critical study by Perry Miller (1949).

EGGLESTON, EDWARD (1837–1902), Indiana-born novelist and historian, was brought up in a strict Methodist environment. After some years as a preacher he abandoned Methodism and devoted himself to writing. He deals realistically with frontier life in *The Hoosier Schoolmaster* (1871) and *The Circuit Rider* (1874). The first displays a keen ear for local dialect, and the second is a vivid picture of backwoods life in Indiana and Ohio in the first half of the 19th century. His *Beginners of a Nation* (1896) and *The Transit of Civilization*

(1901) are pioneer studies in social history. Historians judge their approach as antiquarian but recognize that (like his presidential address to the American Historical Association on 'The New History') they perceive the importance of history that draws upon the lives of ordinary people.

Eight, The, were a group of New York artists who shared a dislike of academicism. Formed in 1908 by ROBERT HENRI, they exhibited paintings of widely different moods and techniques. With Henri were associated the romanticist ARTHUR DAVIES; the impressionists MAURICE PRENDERGAST and WILLIAM GLACKENS; and Henri's then followers JOHN SLOAN and GEORGE LUKS. Stigmatized as the 'Ashcan School,' they were able by their example to lead younger artists away from imitation to the discovery of new aesthetic and social values, and were largely responsible for the famous ARMORY SHOW (1913).

Eighteenth Amendment (1919) to the U.S. Constitution forbade the manufacture, sale, or transportation of liquor. Passage of the Amendment followed the prohibition by Congress during World War I of the manufacture and sale of liquor, allegedly as a measure of economy, a law that was in effect when 46 states ratified the proposed Amendment. The disastrous consequences of the PROHIBITION ERA thus ushered in led to the repeal of the Amendment fourteen years later by passage of the Twenty-first Amendment.

Eighth Amendment to the U.S. Constitution, see *Bill of Rights*.

EINSTEIN, ALBERT (1879–1955), theoretical physicist, while examiner (1902–9) at the patent office in Bern, Switzerland, obtained his doctorate (1905) at the University of Zurich. During this period he studied the motion of atoms, explained the photoelectric effect, and evolved the special theory of relativity. His international fame established, in 1914 he accepted the directorship of theoretical physics at the Kaiser Wilhelm Institute in Berlin. For his work, especially on photoelectricity, he received the 1921 Nobel Prize in physics.

Deprived of post, property, and citizenship in 1933 by the Nazi government, Einstein accepted a chair at the Institute for Advanced Study, Princeton (1933–45), and in 1940 became an American citizen. Having completed his formulation of a general theory of relativity about 1916, in 1929 he proposed a unified field theory, a single mathematical system that places electromagnetism and gravitation in one universal law. Its mathematical expression, applicable to relativity and quantum theories, appeared in 1950, as an appendix to his fourth edition of *The Meaning of Relativity* (1922). His translated works also include *On the Method of Theoretical Physics* (1933), and *Out of My Later Years* (1950). His famous letter to President Roosevelt (1939) regarding the potential of nuclear energy in warfare influenced the Administration to set up the Manhattan Project, which created the atomic bomb.

EISENHOWER, DWIGHT DAVID (1890–), 34th President of the U.S. (1953–61), was born in Denison, Texas, spent his boyhood in Abilene, Kansas, and graduated from the U.S. Military Academy (1915). Continuously in active military service, soon after the U.S. entered World War II he was named (February 1942) chief of the War Plans Division in the Office of the Chief of Staff, and four months later was appointed commander of U.S. forces in the European theater, where he commanded the Allied invasion of North Africa. As Supreme Commander of the Allied Expeditionary Force in Western Europe (1944), he directed the invasion of Europe across the English Channel, and after the surrender of Germany (May 1945) he commanded the U.S. occupation zone.

As general of the army he succeeded General George Marshall as chief of staff (1945), a post he left to accept the presidency of Columbia University (1948). In 1951, on leave of absence from Columbia, he served as Supreme Commander of NATO until he resigned to campaign (1952) as Republican nominee for the presidency against the Democratic candidate, Adlai E. Stevenson. He won the election with the largest popular vote up to that time (34,000,000) and an electoral vote of 442 to 89, a sweeping personal victory. He again defeated Stevenson in 1956, and served out his second term.

A veteran of long service to his country, Eisenhower came to high office as an attractive new personality with an internationalist outlook in foreign policy and a middle-of-the-road orientation in domestic affairs ('Moderate Republicanism'). During his eight years as President he delegated much of his party responsibility to Vice President Richard Nixon, and a large part of foreign policy to Secretary of State John Foster Dulles.

As a soldier Eisenhower had a quick, clear understanding, human insight, and wide experience of the nation and the world. As President, he was able to work with Congress, predominantly Democratic for six of his eight years in office, with noteworthy co-operation. In domestic affairs he promoted a vast national highway program, liberalized the social security laws, and aided urban renewal. With Dulles as his representative in foreign affairs he ended the Korean War, initiated SEATO, and revived rapprochement with Latin America through the Organization of American States.

'Elastic clause,' see *Implied powers.*

El Dorado (Sp. the gilded one) was originally applied to the supposed king of Manoa, a fabled city of enormous wealth on the Amazon. Expeditions from both Spain and England (two led by Sir Walter Raleigh) tried to discover this king, said to be permanently powdered with gold dust. The legend, associated with many Indian tribes of the Southwest, is dealt with in Bandelier's *The Gilded Man* (1893). By extension the name applies to any region of storied wealth.

Election day, established by Congress in 1845 as a unified time of voting for Federal officers, is the first Tuesday after the first Monday in November, and is recognized as a legal holiday in 36 states. Municipal and state elections are generally held at the same time.

Elections, see *Ballot, City government, Congress, Direct primary, Election day, Electoral college, Initiative, National convention, Party government, Popular vote, Presidency, Presidential campaigns, Presidents, Proportional representation, Recall, Referendum, State government, Suffrage, Town meetings, Vice Presidency.*

Elections, presidential, see *Campaign of 1789,* et seq.

Electoral College, established by Article II of the Federal Constitution, is the official means of proclaiming the election of the President and Vice President of the U.S. It has been called 'America's oldest puppet show,' and, although it has been continually criticized by men of all parties for 175 years, it continues to be the method of election. By law each state is entitled to a number of electors equal to the state's total representation in the Senate and House of Representatives. On the first Monday after the second Wednesday in December following ELECTION DAY the electors meet at their respective state capitals to cast their ballots. When there are more than two serious contenders for office, the device quite easily may seat MINORITY PRESIDENTS, and on fourteen occasions has done so.

Its defects are serious. It operates on the winner-take-all principle, and thus a presidential candidate who loses a state even by a narrow margin loses the state's electoral vote. Thus the winner's electoral votes are usually grotesquely inflated. Since electors are not legally bound to vote for the winner of the popular vote, they may cast their ballots as they personally choose. This system with its area of indeterminacy is, as students of government have long pointed out, 'potential dynamite.' Failure to overhaul it stems from the power politics of states, sections, competing parties, and groups, each of which would lose some present advantage by any change that has yet been proposed.

Electoral Commission was established by Congress in January 1877 to determine the validity of the challenged electoral votes for President submitted by Oregon, Florida, Louisiana, and South Carolina in the highly controversial Hayes-Tilden election of the previous autumn. The four states had submitted multiple sets of returns, and in the absence of any constitutional or legislative provisions to rule on the proper set, Congress appointed a bipartisan commission of five Senators, five Representatives, and five Supreme Court justices. Seven of the total number were to be Democrats, seven to be Republicans, and the fifth Justice, presumably independent, was to be chosen by his colleagues. Justice JOSEPH P. BRADLEY, thus selected, invariably voted with the Republicans on a commission where votes were consistently partisan. The result was the election of Hayes (by an electoral vote of 185 to 184), although his Democratic opponent, Samuel J. Tilden, had a majority of the popular votes.

Public indignation was intense and party passions ran high. Later investigations revealed frauds on both sides. The commission undoubtedly subverted the 'will of the people,' but the solution was accepted without resort to violence.

Electricity, though study of it extends back to the 18th century, was at first regarded as little more than an interesting curiosity, since it seemed to have no practical use. Professor JOHN WINTHROP, the most accomplished American scientist of his day, gave laboratory demonstrations of electricity and magnetism (1746) in his Harvard classroom, but only as an exhibition of natural phenomena. Benjamin Franklin's *Experiments and Observations on Electricity* (1751–54) set forth his discovery that lightning and electricity are identical, elucidated the working of the Leyden jar (the earliest form of electrical condenser), and brought to the language several words first used in the technical sense they still retain, including *battery, conductor, discharge, plus* and *minus, positive* and *negative*. His contributions in the field make Franklin one of the very great American scientists.

Electricity could be put to practical use only when the relationship of magnetism and electricity had been established. The pioneer work of JOSEPH HENRY was basic in the development of the generator and other electromagnetic devices (1827–31). The demonstration of the incandescent lamp (1879) by THOMAS A. EDISON introduced electricity into all phases of life. The introduction of steam turbines (1890) to drive dynamos made possible the erection (1894) of the Niagara Falls plant, thereby inaugurating the era of hydroelectric power.

Theoretical as well as practical developments were advanced by the work of ALEXANDER GRAHAM BELL, CHARLES F. BRUSH, and GEORGE WESTINGHOUSE in the application of electrical devices; of NIKOLA TESLA, CHARLES STEINMETZ, ELIHU THOMSON, and E. F. W. ALEXANDERSON in the field of high-tension electricity; of ROBERT A. MILLIKAN, LEE DE FOREST, MICHAEL I. PUPIN, VLADIMIR F. ZWORYKIN, and EDWIN H. ARMSTRONG in electronics.

Eleventh Amendment (1798) to the U.S. Constitution was adopted to protect the states against suits instituted by persons living elsewhere. It removed from the jurisdiction of Federal courts any suit in law or equity against a state 'by Citizens of another State, or by Citizens or Subjects of any Foreign State.' It was adopted after the U.S. Supreme Court decision in CHISHOLM *v.* GEORGIA (1793), which had ruled that such suits were admissible.

ELIOT, CHARLES WILLIAM (1834–1926), born in Boston, after graduation from Harvard (1853) studied chemistry and educational methods in Europe (1863–65). He returned to accept appointment as professor of analytical chemistry at the newly established Massachusetts Institute of Technology (1865–69). Harvard called him as its president when he was thirty-five years old, and he guided its fortunes from 1869 until 1909, making it the pacemaker of American universities.

The changes he effected were revolutionary. He developed a small college into a university by reforming its graduate and professional schools (especially law and medicine), enriching the curriculum, raising the undergraduate standards, and attracting distinguished scholars. He made use of the elective system to allow students more freedom in their choice of studies, and he was influential in securing a greater degree of uniformity in high school curriculums and college entrance requirements. His *Harvard Classics* (1910), a 50-volume selection of world literature, became a 'five-foot shelf,' chosen to further adult education by means of a planned course of study. He combined daring with patience, and valued people whose ideas he respected even when he did not share their views. Regarded as first citizen of the country at the time of his retirement in his late sixties, he was steadily in demand thereafter for a decade as a member of national committees. His *University Administration* (1908) is the distillation of his experience.

ELIOT, JARED (1685–1763), grandson of JOHN ELIOT, after attending Harvard for a year (1699–1700), left to attend Yale, from which he graduated in 1706. He began his lifelong ministry at Killingworth, Connecticut. The ministry was his profession, but he also practiced medicine, and for 50 years he was the most respected physician in New England. His interest in metallurgy led him to erect (1744) the first steel furnace in the province, and to develop a process for smelting iron from black magnetic sand (1762). Scientific agriculture also claimed his attention, and his *Essays upon Field-Husbandry* (1748 and later), the first colonial work on the subject, became well known abroad. The *Essays* inaugurated a correspondence and later a warm friendship with Benjamin Franklin. Eliot is credited with having introduced the cultivation of rhubarb and the white mulberry tree.

ELIOT, JOHN (1604–90), educated at Cambridge, as a staunch Puritan migrated to Boston in 1631 and settled at nearby Roxbury (1632). There as 'Apostle to the Indians,' he devoted his life to missionary work among them, and was the first missionary to preach to Indians in their native tongue. Soon after his arrival he was chosen as chief compiler of the BAY PSALM BOOK (1640). With the help of the Society for the Propagation of the Gospel in New England he established some fourteen villages of PRAYING INDIANS, few of whom survived tribal massacres during King Philip's War (1675). His translation of the Bible into the Natick (Algonquian) language (1661–63) was the first complete Bible printed in the British colonies, and was recognized in Europe at the time as a work of devoted scholarship. That and his *Indian Primer* (1669) have remained a chief source of knowledge about the Massachusetts Indians.

ELIOT, T. S. [THOMAS STEARNS] (1888–1965), poet and critic, was born in St. Louis. Four years after graduation from Harvard (1910) he took up permanent residence abroad, and in 1927 he became a British subject. He attained stature as a critic with his first volume of essays, *The Sacred Wood* (1920). Shortly thereafter he founded and for many years edited (1923–39) the quarterly review *Criterion*. As the leading English critic and poet of the first half of the 20th century, he exerted considerable influence in college classrooms through such poems as 'The Waste Land,' which reflected the disillusionment of the 1920's. Eliot also expressed his concepts in poetic dramas, notably in *Murder in the Cathedral* (1935). In 1948 he was awarded the Nobel Prize in literature. He was an Anglo-Catholic in religion and a classicist in literature.

Elkins Act (1903) supplemented the Interstate Commerce Act of 1887 by providing more specific procedures and penalties for railroad REBATES. The railroads themselves supported the Act, described as 'a truce of the principals to abolish piracy.' By its provisions published freight rates were declared the standard, deviations from them a misdemeanor, and shippers were equally liable with the railroads to prosecution. This regulatory power was further strengthened by the HEPBURN ACT (1906).

Elks, Benevolent and Protective Order of, was formed in New York City (1868) as a society of actors and writers. It later became a social and charitable order. National in scope, in 1965 it reported a membership of 1,333,000.

ELLINGTON, DUKE [EDWARD KENNEDY] (1899–), Negro band leader, and major jazz composer, was one of the first musicians to bring sophisticated musical form to jazz. His compositions drew heavily on Impressionistic composers such as Debussy and Ravel, but were based solidly on the jazz of the 1920's and 1930's. Many of his arrangements were in miniature concerto form, with the soloist developing his own improvisations within Ellington's composition.

Ellis Island, some 27 acres in upper New York Bay, southwest of Manhattan, became government property in 1808, and was long the site of an arsenal and fort. From 1892 to 1943 it served as the chief U.S. immigration station, through which passed millions of immigrants from all parts of Europe. It was abandoned in 1954. In 1965 it was proclaimed a National Historic Site in tribute to American immigrants.

ELLSWORTH, LINCOLN (1880–1951), received his training as a civil engineer at Columbia and Yale, and in 1924 led a geological expedition to the Andes Mountains. With Roald Amundsen he conducted a transpolar flight from Spitzbergen to Alaska (1926), and with Herbert Wilkins carried out a transarctic submarine expedition (1931). His 2300-mile airplane flight across the antarctic (1935) from Weddell Sea to the Ross Sea was followed (1939) by a flight from the Indian Ocean to the interior of Antarctica, both over unexplored territory. His writings include *Search* (1932), and *Beyond Horizons* (1938).

ELLSWORTH, OLIVER (1745–1807), Connecticut-born statesman, after graduation from the College of New Jersey (Princeton) in 1766, practiced law at Hartford. He was a member of the Continental Congress (1777–84), and performed important service as delegate to the Federal Constitutional Convention by advancing the CONNECTICUT COMPROMISE, which ended the struggle between large and small states in the matter of representation. (He coined the term 'United States' in the Constitution.) While serving in the Senate (1789–96) Washington appointed him Chief Justice of the Supreme Court (1796–99), in which capacity he went as principal commissioner to France, where he successfully negotiated with Napoleon on American shipping rights.

While abroad, he felt impelled by failing health to resign from the Court. His greatest contribution as statesman was his part in creating the Federal judiciary. As chairman of the committee charged to organize the courts, he drafted the JUDICIARY ACT of 1789, which established the system that still remains substantially unchanged.

ELY, RICHARD THEODORE (1854–1943), professor of political economy successively at Johns Hopkins (1881–92), Wisconsin (1892–1925), and Northwestern (1925–33), was one of the most influential teachers of his time. His *Outlines of Economics* (with R. H. Hess, 1889; 6th ed., 1937) was instrumental in popularizing study of the subject, and was recognized as a standard text. An early leader of CHRISTIAN SOCIALISM, he advocated public control of resources, prohibition of child labor, and the development of labor unions. He founded the Institute for Economic Research (1920), and influenced much progressive legislation carried out in Wisconsin by La Follette. His many books include *Monopolies and Trusts* (1900), *Hard Times . . .* (1931), and *Ground under Our Feet* (1938).

Emancipation Proclamation, potentially the most revolutionary document in U.S. history since the Declaration of Independence, was prepared by Lincoln independently in the summer of 1862 during a period of gloom and defeat. He first announced it at a cabinet meeting in July of that year. Lincoln's cardinal policy in the early months of the Civil War was to save the BORDER STATES for the Union, and to that end he resisted pressure from antislavery groups to issue an edict of emancipation, and even sought to moderate congressional legislation on confiscation of property. As early as September 1861 he had ordered General Frémont, commanding the Western Department, to modify his military proclamation declaring free the slaves of all Missourians supporting the Confederacy. Until his death, Lincoln used every political pressure to win support for 'compensated emancipation,' a government subsidy to states that would appropriate money to purchase and colonize slaves. He was blocked on the one hand by strict constructionists (defenders of states' rights) on the ground of unconstitutionality; and on the other by abolitionists, who argued that slave owners did not deserve compensation.

Although by midsummer of 1862 Congress had imposed emancipation of slaves as a sweeping penalty upon 'rebels' by confiscatory acts, political considerations as well as national security guided Lincoln in his determination to wait for a military victory before announcing his verdict. That moment came when the battle of ANTIETAM put the Confederate armies on the defensive, and effectively blocked foreign recognition of the Confederacy. On 22 September 1862 Lincoln issued his preliminary declaration, affirming his stand that union, not abolition, was his war aim, and that compensated emancipation was still his policy. He added merely that persons held as slaves in areas 'in rebellion against the United States' would be free as of 1 January 1863, and on that date the definitive proclamation was issued.

The document was not an edict of abolition in fact, since it specifically exempted such border territory as Tennessee and portions of Virginia and Louisiana. Because it declared liberation for areas not under Union control, only a complete Union victory could make it effective. Yet it was a political maneuver timed with acuteness and great wisdom. It brought Lincoln the support of liberal opinion, Congress hailed it, and in the North it became a battle cry, even though a large number of Northern conservatives deplored it as illegal, unwise, and irrelevant. The South viewed it as a fiendish attempt to stir up servile insurrection.

Lincoln saw his act as 'the greatest question ever presented to practical statesmanship,' and bit by bit world opinion came to recognize the document as one of the great milestones of the 19th century, since the cause of the Union had been fused with that of human liberty. Ultimate emancipation was effected as a national measure in the Thirteenth Amendment, and decisive refusal to make compensation for slave property was embodied in the Fourteenth.

See J. H. Franklin, *The Emancipation Proclamation* (1962).

Emancipator, The Great, sobriquet of Lincoln.

Embargo Act (1807), recommended by Jefferson in a brief message to Congress (18 December), and immediately passed (22 December), was an answer to certain restrictive measures by which the belligerents France and England were interfering with U.S. shipping. The NONIMPORTATION ACT of 1806, a protest against British seizure of American ships and the impressment of American sailors, had failed to achieve its end. The Embargo Act, fiercely resented by shipping interests in the North, virtually ended all legitimate commerce with other nations by forbidding U.S. vessels to leave for foreign ports. This attempt to force an issue proved to be the cure that killed. It was futile because it created a brisk smuggling trade, and gave British shippers a monopoly of registered tonnage. It presented Napoleon with the opportunity of impounding $10,000,000 worth of U.S. goods, a procedure justified, he explained, because his confiscation assisted Jefferson's embargo. Northern Republicans revolted, and Federalists charged that the 'Virginia dynasty' was an ally of Bonaparte, and that the Republican party was a greater enemy to American commerce than Britain. The administration was politically in deep embarrassment. Since the embargo failed to influence the policy of either England or France, or to protect the American merchant marine, it proved to be the most costly mistake during Jefferson's eight years in office. In force for fourteen months, in March 1809 it was repealed by passage of the NONINTERCOURSE ACT.

Emergency Banking Relief Act (1933) was introduced and passed on the same day (9 March). It confirmed all the emergency steps taken by President Roosevelt five days before, when he assumed office. The Act gave the President broad discretionary powers over transactions in credit, currency, gold, and silver, including foreign exchange. It forbade hoarding or exporting gold, and thus in effect took the U.S. off the gold standard. But it also quickly checked the money panic, and allowed sound banks to reopen under regulation. A conservator supervised the assets of insolvent banks, and the RECONSTRUCTION FINANCE CORPORATION was empowered to subscribe to the preferred stock of national banks and trust companies. Under these regulations the 'bank holiday,' in effect for eight days, came to an end on 13 March.

Emergency Detention Act, see *McCarran-Wood Act.*

Emergency Fleet Corporation, created by Congress in April 1916, was a reorganization of the U.S. Shipping Board. Given broad powers to requisition, purchase, construct, and operate ships, it was designed to build a 'bridge to France,' in an effort to replace the tonnage which German submarines were destroying at the rate of more than half a million tons monthly. Embarking on a vast program of ship construction, the Corporation laid down two keels for every one sunk by the U-boats. By 1921 it had raised the tonnage of American vessels in foreign trade from 3,000,000 to 11,000,000. In 1927 it became the Merchant Fleet Corporation.

Emergency Railroad Transportation Act (June 1933) was designed to eliminate unnecessary duplication of rail services and facilities, and to promote financial reorganization of the carriers. It placed railroad holding companies under the supervision of the Interstate Commerce Commission, provided for a simpler rule of establishing rates, and created the office of Federal Co-ordinator of Transportation.

EMERSON, RALPH WALDO (1803–82), was son of William Emerson, pastor of the First Unitarian Church in Boston. After his father's death in 1811 he was raised by his mother and an aunt, the eccentric but stimulating Mary Moody Emerson, who led the boy toward his lifelong conviction that a mind stretched by new ideas can never shrink to its former dimensions. The year before graduating from Harvard (1821) he began his famous *Journals,* voluminous records of the thoughts later embodied in his poems and essays. He taught school briefly, and after desultory study at the Harvard Divinity School became minister (1829) of the Old South Church (Second Unitarian) in Boston. In the same year he married Ellen Tucker, who died of tuberculosis in 1831. He resigned his only pastorate in 1832, unable conscientiously to administer the Lord's Supper. Soon thereafter, during a trip to Europe, he began his friendship with the leading English romanticists, Wordsworth, Coleridge, and Carlyle, and his intimate acquaintance with transcendentalism and German idealism. At the same time he enriched his Yankee-Unitarian inheritance with a study of the sacred books of the East, tempered by the idealism of Berkeley and Locke, the skepticism of Montaigne and Hume, and the mysticism of Swedenborg. He began his career as a lecturer upon his return to Boston, and his lyceum appearances were so popular that he was able (1834) to purchase a home in Concord, where he brought Lydia Jackson as his second wife (1835), and where his four children were born. The lectures, presenting the essence of his unsystematic philosophy, set forth his ideas on such topics as 'Human Culture' and 'The Philosophy of History.' They were the basis for his first book, *Nature* (1836), a fundamental document in Emerson's expression of the worth of the individual. At the same time he gave support to the group interested in TRANSCENDENTALISM, and contributed to its magazine, *The Dial,* of which for a time (1842–44) he was editor. Two addresses delivered at Harvard attracted wide attention. In his Phi Beta Kappa oration, 'The American Scholar' (1837), he applied his cultural ideas to national problems by pleading for an American culture free from European domination. It was immediately hailed as an intellectual Declaration of Independence, and remains one of the most stimulating testaments of the 19th century. His 'Divinity School Address' (1838) attacked formalism in religion, and Emerson was not invited to Harvard again until 1866, when the college honored him with a Doctor of Law degree.

Emerson's concern with issues of the day increased during the 1850's, and his annual lecture tours became events of importance. After 1866 he felt himself unable to produce new work, but he continued to be thereafter, as he remains, a spokesman of self-reliance, obedience to instincts, and the spiritual nature of reality.

Biographies include those of George E. Woodberry (1907), and Ralph L. Rusk (1949).

Emigrant aid movement, designed to promote antislavery migration to Kansas Territory, was given impetus by the Massachusetts abolitionist Eli Thayer (1819–99), who organized the New England Emigrant Aid Company (1854) even before the Kansas-Nebraska bill became law. Largely confined to the Northeast, it was a 'crusade' supported by such publicists as Gerrit Smith, E. E. Hale, and Horace Greeley. Though promoters roused northern sentiment, tangible results were negligible; some 2000 colonists were settled, and by 1857 the movement virtually ended. Yet meanwhile, even though it had been bitterly opposed in the South, it had made a deep impression on public opinion, and was a factor leading to BLEEDING KANSAS.

Eminent domain, the power of the government to 'condemn' or take private property for public use with reasonable compensation, is considered the inherent right of sovereign states. The Fifth and Fourteenth Amendments to the U.S. Constitution establish and limit such rights in general terms. The question has risen, chiefly in the matter of flood controls and hydroelectric power, whether the federal government may exercise the right of eminent domain in a state without the state's consent. Since the Supreme Court has never ruled on the principle, there probably exists in the U.S. an undefined region between Federal and state authority regarding eminent domain for purposes not expressed in the Constitution.

EMMETT, DANIEL DECATUR (1815–1904), Ohio-born song writer, founded the Virginia Minstrels (1842), first of the classic four-man MINSTREL SHOW troupes. After 1858 he was associated with Bryant's Minstrels, for which he composed his original and immensely popular *Dixie* (1859) as a walk-around (the comic dance in which the performer describes a large circle). As a Union sympathizer during the Civil War he was dismayed to find that *Dixie* had been appropriated as a Confederate marching song and used as a rallying song for the southern cause. He wrote the words (but not the music) for *Old Dan Tucker* (*c.* 1833).

Empire State Building, in New York City, on Fifth Avenue between 33rd and 34th Streets, is 1472 ft. high and is topped by a 222-foot television tower. It is the world's tallest structure. Completed in 1931, it can house 25,000 tenants and attracts over 1,000,000 annually to its observation stations.

Empiricism, the philosophical doctrine that all knowledge derives from experience (or sense impression), holds that generalizations can yield only a certain degree of probability. Science employs the empirical method. In religion it was the approach used by JONATHAN EDWARDS. Later empiricists were WILLIAM JAMES, JOHN DEWEY, and WILLIAM E. HOCKING.

Employers' liability, see *Workmen's compensation.*

Employment bureau, a public or private agency created for the purpose of finding employment for applicants, originated during the 19th century both in the U.S. and in Europe. Massachusetts was the first state to regulate private employment bureaus (1848), and Ohio established the first state agency (1890). The federal government opened offices in 1907 under the Bureau of Immigration and Naturalization, and in 1918 the Employment Service became a (somewhat ineffective) unit in the Department of Labor. The Wagner-Peyser Act (1933) set up a national system based upon grants-in-aid for states to manage. In 1939 the Service was transferred to the Federal Security Agency and placed with that administration's Bureau of Employment Security.

ENDECOTT, JOHN (*c.* 1599–1665), who preceded John Winthrop as governor of the Massachusetts Bay colony (1628–30), became the first governor of the colony at Salem, and remained important in public affairs after Winthrop established the colony's center at Boston. Though an able administrator, he was a bigot who made the word 'puritan' odious to later generations. He is chiefly remembered for his harshness to heretics, and his zealous persecution of the Quakers.

Engineering began in America as an empirical art in the inventions of OLIVER EVANS, and became an applied science when educational institutions established specialized schools. Pioneers in teaching the young profession were the U.S. Military Academy, and Rensselaer Polytechnic Institute, the first to grant engineering degrees (1835). The Erie Canal, completed in 1825, provided some opportunity for engineers to gain experience, but it was the expansive era of railroad construction after 1850 that gave training and employment to engineers on a major scale.

Thereafter specialization grew, as mining and mechanical problems became complex. Civil engineering was developed with notable success by JOHN A. ROEBLING and JAMES B. EADS in bridge construction. The need for engineers encouraged the formation of scientific schools at Harvard (1847) and Yale (1861), and the founding of Massachusetts Institute of Technology (1865) and other engineering schools. A landmark in engineering management was the construction of the Panama Canal (1907–14) by GEORGE W. GOETHALS.

During the 20th century engineering has moved further from art toward pure science, and emphasis has shifted from empirical application of formulas. Research laboratories are now an integral part of large industries as well as of technical schools. New engineering fields are variously designated as aeronautical, agricultural, chemical, electrical, geological, marine, and metallurgical.

Entail in law is the restriction of inheritance to particular heirs to keep family property undivided. The custom had been common in England for many centuries before the colonizing of America, and was adopted especially in the land tenures in New York and the South. Such leaders as Jefferson, who were stoutly opposed to the perpetuation of political control by a bloc of landed aristocrats, steered the legislation that first abolished entail in Virginia (1776). Soon thereafter most states outlawed the practice.

'Entangling alliances' was a phrase used by Jefferson in his first inaugural address (1801) to express his fear that the nation might become involuntarily committed to a course of action counter to its best interests. He declared his devotion to 'peace, commerce, and honest friendship with all nations, entangling alliances with none.' (Washington had advised against 'permanent alliances.') Jefferson's phrase was later used as the rallying cry of isolationists.

Entertainment, see *Bridge, Burlesque, Circus, Dance, Jazz, Medicine show, Minstrel show, Motion pictures, Night clubs, Operetta (musical comedy), Pantomime, Puppet shows, Radio, Rodeo, Showboats, Sports, Television, Theater,* and *Vaudeville.*

'Enumerated articles,' see *Navigation Acts.*

Enumerated powers, see *Delegated powers.*

Ephrata Cloister, see *Beissel, J. C.*

EPIC, see *Sinclair, Upton.*

Episcopal Church, see *Protestant Episcopal Church.*

E Pluribus Unum (*one from many*) is the Latin motto on the Great Seal of the U.S. It was chosen (1776) by Franklin, Adams, and Jefferson, the committee appointed by the Continental Congress to select the inscription. The words are taken from *Moretum,* a poem attributed to Virgil. They long appeared (1732–1833) as a motto on the cover of the *Gentleman's Magazine* and thus were well known at the time.

Equity law is the system of jurisprudence which seeks to do justice by determining what is equitable and fair, and offering remedies incident to the hardships resulting from the inflexibility of the common-law tribunals. The steady growth of the complexities of property and of business and social relations have increasingly required equitable interference with common-law rules. Both in England and the U.S. doctrines of the common law have been subjected to the modifications introduced by equity, and in the U.S. many states have merged the two systems of rules, which are administered by the same courts. Notable achievements of equity were the mortgage and the trust, and, among remedies, it afforded the injunction. The foundations of equity jurisprudence in the U.S. were laid by JAMES KENT and JOSEPH STORY.

'Era of Good Feelings' was the epithet coined by the Boston *Columbian Centinel* (July 1817) to express the enthusiasm (particularly marked in New

England) for President Monroe's accession to office. Federalists thus extended welcome to the President, whose summer tour was thought to symbolize the triumph of national feeling over party animosities. Although misleading, the phrase became a rallying cry during Monroe's two terms in office (1817–25). Actually sectional rivalries were bitter and economic issues were working basic transformations in national affairs.

Erdman Act (1898), see *Railroad Mediation Acts.*

ERIC THE RED and **ERICSSON,** LEIF, see *Leif Ericsson.*

ERICSSON, JOHN (1803–89), Swedish-born inventor and marine engineer, after coming to New York in 1839, furnished designs (1840) for the screw warship *Princeton,* the first to have its propelling machinery under water and thus out of firing range. He is chiefly remembered as the designer and builder (1861) of the ironclad *Monitor,* which had a circular revolving armored turret. His other contributions were made most notably in ordnance and heat engines.

Erie Canal was opened (1825) as a toll waterway, extending from Albany to Buffalo and connecting the Hudson with Lake Erie. The canal gave the Atlantic port city of New York easy access to the West. The project had long been envisioned and the War of 1812 spurred interest in wresting the Great Lakes trade from Canadian competition. The New York legislature, with the vigorous support of Governor De Witt Clinton, passed the canal bill in 1817, and work on the $7,000,000 project began immediately. Its completion was the occasion of gala observances, including the emptying of a barrel of Lake Erie water into the Atlantic. Connecting branches gave 'Clinton's ditch' large profits and set off a canal-building boom. Of major importance was the practical instruction it furnished young engineers.

Railroad competition after 1860 destroyed the Erie canal's long-haul advantages, but in its time it had proved immensely important. It was a large factor in the development of New York City as a financial center, by opening Eastern markets to the farm products of the Great Lakes region. It fostered emigration to the West and helped create numerous large cities. The modern New York State Barge Canal System (1905) in the main follows the original course and still bears a rich share of Western produce to the markets of the world.

Erie Indians, of Iroquoian stock, in the 17th century lived south of Lake Erie from the Genesee valley to Ohio. Estimated to number some 14,000, they were sedentary farmers and traditional enemies of the IROQUOIS CONFEDERACY, which by 1655 had almost annihilated them. Remnants of the tribe were absorbed by the Seneca, a component group within the Confederacy.

Erie, Lake, fourth in size and shallowest of the GREAT LAKES, is 241 miles long, covers an area of 9910 square miles. It lies between the U.S. and Canada, the northern boundary of Ohio. Its inlet from Lake Huron is the Detroit river, and its outlet is the Niagara, into Lake Ontario. It was named for the Indian tribe (along its southern shore) which was absorbed by the Seneca in 1655. French explorers came to know of its existence about that time. In 1679 at Niagara TONTI launched the *Griffon,* the first ship on the lake.

Its strategic location made Lake Erie the most significant of the Great Lakes during the French and Indian Wars. In 1813 it was the scene of Commodore Perry's victory over the British. With the completion of the Erie Canal (1825), lake commerce contributed to the economic development of the West. Large cities that it helped develop are Buffalo (N.Y.), Erie (Pa.), Cleveland and Toledo (Ohio), and Detroit (Mich.).

Erie Railroad, organized in 1833, by 1851 connected New York City with Lake Erie. It was a 483-mile route, and the longest railroad line in the world at that time. A profitable carrier during the Civil War, it became the subject of a tremendous financial battle (1866–68), when Daniel Drew, Jay Gould, and James Fisk by political and financial chicanery prevented Cornelius Vanderbilt from gaining control. Gould outmaneuvered Drew but was ejected from control when his operations brought the company into bankruptcy (1877). After a series of reorganizations and a long uphill fight, solvency was restored. In 1942 Erie stock yielded a dividend, the first in 69 years.

Erskine agreement, so called, was the effort of President Madison, during his second month in office, to postpone the troublesome subject of impressment. David M. Erskine, the British minister at Washington, entered into an agreement (April 1809) with Robert Smith, the American Secretary of State, whereby Britain agreed to exempt American ships from the Orders in Council of 1807 (directing the British navy to impress British subjects from neutral shipping) if the U.S. would resume commercial relations with England and forbid trade with France. For reasons never explained, George Canning, the British Foreign Secretary, repudiated the agreement and recalled Erskine. He thus lost the chance to break the U.S. ties with France by making the U.S. a silent partner of the Allies. The forces pushing the U.S. into a second Anglo-American war thus were increased.

ESCALANTE, Silvestre Vélez de (*fl.* 1769–79), Spanish missionary in the Southwest, in 1776 led an expedition from Santa Fe into Utah. He was the first white man to penetrate and map the Utah country. His journal (published in 1909) is important source material dealing with the region.

'Escalator clause,' see *London Naval Conference (1930)*.

Esch-Cummins Act (1920), or Railroad Transportation Act, unlike previous railroad regulations, sought to encourage rather than discourage consolidation, now that systems were being restored to private ownership after World War I. It empowered the ICC to evaluate railroad property, set maximum and minimum rates, and exercise complete jurisdiction over the financial operations of the railroads as a protection to stockholders. Its 'recapture clause' provided that all net earnings over 6 per cent should be divided equally between the carrier and the government, the latter to use such earnings as a revolving fund for the benefit of the weaker railroads. The revolutionary character of the Act was its consolidation feature. (Ultimately all railroads throughout the country were combined into regional systems.)

Some features of the Act worked badly. The labor provision set up the Railroad Labor Board, which, unable to prevent the shopmen's strike of 1922, was replaced (1926) by boards of adjustment, mediation, and arbitration with which the federal government had only the most tenuous connection, by amendments adopted in the WATSON-PARKER ACT (1926) and the CROSSER-DILL ACT (1934). In practice the recapture clause proved unworkable and was later repealed; and issues arising from an attempt to fix a 'fair rate' ran afoul of the old difficulty of evaluation and had to await Supreme Court action in 1929. Thus the measure was a subject of controversy for a great many years.

Espionage Act of 1917, indicative of the fear hysteria which gripped the U.S. at the outbreak of World War I, provided severe penalties (up to a $10,000 fine and twenty years' imprisonment) for persons found guilty of interfering with the draft or encouraging disloyalty to the U.S. It was supplemented by the Sedition Act of 1918, which extended the penalty to anyone deemed abusive of the government in writing. Under these harsh laws, the most extreme of their kind ever enacted in the U.S., more than 1500 arrests were made. Those arrested (and in many instances later pardoned) included EUGENE V. DEBS and VICTOR BERGER.

ESPY, James Pollard (1785–1860), as 'meteorologist to the U.S. government' was assigned first to the War Department (1842), then also to the Navy Department (1848). In 1843 he submitted the first annual weather report. His *Law of Cooling of Atmospheric Air* (1843) is a classic contribution in the field of meteorology. He pioneered in scientific weather forecasting, and propounded his convection theory of precipitation.

***Essex* Case** was a diplomatic incident involving the U.S. and Britain. It developed from the British capture in 1804 of the American merchant vessel *Essex*. By the terms of the 'Rule of 1756,' forbidding neutrals to engage during wartime in any trade that was forbidden in time of peace, *Essex* was claimed as a prize for engaging in a continuous voyage between the French West Indies and France, then at war with England. The vessel had used the customary method of evading the Rule by interrupting the voyage with a stop at an American port. (The principle of the 'broken voyage' had been upheld in two British Admiralty decisions.) In this instance British policy was abruptly reversed by an Admiralty decision (1805) that any cargo was subject to seizure unless the shipper could prove that he had originally intended to terminate the voyage at the interim port. Otherwise the voyage was 'continuous.' Thereafter seizures of American vessels increased sharply, exacerbating the tensions that led to the War of 1812.

Essex Junto, so called, was made up of such New England families of 'education and property' as the Pickerings, Cabots, and Lowells. Representing the privileged interests of Essex county, Massachusetts, they gathered in 1778 to oppose the state constitution drawn up that year by the General Court. Their effort was successful to the extent that some of their suggested changes were incorporated by John Adams in his draft of the constitution of 1780. Staunch Federalists, in later years they denounced republicanism, and after passage of Jefferson's Embargo Act (1807) the extremists among them pressed for nullification and secession. Unsupported by popular opinion, they lost influence, and the Treaty of Ghent (1814), which ended the War of 1812, effectively stopped the Junto intrigues.

Established Church of England, see *Protestant Episcopal Church.*

Ethical Culture movement, the most important development of religious HUMANISM, originated in the Society of Ethical Culture, founded (1876) in New York City by FELIX ADLER. It prescribes no definite ethical system, although it asserts 'the supreme importance of the ethical factor' in all relationships. The Society places much emphasis on education, holds its own religious services, and makes clear that members are free to have other religious affiliations. Its groups are organized in many cities throughout the U.S. The total membership is small (5500 as reported in the 1965 census), but the movement is intellectually vigorous.

Ethnology, the branch of anthropology that examines distinctive groups of mankind, has long fascinated students of aboriginal American cultures. From the first, missionaries and explorers made records of their observations, and since the founding of the American Philosophical Society (1743) many learned societies have collected ethnological data. The American Antiquarian Society (est. 1812) gave special attention to ethnic investigations. In 1830 GEORGE CATLIN began his remarkable series of ethnological paintings of Indian tribes. ALBERT GALLATIN created the science of American linguistics with his *Synopsis of the Indian Tribes* (1836), and founded the American Ethnological Society in 1842. The Smithsonian Institution (est. 1846), with its primary interest in scientific research, helped build up the U.S. Bureau of American Ethnology (est. 1879). Pioneer Indian studies conducted by HENRY R. SCHOOLCRAFT and LEWIS MORGAN were followed by the extensive investigations of Indian life in the Pacific states made by H. H. BANCROFT. Interest in western antiquities led to the founding (1879) of the Archaeological Institute of America, and is reflected in the studies of J. C. BOURKE, F. H. CUSHING, and A. F. A. BANDELIER. *The American Race* (1891), by D. C. BRINTON, broke ground for such later research as that of CLARK WISSLER. The ethnological and linguistic contributions of FRANZ BOAS, the most influential American anthropologist of the 20th century, prepared the way for the studies of his pupil RUTH BENEDICT, who helped develop the field of cultural anthropology. In addition to the learned societies named above, field investigations are conducted by major universities and such institutions as the American Museum of Natural History.

European Economic Community (EEC), generally called the Common Market, came into effect by provision of a treaty (1957) signed by six nations (Belgium, France, Italy, Luxembourg,

The Netherlands, and West Germany). The Common Market seeks to work toward a customs union and the free flow of goods and services. The first U.S. trade agreement with the EEC was signed in 1962. It provides a partially reciprocal reduction of tariffs to increase each side's chances of exporting to the other.

European Recovery Program, see *Marshall Plan.*

Eutaw Springs, Battle of (8 September 1781), was the last important engagement in South Carolina during the War of Independence. Some 2000 American Continentals and militia under Nathanael Greene unsuccessfully attacked 2500 British regulars, who, failing to secure their gains, fell back to Charleston, thus leaving the Americans strategically in command of the interior of the state.

Evangelism, see *Revivals.*

EVANS, CHARLES (1850–1935), received his library training at the Boston Athenaeum and was successively librarian of the Public Library of Indianapolis, the Enoch Pratt Free Library in Baltimore, and other institutions. He was admired for his abilities in his field, but was not an administrator. He is especially known for *American Bibliography* (12 vols., 1903–34), a chronological listing of nearly 38,000 titles of books, pamphlets, and periodicals printed in America from 1639 through 1799. A thirteenth volume (compiled by C. K. Skipton, 1955) brings the record to 1800.

EVANS, GEORGE HENRY (1805–56), English-born editor and agrarian reformer, came to the U.S. in 1820. An ardent admirer of Robert Dale Owen and Frances Wright, he supported the WORKINGMEN'S PARTY and established the *Working Man's Advocate* (1829–37, 1844–47), the first important labor paper in the country. His *History of the . . . Workingmen's Party* (1840) opposed FOURIERISM and favored Jefferson's agrarianism. He organized the National Reform Association (with many state branches) to agitate for cheap public lands as a 'safety valve' for eastern labor unrest, thus keeping wages high. As the best means of achieving the ends of labor, he advocated pressure politics: 'Vote yourself a farm.' This movement culminated in the HOMESTEAD ACT (1862).

EVANS, LEWIS (*c.* 1700–1756), English surveyor and geographer, after travels in America through the middle colonies during the 1740's, published maps which were widely used by migrating colonists and by military expeditions into the new West. Distinguished for their excellent detail of the roads, they were reprinted (and plagiarized) seventeen times between 1755 and 1814.

EVANS, OLIVER (1755–1819), Delaware industrialist and inventor, patented such automatic flour-milling devices as an elevator, a conveyor, and a hopperboy (*c.* 1785), machines that, with their intimation of the assembly line, were harbingers of MASS PRODUCTION. As author of *The Young Mill-Wright and Miller's Guide* (1795), which went through several editions, he made his experience available throughout the U.S. A pioneer in constructing high-pressure steam engines, he established the Mars Iron Works (1807), and his steam-powered river dredge was the first to be used in America. With ELI WHITNEY, Evans ranks as an inventor and organizer whose ideas were influential in developing the industrial character of the U.S.

EVARTS, WILLIAM MAXWELL (1818–1901), after graduation from Yale (1837) and study in the Harvard Law School, took up the practice of law in New York City, where he became one of the notable trial lawyers of his day. He handled several prize cases for the government during the Civil War, and his eloquent defense of President Andrew Johnson tore to shreds the case of the prosecution in the impeachment trial. During his last year in office (1868) Johnson appointed Evarts Attorney General, and Evarts served as Secretary of State throughout the Hayes administration (1877–80). Confronted with French interest in constructing an isthmian canal, he formulated the policy, subsequently maintained, that any such canal must remain under American control.

'Ever normal granary,' see *Agricultural Adjustment Act.*

EVERETT, EDWARD (1794–1865), after graduation from Harvard (1811) received an appointment there as professor of Greek literature (1815), and went abroad to travel and study at Göttingen (Ph.D., 1817). He took up his professorship briefly (1819–25), while editing the *North American Review* (1820–23), but abandoned teaching to enter politics as a Whig. Having served as U.S. Representative (1825–35), and governor of Massachusetts (1836–39), he accepted President Tyler's appointment as minister to England (1841–45). For three years Everett occupied the president's chair at Harvard (1846–49), but returned to public life when he was appointed Secretary of State (1852–53) after Webster's death. He was then elected to the Senate (1853–54). In 1860 he ran for the vice presidency as a candidate of the short-lived CONSTITUTIONAL UNION PARTY. The most noted orator of his day, during the Civil War he drew immense audiences, speaking throughout the North for the Union cause. His most famous address, now completely forgotten, was the two-hour-long principal oration delivered at the dedication of the Gettysburg battlefield (November 1863). It was followed by Lincoln's imperishable utterance.

Everglades, covering the greater part of southern Florida, is a swamp area of nearly 5000 square miles, more than half of which has been reclaimed. Everglades National Park (est. 1947) embraces 1,302,000 acres of subtropical flora and fauna, and is known especially for its abundant bird life.

EWELL, RICHARD STODDERT (1817–72), Virginia-born graduate of the U.S. Military Academy (1840), resigned his commission in the army in 1861 to serve in the Confederacy. He succeeded Jackson (May 1863) as corps commander and was in charge of the Confederate left at Gettysburg. Injuries sustained during the Wilderness campaign (1864) compelled his retirement from the field. He commanded the defenses of Richmond when the city fell, and in April 1865 surrendered his forces to Sheridan.

Excess profit tax, first levied by the federal government in 1916 to increase tax revenues, was motivated by the feeling that high war profits were mainly 'windfalls.' Repealed in 1921, the tax was revived in 1933, and has since remained in force.

Exchanges, organized centers for trading in securities and commodities, developed during the 19th century. They regulate trading activities but do not themselves buy or sell or fix prices. STOCK EXCHANGES are associations for the purchase and sale of investment securities, the oldest of which in the U.S. is the New York Stock Exchange (est. 1792). Commodity exchanges deal in such items as grains, lumber, and cotton. The Chicago Board of Trade was organized in 1848, and the New York Produce Exchange in 1850. All exchanges are subject to Federal supervision by such agencies as the FEDERAL TRADE COMMISSION (1914), and the SECURITIES AND EXCHANGE COMMISSION (1934). Regulations are also provided by the Futures Trading Act (1921), the Grain Futures Act (1921), the Commodity Exchange Act (1936), and similar later legislation.

Excise, see *Internal revenue.*

Executive agencies, U.S., presidential advisory boards, in 1965 were nine in number: BUREAU OF THE BUDGET, NATIONAL SECURITY COUNCIL, CENTRAL INTELLIGENCE AGENCY, Council of Economic Advisors, National Aeronautics and Space Council, Office of Economic Opportunity, Office of Emergency Planning, Office of Science and Technology, and Special Representative for Trade Negotiations.

Executive agreements are pacts drawn up by the President of the U.S. and another head of state. They have the effectiveness and validity of a treaty as an international act. Although executive agreements may be made by the sole authority of the President as commander in chief of the armed forces, or by virtue of his executive power under the Constitution, a number have been made under statute or Congressional joint resolutions conferring special power upon the President. They are now more numerous than treaties, and since they do not require Senate ratification, as do treaties, they are frequently negotiated to avoid the cumbersome machinery in the upper House. Generally of lesser importance in content than negotiations which would require a treaty, they have included postal conventions (since 1792), settlement of claims of American citizens, tariff duties, arbitration, and copyright and patent arrangements. Examples of wartime agreements include the Destroyer Transfer Agreement (1940), the Atlantic Charter (1941), and the agreements reached at Teheran (1943), Yalta (1945), and Potsdam (1945).

Executive departments, see *Cabinet.*

Executive orders of the President are rules issued to executive and administrative agencies to carry out provisions of legislative policy. They are legally binding, since the Constitution charges the President to execute the laws of the land. Their multiplicity has increased as the complexity of government has increased. Executive orders and proclamations were edited and distributed by the Department of State until that function was transferred in 1936 to the Division of the FEDERAL REGISTER, National Archives.

Executive powers, see *The Presidency.*

Executive reorganization, in the interest of greater economy and efficiency, had its beginning (1936) when President Roosevelt appointed a three-man Committee on Administrative Management (the Brownlow Committee). In 1937 the Committee reported a bill, which was defeated by Congress, recommending increased staff assistance, the creation of an Executive Office, reorganization of the Bureau of the Budget, and co-ordination of public works, welfare, lending, and social security. A weak law enacted in 1939 gave the President power to establish the Executive Office and the right to create fifteen independent agencies, including the Federal Security Agency, Federal Works Agency, and Federal Loan Agency. The recommendations made to Congress in 1949 by the HOOVER COMMISSION carried executive reorganization much further.

Expatriation, as a voluntary surrender of citizenship, has been explicitly recognized by various congressional enactments. In 1868 Congress announced the right of voluntary expatriation to be a 'natural and inherent right of all people,' and declared an intent to protect naturalized U.S. citizens abroad, even in those countries of which they were formerly citizens. The power of Congress to legislate in this field is set forth in the Constitution (Art. I, sec. 8).

Explorations of America followed the era of discovery (see AMERICA), and established the New World as a potential source of wealth to European nations. Spain was lured by rumors of gold and silver mines, France envisioned a large-scale fur trade with the Indians, and England was interested in establishing colonies and growing silk. Exploration was encouraged not only by the hope of discovering native products that could be marketed in Europe, such as sarsaparilla, sassafras, guaiacum, and tobacco; but especially by the wish to find a NORTHWEST PASSAGE to the Orient. The interior of the continent became known to some extent during the 17th century through the reports and MAPS of missionaries and fur traders, though vast regions remained largely unknown until well into the 19th century. Commercial trapping was a prime factor in stimulating the WESTERN MOVEMENT, since the traders explored the rivers, blazed trails through unmapped forests, learned to counter Indian hostilities, and opened the way for agricultural settlements along the entire American FRONTIER.

The famous LEWIS AND CLARK EXPEDITION (1804–6), the first official American penetration into the Far West, was followed by the scientific explorations of ZEBULON PIKE (1805–7), STEPHEN LONG (1819–20), LEWIS CASS (1820), J. N. NICOLLET (1838–41), and JOHN C. FRÉMONT, who surveyed and mapped the central Rockies. Commerce into the Southwest had been made possible by early expeditions sent out from NEW SPAIN, and by 1822 explorations were conducted by way of the SANTA FE TRAIL. Other notable explorations are described under ARCHAEOLOGY, GEOGRAPHY, GEOLOGY, OCEANOGRAPHY, PALEONTOLOGY, POLAR EXPEDITIONS, and ZOOLOGY.

Export-Import Bank, a government corporation chartered by Congress in 1934, was established by executive order. In 1945 it became an independent Federal agency with increased powers and an authorized capital of $1,000,000,000. It makes or guarantees private loans to finance commerce between the U.S. and foreign nations, and extends credit to firms whose funds are invested in countries with exchange restrictions. In 1960 its loans outstanding amounted to $3,500,000,000, and its annual expenditures exceeded $323,000,000.

Ex post facto law is a law declaring an act illegal which was legal when committed. The Federal Constitution forbids Congress to enact ex post facto laws, and places the same interdict upon state legislatures (Art. I, secs. 9 and 10).

Ex-Presidents of the U.S. have no official standing either by law or by custom, and thus the experience of such leading statesmen has rarely been used effectively. Washington, John Adams, Jefferson, Madison, and Monroe retired to their estates. The political career of J. Q. Adams appeared to be over when he left office in 1829, but his example is unique. He sought and won election to the House of Representatives (1831), where he served ably and effectively until his death seventeen years later. Van Buren twice unsuccessfully sought reelection to the presidency after his term ended in 1841. Although Fillmore lived for 21 years after leaving office in 1853, he exerted little influence. He was the unsuccessful presidential nominee of the Know-Nothing party in 1856, and thereafter took no public share in political affairs. Benjamin Harrison resumed his law practice in 1893, as did Coolidge in 1929. The political counsel of Cleveland in the decade of his retirement (1897–1908) was in constant demand. After his defeat as the Progressive standard-bearer in 1912, Theodore Roosevelt went big-game hunting in Africa, explored the Amazon jungles, and continued his historical writings.

Taft occupied a chair of law at Yale until he was appointed to the Supreme Court as Chief Justice. Wilson, ill and disillusioned after his failure to win ratification of the League of Nations treaty, withdrew entirely from politics. Hoover went into political eclipse after his defeat in 1932, but returned to public affairs in 1947 when he headed the HOOVER COMMISSION on executive reorganization. Truman and Eisenhower as ex-Presidents have often been impelled to speak out on public issues, but they have chiefly had the restricted influence of former party leaders.

In 1958 Congress provided lifetime pensions of $25,000 a year and other perquisites for ex-Presidents, including a $50,000 annual drawing account for office assistants. Widows may draw $10,000 annually. The long-established precedent of ignoring ex-Presidents in government councils was broken in 1963, when Congress provided that former Presidents may at their request address Congress. The courtesy is potentially significant.

Expressionism in painting is a term which originated in Munich (1911) to describe any modern work of art which deliberately distorts form to convey an emotion by spontaneity or intuition. Not concerned with the 'outward effect' of representation, it attempts to grapple with the 'form beneath.' In art expressionism is allied to IMPRESSIONISM, but with a different emphasis, since expressionism is primarily concerned with intellectual conceptions. A tendency rather than a school, expressionism was early developed in painting by Van Gogh and carried into American painting by such artists as JOHN MARIN and FRANKLIN WATKINS. Abstract expressionism, a movement after 1940, has been the method of HANS HOFMANN, WILLEM DE KOONING, and JACKSON POLLOCK.

Extradition, the surrender of an alleged criminal by one state to another, is accomplished between sovereign nations by treaty. The U.S. has negotiated many such treaties, but since each case is decided by the nature and circumstances of the individual crime, nations on occasion contest the terms of a treaty and refuse the demand for extradition. Internationally, a surrender of fugitives by one state to another need not take place if the crime allegedly is 'political' in nature.

Interstate extradition (also called rendition) is provided for in the 'interstate comity' clause of the Constitution

(Art. IV, sec. 2), which specifies that the governor of the state of refuge 'shall' return the prisoner to the state whence he came, upon the demand of the governor of the state having jurisdiction of the crime. The provision, although apparently mandatory, has been held by the Supreme Court to be discretionary, moral not legal, thus justifying the many refusals for extradition that have occurred. No reason need be given by a state for refusing to extradite a fugitive.

Extraterritoriality, an exemption from the jurisdiction of local tribunals, generally pertains only to diplomatic agents in foreign countries. During the 19th century it was often granted as a special right conferred by a government upon citizens of other nations who were residents within the territory of the conferring nation. Such rights included exemption from local laws, privileges pertaining to railroad concessions, harbor rights, and taxation. They were often secured from Eastern governments by Western powers who won unilateral concessions by coercion.

The U.S. participated in many such agreements, including treaties with China, Japan, Siam, Egypt, and Persia. In 1894, following the lead of Great Britain, the U.S. signed a treaty with Japan abolishing nondiplomatic extraterritoriality, which it recognized as an infringement of sovereignty as well as an opportunity for abuses. It was likewise abolished in China (1943) by treaty.

F

Factory system, see *Manufacturing.*

'Fair Deal,' the slogan applied to the Truman Administration, was coined by President Truman in his address to Congress in January 1949. Largely an extension of the Roosevelt 'New Deal,' it proposed legislation on civil rights, fair employment practices, educational appropriations, improvement of public welfare laws, and a POINT FOUR PROGRAM to make 'the benefits of our scientific advances and industrial progress available for the improvement and growth of underdeveloped areas.'

Fair Employment Practices Committee (1941), established by executive order to curb racial discrimination in war industries and government employment, was later strengthened to encompass war contracts. President Roosevelt thus averted a threatened march on Washington. In 1946 a bill for a permanent FEPC was killed in the Senate by a filibuster of Southern Democrats, and the committee was suspended for lack of funds. It was the forerunner of laws passed in many states and cities barring race restrictions in employment.

Fair Labor Standards Act (1938), known also as the Wages and Hours Law, sets minimum and maximum standard wages and a maximum working week for employees producing goods for interstate commerce. It also specifies minimum wages and maximum hours and the nature of labor for children. A far-sighted Act, it established the Wage and Hour Division in the Department of Labor, and was the first permanent minimum wage legislation enacted on a national scale.

Fair Oaks, Battle of (31 May–1 June 1862), also known as Seven Pines, was a major Civil War engagement by which McClellan made an unsuccessful bid to capture Richmond. The Confederates under J. E. Johnston attacked McClellan's two corps on the south bank of the swollen Chickahominy river near Fair Oaks Station, some eight miles east of Richmond. The Confederate attack was not well co-ordinated, and on the first day Johnston was severely wounded. On the second day Robert E. Lee took command. He ordered Jackson to attack McClellan's left flank while Lee attacked the center. McClellan, warned by a premature cavalry attack, withdrew to a base on the James river, and waited for reinforcements. The Union was thus put on the defensive. Lee and Jackson, by their brilliant maneuvering, convinced the Union forces that they had far greater forces than they actually did, and forced the Lincoln Administration to hold thousands of troops far from the combat, ready to repulse an attack on Washington. Each side engaged some 40,000 men, and both sustained heavy losses in a battle that delayed the capture of Richmond until the closing weeks of the war. The engagement was followed by the SEVEN DAYS' BATTLES, which began 26 June.

Fair trade laws were enactments during the 1930's legislated in 45 states to permit manufacturers, wholesalers, and retailers of branded products to establish resale prices. Such gestures toward aiding the independent businessman proved largely a failure, since states without the laws offered loopholes. Mail-order business permitted discount houses in states not requiring fixed prices to function in states where fair trade laws prevailed. Thus the laws proved almost entirely futile and large companies gradually abandoned fair trade as a sales policy.

FAIRBANKS, DOUGLAS [DOUGLAS ELTON ULMAN] (1883–1939), in 1915 abandoned the legitimate theater to begin his career as a motion picture actor. Distinguished by his personal charm, for more than a decade he was a box-office attraction in such movies as *The Mark of Zorro, The Three Musketeers,* and *Robin Hood,* in which he performed with muscular agility. For a time (1920–35) he was the husband of MARY PICKFORD.

FAIRBANKS, ERASTUS (1792–1864), established an iron foundry at St. Johnsbury, Vermont, where he became internationally known as manufacturer of the platform scale, invented (1830) by his brother Thaddeus Fairbanks (1796–1886). Twice governor of Vermont (1852–53, 1860–61), he was among the notable 'war governors' of the North, liberally supporting the Union cause with troops and supplies.

FAIRFAX, THOMAS, 6th Baron Fairfax of Cameron (1693–1781), educated at Oxford, in 1747 settled in Virginia, where he had inherited the vast Northern Neck of the colony (5,280,000 acres) from his grandfather, Baron Culpeper, at one time the colonial governor (1675–83). Patron of the youthful George Washington, who surveyed his property, Fairfax was the only resident peer in America, and remained a Loyalist through the War of Independence. He was never molested by the Americans, but four years after his death Virginia revoked the family's proprietary rights.

FALL, ALBERT BACON (1861–1944), U.S. Senator from New Mexico (1912–21), was Harding's Secretary of the Interior (1921–23). Found guilty (1929) of conspiracy to defraud the government in the notorious TEAPOT DOME oil scandal, he served a brief prison term (1931–32).

Fall line is the junction of the coastal plains of the eastern U.S. (including the TIDEWATER region in a few areas) with the PIEDMONT or foothill area to the west. It is so designated because waterfalls or rapids there mark the eastward passage of streams across the line, which is the head of navigation. The fall line stimulated the growth of towns and industry, because it offered water power and required the building of canals or railroads at the points where the rivers were no longer navigable. On it are located Camden and Columbia (S.C.), Raleigh (N.C.), and Fredericksburg, Petersburg, and Richmond (Va.).

Fallen Timbers, Battle of (20 August 1794), was decisively won by ANTHONY WAYNE, with his mounted Kentucky riflemen, against Indians of several tribes who had been encouraged to fight by the British, then at peace with the U.S. Wayne had built Fort Defiance in the midst of a group of Indian villages in the Northwest Territory, and had offered to make peace with the Indians. They refused, and withdrew toward the British fort, taking a position behind a natural barrier of fallen trees. The Americans attacked, the infantry firing on the center and the mounted riflemen jumping their horses over the logs on the left flank. The entire engagement lasted only forty minutes. The victory hastened the end of Indian resistance in the area and paved the way for the enforcement of JAY'S TREATY on the frontier and the evacuation of the British border forts. The site of the battle is now an Ohio state park.

Faneuil Hall was designed as a market building and public hall by the artist JOHN SMIBERT, and given to the town of Boston (1742) by the merchant Peter Faneuil (1700–1743). This so-called 'cradle of liberty' was the scene of patriotic meetings on the eve of the Revolution. It was almost wholly destroyed by fire in 1761, then rebuilt and used as a theater during the British occupation of Boston (1775–76). In 1806 it was much enlarged according to the design of CHARLES BULFINCH, and is now a historical museum.

Far Eastern Commission, see *Japan, Occupation of.*

Far North, see *North Woods.*

Far West, the region west of the Continental Divide between the PACIFIC NORTHWEST and the SOUTHWEST, includes California, Nevada, Utah, and the western portions of Colorado and Wyoming. Geographically its spine is the rugged Sierra Nevada range, whose western slopes feed streams into the 1200-mile Pacific coastline, and whose barriers create the Nevada desert. Subject to extremes of heat and cold, it is a region of high plateaus to the east, important as large mining and grazing areas.

Although the Pacific coast had been explored by Cabrillo and Drake in the 16th century, the Far West was not occupied by whites until JUNIPERO SERRA founded the California missions (1769). The U.S. seized the region during the Mexican War, and it began to be developed during the gold rush. Completion of the transcontinental railroad (1869) encouraged sheep and cattle ranching, and during the 20th century irrigation has reclaimed large sections.

FARLEY, JAMES ALOYSIUS (1888–), as chairman of the Democratic National Committee (1932–40), managed the first two presidential campaigns of F. D. Roosevelt and served as Postmaster General (1933–40). He opposed Roosevelt's third-term candidacy, was himself an unsuccessful presidential aspirant in 1940, and thereafter retired from national politics.

Farm legislation in the U.S. had its significant beginning with the creation of the Department of Agriculture (1862) and passage of the MORRILL LAND GRANT ACT (1862), which provided for the endowment of agricultural colleges in all the states. The HATCH ACT of 1887 extended subsidies to agricultural experiment stations. Legislation to give direct aid to farmers became a serious concern of Congress when it passed the Federal Farm Loan Act (1916), creating twelve regional districts administered by a Federal Farm Loan Board. A Farm Loan Bank was established in each district to offer long-term loans on farm-mortgage security to co-operative farm loan associations. The Warehouse Act, passed at the same time, authorized licensed warehouses to issue receipts for agricultural commodities, negotiable at banks. In 1929 the Agricultural Marketing Act set up a Federal Farm Board to promote the sale of farm produce through co-operatives.

The epidemic of farm bankruptcies following the PANIC OF 1929 made further legislation imperative. The Agricultural Adjustment Act (1933) sought to stabilize commodity prices, and the Farm Relief and Inflation Act (1933) was passed at the request of President Roosevelt to devalue the currency. This effort to establish a 'commodity dollar' had no appreciable effect in raising commodity prices, and in 1934 the country returned to a modified gold standard.

A new Farm Credit Administration (1933), which absorbed the Federal Farm Board, was set up by Executive Order to handle all Federal units dealing with agricultural credit. Congress immediately passed the Federal Farm Loan Act (1933), authorizing Federal Land Banks to issue bonds up to $2,000,000,000 to refinance farm loans, and the COMMODITY CREDIT CORPORATION began lending money directly to farmers. In 1934 the Farm Mortgage Refinancing Act established the Federal Farm Mortgage Corporation within the Farm Credit Administration as a further aid to farmers. Similar in purpose was the Frazier-Lemke Act (1935), which provided a three-year moratorium against seizure of farm property. In the same decade, to cope with the problems of tenant farmers and sharecroppers, Congress authorized the FARM SECURITY ADMINISTRATION. Since 1939 all Federal farm agencies have functioned within the Department of Agriculture.

Farm Security Administration (1937), established by the Bankhead-Jones Farm Tenant Act, was designed to cope with the steady decline in U.S. farm ownership and the increase in the number of TENANT FARMERS and SHARECROPPERS. Against repeated opposition from southern conservatives, the FSA shaped a program which regulated the supply, wages, and hours of migrant workers, and helped to develop co-operative homestead communities. It took over the work of the Resettlement Administration (1935), which was assisting tenants to become farm owners through easy, long-term loans, and guiding them in matters of soil erosion control, land reclamation, and reforestation. Nearly 40,000 families were thus able to buy farms.

FARMER, FANNIE MERRITT (1857–1915), a graduate of the Boston Cooking School (1889), in 1902 opened Miss Farmer's School of Cookery. As 'the mother of level measurements,' she emphasized accuracy in recipe directions. Her text, *The Boston Cooking School Cook Book* (1896), many times re-edited and translated, still remains standard, and has attained a sale of some 3,000,000 copies.

FARMER, MOSES GERRISH (1820–93), New Hampshire-born inventor, helped build some of the first telegraph lines in Massachusetts. He installed in Boston (1851) the first electric fire-alarm service in any city. Twenty years before Edison, he produced electric lamps (1858–59), and in 1868, with a dynamo of his own invention, he lighted a house, but he never succeeded in perfecting a marketable bulb. He was an electrician for the U.S. Torpedo Station at Newport, Rhode Island (1872–81), and is credited with greatly advancing the art of torpedo warfare.

Farmer-Labor party, formed in 1920 by former members of the older PROGRESSIVE PARTY, was chiefly represented by farmer and labor leaders of the Midwest. It advocated government ownership of public utilities, establishment of government banks, farm-relief measures, and forward-looking labor legislation. Though its candidate for President (P. P. Christensen of Utah) polled a relatively small vote, the party continued to be strong in the West, especially in Minnesota and the Dakotas. In 1924 it joined the La Follette PROGRESSIVE PARTY, and some of its reform measures were incorporated in modified form in the early New Deal legislation.

Farmers' Alliance was the name commonly given to either or both of two powerful agricultural organizations which carried forward (during the 1880's and 1890's) the agrarian revolt after the decline of the GRANGER MOVEMENT. Local organizations were consolidated into two powerful groups. The National Farmers' Alliance (the Northern Alliance) was organized in the farming states of the West from Ohio to the Dakotas. The Farmers' Alliance and Industrial Union (the Southern Alliance) drew its membership from farmers in the Louisiana, Arkansas, and Texas region. Both groups were major political forces in their regions. Their programs for improving farm conditions were nearly identical, but sectional differences frustrated all efforts to amalgamate them. As social organizations they sponsored outings, and their circulating libraries, farm newspapers and magazines made them, in the words of one observer, the farmers' 'national university.' Through their thousands of farmers' exchanges and their cooperative marketing they prospered economically, conducting a business estimated at its peak to exceed $10,000,000 annually.

The historical significance of the Farmers' Alliance derives from its political activities. In general it sought to curb railroad abuses, regulate public utilities, and secure government relief for mortgage indebtedness. Its so-called Sub-Treasury scheme, designed as a measure to gain government support for financing crops, was considered quixotic at the time, but it was adopted as national policy under the WAREHOUSE ACT of 1916. In 1892 the Alliance identified itself with the POPULIST PARTY, whose failure to maintain party unity led to the debacle of both the Alliance and Populist movements, and to an abiding distrust of direct political action by farm organizations.

See S. J. Buck, *The Agrarian Crusade* (1919), and J. D. Hicks, *The Populist Revolt* (1931).

Farmers' associations, see *Granger movement, Farmers' Alliance, Greenback party, Greenback-Labor party, Populist party, Farmer-Labor party.*

Farmers' Non-Partisan League was organized in North Dakota during the Wilson administration to seek legislation for farm relief. In 1916 the League gained control of the government of North Dakota, and by 1920 had spread into fifteen states of the West so effectively that law enactments of a far-reaching nature had provided for state-owned warehouses and grain elevators, insurance benefits, a Home Building Association, and tax readjustments. Such laws, which resembled the Granger and Populist laws of the 1880's, were denounced in the East as 'class' legislation, on the ground that they were not national in character.

Farming, see *Agriculture.*

FARRAGUT, DAVID GLASGOW (1801–70), born in Tennessee, at the age of nine began his naval career as a midshipman on the *Essex,* which was commanded by his guardian, DAVID PORTER. At the outbreak of the Civil War he remained loyal to the Union he had served so long. He first distinguished himself as a national hero when in April 1862, with a fleet of eight steam sloops-of-war and fifteen gunboats, he ran the gauntlet of New Orleans defenses and captured the city. His control of the Mississippi north to Vicksburg contributed to Grant's success in the VICKSBURG CAMPAIGN. In August 1864 his celebrated defeat of a Confederate flotilla in Mobile Bay ('Damn the torpedoes') effectively ended blockade-running there. Easily the outstanding naval commander of the war, he was raised to the newly created ranks of rear admiral (1862), vice admiral (1864), and admiral (1866).

Fast days, or Days of Humiliation, in colonial New England were fixed and official observances, marked by church services and abstinence from secular pursuits. They were decreed upon any public loss or affliction, and during periods of political or social commotion. Since they were looked upon as a means of 'renewing' the church covenant, they contributed to the growth of revivalism. They gradually became habitual, and eventually were established as annual events. They extended into the Revolutionary period, when they were used by the clergy, the states, and the Continental Congress as an effective means to rouse patriot sentiment.

Father of His Country, sobriquet first applied to Washington in Francis Bailey's *Nord Americanische Kalender* in 1779 (Lancaster, Pa.), was applied to the General in many of the adulatory addresses at the time he resigned his commission in 1783. It has persisted ever since.

'Father of Waters' (Mississippi river) is an incorrect translation of the Algonquian *misi sipi* (great water). The term, first heard by the French in the upper reaches, came to designate the entire system.

FAULKNER, WILLIAM [HARRISON] (1897–1962), was a lifelong resident of Oxford, Mississippi, and from his experience and memories created his mythical Yoknapatawpha County, a carefully mapped enclave which was the locale of his most important fiction. Faulkner is a social historian in the sense that the events which occur and the emotions they arouse in the Sartoris clan are based on his knowledge of his great-grandfather, Colonel William Falkner, the original of John Sartoris. The various stories, from *Sartoris* (1929) to *Intruder in the Dust* (1948), weave the genealogies and chronicles of families whose sagas have made up the history of the county from the days of the Chicasaw Indians to the present.

Faulkner's fictional canvas is large; it depicts the break-up of a feudal society of landed gentry and their slaves. Crass newcomers water down old codes and old moralities, and the fortunes of the black and white descendants of this Deep South region are interwoven with compassion.

The development of Faulkner's art was rapid, but so slow was the growth of his reputation that in 1945 all seventeen of his books were out of print in the U.S. The Nobel Prize in literature awarded him in 1949 made his countrymen aware of the esteem in which he was held internationally. At the time of his death Faulkner dominated American fiction, and he had been accorded rank as one of the most fertile masters of his art in the 20th century.

'Favorite son' is a political candidate who has the voting support of his own state delegates at a national convention, but is not well known elsewhere. As a 'presidential possibility' he is chiefly benefited by early recognition as a national favorite, but his main strength lies in his ability to influence the final nomination by transferring the support of his followers to another candidate.

Federal agencies, to execute the laws passed by Congress, have multiplied especially since passage of the Executive Reorganization Act of 1949, pursuant to the report of the HOOVER COMMISSION (1947), which recommended changes to effect a more orderly grouping of government functions and services. In addition to the eight EXECUTIVE AGENCIES, which are presidential advisory boards, are such agencies as the General Services Administration (1949), a governmental 'housekeeping' organization; the Small Business Administration (1953), to promote research and offer counsel; the U.S. Information Agency (1953), to coordinate intelligence distributed in foreign countries; the Commission on Civil Rights (1957), to report on alleged violation of the franchise rights of citizens;

and the Federal Aviation Agency (1958), to supervise civil aeronautics. Older agencies include the CIVIL SERVICE COMMISSION, FEDERAL REGULATORY COMMISSIONS, and the VETERANS ADMINISTRATION.

Federal aid, grants made directly or indirectly to the states, until recently nearly always in the form of land grants, has been forthcoming from the earliest years of the Republic for a variety of purposes, most notably to improve education and assist in extending transportation facilities. In 1785 a portion of the NORTHWEST TERRITORY was set aside 'for the use of schools' by the Congress of Confederation, and after Ohio was admitted to the Union in 1802, Congress regularly made a practice of granting new states a portion of public lands within their boundaries, proceeds from the sale of which were to be used for education. The MORRILL LAND GRANT ACT (1862), with similar purpose, was extended by the HATCH ACT (1887), the SMITH-LEVER ACT (1914), and the SMITH-HUGHES ACT (1917). The numerous grants made before 1860 to the states for turnpikes, canals, and railways furnished precedent for the Federal Aid Road Act (1916), which, with successive extensions, aided postal RURAL FREE DELIVERY. In recent years Federal grants to states for welfare aid, disaster aid, and for the construction of interstate turnpikes have aggregated several billion dollars. The most sweeping example of Federal aid for roads was Eisenhower's Interstate and Defense Highway Act of 1956, in which the federal government contributed nine times the amount granted by each co-operating state for these roads. It was justified on the grounds of national defense, highway safety, and economic growth. In 1963 Congress passed the COLLEGE AID ACT, providing Federal grants and loans directly to colleges. Both Presidents Kennedy and Johnson stressed the Federal grant and matching system in their vocational and educational retraining programs to cope with AUTOMATION and regional poverty, as well as in scientific or scholarly subsidies.

Federal Arts Project, inaugurated in 1935 as part of the WORKS PROJECTS ADMINISTRATION, employed hundreds of artists to decorate public buildings (especially post offices) with murals, circulate art exhibits, teach art appreciation, and compile a vast record of American folk art. Musical performances under the project came to average 4000 a month. Its significance stemmed not only from its accomplishments but from public recognition of the fact that artists could make a contribution to society and that society, in turn, had a responsibility to art. The Project ceased when WPA was abolished in 1942.

Federal Bureau of Investigation (F.B.I.), division of the U.S. Department of Justice, was created (1908) to conduct investigations solely for the Justice Department. After the appointment (1924) of J. EDGAR HOOVER as director, the Bureau gradually added other duties. Reorganized in 1933 with wider powers, it was charged with investigating violations of Federal laws. The F.B.I. currently handles alleged violation of some 120 Federal statutes, including those pertaining to kidnapping, bank robberies, and narcotics traffic. It is responsible for the internal security of the U.S. in matters of sabotage, conspiracy, and treason. Its Identification Division has some 150,000,000 fingerprint cards on file.

Federal Child Labor Law (Keating-Owen Act), see *Hammer* v. *Dagenhart.*

Federal Communications Commission, established as an independent executive agency by the Federal Communications Act of 1934, replaced the Federal Radio Commission (1927). It consists of a board of seven members, appointed by the President with the consent of the Senate. The Commissioners serve seven-year terms, and have jurisdiction over all communication systems: cable, telephone, telegraph, radio, and television industries. The FCC is a quasi-judicial agency with plenary administrative powers, including the issuance of rules, the holding of hearings, and determination of final orders.

Federal Constitution, see *Constitution of the U.S.*

Federal Constitutional Convention (25 May–17 September 1787) was called by

Congress at the invitation of the ANNAPOLIS CONVENTION. It met in the State House (Independence Hall) at Philadelphia to draw up a plan of government to supersede the ARTICLES OF CONFEDERATION. All the states except Rhode Island sent representatives to it, and George Washington presided. It was a notable assemblage of 55 delegates, including Benjamin Franklin, Robert Morris, James Wilson, Gouverneur Morris (Pennsylvania); George Mason, Edmund Randolph, James Madison, George Wythe (Virginia); Elbridge Gerry, Rufus King (Massachusetts); Oliver Ellsworth, Roger Sherman (Connecticut); Charles Pinckney, Charles Cotesworth Pinckney (South Carolina); William Paterson (New Jersey); Alexander Hamilton (New York); and John Dickinson (Maryland).

The principal issue of legislative representation concerned the Large-State or RANDOLPH PLAN, offered by Governor Randolph of Virginia, proposing leadership based on wealth and population, and the Small-State or PATERSON PLAN, offered by William Paterson, recommending equal representation of states in Congress. Since neither the large nor the small states would yield, for a time the convention was threatened with dissolution. In mid July Ellsworth offered the CONNECTICUT COMPROMISE, which gradually won approval by its provision that a lower house would be elected according to population and an upper house would give equal representation to every state, regardless of size.

The convention then proceeded to the Great Debate (6 August–10 September) about specific provisions: the extent and limits of Federal power, checks and balances in the branches of government, the length of terms in office for the President and members of the two houses, and other details. The debate concluded, the instrument was drafted and examined clause by clause. Of the 42 delegates then present 39 signed the draft. (Gerry and Mason abstained because it then lacked a Bill of Rights, Randolph because he preferred his own plan.) The convention formally adjourned on 17 September after submitting the final copy of the Constitution to Congress.

See Max Farrand, *The Framing of the Constitution of the U.S.* (1913); Carl Van Doren, *The Great Rehearsal* (1948); and Broadus and Louise Mitchell, *A Biography of the Constitution of the United States* (1964).

Federal Corrupt Practices Act, see *Hatch Act of 1939.*

Federal Council of Churches, see *National Council of Churches.*

Federal Deposit Insurance Corporation, created by the GLASS-STEAGALL ACT of 1933, was chartered to insure deposits up to a fixed sum in member banks of the Federal Reserve System. This Federal guarantee of deposits is administered through a bipartisan board of two directors plus the Comptroller of the Currency. The Corporation is empowered to act as receiver of closed banks, adopt measures to avoid improper banking practices, and facilitate bank mergers.

Federal Emergency Relief Administration (1933–35) sought to alleviate the condition of some 15,000,000 unemployed, victims of the Great Depression. Under the authority of Harry L. Hopkins it appropriated $500,000,000 for direct emergency relief to state and local agencies, to whom eventually it granted $3,000,000,000. The work of FERA was concluded by passage of the SOCIAL SECURITY ACT.

Federal Government, the form of organization adopted by the states in the Federal Constitution of 1789, is a plan of governance which delegates certain powers to a central government and specifically or by implication reserves other powers to the sovereign states. To this end, the rights of the states were carefully preserved in the Constitution, insofar as such rights might not infringe upon the welfare and safety of the national body.

The framers of the Constitution, seeking to prevent any one branch of the federal government from becoming absolute, provided for a system of CHECKS AND BALANCES (SEPARATION OF POWERS). The departments of the government are thus independently administered: the executive by the President, the legislative by Congress, and the judicial by the Supreme Court. The Constitution specifies and limits the function of each department, lest the liberties of the people be endangered. Inasmuch as a separation of powers principle generally requires an outside authority or influence to make the legislative and executive branches of government work harmoniously, POLITICAL PARTIES developed, which acted as unifying forces.

Federalism in the U.S. has developed parallel to a presidential form of government, in which the President, as elected directly by the people, is expected to influence Congress as a spokesman for the nation as a whole. This executive leadership has come to be the dominant feature of the American Federal system. The Civil War and the growth of a national economy weakened the old states' rights in favor of centralization. Although the states actually have more powerful functions than ever, the advance of centralization, accelerated by the New Deal measures of the 1930's, continues steadily.

Federal Housing Administration (1934) was created by act of Congress to help home owners finance repairs and to stimulate residential construction through Federal mortgages. The Act increased the borrowing power of the HOME OWNERS' LOAN CORPORATION, and by 1940 FHA had covered over $4,000,000,000 in mortgages. Home building was suspended during World War II, but resumed on a large scale after 1950.

Federal Music Project, see *Work Projects Administration.*

Federal Power Commission, established by the Water Power Act (1920), is headed by the Secretaries of War, Interior, and Agriculture, and empowered to develop facilities (dams, reservoirs, transmission lines) on navigable streams. The Commission was an important step in the CONSERVATION MOVEMENT.

Federal Register, official journal of the U.S. government, was authorized by Congress in 1935 as a daily record of executive and administrative orders. It includes such documents as the President may direct or Congress may require to be published, and is edited and distributed in the Division of the Federal Register, National Archives.

Federal regulatory commissions had their inception when the CIVIL SERVICE COMMISSION was established (1883) to administer a merit system in the federal government. The development of such agencies has advanced to a point where by mid-20th century they had in effect become a fourth branch of the executive, legislative, and judicial powers of government. More than 60 independent regulatory agencies in 1965 were employing a personnel of 400,000, and were supported by Congress with a total annual budget of $10,000,000,000.

Many of them exercise quasi-judicial powers, in that they first promulgate regulations which have the force and effect of law, then later adjudicate them. Wide-reaching in their powers are the INTERSTATE COMMERCE COMMISSION (1887), the first effective administrative board; the FEDERAL RESERVE SYSTEM (1913); the FEDERAL TRADE COMMISSION (1914); the FEDERAL POWER COMMISSION (1920); the TENNESSEE VALLEY AUTHORITY (1933); the FEDERAL COMMUNICATIONS COMMISSION (1934); and the ATOMIC ENERGY COMMISSION (1946). Congress entrusts vast powers to these commissions to mediate the claims of rival interests. The procedure of selection to membership is intended to be as free as possible from partisan politics.

Federal Reserve System, established by the Owen-Glass Act (1913), was the first thorough overhauling of the national banking system after the Civil War. Lack of central banking during the period 1863–1913 had made the U.S., in the judgment of a foreign central banker, a great financial nuisance. Bank notes fluctuated in value, financial panics could not be controlled, and stock speculation gravitated to powerful private banks. Creation of the Federal Reserve System substantially carried out President Wilson's program for the banking and currency reform that Wilson outlined to Congress. He asked for a currency elastically responsible to sound credit, with a system not controlled by the decisions of private banks, thus making banks the instruments, not the masters, of business.

The unique national bank thus created was a bank for banks, co-ordinated by a central board in Washington. It consists of twelve regional banks in Boston, New York, Philadelphia, Richmond, Atlanta, St. Louis, Chicago, Cleveland, Minneapolis, Kansas City, Dallas, and San Francisco. Each district has a depository Reserve Bank. To them member banks subscribe to the central system 6 per cent of their capital. These depositories do not engage directly in banking, but act as agents for all national banks and for member state banks and trust companies. Within ten years one-third of the banks of the country, with 70 per cent of the banking resources, were members of the System. They thus replaced the so-called subtreasuries, the national finance disbursing agencies abolished in 1920. At present the Federal Reserve System holds more than 90 per cent of the loans and securities of all insured commercial banks.

The Board of Governors of the FCS, composed of seven members appointed by the President for fourteen-year terms, is authorized to raise or lower the rediscount rate prevailing at the district reserve banks for lending money to member banks on security, and thus directly controls the money supply. The district banks are governed by a board of nine directors, three chosen by the national board. The System's currency is based upon approved rediscount paper deposited by member banks, and against such paper the reserve banks issue Federal Reserve notes (government obligations) as part of the circulating money supply. The System's control over credit and currency has thus become a powerful influence on the nation's economic life, since it operates as an open market for the purchase and sale of large amounts of securities. Its power to raise or lower the gold reserve requirements for note issues is a major factor in credit stability.

Federal Securities Act, see *Securities and Exchange Commission.*

Federal theology, see *Puritanism.*

Federal Trade Commission (1914), created by act of Congress as a part of President Wilson's trust regulation program, was designed to prevent unfair methods of competition in interstate commerce. The nonpartisan commission, consisting of five members appointed by the President for seven-year terms, is empowered to demand annual reports from corporations and to investigate business practices. It is required to investigate and control monopolistic practices, and to prevent the mislabeling or adulteration of commodities, the establishment of combinations for maintaining resale prices, and the making of false claims to patents. Though the FTC is intended to prevent rather than to punish, it is authorized to issue 'cease and desist' orders against corporations found guilty of malpractices. Before 1920 it issued nearly 400 such orders, and its subsequent investigations led to more adequate regulation of public utilities.

Federal Works Agency (1939), established by executive order, became the over-all supervisory policy-making body controlling the functions of its constituent bodies. It administers Federal highway funds, co-ordinates Federal housing activities, and supervises maintenance of U.S. government buildings. It absorbed such relief agencies as WORKS PROJECTS ADMINISTRATION, and PUBLIC WORKS ADMINISTRATION.

Federal Writers' Project, see *Works Projects Administration.*

Federalism, see *Federal Government.*

Federalist Papers are the unique collection of 85 essays gathered and published as *The Federalist* (2 vols., 1788). Seventy-seven of the *Papers* originally appeared in New York newspapers (1787–88) over the signature 'Publius,' and eight were added later. Probably 50 of the essays were written by Alexander Hamilton, some 30 by James Madison, and about 5 by John Jay. They urged adoption of the Federal Constitution, which at that time was before the states for ratification, by stressing the inadequacy of the Articles of Confederation and expounding the principles of republican government embodied in the instrument under consideration. They were widely reprinted in newspapers elsewhere.

Notable as a profound treatise on political science, the *Federalist Papers* were of crucial importance in the founding of the American nation, for they shaped public opinion and won support for the document that became the basic law of the land. Thomas Jefferson pronounced them 'the best commentary on the principles of government which has ever been written.' Justice Joseph Story called them 'incomparable,' and Chancellor James Kent thought them superior to Montesquieu, Milton, Locke, and Burke. As a commentary on the Constitution, again and again they have furnished the abstract principles to which the Supreme Court has resorted for an analysis of government function. Thus they have guided the interpretation of the Constitution itself. In the famous Tenth Number, Madison argues that government must reconcile through a system of CHECKS AND BALANCES the claims of conflicting interest groups into which all societies have been divided of necessity in civilized nations.

Federalist party was organized during the first administration of Washington by men who favored a strong Federal union. The political division in Washington's cabinet shaped itself into the Federalist group, headed by Alexander Hamilton, and the Anti-Federalist DEMOCRATIC-REPUBLICAN group, supporters of Thomas Jefferson, who thought in terms of individual liberties and an agrarian society. Federalists were the majority party in the Senate from 1791 through Adams's administration (1801), and controlled the House during the same period with the exception of the third Congress (1793–95).

Drawn largely from the well-established merchant class and property owners of the North, the Federalists were conservative and looked favorably upon a commercial and industrial expansion. In foreign affairs they were pro-British. The Federalist debacle in the election of 1800, following passage of the ALIEN AND SEDITION ACTS, foreshadowed the end of the party, thereafter led by reactionary New Englanders. During the troubled period culminating in the War of 1812, merchants and shipowners of the North expressed their feelings by opposition to the EMBARGO ACT of 1807, and a disgruntled rump, the ESSEX JUNTO, contemplated secession. The successful prosecution of the war, and the shift of national interest to new issues, outmoded a party which was already moribund. Its last presidential candidate, Rufus King of New York, in the election of 1816 polled only 34 electoral votes, and Monroe was swept into office by a count of 162. But as a minority party, the Federalists continued to elect members to both houses of Congress through Monroe's second term (1821–25), after which the party expired.

See John C. Miller, *The Federalist Era, 1789–1801* (1960); and Shaw Livermore, Jr., *The Twilight of Federalism, 1815–1830* (1962).

FEKE, ROBERT (*fl.* 1741–50), self-taught portrait painter, although his origin and end are unknown, was probably born in America. His figures are flat and lack individuality, but he shows a feeling for tone, observable in the texture of the accurately reproduced costumes. His services were in demand in the chief cities, especially in Boston. He is characteristically represented by *Unknown Lady* (Brooklyn Museum).

Feminism as a reform movement to give women educational, social, and political equality with men, took shape late in the 18th century after publication of the notable *Vindication of the Rights of Woman* (1792) by the English feminist Mary Wollstonecraft. The agitation for political rights of women by MERCY WARREN and Abigail Adams (who urged that the Constitution specifically incorporate such rights) was treated with polite condescension. EMMA WILLARD, a pioneer in feminine education, opened her seminary at Middlebury, Vermont, in 1814, and the opportunity of higher education for women was well advanced when MARY LYON established Mount Holyoke Seminary (1837) in the same year that Oberlin College gave the first college degree to a woman. *Woman in the Nineteenth Century* (1845), by MARGARET FULLER, was an early study of feminism.

The injustice of discriminating against women in abolition organizations led the GRIMKÉ sisters, Sarah and Angelina, to work for the rights of women as well as the rights of the Negro. LUCY STONE was a pioneer worker for women's suffrage, and the movement became predominantly political when LUCRETIA MOTT and ELIZABETH CADY STANTON initiated the first convention for women's rights (1848) in the U.S. The most notable 19th-century leader in the U.S. was SUSAN B. ANTHONY, whose labors were vindicated (1920) by adoption of the Nineteenth Amendment to the Constitution, giving women the right to vote.

See also *Woman Suffrage Movement, Women's Clubs, Women's Educational Movement.*

Fenian uprising (1866–70) was a phase in the republican revolutionary movement in Ireland. Rival secret Irish brotherhoods in New York City mapped plans to seize Canada and hold it as hostage for Irish freedom. The first invasion (April 1866) was nipped by Federal authorities in Maine. Two months later 'General' John O'Neil crossed the Niagara river with several hundred armed Irishmen and fought the 'Battle of Limestone Ridge' with Canadian militiamen before fleeing back to New York state. The leaders were arrested, but promptly set free through political pressure. During the following three years the Fenians collected arms and money, and in the spring of 1870 again moved on Canada. This time U.S. marshals arrested the leaders in northern Vermont, and the 'armies' disintegrated. The episodes put Canada to some expense, for which she was never reimbursed by the U.S.

FENOLLOSA, ERNEST FRANCISCO (1853–1908), after graduation from Harvard (1874) spent twelve years (1878–90) as professor of political economy and of philosophy at Tokyo University. A pioneer in the study of Japanese art, he made himself such a connoisseur that the Japanese government appointed him imperial fine arts commissioner. On his return to Boston he became a prime mover of the great Japanese collection in the Boston Museum of Fine Arts, where he served as curator of the department of Oriental art (1890–96). Besides his own poetry and his translations of Oriental poems, he wrote the authoritative study *Epochs of Chinese and Japanese Art* (2nd ed., 1912).

FERMI, ENRICO (1901–54), Italian-born physicist, after teaching at the universities of Florence and Rome, became professor of physics at Columbia (1939–45) and Chicago (1945–54). In 1938 he received the Nobel Prize in physics for his work on radioactive substances. His early research (1934–38) and active participation (after 1938) in atomic energy problems materially aided in building the atomic bomb. The first to produce artificial radioactivity by bombarding atomic nuclei with neutrons, he later turned his attention to high energy phenomena. He discovered element 93 (neptunium) and formulated the theory of beta-ray emission in radioactivity. His writings include *Thermodynamics* (1937) and *Elementary Particles* (1951).

FERREL, WILLIAM (1817–91), Pennsylvania-born meteorologist, after graduation from Bethany College, West Virginia, worked several years on the *Nautical Almanac,* and on the Coast and Geodetic Survey (1867–82). His meteorological research led him to formulate Ferrel's Law (1856), the theory of atmospheric circulation that expresses the fact that bodies on the earth's surface are deflected to the right in the Northern Hemisphere and to the left in the Southern Hemisphere. His extensive writings include *Tidal Researches* (1874) and *Meteorological Researches* (1875–81).

FESSENDEN, WILLIAM PITT (1806–69), a graduate of Bowdoin (1823), became one of the leading lawyers of Maine, where he helped organize the Republican party. Elected to the U.S. Senate (1854), he remained there until his death, except when he served for nine months (1864–65) as Lincoln's Secretary of the Treasury. His greatest service he performed as chairman of the joint Committee on Reconstruction, for he was a moderate among the RADICAL REPUBLICANS, and his refusal to vote for the impeachment of President Johnson (whom he disliked), though contrary to the expressed wishes of his constituency, was motivated by a high sense of duty.

F.F.V. (First Families of Virginia) was a term applied, somewhat satirically, in the North during the 19th century to

Virginia families proud of their descent from early aristocratic colonists. Actually very few of the great landowners could properly claim more than remote connections with the peerage. Most of them were of the English county squirearchy or prosperous merchant class.

FIELD, David Dudley (1805–94), born in Haddam, Connecticut, was the eldest of the distinguished sons of the Reverend David Dudley Field (1781–1867). After graduation from Williams (1825) he was admitted to the bar in New York City. He became nationally known for his arguments before the U.S. Supreme Court on issues of constitutional law, but his greatest achievement was his labor in behalf of law reform. The codes of civil procedure which he drew up were adopted in many states. His *Draft Outline of an International Code* (2 vols., 1872) strongly influenced the English Judicature Acts of 1873 and 1875.

A younger brother, Stephen Johnson Field (1816–99), likewise graduated from Williams (1837) and practiced law in New York with his elder brother before removing to California (1849). There he drafted codes of civil and criminal procedures that became the basis of mining law in the Far West. He was serving as chief justice (1859–63) of the California supreme court when President Lincoln appointed him to the bench of the U.S. Supreme Court, where he served for 34 years and seven months (1863–97), the longest term in the court's history. He backed his opinions with legal acumen, and as a believer in states' rights was a strict constructionist in matters concerning the implied powers of the Federal Constitution.

A third brother, Cyrus West Field (1819–92), settled in New York as merchant and financier. He promoted the laying of the first (unsuccessful) atlantic cable (1858), and the second, and permanent, cable (1866). His persistence in accomplishing what was judged to be impossible won him a vote of thanks from Congress and many other honors on both sides of the ocean. He later promoted the building of the New York City elevated railway system.

FIELD, Marshall (1834–1906), Massachusetts-born merchant, in 1865 became a partner in the Chicago dry goods firm of Field, Palmer and Leiter, the company which later (1881) became Marshall Field and Company, patronized especially by the carriage trade. Field was a pioneer in modern retailing practices. He organized buying agencies throughout the world, purchased the entire output of manufacturing plants, and established factories of his own. Eventually he amassed a large private fortune. His major philanthropies include donations to the Art Institute of Chicago and to the University of Chicago. In 1893 he endowed the Field Museum of Natural History (since 1943 the Chicago Natural History Museum).

FIELDS, W. C. (1879–1946), stage name of W. C. Dukenfield, made his Broadway appearance as comedian in such musical productions as the Ziegfeld *Follies* and Earl Carroll's *Vanities.* He later starred in motion pictures and on the radio, and was noted for his 'out-and-out crazy' brand of exaggeration.

Fifteenth Amendment to the U.S. Constitution (1870) states that the right of citizens to vote shall not be denied or abridged 'on account of race, color, or previous condition of servitude.' Although intended to confer the right to vote on the Negro, it continued for nearly a century to be a guarantee on paper only, since several southern states by law prescribed poll tax, resident and registration requirements, and literacy tests. Passage of the civil rights acts in the 1960's outlawed such practices.

Fifth Amendment to the U.S. Constitution, adopted in 1791, guarantees that no person shall be tried for a capital crime unless indicted by a grand jury, bans double jeopardy, provides that no person may be deprived of life, liberty, or property without due process of law, and that private property cannot be taken for public use without just compensation. It is best known for its provision that no person may be forced to be a witness against himself in a criminal case. Even though the language of the Amendment makes no distinction between Federal and state cases, the Supreme Court has consistently held that the Amendment does not protect a witness in a state criminal case, since the states are free to adopt their own constitutional provisions. The Court has done so in the belief that the framers of the BILL OF RIGHTS intended such restrictions to extend only to the federal government.

Fifth column, as a term, was first used during the Spanish Civil War (1936–39) by General Mola, who stated in a broadcast that he had four columns of soldiers advancing on Madrid, and a 'fifth column' within the city, sympathizers who would assist the invading army. The term came into wide use at the beginning of World War II, when the Germans invaded Western Europe.

Fifty-four forty or fight was an aggressive slogan adopted by extremists in the OREGON BOUNDARY DISPUTE. It was not used, as has been often alleged, by the Democrats during the presidential campaign of 1844, but became popular after Polk's election.

Filibuster, in U.S. politics, is the attempt by a member of a deliberative body to obstruct action on a bill by the use of delaying tactics, such as speaking to consume time. The term refers especially to the almost unlimited debate allowed in the U.S. Senate. Although that body adopted in 1917 a modified form of CLOSURE, the tradition of unlimited debate is so strong in the Senate that closure is seldom invoked, and a determined minority, skillfully led, can generally force some kind of compromise.

Filibustering in U.S. history refers to the acts of buccaneers who, in the 19th century, organized and led (under private initiative) armed attacks against a country at peace with the U.S. While still a part of Mexico, Texas was a scene of filibustering activities. JOHN A. QUITMAN aided a filibustering expedition to Cuba in 1848, and WILLIAM WALKER led an abortive invasion of Lower California (1853–54). All such expeditions, usually an expression of southern expansionism, ultimately petered out.

FILLMORE, MILLARD (1800–74), 13th President of the U.S. (1850–53), was born in Cayuga county, New York. After a desultory education he was admitted to the bar and practiced law in Buffalo. As a protégé of Thurlow Weed, he was sent to the state assembly (1829–31) on the Anti-Masonic ticket. While serving in the U.S. House of Representatives (1833–35, 1837–43), he joined the Whig party (1834) and became its leader in the House. Defeated as Whig nominee for governor of New York (1844), with the backing of Henry Clay he was elected Vice President (1848) on the ticket with Zachary Taylor, and presided with notable fairness over the Senate during the turbulent debates of 1850.

On Taylor's death (9 July 1850) he succeeded to the presidency, signed the COMPROMISE OF 1850, and sought to enforce its fugitive slave provisions. He appointed Daniel Webster his Secretary of State, approved the treaty opening Japan to Western commerce, and by occupying a middle ground on the slavery issue tried to make the Whigs a national party. But the Whig nomination of 1852 was controlled by the antislavery faction, which ran General Winfield Scott as its candidate. Party division could not be stemmed, and Fillmore's political career virtually ended when he went out of office in 1853. He joined the KNOW-NOTHING PARTY and became its presidential candidate in the election of 1856, but he carried only the state of Maryland. He took no active part in Civil War issues and retired to obscurity.

FILSON, JOHN (*c.* 1747–88), Kentucky pioneer, wrote the first descriptive account of that region, *Discovery, Settlement, and Present State of Kentucke* (1784). Its famous appendix sets forth in orotund prose the 'autobiography' of Daniel Boone, who was so delighted with the portrait that he pronounced 'The Adventures of Col. Daniel Boone' true in every detail. The book went through many editions, and was chiefly responsible for the Boone legend in American history.

Fine arts, see *Architecture, Music, Painting,* and *Sculpture.*

FINK, MIKE (*c.* 1770–1822), was born in Pittsburgh. While serving as keelboatman on western rivers, he became a trapper and hunter on the first of the ASHLEY EXPEDITIONS (1822). He was killed in a brawl. The colorful tales about the incident, and Fink's reputation as narrator of 'tall tales,' have given him rank with Paul Bunyan in frontier legends.

FINNEY, CHARLES GRANDISON (1792–1875), Connecticut-born evangelist and educator, having been licensed as a Presbyterian minister (1824), became immensely successful as a revivalist. Adopting Congregationalism, he went to Oberlin College as a professor of theology (1837) and served there later as president (1851–65). His writings were widely influential in establishing the 'Oberlin theology' (a branch of the New School Calvinism), and he continued to be in great demand as a revival preacher in the U.S. and in England. His emphasis on 'disinterested benevolence' was a factor in shaping the many charitable enterprises of his day.

'Fire-eaters' were southern extremists who advocated secession during the 1850's. They included such hotheads as ROBERT RHETT, EDMUND RUFFIN, and WILLIAM YANCEY. Distrusted by moderates (whom they bored, as well), they seldom were given positions of responsibility after the Confederacy was formed.

First Amendment to the U.S. Constitution, see *Bill of Rights.*

First in War, *First in Peace, and First in the Hearts of His Countrymen,* a phrase characterizing Washington, was part of the resolution written by R. H. Lee and offered by John Marshall in Congress on the occasion of the death of Washington.

First Lady, unofficial title of the President's wife or his designated hostess, gained currency after it was applied to Lucy Webb Hayes in an account of the inauguration of President Hayes (1877). A play (1911) about Dolly Madison by C. F. Nirdlinger was titled *The First Lady of the Land.*

FISH, HAMILTON (1808–93), lawyer and statesman, was the son of Nicholas Fish (1758–1833), a leading Federalist and founder of a family long prominent in New York politics and society. (The son was named for his father's close friend, Alexander Hamilton.) After graduation from Columbia (1827), Hamilton Fish practiced law and entered politics as a Whig, serving as U.S. Representative (1843–45), as lieutenant governor (1847–48), and as governor (1849–50) of New York. A moderate antislavery supporter, while in the U.S. Senate (1851–57) he moved into the Republican party.

He was engaged in private and civil affairs in New York City when President Grant selected him as Secretary of State, an office he conducted with patience and tact through both of Grant's administrations (1869–77). Respected for his probity and political discernment, he proved himself one of the ablest men who have guided American foreign policy. His greatest achievement as Secretary was the liquidation of all outstanding diplomatic controversies with Great Britain, secured by the WASHINGTON TREATY of 1871. He kept filibustering expeditions from the U.S. to Cuba at a minimum, and by his adroit handling of the VIRGINIUS AFFAIR (1873) he averted an unnecessary war with Spain. After 1877 he retired to private life.

See Allan Nevins, *Hamilton Fish: The Inner History of the Grant Administration* (1936).

Fisheries off the Newfoundland coast were known to seafaring Europeans early in the 16th century, but not until the period of settlements did fishing along the North American coast become commercially important. The successful fishing venture of JOHN SMITH in 1614 off New England helped establish that region as a fishing ground, and before the 18th century Boston was a busy trade center for cod and mackerel. The largest fishing grounds in the North Atlantic are in fact off the Canadian shore, and have long attracted American and European fishing fleets. The most valuable yields of American waters are oyster, lobster, and crab on the Eastern seaboard, and salmon, sardine, and tuna on the Pacific. By 1900 San Francisco had become one of the great fishing centers in the world. Fishing rights along the entire Atlantic coast were confirmed to the American colonies in the TREATY OF PARIS of 1783, but the Treaty was abrogated by the British upon the outbreak of the War of 1812. The prolonged friction that developed between Canada and the U.S. on fishing rights was not finally settled until 1910, when the issue was arbitrated at The Hague. (WHALING, from colonial times the source of fuel and tallow, virtually ceased with the development of the petroleum industry.)

FISK, JAMES (1834–72), Vermont-born 'robber baron' of the Gilded Age, gained wealth during the Civil War by trading cotton purchased in occupied areas of the South, and by selling Confederate bonds in England. A notorious New York broker and stock gambler, with Jay Gould he engaged in buccaneering exploits which made them fortunes, and helped to engineer the events that involved the U.S. Treasury in the BLACK FRIDAY scandal of 1869. The subsequent career of 'Jubilee Jim' as steamboat operator, Hudson river 'admiral,' militia colonel, theatrical producer, and *bon vivant,* ended abruptly when he was shot by a rival for his current mistress, the actress Josie Mansfield.

Fisk University (est. 1866), Negro liberal arts institution at Nashville, Tennessee, was chartered by the American Missionary Association. In addition to its college department it embraces a preparatory department, and departments of theology, teacher training, and music. Since 1871 it has been noted for its Jubilee Singers. In 1965, with a faculty of 67, it enrolled 900 students.

FISKE, JOHN (1842–1901), Connecticut-born historian and philosopher, after graduation from Harvard (1863) devoted himself to lecturing and writing. The leading American exponent and popularizer of Darwinism, Fiske attempted to reconcile religion with Spencerian evolution in such studies as *The Outlines of Cosmic Philosophy* (2 vols., 1874), *Darwinism and Other Essays* (1879), and *The Destiny of Man* (1884), works that brought theological liberalism into open conflict with orthodoxy. He vitalized early American history, stressing the European genesis of American institutions in *The Beginnings of New England* (1889), and *The Discovery of America* (2 vols., 1892), applying the Comtean ideas of sociological evolution to American history.

Although not an original thinker, Fiske was a cultural force and the most popular American historian of his day. He wrote with style and movement, and despite his superficiality he influenced historians for a time to accept the 'Cavalier' legend of southern society. Many historians still cling to his theory that the span 1783–89 was the 'critical period' in the founding of the new nation.

FISKE, MINNIE MADDERN (1865–1932), born in New Orleans, for 25 years was the acknowledged leader of the American stage. A star at fifteen, she was admired for her polished technique, and took rank as an interpreter of the intellectual drama. She helped introduce Ibsen to the U.S., and made a memorable tour in Sheridan's *Rivals* shortly before her death.

FITCH, JOHN (1743–98), Connecticut-born inventor, began work in Pennsylvania on a steam engine (1785), and secured exclusive rights to operate steamboats on the inland waterways of New York and most of the Middle Atlantic states. He launched his first vessel, propelled by steam-driven oars, on the Delaware river in 1787, and is generally acknowledged as the inventor of the steamboat. Unable to gain financial backing, Fitch could not develop his invention commercially, and frustration drove him to suicide.

FITZHUGH, GEORGE (1806–81), Virginia lawyer, was the most influential pro-slavery propagandist in the decade before the Civil War. In his *Sociology for the South* (1854) he contended that the laissez-faire capitalism of the North had proved a failure, and in his tract *Cannibals All!* (1857) he justified the slave economy on the ground that the alternative is a cannibalistic system of laissez-faire society, as in the North or in England. Fitzhugh's writings and lectures embarrassed the moderate Southerners, angered Northerners, and were widely quoted for their contention that slavery, black or white, had been normal in history. Lincoln's 'House Divided' speech deliberately reversed Fitzhugh's argument that the slavery principle would inevitably win out everywhere. After the war Fitzhugh served the Freedmen's Bureau as an associate justice of the local Freedmen's Court, but he retained his anti-Negro prejudices.

FITZPATRICK, THOMAS (*c.* 1799–1854), Irish-born trapper and guide, was one of the notable MOUNTAIN MEN. He accompanied the first of the ASHLEY EXPEDITIONS (1823), with Jed Smith located SOUTH PASS (1824), and later became a senior partner of the Rocky Mountain Fur Company (1830–34). Fitzpatrick (whose Indian name was 'Broken Hand') served as guide for the expeditions of Frémont and Kearney. In 1846 he was appointed Indian agent for a large part of present Colorado and was successful in negotiating treaties, most notably the Treaty of Fort Laramie (1851), which permitted the establishment of forts and roads and provided territorial boundaries for Indian tribes.

Five civilized tribes is the term first officially applied in 1876 to those CHEROKEE, CREEK, CHOCTAW, CHICKASAW, and SEMINOLE Indian groups forcibly transferred from Georgia and the Gulf states to Indian Territory (Oklahoma) during the 1830's. By 1838 the 'Trail of Tears' was closed. The group adopted white laws and institutions and intermarried with whites and Negroes. Today it numbers some 65,000 persons.

Five Forks, Battle of, the last important engagement of the Civil War, was fought (1 April 1865) southwest of Petersburg, Virginia. The defeat of Lee's right (under Pickett) by two Union corps (under Sheridan) gave Grant the chance to penetrate the center of the Confederate defenses. It therefore led to the fall of Petersburg, the capture of Richmond, and the surrender (12 April) of Lee's army at Appomattox.

Five nations, see *Iroquois Confederacy*.

Flag Day (14 June), anniversary of the adoption (1777) of the American flag, was so designated in 1895. It has been observed by presidential proclamation since 1949, but it is a legal holiday only in Pennsylvania.

Flag of the U.S. (The Stars and Stripes, Old Glory) was designed according to a resolution of the Second Continental Congress (14 June 1777): 'That the flag of the U.S. be thirteen stripes, alternate red and white, that the union be thirteen stars, white in a blue field representing a new constellation.' The legend that Betsy Ross made the first national banner is generally discredited.

FLAGLER, HENRY MORRISON (1830–1913), in partnership with John D. Rockefeller and others, established a firm in Cleveland which became (1870) the STANDARD OIL COMPANY. During the 1890's he began large-scale development of Florida real estate, railroads, and hotels, and was chiefly responsible for the early growth of Florida resort areas.

'Flapper,' a term originating in the U.S. about 1923, was applied to the young woman of the JAZZ AGE, who bobbed her hair and shortened her skirts, danced the CHARLESTON, smoked cigarettes in public, and sought to be otherwise unconventional with hectic gaiety. She has been memorably portrayed in the fiction of F. Scott Fitzgerald and the illustrations of John Held, Jr.

Flathead Indians, a small tribe of Salishan stock, in the early 19th century inhabited the Bitter Root river valley of western Montana. Unlike neighboring tribes, the Salishan never actually flattened their heads. In 1872 they were moved north to the lake and river bearing their name.

Fletcher* v. *Peck (1810), a case involving claims stemming from the YAZOO LAND FRAUDS, resulted in a unanimous U.S. Supreme Court decision, written by Chief Justice Marshall. An original land grant had been rescinded by the Georgia legislature because the grant had been fraudulently made. The Court held that the original grant was a contract within the meaning of the Constitution, and that the rescinding law was an impairment of the obligation of contracts, whatever the motive may have been. The case established a precedent by invalidating a state law as contrary to the Constitution.

FLEXNER, ABRAHAM (1866–1959), after graduation from Johns Hopkins (1886) and further study, joined the research staff of the Carnegie Foundation for the Advancement of Teaching. His most widely known work, the report on *Medical Education in the United States and Canada* (1910), gave impetus to important reforms in the curricula and standards of medical schools. In *Universities: American, English, and German* (1930) he criticized abuses of the elective system in the U.S., and the trend toward vocationalism. He served as secretary of the General Education Board (1917–25); and, as the first director of the newly organized Institute for Advanced Study, Princeton, New Jersey (1930–39), he profoundly influenced its plan and scope.

FLEXNER, SIMON (1863–1946), elder brother of ABRAHAM FLEXNER, received his medical training at Louisville (1889), and joined the staff of the Rockefeller Institute (1903), which he served for fifteen years as director (1920–35). His work in experimental epidemiology led to his discovery (1907) of a serum for treating cerebrospinal meningitis, and to his demonstration (1909) that poliomyelitis is caused by a virus.

FLINT, TIMOTHY (1780–1840), Massachusetts-born author and editor, after graduation from Harvard (1800) entered the ministry. The record of his missionary journeys in the Ohio and Mississippi valleys (1815–25) he set down in *Recollections of the Last Ten Years* (1826), a pioneer account of the West. The earliest and most prolific writer of western fiction, Flint wrote in the romantic vein of Chateaubriand, and in his day was widely read at home and abroad. The *Western Monthly Review,* which he founded and edited at Cincinnati (1827–30), sought to interpret the West to the East.

Flogging was a common form of punishment for criminals and fractious seamen into the 19th century, although Quakers discontinued its use much earlier on humanitarian grounds. The practice was outlawed in the U.S. navy and merchant marine by Congress in 1850. Flogging is still permitted in Delaware, and is used unofficially in some prisons to maintain discipline.

Flood control in the U.S. began in the colonial period with the construction of levees similar to those on such European rivers as the Danube and the Po. The alluvial plain along the lower Mississippi attracted settlers, but it was subject to periodic floods, and state (and later Federal) aid was needed to meet the mounting cost of construction and maintenance of levees. After 1879 the work of flood protection in the Mississippi valley was taken over by the federal government. Successive and increasingly devastating floods, as the eroded areas of the great central basin allowed heavier runoffs, required higher and higher levees, until in the 1920's a new system of protection had to be devised, not only for the great central continental basin, but for river systems everywhere throughout the U.S. Cutoffs and detention reservoirs on tributary rivers came into general use. The principle of a multipurpose project was first used on HOOVER DAM (1936) on the Colorado river. Since then it has been adopted for similar DAMS AND RESERVOIRS.

Florida was discovered and claimed (as an island) for Spain by PONCE DE LEÓN (April 1513), who named it for the Easter season (Pascua florida). Later explorers, notably NARVÁEZ and DE SOTO, determined the true geography of the region and applied the name to the vast stretches comprising most of the Southeast. Spanish colonization in Florida began with the founding of St. Augustine (1565), and though the soil proved relatively infertile, the Spanish held the region because it lay strategically above the Straits of Florida, through which sailed rich cargo bound for Spain.

The northern boundary was established (1742) when Oglethorpe of Georgia defeated the Spanish in the battle of Bloody Marsh. Seizure by England (1763), when Spain sided with France in the Seven Years' War, was followed by an influx of English settlers, and by the division into EAST FLORIDA and WEST FLORIDA. Both were returned to Spain by the terms of the TREATY OF PARIS of 1783, but the ADAMS-ONÍS TREATY (1819) provided for the sale of Florida to the U.S.

Organized as a territory in 1822, the region was beset by Indian wars. It was admitted to the Union (1845) as the

27th state, with Tallahassee as its capital, in the same year that the Seminole tribes were removed to Oklahoma. Florida seceded from the Union in January 1861, supported the Confederacy during the Civil War, suffered lightly during the Reconstruction era, and was readmitted to the Union in 1868.

Situated entirely within the temperate zone and influenced by the surrounding subtropical waters, Florida has been subject to periodic land booms, precipitated during the 20th century by an influx of winter and year-round residents attracted by the climate. Best known for its resorts and for the citrus fruits it produces, it also has a diversified economy that includes cattle raising and phosphate mining. The draining of the EVERGLADES (a national park since 1947) has contributed greatly to its recent development. The population of three major cities noticeably increased in the decade 1950–60: Miami, 125,000 to 275,000; Tampa, 125,000 to 275,000; St. Petersburg, 97,000 to 181,000. That of Jacksonville (201,000) slightly decreased. Best known among its several institutions of higher learning are the University of Florida (Gainesville, est. 1853), Rollins College (Winter Park, est. 1885), and the University of Miami (est. 1925).

Florida Treaty, see *Adams-Onís Treaty*.

Folger Shakespeare Library, in Washington, D.C., was established (1932) by Henry Clay Folger (1857–1930) and his wife Emily Jordan Folger (a Vassar graduate) to 'help make the U.S. a center for literary study and progress.' After graduation from Amherst (1879) Folger rose to be head of the Standard Oil Company of New York. In college he had been deeply influenced by Emerson, especially by Emerson's 'Remarks at the Celebration of the 300th Anniversary of the Birth of William Shakespeare.' Thereafter he began gathering books until he had assembled the world's largest collection of Shakespeareana. The library is a research institution centering on Anglo-American civilization in the 17th and 18th centuries, and the leading repository in the U.S. of material relating to the drama.

Folklore in the U.S., see *American Folk-Lore Society, Sam Bass, Tony Beaver, Billy the Kid, Daniel Boone, James Bridger, Paul Bunyan, Kit Carson, David Crockett, Mike Fink, Frontier, John Henry, Jesse James, Casey Jones, Pecos Bill, Spirituals, Tall Tales.*

FOLLEN, CHARLES (1796–1840), German-born educator, was dismissed from teaching posts at Jena (1818–20) and Basel (1820–23) for his political radicalism. He then joined the faculty of Harvard (1825), where he taught ethics and history, and there inaugurated the teaching of German. Influenced by the new German calisthenics, he introduced the first college gymnasium at Harvard, an example soon followed by Yale, Williams, Amherst, and Brown. His teaching career ended (1835) when his antislavery activities were not supported by the college. He devoted his remaining years to the Unitarian ministry and reform movements. His wife, Eliza Lee (Cabot) Follen (1787–1860), vigorously supported her husband's causes, and helped promote the education of women.

Follies, in the sense of alleged foolish undertakings, is a term applied in the U.S. to such enterprises as that of Robert Fulton, whose pioneer experiment in steam navigation, the *Clermont,* was called 'Fulton's folly.' The stone arch bridge designed and constructed (1832) by Benjamin H. Latrobe (1806–78) for the Baltimore and Ohio Railroad across the Patapsco river in Maryland was called 'Latrobe's folly' by contemporary engineers, who expected it to fall of its own weight. (The bridge proved to be eminently safe.) When Edward L. Drake tapped petroleum by drilling a well in western Pennsylvania (1859), his venture was ridiculed as 'Drake's folly.' Secretary of State Seward's purchase of Alaska (1867) was 'Seward's folly.' Longwood, the expensive 'great house' on the plantation of Dr. Haller Nutt, near Natchez, Mississippi, was a Moorish extravaganza only half completed at the outbreak of the Civil War. 'Nutt's folly' ended the opulent era of southern architecture.

Folsom culture, early North American culture existing 10,000 to 25,000 years ago, is known by artifacts first excavated (1926) near Folsom, New Mexico. The Folsom points, leaf-shaped flint projectiles (probably javelin heads), are found in association with other stone implements, and the remains of such extinct mammals as bison, camels, and mastodons. No identifiable human remains have been discovered, although sites are numerous elsewhere in the western U.S. and Canada.

Fontainebleau, Treaty of (1762), by the terms of which France ceded all of Louisiana west of the Mississippi to Spain, was repudiated by the secret Treaty of San Ildefonso (1800), and the retrocession was confirmed by the Treaty of Madrid (1801). Jefferson, alarmed after learning of the arrangements, began negotiations leading to the historic LOUISIANA PURCHASE (1803).

Football, as an amateur and professional spectator sport, is rivaled in the U.S. only by baseball. The first intercollegiate football match in America was played (1869) at New Brunswick, New Jersey, by Rutgers and Princeton. The rules drawn up in 1873 by Rutgers, Princeton, Columbia, and Yale laid the foundation for all subsequent matches. Coaching of teams became professional in the 1890's, and despite protests against the death toll of the game, football gained in popularity, with rules steadily reshaped for safety and sportsmanship by such athletic directors as WALTER CAMP and ALONZO STAGG.

The postseason Rose Bowl tournament (Pasadena) has been annual since 1916. Similar tournaments include the Sugar Bowl (New Orleans), the Orange Bowl (Miami), the Sun Bowl (El Paso), and the Cotton Bowl (Dallas). Organized professional football, dating from 1920, in recent years has gained immense popularity. During the 1920's college football became big business, with paid admissions to mammoth stadiums running into millions of dollars. The inevitable subsidizing of players by enthusiastic alumni became an open scandal, and colleges were repeatedly attacked for overemphasizing the sport. Steady effort has been exerted to regularize this unique American institution, created at its best by such athletic directors and coaches (following Camp and Stagg) as POP WARNER, KNUTE ROCKNE, and FRANK LEAHY. Probably the best known player was RED GRANGE.

See Allison Danzig, *The History of American Football* (1956).

Foraker Act, see *Puerto Rico.*

FORCE, PETER (1790–1868), New Jersey-born printer and historian, for many years issued in Washington, D.C., the *National Calendar* (14 vols., 1820–36), annual yearbook of statistical information with historical summaries. His *American Archives* (9 vols., 1837–53), authorized by Congress as a record of Federal affairs from 1774 to 1789, covers only the years 1774–76, since Secretary of State Marcy summarily refused to sanction further subsidy on the ground that the publication had no utility. Force's *Tracts and Other Papers Relating Principally to . . . North America* (4 vols., 1836–46; reissued 1947) are reprints of scarce colonial pamphlets. His important collection of more than 60,000 books and pamphlets was purchased by Congress in 1867, thus partially offsetting Marcy's blow to historical scholarship.

Force acts, so called, are various Federal statutes intended to implement previous laws, and all are sectional in character. That passed by Congress in 1833 empowered Jackson to override South Carolina's ORDINANCE OF NULLIFICATION. Similar were four acts of Congress (1870–75) intended primarily to compel recognition of the CIVIL RIGHTS ACT of 1866, and of the FOURTEENTH AMENDMENT. Eventually Congress repealed most of the later force acts, pursuant to decisions rendered by the Supreme Court in the CIVIL RIGHTS CASES (1883).

FORD, HENRY (1863–1947), born on a farm near Dearborn, Michigan, worked in Detroit (1879–86) as a machinist, and became an engineer with the Edison Company in 1887. He built a gasoline automobile in 1892, and organized (1903) the Ford Motor Company, which produced in 1908 the first 'Model T,' an inexpensive and dependable vehicle which ended the era of rural isolation, introduced factory assembly methods, and came to symbolize American industrial technique. He attracted national attention in 1914 by inaugurating a $5 minimum wage for an eight-hour day.

For some time he refused to alter the Model T, of which he had sold 15,000,000. Then, in 1927, he changed his mind and began manufacturing the Model A, but the delay had cost him the dominance of the market. Although his son, EDSEL BRYANT FORD (1893–1943), assumed the presidency of the company in 1918, Henry Ford remained the deciding power, and for a period of two years after Edsel's death he resumed presidency of the company. In 1945 he relinquished control to his grandson, HENRY FORD II (1917–).

An idealist of an eccentric variety, during World War I Henry Ford was so ardent in his isolationism that in 1915 he sponsored a peace expedition to Europe with the object of 'getting the boys out of the trenches by Christmas.' Ridicule curdled his idealism and may have sharpened his acumen. With Edsel he was able in 1936 to establish the FORD FOUNDATION, by far the world's largest philanthropic endowment. In World War II he turned out military airplanes in his great Willow Run plant, the nation's largest. Mercurial, always hostile to unions, and with few intellectual interests, Ford nevertheless was the genius whose $5 formula of 1914 has been termed 'the greatest single step in the history of wages.'

See Allan Nevins and F. E. Hill, *Ford: The Times, the Man, the Company* (3 vols., 1954–63).

Ford Foundation, established (1936) by Henry and Edsel Ford, administers funds on a worldwide scale for artistic, scientific, educational, and charitable purposes. By far the world's largest endowed FOUNDATION, in 1965 from assets of $2,400,000,000 it disbursed $250,000,000.

Fordham University, Catholic (Jesuit) institution established in New York City (1841) as St. John's College, was rechartered in 1905 under its present name. The eight schools of this largest Roman Catholic university in the world are College, Law, Pharmacy, Social Service, Business, Education, Graduate, and General Studies. In 1965, with a faculty of 485, it enrolled 10,340 students.

Fordney-McCumber Tariff Act (1922) established the highest tariff rates in U.S. history, with increases ranging from 60 to 400 per cent on some commodities. Economically it fostered the growth of monopolies, prevented repayment of European obligations in the form of goods, and provoked foreign tariff reprisals. Though the President was empowered to change tariffs as a way of equalizing the cost of American and foreign products, no effective executive action was taken in the next decade, and the slump in foreign trade was deepened by passage (1930) of the HAWLEY-SMOOT TARIFF ACT.

Foreign affairs, see *State, Department of; Foreign policy.*

Foreign observers who came to America during the 18th and 19th centuries in the course of some official or personal venture on occasion left interesting records of their impressions. The Swedish scientist PETER KALM during his three-year tour (1748–51) found Americans a fascinating miscellany, as did FRANCISCO DE MIRANDA, and the MARQUIS DE CHASTELLUX, traveling in the 1780's. CHATEAUBRIAND, briefly in America a decade later, influenced the entire romantic period with his image of the natural man and the noble savage.

During the 1820's the enthusiastic views of FRANCES WRIGHT were not shared by BASIL HALL or by FRANCES TROLLOPE, whose unflattering accounts were nonetheless widely discussed. The caustic judgments of HARRIET MARTINEAU and FREDERICK MARRYAT aroused deep resentment in the 1830's, but their observations did not begin to approach in importance those of MICHAEL CHEVALIER and of ALEXIS DE TOCQUEVILLE, whose *Democracy in America* (1835) still remains a classic study of American democratic ideas and practices. In the same decade the German prince MAXIMILIAN traveled in the Rocky Mountain region, and left a record chiefly important for the sketches made by the painter Karl Bodmer, who accompanied him.

Other Europeans who reported on their travels in the U.S. before the Civil War include CHARLES LYELL, JAMES BUCKINGHAM, FREDRIKA BREMER, T. C. GRATTAN, and (most indelibly) CHARLES DICKENS, whose strictures for a time put a strain on Anglo-American relations. Since then, studies of American society and institutions have been made by scores of foreign observers, frequently by the type of intellectual called the 'professional European,' who deplored the lack of a cultural tradition and the hectic pace of American living. The most penetrating analyses during the late 19th century are the observations of the French journalist PAUL BOURGET and the British historian JAMES BRYCE, whose study of American political systems, *The American Commonwealth* (1885), remains a classic.

Foreign policy, see *Adams-Onís Treaty, Caribbean policy, Expatriation, Freedom of the seas, Isolationism, League of Nations, Louisiana Purchase, Manifest Destiny, Marshall Plan, Mexican Cession, Monroe Doctrine, Mutual Security Act, North Atlantic Treaty, Open-Door Policy, Panama Canal, Reciprocity, Truman Doctrine, United Nations.*

Foreign Service of the U.S. originated during the War of Independence, when the Continental Congress sent diplomatic representatives abroad. After adoption of the Federal Constitution, Congress made appropriation for salaries of ministers and chargés d'affaires, and defined by law (1792) the power and duties of American consuls, who in the early decades were often political appointees. More definite organization was given during the 1850's, but not until the PENDLETON ACT (1883) was a merit system effectively begun. The Rogers Act of 1924 brought about a major reorganization by combining diplomatic and consular services, and establishing a Foreign Service School within the State Department. The Foreign Service Act of 1946 made use of the merit system mandatory for non-appointive positions, and placed the Service under a director. Ambassadorial posts are outside the merit system, since ambassadors are appointed by the President.

Foreign trade, see *Commerce.*

Forests covered vast expanses of North America when European explorers first arrived. Settlements opened clearings along the eastern seaboard during the colonial period. LUMBERING, an export industry after 1800, began moving west as the timber stands thinned out, but the supply seemed limitless and no thought was given to reforestation. Widespread fires hastened the destruction. Few effective steps were taken before the end of the 19th century to conserve remaining forests or to restore denuded areas. By the Forest Reserve Act (1891) Congress authorized the President to set apart forest reserve lands in the public domain, and closed timber areas to settlers. This important attempt to prevent reckless exhaustion of natural resources was buttressed by two later acts, the CAREY LAND ACT (1894) and the NEWLANDS RECLAMATION ACT (1902).

Soon thereafter the growth of the CONSERVATION MOVEMENT brought a new awareness of the vital importance of forests in preventing floods and erosion. (The Forest Service in the Department of Agriculture, and several agencies in the Department of the Interior, are directly or indirectly responsible for conserving forest resources. Similar bureaus are administered by the states.) Nearly three-fourths of the commercial forest lands are privately owned; the rest are in Federal, state, county, or municipal ownership. Most of the Federal forest lands are in NATIONAL FORESTS and NATIONAL PARKS.

FORREST, EDWIN (1806–72), born in Philadelphia, began his lifelong career as actor by supporting Edmund Kean in Shakespearean roles. His appearance (1826) in New York as Othello began a period of enormous prestige. Forrest's rivalry with the English actor William Macready began when Macready partisans hissed Forrest's *Macbeth* in London, and culminated in New York in the ASTOR PLACE RIOT (1849). Forrest's jealousy and violent temper did not impair his reputation on the stage, where he held audiences by the vigor of his interpretations. He amassed a fortune, largely bequeathed to the Edwin Forrest Home for Retired Actors, which he established in Philadelphia.

FORREST, NATHAN BEDFORD (1821–77), upon the outbreak of the Civil War left his Mississippi cotton plantation and raised a battalion at his own expense. Although he lacked a formal education, he turned his natural abilities to account, leading cavalry troops brilliantly throughout the war, notably at Shiloh, Murfreesboro, and Chickamauga. As lieutenant general in charge of all Confederate cavalry at war's end, he was subsequently judged by the Union general William T. Sherman as 'the most remarkable man the Civil War produced on either side.' Legends of his exploits still persist in the South. He later became Grand Wizard of the KU KLUX KLAN (1867), which he disbanded in 1869.

FORSYTHE, JOHN (1780–1841), born in Virginia, after graduation from the College of New Jersey (Princeton) in 1799, practiced law in Augusta, Georgia, and became attorney general of the state. After serving in the U.S. House of Representatives (1813–18) and the Senate (1818–19), he resigned to become Monroe's minister to Spain (1819–23), where he helped negotiate the ADAMS-ONÍS TREATY, by which Florida was secured for the U.S. Again in the House (1823–27) and Senate (1829–34), he later served both Jackson and Van Buren as Secretary of State (1834–41). During those seven years he dealt with the question of the annexation of Texas, the CAROLINE AFFAIR with Canada, and the dispute over the Maine boundary.

FORTEN, JAMES (1766–1842), Philadelphia sailmaker, was one of the most influential Negro spokesmen in the ABOLITION MOVEMENT. He served as a youth in the Continental navy and in later years as a prosperous businessman was active in philanthropic causes.

Fortunes, Great, in the U.S. were not established until well into the 19th century. Although leading merchants, bankers, and foreign traders in eastern cities had acquired considerable means before 1800, the first great fortune achieved was that of JOHN JACOB ASTOR (furs and New York City real estate), who at his death (1848) left a $30,000,000 estate. CORNELIUS VANDERBILT (railroads and shipping) left the bulk of his $100,000,000 estate (1877) to his son William H. Vanderbilt (1821–85), who doubled the fortune.

In the Middle West the first notable fortunes were established by PHILIP D. ARMOUR (meat packing), MARSHALL FIELD (dry-goods), CYRUS H. MC CORMICK (harvesting machines), and GEORGE M. PULLMAN (sleeping and dining cars). The California gold mines created great wealth only indirectly, but the Pacific railroads gave fortunes to LELAND STANFORD and COLLIS P. HUNTINGTON. Copper mining and smelting built an industrial empire for the GUGGENHEIM family.

At the turn of the 20th century the vast fortune of ANDREW CARNEGIE had been made in steel, and that of the MELLON family had been accumulated in banking. (J. P. MORGAN was a wealthy man, but his fortune, compared with that of other contemporary millionaires, was relatively small.) Pennsylvania oil laid the foundation of the mightiest American fortune, that of JOHN D. ROCKEFELLER. Other great fortunes were established by the DU PONT family (explosives and diversified holdings), JAMES B. DUKE (tobacco), and HENRY FORD (automobiles).

See Gustavus Myers, *History of the Great American Fortunes* (1936).

Forty-niners, see *California Gold Rush.*

FOSDICK, HARRY EMERSON (1878–), Baptist minister and professor of practical theology at Union Theological Seminary (1915–46), was the first pastor of a church built for him, Riverside Church in New York City (1930–46). The most eloquent voice in the American pulpit during the 1920's and 1930's, he was regarded as a somewhat misty theologian, but he dealt directly with the personal problems of his hearers with discernment and rhetorical skill, not only in the pulpit and on the radio (where his audiences were enormous) but in his many books, represented by *As I See Religion* (1932), and *On Being a Real Person* (1943).

His brother, RAYMOND BLAINE FOSDICK (1883–), New York lawyer and an authority on police systems, was active in numerous philanthropic organizations, and for some years (1936–48) served as president of the Rockefeller Foundation.

FOSTER, STEPHEN COLLINS (1826–64), Pennsylvania-born composer, was entirely self-taught. He gained his knowledge of the Negro chiefly from Negro camp meetings and from MINSTREL SHOWS, for which he wrote his songs, many of which have entered into the treasury of American 'folk' music. Melodically simple, they include *Oh! Susannah* (1847), *Old Folks at Home (Swanee River)* (1851), *My Old Kentucky Home* (1853), and *Old Black Joe* (1860). His short life, spent finally in a Bowery lodging house in lower New York, was blighted by poverty and alcohol.

FOSTER, WILLIAM ZEBULON (1881–), Massachusetts-born communist leader in the U.S., was a staunch Marxist when he affiliated himself in 1900 with the SOCIALIST PARTY. Later he identified himself with the IWW, and in 1918 became secretary of the 22 A.F. of L. unions formed to spearhead the great steel strike of 1919. After the organization of the American COMMUNIST PARTY (1919), he thrice ran as the Communist party's presidential candidate (1924, 1928, 1932). Although displaced in party leadership by EARL BROWDER, he again became national head (1945–48), until ill health and legal complications led him to withdraw from political activity.

Foundations, Endowed, administered usually under a Federal or state charter by an independent governing board for charitable, educational, or scientific purposes, had their origin in the U.S. with the two £1000 bequests (1790) of Benjamin Franklin (to Boston and Philadelphia) to accrue for 200 years as loan funds for young men. (They are still accumulating.) Between 1790 and 1900 some half-dozen foundations were set up, notably those of GEORGE PEABODY. The period of large foundations began when John D. Rockefeller set up the GENERAL EDUCATION BOARD (1902), and Andrew Carnegie established the CARNEGIE CORPORATION (1911).

By 1960 some 5000 philanthropic foundations in the U.S. were disbursing grants that annually totaled more than $700,000,000 from assets that aggregated $12,000,000,000. Although they bulk large in themselves and in the public eye, their expenditures account for less than 10 per cent of all American PHILANTHROPY. In general they are concentrated in New York, California, and Texas, with the largest grants subsidizing education (50 per cent), health (15 per cent), scientific research (15 per cent), and social welfare (10 per cent). (Only about 5 per cent support the humanities.) Notable among them, in addition to the Carnegie Corporation, are the RUSSELL SAGE FOUNDATION (1907), ROCKEFELLER FOUNDATION (1913), DUKE ENDOWMENT (1924), GUGGENHEIM FOUNDATION (1925), HARTFORD FOUNDATION (1929), KELLOGG FOUNDATION (1930), and the massive FORD FOUNDATION (1936).

Four Freedoms, as enunciated by President F. D. Roosevelt in his annual message to Congress (6 January 1941), recommending Lend-Lease for the Allies, were freedom of speech and expression, freedom of worship, freedom from want, and freedom from fear. These he termed the 'essential human freedoms' by which a future world order could be secured.

'Four Hundred, The,' see *McAllister, Ward.*

'Four Minute Men,' see *Committee on Public Information.*

Four Power Treaty, see *Washington Conference (1921–22).*

Fourierism, the communal system propounded by the French socialist Charles Fourier (1772–1837), was one element in UTOPIAN SOCIALISM, and was developed from Fourier's idea that the passions of man would in a state of nature attain harmony. Fourier proposed to organize society into so-called 'phalansteries,' units large enough for all social and industrial requirements (estimated at 1620 persons), arranged in groups according to occupations, capabilities, and attractions. These community units would guarantee to every member the means of self-support and the opportunity to develop his interests. An agrarian-handicraft economy, Fourierism was brought to the U.S. about 1840 and vigorously supported by such publicists of the idea as ALBERT BRISBANE and HORACE GREELEY. The most successful colony was the NORTH AMERICAN PHALANX. For a time BROOK FARM adopted the system. But the communities could not be made practicable and the movement declined rapidly after 1850.

Fourteen Points, set forth by President Wilson in an address to Congress (8 January 1918), was in Wilson's judgment 'the only possible program' for peace after World War I. The fourteen points were (1) 'open covenants openly arrived at'; (2) freedom of the seas; (3) removal of trade barriers; (4) reduction of armaments; (5) adjustment of colonial claims with the interest of the populations weighing equally with that of the claimants; (6) evacuation of Russian territory and independent determination by Russia of her own national policy; (7) evacuation and restoration of Belgium; (8) evacuation and restoration of France, and the return of Alsace-Lorraine; (9, 10, 11) readjustment of Austro-Hungarian, Italian, and Balkan frontiers along historically established lines of nationality; (12) freedom of the Dardanelles and self-determination for the peoples under Turkish rule; (13) an independent Poland, with free access to the sea; (14) establishment of 'a general association of nations . . . under specific covenants.'

The proposal was a moral offensive, which speeded the end of the war by driving a wedge between the German people and their government, and it gave Wilson a position of leadership among the Allies. But ten months later, after the Armistice (11 November), opposition to the points quickly crystallized, and the TREATY OF VERSAILLES represented a defeat for many of them. The fourteenth, however, led to the establishment of the LEAGUE OF NATIONS.

Fourteenth Amendment (1868) to the U.S. Constitution is by far the most detailed of the three CIVIL WAR AMENDMENTS. It established Negro citizenship, and, by denying states the right to abridge citizenship privileges (a restraint imposed on the federal government in 1791 by the FIFTH AMENDMENT), it set limits which have given the courts great difficulty in deciding the precise meaning of its DUE PROCESS clause.

Overshadowing all other Supreme Court decisions based on this Amendment is that in BROWN *v.* BOARD OF EDUCATION (1954), the ruling that declared the segregation of Negroes and whites in school to be unconstitutional. This was based on the guarantee of equal protection of the laws, and not on the due process clause.

The Amendment also clarified the meaning of 'dual citizenship,' by making all individuals born in the United States or subject to its jurisdiction citizens of both the nation and of the state in which they resided; it abolished the 'three-fifths' clause, which had counted a slave as three-fifths of a person for both taxation and representation; and it declared the Confederacy's debts illegal and void and made former Federal or state officials who had served the Confederacy ineligible for federal or state office — though Congress could remove this disability by a two-thirds vote of both Houses. It also provided — but this clause was never enforced — that congressional representation of states that denied the right to vote to those eligible to do so could be reduced in proportion to the percentage of those so discriminated against.

Fourth Amendment to the U.S. Constitution, see *Bill of Rights.*

Fourth of March Speech, see *Calhoun, J. C.*

FOX, GEORGE, see *Friends, Society of.*

Fox Indians, see *Sauk and Fox Indians.*

FOXE, LUKE (1586–1635), English navigator, in his search for the NORTHWEST PASSAGE to Asia (1631) explored the west shore of Hudson Bay, and concluded that no such transit was possible. His *North-West Fox* (1635) is an account of his voyage, and made a considerable contribution to geographical knowledge, much more than did the account written by his contemporary, THOMAS JAMES, who received high praise.

France, War with (1798–1800), an undeclared war, rose out of the diplomatic conflicts stemming from the European wars of the French Revolution. It was initiated by the GENÊT AFFAIR and the XYZ AFFAIR. In the spring of 1798 Congress empowered the merchant marine to 'repel by force any assault,' and ordered the navy to seize armed French craft molesting American trade. The aged Washington was called from retirement and appointed commander in chief of the army.

Numerous privateers were captured on both sides. Three small battles were fought by ships of the line in the West Indian area, and won by Americans. President Adams saw the danger into which the nation was drifting, and appointed a commission to meet Napoleon in Paris. The First Consul received the commission cordially, and the CONVENTION OF 1800 brought the war to an end.

Franchise, see *Suffrage.*

Franciscans, among Roman Catholic orders, pioneered in the exploration and settlement of North America. In point of time and extent of the territory they covered they were the most important missionaries among the Indians from the arrival of NARVÁEZ in Florida (1528) to the founding of California missions by JUNIPERO SERRA (1769).

Franco-American Alliance (1778) followed the covert assistance to the American colonies that France had been extending since the outbreak of the War of Independence. The joint diplomatic commission to France (Franklin, Deane, and Lee) sent by Congress in 1776, for two years had sought French recognition of American independence, but the French minister of foreign affairs, Vergennes, pursued a policy of delay until some military event might assure the triumph of the American cause. That occurred when Burgoyne surrendered at Saratoga in 1777.

Vergennes came to a quick decision when he learned that Franklin and Deane were meeting with emissaries of Lord North, ostensibly to arrange peace terms that would tie the colonies to Great Britain. He suggested a treaty of amity and commerce, and a treaty of alliance, the latter to become effective if and when war broke out between France and England. (The two nations were at war in a matter of weeks.) The terms of the treaty were so generous that Congress unanimously ratified it. In the CONVENTION OF 1800 the Alliance was terminated.

FRANKFURTER, FELIX (1882–1965), Vienna-born Justice of the U.S. Supreme Court, was brought to the U.S. in 1894. After graduation from the Harvard Law School (1906) and a brief service as assistant U.S. attorney (1906–10) in New York City and in the Bureau of Insular Affairs (1911–14), he became a professor at Harvard Law School (1914–39). During World War I he directed national labor policy as chairman of the War Labor Policies Board. As a staunch liberal, he helped organize the American Civil Liberties Union and assailed labor injunctions. Appointed by President F. D. Roosevelt to the Supreme Court (1939–62), he continued to support the legal principles which his liberalism invigorated. His writings include *The Case of Sacco and Vanzetti* (1927), *The Labor Injunction* (1930), and his revealing essays in *Law and Politics* (1939).

FRANKLIN, BENJAMIN (1706–90), born in Boston, left school at the age of ten to assist his father, a tallow chandler and soapmaker. Apprenticed at twelve to his half-brother James, a printer, at fifteen young Ben was reading Xenophon, Plutarch, Bunyan, and Locke, and consciously laboring to model his style on Addison's *Spectator* for the squibs he submitted to his brother's newly founded *New England Courant.* At sixteen he anonymously contributed his *Dogood Papers* (1722), sprightly commentaries on local and domestic affairs. A year later, restive under the terms of indenture and puffed by a success he could not profit by at home, he ran off to Philadelphia and entered the printing shop of Samuel Keimer. Under the patronage of Governor Keith (who promptly forgot him) he sailed for England to buy equipment for a printing shop of his own. He returned to Philadelphia (1726) and bought out Keimer's *Pennsylvania Gazette,* which under Franklin's management (1730–66) became one of the most successful news organs of its day, made popular by its editor's terse clarity and prudential wisdom. He had already organized a discussion group, the Junto Club (1727), which developed into the notable Library Company (1731). Meanwhile he 'took to wife' Deborah Read, daughter of his first landlady. They remained devoted throughout life. She assisted him in his shop, bore him two children, and accepted into the household Franklin's two illegitimate children.

The phenomenal success of Franklin's *Poor Richard's Almanack* (1732–57) stemmed in part from the fact that Franklin issued it in three editions, with local data for New England, the Middle Colonies, and the South. But, more importantly, in 'Poor Richard' (or 'Dick Saunders') Franklin created an authentic fictional character, a homespun commentator whose commonsense reflections made 'Poor Richard' a household name.

Franklin began to teach himself languages in 1733. He studied French, Italian, German, and Spanish, and in due course he was able to speak and write French with reasonable facility. During the 1730's his business interests carried him to the fringes of politics. His concern with civic improvements put Philadelphia ahead of other cities in matters of street paving and lighting, and police and fire-fighting organizations. His proposals relating to welfare and learning were soon adopted, and so farsighted that the results are still impressive: the American Philosophical Society (1743), the University of Pennsylvania (1751), and the Pennsylvania Hospital (1752).

Franklin's desire to know more about electricity was all-consuming, and having achieved financial independence he devoted himself to experiments. He entered into correspondence at home and abroad with all who, by exchange of ideas, could further investigation of electrical phenomena. His *Experiments and Observations on Electricity* (1751–54) set forth his discovery that electricity and lightning are identical, elucidated the workings of the Leyden jar (the earliest electrical condenser), described his invention of the lightning rod, and brought to the language several technical terms. These discoveries in the science of electrostatics give Franklin rank among the greatest American researchers in pure science.

Franklin became a member of the Pennsylvania Assembly in 1751, and served for the next twelve years. As Deputy Postmaster-General for the colonies from 1753 until the Revolution, he perceived the need of federation, and in 1754 he drafted the ALBANY PLAN OF UNION, the forerunner of the Federal Constitution. His services abroad began in 1757, when he was sent as agent for the Assembly in an attempt to terminate proprietary government. The selection was made in part because of Franklin's proved skill as a negotiator, but also because he would be received as a distinguished scientist and man of letters. His achievement won public recognition in England, and Oxford conferred on him the degree of Doctor of Civil Law.

After a brief interval at home he was again sent to London by the Assembly in 1764, this time to petition that the colony be made a royal province. Officially an agent for Georgia, New Jersey, and Massachusetts as well, he demanded no rights except those possessed by all British subjects. He worked for repeal of the TOWNSHEND ACTS, but his connection with the affair of the 'Hutchinson Letters' embarrassed Governor HUTCHINSON of Massachusetts, and cost Franklin his postmastership (1772). Certain that war was inevitable, he returned to America (1775) to serve in the Continental Congress, where he was made a member of the committee that drafted the Declaration of Independence.

Late in 1776 Congress sent him to France as one of its representatives to create an alliance with that country. There, with a high reputation well supported by his winning presence, he did much to gain French recognition of the new republic (1778). Appointed plenipotentiary to the French court in that year, he still found time for scientific research, and for amusing his friends with urbane bagatelles, witty trifles which he set up on his private press at Passy, normally used for propaganda releases. In 1785 he made his final voyage from Europe, having signed with John Adams and John Jay the TREATY OF PARIS of 1783, which concluded the War of Independence. He had reached his 80th year, and was the most famous man living. In his last service to his country, as a member of the Federal Constitutional Convention (1787) he signed the Constitution.

Throughout his life Franklin wrote extensively in a style which is always lucid, often memorable, and frequently salty. His pragmatic temper marks him as an exemplar of one aspect of the 18th-century Enlightenment. His classic *Autobiography* (begun in 1771 and sketching his career into his fifties) is a candid record of self-discoveries. When he died in April 1790 he was accorded world-wide honors reserved otherwise only for Washington, and was remembered with an affection extended uniquely to himself.

Biographies include those by James Parton (1864), Carl Van Doren (1938), and Verner W. Crane (1954). The *Papers of Benjamin Franklin* (some 40 volumes), issued under the auspices of the American Philosophical Society and Yale University, are being edited by L. W. Labaree and others.

Franklin, State of, see *Tennessee.*

Fraternal orders, see *Freemasonry, Knights of Columbus, Elks.*

Fraternities, in American colleges, are student societies organized as social groups, which members join by invitation. Also known as Greek-letter societies since they usually are named by the two or three initial Greek letters of their motto, they may be either 'local,' that is, autonomous, or chapters of a national organization. The oldest, Phi Beta Kappa (1776), became a scholarship honor society soon after it was established. The three social groups established at Union College (1825–27) became the model for later organizations. The defects of fraternities stem in large measure from the tendency of many college alumni to regard them as sacred cows. Racial discrimination in the charters of some national organizations has led some local chapters in recent years to become autonomous. Such clubs in women's colleges (sororities) are of relatively recent origin.

Fraunces Tavern, at Broad and Pearl streets in New York City (still used as a restaurant), is a landmark because in its Long Room in December 1783 Washington bade farewell to his officers. Its Negro proprietor, Samuel Fraunces, later became Washington's steward.

FRAZEE, JOHN (1790–1852), self-taught New Jersey sculptor, was trained as a stonecutter and began carving busts about 1825. His portrait of John Wells in St. Paul's Church, New York City, is thought to be the first marble bust executed by a native American. His portraits, including carvings of Daniel Webster and John Marshall, have the interest of chronicle because of Frazee's faithfulness to detail.

Frazier-Lemke Bankruptcy Act, see *Farm legislation.*

Fredericksburg, Battle of, was fought on 13 December 1862 in the wooded heights above Fredericksburg, Virginia. General Burnside with an overwhelming Union force of 113,000 attacked General Lee's army of 75,000 on the south bank of the Rappahannock. The exciting spectacle was the most senseless carnage of the Civil War. Wave after wave of Union infantry was broken and rolled back by the devastating fire of entrenched Confederate artillery and riflemen. The appalling and one-sided slaughter cost Burnside some 12,600 casualties; Lee lost less than half that number. The debacle profoundly depressed the North and encouraged interventionist feeling in Europe. (A French army took Mexico City six months later.) Lincoln replaced Burnside with Hooker, but the political crisis thus created, at home and abroad, was major. Lincoln surmounted the crisis with statesmanship of the first order, but at the time he said: 'If there is a worse place than Hell, I am in it.'

Free enterprise, see *Laissez faire.*

Freedmen's Bureau, created by Congress in 1865, was a government agency formed to deal with some 4,000,000 newly liberated Negroes after the Civil War; and rarely in modern times has a nation tackled a social problem of such magnitude with so little planning. The Act that created the Bureau was ambiguous. It sought to prepare the freedman for responsible citizenship, yet it made possible the ruthless exploitation of his labor. The Bureau thus became a 'mixture of welfare and abuse, of genuine service and shameful corruption.' Backed by military force, it was a powerful instrument of RECONSTRUCTION, and ultimately became little more than a political machine to organize the Negro vote for the Republican party. Its activities ceased in 1874. Although it performed services of relief, it exasperated southern whites more than any other agency. Recent research tends to be more favorable to the contributions of the Bureau.

Freedom of press and speech, see *Civil liberties.*

Freedom of the seas, see *Blockade, Fisheries, Fourteen Points, Navigation Acts, Neutral Rights, Territorial Waters.*

Freedom riders, so called, were the interracial groups of Negroes and whites who in 1961 chartered buses and rode through various states in the Deep South to give publicity to and to challenge the legality of the laws in those states which still required race segregation on common carriers and in restaurants. The incident drew worldwide notice because riots occurred and many of the riders were arrested.

Freehold in English law is fee simple tenure of property, that is, unentailed ownership. Most of the colonies restricted the right to vote and hold office to freeholders. After the Revolution, in general the right to vote ceased to depend upon the freehold.

FREEMAN, DOUGLAS SOUTHALL (1886–1953), a graduate of Richmond College (1904) and Johns Hopkins (1908), was a lifelong editor of the Richmond *News Leader* (1915–53). An authority on military strategy and the military history of the Civil War, he first became widely known for his biography of R. E. Lee (4 vols., 1934–35, Pulitzer Prize), followed by *Lee's Lieutenants* (3 vols., 1942–44). At the time of his death he had nearly completed his life of Washington (6 vols., 1948–54).

Freeman's Farm, Battle of (September 1777), was fought at Stillwater, New York, on the Hudson river above Albany, toward which Burgoyne was pressing during the SARATOGA CAMPAIGN. Moving south from Montreal, he encountered the entrenched position prepared by Gates on Bemis Heights, and was stopped short of his goal by the Yankee militiamen, commanded by Colonel DANIEL MORGAN (British casualties 600, American 300). With rations diminishing, Burgoyne had either to retreat or try again to join forces with Clinton on the lower Hudson. During the first week in October he lost another encounter in the same region, and retreated to Saratoga.

Freemasons (Free and Accepted Masons) are members of a secret society united for fraternal purposes. Claiming great antiquity, the institution of freemasonry in its symbols and rites preserves much of the spirit and form of a medieval guild, stressing a belief in the 'Grand Architect of the Universe, the Bible, and usually (in modern times) rejection of political activities *as Masons.'* Catholics do not join the society, and on the Continent, they look upon Masonry as historically hostile to the Church. Franklin became a Mason in the 1730's, and Washington, who took the oath of office as President upon his Masonic Bible, laid the cornerstone of the national Capitol with a Masonic trowel. (Thereafter participation of Masons in cornerstone layings was strongly opposed by those who objected to secret societies, of which the Masonic is the strongest.) Later Presidents who were Masons include Jefferson, Madison, Monroe, Jackson, Polk, Buchanan, Andrew Johnson, Garfield, McKinley, Theodore Roosevelt, Taft, Harding, F. D. Roosevelt, and Truman.

Anti-Masonic feeling during the 19th century was often bitter, and shared by those who were suspicious of secret societies and opposed extrajudicial oaths. In the 1830's a short-lived ANTI-MASONIC PARTY drew support for its presidential candidate. Higher Masonic degrees are those of the Knights Templar and the Scottish Rite Masons, and only members of those orders are eligible to become SHRINERS. Because obedience to the law of the land is mandatory upon members, no international organization is possible. At present there are some 3,000,000 Masons in the U.S.

Freemen, throughout the colonial period of American history, were those persons who possessed a FREEHOLD. Freemen alone in most of the colonies had the right to participate in the government of the colony and to vote for members of the COLONIAL ASSEMBLIES.

'Freeport doctrine,' so called, stemmed from the most memorable of the

LINCOLN-DOUGLAS DEBATES. At Freeport, Illinois (27 August 1858), Lincoln asked Douglas how he could reconcile the doctrine of 'popular sovereignty' with the DRED SCOTT decision. Douglas answered that the people of a territory could lawfully exclude slavery prior to the formulation of a state constitution. He said that the right to admit or bar slavery existed despite the Supreme Court dictum, 'for the reason that slavery cannot exist a day or an hour anywhere, unless it is supported by local police regulations.'

Douglas was right, since Congress could not force a territorial legislature to pass a law against its will. The 'Freeport doctrine' won Douglas his reelection to the Senate, but since it defied Buchanan and the southern Democrats who were attempting to protect slavery in every territory, it was instrumental in depriving him of southern backing for the presidential nomination in 1860.

Free silver, as a political shibboleth, followed the PANIC OF 1873. The free coinage of silver first became an issue in the presidential campaign of 1876, soon after formation of the GREENBACK PARTY, and for the next quarter-century inflationists sought to re-establish BIMETALLISM. The first of several government subsidies to silver producers was the BLAND-ALLISON SILVER ACT (1878). In 1890 Congress passed the SHERMAN SILVER PURCHASE ACT in an attempt to compromise with gold standard advocates. The PANIC OF 1893 brought repeal of the Sherman Act, and free silver became the chief issue in the 1896 presidential campaign, in which W. J. Bryan, the Democratic standard bearer, nearly impaled McKinley on a 'cross of gold.' The issue was revived in 1900 in a similarly close McKinley-Bryan contest, which the Republicans again won, but increasing gold supplies and returning prosperity thereafter minimized free silver as a political issue.

Free-Soil party, which came into existence in 1847–48, developed from opposition to the extension of slavery into any of the territories newly acquired from Mexico. The Free-Soil forces, consolidated by the struggle over the WILMOT PROVISO, consisted of New York Democrats known as BARNBURNERS, the 'conscience' (antislavery) Whigs, and members of the former LIBERTY PARTY. Formally organized at Buffalo in August 1848 with the slogan 'free soil, free speech, free labor and free men,' it nominated Van Buren and C. F. Adams for President and Vice President. It polled some 291,000 votes, and, by giving New York state to the Whigs, was a decisive factor in swinging the election to Zachary Taylor. Since the COMPROMISE OF 1850 supposedly settled the slavery issue, support of the party dwindled. In 1854 it was absorbed into the Republican party.

FRÉMONT, JOHN CHARLES (1813–90), soldier, explorer, and political leader, was reared in Charleston, South Carolina, where he attended the College of Charleston (1829–31). In 1838 he was commissioned a lieutenant in the U.S. Topographical Corps and accompanied J. N. NICOLLET as chief assistant in mapping the country between the upper waters of the Mississippi and Missouri rivers (1838–41). In 1841 he eloped with Jessie Benton, daughter of Senator THOMAS HART BENTON, who, reconciled to the match, secured for Frémont the command of an expedition (1842) that mapped the region from Kansas City to Fremont Peak in western Wyoming. His second expedition (1843–44) was far more extensive. It covered the region through Utah to Oregon, traversed the length of California, and returned by way of Nevada, Utah, and Colorado. On the third (1845–46) he mapped the central Rockies, crossed into California, and encouraged the Americans there who were attempting to set up the BEAR FLAG REPUBLIC.

Frémont's vivid reports of these expeditions were widely reprinted and stirred up enthusiasm for the West and national expansion. Scientifically the accomplishment was notable. Frémont had covered more ground than any previous explorer of the West and had assembled a great variety of data. His identification and description of the Great Basin remains a geographical achievement.

He then began his ill-starred political career. Appointed governor (1847) of the newly organized civil government of California by Commodore ROBERT STOCK-

TON, he came into the political cross-fire of Stockton and General STEPHEN KEARNEY. He was court-martialed and found guilty of mutiny. President Polk remitted the penalty, but proud and injured, Frémont resigned his commission. He made a fortune in the gold rush and was briefly U.S. Senator from California (1850–51). When the Republican party met in its first national convention (1856), Frémont won the nomination, but he lost the election to Buchanan by an electoral vote of 114 to 174 and a popular vote of 1,341,000 to 1,838,000.

As a major general in the Civil War commanding the Department of the West, he issued an order confiscating the property of Missouri rebels and emancipating their slaves. For this he was promptly removed, lest his action alienate Kentucky and other border states.

Railroad ventures in 1870 cost him his fortune. Beggared, he struggled on, loyally supported by his wife. For a time he was territorial governor of Arizona (1878–83). He was belatedly (1890) restored to his rank of major general but did not live to enjoy his pension. Frémont was the first distinctively scientific American explorer, and one of the greatest; he was painstaking and intellectually wide ranging. One of the most controversial figures of Western history, 'The Pathfinder' did more to publicize the West than any other person. His career after 1846, though prominent, was anticlimactic.

See Allan Nevins, *Frémont: Pathmarker of the West* (1955). Nevins edited Frémont's *Narratives of Exploration and Adventure* (1956).

FRENCH, DANIEL CHESTER (1850–1931), New Hampshire–born sculptor, studied under William Rimmer in Boston and Thomas Ball in Florence. He was twenty-three when he executed his first commission, *The Minuteman,* at Concord, Massachusetts. His bust of Emerson (1879), modeled from life, is vigorous and sensitive. He later devoted his talents to monumental sculpture, executing such works as the John Harvard statue, in the Harvard Yard; the heroic Lincoln, in the Lincoln Memorial, Washington, D.C.; and the six heroic figures in the Minnesota capitol, St. Paul.

French Alliance, see *Franco-American Alliance.*

French and Indian Wars (1689–1763), lasting for the greater part of a century, were the North American campaigns in the world-wide dynastic struggle between France and England. Although the stakes were huge, Europeans regarded the American phase as relatively unimportant. To the American colonists the rivalry of the two powers, with their Indian allies, was of immediate concern. In America it appeared to be a single conflict, occasionally interrupted by truces, with London, Paris, and Madrid as the centers of diplomacy.

KING WILLIAM'S WAR (1689–97) took place principally in Canada and New York, and settled nothing except the return of Port Royal to the French. QUEEN ANNE'S WAR (1702–13) washed the frontier in blood from New England to Florida (especially in the attack on Deerfield, Massachusetts), and created troubles leading to the so-called WAR OF JENKIN'S EAR (1739). The American phase of the War of the Austrian Succession, KING GEORGE'S WAR (1744–48), again involved the border from Nova Scotia to Pennsylvania. (This time the West Indies were especially embroiled.) Rivalries then shifted westward to the Ohio valley, where a group of Virginians who had formed the OHIO COMPANY encountered the French, who were investigating the possibilities of a similar venture.

Soon thereafter began the last and most significant of the series, referred to simply as the French and Indian War (1755–63). The French defeated General BRADDOCK in western Pennsylvania in July 1755, and in turn were repulsed at the battle of LAKE GEORGE in September. In 1756 the Seven Years' War (world-wide in scale) was formally declared. The English planned four campaigns in North America: against Niagara and settlements on Lake Erie, and against Ticonderoga and the stronghold at Quebec. In September 1759, on the PLAINS OF ABRAHAM above Quebec, Wolfe and Montcalm engaged in the mortal combat (both lost their lives) that cost France an empire and secured North America for the English-speaking peoples. The TREATY OF PARIS of 1763 put the seal on the immense victory, so soon to be forfeited in large part by Great Britain through the War of Independence.

The classic works in English on the conflict are those of FRANCIS PARKMAN. See also Edward P. Hamilton, *The French and Indian Wars* (1962).

FRENEAU, PHILIP [MORIN] (1752–1832), born in New York City, after graduation from the College of New Jersey at Princeton (1771) served in the War of Independence as soldier and privateer. He was captured at sea and imprisoned on the brig *Aurora,* an experience which he recorded in his intensely bitter poem 'The British Prison-Ship' (1781). This and other war poems made him known as the 'poet of the American Revolution.'

As editor of the Jefferson-sponsored *National Gazette* (1791–93), Freneau became the first effective crusading newspaperman in America, and he propagandized Republicanism with such gusto that Washington termed him a rascal and Hamilton publicly branded him as a liar. But Jefferson said that Freneau saved the Constitution when it was 'galloping fast into monarchy.' Freneau was frequently involved in editorial quarrels, and none of his journalistic ventures was profitable. Nevertheless, as a commentator on current events he made national issues the subject of debate, and his place is no less secure as the earliest important romantic poet in America.

FREUND, ERNST (1864–1932), professor of jurisprudence and public law at Chicago (after 1902), was a leading authority on American legal systems. His writings include *Police Power* (1904), *Standards of American Legislation* (1917), and *Administrative Powers Over Persons and Property* (1928).

FRICK, HENRY CLAY (1849–1919), Pennsylvania capitalist, after acquiring large coke manufacturing properties, joined Andrew Carnegie and as his plant manager organized and ran Carnegie's great steel mills until 1899. His adamant anti-union stand in labor disputes resulted in the bloody HOMESTEAD STRIKE (1892), one of the bitterest in U.S. history. An associate at various times of Carnegie (who won the issue of controlling interest), and of Mellon, Morgan, and Rockefeller, he built an enormous fortune. His New York mansion, together with his art collection and an endowment of $15,000,000, was willed to the public as a museum.

Friends, The Religious Society of, is a sect founded (1647) by the English religious leader George Fox (1624–91), who rejected clergymen and churches after he had concluded that there is 'that of God in every man.' The name 'Quaker' is said to have been applied to the followers of Fox because at their meetings they shook with emotion, although Fox himself wrote in his journal that the name was first given to the Friends by one Justice Bennet, 'because I bid them, Tremble at the Word of the Lord.' In an era of odd sects, to their 17th-century compatriots the Friends were the queerest of the lot, and no group was treated with more bitter ridicule or vigorous persecution. Some 3000 were imprisoned in the first two years of the Restoration (1660–61).

Guided by an 'Inward Light,' which led them without intermediary rites or instruction directly to the experience of God, they required no church, no creed, and no priesthood. All Friends are lay preachers. They merely gathered at meetings in silence for an hour, unless moved to speech or prayer, adopted plainness in apparel, and addressed each other as 'thee,' a term still in use in the intimacy of their homes. They refused to doff hats except in prayer, or to swear an oath in court, since a man's plain word should be his oath. They have always observed the commandment against murder by refusing to bear arms in wartime, although their dedicated contribution to non-combat service branches has been traditional.

Almost immediately the sect spread throughout Europe, not great in numbers but strong in the conviction of those who cherished the teachings of Christ but cared little for the discipline of theology. In the 1650's Quaker missionaries began arriving in the American colonies. New England Puritans harried them mercilessly, hanging a few who returned after banishment. In the early years all the colonies save tolerant Rhode Island passed severe laws against them. But they continued their passive resistance, and in the colonies as in England they made converts by the same resolute faith that prompted WILLIAM PENN, imprisoned in the London Tower (1669), to defend his convictions in the pamphlet, *No Cross, No Crown*.

Although the Friends in America by 1674 had won a grudging toleration, and had acquired proprietary rights in West New Jersey (Penn was an aristocrat with powerful friends at court), it was not until Penn himself opened up the vast reaches of his 'Holy Experiment' to all who sought religious liberty (1681) that Friends gained an unparalleled opportunity to put their trust in humanity to the test. Within two generations Philadelphia had become a metropolis, with good schools and the best hospitals and charitable institutions in the colonies.

The fundamental tenets of the Friends have altered in no major way, and their ardent humanitarianism, early reflected in the writings of JOHN WOOLMAN, has led them to support all forms of social betterment. The most considerable thinker produced by American Quakerism was RUFUS JONES.

Institutions of higher learning founded by Friends include Haverford (est. 1833), Swarthmore (est. 1864), and Bryn Mawr (est. 1885). In 1965 the various groups in the U.S. totaled some 126,000 members.

See A. C. Thomas, *A History of the Friends in America* (6th ed., 1930); and H. H. Brinton, *Friends for Three Hundred Years* (1952), with emphasis on faith and practice.

Fries's Rebellion, so called, was the 'insurrection' of some hundred or more Pennsylvania farmers who resisted a direct Federal property tax levied by Congress in 1798 in anticipation of war with France. Led by a traveling auctioneer, 'Captain' John Fries (1750–1818), who armed himself with sword and pistol and wore a French tricorn hat, the insurgents chased the Federalist tax collectors out of Bucks county and compelled the liberation of prisoners jailed at Bethlehem. President Adams sent troops to establish order and apprehend Fries. Although convicted of treason and sentenced to death, Fries was pardoned by the President.

FROBISHER, MARTIN (*c.* 1539–94), licensed by Elizabeth I and backed by a group of English merchant venturers, in the late 1570's sought gold in the New World and a NORTHWEST PASSAGE to the Orient. He discovered Hudson Strait (which he named Mistaken Strait), and returned home with shiploads of fool's gold (iron pyrites) and mica, which finally served as road building material. He later commanded a ship in Sir Francis Drake's expedition to the West Indies (1585), and was knighted for his services in the defeat of the Spanish Armada (1588).

FROHMAN, CHARLES (1860–1915), Ohio-born theatrical producer, after successfully producing Bronson Howard's *Shenandoah* in New York (1889), organized his own stock company. In 1896 he formed the first theatrical syndicate. It emphasized the 'star system' and gradually extended its control throughout the U.S. In 1897 he leased a theater in London to exchange successful plays between that city and New York. He thereafter promoted the careers of such leading actors as Maude Adams, John Drew, Julia Marlowe, and Ethel Barrymore. He died in the sinking of the *Lusitania*.

His brother, DANIEL FROHMAN (1851–1940), had preceded him to New York as an impresario. For many years Daniel Frohman managed English and American stars and theatrical companies. He was chiefly associated with the Lyceum Theatre, where his stock company was based.

FRONTENAC, LOUIS DE BUADE, Comte de (1620–98), as French governor of New France (1672–82, 1689–98) embarked vigorously upon a course which, had it not been curbed by Louis XIV, would have resulted in considerable political independence for Canada. Frequently in conflict with the sovereign council, with the Jesuits, with the intendant (royal tax collector), and with the governor of Montreal, he was recalled in 1682, but was sent back in 1689 to handle the Iroquois, who submitted in 1696. He forwarded the explorations of JOLLIET, MARQUETTE, and LA SALLE; aided in the establishment of forts and military posts; and repulsed the attack on Quebec by WILLIAM PHIPS in the course of KING WILLIAM'S WAR (1689–97). One of the great colonial administrators, he was fearless, resourceful, and decisive.

Frontier, in American history, has generally meant the sparsely settled region bordering on the wilderness, whose few inhabitants were chiefly concerned with the pioneer labor of breaking ground and building homes. Its existence has been subject to interpretations by native and FOREIGN OBSERVERS from colonial times. Indeed, the literature dealing with the EXPLORATION and settlement of the American continent is by far the most voluminous body of material touching upon its civilization.

There have been many types of frontier, including those of the discoverer, the missionary, the fur trader, the miner, and the grazer. There were also 'frontiers' of such ventures as TURNPIKES, CANALS, and RAILROADS. But emphasis properly has been given to the achievement of the farmer, whose necessary operations destroyed forever the virgin character of the land.

The tremendous influence of the frontier in shaping American character was first set forth in the famous essay on 'The Significance of the Frontier in American History,' by the historian F. J. TURNER (1893). He believed that the outer limit of agricultural settlement is the beginning of the frontier, and that democracy (defined as the achievement of status for the common man) and characteristic American traits were a direct product of this frontier. In the process of occupying the continent, Americans developed their ideas of government and institutions. For 300 years the frontier as a social process compelled adaptation to the requirements of new environments. It lured the discontented, the dispossessed, the restive, and the ambitious. It encouraged self-reliance, broke down class distinctions, created opposition to coercion, and fostered political individualism. With the closing of the physical frontier in the early decades of the 20th century, as an actuality it ceased to exist, but it had created an image and a myth.

Later historians point out that Turner's thesis won its enormous vogue because it reflected beliefs already long accepted.

As late as 1800 the interior of North America was largely unknown, although it was believed to be an almost limitless expanse of arable terrain capable of supporting millions. The penetration made by the LEWIS AND CLARK EXPEDITION gave warrant for surmise that natural resources would provide for an agrarian society, self-contained and centering in the Mississippi valley, rather than one depending upon maritime commerce between the Atlantic coast and Europe.

The vision that 'westward the course of empire takes its way' had been at the root of Franklin's economic thinking and determined Jefferson's policies of state, especially in his LOUISIANA PURCHASE, a mammoth frontier acquisition. By 1820 the belief in a continental destiny was national in scope, and thus frontier problems became political. Federal support of western exploration and expansion created a fear that the agricultural West might dominate the commercial East. Such eastern statesmen as Daniel Webster gave vigorous support to the myth, created by such Western explorers as ZEBULON PIKE and STEPHEN LONG in their reports, of the GREAT AMERICAN DESERT in the high Plains region.

By 1870 the Continental Divide was proved not to be a barrier to western settlements. The nation thereafter discovered that institutions as well as environment were factors in closing frontiers. Such realization, resulting from a new concept of *how* to occupy virgin territory, thus became a major factor in closing the frontier period of American history.

See R. A. Billington, *Westward Expansion* (1949); R. C. Buley, *The Old Northwest, 1815–1840* (2 vols., 1950); Everett Dick, *Vanguards of the Frontier* (1941); Henry Nash Smith, *Virgin Land* (1950); F. J. Turner, *The Frontier in American History* (reissued, 1950).

FROST, ROBERT (1874–1963), born in San Francisco, for a time attended first Dartmouth, then Harvard, taught school, and worked at various jobs before settling on a farm in New Hampshire. Unable to gain a hearing for his poetry at home, in 1912 he went to England, where he brought out two volumes of poems about New England: *A Boy's Will* (1913), and *North of Boston* (1914). He returned to the U.S. in 1915, and soon won recognition as a poet of the first rank. Four times he was awarded the Pulitzer prize in poetry, for *New Hampshire* (1924), *Collected Poems* (1931), *A Further Range* (1937), and *A Witness Tree* (1943).

Primarily a nature poet, though never a nature mystic, Frost is an expert prosodist whose verses (often dramatic in manner and conversational in tone) are unsurpassed as genre studies of New England character, with a philosophical subtlety especially apparent in such works as the metaphysical blank verse plays, *A Masque of Reason* (1945), and *A Masque of Mercy* (1947). In his later years Frost was accorded honor, by the public and critics alike, seldom matched in the lifetime of an artist. The U.S. Senate adopted a resolution of felicitation for him on his seventy-fifth birthday, an homage accorded no other American poet.

See Sidney Cox, *Swinger of Birches* (1957), and Reuben Brower, *The Poetry of Robert Frost* (1963).

FROTHINGHAM, Octavius Brooks (1822–95), after graduation from Harvard (1843) entered the Unitarian ministry. Too liberal in his doctrines for orthodox Unitarians, he founded at Boston the Free Religious Association (1867). He wrote substantial biographies of his friends Theodore Parker and George Ripley, as well as the widely read *Religion of Humanity* (1872), a classic study of early religious HUMANISM, and *Transcendentalism in New England: A History* (1876).

Fruitlands, an eleven-acre farm at Harvard, Massachusetts, was the site of Bronson Alcott's seven-month experiment in 'consocial' living. With his family and a few other transcendental idealists, in 1843 Alcott sought to restore the 'Orphic life' of communing austerely with nature in its pristine beauty. Winter ended the experiment, and the Alcotts returned to Concord.

FRY, William Henry (1813–64), Philadelphia musician, composed *Leonora* (1845), the first notable American opera, however amateurish in workmanship. His second, *Notre Dame de Paris* (1864), was conducted in Philadelphia by Theodore Thomas. He was a pioneer of music criticism in the U.S., serving on the staff of the New York *Tribune*.

Fugitive slave laws, congressional acts of 1793 and 1850, provided for the return of escaped Negro slaves to their owners. Northern states, having abolished slavery, became lax in enforcing the 1793 law, to the great irritation of the South. The stringent fugitive slave regulations enacted as part of the Compromise of 1850 were aimed at the UNDERGROUND RAILROAD, the network by which slaves were helped to escape into free states.

Harriet Beecher Stowe's *Uncle Tom's Cabin* (1852), spectacularly successful in rousing antislavery sentiment, was inspired by the Compromise law. The fateful decision in the DRED SCOTT CASE (1857) widened the sectional breach, and the actions of northern states in nullifying slave laws were cited by South Carolina as one cause for secession. Both fugitive slave laws were repealed in 1864.

Fulbright Act (1946) provides the financial means for teacher and student exchange between the U.S. and foreign countries. Sponsored by Senator J. William Fulbright of Arkansas and financed at first by the sale of American World War II overseas surplus, the program now is supported by supplementary funds. In its first fifteen years it allowed 22,000 foreign students, teachers, and scholars to visit and study in the U.S., and some 16,000 Americans to study and teach abroad. The federal government was thus committed for the first time to long-term world-wide educational programs, and on a substantial scale.

'Full Dinner Pail,' a Republican campaign slogan in 1900, emphasized the prosperity of McKinley's first term, which followed the depression of 1893–96. It appealed particularly to the labor vote.

FULLER, [Sarah] Margaret (1810–50), born in Cambridge, Massachusetts, was one of the most vivid intellectual personalities of her day. Under the tutelage of her father, Timothy Fuller (1778–1835), a lawyer of some eminence, she began to study Latin at six years, and in early youth she selected Shakespeare, Cervantes, and Molière as her favorite authors. She soon mastered Greek, Italian, and German. As a young woman she identified herself with TRANSCENDENTALISM and became a friend of the intellectual leaders of the time. A stimulating talker, as the 'Priestess of Transcendentalism' for five years she conducted in Boston a series of conversation classes on social and literary topics, and her ability to draw out the unsuspected facilities of those who shared her interests was remarkable. From these talks developed her study, *Woman in the Nineteenth Century* (1845), the first mature consideration of FEMINISM by an American.

For two years she edited *The Dial* (1840–42), a distinguished literary review, and in 1844 accepted Greeley's invitation to become literary editor of the New York *Tribune*. She went abroad in 1846, and while in Italy bore a son (1848) to the Marchése Angelo Ossoli, whom she married in 1849. Ardent followers of Mazzini, they took part in the revolution of 1848–49. She was returning to America when she and her family were drowned in a wreck off Fire Island. Her originalities verged on the eccentric, but she had a compelling power in winning the devotion of those who penetrated beyond her self-esteem.

FULLER, MELVILLE WESTON (1833–1910), born in Maine, after graduation from Bowdoin (1853) practiced law in Chicago, where he rose to a high position at the bar of the Northwest. Long active in Democratic politics, by President Cleveland's appointment (1888) he succeeded Morrison R. Waite as 7th Chief Justice of the U.S. Supreme Court. In 1900 he became a member of the Permanent Court of Arbitration (the Hague Tribunal). As a jurist in temper with the times, he favored a strict construction of the Constitution and economic individualism.

FULTON, ROBERT (1765–1815), Pennsylvania-born civil engineer, artist, and inventor, began his versatile career as an expert gunsmith during the War of Independence. In London (1786–93) he studied painting under Benjamin West. Urged by James Watt and others, he turned to engineering, and invented an apparatus to raise and lower canal boats (the double inclined plane), a device for sawing marble, and a machine for twisting hemp into rope. Taking residence in France (1796), he constructed the *Nautilus,* a steam-propelled 'diving boat,' which in 1801 submerged to a depth of 25 ft. In the same year he published *A Treatise on the Improvement of Canal Navigation,* a prophetic discourse on the political and economic importance of inland waterways.

Upon ending his twenty-year sojourn abroad (1805) he settled in New York, and with the backing of ROBERT R. LIVINGSTON he designed the *Clermont,* a 150-ft. two-sided paddlewheel driven by a Watt engine. On 17 August 1807, with sparks roaring from her smokestack, the snub-nosed vessel steamed up the Hudson from New York to Albany. Fulton completed the round trip in 62 hours of operating time, and thus inaugurated the era of commercial steam navigation. Fulton's importance was not in his originality but in his ability to make effective use of principles established by earlier experimenters.

Fundamental Constitutions of Carolina, see *Carolina Proprietors.*

Fundamental Orders of Connecticut were adopted (1639) by the leading settlements of Hartford, Wethersfield, and Windsor, and remained the basic law of the colony until 1662, when Connecticut became a charter colony. Largely framed by THOMAS HOOKER, JOHN HAYNES, and Roger Ludlow (the lawyer who put them into final form), the statutes were similar to those of other New England colonies, but more compact. They emphasized the welfare of the community rather than that of the individual, and they differed from the laws of Massachusetts by extending the franchise, since they did not make church membership a prerequisite for voting. Even so, they did not make Connecticut a 'commonwealth democracy,' since fewer than half the male inhabitants were freemen. But as a clear statement of government for a commonwealth, they helped the framers of state governments (after 1776) to write their constitutions.

Fundamentalism, a 20th-century movement in American Protestantism, emphasizes as fundamental to Christianity a literal acceptance of traditional interpretations of the Bible, especially in such matters as the Virgin birth, the physical resurrection of Christ, and the inerrancy of the Scriptures. Objecting to the teachings of liberal churchmen, Fundamentalists oppose the teaching of evolutionary science. The extravagantly publicized SCOPES TRIAL (1925) in Tennessee brought into full view the fundamentalist controversy. Though it is still a political and religious factor in rural districts of the South, Fundamentalism has declined as a movement.

Funding Act, see *Assumption Act.*

Fur trade, which began with the first contact between European explorers and the Indians along the shores of North America, was a major factor in opening the continent to exploration and settlement. Furs, especially beaver in the North and deerskin in the South, always commanded a ready market in Europe (beaver supplied the material for most of Europe's hats), and those from the West Coast did so in China.

Since furs were one of the few New World commodities which brought immediate returns, they were the object of fierce rivalries between individual traders as well as nationally sponsored groups. The fur trade, after it was highly organized in the 18th century, founded great fortunes for a few, and therefore attracted many. It involved the colonies and later the U.S. in diplomatic negotiations or military conflict, at one time or another, not only with the Indians but with Spain, England, France, Holland, and Russia. Indeed, there has been scarcely any part of the American continent that has not been the scene of the fur trader's activity. As late as 1892 seal hunting in the Bering Sea involved the U.S. and Great Britain in a dispute requiring settlement by an international tribunal.

The vast Hudson Bay area was continuously exploited after 1670 by HUDSON'S BAY COMPANY, and after 1787 by its powerful rival, the NORTH WEST COMPANY. In the St. Lawrence–Great Lakes and upper Mississippi region the peltry trade flourished on a large scale for some 200 years (roughly from 1640). Until the close of the War of 1812, it centered chiefly in Quebec (and later Montreal). After 1817 its western reaches were monopolized by the AMERICAN FUR COMPANY, chartered by JOHN JACOB ASTOR.

In New England the fur trade began with the settlement of Plymouth (1620) and continued through the colonial period, though its importance declined after King Philip's War (1676). There were no useful waterways, and the presence of New Netherland to the west and New France to the north held the New England fur trade in check. Furthermore, as settlements spread and forests yielded to the ax, trappers were forced farther into the interior.

The Dutch and Swedes, pioneers in the fur trade of the middle region, were supplanted by the English in the latter half of the 17th century. Farther south a three-cornered rivalry among English, Spanish, and French traders extended to the Mississippi. The advance of settlements after the War of Independence doomed the fur trade in the entire eastern U.S., but the explorations thereafter of traders in the Far West became a major factor in the WESTWARD MOVEMENT. Indeed, the abundance and fine quality of the furs to be obtained in the Rocky Mountains made that vast region during the first half of the 19th century the most attractive fur-trading area on the continent.

After the return of the LEWIS AND CLARK EXPEDITION (1806) hunters and trappers in large numbers scoured the great expanse that the Expedition had explored. Of first importance was the organization of the ASHLEY EXPEDITIONS (1822), trading vanguards that discovered and mapped the routes by which settlers later crossed the Continental Divide. St. Louis had become the gateway to the West before 1810, and then and in the succeeding three decades it was the chief market and supply point for such fur traders as MANUEL LISA and the CHOUTEAU FAMILY.

Trade and exploration proceeded hand in hand, and Indian trade and Indian diplomacy were synonymous terms. National rivalries centered on the fur trade, whose regulations from the beginning were a matter of government concern, sometimes at the highest level.

Not least important is the vast body of letters, journals, and diaries left by the traders themselves, a literary heritage that records one of the most savage, dauntless, and picturesque aspects of American history.

General studies include H. M. Chittenden, *The American Fur Trade of the Far West* (3 vols., 1902); C. A. Vandiveer, *The Fur-Trade and Early Western Exploration* (1929); G. L. Nute, *The Voyageur* (1931); and Bernard De Voto, *Across the Wide Missouri* (1948).

Furniture in the colonial period was rarely imported, for joiners and other artisans could supply the early needs, and during the 18th century American craftsmen were producing furniture that rivaled the best contemporary work in London. At first current English styles were reproduced in pine, cherry, and maple. Later experts added walnut and mahogany, notably William Savery (1721–87) and Thomas Affleck (*fl.* 1763–95) of Philadelphia, and John Townsend (1721–1809) and John Goddard (1723–85) of Newport. The architect and builder SAMUEL MC INTIRE executed carvings for the furniture made by Salem cabinetworkers. In New York City during the 1790's DUNCAN PHYFE established a shop noted for the quality of its workmanship. Local characteristics are best represented in the traditional styles and painted designs preserved by the Pennsylvania Germans.

In the 19th century American furniture in general imitated various European styles, principally English and French. Mass production of machine-made furniture late in the century turned out golden oak in rococo designs. Contemporary furniture, often functional in design, makes use of synthetic materials, as well as glass, tubular steel, and wood.

Furuseth Act, see *La Follette Seaman's Act.*

G

GABO, Naum (1890–), Russian-born sculptor, came to the U.S. in 1946. Influenced in his earlier years by cubism, with his brother, Anton Pevsner, he worked out a 'constructivist' principle for art, especially treating space as a material subject, not an abstraction. 'Air which circulates becomes an integral part of the work.' Representative are his *Spiral Theme* (in plastic), and *Study for Construction in Space* (brass net, plastic and stainless steel wire).

GABRILOWITSCH, Ossip (1878–1936), Russian-born pianist and conductor, studied under Anton Rubinstein and Theodor Leschetizky, and made his American debut in 1900. He married the singer Clara Clemens (daughter of Mark Twain) in 1909, and after 1914 resided permanently in the U.S. While conductor of the Detroit Symphony Orchestra (1918–36), he appeared frequently as guest soloist with other orchestras. His playing was distinguished for its brilliant technique.

GADSDEN, Christopher (1724–1805), wealthy English-educated merchant of Charleston, South Carolina, in the STAMP ACT CONGRESS (1765) was a bold and able mobilizer of colonial opinion against Parliament's interference in American internal affairs. As a radical in the struggle over the South Carolina constitution (1778), he favored separation of church and state and the popular election of senators. On national issues in general he shared the views of Samuel Adams (Massachusetts), Thomas Mifflin (Pennsylvania), and Patrick Henry (Virginia).

Gadsden Purchase (1853), an area of 29,640 square miles acquired from Mexico for $10,000,000, now forms the entire southern border of Arizona south of the Gila river, and of New Mexico east to the Rio Grande. The purchase followed Congressional authorization of surveys, under the direction of the war department, of four possible routes for transcontinental railway systems. President Pierce's Secretary of War, Jefferson Davis of Mississippi, was interested in a southern route as a means to rival the Northeast in the struggle made acute by the COMPROMISE OF 1850. Such a route required passage through a large strip of territory in northwest Mexico. Davis persuaded the President to send the South Carolina railroad promoter Senator James Gadsden (1788–1858), who was interested both politically and financially in promoting the purchase, as minister to Mexico to negotiate the transfer. The acquisition, which completed the present BOUNDARIES of the U.S., was made by a treaty which the Senate ratified by a narrow margin in 1854. The treaty also included the privilege to build a road across the Isthmus of Tehuantepec for interocean commerce, with right of transit even in time of war. This concession, never used, was formally abrogated in 1937.

'Gag rule,' so called, is a special order of business sometimes adopted by deliberative assemblies to limit or suppress debate. In U.S. history it was most notoriously used as a proslavery measure. It was first adopted by Congress in 1836. The action tabled all antislavery petitions, then flooding the House. For eight years such 'gag rules,' variously phrased, were eloquently opposed from the floor of the House by John Quincy Adams, though he was no abolitionist, on the ground that they unconstitutionally deprived citizens of the right of petition. Finally the northern states compelled their representatives to support Adams, and no such rule (which requires renewal at each session) was adopted after the last expired in 1844.

GAGE, Thomas (1721–87), British general, after service in the French and Indian Wars succeeded Jeffrey Amherst as commander in chief of British forces in North America (1763). He replaced Thomas Hutchinson as governor of Massachusetts (May 1774), and his attempt, in line of duty, to secure military stores west of Boston (at Concord) precipitated the War of Independence (18 April 1775). In October he resigned and was replaced by SIR WILLIAM HOWE.

GALBRAITH, John Kenneth (1908–), Canadian-born economist, occupied a chair of economics at Harvard (1949–60) while serving as economic adviser to government agencies. In 1961 he was appointed U.S. ambassador to India. Among his studies two have received much attention. *American Capitalism: The Concept of Countervailing Power* (1952; rev. ed., 1956) defends big business in the present American economy and argues that in the American system of oligopoly (in which large enterprises set prices that smaller competitors usually have to follow) the power of capitalism is balanced by that of trade unions and government regulations. In *The Affluent Society* (1958) he suggests an increase in unemployment compensation, sales taxes, and spending for public purposes as a solution to the problems of inflation and unemployment.

GALLATIN, [ABRAHAM ALFONSE] ALBERT (1761–1849), member of an aristocratic and wealthy Swiss family, became imbued with the political enthusiasm of the times, cast off his Genevan ties, and emigrated to Boston (1780). There for a few months he supported himself by teaching French at Harvard. Settling soon on a frontier farm in Pennsylvania, he engaged in profitable land speculation, married, entered politics, and became one of the founders of the DEMOCRATIC-REPUBLICAN PARTY. Chosen by both his party and the Federalists as U.S. Senator in 1793, he was denied his seat on the technicality that his citizenship qualifications had not been fully met. The underlying reason seems to have been a Federalist reprisal for his support of the Pennsylvania frontiersmen on the issues that soon erupted into the WHISKY REBELLION (1794).

In 1795 he was elected to the House of Representatives, and won leadership of his party through tact, industry, and an intellectual keenness which Jefferson recognized by appointing Gallatin his Secretary of the Treasury (1801), a post he held into Madison's second Administration, resigning in 1814. Although Gallatin had been an unsparing critic of Hamilton, on the whole he continued Hamilton's financial methods. He administered his office for thirteen years with skill, guided by the principle that, although federalism should not encroach on the sovereignty of the states, Federal debts were mortgages to be redeemed by the central government.

When the War of 1812 placed a strain on the treasury, he sailed for Europe (1813), to negotiate a speedy end to the conflict by accepting the proffered mediation of Russia. To carry out his assignment effectively he resigned his cabinet post, and he was chiefly responsible for the terms of the TREATY OF GHENT (1814), which ended hostilities with England.

Madison selected Gallatin in 1816 as minister to France, where he remained for seven years. In 1826 John Quincy Adams sent him as minister to England. There he won such major concessions as the renewal of the important commercial treaties of 1815 and 1818 and the continuance of the joint Anglo-American occupation of Oregon. He assured the settlement of the vexing Northeast boundary question by referring it to the king of the Netherlands for negotiation.

Founder and first president (1832–39) of the New York bank later named for him, Gallatin devoted much of his time to science and literature after his return to private life in 1827. His *Synopsis of the Indian Tribes . . . of North America* (1836) stimulated the science of linguistics in the U.S., and he won the title of 'father of American ethnology' by founding the American Ethnological Society (1842). Reserved and austere, Gallatin never drew a close following in politics or warm friendships outside his family, but he was a statesman whose integrity and force of character give him lasting eminence.

Henry Adams's *The Life and Writings of Albert Gallatin* (1879) is a distinguished study.

GALLAUDET, THOMAS HOPKINS (1787–1851), Philadelphia-born graduate of Yale (1805), after studying methods of education for the deaf in England and France, founded (1817) the first institution for deaf-mutes in America at Hartford, Connecticut. His eldest son, Thomas Gallaudet (1822–1902), continued the work in New York City. His youngest son, Edward Miner Gallaudet (1837–1918), opened a similar institution in Washington, D.C., the upper division of which became Gallaudet College (1864).

GALLOWAY, JOSEPH (1731–1803), eminent Philadelphia lawyer, in an effort to tax the land holdings of the Penn family, joined Benjamin Franklin in petitioning the king (1764–65) to substitute royal for proprietary government in the colony. As a member of the First Continental Congress, he submitted a Plan of Union (1774) advocating a written constitution and a continental legislature co-equal with Parliament in dealing with affairs of the colonies. It was so favorably received that it was defeated by only one vote, and had it been presented before the SUFFOLK RESOLVES, which had prior consideration, it probably would have been adopted.

When the Revolution began Galloway remained a Loyalist, and he acted as Sir William Howe's civil administrator while Philadelphia was occupied by the British. He lived in England after 1778, when his estates were confiscated by Pennsylvania. One of the clearest thinkers and ablest political writers on issues of the times, he ranks with Thomas Hutchinson among the American statesmen who opposed the War of Independence.

Gallup Poll, a statistical report of public opinion on newsworthy issues, was originated by George H. Gallup (1901–), who founded the American Institute of Public Opinion (1935) at Princeton, N.J. Its polls, which have had a high degree of accuracy, usually exert considerable influence on the strategy of legislators and politicians.

Gambling, or gaming for diversion, unlike the scheme of LOTTERIES, has always been illegal in most of the U.S. From New Orleans, where the first houses exclusively for gambling games were opened about 1800, the professional sharper moved wherever new regions looked profitable. River gambling on the Mississippi steamboats reached its peak in the 1850's. The Club House at Saratoga Springs, New York, opened in 1867, and later (1894–1906) came under the management of the celebrated gambler Richard Canfield (1855–1914). Nevada still sanctions many types of gambling, and derives a large revenue from such resort cities as Reno and Las Vegas.

In about a third of the states gambling in the form of parimutuel betting (a share in the total stakes) is a source of revenue to states and municipalities. Policy betting (originally called lottery insurance) has grown in popularity during the last hundred years. It postulates that certain numbers will be drawn in a lottery, and now is controlled (with the connivance of corrupt officials) by racketeers. The policy racket and the 'fixing' of sports events by 'bookies' (gambling brokers) led in 1950 to a U.S. Senate investigation of organized crime.

Gangsters is a term (used colloquially in the U.S.) synonymous with 'hoodlums,' or criminals especially engaged in RACKETEERING. They first became well organized during the PROHIBITION ERA of the 1920's, when they began to operate on a national scale. They are chiefly involved in extortion and robberies.

G.A.R., see *Grand Army of the Republic.*

GARBO, GRETA [GRETA LOVISA GUSTAFSSON] (1905–), Swedish-born motion picture actress, came to Hollywood in 1926 and won nation-wide fame for her beauty and the restraint of her acting in such films as *Anna Christie, Queen Christina,* and *Anna Karenina.* She lived in retirement after the release of her last film in 1941.

GARCÉS, FRANCISCO TOMÁS HERMENEGILDO (1738–81), Spanish missionary in the Southwest, accompanied ANZA to California (1774–75), and later by his skill and endurance in exploring the Mohave region won the friendship of the powerful Yuma Indians, for whom he established missions. He was less successful in the Hopi villages, but it was in the Yuma region, during an Indian revolt, that he was clubbed to death. His diary (ed. by Elliott Coues, 2 vols., 1900) is useful source material.

GARCIA, see *Message to Garcia.*

GARDEN, ALEXANDER (*c.* 1730–91), Scottish-born physician, after receiving his medical degree at Edinburgh, in 1752 settled at Charleston, South Carolina. The most accomplished American botanist of his day, he made discoveries of new plant and animal species, including the congo eel and the mud eel. His wide correspondence with European naturalists included Linnaeus, who had great respect for Garden's careful descriptions, and named the gardenia for him. Garden was elected to the Royal Society in 1773. He chose to return to England at the outbreak of the War of Independence.

GARDEN, MARY (1877–), Scottish-born operatic soprano, after voice training in Paris made her debut there in Charpentier's *Louise* with spectacular success (1900). She came to America (1907) to join the Hammerstein Company. She soon began her long association (1910–31) with the Chicago Opera Company, playing her chief roles as Marguerite, Salome, Thaïs, and Louise. During one season (1921–22) she served as general director.

GARDINER, THOMAS (*fl.* 1630–32), arrived in Massachusetts, with a mistress, during the first year of the great Puritan migration (1630). His dramatic career has mystified historians and provided inspiration for poetry and fiction, including Longfellow's *Tales of a Wayside Inn.* Tolerant authorities became unsympathetic when they discovered that Gardiner had deserted two wives and was a Papist. As an agent for FERDINANDO GORGES, Gardiner hastened into Maine, and then returned to England, later testifying for Gorges as star witness against the Massachusetts charter.

GARFIELD, JAMES ABRAM (1831–81), 20th President of the U.S., was born in a frontier log cabin in Cuyahoga county, Ohio. After graduation from Williams College (1856) he became principal of Hiram College (1857–61). He was admitted to the Ohio bar in 1859. He organized an Ohio volunteer regiment (1861), served in the field, and two years later resigned his commission as major general to take a seat in the House of Representatives (1863–80). A regular Republican, he followed the party's program of Reconstruction, hard-money deflation, and opposition to civil service reform. Although unknown nationally, in the 1880 presidential campaign he was chosen on the 36th ballot as a compromise candidate, with Chester A. Arthur as running mate. Elected by a narrow popular vote over his Democratic opponent W. S. Hancock (electoral vote 214 to 155), he selected as his Secretary of State JAMES G. BLAINE, whose nomination for President had been blocked by ROSCOE CONKLING. Thus war was declared between the President and the Republican 'stalwarts,' the controlling faction of the party. After holding office but four months, he was shot (2 July 1881) by a disappointed office seeker, one Charles Guiteau. He lingered through the hot summer and died on 19 September.

A brilliant orator and a charming man, Garfield in his seventeen years as congressman had shown little force or originality, and his early death gave him scant opportunity to demonstrate statesmanship as President. His son, Harry Augustus Garfield (1863–1942), was president of Williams College (1908–34) and U.S. fuel administrator during World War I. Another son, James Rudolph Garfield (1865–1950) was Theodore Roosevelt's Secretary of the Interior.

See the biographies by T. C. Smith (2 vols., 1925), and R. G. Caldwell (1931).

GARRETSON, JAMES EDMUND (1828–95), a pioneer in oral surgery, graduated from the medical school of the University of Pennsylvania (1859), and ten years later published his textbook on dental surgery, the first (and long the standard) work in its field. After 1874 he taught at the Philadelphia Dental School, serving as dean from 1880.

GARRISON, WILLIAM LLOYD (1805–79), most vehement of the Massachusetts abolitionists, for a year (1829–30) edited with BENJAMIN LUNDY the *Genius of Universal Emancipation* at Baltimore. After imprisonment for libel he returned to Boston to edit the *Liberator* (1831–65), a militantly abolitionist weekly which in its first issue carried Garrison's motto: 'I am in earnest — I will not equivocate — I will not excuse — I will not retreat a single inch — *and I will be heard.*' Moved by the zeal of the dedicated, Garrison spurned both force and political aid as a means to achieve the immediate and complete emancipation of slaves. Relying wholly on moral suasion, he used such quotable and inflammatory language that the *Liberator* (with its relatively small circulation) gained both fame and notoriety. He castigated slaveholders, attacked moderate abolitionists, advocated northern secession, and before a Fourth of July gathering in 1854 burned a copy of the Constitution, saying, 'So perish all compromises with tyranny.' The 19th century view that Garrison was the foremost leader of the abolitionist cause still has scholarly adherents. After the Civil War he retired from public activity.

GARY, ELBERT HENRY (1846–1927), Chicago lawyer and industrialist, in association with J. P. Morgan organized and directed both the Federal Steel Company (1898) and the U.S. Steel Corporation (1901), the latter capitalized at what was then the colossal sum of $1,400,000,000. He founded the company town of Gary, Indiana, which by 1910 had a population of 55,000 and by 1920 had nearly doubled in size. In 1919 the U.S. Supreme Court ended the efforts of the government to dissolve the United States Steel Corporation as a monopoly. Though he was adamantly opposed to labor unions, under pressure of public opinion Gary shortened working hours after the bitter but unsuccessful steel strike of 1919.

Gas, the illuminating fuel produced by distillation from coal, but also found as a natural product in association with petroleum, became an important factor in U.S. economy during the first quarter of the 19th century. When it was adopted for city lighting, it made possible a twelve-hour working day the year round. Baltimore pioneered in the gas industry in 1816, and street lighting by gas was soon adopted by Boston (1822) and New York (1823). Although the incandescent bulb had largely replaced gas illumination by 1900, both natural gas (petroleum) and manufactured gas (coal) are still chief sources for heat and power. The nation's pipeline systems for natural gas, which is most plentiful in Texas and Louisiana, exceed 400,000 miles.

Gas Ring, see *Philadelphia Gas Ring.*

GATES, HORATIO (1727–1808), English-born general, arrived in America to fight in the French and Indian War (1755–63). He returned to England in 1765 and resigned from the army. When he next came to America (1772), he joined the patriot cause, and as commanding general in the SARATOGA CAMPAIGN (1777) won national fame. The so-called CONWAY CABAL (which came to nothing) was a maneuver to supplant Washington as commander in chief and replace him with Gates. Gates's stinging defeat in the battle of CAMDEN (1780) led to his replacement by NATHANAEL GREENE, but a congressional investigation was canceled (1782), and Gates served again at the end of the war. He spent the rest of his life in New York.

GATES, SIR THOMAS (*fl.* 1585–1621), as one of the grantees of the VIRGINIA COMPANY, led a fleet of nine ships to Jamestown in 1609. His own flagship, *Sea Venture,* was wrecked on the Bermudas, thus providing Shakespeare with material for *The Tempest.* He was governor of the Jamestown colony for three years (1611–14) before returning to England.

GATLING, RICHARD JORDAN (1818–1903), North Carolina inventor, in 1862 successfully demonstrated for the U.S. Ordnance Department a multiple-firing gun (forerunner of the machine gun). It was not adopted until 1866, but it was thereafter long used by the U.S. army, and gave currency to the slang term *gat,* for a gun or revolver.

GAYARRÉ, CHARLES ÉTIENNE ARTHUR (1806–95), Louisiana historian, was long prominent in state affairs and a leader of New Orleans literary circles. His *History of Louisiana* (4 vols., 1851–66), although somewhat fictionalized, is a monumental study, authentic in its descriptions, and still standard for the colonial and early national periods.

GEHRIG, LOU [HENRY LOUIS] (1903–41), as first baseman (1925–39) for the New York Yankees established the baseball record of playing 2130 consecutive league games. One of the great modern professional players, the 'Iron Horse' had a lifetime batting average of .341. He won the most-valuable-player award four times.

GELL-MANN, MURRAY (1929–), theoretical physicist, became a professor of physics at California Institute of Technology in 1956. He pioneered in the study of weak interactions, a new branch of physical science in which a mathematical quantity called the vector coupling constant has been found to be the same for the decay of the mu meson (muon) and the beta decay of the neutron. He introduced 'strangeness numbers' as part of a scheme for predicting the outcome of the interaction of wayward subatomic particles. This work has helped to clarify an understanding of electromagnetic phenomena.

General Court was the term applied in colonial New England to its bicameral legislatures, a meeting of the governor and his ASSISTANTS (upper house), and the deputies (lower house). The deputies were propertied FREEMEN, who elected the assistants, the inner circle of about twelve men who wielded authority under certain restraints from the deputies. The term first designated the general court or meeting of the ruling members of the Massachusetts Bay Company. It still remains the official name of the legislative assemblies of Massachusetts and New Hampshire.

General Education Board, established in 1903 by John D. Rockefeller, for 60 years made gifts to various educational and research agencies. Beginning as an undertaking to supply the needs of high schools in the South, especially Negro education and agricultural training, it soon was promoting a comprehensive system of higher education in the U.S., and appropriating funds (on a matching basis) to technical and professional schools on terms invited by its beneficiaries. Rockefeller's total endowment of $129,000,000 made it one of the largest philanthropies of its kind in history. Before its virtual liquidation in 1961, the Board had made benefactions of more than $300,000,000.

General Electric Company at Schenectady, New York (incorporated in 1892), is the largest electrical equipment manufacturer in the U.S. As a pioneer in industrial research, it established its Research Laboratory in 1900 under the direction of WILLIS R. WHITNEY. (For many years CHARLES P. STEINMETZ was associated with the company as consulting engineer.) After World War II the company carried out a broad diversification program into household appliances, radio, television, and other electronic devices, as well as plastics, alloys, and diesel engines. The groundwork for this great expansion was laid during the presidency of GERARD SWOPE (1922–39).

General Motors Corporation (1908), the largest manufacturing establishment in the world, is chiefly located in Michigan. It turns out nearly 60 per cent of the automotive vehicles in the nation and a wide variety of motor-powered products, including diesels, airplane engines, refrigerators, and electrical equipment. Its operations are carried on in some 90 plants located in more than 45 cities in the U.S., with affiliates abroad. The development of this vast industrial empire began under the presidency of Alfred P. Sloan (1923–37). In 1965 its net income of $2,000,000,000 was the largest of any corporation.

Genêt Affair (1793–94) occurred when the Girondists, the moderate French republicans, sent Citizen Edmond Charles Genêt (1763–1834) as minister from France to the U.S. He landed at Charleston, South Carolina, in April 1793. His cordial civic welcome was amplified during his progress en route to the capital (Philadelphia) by ANTI-FEDERALISTS, who sought thereby to create pressure favorable to France after Washington's NEUTRALITY PROCLAMATION. The minister became a factor in the political struggle between Hamilton and Jefferson, whom Genêt at first embarrassed and later alienated by improper distribution of French military commissions as a prelude to organized expeditions against Canada, Spanish Florida, and Louisiana.

After Genêt disingenuously ordered the dispatch of an interned French privateer, the administration ordered his recall. He was permitted unofficial residence in the U.S., however, since his return in disgrace to France (by then turned Jacobin) would have meant the guillotine. The failure of Genêt's mission was paralleled by that of Gouverneur Morris in Paris, and gave convincing evidence that the FRANCO-AMERICAN ALLIANCE of 1778 no longer had any meaning. Genêt became an American citizen, married a daughter of

Governor George Clinton of New York, and settled on the Hudson.

Geneva Conference of 1927, a five-power meeting called by President Coolidge, assembled at Geneva, Switzerland (20 June–24 August) to consider further reduction of naval armament pursuant to the WASHINGTON CONFERENCE (1921–22). France and Italy declined the invitation. Japan and Great Britain met with the U.S., but since Great Britain and the U.S. could not agree on cruiser reduction, the conference adjourned without accomplishment.

Geneva Conference of 1932, assembled with U.S. participation to discuss general disarmament, was the first world conference in history to take up the limitation of armaments of every kind. Germany announced her withdrawal from the League of Nations in October, and the conference broke up without accomplishment in the spring of 1934.

Geneva Conference of 1954 dealt with both Korean and Indochinese peace settlements. Practically all the belligerents in Korea, including the U.S., Soviet Russia, Red China, North Korea, South Korea, France, and others tried but failed to unify Korea or to go beyond an armistice. Most of these powers, plus the communist Viet Minh regime of Vietnam, signed an eight-power agreement which compelled defeated France to accept the partition of Vietnam near the 17th parallel, promised elections in 1956, recognized the sovereignty of Cambodia and Laos, and arranged an armistice. However, the Eisenhower administration was unwilling to share the onus of these communist gains and refused to sign, although promising to 'refrain from the threat of force to disturb' the agreements. This Geneva Conference became the focus of debate during the public discussions over the VIETNAM War (1966).

Geneva Conference of 1955 was the 'summit conference' to end the 'cold war' between East and West, and it was attended by the heads of state from Great Britain, France, Soviet Russia, and the U.S. President Eisenhower offered the so-called Open Skies Plan to avert nuclear (and conventional) surprise attacks. This involved international aerial inspection aided by complete blueprints of military centers. Gradual disarmament as well as international inspection were urged. However, Soviet Russia, while willing to accept limited inspection, rejected the plan as a legalization of nuclear weapons which must be prohibited, and demanded the scrapping of NATO and overseas bases. It is surmised that the failure of the Open Skies idea led the U.S. to use secret reconnaissance flights over Soviet Russia by means of the novel Lockheed U-2 plane.

Geneva Conference of 1958 became a long series of meetings of Great Britain, Soviet Russia, and the U.S. in an attempt to formulate a treaty outlawing nuclear tests. Since no agreement could be reached, in 1962 the negotiations were indefinitely suspended.

GENTH, FREDERICK AUGUSTUS (1820–93), German-born chemist, came to the U.S. in 1848 and opened a laboratory in Philadelphia (1850–70) for commercial analysis, research, and instruction. He served as professor of chemistry at the University of Pennsylvania (1872–88), and as an expert on mineral chemistry was the most distinguished analytical chemist of his day.

Geography of America became a serious study late in the 18th century. The first American 'specialist' in geography was JEDIDIAH MORSE, whose pioneer study, *American Geography* (1789), is evidence that 'facts' about areas west of the Appalachians were largely conjectural. The German scholar Christoph Daniel Ebeling (1741–1817) compiled *Erdbeschreibung und Geschichte von America* (7 vols., 1793–1816), the first systematic attempt to cull evidence by studying scores of travelers' observations. Easily first among the pioneers of modern American geography was the German scientist Alexander von Humboldt (1769–1859), whose expeditions to North and South America (1799–1804) inaugurated the era of scientific exploration.

The nation's universities, and such agencies as the AMERICAN GEOGRAPHICAL SOCIETY (1852) and the NATIONAL GEOGRAPHIC SOCIETY (1888), began offering research facilities and sponsoring field investigations in the late 19th century. Notable government topographical and geographical surveys of the West were those conducted during the 1860's and 1870's by F. V. HAYDEN (Nebraska and Wyoming), CLARENCE KING (40th Parallel), G. M. WHEELER (100th Meridian), and J. W. POWELL and CLARENCE DUTTON (Utah, Nevada, and Arizona). The contributions of GEORGE PERKINS MARSH in the 1860's to ecology were major and served as a guide to the 20th-century CONSERVATION MOVEMENT. Geographical concepts today owe much to the groundwork of such American scientists as WILLIAM M. DAVIS, ELLEN C. SEMPLE, and ISAIAH BOWMAN.

Geological Survey, U.S. (est. 1879), was constituted a permanent bureau in the Department of the Interior to unify and centralize the separate surveys already undertaken by F. V. HAYDEN, G. M. WHEELER, CLARENCE KING (its first director, 1879–81), and J. W. POWELL (its second, 1881–94). The work of this division in geological exploration, preparation of maps, examination of natural resources, and study of the problems relating to the land has from the first been carried forward with a remarkably high degree of scientific imagination and economic foresight, and is recorded in many series of published reports.

Geology as a science began in the U.S. with the *Observations* (1809) of WILLIAM MACLURE, who sketched the first geological map of America. A pioneer in the teaching of earth sciences was BENJAMIN SILLIMAN of Yale, who directed the studies (1802–53) of such geologists as AMOS EATON, EDWARD HITCHCOCK, DENISON OLMSTEAD, JAMES DWIGHT DANA, and JOSIAH DWIGHT WHITNEY. In 1879 CLARENCE KING established the U.S. Geological Survey. The transcontinental survey of RAPHAEL PUMPELLY opened up the resources of the Northwest, and the inquiries of NATHANIEL S. SHALER drew attention to the importance of physiography in the study of U.S. history.

The allied field of paleontology had its modest beginning under impressive aegis in 1801, when President Jefferson, then also president of the American Philosophical Society, encouraged the artist CHARLES WILLSON PEALE to recover mastodon bones from a New York farm, and authorized the Army department to loan digging equipment. By mid-19th century LOUIS AGASSIZ, JOSEPH LEIDY, O. C. MARSH, and E. D. COPE had advanced studies in the field. The fossil treasures collected in Nebraska after 1900, among the richest in North America, were turned up by the Morrill Paleontological Expeditions, financed by the Nebraska banker Charles H. Morrill (1842–1928).

GEORGE III [GEORGE WILLIAM FREDERICK] (1738–1820), king of Great Britain and Ireland (1760–1820), began his long reign just at the time the troubles between England and her American colonies were beginning to brew. The legend has long persisted that George III was a corrupt tyrant who acted unconstitutionally and sought to curb English liberties. But the chief measures that provoked the War of Independence were taken largely by the government, although the king's use of his patronage system involved a considerable personal influence. The king had limited abilities, but a strong sense of duty as a parliamentary monarch, with no shadow of doubt about his sovereign constitutionality. He is said to have prolonged the war by insisting on retaining as first minister the unhappy Lord NORTH, who had never wanted the war at all, but stayed on as a buffer between the king and the Whigs. Recurrent sieges of mental illness ultimately incapacitated the king.

GEORGE, HENRY (1839–97), at sixteen left his devoutly religious Philadelphia home to sail as foremast boy to Calcutta, where he was first struck by the contrast between poverty and wealth. Attracted by the promise of work to San Francisco (1857), he struggled for ten years at various occupations, chiefly as a printer and newspaperman. His reformist tendencies led him to a diagnosis of the causes of poverty and inequality that distinguishes him as one of the few original American economic theorists. He elaborated his views in *Progress and Poverty* (1879), a classic in the literature of ideas. He attributed poverty to rent and proposed a tax on land as the remedy for social ills. He set forth the formula of the Single Tax, one that would wipe out unearned income or gain through speculation on land, and by insuring equal access to resources, forestall monopoly and give economic equality to all classes of society.

In 1880 he moved to New York. For the rest of his life he was greatly in demand as a lecturer at home and abroad. He also wrote constantly to amplify his theory. The single-tax doctrine did not succeed in its larger purpose, since it failed to comprehend fully the endless ramifications of the new capitalism. But it was a powerful manifesto of popular aspiration the world over. Some 2,000,000 copies of the book had sold before 1900, and a whole generation of progressives acknowledged their indebtedness to this eloquent reformer. Although he was twice defeated as Democratic candidate for mayor of New York City (he died just before the second election), he was a formidable rival to the Tammany machine, even without party organization. His theories have influenced tax legislation in many nations, including the U.S.

See A. A. DeMille, *Henry George* (1950).

George, Lake, in northeastern New York in the foothills of the Adirondacks, lies in the region that frequently was a battleground during the FRENCH AND INDIAN WAR (1755–63). The ruins of Fort William Henry (1755) and Fort George (1759) are at its southern end. It was discovered by the Jesuit missionary ISAAC JOGUES (1646), and given its present name (1755) by the colonial superintendent of Indian affairs, SIR WILLIAM JOHNSON. The Lake today is the center of a resort area.

Georgetown University (1791) in Washington, D.C., is the oldest U.S. Catholic college, opened by Bishop JOHN CARROLL. It is best known for its schools of foreign service, law, and medicine. In 1965, with a faculty of 1390, it enrolled 6760 students.

Georgia, visited by De Soto in 1540, was part of the grant to the Lords Proprietors of Carolina (1663), and became an independent colony under royal charter in 1732. Designed as a southern bastion against encroachment by Spain in her war against England (1739–48), it was settled under arrangements made by influential and wealthy humanitarians who hoped to better the condition of the deserving poor in England. The venture was administered by JAMES OGLETHORPE, who established the undertaking between the Savannah and Altamaha rivers in the name of George II. Under a benevolent despotism the selected colonists tilled their farms (50 acres per person, 500 acres for a family of six). Slavery was forbidden. But unwise paternalistic rules hampered the economy and at the outbreak of the Revolution, Georgia was the weakest and least populous of the Thirteen Colonies.

The seat of government, until Atlanta became the capital (1868), was chiefly Savannah or Augusta. Although Georgia was a strong advocate of states' rights, it was by unanimous vote the first of the southern states to ratify the Constitution (1788), since it recognized that its relation to Spanish and to Indian problems could profit from a federation. In 1802 it assumed its present boundaries. Slavery had been instituted and the cotton industry flourished. Following the War of 1812 Savannah rivaled Charleston as a commercial and shipping center. Georgia ratified the Confederate constitution in March 1861, and became a major battlefield during the ATLANTA CAMPAIGN (1864). When the state was readmitted to the Union (1870), the large plantations were breaking up, and with slavery abolished, large acreages were worked by SHARECROPPERS and TENANT FARMERS.

Rapid industrial and commercial growth offset agricultural losses, Atlanta became 'the New York of the South' and in recent years diversified farming, with cotton the leading money crop, has replaced the one-crop system. Next to California, Georgia leads in lumber production, and is a chief source of pulp and turpentine. The population increase during the decade 1950–60 from 3,400,000 to 3,900,000 is chiefly concentrated in ATLANTA, the largest city, and in Columbus (80,000 to 117,000), Macon (70,000 to 123,000) and Savannah (120,000 to 150,000). Leading institutions of higher learning include the University of Georgia (Athens, est. 1785), Emory University (Atlanta, est. 1836), and Georgia Institute of Technology (Atlanta, est. 1885).

German mercenaries, see *Hessians.*

Germantown, Battle of (4 October 1777), was the last important engagement conducted by Washington before he wintered at VALLEY FORGE. After the battle of BRANDYWINE the British occupied Philadelphia and the greater part of Howe's army camped at Germantown. Washington's attack failed chiefly because a fog confused his troops, and an unexpected skirmish delayed the arrival of General Nathanael Greene. The Americans suffered some 1075 casualties; the British, 530.

Germany, Occupation of, began after Germany's unconditional surrender to the Allies (7–8 May 1945). Allied military commanders took over the functions of government. The occupation plan was based on Allied military arrangements made at the YALTA CONFERENCE (February 1945) and the POTSDAM CONFERENCE (August 1945). Germany was divided into four occupation zones, each separately administered by Russia, the U.S., Great Britain, and, later, France. Berlin, similarly zoned, became the seat of a four-power control council. Conflicts over the terms of the Potsdam Agreement, and the refusal of the Soviets to establish a 'hard' unified currency, weakened the control council from the start, and in 1948 the Soviet representatives ceased to attend the council meetings.

In April 1949 the Allied High Commission (a three-man body representing the U.S., Great Britain, and France, and exercising supreme authority in the three zones that now constitute the Federal Republic of Germany) drafted an Occupation Statute, defining the terms for a merger of the three zones. In 1948–49 German delegates from their zones met at Bonn, the temporary capital, and wrote a constitution for West Germany. Constant efforts of the Soviet military government to isolate the Allied sectors of Berlin from the rest of Western-controlled Germany by a blockade of the rail and highway connections led to the BERLIN AIRLIFT, which supplied the city until the blockade was abandoned (1949).

A 'peace contract' (1952) between West Germany and the three Western Powers gave nominal sovereignty to the new state, and it gained *de jure* sovereignty in 1955. It would be premature to conclude that the occupation of West Germany had ended, however, considering the presence of Allied garrisons, their reinforcement during later Berlin crises, and the constant danger that the Allied communication with other parts of Germany might be cut. No peace treaty has yet been signed with Germany, and the occupation continues, though unofficially.

GERONIMO (*c.* 1829–1909) was an Apache chief who led several relentless attacks on white settlers in the Southwest. He was captured, but escaped (1883). He finally surrendered in 1886 on condition that his braves might join their families in Florida. They were imprisoned instead, and ultimately were moved to Oklahoma, where Geronimo died. He was an outstanding leader and became a legendary figure in his lifetime. In 1906 he dictated *Geronimo's Story of His Life.*

GERRY, ELBRIDGE (1744–1814), after graduation from Harvard (1762) entered his father's shipping business at Marblehead, Massachusetts. He served in the Continental Congress (1776–85), and was a delegate to the Federal Constitutional Convention (1787). He refused to sign the Constitution and opposed its ratification. His objections were overcome when the first ten amendments (the Bill of Rights) were added. Twice elected to Congress (1789–93), in 1797, with C. C. Pinckney and John Marshall, he undertook the mission to France that culminated in the so-called XYZ AFFAIR.

In the second of his two terms as governor of Massachusetts (1810–11) his Jeffersonian followers, by a political maneuver since known as the GERRYMANDER, sought to retain control of the state. Although Gerry was defeated by Federalists in his third-term bid for governor, he was immediately nominated (and elected) Vice President of the U.S. on the ticket with James Madison, whom he loyally supported in the War of 1812 despite the strong opposition of his Massachusetts constituency. He died in office.

Gerrymander in U.S. politics means the districting of state, county, or local voting units in such a way as to gain partisan advantage. The term originated in 1812, when followers of Governor ELBRIDGE GERRY of Massachusetts, seeking to retain control, rearranged election districts in a grotesque manner, suggesting to a contemporary cartoonist the shape of a salamander.

The practice still persists, although state constitutions usually have some rules controlling the distribution of representatives. Recent Supreme Court rulings on REAPPORTIONMENT have sharply curtailed the power of state legislatures to gerrymander.

GERSHWIN, GEORGE (1898–1937), born in the lower East Side of New York City, received his early musical training in TIN PAN ALLEY. He later studied under the composer and teacher Rubin Goldmark (1872–1936), and in his own idiom produced such masterpieces of their genre as *Lady Be Good* (1924), and *Of Thee I Sing* (1931), the first musical comedy to receive a Pulitzer Prize. His *Rhapsody in Blue* (1924), composed for Paul Whiteman's first concert of 'symphonic jazz,' is the classic example of its type. The orchestral poem *An American in Paris* (1928) was commissioned by Walter Damrosch. His major work, *Porgy and Bess* (1935), a folk opera interpreting the Negro spirit, has been repeatedly performed throughout the world. His brother Ira Gershwin (1896–) wrote the lyrics for most of his best songs.

Gettysburg Address was delivered by Abraham Lincoln (19 November 1863) at the dedication of a national cemetery on the site of the great Pennsylvania battlefield. Lincoln completed it in Washington, although he made minor changes at Gettysburg. He read his three brief paragraphs slowly, and the crowd, weary after the two-hour oration of Edward Everett, applauded without enthusiasm. Although for partisan reasons the address at the time was belittled or denounced, contrary to general belief the speech was judged at once and by many to be one of the noble expressions of American democracy.

Gettysburg, Battle of (1–3 July 1863), was the greatest combat in the Civil War, involving 93,000 Federals and 70,000 Confederates. It decided the outcome of the invasion of Pennsylvania, and with the simultaneous victory of Grant at Vicksburg it forecast the ultimate defeat of the Confederacy.

After his victory at CHANCELLORSVILLE (2–5 May) General Lee continued his invasion of the North. His reorganized army crossed the Potomac. Ewell's 2d Corps swept the Shenandoah valley clear of Union forces. By late June Lee was seriously threatening Harrisburg. His cavalry, under J. E. B. Stuart, was raiding between Washington and the Union forces, commanded by George G. Meade, that were concentrating north of the Potomac. On 1 July a Union advance sent to delay Lee came in contact with a Confederate division west of Gettysburg, which thus became the unintended site of the massive encounter.

The battle was unique in that both Meade and Lee stumbled into it. Neither commander was present on the first day or knew much of what was going on until the first day was over, when the Confederate advantage was so overwhelming that any possibility of a Union victory rested on a feather's edge. Longstreet led the main attack against the Union right on 2 July, but his delay (till 4 p.m.) had given Meade time to assemble his whole force and consolidate its strong position on Cemetery Ridge. Although the Confederates took the Peach Orchard and Culp's Hill, they were repulsed at Round Top and Little Round Top (commanding Cemetery Ridge), and were beaten off at Cemetery Hill.

Meade's counterattack on the morning of 3 July retook Culp's Hill. Lee's order to attack the Union center on Cemetery Ridge engaged 15,000 of Longstreet's men in the culminating event of PICKETT'S CHARGE, which was repulsed with tremendous Confederate loss. Meanwhile Stuart's wild ride around the Federal army had proved futile. Exhausted, both armies held their positions until the night of 4 July, when Lee withdrew.

Although high water in the Potomac delayed Lee's crossing back to Virginia, Meade failed to attack in force, and Lee escaped. The Union casualties totaled 23,000; the Confederate, 20,000. Informed students of the event credit success chiefly to Meade's excellent defense and Lee's poorly co-ordinated attack. The Federal victory at Gettysburg saved the Union.

Ghent, Treaty of, ending the WAR OF 1812, was signed in Belgium (24 December 1814) by Great Britain and the U.S. The five U.S. representatives were James A. Bayard, Jonathan Russell, Henry Clay, John Quincy Adams, and Albert Gallatin, the chief spokesman for this very able group. The treaty restored peace, but it was silent on the issues over which the two nations had clashed. No allusion was made to the impressment of American seamen, indemnities for seizures, or the right of search and visit. The treaty provided for restoration of all conquered territory and for the appointment of commissions to determine the disputed Canada–U.S. boundary. The question of naval forces on the Great Lakes and the issues involved in the OREGON BOUNDARY DISPUTE were tabled. The Senate unanimously ratified the treaty (February 1815), and thus wiped the war off the books.

Ghost Dance, the central ritual of a messianic Indian religion, was instituted about 1888 on a reservation in Nevada among the Paiute by a tribesman, Wovoka, or 'Jack Wilson.' After a hypnotic trance, Wovoka preached the coming of an Indian Messiah who would restore the country to the Indians and reunite the living with their departed friends. The cult spread to other reservations, members falling into trances and talking to 'ghosts.' Tension mounted, and in 1890 the Ghost Dance uprising on the Black Hills Reservation in North Dakota culminated in the battle of Wounded Knee, during which U.S. Army troops massacred some 200 Teton Sioux. Thus ended the so-called Messiah War.

G.I. (general issue) was the term used colloquially in World War II to designate an American soldier. It corresponds to the name 'doughboy' of World War I.

G.I. Bill of Rights, so called, under the Servicemen's Readjustment Act (1944) provided benefits for American veterans after World War II. The law chiefly guaranteed loans, made arrangements to counter veteran unemployment, and offered financial aid for industrial training and liberal arts education. Similar educational and readjustment payments were provided for Korean War veterans (1952). The program was ended in 1956, but meanwhile it had enabled several million veterans to go to college.

GIBBONS, JAMES (1834–1921), Baltimore-born Roman Catholic prelate, was consecrated bishop (1868) of a newly created diocese in North Carolina. In 1877 he became head of the see of Baltimore, and was created a cardinal in 1886. Deeply attached to American institutions and to the people, he greatly altered the attitude of his church toward the KNIGHTS OF LABOR. He laid the cornerstone of the Catholic University of America, Washington, D.C. (1888), and until his death served as its chancellor.

Gibbons* v. *Ogden (1824) was a case resulting in the first broad construction by the U.S. Supreme Court of the nature and scope of congressional power under the commerce clause of the Constitution. In the most difficult and far-reaching of his decisions, John Marshall held that Congress was supreme in all aspects of interstate commerce and could not be limited by state powers in that area. His decision defined commerce as including not only buying and selling but also the means of transportation and the routes. It interpreted the phrase 'to regulate' to mean that Congress could foster, inhibit, or protect interstate commerce. The decision broke the steamboat navigations monopoly of New York and Louisiana which had controlled licenses based on the Livingston-Fulton patents.

GIBBS, JOSIAH WILLARD (1839–1903), after graduation from Yale (1858) and study abroad, returned to Yale as professor of mathematical physics (1871–1903). In 1873 he published his first two papers setting forth equations for the mechanical action of heat. His classic memoir, 'On the Equilibrium of Heterogeneous Substances' (1876–78), remains one of the great achievements in theoretical physics, and it was the foundation of the science of physical chemistry by its formulation of the phase-rule.

Gibbs's papers on vector analysis (1880–84) were followed by others that developed the electromagnetic theory of light (1882–89). His later work in statistical mechanics, describing the movement of subatomic particles, although long unrecognized, has proved to be his most important contribution. The *Collected Works* (1928) reveal the profound originality of Gibbs, who was one of the very few pure scientists in America before the 20th century.

See L. P. Wheeler, *Josiah Willard Gibbs* (1951).

GIBSON, Charles Dana (1867–1945), Massachusetts-born illustrator, established a reputation in the 1890's for his so-called 'Gibson girl,' black and white drawings glorifying American womanhood. They reflect the gaiety of well-bred society of the time and appealed to sentimental tastes.

GIDDINGS, Franklin Henry (1855–1931), a founder of sociology in the U.S., occupied the first chair of sociology at Columbia (after 1894). He demonstrated how statistical tables could serve as analytical devices for reaching abstract generalizations, and under his influence the American community, rural and urban, was examined in its ecological context. His writings include *The Principles of Sociology* (1896), *Democracy and Empire* (1900), and *Studies in the Theory of Human Society* (1922).

GIDDINGS, Joshua Reed (1795–1864), represented the Western Reserve district of Ohio in Congress (1838–59). For his militant abolitionist tactics he was censured by the House (1842), resigned, and was promptly re-elected. Giddings broke with the Whig party, and led the insurgent antislavery bloc which became the FREE-SOIL PARTY (1848). As a congressman he joined J. Q. Adams in fighting the 'GAG RULE,' denounced the annexation of Texas and the Mexican War as a slaveholders' conspiracy, and, while opposed to disunion, urged the President to free the slaves if war came. After 1861 he served as consul general to Canada.

Gideon International, see *Bible Societies.*

GILBERT, Cass (1859–1934), Ohio-born architect, designed the 60-story Woolworth Building in New York (1913), for many years the world's tallest. Its overlay of Gothic motives, carried up to the top of the building, were subordinated to the vertical lines, and thus the edifice became a tower, anticipating the form of later skyscrapers. Gilbert's other designs include the public libraries at St. Louis, Detroit, and New Haven; the U.S. Supreme Court building; and the Minnesota state capitol.

GILBERT, Henry Franklin Belknap (1868–1928), was the first American composer to experiment successfully with native folk music as an art form. His *Comedy Overture on Negro Themes* (1906) was a pioneer orchestration of Negro jazz idioms. *Dance in Place Congo* (1918), scored for ballet and based on Creole themes from New Orleans, brought him national recognition.

GILBERT, Sir Humphrey (*c.* 1539–83), educated at Eton and Oxford, was a half-brother of Sir Walter Raleigh. Authorized by Queen Elizabeth to colonize in the New World, and incidentally to search for the NORTHWEST PASSAGE, in 1583 Gilbert took possession of Newfoundland. He attempted no colonization at the time, and was lost in a storm while returning home. A year later his patents were renewed in Raleigh's name.

Gilded age, so called, was the period from the end of the Civil War to the PANIC OF 1873. It was an era of currency inflation, widespread speculation, loose business and political morals, and it expressed the irresponsible materialism of a victorious North. The phrase is derived from the title of the novel written by Mark Twain and Charles Dudley Warner (1873), castigating the vulgarity of that decade.

GILMAN, Daniel Coit (1831–1908), Connecticut-born educator, after graduation from Yale (1852) and study abroad, returned to Yale as librarian (1858–65) and professor of geography in the Sheffield Scientific School, which he helped found (1861). He served briefly (1872–75) as president of the newly organized University of California, but his great work began when he was installed (1876) as first president of

Johns Hopkins University, established specifically to foster graduate study and research. Here Gilman inaugurated the most fruitful experiment in American higher education. His stimulating personality and emphasis on creative scholarship attracted brilliant scholars to his faculty, and before his retirement (1901) Gilman had made Johns Hopkins an important university and medical center. His writings include *University Problems* (1898), and *The Launching of a University* (1906).

GILMORE, PATRICK SARSFIELD (1829–92), Irish-born bandmaster, organized his own band in Boston (1859), and conducted the first of his spectacular music festivals in New Orleans (1864). He organized still bigger ones in Boston at the National Peace Jubilee (1869), and the World Peace Jubilee (1872), but the 20,000-voice chorus in the latter proved unwieldy. He wrote the words and music for the popular Civil War song, *When Johnny Comes Marching Home*.

GIRARD, STEPHEN (1750–1831), French-born banker and philanthropist, settled in Philadelphia (1776) as shipowner and merchant. He established his own banking house and helped finance the U.S. in the War of 1812. He bequeathed several million dollars to found Girard College, an educational institution (still functioning under the terms of his will) for poor white orphan boys.

GIST, CHRISTOPHER (*c.* 1706–59), frontiersman in the employ of the OHIO COMPANY (1750), penetrated the Kentucky region eighteen years before Daniel Boone. In 1753–54 he accompanied George Washington on a journey to warn the French out of the Ohio valley, and later guided Braddock's expedition (1755) against Fort Duquesne. Gist was highly regarded by his contemporaries as a woodsman and surveyor. His *Journals,* covering his experiences in Ohio and Kentucky during 1750–53, were published in 1893.

Glacier National Park (1910), 1,000,000 acres in northwestern Montana, straddling the Continental Divide, is a rugged mountain region of scores of glaciers, snow-capped precipices, waterfalls, lakes, and densely forested slopes. It adjoins the Canadian Glacier National Park.

GLADDEN, WASHINGTON (1836–1918), Pennsylvania-born clergyman, graduated from Williams (1859) and from 1882 until his death was pastor of the First Congregational Church in Columbus, Ohio. His many books, including *Who Wrote the Bible?* (1891) and *Social Salvation* (1902), helped to popularize 'modernist' views. He was a leading figure in the CHRISTIAN SOCIALISM movement, and built his philosophy upon an application of Christian principles to social problems.

GLASGOW, ELLEN [ANDERSON GHOLSON] (1874–1945), was born in Richmond, Virginia, where she lived most of her life. Her many novels, which were sympathetic depictions of the decline of an aristocratic culture, follow the theme of her motto: 'What the South needs is blood and irony.' In revolt against the romantic treatment of southern life, she wrote novels of the city (Richmond) and the country (the rural western part of her state). Her work constitutes a social history of Virginia since 1850, and her impressive achievements include *The Battle-Ground* (1902), *Barren Ground* (1925), and *The Romantic Comedians* (1926).

Glass was made by American colonists from the time of the early settlements, but it was not commercially manufactured until the 18th century, when small bottle works were set up in various places. By 1740 flint hollow ware and window glass were produced in New Jersey, and before the Revolution HENRY STIEGEL had made Philadelphia a glassmaking center. By 1812 Pittsburgh had become foremost in the industry, with five factories in operation. After 1820 American makers perfected the technique of manufacturing pressed glassware, thereby lowering the cost and increasing the demand. Household canning (begun about 1850) further extended the glass industry. Plate glass, widely adopted after the Civil War, ultimately altered the character of urban architecture and display merchandising.

Glass-Owen Act, see *Federal Reserve System.*

Glass-Steagall Banking Act (1933), the most important banking measure since the Federal Reserve Act of 1913, provided for the separation of COMMERCIAL and INVESTMENT BANKING. It severely limited the use of bank credit for speculation, extended the FEDERAL RESERVE SYSTEM, and permitted branch banking. To prevent a recurrence of the epidemic of bank failures in the 1920's, it created the Federal Bank Deposit Insurance Corporation for guaranteeing individual bank deposits up to a fixed sum. To the general public the deposit guarantee was the striking feature of the statute.

GLIDDEN, JOSEPH FARWELL (1813–1906), New Hampshire–born farmer, invented the form of twisted BARBED WIRE now in common use. He received a patent in 1874, and by 1883 his company, in DeKalb, Illinois, was turning out 600 miles of barbed wire daily, thus reducing the expense of fencing to a fraction of its former cost and revolutionizing ranching on the Great Plains.

GLUECK, SHELDON (1896–), Polish-born criminologist and professor of law at Harvard (after 1931), made comprehensive diagnoses of the entire American system of criminal justice in such works as *Crime and Justice* (1945) and *Unraveling Juvenile Delinquency* (1950). As an adviser to many government law agencies, he sought to make officials aware of the need to reach problems in the field of social pathology, especially in the area of family disintegration.

Gobbledygook, a term coined by U.S. Representative Maury Maverick (1895–1954) of Texas, is used to describe the verbiage often employed in the directives of officialdom. The term was derisively applied to NEW DEAL measures.

GODDARD, ROBERT HUTCHINGS (1882–1945), professor of physics at Clark University (1919–43), began his work on rocketry in 1912. In 1926 he successfully launched the world's first liquid-fuel rocket, and during World War II he directed research in jet propulsion for the U.S. Navy. His accomplishments won him the sobriquet 'father of the modern rocket.' In 1960 the U.S. government paid $1,000,000 to Goddard's assigns for the use of his patents.

Godey's Lady's Book, see *Hale, Sarah J.*

GODFREY, THOMAS (1704–49), glazier and self-taught mathematician, grew up in Philadelphia without formal education. From cutting glass and fitting panes with precision he developed an interest in advancing his mathematical knowledge. He secured access to the personal library of JAMES LOGAN and there pored over books on mathematics and astronomy. This study he turned to a useful end by inventing (1730) a new mariner's quadrant, the theodolite, for which he later received a prize from the Royal Society.

GODKIN, EDWIN LAWRENCE (1831–1902), born in Ireland of English parents, in 1856 came to New York, where nine years later he founded the *Nation,* a weekly journal which for the next 30 years was a powerful leader of opinion in the U.S. Concerned with public affairs, literature, and the arts, it expressed the ideas of a fearless, sensitive, widely erudite, and acidulous critic with a distinguished literary style. He later edited the New York *Evening Post* (1883–99), as successor to Carl Schurz.

Godkin was an economist of the school of J. S. Mill, a champion of property rights, and a critic of agrarianism and organized labor. He insisted that socialism could not improve economic conditions. William James observed that Godkin 'couldn't imagine a different kind of creature from himself in politics,' and that he tended to identify good taste with righteousness. Yet Godkin, an economic and political conservative, had the power to stir sympathy for liberal reforms among an intellectual elite who were devoted to public honesty.

GODWIN, PARKE (1816–1904), after graduation from Princeton (1834) began his long literary career in association on the New York *Evening Post* with William Cullen Bryant, whose daughter he married. His *Popular View of the Doctrines of Charles Fourier* (1844), an exposition of FOURIERISM, became a standard American reference on the subject. He succeeded his father-in-law (whose biography he published in 1883) as editor of the *Evening Post* (1878–81). Godwin was a consistent defender of human rights, fought political corruption, and carried on the journal's independent tradition.

GOETHALS, George Washington (1858–1928), a graduate of the U.S. Military Academy (1880), as a lieutenant colonel was appointed (1907) chief engineer of the PANAMA CANAL. There he surmounted huge difficulties, involving not only engineering, but also labor, housing, sanitation, and law enforcement. The completion of his work ahead of schedule was a triumph of engineering and administration. In 1915 he received the thanks of Congress and the rank of major general.

Gold Bullion Depository, see *Knox, Fort.*

Gold Democrats, see *National Democratic Party.*

GOLDMAN, Emma (1869–1940), Russian-born anarchist, in 1886 came to the U.S., where her inflammatory speeches led to riots and to her imprisonment (1893). She edited the anarchist journal *Mother Earth* in collaboration with Alexander Berkman (1870–1936), the anarchist who attempted to assassinate the industrialist HENRY C. FRICK. Imprisoned in 1916 for publicly advocating birth control, and again for obstructing the draft (1917), she was deported to Russia in 1919, but left there two years later because she objected to Bolshevism. A woman without a country during the 1920's, she was permitted to return to the U.S. in 1934 on a 90-day visa. In 1936 she published her autobiography. Unable to resist the ferment of revolution, she went to Spain during its years of civil war (1936–39). She died in Toronto, Canada.

GOLDMAN, Edwin Franko (1878–1956), began as cornetist in the Metropolitan Opera House orchestra (1895–1905), taught band instruments, and established (1918) in New York the Goldman Band Free Summer Concerts, which he annually conducted for many years. He pioneered in presenting symphony music by all-wind bands, and composed numerous marches and a large number of solos for various wind instruments.

Gold mining in the U.S. was carried on in a limited way after the discovery of gold in North Carolina (1799) and Georgia (1828). The dramatic gold strike which touched off the CALIFORNIA GOLD RUSH (1848) resulted in the extraction of some $550,000,000 worth of gold within a decade. The COMSTOCK LODE, discovered (1859) in Nevada, yielded more than $300,000,000 in gold and silver before it was exhausted in 1879. By 1870 other gold camps had been established in Colorado, Idaho, and Montana. During the 1880's gold fields were discovered in South Dakota and Alaska, but by 1920 high grade ores in the U.S. were largely exhausted. Today only in South Dakota is gold the principal mineral in order of value. The U.S. Bureau of Mines has estimated that from 1493 to 1957 the U.S. produced some $7,500,000,000 worth of gold, about 15 per cent of the world's supply.

Gold Reserve Act (1934), see *Gold Standard.*

Gold Rushes, see *California Gold Rush, Klondike,* and *Mining.*

Gold standard is the monetary system in which the basic unit is defined by a fixed quantity of gold. In the U.S. the COINAGE ACT of 1873, by demonetizing silver, legally ended BIMETALLISM. The GOLD STANDARD ACT of 1900 declared that the gold dollar 'shall be the standard unit of value.' The gold standard continued until the bank crisis of 1933, precipitated by the PANIC OF 1929. The Gold Reserve Act of 1934 nationalized all gold in order to increase commodity prices without recourse to inflationary measures, discontinued the coinage and circulation of gold, and made the ownership of gold as a commodity (except under license) a criminal offense.

Gold Standard Act (1900) declared all forms of money redeemable in gold and reduced the redemption fund to $150,000,000. It fixed the gold dollar at 25.8 grains (nine-tenths pure), established the price of gold at $20.67 an ounce, and made gold the monetary standard for all currency issued.

Golf was first taken up as a sport in the U.S. when the Foxburg Golf Club was formed (1887) at Foxburg, Pennsylvania. Since then golf courses have been established by the thousands throughout the country. The U.S. Golf Association (1894) is the governing body of annual championship tournaments, conducting the National Amateur, the National Open (for professionals), and the National Women's Amateur. Trophies include the Walker Cup (amateur), the Ryder Cup (professional), and the Curtis Cup (women).

The championship feats of BOBBY JONES in 1930 have never been equaled. Other outstanding figures in golf include Walter Hagen (1892–), who won several championships in the period 1914–31; Gene Sarazen (1901–), a valued member of Ryder Cup teams during the 1920's; and Ben Hogan (1912–) and Sam Snead (1912–), two of the biggest tournament money winners.

GOMPERS, SAMUEL (1850–1924), English-born labor leader, whose Jewish parents came from the working class of Holland, was brought as a boy to New York, where at thirteen he joined the Cigarmakers' Union. He later became its president (1874–81), and took the lead in organizing the AMERICAN FEDERATION OF LABOR (1886), of which group he remained president (except in 1895) until his death.

Determined to divorce unionism from politics and from 'socialistic' theories, Gompers worked tirelessly to keep the ranks of the skilled workers solid by using salaried organizers and a labor press. He stressed practical demands in wages and hours. Throughout his lifetime he remained the acknowledged head of the American labor movement, and during World War I he was labor's spokesman in the cause of national unity. *Seventy Years of Life and Labor* (2 vols., 1925) is his autobiography.

Good Neighbor Policy was the popular phrase applied to the Latin American policy of the early Administrations of President F. D. Roosevelt. It reversed the so-called 'Big Stick' and 'Dollar Diplomacy' trend dating back to the Administrations of Theodore Roosevelt and Taft. It was implemented by the withdrawal of U.S. marines from Latin American countries and the abrogation of the PLATT AMENDMENT. The MONTEVIDEO CONFERENCE (1933) explicitly declared that 'no state has the right to intervene in the internal or external affairs of another.'

GOODHUE, BERTRAM GROSVENOR (1869–1924), for many years (1891–1914) was an associate of the Boston architect RALPH ADAMS CRAM. He was known especially for his ecclesiastical and university buildings, predominantly Gothic in style, represented by St. Thomas Church in New York and the buildings of the U.S. Military Academy at West Point. His later and more contemporary structures include the National Academy of Sciences in Washington, D.C., and the Nebraska state capitol.

GOODMAN, BENNY [BENJAMIN DAVID] (1909–), began his musical career as a clarinetist during the 1920's in Chicago, then a flourishing center of jazz. In 1934 he organized his own orchestra in New York, and led the development of SWING music. BELA BARTOK wrote *Contrasts* (1938) for Goodman.

GOODRICH, SAMUEL GRISWOLD (1793–1860), Boston publisher, founded the annual gift book *The Token* (1827–42), to which the best-known American writers of the day (including Hawthorne, Longfellow, and Lowell) contributed. Under the pseudonym of Peter Parley, Goodrich published 116 juvenile items, beginning with *The Tales of Peter Parley about America* (1827). They were moralistic in tone but free from religious didacticism. (He was sole author of only a few.) He wrote other books and edited a total of 170, which sold some 7,000,000 copies and brought him a fortune. His *Recollections of a Lifetime* (1856) is an autobiography of the most prolific American publisher of his generation.

GOODWIN, NAT [NATHANIEL] (1857–1919), began his stage career as a vaudeville actor at Tony Pastor's Theatre in New York. He later won recognition in the U.S. and abroad playing serious parts, notably as Fagin in Dickens's *Oliver Twist.* In 1911 he returned to vaudeville.

GOODYEAR, Charles (1800–1860), Connecticut-born inventor of vulcanized rubber, discovered the process in 1839 when by accident he dropped some rubber treated with sulphur on a hot stove. He improved and patented the process (1844), which involved him in costly litigation against infringement. He won his suit in 1852, but he was a poor business manager. He canceled his mounting debts by selling his royalty rights for a fraction of their value, and sought unsuccessfully to establish a factory in England. He was imprisoned for debt in France when a company there using his process failed. He returned to New York in 1858 and died two years later, never having realized profits from the invention that created the vast RUBBER INDUSTRY.

GOOKIN, Daniel (1612–87), an ardent Puritan, left his father's Virginia plantation in 1644 to settle in Massachusetts, where thereafter he was constantly in public employment. He compiled *Historical Collections of the Indians in New England* (completed 1674, published 1792) because he wished to describe the customs of the Indian nations that he knew. His *Historical Account of the Doings and Sufferings of the Christian Indians* (completed 1677, published 1836) is a vindication of Indian tribes during King Philip's War. Gookin wrote these early accounts with dispassionate authority.

GORGAS, William Crawford (1854–1920), as a surgeon in the U.S. Army Medical Corps was placed in charge of sanitation in Cuba in 1898. By applying the discoveries of WALTER REED, he destroyed the breeding places of the mosquito that carried yellow fever. For his work after 1904 in ridding the Panama Canal Zone of the disease he won a world-wide reputation as sanitation expert. In 1914 he was appointed surgeon general of the U.S. Army.

GORGES, Sir Ferdinando (*c.* 1568–1647), British colonizer, was a younger son of a well-connected Somerset family. He entered the army, was knighted for his services at the siege of Rouen (1591), and while serving as military governor of Plymouth, became a leading organizer of the PLYMOUTH COMPANY (1606). Hoping to plant settlements on the New England coast, he backed fishing and trading expeditions. Most were unsuccessful. A ship largely paid for by Gorges returned in 1615, having done 'little or nothing but lost her time.' The one he sent in 1616 fared better. Even though the ship's company refused to explore, the men traded along the coast and wintered there. In 1620 Gorges took the lead in establishing the COUNCIL FOR NEW ENGLAND. Although the attempts of the Council at settlement generally failed, from its grants developed the PLYMOUTH COLONY and the MASSACHUSETTS BAY COMPANY. In succeeding years both Plymouth and Massachusetts managed to circumvent the authority of the Council, although after litigation Gorges was able to secure title (1639) to the province of Maine. He could not raise funds to colonize it, and ultimately his domain was sold to Massachusetts (1677) by his grandson, Ferdinando Gorges (1630–1718). The career of Sir Ferdinando has usually been regarded as a failure, but the fact remains that the actual colonization of New England owes much to him.

Gorman-Wilson Tariff Act, see *Wilson-Gorman.*

GORTON, Samuel (*c.* 1592–1677), seeking religious asylum, arrived in New England (1637) and was successively banished from Boston and Plymouth for teaching heretical doctrines. After turbulent stays in various Rhode Island towns, he founded Shawomet on Narragansett Bay. Imprisoned by Massachusetts authorities (1644) and soon exiled to England, he returned four years later to live peaceably at Shawomet, which he renamed Warwick in honor of his powerful protector. There he preached for the rest of his life to colonists and Indians.

Gorton adhered to a species of ANTINOMIANISM which denied the Trinity and the actuality of heaven and hell. He asserted that immortality depended upon individual character, since every man should be his own priest. His followers (Gortonists or Gortonites) remained a distinct group for several decades.

GOSNOLD, Bartholomew (*fl.* 1572–

1607), English navigator, commanded an exploring expedition in 1602 along the New England coast from Maine to Narragansett Bay. He gave Cape Cod its name because of the abundance of fish in its waters, and thereby opened the eyes of his countrymen to the possibility of trade and colonization. In 1606, in the *God Speed,* he brought a number of the first settlers to Jamestown, Virginia. He died there of malaria.

Gotham, as a term applied to New York City, was first used jocularly by Irving in *Salmagundi* (1807–8). The 'wise men' of Gotham (England) traditionally were noted for their stupidity.

Gothic Revival, see *Architecture.*

GOTTSCHALK, LOUIS MOREAU (1829–69), New Orleans–born pianist and composer, after study under Chopin and Berlioz appeared successfully in Europe, the U.S., and South America. As a musical prodigy whom Berlioz termed a 'consummate pianist,' Gottschalk was in time as in talent the first American pianist. In their day such simple piano pieces as *The Last Hope* and *The Dying Poet* were immensely popular. He was also a member of the New York circle of FREDERICK CHURCH, the landscape painter.

GOUGH, JOHN BARTHOLOMEW (1817–86), born in England, was a reformed drunkard and the most sensational temperance lecturer of his day. For 40 years after 1845, both in England and America, he drew immense crowds. He is said to have made thousands of converts take the pledge by the pathos of his dramatic lectures.

GOULD, JAY (1836–92), New York financier, with James Fisk and Daniel Drew gained control (1868) of the ERIE RAILROAD by political and financial chicanery. His attempt (with Fisk) to corner the gold market in 1869 brought on the notorious BLACK FRIDAY panic. In the 1870's and 1880's, after having been ejected from control of the Erie, Gould moved his operations westward. He then possessed a fortune estimated at $25,000,000. At the time of his death the so-called Gould group in the trans-Mississippi West was one of the six railroad combinations controlling the major part of the railroad business in the U.S. Among his other large possessions at different times were the New York *World,* the New York elevated railways, and the Western Union Telegraph Company. However unjustified the term 'Robber Baron' may be as applied to an entire generation of entrepreneurs, it seems fully descriptive of Jay Gould.

'Government by Injunction' was a denunciatory phrase that gained currency during the PULLMAN STRIKE (1894), when the Federal circuit court served a 'blanket injunction' to break the strike. It was later used as a slogan to express opposition to the widespread use of injunctions to enforce the SHERMAN ANTITRUST ACT in labor disputes. The misuse of the injunction was prevented by passage of the Norris–La Guardia Anti-Injunction Act (1932).

GRADY, HENRY WOODFIN (1850–89), a graduate of the University of Georgia (1868), as editor of the Atlanta *Constitution* (1879–89) became an eloquent spokesman for the South. He led the group that took over the doctrines of northern capitalism and set about industrializing the South. He achieved a national reputation for his adroit speech titled 'The New South,' which he delivered in New York in 1886. In that remarkable feat of oratory Grady won over a suspicious audience, including such financiers as J. P. Morgan and Russell Sage, convincing his listeners that the reconstructed South warranted the investment of northern capital and that the South should be trusted to solve its own race problems.

GRAHAM, MARTHA (1902–), made her debut as dancer in Ted Shawn's *Xochitl* (1920). In 1932 she received a Guggenheim Fellowship to study the native dances of Mexico and Yucatan. At her Bennington (Vermont) School of the Dance (1935–41) she worked on ideas that made her larger productions possible. Her solo performances were accompanied by such orchestral scores as *Letter to the World* (1940), *Death and Entrance* (1943), and Aaron Copland's *Appalachian Spring* (1945). One of the notable artists of her time, she is the creator of such dance compositions as

Phaedra (1962) and *A Look at Lightning* (1962).

GRAHAM, BILLY [WILLIAM FRANKLIN], see *Revivals.*

Grand Army of the Republic was formed (1866) after the Civil War by veterans of the Union armies. By the mid-1880's, with a membership of more than 400,000, the G.A.R. had become one of the most powerful pressure groups in the country, intimately allied with the Republican party. It flooded the country with propaganda, censored textbooks, intimidated congressmen, and threatened Presidents. In 1887 Congress passed the Dependent Pension bill, granting pensions to all veterans suffering from disabilities of any nature. President Cleveland's veto of the bill was an important factor in his failure to be re-elected in 1888. In 1890 Congress passed and President Harrison signed a Disability Pension Act embodying the features of the earlier bill. By 1949, when the G.A.R. held its eighty-third (and final) encampment, Civil War pensions totaled nearly $8,000,000,000. The last member of the G.A.R. died in 1956.

Grand Bank is the submerged tableland off Newfoundland, stretching south to the latitude of Boston, and eastward some 300 miles. It is covered by an average of 240 ft. of water. It is an important cod-fishing region. Its resources were first discovered by John Cabot in 1497. The area is persistently foggy, since the Arctic current and the Gulf Stream meet here. Icebergs carried down by the Labrador current have always made fishing hazardous.

Grand Canyon, in northwestern Arizona, is the vast gorge of the Colorado river, discovered (1540) by García Cárdenas, a member of Coronado's expedition. It is roughly a mile deep, 4 to 18 miles wide, and 217 miles long. Grand Canyon National Park (1919), a spectacular example of erosion, includes 105 miles of the Canyon.

Grand Coulee Dam, on the Columbia river 70 miles west of Spokane, Washington, was completed in 1942. It is the nation's largest concrete dam (4173 ft. long and 550 ft. high), and the key water-control structure in the million-acre Columbia Basin Project. Its power plant supplies electricity on a vast scale. Its reservoir, Lake Roosevelt (151 miles long), is a chief link in flood control for the region.

Grandfather clauses, so called, were the provisions enacted between 1895 and 1910 in the state constitutions of Alabama, Georgia, Louisiana, North Carolina, Oklahoma, South Carolina, and Virginia in an effort to disfranchise Negroes, despite the Fifteenth Amendment. The clauses restricted the voting right to those who were lineal descendants of persons who had the right to vote as of 1 January 1867. Negroes in those states could not vote at that time. In 1915 the U.S. Supreme Court declared the clauses unconstitutional.

Grand Teton National Park (est. 1929), 300,000 acres in northwestern Wyoming, embraces the most scenic portion of the Teton Range, a region of towering, snow-capped peaks and glacier-fed lakes. It lies just south of Yellowstone National Park.

GRANGE, RED [HAROLD E.] (1903–), after playing high school football at Wheaton, Illinois, became the 'Galloping Ghost' of the University of Illinois team during 1923–25. Called by coach R. C. Zuppke 'the greatest name in football,' Grange once made four long touchdown runs in twelve minutes. Thereafter for a decade he was the mainstay of the professional Chicago Bears. He later became a radio and TV sportscaster.

Granger cases were those cases that resulted in a series of rulings by the U.S. Supreme Court, testing the constitutionality of state laws enacted in the interests of the GRANGER MOVEMENT. The first and most important was the case of MUNN *v.* ILLINOIS (1876), in which the Court upheld the Illinois law regulating grain elevators. Others in the same year included cases against railroads, and involved the validity of Granger laws establishing maximum freight and passenger rates. The Court affirmed the state's right to regulate property affecting the public interest and denied that the laws violated the Fourteenth Amendment or the interstate commerce clause of the Constitution. Thus was inaugurated the period of governmental regulation of public utilities.

Although branded as socialistic and revolutionary, and a blow to private initiative, the decisions remain a landmark in American constitutional law and in the history of public regulation. In 1886 (with Chief Justice Waite dissenting) the Court reversed the direction of its former rulings in the case of *Wabash, St. Louis & Pacific Railroad* v. *Illinois,* on the ground that the Illinois statute infringed upon the power of Congress over interstate commerce. That decision virtually ended state regulation of roads and rates, and Congress responded to the imperative need for action by passing the INTERSTATE COMMERCE ACT (1887).

Granger movement, beginning as a social and educational association of Midwestern farmers, soon became an organized protest against economic abuses. Membership in the National Grange of the Patrons of Husbandry (1867) reached its peak in 1875, soon after IGNATIUS DONNELLY began editing his influential weekly *Monopolist* (1874–79). The first Granger legislation, passed in Illinois (1871), empowered a railroad and warehouse commission to fix maximum rates. Wisconsin and Iowa regulated interstate railroad freight rates in 1874, by which time independent farmers' parties had been organized in nine prairie states and in Oregon and California.

The constitutionality of the laws was challenged in the GRANGER CASES, but upheld by the U.S. Supreme Court on the principle that private property devoted to public use should be subject to public regulation. With the rise of the GREENBACK PARTY (1876) and other political organizations of agrarian protest, the granges again became social organizations, especially active (into the 20th century) in New England, where they had been least organized politically.

GRANT, ULYSSES SIMPSON (1822–85), 18th President of the U.S. (1869–77), was raised on an Ohio farm. After graduation from the U.S. Military Academy (1843) he served creditably in the Mexican War. His intemperate drinking led to his resignation from the army in 1854, and for the next six years he lived in St. Louis, Missouri, earning a scanty subsistence by farming and dealing in real estate. In 1860, regarded by his friends as a failure, he moved his family to Galena, Illinois, where at the outbreak of the Civil War he was clerking in his father's leather store. Commissioned a colonel of volunteers, he shortly became a brigadier general. His capture of Fort HENRY and Fort DONELSON in the Western theater, the first major Union victories, brought him to the attention of Lincoln, who made him a major general.

Grant's conduct of the VICKSBURG CAMPAIGN (1862–63), ending with the capture of the city, although overshadowed at the time by the simultaneous victory at Gettysburg, was fully as much a turning point of the war. Historians generally agree that from a purely strategic point of view it was one of the best-conducted campaigns in military history. In October Grant took over supreme command in the West, and in March 1864 the President made him General in Chief of the Union army with the rank of Lieutenant General, a grade especially revived for him by Congress. Grant himself conducted the WILDERNESS CAMPAIGN (1864) and directed the strategy that ended the war with Lee's surrender at APPOMATTOX.

By then a folk-hero, Grant was made a full General in 1866 (the first since Washington), and became the inevitable choice of the Republicans for President. In the bitter campaign of 1868 Grant defeated the Democratic candidate, New York's former governor Horatio Seymour, by an electoral vote of 214 to 80. He entered the White House facing complex problems. But a seemingly incredible character change had taken place. The resolute, direct, and intellectually honest soldier became a vacillating, naïve, and petty politician. The able leader of men in the field chose his advisers in office sometimes with bizarre irresponsibility. During his eight years as President he appointed 25 men to his cabinet. A few, like his Secretary of State, HAMILTON FISH, were men of talent. Some, like E. R. Hoar, J. D. Cox, B. H. Bristow, and Marshall Jewell, were intelligent and honest. Grant dismissed all except Fish. With a profound faith in his friends, Grant was duped and betrayed by disreputable financiers and politicians whose corruption made his Administrations a national disgrace. Serious scandals (among them the BLACK FRIDAY swindle) involved such cabinet members as G. S. Boutwell (Treasury, 1869–73), W. W. Belknap (War, 1869–76), Columbus Delano (Interior, 1870–73), and G. H. Williams (Attorney General, 1871–75).

Although the nation had had ample opportunity to see that it had elected to highest office the most ill-fitted man imaginable, in 1872 it again decided in favor of its indestructible legend. Grant won re-election over Horace Greeley, the candidate of the Democrats and the Liberal Republicans, by an electoral vote of 292 to 66.

Upon retirement Grant made a two-year triumphal tour of the globe before taking up residence in New York City. There he invested his money in a private banking house, which collapsed (1884), leaving him bankrupt. Mortally ill from cancer of the throat, he set about writing his *Personal Memoirs* (2 vols., 1885–86) in order to provide for his family and to pay his debts. He completed the *Memoirs* a few days before his death. Unassuming in tone and direct in style, they take their place among the great military reminiscences of history.

Grant himself ranks with the notable captains. In the field he was a man of zeal and imagination, who executed his campaigns with a clear perception of the elementary military doctrine that the destruction of the enemy's armies, not the capture of its cities, brings a war to its end.

The *Personal Memoirs* have been edited with notes by E. B. Long (1952). Biographies include those by W. B. Hesseltine (1935); and Lloyd Lewis (1950), continued by Bruce Catton (2 vols., 1954–60).

GRASSE, FRANÇOIS JOSEPH PAUL, Comte de (1723–88), chief of squadron of the French navy, was dispatched from France (1781) with a powerful fleet to assist the Continental force in the American Revolution. His blockade of the York and James rivers, superbly co-ordinated with the land operations conducted by Washington, was crucial to the victory of the YORKTOWN CAMPAIGN.

GRATTAN, THOMAS COLLEY (1792–1864), British consul at Boston (1839–46), wrote *Civilized America* (2 vols., 1859). Although sharply critical of U.S. social standards, Grattan was a shrewd observer who admired the energy and independence of the American character.

GRATZ, BARNARD (1738–1801), German-born Philadelphia merchant, came to America in 1754, and in partnership with his brother Michael Gratz (1740–1811) within two decades had become one of the great landowners and land-promoters beyond the Alleghenies. He gave invaluable financial aid to the patriot cause during the Revolution, and later helped amend the Pennsylvania and Maryland constitutions to give Jews the right to hold office.

GRAUPNER, [JOHANNES CHRISTIAN] GOTTLIEB (1767–1836), German-born musician, in 1797 settled in Boston, where he and his wife, who was an English actress and singer, became the center of the musical life of the city. (He became a U.S. citizen in 1808.) A teacher and publisher of music, Graupner performed a cultural service by organizing the Boston Philharmonic Society (1810–24), the first regular orchestra in the U.S., and by founding (1815) the still-surviving choral group, the Handel and Haydn Society. Music historians have hailed Graupner as 'the father of American orchestral music.'

GRAVES, MORRIS COLE (1910–), Oregon-born artist, was strongly influenced by the modes and techniques of the Far East. He is best known for his paintings of the birds and small animals that were the companions of his temporary hermit existence on the remote Anacortes seacoast of the state of Washington. Graves is respected for his subtle and restrained style.

GRAY, ASA (1810–88), as a boy began collecting and identifying plants near his home in Oneida county, New York. After graduation from Fairfield (Massachusetts) Medical School (1831), he set to work on the first of his botanical texts, *Elements of Botany* (1836), followed by many others influential in the development of descriptive botany. While working as a professor of natural history at Harvard (1842–73), he devoted himself to preparing his *Synoptical Flora* (1878), and his labors gave him rank as one of the foremost botanists of his century. He was a leading supporter of Darwin at a time when Darwin's theories were anathema to many, especially to his famous colleague Louis Agassiz.

'Great American Desert' was the term applied during the first half of the 19th century to the High Plains region east of the Rocky Mountains. It was not at first applied to Utah and the Great Basin of the Southwest, because those areas were not known. ZEBULON PIKE used the term in his account (1810) of an expedition across the plains to the upper Rio Grande valley. STEPHEN H. LONG confirmed Pike's impression in the narrative (1823) of his journey to the Rockies, and thereafter for three decades school geographies in their maps labeled the region 'Great American Desert.' Travelers repeatedly asserted that the aridity and desolation of the High Plains rendered them uninhabitable by civilized man, and that those who sought to take up a pastoral life west of present central Nebraska would become nomadic brigands, a menace to more eastern agricultural communities. In fact, when the Union Pacific Railroad was chartered in 1862, it was expected to be the means of connecting the Mississippi valley with the Pacific West by offering transportation through the desert barrier.

The mythical character of the term was first emphasized during the 1840's by the Santa Fe traders. JOSIAH GREGG in his classic account of *Commerce of the Prairies* (1844) envisioned agricultural settlements in the region, and the migration of the Mormons to Utah in 1847 confirmed Gregg's prediction. In 1867 FERDINAND V. HAYDEN made the first of his official reports to the Secretary of the Interior, substantiating the new view. Thereafter irrigation systems and other means of tapping the resources of the large region disproved the reality of a 'desert.'

Great Awakening was the series of religious revivals which swept over the American colonies during the second quarter of the 18th century, almost simultaneously in New England, the Middle Colonies, and the South. It seems to have started in New Jersey, when the German immigrant pastor of the Dutch Reformed Church, Theodore Frelinghuysen, led revival meetings (1719) in the Raritan valley. WILLIAM TENNENT became a leader of the movement among Presbyterians in frontier Pennsylvania when he established his Log College (1736), the prototype of schools that drilled their pupils with evangelical zeal. The stirring sermons of JONATHAN EDWARDS at Northampton, Massachusetts, soon became known abroad. His description of the revival that he sponsored, set forth in *A Faithful Narrative* (1737), influenced John Wesley, who started the Methodist movement in England. GEORGE WHITEFIELD read the account in 1738 at Savannah, Georgia, and his triumphal tour as a revivalist dates from that moment.

The second phase of the Awakening, the violent 'saving' of sinners, began with Whitefield's journey (1739–41) north to Maine. His method infected scores of lay exhorters and itinerant preachers, notably GILBERT TENNENT, William's son. The Awakening led JONATHAN DICKINSON to found the College of New Jersey (Princeton, 1746). It reached a peak in Virginia (1748–49) with the preaching of SAMUEL DAVIES, and it accounts for the great success among Baptists and Methodists before 1770. In New England the movement died rapidly, but not without leaving bitter doctrinal disputes between the 'New Lights' and the 'Old Lights,' the latter group opposing revivalism as extravagant and impermanent. In the Middle Colonies 'New Sides' and 'Old Sides' divided the Presbyterian Church.

Although the effect of the Awakening in terms of pure religion is impossible to estimate, its social significance was immense. It brought more people into Protestant churches, which it also helped to splinter (but such divisions were hardly new to Protestantism). Before the Revolution nearly every major religious sect had its own institution of higher education, and each college founded by a sect was an inducement to other sects to found a college which would thereby save Americans from the untruths of rival institutions. Dickinson at Princeton supported the New Side Presbyterians. Anglicans and Old Side Presbyterians worked together to establish King's College (Columbia, 1754). Revivalist Baptists supported the College of Rhode Island (Brown, 1764), and Dutch Reformed revivalists founded Queen's College (Rutgers, 1766).

The Awakening also resulted in the outburst of missionary effort among the Indians, notably in the establishment of Dartmouth College (1769), and it therefore served in a larger way to build up intercolonial interests. Before the Revolution it was something of a factor in creating opposition to royal officials, who generally supported the Anglican church. It certainly created a democratic spirit in religion similar to that which, in other areas of colonial life, was urging the colonists toward political independence.

See W. W. Sweet, *Revivalism in America* (1944), and B. A. Weisberger, *They Gathered at the River* (1958).

Great Basin is an interior region of the western U.S., lying between the west wall of the Rocky Mountains and the east wall of the Sierra Nevada. The initial explorations of B. L. E. BONNEVILLE (1832–34), and of JOHN C. FRÉMONT (1843–45), who named it, furnished general knowledge, which was rounded out by the field work of the U.S. Geological Survey (1879–83) under the direction of Grove Karl Gilbert (1843–1918).

The Basin, which covers an area of some 200,000 square miles, is roughly triangular, and widest in the north. It includes most of Nevada, the western half of Utah, a portion of southeastern California, and areas in Oregon, Wyoming, and Idaho. Its rugged north-south ranges are divided by deep, flat valleys. The altitude varies from peaks that are thousands of feet above sea level to DEATH VALLEY, 282 ft. below. Little rain falls in the Basin, and its rivers, which find no outlet to the sea, either disappear in alkaline sinks or drain into saline lakes. In early geological ages two great lakes, Bonneville and Lahontan, covered most of the northern section. (Great Salt Lake is a remnant of Lake Bonneville.) Today some areas of the Basin are irrigated and have been successfully developed for farming.

Great Depression, see *Panic of 1929.*

Great Divide, see *Continental Divide.*

Great Lakes, the largest body of fresh water in the world, are the group of five lakes in central North America: SUPERIOR, HURON, MICHIGAN, ERIE, and ONTARIO. They cover 94,710 square miles, and drain 287,900. From Duluth, Minnesota, they stretch eastward 1160 miles, emptying by their natural course into the St. Lawrence river. All are subject to sudden and violent storms. Canals and waterways divert some lake traffic south to the Mississippi and southeasterly to the Hudson. The international boundary between Canada and the U.S. passes approximately through the center of all except Lake Michigan, which is entirely within the U.S. The region was long disputed in the struggle between Great Britain and France for the interior of the continent, and came under British control after the TREATY OF PARIS of 1763. By the terms of the RUSH-BAGOT TREATY (1817), still in force, the Great Lakes have been free from naval armaments. The St. Lawrence Seaway, opened for commerce in 1959, provides ocean navigation through the Lakes for a score of large cities in the heart of the North American continent.

Great Plains, see *Plains region.*

Great Salt Lake, in northwestern Utah, is the largest body of water (35 by 75 miles) west of the Mississippi river. It is a remnant of ancient Lake Bonneville. It has an average depth of 20 ft., no known outlet, and a salt density six times that of the ocean. The only life it supports are brine shrimp.

Great Smoky Mountains, with peaks rising to 6,000 ft., are that part of the Appalachian system located in western North Carolina and eastern Tennessee. In 1930 some 500,000 acres were set aside as a national park.

'Great White Way,' see *Broadway.*

Greek Revival, see *Classic Revival.*

GREELEY, HORACE (1811–72), born in New Hampshire, ended his irregular schooling at fifteen. After an apprenticeship on a country newspaper in Vermont (1826–30), he founded and edited the *New Yorker* (1834–41), a journal of criticism. Encouraged by his friends Thurlow Weed and William H. Seward, in 1841 he began publication of a penny daily, the New York *Tribune,* which during the next 30 years Greeley made into a liberal journal of the first magnitude, with a circulation of 200,000 by 1860. To it he attracted Charles A. Dana as managing editor and George Ripley as book reviewer. He persistently championed the cause of the farmer, the worker, and the underprivileged. He supported the formation of the Republican party (1854) and even urged forcible resistance to the Fugitive Slave Act. The *Tribune* advocated Fourier cooperatives, trade unions, 'land for the landless' (the later Homestead Act), antislavery strategies, and opposition to the Mexican War. Thousands acted on his advice to 'Go West, young man, go West.'

As a War Radical, he publicized his famous editorial rebuke, 'The Prayer of Twenty Million' (1862), criticizing Lincoln for 'the policy you seem to be pursuing.' To this Lincoln replied frankly that his first objective was to save the Union, whether he could do it without freeing the slaves, by freeing them, or by freeing some and leaving others in bondage.

After the Civil War Greeley encouraged resistance to spoilsmen in politics, and as the presidential nominee of the Democrats and the Liberal Republicans in 1872, he tried but failed to block Grant's re-election. Impulsive and unpredictable, in his campaign Greeley cultivated his fads and idiosyncrasies to an extent that laid him open to ridicule. He lost the election by a large electoral margin (292 to 66), and three weeks later he died insane. Yet Greeley was farseeing, and his autobiography, *Recollections of a Busy Life* (1868), is the portrait of one of the most influential journalists of the 19th century. Although he regarded his account of *An Overland Journey from New York to San Francisco* (1860) as ephemeral, it is an astute assessment of the potential of the regions through which he traveled. He was pre-eminent among editors for the terse persuasiveness of his style and for his development of the editorial page.

Biographies include those by D. C. Seitz (1926), and W. H. Hale (1950).

GREELY, ADOLPHUS WASHINGTON (1844–1935), as an army lieutenant in 1881 explored and mapped unknown segments of Greenland and Ellesmere Island. Because relief ships were unable to reach Greely's party until 1884, all except Greely and six others perished of starvation. Promoted to the rank of brigadier general (1887), Greely in the next two decades did notable work by establishing telegraph communications in outlying U.S. possessions. In 1906 he directed relief operations after the San Francisco earthquake. He retired in 1908 with the rank of major general, and in 1935 was awarded the Medal of Honor.

GREEN, HETTY HOWLAND ROBINSON (1834–1916), New York financier, was born in New Bedford, Massachusetts. She inherited something of a fortune from her father (1865), and invested so shrewdly that at her death she was reported to be the ablest woman financier in the world, and, with an estate of $100,000,000, was presumably the wealthiest. Her eccentricities became legend, and, though exaggerated, are confirmed by the fact that from time to time she obscured her identity by living in tenement houses, and often sat on the floor in a semi-reserved area of her banking firm to review her financial data.

GREEN, WILLIAM (1870–1952), after serving as secretary-treasurer (1912–24) of the United Mine Workers of America, succeeded SAMUEL GOMPERS as president of the American Federation of Labor (1924–52). Green was elected at a time when the U.S. and the labor movement were in a conservative phase, and the A.F. of L. reflected the mood. In 1935 the A.F. of L. was challenged by the formation of a Committee for Industrial Organization, which under JOHN L. LEWIS became in 1938 the Congress of Industrial Organizations. Despite Green's apparent timidity, the A.F. of L. reached its greatest membership under his management.

Green Mountain Boys, irregular militiamen led by ETHAN ALLEN, were originally organized (1771) to defend the New Hampshire Grants in Vermont against New York land speculators. In 1775 Allen used these troops for his dramatic capture of Fort Ticonderoga.

Green Mountains, that part of the Appalachian system extending as a spine through Vermont, reach their highest elevation in Mt. Mansfield (4393 ft.). They are generally low and well forested. Much of the area is a national forest reserve.

Greenback party (1874), also known as the National Greenback party, was a minority group supported chiefly by the farmers in the prairie states and the South who had gone into debt after the PANIC OF 1873. It sought inflation, especially by the repeal of the RESUMPTION ACT of 1875, which provided for the redemption of GREENBACKS in gold. With Peter Cooper as presidential candidate, the party polled 81,000 votes in 1876. Two years later some labor organizations, embittered by the labor troubles of 1877, joined the group to form the Greenback-Labor party. In the congressional elections of 1878 the party polled over 1,000,000 votes and elected fourteen Representatives to Congress. By 1880 the labor element had shifted its interests, and the party's nominee for President, James B. Weaver, received only 307,000 votes. The party did not survive the decade.

Greenbacks, the popular name for U.S. government legal tender notes irredeemable in coins, were first issued in 1862 to meet the exigencies of war, and were placed on a par with notes backed by specie. By the war's end (1865) greenbacks had depreciated and were outstanding to an amount exceeding $400,000,000. After the PANIC OF 1873, hard-hit farmers sought to inflate the currency with more greenbacks. When President Grant vetoed the inflation bill that Congress had passed in 1874, the GREENBACK PARTY formed, but conservatives triumphed with the RESUMPTION ACT (1875). In 1878 Congress made the greenbacks then outstanding ($346,681,000) a permanent part of the currency.

GREENE, NATHANAEL (1742–86), Rhode Island-born Revolutionary general, commanded militia at the siege of Boston and was in charge of the city after the British evacuation. As a major general he commanded troops at Trenton, Brandywine, Germantown, and Monmouth (1776–78). After Horatio Gates lost the battle of Camden (1780), Greene took command of the CAROLINA CAMPAIGN. In 1785 the people of Georgia gave him Mulberry Grove, the Savannah plantation on which Eli Whitney later invented the cotton gin. Although self-trained as a soldier, Greene was a gifted leader and among Revolutionary generals is generally ranked next to Washington in military acumen.

GREENOUGH, HORATIO (1805–52), the first professional American sculptor, was the son of a Boston merchant. Upon graduation from Harvard (1825) he embarked for Italy to study under Thorvaldsen. Thereafter (1829–51) he lived chiefly in Florence, where he executed the colossal marble half-draped, seated *Washington* (1833), commissioned for the rotunda of the National Capitol. (It was so imperfectly lighted that it was later transferred to the Capitol grounds, and is now in the Smithsonian Institution.) Because it depicted Washington as an Olympian god, it aroused both indignation and jocose criticism. Greenough's group *The Rescue* was made for the east stairway of the Capitol.

More impressive than Greenough's works, which exhibit the sentimental classicism of the time, are his theories of art, set forth in *Aesthetics in Washington* (1851), vivid and farseeing. He formulated the idea that 'form follows function,' now commonly associated with the architecture of Louis Sullivan and Frank Lloyd Wright. Among his published works are *Experiences of a Yankee Stonecutter* (1852), and *Letters* (1887).

Greenville, Treaty of (1795), following the battle of FALLEN TIMBERS, ended almost twenty years of fighting in the West. It was signed by Anthony Wayne and the chiefs of twelve Indian tribes. By its terms, which were scrupulously observed by the Indians, the tribes ceded to the U.S. the southeastern corner of the NORTHWEST TERRITORY, together with sixteen enclaves including Detroit and the present site of Chicago, in return for annuities to the value of $10,000. Thus presumably a boundary had been set between the Indian lands and those available to settlers. But the insatiable greed of the pioneers for land soon made the treaty meaningless. By 1809 the Indians of the region had parted with nearly 50,000,000 acres, largely under duress.

Greenwich Village, situated in lower Manhattan, New York City, was a separate village in the colonial period, and later became an exclusive residential section. By 1900 it had become known chiefly as a colony of artistic and literary Bohemians.

GREENWOOD, ISAAC (1702–45), after graduation from Harvard (1721) and study in England, was appointed (1727) to the newly created chair of mathematics at Harvard, the first endowed professorship of science in America. His lectures stimulated interest in science, but after ten years chronic alcoholism led to his retirement and to his early death.

GREGG, JOSIAH (1806–50), born in Tennessee, in 1831 became a trader on routes east and southeast from Santa Fe. During his journeys to Texas and Mexico he blazed new trails and assembled the most complete and reliable maps of the area then available. He recorded his observations in *Commerce of the Prairies* (1844; ed. by M. L. Moorhead, 1954), a classic of American frontier history. He died of exposure while on an expedition across the Coast Range in California. His recently published *Diary and Letters* (2 vols., 1941–44) supply further frontier data.

GRENVILLE, GEORGE (1712–70), held various cabinet posts in the British government before becoming prime minister (1763–66) during the period when the ill-advised SUGAR ACT (1764) and STAMP ACT (1765) were promulgated. An administrator rather than a statesman, he was judged in his day to be the ablest man of business in British politics. His government did not fall because the American colonies opposed the Stamp Act, but because he tried to remove one of the 'king's friends' from the ministry. ROCKINGHAM then formed a coalition.

GRIFFES, CHARLES TOMLINSON (1884–1920), after studying composition with Humperdinck in Berlin, taught music at the Hackley School in Tarrytown, New York. His own music, incorporating elements of the impressionist idiom, is remarkable for its fantasy-like quality, well represented by the symphonic poem *The Pleasure-Dome of Kubla Khan* (1919). His other large works include a string quartet and a piano sonata.

GRIFFITH, D. W. [DAVID LEWELYN WARK] (1873–1948), Kentucky-born motion picture director, was first associated with the industry as an actor (1907). He became a director in 1908. He formed the patterns of movie techniques more than any other producer of his day, developing such effects as soft focus, mist photography, the flash back, the long shot, the close-up, the fade-in, and the fade-out. He directed some 500 pictures, and his filming of *The Birth of a Nation* (1915) is a landmark in motion picture history since in it his techniques were fully exploited. However, the racist quality of the film, which was based on Thomas Nixon's novel *The Clansman,* a story of Reconstruction days, aroused a great liberal outcry, and possibly in expiation Griffith then produced *Intolerance* (1916), a $1,900,000 spectacle that broke all records for costly movies of that day.

GRIMKÉ, see *Weld, T. D.*

Gringo, among Spanish-Americans, was a term of contempt for Anglo-Americans. It was first used in the late 18th century to designate those who 'talk Greek' (*griego*) or gibberish.

GROPIUS, WALTER ADOLF (1883–), German-born architect, was a pioneer in the design known as the functional or INTERNATIONAL STYLE. After World War I he reorganized the Weimar School of Art as the Staatliches Bauhaus (1918), a socially minded group that made art a partner of science, technology, and humanism. After working independently in Germany and England, Gropius came to the U.S. (1937), where he headed the Harvard School of Architecture (1938–48). His writings include *Rebuilding Our Communities* (1946).

GROSEILLIERS, MÉDARD CHOUART, Sieur des, see *Radisson.*

GROSS, SAMUEL DAVID (1805–84), after graduation from Jefferson Medical College, Philadelphia (1828), taught in the medical colleges of several universities before returning to Jefferson, where he occupied the chair of surgery (1865–82). He was one of the most influential physicians in 19th-century America through his constantly revised *System of Surgery* (1859), a work which was based on his experience as a teacher of surgery, pathology, and anatomy. He was a founder of the American Surgical Association (1880).

Guadalcanal, Battle of (12–15 November 1942), during the SOLOMON ISLANDS CAMPAIGN in World War II, followed the defeat of U.S. naval forces by Japanese cruisers in the battle of SAVO ISLAND (9 August), after which ensued a six-month contest for the island of Guadalcanal, on which a key U.S. air base, Henderson Field, had been established. Scores of ground actions on a major scale took place in jungles and on mountains, and air fights were continuous.

By November Admiral WILLIAM F. HALSEY was ready to engage his South Pacific fleet in a naval battle of tremendous dimension, and his decisive victory, by preventing the Japanese from landing reinforcements, made possible the conquest of Guadalcanal by U.S. troops. Two U.S. cruisers and seven destroyers were lost. The action cost the Japanese two battleships, one cruiser, two destroyers, and ten transports. In February 1943 the Japanese abandoned the island, and the defensive period in the war with Japan ended.

Guadalupe Hidalgo, Treaty of (1848), closed the MEXICAN WAR. By its terms Mexico relinquished all claims to Texas above the Rio Grande and ceded New Mexico and Upper California to the U.S. (Ultimately the region formed the states of California, Arizona, New Mexico, Nevada, Utah, and parts of Colorado and Wyoming.) The U.S. paid $15,000,000 and assumed the unpaid claims against Mexico. Thus the nation rounded out its mid-continental BOUNDARIES, which were finally completed by the GADSDEN PURCHASE (1853).

Guam, largest of the Mariana Islands (originally called the Ladrones) in the Pacific, is an unincorporated territory of the U.S., 209 square miles in area with a population (1965) of some 73,000. Ceded to the U.S. by Spain (1898) after the Spanish-American War, it was administered by the Department of the Navy until 1950, when the administration was transferred to the Department of the Interior. Local affairs are conducted by a governor and a unicameral legislature. Guam is the chief Pacific base of the USAF Strategic Air Command.

Guerrière, see *Constitution.*

Guffey-Snyder Coal Act, see *Bituminous Coal Act.*

GUGGENHEIM, DANIEL (1856–1930), industrialist and philanthropist, in 1884 became actively engaged in the copper mining and smelting business in which his father, Meyer Guggenheim (1828–1905), had made heavy investments. As head of the American Smelting and Refining Company (1901–19), Daniel Guggenheim, with his six brothers, created a world-wide industrial empire, including nitrate fields, tin mines, rubber plantations, and diamond fields. In 1924 he established the Daniel and Florence Guggenheim Foundation for benevolent activities. He also created the Daniel Guggenheim Fund for the Promotion of Aeronautics.

Guggenheim Foundation (John Simon Guggenheim Memorial Foundation), established (1925), in memory of a son, by John Simon Guggenheim (1867–1941), a brother of DANIEL GUGGENHEIM, annually awards fellowships for creative work in the arts and for research in all branches of knowledge. In 1965 from assets of $57,200,000 it disbursed $1,996,000 in support of some 500 undertakings.

Guilford Courthouse, Battle of (March 1781), near the close of the CAROLINA CAMPAIGN in the War of Independence, took place two months after COWPENS. General Greene with a force of 4400 North Carolinians offered battle. Cornwallis won the field but at such a loss that he was unable to continue the campaign without reinforcements by sea. The YORKTOWN CAMPAIGN opened in August.

Gulf States, bordering on the Gulf of Mexico, are Florida, Alabama, Mississippi, Louisiana, and Texas.

H

Habeas corpus is the common-law writ by which a judge directs that a person detaining another bring the detained person before the court for a hearing. As a device for the preservation of civil liberties, it has for some centuries been incorporated in English jurisprudence. In America before the War of Independence it was especially invoked against the government for wrongful imprisonment. As a result, the U.S. Constitution (Art. 1, sec. 9) declares that the privilege of the writ can be set aside only in case of rebellion or invasion, when suspension may be required for the public safety. In 1833 Congress authorized Federal courts to issue such writs to state officials, but in ABLEMAN *v.* BOOTH (1859) the Supreme Court denied the right of a state judiciary to interfere in Federal cases.

The Constitution does not say who has the right to suspend the writ. Lincoln met the Civil War emergency by promptly suspending the writ in parts of Maryland. In the MERRYMAN CASE (1861) Chief Justice Taney ruled that Congress alone had that right, although Lincoln, then faced with a crumbling nation, ignored the judgment and acted on the opinion of his attorney general that the President has the power to act in the absence of legislation. The Ku Klux Klan Act of 1871 authorized the President to suspend the writ as part of a program to suppress violence by military force. Complicating the issue is the fact that there are several kinds of writs of habeas corpus with various uses.

HACKETT, JAMES HENRY (1800–71), was one of the earliest American actors to succeed both in the U.S. and England. He played American comedy types, and in later years starred as Falstaff.

His son, JAMES KETELTAS HACKETT (1869–1926), who married Mary Mannering, leading lady in Daniel Frohman's stock company, was one of the first matinee idols, especially popular as a star in such romantic plays as *The Prisoner of Zenda* (1894). He later won acclaim for his productions of *Macbeth* and *Othello* in New York, London, and Paris, and received public honors in England, France, and the U.S., which were bestowed on him as the leading American actor of his day.

HADLEY, ARTHUR TWINING (1856–1930), son of the Yale philologist James Hadley (1821–72), taught political economy at Yale for twenty years. His *Railroad Transportation* (1889), long a standard work, was the first comprehensive treatment of the subject. As president of Yale (1899–1921) he guided the wide expansion of the university. His social philosophy is set forth in *Freedom and Responsibility* (1903), *The Moral Basis of Democracy* (1919), and *The Conflict between Liberty and Equality* (1925).

Hague Conference of 1899 was a meeting in Holland at The Hague of 26 nations (including the U.S.), convened to discuss disarmament and the limitation of methods of warfare. No agreements were reached on the issues discussed, but the Conference established the PERMANENT COURT OF ARBITRATION.

The second Hague Conference (1907) was attended by 46 nations. The efforts of the U.S. to establish a world court were unsuccessful, but the Conference adopted a series of resolutions touching on humane procedure in the conduct of war. These attempts to formulate rules of international law foreshadowed the LEAGUE OF NATIONS and the UNITED NATIONS.

Hague Tribunal, see *Permanent Court of Arbitration.*

Hail, Columbia!, see *Hopkinson, Joseph.*

HAINES, CHARLES GROVE (1879–1948), professor of political science at the University of California at Los Angeles (after 1925), was a leading authority on American jurisprudence. His earlier writings include *The Conflict Over Judicial Powers in the U.S. to 1870* (1909), and *The American Doctrine of Judicial Supremacy* (1932). His major work, covering the period 1789–1864, is *The Role of the Supreme Court in American Government and Politics* (2 vols., 1944–57), completed by

F. H. Sherwood. It explores the extent to which the Court participated in and influenced 'the political and partisan activities of the time.'

Haiti, with a population (1965) of 4,552,000 Negroes, is a French-speaking republic (with Port-au-Prince as capital) which occupies the western third of the Caribbean island of Hispaniola, discovered by Columbus in 1492. Ceded by Spain to France in 1697, Haiti first became strategically important to the U.S. when Admiral Comte de Grasse landed there in 1781 and made it the base of naval operations in the War of Independence. It next figured prominently when Bonaparte dispatched an expeditionary force to Santo Domingo in 1801, with orders to suppress the insurrection of Toussaint l'Ouverture, then to take possession of New Orleans and Louisiana. When he failed, he decided to sell Louisiana to the U.S. Haiti won its independence from France in 1804.

The republic was not thereafter seriously involved in U.S. diplomacy until the U.S. intervened during major disorders in 1915 to prevent European occupation in the strategic canal area and to protect American investments. The U.S. exercised political control until 1930. The period of American occupation was marked by great material advances, but also by severe clashes. American public opinion reacted against 'dollar diplomacy,' and with the advent of the 'Good Neighbor policy' American military forces were withdrawn in 1934. Political turbulence in this poverty-stricken nation became especially violent during the 1950's, and the future of the republic remains politically uncertain. In 1963 the U.S. suspended diplomatic relations with Haiti, and the Organization of American States appealed to the government of Haiti to cease its political terror and repression.

HAKLUYT, RICHARD (*c.* 1552–1616), was graduated from Oxford (1574), where he later lectured on geography. He was a scholar and collector, and a propagandist who made the doctrine of colonial expansion a religion. He sincerely believed that England had an obligation to carry the Protestant gospel to the Indians. To enforce his argument he emphasized every theme of self-interest in his demand for colonies overseas. His *Divers Voyages* (1582) introduced the English-speaking world to the discoveries made in North America by the Cabots, Verrazano, and Ribaut. In 1589 he compiled *The principal navigations, voyages, traffiques and discoveries of the English nation* (enlarged, 3 vols., 1598–1600), a work of transcendent importance in promoting English discovery and colonization in America, because it gathered firsthand narratives of exploration and made them available to posterity. His mass of unused material was bequeathed to SAMUEL PURCHAS, who carried on the work of publication.

HALE, EDWARD EVERETT (1822–1909), Boston Unitarian clergyman, author, and philanthropist, was a nephew of Edward Everett. His travel books, represented by *Ninety Days' Worth of Europe* (1861), are sentimental in appeal, but they were remarkably open-minded for a period when many Americans believed that one's Americanism was corrupted by foreign travel. The declaration of the Ohio 'peace' Democrat (Copperhead), Congressman Clement L. Vallandigham, that he did 'not want to belong to the U.S.,' inspired Hale to write 'The Man Without a Country,' which was first published in the December 1863 issue of the *Atlantic Monthly*. Widely republished, it kindled more patriotic fervor than any other writing during that period of the Civil War when defeatists were organizing formidable societies to force a negotiated peace. Hale's *Franklin in France* (2 vols., 1887–88) is a substantial work of scholarship.

His sister, LUCRETIA PEABODY HALE (1820–1900), is still remembered for *The Peterkin Papers* (1880), a sprightly satire on a Boston culture bent on education.

HALE, GEORGE ELLERY (1868–1938), an authority on solar vortices and magnetic fields, first successfully photographed a solar prominence with his invention of the spectroheliograph (1891). He organized and directed the Yerkes Observatory (1895–1905), and the Mt. Wilson Observatory (1904–23). He was the leading spirit behind the construction of the great 200-inch reflecting telescope, later named for him, on Mt. Palomar.

His writings include *Beyond the Milky Way* (1926) and *Signals from the Stars* (1932).

HALE, NATHAN (1755–76), having graduated from Yale (1773), was teaching school when the War of Independence began. Commissioned a captain in the Connecticut militia, he volunteered to serve as a spy among British troops on Long Island. He disguised himself as a schoolmaster, and got the information for which he had been sent, but on his way back to the American lines he was discovered and hanged without trial. On the gallows his last words were (improving a phrase from Addison's *Cato*): 'I only regret that I have but one life to lose for my country.'

HALE, SARAH JOSEPHA [BUELL] (1788–1879), born near Newport, New Hampshire, in 1811 married a young lawyer, David Hale, reared a family of five, and six years after the death of her husband in 1822 settled with her children in Boston. There she made a name for herself as editor of the *Ladies' Magazine* (1828–37), a potpourri of fiction and poetry, embellished by colored fashion plates. When the Philadelphia publisher Louis Antoine Godey purchased the magazine, he renamed it *Godey's Lady's Book*. With Mrs. Hale as editor (1837–77), *Godey's* over the next 40 years gained a then impressive circulation of 150,000 subscribers. She incorporated departments on domestic art, cooking, and household hints, set a pattern for today's women's magazines, and deeply influenced two generations of American wives and mothers.

The magazine became in fact the leading authority in the nation on matters of fashion, etiquette, and cookery. It espoused the cause of child welfare and humanitarian reforms, and it numbered among its contributors such American writers as Hawthorne, Longfellow, Poe, Holmes, and Lowell. Although she was not a 'feminist,' Mrs. Hale gave important support to the higher education of women. At her urging President Lincoln issued the first national proclamation of Thanksgiving Day (1864). Her later works include novels, plays, and short stories, but as an author she is chiefly remembered for the nursery rhyme, 'Mary had a little lamb' (1830).

See R. E. Finley, *The Lady of Godey's* (1931).

'Half-breeds' was the contemptuous epithet applied by the 'STALWARTS,' during the Hayes and Garfield Administrations, to the wing of the Republican party that favored a conciliatory policy toward the South and advocated civil service reform.

Half-Way Covenant, approved by a Massachusetts church synod in 1662, was devised as a means of extending 'half-way' membership in the New England churches to the children of first-generation Congregationalists, who were full members by virtue of their personal experience of conversion. It granted church membership, but withheld participation in the Lord's Supper as well as the privilege of voting on church affairs until an acceptable proof of 'regeneration' was forthcoming.

This was a practical plan for keeping the church benches filled at a time when the ranks of 'Visible Saints' were thinning. It also insured that the privileges of sharing political control would remain within the respectable families, since only church members had the franchise. The compromise was carried even further in the Connecticut valley, dominated by SOLOMON STODDARD, who treated the Lord's Supper as a 'converting ordinance,' and extended it to all who desired church membership. The issue that Stoddard created was never resolved, though it was largely forgotten a century later.

HALIFAX, GEORGE MONTAGU DUNK, 2nd Earl of (1716–71), after his appointment (1748) as president of the British BOARD OF TRADE AND PLANTATIONS, helped focus administrative attention on colonial problems by compiling reports of enterprises in America during the previous 30 years. He outlined plans to strengthen the position of royal governors, secured control of colonial patronage, and on entering the cabinet at forty (in 1756), became in effect a secretary of state for the colonies. Younger members of the Board received useful political training under him, and he continued to be a powerful influence in colonial affairs after his retirement from active service (1761).

HALL, Basil (1788–1844), retired British naval officer, in his widely read account of *Travels in North America in the Years 1827 and 1828* (3 vols., 1829) nettled a growing national self-consciousness by his Tory intransigence. Seldom captious, his criticism merely rose from his conviction that democracy is an inferior form of government and society. The letters of his wife, Margaret Hunter Hall (1799–1876), written at the time of their tour, were published in 1931 as *The Aristocratic Journey*.

HALL, Granville Stanley (1846–1924), after graduation from Williams (1867) studied experimental psychology in Germany, took his Ph.D. under William James at Harvard (1878), and founded a psychological laboratory at Johns Hopkins (1882), which soon became the leading U.S. research organization in its field. (Outstanding among his students was john dewey.) He established the *American Journal of Psychology* (1887), and served as first president of the American Psychological Association (1891).

He was the first president of Clark University (1888–1920), and under his guidance that institution was widely known and admired for its graduate courses in education and psychology. He inaugurated the child-study movement in the U.S. with *The Contents of Children's Minds on Entering School* (1894). His other writings include pioneer studies in the field of sex education, industrial education, and social problems, notably in *Adolescence* (2 vols., 1904), *Educational Problems* (2 vols., 1911), and *Senescence* (1922).

HALL, James (1793–1868), born in Philadelphia, in 1820 settled as a lawyer (later a judge) in Illinois, which had recently (1818) acquired statehood. As state treasurer and as trustee of Illinois College (founded 1829), he was a leader in organizing the financial and educational system of the state. He established the first literary periodical west of Ohio, the *Illinois Monthly Magazine* (1830–32), continued, after Hall moved to Cincinnati, as the *Western Monthly Magazine* (1832–36). The history of the Ohio valley was his lifelong interest, and his *Legends of the West* (1832; rev. ed., 1853), chiefly a collection of short tales and sketches, gave Easterners an awareness of western lore and its significance in the image of America. His *Notes on Western States* (1838) was important as a guide to pioneer farming.

HALL, James (1811–98), professor of geology at Rensselaer Polytechnic Institute (after 1836), became an authority on invertebrate paleontology. His *Palaeontology of New York,* published in a series of volumes (1847–94), is a basic study among North American geological histories.

HALL, Samuel Read (1795–1877), educator and clergyman, founded (1823) a training school for teachers, one of the first in the U.S., at Concord, Vermont. He later became principal of the teachers' seminary at Phillips Academy in Andover, Massachusetts (1830–37), and of Craftsbury Academy (Vermont), to which he added a teachers' training department (1840). He published many textbooks, and his *Lectures on School-Keeping* (1829) was republished in 1929.

Hall of Fame for Great Americans, established in 1900 on the University Heights campus of New York University, is an open-air colonnade with busts and tablets of persons honored for national achievements. New names are voted every five years from a list of men and women (dead more than 25 years) submitted from every state. In 1965 the selections totaled 93.

The National Baseball Hall of Fame (1939) at Cooperstown, New York, commemorates a similar number of baseball heroes. Its museum displays such relics as bats, balls, and uniforms.

HALLECK, Henry Wager (1815–72), born in upper New York, after graduation from the U.S. Military Academy (1839) served in California during the Mexican War and helped frame the constitution of that new state (1850). After the outbreak of the Civil War he was placed in charge of the Department of the Missouri (August 1861), to which command the departments of Ohio and Kansas were added (March 1862). An able organizer, in July 1862 he was appointed general in chief of the Union forces with headquarters in Washington, but his inability to deal in any large way with military problems led Lincoln (March 1864) to replace him with Grant, whose chief of staff Halleck then became. After the war and until his death he commanded the Division of the South, with headquarters at Louisville.

HALSEY, William Frederick (1882–1959), a graduate of the U.S. Naval Academy (1904), commanded the South Pacific fleet during the Solomon Islands campaign (1942–43) in World War II. His decisive victory in the battle of GUADALCANAL (November 1942) ended the defensive period in the war with Japan. As commander of the U.S. Third Fleet (1944–45), 'Bull' Halsey led the naval assault on the Philippines, and the carrier-based attack on Japan (July 1945). Later that year he was raised to the rank of admiral of the fleet.

HALSTED, William Stewart (1852–1922), after graduation from the College of Physicians and Surgeons (1877), became the first professor of surgery at Johns Hopkins (1886), and one of the most notable American surgeons of his time. His contributions include operative techniques that reduce tissue injury, the anesthetizing of nerves by cocaine injection, and the introduction of rubber gloves in surgery. He was a pioneer in the treatment of breast cancer by the massive excision of the breast and lymph glands, and in the surgery of inguinal hernia.

Hambletonian, a muscular bay horse with well-formed hind legs, sired at Chester, New York, in 1849, lived 27 years, and was the foundation sire of the famous strain of trotting horses bearing his name. The Hambletonian races for three-year-old trotters, held annually since 1926, were first run at Goshen, New York, and are currently held (since 1957) at Du Quoin, Illinois.

HAMILTON, Dr. Alexander (1712–56), Scottish-born physician trained at Edinburgh, after 1738 practiced in Maryland. A founder of the intellectual group called the Tuesday Club of Annapolis (1745–56), he is best known for his *Itinerarium* (1744), a sharply observant picture of men and manners, written after a journey through the northern colonies. It is especially important as a report on medical practices.

HAMILTON, Alexander (1755–1804), statesman, was born in Nevis, West Indies, the illegitimate son of a Scottish merchant. Friends who recognized his brilliant promise sent him to New York (1772), where he entered King's College (Columbia) in 1774. The two anonymous pamphlets that he wrote at seventeen defending the patriot cause, *A Full Vindication of the Measures of Congress* (1774) and *The Farmer Refuted* (1775), answer arguments of the influential Loyalist Samuel Seabury, and are an impressive display of the mature grasp of the principles of constitutional government that distinguish all Hamilton's later political discourses. During the War of Independence he served first in the field (1776), four years as Washington's secretary and confidential aide (1777–81), and again as commander of troops (1781) in the final assault at Yorktown. In 1780 he married Elizabeth, daughter of General Philip Schuyler.

After serving briefly in the Continental Congress (1782–83), Hamilton took up the practice of law in New York, where he raised a family of eight children and took a prominent part in the social life of the city. As a delegate to the Annapolis Convention (1786), he drafted the call for the Federal Constitutional Convention (1787). He was a keen advocate of centralized government and the principal author of the series of articles arguing for ratification of the proposed constitution, known as *The Federalist* (1787–88), a gathering of essays that has become the classic commentary on American constitutional law. His labors were of first importance in winning support for adoption of the Constitution.

The new government inaugurated, Washington chose Hamilton as his Secretary of the Treasury (1789–95), in which post Hamilton presented a succession of papers far-reaching in their influence on public credit. First, he recommended funding of the foreign and domestic debt at par, to establish a standard of exchange. He then proposed that the federal government assume the debts incurred by the states during the war. He asked further that an excise tax be levied to provide revenue, and that a national bank be established, modeled on the Bank of England. His famous *Report on Manufactures* (1791) called for a protective tariff to encourage 'infant industries.' This 'Hamiltonian system' was designed to increase the interdependence of the states, and because it was allied with the conservative mercantile-shipping-financial interests of the North, it created political opposition to the 'Jeffersonian system,' which favored states' rights and an agrarian economy.

Although Washington had hoped to avoid parties, two groups inevitably formed, crystallized during the Adams administration into the FEDERALIST PARTY, led by Hamilton, and the REPUBLICAN-DEMOCRATIC PARTY, under Jefferson. Most of Hamilton's key proposals were adopted in Washington's Administration, during which period both Hamilton and Jefferson resigned, each having failed to win support on his partisan principle, Hamilton because he did not obtain his protective tariff. Indeed, today historians feel that Hamilton's communications with a British agent, aimed to thwart Jefferson's avowed policies of state, and conducted without Washington's knowledge, overstepped the bounds of loyalty to his chief.

Hamilton resumed his law practice in New York, and in the sweeping victory of the Republicans in the election of 1800, in which Jefferson and Burr tied for office, Hamilton's influence gave Jefferson first place. Burr was disgruntled, and when Hamilton again thwarted Burr in 1804 by keeping him from the New York governorship, Burr accused Hamilton of publicly calling him a 'despicable' person. In the ensuing duel (11 July 1804), which Burr fought in deadly earnest, Burr killed Hamilton.

Hamilton lacked Jefferson's trust in local self-government and the democratic process, but at a time when American nationalism was a new concept he dedicated himself to its realization. Opinionated and impolitic, he was at the same time a towering figure, whose intellectual powers and administrative skills were of the first order. Hamilton is judged to be the one person, next to Washington, to whom the foundation of American federalism owes most.

See the biographies by Louis M. Hacker (1957), John C. Miller (1959), and Broadus Mitchell (2 vols., 1957–62).

HAMILTON, ANDREW (1656–1741), Scottish-born lawyer, settled in Philadelphia. As one of the most respected attorneys in the colonies, he was called to New York in 1735 to plead for JOHN PETER ZENGER in the famous newspaper libel case. His brilliant defense, resulting in acquittal, urged the doctrine that 'truth is a defense against libel,' and was a landmark in the development of the principle of a free press.

Hamilton College, at Clinton, New York, was founded (1812) as a liberal arts college for men. It stems from Hamilton Oneida Academy (1793), established by the Connecticut missionary to the Oneida Indians, Samuel Kirkland, who received (through the aid of Alexander Hamilton) a charter from New York state to educate Indian and white boys. In 1965, with an endowment of $14,600,000 and a faculty of 84, it enrolled 790 students.

Hammer* v. *Dagenhart (1918), a case resulting in a 5 to 4 decision of the U.S. Supreme Court, invalidated the Keating-Owen Act of 1916, which forbade interstate shipment of the products of child labor. It did so on the ground that the Act was not a regulation of commerce, but an attempt to regulate the conditions of manufacture, a matter reserved to the states. (Holmes's dissent upheld the unqualified right of Congress to regulate interstate commerce, including the power to prohibit.) The unrealistic limitation which the Court thus wrote into the Constitution on the power of Congress to legislate was repudiated (1941) in *U.S.* v. *Darby,* a decision that unanimously overruled the Hammer case by upholding the FAIR LABOR STANDARDS ACT (1938).

HAMMERSTEIN, OSCAR (1847–1919), German-born impresario, having built two opera houses in New York (1888–92), in 1906 built the second Manhattan Opera House, where he introduced some of the leading singers of the day, and operas by Debussy and Richard Strauss. In 1910 his interests were bought out by the Metropolitan Opera Company. His grandson, OSCAR HAMMERSTEIN II (1895–1960), wrote the lyrics for such musicals as *Oklahoma!* (1943), *Carousel* (1945) and *South Pacific* (1949), with music composed by RICHARD RODGERS. The musicals made theatrical history by the length of their runs, and are notable in that, contrary to tradition, their plots have a serious strain and at times employ tragic overtones.

Hampden-Sydney College, in Virginia, was one of four Presbyterian colleges founded in the 1780's. First opened as an academy in 1776, it was chartered as a college in 1783. Although it is still a small institution (with an enrollment in 1965 of some 490), many of its graduates have become prominent in public service, among them President William H. Harrison.

HAMPTON, WADE (1751–1835), South Carolina planter, was reputedly the wealthiest plantation owner in the U.S. As a major general in the War of 1812, he was turned back from his attempt to invade Canada by the skirmish at CHATEAUGAY. Accused by General James Wilkinson of losing the campaign, he resigned his command.

HAMPTON, WADE (1818–1902), grandson of Wade Hampton (1751–1835), graduated from South Carolina College (1836). During the Civil War he served as a general officer in the Confederate army, and succeeded to the command of the cavalry corps after the death of Jeb Stuart (1864). After the war he dominated South Carolina politics. He was twice elected governor and later served as U.S. Senator (1879–90). He was defeated for re-election by the followers of BENJAMIN TILLMAN.

Hampton Institute, Virginia, opened (1868) as a co-educational teacher training and agricultural school for Negroes. In 1920 it became a college with a humanities program. Many early Tuskegee teachers, including BOOKER T. WASHINGTON, were trained at Hampton, which is the best endowed Negro institution and the first to become internationally known. In 1965, with an endowment of $26,000,000 and a faculty of 160, it enrolled 1900 students.

Hampton Roads, Battle of (9 March 1862), though small in scale was revolutionary in effect. It was the first engagement between armored naval vessels, 'ironclads,' and introduced the revolving gun turret. Union forces had scuttled the frigate *Merrimac* when they abandoned the navy yard at Portsmouth, Virginia, at the outbreak of the Civil War. The Confederates raised the ship, renamed it *Virginia,* and converted it into a formidable ironclad. It closed the James river to the Union navy during the first weeks of the PENINSULAR CAMPAIGN. But the *Virginia* met her equal in the *Monitor* in Hampton Roads, where the two engaged in a five-hour close-range duel. The battle was a draw, but thereafter several thousand Confederate troops were tied up in look-out duty, and thus the Union gained some advantage.

Hampton Roads Conference (3 February 1865), held on board a Union steamer in Hampton Roads, was a design of Jefferson Davis 'to secure peace to the two countries' at that time when the collapse of the Confederacy was imminent. Lincoln met with A. H. Stephens, the vice president of the Confederacy, whose credentials gave him authority to negotiate peace if he were recognized as the envoy of a sovereign state. Lincoln patiently repeated his refusal to negotiate except on terms already known: reunion and abolition of slavery. He rejected Stephens's suggestion that if an armistice could be arranged, Confederate troops might secretly be used to assist the nationalist movement in Mexico. Lincoln reminded Stephens that the terms required the disbanding of all rebel forces. Thus the strange conference ended.

HANCOCK, JOHN (1737–93), Revolutionary patriot, was born in Braintree, Massachusetts. After graduation from Harvard (1754) he inherited from an uncle Boston's leading mercantile firm and thus took a prominent part in affairs of the town. Strongly opposed to such British trade restrictions as the Stamp Act (1765), he gave generous financial support to the SONS OF LIBERTY. The seizure and burning by customs officials of his sloop *Liberty* in 1768, on the ground that it had been trading illegally, led to law suits but enhanced his popularity. He was elected to the General Court (1769) and was serving as president of the Massachusetts Provincial Congress (1774–75) at the outbreak of the War of Independence. He presided at the Second Continental Congress (1775–77), and was the first to sign the Declaration of Independence. By virtue of his liberal public spirit, and his wealth and social position, he wielded great influence, and was chosen the first governor of Massachusetts, a post he filled almost continuously from 1780 until his death.

HANCOCK, WINFIELD SCOTT (1824–86), Pennsylvania-born Union general, after graduation from the U.S. Military Academy (1844) served in the Mexican War and throughout the Civil War. The greatest fighting general in the Army of the Potomac, Hancock commanded the 2d Corps at Gettysburg, and in the last two days of that battle was foremost in repulsing the Confederate attacks. Later he served as chief of the military department of Louisiana and Texas. Because of his outstanding military record, the Democrats ran him as presidential candidate in the 1880 election. Although Garfield won handsomely in the electoral vote, his popular plurality over Hancock was less than 10,000 in a total of more than 9,000,000 votes.

HAND, LEARNED (1872–1961), after graduation from Harvard (1893) began the practice of law at Albany, New York. As judge of the U.S. Southern District of New York (1909–24) and of the U.S. Court of Appeals, Second Circuit (1924–51), he wrote more than 2000 opinions, noted for their clarity and eloquence. Many of them became standard for law schools, and they gave Hand a reputation as an outstanding liberal. His *Spirit of Liberty* (1952), a defense of freedom against extremists of all persuasions, embodies the spirit of the man himself, who was by many called the greatest jurist of his time.

HANDY, W. C. [WILLIAM CHRISTOPHER] (1873–1958), Negro composer, first toured as a minstrel show cornetist. He was the first jazz composer to exploit the BLUES. His *Memphis Blues* (1911) was soon followed by his most famous piece, the *St. Louis Blues* (1914). His numerous compositions exploit the Negro musical idioms. *Father of the Blues* (1941) is his autobiography.

HANNA, MARCUS ALONZO (1837–1904), Cleveland industrialist, became active in politics and by 1890 was the ruling Republican power in Ohio. No figure in American political history has more typically represented the national 'boss.' He was genuinely convinced that business interests should govern (as honestly as possible) in the interest of national well-being, and he was an ardent missionary in the cause of the Republican party. Shrewd, intelligent, and personally upright, he enjoyed manipulating political situations.

'Uncle Mark' selected William McKinley for high authority and he steered McKinley into the Ohio governorship in 1891 and again in 1893. As chairman of the Republican National Committee in 1895, he secured the presidential nomination of McKinley on the first ballot, and his persuasions in the matter of large campaign contributions (colossal for that time) were effective in McKinley's defeat of Bryan. As a U.S. Senator (1897–1904) he stood with organized labor while championing political 'standpattism.' In 1901 his local power waned when TOM JOHNSON was elected mayor of Cleveland, and his national influence ebbed when, at McKinley's death, 'that cowboy' Theodore Roosevelt took the seat of government and deprived Hanna of control of the party machine. Yet he continued to be a well-liked and enlightened employer for the numerous employees of his extensive mining and street railway properties, and he was able to persuade the ultraconservative coal operators to make substantial concessions in the national anthracite coal strike of 1902. His death a year later ended the career of one of the most powerful political organizers of modern times.

HANSEN, MARCUS LEE (1892–1938), professor of history at Illinois after 1930, projected a trilogy on immigration which began with *The Atlantic Migration, 1607–1860* (1940, Pulitzer Prize 1941). From his papers were also assembled *The Immigrant in American History* (1940), and *The Mingling of* *the Canadian and American Peoples* (1940). Hansen was the first to treat the 19th-century immigration to America as an immense but unitary historical process.

HANSON, HOWARD (1896–), Nebraska-born composer and educator, was the first student of music to be enrolled in the American Academy in Rome (1921–24). Upon his return (1924) he became director of the Eastman School of Music at the University of Rochester. His many compositions include the opera *Merry Mount,* performed by the Metropolitan Opera Company (1934), and *Symphony No. 4,* awarded the Pulitzer Prize in 1944. He has often conducted the works of American composers, and has recorded an extensive series of native orchestral pieces.

HARDING, WARREN GAMALIEL (1865–1923), 29th President of the U.S. (1921–23), after attending Ohio Central College (1879–82), and briefly studying law, became owner and editor of a newspaper in Marion, Ohio. He entered politics, and while serving in the U.S. Senate (1915–21) was nominated for President by the Republican National Convention after a deadlock in the balloting between General Leonard Wood and Illinois governor Frank O. Lowden. Instructed to straddle the issue of whether or not the U.S. should join the League of Nations, in his campaign Harding pledged a 'return to normalcy,' and was elected by a landslide vote that defeated his Democratic opponent, Governor James M. Cox of Ohio, who had strongly endorsed the League.

Despite appointments to his Cabinet of such men of standing as Charles E. Hughes and Herbert Hoover, he opened the way to corruption by making the OHIO GANG his confidants. Harry Daugherty (later dismissed) was his Attorney General. Albert Fall (later imprisoned) headed the Department of the Interior. Edwin Denby (Navy), with Fall, Daugherty, and others, was implicated in the notorious TEAPOT DOME oil scandal.

Demoralized by the betrayal of his friends, and humiliated by an inevitable exposure, Harding, though not officially involved, was under acute tension. He died in office (2 August 1923) while returning from a trip to Alaska. Simple, friendly, and easy-going, he could not resist more unscrupulous wills, and his sudden death spared him from the aftermath of events which had revealed an Administration both incompetent and corrupt.

See Andrew Sinclair, *The Available Man: Warren Gamaliel Harding* (1965).

HARIOT, THOMAS (1560–1621), professor of mathematics at Oxford, was persuaded by Walter Raleigh to accompany Grenville to ROANOKE ISLAND in 1585 to observe and report. Hariot's *A brief and true report of the new found land of Virginia* (1588) is the first English book on the first English colony in what is now the U.S. Promptly translated into Latin, French, and German, in its 1590 (THEODOR DE BRY) edition this famous statistical survey contains the equally notable watercolors of JOHN WHITE, reproduced by De Bry's engravings. The influence of the volume was immense, and no other English colony in America ever produced anything comparable to it. The text was republished by HAKLUYT.

HARLAN, JOHN MARSHALL (1833–1911), Kentucky-born jurist, was practicing law in Louisville when President Hayes appointed him (1877) an Associate Justice of the U.S. Supreme Court, where for 34 years he served with distinction. Of liberal and independent convictions, he dissented in several notable instances, including the CIVIL RIGHTS CASES (1883), POLLOCK *v.* FARMERS' LOAN (income tax cases, 1895), and the INSULAR CASES (1901). His interest in the welfare of society led him steadily to oppose the narrow interpretations of the commerce power, the so-called RULE OF REASON, and to uphold the POLICE POWER of the states, a view that later Court decisions adopted.

Harlem, the congested residential and business section of upper Manhattan, centers on New York's 125th Street. It was originally the Dutch settlement Nieuw Haarlem (1658), and remained a rural area into the 19th century. In 1880 it was a fashionable residential section. The heavy influx of Negroes (after 1910) and of Puerto Ricans (after

1940) has created tremendous problems associated with poverty, discrimination, and overcrowding in what today is the nation's most populous slum area.

Harmony Society was established (1804) in western Pennsylvania by some 600 German Separatists under the leadership of George Rapp (1757–1847). In 1815 the colony moved to Indiana, where it prospered. In 1825 it sold the Indiana site to the British socialist Robert Owen, who there established his Utopian community of NEW HARMONY. The Rappists then settled permanently twenty miles below Pittsburgh on the Ohio river, where they continued to adhere to communal living and celibacy. In 1906 the society became extinct.

HARNETT, WILLIAM MICHAEL (1848–92), self-taught Philadelphia painter, was amazingly adept at the *trompe l'oeil* still life. In his day he was applauded by the public but treated contemptuously by critics. His oft-reproduced *After the Hunt* (1885) represents his skill in composition, and Harnett's work is now recognized as a forerunner of the most highly polished surrealist technique.

HARPER, WILLIAM RAINEY (1856–1906), resigned his chair of Semitic languages at Yale (1886–91) to accept the presidency of the newly established University of Chicago, and under his leadership that institution immediately became a center of research and graduate study, and the most vigorous university west of the Alleghenies. Harper was interested in the CHAUTAUQUA MOVEMENT, and as principal of the Chautauqua College of Liberal Arts (1885–91), he furthered adult education by making the Chautauqua system a force for general culture. He was author and editor of many works in the field of Biblical studies, and the quality of his intellectual keenness as an academic administrator is displayed in *The Trend of Higher Education* (1905).

Harpers Ferry, in easternmost West Virginia, is a small village situated on the bluffs above the confluence of the Potomac and Shenandoah rivers. In 1796 a U.S. arsenal was located there, and in 1859 it was seized briefly by JOHN BROWN in his quixotic raid. Because the town is a key to the Shenandoah valley, it was repeatedly the scene of Civil War engagements.

Harper's Monthly Magazine, founded (1850) as an eclectic literary periodical by Harper and Brothers, at first drew heavily upon the fiction of the best-known British authors. During the long editorship (1869–1919) of Henry Mills Alden it became more diversified, publishing discussions of social problems and contemporary politics, a policy it still pursues. Named *Harper's Magazine* in 1925, in 1960 it had a circulation of 232,000.

Harper's Weekly (1857–1916), chiefly a pictorial family magazine founded by Harper and Brothers, exerted popular political influence through the illustrations of its staff artist, THOMAS NAST. His cartoons helped to overthrow the TWEED RING in 1872, when the *Weekly* was at the height of its power. It also published stories by the best-known writers of the day, from Dickens and Wilkie Collins to Kipling and Henry James. Notable among its editors were G. W. CURTIS (1863–92), and CARL SCHURZ (1892–94). In 1916 it was consolidated with the *Independent.*

HARRIMAN, EDWARD HENRY (1848–1909), had made a fortune in Wall Street before he was thirty, and in the 1880's began to organize railroad systems. By 1900 he controlled 20,245 miles of railroad, including the Illinois Central and the Union Pacific. His attempt to add control of the Chicago, Burlington & Quincy in 1901 as a key connection into Chicago was blocked by J. J. HILL in a titanic struggle, one of the most famous battles in American financial history. Although Hill won the contest, Harriman used the strength of his roads to extend his domain, until in 1907 his financial practices were condemned by the Interstate Commerce Commission as 'indefensible.' But his constructive energies were immense, and on a national and even global scale, for he saw all ramifications of a complex situation at a glance. He established not only a steamship line to the Orient, but planned a round-the-world transportation system (which, however, missed fulfillment because of political conditions).

His son, WILLIAM AVERELL HARRIMAN (1891–), took over the business interests. He served as ambassador to Soviet Russia (1943–46), as Secretary of Commerce (1946–48), as governor of New York (1955–58), and later acted as a high-ranking government servant on special missions abroad.

HARRIS, CHAPIN AARON (1806–60), a founder of dentistry as a profession, established a dental periodical (the first anywhere in the world), the *American Journal of Dental Science* (1839), and founded the Baltimore College of Dental Surgery (1840), for the systematic training of dentists. (It is now part of the University of Maryland.) His pioneer study, *The Dental Art* (1839), was later expanded as *Principles and Practice of Dental Surgery,* widely used in its day.

HARRIS, ROY [ELLSWORTH] (1898–), Oklahoma-born composer, studied with Arthur Farwell, Arthur Bliss, and briefly with Nadia Boulanger (1926). A prolific composer (especially during the 1930's and 1940's) in all media except opera, he often employs native themes in his larger works, which include *Folksong Symphony* (1940), *Cimarron* (1941), and *Gettysburg Address Symphony* (1944). His music is distinguished for its melodic invention and emotional vitality.

HARRIS, TOWNSEND (1804–78), New York merchant, as a member of the board of education launched a vigorous campaign to establish a free city college, and was largely responsible for the legislation chartering the College of the City of New York (1847). President Buchanan sent him as the first American consul to Japan (1855), where he negotiated the earliest U.S.–Japanese commercial treaty (1858). A genuine admirer of Japanese culture, and a highly influential adviser to their government, he established the tradition of friendship between the two nations which, briefly broken during the 1940's, has continued to the present.

HARRIS, WILLIAM TORREY (1835–1909), Connecticut-born educator, attended Yale into his junior year in the class of 1858. As superintendent of the St. Louis school system (1867–80) and U.S. Commissioner of Education (1889–1906), he advanced vocationalism and became the leading educational philosopher in the country. He was the foremost exponent of Hegel in the U.S., and in 1867 founded the St. Louis school of IDEALISM, thereby initiating the systematic study of German thought in America. He founded and edited (1867–93) the *Journal of Speculative Philosophy,* the first periodical in the English language devoted exclusively to philosophy, and the one that published the early writings of Peirce, James, Royce, and Dewey. With Bronson Alcott he founded the CONCORD SCHOOL OF PHILOSOPHY (1880).

In Harris's optimistic idealism the security and destiny of individuals lies in their willing subordination of self to the dominant aspects of society (family, school, church, state), and for Harris no conflict existed between the values of capitalism and those of mind and spirit. Although no measure can be taken of the effect of his teaching in reinforcing the conservative tenor of American thinking, by his official positions and through the prodigious number of his essays and lectures he became one of the most influential intellectual leaders of his day.

Harrisburg Convention (1827) was called at Harrisburg, Pennsylvania, by advocates of a higher tariff. Led by Henry Clay, 100 delegates from 13 states drew up and submitted to Congress a statement recommending a tariff favorable to manufacturers. The result was the passage of the TARIFF OF 1828, the so-called 'Tariff of Abominations.'

HARRISON, BENJAMIN (1833–1901), 23d President of the U.S. (1889–93), was born in Ohio, and was the grandson of President William Henry Harrison. Soon after graduation from Miami University (1852) he was admitted to the bar in Indianapolis, where he became a well-established corporation lawyer. Having faithfully served his party as a Republican in the U.S. Senate (1881–87), he was chosen (1888) as the most 'available' and least offensive presidential candidate to oppose Grover Cleveland. Cleveland received a popular plurality of 100,000, but Harrison won the electoral vote (233 to 168).

Dignified, honest, and conscientious, but unskillful in arousing public opinion, Harrison lacked the ability to check the spoilsmen of a party controlled largely by his very astute Secretary of State, JAMES G. BLAINE. With 'Czar' Reed as Speaker of the House, and with a majority of both Houses obligated to the machine that had placed them in office, the connection between government and business during the Harrison administration was frankly avowed. During his term the high McKinley Tariff Act (made palatable by his reciprocity provision) and the Sherman Silver Purchase Act (which he hoped would help the silver industry) were passed, Civil War pensions were augmented, and imperialist policies were pressed in the Pacific. Defeated for reelection in 1892 by Cleveland, Harrison returned to his law practice.

HARRISON, PETER (1716–75), Newport, Rhode Island, merchant, born in England, has won recognition as the foremost architect in colonial America. Although an amateur, Harrison designed with cultivated ingenuity. He trained himself principally by studying sketches and plates in the works of the English architect James Gibbs, and was a close student of Sir Christopher Wren. He executed most commissions without pay, and built King's Chapel in Boston (1754), and the Redwood Library (1749) and Touro Synagogue (1763) in Newport. His design of the Redwood Library introduced the Palladian style in America.

HARRISON, WILLIAM HENRY (1773–1841), 9th President of the U.S. (1841), was born in Virginia and attended Hampton-Sydney College (1787–90). The death of his father compelled him to abandon his study of medicine in Philadelphia (1791). He joined the army and took part in Indian campaigns in the Old Northwest. While secretary of the Northwest Territory (1798) he won election as territorial delegate to Congress, where he helped form the new divisions of Ohio and Indiana. Thereafter for twelve years he served as governor of Indiana Territory (1800–1812).

He won the battle of TIPPECANOE (1811), and in the War of 1812, after the debacle of General WILLIAM HULL, took command in the Northwest. He captured Detroit in September 1813, and three weeks later established American hegemony in the West by the battle of the THAMES. As a Whig supporter of Clay he served in the House (1816–19) and the Senate (1825), but suffered eclipse during the Jackson era. In 1836 a group of Anti-Masonic Whigs ran him for President, and his unexpected strength in that campaign turned the attention of the Whig party to him in 1840. The support of Webster was chiefly responsible for his capturing the nomination from his formidable opponent, Henry Clay.

The election campaigns of 1840 are unique in American history for their carnival atmosphere. Neither party adopted a platform or presented real issues. The General and his running mate JOHN TYLER were presented to the public as 'Tippecanoe and Tyler too,' the rugged frontiersman and his loyal supporter. The Democrats derisively called Harrison the 'Log Cabin and Hard Cider' candidate, a challenge the Whigs turned to profit by forming log cabin clubs and serving hard cider at their rallies. In their turn they created an image of President Van Buren, the Democratic candidate, as a wealthy, effete New Yorker, drinking wine 'from his coolers of silver.' Harrison carried the election by a four-to-one majority, 234 electoral votes to Van Buren's 60, although the popular vote was close (roughly 1,275,000 to 1,128,000). The tide that ran against the organized party in power, and that for the first time since 1800 favored a diffuse coalition, in part stemmed from the PANIC OF 1837.

Harrison selected a Whig cabinet headed by Webster and followed a program outlined by Clay. But the strain of the campaign had exhausted the general, then sixty-eight, and he succumbed to pneumonia one month after his inauguration. He was the first President to die in office. Harrison's nomination was significant in the evolution of the presidency, for it demonstrated to politicians that, in general, when factional issues threaten national parties, the winning candidate can be a military hero or a relatively obscure figure free from commitments on matters of principle. Harrison was a man of commonplace mind and obstinate views, but he was a leader in fashioning the new West. His grandson, Benjamin Harrison, was the 23rd President.

See Freeman Cleaves, *Old Tippecanoe* (1939).

Harrison Land Act, see *Public land sales.*

HART, Albert Bushnell (1854–1943), professor of history and government at Harvard (1897–1926), was especially known as an organizer of such undertakings as the 'American Nation' series (28 vols., 1904–18), a co-operative history, representing the result of the first generation of American scientific historiography. A prodigious worker, Hart was responsible for the publication of some 100 volumes, and wrote extensively himself on many aspects of American government and history.

HART, William S. (1870–1946), after a career as an actor on Broadway and in road companies (1895–1914), starred in motion pictures. Prototype of the 'strong, silent man of the West,' he was famous for such films as *Wild Bill Hickok,* and *Square Deal Sanderson.*

HARTE, Bret [Francis Brett] (1836–1902), went to California from Albany, New York, in 1854, worked at various jobs, and settled (1860) in San Francisco. There he became a printer and journalist, and the leader of a brilliant literary group that included Mark Twain, Ambrose Bierce, Joaquin Miller, Clarence King, and Ina Coolbrith. As first editor (1868–71) of the *Overland Monthly,* he made that magazine the most distinguished of all western periodicals. Publication of *The Luck of Roaring Camp and Other Sketches* (1870) brought him into national prominence. They were the earliest of all western local color stories, romantic and picturesque, and their influence on the genre was immense. He was also a pioneer in writing humorous or sentimental vernacular poetry glorifying people or events on the frontier, and his 'Pike' verses, issued as *The Heathen Chinee* (1871), begot a progeny of dialect poems.

His triumphal trip East at that time was undertaken to fulfill a $10,000 contract with the *Atlantic Monthly* for twelve contributions. The demand for his stories forced him into a mold, and thereafter he imitated himself, turning out stories to order, and adding a volume every year or so to his collected works. During the last 24 years of his life he lived abroad, chiefly in London, where he died.

See G. R. Stewart, Jr., *Bret Harte* (1931).

Hartford Convention (1814–15) was inspired by mercantile interests opposed to Republican policy. At the invitation of the Massachusetts legislature it assembled in secret session at Hartford, Connecticut, in December 1814, to consider measures that would strengthen Federalist control in a period of Republican domination in domestic and foreign affairs. Its delegates were all from New England, chiefly from Massachusetts, Rhode Island, and Connecticut (the mercantile states), and it adopted a set of resolutions calling among other things for (1) nullification of the conscription bill then before Congress, should that bill pass; (2) an independent interstate defense machinery, to be supported by Federal taxes collected within the states; and (3) prohibition of all embargoes lasting more than 60 days. Moderates controlled the convention, and contrary to popular belief, secession was not seriously considered.

A committee was appointed by the Massachusetts legislature to negotiate with Congress, but the signing of the Treaty of Ghent, which concluded the War of 1812 nine days after the convention met, brought an abrupt end to the work of its committees. The convention was dissolved early in 1815. The ridicule heaped on it was one factor in the decline of the Federalist party's national importance.

Hartford Foundation (John A. Hartford Foundation) was established (1929) by John A. Hartford (1872–1951), pioneer promoter of supermarkets. Its funds, which have been applied to religious, charitable, literary, and scientific purposes, most recently have been granted chiefly for medical education and research. One of the largest endowed foundations in the world, in 1965 from assets of $397,000,000 it disbursed $13,800,000.

Hartford Wits, see *Connecticut Wits.*

Harvard University, the oldest institution of higher learning in the U.S., was founded (1636) as 'a schoale or colledge' at Cambridge, Massachusetts, under a grant of £400 made by the General Court. It opened (1638) under a board of overseers in whom the young colonist John Harvard (1607–38) placed his confidence, and they in turn honored his benefactions by giving the college his name. In 1642 it graduated its first class, bestowing degrees upon nine bachelors, ranging in age from seventeen to twenty-three.

Like later COLLEGE CHARTERS, the degree-giving power of Harvard was 'prescriptive,' that is, while it was not specifically sanctioned by Parliament (which long had given Oxford and Cambridge a monopoly), it was never challenged. In 1650 the college received its charter from the General Court and became a corporation, consisting of the president, five fellows, and the treasurer; since that time the control has been vested jointly in the Corporation (the administrative body) and the Board of Overseers (officials, once elected by the legislature, who have revisory power over the acts of the Corporation). Closely allied with the church in its early years, in 1851 the college ceased to require representation of the clergy on its Board of Overseers, whose members since then have been chosen by the alumni.

Early presidents whose names are especially honored include HENRY DUNSTER (1640–54), who gave the college its true beginning; JOHN LEVERETT (1708–24), under whose aegis a liberal tradition was established; and EDWARD HOLYOKE (1737–69), during whose administration scientific instruction was built up. Schools of medicine (1782), law (1817), divinity (1819), and engineering (1847) gave increased stature to the institution, and under the long administration of CHARLES W. ELIOT (1869–1909), Harvard added the elective system of studies (imitated elsewhere), adopted the casebook method of legal studies inaugurated by Dean C. C. LANGDELL, and was in fact transformed from a college into a university, thus living up to the name given to it in the Massachusetts constitution of 1780.

Its present undergraduate instruction, introduced by A. LAWRENCE LOWELL (1909–33), functions under the tutorial plan organized around the houses, which in effect are small colleges within the larger body. The university's library resources and research facilities are unrivaled in the academic world. Throughout its history Harvard has played an important role in the cultural life of America, and its faculty has included many persons of distinction in public life. In 1965, with an endowment of $621,000,000 (the largest in the U.S.) and a faculty of 5680, it enrolled 11,950 students.

HASSAM, CHILDE (1859–1935), Boston painter and etcher, studied in Paris under Lefebvre and G. R. Boulanger. His landscapes and interiors, strongly influenced by impressionism, are represented by *July 14th, Rue Daunou* (Metropolitan Museum). He avoided real painting problems in a successful effort to be salable, but he made the style of Monet popular.

HASSLER, FERDINAND RUDOLPH (1770–1843), Swiss-born geodesist, came to the U.S. in 1805. At the invitation of President Jefferson he organized the U.S. COAST AND GEODETIC SURVEY (1807), spent several years abroad to supervise the design and construction of precision instruments, and when field work got under way he served as superintendent (1816–18). Excluded for a time from his task by a law requiring that only military and naval personnel might be employed in the work, he was reappointed in 1832, and served with distinction until his death. His standards of precision are still followed.

HASTIE, WILLIAM HENRY (1904–), Tennessee-born Negro jurist, graduated from Amherst (1925) and Harvard Law School. After private practice, he served as judge of the District Court of Virgin Islands (1937–39), as dean of Howard University School of Law (1939–46), and as governor of the Virgin Islands (1946–49). In 1949 he was appointed to the bench as judge of the Third U.S. Circuit Court of Appeals.

HASTINGS, THOMAS (1784–1872), born in Connecticut, was long associated with church music in New York City, where he conducted choirs and composed words and music for hymns. His hymnals include *Musica Sacra* (1816), *Spiritual Songs* (with Lowell Mason, 1831), and *Devotional Hymns* (1850), in which first appeared his well-known setting for Toplady's 'Rock of Ages.'

Hat Act (1732) was passed by Parliament at the insistence of London's Worshipful Company of Hatters, who feared that Americans were not importing all their headgear from London. The law limited the number of hatter apprentices in the colonies and forbade colonial exportation of hats. Soon thereafter the hats exported from New York bore the label 'British.'

Hatch Act (1887), most important of its kind after the MORRILL ACT (1862), made Federal subsidies (providing the states matched the appropriations) for the creation of agricultural experiment stations for research in every state of the Union.

Hatch Act (1939), as a result of alleged political malpractices involving the votes of WPA workers during the elections of 1938, prohibited Federal office holders from active participation in political campaigns, and, in an amendment (1940), limited the annual expenditures of political parties to $3,000,000 and of individuals to $5000. Exactly how to define the term 'pernicious political practices,' as the Act phrased it, has never been determined, and expenditures and contributions have often greatly exceeded the amounts stipulated by the law.

Haverford College was founded (1833) at Haverford, Pennsylvania, as a school by the Society of Friends, and in 1856 it became the first Quaker liberal arts college for men. As a Quaker institution, Haverford stresses community service. In 1965, with an endowment of $14,000,000 and a faculty of 70, it enrolled 500 students.

Hawaii, admitted to the Union as the 50th state (1959), is the first overseas and the second non-contiguous state. (Alaska had previously been admitted in the same year.) It comprises twenty islands (seven inhabited) in the central Pacific, 2090 miles west of San Francisco, which is the nearest mainland port. The islands, with a notably fine climate, are volcanic in origin, and are fringed with coral reefs. Those inhabited are fertile and all are mountainous. They rise from the ocean floor to an altitude of 13,796 ft. above sea level at Mauna Kea, an extinct volcano on the largest island, Hawaii. Mauna Kea's twin, Mauna Loa, almost as high, is the world's largest active volcano.

When the British navigator JAMES COOK in 1778 discovered the Sandwich Islands, as he named them, they were ruled by native warring kings, but under the sole sovereignty (1795–1819) of Kamehameha I and his successors (to 1893) agriculture and commerce flourished. American missionaries became prominent in local affairs after 1820, and helped evolve a written language and the first constitution (1839). Hawaii had become so important an American outpost in those two decades that in 1844 the U.S. sent a foreign affairs representative there, the first government to do so. The increasing interest of many foreign powers in the mid-Pacific made a 'reform' agitation inevitable. Queen Liliuokalani was deposed in 1893. In 1900 Hawaii became the last U.S. Organized Territory.

The original culture of the Hawaiians, one of the most advanced of Polynesian civilizations, was overlaid in the latter part of the 19th century by immigrant groups from China and Japan, and later by cultural traces from seafaring nations throughout the world. No state in the U.S. has so eclectic a culture.

Its industries center upon sugar and pineapple production, but the largest part of its income is from tourism. Honolulu, on the island of Oahu, is the capital. It is a cosmopolitan city, with a population (1960) of 294,000. Nearby are the large naval installations at Pearl Harbor.

Hawaii National Park (est. 1916) is a volcanic region on the island of Hawaii, with luxuriant flora ranging in variety from tropical to semi-arctic specimens. The University of Hawaii (Honolulu, est. 1907) is the leading institution of higher learning; in 1965, with a faculty of 755, it enrolled 14,700 students.

***Hawaii* v. *Mankichi*,** see *Insular Cases*.

HAWKINS, Sir John (1532–95), British admiral, having found how profitable Negroes were as merchandise, introduced the slave trade in America. During the 1560's he inaugurated the so-called 'triangular trade' by loading 'black ivory' in Africa, selling his cargoes of slaves to planters in Haiti (in violation of the laws of Spain), and returning to England with such salable commodities as cow hides, sugar, and pearls. His voyages so profited the investors, including Queen Elizabeth, that he was granted arms with a chained 'demi-Moor' as a crest. He later held office as treasurer of the navy and commanded a vessel in the defeat of the Spanish Armada (1588), for which service he was knighted. He died at sea while on a treasure hunt in the West Indies. Hawkins combined dauntless seamanship with business acumen, and in collaboration with his kinsman FRANCIS DRAKE was instrumental in preventing the Spanish from establishing a monopoly in the New World.

Hawley-Smoot Tariff Act (1930), the highest in U.S. history, raised duties even above those of the excessive FORDNEY-MC CUMBER TARIFF ACT (1922). Vigorous protests from economists, unanimous in their disapproval, had no effect on President Hoover, who signed the bill in the belief that it would help the hard-pressed staple farmer. Levied on all imported goods and materials, it increased tariffs especially on minerals, chemicals, dyestuffs, and textiles. The Act aroused deep resentment abroad. Within two years 25 countries had established retaliatory tariffs, and foreign trade, already declining, slumped still further.

HAWTHORNE, Nathaniel (1804–64), novelist and writer of tales, was born at Salem, Massachusetts, where his Puritan forebears had lived as magistrates and seafarers for five generations. After graduation from Bowdoin (1825) he returned to Salem and a life of isolation, devoting himself to writing. To earn a living he engaged in hack work and for a time (1839–41) served as a measurer in the Boston customhouse. After trying out the communal life of BROOK FARM (1841–42), which proved uncongenial, he married Sophia Peabody, a sister of ELIZABETH PEABODY, and one of Hawthorne's earliest admirers. They lived briefly in Concord (1842–45), where Hawthorne wrote *Mosses from an Old Manse* (1846), tales in which the themes and characters anticipate the enduring fabric of the longer narratives soon to follow.

He was working as surveyor of the port of Salem (1846–49) when he began his masterpiece, *The Scarlet Letter* (1850), immediately followed by the story which he liked best of his works, *The House of the Seven Gables* (1851). These novels, which search out the play of evil and the ramifications of sin, guilt, and remorse, established Hawthorne as the classic interpreter in fiction of the Puritan mind. The months that he spent at Brook Farm furnished the setting for *The Blithedale Romance* (1852).

For four years Hawthorne served as U.S. consul at Liverpool (1853–57), and after leisurely travel in France and Italy returned home in 1860. This seven-year sojourn abroad gave him an opportunity to consider America in relation to its past and to speculate about the future. These related themes are adumbrated in *The Marble Faun* (1860) and woven into *Our Old Home* (1863). The latter remains the most moving autobiographical record left by any of the large number of travelers who at that time were setting down their impressions of the Old World.

One of the masters of English prose style as well as a craftsman of the first order, Hawthorne used the psychological method to probe the depths of human iniquity. He was recognized in his lifetime as a notable writer, but his 'unmalleable nature' made him seem aloof, and he formed few literary friendships either in England or America. It is significant that *Moby-Dick,* a study in evil and Melville's greatest work, was dedicated in admiration to Hawthorne.

See the biographies by Newton Arvin (1929) and Randall Stewart (1948).

HAY, John [Milton] (1838–1905), born in Indiana, after graduation from Brown (1858), studied law in Springfield, Illinois, where he met Lincoln, whom he accompanied to Washington as private secretary (1860–65). After holding minor posts in foreign legations and engaging in journalism in New York City, he re-entered government service as assistant secretary of state under Hayes (1879–81). Sent as McKinley's ambassador to England (1897), from 1898 until his death he was Secretary of State under McKinley and Theodore Roosevelt. He was responsible for the OPEN DOOR POLICY in China (1899), and concluded the HAY-PAUNCEFOTE TREATY with Great Britain (1900–1901), and the HAY-HERRÁN and HAY-BUNAU-VARILLA treaties with Colombia and Panama, respectively. Under McKinley Hay directed foreign affairs; the interventionist policies after 1901 were largely shaped by Roosevelt.

Although his accomplishments were chiefly in the field of diplomacy, Hay was distinguished as a man of letters. His novel *The Breadwinners* (1884) sought to deal with economic problems of the day. His vernacular poems, *Pike County Ballads* (1871), portray real Midwestern themes and people, and 'Jim Bludso' is an authentic folk expression. In collaboration with John G. Nicolay (Lincoln's other private secretary) he wrote the monumental *Abraham Lincoln: A History* (10 vols., 1890).

See Tyler Dennett, *John Hay: From Poetry to Politics* (1933).

Hay treaties. Secretary of State John Hay negotiated three treaties bearing his name, all dealing with the construction and management of an isthmian canal. The **Hay-Pauncefote Treaty** (November 1901), signed by Hay and the British ambassador Sir Julian Pauncefote, superseded the CLAYTON-BULWER TREATY of 1850, and provided that the U.S. might have the exclusive right to construct, manage, and fortify a canal to join the Atlantic and Pacific oceans, open to ships of all nations on equal terms.

The **Hay-Herrán Treaty** (January 1903), negotiated with Minister Herrán of Colombia, provided that Colombia would lease to the U.S. a strip of land across the isthmus of Panama for the construction of a canal. The Colombian senate, however, refused to ratify the agreement, demanding a larger sum in payment than the $10,000,000 stipulated. The refusal resulted in the bloodless PANAMA REVOLUTION, which gave the Isthmus of Panama its independence from Colombia. Roosevelt's later public statement, 'I took Panama,' was very costly in hemispheric good will. Twelve days after the U.S. recognized the new Republic of Panama (6 November 1903), Hay signed the **Hay-Bunau-Varilla Treaty** with minister Philippe Bunau-Varilla of Panama. It granted to the U.S. the use and control of the 10-mile-wide CANAL ZONE in perpetuity. Agitation for revision of this treaty had become so vigorous by 1964 that the Republic of Panama broke off diplomatic relations with the U.S. and placed the issue before the Organization of American States. The following year President Johnson promised a new treaty.

HAYDEN, FERDINAND VANDIVEER (1829–87), Massachusetts-born geologist, after graduation from Oberlin (1850) studied medicine. His interest soon turned to geology, and in 1856 he began his series of investigations of the Far West, summarized first in *Geological Report of the Exploration of the Yellowstone and Missouri Rivers in 1859–60* (1869). During the Civil War he served as an army surgeon. He was teaching geology at Pennsylvania (1865–72) when in 1867 he began his twelve years of labor as geologist-in-charge of the U.S. Geological and Geographic Survey of the territories, especially in the Rocky Mountain region, where he found extensive mineral resources and botanical specimens. The work resulted in a series of monographs in all branches of natural history and economic science, including his *Geological and Geographical Atlas of Colorado* (1877). As head of the Montana division (1879–86) of the reconstituted U.S. Geological Survey, he was largely responsible for creating Yellowstone National Park.

HAYES, HELEN [MRS. CHARLES MACARTHUR] (1900–), made her Broadway debut as a child in the musical comedy *Old Dutch* (1908). An actress of the first rank, she has given notable performances in *Dear Brutus, Mary of Scotland, Caesar and Cleopatra,* and especially in Laurence Housman's *Victoria Regina,* 1937–38. More recent productions have included *My Son John* (film), 1951; *Skin of Our Teeth* (Europe and U.S.), 1955; and *Time Remembered,* 1958.

HAYES, Rutherford Birchard (1822–93), 19th President of the U.S. (1877–81), was born in Ohio. After graduation from Kenyon College (1843) and Harvard Law School, he practiced law in Cincinnati, served as a Union general during the Civil War, and became a Republican member of Congress (1865–67). He served three terms as governor of Ohio, where his 'sound-money campaign' attracted national attention and marked him out as a candidate for the presidency. In 1876 he obtained the Republican nomination, and after the famous Hayes-Tilden dispute over the balloting, settled by the ELECTORAL COMMISSION, was declared duly elected.

His first important act was to end Reconstruction by withdrawing Federal troops from southern state capitals. This conciliatory policy toward the South, and his effort to restrict the 'spoils system,' alienated the party boss ROSCOE CONKLING, who was able to thwart Hayes's effort to inaugurate civil service reforms. Since many even among his own party believed that he had achieved office through fraud, Hayes was never able to count on the moral support of the country. Thus a second term, in which he might have consolidated his position, was out of the question. Furthermore, by 1878 the Democrats controlled both Houses of Congress, thereby effectively blocking the President in his political strategy.

His cabinet, headed by William M. Evarts (State), included CARL SCHURZ (Interior), who cleaned up the scandalous corruption of the Indian Bureau. To dramatize the reconciliation of the sections, the President brought an ex-Confederate Tennessee jurist, David M. Key (1824–1900), into his cabinet as Postmaster General. But Hayes was surprisingly obtuse in refusing to countenance repeal of the hated FORCE ACTS, and he seriously compromised himself with his reform group by the number of appointments he continued to make as political awards. Yet the fact remains that his adamantine stubbornness in dealing with spoilsmen had an important effect in restoring to the executive branch of government the prerogatives which had been usurped by Congress during the previous three administrations, and thus re-established the normal and constitutional relationship between the President and Congress. But he paid little attention to railroad malpractices or to land frauds, and his only solution of the labor unrest that erupted in the RAILROAD STRIKES OF 1877 was to call out Federal troops. His administration, despite its political drama, lacked statesmanship.

Biographies include those by C. R. Williams (2 vols., 1914); H. J. Eckenrode (1930), and Harry Barnard (1956).

Haymarket Riot (4 May 1886), growing out of labor strikes in Chicago for an eight-hour working day, occurred in Haymarket Square. On 3 May the police in attempting to curb a melee had killed or wounded some half dozen strikers. When a street meeting was called on 4 May to protest the 'massacre,' someone (never identified) threw a bomb into the ranks of the police called out to break up the assembly.

A panic followed, in which seven policemen were killed and some three score injured. Declaring that those who incited the deed were equally guilty of murder, Judge Joseph E. Gary sentenced seven of the rioters to death and one to prison. Four were hanged, and one committed suicide. The sentence of two was commuted to life imprisonment by Governor Oglesby. In 1893, when Governor JOHN P. ALTGELD came into office, he charged a miscarriage of justice and pardoned the remaining three. Altgeld was denounced as an abettor of anarchy, and the incident contributed to the delay for a generation of the adoption of an eight-hour day.

HAYNE, Robert Young (1791–1839), South Carolina statesman, was serving in the U.S. Senate (1823–32) when he gained attention as the leading southern spokesman for the doctrine of states' rights. In his famous debate (1830) with Daniel Webster, he argued that questions of sovereignty are not subject to judicial review. He was serving as governor of South Carolina (1832–34) when that state passed its ORDINANCE OF NULLIFICATION in defiance of the Tariff of 1832.

HAYNES, Elwood (1857–1925), a graduate of Worcester Polytechnic Institute (1881), while working for an Indiana gas company designed the first 'horseless carriage' successfully driven in the U.S. (4 July 1894). A pioneer automobile manufacturer, he formed his own company in 1895, and in 1910 presented his first car (reputedly the oldest in the U.S.) to the Smithsonian Institution. He developed alloys of cobalt, chromium, and tungsten, made many improvements in the structure of metals, and in 1919 patented stainless steel.

HAYNES, John (*c.* 1594–1654), emigrated to Massachusetts (1633), and as governor (1635) banished Roger Williams. In 1637 he moved to Hartford, Connecticut, where he became first governor of the colony under the FUNDAMENTAL ORDERS (1639), and continued so to serve on alternate years until his death.

HAYS, Arthur Garfield (1881–1954), distinguished himself as a lawyer in cases involving civil liberties, notably in the SCOPES TRIAL (1925) and the SACCO-VANZETTI CASE (1927). For many years he was general counsel and later director of the American Civil Liberties Union. *City Lawyer* (1942) is his autobiography.

HAZARD, Ebenezer (1744–1817), after graduation from the College of New Jersey (Princeton, 1762), became a publisher in New York City, and for a time served as postmaster general (1782–89). With the encouragement of the Continental Congress, and influenced by the work of his friend JEREMY BELKNAP, he began to assemble the material issued as *Historical Collections, State Papers, and Other Authentic Documents* (2 vols., 1792–94). The work is significant as a pioneer effort to collect and publish historical records.

Head tax, see *Poll tax*.

Health, Education, and Welfare, U.S. Department of, was established by Congress (1953) as the tenth unified department of cabinet rank. Its major divisions include Public Health Service, Office of Education, Social Security, Welfare, and Food and Drug Administration. Secretaries of the department and the Presidents under whom they served are as follows.

Eisenhower

Oveta Culp Hobby (Texas) 1953
Marion B. Folsom (N.Y.) 1955
Arthur S. Flemming (Ohio) 1958

Kennedy

Abraham A. Ribicoff (Conn.) 1961
Anthony J. Celebrezze (Ohio) 1961

L. B. Johnson

Anthony J. Celebrezze (Ohio) 1963
John W. Gardner (N.Y.) 1965

Health insurance, a field in which the U.S. federal and state governments have greatly lagged behind Europe since Bismarck's time, became a national political issue in the 1960's. Strenuous New Deal efforts to promote health insurance were defeated as 'socialized medicine' through the lobby of the American Medical Association. As a result, middle-class private programs such as Blue Cross and Blue Shield, paid wholly by the insured, flourished, and by the mid 1950's there had developed the very successful group major medical expense insurance, paid in part by the company and in part by the worker, which protected employees and their families against catastrophic expenses of disability by offering hospital, surgical, and medical expenses for long periods. Labor unions also pressed successfully for fringe benefits that included plant health insurance.

But conservatives continued to resist federally supported health insurance, even defeating the modest effort of Eisenhower in 1954 to secure Federal funds to expand private voluntary health insurance systems. In 1960, President Kennedy made a campaign issue of 'Medicare' to tie health insurance to the social security system. This idea in modified form became law on July 30, 1965. The health insurance law, popularly called Medicare, offered two kinds of insurance for those over sixty-five. One was hospital insurance, financed by equal contributions from employers and employees; the other, a voluntary measure, gave medical insurance covering doctor's expenses and certain other costs to be paid equally by the insured and the federal government. By the first, the insured received hospitalization for up to 90 days in a 'spell of illness,' outpatient diagnostic services, skilled nursing-home care, home health care after hospitalization, as well as various hospital services. In the campaign of 1964, Medicare was denounced by the Republican party as grossly inadequate; they preferred full medical and hospital costs for the needy rather than a general coverage. The Kennedy-Johnson victory in the passage of Medicare closed the long-existing gap between Europe's various health insurance systems and the individualistic private American plans.

HEARN, LAFCADIO (1850–1904), of Irish-Greek parentage, was born in the Ionian Islands, and educated in Ireland, England, and France. He emigrated to the U.S. in 1869, and, as a 'civilized nomad,' lived briefly in New York and New Orleans before he became a citizen of Japan (1893), married a Japanese woman, and taught English literature in the Imperial University at Tokyo. His exotic, highly polished tales, dealing with Creole life in New Orleans and the West Indies, are best represented by *Chita* (1889), and the posthumous *Creole Sketches* (1924). His books and lectures on Japan are somewhat romanticized, but his sympathetic interpretations are credited with promoting amity between East and West.

HEARST, WILLIAM RANDOLPH (1863–1951), son of George Hearst (1820–91), California mining magnate and U.S. Senator, after attending Harvard (1882–85) began his journalistic career in charge of his father's San Francisco *Examiner*. In 1895 he purchased the New York *Journal* and began a spectacular circulation war with Joseph Pulitzer. Both used the techniques of YELLOW JOURNALISM. (Pulitzer lost.) By whipping up a popular demand for war with Spain, Hearst fed the flames of chauvinism and greatly increased the circulation of his paper. A showman and a propagandist with colossal ego, he created an immense newspaper chain, noted for its high-salaried staff and notorious for its sensationalism. Backed by the power of his wealth, seemingly indifferent to truth, and ruthlessly dictatorial, Hearst debased the standards of American journalism with appalling irresponsibility. His empire later came to include such properties as motion pictures and radio companies.

Hearst ran his enterprises from his incredible San Simeon estate, on which he annually lavished millions, buying art objects of great value to furnish it. Late in life his debts threatened him with financial ruin, and he recouped his fortune by making large private sales of his by then enormous accumulation of art treasures, which even included Spanish castles, carefully dismantled and crated.

Hearst's baffling perversities of character were matched by his undoubted abilities as a journalist and businessman.

One of the many biographies is W. A. Swanberg, *Citizen Hearst* (1961).

HECKER, ISAAC THOMAS (1819–88), born in New York, was early influenced by Orestes Brownson and the transcendentalist movement, and for six months joined the group at BROOK FARM. He was ordained a Catholic priest in 1849, and soon after went to Europe as a Redemptorist missionary. A zealot, he proceeded in ways that led to his expulsion from the order in 1858, but in the same year the Pope dispensed his vows and Hecker founded the missionary Priests of St. Paul the Apostle (the Paulist Fathers), of which group Hecker was the Superior until his death. He also founded the eclectic monthly *Catholic World* (1865), still important, which he edited until his death.

HEDGE, FREDERIC HENRY (1805–90), son of Dr. Levi Hedge, professor of philosophy at Harvard, studied for four years in Germany under the tutelage of George Bancroft before he entered Harvard, from which he graduated in 1825, when he was just past twenty. He was serving a Bangor, Maine, parish as a Unitarian minister when he became a moving spirit in forming the TRANSCENDENTAL CLUB (1836), sometimes called the Hedge Club because it met when Hedge found the opportunity to come to Boston. He established himself as a scholar with *Prose Writers of Germany* (1848), important as a work that introduced German literature into America. He later taught at Harvard as professor of ecclesiastical history (1857–76) and of German (1872–84) until his retirement. Thus his considerable earlier achievement in awakening interest in the field of German literature received academic recognition.

HELBURN, Theresa [Mrs. John B. Opdycke] (1887–1959), a graduate of Bryn Mawr (1908), served as director of the THEATRE GUILD for many years after 1919. As a force in the LITTLE THEATER MOVEMENT she stimulated new techniques in stage design and acting. Her productions include *Mary of Scotland* (1933), *The Philadelphia Story* (1939), *Oklahoma!* (1943), and *The Iceman Cometh* (1946).

HELD, John, Jr. (1889–1958), cartoonist and illustrator, was considered the leading interpreter of the younger generation of the JAZZ AGE. After 1928 he devoted himself largely to writing.

'Helderberg War,' see *Anti-Rent War.*

Hell's Kitchen, a district on the west side of Manhattan, was named for Dutch Heinrich's Hell's Kitchen Gang, which raided freight yards in the area during the late 1860's. It became a hangout for gunmen and thieves until the gangs were broken up in 1910.

HELPER, Hinton Rowan (1829–1909), born in North Carolina into an impoverished household, spoke for the nonslaveholding poor whites of the South in *The Impending Crisis* (1857), which was a violent attack on slavery. Although abusively abolitionist, it was not written with sympathy for Negroes, whom Helper despised. It was directed against a system that he believed was bringing economic ruin to the small farmer. The book aroused fierce controversy. To circulate it in the South was a crime. In the North, Horace Greeley prepared a version (1858) as a campaign book for the Republican party. Some 100,000 copies were distributed, thereby creating so bitter a cleavage that in December 1859 John Sherman was denied the House Speakership because he had endorsed the book. After the Civil War Helper continued to pour his vitriol in racist attacks, disseminated in such books as *Nojoque* (1867) and *The Negroes in Negroland* (1868). Finally bankrupt, and declaring that 'There is no justice in this world,' Helper committed suicide at eighty.

HEMINGWAY, Ernest [Miller] (1898–1961), Illinois-born novelist, first won critical acclaim for *The Sun Also Rises* (1926), a story concerned with the moral collapse of expatriate Americans after World War I. His fictional craftsmanship, which greatly influenced younger writers, is typified by clipped, curt statements of what his reporter's eye observed. His power to evoke poignant emotion is displayed in many later books, including *A Farewell to Arms* (1929), *Death in the Afternoon* (1932), *For Whom the Bell Tolls* (1940), and *The Old Man and the Sea* (1952). His volunteer ambulance corps experiences in World War I, especially in France and Italy, gave him indispensable background for his novels of the 1920's. With the Great Depression and the rise of fascism, his novels reflected increasing social consciousness. In 1954 he won the Nobel Prize in literature. Often concerned in his stories with the hunter, the hunted, and death, he died from a self-inflicted gunshot wound.

HENNEPIN, Louis (1640–1701), Belgian-born Franciscan Recollect friar, in 1678 became chaplain of La Salle's proposed western expedition. He accompanied Michel Aco into the upper Mississippi valley and discovered St. Anthony's Falls (Minneapolis, 1680). After returning to France he published *Description de la Louisiane* (1683), which was a best seller in its day. Its trustworthy geographical observations (including the first description of Niagara Falls) are enlivened by comments on Indian customs and manners. His later *Nouvelle Découverte* (1697) is the story of a journey to the mouth of the Mississippi. It is believed to have been plagiarized from descriptions by a fellow Recollect, Zenobius Membré, who had accompanied La Salle in 1682. The Hennepin books ran to 35 variant editions in five languages.

HENRI, Robert (1865–1929), Ohio-born painter, attracted talented students to his studio, first in Philadelphia and later in New York. As the most stimulating member of the realists known as THE EIGHT, he was distinguished for his inspired teaching and for his dramatic portraits, represented by *Spanish Gypsy* (Metropolitan Museum), and *Young Woman in Black* (Art Institute, Chicago).

HENRY, Alexander (1739–1824), New Jersey-born fur trader in the Old Northwest, was one of the group that eventually became the powerful North West Company. As early as 1760 he had visited the site of Milwaukee and soon thereafter obtained a monopoly of the Lake Superior trade. (Henry started John Jacob Astor on his career in the West.) Henry's *Travels and Adventures in Canada and the Indian Territories* (1809) is one of the notable source books for the fur trade, a vivid picture of life in the woods and the ways of the Indians and trappers in the late 18th century. Francis Parkman drew from it in writing *The Conspiracy of Pontiac,* and Thoreau regarded it (in *A Week on the Concord*) as 'a sort of classic among books of American travel.' In his early youth Washington Irving had dined at Montreal with Henry and other 'mighty Northwesters,' whose enthralling stories Irving never forgot.

HENRY, Joseph (1797–1878), physicist, was educated at Albany Academy, where he later taught mathematics and natural philosophy (1826–32), and began his notable researches in the field of electromagnetism. By producing (1830) a multi-turn multi-layer coil, he discovered the phenomenon of self inductance, and in his honor the electrical unit of inductance is called the henry. His achievement, prior to and independently paralleling that of Faraday, was basic to the development of the electric motor, generator, dynamo, and transformer. Henry credited Faraday with priority in detection of the induced current, because Faraday published his results first. In 1832 Henry became the first professor of natural philosophy at Princeton.

Henry was called to Washington in 1846 as the first secretary and director of the Smithsonian Institution, and he formulated the broad policies of research and diffusion of knowledge still carried on there. His introduction (*c.* 1850) of the telegraph to transmit weather reports and to forecast weather conditions laid the foundation for the U.S. Weather Bureau.

HENRY, Patrick (1736–99), statesman and orator, was born in up-country Virginia and educated at home. Admitted to the bar in 1760, he became famous and wealthy as a trial lawyer after he won the case against the established church in the so-called PARSONS' CAUSE. In 1765 he stirred up the Virginia Assembly with his 'supreme torrents of eloquence' on the menace to individual liberties of the STAMP ACT. To the Tidewater gentry this red-headed, raw-boned frontiersman was a dangerous demagogue, with his cry: 'If *this* be treason, make the most of it.' But the Piedmont democrats regarded the impetuous radical as an inspired genius when he concluded his speech in the Assembly (1775) with the flaming words: 'I know not what course others may take, but as for me, give me liberty or give me death.' Thenceforth this 'forest-born Demosthenes' ranked as the foremost orator of the American Revolution.

As a leader who took an uncompromising stand against British claims, Henry won election as the first governor of the State of Virginia (1776–79), during which period he sent George Rogers Clark into the Old Northwest. In the state convention called (1788) to decide whether Virginia should ratify the Federal Constitution, Henry led the opposition, contending that the instrument endangered state and individual liberties.

Henry was by temperament averse to the routine of public duties, and after 1794 he declined in succession several high offices, including election to the U.S. Senate (1794), and Washington's offer to appoint him Secretary of State (1795) or chief justice of the U.S. Supreme Court (1795). He refused election as governor of Virginia in 1796, and appointment as envoy to France in 1799. But in his closing years he had become a Federalist, and in 1799 he consented to serve again in the state legislature, in order to combat the VIRGINIA RESOLVES. He died on his Charlotte county estate before the legislative session opened.

See Jacob Axelrad, *Patrick Henry* (1947).

Henry E. Huntington Library and Art Gallery, at San Marino, California (near Pasadena), is on the estate of its founder (1850–1927), who was the nephew of C. P. HUNTINGTON. An endowed educational institution, it is unique in the combination of its facilities for research, and its extensive collections of incunabula, rare books and manuscripts of English and American literature, Americana, and Spanish-American history (especially West Coast material). Its art treasures include a notable collection of English paintings.

Henry, Fort, on the Tennessee river, was the first stronghold captured (6 February 1862) during the Civil War in the Union advance to deny the Confederacy any control of the Mississippi river. It was a preliminary move in Grant's successful VICKSBURG CAMPAIGN. Ten days later Grant captured FORT DONELSON.

Henry Street Settlement, see *Wald, Lillian.*

Hepburn Act (1906), adopted after President Theodore Roosevelt's demand for stricter railroad regulation, increased the membership of the Interstate Commerce Commission from five to seven, and gave that body authority to fix maximum rates. It extended regulations to storage, refrigeration, and terminal facilities, cut down free passes, and prohibited railroads from carrying commodities produced by companies in which they had an interest. Appeals were admissible to Federal courts, with the burden of proof on the carrier, not on the Commission as theretofore, a situation which had allowed carriers to delay rate changes by lengthy legal proceedings. Though it represented a substantial advance in railway regulation, it failed to authorize the Commission to evaluate railroad properties or the cost of service. Provision for valuation was made in 1913, but another decade elapsed before such valuation was used for the purpose of rate-making.

***Hepburn* v. *Griswold*,** see *Legal Tender Cases.*

HERBERT, VICTOR (1859–1924), Irish-born cellist, conductor, and composer, came to the U.S. in 1886. His two grand operas *Natoma* (1911) and *Madeleine* (1914), as well as his earlier symphonic music, are overshadowed by his enormously successful operettas *Babes in Toyland* (1903), *Mlle. Modiste* (1905), and *Naughty Marietta* (1910). He was founder (1914) of the American Society of Composers, Authors, and Publishers (ASCAP), which he served as vice president until his death. His most important post as conductor was with the Pittsburgh Symphony, which he directed for six years (1898–1904).

HERKIMER, NICHOLAS (1728–77), appointed a brigadier general in the New York militia (1776) during the War of Independence, was leading a relief party to the Americans besieged at Fort Stanwix, the site of Rome, New York, when he was ambushed by a British contingent. Herkimer was killed and his force compelled to retreat, but his action delayed British troops on their way to join Burgoyne and thus contributed to the defeat of Burgoyne at SARATOGA.

Hermitage, The, a plantation near Nashville, Tennessee, was bought by Andrew Jackson in 1795. In 1819 he replaced the log cabin with a brick mansion, which burned in 1834. The present building, erected on the old site in the following year, has been preserved as a shrine since 1856.

HERNDON, WILLIAM HENRY (1818–91), in 1843 became a junior member of the Springfield (Illinois) law firm of Lincoln and Herndon, a partnership that was never dissolved. After Lincoln's assassination Herndon collected reminiscences of the early years and (with Jesse Weik) wrote *Herndon's Lincoln: The True Story of a Great Life* (3 vols., 1889). The book was savagely attacked at the time, because many of the stories ran counter to the growing Lincoln legend. However, the volumes remain a classic picture of Lincoln's prairie years.

'Herrin Massacre' (June 1922) was the bloody climax of the struggle in the coal mines of southern Illinois. Nonunion labor had been brought in during a coal strike. Under promise of safe conduct, 47 of the strikebreakers surrendered to an armed force of several hundred striking union miners. They were marched to a spot near Herrin and ordered to run for their lives under fire. More than twenty were killed. Although a grand jury returned 214 indictments for murder, local sentiment made convictions impossible, and after April 1923 further court action was dropped.

HERRON, George Davis (1862–1925), an ardent supporter of CHRISTIAN SOCIALISM, resigned his post as professor of applied Christianity in Iowa State College (1893–1900) because the trustees objected to his teaching. Thereafter he lectured upon the relations of Christianity to existing social conditions. Representative of his writing is *Social Meanings of Religious Experiences* (1895).

HERSKOVITS, Melville Jean (1895–1964), professor of anthropology at Northwestern after 1935, pioneered in the field of psycho-cultural studies. The results of his investigations, which have led to fresh assessments of the manner in which cultures are transmitted, are set forth in such books as *Acculturization* (1938), *The Myth of the Negro Past* (1941), and *Cultural Anthropology* (1955). Herskovits was an influential disciple of FRANZ BOAS and a leading Africanist. He headed the national scholarly associations in both physical and cultural anthropology at various times.

HESSELIUS, Gustavus (1682–1755), Swedish-born artist and organ builder, emigrated to Delaware in 1712. He was the earliest talented portrait painter in America and the first to receive an important commission. He painted *The Last Supper* (1721) for the Vestry of St. Barnabas Church, Prince George's county, Maryland. At the request of the Pennsylvania authorities he made a painting of Indian chiefs during a parley. His portrait (1735) of *Lapowinsa* (Pennsylvania Historical Society) catches the expression of a noble but deeply troubled aborigine. Few portraits attributed to Hesselius are authentic.

Hessians, the German mercenaries hired by the British during the War of Independence, were the 30,000 soldiers recruited principally from Hesse-Cassel and Hesse-Darmstadt. They were well drilled and ably commanded, and they took part in almost all the campaigns of the war. Respected by the Americans for their fighting ability, they were often better treated as prisoners than were the British soldiers. Over half the survivors returned to Germany after the war, but many remained as farmers and artisans.

HEWITT, Abram Stevens (1822–1903), after graduation from Columbia (1842) married a daughter of PETER COOPER, who set Hewitt up in iron manufacture. Hewitt was one of the first great American ironmasters. He supplied guns and armor to the Union forces during the Civil War, and by introducing the open-hearth process of smelting (1868) he helped to expand the U.S. steel industry on a major scale. (Incidentally, he built up one of the great fortunes of his day.) As a leader of the Democratic party he directed Tilden's presidential campaign in 1876, and later served in Congress (1876–86) and as a reform mayor of New York (1887–88). The great age of American capitalism is seen at its best in the achievements of Cooper and Hewitt.

HIAWATHA, 16th-century Mohawk Indian chief, is credited with having been largely responsible for creating the IROQUOIS CONFEDERACY, which originally sought to achieve universal peace by binding the tribes together. (Actually the league became one of the most formidable military powers in North America.) The studies of HENRY SCHOOLCRAFT were the basis of Longfellow's *Hiawatha,* a poem that turned legend into romance and gave no hint of the statesmanship of this early empire builder.

HICKOK, Wild Bill [James Butler] (1837–76), Illinois-born scout and stagecoach driver, served as a U.S. marshal in the West after the Civil War. For a year he toured the East with Buffalo Bill (1872–73). The legend of his invincibility in his encounters with frontier desperadoes became something of a challenge to gunmen, and he was murdered at Deadwood, South Dakota.

HICKS, Edward (1780–1849), Pennsylvania carriage-painter, became an itinerant Quaker preacher. Convinced that his power to attract large audiences resulted only in pride in his own accomplishment, he abandoned preaching and took up easel painting, always on wood panels. His moral allegory, *The Peaceable Kingdom* (of which he made nearly 100 versions), though primitive in technique, conveys, like his other works, the arresting originality of an artist excited by his convictions. Almost all his pictures are copies of works by well-known artists, yet they retain their individuality.

HICKS, Elias, see *Friends.*

Hidatsa Indians, of Siouan stock, were a village tribe on the northern Plains, culturally allied to their neighbors, the ARIKARA and the MANDAN Indians. Numbering some 2000 when Lewis and Clark visited them (1804), they were later decimated by smallpox. Remnants now live on a reservation in North Dakota. The spreading eagle feather headdress, used today by Indians on ceremonial occasions, probably originated among the Hidatsa and Mandan.

High schools (with free education supported by taxes) developed in the U.S. during the 19th century to complement the education that ACADEMIES offered at the secondary level. In the East they did not at first compete with academies in preparing youth for college, but in the West from the beginning they were the stepping stone to further education.

In about 1910 the unit of four grades (9–12) began in some instances to absorb grades 7–9 into a junior high school. Similarly the senior high schools sometimes included grades 13–14, the upper years becoming a junior college. The typical high school today is co-educational and comprehensive, with college preparatory and vocational departments. In the U.S. it has an importance in the education of all youth quite unparalleled elsewhere. In 1965 more than 15,000,000 pupils were enrolled in high schools.

Highways, see *Transportation.*

HILDRETH, Richard (1807–65), Massachusetts-born journalist and historian, graduated from Harvard (1826), and was admitted to the bar in 1830. He helped found and edit the Boston *Daily Atlas* (1832), wrote on a variety of social and economic themes, and after travel in the South became widely known for one of the earliest antislavery novels, *The Slave: or Memoirs of Archy Moore* (1836), savagely satiric and surprisingly frank in its depiction of sexual abuses incident to slavery.

His fame rests, however, upon his *History of the U.S.* (6 vols., 1849–52), covering the period 1492–1821. It is notable for its accuracy and candor, and its acute insights into the relationship between politics and economics. Consciously antiliterary in style, with a strong Federalist bias, it was hailed by later historians for its pioneer 'scientific' approach. Although Hildreth could not compete in sales with his rival, George Bancroft, he won followers for decades.

HILL, Ambrose Powell (1825–65), Virginia-born graduate of the U.S. Military Academy (1847), in 1861 resigned his commission in the U.S. Army to join the Confederate forces. He commanded a division under Jackson, whom he succeeded as corps commander after Jackson's death at Chancellorsville (May 1863). During the first day's fighting at Gettysburg he was in full command of the Confederate forces until the arrival of Lee. He was killed (2 April 1865) at Petersburg, while rallying his men with characteristic impulsiveness. As a troop leader, Hill is judged unmatched among the generals of either side.

HILL, Daniel Harvey (1821–89), South Carolina-born graduate of the U.S. Military Academy (1842), was superintendent of the North Carolina Military Institute at the outbreak of the Civil War. Joining the Confederacy, he served continuously, and as corps commander at Chickamauga his leadership was conspicuous. At the war's end, with General J. E. Johnston, he surrendered to General Sherman.

HILL, James Jerome (1838–1916), Ontario-born railroad executive, in 1856 moved to St. Paul, Minnesota, where he settled and became the leading financier of the Northwest. After he purchased the St. Paul & Pacific Railroad (1878), he undertook what is generally considered the greatest feat of railroad building in U.S. history. He extended the line across Montana (1887) to Seattle (1893), despite the appalling difficulties of terrain, and without the Federal assistance that had been showered on other transcontinental railroad projects. In 1890 he consolidated his properties into the Great Northern Railway, and after 1893, by reorganizing the Northern Pacific, he controlled 10,000 miles of railroads from Lake Superior to Puget Sound.

As an 'empire builder,' he began settling his great domain by scouring Europe for homesteaders, whom his agents met on their arrival at the piers in New York City. He introduced scientific farming, supported schools and churches, and gave paternalistic direction to the development of the entire Northwest.

In 1901 he was victor in the titanic financial struggle with E. H. HARRIMAN for control of the Chicago, Burlington & Quincy line into Chicago. Though the security company that he then organized to consolidate his holdings was outlawed (1904) by the U.S. Supreme Court, Hill continued to wield great financial power.

See J. G. Pyle, *The Life of James J. Hill* (2 vols., 1917).

HILLMAN, SIDNEY (1887–1946), Lithuanian-born labor leader, came to the U.S. in 1907 and began working with the Chicago clothing firm of Hart, Schaffner, and Marx. The collective bargaining agreement for reaching labor settlements that he negotiated with that company in 1910 was adopted by other companies. In 1914 he became president of the Amalgamated Clothing Workers, and promoted such pioneer union practices as co-operative housing and banking. He helped found the Congress of Industrial Organizations (1935), and as its delegate to world labor parleys was prominent in establishing the World Federation of Trade Unions (1945).

HILLQUIT, MORRIS (1869–1933), Latvian-born lawyer and socialist leader, in 1886 settled in New York City, where he became a prominent labor lawyer and the dominant theorist and tactician of the SOCIALIST PARTY. His *History of Socialism in the U.S.* (rev. ed., 1910) is a standard text.

HILLSBOROUGH, WILLS HILL, Earl of (1718–93), as president of the BOARD OF TRADE AND PLANTATIONS (1763–66) and as the first British secretary of state for colonies (1768–72), was directly responsible for the policies of the government on the eve of the War of Independence. His limited understanding of Britain's IMPERIAL PROBLEMS widened the breach between the American colonies and England.

HINDEMITH, PAUL (1895–1963), German-born composer, conductor, and aesthetician, contributed significantly to American musical life during his fifteen-year residence in the U.S., where he taught at the Berkshire Music Center (1938–39), at Yale (1940–53), and at Harvard (1950–51). He became an American citizen in 1946, but after 1953 was associated with the University of Zürich, where a less onerous academic program allowed him more opportunities to conduct.

During his 'American period' he became progressively more interested in the aesthetics and philosophy of music, crystallized in a revision (1948) of his early song cycle *Das Marienleben* (1923), now published with explanatory analyses. His *A Composer's World* (1952) discusses his philosophy. His strongly personal style of composition is represented by *Ludus Tonalis* (1943), and *When Lilacs Last in the Door-Yard Bloomed* (1946). He completed his huge opera on the subject of Kepler, *Die Harmonie der Welt* (1951–57), after he returned to Europe.

Hiroshima, Japanese city on the island of Honshu, was a World War II military and naval center. It was the target (6 August 1945) of the first atomic bomb to be dropped on a populated area. Some 130,000 casualties were inflicted, and three-fourths of the buildings were demolished. A second bomb, dropped three days later, devastated Nagasaki. On 15 August the Japanese entered into a cease-fire agreement.

HISS, ALGER (1904–), began his promising law career in the 1930's attached to government agencies. In the State Department after 1936 he became adviser at international conferences. Having resigned his high government post in 1947 to serve as president of the Carnegie Endowment for International Peace, he was accused by a confessed communist party courier, Whittaker Chambers, of transmitting government documents to the Russians. Hiss was indicted for perjury, found guilty (1950), and served a five-year prison term.

Historical Records Survey, functioning under the Works Progress Administration, during the 1930's prepared inventories of historical collections in every state, listing public archives, private collections, church archives, early American imprints, and portraits. Though the compilations are uneven (for many field workers were not trained professionally), they are of great importance because of their accumulation of material and identification of items. The work of the Survey was a part of the expansion of archival interest stimulated in 1934 by the establishment of the NATIONAL ARCHIVES.

Historical societies, as organizations in the U.S. for the preservation and study of state and local data, began with the formation of the MASSACHUSETTS HISTORICAL SOCIETY (1791). Others soon followed: New York (1804), AMERICAN ANTIQUARIAN SOCIETY (1812), Rhode Island (1822), Maine (1823), New Hampshire (1823), Pennsylvania (1824), Connecticut (1825), Indiana (1830), Ohio (1831), Virginia (1831), Louisiana (1836), Vermont (1838), Georgia (1839), Maryland (1844), Tennessee (1849), Wisconsin (1849), and Minnesota (1849). By 1884, when the American Historical Association was founded, more than 200 such groups had been organized, some specializing in particular fields of interest such as genealogy, science, or religion. By the end of the century academic historians had helped transform many of the older societies into instruments of scholarship, a task notably accomplished by C. W. ALVORD, L. C. DRAPER, and R. G. THWAITES, among others. The important MISSISSIPPI VALLEY HISTORICAL SOCIETY (1907) broadened the base of regional studies.

Today the number of societies (reported to be 1750 in 1959) continues to increase, with historical house museums often an added feature. Though there is little uniformity among them, a principal function of the larger and well endowed institutions is the publication of transactions or proceedings (articles, documents, and memoirs), which total many thousands of volumes. Some issue quarterly reviews. Through them the federal government during the 1930's carried out its HISTORICAL RECORDS SURVEY. The U.S. has studied its own history, through the productivity of its historical societies, in a manner unrivaled elsewhere.

Historical Sources and Archives were first given national attention when EBENEZER HAZARD, encouraged by the Continental Congress during the 1770's, began assembling items which he published as *Historical Documents* (2 vols., 1792–94). Meanwhile JEREMY BELKNAP had founded in Massachusetts (1791) the first of the great number of American HISTORICAL SOCIETIES, organizations primarily concerned with historiography. Guided chiefly by JARED SPARKS, from 1829 to 1861 the federal government spent $130,000 to purchase manuscripts of early statesmen and to support the publication of public documents. But the lack of any settled plan resulted in such unfortunate instances as the withdrawal of support from the work of PETER FORCE. The importance of professional planning was first made clear by J. F. JAMESON, the leading contributor to historiography until his death in 1937. In 1934 Congress created the NATIONAL ARCHIVES. The LIBRARY OF CONGRESS conducts the major Federal activities in the study of history, and is the leading depository of manuscripts and the nation's publications.

The high standard of scholarship set by Julian P. Boyd in editing the papers of Thomas Jefferson, begun during the 1940's, has influenced similar projects on the Adamses, Franklin, Hamilton, Madison, and other statesmen.

History in America, as a written record of the New World, began with Columbus's famous 'Letter' (1493), describing his first voyage. It was followed by the accounts by PETER MARTYR and OVIEDO, and by letters written by the hosts of explorers and settlers who wrote to acquaint the people at home with their experiences, or to attract newcomers and potential investors. Such was the purpose of THOMAS HARIOT and JOHN SMITH in writing the earliest histories of 'Virginia' (which in 1600 meant the entire seaboard north to the Maine coast). Since the Puritans of New England viewed their coming to America as part of a divine plan, they wrote the story of their migration and new establishments with the dedicated purpose of recording for posterity God's 'wonder-working providence,' a concept which dictated the form given to the accounts written by WILLIAM BRADFORD, EDWARD JOHNSON, JOHN WINTHROP, and later by COTTON MATHER and THOMAS PRINCE.

In the newer colonies of the 18th century, histories continued to be somewhat promotional in character, but most of them were shaped by the concept, made familiar by the Enlightenment, that regularity of natural law operates in a continuous chain of events. Thus by their rationalist outlook, which replaced the earlier supernaturalism, and by their attempt to give documentary objectivity, they pointed the way toward modern historiography. Such are the works, usually local in their concern, by ROBERT BEVERLEY and WILLIAM STITH of Virginia; WILLIAM SMITH and CADWALLADER COLDEN of New York; and THOMAS HUTCHINSON, JEREMY BELKNAP, and ISAAC BACKUS of Massachusetts.

Although writers well into the 19th century followed the method of their predecessors, their tone caught the spirit of nationalism reflected in the paintings of John Trumbull, the poetry of Joel Barlow, and the oratory of Daniel Webster. Favorite subjects for history are typified by the story of the Revolution, told with patriotic fervor by MERCY WARREN. Both JOHN MARSHALL and WASHINGTON IRVING in their multivolumed biographies of Washington draped him in a toga. Many of the early 19th-century historians of the Revolution, including Marshall and DAVID RAMSAY, plagiarized much of their narrative from such Whig sources as Edmund Burke's *Annual Register*.

Throughout his life GEORGE BANCROFT (1800–1891) wrote an idealistic type of history, which espoused 'manifest destiny' and stressed the role of ideas and principles as causes of historical development. He used the detailed exactness of German scholarship, which was the best historiography of his day, and by a strict adherence to chronology he let events demonstrate their providential character. The narrative method was also used by Bancroft's widely read contemporaries, RICHARD HILDRETH, JOHN PALFREY, WILLIAM H. PRESCOTT, and JOHN L. MOTLEY. It was used at its best by FRANCIS PARKMAN, the vigor of whose historical reconstruction is unexcelled. The style, though not the power, continued into the 20th century in the work of JAMES F. RHODES, THEODORE ROOSEVELT, and JAMES SCHOULER.

Although JARED SPARKS broke ground for the first systematic study of history when (at Harvard) he became the first American professor of the subject (1839), only toward the end of the century did the writing of history in the U.S. become a disciplined profession. CHARLES K. ADAMS pioneered in the history seminar at Michigan, as did HENRY ADAMS at Harvard and HERBERT B. ADAMS at Johns Hopkins in the 1870's. H. E. VON HOLST did the same at Chicago in 1892. By persistently accumulating source materials and working with historical societies, JUSTIN WINSOR as librarian and editor tied antiquarianism into scholarship, and in the field of bibliography JOSEPH SABIN and CHARLES EVANS worked to the same end. MOSES COIT TYLER was a pioneer in the scholarly study of American literature.

Scientific accuracy, which became a dominant factor in historiography, was the major contribution of the graduate seminars, and discursive narratives were replaced by footnoted monographs, a method encouraged by such notable scholars as EDWARD CHANNING and CHARLES M. ANDREWS. Collaborative undertakings, such as the 'American Nation' series (28 vols., 1904–18) under the editorship of ALBERT B. HART, drew upon the specialized knowledge of a galaxy of scholars.

A variety of concepts gradually gave new forms to historical writing. An evolutionary school drew upon such scientific disciplines as biology and physics. The importance of institutions as forms of organized social action underlay the thinking of many. FREDERICK J. TURNER stressed the influence of the frontier. As in Great Britain, history-writing in the U.S. was dominated by an Anglo-Saxon Protestant ethnic predisposition.

Soon the institutional approach began to extend far beyond political subjects to include all aspects of history, ecological and artistic, psychological and intellectual. N. S. SHALER opened fruitful inquiry into physiographic problems. JOHN W. BURGESS stressed the idea of Union. Turner examined the role of sections in shaping the American character. The Marxist interpretation lived briefly. The sense that the whole life of a people constitutes history (ideas, economy, and social form) was to one extent or another central in the teaching of the 'New History,' represented in the writings of J. H. ROBINSON and CHARLES A. BEARD. J. B. MC MASTER and EDWARD EGGLESTON were pioneers in social history, a field in which ARTHUR SCHLESINGER was a leader after 1925. Intellectual history was the province of V. L. PARRINGTON, MERLE CURTI, and HENRY S. COMMAGER. ALLAN NEVINS led in the large-scale use of business archives. The broader approach is clear in the writings of CARL BECKER, SAMUEL E. MORISON, and, most recently, ARTHUR SCHLESINGER, JR. The *History of American Life* (13 vols., ed. by A. M. Schlesinger and Dixon R. Fox) covers the period to 1941, and views history as the sum total of human activity. The latest co-operative history, *The New American Nation Series* (ed. by H. S. Commager and R. B. Morris) will cover the period to 1960 in some 50 volumes.

Since history is the study of human experience, its relation to BIOGRAPHY is a blood tie.

HITCHCOCK, ALFRED JOSEPH (1899–), English-born motion picture director, began his career as a technician (1920). A director of British films after 1925, he came to the U.S. during the 1930's. His technique in creating suspense is notably evident in such movies as *The Lady Vanishes* (1938), *The Paradine Case* (1947), and *Strangers on a Train* (1951).

HITCHCOCK, EDWARD (1793–1864), after graduation from Yale Theological Seminary (1820) served briefly in a pastorate, but returned to Yale to study science under Benjamin Silliman. Called to the newly created chair of chemistry at Amherst (1825), he was appointed state geologist of Massachusetts in 1830, and began his notable reports on the geology of New England, the first of their kind to be published (1833–41). As president of Amherst (1845–54) he continued his field studies in geology, zoology, and botany, and later acted briefly as state geologist of Vermont (1857–61). His labors encouraged other states to institute similar surveys, and his *Elementary Geology* (1840) became a widely adopted textbook, passing through 30 editions.

HITCHCOCK, THOMAS, JR. (1900–1944), a graduate of Harvard (1922), while still in college began winning polo tournaments, and became so expert that for eighteen years the U.S. Polo Association gave him its highest rating, a ten-goal handicap. One of the outstanding polo players of all time, he was a banker by profession. He served as an aviator in both World Wars, and was killed in a crash during World War II.

HOAR, GEORGE FRISBIE (1826–1904), after graduation from Harvard (1846) practiced law at Worcester, Massachusetts, and entered politics. As a Republican member of the U.S. House of Representatives (1869–77) and the U.S. Senate (1877–1904), he advanced civil service reform, helped draft the Sherman Antitrust Act (1890), and strongly opposed McKinley's expansionist policy. He was one of the group of men at that time whose sense of political responsibility often transcended party interest. His *Autobiography* (2 vols., 1903) is significant commentary.

HOBAN, JAMES (1762–1831), Irish-born architect, in 1792 won the competition for design of the White House. He supervised its construction (1792–99), and rebuilt it after it was burned by the British during the War of 1812. In government employ for 25 years, he later supervised the erection of the State and the War offices.

Hockey, usually referring to ice hockey, is a fast, rugged game played exclusively by men. It has been popular in Canada since the 1870's, but was not introduced into the U.S. until 1893, when it was played at Yale and at Johns Hopkins. The Amateur Hockey League (1896) helped spread interest in the sport. Professional hockey, played since 1903, like amateur hockey has progressively gained in popularity. Among trophies is the coveted Stanley Cup (1912).

Field hockey, played in the U.S. since 1890, is especially popular among college girls. The U.S. Field Hockey Association (1922) is the ruling body.

HOCKING, WILLIAM ERNEST (1873–1966), professor of philosophy at Harvard (1914–43) and elsewhere, wrote illuminatingly on a broad range of subjects, including logic, psychology, ethics, politics and religion, and especially metaphysics. He made his most original contribution in *The Meaning of God in Human Experience* (1912), where he applied his idealist principles to the religious life, interpreting religion largely as an 'idea in the process of being born.' He interpreted mysticism as part of the rhythm which alternates between vision (feeling) and detail (action). In the same vein are his *The Spirit of World Politics* (1932) and *Science and the Idea of God* (1944). Hocking was commissioned during World War II by the Armed Forces Institute to write a textbook on philosophy, and his popularized *Preface to Philosophy* (1945) is a summary for laymen of his lifework.

HODGE, Charles (1797–1878), a graduate of the College of New Jersey (1815), in 1820 began his lifelong teaching at Princeton Theological Seminary. His chief monument, *Systematic Theology* (3 vols., 1872–73), in its day was regarded as the classic statement of Calvinist orthodoxy. During his 58 years in the classroom he trained more divinity students, Presbyterian and otherwise, than any other American of the 19th century, and his influence on the religious life of the country was far-reaching.

HODGE, Frederick Webb (1864–1956), English-born anthropologist, became associated with the Bureau of American Ethnology in 1889, led several of its expeditions into the Southwest, and edited its *Handbook of the American Indians, North of Mexico* (2 vols., 1907–10). It is a systematic and meticulous compilation, and remains basic in its field. Hodge was in charge of the Bureau for eight years (1910–18), and was later associated with the Museum of the American Indian, New York City (1918–31), until he became director of the Southwest Museum, Los Angeles (after 1931).

HOE, Richard March (1812–86), entered his father's New York printing press manufacturing business, and there invented the rotary press (1846). By thus quadrupling the speed of printing, Hoe created the means of mass communication. His later improvements, especially his invention of a device to fold papers as they issued from the press, completed the principal steps in the evolution of the machinery by which modern newspapers are printed.

HOFFMAN, Malvina (1887–1966), New York sculptor, has executed portraits of prominent persons, and designed groups and panel façades for public buildings here and abroad. She made her unique anthropological gallery of 100 portraits of racial types (Chicago Natural History Museum) after five years of study and world travel. Representative of her spirited figures are *Bacchanale russe* (Luxembourg Museum) and *Pavlova gavotte* (Stockholm).

HOFMANN, Hans (1880–1966), German-born painter, studied in Paris before founding his own school in Munich (1915) and later in New York (1933). Notable as a teacher of artists, Hofmann is recognized as a leading abstract expressionist. (His 'drip' technique anticipated Jackson Pollock as early as 1940.) His paintings are distinguished for their exuberant color, and are represented by *Spring* (1940), *Cataclysm* (1945), made just before the bomb fell on Hiroshima, and *Orchestral Dominance in Yellow* (1954).

HOFMANN, Josef Casimir (1876–1957), Polish-born pianist, after study under Anton Rubinstein, toured Europe as a child prodigy, making his American debut (1887) playing Beethoven's *Piano Concerto No. I* at the Metropolitan Opera House. Under the pseudonym 'Michel Dvorsky' he composed extensively, but he was esteemed primarily as a performer. Hofmann served at the Curtis Institute of Music as head of the piano department (1924–26); later he became director of the Institute (1926–38).

HOLBROOK, Josiah (1788–1854), after graduation from Yale (1810), devoted his life to promoting his scheme for a national adult system of popular education. In 1826, at Millbury, Massachusetts, he organized the first LYCEUM, and thereafter went about the country lecturing on geology and natural history, and urging villages to make exhibits of their collections, however unscientifically displayed. His crusade resulted in 100 branches of the American Lyceum, which in two years had spread to every state in the Union.

HOLC, see *Home Owners Loan Corporation.*

Holding companies are organizations in which a corporation holds enough shares of other companies to control their operations. By pyramiding, costs are reduced, and the last company created can control all. Because stock is scattered among many small holders, the ownership of not more than 10 or 20 per cent of the stock available may control an industry. New Jersey first permitted holding companies in 1889.

For many years the U.S. STEEL CORPORATION was the largest holding company in the U.S. Holding companies were partially curbed after the Supreme Court's dissolution of the Northern Securities Company (1904), the American Tobacco Company (1911), and the STANDARD OIL COMPANY (1911). The Wheeler-Rayburn Holding Company Act (1935) ended the pyramiding of public utility companies. In 1961 the Supreme Court, with similar intent to dissolve the monopoly devices in big business, ruled that the du Pont Company must divest itself of its General Motors Corporation holdings.

Holidays are not national in the U.S. Federal 'legal public holidays' are New Year's Day (1 January), Washington's Birthday (22 February), MEMORIAL DAY (30 May), INDEPENDENCE DAY (4 July), LABOR DAY (first Monday in September), VETERANS' DAY (11 November), THANKSGIVING DAY (fourth Thursday in November), and Christmas. Numerous other holidays are legally recognized in the various states, but only as states select them for particular reasons.

HOLLAND, JOHN PHILIP (1840–1914), Irish-born inventor, bent upon the destruction of the naval supremacy of Britain, in 1891 constructed a cigar-shaped submarine, 55 ft. long, the most practical underwater torpedo boat of its day. Adopted by the U.S. navy in 1900, it was the first to use an internal combustion engine (when surfaced) in conjunction with an electric motor (when submerged). After World War I it was superseded by the even-keel submarine invented by SIMON LAKE.

HOLLEY, ALEXANDER LYMAN (1832–82), an expert on locomotives, after graduation from Brown (1853) purchased the American rights to the Bessemer steel process, and in 1865, at Troy, New York, built the first steel plant of commercial significance in the U.S. By applying the processes of Bessemer and of WILLIAM KELLY, he laid the foundations of an industry that was nurtured to giant growth by ANDREW CARNEGIE.

Hollywood, see *Motion pictures.*

HOLMES, OLIVER WENDELL (1809–94), after graduation from Harvard (1829) and medical study at Harvard and in Paris, returned to Boston and shortly began his long association with the Harvard Medical School (1847–82), where throughout his career he was a stimulating teacher. Although never eminent in original medical research, he wrote a notable essay on 'The Contagiousness of Puerperal Fever' (1843), assailing the bigotry of medical doctors who were unwilling to accept the evidence of the causes of the infection.

Holmes is deservedly remembered as a discursive essayist; the urbane wit of his *Autocrat of the Breakfast-Table* (1858) still sparkles. His understanding of abnormal psychology, best represented by his novel *Elsie Venner* (1861), was ahead of its time. His popular poems endeared him to a large audience. Constantly in demand as a lyceum lecturer, he combined a zeal for scientific rationalism with an aristocratic amicability.

HOLMES, OLIVER WENDELL (1841–1935), son and namesake of the Boston physician, after graduation from Harvard (1861) served as a junior officer in the Civil War. He was teaching law at Harvard when he was appointed to the bench of the Massachusetts Supreme Court, where he served as associate justice (1882–99) and as chief justice (1899–1902). President Theodore Roosevelt appointed him to the U.S. Supreme Court, where for 30 years (1902–32) he consistently defended human rights.

The philosophy that underlay all his decisions is expressed fully in his great treatise on *The Common Law* (1881). To Holmes the law was a living and growing organism, to be molded to the needs of a changing society. 'The life of law has not been logic; it has been experience.' He argued that law is a product and function of society, not its principle. Since many of his opinions were handed down when he seemed to be speaking for a minority, he was called 'the great dissenter.'

Most influential upon American law and liberalism was the Holmes doctrine of free speech, notably expressed in SCHENCK *v.* U.S. (1919), a case in which the Court gave a unanimous decision. Holmes argued that while no one has a right falsely to cry fire in a crowded theater, he rejected the belief that a 'remote bad tendency' in a speech or pamphlet was enough to convict a defendant. Instead he urged 'free trade in ideas' as a pragmatic way to discover truth. Only an immediate danger, 'a clear and present danger,' could justify congressional interference with freedom of speech. The influence of Holmes on younger lawyers and judges was immense, and he is generally thought of as the most distinguished of all American jurists.

HOLST, HERMANN EDUARD VON (1841–1904), the first professor of history at Chicago (1892–1900), was born in Russia of German parentage. He emigrated to the U.S. in 1867, where he studied American institutions. In 1872 he returned to Europe to teach at Strasbourg (1872–74) and Freiburg (1874–92). His chief historical study, *The Constitutional and Political History of the U.S.* (7 vols., 1876–92), covering the period 1750–1861, finds slavery a keystone to the development of American constitutional doctrines, and the annexation of Texas as well as the Mexican War to be a conspiracy by the 'slavocracy.' He was severely critical of the southern doctrine of state sovereignty. His biographies of Calhoun (1882) and John Brown (1888) reflect these ideas.

HOLT, LUTHER EMMETT (1855–1924), while clinical professor of diseases of children at New York Polyclinic Hospital (1890–1901), wrote his classic study on *The Care and Feeding of Children* (1894). It achieved a popular success unrivaled by any previous medical study, and established scientific common sense in the American nursery. After 1901 he taught at Columbia.

HOLYOKE, EDWARD (1689–1769), a graduate of Harvard (1705), served his college as president for more than 30 years (1737–69), during which period he built up instruction in mathematics and science, and established the first laboratory of experimental physics in the U.S. Though he was not regarded by his contemporaries as a commanding figure, he administered the college with a foresight that helped liberalize the traditions of its curriculum.

Holyoke, see *Mount Holyoke College.*

Home Owners' Loan Corporation, created by the Home Owners' Refinancing Act (1933), was empowered to refinance small mortgages on privately owned homes. The HOLC granted over $3,000,000,000 at low interest to stabilize the value of real estate that had depreciated during the Depression. By the time its work was terminated in 1936 it had made some 1,000,000 loans.

Home relief, see *Federal Emergency Relief Administration.*

HOMER, WINSLOW (1836–1910), Boston-born artist, won international popularity during the Civil War as illustrator for *Harper's Weekly*. Many of his genre studies, such as *Crack the Whip* (Metropolitan Museum), date from that period. The realism and fine draftsmanship of his anecdotal studies of Negro life, painted shortly after a trip to Europe (1867), foreshadow the emphasis on structure that distinguishes *Eliphalet Terry Fishing from a Boat* (Century Association, N.Y.).

In 1876 he abandoned illustration, and, impervious to outside influence, began to depict aspects of the American scene in oils and water colors, particularly as he observed them on the Maine coast, in the Adirondacks, and in Florida and the Bahamas. Such are *Breezing Up* (National Gallery), with its deliberate ruggedness conveyed by the effect of dark on light colors; and *Gulf Stream* and *Moonlight, Wood's Island Light* (Metropolitan Museum), which emphasize the impersonal forces and grandeur of nature. To the end Homer remained faithful to the concepts of the HUDSON RIVER SCHOOL.

Homestead Act (1862), as an inducement to westward migration and the opening up of prairie wheatfields, offered any enterprising farmer 160 acres of surveyed public domain for a nominal fee. The settler had complete ownership after five years' residence, or after six months with payment of $1.50 an acre. Some 15,000 homesteads were thus pre-empted during the Civil War. Although the Act was intended in part as a safety valve for urban labor problems in the East, it failed in that purpose because it provided impetus for land speculators and it was incompatible with the Industrial Revolution then beginning. Steam-driven tractors and threshing machines all but wiped out the small-scale commercial farms.

Homestead Strike (1892) was one of the most bitterly fought industrial disputes in U.S. labor history. It took on a violent aspect when strikers at the Carnegie Steel Company plant at Homestead, Pennsylvania, fired upon two barges being towed up the Monongahela with 300 Pinkerton detectives aboard, who had been engaged by the company's president, H. C. FRICK, to protect nonunion workers. On 6 July infuriated strikers engaged with the Pinkerton army in a pitched battle that resulted in a number of deaths. State troops restored order and the strike was broken.

HONE, PHILIP (1780–1851), New York businessman, Whig politician, and socialite, retired with a fortune in 1820. He became mayor of New York in 1826. He was concerned with the cultural development of the city and made his town house, overlooking City Hall park, a gathering place for artists, actors, and musicians. His *Diary* (1828–51) (2 vols., ed. by Allan Nevins, 1927) is shrewd, opinionated, and a valuable record of the social and political life of the city during the second quarter of the 19th century.

HOOD, JOHN BELL (1831–79), Kentucky-born graduate of the U.S. Military Academy (1853), in 1861 joined the Confederacy. A division commander under Longstreet, he replaced J. E. Johnston as corps commander in the ATLANTA CAMPAIGN, but fared no better than Johnston. His force was virtually annihilated by G. H. Thomas in the battle of NASHVILLE (December 1864), and he resigned his command soon thereafter. He was a bold and energetic leader, admired as a fighting general.

HOOKER, JOSEPH (1814–79), Massachusetts-born graduate of the U.S. Military Academy (1837), joined the Union as a division commander at the outbreak of the Civil War. After the battle of Fredericksburg he succeeded Ambrose Burnside in command of the Army of the Potomac (January 1863). At Chancellorsville 'Fighting Joe' Hooker was repeatedly outmaneuvered by Lee. In June 1863, after a squabble with Halleck, the general in chief, Hooker resigned his commission. He took part in later campaigns, and after the war he commanded various military departments until his retirement. Brave, vain, and unreliable, Hooker never won the confidence of other Union commanders.

HOOKER, THOMAS (1586–1647), after taking his degree at Cambridge (1608), became a fellow of Emmanuel College (1609–18). Forced by Laud to leave his post when he became one of the conspicuous Puritan leaders in England, Hooker came to New England (1633) and soon migrated from Boston to Hartford (1636), where he was pastor of the church and for the rest of his life virtual dictator of Connecticut. A dominating figure and the most eloquent of Puritan preachers, he was described by Cotton Mather as a man who could put a king in his pocket. His *Survey of the Summe of Church Discipline* (1648) is the supreme exposition of the Congregational church polity, expressing not merely New England ecclesiastical theory but political doctrine and concepts of law, nature, and reason.

The claim that he was an exponent of a liberal democratic social philosophy is unfounded. Hooker's religious and political opinions show him to have been essentially a medieval church autocrat.

As he made clear in the FUNDAMENTAL ORDERS of Connecticut (1639), for which he was largely responsible, he believed that authority should be vested in such part of the people as are deemed competent to exercise it. That is to say, the people may choose, but those chosen, elders in the church and magistrates in the state, will rule.

Hoosier, a term applied to the inhabitants of Indiana since pioneer days, is assumed to be of some local origin, but no explanation of it has common acceptance among scholars. It appeared first in print in 1830, in a poem printed in the Indianapolis *Journal.*

HOOVER, HERBERT CLARK (1874–1964), 31st President of the U.S. (1929–33), was born at West Branch, Iowa, and graduated from Stanford (1895). Until 1914 he engaged in a world-wide mining and engineering career, earning a fortune which enabled him thereafter to devote himself to public service. A Quaker, as chairman of the U.S. Commission for Relief in Belgium (1915–19) he won wide recognition for his humanitarian efforts, and Wilson appointed him to the critical post of U.S. Food Administrator during World War I (1917–19). His administrative skill in insuring the feeding of our near-bankrupt allies, as well as ourselves, was credited as a major contribution to winning the war.

As Secretary of Commerce under Harding and Coolidge (1921–28), he persuaded large firms to adopt simplification and standardization of production goods and a system of planned economy. Esteemed as a moderate liberal, in 1928 he received the Republican nomination for President. His easy defeat of his Democratic rival, Alfred E. Smith, by an electoral vote of 447 to 87, is largely attributed to the fact that the election year had been unusually prosperous.

Few informed persons in the spring of 1929 chose to read the signs pointing to the massive stock crash of October, and Hoover's announcement that 'in no nation are the fruits of accomplishment more secure' reflected a judgment shared by most of the nation. As the country drifted into the Great Depression, the government adopted measures that proved inadequate to stop the increasing number of commercial and farm failures, the rising number of the unemployed (12,000,000 or more by 1932), and a sharp decline in foreign trade.

Few Presidents have ever faced more melancholy prospects for re-election, and Hoover's defeat at the polls by F. D. Roosevelt, who received more than 57 per cent of the popular vote (electoral vote 472 to 59), was a mandate for change. The final months of Hoover's term were tragic. During that interim period a 'lame duck' session of Congress was virtually controlled by the Democrats, and President-elect Roosevelt refused to jeopardize his New Deal program by joint action with the defeated President. The fact is, however, that Hoover had anticipated certain New Deal measures, and his Reconstruction Finance Corporation even became a major anti-depression engine for Roosevelt.

During the many years of his retirement Hoover wrote *The Challenge to Liberty* (1934) and *The Basis of Lasting Peace* (1945).

Hoover returned to public affairs when he headed the HOOVER COMMISSION (1947–49, 1953–55), which was empowered by Congress to advise on reorganizing the executive branch of the government. A man of intelligence, integrity, and humanitarian principles, with administrative skill of the highest order, as President he envisioned an 'American system,' as he termed it, in which laissez faire methods could be balanced by economic planning.

HOOVER, JOHN EDGAR (1895–   ), was born in Washington, D.C., and graduated from George Washington University in 1916. As chief of the FEDERAL BUREAU OF INVESTIGATION (after 1924) he built up and for more than four decades directed an impressive crime-detection agency within the Department of Justice. He is considered to be an uncommonly capable executive.

Hoover Commission, officially named the Commission on Reorganization of the Executive Branch of the Federal Government, was established by Congress (1947) as a committee headed by former President Hoover to study and advise on matters of executive organization. Its report (1949) led to the important Reorganization Act of 1949, by which the President was authorized to create a more orderly grouping of functions within departments and agencies with clear lines of control and strong staff services. Later legislation to the same end (1952) extended to the Bureau of Internal Revenue and to the Civil Service.

Hoover Dam, on the Colorado river at the Nevada-Arizona border, was completed in 1936, and was then named Boulder Dam. It is the highest concrete dam in the U.S. (726 ft.), the principal source of hydroelectric power in the Southwest, and a major flood control and water storage basin, holding back Lake Mead, 115 miles long, which it created.

Hoover moratorium, so called, was a proposal, made by President Hoover in 1931, that payments on all intergovernmental debts be suspended, including the debt payments of European nations to the U.S. as well as German reparations due England and France. This step was taken after major German and Austrian bank crashes compelled the German President, Paul von Hindenburg, to appeal directly to Hoover. The worsening world-wide Depression ended most war debt payments to the U.S. thereafter.

Hopedale Community (1842–56) was organized by Adin Ballou (1803–90) and other Universalists at Milford, Massachusetts. One of the religious utopian communities of the time, it shifted between extremes of communal and individual management, and finally collapsed.

Hopi Indians, formerly called Moqui, live in mesa pueblos in northeastern Arizona. Of Uto-Aztecan stock, they speak a Shoshonean dialect, and are Pueblo in culture. They were especially resistant to the efforts of early Spanish missionaries. Peaceful, sedentary farmers with special skills in pottery, basketry, textiles, and water-color work, they alone among Indians of the Southwest have preserved the ceremonial Snake dance.

HOPKINS, Esek (1718–1802), brother of the Rhode Island patriot STEPHEN HOPKINS, was appointed (December 1775) commander in chief of the newly created Continental navy. He had made his reputation as a leading colonial seaman while commanding a privateer during the French and Indian War (1755–63). In January 1776 he hoisted his flag as commodore of the eight converted merchantmen that constituted the U.S. naval force. During that year he made a successful raid on British shipping in the Bahamas and directed naval depredations elsewhere. But he failed to observe the orders of Congress, and was censured. The distrust was mutual, difficulties increased, and in January 1777 Congress summarily dismissed Hopkins from his command.

HOPKINS, Harry Lloyd (1890–1946), having devoted himself to a career as social worker, was appointed by President F. D. Roosevelt to head the FEDERAL EMERGENCY RELIEF ADMINISTRATION (1933), the CIVIL WORKS ADMINISTRATION (1933), and the WORKS PROJECTS ADMINISTRATION (1935). He later served Roosevelt as Secretary of Commerce (1938–40). He was an intimate associate of the President during World War II, and he administered LEND-LEASE (1941) and held high posts as special assistant to Roosevelt both at home and abroad. Much social legislation enacted at the time and still in effect was generated by Hopkins.

HOPKINS, Mark (1802–87), born in Stockbridge, Massachusetts, was graduated from Williams (1824) and Pittsfield Medical College (1829) before joining the Williams faculty, where he became a lifelong professor of philosophy (1830–87). As president of Williams (1836–72), he won respect as an administrator and renown as a teacher, which was expressed by President Garfield: 'Give me a log hut, with only a simple bench, Mark Hopkins on one end and I on the other, and you may have all the buildings, apparatus, and libraries without him.'

HOPKINS, Samuel (1721–1803), Connecticut-born Congregational minister, after graduation from Yale (1741) became the leading disciple of Jonathan

Edwards, on whose philosophy he built his own 'Hopkinsianism,' a doctrine of 'disinterested benevolence' sometimes described as the 'willingness to be damned.' A prolific writer, he was best known for his *System of Doctrines Contained in Divine Revelation* (2 vols., 1793), which was influential in American religious life for 70 years and the first systematic treatise by an American theologian.

HOPKINS, STEPHEN (1707–85), elder brother of ESEK HOPKINS, was prominent in Rhode Island affairs and was elected governor of that colony nine times between 1755 and 1768. He was a strenuous defender of natural rights and one of the most effective pamphleteers in the cause of American independence. His *Rights of Colonies Examined* (1765) was widely read and is a vigorous essay on the origin and nature of law. He later (1774–76) was a delegate to both the First and the Second Continental Congress, and served on committees of correspondence.

HOPKINSON, FRANCIS (1737–91), statesman, jurist, man of letters, and musician, was born in Philadelphia, where he was the first student to graduate from the College of Philadelphia (1757). An eminent lawyer, he served on the New Jersey governor's council (1774), represented New Jersey in the Continental Congress (1776), and signed the Declaration of Independence. During the Revolution he contributed to the patriot cause with a series of political satires in prose and verse, including *A Pretty Story* (1774), an allegory that traces events leading to the first Congress. His rollicking ballad *The Battle of the Kegs* (1778) was one of the most popular poems of the war period. During 1776–77 he served as chairman of the navy board, and in 1778 as treasurer of the Continental loan office. For ten years he was judge of the Admiralty Court of Pennsylvania (1779–89). Thereafter, as judge of the U.S. district court, he staunchly supported the Federalists in his decisions and his contributions to magazines.

Hopkinson was not only talented as a writer of essays and light verse, he was leader of Philadelphia musical society, a skillful harpsichordist, and organist of Christ Church. His *Seven Songs* (1788), for which he composed both words and music, is the first book of secular music published by an American, and but one of a number of his compositions. This 'pretty, little, curious, ingenious' man, as John Adams characterized him, was a creditable amateur in portraiture, who designed the American STARS AND STRIPES as well as coins and the seals for various government departments.

His son, JOSEPH HOPKINSON (1770–1842), a distinguished lawyer and jurist, is remembered today as author of the earliest American national anthem, *Hail, Columbia!* (1798), the song that stirred patriotic fervor when war with France seemed imminent.

HOPPE, WILLIE [WILLIAM FREDERICK] (1887–), won his first world championship in billiards in Paris (1906). He subsequently won many balk-line and three-cushion championships, and is generally rated the foremost billiards player of all time.

HOPPER, EDWARD (1882–), New York painter and engraver, trained in the humanism of Henri, developed his own original style. His landscapes as well as his urban scenes are realistic, clear-cut figures. Hopper evokes the loneliness and contrasts of a great city in such oils as *Nighthawks* (Chicago Art Institute), and *Early Sunday Morning* (Whitney Museum).

Horizontal unions, see *Trade unions.*

Horse racing, see *Racing.*

Horses had become extinct in the Western Hemisphere in prehistoric times. The Spanish brought horses to the West Indies, and by 1530 they had multiplied sufficiently to supply most of the transportation for mainland expeditions. A century later horses from Mexico (especially the MUSTANG) became plentiful in the Southwest, and by 1660 the Indians had begun to find them of value. At the same time the foundation stock of the southern Atlantic coast was introduced from the West Indies to Florida, and spread north into the English colonies.

New England carried on extensive breeding from English and Flemish stock, and after 1650 exported horses to other colonies and especially back to the West Indies, where the sugar industry created a steady demand. Horses were essential for inland travel. They were chiefly valued for riding, hunting, and RACING. Until well into the 19th century OXEN and MULES were generally preferred for draft purposes, although the Pennsylvania German farmers developed the famous Conestoga breed, distinguished for size, strength, and endurance. During the 1850's the Percheron was widely imported from France as a work animal.

The post-rider, stagecoach, and the horse- or mule-drawn canal boat opened interior commerce and travel, and the horse was a necessity to the peddler, the doctor, and the circuit-riding parson. The Western pony served the hunter, trapper, and miner, and pack horses and express ponies preceded the railroad for transportation in the Far West. So essential was a horse to life itself in the West and Southwest that horse thieves were summarily hanged without jury trial.

Until automotive power replaced them, horses served universally for adjuncts in military campaigns and city distributive systems. The corn belt from Ohio to Iowa became the center of draft-horse supply after 1870, furnishing such breeds as the Belgian, Clydesdale, and Shire. Notable as saddle horses were the easy-gaited Narragansett pacers and the breeds sired by HAMBLETONIAN and JUSTIN MORGAN.

Horseshoe Bend, Battle of (March 1814), took place when Major General Andrew Jackson with 2000 militia and regulars defeated (and all but wiped out) 1000 Creek Indians strongly entrenched at Horseshoe Bend on the Tallapoosa river in Alabama. Thus the military power of the Indians in the Old Southwest was broken. After the Treaty of Fort Jackson (August 1814), by which the Creeks ceded large tracts in Mississippi Territory, the region was opened to white settlements.

HOSMER, HARRIET GOODHUE (1830–1908), Massachusetts-born sculptor, after 1852 lived chiefly in Rome, where she created graceful figures that were very popular in their day. Representative of her work are *Beatrice Cenci* (St. Louis), *Zenobia* (Metropolitan Museum), and the spirited *Puck* (1860), which was purchased by the Prince of Wales, and in such demand that the sculptor employed several marble workers to chisel reproductions. Her example opened the field of sculpture to women, who had been traditionally excluded from it.

Hospitals, see *Medicine.*

Hot Springs National Park (est. 1921), 1000 acres in central Arkansas, was set aside as a Federal reservation in 1832. Its hot springs are visited for their therapeutic value. The bathhouses are run under government supervision.

HOUDINI, HARRY (1874–1926), stage name of Ehrich Weiss, was internationally celebrated as a magician. Skillful in exposing fraudulent spiritualistic mediums, as a performer he specialized in escapes from locked handcuffs, strait jackets, and sealed chests under water. He bequeathed his large library on magic to the Library of Congress.

HOUDON, JEAN ANTOINE (1741–1828), French sculptor, was famous for his 200 marble portraits, which still remain unsurpassed for their grace and vigorous lifelikeness. Accompanying Franklin to America in 1785, he visited Mount Vernon, where he modeled a bust of Washington from which he later made the famous statue in the capitol at Richmond. His busts of Jefferson and Franklin are well known.

HOUSE, EDWARD MANDELL (1858–1938), having become a power as 'Colonel House' in Texas politics, helped swing the Democratic presidential nomination to Wilson in 1912. He thereafter enjoyed Wilson's confidence to a degree that made House one of the most influential persons in the country. Wilson selected his cabinet with the advice of House, who acted as the ubiquitous political liaison officer of the Wilson administration both at home and abroad (an 'alter ego,' according to the President). He accompanied Wilson to Paris and helped draft the covenant of the League of Nations, but after returning to the U.S. he and Wilson quarreled over issues that the peace settlement had created, and House retired from public life. In 1911 House had almost forecast Wilson's career in a political novel, *Philip Dru: Administrator,* in which a beneficent dictator destroys the 'credit trust,' imposes a corporate income tax, and abolishes the protective tariff — not all too far from the actuality.

House of Representatives, U.S., the lower house of CONGRESS, is the popularly elected body provided for in the Federal Constitution. Composed of members chosen every two years, it is presided over by a Speaker. Although the House shares with the Senate general legislative functions, it exercises several exclusive powers, including the power to initiate revenue bills, impeach Federal officers, and elect the President in the event of a tie or lack of majority in the ELECTORAL COLLEGE. Membership is based on the population of each state as determined by the census required by law every ten years. (The first House had 65 members.) Its size expanded as the population grew, but since 1929 the total membership has been fixed by action of Congress at 435. Each state is assured constitutionally of at least one seat and one vote; as of the 1960 census each Congressman has represented more than 410,000 constituents.

Leadership in the House is vested chiefly in the Speaker, the Committee on Rules, the chairmen of important standing committees, and the floor leaders. The Committee on Rules is especially powerful since it has the right to be heard on almost any occasion, determines what measures shall be considered, how long the debate may last, and when the votes shall be taken. Important committees include Banking and Currency, Foreign Affairs, Government Operations, House Administration, Interstate and Foreign Commerce, Judiciary, and especially Ways and Means, the committee that prepares tariff and tax bills. It is within the power of a House committee to recommend the adoption of a bill under its consideration, with or without amendments, report adversely, delay the report indefinitely, or ignore the bill entirely. So enormous is the authority of committees that to a degree the House is a ratifying rather than a deliberative assembly, since debate is strictly limited by CLOSURE and is usually perfunctory.

Each party has a floor leader, who organizes party strategy. So important has the function of the floor leader in the House become that he is relieved of service on committees. He is influential in determining who will speak on bills and whom the presiding officer will recognize. Today the majority floor leader has succeeded to many of the prerogatives formerly exercised by the Speaker, to whom he is second in power. With the exercise of tact and with the aid of his 'whip,' a member charged with keeping party members in step, and his steering committee, the majority leader seeks to keep the machine running smoothly.

The Speaker is always a member of the majority party, nominally elected by the entire body, but generally chosen by the majority party leaders. At one time the Speaker exercised autocratic control, appointing members of the standing committees, and as chairman of the Committee on Rules, determining the agenda and methods of debate. The congressional 'revolution' of 1910 against 'Czar' CANNON eliminated much of this power, although the Speaker still has the power of recognition in floor debates. He refers bills to committee, puts questions to a vote, signs all bills passed by the chamber, and rules on points of order. The House itself appoints all committees, and the Speaker may not serve on the Committee on Rules. He is thus only one of several leaders in the chamber.

SPEAKERS OF THE HOUSE
(Names in small capitals are persons separately treated.)

Frederick A. C. Muhlenberg (Pa.) 1789–91
JONATHAN TRUMBULL (Conn.) 1791–93
Frederick A. C. Muhlenberg (Pa.) 1793–95
Jonathan Dayton (N.J.) 1795–99
Theodore Sedgwick (Mass.) 1799–1801
Nathaniel Macon (N.C.) 1801–7
Joseph B. Varnum (Mass.) 1807–11
HENRY CLAY (Ky.) 1811–14
Langdon Cheves (S.C.) 1814–15
HENRY CLAY (Ky.) 1815–20
John W. Taylor (N.Y.) 1820–21
Philip P. Barbour (Va.) 1821–23
HENRY CLAY (Ky.) 1823–25
John W. Taylor (N.Y.) 1825–27

Andrew Stevenson (Va.) 1827–34
JOHN BELL (Tenn.) 1834–35
JAMES K. POLK (Tenn.) 1835–39
Robert M. T. Hunter (Va.) 1839–41
John White (Ky.) 1841–43
John W. Jones (Va.) 1843–45
John W. Davis (Ind.) 1845–47
Robert C. Winthrop (Mass.) 1847–49
HOWELL COBB (Ga.) 1849–51
Linn Boyd (Ky.) 1851–55
NATHANIEL P. BANKS (Mass.) 1856–57
James L. Orr (S.C.) 1857–59
William Pennington (N.J.) 1860–61
Galusha A. Grow (Pa.) 1861–63
Schuyler Colfax (Ind.) 1863–69
JAMES G. BLAINE (Me.) 1869–75
Michael C. Kerr (Ind.) 1875–76
Samuel J. Randall (Pa.) 1876–81
Joseph W. Keifer (Ohio) 1881–83
John G. Carlisle (Ky.) 1883–89
THOMAS B. REED (Me.) 1889–91
Charles F. Crisp (Ga.) 1891–95
THOMAS B. REED (Me.) 1895–99
David B. Henderson (Iowa) 1899–1903
JOSEPH G. CANNON (Ill.) 1903–11
CHAMP CLARK (Mo.) 1911–19
Frederick H. Gillett (Mass.) 1919–25
Nicholas Longworth (Ohio) 1925–31
John N. Garner (Texas) 1931–33
Henry T. Rainey (Ill.) 1933–35
Joseph W. Byrns (Tenn.) 1935–36
William B. Bankhead (Ala.) 1936–40
SAM RAYBURN (Texas) 1940–47
Joseph W. Martin, Jr. (Mass.) 1947–49
SAM RAYBURN (Texas) 1949–53
Joseph W. Martin, Jr. (Mass.) 1953–55
SAM RAYBURN (Texas) 1955–61
John W. McCormack (Mass.) 1961–

For studies on the House and the Speaker, see M. P. Follett, *The Speaker* (1896); D. S. Alexander, *The History and Procedure of the House of Representatives* (1916); and Neil MacNeil, *Forge of Democracy: The House of Representatives* (1963).

Housing, as a problem, was first recognized in the U.S. by a New York City tenement law (1867) whose meager requirements were somewhat extended twelve years later to prohibit windowless rooms. In 1901 the city became an example for other municipalities by requiring better ventilation, fire protection, and sanitation. In 1916 it enacted the first zoning laws in the country. Though CITY PLANNING dates from the design of William Penn for Philadelphia (1692), not until the 1930's did federal, state, and city governments give immediate attention to the housing question, aimed at eliminating slums, those congested areas that had been created in all major U.S. cities especially by the unrestricted immigration from Europe during the first half of the 19th century.

The Housing Act of 1934 set up the FEDERAL HOUSING ADMINISTRATION, and low-rental housing projects were coordinated by the WAGNER-STEAGALL ACT (1937). After World War II large-scale home-building projects were speeded by mass-production methods, especially prefabrication, and by Federal grants for redevelopment and rehabilitation of blighted areas. By 1960 suburbia had become a 'problem area,' and racial discrimination a major issue.

In the three-year period 1960–62 the number of new housing units begun each year (according to the Bureau of the Census) averaged 1,350,000, with an annual increase of 100,000. Regionally the largest number of these units has been in the South and West. The estimated value of such construction each year has averaged $15,000,000,000.

Housing and Urban Development, Department of, created by Congress in 1965, in effect gave cabinet status to the Housing and Home Finance Agency, which had been established in 1947 to bring related but separate programs of housing, urban renewal, and Federal mortgage activities under unified direction. The new department authorizes top level Federal participation in the fast-growing problems of city dwellers in the U.S. Secretaries of Housing and Urban Development and the Presidents under whom they served are as follows.

L. B. JOHNSON
Robert C. Weaver (S.C.) 1966

HOUSTON, DAVID FRANKLIN (1866–1940), North Carolina-born educator and government executive, was president of the University of Texas (1905–8) before serving as chancellor of Washington University at St. Louis (1908–16). President Wilson first appointed him Secretary of Agriculture (1913–20), then Secretary of the Treasury (1920–21). Houston's *Eight Years with Wilson's Cabinet* (2 vols., 1926) is a personal record of events during the period of the 'New Freedom.'

HOUSTON, SAMUEL (1793–1863), Virginia-born general and statesman, after moving with his family to the Tennessee frontier spent much of his youth with the Cherokee Indians. He captured the public imagination by his swashbuckling exploits in Jackson's campaign against the Creek Indians (1814). On his return home he practiced law, entered politics, and served as a Democrat in the U.S. Congress (1823–27). Elected governor of Tennessee (1827), he seemed on his way to a bright political future when his bride suddenly left him. He resigned his office (1829) and went to live among the Cherokee in Oklahoma, where he was formally adopted into the tribe as 'The Raven,' and took an Indian wife.

In 1835 Houston moved to Texas, and in 1836 as commander of the revolutionary troops again entered the limelight when he captured Santa Anna at SAN JACINTO. He became the first president of the Lone Star Republic (1836–38, 1841–44), and when Texas joined the Union, he was sent to the U.S. Senate for two terms (1847–59). He lost his seat by his uncompromising Union stand, but his great popularity again won him election as governor (1859). When Texas voted to secede from the Union (February 1861), he was deposed. Tall, vigorous, and dramatic in speech and action, Sam Houston as a personality remained curiously aloof and cold throughout his life. But for his state he came to symbolize the intrepid soldier and fearless, candid legislator.

See Marquis James, *The Raven* (1929), and M. K. Wisehart, *Sam Houston, American Giant* (1962).

Houston, named for the Texas general, was founded in 1836 on the Gulf Coast plain northwest of Galveston Bay. It served briefly (1837–39) as capital of the Texas republic. First a railroad center for transportation of cotton, lumber, rice and other products of the region, after the opening of a ship channel (1914) it became one of the great seaports of the nation (now second to New York) and the largest city in Texas. The development of nearby oil fields brought wealth to the city, which mushroomed from a population of 80,000 in 1910 to 938,000 in 1960. It is the seat of the extensive Texas Medical Center, and of Rice University (est. 1891) and the University of Houston (est. 1934).

HOWARD, LELAND OSSIAN (1857–1950), chief of the U.S. Bureau of Entomology (1894–1927) and its principal entomologist (1927–31), profoundly influenced the development of economic and medical entomology in the U.S. by his contributions to the study of insect parasites and crop pests. His writings include *Mosquitoes* (1901), *The House Fly* (1911), and *The Insect Menace* (1931).

HOWARD, OLIVER OTIS (1830–1909), Maine-born Union general in the Civil War, was a graduate of Bowdoin (1850) and the U.S. Military Academy (1854). From the first battle of Bull Run he took part in engagements, and at the war's end he was in command of the Army of the Tennessee. President Johnson made Howard, the 'Christian soldier,' chief commissioner of the FREEDMEN'S BUREAU (1865). As a leader in Negro education, Howard founded and served as first president (1869–73) of the university which bears his name. He later directed Indian campaigns, and from 1886 until his retirement (1894) he commanded the Division of the East in the U.S. Army.

Howard University, co-educational institution at Washington, D.C., was chartered by Congress (1867) and opened by the Freedmen's Bureau, then headed by General O. O. HOWARD, who served as its first president. Although it is open to all races, it has a predominantly Negro student body. With an annual congressional appropriation (since 1928), it offers a variety of courses at the undergraduate and graduate level. In 1965, with a faculty of 740, its enrollment exceeded 7000.

HOWE, ELIAS (1819–69), while employed in a Boston machine shop, invented a sewing machine, which he patented in 1846. Unable to secure financial backing in the U.S., he took an improved model to England (1847–49), where he gained all British rights. On his return he brought suit for an infringement of his patent, and won final judgment in 1854. With the large royalties thus earned he supported through the Civil War an infantry regiment in which he served as a private.

The Howe sewing machine was popularized during the 1860's by the inventor Isaac Singer (1811–75), whose first patent claims were disallowed but whose later improvements were important. Howe's invention generated a revolution in industry second in magnitude only to that wrought by the telegraph, for by it clothing could be mass produced.

HOWE, Julia Ward (1819–1910), was a daughter of the New York financier Samuel Ward (1786–1839). As a New York belle, Miss Julia Ward was welcomed in Boston society, where she shocked and fascinated her father's Boston friends with her trained operatic voice and adroit wit. In 1843 she married the philanthropist SAMUEL GRIDLEY HOWE, and with him conducted the Boston *Commonwealth,* an antislavery journal. They shared a deep interest in reform causes, for which she continued to write and lecture after she was widowed in 1876. She became most widely known as author of 'The Battle Hymn of the Republic' (1861), which was enormously popular throughout the Union during the Civil War. She was the first woman member of the American Academy of Arts and Letters.

HOWE, Samuel Gridley (1801–76), reformer and philanthropist, after graduation from Brown (1821) and Harvard Medical School (1824) began his lifework when he became director (1829–73) of the New England Asylum for the Blind at Boston (now the Perkins Institution in Watertown), the first school for the blind in the U.S. There his sensational success in communicating with and training the blind deaf-mute LAURA BRIDGMAN gave new hope to those so handicapped.

He worked with HORACE MANN in progressive education, and aided DOROTHEA DIX in her treatment of the feebleminded (though he encouraged an overoptimism in the matter of rehabilitation). For ten years he was chairman of the Massachusetts Board of Charities (1865–74), the first such state organization. A champion of oppressed people, late in life he assisted the Cretans in their struggle against the Turks, as early in life he had supported the Greeks in their War of Independence. The inherited wealth of his wife, JULIA WARD HOWE, made possible their philanthropies, which they devoted to liberal causes.

HOWE, Sir William (1729–1814), served with distinction in the last French and Indian War under General James Wolfe at Quebec (1760). In 1775 at the outbreak of the War of Independence he arrived at Boston with British reinforcements for General Gage, and commanded at Bunker Hill. Knighted soon thereafter, he succeeded Gage in authority, and in October was appointed commander in chief of British forces in America. He won the battle of Long Island (1776), occupied New York City, and after the battle of White Plains was in control of southeastern New York and much of New Jersey. Having defeated Washington at Brandywine and Germantown (1777), he wintered gaily in Philadelphia while Washington's barefoot army mustered at Valley Forge. In the next spring, still unable to win decisive battles, he was recalled. He was succeeded by Sir HENRY CLINTON.

HOWELLS, William Dean (1837–1920), Ohio-born novelist and critic, was largely self-taught, for he was taken from school at the age of nine to set type in his father's printing shop. But he became in his youth an avid reader, and his five years as newspaper reporter (1856–61) developed his skill in observation and writing. So impressive was his campaign biography of Lincoln that it won him appointment as U.S. consul in Venice (1861–65). Upon his return he settled in Boston, joined the staff of the *Atlantic Monthly,* and for ten years as its editor (1871–81) was the mentor of promising writers. During this period he began one of the most prolific literary careers of the century, with his novel of manners, *Their Wedding Journey* (1872). (Between 1860 and 1920 he wrote 5 volumes of poems, 20 plays, 43 volumes of prose fiction, 33 volumes of essays, and 6 volumes of criticism.)

In those years he formulated his theory of literary realism, the first to be well defined in the U.S. He believed that fiction as an art must deal with what is actual and observable, not what is romanticized or genteel. He exemplified this concept in his masterpiece (dealing with the self-made man), *The Rise of Silas Lapham* (1885). In the year of its publication he moved to New York, a transfer significant in American literary history. Thereafter as a member of the editorial staff of *Harper's* he gave attention to the problems of industrial society, highlighted in *A Hazard of New Fortunes* (1889). His realism deepened into naturalism, and his notable achievement *The Landlord at Lion's Head* (1897) sketches a bleak picture of New England life.

By this time Howells was regarded as the pre-eminent American man of letters. His fiction and criticism, represented in *Literature and Life* (1902), gave encouragement to such young realists as Frank Norris, Stephen Crane, and Hamlin Garland. Howells's books have been called the documents of the cultural and social history that he interprets. By his accomplishments he influenced the art of fiction more than any other American writer of his time.

'Hub of the Universe,' as a term applied to Boston, was given currency by Oliver Wendell Holmes in *The Autocrat of the Breakfast Table* (1858), and is actually a misquotation: 'Boston State-house is the hub of the solar system.'

HUBBARD, ELBERT (1856–1915), in 1891 established an artist colony at East Aurora, New York, where he set up his Roycroft Shop, devoted to making de luxe editions of the classics. He edited an inspirational magazine, the *Philistine* (1895–1915), and wrote a series of 170 *Little Journeys* to the homes of successful men. He is chiefly remembered for his essay, A MESSAGE TO GARCIA, extolling the virtues of steadfastness and unquestioning service to one's employer.

HUBBARD, WILLIAM (1621–1704), born in England, graduated from Harvard in the first class (1642), and settled as minister at Ipswich. At the request of the General Court he wrote *A General History of New England,* completed in 1682 but not published until 1815. It was the manuscript source of the 18th-century histories written by Cotton Mather and Thomas Prince. His *Narrative of the Troubles with the Indians in New-England* (1677), the fullest account of King Philip's War (1675–76), remained popular for two centuries.

HUBBELL, CARL OWEN (1903–), as pitcher for the New York Giants won the 1934 All-Star game by his famous 'screwball' hurling. In the 1934–35 seasons 'The Meal Ticket' pitched 24 consecutive victories, and before 1947 had won 253 games.

HUBBLE, EDWIN POWELL (1889–1953), astronomer at the Mt. Wilson Observatory (1919–53), put forward the idea of an expanding universe, which had been suggested by his work on extragalactic nebulae, using the great 100-inch telescope. He worked out measurements of nebular distance and speed with his colleague, M. L. Humason. Hubble's writings include *The Realm of Nebulae* (1936) and *The Observational Approach to Cosmology* (1937).

HUDSON, HENRY (*fl.* 1607–11), English navigator, was employed (1607) by the Muscovy Company of London to find a northeast or northwest passage to the Orient. In his first two explorations he failed to get beyond Greenland. In 1609 he undertook his third voyage for the Dutch East India Company in the *Half-Moon.* Reaching Virginia waters, he followed the coastline north until he found himself in a wide 'lake,' the mouth of the noble river which bears his name, and his passage up to the present site of Albany gave the Dutch their claim to the region. His fourth expedition (1610), financed by English adventurers, took him far north through Hudson strait into the mighty bay, where in the following summer he was set adrift by a mutinous crew and perished. But his discoveries had given England claim to the vast Hudson Bay region.

Hudson river, 306 miles long, rises in the Adirondacks and flows south to enter New York Bay. One of the important waterways of the world, it is tidal to Albany and navigable for ocean vessels to that point. First explored by

Henry Hudson in 1609, the river was the highway for fur traders and early settlers. It was of strategic importance through the period of the Indian wars, the Revolution, and the War of 1812. Canals built in the 1820's and 1830's (chiefly the ERIE CANAL) joined the Hudson with other important waterways, and until the advent of the railroad these canals were the principal means of inland transportation. The modern New York Barge Canal, which bears heavy traffic, connects the Hudson with the Great Lakes and with Lake Champlain and the St. Lawrence river.

Hudson River School, reflecting the romanticism of the early 19th century, was the first native school of landscape painting in America (1825–75). The scenic grandeur of the Hudson river valley, the Catskills, Niagara Falls, and the White Mountains attracted artists who rebelled against the 18th-century classical tradition of idealized portraiture. (Coinciding with the rise of nationalism, the movement in art was paralleled in literature by the novels of Cooper and the poetry of Bryant.) The leader of the school, THOMAS COLE, drew a following of such artists as THOMAS DOUGHTY, ASHER DURAND, and JOHN KENSETT. In the next generation FREDERICK CHURCH and ALBERT BIERSTADT extended the range by depicting scenes in the Far West and elsewhere. GEORGE INNESS began his career in the vein of the Hudson River School, for whom the love of nature was a passion, and WINSLOW HOMER, who lived into the twentieth century, remained faithful to its concept that emotion should appear to spring from subject matter.

Hudson's Bay Company is the oldest incorporated trading company in the world. Chartered by Charles II in 1670, it was a monopoly that virtually exercised sovereign trading rights in the basins drained by the rivers flowing into Hudson Bay. In so vast a frontier 'the Bay' rights could be enforced only by the law of the jungle, since traders, French and English, constantly encroached on one another. In 1787 the North West Company was formed farther west (north to the Arctic and south to ASTORIA), and within 30 years the rivalry of the two groups had become so bloody that Parliament forced a merger (1821), under the name of Hudson's Bay. Thus began a period of true monopoly, whereby the Company (except for the eastern segment) virtually ruled Canada, with its sovereignty extending into disputed areas of the U.S. south of the Columbia river. After a parliamentary investigation (1857), ownership of stock became public, and since 1869 the Company's interests, still vigorous, have been transferred largely to diversified commercial enterprises.

HUGHES, CHARLES EVANS (1862–1948), after graduation from Brown (1881) practiced law in New York City, where he achieved nationwide prominence by exposing (1905–6) the abuses of insurance companies. While he was governor of New York (1906–10), his administration was notable for its reform legislation, including the establishment of a Public Service Commission. Appointed to the U.S. Supreme Court (1910), he resigned in 1916 to accept the Republican nomination for President. Hughes lost to Wilson in one of the closest contests in U.S. history, by an electoral vote of 277 to 254 (and a popular plurality of 600,000).

Hughes served as Secretary of State in the administrations of Harding and Coolidge (1921–25), during which period he organized the Washington Conference on naval limitation (1921–22) and negotiated a series of multipartite treaties. He was a judge on the Permanent Court of International Justice (1930) when he accepted an appointment to succeed Taft as Chief Justice of the U.S. Supreme Court, a post he held until his retirement (1941). In that decade he enhanced the efficiency of the Federal court system, and gave firm support to the freedoms guaranteed to citizens against state actions under the First Amendment. In the alignment between liberals and conservatives he held a middle ground, at the same time helping to reshape the law to meet social change. He displayed political acumen of high order when he led the masterly retreat of the Court during the debate (1937) on President Roosevelt's court reorganization plan.

See the biographies by M. J. Pusey (2 vols., 1951) and Dexter Perkins (1956).

HUGHES, John Joseph (1797–1864), Irish-born Catholic prelate who emigrated to the U.S. in 1817, was the first archbishop of New York (1850). He was ordained in 1826, and as a fighting Irish priest began a crusade for adequate parochial schools for all Catholics, regardless of national origin. In 1841 he founded St. John's College (now Fordham University). To Catholics abroad Archbishop Hughes became the foremost interpreter of the American religious situation. He visited Europe and the Vatican frequently, and helped establish the North American College in Rome. At Lincoln's request he became a personal agent abroad for the Union cause, especially in Catholic countries. Seldom has an American prelate held such extraordinary influence over the laity on so wide a range of issues — social, political, and educational.

Huguenots were French Protestants, Calvinistic in doctrine and Presbyterian in government. Henry IV granted them religious toleration by the Edict of Nantes (1598), but the Edict was revoked in 1685 by Louis XIV, and some 300,000 of the persecuted Huguenots fled the country. Although relatively few came to America, those who did were frequently persons of ability, and the Huguenots acquired power and influence quite out of proportion to their numbers. Among the Huguenot families that settled in colonial America were the Legarés and Petigrus of South Carolina, the Maurys of Virginia, the Jays and De Lanceys of New York, and the Reveres of Massachusetts. The only surviving Huguenot church is in Charleston, South Carolina, a city they helped found and develop as one of the leading cosmopolitan and commercial centers of the southern colonies.

HULL, Cordell (1871–1955), Tennessee-born statesman, was for many years a member of the U.S. House of Representatives (1907–21, 1923–31), where he sponsored important tax legislation, including the Federal income tax section of the tariff law of 1913. Elected to the Senate in 1931, he resigned his seat to become Roosevelt's Secretary of State (1933–44), in which post he applied his economic principles through a program of reciprocal trade agreements, intended to reduce the existing high tariff barriers. Through his efforts reciprocal agreements were signed with many nations under the important TRADE AGREEMENTS ACT (1934). His Good Neighbor policy in Latin America resulted in the withdrawal of American marines from Haiti (1934), the cancellation of the PLATT AMENDMENT (1934), and the calling of three PAN-AMERICAN CONFERENCES. He favored aid to the Allies from the beginning of World War II, and worked steadily for modification of the isolationist NEUTRALITY ACTS (1935–37). In 1945 he received the Nobel Peace prize for his work in building the world organization that resulted in the United Nations.

HULL, Isaac (1773–1843), Connecticut-born commodore in the U.S. navy, commanded vessels early in the Tripolitan War (1803–5). As captain of the frigate *Constitution* during the War of 1812, he forced the surrender of the British frigate *Guerrière* (19 August 1812) off Nova Scotia. The victory was as important in bolstering sagging morale as it was as a naval engagement. His high reputation for practical seamanship was deserved, and as commodore he later commanded the U.S. Pacific squadron (1824–27).

HULL, John (1624–83), born in England, became the wealthiest Boston merchant and shipowner of his day. As mintmaster, with his partner Robert Sanderson, he coined the willow-, oak-, and pine-tree shillings, but his lasting contribution was made as master goldsmith and teacher of a long line of colonial goldsmiths and silversmiths, who enriched the churches and homes of New England with beautiful examples of their art.

HULL, William (1753–1825), a graduate of Yale (1772), served in the War of Independence and in 1805 became governor of the newly established Michigan Territory. During the War of 1812 as the commanding general at Detroit, he was expected to lead the westernmost force of the three-pronged invasion into Canada. His timidity was so great that the Canadian general, Isaac Brock, secured the surrender of Detroit and captured a large store of supplies even before Hull embarked. Court-martialed and convicted of cowardice and neglect of duty, Hull was sentenced to be shot, but his Revolutionary War record prompted a stay of execution.

Hull-House, see *Addams, Jane.*

Humane societies were first organized in America during the 18th century at Philadelphia and Boston as lifesaving services. The Humane Society of New York (1814) extended aid to destitute debtors and other poor in prisons. The work assumed a new direction with the creation of Societies for the Prevention of Cruelty to Animals (1866) and to Children (1875). The American Humane Association (1877) gradually took on the function of a co-ordinating agency for all state and local human activities.

Humanism in religion (or *modernism* as it is sometimes called), first appeared in the U.S. late in the 19th century within the liberal wing of Protestant denominations. It was an attempt to reconcile science with historic Christianity. In general it repudiated the supernatural. It viewed God as indwelling spirit rather than as Creator, and the Gospels as symbolic rather than historic truth. The classic statement in the U.S. of early religious modernism is *The Religion of Humanity* (1872), by O. B. FROTHINGHAM. It shows a vestige of theism and a dependence on divergent ethical ideals. The most important humanist development originated in the ETHICAL CULTURE MOVEMENT (1876). Reaction to optimistic modernism stems largely from Germany, and has been made explicit in existentialism.

Humanism, New, was a critical movement in literature that flourished in the U.S. during the 1920's. Though the term had diverse meanings, under the leadership of IRVING BABBITT and PAUL ELMER MORE it emphasized universal, ethical human values, which find their ultimate principle in restraint and reason, as exemplified in the classics. It was an attempt to establish a code and a standard for measuring artistic achievement, particularly in literature.

Humanitarianism, see *Abolition movement, Antislavery societies, Humane societies, Philanthropy, Prison reform, Settlement houses, Slums, Temperance movement.*

Humphrey's Executor* v. *U.S. (1935) was a case resulting in a ruling of the U.S. Supreme Court declaring that the President's power of removal was limited to purely executive officers. The Court held that William E. Humphrey, a Federal Trade Commissioner, was an administrative officer as determined by Congressional Act, with quasi-legislative and quasi-judicial powers, and hence was removable only for cause as provided in the statute establishing the position.

Hundred, in England a division or subdivision of a county, was introduced into the colonies of Pennsylvania, Virginia, Maryland, and Delaware, where it served for election districts or for the administration of fiscal matters. It was the first English local division instituted in America. It gradually lost its significance except in Delaware, where it still exists. The origin of the term is not known, but some authorities hold that in Anglo-Saxon times it denoted a group of 100 families.

HUNEKER, JAMES GIBBONS (1857–1921), Philadelphia-born music critic and essayist, after piano study in Paris with Georges Mathias returned to the U.S., where he became a music, art, and drama critic. He was principally associated with the New York *Sun* (1902–17), the *Times* (1917–19), and the *World* (1919–21). He wrote with gusto and originality on a variety of subjects dealing with the arts, and was highly respected as a music critic at home and abroad. His criticisms, eclectic and expressionistic, directed American interest in the arts toward European modernism, exemplified by Ibsen, Shaw, D'Annunzio, Strindberg, Cézanne, and Debussy. Chief among his twenty books are *Mezzotints in Modern Music* (1899), essays on Brahms, Liszt, and others; and *Chopin: The Man and His Music* (1900), which is still highly regarded. His autobiography, *Steeplejack* (1920), pictures his years in Paris among the giants of art and literature.

Hunkers, the conservative faction of the Democratic party in New York during the 1840's, were so named because their antagonists saw them as politicians who wished to retain the whole 'hunk' of party patronage and policy, especially on slavery. The radical faction were called 'BARNBURNERS.'

HUNT, RICHARD MORRIS (1828–95), Vermont-born architect, was the first American to study architecture at the Beaux-Arts in Paris. He began his apprenticeship under T. U. WALTER, and in 1857, in New York, he founded the first American studio for training architects. In the same year he helped organize the American Institute of Architects. Although his work was imitative, it was eclectic. He designed many of the lavish French Renaissance chateau-style New York and Newport mansions built for merchant princes during the 1870's. His influence was limited.

His brother, WILLIAM MORRIS HUNT (1824–79), after study abroad established himself as a painter in Boston, where he introduced the Barbizon school to America. As a teacher and painter he exerted an influence on American art by turning the rising generation toward Paris. Strongly influenced by Millet, his lifelong friend, he is represented by *Peasant Girl at Barbizon* (Boston Fine Arts) and *The Bathers* (Metropolitan Museum).

HUNTINGTON, COLLIS POTTER (1821–1900), Connecticut-born railroad builder, laid the grounds of his fortune as a merchant in Sacramento after the California gold rush (1849). He guided the building of the CENTRAL PACIFIC RAILROAD, and with Leland Stanford consolidated industrial power by forming the SOUTHERN PACIFIC RAILROAD, of which Huntington was president after 1890. Notable among the 'robber barons,' he obtained favorable legislation from Congress by his lobbying, and through bribery of his state's legislature he gained virtual control of transportation in the West. He left most of his large estate to his nephew, Henry E. Huntington (1850–1927), who was associated with him in business and who founded the HENRY E. HUNTINGTON LIBRARY.

Huntington Library, see *Henry E. Huntington Library.*

Huron Indians, a confederacy of nomadic Iroquoian tribes, originally inhabited Ontario. When Champlain visited Lake Huron (1615) they were estimated to number some 25,000. Their traditional enemies were the Iroquois to the south, who, coming into the possession of firearms, virtually exterminated the Hurons (1648–50). Remnants fled to Quebec and elsewhere. In Michigan and Ohio they were known as the Wyandot Indians, and were allied with the British in the Revolution and the War of 1812. The few that remained were later moved to Oklahoma.

Huron, Lake, second largest of the GREAT LAKES, is 206 miles long, covers an area of 23,000 square miles, and forms most of the eastern boundary of Michigan. It is twenty feet lower than Lake Superior, whose waters it receives (together with those of Lake Michigan, flowing north) at its westernmost extremity. Its waters flow down the Detroit river to Lake Erie. ETIENNE BRULÉ visited Georgian bay in 1612, and in 1615 Champlain explored part of the lake. It later became the route of explorers, missionaries, and fur traders to the Mississippi and the western plains. The Michigan cities Port Huron and Bay City are both ports of entry.

Hurricanes are the vast marine storms that in the Northern Hemisphere begin as tropical gales in the vicinity of the West Indies. They travel slowly northward in an unpredictable manner, often gathering momentum, and generate winds within a 600-mile area that may average more than 100 miles an hour. Some half dozen hurricanes strike the North American mainland annually, usually along the Gulf or the Atlantic coast between August and October, traveling north, sometimes into Canada. Though much progress has recently been made in hurricane warnings, large hurricanes inevitably cause enormous damage.

HUTCHINS, ROBERT MAYNARD (1899–), as president (1929–45) and chancellor (1945–51) of the University of Chicago, put into effect the 'Chicago plan,' a four-year junior college and liberal arts university divorced from professional schools. (He also abolished compulsory courses and conventional grading systems.) He attacked narrow factualism, exaggerated vocationalism, and the intellectual disorder of the elective system, and emphasized the study of great books as a method of discovering a unified philosophical idea of the universe. In 1951 he became an associate director of the Ford Foundation, a post he held until he became president (1954) of the Fund for the Republic.

HUTCHINSON, ANNE (1591–1643), soon after migrating with her husband and family from England to Massachusetts (1634), began holding informal weekly meetings to discuss the sermons of the previous Sunday. Admired for her keen mind, she nevertheless came into sharp conflict with John Cotton and John Winthrop by her defiant espousal of the covenant of grace as opposed to the covenant of works. (That is, she insisted that faith alone is necessary for salvation.) She thus opened up the ANTINOMIAN CONTROVERSY, was tried by the General Court, and sentenced to banishment (1637) for 'traducing the ministers.' She and her family settled in Rhode Island with WILLIAM CODDINGTON and others, but even there her life continued to be stormy. She sought new asylum in New York (1642), but she and all other members of her family but one were massacred by Indians.

HUTCHINSON, THOMAS (1711–80), son of a wealthy Boston merchant, and a descendant of Anne Hutchinson, after graduation from Harvard (1727) began his notable public career as a member of the Massachusetts General Court (1737). As lieutenant (acting) governor (1758–71), he was the most influential man in the colony, but his 'hard money' policy and Tory leanings made him unpopular with the radical faction led by Samuel Adams and James Otis. His effort to enforce the Stamp Act (1765) was so bitterly resented that a mob sacked and burned his mansion and dumped his precious historical manuscripts into the street.

His unpopularity after he became governor (1771–74) was made acute by the publication of the so-called 'Hutchinson letters.' In the late 1760's Hutchinson had written privately to English friends, expressing the hope that the ministry would take drastic action to curb 'what are called English liberties.' The letters came into the possession of Benjamin Franklin, who sent them to Boston with instructions to keep them private. Franklin's instructions were ignored, and the resulting scandal, when Samuel Adams read them in the House of Representatives, clearly impaired Hutchinson's effectiveness as governor. Later in that year (1773), when he refused to allow the tea-laden ships to clear Boston Harbor, he precipitated the BOSTON TEA PARTY. He was replaced by a military governor, General Thomas Gage. Hutchinson was the last royal governor of the colony. In 1774 he sailed for England, where he remained.

Intelligent and learned, Hutchinson was a man of integrity, and his high rank as a scholar is manifest in his *History of the Colony of Massachusetts-Bay* (3 vols., 1764–1828; ed. by L. S. Mayo, 1936). These very readable volumes reflect his dislike of colonial intolerance (although he felt that Anne Hutchinson had threatened the Puritan order), his enlightened attitude toward the Indians, and his underlying desire to achieve conciliation with England. Long vilified for his Tory sympathies and economic conservatism, after the passage of a century he was accorded memorial honors in Boston suggestive of an apology, and the weight of scholarly opinion today inclines to the belief that Hutchinson is more deserving of respect than defense.

Hydrogen bomb, see *Nuclear energy*.

Hymns have been a part of all American Protestant church services from the founding of the colonies. Puritans restricted their church music to the singing of traditional psalms, beginning with the Ainsworth-Hopkins-Sternhold version, which so offended the trained scholars of the infant colony that several of them published the first American collection, generally known as the BAY PSALM BOOK (1640). Since written music was practically unknown in the colonies, John Tufts (1689–1750), a young New England minister, effected a revolution in social history when he issued the first singing book in America, *An Introduc-*

tion to the Singing of Psalm Tunes (*c.* 1712). The modern system of musical notation was introduced in *The Grounds and Rules of Music Explained* (1721), by Thomas Walter (1696–1725), a nephew of Cotton Mather, who himself had undertaken to refine meters in *Psalterium Americanum* (1718).

The first hymn book (as distinguished from a psalm book) printed in America was *Collection of Psalms and Hymns* (Charleston, 1737), prepared from English tunes and verses by John Wesley during his missionary residence in the South. American hymnody has always been stimulated by English usage, and, apart from psalmody, dates from the compilations of Isaac Watts, whose influence in America began about 1715. A new epoch in church music, which lasted for a century and coincided with the passing of the *Bay Psalm Book,* was inaugurated by *Urania* (1761), compiled by James Lyon (1735–94) shortly after his graduation from Princeton. It included anthems. During the Revolution the hymns of WILLIAM BILLINGS, America's first professional musician, were especially popular.

The considerable body of Lutheran hymnody, traditional among the Pennsylvania Germans (and in some degree among the Swedish settlers), dates from the late 17th century and includes the first original tunes and hymns produced in America. The highest level of musical activity in the colonies was attained by the Moravians at Bethlehem, Pennsylvania, where varied instruments and original compositions have always been traditional. Patriotic hymns include the national anthem, 'THE STAR-SPANGLED BANNER'; 'America' (1831), by Samuel F. Smith; and 'The Battle-Hymn of the Republic' (1861), by Julia Ward Howe.

The best known American composers of hymns and compilers of hymnals during the 19th century were THOMAS HASTINGS and LOWELL MASON. Almost every poet wrote verses either intended for solemn community singing or adaptable to it, among them SAMUEL LONGFELLOW, J. G. WHITTIER, and PHILLIPS BROOKS. The gospel song tradition of the Negro SPIRITUALS is uniquely American. Folk hymnody has survived in REVIVAL MEETINGS.

The 20th-century revival of interest in Lutheran hymnody and in the plain song (the nonmetrical chant melody of church services) has extended the range and enhanced the quality of many hymn books, notably the *Protestant Episcopal Hymn Book* (1940), the *Hymn Book for School and College Use* (Yale, 1956), and the *New Lutheran Hymn Book* (1957). Distinctive contributions to 20th-century hymnody have been made by the American composer and organist Leo Sowerby (1895–), and by the English composer Ralph Vaughan Williams.

See Henry W. Foote, *Three Centuries of American Hymnody* (1940), and George P. Jackson, *White and Negro Spirituals* (1944).

I

IBERVILLE, Pierre le Moyne, Sieur d' (1661–1706), Canadian soldier and colonizer, was son of the Sieur de LONGUEUIL. He commanded four expeditions against British trading posts during KING WILLIAM'S WAR (1689–97), interfering with British trade in the Hudson Bay area, and capturing St. John's, Newfoundland. In 1699, with his brother, Sieur de BIENVILLE, he established the earliest settlements in the Mississippi delta, principally at Mobile and Biloxi (1702). During QUEEN ANNE'S WAR, which began in 1702, he captured Nevis and St. Christopher in the West Indies, but he died of a fever before he could carry out his long-planned venture to attack New York and Boston. The accomplishments of this 'first great Canadian,' were considerable, especially by increasing the domain of New France in America.

Icarian colonies, see *Cabet, Étienne.*

I.C.C., see *Interstate Commerce Commission.*

ICKES, Harold L. (1874–1952), after graduation from Chicago (1897) practiced law and entered Illinois reform politics. For thirteen years he served as Secretary of the Interior (1933–46) in the cabinets of Roosevelt and Truman, during which period he directed the PUBLIC WORKS ADMINISTRATION. 'Honest Harold' administered huge sums efficiently without waste or scandal, and he rejected shoddy projects, but critics complained that he moved too slowly to make an immediate impact on the Depression. However, he quickly responded to changes that the Truman administration was effecting, and he resigned in 1946 when the President nominated Edwin W. Pauley, a California oil company executive, as undersecretary of the Navy, publicly charging that such an appointment had an odor reminiscent of TEAPOT DOME dealings.

Outspoken and blunt, especially on Hitler, racial discrimination, and sometimes on petty issues, Ickes was a respected and colorful administrator who summarized much of his career in *The Autobiography of a Curmudgeon* (1943). His posthumously published *Secret Diary* (3 vols., 1953) is an intimate history of the Roosevelt administration for the years 1933–41.

Idaho, in the heart of the Rocky Mountains, was first penetrated by white men when Lewis and Clark crossed it in 1805. (The name derives from Shoshone *ida-ho:* salmon tribe.) With a mean elevation of 5000 feet, it has vast areas of NATIONAL FORESTS (one-third of its 83,557 square miles), massive peaks, deep canyons, and great game preserves and wildernesses. A series of high plains is formed in the SNAKE RIVER region by sheets of lava, several thousand feet deep. Some areas of the state are still largely inaccessible.

Rival fur companies penetrated Idaho after 1810, and during the 1830's and 1840's emigrants on the OREGON TRAIL crossed its full width. Gold seekers in the Oregon Territory helped determine its independent status as Idaho Territory in 1863, and it was admitted to the Union in 1890 as the 43d state, with Boise as its capital.

Long one of the leading silver-producing areas in the world, today Idaho is being tapped for its enormous hydroelectric potential, especially along the turbulent and previously untamed Snake. Lumbering and agricultural advantages are likewise under development. Boise is the commercial center, and such recreation areas as Sun Valley have become important factors in the state's economy. In the decade 1950–60, although the population of Boise remained stationary (34,000), that of the state increased from 588,000 to 667,000. The leading institution of higher learning is the University of Idaho (Moscow, est. 1889), a pioneer organization in cooperative student living.

Idealism, in philosophy, is the metaphysical doctrine that the real is of the nature of thought. As developed by the English philosopher George Berkeley (1685–1753), it holds that there is no existence of matter independent of perception. The principal exponent in America of Berkeleian idealism was the educator SAMUEL JOHNSON. In *transcen-*

dental idealism, the doctrine of the German metaphysician Immanuel Kant (1724–1804), the things to which the conceptions of reality are applicable are merely appearances and not things-in-themselves, since things-in-themselves are held to be absolutely unknowable. TRANSCENDENTALISM developed as a movement in the U.S. chiefly in the period 1836–60.

Absolute idealism, the doctrine of the German philosopher G. W. F. Hegel (1770–1831), supposes that things derive their reality from one Mind to which all other minds are related as parts to the whole. Since man is endowed with a moral will and independence, he has an ethical obligation to contribute to the moral order. American exponents of Hegelian ethical idealism include W. T. HARRIS and JOSIAH ROYCE.

'I do not choose to run,' see *Coolidge, Calvin.*

'I had rather be right than be President,' see *Clay, Henry.*

'I have not yet begun to fight,' see *Jones, J. P.*

Illinois, originally part of the NORTHWEST TERRITORY, was first visited by MARQUETTE and JOLLIET (1673), and soon after by LA SALLE (1679). The name (as rendered by the French) derives from the Illini, the Algonquian tribe then inhabiting the region. The area remained under French control until ceded to the British in 1763. As part of Indiana Territory, during the War of Independence it was associated with the exploits of George Rogers Clark in the OLD NORTHWEST. Illinois Territory was established in 1809. Settlements after the War of 1812 were rapid, and in 1818 Illinois was admitted to the Union as the 21st state, with its capital first at Kaskaskia (1818–20), then Vandalia (1820–39), and (permanently thereafter) at Springfield.

A rolling, fertile prairie drained by some 275 rivers, Illinois has an average elevation of 600 ft. above sea level. The state first won national attention when Stephen Douglas and Abraham Lincoln debated the slavery issue in their famous senatorial race (1858). With the building of railroads in the 1850's, and the growth of Cyrus McCormick's agricultural-implement factory at CHICAGO in the same decade, industries sprang up, soon growing to enormous proportions.

Today Illinois is one of the great agricultural and industrial states of the Union, and Chicago is the cultural and financial center of the Midwest. During the decade 1950–60 Illinois had a population growth of nearly 2,000,000. That of Chicago's inner city dropped somewhat. The rise appeared chiefly in small towns and cities, many of which doubled or trebled in size. Illinois has long given liberal support to education, and its 80 institutions of higher learning include such leading universities as Northwestern (Evanston, est. 1851), Illinois Institute of Technology (est. 1892), and Chicago (est. 1892).

IMLAY, GILBERT (1754–1828?), author and adventurer, took part in the War of Independence before leaving New Jersey for Kentucky, where he became a surveyor and land speculator. After 1786 he lived abroad. In Paris during the French Revolution he moved in the circle of Tom Paine and formed a temporary liaison with the feminist Mary Wollstonecraft, whom he deserted after she bore his daughter. His widely read *Topographical Description of the Western Territory of North America* (1792) is permeated with the clichés of contemporary European radicalism, as is his sentimental romance *The Emigrants* (1793), contrasting the enchantment of the American frontier with the debased culture of Europe. His subsequent career is obscure.

Immigration, as the word describes the first settlements in America, first began with the Spanish settlements of the Southwest in the early 1500's, though immigration from Spain was limited at that time. English colonization of the Atlantic seaboard from Virginia to New England started soon after 1600, the Dutch arrived in NEW NETHERLAND in 1624, and the Swedes and Finns settled in NEW SWEDEN in 1638. German settlements in Pennsylvania followed the arrival of WILLIAM PENN in 1682. French culture in the Mississippi valley stemmed from the colonies planted by LA SALLE and IBERVILLE late in the 17th century. Scotch-Irish emigrants opened frontiers in western Pennsylvania, Virginia, the Carolinas, and Georgia soon after 1700; and later in the century Spanish settlements were developing the Southwest. From 1820 to 1920 the image of America, first as an agricultural promise and later as an industrial reality, jarred some 38,000,000 Europeans from their moorings, set them free from the political, economic, social, and religious trammels of the Old World, and brought them to the U.S. in the greatest migration in history.

The 'Old Migration' began as a constant stream in the 1820's (mainly Irish, German, and Scandinavian) and reached its peak during the years 1840–80. The Irish, who arrived in immense waves, were abjectly poor peasants, and, though large numbers were absorbed into eastern cities (causing labor dislocations and rousing the strong prejudices expressed in NATIVISM), they provided the great body of manpower for the tasks of industrialization and for the canal and railroad construction as the nation moved its frontier westward. Scandinavians were principally attracted to frontier farms in the general area of Wisconsin, Minnesota, and Nebraska. The German emigrants, uprooted like the Irish by economic distress (some 4000 were directly affected by the political revolution of 1848), formed colonies in New York, Baltimore, Cincinnati, and St. Louis, and by 1858 had virtually made Milwaukee a German city. In the same period (especially 1854–68) Chinese immigrant labor, attracted by the CONTRACT LABOR ACT of 1864, were laying tracks in the Far West for the railroads that were linking the continent. The degree to which social and economic problems were thus created by the rapid influx of Chinese labor is manifest in the BURLINGAME TREATY (1868), the subsequent CHINESE EXCLUSION ACTS, and the CONTRACT LABOR ACT of 1885, which reversed the labor law of 1864 by forbidding further importation of contract workers. (JAPANESE EXCLUSION was not an issue until the 20th century.)

The 'New Immigration' from eastern and southern Europe developed in the 1880's, and a heavy flow at the turn of the 20th century from Russia, Poland, Austria-Hungary, the Balkans, and Italy concentrated sizable foreign-born blocs in the larger cities: Boston (Irish), New York (Jews, Italians), and Chicago (Poles, Hungarians, Bohemians). Of the total U.S. population in 1900 (76,000,000) more than 10,000,000 had been born in Europe and some 26,000,000 were of foreign parentage. Most numerous were those who settled in New York.

Whereas earlier groups had been largely absorbed by the land, by 1900 the new concentration in the cities sharpened the pains of readjustment. The immigrant still subscribed to the 'melting pot' theory that his native gifts and language would be distilled into the new American race (an idea as old as Crèvecœur and Jefferson), but by 1920 he was aware that such fusion had not been achieved. At the same time the older Americans in alarm launched a strident movement for a 'quota law' lest native-born laborers should be put out of jobs. The JOHNSON-REED ACT of 1924 almost stopped all immigration to the U.S. The act allayed fear by 'natives' of 'foreigners,' but it intensified the racial pride of national groups who, in fact, by their various and lively regional cultures have given an immense vitality to the character of the nation.

In 1948 the immigration law authorized the admission of 205,000 European displaced persons, including 3000 nonquota orphans, and the number was increased in 1950. The McCarran-Walter Act of 1952 codified U.S. immigration laws, in general retaining the provisions of the 1924 Act on maximum immigration and the quota system, but removing the ban against immigration of Asian and Pacific people. In 1965 the largest annual quotas applied to Great Britain (65,000), Germany (25,800), and Ireland (17,700). Other European quotas ranged from 6500 (Poland) to 225 (Turkey). Asian and African national quotas are almost uniformly limited to 100. The total number admitted from all countries in 1965 was 296,697, about one-third of the number annually admitted in the peak decade 1900–1910. In 1965 Congress enacted a new immigration law abolishing the national-origins quota system as of June 1968, thus wiping out racial discrimination in immigration.

See Carl Wittke, *We Who Built America* (1939) M. L. Hansen, *The Immigrant in American History* (ed. by A. M. Schlesinger, 1941), and Oscar Handlin, *Immigration as a Factor in American History* (1959).

Impeachment, a method for removing civil and judicial officers before the expiration of their terms, is provided for in the Federal Constitution (Art. I, sec. 5). By a majority vote the House of Representatives may adopt an impeachment resolution (that is, bring charges against an official), and the Senate, which tries the impeachment, may convict by a two-thirds vote. A conviction can lead to criminal proceedings in the lower courts. The President's pardoning power does not extend to impeachment convictions.

In U.S. history impeachment proceedings have been instituted on numerous occasions, chiefly against lower court judges, whose removal cannot otherwise be effected. (Very few have been convicted.) On occasion impeachments have been instruments of party warfare, notably in the cases of Justice SAMUEL CHASE and President ANDREW JOHNSON. Grant's corrupt Secretary of War, W. W. Belknap, was unanimously impeached but resigned before the Senate convened for trial. In some states and municipalities, legislative impeachment is supplemented by popular RECALL.

Imperial problems, as Great Britain faced them in America after the TREATY OF PARIS of 1763, were of unprecedented magnitude. By excluding France from the continent, Britain had more than doubled the extent of her possessions in the Western Hemisphere. Moreover, she had brought into the Empire the American Indians, a race alien in language, religion, and customs. Baffling questions were raised in matters of Indian relations, fur trade, land policy, and military and political administration. Organization of this vast territory soon presented more problems than the British government could handle.

The PROCLAMATION OF 1763 placed Indian trade under royal control, which in effect barred settlements west of the Alleghenies. Though motivated by good intentions, this attempt to impede westward migration was unrealistic. The Indian uprising under PONTIAC (1763–64) made frontier problems acute, since military establishments had to be restored, and the Treasury was already severely strained after the Seven Years' War. Might not the American colonies reasonably be expected to bear part of the Empire's financial burden? Parliament thought so. The NAVIGATION ACTS were more vigorously enforced, and efforts made to curb smuggling and illegal trade. Passage of the SUGAR ACT (1764) and the STAMP ACT (1765) was bitterly resented in the colonies, for the levies were internal taxes, an encroachment on the rights of colonial assemblies. Opposition was crystallized by what seemed a highhanded method of coercion, although at the time the colonists had no thought of revolution.

The immediate repeal of the Stamp Act ushered in a decade of Government drifting and muddling. Indeed, the TOWNSHEND ACTS (1767), by helping to create grave constitutional issues, compounded the injury. The colonies, now rapidly becoming a dominion, were increasingly treated as wayward dependencies. Had the policy makers in Whitehall abandoned the legal fiction of central authority and recognized the actuality of federalism, the imperial disorganization certainly would have been postponed, and the War of Independence might have been avoided.

See L. H. Gipson, *The Coming of the American Revolution, 1763–1775* (1954).

Imperial wars, see *French and Indian Wars.*

Imperialism, the domination of one people by another, in modern history began in the 16th century, when national states began to build 'trading' empires by establishing colonies. Early settlements in North America were created by European nations in their attempts to find areas for capital investments, to exploit raw material, and to build up markets for home exports. (Emigration of settlers is called colonialism.) These empires were erected according to theories of MERCANTILISM, the pursuit of economic power through national self-sufficiency.

In the U.S. imperialism has never consistently commanded support, although the impulse that led to the Mexican War (1846), called 'MANIFEST DESTINY,' was clearly imperialistic. After the Civil War Secretary of State Seward inaugurated an imperial policy in the Pacific by his purchase of Alaska (1867). Other moves in the international struggle for new markets and sources of supply called for the cementing of friendly relations with China (later called the OPEN DOOR POLICY), the building of an Isthmian canal, the annexation of Hawaii, and control over selected Pacific islands as coaling stations. The war with Spain in 1898 led not only to the destruction of Spain's 'sovereignty' in Cuba, but to the annexation by the U.S. of Puerto Rico, the Philippines, and Guam.

The word 'imperialism' as a political slogan was first used in the U.S. to attack Republican expansionist policies during the McKinley campaign of 1900. (The Republicans won the election, however.) The U.S. established imperialistic protectorates over Cuba (1901), Panama (1903), the Dominican Republic (1905), Nicaragua (1912), and Haiti (1915). In 1916 it purchased the Virgin Islands from Denmark.

After 1929 the U.S. largely modified or abandoned its imperialistic policy, in part because imperialism never paid the expected dividends, but chiefly because the demand for independence among colonial peoples everywhere met increasing response in a nation once itself a colony. The U.S. no longer acts in the role of protector to the above-named territories. The Philippines became a republic in 1946, and Alaska and Hawaii gained statehood in 1959.

Imperialism as an expansion of influence seeking to control or manipulate the internal and external policies of a nation can also be cultural, economic, linguistic, political, or religious in nature. Russian power in Hungary, U.S. control over the economy of Guatemala, and Portuguese hegemony over Angola are instances of 'imperialism' beyond the limited definition of physical annexation.

Implied powers of Congress, as a doctrine finds its basis in the final clause of Article I, section 8 of the Constitution, the so-called 'elastic clause,' by which Congress is provided with all powers necessary to execute the DESIGNATED POWERS there enumerated. As soon as the Constitution went into effect, Anti-Federalists (rigid interpreters of the document, called strict constructionists) favored limiting the powers of the central government. Under Hamilton's leadership, supported by decisions of the U.S. Supreme Court under Chief Justice Marshall, the Federalists (broad or 'loose' constructionists) made liberal use of the elastic clause, notably in the case of MC CULLOCH *v.* MARYLAND (1819), to strengthen centralized government in the early years of the Republic.

In recent times the decisions of the Court have greatly expanded the powers of the federal government to undertake national services and determine public standards, notably in the WAGNER-CONNERY ACT (1935), the SOCIAL SECURITY ACT (1935), and the SMITH ACT (1940). Thus Congress, backed by Supreme Court interpretations of the Constitution, has augmented its interstate commerce and taxing powers so extensively that few economic facets of American life remain outside its control.

Impressionism, as an aesthetic movement in painting, music, and literature, arose in France during the 1860's. An extension of earlier romanticism, it was an attempt to portray the effect of 'impressions' of an experience upon the consciousness of the artist. In painting it sought primarily to render atmospheric effects of light as observed out of doors, and its chief subjects were landscapes of nature scenes in which fragmentary components of light and shade were made to convey the pattern. The paintings of the Europeans Monet, Manet, Pissarro, and Sisley were deeply influential on the style of many American painters, including WHISTLER, TWACHTMAN, WEIR, and MARY CASSATT. Postimpressionism is the theory or practice of artists (Cézanne, Gauguin, Van Gogh, Seurat) who sought in their work a stronger spatial construction or a more personal expression than Impressionists at first achieved.

In music impressionism tried to evoke a mood, with emphasis upon the individual sonorities of chords. Originating in France, notably in the music of Debussy, as a reaction against Wagnerian romanticism, the movement influenced such American composers as GRIFFES and LOEFFLER.

In poetry and fiction, impressionism

in the U.S. expressed itself in a variety of trends, but chiefly by depicting scenes and emotions without detailed elaboration. Its leading proponents among critics were HUNEKER and NATHAN. Among poets, EZRA POUND was for a time in the vanguard, with a large and important following. Scarcely a leading novelist has been untouched by its influence.

Impressment of American sailors into service in the British navy became an Anglo-American issue during the Napoleonic Wars (1803–15), when British seamen often deserted to sign up in the American merchant marine. 'Press gangs' claimed the right to board American merchantmen to retrieve deserters, and in the process they frequently impressed any sailor who could pass as a Briton, unless he could prove American citizenship. In the beginning of that period some 90 per cent of the correspondence of American ministers at the Court of St. James's had to do with attempts to validate the nationality of American seamen.

The impressment issue became acute in the CHESAPEAKE-LEOPARD INCIDENT (1807), a forceable boarding of an American frigate by a British naval contingent, which brought the two nations to the verge of war. Of the 10,000 persons estimated to have been impressed from the American merchant marine, about 1000 proved to be British subjects. Congress cited impressment as one of the causes of the War of 1812.

Income tax was first imposed by Congress in 1861 (3 per cent on incomes over $800). Twice increased during the Civil War years, it was terminated in 1870. The Wilson-Gorman Tariff Act of 1894 imposed a 2 per cent tax on incomes over $4000, but that clause of the Act was declared unconstitutional a year later. Adoption of the Sixteenth Amendment (1913) enabled Congress to enact a third income tax law, since which time individual income tax receipts have steadily increased in importance as a revenue source, yielding in 1965 more than $70,000,000,000. Wisconsin imposed the first state income tax in 1911. Today almost all states, as well as the District of Columbia, levy some form of income tax.

Indentured servants, or bound laborers, were used principally in the Middle Colonies and the tobacco provinces during the colonial period. Voluntary servants (redemptioners or 'free willers') were white immigrants who bound themselves to service for a period of years (usually two to seven) in return for passage to America. This group, which may have accounted for three-fourths of the total immigration before 1775, also included apprentices, minors who were provided training in specified trades. Involuntary workers comprised those in servitude for debt, or British convicts transported to the colonies (principally to Maryland, Virginia, or the West Indies). Some 50,000 such workers were sent from England before the Revolution. Unlike slavery, indentured servitude, whether voluntary or involuntary, bound the laborer only for a specified time.

Independence Day (the Fourth of July) is the chief patriotic holiday in the U.S., and commemorates the adoption of the Declaration of Independence (1776). Although John Adams on the day following the vote for independence called for popular celebrations at every anniversary thereafter, partisan spirit during the Federal era excluded Anti-Federalists from official observances. The situation was reversed when Republicans came to power in 1800. The Fourth of July was not celebrated on a national scale until about 1815. Thereafter the jubilee day was traditionally observed by fireworks, parades, and oratory. Those features have gradually become less conspicuous.

Independence Hall, in Philadelphia, is the chief national shrine in the U.S. In it the Declaration of Independence was proclaimed (4 July 1776), Washington accepted command of the Continental army, and the Constitution of the U.S. was adopted (1787). It was made a national museum in 1876, and the LIBERTY BELL is in its central rotunda.

Independent Republicans, see *'Mugwumps.'*

Independent Treasury Act (1840), established under pressure of the Van Buren Democrats, entrusted the government with the exclusive care of its own funds, which previously had been held first in the BANK OF THE U.S. and then (after 1833) in President Jackson's so-called 'PET BANKS.' The Act also created subtreasuries at New York, Boston, Philadelphia, Washington, Charleston, St. Louis, and New Orleans. It was repealed a year later by a Whig majority, who hoped to re-establish a national bank, and for five years the Whigs defeated efforts of Democrats to re-establish subtreasuries. During that period the Secretary of the Treasury used state banks as depositories. In 1846 the Democrats were able to revive the Act, which served as the basis of the U.S. fiscal system until creation of the FEDERAL RESERVE SYSTEM (1913). The subtreasury system was finally abolished in 1920.

Independents, see *Separatists.*

Indian captivities, a separate and extensive body of literature, are peculiar to the American frontier. Whether true or fictionalized, they were a steadily profitable publishing venture as long as the border Indian existed, and they were popular among readers eager for narrative accounts of frontier life set down in the picaresque tradition. Religious groups sponsored them as examples of Christian fortitude and martyrdom, and promoters used them to call the attention of prospective settlers to Indian territory. Such captivity accounts as those by MARY ROWLANDSON and JOHN WILLIAMS became the best sellers of their day. Indian captivities were in part responsible for engendering a hatred of Indians, and must be taken into account in speaking of the romantic revolution in fiction which idealized the character of the 'noble savage.'

Indian missions were first established in Spanish North America by FRANCISCANS (1528), and their 17th- and 18th-century missions of New Mexico, Arizona, California, Texas, and Florida compose a whole chapter in frontier missionary endeavor. During the 17th century the JESUITS founded missions throughout New France, and Protestants in the English, Dutch, and German settlements carried on missionary work among the various tribes. Such men as ROGER WILLIAMS, JOHN ELIOT, and ELEAZAR WHEELOCK are especially associated with the PRAYING INDIANS.

Indian reservations, land set aside for the occupancy and use of Indian tribes, were first created by a policy inaugurated in 1786. Ultimately some 200 were established in more than 40 states. Indian land holdings, which were some 137,000,000 acres in 1887, by 1960 had shrunk to about 54,000,000 acres. Today the Indian population, which increased from 357,000 in 1950 to 524,000 in 1960, is situated chiefly in Arizona (83,000), Oklahoma (65,000), New Mexico (56,000), California (40,000), North Carolina (38,000), Washington (27,000), South Dakota (25,000), Montana (21,000), New York (16,000), and Minnesota (15,000). Those who live on reservations eke out their existence on government doles. They are the tragic remnants of the race that helped the white man gain his first foothold in the New World.

Many Indians have left the reservations and are being assimilated. The Iroquois, for example, now have created a tradition of becoming professional steel-workers in skyscraper construction throughout the state of New York.

Indian Territory, originally the eastern part of present Oklahoma north of the Red river, was set aside in 1834 for the FIVE CIVILIZED TRIBES. It never received formal organization, but with the subsequent settlement of western portions, the eastern part was organized as Oklahoma Territory (1890), into which other tribes were settled. In 1907 Indian Territory and Oklahoma Territory were merged to form the state of Oklahoma.

Indian treaties are a body of material unique in the literature of the world. Composed by no single author, they occupy a place in prose comparable in many ways to that of the popular ballad in poetry, especially in their provenance, structure, the metaphors and even the rites of their composition and style. Since Indian tribes acted as buffer states between French and British colonies and were invaluable allies in time of war, colonial governors always sought to make treaties of friendship with the Indians. A large number were printed, but the issue of each text was very limited. No single person in the history of Indian diplomatic relations was more important than CONRAD WEISER, who gained the allegiance of the Iroquois for the British in the French and Indian Wars.

The subsequent history of Indian treaties, which offered a guarantee of tribal lands 'as long as grass shall grow and water run,' is a sorry chapter in American history, best characterized by Helen Hunt Jackson in *A Century of Dishonor* (1881).

Indian tribes, see *Abnaki, Algonquian Family, Apache, Arapaho, Arikara, Assiniboin, Blackfoot, Cherokee, Cheyenne, Chickasaw, Chinook, Comanche, Cree, Creek, Crow, Dakota, Delaware, Flathead, Hidatsa, Hopi, Huron, Iroquois Confederacy, Kickapoo, Kiowa, Mahican, Mandan, Miami, Mohave, Mohawk, Mohegan, Massachuset, Narragansett, Natchez, Navaho, Nez Percé, Ojibwa, Omaha, Osage, Ottawa, Paiute, Pawnee, Potawatomi, Pueblo, Sauk and Fox, Seminole, Shawnee, Shoshone, Siouan Family, Snake, Ute, Zuñi.*

Indian wars, prosecuted under Federal authority, began with those early campaigns which, in the process of westward expansion, culminated in the battle of FALLEN TIMBERS (1794), and the consequent opening of the NORTHWEST TERRITORY to settlement. The SEMINOLE WARS of 1816–18 led to the acquisition of Florida, and thereafter everywhere along the American frontier for 70 years the story repeated itself. The Seminole Wars of 1835–42 forcibly removed large numbers of Indians in the southern states into the West. Those who would not go were gradually eliminated. The BLACK HAWK WAR (1832) was the final Indian conflict on the northwestern frontier east of the Mississippi.

But most of the Indian 'wars' came later. During the Civil War the Sioux and Cheyenne fought back with considerable success. Thereafter the broad classification of the numerous engagements is threefold: those of the Great Plains, the Southwest, and the Northwest. As a lieutenant colonel commanding a cavalry unit, GEORGE A. CUSTER for a decade campaigned against the Plains Indians (1867–76), until he was killed in the battle of Little Bighorn. General Edward R. S. Canby (1817–73), in command of the Department of the Columbia on the Pacific coast, brought an end to the Modoc War (1872–73), though he was treacherously killed while negotiating peace with the MODOC INDIANS. General George Crook (1828–90) operated with success and great tact in the Southwest, ending the authority of GERONIMO (1884). The last significant campaigns were those against the Sioux (1890–91), the so-called 'Messiah War' initiated by the GHOST DANCE uprising, brought to conclusion under the command of General Nelson A. Miles (1839–1925). Thus the 'Indian problem' was largely ended, since full-blooded Indians for the most part had been killed or confined to reservations.

Indiana, first explored by LA SALLE (1670), was part of the French Empire in North America until it was ceded to Great Britain by the TREATY OF PARIS of 1763. Organized in 1787 as part of the NORTHWEST TERRITORY, it was opened to settlements by the victory of Anthony Wayne at FALLEN TIMBERS (1794). It became a separate territory in 1800, and was admitted to the Union in 1816 as the 19th state.

The frontier characteristics of the people of the region, independence and self-respect, were maintained even after the Civil War and into the period when Indiana began to develop an industrial economy. The state remains important for its diversified farming, and ranks high in the production of coal and limestone. Indianapolis, capital since 1825, a cultural and commercial center, is rapidly becoming a metropolis, with a population (in 1960) approaching 500,000. Among the state's two score institutions of higher learning are the universities of Indiana (Bloomington, est. 1824), Notre Dame (South Bend, est. 1844), and Purdue (est. 1874).

Indians, American, as migratory bands of Siberian Mongoloids, began to penetrate the Western Hemisphere by way of Seward Peninsula in Alaska between 25,000 and 35,000 years ago. The migrations extended through South America and had reached Patagonia by 8000 B.C. These prehistoric peoples were racially akin to those people whom Columbus by misapprehension called Indians.

There is no evidence of earlier human life in the New World. In what is now Canada and the U.S. these Asian stocks developed into a large number of differentiated linguistic families. Indian languages have no tie with any known European or Asian tongues, though the dialects within linguistic families have enough kinship to suggest 'family' groups. Historically important among the families have been the IROQUOIS (Northeast), ALGONQUIAN and SIOUAN (Northeast and Plains), NATCHEZ-MUSKHOGEAN (Deep South), ATHAPASKAN and YUMAN (Southwest), and UTO-AZTECAN (Plains, Southwest and Far West).

The Indian population during the colonial period was not evenly distributed over the present continental U.S. It was dense on the margins and sparse in the Great Basin and on the arid Great Plains. The total population may have been something under 900,000. By 1865 it was estimated to be about 340,000, a figure that remained relatively unchanged for 80 years. The 1960 census placed the Indian population at 524,000.

Indian villages were always small, and when communities numbered more than 150 they were usually divided, probably for economic welfare. Only the Plains Indians were nomadic, pursuing buffalo herds for food and clothing. Some tribes, notably the Iroquois, were bound by formally organized confederacies. Others, like the Abnaki (Northeast), Creeks (Southeast), Pawnee and Dakota (Plains), were less closely tied. But all tribes reserved the right of independent action at any time. For the most part the tribes were predatory and hostile to each other, for war was a part of the social code, which demanded that the young brave certify his manhood by bringing in a scalp. Such a situation made conquest by the whites relatively easy, since this internecine strife was more deadly to the Indians than warfare with the white man. In fact, tribes seldom co-operated with each other against white intruders. The two notable exceptions were the battles of FALLEN TIMBERS (1794) and LITTLE BIGHORN (1876). During the French and Indian Wars (1689–1763), the tribes were used as buffers between colonies, and by means of INDIAN TREATIES colonial governors secured invaluable allies.

Excepting the village tribes of the Southwest, the Indians of the U.S. were primarily hunters, and agriculture was a secondary means of subsistence. The coming of Europeans speeded the tempo of Indian warfare by introducing the gun and the horse. As a social amenity Indians exchanged tobacco for the white man's distilled liquor, never previously known to them. In the colonizing of the nation Indians were important economically as a market for manufactured items bartered for hides and furs. They also contributed knowledge about medicinal plants and food (tomatoes, corn, beans, squash, and maple sugar).

The cultural areas, in which tribes had somewhat similar ways of living, are customarily divided into geographical regions, since the character of a region would determine tribal economy. These are the Northeastern Woodland (DELAWARE, IROQUOIS, OJIBWA, MIAMI, SAUK AND FOX, SHAWNEE); Southeast (CHEROKEE, CHOCTAW, CHICKASAW, CREEK, SEMINOLE); Great Plains (BLACKFOOT, CHEYENNE, ARAPAHO, COMANCHE, CROW, DAKOTA, PAWNEE); Southwest or Desert (APACHE, HOPI, ZUÑI, NAVAHO); Far West (PAIUTE, MODOC); Pacific Northwest (CHINOOK); and Mountain or Plateau (NEZ PERCÉ).

In the 1890's the long struggle between whites and Indians, dating back to the Spanish conquests in the 16th century, was brought to an end by the last of the INDIAN WARS, and by 1900 all tribes had been settled on INDIAN RESERVATIONS. Improving the lot of the Indian is still one of the nation's most baffling problems, since the Indian has been largely ignored even by people dedicated to minority causes, and few Indians have been brought into the main cultural stream of the nation. Yet the fact that a very large number of Indian names have been given to states, counties, cities, lakes, rivers, and other localities is testimony of the incalculable influence of the Indians, whose rugged independence long kept them in tribal isolation. The story of the penetration of Europeans into a New World inhabited by a highly capable but (except for such groups as the Aztecs, Mayas, and Incas) primitive civilization is long, complex, and usually tragic. Congress granted Indians citizenship in 1924, and in recent times it has become something of a distinction in the U.S. to claim descent from Indian forebears.

The largest collection of Indian culture is that in the Museum of the American Indian (New York City). See Clark Wissler, *Indians of the U.S.* (1946), and *The American Indian* (3rd ed., 1950); and J. R. Swanton, *The Indian Tribes of North America* (1952).

Indigo culture was introduced into South Carolina in the early colonial period, and by 1748 indigo had become one of the STAPLE CROPS, as the British government granted a bounty of sixpence a pound for indigo shipped to England. By 1770 more than 1,000,000 pounds were being exported annually. After the War of Independence indigo culture sharply declined, chiefly because the new American government offered no bounty, and cotton was proving to be the more profitable export.

Industrial management, or scientific management, is the term applied to the highly organized methods employed in commercial and industrial production. The development of automatic machinery after the Civil War, together with increased competition, led American engineers to study means of improving efficiency. The first to make detailed time and motion analyses, F. W. TAYLOR, based his reports on observations he made during the 1880's as foreman in a steel mill. The assembly line method of production led to the study of such problems as distributing processes, labor specialization, flow of material, and methods of accounting.

Soon after 1910 H. L. GANTT pioneered in advocating on-the-spot training courses, as did LILLIAN and FRANK GILBRETH, who made studies of fatigue and of personnel relations. Such inquiries led to the widespread use of psychological tests, and to the famous Hawthorne Experiment of ELTON MAYO during the 1920's, from which developed the 'human relations school' of industrial management, whose techniques were absorbed during the 1950's into the processes of AUTOMATION.

Industrial unions, whose organization is sometimes called 'vertical,' are labor unions that organize all workers, whether skilled or unskilled and irrespective of occupation, in contrast to TRADE UNIONS, which organize on the basis of craft. In 1879 the KNIGHTS OF LABOR became an industrial union. More militant were the INDUSTRIAL WORKERS OF THE WORLD (1905), committed to the principle of class warfare. In the 1930's when the Committee on Industrial Organization seceded from the craft-dominated AMERICAN FEDERATION OF LABOR, the leaders concentrated upon a type of union that could meet the threat of the machine in mass production industries, and formed the CONGRESS OF INDUSTRIAL ORGANIZATIONS. In 1955 the two were merged into the A.F.L.–C.I.O.

Industrial Workers of the World (I.W.W.) was a revolutionary labor union launched at Chicago in 1905 by delegates from 43 organizations under the leadership of EUGENE V. DEBS, DANIEL DE LEON, and others. Its program was anarchist-syndicalist-socialist in nature, demanding the overthrow of capitalism through political and economic action, including strikes, boycotts, and sabotage. Until World War I this union of 'Wobblies' (sometimes called 'the Bummery') was particularly strong among textile workers, migratory farmers, dock workers, and Western miners and lumberjacks. In 1912 it reached a peak membership of 100,000. Its propaganda pamphlets included *I.W.W. Songs* (1918), with such popular pieces as 'Hallelujah, I'm a Bum,' and 'Casey Jones, the Union Scab.' Most famous was the 'Pie in the Sky' phrase from 'The Brother and the Slave.'

It was the first large labor organization to be formally committed to the principle of class warfare, and was relatively early among INDUSTRIAL UNIONS. But as a result of vigilante action and Federal prosecutions beginning in 1917 its already reduced membership rapidly dwindled, a disintegration hastened by the hysteria against 'radicalism.' It contributed, however, to the U.S. labor movement by insisting on a union of skilled and unskilled workers, the typical structure of present labor unions. Although virtually inoperative after 1918, it held its twenty-seventh convention in 1955.

Industry, see *Manufacturing.*

Inflation, a condition created by rapidly rising prices, may be caused by a short supply of commodities, an increased demand for goods, a large supply of money and credit, or the printing of FIAT CURRENCY. In the colonial period the chronic shortage of coins encouraged unorthodox monetary experiments. The improvised nature of the War of Independence made sound financing difficult and led Congress to issue unsecured CONTINENTAL CURRENCY. The states also printed fiat money copiously, thus encouraging a runaway type of inflation.

The tight British blockade of imports during the War of 1812 exhausted credit, made currency often irredeemable, and led to suspension of payments in 1814 and inflated prices. Out of the great land boom of the 1830's, fed by irresponsible state bank policies of credit, came the PANIC OF 1837.

Only 20 per cent of the Union's bills were paid by taxes during the Civil War, and the heavy reliance upon unsecured GREENBACKS produced inflation. In 1914–17 Allied purchases cheapened the dollar by bringing half the world's gold to the U.S. A near-runaway boom began in 1919, based on such demand factors as deferred orders and reconstruction. Thus the cost of living, which had climbed in 1919 to 77 per cent above the 1914 level, rose to 105 per cent in 1920.

The price rise of 30 per cent during 1938–45 was modest by the 1914–20 standards, largely because the government enacted wartime price controls, checked wages, and resisted farm bloc pressures. But the postwar demand for houses and automobiles, and for quick decontrol so that the classic laws of supply and demand could presumably end all shortages, resulted in inflation. Food prices alone rose by 34 per cent in 1946. The Korean War of 1950 revived an inflationary spiral for a brief period, but at a moderate pace that was offset by the rapidly rising Gross National Product and an ever higher standard of living.

INGERSOLL, ROBERT GREEN (1833–99), nationally known in his day as a religious skeptic, was the son of a revivalist preacher, yet their relationship was warmly affectionate. Ingersoll practiced law in Illinois, married a free-thinking young woman, served gallantly at Shiloh as a Union cavalry colonel, and after the Civil War was attorney general of Illinois (1866–69). He became a fervent Republican, and as a spellbinding orator in 1876 nominated James G. Blaine for the presidency in his famous 'plumed knight' speech. Thereafter for twenty years the forensic triumphs of 'Royal Bob' in his attacks on any variety of anthropomorphic god attracted audiences of unprecedented size. Seeking to 'rescue the reputation of the Deity from the aspersions of the pulpit,' he was regarded by millions of the pious as a notorious infidel. To other millions he was an evangel releasing mankind from bigotry and superstition. To his lecture manager he was a person who could attract more money at the box office than anyone 'since lecturing began.' As an economic conservative he avoided the issue of poverty and unemployment, and he swayed election-year audiences with 'bloody shirt' oratory to remind them that the Confederates had been Democrats.

Incomparable in moving juries and convincing judges, he won note for his defense in the STAR ROUTE mail scandals involving frauds against the government. Few men in public life have had so many vociferous adherents and detractors on a national scale.

See Orvin Larson, *American Infidel* (1962).

In God We Trust first appeared as an inscription on U.S. coins in 1864 by authorization of Congress. In 1956 Congress designated it the U.S. National Motto and ordered it placed on all paper money and all coins.

INGRAHAM, PRENTISS (1843–1904), son of the historical romancer Joseph Holt Ingraham (1809–60), became one of the most prolific writers of dime novels. Some 200 of the 600 that he turned out had as hero his friend Buffalo Bill. He worked at great speed, on one occasion allegedly completing a 35,000-word story in 24 hours.

Initiative, the device whereby legislation may be enacted directly by the people, was introduced by South Dakota in 1898. The system permits any group of persons to propose a law by securing a specified number of signatures of the voters. Similar to the RECALL, the method has been adopted by a score of states, but does not exist on the Federal level.

Injunction, in law, is a judicial order requiring the person to whom it is directed to do or to refrain from doing a particular thing. As applied in the U.S., it was a serious impediment to labor organization so long as courts could compel strikers to return to work. It was first used in the 1880's and became well known in labor disputes during the PULLMAN STRIKE (1894). The CLAYTON ANTITRUST ACT (1914) largely exempted unions from antitrust laws, but the injunction remained a rigorous antitrust weapon, and it was used especially during the 1920's. The NORRIS-LA GUARDIA ANTI-INJUNCTION ACT (1932) specified union actions that might not be enjoined, and similar laws in many states soon legalized union objectives previously deemed unwarrantable. The TAFT-HARTLEY ACT (1947) restored to the courts some power over injunctions, but only the government can request their issuance against secondary boycotts and strikes that are outside its jurisdiction. Like the WRIT OF MANDAMUS, which it resembles, the injunction is now usually applied only as an extraordinary remedy.

INNESS, GEORGE (1825–94), New York landscape painter, began his career in the literal, romantic vein of the Hudson River School. In his European travels he absorbed the techniques of the Barbizon group, with its insistence upon unpretentious rendering of landscape. His own style became increasingly free and rich in color, developing a wide range of light effects and conveying his mystical vision of the world of nature. Characteristic of his ability to control different intensities of light are *Delaware Water Gap* (Metropolitan Museum), and *Rainbow after a Storm* (Chicago Art Institute).

Institute for Advanced Study, at Princeton, New Jersey, was chartered (1930) as a research center of study beyond the graduate level, and opened (1933) under the direction of ABRAHAM FLEXNER. Endowed by Louis Bamberger and his sister Mrs. Felix Fuld, it includes schools of politics, economics, mathematics, and the humanities. In 1965, with an endowment of $30,811,000 and a faculty of 31, it enrolled 105 research scholars.

Instrumentalism is the philosophical view which holds that man, through the use of ideas, can create his own world. That is, in the course of evolution thought becomes an instrument for adjustment and survival. Among Americans the thesis was most fully developed by JOHN DEWEY and GEORGE H. MEAD.

Insular Cases, a series of U.S. Supreme Court decisions from 1901 to 1922, defined the constitutional status of the outlying possessions of the U.S. American dependencies were judged either 'incorporated' or 'unincorporated,' and the question of what constitutes incorporation depends on the basis of fact and intention as revealed in Congressional legislation. Thus Hawaii and Alaska were declared incorporated (*Hawaii* v. *Mankichi,* 1903; *Rasmussen* v. *U.S.,* 1905), but Puerto Rico was unincorporated (*Balzac* v. *Porto Rico,* 1922) despite the fact that its inhabitants had been U.S. citizens since 1917. But unincorporated territories are not foreign, and their exports are not controlled by American customs duties unless by special act of Congress (*De Lima* v. *Bidwell,* 1901). Congress may impose these duties as it sees fit (*Dorr* v. *U.S.,* 1904). This situation gave Congress, in the words of Chief Justice Fuller, the power to acquire a province and 'keep it like a disembodied shade, in an intermediate state of ambiguous existence.'

The Court further distinguished between 'fundamental' rights and 'procedural' rights. Fundamental rights were extended to all who come under the sovereignty of the U.S., but procedural rights (such as trial by jury) were extended to inhabitants of unincorporated territories only when Congress so specified. No Colonial Office was ever established in the U.S., since the government was reluctant to admit the existence of an Empire. Thus the advocates of both high tariff and territorial expansion, when they were in power, could eat their cake and have it, by maintaining a tariff wall against insular products that competed with home-grown products. During the brief period of their existence, the nation's colonies were administered with a degree of improvisation.

Insular possessions of the U.S., see *Territories;* also *Trust Territory.*

INSULL, SAMUEL (1859–1938), English-born public utilities financier, was high in management of the Edison industrial holdings before he gained control (1910) of the transit system of Chicago. He then began to build a mammoth interlocking directorate, ultimately controlling one-eighth of the nation's electric power. He was chairman of 65 companies and director of 85 when his utilities empire collapsed (1932), taking down with it thousands of small investors. Insull fled to Greece, which had no extradition treaty with the U.S. Upon his return he was vindicated of the charge of embezzlement, but the methods he had employed raised doubts whether those in control of the corporate life of America were motivated by ideals of honorable conduct.

Insurance companies, on a very modest scale, were first established in the American colonies at Philadelphia (1721) and Boston (1724), chiefly for underwriting marine policies. At Charleston a mutual fire insurance society was organized in 1735, and the first life insurance group was formed at Philadelphia in 1759. Little attention was paid to mortality statistics until Professor Edward Wigglesworth of Harvard in 1789 compiled the earliest American mortality table. By 1800 more than 30 insurance companies were writing policies on a variety of risks. New York was the first to enact state laws (1849) to regulate insurance practices, because poorly financed or badly managed organizations had often gone into bankruptcy due to lack of such regulation.

Massachusetts established the first state insurance department in 1855, headed (1858–66) by ELIZUR WRIGHT, who instituted important reforms, especially in the building of sound reserves to give stability to the business. New York set up a like department in 1859. By 1900 insurance companies were among the most important financial institutions in the U.S., with assets aggregating many hundreds of millions of dollars. At the same time, the need for more strictly regulated state insurance commissions was dramatically revealed after CHARLES E. HUGHES in New York (1906–7) and LOUIS D. BRANDEIS in Massachusetts (1906) had conducted investigations of corrupt insurance practices.

At the present time insurances include life, health, savings, education, property loss, unemployment, and social security, with total assets under Federal, state, and private administration reaching astronomical figures. In the U.S. insurance now influences family financial planning from the cradle to the grave.

'Insurgents,' see *Progressive party.*

Integration, see *Brown* v. *Board of Education.*

Interchangeable parts, see *'American system,' Invention.*

Intercolonial relations, see *New England Confederacy* (1643); *Albany Plan of Union* (1754); *Stamp Act Congress* (1765); *Committees of Correspondence* (1772); *Continental Congress* (1774–89); and *Articles of Confederation* (1781–89).

Interior, Department of the, established in 1849 as the sixth department of cabinet rank, is primarily concerned with the development and conservation of the natural resources of the nation. Its chief divisions include the GEOLOGICAL SURVEY, National Park Service, and bureaus of Reclamation, Land Management, and Mines. Secretaries of the Interior and the Presidents under whom they served are as follows.

TAYLOR

Thomas Ewing (Ohio) 1849

FILLMORE

James A. Pearce (Md.) 1850
Thomas M. T. McKennan (Pa.) 1850
Alexander H. H. Stuart (Va.) 1850

PIERCE

Robert McClelland (Mich.) 1853

BUCHANAN

Jacob Thompson (Miss.) 1857

LINCOLN

Caleb B. Smith (Ind.) 1861
John P. Usher (Ind.) 1863

A. JOHNSON
John P. Usher (Ind.) 1865
James Harlan (Iowa) 1865
Orville H. Browning (Ill.) 1866

GRANT
Jacob D. Cox (Ohio) 1869
Columbus Delano (Ohio) 1870
Zachariah Chandler (Mich.) 1875

HAYES
Carl Schurz (Mo.) 1877

GARFIELD
Samuel J. Kirkwood (Iowa) 1881

ARTHUR
Henry M. Teller (Colo.) 1882

CLEVELAND
Lucius Q. C. Lamar (Miss.) 1885
William F. Vilas (Wis.) 1888

B. HARRISON
John W. Noble (Mo.) 1889

CLEVELAND
Hoke Smith (Ga.) 1893
David R. Francis (Mo.) 1896

MCKINLEY
Cornelius N. Bliss (N.Y.) 1897
Ethan A. Hitchcock (Mo.) 1899

T. ROOSEVELT
Ethan A. Hitchcock (Mo.) 1901
James R. Garfield (Ohio) 1907

TAFT
Richard A. Ballinger (Wash.) 1909
Walter L. Fisher (Ill.) 1911

WILSON
Franklin K. Lane (Calif.) 1913
John B. Payne (Va.) 1920

HARDING
Albert B. Fall (N.M.) 1921
Hubert Work (N.M.) 1923

COOLIDGE
Hubert Work (N.M.) 1923
Roy O. West (Ill.) 1928

HOOVER
Ray Lyman Wilbur (Calif.) 1929

F. D. ROOSEVELT
Harold L. Ickes (Ill.) 1933

TRUMAN
Harold L. Ickes (Ill.) 1945
Julius A. Krug (Wis.) 1946
Oscar L. Chapman (Colo.) 1949

EISENHOWER
Douglas McKay (Ore.) 1953
Fred A. Seaton (Neb.) 1956

KENNEDY
Stewart L. Udall (Ariz.) 1961

L. B. JOHNSON
Stewart L. Udall (Ariz.) 1963

Interior decoration, comprising adornment and furnishings of buildings, for the early American colonists was usually a matter of adapting native woods and homespun fabrics to household needs. Only the wealthy could afford the imported craft or fabric of silversmith, cabinetmaker, and linen draper. Dishes were of wood or pewter. The styles adopted customarily followed traditional patterns, and some, such as those of the Pennsylvania Germans, of the French settlers in Louisiana, and of the Spanish in the Southwest, have persisted into the 20th century. In the late colonial period the skill of such craftsmen as PAUL REVERE (silversmith) and SAMUEL MC INTIRE (woodcarver) supplemented the importations, especially from France and England. The styles of the 19th and 20th centuries have been displayed in various WORLD'S FAIRS. See *Furniture*.

Interlocking directorate is a method of potential monopoly control, since it is a system in which a member of the board of directors of one corporation is simultaneously a member of similar boards in related industries. The PUJO COMMITTEE (1912) was set up by Congress to investigate such 'money trusts.' Its nationally publicized revelations inspired Louis Brandeis's book, *Other People's Money,* and the CLAYTON ANTITRUST ACT (1914), which Brandeis influenced. But though the Act sought to curb the interlocking directorates of banks and industrial combinations, the complicated exceptions to its restrictions have led to court interpretations that have reduced the importance of the law.

Internal improvements, the program for building turnpikes, bridges, canals, and railroads, first became a serious political issue when the question was raised whether such construction should go forward at Federal expense, since the Constitution made no specific provision in such matters. The first congressional appropriation for interstate internal improvements was provided in 1806 for construction of the CUMBERLAND ROAD.

Monroe (in 1822) and Jackson (in 1830) vetoed road bills on the ground of unconstitutionality, and although Clay, Webster, and the Whig party in general favored such government spending, the states usually met the expense.

After the Mexican War (1848) railroad surveys and the Federal program for the construction of transcontinental wagon roads increased the awareness of Congress to the growing need of Federal support in such ventures, and before the Civil War the government allotted subsidies to mail carriers to build roads. Today the cost of constructing and maintaining the links that bind the nation together is apportioned among Federal, state, and local authorities.

Internal revenue is an excise tax derived from goods produced and consumed inside a country. First developed by Holland in the 17th century, such taxes were established by law in England in 1643 and introduced into the American colonies. The federal government used them first in 1791, but strong opposition led to their repeal in 1802. They were levied again during the War of 1812 and again repealed (1817). Although widely applied during the Civil War, by 1883 only liquor and tobacco were taxed. The temporary increase during the Spanish-American War was greatly extended during both World Wars. At present both Federal and state excise taxes are widely applied on a great variety of items. U.S. Internal Revenue collections in 1965 exceeded $14,700,000,000.

Internal Security Act (1951), see *McCarran Act.*

International Bank, see *World Bank.*

International Broadcasting Service, see *Voice of America.*

International Court of Justice, the principal judicial body within the United Nations, superseded the World Court of the LEAGUE OF NATIONS. Its fifteen judges are elected for nine-year terms by the General Assembly and the Security Council, voting independently. Its competence is limited to disputes concerning the interpretation of treaties, questions of international law, and alleged breaches of obligation.

International Geophysical Year was the eighteen-month period (1 July 1957—31 December 1958) during which 60,000 scientists from all nations participated in studies of the earth, the oceans, the atmosphere, and the sun. Discovery of the VAN ALLEN BELTS of radiation has been called the most significant find of the I.G.Y. U.S. scientists who participated were supported by a $39,000,000 grant from Congress to the National Science Foundation. A summary report was published as *Assault on the Unknown* (1961).

International Labor Organization, see *League of Nations.*

International Monetary Fund (1945) was authorized by Congress following the BRETTON WOODS CONFERENCE. It is an agency related to the United Nations and is designed to maintain stable exchange rates and discourage restrictions on the transfer of funds from nation to nation. (Without a central agency such restrictions become haphazard.) With more than $15,000,000,000 in gold and national currencies, the I.M.F. is the world's largest source of quickly available international credit. In 1965 its resources were obtained from payments by 102 member nations.

International News Service, founded (1906) by W. R. HEARST as a service to his own papers, subsequently sold its services to other newspapers, and by 1948 was serving 2400 papers and radio stations throughout the world. The INS ranked in size next to the ASSOCIATED PRESS and the UNITED PRESS. In 1958 it merged with the United Press to form the United Press International.

International style in architecture combines an interest in modern materials (reinforced concrete, steel, opaque walls replaced by glass) with functional design. It began to affect American architecture during the 1920's. A leading German practitioner of the International style, WALTER GROPIUS, came to the U.S. in 1937. The wide popularity of the style derived from the appeal of new materials and techniques, although it has been criticized for its impersonality.

Interstate Commerce Commission (ICC), the second permanent FEDERAL REGULA-

TORY COMMISSION, was created by Congress (1887) to regulate commerce among the states. It provided that all railroad charges should be 'reasonable and just,' and specifically prohibited pooling, rebates, discrimination, and higher charges for short hauls than for long ones. The Commission was authorized to investigate the management of railroads, summon witnesses, and compel the production of company books and papers, but its orders did not have the binding force of a court decree. The immediate practical results of the Interstate Commerce Act were feeble, since the railroads used a variety of devices to circumvent its provisions, and decisions of the Commission (which did not have the power to fix rates) met serious reversals in Supreme Court decisions. By 1898 the body was reduced to an agency chiefly engaged in collecting and publishing statistics.

The ELKINS ACT (1903) was aimed at the rebate evil, but it did not go very far. Incessant demands led to amendments that steadily increased the authority of the Commission. Such were the HEPBURN ACT (1906), the MANN-ELKINS ACT (1910), the ESCH-CUMMINS ACT (1920), the EMERGENCY RAILROAD TRANSPORTATION ACT (1933), and the MOTOR CARRIER ACT (1935). By the REED-BULWINKLE ACT (1948) regulation of all monopoly business practices came under the jurisdiction of the eleven-member board, whose powers today extend over all carriers of interstate commerce.

Interventionist movements, the attempts of European states to intervene in the affairs of American sovereignties, occurred overtly three times during the 19th century. In 1825 England's foreign minister, George Canning, by his official recognition of Mexican and Colombian regimes, sought to create a balance of power in Latin America. Writing of the event, he said, 'Spanish America is free, and if we do not mismanage our affairs sadly, she is English.' Mexico signed a commercial treaty with England, but the death of Canning (then prime minister) in 1827 forestalled the development of spheres of influence, since his successor, Lord Goderich, was both conciliatory and inept.

In 1843 France and England urged Mexico to recognize the independence of Texas, but since the Mexican cabinet was in no position to recognize a separate Texas state, the matter, as far as European influence was concerned, came to an end. The third effort occurred in 1864, when a French army, occupying Mexico City, put Maximilian of Austria on the imperial throne. The U.S. government refused to recognize the puppet emperor, who was later ousted and shot by a republican army (1867). The real tide that turned events against European influence was the sentiment that welled up throughout Europe favoring the Union cause after publication of Lincoln's Emancipation Proclamation. At the time Spain was toying with the idea of converting Santo Domingo into a province. But so powerful was the sentiment abroad for the Union cause that European governments could not negotiate a balance of power by playing Confederate interests against those of the Union, and the Spanish, French, and English interventionist movements collapsed.

Intolerable Acts, see *Coercive Acts.*

Invention, as a technological innovation applied to agriculture and the industrial arts, has a history in the U.S. closely associated with population and territorial expansion. The flour mill (1780) of OLIVER EVANS was an early response to labor shortage in a period of land exploitation. When SAMUEL SLATER first spun cotton by a power loom (1790), he created the means by which New England developed its large textile industry. The cotton gin of ELI WHITNEY not only helped to build a 'cotton kingdom' in the South after 1793, but enormously sharpened political issues by extending slave territory. Whitney's invention (1798) of machine tools to manufacture interchangeable parts doomed the artisan era, and by pointing the way toward mass production, it became the most revolutionary technical achievement in American history. JOHN FITCH successfully launched a steam vessel in 1787, and the improvements of JOHN STEVENS and ROBERT FULTON made upstream river transport commercially feasible by 1807.

The steamboat bred industrial centers along inland waterways, and inspired PETER COOPER to apply the principle of steam locomotion to railroads. In the expanding West after 1831 farming was converted into a large-scale enterprise by the grain reaper of CYRUS MC CORMICK, whose invention was a factor in making the East dependent on the West for wheat, and in creating an additional necessity for union. But the greatest stimulus to unity, next to the railroad, developed from the discoveries of JOSEPH HENRY, who as physicist demonstrated that induced currents could operate an electromagnetic telegraph. SAMUEL F. B. MORSE put Henry's ideas into commercial operation (1844), and thence grew concepts of the first successfully built dynamo (1881), now developed into the huge turbines of hydroelectric plants.

Four other inventions of the 1840's have special significance. CHARLES GOODYEAR, by improving his process for vulcanizing rubber, made possible the vast rubber industry. The invention of the rotary press by RICHARD HOE created the means for mass communication. JOHN ERICSSON designed the screw propeller, and the sewing machine devised by ELIAS HOWE opened the way for the ready-made garment industry. Other inventions of that time include the passenger elevator (1854) of ELISHA OTIS, which made the skyscraper feasible; and the typewriter (1868), patented by CHRISTOPHER SHOLES, which improved business efficiency. Ranching on the Great Plains was revolutionized after JOSEPH GLIDDEN created BARBED WIRE, and when OTTMAN MERGENTHALER invented the linotype (1884), mass circulation of newspapers became possible.

The social and cultural shape of the 20th century was foreshadowed by the invention of the telephone (ALEXANDER BELL, 1876), the microphone (EMILE BERLINER, 1877), the phonograph and the incandescent lamp (THOMAS EDISON, 1877–79), and photographic processing (GEORGE EASTMAN, 1880). Later inventions, especially in the field of electricity and electronics, have proliferated to create the mass media of motion pictures, radio, and television. Developments in metallurgy and improvement in combustion engines have built the automobile industries and transformed the flying machine of the WRIGHT brothers into airliners driven by JET PROPULSION.

The individualistic inventor no longer exists. Edison first created a 'factory' for the manufacture of ideas in his laboratories, but the concept of team research and development was inaugurated (1900) when WILLIS WHITNEY became director of the research laboratory of General Electric Company. Such teams of highly skilled technicians, under the guidance of research scientists, pool their knowledge, and their combined efforts enormously increase the rate of discovery of new scientific principles and their application in new products.

Investment banking, developed as a means of furthering commerce, acts primarily to finance new enterprises by the sale of securities. (Such in effect was the function of the JOINT-STOCK COMPANIES organized to finance American colonization.) JAY COOKE, the first large-scale U.S. private investment banker, acted as the Treasury's fiscal agent during the Civil War. Soon thereafter A. J. DREXEL and J. P. MORGAN, operating in the field of railroads, helped establish the means of trade that support COMMERCIAL BANKING.

Investment business reforms, see *Truth in Securities Act (1933)* and *Securities and Exchange Commission (1934)*.

Iowa, first explored by MARQUETTE and JOLLIET (1673), was long dominated by Sioux Indians, and it derives its name from a Siouan tribe. It was part of the Louisiana Purchase (1803), and after BLACK HAWK was subdued (1832) a rush of settlers established homesteads. It became Iowa Territory in 1838, and in 1846 was admitted to the Union as the 29th state. European immigration after 1850, chiefly from Germany and Scandinavia, helped create an agricultural commonwealth of small towns and independent farmers. Their antislavery sympathies not only supplied a large number of troops to the Union forces but made it one of the chief breadbaskets for the North during the Civil War.

With a soil of remarkable fertility, Iowa remains 95 per cent farmland today, and is the nation's leading producer of corn and hogs. It is second in the production of cattle, soybeans, and oats. Des Moines, the capital since 1857, is the commercial center, with a population (1960) of 209,000. Since World

War II industries have rapidly multiplied, ranging in a wide diversity of products from railroad equipment to vending machines, and bringing in a gross income (1965) of several billion dollars. Among the state's score of institutions of higher learning are the nationally eminent University of Iowa (Iowa City, est. 1847), and the Iowa State University (Ames, est. 1858).

IRELAND, JOHN (1838–1918), Irish-born Roman Catholic prelate, was taken in his boyhood to St. Paul, Minnesota, educated by French missionaries, and after his ordination (1861) served as a chaplain in the Civil War. Coadjutor bishop of St. Paul (after 1875), and archbishop (1888), he exercised considerable influence over the immigrant Irish, whom he urged to leave the slums of the East for cheap land in the West. He organized settlements and a Catholic Colonization Bureau for these newcomers. Always independent and outspoken, he declared his preference for state schools if they would teach morals and religion, and he experimented with a combination of parochial and state instruction. As a leading churchman helping to shape the social growth of the nation he was consulted by Presidents and business leaders alike.

Iron Act (1750), passed by Parliament, sought to maintain the colonial supply of iron for English Midland industries by forbidding further erection of iron-finishing mills in the colonies. The injunction was flagrantly disregarded.

Ironclads, see *Hampton Roads, Battle of.*

'Iron curtain,' as a term connoting Soviet control in communist countries, gained currency after Winston Churchill used it in an address at Fulton, Missouri (March 1946), saying that Russia was manipulating affairs in eastern Europe behind an 'iron curtain.' By extension, 'bamboo curtain' came to signify communist control in China.

Iron manufacture began in the colonies when JOHN WINTHROP, JR., built furnaces and forges at Saugus (Lynn), Massachusetts in 1644. Other ironworks followed in New England and New Jersey, but the industry made little progress during the 17th century. After 1720 its development was remarkably rapid, and by 1760 it was thriving wherever waterpower and wood (charcoal) for smelting were near surface deposits of iron ore. At the outbreak of the War of Independence (1775) the colonies were manufacturing more iron than England and Wales together. Though usually employing no more than a few dozen hands, the companies were averaging 300 tons of pig iron annually for each furnace, and 150 tons of bar iron for each forge, and they were spread from New Hampshire to South Carolina and westward to the frontier. Southeastern Pennsylvania had already become a highly industrialized region.

As anthracite fuel became available after 1850, the iron industry moved into western Pennsylvania, and to Ohio, Kentucky, and Tennessee. Railroad expansion then revolutionized the industry by creating the era of large integrated iron mills. The Bessemer method of converting iron to steel (1856) was put into commercial use in the U.S. (1865) by A. L. HOLLEY and WILLIAM KELLY, who laid the foundations of the STEEL INDUSTRY. The chief resources in the U.S. today for iron manufacture are located in Michigan and Minnesota.

Iroquois Confederacy was a league of the MOHAWK, Oneida, Onondaga, Cayuga, and Seneca Indian tribes (known as the Five Nations), whose territory in 1609 extended across New York state from the Hudson river to Lake Erie. After the Tuscaroras in the Carolinas joined the league in 1722, it became the Six Nations. According to tradition this federation dated from the early 16th century, when various chiefs, including HIAWATHA, formed a loose union. After procuring firearms from the Dutch the Five Nations made war upon all neighboring tribes, especially the Algonquin, ERIE, and HURON, driving off some and making tributary or incorporating others.

During the 17th century and later the confederacy became the most remarkable political organization in North America, and its rule was acknowledged from the Ottawa river to the Tennessee, and from the Kennebec to Lake Michigan. It exerted an influence on American history out of all proportion to its numbers. Although the tribes probably never exceeded 15,000 at any one time, until well into the 18th century they held two mighty European empires in check.

Intelligent and brave, during the French and Indian Wars the Iroquois were allies of the British and warm admirers of SIR WILLIAM JOHNSON, under whose control they stemmed French penetration westward through the Mohawk valley. All except the Oneida and the Tuscarora supported the Loyalists in the War of Independence. Notable leaders include SEQUOYA, CORNPLANTER, LOGAN, JOSEPH BRANT, and RED JACKET. Today many Iroquois Indians are established in professional careers, and their skilled artisans are especially adept as steelworkers in the construction of skyscrapers.

Irrigation, see *Conservation movement; Flood control.*

IRVING, WASHINGTON (1783–1859), was the gifted son of an affluent New York merchant. His elder brothers, William Irving (1766–1821), who was influential in state politics, and Peter Irving (1772–1838), physician and journalist, affectionately guided the career of their much younger brother who, while studying for the law, amused himself by writing essays about the city's past and present. After the appearance (1809) of 'Knickerbocker's' burlesque *History of New York,* Washington Irving dominated the KNICKERBOCKER GROUP of writers for a decade. With publication of *The Sketch Book* (1820) he was acclaimed at home and abroad as the leading American man of letters.

While attached to the American legations in Madrid and London (1826–32), he wrote his biography of Columbus (1828; rev. ed., 3 vols., 1848–49), and of the companions of Columbus (1831), still regarded as important, if uncritical, biographies of the discoverers. His journey into the Western frontier across Oklahoma he recorded factually in *A Tour on the Prairies* (1835), a narrative more detailed and alive than any other dealing with that region.

From his reading about the Far West and from records furnished him by John Jacob Astor, Irving wrote *Astoria* (1836), and *Captain Bonneville* (1837), works still useful as studies of the fur trade. When Irving learned that Prescott was undertaking a history of the conquest of Mexico, he abandoned his own project on the subject. A literary idol in his lifetime as creator of such characters as Diedrich Knickerbocker and Rip Van Winkle, Irving remains important even now as a literary historian and biographer. Much of his research was derivative, but his considerable talents as a writer of history reveal a rare combination of scholarship and good writing.

The standard biography is that by Stanley T. Williams (2 vols., 1935).

Isle Royale National Park (est. 1940), 133,000 acres, is the largest island in Lake Superior, and a part of Michigan. It is a rugged, forested wilderness with a large moose herd and pre-Columbian copper mines.

Isolationism, the term applied to that foreign policy of the U.S. which has advocated nonparticipation in alliances or in the affairs of other nations, derives its spirit from Washington's proclamation of neutrality in 1793. His Farewell Address (1796) enunciated the doctrine generally acknowledged as the foundation of U.S. isolationist policy, which endured until World War II: 'Europe has a set of primary interests, which to us have none, or a very remote relation . . . It is our true policy to steer clear of permanent alliances, with any portion of the foreign world.' His principle (which did not exclude temporary alliances) was further confirmed by the MONROE DOCTRINE (1823).

Avoiding diplomatic commitments was relatively easy in the early days of the Republic, when economic and political rivalries between the U.S. and other nations were of little consequence, but conditions had greatly altered 90 years later. In his message to Congress on 4 September 1914 President Wilson said of World War I: 'We had no part in making it. But it is here. It affects us directly and palpably almost as if we were participants in the circumstances which gave rise to it.' The strong desire throughout the nation to remain neutral, which ended when the U.S. joined the Allies, became almost an obsession when the war was over in 1918. Republicans (except for their internationalist wing) were convinced that alliances of any sort would lead to involvement in future wars, and defeated Wilson's hope that the U.S. would join the LEAGUE OF NATIONS. Isolationist sentiment, strongly supported by German and Irish communities (especially in the Middle West), continued to shape American foreign policy almost to the brink of World War II. The activities of the NYE COMMITTEE (1934–36) strengthened such feeling and set the domestic background for a series of NEUTRALITY ACTS when Italy attacked Ethiopia (1935), the Spanish Civil War erupted (1936), and World War II began (1939).

But in 1941, as in 1917, the U.S. was swept into global war, and in 1945 it was the U.S. that proposed formation of the United Nations to succeed the moribund League of Nations. The ablest leader of the isolationist bloc during the 1930's, Senator ARTHUR VANDENBERG, then reversed himself, became the champion of the interventionist wing of the Republican party, and supported the bipartisan effort of President Roosevelt to relinquish traditional isolationism. Once the principles set forth in the TRUMAN DOCTRINE (1947), the MARSHALL PLAN (1947), and similar programs had become established, the influence of isolationism in national policy greatly decreased. Present-day isolationists favor political and military withdrawal from overseas bases as well as the establishment of a 'fortress America,' unhampered by the pressures and obligations of alliances and international associations. But with all nations rapidly increasing their ties and commitments on a global scale in an age when nuclear warfare can be touched off at a moment's notice, the question rises whether isolationism can in the future be a political issue.

Item veto, see *Veto.*

IVES, CHARLES [EDWARD] (1874–1954), Connecticut-born composer, received his first musical instruction from his father, George Ives, a distinguished bandmaster. Strongly influenced by his father's acoustical experiments, he began composing before his admission to Yale (1894), where he studied with Parker and Buck. He soon realized that a career in music was impractical, for he was already composing in a style that baffled his teachers and the public. From the time of his graduation (1898) until 1930 he very successfully conducted an insurance brokerage in New York.

His mature music, all written between 1898 and 1921, has deep roots in American institutions, letters, and geography. Hymn-tunes, folk-songs, patriotic marches, and popular ragtime often generated his larger pieces, such as the four *Violin Sonatas* (1908–15) and the *Second Quartet* (1913), with their polytonal or polymetric situations. Although much of Ives's music is serious in purpose, it is streaked with a rough humor expressed in *non sequiturs,* false conclusions, parody, and elisions. In 1919 Ives privately published his *Second Piano Sonata: Concord, Massachusetts, 1840–60* (1915), which John Kirkpatrick first publicly performed (1939) in New York. A monumental and characteristic work, like many others it is accompanied by a discerning essay setting forth the artistic plan. In 1922 Ives published *114 Songs,* the core of some 150 melodies, which show a broad gamut of expression and style. Ives did not participate in musical life and rarely attended concerts. Recognition of Ives by the general public came after 1940; in 1947 his *Symphony No. 3* (1904) belatedly won the Pulitzer Prize in music. A large collection of his manuscripts, of which at present only a small fraction has been published, is at Yale.

Iwo Jima, Battle of (19 February–17 March 1945), one of the famous engagements in the 'stepping-stone' operation leading to the end of the Pacific campaign in World War II, was begun when two divisions of U.S. Marines landed on the most important of the Volcanic Islands, site of a Japanese air base 750 miles from Tokyo. After bitter fighting the U.S. forces took Mt. Suribachi on 23 February, scene of the famous flag-raising memorialized by the bronze statue in Arlington National Cemetery. Conquest of the island was completed three weeks later, after a steady, bloody advance against the holed-up enemy. The Marine casualty list (nearly 5000 killed and 15,000 wounded) is a measure of the determined resistance of the Japanese.

I.W.W., see *Industrial Workers of the World.*

J

JACKSON, ANDREW (1767–1845), 7th President of the U.S. (1829–37), was born on the South Carolina frontier to immigrant parents from northern Ireland. As a lad of thirteen he fought in the Revolution. Orphaned at fourteen by the death of his mother, he educated himself by reading law, was admitted to the bar (1787), and upon his appointment in 1788 as solicitor for the western district of North Carolina (now Tennessee), settled at Nashville. There he built his home, 'The HERMITAGE,' where he lived as a cotton planter in the intervals of his political career, and where he died and is buried. His marriage to Rachel Donelson before she was technically divorced from her first husband gave his enemies an opportunity to attack his 'scandalous' behavior, a circumstance which long continued to prove vexatious.

He entered politics by helping to draft the Tennessee constitution, and served as the new state's first Representative in Congress (1796). He left the Senate (1797–98) to become judge of the Tennessee Supreme Court (1798–1804), and in 1802 was appointed major general of the state militia. Personal feuds led to his temporary political retirement, but after his militia forces had suppressed a rebellion of the Creek Indians in Mississippi Territory (1814), he was commissioned major general in the U.S. Army. His decisive defeat of the British in the battle of New Orleans (1815), although it had no effect on the outcome of the War of 1812 (the peace treaty had already been signed), won him national attention as a military hero and put him in line for high office should he seek it.

While commanding in the Seminole War he invaded Florida, and created an international incident in the ARBUTHNOT AND AMBRISTER AFFAIR (1818). But his seizure of Spanish Pensacola and other towns led to the signing of the ADAMS-ONÍS TREATY (1819) by which Florida was purchased, and thus gave 'Old Hickory,' as his western admirers then called him, an opportunity to move onto the national scene. He became a standard-bearer of the Democratic party and the leader of what was later designated JACKSONIAN DEMOCRACY. In the presidential election of 1824 he polled the largest popular vote, but since no candidate had an electoral majority (Jackson 99, Adams 84, Crawford 41, Clay 37), the House, influenced by Clay, voted for Adams. Four years later Jackson was swept into office by a decisive electoral vote (Jackson 178, Adams 83). The inauguration of this backwoodsman brought the 'rabble' to the White House reception, and Washington society shuddered.

Jackson's inaugural address summed up his policy in a sentence: 'The Federal Constitution must be obeyed, state rights preserved, our national debt must be paid, direct taxes and loans avoided, and the Federal Union preserved.' His eight years in office took the stamp of his personality, a compound of loyalties and credulity, honesty and quarrelsomeness. On occasion his policies were determined by his 'KITCHEN CABINET,' a small group of favorite advisers. Party was paramount, the SPOILS SYSTEM was developed, and personal relationships were of utmost importance. The affair of PEGGY EATON helped break up his cabinet, but there were other issues more fundamentally important. Calhoun, who had vigorously opposed the protective Tariff of 1832, promulgated the doctrine of NULLIFICATION and resigned the vice presidency. Standing firmly for union, Jackson steered passage of the FORCE BILL (1833). The cleavage was partly bridged by the COMPROMISE TARIFF OF 1833, but meanwhile the question whether the BANK OF THE U.S. should be rechartered had been made the big issue in the campaign of 1832. Jackson won overwhelmingly in the electoral vote (Jackson 219, Clay 49).

Jackson's second Administration, more bitterly resented by conservatives than his first, was dominated by the bank issue. He selected his so-called 'pet banks' by allocating Federal money to selected state banks, but the issuance of his SPECIE CIRCULAR (1836), and events leading to the PANIC OF 1837, made his willingness to retire to 'The Hermitage' in 1837 more certain. In that year he failed in his effort to annex Texas after its revolution, an acquisition that would have gratified expansionists.

Self-willed and capricious, Jackson was a powerful democratic leader. With all the virtues and many of the faults of the American frontiersman, he was personally dignified and courteous, and he maintained to the end the 'gentleman's code' that had led him in earlier years to fight several duels. He virtually remade the presidency, which under his predecessors had become closely identified with the cabinet and dependent upon Congress. He was the first President to make bold use of the veto power. Few Presidents have accomplished so much, and only Lincoln has surpassed him as the image of the democratic hero. He was indeed the symbol of an age.

Biographies include those by John S. Bassett (2 vols., 1925), and Marquis James (2 vols., 1933–37). See also A. M. Schlesinger, Jr., *The Age of Jackson* (1945).

JACKSON, Helen Hunt (1831–85), was born in Amherst, Massachusetts, married an army engineer, and some years after the tragic deaths of her husband and two children she remarried and moved to Colorado Springs. Becoming deeply interested in the wrongs done to the Indian, she published a severe attack on Federal violations of Indian treaties in *A Century of Dishonor* (1881). This earned her an appointment as a special commissioner to investigate the situation of the Mission Indians of California. She became the Harriet Beecher Stowe of the Indians when she wrote her popular romantic novel, *Ramona* (1884), which depicted the violent disruption of a Spanish-Indian paradise by brutal gold seekers. Her writings stimulated the rise of Indian Rights Associations in various cities and finally the passage of the Dawes Act of 1887, which aimed to assimilate the Indian and ultimately to grant him citizenship.

JACKSON, Robert Houghwout (1892–1954), a strong advocate of New Deal policies, was appointed U.S. Solicitor General (1938), U.S. Attorney General (1940), and Associate Justice of the U.S. Supreme Court (1941), where his opinions continued to reflect his opposition to vested interests. In 1945–46 he was chief counsel for the prosecution in the International Military Tribunal at the Nuremberg WAR CRIMES TRIALS. One of the Supreme Court's greatest opinion writers, Jackson expressed his legal philosophy in *The Struggle for Judicial Supremacy* (1940), and *The Supreme Court in the American System of Government* (1955).

JACKSON, Thomas Jonathan ['Stonewall'] (1824–63), born in West Virginia, graduated from the U.S. Military Academy (1846), served in the Mexican War, and taught mathematics at Virginia Military Institute (1851–61). At the outbreak of the Civil War he served as a field officer in the Confederate army until as commander of a brigade at the first battle of BULL RUN he earned his sobriquet by standing (in the words of a fellow officer) 'like a stone wall.' Given command in the Shenandoah campaign (1861–62), he handled his strategy so expertly that he immobilized a large Union force. Although his offensive tactics in the SEVEN DAYS' BATTLES before Richmond were disappointing (June–July 1862), he redeemed himself brilliantly in the second battle of Bull Run (August) and ANTIETAM (September), and he assumed corps command at FREDERICKSBURG in December. He was at the pinnacle of his capabilities at CHANCELLORSVILLE (May 1863), where the well-earned southern victory was too dearly won. Reconnoitering in semidarkness between the lines, he was mortally wounded by one of his own sharpshooters.

This devout Calvinist, with his arresting personal quirks, was Lee's ablest lieutenant, and next to Lee the South's greatest and most loved general. At the head of his troops, who idolized him, Jackson was a Cromwell, and the supreme realist who could answer the query whether he regretted seeing brave Yankees fall: 'No. Shoot them all. I do not wish them to be brave.'

Jacksonian Democracy grew up within the Republican party, which appeared to be united during the 'era of good feelings' under Monroe (1817–25). Actually the party was breaking up into factions, conservative (Jeffersonian) and democratic (Jacksonian), and the presidential nomination of Jackson in 1824 was largely the result of state politicians angling for national power. Although the differences of the factions varied from region to region, in general the Jacksonian group wished to level all political inequalities that still remained in the state constitutions. In the northern states this political temper had largely abolished property qualifications for the franchise and created an electorate at odds with the Jeffersonian school. Jacksonians were a new breed of professional politicians, who, having enjoyed state patronage, wished to banquet on the emoluments of Federal office. At their best they represented a genuine aspiration toward equality, but the nature of such a leveling process invites the demagogue.

Able and ingratiating men of humble origin, such as James Buchanan of Pennsylvania and Martin Van Buren of New York, followed the obvious strategy of consolidating the democratic factions of other states, and looked for a national figure to carry their junto to victory. In the person of Andrew Jackson, hero of New Orleans, self-educated Westerner, and an aggressive leader, they had the ideal standard-bearer for democracy. Although the Jackson democrats narrowly lost the 1824 election, they won it handsomely four years later in the 'revolution' of 1828. This was not a triumph of western radicalism over eastern capitalism, but the emergence of noncapitalists (farmers and artisans) in all sections, supported by the leading intellectuals of the day. The movement continued in diluted form into the administration of Andrew Johnson.

Jacobin clubs were democratic societies formed at Philadelphia and elsewhere after the arrival of Citizen GENÊT in 1793. Modeled on the Jacobin Club in Paris, they sought to arouse sympathy for the French Revolution. Representative of all intellectual 'leftist' groups, they opposed the Federalist faction in Washington's administration and vilified Washington himself. At various periods in American politics those whom their opponents have judged unduly liberal have been called Jacobin.

JAMES, EDMUND JANES (1855–1925), while professor of political and social science at Pennsylvania (1884–95), founded the American Economic Association (1885) and the American Academy of Political and Social Science (1889). At Chicago from 1896 to 1901, he later was president of Northwestern University (1902–4), and of the University of Illinois (1904–20). His many studies of national and municipal economic programs include *Growth of Great Cities* (1900), and *The Land Grant Act of 1862* (1910).

JAMES, HENRY (1811–82), was a lecturer and writer on religious and social themes. Son of a wealthy Albany merchant, he rebelled against his Princeton Theological School training and for a time found a solution to his philosophical problems in the teachings of Swedenborg. Intimately associated with FOURIERISM, he was respected by such independent thinkers as Emerson and Carlyle, on whom he frequently lectured. He desired his sons to be 'citizens of the world' and gave them a remarkably eclectic education by way of travel and private tutors, and both Henry and William James made international reputations.

JAMES, HENRY (1843–1916), son of the elder HENRY JAMES, determined on a career of letters. A detached spectator of life, sensitive, cultivated, and brilliant, he is now recognized as one of America's foremost novelists and a literary critic of the first rank. In his own day, however, his brother WILLIAM JAMES thought him too Europeanized (Henry James became a British subject in 1915), and Mark Twain said that he would rather be condemned to John Bunyan's heaven than read a James novel.

James was a pioneer in psychological realism and looked upon Hawthorne as his master. He deliberately invoked the profession of what he called the 'obstinate finality' of the artist, whom he depicted as writer, painter, or actor, by placing him as a pilgrim into situations, and his acute moral sense predominates in his stories and plays. His achievements extend from *Daisy Miller* (1879) to *The Golden Bowl* (1904). His literary criticisms were gathered by R. P. Blackmur in 1934.

JAMES, JESSE [WOODSON] (1847–82), born in Missouri, at fifteen joined the

Quantrill gang during the Civil War and with his brother Frank (1843–1915) led the most notorious band of outlaws in U.S. history. As specialists in train and bank robberies they inspired melodramatic legends and quantities of dime-novel literature. The reward offered for the capture of the James brothers corrupted one of the gang, who shot Jesse. Frank lived out his life in respectable obscurity on a Missouri farm.

JAMES, THOMAS (*c.* 1593–1635), English navigator, sailed from Bristol (1631) in search of the NORTHWEST PASSAGE to Asia. He explored James Bay (the southern extension of Hudson Bay) and wintered on Charlton Island. His *Strange and Dangerous Voyage* (1633) remained popular for many years, but its contribution to geographical knowledge was inconsequential. The return of James ended the first great period of Arctic explorations.

JAMES, WILLIAM (1842–1910), son of the elder HENRY JAMES and brother of HENRY JAMES the novelist, was the most distinguished American philosopher and psychologist of his time. After graduation from Harvard Medical School (1869) he joined its faculty (1872) as lecturer on physiology and anatomy. His interest began to center on physiological psychology, and he transferred to the philosophy department, where he created the first psychological laboratory in the U.S. (1876). He thus altered the character of psychology by making a laboratory science of what until then had been termed mental philosophy. The publication of his *Principles of Psychology* (1890) was epoch-making, because the work established the 'functional' approach to the subject. James held that basically mind and body are inseparable, and that since mind is a function of the physical organism, the individual as a whole adjusts to environment. In such a concept of mind as instrument, the 'deterministic' forces of biology and heredity are reconciled with choice, effort, and indeed with free will itself.

With the *Principles* behind him, James turned to problems of religion and philosophy, the field that had always basically interested him, and one in which his experience in psychophysics dictated his entirely empirical method. In *The Will to Believe* (1897) James acknowledged his debt to CHARLES SANDERS PEIRCE and the tradition of British empiricism. There and in other writings he developed Peirce's concept of PRAGMATISM, holding that the truth of an idea can be known only by the consequences to which it leads, and that in matters of faith the criterion for acceptance is the will to believe; ideas are instruments, and truth is 'only the expedient in our way of thinking.'

In *The Varieties of Religious Experience* (1902), he attempted to harmonize the conflict between religion and the apparently deterministic implications of science. There he carried forward his pragmatic theory of method, arguing that for all practical purposes items of religious faith are true when they provide emotional satisfactions. He concluded that faith harmonizes with scientific knowledge and method by denying that conflict is necessary in this never-finished universe. The psychology and philosophy of James are inseparable, and the meaning of *Varieties* cannot be understood apart from his later philosophical discussions, set forth in *Pragmatism* (1907), *A Pluralistic Universe* (1909), and especially *Essays in Radical Empiricism* (1912).

In the *Essays* James postulated that relations between things, whether binding or repelling, have functions as real as the things themselves; that sense experience is as important as the object that creates it; that ideas about things thus gain importance by virtue of the status given to the relationship. The *Essays* are radical because James opened the way still further to reconcile faith with science by viewing the universe without fixed moorings. The philosophy of James, optimistic and individualistic, and predicated on faith in human progress, was deeply related to the American faith and experience. Translated by the instrumentalism of JOHN DEWEY to the plane of social reconstruction, for nearly half a century it dominated American education.

A writer who commanded a literary style of great clarity and vigor, James championed the convictions of those who value the effort to achieve, have faith in melioration, and believe that human environment is subject to control by social intelligence. In his day his influence was compelling because his thought epitomized the dominant theme in the literature of ideas. In the light of present scientific advances, many leaders of speculative thought believe that he may yet prove to have been closer to great truth than many philosophers whose systems lead to settled conclusions.

See R. B. Perry, *The Thought and Character of William James* (2 vols., 1935).

James River, 340 miles long, rises in the Allegheny Mountains in West Virginia and winds east across Virginia to enter Chesapeake Bay. Jamestown was founded on its lower course in 1607. A tidewater estuary to Richmond, it offered the means for the development of early plantation settlements. Canals built after 1785 connected the PIEDMONT region of western Virginia with the Atlantic. In the Civil War the river figured prominently in Union attempts to capture Richmond.

JAMESON, JOHN FRANKLIN (1859–1937), after teaching history at Brown (1888–1901) and Chicago (1901–5) became director (1905–28) of the department of historical research of the Carnegie Institution, Washington, D.C. During this period he evolved the first plan for a comprehensive program of historical documentary publication by the federal government under professional guidance. Chief of the manuscript division of the Library of Congress (1928–37), he also served as chairman of the committee of management of the *Dictionary of American Biography,* and thus was largely responsible for the inauguration and completion of that monumental work. In his leadership of many historical undertakings he exercised a more profound influence on American historiography than any other scholar before or since his time. Best known of his writings is *The American Revolution Considered as a Social Movement* (1926).

Jamestown, on a peninsula near the mouth of the James river in Virginia, was established (1607) as the first permanent English settlement in America. The efficient leadership of JOHN SMITH held the colony together during the first three years, when survival demanded uncommon resourcefulness. In 1619 the first representative government in the New World (the house of burgesses) met at Jamestown, which remained the capital of Virginia until 1699, though only nominally so after 1676, when it was burned during BACON'S REBELLION. Jamestown fell into decay after the seat of government was officially shifted to Williamsburg in 1699, and today few relics remain. Since 1936 Jamestown has been a part of the Colonial National Historical Park. Archaeological discoveries on the peninsula since 1955 are leading to reconstructions and interpretations of aspects of life in 17th-century America.

JANSKY, CARL GUTHE (1905–50), after graduation from Wisconsin (1927), became a radio research engineer with the Bell Telephone Laboratories. He specialized in the study of atmospheric interference and radio waves of interstellar origin. By establishing the extra-territorial source of certain static noises, he inaugurated radio astronomy (1931), one of the great scientific innovations of the 20th century, recognized for its true significance only after World War II.

Japan (occupation of and treaties with after World War II). In accordance with the terms of the POTSDAM CONFERENCE the occupation was relatively simple, for under General Douglas MacArthur the occupation force controlled Japan through the existing machinery of the Imperial government, effecting in the process a revolution in Japanese government, education, and business. The occupation ceased when the Japanese Peace Treaty, recognizing Japan's full sovereignty, was signed at San Francisco (September 1951) by 49 nations, not including the U.S.S.R. In turn Japan acknowledged the independence of Korea, and renounced all claim to the Pacific islands formerly under her mandate.

By the U.S.–Japanese Security Treaty, signed at the same time, Japan granted the U.S. the right to maintain armed forces in Japan to provide for the security of Japan against armed attack by a third party. In 1960 this Security Treaty was amended to increase the degree of mutual co-operation in the event the peace and safety of Japan is threatened.

Japanese exclusion, notably in California, by way of discriminatory state laws during the period 1906–24, was in fact a national policy under Theodore Roosevelt's 'Gentleman's Agreement' of 1907. With the passage of the Immigration Act of 1924 such exclusion was enforced by a statute that remained in effect until the McCarran-Walter Act of 1952.

JARVES, JAMES JACKSON (1818–88), Boston-born art critic, collector, and world-traveler, began his career as editor of the weekly *Polynesian* (1840–48), the first Hawaiian newspaper. He settled in Florence soon after. His European travel books are important 'documentaries,' written to convince American travelers that their prejudices blinded them to the significance of the civilizations they were observing. They include *Parisian Sights* (1852), and *Italian Sights* (1856). *Art Hints* (1855) was his pioneer study of art teaching and schools of design, followed by others notable for their acuteness. In 1871 he deposited his distinguished collection of Italian primitives at Yale.

Jay, JOHN (1745–1829), born in New York City, was graduated from King's College (Columbia) in 1764, and practiced law in partnership with ROBERT R. LIVINGSTON. He energetically supported the patriot cause, and while a member of both Continental Congresses, wrote his notable *Address to the People of Great Britain* (1774), and served on COMMITTEES OF CORRESPONDENCE. He helped draft the constitution of New York, and later became its governor (1795–1801).

His important service in the federal government began with his appointment as minister to Spain (1780–82), peace commissioner to England (1783), and Secretary of Foreign Affairs for the Continental Congress (1784–89). His five FEDERALIST PAPERS (nos. 2, 3, 4, 5, 64) deal chiefly with the Constitution in relation to foreign affairs. Washington appointed him the first Chief Justice of the U.S. Supreme Court (1789–95), during which period Jay went to England to negotiate JAY'S TREATY. He resigned his post to conclude his years in politics as New York's governor (1795–1801).

Jay Hawks, see *Bleeding Kansas*.

Jay's Treaty (1794) was negotiated by Chief Justice JOHN JAY as minister extraordinary to London to solve friction between the U.S. and Britain that was bringing the two countries to the verge of war. Despite the TREATY OF PARIS of 1783, the British had not evacuated their military posts in the Old Northwest. Thus they still controlled the lucrative fur trade and prevented settlements in the Ohio valley. Their interference with neutral shipping by seizure and impressment was endangering Hamilton's fiscal structure by cutting off British exports to the U.S.

The treaty provided for British evacuation of the Northwest posts by 1796. It opened a limited West Indies trade to U.S. vessels, gave the U.S. a 'MOST-FAVORED-NATION' commercial status, and referred pre-Revolutionary debt claims to mixed commissions. (It ignored the issues of impressment and stolen slaves.) The treaty enraged pro-French Republicans, who felt that Jay's self-esteem had left him open to blandishments. After lengthy debate Congress ratified it and Washington signed it. In the light of history the treaty is not regarded as a notable victory for British diplomacy.

Jazz, the result of a 300-year blending of European and West African musical traditions, is an art form indigenous to the U.S. It originated during the 19th century in New Orleans, where predominantly European music patterns drew upon rhythms brought in from the West Indies. Jazz rhythms are basically marching rhythms. Military bands were immensely popular everywhere in the U.S. in the early years of the Republic, and no parade, picnic, riverboat excursion, or (in many instances) funeral was complete without a brass band. The number of such bands formed in New Orleans by Negroes, with their highly organized fraternal societies, greatly exceeded those elsewhere. Negro funerals in the city, ritualistic with tribal and illegal *vodun* drumming and chanting imported from Haiti, were major affairs among the less-educated and darker-skinned Negroes of uptown New Orleans. Although the brass-band march to the grave was solemn and formal, its return became a happy dance. The instrumentalists sang their moods by way of 'swinging' their march tunes, improvising rhythms, and thus the element of jazz was created.

In the official red-light district of New Orleans, Storyville, jazz became a full-time profession (1897–1917). There the solo pianist was established, notably JELLY ROLL MORTON, and Negro bands created the New Orleans style of jazz. The BLUES developed after 1911. Allied to jazz, RAGTIME was introduced from the Midwest after 1896.

In the early 1920's a new style emerged, represented by BIX BEIDERBECKE and labeled 'Chicago.' It substituted tension and drive for the relaxed ease of DIXIELAND playing. LOUIS ARMSTRONG gave a new dimension to improvisation when he broke away from New Orleans ensemble style. The 'jazz age' ended about 1926, but jazz rhythms had infiltrated every form of music, emerging in popular music during the 1930's as SWING and BOOGIE WOOGIE, and after World War II as BOP.

Jazz Age, the derogatory term applied to the post–World War I era of the 'LOST GENERATION,' was characterized by a determined unconventionality and glorification of youth. Such frenetic dances as the BLACK BOTTOM and the CHARLESTON are associated with this period of SPEAKEASIES and the 'shocking' behavior of the FLAPPER. Scott Fitzgerald and John Dos Passos portrayed it in fiction, John Held, Jr. in illustrations, and Hart Crane in poetry.

JEFFERSON, JOSEPH (1829–1905), born into a family of actors, spent the first twenty years of his professional life as a strolling player. He won his earliest success on the legitimate stage (1858) in comic roles as a member of Laura Keene's company. Collaborating with Dion Boucicault in 1865, he staged in London a dramatic version of *Rip Van Winkle,* which he brought to New York in 1866, and thereafter delighted two generations of theater-goers in the title role of Irving's story. He was one of the earliest American stars to establish his own road company. Although his repertory was limited chiefly to Rip and to Bob Acres in Sheridan's *The Rivals,* his performances were memorable and won him rank as the most famous 19th-century American comedian.

JEFFERSON, THOMAS (1743–1826), 3rd President of the U.S. (1801–9), was born at 'Shadwell' in Albemarle county, Virginia, a frontier wilderness in the Blue Ridge. His father Peter Jefferson, a civil engineer, was a thorough democrat, who had married into the prominent Randolph family. The vicinity remained Jefferson's lifelong home, and from that environment he absorbed his devout agrarianism. By the time he had graduated from William and Mary (1762), he had deepened his knowledge of Greek, Latin, and French (to which he soon added Anglo-Saxon, Italian, and Spanish), and developed an abiding interest in the natural sciences. He studied law with GEORGE WYTHE, was admitted to the bar (1767), and after entering the House of Burgesses (1769) was almost continuously in political service until his retirement from the presidency. His marriage (1772) to Martha Skelton was singularly happy. After her early death ten years later, he devoted his affections to their two daughters, whom he adored.

Jefferson identified himself with the aggressive anti-British group who believed that Parliament lacked authority in the colonies, which owed allegiance in their judgment only to the crown. His brilliant and widely read pamphlet, *A Summary View of the Rights of America* (1774), gave him leadership in the Revolutionary cause, and procured him the honor, as a member of the Continental Congress (1775–76), of drafting the Declaration of Independence. He then resumed his seat in the Virginia legislature, where he sought to enact laws that would replace aristocratic authority with republican ordinance. He wished to abolish entail, primogeniture, and an established church, and he hoped to create a system of general education. The first three objectives were soon secured, but Jefferson's vision of grammar and classical schools for the poor, a free state library, and a state college, was not then shared by the legislative body, which chiefly represented the planter class. He was unable to win support for his plan to manumit slaves, though he secured a humanitarian revision of the penal code.

He was twice elected governor of his state (1779–81), directing its affairs through the gloomiest period of the Revolution, when Virginia was overrun by British expeditions. To the attacks upon his administration was added the burden of his wife's illness and death. He declined renomination, occupying the interim (1781–82) by setting down his *Notes on the State of Virginia* (1784), informal essays on scientific, social, and political topics, which take rank for their speculations about geography, customs, and race.

The war was over and the need for experienced counsel in negotiating settlements was urgent. Jefferson returned to Congress (1783), where he headed the committee to consider the treaty of peace, drafted the plan for decimal coinage, and outlined the basis for the important ORDINANCE OF 1787. Congress then sent him to France (1784) to assist Franklin and Adams in drawing up treaties of commerce, and there Jefferson remained as minister (1785–89). When the new American government was formed, Washington brought Jefferson into his cabinet as the first Secretary of State (1789–94).

Although the irreconcilable differences between Jefferson and Secretary of the Treasury Alexander Hamilton were never personal, the two were antipodal in temperament and political belief. Hamilton, brisk and energetic, was a specialist in finance who envisioned the future of America as a more complex society than Jefferson hoped was necessary. Jefferson was an experienced administrator, trained abroad as well as at home, who feared tyranny more than 'mobocracy.' The schools of thought that these two great statesmen represented crystallized in the formation of political parties. Jefferson thought in terms of individual liberties, mild laws, and an agrarian society, and those who founded the DEMOCRATIC-REPUBLICAN PARTY gravitated to him. Hamilton was spokesman for those commercialist and mercantile interests that created the FEDERALIST PARTY. The disagreement of the two was made evident in December 1790 when Washington called for a cabinet opinion on Hamilton's report recommending a national bank, which Jefferson thought unconstitutional. Washington gave authority to Hamilton's judgment.

Party alignments were clearly drawn by 1793, when war broke out between England and France, and all agreed that Jefferson handled the NEUTRALITY PROCLAMATION admirably. Those who saw the French Revolution as a contest between republicanism and monarchy joined the Republican party. Those who viewed it as a phase of the age-old struggle between property and destitution (order and anarchy) became Federalists. Now antagonistic to what he believed was Hamilton's scheming, Jefferson made issues, and harmony became impossible when differences were carried by partisans into the newspapers. Washington reluctantly accepted Jefferson's resignation (December 1793), and Jefferson retired to his home, 'Monticello.'

Jefferson re-entered public life as Republican candidate for the presidency in 1796. Next to John Adams, the Federalist candidate, he received the largest number of votes, and thus (under the existing laws) became Vice President. He took little part in the Administration, but as president of the Senate he gave skillful direction to the growth of his party.

The defeat of the Federalists at the polls in the 'Revolution of 1800' was largely the work of Aaron Burr, who swung New York to the Republicans. Jefferson and Burr tied for first place with 73 electoral votes (with 65 and 64 respectively to the Federalists Adams and C. C. Pinckney). Such close party division made final selection by the House of Representatives a partisan maneuver. Finally in mid-February 1801, after 35 ballots (and through the influence of Hamilton, who persuaded three Federalists to cast blank ballots), the House gave the election to Jefferson.

For his two key cabinet posts, state and treasury, Jefferson selected JAMES MADISON and ALBERT GALLATIN, and set himself the task of republicanizing the government and public opinion by adopting the simplest possible protocol for official functions and reducing government expense. He chose Republicans for office. The notable events during his first Administration include the LOUISIANA PURCHASE (1803), the LEWIS AND

CLARK EXPEDITION (1804–6), and the prosecution of the TRIPOLITAN WAR (1801–5), which ended tribute payment to Mediterranean pirates.

Jefferson's second term is especially remembered for the NON-INTERCOURSE ACT (1806), and the EMBARGO ACT (1807). They were designed to stop British seizure of American ships during the Napoleonic Wars, and because they sharply curtailed trade in sections of the country that had supported him (especially in New England), they revived partisan opposition. He refused a third nomination in 1818, but was closely consulted by his successors and neighbors, Madison and Monroe. Thus for 24 years he managed the political principles of the 'Jeffersonian system.' His ideas became the foundation of American republicanism and his Administrations ended the possibility of a class government.

Jefferson, like Franklin, was a promoter of scientific inquiry. As president of the American Philosophical Society (1797–1815), he gave support to the first organized scientific expeditions in the U.S., beginning with the modest paleological enterprise of the painter CHARLES WILLSON PEALE. A lifelong concern with education led Jefferson to establish the University of Virginia (chartered 1819), for which he planned the curriculum and in which he served as first rector. Easily the first American architect of his day, he designed his home, 'Monticello,' as well as the homes of neighboring friends. He laid out the Virginia state Capitol (1785–89), and the buildings of the University (1817–26), a high mark of classical revival, and the most notable unit of collegiate architecture in the U.S.

The importance of Jefferson can scarcely be overestimated. He would have won enduring rank among American statesmen had he done no more than write the Declaration of Independence. But equally notable were the legal and constitutional reforms he instituted in his native Virginia, his role as father of the nation's territorial system, and his acquisition of Louisiana Territory. The very success of his highly personal methods as a politician in dealing with Congress weakened the office of President for his less skillful followers.

He was unswerving in his faith that man can be reached by reason and that ignorance is dispelled by education, and he was author of an educational plan more farseeing than any existing elsewhere. The epitaph he chose for his tomb gives substantial evidence that he approximates Plato's philosopher-king: 'Here was buried Thomas Jefferson, Author of the Declaration of Independence, of the Statute of Virginia for Religious Freedom, and Father of the University of Virginia.'

The projected edition of the Jefferson Papers (52 vols., ed. by Julian Boyd, 1950–) is well advanced, as is the inclusive biography by Dumas Malone (5 vols., 1948–).

Jefferson Memorial, see *Thomas Jefferson Memorial.*

Jefferson Territory came into existence (1859) as a spontaneous provisional government in Colorado, following the discovery of gold near the site of Denver in 1858. It was dissolved upon creation of the Territory of Colorado in 1861.

Jeffersonian Democracy was the conservative faction within the Republican party, as distinguished from JACKSONIAN DEMOCRACY, the democratic faction. It took form during the 'era of good feelings' under Monroe (1817–25). Jefferson had long since expressed his fear that the growth of large cities with an industrial-centered economy would endanger a democracy that he believed should be based on agriculture and developed by a citizenry of educated, independent freeholders. His fears were justified to the degree that after 1815 a new breed of professional machine politicians made their way, demagoguery flourished, and the SPOILS SYSTEM was extended to Federal office.

JEFFRIES, JAMES J. (1875–1953), Ohio-born pugilist, in 1899 won the world heavyweight boxing championship from the English prizefighter Bob Fitzsimmons (1862–1917) at Coney Island, New York. He retired from the ring undefeated in 1905 for lack of a challenger. Public clamor brought him back to the ring in 1910, when he lost the title to JACK JOHNSON at Reno, Nevada.

Jehovah's Witnesses, a religious sect organized in 1872 at Pittsburgh, Pennsylvania, by Charles Taze Russell (1852–1916), were known as Russellites for many years. Without churches or ministers, adherents gather in assemblies to await the second coming of Christ at any moment; hence their slogan 'Millions now living will never die.' In the past they were frequently in conflict with municipal, state, or Federal authorities because of their methods of assembly and their refusal to engage in military service. In recent years the Supreme Court has affirmed their rights as a religious body to forbid their children to salute the flag in school and to distribute religious literature freely. In 1965 the denomination reported a membership of 315,500.

Jenkins' Ear, War of (1739–42), was a struggle in the commercial rivalry of England and Spain. The appearance in the House of Commons of a merchant seaman, Robert Jenkins, who showed an ear lopped off in a brush with the Spanish off Florida, had immense propaganda effect. A restive public opinion and a desire to loot the Spanish empire led England to a declaration of war. allegedly for a series of such mistreatments as that suffered by Jenkins. Hostilities were chiefly naval engagements in the Caribbean. On land, the Spanish attacked Georgia in 1742, but were repulsed. Thereafter the struggle merged into the War of the Austrian Succession, of which KING GEORGE'S WAR (1743–48) was the American phase.

JENNEY, WILLIAM LE BARON (1832–1907), studied engineering at Harvard and architecture at the Beaux-Arts in Paris. He served as chief engineer on General Sherman's staff during the Civil War. A pioneer of skyscraper construction, he used cast-iron columns and wrought-iron beams to erect the ten-story Home Insurance Building in Chicago (1885). It was the first true steel-skeleton building in which both floors and exterior masonry walls hung on structural framework.

Jesuit Relations were the reports prepared by Jesuit missionaries of their work in New France, annually published after 1632 to announce the great work 'ad majoram Dei gloriam.' They deal with the Great Lakes region and are documents of unique historical importance. Written by men who combined the physical endurance of explorers with the scholarship of trained seminarians, they are vivid observations of the traditions and economic life of the Indian civilizations now vanished.

Francis Parkman wrote the important and widely read history of *The Jesuits in North America* (1867), and the Canadian government published a 73-volume edition of the *Relations* (1896–1901) with an English translation, compiled by REUBEN G. THWAITES.

Jesuits, religious order of the Roman Catholic Church (founded in 1534 by Ignatius Loyola), were influential in the French, Spanish, and Portuguese possessions of America. Distinguished for their missionary work, first among the Florida Indians (1566–72), but especially in the Great Lakes region, the Mississippi valley, and the Southwest, they were well-trained scholars, numbering among their leaders MARQUETTE and JOGUES (French), KINO (Spanish), and DE SMET (Belgian). Their reports, known as the JESUIT RELATIONS, have great historical importance. They were associated with the Calverts in founding Maryland, and in the post-colonial period they opened missions in the Middle West and the Far West. Their major interest was in education, and they gained distinction in the natural sciences. Among the score of learned institutions that they founded in the U.S. are GEORGETOWN (1791) and FORDHAM (1841).

JEWETT, CHARLES COFFIN (1816–68), a graduate of Brown (1835) and Andover Theological Seminary (1840), having served as librarian at both Andover and Brown, became librarian of the Smithsonian Institution (1848), where he published a survey of U.S. libraries, and devised a duplicating system for catalog entries. The catalog rules that he worked out as superintendent of the Boston Public Library (1858–68) came into international use.

Jews first arrived in America at New Amsterdam (1654) in small numbers, some of them refugees from Brazil after the Portuguese capture of Pernambuco. Since Rhode Island was the only colony offering complete religious toleration, the first synagogue in America (1658) was built at Newport, which during the 17th century became a noted Jewish center. (Touro Synagogue, built in 1763, and the oldest place of assembly for Jews in the U.S., was designated a national historic site in 1946.)

At the outbreak of the Revolution some 2000 Jews, scattered throughout the colonies, formed tiny communities with an elite of merchants and bankers and a majority of artisans. (HAYM SALOMON and BARNARD GRATZ gave invaluable aid in helping to finance the patriot cause.) Such groups, while maintaining an ethnic separateness, progressively gained *de facto* recognition of civil equality and religious freedom, and these rights were written into the Federal Constitution and most early state constitutions. The last legal limitations on the full political equality of the Jews (among other non-Christians) were removed in North Carolina in 1868.

The three main waves of Jewish immigration to the U.S. were those of the Sephardic (Spanish-Portuguese) Jews before 1840, the Ashkenazic (German) Jews during most of the 19th century, and the Russian and Polish Jews after 1880. The large-scale immigration of refugees from the German ghettos (1825–80) was motivated by the same economic, social, and political factors that brought great numbers from central Europe generally. (Reactionary Bavaria even restricted Jewish marriages and extorted high ghetto taxes.)

The German Jews differed from their predecessors by dispersing geographically, assuming new entrepreneurial roles in the growing economy, and organizing religious communities that were far less rigidly disciplined. The picture of the German Jewish peddler whose services in frontier towns culminated in the establishment of retail department stores dates from this period. Many German Jews rejected the oriental customs of the synagogue and brought with them the new concepts of Reform Judaism, which tends toward complete assimilation into community life. The Reform movement was given formal expression in the establishment of the Union of American Hebrew Congregations (1873) and the founding of Hebrew Union College (Cincinnati, 1875) by ISAAC M. WISE.

The character of American Jewry was radically influenced by the flood of immigrants from Eastern Europe during the period 1880–1924, when some 2,350,000 Jews sought freedom in the U.S. from Czarist persecution in Russia and Romania. Their beliefs ranging from rigid orthodoxy to militant secularism, they swelled the ranks of the proletariat, especially in the needle trades, and many contributed actively to organizing the ranks of the labor movement and the new socialist parties. Culturally they brought their Yiddish language, interest in the renascent Hebrew language and Jewish scholarship, an ardent hope for a revived Jewish homeland (Zionism), and above all a keen attachment to Jewish traditions. In the decades between the two World Wars, the new arrivals and their children were rapidly assimilated into American life, chiefly among the urban middle class, where they concentrated in business and the professions.

With the outbreak of World War II a religious and cultural awakening led to a tremendous increase in affiliation with synagogues and other Jewish organizations. In the process of integrating their ancient loyalties with the new pattern of American life, these Jews have made up the bulk of Conservative Judaism, and have augmented as well as influenced the Reform movement. Their ranks were filled by immigrants fleeing Nazi persecution during the 1930's, and by the arrival after 1945 of survivors of the Nazi decimation of European Jewry.

The major streams of American Judaism are represented in three principal theological schools: Hebrew Union College (Reform), already mentioned; Yeshiva University, in New York (Orthodox, est. 1886); and the Jewish Theological Seminary of America, in New York (Conservative, est. 1887), of which the Talmudist SOLOMON SCHECHTER was at one time president. Zionism was given particular emphasis by STEPHEN S. WISE.

In 1965 the Jewish population of the U.S. was estimated at 5,585,000, located chiefly in the urban and suburban areas of New York City (1,836,000), Los Angeles (435,000), Philadelphia (330,000), Chicago (285,000), Boston (160,000), and Newark, N.J. (100,000). No country in the world has so large a Jewish population.

Jim Crow, generic name for a Negro, derives from the minstrel-show 'Jim Crow,' introduced by T. D. Rice about 1828. By extension the term implies discriminatory statutes ('Jim Crow laws').

Jingoism, the term applied to bellicose nationalism, was first widely used in the U.S. when the 'jingo press' incited public opinion against Spain in the period leading to the Spanish-American War (1898).

JOGUES, Isaac (1607–46), French Jesuit missionary in North America after 1636, first worked among the Huron and Mohawk Indians. He was the earliest to penetrate into the region of Lake George, and by 1641 his westward journeys had brought him to Sault Ste. Marie, which he named. His important narrative reports are in the JESUIT RELATIONS. Murdered by Indians, he is one of the Martyrs of North America canonized in 1930.

John Henry is the hero of Negro ballads and tales that originated about 1870, possibly in West Virginia. He is depicted as a rugged railroad steel driver who outdoes a steamdrill but dies exhausted 'with his hammer in his hand.' His counterpart in legends of the West is PAUL BUNYAN.

Johnny Appleseed, see *Chapman, John.*

Johns Hopkins University, chartered at Baltimore in 1867, was endowed by the financier Johns Hopkins (1795–1873). It opened in 1876 under the presidency of DANIEL COIT GILMAN, who introduced in the U.S. the seminar method of teaching and made the university a leading center for graduate study and research. The affiliated medical school, founded in 1893, immediately became world renowned under the aegis of WILLIAM OSLER. Its press was the first to be established in an American university and pioneered in publishing learned journals and monographs. In 1965, with an endowment of $109,650,000 and a faculty of 1738, it enrolled 8700 students.

JOHNSON, Andrew (1808–75), 17th President of the U.S. (1865–69), was born at Raleigh, North Carolina, and at fourteen was apprenticed to a tailor. In 1826 his family moved to Tennessee, where the youth set up his own shop at Greenville. He had no formal schooling, but with perseverance and the aid of his wife Eliza McCaudle, whom he married in 1827, he learned to write. The best debater in the community, he became the acknowledged leader among farmers and artisans in a region only loosely controlled by the slaveholding gentry.

From 1830 he was almost continuously in public office, at first locally, then as representative and senator, as Congressman (1843–53), governor of Tennessee (1853–57), and U.S. Senator (1857–62). A Democrat and champion of the laboring class, he fought for a Homestead bill to aid settlers. When Tennessee seceded (June 1861), he remained in the Senate, the only Southerner there. He vigorously supported Lincoln, who appointed him military governor of the important border state which Johnson had so long and ably served, and Johnson managed his assignment with the skill of instinct and political knowledge. The fact that he was a Southerner and a war Democrat made him the inevitable choice as Lincoln's running mate on the successful Union ticket in 1864.

Succeeding to the presidency on the day after Lincoln was shot (15 April 1865), Johnson continued to follow the RECONSTRUCTION program that Lincoln had inaugurated. He believed the task to be an executive function, not a legislative one, and set about restoring civil government in the ex-Confederate states. At this point he came into mortal conflict with the radical Republicans. He was conservative on race relations and was unwilling to grant equal civil rights to Negroes. He therefore vetoed (February 1866) the bill extending the life of the FREEDMEN'S BUREAU. It was passed over his veto. Again over his veto Congress passed in 1867 a series of Reconstruction Acts and the TENURE OF OFFICE ACT. Johnson's dismissal from his cabinet of Secretary of War Stanton defied the Act and set the stage for the impeachment proceedings against the President.

Johnson had long since lost all ability

to interfere substantially with the legislative programs of the Radicals who controlled Congress. The end of his term was but months away and he had no political future. The fact that Congress went to the enormous bother of trying to depose him was a political maneuver. Johnson's very weakness was a spur to the ambitions of BENJAMIN WADE, THADDEUS STEVENS, BENJAMIN BUTLER, and GEORGE BOUTWELL. Led by such men, the radicals sought to test the possibility of suspending the presidential system.

Alleging violation of his oath of office on the ground that Johnson had committed 'high crimes and misdemeanors,' Congress opened trial on 30 March 1868, and during its three-month course the President's able counsel, including William M. Evarts, tore the case of the prosecution to shreds. Yet the radicals would have succeeded in their purpose but for Chief Justice Chase, who insisted upon legal procedure, and seven Republican Senators who sacrificed their political future by voting for acquittal. One more affirmative vote, and Ben Wade, president pro tempore of the Senate, would have been installed in the White House. Johnson served out his term and retired to private life. In 1875 he was returned to the Senate from Tennessee, but died a few months after taking his seat.

Self-educated and self-trained, Johnson possessed many of Lincoln's virtues but lacked his ability to handle men. Retaining many of his early social prejudices, Johnson was the ablest spokesman for southern white populism. He was honest, courageous, and intellectually astute, and, according to 'revisionist' historians, was the most maligned and misunderstood of all Presidents. He held office at a crucial period in the history of the federal government, and no President has ever been placed in a more difficult situation. His social philosophy and outlook, however, have come under sharp attack.

JOHNSON, EDWARD (1598–1672), having migrated (1630) to Massachusetts Bay, in 1642 became a founder of Woburn. A stalwart militia captain and devout Puritan, he published *A History of New-England* (London, 1653, dated 1654), better known by its running-title: *The Wonder-Working Providence of Sions Savior in New England,* the earliest general history of the Bay colony. It is a classic (if homely) example of the Puritan view of history: that the New England leaders were servants of Christ, and the settlements had prospered because Christ's soldiers were advancing against the wilderness and its pagans.

JOHNSON, HIRAM WARREN (1866–1945), first came into prominence when, as a prosecuting attorney in California, he secured the conviction (1909) of ABE RUEF and other political grafters. As governor of California (1911–17), he shattered the domination of the railroads over state politics, and inaugurated important social and political reforms. He was a founder of the Progressive party (1912), and in that year ran for Vice President on the unsuccessful Progressive ticket, which nominated Theodore Roosevelt for President. Johnson entered the U.S. Senate as a Progressive in 1917, and as a Republican after 1920 remained in that body until his death. A stubborn opponent of the League of Nations, he was a consistent isolationist, fighting F. D. Roosevelt's foreign policy, and voting (1945) against ratification of the charter of the United Nations.

JOHNSON, JACK [JOHN ARTHUR] (1876–1946), formidably built Negro pugilist, in 1910 won the world heavyweight boxing championship from JAMES J. JEFFRIES at Reno, Nevada. The remark of his mother after the match: 'He said he'd bring home the bacon, and the honey boy has gone and done it,' added a new phrase to the vernacular. He retained the title until knocked out by JESS WILLARD at Havana, Cuba, in 1915.

JOHNSON, JAMES WELDON (1871–1938), the first Negro to be admitted to the Florida bar (1897), practiced law in Jacksonville until 1901, when he moved to New York to collaborate with his brother, J. Rosamond Johnson, in writing light opera. He later served as American consul in Venezuela (1906–9) and Nicaragua (1909–12). As field secretary of the National Association for the Advancement of Colored People after 1916 he was a key figure in advancing the cause of civil liberties. In 1920, when he investigated abuses by U.S. Marines of Haitians under American occupation, his charges of brutality created a major issue in the presidential election. After 1930 he occupied a chair in creative literature at Fisk University. A talented writer, he was one of the most distinguished Negro poets. He wrote a pioneer treatment of Negro 'passing' in the novel *The Autobiography of an Ex-Colored Man* (1912), and the poem 'Lift Every Voice and Sing,' which rated as a Negro national hymn.

JOHNSON, Lyndon Baines (1908–), 36th President of the U.S. (1963–), was born near Stonewall, Texas. After graduation from Southwest State Teachers College (1930) he taught school and studied law. In the same decade he entered politics as a Democrat. He was elected to Congress and served his Texas district (1937–49) before entering the Senate (1949–61). During the Eisenhower Administration, first as minority leader (1953–55) and thereafter as majority leader (1955–61), he proved himself a political tactician of the first order.

With passage in 1957 of the civil rights bill, which he had sponsored, he became a contender for the presidency in 1960. At the Democratic convention Senator John F. Kennedy won the nomination, and he persuaded Johnson, as representative of the moderate southern wing of the party, to act as his running mate. The Democrats won the election. Both men were together on a speech-making tour in Texas when President Kennedy was assassinated (22 November 1963). Johnson was immediately sworn in as President.

Johnson entered the White House as a man basically different from his predecessor. Though both were men of means, Kennedy was identified with the urban, industrial, and international-minded Northeast, and Johnson was allied with the rural, agricultural, and regional interests of the Southwest. But as a political craftsman with many years of Senate leadership Johnson carried to the office a tested experience and a liberal program similar to Kennedy's.

When the 89th Congress adjourned in October 1965 it had enacted at Johnson's behest social and economic legislation of a far-reaching character, including the planned expenditure of billions of dollars for Federal assistance to schools, to the depressed Appalachian region, and to medicare for the elderly. It also had assured voting rights to the Negro and enacted Johnson's request for legislation to wipe out discrimination in immigration. These were major goals of his 'Great Society' program.

JOHNSON, Samuel (1696–1772), Connecticut-born clergyman and philosopher, graduated from Yale in 1714. A leading Congregational minister in his colony, in 1722 he sailed for England, where he was ordained as an Anglican minister. In 1724 he opened the first Anglican church in Connecticut at Stratford. He remained there as minister until he became the first president of King's College (Columbia) in New York City (1754–63). He was a friend and correspondent of the English philosopher george berkeley, and became the principal exponent in America of Berkeleian idealism. His *Elementa Philosophica* (1752), the earliest philosophy textbook written and published in the country, follows Berkeley in postulating spirit as the only substance, insisting that matter exists only in the mind of the perceiver and that nature is simply the succession of ideas that God presents to the mind.

JOHNSON, Tom Loftin (1854–1911), born in Kentucky, became a wealthy Ohio manufacturer. In the 1880's he devoted himself to reform under the influence of the writings of henry george. He served in Congress (1891–95), but it was as mayor of Cleveland (1901–9) that he became a national figure, because of his effort to rescue that city from the grip of the utilities (especially the street railway interests) and the domination of mark hanna. Although he was only partially successful, for a time he made Cleveland the best governed city in the country and did more than any public figure of his time to create a civic consciousness.

JOHNSON, Walter Perry (1887–1946), as pitcher for the Washington Senators after 1907, is acknowledged to be the fastest hurler in the history of baseball. Before retiring from active play in 1927, the 'Big Train' established several records, including the greatest number of shutouts (113), strikeouts (3497), and consecutive scoreless innings pitched (56).

JOHNSON, Sir William (1715–74), Irish-born fur trader, administrator, and militia commander, came to America to manage the Mohawk valley lands of his uncle, Peter Warren (later Admiral Sir Peter), who had married into the De Lancey clan. On the Mohawk river (at the site of Amsterdam, New York) in 1738 Johnson set up a trading post, and among traders and colonial administrators his was a singularly interesting personality.

He became owner of an immense domain and the wealthiest colonist of his day, but he was not a land speculator. His largest single holding (100,000 acres) was the gift of a Mohawk tribe, and was given on condition that he protect their hunting grounds, which he did. He associated with Indians as an equal, wore their clothes, spoke their language, and throughout his life enjoyed their implicit trust. He exercised a feudal authority unparalleled in American history, living in baronial if untidy splendor at Johnson Hall, where Indians at will overflowed his house and grounds, to the scandal of white visitors, who disapproved of his casual hospitality to Indians and his intimacy with their squaws.

The Mohawk valley was the key to the West, and for twenty years, until the end of the French and Indian Wars (1763), through his control of the IROQUOIS CONFEDERACY, Johnson held that key. After he won the battle of LAKE GEORGE (1755), as the sole successful military leader in the year of Braddock's defeat he was created a baronet, the second in America.

As Superintendent of Indian Affairs (after 1756) he held an office of importance in the struggle against France. He died on the eve of the War of Independence (for which he had no stomach) after an impassioned two-hour speech, promising the Indians protection from white aggressors. His loyalties, foibles, and abilities were uniquely combined, and his service to the crown was considerable.

Johnson-Clarendon Convention (1869), negotiated by Secretary Seward, covered the U.S. claims against Great Britain for damage done to the U.S. merchant marine by British-built Confederate raiders during the Civil War. British concessions were so slight that the Senate rejected the Convention, and the claims were finally settled by the TREATY OF WASHINGTON (1871).

Johnson-Reed Act (1924), replacing the QUOTA ACT of 1921, limited IMMIGRATION (with a few exceptions) by establishing a quota of 2 per cent of the nationals of any country residing in the U.S in 1890. By abrogating the 'Gentlemen's Agreement' of 1907, it prohibited all immigration from Japan. The law further provided that the quota should remain in force until 1927, when a National Origins quota (on the basis of the ratio of each country's nationals in the U.S. in 1920) should be substituted. The intent of the law was to discourage the 'new immigration' from southern and eastern Europe and encourage a greater number of the 'old immigration' from Scandinavia and western Europe. By 1930 the law clearly had accomplished its purpose of altering the immigration pattern.

JOHNSTON, Albert Sidney (1802–62), born in Kentucky, after graduation from the U.S. Military Academy (1826) served in the Black Hawk War. In 1834 he resigned from the U.S. army and settled in Texas, where he commanded troops during the Mexican War. Re-entering the U.S. army in 1849, he was assigned to command the Department of Texas (1856–58), Utah (1858–60), and the Pacific (1860–61). Regarded as one of the foremost soldiers in the country, he resigned his commission at the outbreak of the Civil War and as a full general in the Confederate army commanded operations in the West. Concentrating his forces at Corinth, Mississippi, he took the offensive against Grant, and in the battle of SHILOH (April 1862), at the full tide of his success, Johnston was mortally wounded.

JOHNSTON, Joseph Eggleston (1807–91), Virginia-born graduate of the U.S. Military Academy (1829), was serving in the U.S. Army as quartermaster general at the outbreak of the Civil War.

Transferring his loyalty to the Confederacy, he helped secure the victory at BULL RUN (July 1861). As a full general commanding the Army of Northern Virginia, he opposed McClellan in the Peninsular Campaign until he was wounded at FAIR OAKS (May 1862). Upon recovery he commanded the Department of the West during the Vicksburg Campaign, but failing to satisfy President Davis, he was replaced in the Atlanta Campaign by Hood, who fared no better. Restored to command by Lee in February 1865, in the closing weeks of the war he obstructed Sherman's advance into North Carolina, and only capitulated after Lee had surrendered to Grant. Dogmatic in judgment and choleric in temper, Johnston lacked the daring of Lee and Jackson, but was peerless in defensive tactics. The duel waged by Sherman and Johnston was a contest between two great captains.

Johnstown Flood occurred in May 1889, when during a heavy rainstorm a dam above the manufacturing city of Johnstown, Pennsylvania, gave way, releasing waters that destroyed four valley towns before drowning Johnstown in 30 ft. of silt and debris. Some 2200 lives were lost in the disaster.

Joint Committee of Fifteen (December 1865–March 1867), the popular name of the Joint Congressional Committee on Reconstruction, was appointed on the recommendation of THADDEUS STEVENS, and consisted of six Senators and nine Representatives. Although under the chairmanship of the moderate WILLIAM P. FESSENDEN, it was dominated by Stevens and a majority of RADICAL REPUBLICANS, who proved themselves the shrewdest body of parliamentarians in American history. The Committee drafted the FOURTEENTH AMENDMENT and the RECONSTRUCTION ACTS, which in modified form the Congress adopted. Having achieved its aim of setting the pace of RECONSTRUCTION, and dictating the tactics in the struggle against President Johnson, the Committee expired with the end of the 39th Congress.

Joint Resolutions, see *Legislative Resolutions.*

Joint-stock companies, associations organized to conduct business with a capital stock owned by private holders, were the groups that financed the exploration and settlement of the American colonies. Chartered by European governments from the 16th to the 18th century, they combined the capital of the many under the management of the few, chosen by the stockholders. Each company received monopoly rights in specified locations, with full control over whatever trading posts or colonies it might see fit to establish. Such were the LONDON COMPANY (1606), the PLYMOUTH COMPANY (1606), the DUTCH WEST INDIA COMPANY (1621), the MASSACHUSETTS BAY COMPANY (1628), and HUDSON'S BAY COMPANY (1670). PROPRIETARY COLONIES inevitably superseded the chartered companies, whose purpose had been primarily to establish settlements.

JOLLIET, LOUIS (1645–1700), French-Canadian explorer, in collaboration with JACQUES MARQUETTE led the expedition that discovered the upper Mississippi river (1673). After discovering that the great waterway led to the Gulf of Mexico, they ascended the Illinois to the present site of Chicago and portaged to Lake Michigan. Returning east to make his report, Jolliet was caught in the rapids near Montreal, his records were lost, and Marquette's journal became the sole official account of the voyage. An expert mapmaker, Jolliet later was named the hydrographer of New France.

JOLSON, AL (1886–1950), stage name of Asa Yoelson, began his career as singer in vaudeville. He later starred in such musicals as *Hold on to Your Hat* (1940). His motion picture *The Jazz Singer* (1927) made history as the first feature film to synchronize speech with music.

JONES, CASEY, hero of popular ballads and folk tales, was presumably John Luther Jones (1864–1900) of Cayce, Kentucky, the railroad engineer who died at the throttle while slowing down his crashing *Cannon Ball,* the crack passenger train running south from Memphis. His passengers were saved. His statue stands at Cayce, but his most enduring monument may be the ballad 'Casey Jones.'

JONES, Hugh (*c.* 1670–1760), a clergyman in Jamestown, Virginia, in 1717 was called to the first colonial chair in mathematics, at William and Mary. He wrote an able historical survey, *The Present State of Virginia* (1724), largely to attract financial aid from friends in London (where the tract was published) for the young and impoverished college. His *Accidence to the English Tongue,* issued at the same time, is the first American grammar of the English language.

JONES, John (1729–91), after study in the principal medical centers in Europe, practiced medicine in New York and became a member of the original medical faculty of King's College (Columbia) in 1767. His surgical textbook on the *Treatment of Wounds and Fractures* (1775), indispensable for doctors during the Revolution, was the first American handbook on surgery.

JONES, John Paul (1747–92), born of humble parentage in Scotland, was christened John, and later added Jones to his surname Paul. In 1761, at the age of thirteen, John Paul, Jr., with his parents' blessing, embarked as ship's boy on a brig plying the Atlantic. Eight years later he became master of a merchant vessel in the West Indies trade, but having run a mutinous seaman through with a sword, had to flee the island of Tobago in 1773. He changed his name to John Jones, and in December 1775 as John Paul Jones was commissioned a first lieutenant in the Continental navy. The flag he hoisted on the armed ship *Alfred* was the 'Grand Union Stripes' (the Union Jack and Stripes), symbolizing resistance to tyranny but loyalty to the crown. In May 1776 with the temporary rank of captain he was given command of the sloop *Providence,* and his indecision over independence vanished.

In 1777 he was sent to France in *Ranger* to announce the capture of Burgoyne. With Brest as his base he raided English shipping, spiked the guns at Whitehaven, near his old home, and in April 1778 captured *Drake* in the most spectacular battle up to that time between ships of rival navies. This was prelude to the event that has deservedly given him stature among those who have won sea battles.

He took command of a squadron of five ships headed by one he named *Bonhomme Richard* to honor Benjamin Franklin. In September he encountered British merchantmen at Flamborough Head, convoyed by *Serapis* and a smaller warship. Seeing the superiority of *Serapis,* without hesitation he sailed in close and ran *Richard's* bow into the stern of *Serapis.* The enemy seemed to have locked *Richard* in deadly embrace, but to the British captain's query 'Has your ship struck?' Jones made his immortal reply: 'I have not yet begun to fight.' Then ensued a three-hour moonlit battle, one of the most inspiring in naval annals. With the hull of *Richard* pierced, her decks ripped, her hold filling, rudderless, and with fires out of control, Jones fought on. It was *Serapis* that struck. Two days later *Richard* sank.

Feted in France, Jones became the hero of countless ballads and of legends that have been repeated far into the 20th century. But since his exploits had slight military value, after the French entered the war Congress dismantled the CONTINENTAL NAVY and had no further use for his services. In 1788 he accepted the invitation of Catherine II of Russia to serve as rear admiral in her imperial navy. He successfully commanded against the Turks, and in 1789 returned to Paris, where he died obscurely. His forgotten grave was identified in 1905 and his remains were brought to America, where since 1913 they have been enshrined in a crypt at the U.S. Naval Academy. He was without peer as a tactician and in the tradition of the U.S. Navy has a place comparable to that of Nelson in the Royal Navy of Great Britain.

The only trustworthy biography is that by S. E. Morison (1959).

JONES, Bobby [Robert Tyre] (1902–), golfer, after graduation from Harvard (1924), took up the practice of law in Atlanta, Georgia. The greatest golf player of his day, in 1930 Jones became the only player ever to make the 'grand slam' in golf, by winning the National Amateur, the National Open, the British Amateur, and the British Open championships, after which he retired from tournament play.

JONES, Rufus [Matthew] (1863–1948), a lifelong professor of philosophy and ethics at Haverford (1893–1934), was the most considerable exponent of American Quakerism during his lifetime. In *Studies in Mystical Religion* (1909), *New Studies in Mystical Religion* (1927), and many other works, he developed a religious philosophy which (much like Emerson's) was that of the homespun moralist, elevated and serene: a practical mysticism that saw the human mind, so far as it embodies the great values, as the channel through which the divine mind finds expression.

JONES, Samuel Milton (1846–1904), Welsh-born political reformer, after establishing a lucrative business in oil-drilling machinery in Toledo, Ohio, with an advanced program of management-employee relations, entered local politics. Elected mayor on a Republican ticket (1897), he put into operation so broad a program of municipal reform, including an eight-hour day and a minimum wage, that in 1899 he was refused renomination by his party. When he ran as an independent he overwhelmingly defeated both political machines, was re-elected in 1901 and 1903, and died in office. He was succeeded by BRAND WHITLOCK, who carried on the work of reform. Whitlock portrays the picturesque career of 'Golden Rule' Jones in his autobiography, *Forty Years of It* (1914).

Jones Act (1916), also known as the Organic Act of the Philippine Islands, reaffirmed the U.S. intention to withdraw its sovereignty and to recognize their independence. It inaugurated far-reaching political reforms by providing for Filipino citizenship and self-rule.

The Jones Act of 1917 (the Organic Act for Puerto Rico) made Puerto Rico a U.S. territory and conferred U.S. citizenship upon its inhabitants.

The Jones Act of 1920 (the Merchant Marine Act) repealed World War I emergency legislation relating to shipping, reorganized the U.S. Shipping Board, and provided heavy mail subsidies to private shipping companies. It authorized preferential tariffs on goods imported in American vessels, restricted trade with American colonies to American ships, and permitted the Board to sell the government-owned fleet on extraordinarily liberal terms. It was supplemented by the JONES-WHITE ACT of 1928.

Jones-White Act (1928), also known as the Merchant Marine Act of 1928, authorized the sale of government-owned vessels not yet disposed of under the JONES ACT of 1920. It increased mail subsidies and appropriated $250,000,000 for loans for construction of private shipping. The reduction of international trade arising from the world depression (1929) impeded its effectiveness.

JOPLIN, Scott (1868–1917), Texas Negro, after a period of itinerant piano playing in honky-tonks, starting at Sedalia, Missouri, arrived in St. Louis (1885), where he became one of the chief composers and performers of RAGTIME. His *Maple Leaf Rag* (1899) started a vogue in syncopated melody.

JORDAN, David Starr (1851–1931), was head of the natural science department at Indiana University (1879–85) when he became its president (1885–91). As first president of Stanford (1891–1913) and its chancellor (1913–16), he gathered a notable faculty and made that institution one of the leading American universities. One of the greatest ichthyologists of his day, he is represented by *The Fishes of North and Middle America* (4 vols., 1896–1900). He was a prolific writer and an ardent pacifist, contending in *War's Aftermath* (1914) that war acts as a reverse selective agent to perpetuate the unfit at the expense of the fit.

JOSEPH (*c.* 1840–1904), Nez Percé chief, defied efforts of the U.S. government to move his people from their traditionally open Oregon lands and was one of the leaders in a campaign (1877) against overwhelming odds. He was finally captured, just short of his objective, during a retreat that would have taken him to Canada. Saddened by his losses but unbroken in spirit, he made a brief but haunting surrender speech: 'From where the sun now stands I shall fight no more forever.' He spent his later years on a reservation, devoting himself to the welfare of his people.

JOSSELYN, John (*fl.* 1638–75), English naturalist and traveler, first visited New England in 1638–39, when his brother was the representative of Gorges in Maine. After a later prolonged stay (1663–71) he wrote *New-Englands rarities discovered* (1672), a work whose notice by the Royal Society encouraged him to publish *An account of two voyages to New-England* (1674). Josselyn combined scientific lore (including reports of mermen and accounts of Indians who speak 'in perfect hexameter verse') with general descriptions, hints to settlers, and digs at the Puritans. As herbalist, Josselyn was the first botanizer in the region and recorded several genera peculiar to American flora.

Journalism, as writing designed to present facts or describe events through such media as newspapers and magazines, was slow in developing in America (as in Europe). The severity of libel laws in all the colonies forced journalists to criticize governments by innuendo rather than directly. JOHN PETER ZENGER, whose New York newspaper had attacked Governor Cosby, was tried for seditious libel in 1735. His acquittal on the principle that truth is a defense against libel was a landmark in the long struggle for freedom of the press, although it did not appear as such until, on the eve of the Revolution, liberty of discussion became a burning issue.

But even after such upheavals as the revolutions in America and France, journalism in the U.S. continued to serve as the handmaid of politics, with no independent standards or aims. For some time NEWSPAPERS were largely party house-organs. By mid-19th century the spread of universal education had fostered a growing support of newspapers and periodicals. The invention by R. M. HOE of the rotary press (1847) and that by OTTMAR MERGENTHALER of the linotype (1884) vastly increased the prestige of the 'fourth estate.' Meanwhile individual leadership of such great editors as WILLIAM CULLEN BRYANT, HORACE GREELEY, SAMUEL BOWLES, CHARLES A. DANA, and HENRY J. RAYMOND made the newspaper influential in American politics. In 1898 the YELLOW JOURNALISM of WILLIAM RANDOLPH HEARST and JOSEPH PULITZER almost made the Spanish-American War a by-product of their circulation war.

Leading journals of opinion in the U.S. during the 19th century included the democratic *Harper's Weekly,* edited by G. W. CURTIS; the *Independent,* guided by the preacher and reformer HENRY WARD BEECHER; and the brilliant *Nation* of E. L. GODKIN.

When newspapers became large business enterprises, late in the 19th century, most of them subordinated the personal element to editorial anonymity, and attempted to restrict opinion to the editorial page. News gathering and reporting assumed great importance, and before 1900 such journalists as HENRY STANLEY and RICHARD HARDING DAVIS were internationally known. No journalist since WILLIAM ALLEN WHITE (who died in 1944) has won a national reputation as a writer of editorials.

The University of Missouri established the first school of journalism in 1908, and by the bequest of Joseph Pulitzer a similar school was opened four years later at Columbia. Since then schools of journalism have been instituted widely throughout the country.

In 1914 HERBERT CROLY launched the *New Republic,* with such political commentators as WALTER LIPPMANN on its editorial board. In 1918 OSWALD GARRISON VILLARD transformed the *Nation* into a similar journal of opinion. But by mid-20th century such MAGAZINES, with their relatively small circulation, were faced with a radical change of emphasis in American journalism. In 1923 *Time* inaugurated an era of news weeklies, which combine fact and opinion in their articles, and have no regular editorial page. With staffs of researchers, and subeditors who rewrite articles which cover news in all fields, including the arts, science, and business, they have reversed the procedure of the editorial analyst. They do publish editorials as brief or occasional special features.

The competition of television and radio, prolonged labor disputes, rising costs, and advances in technology have accelerated the rate of mergers and the emergence of the one-newspaper cities. These factors have enhanced the conservative complexion of the metropolitan press, especially since the advent of the New Deal in the 1930's. Thus the liberal Chicago *Sun* with its distinguished feature articles was soon absorbed by a merger, while the anti–New Deal and isolationist Chicago *Tribune* of Colonel Robert McCormick (and his successors) thrived. There remained, however, the unusual high quality of Adolph Ochs's *New York Times,* and certain other major newspapers that enjoy an international reputation.

JUDD, CHARLES HUBBARD (1873–1946), for many years head of the department of education at Chicago (1909–38) and a consultant in psychology for many institutions, made important school surveys throughout the nation, and helped direct planning of educational policy boards. A follower of the experimental method of Wundt, under whom he had studied at Leipzig, he was a prolific writer who influenced the trend of education with such books as *Measuring the Work of the Public Schools* (1916), *Problems of Education in the United States* (1933), and *Educational Psychology* (1939).

Judicial review in the U.S. is the term applied to the power of the Supreme Court to review the constitutionality of the acts of Congress and the states. Such power was not specifically conferred upon the Court by the framers of the Constitution. But, in the early days of the Republic, lawyers trained in the tradition of English courts were familiar with a review by the Privy Council, which could deem some acts 'contrary to the laws of England,' and state courts had already in several instances declared acts of state legislatures void, as contrary to the state constitutions or to 'natural rights.'

The Court first held an act of Congress void in MARBURY *v.* MADISON (1803). The decision and the mode of reasoning used to support it were criticized, but no attack then or later on the constitutional power of the Court to review acts of Congress ever approached success. The case of FLETCHER *v.* PECK (1810) likewise established a precedent by invalidating a state law as contrary to the Constitution. MARTIN *v.* HUNTER'S LESSEE (1816) and COHENS *v.* VIRGINIA (1821) extended the power of review to state courts.

The most significant period in the history of judicial review was the years 1935–37, when in twelve decisions the Court invalidated much of the NEW DEAL legislation. In recent years the Court has been sharply divided on the exercise of judicial review. Those advocating restraint do so on the ground that congressional or executive authority should not be infringed. The 'judicial activists' argue that the liberties of the people are endangered by government encroachments. The issue is not new, since the Court has always faced the dilemma of preserving the Federal system and at the same time upholding minority rights. The majority on the bench since 1950 has tended to support judicial restraint. The striking exception occurred in 1954, when the Court, in its historic decision in BROWN *v.* BOARD OF EDUCATION, unanimously ruled that segregation in public schools was unconstitutional.

Judiciary, see *Courts.*

Judiciary Act of 1789, implementing the judiciary clause of the Constitution, first organized the Federal judiciary. It provided that the Supreme Court of the U.S. consist of six members, and established three circuit courts and thirteen district courts. Most significantly, it gave Federal courts the power of JUDICIAL REVIEW of state courts.

Judiciary Act of 1801, long under careful consideration, reduced to five the number of Supreme Court justices, created six circuit courts, and established five new district courts. The incoming Republicans derided the incumbents as MIDNIGHT JUDGES, and in partisan zeal repealed the Act.

JUDSON, EDWARD ZANE CARROLL (1823–86), adventurer and writer of dime novels under the pseudonym Ned Buntline, first won notoriety on a national scale when in New York City he led the mob in the ASTOR PLACE RIOT (1849). In the same year he helped found the KNOW-NOTHING PARTY. After being dishonorably discharged from the Union army (1864), he met W. F. CODY, whom he endowed with the name Buffalo Bill, and made the hero of a series of thrillers. A prolific author, Judson turned out some 400 novels.

Juilliard School of Music, in New York City, was chartered (1926) with a foundation established by a legacy of the New York industrialist Augustus D. Juilliard (d. 1919). It aids in completing the musical training of talented students. In 1965, with a faculty of 152, it enrolled 990.

Julliard* v. *Greenman (1884), see *Legal Tender Cases.*

Junto Club (The Junto) was a 'mutual improvement' society organized in 1727 at Philadelphia by Benjamin Franklin. Its membership was originally restricted to artisans. An important cultural influence, in 1731 it formed a subscription library (the first public library in America), and from it developed the AMERICAN PHILOSOPHICAL SOCIETY.

Justice, Department of, was created by Congress in 1870. The office of ATTORNEY GENERAL, the nucleus of the Department, had been established in 1789, but not until after the Civil War did the duties of the Attorney General become so burdensome as to require a law department of the federal government. The Solicitor General, whose office was created when the department was organized, assumes principal responsibility for representing the federal government in cases before the Supreme Court.

The expansion of divisions and bureaus has given large scope to the work of this executive branch. A staff of Assistant Attorneys General now head such departments as Antitrust, Civil Rights, Internal Security, Lands, Tax, Prisons, Immigration and Naturalization, and the FEDERAL BUREAU OF INVESTIGATION.

Justices of the U.S. Supreme Court have been appointed by Presidents as follows: (The names of Chief Justices are starred; names in small capitals are of persons treated in separate articles.)

WASHINGTON

*JOHN JAY (N.Y.) 1789–95
John Rutledge (S.C.) 1789–91
William Cushing (Mass.) 1789–1810
JAMES WILSON (Pa.) 1789–98
John Blair (Va.) 1789–96
Robert H. Harrison (Md.) 1789 (nominated and confirmed, but never served)
James Iredell (N.C.) 1790–99
Thomas Johnson (Md.) 1791–93
WILLIAM PATERSON (N.J.) 1793–1806
*JOHN RUTLEDGE (S.C.) 1795 (appointment not confirmed)
SAMUEL CHASE (Md.) 1796–1811
*OLIVER ELLSWORTH (Conn.) 1796–99

J. ADAMS

Bushrod Washington (Va.) 1798–1829
Alfred Moore (N.C.) 1799–1804
*JOHN MARSHALL (Va.) 1801–35

JEFFERSON

William Johnson (S.C.) 1804–34
Henry Brockholst Livingston (N.Y.) 1806–23
Thomas Todd (Ky.) 1807–26

MADISON

JOSEPH STORY (Mass.) 1811–45
Gabriel Duval (Md.) 1811–36

MONROE

Smith Thompson (N.Y.) 1823–43

J. Q. ADAMS

Robert Trimble (Ky.) 1826–28

JACKSON

John McLean (Ohio) 1829–61
Henry Baldwin (Pa.) 1830–44
James M. Wayne (Ga.) 1835–67
*ROGER B. TANEY (Md.) 1836–64
Philip P. Barbour (Va.) 1836–41
John Catron (Tenn.) 1837–65
John McKinley (Ala.) 1837–52

VAN BUREN

Peter V. Daniel (Va.) 1841–60

W. H. HARRISON

none

TYLER

Samuel Nelson (N.Y.) 1845–72

POLK

Levi Woodbury (N.H.) 1845–51
Robert C. Grier (Pa.) 1846–70

TAYLOR

none

FILLMORE

Benjamin R. Curtis (Mass.) 1851–57

PIERCE

John A. Campbell (Ala.) 1853–61

BUCHANAN

Nathan Clifford (Me.) 1858–81

LINCOLN

Noah H. Swayne (Ohio) 1862–81
SAMUEL F. MILLER (Iowa) 1862–90
David Davis (Ill.) 1862–77

STEPHEN J. FIELD (Calif.) 1863–97
*SALMON P. CHASE (Ohio) 1864–73

A. JOHNSON
none

GRANT
William Strong (Pa.) 1870–80
JOSEPH P. BRADLEY (N.J.) 1870–92
Ward Hunt (N.Y.) 1873–82
*MORRISON R. WAITE (Ohio) 1874–88

HAYES
JOHN M. HARLAN (Ky.) 1877–1911
William B. Woods (Ga.) 1881–87

GARFIELD
Stanley Matthews (Ohio) 1881–89

ARTHUR
Horace Gray (Mass.) 1882–1902
Samuel Blatchford (N.Y.) 1882–93

CLEVELAND
LUCIUS Q. C. LAMAR (Miss.) 1888–93
*MELVILLE W. FULLER (Ill.) 1888–1910

B. HARRISON
David J. Brewer (Kan.) 1889–1910
Henry B. Brown (Mich.) 1890–1906
George Shiras, Jr. (Pa.) 1892–1903
Howell E. Jackson (Tenn.) 1893–95

CLEVELAND
Edward D. White (La.) 1894–1910
Rufus W. Peckham (N.Y.) 1895–1909

MCKINLEY
Joseph McKenna (Calif.) 1898–1925

T. ROOSEVELT
OLIVER WENDELL HOLMES (Mass.) 1902–32
William R. Day (Ohio) 1903–22
William H. Moody (Mass.) 1906–10

TAFT
Horace H. Lurton (Tenn.) 1910–14
*EDWARD D. WHITE (La.) 1910–21
Charles E. Hughes (N.Y.) 1910–16
Willis Van Devanter (Wyo.) 1911–37
Joseph R. Lamar (Ga.) 1911–16
Mahlon Pitney (N.J.) 1912–22

WILSON
James C. McReynolds (Tenn.) 1914–41
LOUIS D. BRANDEIS (Mass.) 1916–39
John H. Clarke (Ohio) 1916–22

HARDING
*WILLIAM H. TAFT (Conn.) 1921–30
George Sutherland (Utah) 1922–38
Pierce Butler (Minn.) 1922–39
Edward T. Sanford (Tenn.) 1923–30

COOLIDGE
HARLAN F. STONE (N.Y.) 1925–41
*CHARLES E. HUGHES (N.Y.) 1930–41

HOOVER
Owen J. Roberts (Pa.) 1930–45
BENJAMIN N. CARDOZO (N.Y.) 1932–38

F. D. ROOSEVELT
HUGO L. BLACK (Ala.) 1937–
Stanley Reed (Ky.) 1938–57
FELIX FRANKFURTER (Mass.) 1939–62
WILLIAM O. DOUGLAS (Conn.) 1939–
Frank Murphy (Mich.) 1940–49
*HARLAN F. STONE (N.Y.) 1941–46
JAMES F. BYRNES (S.C.) 1941–42
ROBERT H. JACKSON (N.Y.) 1941–54
Wiley B. Rutledge (Iowa) 1943–49

TRUMAN
Harold H. Burton (Ohio) 1945–58
*FRED M. VINSON (Ky.) 1946–53
Tom C. Clark (Tex.) 1949–
Sherman Minton (Ind.) 1949–56

EISENHOWER
*EARL WARREN (Calif.) 1953–
John M. Harlan (N.Y.) 1955–
William J. Brennan, Jr. (N.J.) 1956–
Charles E. Whittaker (Mo.) 1957–62
Potter Stewart (Ohio) 1958–

KENNEDY
Byron R. White (Colo.) 1962–
Arthur J. Goldberg (Ill.) 1962–65

L. B. JOHNSON
Abe Fortas (Tenn.) 1965–

Justices of the Peace are the local or inferior judges in counties, towns, or other districts, elected to preserve order, to try minor cases, and to discharge other specified functions. While the institution of justice of the peace still exists in most states, in urban centers the trend has been toward abolition of the office.

Justin Morgan was a horse, foundation sire of the breed of Morgan horses, and named for his original owner, Justin Morgan (1747–97). The Vermont-bred stallion, with short neck, chestnut hair, delicate head, and remarkable endurance, was twenty-nine years old when it died in 1821. It was the only horse to sire a distinctive breed in the U.S. The strain preceded that of HAMBLETONIAN as the favorite among trotting horses in the U.S.

Juvenile courts, set up in response to a growing concern for CHILD WELFARE, took on their present form when Illinois and Colorado enacted statutes providing for them in 1899. They introduced a new legal concept in American jurisprudence by regarding a child who broke the law not as a criminal, but as a ward of the state, subject to the care and control of the courts. The Colorado court, under the administration of Judge BEN LINDSEY (after 1900), attracted nation-wide attention and helped develop similar institutions throughout the country. Such courts now generally handle cases with a view to welfare rather than punishment: the act is a crime, but judgment is reserved on the issue of whether the perpetrator is a criminal.

K

KALB, Johann de (1721–80), German general in the War of Independence, after long service with the French army came to America in 1768 as a French secret agent. In 1776 as 'Baron de Kalb' he was given rank as a brigade commander in the Continental army, took part in the Philadelphia campaign, and served with Washington at Valley Forge. Second in command to Gates during the Carolina campaign, he fought in the Battle of CAMDEN, and died there of his wounds.

KALM, Peter (1716–79), Swedish scientist trained by Linnaeus, was sent to America by the Royal Academy of Science at Stockholm to visit the Middle Colonies (1748–51). Upon his return he published an account of his journey (3 vols., 1753–61), translated as *Travels into North America* (1770–71). (The manuscript of his fourth volume was destroyed, but notes for it were discovered and published in 1929.) The work dealt chiefly with botanical studies of America, and it was the first of its kind written by a trained scientist. But the account is also shrewd in its observations of people and institutions.

KALTENBORN, H. V. [Hans] (1878–1965), radio news analyst, after graduation from Harvard (1909) was long associated with the *Brooklyn Eagle* as an editorial writer (1910–30). He began his career as a radio commentator in 1922, during the infancy of broadcasting, and for more than 30 years enjoyed a worldwide reputation for the incisiveness and vigor of his news reports.

Kanagawa, Treaty of (1854), the epochmaking alliance of commerce and amity opening Japan to the Occident, was signed by Commodore Perry at Yokohama. The U.S. was allowed to establish a consulate, and American vessels were permitted to visit designated Japanese ports for supplies and a limited trade.

Kansas, in the center of the continental U.S., was the 34th state to be admitted to the Union (1861). Coronado, searching for gold in the 1540's, found the region occupied by Indian tribes, including the Kansa, for which the state is named. The region was later explored by Spanish and French traders. It was transferred to the U.S. by the Louisiana Purchase (1803), and in 1817 it became part of the unorganized INDIAN TERRITORY.

To the east it is a rolling prairie. Its semi-arid western plains are cut by river valleys, the highways along which traders could move to the Southwest over the Santa Fe Trail, and settlers emigrating to California and Oregon could fork north. During the five-year Border War (1854–59) following the Kansas-Nebraska Act, BLEEDING KANSAS became a national issue in the sectional struggle. Three years after popular rejection of the LECOMPTON CONSTITUTION (1857), Kansas entered the Union as a free-soil state, with Topeka as its capital.

Railroads encouraged the growth of such cow towns as Abilene and Dodge City as shipping points, and the introduction of machinery gave its western lands to wheat, which is still the state's leading commodity. Subject to temperature extremes, Kansas is prone to blizzards, droughts, and dust storms. Primarily an agricultural state with a major stockyard industry, since World War II Kansas has developed large aircraft manufacture and petroleum production. In the decade 1950–60 Kansas City, Kansas — closely tied to Kansas City, Missouri — dropped in population from 129,000 to 121,000. But its other two chief cities, Wichita and Topeka, grew respectively from 168,000 to 254,000 and 78,000 to 119,000. The leading institution of higher learning is the University of Kansas (Lawrence, est. 1865). In 1965, with a faculty of 945 it enrolled 12,000 students.

Kansas City, Missouri, with a population (1960) of 476,000, is at the junction of the Missouri and Kansas rivers, and adjacent to Kansas City, Kansas (121,000). Together they form a commercial, industrial, and cultural center for the heart of the fertile mid-continent. The Kansas City *Star* has a national circulation. The Missouri city is the site of Rockhurst College (est. 1910), and the Junior College of Kansas

City (est. 1915), with enrollments, respectively, of 1824 and 4212 in 1965.

Kansas-Nebraska Act, passed on 30 May 1854 after three months of bitter debate, had been introduced by Senator STEPHEN A. DOUGLAS as a bill intended to ease tension in the struggle for domination between North and South. The measure allowed residents of Kansas and Nebraska territories to decide whether or not they would have slavery on the principle of 'popular' or (derisively) 'squatter' sovereignty. The act repealed the MISSOURI COMPROMISE, and thus formally established the doctrine of congressional nonintervention in the territories. The hasty influx of advocates and opponents of slavery racked BLEEDING KANSAS, and opposition to passage of the bill resulted in the EMIGRANT AID MOVEMENT and formation of the Republican party, both in the same year.

Antislavery historians like Rhodes and von Holst charged that Douglas was motivated by a desire to win southern votes for the presidency. A generation later Frank Hodder and others argued that, as a substantial Chicago land investor, Douglas wanted a central trans-Mississippi railroad. 'Revisionist' writers have held that this bill was part of a statesmanlike plan to promote compromise and avert war.

KARLSEFNI, THORFINN (*fl.* A.D. 1010–13), Icelandic trader and kinsman of LEIF ERICSSON, according to the 'Saga of Eric the Red' (in the *Hauksbók*) and the 'Saga of Olaf Tryggvason' (in the *Flateyjarbók*), with three ships and 160 men attempted to colonize the North American mainland, west of Greenland.

KEARNY, STEPHEN WATTS (1794–1848), fought gallantly in the War of 1812 and commanded the Army of the West in the Mexican War. He captured Santa Fe (1846) and continued to California, where he combined his force with Commodore Stockton's men but quarreled over the chief command. Frémont, as civil governor under Stockton, refused to obey Kearny's orders. Kearny was sustained from Washington, and Frémont was court-martialed. Kearny served briefly (March–June 1847) as military governor of California. He was noted as a rigid disciplinarian.

Keating-Owen Act, see *Hammer* v. *Dagenhart* (1918).

KEELER, JAMES EDWARD (1857–1900), as director of Allegheny Observatory (1889–98), confirmed the theory of Clerk Maxwell that the rings of Saturn consist of meteoric particles. While director of Lick Observatory (1898–1900), he photographed large numbers of nebulae previously unidentified, and his papers on spiral nebulae greatly advanced astrophysical knowledge.

KEENE, LAURA (*c.* 1820–73), English-born actress and manager, established (1855) Laura Keene's Theatre in New York City. Hospitable to American plays, she produced Tom Taylor's *Our American Cousin,* which Lincoln was witnessing at Ford's Theater in Washington when he was shot. At one time JOSEPH JEFFERSON was a member of her company.

Kefauver Investigation was the series of hearings (1950–51) before the Senate Subcommittee to Investigate Organized Crime in Interstate Commerce, headed by the Tennessee senator, Estes Kefauver (1903–63). It exposed nation-wide crime syndicates whose huge illegal profits were used to enter legitimate businesses and to gain control over state and local political machines, thus circumventing prosecution. Gambling was found to be a $20 billion a year racket. The hearings attracted national attention not only because of the nature of the findings but because they were televised. The evidence of widespread corruption among Federal tax officials led to the removal of several, and to the resignation of the commissioner of Internal Revenue, George J. Schoeneman.

KEITH, GEORGE (*c.* 1638–1716), Scottish-born clergyman, became principal of the Penn Charter School (1689), where his contentious difference of opinion with William Penn led him to form a strong separatist party of Christian, or Baptist, Quakers ('Keithians'). In 1700 he was ordained in the Church of England, which his ardent followers also joined.

KELLER, HELEN [ADAMS] (1880–), Alabama-born writer, though blind and deaf from early childhood, was educated by the remarkable Anne Sullivan Macy (1866–1936), who remained Miss Keller's constant companion. Helen Keller graduated with honors from Radcliffe (1904), and thereafter devoted her life to writing and lecturing in behalf of the blind. Her books include *The Story of My Life* (1902), *The World I Live In* (1908), *Out of the Dark* (1913), and *The Open Door* (1957).

KELLEY, FLORENCE (1859–1932), social worker, graduated from Cornell (1882) and from Northwestern University law school (1894). For nine years (1891–99) she resided at Hull-House in Chicago, where she worked to improve community life in the slums. Thereafter as resident at Henry Street Settlement in New York City (1899–1924) she turned most of her energies to securing protective labor legislation, especially for women and children, an effort that resulted in the establishment of the U.S. Children's Bureau.

KELLOGG, FRANK BILLINGS (1856–1937), after admission to the bar (1877) gained a reputation as corporation lawyer in St. Paul, Minnesota. He served as special counsel (1904) to the U.S. Attorney General in the prosecution of trusts. Elected to the U.S. Senate (1917–23), he soon thereafter became President Coolidge's ambassador to Great Britain (1924–25), and Secretary of State (1925–29). For his part in negotiating the KELLOGG-BRIAND PACT (1928) outlawing war, he was awarded the 1929 Nobel Peace prize. He later sat on the bench of the Permanent Court of International Justice.

Kellogg-Briand Pact, or Pact of Paris (1928), grew out of a proposal of the French Premier, Aristide Briand, to the U.S. government for a treaty outlawing war between the two countries. Secretary of State FRANK B. KELLOGG countered with the suggestion of a multilateral treaty of the same character. In August 1928, fifteen nations signed an agreement condemning 'recourse to war for the solution of international controversies.' This most thoroughgoing commitment to peace ever made by great powers was ratified by the U.S. in January 1929, and adhered to eventually by 62 nations. Since the sanctions of the pact rested solely on the moral force of world opinion, most leaders understood how insignificant the pact was in political terms. Yet the pact was cited by Justice ROBERT H. JACKSON as a legal basis (in part) for the Nuremberg War Crimes trial of 1945–46.

Kellogg (W. K.) Foundation (1930) was established by Will K. Kellogg (d. 1951), Michigan manufacturer of cereal products. Its funds support agricultural, scientific, and educational programs. One of the largest endowed FOUNDATIONS in the world, in 1965, with assets of $460,500,000, it disbursed $11,338,000.

KELLY, HOWARD ATWOOD (1858–1943), a member of the original medical faculty at Johns Hopkins, served there as professor of gynecology and obstetrics for 30 years (1889–1919). He made notable contributions to abdominal and pelvic surgery techniques. His extensive writings began with *Operative Gynecology* (2 vols., 1898–1906), and include the compilation of medical cyclopedias and dictionaries, and some 500 scientific articles in his field.

KELLY, WILLIAM (1811–88), Kentucky ironmaster, by chance discovered (1851) that pig iron could be converted into steel by directing a blast of air through molten iron. Although the English inventor Henry Bessemer, who perfected the technique in 1856, secured a U.S. patent in 1857, Kelly officially won priority rights, and the Bessemer-Kelly conflict was settled by consolidation of interests. The Bessemer process was put to commercial use in 1865 by A. L. HOLLEY, and the name, already famous in England, continued to prevail both there and in America, while Kelly's name was forgotten.

KEMBLE, FANNY [FRANCES ANNE] (1809–93), was a member of the famous English stage family. With her father, Charles Kemble, she made an American theatrical tour (1832–34), at the conclusion of which she married Pierce Butler of Philadelphia, and settled with him on his Georgia plantation. There she wrote her *Journal of Frances Anne Kemble* (2 vols., 1835), a record of her tour, highly critical of American manners. (Her *Journal of a Residence on a Georgia Plantation,* written in 1838–39, was not published until 1863, and was intended to influence British opinion against the South, whose slave economy she despised.) In 1846 she left her husband, whom she later divorced, and thereafter resided alternately in the U.S. and England, writing plays and poetry, and giving public readings of Shakespeare.

KENDALL, Amos (1789–1869), a graduate of Dartmouth (1811), as an able and influential journalist went to Washington, where he vigorously defended the policies of Andrew Jackson in the *Globe,* the administration journal edited by FRANCIS P. BLAIR. Kendall provided the Jacksonians their watchword: 'The world is governed too much.' A leading member of the President's 'KITCHEN CABINET,' he served as Postmaster General (1835–40) under both Jackson and Van Buren, and thoroughly reorganized the then badly managed department. He later became the business manager for SAMUEL F. B. MORSE.

KENNEDY, John Fitzgerald (1917–63), 35th President of the U.S. (1961–63), was born in Brookline, Massachusetts, second of nine children of the financier Joseph P. Kennedy (1888–). During his junior year at Harvard (from which he graduated *cum laude,* 1940), he spent six months working in the London embassy while his father was ambassador to Great Britain (1937–40). The observations he made at that time are set forth in his first book, *Why England Slept* (1940). His second, *Profiles in Courage* (1956), won a Pulitzer Prize in biography.

After war service in the Navy (1941–45), he entered politics as a Democrat, serving in the U.S. House of Representatives (1947–53), and in the Senate (1953–61). As his party's candidate for President in 1960, with Lyndon B. Johnson as running mate, he campaigned against Vice President Richard M. Nixon, and won the election in the closest presidential race since 1884. Kennedy was the first Roman Catholic to be elected President, and, at forty-three, the youngest man ever elected. (Theodore Roosevelt was forty-two when he assumed office after the death of McKinley.) Kennedy served less than three years of his elected term. On 22 November 1963, while on a speechmaking tour in Texas, he was felled at Dallas by an assassin's bullet. He was succeeded by Vice President Johnson.

The administration of President Kennedy was organized to fit his strong personal views on foreign and domestic policy, and he surrounded himself with young men recruited from the nation's leading universities. He accented the new rather than the traditional in national life, and in the intellectual tradition of Woodrow Wilson, he believed in the power of ideas. Congress supported much that he asked for to expand foreign aid and to carry out his defense and space program, but balked at his program of social reform. In October 1962 he acted decisively in the Cuban missile crisis, compelling the Soviets to abandon their effort to establish long-range missile bases in Cuba, which were well within the range of most U.S. cities. He took the initiative in securing the NUCLEAR TEST-BAN TREATY (1963). His proposed tax cut and civil rights bill were issues pending at the time of his death. Kennedy was gifted with a keen intelligence, and as President had become the chief spokesman for a new generation of leaders in public life.

KENSETT, John Frederick (1818–72), New York painter of the Hudson River School, in 1840 went abroad, where his five years of study in Paris, Düsseldorf, and Rome increased his technical proficiency. His poetic landscapes, represented by *Lake George* and *River Scene* (Metropolitan Museum), are distinguished for their delicate coloring, and brought him wealth and some degree of fame.

Kensington rune stone is the slab found in 1898 on a farm near Kensington, Minnesota. On it inscribed in runic letters is an account of the journey from Vinland of Norse explorers, who allegedly camped nearby in 1362. Historical and philological disputes have long waged over the authenticity of the stone, but the possibility of its genuineness still cannot be dismissed. Recent discoveries in western Ontario of a sword, ax-head, and shield grip (*c.* A.D. 1000) have been pronounced authentic by some scholars.

KENT, James (1763–1847), a graduate of Yale (1781), became the first professor of law at Columbia (1794–98), a post to which he later returned (1824–26). As chief justice of the New York Supreme Court (1804–14) and chancellor of New York (1814–23), he laid the foundations of equity jurisprudence in the U.S. He modified English chancery practice to conform to American institutions, and his reputation derives both from his written opinions and his *Commentaries on the American Law* (4 vols., 1826–30), a systematic treatment called by Justice Story 'our first judicial classic.' It was immediately accepted as an authoritative exposition of the English common law in the U.S., and a standard (Federalist) interpretation of the Constitution. (In 1873 it was edited, with supplementary essays, by O. W. Holmes, Jr.) A rigid conservative, Kent fought the proposed abolition of property qualifications for voting at the New York Constitutional Convention of 1821, denouncing the idea as a threat to property rights and to the principles of liberty.

Kentucky was inaccessible country beyond the Alleghenies in the 17th century. It was first effectively explored in the 1750's and opened to settlement in 1774. A year later the TRANSYLVANIA COMPANY employed Daniel Boone to carve out the WILDERNESS ROAD, along which (after 1800) pioneers moved west in one of the greatest migrations in American history. During the Revolution the region became the 'dark and bloody ground' of Indian warfare, but population grew as trade down the Ohio increased. (The census of 1790 estimated a population of 73,677.) In 1792, after Virginia ceded title and jurisdiction over her western lands, Kentucky was admitted to the Union as the 15th state, the first west of the Appalachians, with Frankfort as its capital. Kentucky did not pass through a territorial stage; its political organization was well advanced when the new nation was formed.

Canals and roads funneled commerce to the Ohio, which forms its long northern and northwestern border (between Ohio, Indiana, and Illinois), and by 1830 Louisville had become an important river port. Kentucky was primarily a state of small farms and thus had little use for slave labor. But after 1840, as a trading region along the great reaches of the Ohio, it became a huge slave market for the lower South.

For Kentucky, a border state on slavery issues, the War Between the States was indeed a civil war, dividing neighbors, friends, and even families in their loyalties. Some 30,000 Kentuckians fought for the Confederacy, and twice that number served in the Union ranks. The readjustments during the Reconstruction period therefore engendered nearly as much bitterness as the war itself. The intensity of feeling had various and seemingly unrelated associations. It expressed itself not only in politics, but in industrial disputes, and in the family feuds of the Cumberland mountaineers.

With an equable climate and abundant rainfall, Kentucky remains predominantly agricultural. The bluegrass region, some 8000 square miles of east central Kentucky, is the country that first attracted settlers across the Alleghenies. With its prosperous villages and towns, its well-kept stud and training farms (and its production of distilled liquors), it is an environment unique in the Mississippi valley.

Coal mining is a major industry. Agriculture gets its largest income from burley tobacco. Its natural wonder, Mammoth Cave, has been a national park since 1936. Louisville, at the Falls of the Ohio, is the largest city, with a population (1960) of 390,000. It is a port of entry, an industrial and financial center, and site of the Kentucky Derby, held since 1875. The University of Kentucky (Lexington, est. 1865) in 1965 enrolled 13,360 students. The oldest institutions are Transylvania (Lexington, est. 1780), the first college west of the Alleghenies, and the University of Louisville (est. 1798).

Kentucky and Virginia Resolves (1798) were two startling protests from state legislatures, and sought to clear an unwholesome atmosphere of the persecution inherent in the ALIEN AND SEDITION ACTS. Those of Kentucky were drafted by

Thomas Jefferson; those of Virginia, by James Madison. Both invoked the compact theory of the Constitution, and maintained that the Acts were unconstitutional. The Kentucky resolves held that when the national government exercises powers not specifically delegated to it, each state 'has an equal right to judge for itself, as well of infractions as of the mode and measure of the redress.' Virginia's resolves were in one set. The second set of the Kentucky resolves (1799) was enacted after several northern states repudiated the position the two states had taken; the opposition maintained that the Federal judiciary was the sole arbiter of constitutionality. Kentucky had added that 'a nullification of these sovereignties . . . is the rightful remedy' in instances where unauthorized acts are legislated. Both states declared firm attachment to the Union, and neither took steps to obstruct execution of the laws they disapproved.

The theory rather than the argument of the resolves is important. It formulated anew the principle of the Revolutionary era that tyranny often exists within the structure of states, and is not necessarily imposed from without. The rationalizations which John Calhoun and other southern particularists drew from these arguments to defend slavery and secession were later issues.

Kenyon College (1824) at Gambier, Ohio, is a liberal arts college for men. Founded by Philander Chase (1775–1852), the first bishop of Ohio, it continues a close association with the Episcopal Church, though it is nondenominational. It is a small institution, with a faculty in 1965 of 68 and an enrollment of 650. Since the establishment of the *Kenyon Review* (1939), a literary quarterly founded by the poet John Crowe Ransom (1888–), its name has become nationally known.

KEOKUK (*c.* 1780–1848), chief of the Sauk and Fox tribes, refused to join BLACK HAWK, who supported the British in the War of 1812. A friend to white settlers, he was later given a large tract of land in Iowa, where a town was named for him and a monument raised in his memory.

KERN, JEROME (1885–1945), born in New York City, after studying composition abroad, wrote such successful operettas as *Very Good Eddie* (1915), *Sally* (1920), and *Roberta* (1933). *Show Boat* (1929), his outstanding success, was prepared from a text made by Edna Ferber from her 1926 novel. After 1931 Kern wrote scores for several motion pictures.

KETTELL, SAMUEL (1800–55), was a self-taught scholar and an early associate of the Boston publisher S. G. GOODRICH ('Peter Parley'). He compiled *Specimens of American Poetry, with Critical and Biographical Notices* (3 vols., 1829), the first important anthology of American verse, a collection of the work of 189 writers, from Cotton Mather to Whittier. It concludes with a 'Catalogue of American Poetry,' a pioneer bibliography of some 500 titles.

KETTERING, CHARLES FRANKLIN (1876–1958), engineer and research consultant, after graduation from Ohio State (1904), began his work in Dayton, Ohio, on automotive ignition systems. By perfecting the electric self-starter in 1911 (invented by C. J. Coleman in 1899), he stimulated automobile production. In 1920 he joined General Motors Company, and for 27 years was in charge of its research laboratories. Highly skilled in automotive technology, he held 140 patents on inventions and improvements, and guided important work on diesels, paints, ethyl gas, and refrigerants.

KEY, FRANCIS SCOTT (1779–1843), Maryland lawyer and poet, was author of the text of the 'STAR-SPANGLED BANNER.' The patriotic verses were inspired by his anxious watch during the British bombardment of Fort McHenry. For eight years he was the U.S. attorney of the District of Columbia (1833–41).

Kickapoo Indians, an Algonquian tribe formerly living in Wisconsin, later moved into Illinois and Indiana, where its members fought with TECUMSEH against the Americans in the War of 1812. By the Treaty of Edwardsville (1819) the tribe ceded all their lands in Illinois to the U.S., some members then settling in Missouri and Kansas, and the rest moving into Mexico (*c.* 1852). Today small Kickapoo bands live on reservations in Kansas and Oklahoma.

KIDD, WILLIAM [CAPTAIN] (*c.* 1645–1701), British privateer, for a time during the 1690's made his headquarters in New York, where in 1697 he was authorized by the governor to proceed against pirates. Forced (he alleged) to turn pirate to save himself from a mutinous crew, he returned home expecting to be pardoned. Instead he was sent to England under guard and hanged. The fact that his estate was surprisingly small created legends of buried treasure, none of which has ever been found, although it continues to be sought.

KILPATRICK, WILLIAM HEARD (1871–1965), professor of the philosophy of education at Teachers College, Columbia (1918–38), was a major reformer. He championed John Dewey's progressive education ideas, going even further in attacking subject matter 'fixed in advance,' and urging the goal of child adaptability and self-reliance. His writings include *Foundations of Method* (1925), *Remaking the Curriculum* (1936), and *Philosophy of Education* (1951).

KING, CLARENCE (1842–1901), Rhode Island-born geologist, after graduation from Yale (1862) for a year studied glaciology under Louis Agassiz and geology under Josiah Whitney. He served as a volunteer geologist in the California state geological survey (1863–66), and won congressional support for the Fortieth Parallel Survey, which he organized and led (1867–72) to map systematically the cordilleran ranges from eastern Colorado into California. His narrative sketches in *Mountaineering in the Sierra Nevada* (1872) are immensely vital. This survey, which was accomplished with enormous difficulties, is set forth in his official account, the co-operative *Report* . . . (7 vols., 1870–80), a masterpiece of scientific exposition. The DIAMOND FRAUD, which he exposed (1872), brought him to public notice. He was a prime mover in establishing the U.S. Geological Survey, and served as its first director (1879–81). Thereafter he became a mining engineer.

Men of such diverse interests as John Hay, Henry Adams, and William Dean Howells praised King extravagantly as the 'universal man.' Yet his later years were tragic. The fortune he seemed on the verge of making during the 1880's eluded him. He was the father of five children after his 'marriage' to a Negro woman, whom he deeply loved, although she did not know his actual identity until he died of a pulmonary disorder in Arizona, by his own wish virtually unattended.

KING, ERNEST JOSEPH (1878–1956), a graduate of the U.S. Naval Academy (1901), during World War II served first as commander in chief of the U.S. Fleet (1941), then as chief of naval operations (1942–45). As a naval officer he had a global view of strategy, and in the light of history his judgments have been found remarkably correct. He was a vital member of the Joint Chiefs of Staff throughout the war, together with the army chief of staff, GEORGE C. MARSHALL, and the chief of the air forces, H. H. ARNOLD. In 1944 he was appointed fleet admiral.

KING, MARTIN LUTHER (1929–), Baptist minister, after earning a doctorate in systematic theology (Boston University, 1954), served as pastor of a Negro church in Montgomery, Alabama, before returning to his native city of Atlanta, Georgia, in a like pastorate. As a follower of the teachings of Thoreau and Gandhi, he organized in the South the 'nonviolent army' of Negroes seeking to implement Federal civil rights laws. After the huge demonstrations in Birmingham had taken place in 1962 (King was arrested fifteen times), he became the recognized leader of the Negro movement in the U.S. In 1964 he received the Nobel Peace award.

KING, RICHARD (1825–85), New York-born Texas rancher, made a fortune in blockade running during the Civil War. Because his fleet of river steamboats ferried cotton from the Rio Grande to Tampico and Vera Cruz under the Mexican flag, they plied with impunity. The King Ranch, originally 75,000 acres in Nueces county when King founded it in 1853, at the time of his death stretched across more than 500,000 acres between the Nueces and the Rio Grande, a fabulous expanse of grassy plains on which herds of beef cattle were fatted for the market. It still remains the largest cattle ranch in the U.S.

KING, RUFUS (1755–1827), a graduate of Harvard (1777), was practicing law at Newburyport when he was sent to represent Massachusetts in the Continental Congress (1784–87), where he helped to draft the ORDINANCE OF 1787. After moving to New York (1788), he served for many years as a staunch Federalist in the U.S. Senate (1789–95, 1813–25). There he became an eloquent antislavery spokesman, resisting the Missouri Compromise of 1820 for its concessions to the slaveholders and urging compensated emancipation financed by the sale of public lands. He was twice the Federalist candidate for Vice President (1804, 1808) and ran for President in 1816, but he was defeated each time. An able negotiator, he performed his most important service as minister to England (1796–1803, 1825–26).

King George's War (1744–48), part of the FRENCH AND INDIAN WARS, was the American phase of the War of the Austrian Succession, and followed the so-called War of JENKINS' EAR. The audacious commando tactics of New Englanders under WILLIAM PEPPERRELL in 1745 led to the capture of Fort Louisbourg in Nova Scotia. In the Mohawk valley the Iroquois were put on the warpath against the French by WILLIAM JOHNSON. The inconclusive Treaty of AIX-LA-CHAPELLE (1748) restored the *status quo ante* and returned Louisbourg to France.

King Philip's War (1675–76), the most devastating period of hostilities in the entire history of New England, began when the Mohawk nation of the IROQUOIS CONFEDERACY took action against the English settlements that had been established in the interior. It was in fact a war of survival, for the Indians as well as the colonists. Now skilled in the use of firearms, the Indians attacked frontier villages and destroyed crops and cattle with the intent of recovering a region they believed had originally only been 'loaned' to the white man. But the Indians were not united, while the settlers had organized the NEW ENGLAND CONFEDERACY. Gradually the tough, disciplined militia, aided by Praying Indians, broke up the hostile Indian concentrations.

King Philip (*c.* 1640–76) was the English name of Metacomet, chief of the Wampanoag and son of MASSASOIT. When he was betrayed and killed by another Indian in 1676, the power of the natives in southern New England was permanently broken. But with aid from the French in the northern area, the Abnaki kept the English at bay for another 75 years. Not until 1720 did New England recover the frontier it had penetrated 50 years earlier, for the losses in men and property had been severe.

King William's War (1689–97), part of the FRENCH AND INDIAN WARS, was the American phase of the War of the League of Augsburg, and took on the character of a series of winter attacks on frontier settlements. Hostilities involved the English and French in the Hudson Bay region, and the Iroquois and the French in New York from the Mohawk river to the St. Lawrence. Schenectady was the first settlement destroyed. Raids followed on the Maine and New Hampshire frontier, while Canadian privateers preyed on Yankee fishermen and traders. The only successful English operation was the seizure of Port Royal (1690) by an expedition of Massachusetts troops under Sir WILLIAM PHIPS. That Nova Scotia stronghold was recaptured a year later, and the inconclusive TREATY OF RYSWICK (1697) restored the *status quo ante* in the colonies. In New England the war dragged on until 1699, when, with scarcely a white settlement left in Maine, Governor Bellomont made peace with the Abnakis.

King's Canyon National Park (est. 1940), 453,000 acres in eastern California, is a Sierra wilderness of towering, snow-capped peaks and groves of giant sequoias. The park, large sections of which are inaccessible except on foot or by pack animal, adjoins Sequoia National Park.

King's College, see *Columbia University.*

King's Mountain, Battle of, was the patriot revenge for the American loyalist victory at the Battle of CAMDEN (August 1780). In October a loyalist force of 1100, screening Cornwallis's left flank, was caught atop King's Mountain, on the border between the Carolinas, by a 900-man force of American frontiersmen. The marksmanship of the backwoodsmen, firing from every rock and bush, prevailed over the bayonet charges of the Loyalists, half of whom were killed. The rest surrendered, and Cornwallis retreated back into South Carolina where he took up winter quarters.

KINO, EUSEBIO FRANCISCO (*c.* 1644–1711), Italian mathematician and astronomer, in 1681 went to New Spain as a Jesuit missionary. He explored Lower California, and later, working out from his base at Sonora, pushed the frontier of missionary work northward to the Gila and Colorado rivers in Arizona. He was a superb church-builder, and he also helped create a cattle kingdom by establishing stock ranches at his missions. His map (1705) remained the basis of maps of the Southwest for a century. H. E. Bolton translated and published his autobiographical chronicle, *Historical Memoir* (1919; reissued, 1948).

Kiowa Indians, a small but extremely warlike Plains tribe of Uto-Aztecan stock, were driven from Montana by the Sioux and Cheyenne, then confederated with the Comanche, with whom they raided the frontier from Kansas to Mexico. After 1875 the remnants were settled in Oklahoma.

'Kitchen cabinet' was the popular name for Andrew Jackson's group of intimate advisers, including AMOS KENDALL, F. P. BLAIR, MARTIN VAN BUREN, and J. H. EATON. Their informal meetings with the President shaped administrative policy, while the members of his formal cabinet were expected merely to execute departmental duties.

Kiwanis International (1915) is a luncheon club for businessmen. The Indian word *Keewanis* ('to make oneself known') is applied to services in support of civic betterment. At present some 4000 clubs in the U.S. and Canada report a membership of about 260,000.

Klamath Indians, the northern branch of the Lutuamian stock (of which the neighbors, the Modoc, belong to the southern branch) in the 19th century lived in southwestern Oregon. Though they were peaceful toward the whites, they periodically raided the North California tribes, taking captives whom they kept or sold as slaves. The practice was discouraged by a treaty with the U.S. in 1864. Today they are farmers in Oregon, and number some 1200.

Klondike Gold Rush, in the YUKON territory of northwest Canada, was a stampede (1897–98) into the region after the discovery of rich gold diggings on Klondike Creek in 1896. The estimated number of 18,000 people in the area by 1898 created a near famine. The hardships of the trails and the color of the Klondike days are described in many personal narratives, notably in the fiction of JACK LONDON.

KNAPP, SEAMAN ASAHEL (1833–1911), was a leader in scientific agricultural education. After serving as professor of agriculture and president at Iowa State Agricultural College (1879–86), he became a special government agent to promote better farming methods in the South. He also traveled widely in the Orient, investigating its resources. From his impressive demonstration of methods to fight the boll weevil, which appeared in Texas in 1903, he helped develop the Farmers' Co-operative Demonstration Work of the U.S. Department of Agriculture, a division that he headed (1902–10). His idea of farm experimental stations with agents who presented concrete lessons to the farmer influenced passage of the HATCH ACT of 1887 and inspired innumerable boys' and girls' rural clubs.

KNEELAND, ABNER, see *Universalism.*

Knickerbocker Group, which took its name from Washington Irving's *A History of New York . . . by Diedrich Knickerbocker* (1809), was a school of some dozen writers associated by their proximity to the city of New York. Through their humor and realism, their interest in native materials, and their unity of purpose, as a group they made a distinctive contribution to American literary history. Irving dominated the group until 1820, when FITZ-GREENE HALLECK and JAMES KIRKE PAULDING took the leadership. Poe's critical review, 'The Literati of New York City,' in *Godey's Lady's Book* (1846) ridiculed the pretentiousness of several of its later members. For a time Bryant was identified with the school, which was important chiefly during the first two decades of its existence.

KNIGHT, SARAH KEMBLE (1666–1727), a woman of substantial position in Boston, kept a writing school. As official recorder of public documents she was known as Madam Knight. Her knowledge of court procedures gave her employment in the settlement of estates. Called to New York for such an undertaking, she made the unprecedented decision to journey there alone on horseback. Her *Journal* of the five-month trip in 1704–5 (published in 1825 and several times reissued) is written with humor, gusto, and earthiness. It furnishes an observant commentary on manners and conditions along the New England shore at the beginning of the 18th century.

Knights of Columbus, an American Roman Catholic society for men, was founded at New Haven, Connecticut (1882), to encourage benevolence and civic loyalty among its members, and to promote the interests of the Roman Catholic Church. Its membership in 1965 was reported as 1,173,500.

Knights of Labor was founded (1869) as a secret order at a tailors' meeting in Philadelphia called by Uriah S. Stephens (1821–82). By far the most important of the early labor groups, in 1879 under the leadership of TERENCE V. POWDERLY it was organized as an industrial (vertical) union on a national basis under central control, with membership open to all workers. Its growth was phenomenal. The Knights helped push the CHINESE EXCLUSION ACT (1882) through Congress, and were largely responsible for the CONTRACT LABOR ACT of 1885.

When the New York financier Jay Gould conferred with the Knights' executive board in 1884 and conceded their demands during a great railroad strike in the Southwest, capital for the first time met labor on equal terms. Events culminating in the HAYMARKET RIOT (1886) cost the loss of its prestige, and factional disputes slowed its aims in securing an eight-hour day, abolition of child labor, and equal pay for equal work. Its membership dropped rapidly from a peak of 702,000 in 1886, the year the AMERICAN FEDERATION OF LABOR was founded, and by 1900 it was virtually extinct.

Knights of St. Crispin, a union of shoemakers in Milwaukee, was organized in 1867 to protest the increasing mechanization of shoe manufacture, whereby unskilled factory labor was cutting down the output of skilled workers. Through a series of successful strikes, the Order became for a time the largest trade union in the country, with a membership of 50,000, but its policy went against the trend of the times, and by 1878 it was defunct. Many of its members joined the KNIGHTS OF LABOR, in which body they became the largest craft element.

Knights of the Golden Circle, a secret order of southern sympathizers powerful in the Middle West during the Civil War, had been organized during the 1850's. At its peak, numbering some 200,000, it was largely composed of 'peace' Democrats and COPPERHEADS, and later reorganized as the Order of American Knights, and the Sons of Liberty. With mounting Union victories, its activities became ridiculous, and it dissolved.

Know-Nothing party (officially after 1854 the American party) was organized in New York City (1849) as a secret, oath-bound society calling itself the Order of the Star-Spangled Banner, whose aim was the political exploitation of NATIVISM. The rising flood of Germans in the Middle West and of Irish Catholics in the East encouraged an anti-immigrant movement which became a party program calling for the exclusion of Catholics and other 'foreigners' from public office. In cities where the catering of Democrats to the immigrant vote was regarded as a menace, the societies briefly enjoyed a phenomenal growth, and baffled political managers of the older parties because initiates of such groups, when questioned by outsiders, answered, 'I know nothing.'

After 1852 the Know-Nothings captured local and state elections everywhere from New Hampshire to Texas. With the passage of the KANSAS-NEBRASKA

ACT (1854) they abandoned secrecy to become the American party. Seceding Whigs led by ex-President Millard Fillmore joined the party, and in 1856 Fillmore was the party's presidential candidate. But the group's affiliation with proslavery Southerners doomed it, and in the election Fillmore carried only the state of Maryland.

KNOX, HENRY (1750–1806), who had started out as a Boston bookseller, without benefit of formal instruction gathered enough technical knowledge from manuals to command with competence Washington's artillery during the War of Independence. General Knox first came into prominence (1775) when he transported many tons of desperately needed cannon from Ticonderoga across the frozen Hudson, over Berkshire trails that had never borne heavy loads, in time to post his artillery atop Dorchester Heights and thus compel the evacuation of Boston by the British. He fought dependably throughout the war, and enjoyed Washington's complete trust. (Washington embraced Knox first when he bid farewell to his officers at FRAUNCES TAVERN in 1783.) He was made Secretary of War under the Articles of Confederation, when he made his most important contribution to civilian administration, and under the Constitution he was the only member of Washington's cabinet to carry over his department headship (1785–94). A genial personality, with an immense girth, Knox was a zealous Federalist and a principal founder of the Society of the CINCINNATI.

KNOX, PHILANDER CHASE (1853–1921), after building a reputation as a corporation lawyer in Pittsburgh, served in the cabinets of McKinley and Theodore Roosevelt as Attorney General (1901–4). There he was identified with trust prosecutions, and succeeded in dissolving the Northern Securities Company. While in the U.S. Senate (1904–9) he accepted Taft's appointment as Secretary of State (1909–13), in which post he initiated the policy referred to as DOLLAR DIPLOMACY by his method of protecting U.S. financial interests abroad. Again in the Senate (1917–21), he joined the irreconcilables in his opposition to ratification of the Treaty of Versailles and U.S. participation in the League of Nations.

Knox, Fort, U.S. military reservation near Louisville, Kentucky, was established as a training camp during World War I, and became a permanent post in 1932. Since 1936 the bulk of the nation's gold bullion has been stored here in the massive steel and concrete vaults of the U.S. Depository.

Knox* v. *Lee, see *Legal Tender Cases.*

Korean War (1950–53), crucial and epoch-making, was the first war in history fought by members of an international organization dedicated to peace. It was an aftermath of situations rising out of the agreements reached at the CAIRO CONFERENCE (1943) and the POTSDAM CONFERENCE (1945), which were not broad enough to encompass global problems. Five years later the major powers were still unable to reconcile their political differences. On the day that communist forces invaded South Korea (25 June 1950) President Truman ordered General Douglas MacArthur into the area, and the United Nations supported the move with forces supplied by fifteen other nations. Fighting centered mainly at the 38th parallel, the previously negotiated division between North Korea (industrial and communist) and South Korea (primarily agricultural).

The war fell into four major divisions. The successful attack of the North Koreans drove the South Koreans and Americans back nearly to the tip of the peninsula and the defense perimeter of Pusan. The triumphant amphibious landing at Inchon, near the 38th parallel, made possible the northward drive of the United Nations forces to the Yalu river, the boundary between North Korea and China. The intervention of the Chinese, however, led to the reconquering of North Korea by the communists. Then followed the 'talking war,' during which both truce negotiations and fighting dragged on. An armistice was signed at Panmunjom in 1953, but no peace was ever made. But communism had suffered its first defeat in this limited war, by which invasion was repelled. (President Truman had dismissed General MacArthur in April 1951 for publicly advocating an attack on Red China contrary to orders from his commander in chief. General Matthew B. Ridgway was thereafter in command.) U.S. casualties totaled 137,000; other U.N. losses, 263,000. North Koreans lost 520,000. The Republic of Korea (South) then signed a mutual defense treaty with the U.S., and North Korea allied itself with communist China.

KOSCIUSZKO, THADDEUS (1746–1817), Polish military leader and statesman, was stirred by the American patriot cause. He came to America in 1776, and as a colonel of engineers served throughout the War of Independence. For his gallant participation Congress thanked him and commissioned him a brigadier general (1783). He revisited the U.S. in 1796–98, during which period Congress appropriated some $15,000 due him and granted him 500 acres of land in Ohio. His later bid for Polish independence against 'Muscovite tyranny' was unsuccessful and he died in exile, but his remains were carried to Cracow and he is revered in Poland as a national hero.

KOSSUTH, LOUIS (1802–94), Hungarian patriot, led the forces that secured the short-lived Hungarian independence from Austria in 1849. He fled the country, and on his visit to the U.S. (1851–52), as a guest of the nation he received tumultuous ovations from New York to New Orleans. European historians are divided in their estimate of his political significance. In the U.S. only Lafayette had expressed the same image of a new hope for national independence abroad.

KOUSSEVITZKY, SERGE (1874–1951), Russian-born conductor, made his debut in Berlin (1908). He came to the U.S. in 1924 as director of the Boston Symphony Orchestra, and remained its conductor for 25 years. One of the ablest musicians of his day, he was imaginative as musical interpreter and alive to new musical forms, giving new works their initial performances and repeated hearings. In 1936 he began conducting the Berkshire Symphonic Festivals, and in 1940 he organized the Berkshire Music Center.

KREISLER, FRITZ (1875–1962), Austrian-born violinist, first played in a concert in the U.S. in 1888. He later studied medicine, then art, but returned to the violin in 1899. One of the greatest instrumentalists of the century, he was acclaimed alike by professional musicians and the public as an artist whose imagination and sensitivity gave the classics unusual range.

Ku Klux Klan is the name of two distinct secret societies. The original Klan was an organization of Confederate veterans who sought to oppose radical Republicans and maintain 'white supremacy' in the South after the Civil War. Local governments were weak and the fear of Republican-inspired Negro insurrections (at the ballot box) led committees to take the law into their own hands. Among such groups the Klan was the best known. It was a social *kuklos* (circle) of young men whose initiation garb of sheets and pillow cases was intended to spread fear among Negroes that authentic spirits of the Confederate dead were riding the countryside. The political implications were evident, and by 1867 the 'circles' had organized as the 'Invisible Empire of the South.' Such lawlessness, always a cloak for petty persecution, revolted responsible Southerners, and the Klan was formally disbanded in 1869. Its activities led to the FORCE ACTS (1870–75), and though some 7000 indictments were handed down, very few convictions were obtained.

The nativist secret society organized in Georgia in 1915, which adopted the name Ku Klux Klan, during the 1920's spread into the North and Middle West, and dedicated itself to a program of hostility to minority and nonconformist groups. Its gaudy paraphernalia and fiery crosses blazed for a decade, and at its height it boasted a membership of some 4,000,000. In Indiana it managed to elect governors and senators friendly to its cause, but its fascist planting took no root, except among confirmed nativists in the Deep South, and various scandals contributed to its decline. Its headquarters in the 1960's was in Tuscaloosa, Alabama, and estimates of its strength ranged from 10,000 to 40,000. Local southern juries seldom convict Klansmen, whatever the accusation.

L

Labadists, followers of the French mystic Jean de Labadie (1610–74), theologically were Calvinists. They were independent of church discipline, and they held their goods and children in common. A group settled in Maryland (1683) and another in New York at about the same time, but the colonies failed before 1730.

Labor Day, observed on the first Monday in September in all states and territories of the U.S., was first celebrated in New York state (1882) under the sponsorship of the Central Labor Union at the suggestion of Peter J. McGuire of the KNIGHTS OF LABOR. Congress made it a legal holiday in 1894.

Labor legislation, see *Child Labor, Fair Labor Standards Act, Social Security Act, Unemployment Compensation, Workmen's Compensation.*

Labor-Management Relations Act, see *Taft-Hartley Act.*

Labor-Management Reporting and Disclosure Act (1959) was the third piece of major Federal labor legislation, preceded by the NATIONAL LABOR RELATIONS ACT (1935) and the TAFT-HARTLEY ACT (1947). Adopted to oust racketeers from unions, and to end various union abuses revealed by the McClellan Committee, the law requires that all labor bodies make a full report of finances, organization, and activities to the Secretary of Labor, and that these reports become public information. A special bill of rights protects secret ballots, free speech, and eliminates oppressive 'trusteeships' by the international unions. Union financial officers serve under bond and may not borrow large sums from the unions. The Taft-Hartley list of 'unfair labor practices' was expanded in deference to management.

Labor movement in the U.S., as in England, was initiated by urban artisans rather than by factory workers, and its early history is not unlike that in the British Isles, though the Industrial Revolution came to the northern states a generation later than to England. In an effort to exploit the western market opened by canals, merchant-capitalists organized trading on a large scale after 1825, with systems of credit, division of labor, and wholesale marketing which threatened small business; and the old-time master workman became a foreman under an entrepreneur.

LABOR UNIONS, as the term is now understood, had been formed before 1800, but until the 1850's they were local, sporadic, and not effective in pressing their demands. Indeed, the ranks of labor were so constantly diluted by immigrants and women (increasingly employed during the 1830's) that trained artisans were alarmed about their declining status. The pioneer labor WORKINGMEN'S PARTY (1828), organized in Philadelphia, spread to other cities, and when small groups of it supported the Democrats, they obtained such reforms as protection against prison contract labor and the abolition of imprisonment for debt. In 1833, with increasing prosperity and rising costs, the American labor movement (like the British) abandoned politics in favor of TRADE UNIONS, the CLOSED SHOP, and STRIKES to win concessions. The introduction of gas lighting in the late 1830's provided means for a twelve-hour working day the year round, and in general wages and working conditions had improved. In many cities, and in the navy yards, by 1836 municipal and navy employees had won a ten-hour day. But the PANIC OF 1837 brought the collapse of unions, and years of recurrent, desperate, and futile strikes.

American workers thus learned that unions offered no help in labor problems. When eager idealists in the 1840's approached them with schemes of UTOPIAN SOCIALISM, instead of trying to assimilate the new industrial order the workers dissipated their energy in efforts to escape it. So firmly grounded was Jefferson's ideal of a simple agrarian society that many Americans regarded industrialism as alien and perilous. There was no inkling that government could be used as an instrument for social betterment. No provision was made for factory inspection before 1865, and not until 1869 was the first state labor bureau established (in Massachusetts).

The effort of labor to adjust itself to the rise of big business and the nationalization of industry was long hampered by contention within its own ranks. Should it fight or accept capitalism? Should it welcome or reject inventions, seek government patronage or trust laissez faire, organize on a craft or an industrial basis? The westward movement and the continuing flow of immigration acted as deterrents against the growth of unions, which were first organized on a national scale by the NATIONAL LABOR UNION (1866). But the nation as a whole persistently refused to regard labor problems realistically. The benefits of invention led to a vast increase in productivity, although labor felt that it shared but a small proportion of these advantages in the form of wages. Giant corporations, representing the combined wealth of thousands of stockholders, could lobby skillfully. They could afford to fight a strike for months, carry their battles through expensive litigation, or close their plants and starve workers into submission.

Reassessment of the entire economic pattern was speeded by events leading to and following World War I. After the PANIC OF 1929, which created the greatest industrial dislocation in U.S. history, the Federal and state legislatures took enormous strides to meet the problems. In the one decade of the 1930's they gave the labor movement more solid gains than would have been conceivable a century before.

Studies of the labor movement include J. R. Commons and others, *History of Labor in the U.S.* (4 vols., 1918–35); F. R. Dulles, *Labor in America* (1949); and Philip Taft, *Organized Labor in American History* (1964).

Labor parties, as groups organized with a platform for workers' benefits, have never exercised much influence in American politics. The pioneer among them was the WORKINGMEN'S PARTY (1828), which achieved modest success only after some of its principles were adopted by the Democrats. It did not survive the PANIC OF 1837. Until the 1850's workers' political activities were restricted because their various nationalities, classes, and religions made cohesion difficult. The Marxist SOCIALIST LABOR PARTY (1877) became the first Socialist party in the U.S. formed on a national scale, and though never able to attract a wide following, it regularly supported candidates for President from 1896 until 1944. The UNION LABOR PARTY (1887) achieved little success because organized labor was reluctant to support a farmer-dominated leadership. The SOCIALIST PARTY (1901) was formed from a merger of dissidents within the Socialist Labor group and the socialists who were not much concerned with the theoretical niceties expounded by the SOCIAL DEMOCRATIC faction. At this time most labor groups rejected either direct political action or affiliated with such protest groups as the FARMER-LABOR PARTY (1920), the PROGRESSIVE PARTY of 1924, and the PROGRESSIVE PARTY of 1948. Ideological left-wingers in 1919 organized as the Workers' party (COMMUNIST), and ran candidates for President for several years.

Organized labor at present maintains powerful lobbies in Washington and makes its influence felt within the major parties. The merger of A.F.L.–C.I.O. (1955), with its 15,000,000 membership, in effect created a substantial political pressure group.

Labor problems in the U.S. until the 20th century were generally negotiated privately, in line with the prevailing belief in laissez-faire individualism. (The CHINESE EXCLUSION ACTS, after 1882, chiefly benefited native labor in the Far West. The RAILROAD MEDIATION ACTS, after 1898, dealt only with train service cases.) In 1884 Congress created a Bureau of Labor, but the bureau did not become a separate Department of Labor with cabinet rank until 1913.

As the technological structure of modern industry multiplied in complexity, state and Federal legislatures attempted to bring public aid to the solution of labor problems. Such was the CLAYTON ANTITRUST ACT of 1914. But not until the 1930's did Federal laws begin to cope with such problems on all fronts. That decade saw passage of the NORRIS–LA GUARDIA ANTI-INJUNCTION ACT (1932), the WAGNER-CONNERY ACT (1935), the SOCIAL SECURITY ACT (1935), the WALSH-HEALY ACT (1936), and the FAIR LABOR STANDARDS ACT (1938). Other legislation at the time dealt with UNEMPLOYMENT, COLLECTIVE BARGAINING, HOME RELIEF, and CHILD LABOR. During the 1930's MIGRATORY LABOR also became a special problem.

Labor unions in the U.S. had their beginning when shoemakers in Philadelphia organized (1792), and by strikes and boycotts gained wage increases in the prosperous years of neutral trade. (In 1805 a strike occasioned the first labor CONSPIRACY case in America.) Such TRADE UNIONS were local and craft-conscious, and were formed to secure mutual benefits and standards of apprenticeship, hours, and wages. The first inter-union group was the Mechanics' Union of Trade Associations (1827), organized in Philadelphia, and their demands included a ten-hour day, restriction of child labor, abolition of imprisonment for debt, and abandonment of sweatshops. Panics, such as those of 1837 and 1857, weakened the bargaining power of unions, for the depressions were especially serious in the growing industrial areas.

After the Civil War, trades' assemblies sprang up with a nation-wide membership. The first attempt to combine the different groups into a federation was the NATIONAL LABOR UNION (1866), and though it lasted but six years, it attained a considerable membership. For a time the KNIGHTS OF ST. CRISPIN (1867) was a vigorous union of shoemakers. By far the most important early union, the KNIGHTS OF LABOR (1869), opened membership to all workers, men and women, skilled and unskilled; but after the AMERICAN FEDERATION OF LABOR was organized (1886), the prestige of the Knights declined. The revolutionary INDUSTRIAL WORKERS OF THE WORLD (1905), emphasizing organization on an industrial (VERTICAL) basis, was active before World War I, but waned rapidly thereafter. The largest and most influential of the industrial unions, the CONGRESS OF INDUSTRIAL ORGANIZATIONS, merged in 1955 to form the A.F.L.–C.I.O., the world's largest labor federation, with a membership of 15,000,000. The best known among the independent unions today are the TEAMSTERS and the UNITED MINE WORKERS, both in the old A.F. of L. for many years.

Labor, U.S. Department of, began as the Bureau of Labor (1884) in the Department of the Interior. It became an independent Labor Department in 1888 but without cabinet status. In 1903 it was combined into the Department of Commerce and Labor, headed by a cabinet officer. In 1913 Congress created a separate Department of Labor with its own cabinet head. Its major divisions include a Bureau of Employment Security, Bureau of Labor Statistics, Office of Labor-Management, and Office of Manpower, Automation, and Training. Secretaries of Labor and the Presidents under whom they served are as follows.

WILSON
William B. Wilson (Pa.) 1913

HARDING
James J. Davis (Pa.) 1921

COOLIDGE
James J. Davis (Pa.) 1923

HOOVER
James J. Davis (Pa.) 1929
William N. Doak (Va.) 1930

F. D. ROOSEVELT
Frances Perkins (N.Y.) 1933

TRUMAN
L. B. Schwellenbach (Wash.) 1945
Maurice J. Tobin (Mass.) 1948

EISENHOWER
Martin P. Durkin (Ill.) 1953
James P. Mitchell (N.J.) 1953

KENNEDY
Arthur J. Goldberg (Ill.) 1961
W. Willard Wirtz (Ill.) 1962

L. B. JOHNSON
W. Willard Wirtz (Ill.) 1963

LACHAISE, GASTON (1882–1935), French-born sculptor, studied at the Beaux-Arts, and in 1906 came to the U.S. The vitality he sought to express is typified in such bronzes as *Standing Woman* (Albright Gallery, Buffalo) and *Floating Figure* (Museum of Modern Art). He emphasizes rhythmic relationships by giving roundness to the elements of form.

Lacrosse, national sport of Canada, was adopted from North American Indians. Its rules were standardized by 1860. In the 1880's it gained a following in the U.S., and under rules laid down by the U.S. Intercollegiate Lacrosse Association the game is played in many colleges, especially in the northeast.

LADD, WILLIAM (1778–1841), graduated from Harvard (1797) and soon gained wealth as a merchant and shipowner.

After he retired from business in 1812 he devoted his philanthropies to the cause of peace. In 1828 he organized the powerful AMERICAN PEACE SOCIETY, of which he was a lifelong president. His *Essay on a Congress of Nations* (1840) projected a plan for an international court of arbitration that anticipated the Hague Tribunal by 80 years. The essential features of its proposed institutions were incorporated in the League of Nations.

LA FARGE, JOHN (1835–1910), artist and writer, was born in New York City, the son of wealthy French parents. He studied landscape painting (1856) in Paris, where he mingled with the intellectual and artistic leaders of the day. After returning to the U.S. (1858), he experimented with luminism in painting, anticipating the colorist treatment of the French Impressionists. In 1876 he was commissioned to decorate Trinity Church, Boston, and thereafter he devoted himself to mural painting and to the design and manufacture of stained glass, reforming the art of the glass-stainer by new methods known in Europe as 'American.' With Henry Adams he visited Japan and the South Seas (1886), recording his impressions in *An Artist's Letters from Japan* (1897), and his posthumous *Reminiscences of the South Seas* (1912), illustrated by his watercolor sketches.

Two grandsons won notice as writers. The architect CHRISTOPHER LA FARGE (1897–1956) devoted himself to literature after 1932. Representative novels include *Each to the Other* (1939), and *The Sudden Guest* (1946). OLIVER LA FARGE (1901–63) conducted ethnological investigations in the Southwest. His *Laughing Boy* (1929) and *The Enemy Gods* (1937) are authentic fictional studies of the Navaho Indians.

LAFAYETTE, MARIE JOSEPH PAUL, Marquis de (1757–1834), began his career in the French army, and was so stirred by the American cause of independence that in 1777 he came to Philadelphia, where Congress commissioned this wealthy nineteen-year-old nobleman a major general. He quickly won the trust and warm friendship of his idol Washington, with whom he shared the hardships of Valley Forge. Following a trip to France (1779–80) to negotiate for naval support, he distinguished himself by his energy at Monmouth and in the YORKTOWN CAMPAIGN. In 1784 the Maryland General Assembly conferred citizenship in perpetuity upon him and his male heirs. (He thus legally became a U.S. citizen when the states were federated, and was the only foreigner so honored in the nation's history until Congress conferred citizenship on Sir Winston Churchill in 1963.) The war over, he returned to France, where he associated himself with the French Revolution, was a state prisoner for five years (1792–97), and lived in retirement during the First Empire.

The warmth of his sixteen-month triumphal tour of the U.S. in 1824–25 is without parallel in the nation's reception of a foreigner. Ebullient, and with the easy self-confidence of the born aristocrat, he captivated men and women of all ranks with his charm of manner, and was overwhelmed with popular applause. Congress awarded him the sum of $24,424 and a township of land. (His own fortune had long since been forfeited to the French government.) A consistent liberal of unswerving courage and integrity, Lafayette was unable to transmit the republican methods of the new American nation to Continental politics, though he continued to exert influence through the respect in which he generally was held.

LAFITTE, JEAN (*fl.* 1780–1825), French pirate and smuggler, with his brother Pierre operated in the Barataria region off the Louisiana coast. During the War of 1812 he refused a commission in the Royal Navy and a handsome cash offer to support the British attack on New Orleans. Instead he aided the Americans, and those among his crew who participated in the battle were subsequently pardoned by President Madison. Lafitte later gathered a thousand followers and resumed his operations off the Texas coast. His end is not known, but his adventures and the rumors of his buried treasure are legendary.

LA FOLLETTE, ROBERT MARION (1855–1925), after graduation from the University of Wisconsin (1879) took up law practice, but most of his life was spent in public service: as U.S. Representative (1885–91), governor of Wisconsin (1900–

1904), and U.S. Senator (1906–25). Crusading, courageous, and independent, he fought the railroad and lumber interests that controlled Wisconsin, and introduced the 'Wisconsin Idea' of a direct primary, tax reform, and anticorruption measures. Although a Republican, he generally supported the reform measures of the Wilson administration. He sponsored the LA FOLLETTE SEAMAN'S ACT (1915), which gave sailors the same rights as factory workers.

Keenly isolationist, he voted against the entry of the U.S. into World War I, an act for which the legislature of his state formally censured him. After the war he was leader of the group that held the balance of power in the Senate, and he opposed the entry of the U.S. into the League of Nations. A lifelong liberal in domestic legislation, he opposed trusts and monopolies. In 1924, as candidate for President on the PROGRESSIVE PARTY ticket, he polled nearly 5,000,000 votes, but he carried only his state.

After his death the La Follette machine in Wisconsin was run by two sons: ROBERT M. LA FOLLETTE (1895–1953), who succeeded his father in the Senate (1925–47); and PHILIP F. LA FOLLETTE (1897–), who served as governor for three terms during the 1930's.

La Follette Seaman's Act (1915) regulated the conditions of employment in the merchant marine and for the first time gave seamen the same basic rights as those of factory workers. It abolished the crime of desertion when the ship was in safe harbor, and radically altered wage rates and minimum standards for food and living quarters. The Act also assured safety measures, a nine-hour day when in port, and the right to join a union.

LA GUARDIA, FIORELLO HENRY (1882–1947), after graduation from New York University (1910) began law practice in New York City. He entered Congress (1917), but resigned to engage actively in World War I. As a major he commanded American bombing squadrons on the Italian front. Again in Congress (1923–33), he became a leader of the progressive bloc and co-sponsor of the NORRIS–LA GUARDIA ANTI-INJUNCTION ACT (1932). He was elected mayor of New York City on a fusion ticket (1933–45), and in that office he executed a vast program of reforms. La Guardia was one of New York's most colorful mayors, and his administration was notable for its reduction of political corruption.

LAHONTAN, LOUIS-ARMAND, Baron de (1666–1713), French explorer, came to New France (1683) and made a close study of Indian life. He recorded his journey into the region of the upper Mississippi in *Nouveaux Voyages* (1703; critical English text, 1905), one of the first extended accounts of the West, and accurate except for his 'discovery' of a mythical River Long.

While the Jesuits and Recollects were minutely describing the American Indian, Lahontan philosophized about him, and his imaginary dialogue with the 'noble savage' Adario greatly influenced European ideas by helping to create the 'natural man' tradition. A measure of its importance is the fact that it went through 52 editions in five languages. French critics have pointed out that Montesquieu and Rousseau drew their ideas of primitivism from such chronicles as Lahontan's, and have suggested that the French Revolution took its origin from Lahontan's concept of the Hurons.

Laissez faire is the doctrine that an economic system functions best when it is free from governmental interference. Historically laissez faire was a reaction against MERCANTILISM, the system of commercial controls imposed, especially upon foreign trade, as a means of strengthening the state. The laissez-faire idea as set forth late in the 18th century by the French physiocrats and by Adam Smith in *Wealth of Nations* (1776) envisioned a system of free enterprise based on private ownership of industry supported by capital invested for profit. Its proponents hold that a 'natural' economic order, when undisturbed by artificial stimulus or regulation, will secure the maximum of well-being for the individual and thus for the community as a whole.

Americans only gradually adopted laissez-faire practices. Alexander Hamilton, although he praised Smith, insisted that 'infant industries' required protection. Southern planters on the other hand, dependent upon tobacco and cotton exports and cheap imports for everyday needs, naturally leaned toward free trade. (Slavery of course broke with the laissez-faire idea of a free wage system.)

In 19th-century America laissez faire thrived upon a vast domestic market, an efficient industry, and rich resources. But as capitalist enterprise evolved, businessmen found their interests best served by combining with their competitors in huge trusts as a means of eliminating waste and controlling price and production. The issue of monopolistic practice was forced into politics late in the 19th century by labor spokesmen and a vocal citizenry. ANTITRUST LAWS, following the efforts of Theodore Roosevelt and Wilson to check bigness in business, met only partial success. Indeed, Republicans of the 1920's coined the formula, 'More business in government, less government in business.'

The New Deal, assuming during the 1930's that 'mature capitalism' and a great depression had made laissez faire obsolete, suspended the antitrust laws for a time in order to create 'fair codes of competition' and fair labor standards, both of which survived despite adverse Supreme Court decisions on the National Industrial Recovery Act and the Agricultural Adjustment Act. By mid-20th century the general theory prevailed that the state must protect individual initiative, the profit motive, and those economic freedoms formerly left to pure laissez-faire individualism, the marketplace, and chance.

LAKE, SIMON (1866–1945), having invented an even-keel submarine torpedo boat (1894), built his *Argonaut,* the first submarine to operate successfully in the open sea (1897). (It was originally intended to salvage sunken treasure.) His models were rejected by the U.S. Navy in favor of the type designed by J. P. HOLLAND, but they were used with success by Germany during World War I, and were adopted later by the U.S. He became a consultant in submarine construction in Russia, Germany, and England. Lake was one of the first to use an internal combustion engine in a submarine. His later inventions included apparatus for recovering submerged cargoes and for carrying freight under water.

Lake Champlain, Battle of, see *Plattsburg.*

Lake Erie, Battle of (10 September 1813), was a curious naval engagement during the War of 1812, fought off Put-in-Bay between vessels hastily built of green wood and manned largely by nondescript crews of scouts, militiamen, and Canadian *voyageurs.* The American fleet of ten ships, led by Commodore OLIVER HAZARD PERRY, defeated a British squadron of six ships commanded by Captain Robert Barclay. Perry's terse report to General William Henry Harrison, 'We have met the enemy and they are ours,' was literally true. The victory insured immediate American control of Lake Erie, and freedom to invade Canada.

Lake George, Battle of (September 1755), was fought by 1200 colonials and 400 Indians, commanded by the major general of New York militia, WILLIAM JOHNSON, and 1400 French and Indian troops under Baron Dieskau. Johnson won the battle and his capture of Dieskau stopped the French offensive, but poor morale among his New England militiamen (the largest contingent) prevented him from moving on to Crown Point, his objective. The battle therefore was a draw in the strategy of the campaign, but it was the only English victory in the year of Braddock's disastrous defeat, and it won Johnson a baronetcy, the second created in America. (Colonel Ephraim Williams, whose estate by will created Williams College, was killed in the battle.)

LALEMANT, GABRIEL (1610–49), French Jesuit missionary in North America (1632–49), assisted JEAN DE BRÉBEUF among the Huron Indians. His important reports home are set down in the JESUIT RELATIONS. With Brébeuf he was tortured to death by the Iroquois in a Lake Ontario village, and is one of the six Martyrs of North America canonized in 1930.

LAMAR, LUCIUS QUENTIN CINCINNATUS (1825–93), after graduation from Emory College (1845) practiced law in Oxford, Mississippi. He represented his state in two Congresses before the Civil War, during which he served in the field and went to Europe as a Confederate commissioner. After the war he was elected to the House of Representatives (1873–77) and to the Senate (1877–85). President Cleveland was criticized for appointing this ex-Confederate Secretary of the Interior (1885–88), in which office Lamar dealt vigorously with the predatory interests that were despoiling lands and forests of the West. He resigned to become an Associate Justice of the U.S. Supreme Court (1888–93). In the rancorous postwar years, Lamar was a statesman whose sense of duty transcended sectional or personal interests, and he came to symbolize restored national harmony.

LAMB, JOHN (1735–1800), as leader (1765) of the SONS OF LIBERTY in New York, gave strong support to the patriot cause. He helped form the New York COMMITTEE OF CORRESPONDENCE, and led the seizure (1774) of the New York customhouse. He commanded troops during the War of Independence, and later served as collector of the port of New York.

'Lame Duck' Amendment, see *Twentieth Amendment.*

Land Acts, see *Public Land Sales.*

Land banks, so called, in the colonial period operated under a system whereby people mortgaged real estate for negotiable bills of credit. Pennsylvania's public loan offices, organized in the 1720's, were well managed, but in Massachusetts the situation was different. There such operations (in effect loans to farmers) held no promise for the country storekeeper or seaport merchant. So violent was local opposition to such a bank organized in 1740 that in the following year Parliament was induced to extend the South Sea Bubble Act of 1720 to similar ventures, thus declaring them illegal. This inept act led to litigation, ruined many stockholders, and left much embittered radicalism in New England. (Sam Adams's father was a victim.) It was in part responsible for the clause in the Federal Constitution forbidding ex post facto laws.

Land bounties, see *Bounties.*

Land commissions, see *Colonial Administration.*

Land Grant colleges, see *Morrill Land Grant Act* (1862).

Land Grants, see *Public Domain.*

Land Ordinances, see *Ordinances.*

Land tenure and land grant policies helped determine the organization of farm production in the American colonies. Property was generally acquired from the proprietor by FREEHOLD. Such grants in New England were made by the colonial governments to towns, who issued deeds to settlers; land was inherited by the children equally (except in Rhode Island), with a double portion reserved for the eldest son. New York fostered large grants to proprietors or promoters, and unlike New England, discouraged settlement. New Jersey and Pennsylvania followed a more democratic system by granting land to settlers in small parcels.

In the South large land accumulation was encouraged during the 17th century by the system of headrights, whereby each person who transported an emigrant at his own expense received some 50 acres per head. Both in New York and in the South land was accumulated by entail, the legal device by which land is settled inalienably upon the owner and his descendants. Jefferson fought the system, which Virginia abolished in 1776, as did most of the states soon thereafter. Likewise PRIMOGENITURE (the descent of land to the eldest son), long widely accepted in the colonies, ceased to operate before 1800, as did the double portion (in Pennsylvania and most of New England) to the eldest son.

Land grant policies affecting settlement of the back country were determined by the colonies laying claim to such lands. They might issue warrants to individuals or to groups. Notable among such grants were those made to the OHIO COMPANY (1747) and to the TRANSYLVANIA COMPANY (1775), whose members were interested in western land speculation.

LANDIS, KENESAW MOUNTAIN (1866–1944), Chicago lawyer and judge, was appointed (1920) by a committee of baseball executives to the newly created post of baseball commissioner as the result of a scandal. Eight members of the Chicago White Sox had accepted bribes to throw the 1919 World Series. 'Czar' Landis not only meted out severe penalties to the 'Black Sox' involved, but imposed strict discipline on players and management to restore public faith in the national pastime. During his long reign club owners introduced night baseball, radio broadcasts, and the farm system for training rookies.

LANGDELL, Christopher Columbus (1826–1906), jurist and law teacher, graduated from Harvard Law School (1853) and practiced law in New York City (1854–70). Called back to the Law School, he taught there for 30 years, serving as dean of the law faculty. He believed that the principles of law are best learned by a study of specific court decisions and introduced the 'case method' of law study, a procedure that gained wide popularity and thus greatly influenced the study of law in the U.S.

LANGLEY, Samuel Pierpont (1834–1906), Massachusetts-born aeronautical engineer, did not attend college and was largely self-taught in science. He became professor of physics and astronomy at present Pittsburgh University and director of the Allegheny Observatory (1867–87). He devised the bolometer for measuring minute quantities of radiant heat, pioneered in the field of infrared radiations, and did much to popularize astronomy, especially with his text *The New Astronomy* (1888). As secretary of the Smithsonian Institution (1887–1906), he established its Astrophysical Observatory, continued his mapping of the solar spectrum, and made important studies of solar eclipses. He constructed the first power-driven heavier-than-air machine to fly successfully (1896). His experiments thereafter with piloted machines were failures, but they later came to be recognized as of great importance, and have given him high rank among the pioneers of aviation.

LANGMUIR, Irving (1881–1957), had lifetime association (1909–51) with the Research Laboratory of General Electric Company at Schenectady, New York, where as a physical chemist he pioneered in the study of surface tensions. In 1932 he received the Nobel Prize in chemistry for his investigations and discoveries in surface chemistry. With G. N. LEWIS he formulated the Lewis-Langmuir theory of atomic structure and valence. His concentric shell theory (1919) explained chemical activity of an element in terms of the completeness of its outer shell of electrons. He developed gas-filled tungsten lamps as an accompaniment to basic research. His interest in artificial rainmaking gave powerful impetus to the scientific reputability of research in that field, thus advancing studies in METEOROLOGY.

LANGNER, Lawrence (1890–1962), Welsh-born patent agent and theater director, organized the Washington Square Players in New York City (1915) and founded the THEATRE GUILD (1919), of which he was a lifelong director. He was founder and first president of the Shakespeare Festival Theatre and Academy, Stratford, Connecticut, and throughout his career he fostered production standards of high order. His knowledge of patent law was often called on by civic and Federal departments, especially for advice in the area of problems involving literary ownership.

Language, American, see *American Language.*

LANSING, Robert (1864–1928), born in Watertown, New York, graduated from Amherst (1886), was admitted to the bar (1889), and became an authority on international law. He founded the *American Journal of International Law* (1907), which he helped edit until his death. As President Wilson's Secretary of State (1915–20), he concluded the LANSING-ISHII AGREEMENT (1917) with Japan. Wilson took Lansing to the Paris Peace Conference in 1919 but Lansing did not regard the covenant of the League of Nations as part of the peace treaty. The breach widened when Wilson, during his later illness, learned that on several occasions Lansing had called the cabinet together for consultation. At Wilson's request, Lansing resigned.

Lansing-Ishii Agreement (1917), negotiated between the U.S. and Japan, was a pact whereby the U.S. was willing to recognize Japan's 'special interest' in China providing Japan would respect the American OPEN DOOR POLICY. The phrase was ambiguous, for in Chinese the word 'special' was rendered 'paramount.' The U.S. sought relief from this embarrassment through the WASHINGTON CONFERENCE (1921), soon after which the agreement was abrogated.

LA SALLE, René Robert Cavelier, Sieur de (1643–87), after arriving in New France (1666) established a fur-trading post above Montreal facetiously named Lachine, since La Salle here intended to outfit an expedition to China. He spent the years 1669–71 exploring the Ohio and Great Lakes region, and probably penetrated Illinois and Michigan, although the exact extent of these travels is not known.

After Marquette and Jolliet had established (1673) the existence of a water highway from the St. Lawrence to the Gulf of Mexico, La Salle determined to extend French power to the Mississippi delta. The French governor, the Comte de Frontenac, encouraged his venture, and on two visits to France (1674, 1677) La Salle obtained from Louis XIV grants of land and a patent to build forts, trade, and explore. From his blockhouse at Niagara he set out (1679) with his lieutenant HENRI DE TONTI across the Great Lakes in the *Griffon* (the first sailing vessel on those waters), landing at Green Bay in Wisconsin. In 1682 he descended the Mississippi river to its mouth and took possession of the whole valley, naming this stupendous accession Louisiana to honor his king.

Again in France (1684) he obtained from Louis four ships, a few score colonizers, and the authority to govern the vast region from Michigan to the Gulf. But the return to America was disastrous. La Salle could not find the mouth of the Mississippi, and his boats were separated. One was wrecked, one captured by the Spanish, and a third returned to France. After landing (1685) on Texas shoals, he began an overland crossing to the east. The attempt to reach any guiding landmark proved futile, and La Salle was murdered by his own men, who soon met a similar fate from the Indians. But this indomitable figure takes rank as the most notable early explorer of the North American continent.

See the biographies by Francis Parkman (1879), and Maurice Constantin-Weyer (1931).

LAS CASAS, Bartolomé de (1474–1566), Spanish historian and 'Apostle of the Indies,' was born in Seville. As a gentleman-adventurer in 1502 he went to the New World to make his fortune. (It was his father who accompanied Columbus in 1493.) He underwent a revolutionary change of character, became an ecclesiastic, and bent all the efforts of his later life to insisting that the primary task of establishing a Spanish Empire in America demanded the peaceful conversion of Indians to the Christian faith. To that end he began his missionary labors (1514), striving to abolish Indian slavery. He wrote copiously and was influential in effecting laws that protected Indians from enslavement. After his final return to Spain in 1547 (aged seventy-three and almost a generation older than the new conquistadors) he published his *Very Brief Account of the Destruction of the Indies* (1552). Its many translations circulated throughout Europe and shocked his countrymen. It was a thundering denunciation (illustrated by Bry) of man's inhumanity to man.

Intended as a pamphlet to shame the Spanish conscience, it was used as a propaganda document to spread the belief that Spaniards are inherently cruel (the so-called 'Black Legend'). Las Casas concluded his long protest against enslavement with *Historia de las Indias* (published in 1875–76), used in manuscript by early historians of Spanish discoveries. It remains a basic document about the early Spanish explorations in the New World.

Lassen Volcanic National Park (est. 1916), 104,000 acres in northern California, is in a volcanic area of the Cascade Range. Lassen Peak (10,453 ft.), intermittently active in the period 1914–21, is the one volcano not yet extinct.

Latin grammar schools, the earliest type of college preparatory schools in the colonies, were established on the English model. The first, the Boston Latin School (1635), is still one of the principal schools in that city. Similar institutions, supported by tuition, quickly followed elsewhere. Boys entered at the age of eight or nine, were grounded chiefly in Latin and Greek for six years, and then were ready for Harvard (or for William and Mary after 1693), although for many boys such training completed their formal education. By mid 18th century Latin schools were supplanted by ACADEMIES.

LATROBE, BENJAMIN HENRY (1764–1820), born and educated in England, was a pivotal figure in the history of American architecture and the first professional American architect. After successful practice in London, he came to the U.S. (1796) and settled in Philadelphia. There, as a leading exponent of the GREEK REVIVAL, he designed (1799) the Bank of Pennsylvania, a structure that inaugurated the widely used temple form for banks. President Jefferson named him surveyor of public buildings (1803), in which capacity Latrobe revised the plans for the national capitol, originally designed by WILLIAM THORNTON, and helped rebuild it (1814–17) after it was burned by the British. He also designed the Cathedral in Baltimore (1818), and St. John's Church in Washington (1816).

A superb draftsman, who had surveyed large tracts from New York to New Orleans, Latrobe made sketches which have been called 'the most authentic existing presentation of the America of his time.' He was deeply cultivated and warmly admired by his contemporaries. No American of the period did more to raise architectural practice to the status of a profession.

Latter-Day Saints, see *Mormons.*

LAUDONNIÈRE, RENÉ GOULAINE DE (*fl.* 1562–82), French Huguenot colonizer, accompanied JEAN RIBAUT on the first French expedition to Florida (1562), and led a second in 1564. The attempt was tragically unsuccessful (the settlement was wiped out by the Spanish colonizer MENÉNDEZ), but Laudonnière managed to return to France, where he published *L'histoire notable de la Floride* (1586), translated and included in Hakluyt's *Principal Navigations* (1587). Laudonnière had been accompanied by the artist Jacques Le Moyne, whose famous drawings of natives and animals also survived and were published by THEODOR DE BRY.

LAUGHLIN, JAMES LAURENCE (1850–1933), as head of the department of political economy at Chicago (1892–1916) developed it into a significant teaching discipline at university level. Although he was a conservative follower of John Stuart Mill in economic theory, he gave encouragement to younger unorthodox theorists, such as THORSTEIN VEBLEN, whom he brought to the university as an instructor. He served as adviser on currency matters to state and Federal agencies, and for 40 years edited the *Journal of Political Economy.* His writings include *History of Bimetallism in the U.S.* (1886), *Facts about Money* (1895), and *Reciprocity* (1903).

LAURENS, HENRY (1724–92), wealthy South Carolina merchant, was a leader in promoting colonial opposition to British coercive demands on the eve of the War of Independence. He served as president of the Second Continental Congress (1777–78). On his way to Holland to negotiate a treaty and a loan, he was captured by the British and imprisoned for more than a year in the Tower of London, until he was exchanged for Cornwallis in 1781. At the war's end he served as peace commissioner with Franklin, Adams, and Jay in negotiating the TREATY OF PARIS of 1783.

His son JOHN LAURENS (1754–82) served Washington as confidential secretary and repeatedly engaged in active service. The abusive criticism of Washington by General CHARLES LEE drew from Laurens a challenge to an inconclusive duel. Laurens was designated to arrange the terms for the surrender of Cornwallis at Yorktown (1781). On a mopping-up operation in the Carolinas the intrepid young man was killed in a minor skirmish. He came to be known as 'the Bayard of the Revolution,' because his gallantry so resembled that of the French military hero of memory.

Lausanne Conference (1932), see *Young Plan.*

LA VÉRENDRYE, PIERRE GAULTIER DE VARENNES, Sieur de (1685–1749), French-Canadian explorer, after military service in Canada and Europe, obtained a monopoly of the fur trade in the West and began a search for an overland route to the Pacific. With his three sons and a nephew he built a fort on the site of Winnepeg (1738), and in that year undertook his memorable journey to the upper Missouri, where he ventured into the Black Hills and may have entered Wyoming. He was the first explorer to reach the northwest plains.

Law in the U.S. developed from English precedent, except in Louisiana, where French civil law prevailed. It did not gain status as a profession in any of the colonies until late in the 18th century. Even judges commonly lacked legal training, and courts were loosely organized. The colonists looked upon lawyers as 'mercenary attorneys,' too expensive for ordinary people, and believed that every man should be able to plead his own cause. But as commercial life became more intricate, communities came to accept the idea that some men should make the law a special business. Well into the 19th century most lawyers received an informal training through apprenticeship, and admission to legal practice was haphazard.

While the colonists could prosper with lay judges and courts manned predominantly by unspecialized lawyers, they could not live without law. In fact, the distrust of lawyers bred a widening respect for law. The Massachusetts *Body of Liberties (*1641) and *General Lawes* (1648) are uniquely significant because they embodied the Puritan 'federal' theology's emphasis upon a 'covenant' or contract in social relationships, and anticipated fundamental elements in American constitutional law. The pervasiveness of legal competence among American men of affairs is evidenced by the fact that of the 56 signers of the Declaration of Independence, 25 were 'lawyers,' as were 36 of the 55 members of the Federal Constitutional Convention.

The first legal society in America was the New York Bar Association (1747). In Massachusetts a similar group was formed in 1761. In the South, where ties with British institutions were closer, the leading practitioners usually attended the Inns of Court in London. William and Mary College in Virginia was the first American institution to offer systematic legal instruction (1779), but the earliest law school was the Litchfield (Connecticut) Law School (1784), established by TAPPING REEVE. Other early colleges to create departments of law were Transylvania (1799), Harvard (1817), Yale (1824), and Virginia (1826). By 1860 law degrees were granted by 22 schools.

In the 18th century English jurisprudence stressed natural law, the theory that law must incorporate the natural rights of man. The *Commentaries* (1765–69) of Sir William Blackstone (1723–80), which exemplify the theory, were the most important influence in American jurisprudence until the last quarter of the 19th century. Blackstone greatly aided the American reception of the COMMON LAW, which was resisted by Jeffersonians as an expensive system of technicalities useful primarily for landowners and well-to-do merchants who could afford litigation and profited from its condemnation of unions and strikes as combinations or conspiracies in restraint of trade.

Leaders among those who helped develop the American concept of law in the early days of the Republic were JAMES KENT, who modified English chancery practice to conform to American institutions; JOSEPH STORY, who codified EQUITY LAW; and EDWARD LIVINGSTON, who first effectively codified procedure law in the U.S. The decisions of JOHN MARSHALL have had a lasting effect in constitutional law. A distinctive feature in the U.S. is the coexistence of Federal and state jurisdiction.

The impact of DARWINISM and of PRAGMATISM upon the American mind is vividly illuminated in the history of legal thinking after 1870. The idea emerged that even fundamental law is an organic growth that must be shaped to the needs of a changing society. Historical jurisprudence gave way to sociological jurisprudence, emphasized in the writings and legal opinions of Justice OLIVER WENDELL HOLMES, America's most distinguished jurist. The creation of a science of law was a special function of the maturing law schools, first notably revitalized when C. C. LANGDELL introduced the case method at Harvard during the 1870's. Eminent American jurists and legal scholars in the 20th century include SAMUEL WILLISTON, LOUIS BRANDEIS, BENJAMIN CARDOZO, ROSCOE

POUND, LEARNED HAND, JOHN WIGMORE, and FELIX FRANKFURTER.

See Homer Cummings and Carl McFarland, *Federal Justice* (1937); J. W. Hurst, *The Growth of American Law* (1950); and Charles Warren, *A History of the American Bar . . . to 1860* (1911).

LAWRENCE, ERNEST ORLANDO (1901–58), director of the Radiation Laboratory (1936–58) at the University of California at Berkeley, conducted pioneer research in nuclear physics and in the application of physics to biology and medicine. In 1930 he devised a 'magnetic resonance accelerator' (cyclotron), which produced high energy particles by bombarding nuclei in a magnetic field. He thus provided a tool for the creation of new elementary particles, and laid the experimental foundation of high energy physics. In 1939 he received the Nobel Prize in physics for the invention and development of his device.

LAWRENCE, JAMES (1781–1813), having served with gallantry in the Tripolitan War, at the outbreak of the War of 1812 commanded the *Hornet,* which after a close fight of fifteen minutes off the Demerara river in British Guiana sank the enemy brig of war *Peacock* (February 1813). Promoted to captain, he was commanding the unlucky *Chesapeake,* with a green and mutinous crew, when in June on his way out of Boston harbor to intercept ships from Canada, he unwisely accepted challenge from the frigate *Shannon*. The *Chesapeake* was captured, but Lawrence's words 'Don't give up the ship,' allegedly uttered as he was being carried from the deck, mortally wounded, became a popular naval battle cry.

LAWSON, THOMAS WILLIAM (1857–1925), multimillionaire Boston stockbroker, made an important contribution to the MUCKRAKING movement by his article on 'Frenzied Finance' for *Everybody's* (1904–5), and by other writings on the subject, including a novel, *Friday the Thirteenth* (1907). Angry clients turned on him as a renegade to his class, and Lawson died in relative poverty. His sensational attacks on the 'money kings,' stock market abuses, and the irresponsible practices of the large insurance companies influenced the significant insurance investigation of 1905 and undoubtedly other financial reforms as well.

Lea-McCarran Act (1938), see *Civil Aeronautics Authority*.

League of Nations (1920–46), with headquarters at Geneva, Switzerland, was the first major world organization dedicated to international co-operation and the prevention of war. It was first formally proposed in President Wilson's FOURTEEN POINTS (1918), and its Covenant was incorporated in the VERSAILLES TREATY (1919). The League's organization and power were subject to untried international sanctions. Although Wilson fought the greatest battle of his political career to win Senate ratification of the Treaty, he failed to gain it and the U.S. never joined the League.

The absence from the League of the U.S. (and, until late in its existence, of Germany and the Soviet Union) contributed to its decline. It was generally successful in settling disputes among smaller nations, but it foundered because the great ones could not be coerced. The U.S. sat in on various humanitarian activities and was represented at its WORLD DISARMAMENT CONFERENCE (1932). But the Japanese invasion of Manchuria (1932), and the accession of the Nazis to power in Germany (1933), which then withdrew from the League, spelled its doom. In 1946 it surrendered its property and records to the UNITED NATIONS.

League of Women Voters was organized (1920) by CARRIE CHAPMAN CATT with the purpose of educating American women to the responsible use of their newly won suffrage. It continues to function on local, state, and national levels.

Learned societies in the U.S. have generally reflected the social and intellectual characteristics of the period of their foundation. Thus the earliest, such as the AMERICAN PHILOSOPHICAL SOCIETY (1743) and the AMERICAN ACADEMY OF ARTS AND SCIENCES (1780), were broadly based, with members chosen from the leaders in science, statecraft, and letters. Later groups tended to limit themselves to fewer disciplines. Thus were formed the regional HISTORICAL SOCIETIES, and such specialized groups as the AMERICAN ANTIQUARIAN SOCIETY (1812), AMERICAN GEOGRAPHICAL SOCIETY (1851), MODERN LANGUAGE ASSOCIATION (1883), AMERICAN HISTORICAL ASSOCIATION (1884), AMERICAN FOLK-LORE SOCIETY (1888), and scores of others covering restricted fields. Important also are such co-ordinating agencies as the National Research Council (1916, natural sciences), American Council of Learned Societies (1919), and the Social Science Research Council (1923).

LEASE, MARY ELIZABETH (1853–1933), agrarian reformer and temperance agitator, as a young woman was admitted to the Kansas bar. Active as a Populist in the campaign of 1890, the sad-faced 'Kansas Pythoness' went about advising farmers to 'raise less corn and more Hell,' and four years later warned the East that 'the people are at bay, let the bloodhounds of money beware.' She retired from political activity in 1918.

Lecompton constitution, formulated at a convention dominated by proslavery Kansans, was approved in December 1857, after Free-Soilers declined to vote. When President Buchanan urged Congress to admit Kansas to the Union under the Lecompton constitution (February 1858), he precipitated a party crisis. Northern Democrats, following the lead of Stephen A. Douglas, condemned the constitution as a violation of POPULAR SOVEREIGNTY and a mockery of justice. Both the Senate and the House decided to submit the constitution to popular vote, and in August Kansas voters rejected it (11,812 to 1926). The decision to remain in territorial status brought the disturbance virtually to an end, since, under the DRED SCOTT decision, slavery was legal in Kansas. But the controversy had given the Republicans a powerful campaign issue. It split the Democratic ticket, and won Lincoln the election in 1860. (In 1861 Kansas was admitted to the Union as a free state.)

LEDYARD, JOHN (1751–89), Connecticut-born explorer, abandoned his studies at Dartmouth, shipped as a sailor, and in 1776 joined Captain James Cook's last voyage to the Sandwich Islands (Hawaii), an account of which he published (1783). He conceived of the American colonies as a potential nation extending to the Pacific Ocean. In France he received encouragement from Thomas Jefferson to seek a practical route overland to the Pacific Northwest, but he was unable to raise funds to finance the venture. Instead, in 1787 he crossed Europe on foot to St. Petersburg, then to Irkutsk in Siberia (1788) where, imprisoned as a spy, he wrote a journal of his Russian travels. While organizing a trek into central Africa, with the blessing of the Royal Society of London, this restless adventurer was delayed in Cairo, where he committed suicide.

Lee Family of Virginia was founded by RICHARD LEE (d. 1664), a wealthy tobacco planter. The family first came into prominence during the 18th century, when four brothers served the patriot cause as statesmen: RICHARD HENRY LEE, FRANCIS LIGHTFOOT LEE, WILLIAM LEE, and ARTHUR LEE. HENRY LEE ('Light-Horse Harry') was a cousin, likewise distinguished, and father of ROBERT E. LEE. R. E. Lee's two sons, GEORGE WASHINGTON CUSTIS LEE and WILLIAM HENRY FITZHUGH LEE ('Rooney'), served the Confederacy as general officers and later occupied positions of responsibility, as did their cousin FITZHUGH LEE.

General CHARLES LEE, a thorn in Washington's flesh, also a Virginian, was not a member of this family.

LEE, ANN (1736–84), religious visionary and founder of the SHAKERS in America, led a band of eight from England in 1774. She was illiterate, but in the eyes of a growing number of adherents she had the power to work miracles. The tour through New England of Mother Ann, or Ann the Word, was disquieting to many, since her followers greeted her appearance as the Second Coming of Christ.

LEE, ARTHUR (1740–92), born at 'Stratford,' Westmoreland county, Virginia, was a brother of Richard H., Francis L., and William Lee. Educated at Eton and Edinburgh (M.D., 1764), he returned home to practice medicine, but decided to study law and set out for London. There, like his brother William, he became a supporter of John Wilkes, and likewise a political pamphleteer.

As agent for the Continental Congress,

he gained the aid of the playwright Beaumarchais (acting in Paris as a secret agent for the French monarchy), whose mock firm, Hortalès & Cie, furnished arms to the Americans (1776–77). Late in 1776 Congress sent Lee and Benjamin Franklin to join Silas Deane, and together they arranged the FRANCO-AMERICAN ALLIANCE. Lee quarreled with both Deane and Franklin, and his reports to Congress resulted in the recall of Deane. In 1777 he acted first as commissioner to Spain, then to Prussia, without receiving official recognition in either post. His unpopularity abroad was such that in 1779 Congress recalled him.

LEE, CHARLES (1731–82), British-born Revolutionary general, served in America during the French and Indian War (1755–61). He was later with the British in Portugal, but in 1773 he settled in Virginia. At the outbreak of the Revolution Congress commissioned him a major general with what amounted to an independent command. Ambitious for supreme authority, he repeatedly disregarded Washington's orders to cross the Hudson after the battle of White Plains, intent on achieving a personal success that would convince Congress that he should replace Washington.

When at last he crossed into New Jersey (December 1776), he was fortunately captured by the British, and his army was placed under Washington. Unfortunately he was later exchanged, and his order to retreat at the battle of Monmouth (1778) led to an American rout until it was stopped by Washington. (The documents revealing his treasonable assistance to General Howe in planning the capture of Philadelphia in 1777 later came to light.) Court martialed for disobeying orders, and suspended from service for a year, he so fulsomely criticized Washington that young JOHN LAURENS challenged him to an inconclusive duel. His abuse of Washington became an affront to Congress, and in 1780 he was dismissed from service.

LEE, FITZHUGH (1835–1905), nephew of Robert E. Lee, graduated from the U.S. Military Academy (1856). He served as a general officer in Stuart's cavalry corps with his cousin, 'Rooney' Lee, and in March 1865 became chief of cavalry for the Army of Northern Virginia. He was later governor of Virginia (1886–90). He served as consul general at Havana (1893–98), and became its military governor after the Spanish-American War. Thereafter for a time he commanded the Department of the Missouri.

LEE, FRANCIS LIGHTFOOT (1734–97), born at 'Stratford,' Westmoreland county, Virginia, was a brother of Richard H., William, and Arthur Lee. Like Richard he served in the Continental Congress (1775–80), signed the Declaration of Independence, and later supported the adoption of the Federal Constitution.

LEE, GEORGE WASHINGTON CUSTIS (1832–1913), eldest son of Robert E. Lee, graduated from the U.S. Military Academy (1854), and during most of the Civil War served as aide-de-camp to President Davis. As major general he commanded in the field after 1864, and was captured at the war's end in the fighting at Sailor's Creek. He succeeded his father as president of Washington and Lee (1871–97).

LEE, HENRY (1756–1819), famed as a cavalry leader in the Revolution, and known as Light-Horse Harry Lee, was born at 'Leesylvania,' Prince William county, Virginia. He was a cousin of Richard A., Francis L., William, and Arthur Lee, and father of Robert E. Lee. A graduate of the College of New Jersey at Princeton (1773), he served brilliantly in the CAROLINA CAMPAIGN. As a member of the Continental Congress (after 1785), he led in the struggle to ratify the Constitution. He served as governor of Virginia (1792–95) and led the troops that quelled the WHISKY REBELLION (1794). As a member of Congress (1799–1801), he wrote the *Resolutions* declaring Washington 'first in war, first in peace, and first in the hearts of his countrymen.'

LEE, RICHARD (d. 1664), founder of the LEE FAMILY of Virginia, migrated from Shropshire, England, to York county, Virginia, where he became a substantial tobacco planter. He was a leader of affairs in the colony, serving at various times as burgess, member of the council, attorney general, and secretary of state.

LEE, Richard Henry (1732–94), born at 'Stratford,' Westmoreland county, Virginia, was a brother of Francis L., William, and Arthur Lee. A discontented aristocrat, he protested the Stamp Act (1765), gave support to the radical measures of Patrick Henry and Thomas Jefferson, and helped form the important intercolonial COMMITTEES OF CORRESPONDENCE. As a member of the Continental Congress (1774–80, 1784–87) he was active in promoting an agreement to halt the importation of slaves. He was a member (with John Adams and Edward Randolph) of the committee that placed Washington in charge of the Continental army, and he introduced the motion that led to the Declaration of Independence. Vigorous in support of states' rights, he opposed the Federal Constitution, but after its adoption, as U.S. Senator (1789–92) he was instrumental in the passage of the Bill of Rights and was author of the Tenth Amendment.

LEE, Robert E. [Edward] (1807–70), general in chief of the Confederate armies in the Civil War, inherited a long and distinguished tradition of arms and service to the nation. Son of HENRY LEE (Light-Horse Harry Lee), of Westmoreland county, Virginia, he graduated from the U.S. Military Academy (1829), joined the Corps of Engineers, and married Mary Custis (1831), whose father's estate, Arlington House, across the Potomac from Washington, D.C., became their home until the Civil War. He served under Winfield Scott in the Mexican War (1846–47), and as superintendent at West Point (1852–55). On leave while commanding a regiment in Texas (1857–61), he directed the capture of John Brown at Harpers Ferry (1859).

When Scott called him back from Texas after the Lower South had seceded in February 1861, the decision forced upon him was agonizing. Lee had no sympathy either for secession or slavery, and he loved the Union and the army he had served. Moreover, on Scott's urgent recommendation, Lincoln offered Lee the field command of the Union army. But Lee could not fight against his own. In April he resigned his commission and assumed command of the military and naval forces of Virginia.

President Davis appointed Lee his military adviser with the rank of general, and when J. E. Johnston was wounded, Lee assumed command of the Army of Northern Virginia (June 1862). His leadership of that army through the next three years placed him among the world's great captains.

Lee immediately took the offensive. He ended McClellan's threat to Richmond in the SEVEN DAYS' battle, and routed Pope at second BULL RUN (August 1862). Checked at ANTIETAM, he defeated Burnside at FREDERICKSBURG in December, and Hooker at CHANCELLORSVILLE (May 1863). His defeat at GETTYSBURG two months later was the turning point of the war. He opposed Grant during the WILDERNESS CAMPAIGN, but his appointment as general in chief (February 1865) could not stem the tide. He surrendered at APPOMATTOX in April 1865, and thereafter served as president of Washington College, renamed Washington and Lee University in the year following his death.

Like George Washington, Lee was a great and simple person. His character offers historians no moral flaws to probe. Whichever choice of allegiance Lee made would have been right. He was idolized by his soldiers and by the South. He has always had the deep admiration of the North, and is a national hero.

See the biography by Douglas Freeman (4 vols., 1934–35).

LEE, William (1739–95), born at 'Stratford,' Westmoreland county, Virginia, was a brother of Richard H., Francis L., and Arthur Lee. He opened a business house in London (1768), became a partisan of the liberal politician John Wilkes, an alderman of London (1775), and accepted appointment by the Continental Congress as a diplomatic agent to win foreign support for the patriot cause. Unable to obtain aid from either Austria or Prussia, he and an unauthorized Dutchman drew up a possible U.S.–Dutch treaty. A copy of this unsanctioned document, on its way to America, was seized when the British captured HENRY LAURENS, and it was used as a cause for the warfare between Great Britain and the Netherlands (1780–84).

LEE, WILLIAM HENRY FITZHUGH (1837–91), known as 'Rooney' Lee, was the son of Robert E. Lee. While a junior at Harvard (1857), he accepted a commission in the U.S. Army. Like his father, at the outbreak of the Civil War he transferred his allegiance to the Confederacy, and most of his service was with Stuart's cavalry. Wounded (1863) and subsequently captured by Federals, upon exchange in 1864 he was promoted to major general. He served as a Democrat in Congress after 1887.

LEEDS, DANIEL (1652–1720), established in Philadelphia a family business as almanac maker with his *American Almanack,* begun in 1687, and carried on by his son, TITAN LEEDS (1699–1738). After 1733 Titan Leeds was in friendly rivalry with Benjamin Franklin. Imitating the 'Bickerstaff' hoax of Swift, Franklin's *Poor Richard* annually claimed that his prediction of Leeds's death had indeed proved true, and Leeds annually denied it.

Legal Tender Cases, testing the constitutionality of the Legal Tender Acts of 1862, 1863, and 1864, were brought before the Supreme Court in the early 1870's. The Acts had authorized the issuance of GREENBACKS. In *Hepburn* v. *Griswold* (1870) by a 5 to 3 decision the Court held the acts unconstitutional, on the ground that they violated the obligation of contracts as set forth in the Fifth Amendment.

In the second case (1871), *Knox* v. *Lee* and *Parker* v. *Davis,* heard before the Court, to which Grant had appointed two new justices, the decision was reversed, and the Court declared that any legal tender was valid when Congress so declared in a time of emergency. The cry rose that Grant had packed the Court, since Grant had made no secret of his disapproval of the *Hepburn* decision and knew how his appointees stood on the issue.

In a still later decision (1884), *Julliard* v. *Greenman,* the Court upheld the Acts without reference to emergency, on the ground that Congress has the constitutional power to borrow money.

Legislative power, the power to make law, is generally the authority to establish policy. In the Federal Constitution of the U.S. (Article I) such authority is delegated to Congress. Under the principle of SEPARATION OF POWERS, legislation is theoretically exercised only by Congress. In fact, however, the President exercises considerable legislative authority by his ordinance-making power, the EXECUTIVE AGREEMENT. The Supreme Court does so by JUDICIAL REVIEW.

Legislative Reorganization Act (1946) (La Follette-Monroney Act) dealt with internal congressional organization and procedure. Standing committees were reduced, in the House from 48 to 19; in the Senate from 33 to 15. Salaries were increased from $10,000 to $12,500 a year, with a tax-exempt expense allowance of $2500. A retirement system was instituted for members of Congress, and improvements were made in the Legislative Reference Service.

Legislative resolutions in the U.S. Congress and in many state assemblies are of three kinds. Simple resolutions are those by which rules of procedure are adopted or committees appointed. Concurrent resolutions embody agreements between the two Houses, and deal chiefly with minor issues of concern to the Houses alone. Joint resolutions are a form of subsidiary legislation of a special or unusual nature. These last are subject to executive veto or approval, and if approved they have the force of law.

LEHMAN, HERBERT HENRY (1878–1963), statesman and philanthropist, after graduation from Williams (1899) became a member of the New York banking firm of Lehman Brothers. As Democratic governor of New York (1932–42) he effected reforms in the state administration and sponsored liberal social welfare legislation. He vigorously inaugurated leadership of the United Nations Relief and Rehabilitation Administration (UNRRA) (1943–46), which fed starving millions in war-torn Europe. For eight years he served his state in the U.S. Senate (1949–57), where he was aligned with the liberal, international bloc. His substantial contributions in politics for 40 years were seldom headlined, but they placed him in the forefront of those working for liberal and humanitarian causes.

LEIDY, Joseph (1823–91), professor of anatomy (1853) and botany (after 1884) at Pennsylvania, was the pre-eminent American anatomist of his day. He classified the fossils collected by F. V. HAYDEN, and his monographs on the fauna of Hayden's surveys of the Far West are landmarks in American paleontology. Leidy was the first to identify extinct species of the horse, tiger, rhinoceros, camel, and sloth in the U.S., and he broke ground in the field of parasitology with *Flora and Fauna within Living Animals* (1853). He was a pioneer elucidator of the sequence of horse forms, a study in which he was followed by E. D. COPE and O. C. MARSH. His *Fresh Water Rhizopods of North America* (1879) includes his own drawings, and remains a permanent contribution to the study of protozoans.

LEIF ERICSSON (*fl.* A.D. 999–1003) was son of Eric the Red, the Norseman from Iceland who discovered Greenland and founded a colony on its southwest coast. About A.D. 1000, 'Leif the Lucky' reached the coast of 'Vinland.' Though long identified by historians with the New England coast, in 1963 this Vinland was discovered to be at L'Anse aux Meadows, a Newfoundland fishing village, where ruins of a Viking settlement were unearthed. Radiocarbon datings of charcoal show that the site was occupied about A.D. 1000. This ancient community, yielding Viking artifacts, may have been settled by Leif or by his kinsman THORFINN KARLSEFNI. The narratives of these voyages, preserved in the 14th-century manuscript sagas *Hauksbók* and *Flateyjarbók,* are thus authenticated.

Leisler's Revolt (1689) was one of a succession of popular revolutions in the American colonies during the 'Glorious Revolution' of 1688, which brought William and Mary to the English throne. A German-born New Yorker, Jacob Leisler (1640–91), attempted to preserve the political status of the ousted James II. For a time Leisler managed to act as *de facto* governor of New York, but he was maneuvered into a position where he could be accused of treason, and he was hanged. In 1695 Parliament repudiated the judicial murder and indemnified Leisler's heirs. The rebellion was one of the earliest attempts to abolish autocratic rule, as it supported the rights of the people.

Lend-Lease Act (1941) gave the President authority to lend or lease equipment to any nation 'whose defense the President deems vital to the defense of the U.S.' It thus made the U.S. an 'arsenal of democracy' after the outbreak of World War II. Its farsighted provisions at once made available $7 billion worth of arms, foodstuffs, and services, which were increased to $50 billion by 1945. By gearing U.S. production to war needs, it officially abandoned any pretense at neutrality. The law also provided for 'reverse lend-lease,' which accounted for $17 billion worth of supplies later needed by American troops abroad.

L'ENFANT, Pierre Charles (1754–1825), French-born engineer, emerged from the War of Independence with the rank of major, and won Washington's attention by designing the insignia for the Society of the CINCINNATI. Having remodeled Federal Hall in New York, where Washington was inaugurated, in 1791 at Washington's request L'Enfant submitted plans for a proposed national capital on the Potomac. His inherently excellent radial design, based upon the great baroque schemes for Rome, Versailles, and London, was beyond the financial ability of Congress to execute, and Washington regretfully terminated L'Enfant's services. L'Enfant then refused what he regarded as an inadequate fee for his labors, declined (in 1812) a professorship at West Point, and thereafter lived an embittered existence on the bounty of compassionate friends.

The haphazard growth of the city of Washington was abruptly altered by congressional action in 1901, when L'Enfant's plans, taken from archives, were used to give the avenues of the city their present axial relations. In 1909, with fitting honors, L'Enfant was given burial in Arlington National Cemetery.

LEUTZE, Emanuel (1816–68), German painter, trained in Düsseldorf, is chiefly known for the theatrically posed *Washington Crossing the Delaware* (Metropolitan Museum, on display at Washington's Crossing, Pennsylvania). He settled in the U.S. (1859), and painted such allegories as *Westward the Course of Em-*

pire Takes Its Way, on the wall of the west stairway of the national Capitol.

Levelers were members of an extremist English Puritan party which arose in the army of the Long Parliament (about 1647). Their ideals of complete political, religious, and social equality were not shared by Cromwell, who crushed the movement (1649). Roger Williams sympathized with their aims, which to some degree were those of Baptists and Quakers.

Lever Act (1917), mobilizing food and fuel resources for World War I, authorized price fixing and control of production and distribution. Herbert Hoover became Food Administrator, and Harry A. Garfield was named Fuel Administrator. Under this conservation act, Congress introduced the first phase of prohibition by forbidding the use of foodstuffs for producing distilled spirits and outlawing the importation of liquor.

LEVERETT, JOHN (1662–1724), after graduation from Harvard (1680) served for twelve years as tutor in the college. He then practiced law, and in 1702 was appointed judge of the Superior Court. Five years later, to the chagrin of the Mather dynasty, he was chosen as the first lay president of Harvard (1707–24), where he established a liberal tradition in spite of clerical conservatism. His election to membership in the Royal Society (1714) probably signalized his support of the Newtonian 'new science.'

LEWIS, CLARENCE IRVING (1883–1964), graduated from Harvard in 1906 and taught philosophy there after 1920. He pioneered in the study of modal logic, dealing with the relationships between such concepts as necessity and possibility. He was a leader in early work on semantics, and his *Analysis of Knowledge and Valuation* (1947) became a landmark in philosophy by its combination of symbolic logic with an essentially pragmatic epistemology. Later works were *The Ground and Nature of the Right* (1955), and *Our Social Inheritance* (1957).

LEWIS, GILBERT NEWTON (1875–1946), professor of physical chemistry at the University of California at Berkeley (after 1912), made basic pioneer contributions to atomic research. He preceded IRVING LANGMUIR in enunciating (1916) the electron theory of valence (that the chemical properties of compounds are explained in terms of their outer shell of electrons), and with Langmuir formulated the Lewis-Langmuir theory of atomic structure and valence. He evolved the 'octet' theory of molecular structure, and improved thermodynamic methods by the concepts of 'fungacity' and 'activity.' His writings include *Valence and the Structure of Atoms and Molecules* (1923), and *The Anatomy of Science* (1926).

LEWIS, JOHN LLEWELLYN (1880–), son of a Welsh immigrant coal miner, rose through the union ranks to become president (1920) of the UNITED MINE WORKERS, an office he held for 40 years. Forceful and determined, Lewis championed every cause that might advance the welfare of the miners, and as president of his union was one of the important figures in the AMERICAN FEDERATION OF LABOR until differences with WILLIAM GREEN on industrial organization led him to break from the A.F. of L. and form the CONGRESS OF INDUSTRIAL ORGANIZATIONS (1935). In 1942, differing with Philip Murray, the new head of the C.I.O., Lewis withdrew his union from it. He subsequently returned to the A.F. of L., and again withdrew in 1947 over differences on the signing of the non-communist affidavit required by the Taft-Hartley law.

Although he helped pave the way for antistrike legislation by striking during the 'no strike' period of World War II, he won the demands of the miners. Similar tactics employed in 1948 led to a heavy fine, but the method again proved successful. The name of John L. Lewis thereafter was synonymous with militant labor leadership.

LEWIS, MERIWETHER (1774–1809), Virginia-born army captain, became secretary to his friend President Jefferson, who selected him to lead the notable LEWIS AND CLARK EXPEDITION. (Lewis chose WILLIAM CLARK as associate in command.) In 1807 Lewis became governor of Louisiana Territory, with headquarters at St. Louis, and while traveling to Washington to prepare the report of the expedition for official publication, he died suddenly at an obscure inn in central Tennessee. He may have been murdered, although Jefferson assumed that his death was a suicide.

LEWIS, [HARRY] SINCLAIR (1885–1951), Minnesota-born novelist, after graduation from Yale (1907) served an apprenticeship as a journalist and hack writer. His first six novels received little attention, but *Main Street* (1920) and *Babbitt* (1922) brought him wide recognition. Intimate pictures of American social behavior, they criticize uncritical conformity, commercialism, and ugly materialism, and their titles soon came to epitomize averageness. His dozen later novels are variants and extensions of the same theme, and have a remarkable ability for reproducing the rhythm and idiom of conversation. As the first American to receive the Nobel Prize in literature (1930), he gained an extensive reputation.

Lewis and Clark Expedition (1804–6), the most significant transcontinental journey in U.S. history, is one of the epics of exploration. Even before President Jefferson had acquired the vast territory of Louisiana from France, he appointed his secretary, MERIWETHER LEWIS, to command an exploring party, and Lewis chose his army friend WILLIAM CLARK to share the leadership. After rigid training outside St. Louis during the winter of 1803–4, the party of 34 soldiers and 10 civilians moved up the Missouri in a 55-foot keelboat and 2 flatboats to the Mandan and Arikara villages near the present site of Bismarck, North Dakota, where they wintered. Having built a fleet of dugout canoes in June 1805 above the Great Falls in Montana, the party reached the foothills of the Rocky Mountains in what is now southwestern Montana. Here their remarkable Indian woman guide, SACAJAWEA, made friendly contact with the Shoshone Indians, who supplied horses for the men, and squaws for the baggage portage, over the Continental Divide at Lemhi Pass, Idaho. The party moved north down the Bitter Root valley to the Nez Percé country, and by following the Clearwater to the Snake they reached the Columbia. On 8 November 1805 they gazed upon the Pacific Ocean.

After a miserable winter spent in a crude shelter named Fort Clatsop, near present Astoria, they began their return journey in March 1806. With an eye to more extensive exploration, the party divided after crossing the Rockies. Lewis went back along the outward route and made a side trip up the Marias, a tributary of the Missouri, while Clark headed for the Yellowstone. They reunited at the site of Fort Union, near the junction of the Yellowstone and the Missouri. They then descended the Missouri, arriving at St. Louis on 23 September 1806. By a rare combination of skill, perseverance, and luck the 4000-mile journey was completed. In the face of almost insuperable difficulties Lewis and Clark were able to bring botanical and geological specimens back to Washington, and report to the President that the objective had been accomplished without a single hostile encounter with Indians, and with the loss of two men — one had died and one deserted. Although their scientific instruments (sextant, chronometer, and spirit level) of necessity limited the accurate fixing of positions, they made careful observations of weather and temperature, and notes on flora and fauna. Lewis's descriptions of Indian customs have high value. These explorers brought back knowledge of vast new territories, and they remain unrivaled among American pathbreakers. Their expedition incalculably influenced the history of the West.

The official journal (2 vols., 1814) was edited by NICHOLAS BIDDLE. The definitive work is that edited by R. G. Thwaites, *Original Journals of the Lewis and Clark Expedition* (8 vols., 1904–5). See also John E. Bakeless, *Partners in Discovery* (1947).

Lexington and Concord, Battle of (19 April 1775), in which the first blood of the War for American Independence was shed, began in the village of Lexington, Massachusetts. General Thomas Gage, the amiable commander of the garrison in Boston, felt duty bound to enforce the COERCIVE ACTS, and learning that patriots were collecting military stores at Concord, he sent a strong detail to confiscate them. But already Paul Revere and one or two others had roused the countryside, and when the detail reached Lexington it was met by a grim band of volunteers, the minutemen, lined up across the common. Which side was first to fire 'the shot heard round the world' remains one of the unsolved riddles of history, but eight Americans lay dead on the green when the British continued their march to Concord, where at the North Bridge they met the 'embattled farmers.' After partially accomplishing their purpose, the British regiments began their return to Boston, but their bright red coats made easy targets for the American marksmen. British casualties totaled 273 (American, 93). Within a week Boston was a beleaguered town.

Leyte Gulf, Battle of (25 October 1944), the greatest naval engagement in history and the last significant one in World War II, climaxed the PHILIPPINES CAMPAIGN. MacArthur had returned to the Philippines with a massive expeditionary force on 20 October, and the Japanese high command, hoping to pin down the American army, brought its entire fleet to bear, concentrating it in the vicinity of Leyte Gulf. Then ensued a tripartite action over a very large area.

In the first phase Admiral Kincaid's search plane tracked down Admiral Nishimura's southern force, heading north from Borneo, in time for Admiral Oldendorf to deploy all the naval strength that had supported the Leyte landings five days before. Nishimura was caught as he approached Leyte through Surigao Strait in the early hours and his force was effectively wiped out.

Then began the most critical action, the battle of Samar, in which Admiral Sprague, by repeated attacks in a running fight that lasted 90 minutes, forced Admiral Kurita to break off action. American casualties totaled 2000 in that engagement, which naval historians call the most gallant in U.S. naval history. An enemy force with ten times the firepower of the American fleet was forced to retire.

Meanwhile the carriers of Admirals Halsey and Mitscher, at the northern end of Luzon, sank major and supporting Japanese ships in the battle of Cape Engaño. These decisive engagements, which destroyed most of Japan's remaining sea power, gave the U.S. Navy complete command of the sea approaches to the Philippines.

LIBBY, WILLARD FRANK (1908–), professor of chemistry at Chicago (1945–59) and at California (Los Angeles) after 1959, served as a member of the Atomic Energy Commission (1954–59). His discovery of radioactive carbon dating, now used in archaeology, geology, geophysics and other sciences, furnished a powerful tool for dating organic materials of the relatively remote past (1000 to 30,000 years ago). For that work he received the 1960 Nobel Prize in chemistry.

Liberal Republican party, which met in convention at Cincinnati in May 1872, was a movement of opposition rather than of positive reform, animated by distrust of President Grant. Started by liberals and reformers, it soon attracted disappointed factional leaders, and its heterogeneous character became its weakness. Gathered in one political group were free-traders (David A. Wells), high protectionists (Horace Greeley), eastern conservatives (Charles Francis Adams), western radicals (Ignatius Donnelly), reformers (Carl Schurz), and old-line politicians (Reuben Fenton). Its platform finally called for withdrawal of troops from the South, civil service reform, and a resumption of specie payments. Greeley headed the ticket. The selection of Greeley, who for years had opposed the Democratic party, though it dismayed the Democrats, seemed to offer them their best choice among evils, for his name carried weight, and at Baltimore those who did not bolt adopted the Liberal's slate. They lost the election, 66 electoral votes to Grant's 292, and the Liberal Republican party came to an end.

Liberalism, as a religious, political, or social philosophy, in the U.S. has no specific or objective meaning, and like a host of other ideological concepts it has undergone a series of basic changes in the past 300 years. Applied to general attitudes, it presumably lies somewhere between conservatism and radicalism, both of which incline toward fixed opinions. In the 18th century ARMINIANISM was considered a liberal religious doctrine, as was CHRISTIAN SOCIALISM in the 19th century and HUMANISM in the 20th century.

In political philosophy the liberal

idea was concerned with the notion of life, liberty, and happiness of the individual. The concept was therefore written into the early state constitutions in the form of checks and balances on governmental authority. Thus the idea that 'that government is best that governs least' became a credo leading to the doctrine of LAISSEZ FAIRE, which endeavored to minimize the role of government in the economic regulation of day-to-day activities.

The liberal social philosophy that underlay all the decisions of the immensely influential jurist OLIVER WENDELL HOLMES envisioned law as a growing organism, to be molded to the needs of changing society. The present-day standard of the liberal emphasizes the welfare of society as a whole, and is particularly concerned with the underprivileged members of the community. Governmental indifference to the status of the individual has given way, especially since the monumental Supreme Court decisions in the late 1930's, to a new philosophy that can be summarized, in the economic sphere, as implying that 'he who cannot help himself may look to society for assistance.' Thus laissez faire is viewed as reactionary by present-day liberals, who hold that man has a positive obligation to help his fellow man.

Liberator, see *Garrison, W. L.*

Liberia, see *American Colonization Society.*

Liberty Bell proclaimed American independence (1776) from the State House (now INDEPENDENCE HALL) in Philadelphia. Originally cast in London for the golden jubilee of Penn's Charter of Privileges, it was cracked before arrival, repaired, and hung in the wooden steeple of the State House. Rung frequently for celebrations, it was strained while tolling for the funeral of Chief Justice Marshall (1835), and then fatally cracked and silenced while pealing on Washington's birthday in 1846. It now rests in the tower hall of Independence Hall.

Liberty loans were a series of five bond issues (the last called a 'Victory Loan') floated by the U.S. Treasury Department to help finance World War I (1917–19). They were oversubscribed, partly as a result of high-powered sales talks at every kind of public gathering, including church meetings.

Liberty party, the first antislavery political party, was formed (1840) at Albany, New York, and cast 7059 votes for J. G. BIRNEY. Its success in splitting the Whig party in 1844, when Birney polled 62,300 votes, carried Polk into the White House. In 1848 it merged with the FREE-SOIL PARTY.

Liberty poles, see *Sons of Liberty.*

Liberty, Statue of, the gigantic copper figure executed in Paris by Frédéric Auguste Bartholdi, was a gift of the French people to commemorate the centennial of American independence. In 1886 it was placed on a 154-ft. pedestal on Bedloe's Island (renamed Liberty Island in 1956), in New York harbor. The statue rises 305 ft. from the base of the pedestal to the torch. It is the loftiest statue in the world. The left hand of 'Liberty Enlightening the World' bears a book of laws, while the right holds aloft a torch. A sonnet by the New York–born poet Emma Lazarus (1849–87), prominent for her part in organizing relief for Jewish immigrants, is inscribed on the pedestal.

Libraries in the U.S., as public institutions, had their origin when John Harvard (1607–38) bequeathed some 300 volumes to the college which bears his name. Sixty years later THOMAS BRAY developed his idea of parochial libraries throughout the colonies. Franklin conceived the subscription Library Company of Philadelphia (1732), and not long after, in 1747, the Redwood Library at Newport, Rhode Island, erected the first library building. The New York Society Library (1754), like the other two, is a general library also strong in Americana. Likewise notable among early incorporated associations is the BOSTON ATHENAEUM (1805). The oldest free public library (supported by public funds) in continuous use is that at Peterborough, New Hampshire (1833). Until the end of the 19th century the largest was the Boston Public Library (1852), known today for its steadily increasing special collections.

With the formation of the American Library Association (1876) free library service was nationally recognized as a corollary of the free public school, and Andrew Carnegie accelerated the movement by endowing more than 2800 libraries throughout the country. In the 1890's state library extension agencies were organized to make library services available to rural communities. Today most states require library service in public schools, and in some states librarians serving tax-supported schools must hold professional certificates. Today more than 7500 public libraries are established in the U.S.

In the U.S., as in no other country, great private libraries have tended to become public property through gift or bequest. The collection of THOMAS PRINCE, for instance, is incorporated in the Boston Public Library. That of Thomas Jefferson became the nucleus of the LIBRARY OF CONGRESS. The great resources of the NEW YORK PUBLIC LIBRARY have been built around the collections of Lenox, Tilden, and Astor. Other notable holdings are those in the Widener and Houghton libraries of HARVARD UNIVERSITY, the JOHN CARTER BROWN LIBRARY of Brown University, the HENRY E. HUNTINGTON LIBRARY in California, the MORGAN LIBRARY in New York City, the CLEMENTS LIBRARY at Ann Arbor, Michigan, and the FOLGER SHAKESPEARE LIBRARY in Washington, D.C.

Notable contributions to American bibliography have been made by JOSEPH SABIN, L. C. DRAPER, JUSTIN WINSOR, and CHARLES EVANS; and to library science by CHARLES JEWETT, MELVIL DEWEY, CHARLES CUTTER, and J. C. DANA. The librarianship of JOHN SHAW BILLINGS was uniquely important.

Library of Congress, established by act of Congress in 1800, is the national library in Washington, D.C., and one of the greatest research libraries in the world. The nucleus of its collections began with the purchase (1815) of Jefferson's library, some 6000 volumes. Other important early collections include the manuscripts of Washington, Jefferson, Hamilton, and Madison, and the books and papers assembled by PETER FORCE. In 1870 the Library became the repository for materials deposited for copyright.

It thrice suffered from fires (1814, 1825, 1851) and did not play an important role until 1899, when Herbert Putnam (1861–1955) became librarian. During his 40 years as director the library built its magnificent collections. By mid-20th century the library, with immense resources and services unmatched in the U.S., contained more than 40 million items, including books, pamphlets, newspapers, music, maps, prints, photographs, recordings, and microfilms. Its collections now multiply by some two million items a year. It presents concerts and lecture programs in its auditorium, and sponsors a chair of poetry. Its printed catalog cards are used in libraries throughout the country.

License Cases (1847), settled by the U.S. Supreme Court, set forth the principle that a tax imposed as an exercise of the state POLICE POWER is valid, even though the levy impinges on interstate commerce. It reflected the Court's reaction, under Chief Justice Taney, in favor of states' rights by somewhat modifying Marshall's decision in GIBBONS *v.* OGDEN (1824).

LIEBER, FRANCIS (1798–1872), German-born political philosopher, emigrated to the U.S. (1827) after his liberal ideas led to difficulties in Germany. He originated and edited the *Encyclopaedia Americana* (13 vols., 1829–33). While professor of history and political economy at South Carolina College (1835–56), he wrote the books that established his reputation as a political theorist, including *A Manual of Political Ethics* (2 vols., 1838–39), and *On Civil Liberty and Self-Government* (2 vols., 1853). Ardently opposed to secession, he left the uncongenial South in 1856 to take a chair at Columbia (in the law school after 1865), and lend his pen to glorifying the organic unity of the U.S. *A Code for the Government of Armies* (1863), reissued by the War Department as *General Orders No. 100,* became a standard international work on military law and the conduct of war.

Lima, Declaration of (1938), one of the steps taken during the 1930's to insure hemispheric solidarity in the face of rising fascist and totalitarian regimes in Europe, was adopted at the Lima Conference. It reaffirmed the absolute sovereignty of the American states and provided for consultation between them. In the declaration the U.S. in effect repudiated the ROOSEVELT COROLLARY (1904) to the Monroe Doctrine, by which the U.S. had assumed the right to police Caribbean areas.

LILIUOKALANI (1838–1917), last reigning queen of the Hawaiian Islands, ascended the throne in 1891 and inaugurated a policy intended to eliminate American influence and restore autocracy. With the connivance of the American minister, John L. Stevens, a 'Committee of Safety' and a contingent of American marines deposed the hapless Queen (1893). In 1895 she formally renounced her royal claims; she was powerless to do otherwise. Author of many songs, she is best remembered for the popular *'Aloha Oe.'*

LINCOLN, ABRAHAM (1809–65), 16th President of the U.S. (1861–65), was born in a log cabin in the backwoods of Kentucky, and grew up on frontier farms as the family moved westward. His father, Thomas Lincoln, was a restless, barely literate frontiersman. His mother, Nancy Hanks Lincoln, who died when he was nine, and about whom little is known, taught him to read. Thereafter for the most part young Abe had to teach himself. When the family moved into Illinois in 1830 (Thomas Lincoln had remarried), the nineteen-year-old youth was a remarkably strong, easy-going, lanky backwoodsman.

In the village of New Salem, near Springfield, for six years (1831–37) he worked at odd jobs. In his spare time he read with eager curiosity such classics as he could lay his hands on, studied law, widened his acquaintanceship, and took an interest in politics. After 1834 he served for seven years as a Whig in the state legislature. (Scholars now dismiss the story that he wooed Ann Rutledge, who died in 1835.) Admitted to the bar in 1836, he moved in the following year to Springfield, where he practiced with various partners, notably with William H. Herndon (1818–91), who was later his biographer, and won a reputation for his succinct argument and pithy humor. He married Mary Todd, the belle of Springfield, in 1842. Of their four sons, only ROBERT TODD LINCOLN lived to manhood.

Lincoln won election to Congress for one term (1847–49), but his opposition to the Mexican War made him unpopular with his constituents. He again settled down to law practice, winning a statewide recognition as attorney for his ability to win cases. During the 1850's as agitation over the slavery issue mounted, Lincoln found himself drawn back into politics. In 1855 he lost his bid for the U.S. senatorship from Illinois. He joined the newly formed Republican party in 1856, and made such effective speeches that he was prominent in that party's councils when it first met in national convention and nominated Frémont for President. In 1858, when the Democratic senator from Illinois, Stephen A. Douglas, sought re-election, the Republican state convention chose Lincoln to oppose him. The choice was significant in that it unanimously nominated a relatively inexperienced contender to a contest against one of the greatest national political leaders in the country. It demonstrated, in other words, a confidence in Lincoln's vote-getting ability. Two sentences in his acceptance speech are still remembered, for he planned to oppose Douglas on the issue of POPULAR SOVEREIGNTY: 'A house divided against itself cannot stand. I believe this government cannot endure permanently half-slave and half-free.'

The LINCOLN-DOUGLAS DEBATES that followed were fought with a conviction that impressed hearers. Douglas won the election but Lincoln had gained national attention. He was invited to give an address at Cooper Union in New York City (February 1860), which won him a large following in all the anti-slavery states and led to his nomination in May at the Republican National Convention, where he defeated the leading contender, William H. Seward, on the third ballot. The split in the Democratic party, whose leading contender was Douglas, made possible the election of Lincoln. To Southerners the Republican victory spelled doom, since the party had pledged nonextension of slavery. They knew that the President-elect was unalterably opposed to the

CRITTENDEN COMPROMISE, which would extend it, and thus the secession movement was well advanced when Lincoln took office in March 1861.

Lincoln curtailed his public utterances as far as possible between his November election and March inauguration lest he embarrass his predecessor, the Democratic incumbent Buchanan, who was vainly trying to compose a settlement, which, in those months of tension, kept him virtually in a state of paralysis. When Lincoln took office he acted swiftly and adhered to one policy: 'My paramount object is to save the Union, and not either to save or destroy slavery.' After Fort Sumter was fired on in April the North responded with enthusiasm to his war proclamations and Congress gave him broad authority. No chief executive in U.S. history, except F. D. Roosevelt, has ever wielded such great power throughout a war. (In English history since the 16th century such authority has been exercised only by Cromwell and Churchill.) With the Union crumbling, Lincoln used his executive authority to such a degree that he violated individual rights under the Constitution, and although his acts were frequently condemned, he did not alter his view that preservation of the Union was paramount, and to that end he ignored Chief Justice Taney's civil rights ruling in the MERRIMAN CASE. He faced not only the issues incident to gearing the nation to total war, but those created by political maneuvering within his cabinet, the hostility of abolitionist spokesmen, and the absence for many months of any distinguished leadership in the field. The patience that Lincoln displayed throughout takes on the quality of genius.

When the Confederate armies were placed on the defensive after the battle of Antietam (September 1862), Lincoln took political and diplomatic advantage of the Union victory. Few assertions of presidential authority have ever been so bold as his issuance of the EMANCIPATION PROCLAMATION. It gave a high moral tone to the northern cause and effectively blocked any chance of foreign recognition for the Confederacy. But he still insisted that union, not abolition of slavery, was the aim of the government.

Lincoln had now risen to full stature as commander in chief and statesman, for he had in fact made the cause of the Union that of human liberty. The same characteristics are displayed in a different vein in his brief GETTYSBURG ADDRESS (1863), one of the noble expressions of American democracy. Lincoln had now become a leader no longer uncertain in performance. Although beset in 1864 by criticism so sharp that he actually expected to be defeated for reelection, he was in fact at the peak of his greatness, and no man who ever occupied the White House has fused such noble qualities with so few defects. Infinitely humble, he had become a master of men. Always sure in vision, he now revealed poise, mental audacity, and astuteness. His public and private utterances were magnetic.

By the autumn of 1864 the successes of Grant and Sherman in the field contributed both to political and popular support, and Lincoln defeated George McClellan, the Democratic candidate, by an electoral vote of 216 to 21, although his popular majority was only 400,000 in a total of 4,000,000 votes. Lincoln's notable second inaugural address (4 March 1865) asked his countrymen to 'finish the work we are in . . . with malice toward none, with charity for all,' and looked forward to a RECONSTRUCTION without vengefulness. Five days after the war ended, Lincoln was shot by John Wilkes Booth while attending Ford's Theater in Washington (14 April). He died the next morning.

More has been written about Lincoln than about any other American, much of it constituting a 'Lincoln legend' adulating a martyred President. Yet the fact remains that no President surpasses him as a symbol of the Union and the American democratic structure.

The best biographies include those by A. J. Beveridge (to 1858) (2 vols., 1928), Carl Sandburg (6 vols., 1926–39), and James G. Randall (5 vols., 1945–55).

LINCOLN, BENJAMIN (1733–1810), as a major general commanding Massachusetts militia, was instrumental in breaking Burgoyne's communications with Canada in the battle of Saratoga (1777). Placed in command of the southern department of the Continental army, he was forced to surrender Charleston (1780) when he was trapped by Clinton.

Exchanged as a prisoner of war, he joined Washington in the siege of Yorktown and received Cornwallis's sword at the surrender.

Lincoln was appointed Secretary of War (1781–83), and later commanded and even financed the militia that suppressed SHAYS'S REBELLION (1787). In 1788 he worked for his state's ratification of the Federal Constitution. Thereafter he served as a Federal commissioner to negotiate with the Creek Indians in the South and with the tribes north of the Ohio.

LINCOLN, MARY TODD (1818–82), member of a genteel Kentucky family, was living in Springfield, Illinois, with her sister when she met Abraham Lincoln. After a series of breaks and reconciliations they were married in 1842. The legends of the unhappiness of their married life have at least some substance, for she cherished the memory of her southern background, and did not share her husband's zeal for the Union. The early death of two of their four sons, the assassination of her husband, and the death of a third, 'Tad,' in 1871, unbalanced her mind. Her uncontrollable extravagance led her son Robert to allow her to be committed for treatment, but she was later adjudged sane.

LINCOLN, ROBERT TODD (1843–1926), the only one of the four sons of Abraham Lincoln to live to manhood, after graduation from Harvard (1864) served on Grant's staff in the closing months of the Civil War. He practiced law in Chicago, served as Secretary of War under Garfield and Arthur (1881–85), and was Harrison's minister to Great Britain (1889–93). He was later president of the Pullman Company (1897–1911). He gave his father's papers to the Library of Congress, where they became available to the public in 1947.

Lincoln Center for the Performing Arts, in New York City, is a fourteen-acre quadrangle in mid-Manhattan at Lincoln Square. The $160,700,000 cultural complex was financed from many sources, chiefly by gifts and private enterprise. The center includes Philharmonic Hall, for concerts (1962); the New York State Theater, for operetta and ballet (1964); Vivian Beaumont Theater, for repertory (1965); Library-Museum, for archives, musical scores, and recordings (1965); Damrosch Park, for open-air concerts (1965); Metropolitan Opera (1966); and Juilliard Music School Building (1967).

Lincoln-Douglas Debates, among the best known in history, were the central events in Abraham Lincoln's senatorial campaign in Illinois against Stephen A. Douglas. They were a series of seven encounters (August–October 1858) throughout the state. Preceded and followed by parades and blaring bands, they attracted crowds upward of 10,000; often entire families arrived in wagons. Each of the debaters was fully aware of the image he brought to the platform. Douglas, the short, stocky 'Little Giant,' meticulously dressed, exuded vigor; Lincoln was shambling, ill-groomed, and awkward. Both were profoundly earnest in their exposition of vital issues.

Douglas in the opening debate at Ottawa argued that the sectional bias of the Republicans would lead to strife, and he firmly adhered to his doctrine of POPULAR SOVEREIGNTY, and denounced the LECOMPTON CONSTITUTION. At Freeport Lincoln argued that Douglas must either accept the DRED SCOTT decision that slavery could go anywhere, or cease urging the sanctity of Supreme Court rulings. Douglas, in his so-called FREEPORT DOCTRINE, answered that Congress could not force a territory to pass a law against its will. The contestants were evenly matched as political debaters, and their language was keen in its give and take, but judged as dialectics the debates had more verbal artifice than lasting substance.

Lincoln Memorial, in West Potomac Park, Washington, D.C., is a large open marble hall, enclosing a heroic statue of Abraham Lincoln, seated in meditation. On the north wall is inscribed a passage from Lincoln's Second Inaugural Address; on the south wall, his Gettysburg Address. Designed and sculptured by Daniel Chester French, the monument was dedicated on Memorial Day, 1922.

LIND, JENNY (1820–87), Swedish soprano, having established her career in opera and concert, under the management of P. T. Barnum toured the U.S. (1850–52) with unprecedented success. Tickets were auctioned and often sold at fantastic prices. The 'Swedish nightingale' was the most celebrated coloratura soprano of her day, with a phenomenal range and remarkable quality of tone. In 1852 she married the conductor and composer Otto Goldschmidt, and later settled in England.

LINDBERGH, CHARLES AUGUSTUS (1902–), was son of Charles Augustus Lindbergh (1859–1924), an outspoken Minnesota Republican liberal in Congress (1907–17) and a staunch pacifist. The son was commissioned in the Air Corps Reserve in 1925. In one of the spectacular feats of the century he took off alone (20 May 1927) in his monoplane, *Spirit of St. Louis,* on a nonstop 3600-mile flight from New York to Paris (33½ hours). This first solo across the Atlantic made 'the lone eagle' an international hero and won him unprecedented honors from many nations. In 1936 with ALEXIS CARREL he invented a perfusion pump that could be used as a mechanical heart. When he was invited in 1938 to inspect the German air force, he was so impressed by Nazi technological developments that he returned to urge appeasement, and resigned from the National Advisory Committee on Aeronautics to protest criticism of his widely publicized views. However, during World War II and later he gave valuable service to the government as a civilian aeronautics consultant.

His wife, ANNE MORROW LINDBERGH (1906–), is author of *North to the Orient* (1935), *Gift from the Sea* (1955), and other books.

LINDSAY, [NICHOLAS] VACHEL (1879–1931), born at Springfield, Illinois, after attending Hiram College (1897–1900), and studying art in Chicago and New York (1900–1905), made tramping tours of the U.S. as a minstrel, exchanging his verses for bed and board. Combining idealism, mysticism, and fundamentalist ideas (he had once studied theology), he expressed deep sympathy for the plain people. In demand as a public reader of his poems, as an exponent of what he called 'the higher vaudeville' he emphasized his strong rhythms by chanting the verses and using gestures. Collections of his poems include *The Chinese Nightingale* (1917), *The Daniel Jazz* (1920), and *Johnny Appleseed* (1928). His moving poem 'The Eagle That Is Forgotten' was written in tribute to the humane Illinois governor John P. Altgeld.

LINDSEY, BEN [BENJAMIN BARR] (1869–1943), an international authority on juvenile delinquency, for many years (1900–1927) was judge of the juvenile court at Denver, Colorado, one of the first such courts in the U.S. He became a judge of the Superior Court of California in 1934. His advocacy of trial marriage in *The Companionate Marriage* (1927) raised more smoke than fire.

Lions, a luncheon club founded (1917) for business men, seeks 'to serve most and to serve best,' an ideal which the members feel is 'caught — not taught.' It presently lists a membership of about 600,000.

LIPPMANN, WALTER (1889–), after graduation from Harvard (1909) began his career in journalism as associate editor of the *New Republic* (1914–17). He was a leading editorial commentator for the New York *World* (1921–31) before starting his long association with the New York *Herald Tribune* and other newspapers. His oft-quoted *Public Opinion* (1922) popularized the term 'stereotypes,' fixed preconceived opinions, a word he borrowed from the printer's mold.

As a philosophical humanist, in *A Preface to Morals* (1929) he holds that the entire framework of traditional theology has collapsed, and that the cultivated and disinterested mind can find in purely mundane virtues an end that may enlist wholehearted devotion. By his expert knowledge of world affairs, expressed with clarity, he has gained a national reputation as a social analyst. His later books include *The Public Philosophy* (1955), and *The Communist World and Ours* (1959).

LISA, MANUEL (1772–1820), New Orleans–born fur trader, by 1800 had become well established at St. Louis, where he held a monopoly for trade with the Osage Indians. The favorable reports of the Lewis and Clark expedition gave Lisa incentive to lead commercial ventures into the upper Missouri region in 1807. At the junction of the Bighorn and the Yellowstone he built Fort Manuel, the first trading post in Montana. In 1809, with members of the CHOUTEAU FAMILY, Lisa formed the Missouri Fur Company, of which he was the recognized head. During the War of 1812 he successfully countered British commercial feelers in the region of North Dakota. No other fur trader in his day organized and administered peltry commerce more astutely.

Litchfield Law School, see *Reeve, Tapping.*

Literacy tests, as criteria for voting in the U.S., in 1964 were required in twenty states. The provisions varied widely but all usually expected those applying for the ballot to write their names and read a simple prose passage. In the seven southern states where application of the test was administered by election officers, literacy requirements usually barred Negroes from voting. Passage of the Voting Rights Act of 1965 outlawed literacy tests to determine qualification of voters.

Literacy tests supplement the quota system as a means of restricting immigration. Congress sought the enactment of bills requiring such tests in 1896 (vetoed by Cleveland) and in 1913 (vetoed by Taft), but such a bill passed over Wilson's veto in 1917, requiring aliens over sixteen to read 'not less than 30 nor more than 80 words in ordinary use' in some language or dialect.

Little America, so named in 1929 by RICHARD E. BYRD, was a base for Antarctic expeditions. Located on an inlet of Ross Sea south of the Bay of Whales, it continued to be a base for subsequent explorations, particularly those led by Byrd in 1946–48.

Little Bighorn, Battle of the, see *Custer.*

'Little Giant,' see *Douglas, S. A.*

Little Steel Formula, so called, was a measure adopted by the National War Labor Board in 1942 to tie wage increases to the rise in living costs. The plan grew out of a wage dispute in the steel industry, and permitted a 15 per cent increase. When John L. Lewis and his United Mine Workers threatened a nation-wide strike in protest, President Roosevelt ordered the seizure of the mines. Anti-union congressmen passed the stringent Smith-Connally Act (over Roosevelt's veto) not only authorizing presidential seizure of essential war plants but also forbidding unions to make campaign fund contributions.

Little theater movement started in France in the late 19th century as a protest against traditionalism in the established commercial theater. In 1915 three important Little Theaters were formed in the U.S. In February the Neighborhood Playhouse opened on Grand Street, New York City, presenting new American and European experimental drama. A week later the Washington Square Players began similar productions at the Bandbox Theater on 57th Street. The Players reorganized in 1919 as the THEATRE GUILD. In the summer on Cape Cod a colony of artists from Greenwich Village formed themselves into the Provincetown Players, improvised a stage, and offered plays by unknown dramatists. It was this latter group, continuing an association through the 1920's, that gave the early plays of Eugene O'Neill their first performance.

These new groups, stimulated by ideas emanating from the 47 Workshop conducted at Harvard by GEORGE P. BAKER, encouraged the establishment of Little Theaters throughout the country, notably in Cleveland, Detroit, Dallas, and Los Angeles. In 1936–39 the U.S. government sponsored the Federal Theatre Project, which brought the theater into many communities that had come to know drama solely through motion pictures.

LITTLE TURTLE (*c.* 1752–1812), Miami Indian chief, commanded his tribe in its victorious wars against Josiah Harmar and General Arthur St. Clair in the Northwest Territory (1790–91). When ANTHONY WAYNE defeated these Indians at Fallen Timbers (1794), near present Toledo, Chief Little Turtle, who had refused the command at that battle, nevertheless signed the Treaty of GREENVILLE (1795), ceding a large portion of Ohio to the U.S.

Livingston Family of New York was founded by ROBERT LIVINGSTON (1654–1728), who emigrated from Scotland and became a fur trader and a power in the affairs of the colony. Of his two sons, Robert and Philip, the elder was father of Robert R. Livingston (1718–75), a justice of the New York Supreme Court (1763–75) and chairman of the colony's Committee of Correspondence. Among the latter's children, ROBERT R. LIVINGSTON (1746–1813) and EDWARD LIVINGSTON (1764–1836) became prominent jurists and statesmen.

Peter Van Brugh Livingston (1710–92) and Philip Livingston (1716–78), sons of the first Philip, were both graduates of Yale and leaders in the patriot cause during the Revolution. Their younger brother, WILLIAM LIVINGSTON (1723–90), became New Jersey's first governor. William's son, Henry Brockholst Livingston (1757–1823), a graduate of the College of New Jersey (1774), served in the Revolution, was admitted to the New York bar (1783) and in 1806 became Associate Justice of the U.S. Supreme Court.

LIVINGSTON, EDWARD (1764–1836), jurist and statesman, was perhaps the most distinguished member of the New York LIVINGSTON FAMILY, which for several generations contributed notably to public affairs in America. After graduation from the College of New Jersey (1781) he practiced law in New York City. As a Jeffersonian Republican in Congress (1795–1801), he opposed Jay's Treaty and the Alien and Sedition Acts. During his service as mayor of New York City (1801–3) a confidential clerk misappropriated public funds, and Livingston resigned his office, met the deficit, and moved to New Orleans, where he resumed law practice. He served President Jackson as Secretary of State (1831–33), minister to France (1833–35), and as a trusted adviser.

Livingston's penal code for Louisiana (published in 1833), although not adopted by the state that had requested it, brought him international fame, and became the model of state penal codes in the U.S. and elsewhere. It was remarkable in its provisions for remedies rather than vindictive punishment. The eminent legal historian Sir Henry Maine called Livingston 'the first legal genius of modern times.'

LIVINGSTON, ROBERT (1654–1728), born in Scotland, came to America in 1673, and settled at Albany, New York. In 1679 he married Alida Van Rensselaer, daughter of a wealthy Dutch patroon. Through his fur trade with the Indians he himself soon gained a position of wealth and influence, living at Livingston Manor, a property of 160,000 acres spread through Dutchess and Columbia counties. The early governors of New York were careful to retain Livingston's favor, and in the century after his death no family was more prominent, through ability and intermarriage, in the affairs of the colony and the state.

LIVINGSTON, ROBERT R. (1746–1813), son of the New York Supreme Court judge Robert R. Livingston (1718–75), after graduation from King's College (Columbia) in 1765 became a law partner of John Jay. Livingston was a member of the Continental Congress, helped draft the Declaration of Independence, and was the first secretary of the department of foreign affairs (1781–83). As chancellor of New York (1777–1801), he administered the oath to George Washington. One of the best legal minds of his time, and a firm Democrat, he was Jefferson's minister to France (1801–4), where he conducted negotiations for the Louisiana Purchase. He held a monopoly on steamboating in New York waters, and financed the experiments of ROBERT FULTON.

LIVINGSTON, WILLIAM (1723–90), a grandson of ROBERT LIVINGSTON, after graduation from Yale (1741) became one of the leading lawyers in New York. After moving to New Jersey, he commanded the state militia (1776), and he became New Jersey's first governor (1778–90). His strong sense of social responsibility led him to place his considerable literary gifts at the service of liberal causes, and one of the two undergraduate literary societies at the College of New Jersey was named after Livingston's pseudonym, 'The American Whig.'

LLOYD, HENRY DEMAREST (1847–1903), a graduate of Columbia (1867), worked on the editorial staff of the Chicago *Tribune* (1872–85), from which he resigned to study social problems. His *Atlantic Monthly* article portraying the methods of the Standard Oil Company, 'The Story of a Great Monopoly' (1881), was a broadside against trusts, and did as much to inaugurate the 'literature of exposure' as any other single piece of writing. This essay he elaborately documented in *Wealth Against Commonwealth* (1894), a classic in the literature of protest. His impassioned plea for industrial justice to Illinois' coal miners, *A Strike of Millionaires Against Miners* (1890), was an effective instrument of the MUCKRAKING movement in supporting the cause of the underprivileged.

Lobbying, the practice of influencing legislation by agents serving special interests, has become an accepted part of the U.S. political system. It is defended as a method by which associations register their opinions, and attacked for its unregulated pressures. Lobby groups include chambers of commerce, trade associations, labor unions, and public welfare groups, all of which maintain permanent offices in Washington and in state capitals. The Regulation of Lobbying Act (1946) requires registration of lobbyists, with a statement of purpose and reports of expenditures.

Lochner* v. *New York (1905) was a decision by a bare majority of the U.S. Supreme Court, which held invalid a New York maximum-hours law for bakers, adjudging it an unreasonable interference with the right of free contract and an excessive use of the state's POLICE POWER. Justice Holmes entered a vigorous dissent; he criticized the majority opinion as 'decided upon an economic theory which a large part of the country does not entertain. . . . The Fourteenth Amendment does not enact Mr. Herbert Spencer's *Social Statics.*' Three years later the Court reversed its opinion as far as women were concerned in MULLER *v.* OREGON.

LOCKE, DAVID Ross (1833–88), during the Civil War won a reputation as humorist, writing for Ohio newspapers under the pseudonym Petroleum Vesuvius Nasby. Using such popular devices as ridiculous spelling, fractured grammar, and foolish arguments, Locke commented on political events of the day. The cartoonist Thomas Nast supplied illustrations for some of the pieces, and Senator Charles Sumner wrote an introduction for one collection. On the lyceum circuit Locke was immensely popular. For one nine-month lecture season he was paid $30,000, said to be the most lucrative tour in the annals of 19th-century lyceum entertainment. President Lincoln read a Nasby letter as comic relief before presenting his Emancipation Proclamation to his cabinet, but some of the less susceptible members thought the gesture inappropriate.

LOCKE, JOHN (1632–1704), English philosopher and founder of British empiricism, ranked as the greatest single authority on political thought at the time the American nation was being founded. His *Two Treatises on Government* (1690) deeply influenced the thinking of the Revolutionary generation. He maintained what Jefferson assumed as basic in the Declaration of Independence: that life, liberty, and property are the inalienable rights of every individual, and that man's happiness and security are the ends for which government came into existence. His *Letters on Toleration* (1689–92) declare that revolution in some circumstances is not only right but obligatory.

Locke's association with American institutions is even more direct, in that in 1669 he drew up a constitution for the CAROLINA PROPRIETORS. That instrument (which sanctioned an aristocratic social order) never became operative as law, but its articles providing for religious toleration were in large part adopted. His principal work, *Essay concerning Human Understanding* (1690), developed the theme that sense perceptions are the basis of reason. This philosophical doctrine of sensationalism influenced the thought of Jonathan Edwards, and has continued as part of American intellectual history.

Lockout, the refusal of an employer to allow employees to enter his plant, is a method used to resist labor demands or break strikes by importing new workers. Courts have generally regarded them as legal unless they violate the terms of a joint agreement. Lockouts are regulated, though not prohibited, by the TAFT-HARTLEY ACT (1947).

'Loco-focos' (1835), an outgrowth of the old WORKINGMEN'S PARTY (1829), were the radical wing of the New York Democratic party. When their opponents turned off the gas at a meeting, the 'loco-focos' wrested control of the city caucus from the conservatives (the HUNKERS) by producing candles, lighting them with the new loco-foco matches, and continuing the meeting. The group included many idealists and reformers, but it had little influence after 1837. The name, however, for many years was derisively applied to all Democrats.

LODGE, HENRY CABOT (1850–1924), member of a prominent Boston family, graduated from Harvard in 1871. Before beginning his long career as U.S. Senator from Massachusetts (1893–1924), he edited the *North American Review* (1876–79), lectured on American history at Harvard (1876–79), and wrote biographies of several American statesmen, including Washington, Hamilton, and Webster. A conservative party-line Republican, he was one of the most nationalistic of American politicians. He was a bitter foe of Wilson's peace policy, and as chairman of the Senate Foreign Relations Committee led the isolationists in the attack on the Treaty of Versailles and the League of Nations.

His grandson, HENRY CABOT LODGE (1902–), after serving as a Republican in the U.S. Senate (1936–53), became the chief U.S. representative to the United Nations (1953–61). In 1963 President Kennedy appointed him ambassador to Vietnam.

'Log Cabin and Hard Cider,' see *Harrison, W. H.*

Log cabins, unknown in England, were introduced by the Swedes (or Finns) on the lower Delaware (1638). They became the typical pioneer American home along the Scotch-Irish frontier. They were one- or two-room buildings, made of round logs, flattened, well mortised together, and chinked with chips and clay.

Log College, see *Tennant, William.*

LOGAN, JAMES (1674–1751), Irish-born statesman and scholar, came to Philadelphia in 1699 as the secretary and confidential adviser of William Penn. He was prominent thereafter in the affairs of the colony as a leader of the aristocratic Proprietary party. He developed a lucrative Indian trade, and lived on a vast estate, where his hospitality to the Indians established their long-lasting friendship with the colony.

Logan was the earliest important botanical experimenter in the British colonies, and the first in the world to demonstrate conclusively the manner of fertilization in corn. He was also a writer on optics, and was the first American known to have purchased a copy of Newton's *Principia* (in 1708). A scholar of discriminating taste, he bequeathed his large classical and scientific library to the city of Philadelphia.

LOGAN, JOHN [or JAMES] (*c.* 1725–80), believed to have been of full French ancestry, is said to have been captured as a child and brought up as an Indian. Generally known as Logan, he led Iroquois tribes on the Ohio and Scioto rivers, and was a staunch friend of the whites until members of his family were victims during a massacre of Indians by white settlers (1774). The Indians retaliated, and when Governor Dunmore sought to adjust the matter, Logan delivered a speech so eloquent that Jefferson ranked it with the orations of Demosthenes and Cicero. It concludes, 'Who is there to mourn for Logan? Not one.' The city of Auburn, New York, erected a monument in his memory.

Logan Act (1798), still on the statute books, was passed as part of the crop of ALIEN AND SEDITION ACTS, after Dr. George Logan (1753–1821), a Philadelphia Quaker, had gone to Paris hoping to preserve the peace. The Act forbids a private citizen to undertake diplomatic negotiations with a foreign nation on the subject of a dispute between it and the U.S.

Logrolling, in U.S. politics, is a term applied to reciprocal political assistance: 'You help me roll my log, and I'll help you roll yours.' The practice generally applies to appropriation measures of local interest, such as road or waterway improvements.

LONDON, JACK [JOHN GRIFFITH] (1876–1916), born in San Francisco, had no exact knowledge of his parentage and was reared by a family without fixed occupation or residence. After tramping through the U.S. and Canada, he joined the Klondike gold rush (1897), an adventure which furnished him with material for such popular stories as *The Son of the Wolf* (1900), and *The Call of the Wild* (1903). Similar tales, such as *The Sea-Wolf* (1904) and *White Fang* (1906), are likewise preoccupied with physical energy and primitive violence. *Martin Eden* (1909) and *John Barleycorn* (1913) are semi-autobiographical.

An impartial worshiper of both Marx and Nietzsche, he produced a large number of stories stressing either an eventual equalitarian golden age or brute instincts as the dominant motive power in man's life. (Almost forgotten in America in mid-20th century, he is still deeply admired in Europe.) He lived his own life with much the same recklessness that he portrayed in his fiction. Plagued by alcoholism and financial disasters, he committed suicide.

London Company was one of two interrelated TRADING COMPANIES that were granted a patent (1606) by the English crown for colonizing America. Under terms of the grant two Virginia companies were established. The London (or South Virginia) Company might plant itself anywhere from present South Carolina to New York, and the PLYMOUTH COMPANY (or North Virginia) might do so from Virginia to Maine, but neither 'planting' was to be within 100 miles of the other. In 1607 the London Company founded JAMESTOWN. In 1609 the Virginia Company chartered a group headed by SIR THOMAS SMITH, one of the most active promoters of his day, but misfortunes dogged the enterprise and in 1619 control passed to SIR EDWIN SANDYS. Two years later Sandys was replaced by SIR FRANCIS WYATT. The unprofitable venture forced the company into receivership, and in 1624 its charter was annulled.

London Economic Conference (1933) convened to deal with international fiscal problems. Since President Roosevelt forbade the U.S. delegation to deal with stabilization issues (the U.S. had just been removed from the GOLD STANDARD), the conference accomplished little. Thus the President hoped to keep his hands free for currency experiments intended to raise price levels and reduce the burden of private debts.

London Naval Conference (1930) was intended to further the cause of peace. By the terms of its Treaty, the U.S., Great Britain, and Japan adopted a program of cruiser limitation at a ratio of 5-5-3. An 'escalator' or escape clause permitted Britain to start construction should France and Italy threaten her naval superiority. The concessions which the U.S. and Great Britain made to induce Japan to accept the ratio actually greatly strengthened Japan's strategic power in the Pacific, but Japanese militarists used the slogan '5-5-3' to discredit the liberal government, and when the militarists came into power in 1934 Japan denounced the treaties and began a frenzied building program. Actually no well-meaning reform of the 20th century proved more dangerous and costly to the U.S. than naval limitation.

LONG, CRAWFORD WILLIAMSON (1815–78), after taking his medical degree at Pennsylvania (1839), practiced medicine at Jefferson, Georgia. Between 1842 and 1846 he performed eight operations using ether anesthesia. W. T. G. MORTON received major credit for his independent discovery of the anesthesia, though it was three years later than Long's, for Morton was the first to make a public demonstration, and he assumed full responsibility.

LONG, HUEY PIERCE (1893–1935), Louisiana lawyer, first as governor of the state (1928–31), then as U.S. Senator (1931–35), built up one of the most ruthless political machines in American history. A clever demagogue with an insatiable lust for power, as governor 'The Kingfish' bludgeoned a supine legislature into passing his laws. Long's regime resulted in many badly needed reforms, but his overbearing methods led many to fear that his Share-the-Wealth program might result in a fascist dictatorship. The presidency was his next goal, and his welfare promises lured a steadily increasing national following, but he was halted in full career by an assassin's bullet.

LONG, STEPHEN HARRIMAN (1784–1864), New Hampshire–born explorer, after graduation from Dartmouth (1809) entered the engineer corps of the U.S. Army (1814). In 1820 he led a party into Colorado, encamped at the present site of Denver, discovered Longs Peak, and was the first white man to scale Pikes Peak. The *Account of an Expedition from Pittsburgh to the Rocky Mountains* (2 vols. and atlas, 1822–23) was compiled chiefly by the botanist and geologist of Long's staff, Dr. Edwin James. Later, as a surveyor for the Baltimore and Ohio railroad route, Long compiled an authoritative topographical manual. He devised the first scientific wooden-truss bridge in America.

'Long drive,' see *Cattle drives.*

LONGFELLOW, HENRY WADSWORTH (1807–82), born in Portland, Maine, after graduation from Bowdoin (1825) traveled in Europe before teaching modern languages at Bowdoin (1829–35). As successor to George Ticknor in the modern language chair at Harvard (1835–54) he became a significant figure in the cultural development of the nation. He was a remarkable linguist who not only knew the principal languages of Europe but also studied such little-known ones as Icelandic and Finnish. His translations from eleven different languages opened the rich heritage of European poetry to generations of Americans.

His own first volume of poetry, *Voices of the Night* (1839), was succeeded by *The Spanish Student* (1843), *The Belfry of Bruges* (1845), *Evangeline* (1847), and *Hiawatha* (1855). These works gave him so great a popularity throughout the English-speaking world that on publication of the *Courtship of Miles Standish* (1858) more than 15,000 copies were sold during the first day in Boston and London.

During his lifetime Longfellow was the most popular poet in America or in the world, and his seventy-fifth birthday was celebrated in every schoolhouse in the U.S. After his death he became the only American ever to be honored with a bust in the Poet's Corner of Westminster Abbey. He was a serene optimist, with a tendency (in his early writings) to moralize. He was not gifted with high imagination, and his overblown literary reputation in his own day was bound to be deflated. But he had great metrical skill and did much to popularize American folk themes abroad. His poetry is part of the national heritage.

Biographies and critical studies include those by Lawrance Thompson (1938), Edward Wagenknecht (1955), and Newton Arvin (1963).

Long Island, extending 118 miles eastward from the mouth of Hudson river, was settled in 1635 by Dutch farmers at its western end, and by New England Puritans (after 1640) along its eastern shores, under Connecticut jurisdiction. In 1674 the whole island became part of the colony of New York. One of the most prosperous and populous areas of its size in the U.S., it has long been known for its large estates, its suburban character, and its numerous summer resorts and beaches. The entire western end (Brooklyn and Queens) is incorporated into the City of New York.

Long Island, Battle of (August 1776), took place when 20,000 British and Hessian troops under Howe's command laid siege to the American fortifications on Brooklyn Heights. The outnumbered Americans fought well, but the plans were faulty and the generals did not execute their assignments. Washington, seeing that his position was hopeless, maneuvered a masterful retreat to Manhattan. Had Howe prevented the movement (which he easily could have done had he known what was happening) he would have ended the war, for if Washington's army had been captured Congress could not have raised another.

LONGSTREET, JAMES (1821–1904), a graduate of the U.S. Military Academy (1842), was in army service at the outbreak of the Civil War. He resigned his commission, joined the Confederacy, and served as brigade, division, and corps commander through most of the major engagements from Bull Run to Antietam. He commanded Lee's right wing at Gettysburg, where his delay in taking the offensive until late on the second day is generally said to have cost Lee the battle. He later took part in the Chattanooga and Wilderness campaigns. During the Reconstruction era he was a Republican and supported Grant, and was thus disliked by Southerners. In later years he served as Federal commissioner of railroads. As a commander he is considered to have been a fine tactician but a poor strategist.

LONGUEUIL, CHARLES LE MOYNE, Sieur de (1625–85), colonizer of New France and founder of a famous Canadian family, after 1641 worked for the Jesuits as trader and interpreter among the Hurons, and helped to found Montreal. Of his eleven sons, all distinguished, the best known are the Sieur d'IBERVILLE and the Sieur de BIENVILLE.

Lookout Mountain, Battle of (24 November 1863), near the close of the CHATTANOOGA CAMPAIGN, was Grant's first move to raise the siege of Chattanooga. Hooker's troops scrambled up the mountain, and in the 'battle of the clouds' drove off Longstreet's men, thereby preparing the way for the final assault on MISSIONARY RIDGE.

Loop, The, so called, is the center of Chicago's financial, shopping, hotel, and theater district. It takes its name from the fact that elevated railroad tracks in that area since 1897 have 'looped' the section.

Loose construction of the Constitution, see *Implied Powers.*

Lords of Trade and Plantations, see *Board of Trade and Plantations.*

Lords Proprietors, see *Proprietary Colonies.*

Los Angeles, third largest city in the U.S. (2,500,000), is the industrial and cultural center of southern California. Founded in 1781 by the Spanish, it became a center of cattle ranching. In 1846 it came under U.S. military control and was incorporated as a city in 1850. Its growth began with the discovery of oil (1890) and the development of the motion picture industry (after 1910). The establishment of advanced technological industry, especially of aircraft factories during World War II, led to a phenomenally rapid population expansion. In the decade 1950–60 its population increased by more than 500,000. Los Angeles embraces an area of 452 square miles and surrounds the independent cities of San Fernando, Culver City, and Beverly Hills. The cultural life of the city is rich in music, theater, and art. Among its important institutions of higher learning are the Henry E. Huntington Library, the University of Southern California (est. 1880), California Institute of Technology (est. 1891), and the University of California at Los Angeles (est. 1919).

'Lost generation' was the phrase Gertrude Stein applied to the young expatriate intellectuals who, having served in World War I, were writing their first and bitter books. Their disillusion is set forth in Ernest Hemingway's *The Sun Also Rises* (1926). The era as a whole is described in Malcolm Cowley's *Exile's Return* (1934).

After 1956 a 'beat generation' of writers was looking for directional signs to return them to reality. The effort has given peripheral popularity to such books as Allen Ginsberg's *Howl and Other Poems* (1956), with its opening keynote 'I saw the best minds of my generation destroyed by madness, starving hysterical naked'; and Jack Kerouac's *On the Road* (1957).

Lotteries, until well into the 19th century, were considered by Americans to be an appropriate means of raising money for public improvements. Lotteries for church benefits were customary during the colonial period, many colleges raised building funds by lotteries, and early improvements in the city of Washington were made through them. The earliest antilottery society (1833), in Philadelphia, spurred efforts in many states to end them on the ground that gambling was immoral. Lotteries were legally abolished in Pennsylvania and Massachusetts in 1833, and by 1850 they had become illegal in most states.

The most spectacular lottery in U.S. history was the Louisiana Lottery (1868–90), a monopoly chartered by the state legislature. It was immensely profitable and continued to do business in New Orleans until 1895, when it was forced to transfer its domicile to Honduras. It finally was harried out of existence in 1906. In 1890 Congress denied the U.S. mails to lottery activities, and in 1895 excluded them from interstate commerce. The nation's first state lottery in the 20th century was established in 1963 by New Hampshire as a means of providing state aid for education.

Parimutuel, or policy betting on horses, in which the winner shares in the total stakes, was originally called 'lottery insurance.' It is now a legalized form of GAMBLING in about a third of the states.

LOUDOUN, JOHN CAMPBELL, Earl of, see *Campbell.*

LOUIS, JOE [JOSEPH LOUIS BARROW] (1914–), Alabama-born boxer, in 1937 won the world heavyweight boxing championship from James J. Braddock in the eighth round at Chicago. A powerfully built Negro, the 'Brown Bomber' defended his title 24 times before retiring undefeated in 1949. His defeat by the German boxer, Max Schmeling, took place in 1936, before he won the championship. In 1938 Louis knocked out Schmeling in a one-round bout. The two Louis-Schmeling fights attracted international attention, because of the Nazi racist theories of the time.

Louisbourg Expedition, see *Pepperrell.*

Louisiana, first organized as the Territory of Orleans (1804), was admitted to the Union (1812) as the 18th state, with NEW ORLEANS as its capital (until 1849). The region was named by LA SALLE (1682) for Louis XIV, and became a French crown colony in 1731. Some 2000 of the ACADIANS expelled by the British from Nova Scotia (1755) ultimately made their way to Louisiana and settled the 'Cajun country' near Bayou Teche. Louisiana was ceded by France to Spain in 1762, and it became the refuge of Royalists fleeing the French Revolution (1789–92). It was returned to France in the Treaty of Madrid (1801), and came into the possession of the U.S. in 1803 as part of the Louisiana Purchase.

The victory of Andrew Jackson at the battle of New Orleans (1815) helped mold the diverse cultures (including German) to a more common pattern, as settlers with English traditions began pouring in from other southern states to develop great sugar and cotton plantations. New Orleans was carried to almost fabulous success as a port (second in the nation by 1835) and as a market for cotton and slaves. The state joined the Confederacy in 1861, suffered heavily from race riots and radical Republican domination during Reconstruction, and for a time became the focus of Ku Klux Klan activity (1866–71). It was readmitted to the Union in 1868, and the broken plantation system was gradually replaced by farm tenancy and sharecropping.

Although the soil of the northern part of the state is relatively unproductive, eastern Louisiana is a vast alluvial plain, much of it semitropical marsh land along which the Mississippi river, now held behind continually rebuilt levees, created a lush delta. It is a region of great sugar plantings and rice fields. Louisiana produces abundant harvests of shellfish in its gulf area, and is an important source of muskrat fur. Discovery of large oil fields in the 20th century helped restore the solvency of the state. In 1960, Louisiana was producing 12 per cent of the nation's mineral wealth (chiefly petroleum products), and ranked second to Texas in such production. Since 1849, Baton Rouge has been the capital, but New Orleans remains the metropolis of the Deep South. The leading institutions of higher learning are Tulane (New Orleans, est. 1834), and Louisiana State University (Baton Rouge, est. 1860).

Louisiana Purchase (1803), the greatest bargain in U.S. history, was also the greatest strain on the Constitution, which said nothing about acquiring new territory or of promising statehood to it. 'Louisiana' was the vast region stretching north from the mouth of the Mississippi river to its source, and west to the Rockies, a tract of some 828,000 square miles. Nobody knew its exact boundaries. Its purchase increased the national territory by 140 per cent and made possible the creation of thirteen states.

In 1802, when President Jefferson learned of the Spanish transfer of Louisiana to France, he was concerned over the threat posed to American security, since Spain had recently closed the Mississippi to Western commerce, and an aggressive France in possession of New Orleans presumably would do likewise. He therefore instructed his minister in Paris, Robert R. Livingston, to negotiate for an irrevocable guarantee of free navigation and trading rights on the river. In January 1803 he sent James Monroe to France to assist in the negotiations, with authority to purchase New Orleans and West Florida for $2,000,000, the sum provided by Congress. Monroe was secretly empowered to offer five times that amount if necessary.

But even before Monroe embarked, events in Europe were altering French territorial interests. Having renewed war with Great Britain, Napoleon welcomed an opportunity to avoid having to defend New Orleans against a British naval attack. Therefore, when Livingston approached Talleyrand in April to repeat the standing offer, the French minister suddenly asked: 'What will you give for the whole of Louisiana?' By the end of the month the treaty of cession, which made possible a continental nation, was signed. This vast transfer cost $15,000,000, or four cents an acre. Federalists, and some Republicans, grumbled at Jefferson's broad view of the Constitution, but the Senate promptly confirmed the agreement, and in December the territory was formally transferred.

LOVEJOY, ARTHUR O. (1873–1962), professor of philosophy at Johns Hopkins, was a critical realist, and though he was little known to the general public, he won the respect of his peers for his chief work, *The Revolt Against Dualism* (1930), an achievement in technical reasoning. His later classic, *The Great Chain of Being* (1936), studies the evolution of a concept by wedding philosophy to historical method, and helped establish the 'history of ideas' approach to the study of culture.

LOVEJOY, ELIJAH PARISH (1802–37), Maine-born abolitionist, was editing the St. Louis *Observer* (1833–36), when he was forced to move to Alton, Illinois. There the press on which he printed the Alton *Observer* was attacked four times, and Lovejoy was killed defending it. His death made it dramatically evident that slavery and the free discussion of slavery could not exist side by side.

LOVEWELL, JOHN (1691–1725), Massachusetts Indian fighter, with a company of volunteers was out for scalp bounty when he and his party were ambushed by Pigwackets in Fryeburg, Maine. Lovewell fell at the outset of the skirmish. The story of 'Lovewell's Fight' is stirringly told in Parkman's *A Half-Century of Conflict,* and has been the subject of ballads.

LOW, SETH (1850–1916), educator and public servant, after graduation from Columbia (1870) entered his father's tea-importing house. As reform mayor of Brooklyn (1882–85) he demonstrated that the MERIT SYSTEM was practicable. (Brooklyn became the first municipality in the U.S. to adopt civil-service rules.) During his presidency of Columbia (1890–1901) the institution greatly expanded its facilities and officially became a university. He later served as mayor of the City of New York (1902–3).

LOWELL, ABBOTT LAWRENCE (1856–1943), brother of PERCIVAL LOWELL, was a Boston lawyer and professor of political science at Harvard (1900–1909) before succeeding Charles Eliot as president of that institution (1909–33). During his term of office he revised the undergraduate curriculum to combat specialization and introduced the 'house system' to secure the advantages of intellectual and social cohesion. He wrote such studies in his field as *Public Opinion and Popular Government* (1913), and summed up his academic career in *What a University President Has Learned* (1938).

LOWELL, FRANCIS CABOT (1775–1817), Boston textile manufacturer, after graduation from Harvard (1793) gathered information in England about power looms and then invented one of his own. In 1814, at Waltham, Massachusetts, he equipped the first American factory to include both spinning and weaving machinery. It thus became the first factory in the world to manufacture cotton cloth by power machinery enclosed in one building. As an employer concerned with the welfare of his workers, he provided chaperoned boarding houses for the girls who worked in the cotton factories of the city of Lowell (named for him), and their deportment in dress and behavior drew national attention, since nowhere else in America were factory workers guided by such paternal solicitude.

LOWELL, James Russell (1819–91), born in Cambridge, Massachusetts, soon after graduation from Harvard (1838) began his long career as magazine editor and contributor. For many years he was professor of modern languages at Harvard (1855–86). In 1857 the *Atlantic Monthly* was founded under his editorship. He resigned that post in 1861 and three years later became joint editor with Charles Eliot Norton of the *North American Review* (1864–72). President Hayes appointed him minister to Spain (1877–80), and to Great Britain, where he remained through the administrations of Garfield and Arthur (1880–85). As a writer he set himself the task of 'transplanting European culture,' and made a contribution to American life by communicating his own enthusiasm for reading books.

LOWELL, Josephine Shaw (1843–1905), a pioneer of charity organization, helped found the influential New York Charity Organization Society, and introduced notable reforms in hospitals, asylums, and prisons. Her *Public Relief and Private Charity* (1884) was an early and important study in the field of social service. For some years (1877–89) she was a member of the New York State Board of Charities, from which she resigned to emphasize her conviction that a realistic attitude toward the problems of social reform demanded not humanitarianism, but political and legislative action.

LOWELL, Percival (1855–1916), brother of A. LAWRENCE LOWELL, graduated from Harvard in 1876. In 1894 he established the Lowell Observatory at Flagstaff, Arizona, where he served (after 1902) as nonresident professor of astronomy at Massachusetts Institute of Technology. In 1914 he predicted the discovery of a planet, which in 1930 was verified as Pluto. Later studies suggest that the 'verification' was accidental, and that Pluto is an escaped satellite, not a planet. Throughout his life Lowell remained firm in his conviction that life exists on Mars.

Lowell Institute, one of the earliest and most influential of the LYCEUMS, was founded (1839) at Boston by endowment of the philanthropist John Lowell (1799–1836). It continues to offer free public lectures by outstanding scholars in all branches of learning.

Loyalists, called Tories by their enemies, were those American colonists who at the time of the War of Independence were opposed to separation from Great Britain. Families were often divided in their sympathies, for this conflict was a civil war. Loyalists were to be found in all the colonies and in every walk of life, but they were proportionately more numerous among the well-to-do, the Anglicans, officeholders, and other conservatives. Loyalist sympathy was strong in New York, New Jersey, and Georgia, and it was effective also in other regions where British arms were most successful, as in Pennsylvania and the Carolinas. It was weakest in such regions of proud tradition as Massachusetts, Connecticut, Maryland, and Virginia. Informed estimates set the over-all actively loyalist population at 10 per cent and the actively patriot at 40 per cent; the remaining 50 per cent were indifferent.

Many who could do so (some 80,000) left the country, and those who removed to Canada were called United Empire Loyalists, a name that became a badge of distinction for them after 1789. The greater number, having no place to go, took the required oath of allegiance to the U.S., and resigned themselves to their exclusion from the professions and public office, and to their heavy taxes.

Through the war years some 30,000 served in the British army, a number equal to the largest force that Washington had under his command at any one time. Many acted as espionage agents for the British and gave financial and material assistance to Great Britain. But the old popular view that Loyalists were perfidious traitors is false. Those who sought to hold the Empire together in 1775 were as intellectually honest as such southern Unionists as General Thomas and Admiral Farragut in 1861. They included such statesmen as THOMAS HUTCHINSON and JOSEPH GALLOWAY. Among churchmen there were SAMUEL SEABURY, JONATHAN BOUCHER, and JONATHAN ODELL; among educators, the president of King's College, MYLES COOPER, and the provost of the College of Philadelphia, WILLIAM SMITH. The extreme disfavor into which Loyalists fell at the outbreak of hostilities created such a bias that a century passed before the writings of Loyalists began to receive the attention they deserved.

The treatment of Loyalists during and after the war is generally thought by historians to have been reasonable, and punishments were meted out by courts of law. The property appropriated from citizens who forfeited 'the right to protection' helped finance the patriot cause. New York, for instance, which had had a large Tory population, obtained over $3,600,000 from the sale of Loyalists' property. Although the peace treaty stipulated the return of that property, and Congress pressed the states to do so, the recommendation for the most part fell on deaf ears, for friendship with the Loyalists was slow in returning.

See C. H. Van Tyne, *The Loyalists in the American Revolution* (1929), and Lewis Einstein, *Divided Loyalties* (1933).

Lumbering, the term used in Canada and the U.S. for the business of cutting timber into boards, remained a local concern until the 19th century, although it was one of the earliest industries. After 1800 Bangor, Maine, became the first of the great 'lumber cities,' providing ship timber for export. By 1850 the industry had begun moving west. It paused briefly in New York and Pennsylvania, until the vast stands of white pine in Michigan made that state the chief source during the 1870's. The 'State of Maine' logging system then moved to the upper Mississippi valley. Massive tree trunks were dragged to the river banks, cut into logs, and floated in huge rafts down the rivers or lakes. When the pine was gone, the lumberjacks migrated to Wisconsin, then to the Pacific Northwest and to Louisiana. The inroads of other building material after 1900 began to cut down the market for lumber.

Logging (the felling and preparation of timber for shipment to sawmills) was a frontier industry, and the work was rough, dangerous, and difficult. Legends, tales, and ballads of the feats of the lumberjack are a colorful chapter in American folklore, especially associated with the NORTH WOODS.

See J. E. Defebaugh, *History of the Lumber Industry of America* (2 vols., 1906–7).

LUNDY, BENJAMIN (1789–1839), Quaker reformer, early determined to devote his life to the cause of abolition. His antislavery lectures, delivered in the 1820's, are said to have been the earliest platform pleas for the emancipation of slaves in the U.S. In 1821, in Ohio, he established the *Genius of Universal Emancipation,* an irregularly published weekly abolitionist journal. Moved from place to place, the *Genius* was issued for fourteen years, during which time Lundy was indefatigable in his effort to find suitable places outside the U.S. to colonize freed Negroes. His pamphlet, *The War in Texas* (1836), had widespread appeal to Northerners who were opposed to the political dominance of the South and extension of slave territory.

Lundy's Lane, Battle of (25 July 1814), was fought three weeks after General Jacob Brown defeated the British at CHIPPEWA. It was the most stubbornly contested engagement in the War of 1812, and took place when Brown's 2600 men, invading Canada, encountered 3000 British troops at Lundy's Lane, near Niagara Falls. The five-hour battle ended in a draw, and although both sides claimed victory, the British remained in possession of the field. The U.S. suffered some 850 casualties, and the British a like number.

Lusitania was the British-owned Cunard liner that was torpedoed without warning by a German submarine and sank off the coast of Ireland (May 1915). It was no mitigation of the act (by rules of international law then in effect) that the German embassy in Washington had inserted an advertisement in American newspapers warning passengers not to sail on Allied ships. The catastrophe, which took the lives of 128 Americans among a total of 1153 passengers lost, created intense indignation throughout the U.S. Public leaders like Theodore Roosevelt clamored for war, and the press took up the cry.

President Wilson's notes to the German government, demanding specific pledges, brought the resignation of Secretary of State Bryan, who feared that the peremptory demands would lead the nation into war. No settlement of the question was reached, although the

Germans offered informal assurances against recurrence, and not until February 1917 did the U.S. sever diplomatic relations with Germany following her resumption of unrestricted submarine warfare.

Lutherans are Protestant adherents to the teachings of the Reformation leader Martin Luther (1483–1546), who emphasized the responsibility of the individual conscience to God alone, the dependence upon Scripture as the one necessary guide to truth, and the necessity of baptism for regeneration. Although church organization is synodical (each church making its own decisions), the church is unified through its doctrine.

Lutherans came first to New York from Holland (1623), and to Delaware from Sweden (1638). The tolerance of Quakers attracted Lutherans to Pennsylvania, and the first Lutheran synod independent of European affiliations resulted from the work of the German-born minister HEINRICH MÜHLENBERG (1748). The large influx from Germany after 1830, and the great immigration from Scandinavia after 1860, led to the formation of numerous independent Lutheran bodies, all of which maintain colleges and theological seminaries. In 1965 members of Lutheran bodies exceeded 8,500,000 in number.

Lyceum movement developed in the U.S. during the 19th century in response to a growing interest in popular education. Associations were formed to provide lectures, concerts, debates, scientific demonstrations, and entertainment. The first such group, established by JOSIAH HOLBROOK in 1826, became so popular that the movement spread to nearly every state in the Union, and before 1890 some 3000 lyceums were founded. The lyceum thus became a powerful force in adult education, social reform, and political discussion.

With the rise of public school systems and the increase in the number of institutions of higher learning, for which the lyceum movement was directly responsible, local groups became forums supplied with lecturers from a central booking office, such as that conducted by JAMES REDPATH. Two distinguished establishments, the LOWELL INSTITUTE of Boston, and COOPER UNION in New York, began as lyceums. After 1890 the movement waned, but its function survived in the CHAUTAUQUA MOVEMENT.

See C. B. Hayes, *The American Lyceum* (1932).

LYELL, SIR CHARLES (1797–1875), the foremost English geologist of the 19th century and a principal founder of the modern science, made two extensive tours through North America during the 1840's. He set forth his observations in *Travels in North America* (2 vols., 1845), and *A Second Visit to the U.S.* (2 vols., 1849). In bringing a knowledge of European geology to bear upon formations in North America, he rendered immense service. He was unique among foreign travel-writers in that he was a trained scientist who observed American social and domestic situations with sympathetic detachment. His study, *The Geological Evidence of the Antiquity of Man* (1863), was very unsettling to the orthodox belief as to the date of creation.

Lynch law in the U.S. is the capital punishment of alleged criminals by private persons (usually mobs) without due process of law. The term probably derives from the name of Charles Lynch (1736–96), who, as a Virginia justice of the peace, employed such extralegal methods to suppress Tory activities during the Revolution.

Under frontier conditions lynch law was carried out by VIGILANTES, and served as a substitute method of social control in regions where legal institutions were unorganized or distrusted. In the South it crystallized into a traditional method of summary execution of Negroes. Southern legislators have been able to block Federal antilynching bills, but public sentiment against the practice has nearly eliminated lynching as a means of 'carrying out the law.'

LYND, ROBERT STAUGHTON (1892–), professor of sociology at Columbia after 1931, with his wife Helen Merrell Lynd, made a sociological study of Muncie, Indiana, published as *Middletown: A Study in Contemporary American Culture* (1929). It was followed by *Middletown in Transition* (1937). Both studies were pioneer efforts to develop a general theory of social-structure stratification by breaking down divisions of the community into classes.

LYON, James, see *Hymns.*

LYON, Mary (1797–1849), while teaching school in Ipswich, Massachusetts, became interested in promoting higher education for women. She devised a plan to establish a seminary for girls of moderate means, raised the funds, and shaped a curriculum modeled on that of Amherst College. In 1837 at South Hadley, Massachusetts, she opened Mount Holyoke Female Seminary (Mount Holyoke College), which she served as principal until her death. She thus founded the first permanent college for women in the U.S.

M

Mc. *Names beginning with 'Mc' are placed as though beginning with 'Mac.'*

McADOO, William Gibbs (1863–1941), Georgia-born political leader, while practicing law in New York became active in Democratic politics. In 1912 he managed Wilson's presidential campaign, and while serving as Wilson's Secretary of the Treasury (1913–18) he married one of Wilson's daughters. During Wilson's Administration the Federal Reserve System was inaugurated (1913), and McAdoo served as the first chairman of the Federal Reserve Board. During World War I he was director general of railroads in the period of government operation. (In 1904 his corporation, the Hudson and Manhattan Railroad Company, had completed the first tunnel under the Hudson river.) He continued to be active in politics and was a prominent contender for the Democratic presidential nomination in 1920 and again in 1924. He later served as senator from California (1933–39). His autobiography, *Crowded Years* (1931), ends with his resignation from the cabinet.

MacARTHUR, Douglas (1880–1964), son of Lieutenant General Arthur MacArthur (1845–1912), graduated from the U.S. Military Academy (1903), and served in World War I as a brigade commander. He was chief of staff (1930–35) when President Roosevelt sent him to the Philippines to direct the defense reorganization of that Commonwealth. Following the Japanese attack on the Philippines (December 1941), MacArthur led a skillful defense of the Islands. After their capture in February 1942 the President appointed him Supreme Commander of forces in the southwest Pacific and ordered him to Australia. As a General of the Army (after 1944), MacArthur directed the campaign that liberated the Philippines (July 1945), accepted the formal surrender of Japan, and served as supreme commander for Allied powers during the occupation of that nation (1945–51). He succeeded brilliantly, with government approval, in carrying out much of his plan to demilitarize and neutralize the Japanese islands. Historians regard that accomplishment as a major achievement in 20th century statesmanship.

MacArthur was given command of United Nations forces in the KOREAN WAR (1950–53), and his handling of the amphibious Inchon landings has been called 'one of the great strategic counterattacks of all time.' But President Truman dismissed him (April 1951) during the conflict because he believed that MacArthur had pushed his eagerness to decide issues in the field by publicly advocating an attack on Red China, and thereby possibly risked a full-scale war with Red China and her ally Russia, against Administration policy. He had thus overstepped the constitutional authority of a military commander. Though he was autocratic and immensely egotistical, MacArthur is nevertheless judged to have been one of the great military leaders of his time.

McALLISTER, [Samuel] Ward (1827–95), born in Georgia, after practicing law in San Francisco in the early boom years (1850–52), retired at the age of twenty-five with a comfortable fortune. He married a millionaire's daughter, established residences in New York and Newport (Rhode Island), and organized the Patriarchs (1872), heads of New York's oldest families, from whom, in order to accommodate Mrs. William Astor's ballroom, he sifted out (1892) 'The Four Hundred,' the 'true' New York society. His snobbish record is interestingly set down in *Society As I Have Found It* (1890).

McCarran Act (Internal Security Act), passed over President Truman's veto in 1951, required the registration of communist and communist-front organizations. It prohibited employment of communists in national defense work, and denied entry into the U.S. of members of totalitarian organizations. In 1965 the U.S. Supreme Court unanimously ruled that individuals may refuse to register with the government as members of the Communist party by invoking their constitutional privilege against self-incrimination.

McCarran-Walter Act (1952), see *Immigration*.

McCarthyism was the term applied to the frenetic attacks on the 'Red Menace,' which Joseph R. McCarthy (1908–56), Republican senator from Wisconsin after 1947, alleged was a communist infiltration at high government levels. He charged publicly that there were 205 card-carrying communists in the State Department. The tactics he employed included half truths, unsupported assertions, and smears. His senatorial immunity blocked suits for libel by those attacked. After 1953, as chairman of the Senate permanent investigations subcommittee, McCarthy conducted widely publicized and televised hearings in which he accused the able Secretary of the Army, Robert T. Stevens, of attempting to cover up evidence of communist espionage activities within his department. In 1954, after President Eisenhower had denounced McCarthy as one who tried 'to set himself above the laws of our land,' the Senate voted a motion censuring McCarthy for his conduct as a Senator. His success in breeding suspicion of treason in the highest echelons of government has been compared with that of Jean Paul Marat during the French Revolution.

McCLELLAN, GEORGE BRINTON (1826–85), son of Dr. George McClellan (1796–1847), a distinguished Philadelphia surgeon, graduated from the U.S. Military Academy (1846) second in his class, served with distinction in the Mexican War, and subsequently became chief engineer of the Illinois Central Railroad. In May 1861 Lincoln gave him command of the Department of the Ohio. Personal magnetism and some successes in western Virginia in June made McClellan a popular hero, and in November he succeeded the aging Scott as general in chief of the Union armies. Frictional differences caused him to be relieved of that office in the following March, but he retained command of the Army of the Potomac. The failure of his PENINSULAR CAMPAIGN was charged to his overcaution. After Second BULL RUN (August 1862) he reorganized the Union forces and checked Lee at ANTIETAM, but he failed to press his advantage in this nearly decisive battle. Lincoln was now fully aware that 'Little Mac,' vacillating and slow, had little capacity for offensive action, and removed him from command.

McClellan ran unsuccessfully on the Democratic ticket against Lincoln in the presidential campaign of 1864. He later resumed his career in engineering and served as governor of New Jersey (1878–81). As a general he was an expert organizer, capable of transforming raw recruits into effective fighting men, but in the view of most competent historians he had no large view of strategy.

McCORMICK, CYRUS HALL (1809–84), invented a successful reaping machine in his father's Virginia blacksmith shop in 1831, using the principle of a moving knife against a fixed finger. His improvements included a platform, a main wheel and gearing, and guards. He demonstrated and patented his invention in 1834, a year after Obed Hussey of Cincinnati, working independently, had patented a similar device, but McCormick was able to outstrip a growing number of competitors. He built his Chicago factory in 1847, and by 1851 had introduced his reaper into Europe at the International Exposition in London. McCormick pioneered in the mass production of factory machinery. During the Civil War he exported grain to Europe on a scale that bolstered the finances of the federal government and helped to make a reality of the observation that King Corn had defeated King Cotton. One of the ablest industrialists of his day, he built a great manufacturing dynasty in Chicago.

McCORMICK, ROBERT SANDERSON (1849–1919), a nephew of C. H. MC CORMICK, married Katherine Van Etta Medill, daughter of the Chicago journalist, JOSEPH MEDILL. McCormick entered the diplomatic service, successively heading U.S. missions to Austria-Hungary (1901–2), Russia (1902–5), and France (1905–7).

His son, JOSEPH MEDILL MCCORMICK (1877–1925), after graduation from Yale (1900) assumed managerial interest in the CHICAGO TRIBUNE. Joseph McCormick was a leading figure in Theodore Roosevelt's Progressive party campaign (1912), and later served in the U.S. House of Representatives (1917–19), and in the Senate (1919–25), where he vigorously opposed entry of the U.S. into the League of Nations. MRS. JOSEPH

McCormick [Ruth Hanna McCormick] (1880–1945), a daughter of mark hanna, participated actively in Republican politics, and served briefly in the House of Representatives (1929–31).

A younger son, Robert Rutherford McCormick (1880–1955), also graduated from Yale (1903), and in 1914 became sole owner of the *Tribune*. In that capacity, he followed his grandfather's personalized journalism, and by extending his newspaper holdings came to dominate the field of journalism in the Midwest. Under his management the *Tribune* became vehemently isolationist and anti–New Deal.

McCOSH, James (1811–94), Scottish-born philosopher, was called to the U.S. as president of the College of New Jersey (1868–88), and his work laid an enduring foundation for the liberal development of the institution. In the U.S. he represented the 'common sense' philosophy of Intuitionism, which opposed the teachings of Kant and J. S. Mill. He maintained that intuitions have their beginnings in simple cognition, take on concrete forms, and pass into beliefs that become principles. He was a champion of Darwinism as evidence of God's method of creation.

McCULLOCH, Hugh (1808–95), Maine-born financier, while president of the State Bank of Indiana was called to Washington (1863) as U.S. Comptroller of the Currency, in which post he launched a new national banking system. Lincoln soon appointed him Secretary of the Treasury, a post he occupied throughout Johnson's term (1865–69). Congress would not adopt his hard money program for retiring greenbacks and the early resumption of specie payments to check high prices. For some years thereafter McCulloch was a partner in the London branch of Jay Cooke and Company, which weathered the Panic of 1873 when the home bank in Philadelphia went bankrupt. He later served briefly as Arthur's Secretary of the Treasury (1884–85). He left a useful autobiography in *Men and Measures of Half a Century* (1888).

McCulloch* v. *Maryland (1819), was a case that resulted in a decision by the U.S. Supreme Court upholding the constitutionality of the second bank of the u.s. It was a milestone in American nationalism. The case is important because it gave high judicial sanction to the implied powers of Congress. Chief Justice Marshall declared that no state possessed the right that had been exercised by the Maryland legislature when it taxed a Federal branch bank, because Congress held implied powers to establish a bank and because 'the power to tax involves the power to destroy.' He thus held the Maryland act unconstitutional. This forthright assertion of national doctrine is generally regarded as Marshall's most brilliant constitutional opinion, but it set off a nationwide controversy that is still unresolved. Issues continue to arise concerning the reciprocal powers of federal and state governments to collect taxes.

MacDONOUGH, Thomas (1783–1825), Delaware-born naval officer, served under Stephen Decatur in the Tripolitan War. During the War of 1812 he commanded a small fleet on Lake Champlain. By superior skill and planning he defeated a larger British fleet in the battle of plattsburg, the most decisive naval engagement of the war. In gratitude Congress gave him a gold medal, and New York and Vermont granted him estates.

McDOUGALL, Alexander (1731–86), Scottish-born Revolutionary Patriot, helped organize the sons of liberty in New York (1765), and was jailed (1771) for issuing a broadside, entitled 'To the Betrayed Inhabitants of the City and Colony of New York,' which criticized the Assembly. He served as a major general during the Revolution, and commanded West Point after Benedict Arnold's treason (1780). He was later a member of the Continental Congress (1781–82, 1784–85).

McDOUGALL, William (1871–1938), English-born psychologist, was professor of psychology at Harvard (1920–27), and thereafter at Duke. He was a student of eugenics and heredity, and had a biological approach to problems in his field. For many years he conducted experiments on the inheritance of acquired characteristics. His *Social Psychology* (1908) was a pioneer study in physiological psychology. Other writings include *The Group Mind* (1920), and *Outline of Psychology* (1923). He explained human behavior in terms of inherited instincts, each coupled with a primary emotion.

Most unfortunate for his reputation were his racist Lowell Lectures, *Is America Safe for Democracy?* (1921). The book cited the army mental tests for alleged proof of Nordic superiority and argued the inherent superiority of children in upper social classes. He disposed of the fact that there were gifted Negroes by concluding that they had a large admixture of white 'blood.'

MacDOWELL, Edward Alexander (1861–1908), born in New York City, studied piano (1875–81) with Teresa Carreño in New York, Marmontel in Paris, and Heymann in Frankfurt. He taught and gave concerts in Germany before returning (1888) to Boston, where he wrote much of his orchestral music during the next eight years. He was called to a newly created chair of music at Columbia (1896–1904), where he continued to compose songs, orchestral pieces, and such piano works as the popular *Woodland Sketches* (1896) and *Sea Pieces* (1898); and the important *Norse* and *Keltic* sonatas (1900–1901), both dedicated to Edvard Grieg. His *Indian Suite* (1897) drew upon authentic Indian melodies. A mental breakdown led him to resign his post.

MacDowell was the leading American composer in the romantic tradition, and the first American composer to attract attention abroad. He often drew his inspiration from the neighborhood of his summer home at Peterborough, New Hampshire, where his widow, the pianist Marian Nevins MacDowell, in 1910 established the MacDowell Colony for composers, artists, and writers.

McDOWELL, Ephraim (1771–1830), after studying medicine for a year with John Bell at Edinburgh, practiced in Danville, Kentucky. A pioneer surgeon in the U.S., McDowell made surgical history by performing the first ovariotomy on record (1809, reported 1817).

McGILLIVRAY, Alexander (1759–93), son of a Scots trader and his half French, half Creek Indian wife, was given a classical education at Charleston. Upon the outbreak of the War of Independence Georgia confiscated the property of his Loyalist father, who returned to Scotland. McGillivray returned to his mother's people. As a British agent during the war, the young chief maintained Creek loyalty to the crown. Later he became a Spanish commissary.

Hoping to end Creek depredations, Secretary of War Knox invited McGillivray to New York, made him a brigadier general, gave him a handsome pension, and concluded the Treaty of New York (1790), by which the Creeks acknowledged U.S. sovereignty over part of their territory. But soon thereafter the Spaniards outbid Knox in subsidizing McGillivray, and the Indian attacks were resumed.

McGRAW, John Joseph (1873–1934), was the star third baseman (1891–1900) for the Baltimore Orioles, before becoming manager (1902–32) of the New York Giants. One of the outstanding figures in baseball, he brought the Giants ten pennants and three world series victories (1905, 1921–22). His world-wide tours (1914, 1924) with groups of baseball players helped popularize the sport in Europe and the Orient.

McGREADY, James (*c.* 1758–1817), during the late 1790's, by his evangelical preaching in Logan county, Kentucky, kindled the flame of the great religious revival which, in 1800, swept over the South and the West, and thus created the first of the so-called camp meetings. He later founded Presbyterian churches along the Indiana frontier.

McGUFFEY, William Holmes (1800–1873), after serving as president of Cincinnati College (1836–39) and Ohio University (1839–43), was for many years professor of moral philosophy at the University of Virginia (1845–73). He is chiefly remembered as compiler of the famous *Eclectic Readers,* which molded American literary taste and concepts of morality, particularly in the Middle West, for 60 years after publication of the *First Reader* (1836). In an age when schools did not have libraries, and when few teachers were well-read, the McGuffey *Readers,* by introducing children to selections from the best British and American writers, performed a service of incalculable value and set the popular literary standard for two generations. The *Readers* carefully adapted their substance and obvious moral teachings to frontier interests. When the *Sixth Reader* was issued in 1857, there was a *Reader* for every school-age group. Total sales of the *Readers* reached some 122,000,000 copies, a number approached in the U.S. only by the Bible and Webster's Spelling Book.

McINTIRE, SAMUEL (1757–1811), Salem, Massachusetts, woodcarver and architect, displayed his talent by creating houses in the Adam style, noted for their slender, well-proportioned columns, and carved mantelpieces and cornices. These houses were designed for the wealthy shipowners of the town. He also executed fine carvings on furniture made by Salem cabinetworkers. His public buildings in Salem include Assembly Hall and Washington Hall.

McINTOSH, WILLIAM (*c.* 1775–1825), Creek Indian chief and son of a British army captain and a Creek woman, was made a brigadier general for his aid to Americans in the War of 1812. After serving with Jackson against the Seminole (1817–18), he persuaded the Lower Creeks to cede lands to Georgia. He was slain by the Upper Creeks, who opposed the cession.

MACK, CONNIE [CORNELIUS McGILLICUDDY] (1862–1956), having played baseball for the Washington Senators (1886–89) and the Pittsburgh Pirates (1891–94), became manager (1901) and later chief owner of the Philadelphia Athletics, which he continued to lead for 50 years. Under his guidance the team won nine pennants and five world series (1910–11, 1913, 1929–30).

McKAY, DONALD (1810–80), Boston shipbuilder, was noted as designer and builder of some of the finest ships of his time, including the famous CLIPPER SHIPS. His three-decker, *New World* (1845), was the largest of its day, and his clipper, *Flying Cloud,* made a record voyage from Boston to San Francisco in 1851. In 1873, unable to compete with iron vessels, he closed his shipyard.

MACKAY, JOHN WILLIAM (1831–1902), Irish-born capitalist, joined the rush to Nevada in 1860, shortly after the COMSTOCK LODE was opened. With J. G. Fair and J. C. Flood he acquired a large share in 'Bonanza' silver mines, which yielded him an immense fortune. In 1886 he formed the Postal Telegraph Cable Company.

MacKAYE, [JAMES MORRISON] STEELE (1842–94), studied acting with Delsarte in Paris, and made his debut (1873) as Hamlet in London. Returning to the U.S., he wrote some twenty plays, notably such domestic melodramas of humble life and eccentric character as *Hazel Kirke* (1880). He introduced the Delsarte system of acting, which stressed co-ordinating the voice with movement of all parts of the body, a technique to which he added the professional study of gymnastics. He devised the first moving or double stage, and folding seats.

MACKENZIE, SIR ALEXANDER (1763–1820), Scottish-born fur trader and explorer, went to Canada (1779), where he built trading posts in the West. He became a partner in the NORTH WEST COMPANY (1787), and in 1789 led an expedition from his headquarters on Lake Athabaska along the Mackenzie river to the Arctic Ocean. In 1793, using water routes, he guided a party across northern Canada to the Pacific, thus completing the first transcontinental journey north of Mexico. His *Voyages . . . to the Frozen and Pacific Oceans* (1801) won him wide recognition and a knighthood.

McKim, Mead and White was the New York architectural firm established (1879) by CHARLES FOLLEN McKIM (1847–1909). Over the years the group came to exercise a greater influence on the course of American architecture than any other firm. After study in Paris McKim began his profession in the architectural office of H. H. RICHARDSON, and during the 1880's McKim, Mead and White reflected Richardson's taste in Romanesque designs. But the firm soon adopted (and adhered to) classic and Renaissance styles in which it executed a large number of commissions, including the Boston Public Library (1888), the Columbia (Low Memorial) Library (1893), the Morgan Library (1906), and the Pennsylvania Railroad station (1910). The

American Academy in Rome was founded (1894) largely through the efforts of McKim, who served as its first president.

WILLIAM RUTHERFORD MEAD (1841–1928), a graduate of Amherst (1867), studied architecture in the New York office of Russell Sturgis (1836–1909) before commencing practice (1872) with McKim, whom he succeeded (1910) as president of the American Academy.

STANFORD WHITE (1853–1906), son of the New York critic Richard Grant White (1821–85), after study abroad and training (like McKim) under Richardson, joined the firm at its founding. He was especially influenced by sculptured Renaissance ornament, and concentrated upon decorative effects and interior design. He was fatally shot by Harry K. Thaw, who alleged that White had alienated the affections of his wife.

McKINLEY, WILLIAM (1843–1901), 25th President of the U.S. (1897–1901), was born at Niles, Ohio. After service in the Union army during the Civil War, from which he emerged a major, he returned to his state and practiced law at Canton. Entering politics, he was elected as a Republican to Congress (1876) where, except for one term, he served until 1891. Although he voted for the BLAND-ALLISON SILVER ACT (1878) and advocated the original FREE SILVER bill of 1890, both favoring subsidies to silver producers, he pleased Ohio industrialists by his ardent support of protection in the MCKINLEY TARIFF ACT (1890). He thus gained the attention of the powerful capitalist-politician MARK HANNA, who steered McKinley into the Ohio governorship (1892–96) and secured the presidential nomination for him on the first ballot in 1896. By making an endorsement of the gold standard his chief campaign issue, McKinley fought Bryan on free silver. The popular vote was close, but by Hanna's masterful adroitness (he persuaded McKinley not to vie with Bryan's oratorical platform appearances, but to receive delegations at his own front porch), McKinley was carried into office by an electoral vote of 271 to 176. With the Republicans in control of Congress, and a thoroughgoing Republican tariff in effect, McKinley could turn his attention to foreign affairs.

Yielding to popular hysteria, McKinley directed Congress in entering the brief and needless Spanish-American War (1898), asked the peace commissioners to demand the Philippines for the U.S., and imposed a tight control on Cuba. He signed the bill annexing Hawaii, supported the OPEN DOOR POLICY promulgated by his Secretary of State John Hay to deal with China, and thus was carried along with the imperialist trend of the times. Defeating Bryan again in 1900 (292 to 155 electoral votes), he had time only to organize his new administration. While attending the Pan-American Exposition at Buffalo, McKinley was shot (6 September 1901) by the anarchist Czolgosz. He died nine days later. A gentle man, simple and friendly, McKinley himself formulated no distinctive policy.

See C. S. Olcott, *The Life of William McKinley* (2 vols., 1916), and Margaret Leech, *In the Days of McKinley* (1959).

McKinley Tariff Act (1890) was pushed through Congress as a result of a bargain between western Republicans who wanted FREE SILVER legislation and eastern Republicans who wanted tariff legislation. It sought not only to protect established industries, but to foster 'infant industries' and by prohibitory duties to create new industries. It was immensely unpopular, and many of its proponents were defeated in the elections of 1892.

This tariff dealt a severe blow to Hawaii by putting a bounty of two cents a pound upon home-grown sugar cane, thus bringing about the collapse of prices and inspiring the island's sugar interests to lobby for annexation to the U.S. However, the law did aid Secretary of State Blaine's idea of Pan-Americanism by authorizing a policy of reciprocal tariffs by executive agreement. President McKinley's last speech, just before his assassination (1901), revealed the conversion of this former arch-protectionist to reciprocity.

MACLURE, WILLIAM (1763–1840), Scottish-born merchant, became a U.S. citizen in 1796. He was a liberal patron of science. His own *Observations on the Geology of the U.S.* (1809, rev., 1817), with an extended text, was the first geological map of America, described by the eminent geologist, George P. Merrill, as 'the first map of its scope in the history of geology.' Maclure was president of the

Philadelphia Academy of Natural Science (after 1817), participated in Robert Owen's NEW HARMONY socialistic community, and later went to live in Mexico. Benjamin Silliman called him the 'father of American geology.'

McMahon Act, see *Atomic Energy Commission.*

McMASTER, JOHN BACH (1852–1932), while a teacher of engineering at Princeton (1877–78), made a trip to collect fossils in Wyoming, where he came under the spell of the frontier. He was determined to write a history of the Common Man, and he is chiefly remembered for his *History of the People of the U.S.* (8 vols., 1883–1913). Upon publication of the first volume he was offered a newly created chair in American history at Pennsylvania. He remained there until his retirement in 1920. The *History,* which covers the period 1784–1861, is a valuable collection of previously neglected facts and records (much of it from newspapers), with unusual attention to the West. It is topical in approach and rambling in style. This and his other books reflect the bias of the time against the newer immigrants and the unions, and an ardent expansionism, but his pioneer work in social history remains significant.

MacMILLAN, DONALD BAXTER (1874–), Massachusetts-born explorer, after graduating from Bowdoin (1898) taught school for a time. He left teaching to accompany Peary to the North Pole (1908–9). His notable trip from Etah, Greenland, to Ellesmere Island (1913–17) proved the nonexistence of what Peary had supposed was Coker Land. In 1925 MacMillan directed a polar expedition for the navy, with an air unit commanded by RICHARD BYRD. During his 27 voyages of exploration to Greenland, Baffin Island, and Labrador (before 1950), MacMillan collected some 40,000 arctic plants, made extensive air surveys, and gathered rare zoological specimens. In 1944 he was awarded the Medal of Honor.

McMILLAN, EDWIN MATTISON (1907–), professor of physics at the University of California at Berkeley, in 1958 became director of its radiation laboratory. By discovering neptunium (element 93), the first transuranic element to be identified, he laid the foundation for the discovery of other elements that are heavier than uranium, and for this research he shared with GLENN T. SEABORG the 1951 Nobel Prize in chemistry. His theory of phase stability led to the development of modified cyclotrons (synchrotrons), which have greatly increased atom-smashing capacity. For his concept of 'phase stability,' first enunciated in 1950, he shared the 1963 Atoms for Peace Award with the Russian nuclear physicist Vladimir I. Veksler.

Macon's Bill No. 2 (1810), so called, was an Act of Congress sponsored by Senator Nathaniel Macon of North Carolina, designed as a substitute for the unsuccessful NONINTERCOURSE ACT. It offered each of the belligerents, France and Great Britain — whichever first recognized American neutral rights — the bait of exclusive trade rights. American shipping was soon engaged in profitable commerce with Great Britain. When President Madison accepted an ambiguous French statement as a bona fide revocation of the Napoleonic decrees on trade, he resumed trade with France, declaring that commerce with Great Britain would come to a halt. The British responded (1811) by a renewal of the blockade of New York and a more vigorous impressment of American seamen. All this diplomatic maneuvering stemmed from Madison's blunder of trying to negotiate from weakness. The War of 1812 was declared before Madison learned that Parliament had repealed the ORDERS IN COUNCIL on commercial restrictions.

MADISON, JAMES (1751–1836), 4th President of the U.S. (1809–17), born in King's county, Virginia, was reared on his father's plantation and educated at the College of New Jersey (Princeton), graduating (1771) as a classmate of Brackenridge and Freneau. Like many of the planter class he took the Patriot side, and he used his store of knowledge about constitutional law to help draft a constitution for the new state of Virginia. In the Continental Congress (1780–83) he favored increasing the power of the central government. As a delegate to the Federal Constitutional Convention (1787) he drew up the 'Virginia Plan,' and by his leadership he won the name 'father of the Constitution.' His *Journals* (3 vols., 1840) are the principal source of knowledge about that assembly. With Hamilton and Jay he contributed to the FEDERALIST PAPERS, led his state in ratifying the Constitution, and was a chief proponent of the Bill of Rights. Indeed, he made his most lasting contribution in his concept of liberty and republican theory. He fought against all government control over thought. To him opinions were not legitimate objects of legislation, and it was he who laid down the rule that 'the censorial power is in the people over the Government, and not in the Government over the people.'

In Congress (1789–97) Madison was a steadfast supporter of Jefferson, with whom he prepared the KENTUCKY AND VIRGINIA RESOLVES, and under whom he served as Secretary of State (1801–9). He was Jefferson's choice for the presidency. During his two terms in office Madison dealt with the results of the foreign policy he had tried previously to shape.

Although Madison surpassed Jefferson in knowledge of political science, he had no special talent as politician or administrator. Slight in stature, with wizened features, he lacked personal magnetism, and had small capacity for inspiring loyalty or rousing national enthusiasm for his ideas. He selected men of mediocre ability for his cabinet, except for Gallatin, whom he retained in the Treasury. Yet after he had concluded the ERSKINE AGREEMENT (1809) with Britain in his second month in office, he was hailed as a skillful negotiator. Its failure led to MACON'S BILL No. 2, an unsuccessful effort to solve the problem of noninterference with American trade during the period of mounting tension between France and England. At the same time the frontiersmen were avid for free land, obtainable only at the expense of the Indians and the British Empire. The 'war hawks,' led by Clay and Calhoun, were hungry for conquest and clamoring for action. British impressment of American seamen continued, and in June 1812 Madison acceded to the popular demand for war with Great Britain. Since New England merchants had already been hard hit commercially, Madison's Federalist opponents at the HARTFORD CONVENTION bitterly opposed 'Mr. Madison's war.'

In the 1812 presidential election Madison was opposed by the New York Federalist, De Witt Clinton. Madison was returned to office by 128 to 89 electoral votes, but the Federalists doubled their strength in Congress. His second Administration was chiefly devoted to prosecuting the war, which went badly. Only the Treaty of Ghent (1814), which ended it, and Jackson's postwar victory at New Orleans, saved the President from extreme unpopularity. In 1816 he signed the bill chartering the second BANK OF THE U.S. and the bill that introduced the TARIFF OF 1816, the first protective tariff in U.S. history.

Madison retired in 1817 to his Virginia estate, Montpelier. There for many years he and Dolley Madison (*nee* Dorothea Payne, 1768–1849) entertained with liberal hospitality, until heavy debts forced him to retrench. Historians accord Madison rank as a great statesman for his contribution to the Federal Constitution, but his stubbornness as an executive and his lack of political flair in dealing with Congress prevented him from exercising leadership as President.

See the biography by Irving Brant (6 vols., 1941–61).

Madison Square Garden, the name given to the New York auditorium (1879) in Madison Square Park, run by P. T. Barnum, was rebuilt in 1890 by McKim, Mead and White. It was demolished in 1925, and a third building was erected uptown, at Eighth Avenue and 50th Street. It is the city's largest indoor stadium, seating 20,000 persons, and it is chiefly used for sporting events, circuses, and large conventions. In 1963 a new Madison Square Garden Sports Center, costing about $116,000,000, with one arena of 22,000 seats and another of 4000 seats, was begun on the site of the Pennsylvania Station.

Mafia, organized bands of Sicilian 'tough guys' (*mafiosi*), dates from Napoleon's invasion of Sicily (1799), when wealthy landowners hired such thugs to safeguard their property from marauders. They not only turned on their employers to extort tribute for the protection, but terrorized the peasants to collect kickbacks on crops. A blood-rite society, it gained a stranglehold of extraordinary power on the social and economic life of Sicily. It remains one of the world's oldest continuous criminal conspiracies.

Italian immigration brought members of the Mafia to the U.S. during the 19th century, but their power began to be felt chiefly in the second quarter of the 20th century. A shadowy organization, cloaked in secrecy, its members are part of *Cosa Nostra* ('our thing'), the mob, or the syndicate. Its kingpins direct operations that have amassed incomes amounting to billions of dollars a year, derived by usury and extortion chiefly from purveyors of narcotics, prostitution, and gambling. The police make no serious dent in the combine, largely because the Mafia enforces its own laws with speedy and brutal death for members who betray its code. In 1957 a raid by government agents on the Apalachin, New York, estate of Joe Barbara broke up an extraordinary top-level convention of 75 members of the Mafia. In 1963 Congress (at the request of Attorney General Kennedy) relaxed the stringent wiretapping regulations and granted immunity to informers.

Magazines in America had their beginning with the nearly simultaneous issue (1741) of Andrew Bradford's *American Magazine* and Franklin's *General Magazine,* both shortlived. The 18th century magazine remained a perilous venture, and such as made their way did so chiefly by reprinting British material. As publishing processes improved and population grew, magazines became something of a factor in the life of the new nation. Two important early periodicals were the *Port Folio* (1801–27), established by JOSEPH DENNIE in Philadelphia, and the Boston *Monthly Anthology* (1803–11), predecessor of the famous and longlived NORTH AMERICAN REVIEW (1815–1939). Other early successes include *Godey's Lady's Book* (1830–98), a fashionable boudoir journal edited for 40 years by SARAH J. HALE, the *Knickerbocker Magazine* (1833–65), and the New York *Ledger* (1855–1903).

Two eclectic literary periodicals antedating the Civil War still lead the field: *Harper's Magazine* (1850–current), and the *Atlantic Monthly* (1857–current). Three magazines established during the 1880's became well known: *Century* (1881–1930), *Forum* (1886–1950), and *Scribner's* (1887–1939). Improved postal organization helped to increase circulation, but until late in the 19th century advertising was a relatively negligible source of revenue. In 1864 *Harper's* carried only notices of Harper books, and the publishers were insulted when a sewing-machine firm offered them a generous fee for an advertisement.

The 'muckraking' magazines of 1890–1910 were able to cut their prices as a result of cheap photoengraving, and they reached for a mass market beginning with *Munsey's Magazine*'s policy of 1893. *McClure's* published Steffens's articles on city corruption. The *American Magazine* was an outlet for Ray Stannard Baker's exposés, and *Collier's* published Mark Sullivan's attack on patent medicine frauds and Upton Sinclair's revelations of loathsome meat packing conditions. Such articles, usually of a high level, aided the passage of key progressive laws such as the Pure Food and Drug Act (1906), the Meat Inspection Act (1906), and the Seventeenth Amendment (1913) for the direct election of senators.

Longest lived among the 'slicks,' which pay highly for popular and timely articles, is the *Saturday Evening Post* (1821), which reflects middle-class conservatism. The *New Yorker* (1925) is widely known as a weekly of sophisticated wit. No less noted among the intelligentsia were *The Smart Set* (1914–23) and *The American Mercury* (1924–33) of the iconoclastic H. L. Mencken and George Jean Nathan. The *Literary Digest,* founded in 1890, attracted a mass clientele for its 'scissors-and-paste' selections of newspaper and magazine opinions. Its famous public opinion polls fell from grace in 1936, when the publishers predicted Landon's victory, using samples from telephone directories and auto registrations.

A comparatively recent development has been the weekly news magazine, of which *Time* (1923) and *Newsweek* (1933) are representative. The photojournals, *Life* and *Look,* still more recent, have immense circulation, each printing about 7,000,000 copies a week in 1965. *Reader's Digest* (1922), which popularized condensations of magazine articles and books, with its foreign-language issues reaches the staggering monthly total of 18,000,000 copies. PULP MAGAZINES and 'comics' are featured on thousands of news stands. At present magazine advertising, costing annually some $600,000,000, makes magazine publishing a profitable venture for such as survive in this highly competitive industry.

See F. L. Mott, *A History of American Magazines* (4 vols., 1930–38).

MAGELLAN, FERDINAND (*c.* 1480–1521), Portuguese navigator, with a fleet of five ships given to him by the king of Spain (Charles I, later the Emperor Charles V), sailed west from Seville in August 1519, skirted the coast of South America, and by November 1520 (with his three remaining ships) rounded Cape Horn and reached the Pacific. In March 1521 he arrived in the Philippines, where he was killed during a brush with natives. Ultimately one of his vessels, crossing the Indian Ocean and rounding the Cape of Good Hope, completed the first voyage around the world (1522). Although Magellan did not live to complete the voyage, his skill and determination were responsible for accomplishing one of the greatest feats in the history of ocean travel. He did not touch upon the Northern Hemisphere, but by revealing the Americas as a new continent, separate from Asia, he revolutionized ideas about the size of the globe.

MAHAN, ALFRED THAYER (1840–1914), a graduate of the U.S. Naval Academy (1859), as president of the Newport War College (1886–89), and the Naval War College (1892–93), gave lectures on naval history and tactics from which grew his notable studies, *The Influence of Sea Power upon History, 1660–1783* (1890), and *The Influence of Sea Power upon the French Revolution, 1793–1812* (2 vols., 1892). As a philosopher of the new imperialism, he rejected liberal internationalism in foreign policy for the grim realism of the struggle for power and national self-interest. He stressed the importance of navies in determining political history. Because he wrote at a time when manifestations of imperialism were world-wide, he influenced the policies of Germany, England, Japan, and the U.S.

Mahican Indians (also called Mohican) were an Algonquian confederacy that originally occupied both banks of the upper Hudson river. (The MOHEGAN Indians are to be distinguished from the larger group, though Cooper confused the two in *The Last of the Mohicans.*) Crowded by the Mohawks who were aided by the Dutch, the Mahicans moved west to join the Delawares in the Ohio region, where they lost their identity. Those remaining in western Massachusetts preserved their tribal homogeneity as the so-called Stockbridge Indians.

Mail-order houses, so called because they receive most of their business by mail, sprang up in the 1870's and 1880's, when railroads began to offer quick and cheap transportation. Their real growth followed the establishment of RURAL FREE DELIVERY (1896) and PARCEL POST service (1913), since their business depended largely upon customers in small towns and rural areas. The mail-order catalog, with its enticing variety of illustrated merchandise, became the 'wish book' for thousands who seldom could reach a metropolis, and it remained so until the mid-1920's, when automobiles began to alter transportation methods. Since then, the larger mail-order houses, such as Montgomery Ward (1872), and Sears, Roebuck and Company (1895), have opened chains of retail stores. General Robert E. Wood (1879–) while president of Sears (1928–39) converted it into the world's largest retailer of general merchandise.

Maine, in the extreme northeastern corner of the U.S., was visited by Sebastian Cabot (1496), and during the 16th century its irregular, rocky coast was known to European mariners. Although FERDINANDO GORGES sponsored a short-lived colony (1607–8), permanent settlements were first made during the 1630's under grants from Charles I, whose queen, feudal proprietor of the province of Maine in France, was honored by the name of the region. In 1677 the Massachusetts Bay Company purchased the proprietary rights, and settlements spread along the coast and the larger rivers. The ties between the settlements were made stronger during the period of French and Indian Wars, and the War of Independence. The sectional balancing of interests between the North and South brought Maine into the Union (1820) as the 23rd state under terms of the MISSOURI COMPROMISE. Its thriving commercial center, Portland, was the capital until Augusta became its permanent legislative site (1832). Long an important lumbering region (and still three-quarters forested), during the first half of the 19th century Maine carried on a prosperous timber trade with Europe and Asia.

The relatively slow population growth (to 969,000 in 1960) has given homogeneity to the people of the state, who still preserve their 'Down East' self-sufficient individualism. The poor soil and brief growing season have confined agriculture to local needs, with the exception of potato production. Pulpwood manufacture is important, and lobster fishing, always a source of income, had become big business by mid-20th century. The 2200 glacier-formed lakes and the 5000 watercourses have made tourist trade and summer residence an economic factor. Acadia National Park (est. 1920) embraces chiefly the granite mountains of Mount Desert Island. Institutions of higher learning include Bowdoin (Brunswick, est. 1794), Colby (Waterville, est. 1813), Bates (Lewiston, est. 1864), and the University of Maine (Orono, est. 1865).

***Maine,* Destruction of the** (15 February 1898), occurred three weeks after the American battleship had been moored in Havana harbor, where she had been sent, ostensibly to protect American life and property. The explosion, which killed 260 officers and men, was judged by a careful naval court of inquiry in 1911 to have been caused by the detonation of an underwater mine, not internal sabotage. Actually the cause has never been determined with certainty, though some historians believe that Cuban rebels sought thereby to embroil the U.S. with Spain. In the weeks following the explosion, the U.S. government urged the public to reserve judgment, but the yellow press attributed the disaster to enemy agents, and 'Remember the *Maine!*' became the popular slogan of those demanding war with Spain.

MAKEMIE, FRANCIS (1658–1708), Scotch-Irish clergyman and missionary, was the first conspicuous Presbyterian leader in America. He arrived in Maryland from Scotland (1683), traveled and preached from the Carolinas to New York, and directed the organization of the first presbytery in the country at Philadelphia (1706). In New York he was arrested and imprisoned (1707) for preaching without a license. Religious freedom owed much to his trial, for the court freed him, and the assembly enacted laws designed to prevent such religious persecution.

'Malefactors of great wealth' was a phrase used by President Theodore Roosevelt in an address (20 August 1907) attacking those whom he considered responsible for the PANIC OF 1907.

MALL, FRANKLIN PAINE (1862–1917), one of the notable American anatomists, briefly occupied chairs in vertebrate anatomy at Clark (1889–92), and at Chicago (1892–93), when those institutions first opened. He went to Johns Hopkins in 1893, where he headed the department of anatomy until his death. There he founded (1914) the principal institution for the study of experimental embryology, and under his guidance cytology, histology, embryology, and adult structure were first correlated.

Mammoth Cave in Kentucky is a series of caverns with spectacular onyx formations. It is believed to have been occupied by prehistoric people. It was 'discovered' in 1799, became a tourist attraction in the 1830's, and was made a national park in 1936.

Manassas, see *Bull Run.*

Manchuria first became a region about which the U.S. defined a specific policy when Secretary of State Hay enunciated his OPEN DOOR POLICY (1899). The TREATY OF PORTSMOUTH (1905), the ROOT-TAKAHIRA AGREEMENT (1908), the LANSING-ISHII AGREEMENT (1917), and the NINE POWER TREATY (1922) expressed continuing U.S. interest in the sovereignty of China over Manchuria as well as elsewhere.

After Japan invaded Manchuria (1931), it was renamed Manchukuo and became a puppet nation. This led Secretary of State Stimson to proclaim the doctrine of nonrecognition (1932). At the end of World War II Manchuria was returned to China under its original name.

Mandamus, see *Writ of Mandamus.*

Mandan Indians, of Siouan stock, were a village tribe on the northern Plains, culturally allied to their neighbors on the Missouri river, the ARIKARA and the HIDATSA. They were known to all exploring parties in the 18th century, and when Lewis and Clark visited them (1804) they numbered some 1200. They were later the subject of a study and many paintings by GEORGE CATLIN. Decimated during the 19th century by smallpox, the remnants of the tribe live on a reservation in North Dakota. The spreading eagle feather headdress, used today by Indians on ceremonial occasions, probably originated among the Mandan and Hidatsa.

Manhattan, an island about thirteen miles long and two miles wide, separated from the mainland to the north by the Harlem river and on the west by the Hudson, forms the principal part of NEW YORK CITY. Discovered by Verrazano (1524), it was visited by Hudson (1609) and first occupied as part of New Netherland by the Dutch, who named the island after the local Indians. A semblance of legality for the accomplished fact of its occupation was given (1626) when the Dutch paid the Indians 60 guilders ($24) for it. The chief of the city's five boroughs, it includes such well-known areas as the BATTERY, the BOWERY, BROADWAY, the EAST SIDE, GREENWICH VILLAGE, HARLEM, and WALL STREET.

Manhattan Project, which developed the materials of the atomic bomb, was created in August 1942, when Oak Ridge, Tennessee, was chosen as the site for the work of the 'Manhattan District.' Under its sponsorship the first chain reaction in nuclear fission was achieved in a converted squash court at the University of Chicago late that year. In May 1943 the project, under control of the U.S. Corps of Engineers and administered by General Leslie R. Groves, took over all work connected with the bomb.

The existence and purpose of the large community of workers at Oak Ridge was kept secret from most of the country until an atomic bomb was dropped on Hiroshima (August 1945), although the first such bomb was experimentally exploded in July 1945, at Alamogordo, New Mexico. Meanwhile scientific research was being conducted at California (Berkeley), Chicago, Columbia, and Los Alamos. In 1946 the project was transferred to the ATOMIC ENERGY COMMISSION, and in 1948 the site of the 'District' became the Oak Ridge National Laboratory, whose plants make radioactive isotopes for medical and industrial uses, and the uranium (U-235) that is used in atomic bombs.

The Manhattan Project is noteworthy as an example of international scientific co-operation, in that England and Canada joined the U.S. in pooling their previously separated efforts. During the war nearly $2,000,000,000 was spent and 125,000 scientists and workers were employed in the secret race against Nazi Germany, whose scientists had split the uranium nucleus in 1939 and were also working on the development of an atomic bomb.

'Manifest Destiny' was a term that gained currency in the 1840's. It implied the inevitability of the continued territorial expansion of the U.S. into undeveloped continental areas to the west and south. (The concept was linked to the idea of IMPERIALISM.) It became the theme of numberless orations, editorials, and political speeches. It was cited as a reason for the annexation of Texas and was caught up by expansionists in the dispute with Great Britain over the boundary of Oregon. Under the leadership of Democrats in the South it became a sectional slogan aimed at the acquisition of slave territory, and its proponents in Congress mustered enough votes to declare war on Mexico in 1846.

'Manifest Destiny' began chiefly as a tenet of the Democratic party, but it had devotees among Whigs and later was implemented by the Republicans. Secretary of State Seward purchased Alaska in 1867 and sought (vainly) to annex sundry Caribbean and Pacific islands. The doctrine was revived and amplified in the 1890's (stimulated by chauvinism and racialism) when Hawaii was annexed and various islands were acquired from Spain.

Manila Bay, Battle of (1 May 1898), was fought in the Philippines during the Spanish-American War. The Asiatic squadron (four cruisers and two gunboats), commanded by Commodore GEORGE DEWEY, had left its base at Hong Kong on 27 April, with orders to capture or destroy the Spanish fleet in Manila Bay, which Dewey entered on the evening of 30 April. At 5:40 a.m. on the following day Dewey engaged the Spanish squadron of ten vessels, methodically raking the Spanish line from end to end with powerful broadsides. By noon all of the Spanish craft had been smashed. No American ships were damaged, and American casualties totaled but eight wounded. (The city of Manila was not taken until 13 August, one day after the signing of the peace protocol.)

MANN, Horace (1796–1859), Massachusetts-born educator, after graduation from Brown (1819), practiced law in Boston until 1837. As secretary of the newly organized Massachusetts Board of Education (1837–48), he opened the first normal school in the U.S. (at Lexington, 1839), and reorganized the entire public school system of the state, setting a national model of longer terms, better schoolhouses, higher teaching salaries, a more scientific pedagogy, and a revived high school movement. By propaganda and legislative reform (he served in Congress, 1848–53) he led the crusade that established the principle of a common-school education at public expense for all children in the U.S. Churchmen attacked his nonsectarian moral instruction in the 'godless' public schools, but Mann, a Unitarian, rejected catechism and proselyting.

Mann published the first of his series of *Annual Reports* in 1838. They are still considered remarkable documents in the history of education. In 1853 he became president of the then recently established Antioch College in Ohio, where his concepts took root at the college level. He identified himself with the liberal movements of his day, and gained legislative support to a unique degree in the treatment of the feeble-minded and the insane. No American of the 19th century contributed more to educational reform.

Mann Act (1910), also called the White Slave Traffic Act, prohibits interstate transportation of women for immoral purposes. The Act is significant as an early extension of Federal control over social welfare.

Mann-Elkins Act (1910), recommended by President Taft, placed communication systems under the jurisdiction of the Interstate Commerce Commission, which it empowered to suspend any rate increases until it investigated the reasonableness of the changes asked. It also provided effective enforcement of the clause in the original interstate commerce act prohibiting the railroads from charging more for short hauls than for long ones over the same route. Its Commerce Court, set up to hear appeals from the Commission, was short-lived. Nevertheless, the Mann-Elkins Act, by giving quasi-judicial control over communications to the ICC, allowed the Commission to become the most powerful administrative agency in government.

Manors in England were landed estates, administered as a unit, over which the proprietor exercised well-defined rights of lordship. In colonial America they were tracts occupied by tenants who paid a fee-farm rent to the proprietor. The feudal character of the old manorial organization was breaking down at the time of the settlement of America, but the system of securing landholdings by patents with manorial rights was observed in the proprietary colonies, chiefly in New York, Maryland, and South Carolina. (The FREEHOLD did not confer a manorial right.) The PATROONS of New York exercised feudal rights and controlled local offices and civil and criminal courts. Early governors of the province created manors along the Hudson and on Long Island.

Among all the English colonies Maryland was unique in the degree to which it was a land of actual manors, demesne lands, freehold tenements, rent rolls, and quit-rents. There the organization was more than social and tenural; it was political and administrative. The proprietor enjoyed the *jura regalia* of his palatinate, and these rights he retained throughout the colonial period. The seignorial life envisioned by the CAROLINA PROPRIETORS never went into effect, although Charleston became the center of a landed aristocracy. Actually, however, such gentry were the heads of large agricultural plantations.

Manufacturing in the U.S. during the colonial period was severely restricted by Parliament, since English merchants expected to have a monopoly of the colonial market. Thus the WOOLENS ACT (1699), the HAT ACT (1732), and the IRON ACT (1750), although they were flagrantly disregarded, were brakes on colonial manufacturing enterprise. IRON MANUFACTURE, however, was far advanced by 1775, even if, on the whole, manufacturing was slow to develop thereafter, chiefly for lack of capital, skilled labor, and easy transportation.

SAMUEL SLATER, using Arkwright machinery, pioneered in the factory system when he first spun cotton by power (1790), and by 1800 seven Arkwright mills were in operation. The system of interchangeable parts, which ELI WHITNEY devised for his firearms factory (1798), proved the most revolutionary invention in American history, by paving the way for MASS PRODUCTION. In 1807 OLIVER EVANS opened a shop to turn out steam engines. The nonintercourse acts, followed by the War of 1812, made the decade 1808–18 a boom period for domestic manufacturing. In 1814 FRANCIS CABOT LOWELL built his factory at Waltham, Massachusetts, where he created the first integrated textile mill in the world. Steam power was not widely adopted in factory work until 1850, when machine shop products multiplied in variety on the basis of standardized parts and quantity production. At the outbreak of the Civil War the chief activity of the Northeast was manufacturing.

Manufacturing activities were spurred by the war effort, and at the war's end the industrial states of the North had control over Federal policies, inaugurating a period of high tariff protection and attracting new branches of manufacture from Europe. The modern industrial era was then under way, with development of the STEEL INDUSTRY, the OIL INDUSTRY, the opening of new mines, the growth of cities, the immigration of labor, and the disappearance of the frontier. All these events quickened the phenomenal technological developments in large-scale business organization. The decade of the 1890's began the industrial use of the internal combustion engine, and the foundation of such giant enterprises as the manufacture of automobiles and airplanes. The steam turbines designed to drive dynamos for the generation of electric power, which so amazed visitors to the Chicago World's Fair (1893), did in fact alter the course of history, as Henry Adams thought they would. Hydroelectric power, inaugurated at Niagara Falls (1894), by 1950 had revolutionized industrial power supply. The vast amounts of energy made available by mammoth dams on the COLORADO, COLUMBIA, and MISSOURI rivers, and created in the South by the TENNESSEE VALLEY AUTHORITY, transformed the face of the nation by making regions that were formerly rural or arid into industrial centers. Manufacturing assets in the U.S. at present total hundreds of billions of dollars.

See V. S. Clark, *History of Manufactures in the U.S., 1607–1928* (3 vols., 1929); and J. G. Glover and W. B. Cornell, eds., *The Development of American Industries* (3d ed., 1951).

Maps are documents that speak a language common to all races and nations, expressing the relationship of society to its geographic environment. Even when maps have been mythical, they have fired the imagination of explorers and have been factors in shaping policies of state. Columbus depended upon charts prepared by Cardinal d'Ailly (1350–1420), whose compendium, *Imago mundi,* reinterpreted the charts drawn by the second-century geographer Ptolemy.

Maps of the coastal areas of the Americas were sketched by 16th-century explorers probing the coastlines of both continents in an attempt to find a passage through the land barrier to the Orient. The natural difficulties of accurate mapping were compounded at first by the unwillingness of rival navigators (and nations) to exchange information. By mid-16th century, however, several map publishing firms had sprung up in Europe, and were issuing hundreds of maps of America, combining fact with legend. The publication of Gerard Mercator's large-scale projection of the world in 1569 inaugurated the science of cartography, and thereafter mariners could navigate with some degree of certainty.

The California coast had been known

in a general way since the discoveries of Cortés in the 1530's, but it was not fully mapped until a century later. The maps that Captain JOHN SMITH made early in the 17th century greatly added to knowledge of the Atlantic seaboard. In the same period SAMUEL CHAMPLAIN was charting the northeast coast, and pioneering in the TOPOGRAPHICAL MAPPING of North America.

In the 18th century the British government projected an elaborate survey of the Atlantic coast. The work resulted in publication of a series of atlases, the *Atlantic Neptune* (1774–81). The first accurate maps of the north Pacific coast were those published (1798), after a three-year survey, by the explorer GEORGE VANCOUVER.

The Coast Survey was authorized by Congress in 1807, and its field work since has been continuous. After the Civil War, Congress enlarged the Survey's functions to cover inland operations. In 1878 it became the Coast and Geodetic Survey, now a bureau of the Department of Commerce. It keeps accurate data on nearly 100,000 miles of coastline, and publishes nautical and aeronautical charts and tables.

In addition, there are scores of other varieties of maps put forth by the federal government as a basis for economic planning. The manifold relationship of cartography to history can be studied in such compendiums as C. O. Paullin, *Atlas of the Historical Geography of the U.S.* (1932), the most elaborate one-volume presentation, and C. E. LeGear, *U.S. Atlases* (1950), a listing under captions such as boundaries, canals, climate, forests, industries, railroads, states, counties, and cities.

Marbury* v. *Madison (1803), a case that resulted in a Supreme Court ruling delivered by Chief Justice Marshall, affirmed the doctrine of JUDICIAL REVIEW, and thus balanced the powers among the legislative, executive, and judicial branches of the government. Marbury had been appointed a justice of the peace for the District of Columbia by President John Adams in the last hours of his administration. Madison, the new Secretary of State, under orders of President Jefferson refused to deliver the commission to Marbury, who applied to the Supreme Court for a WRIT OF MANDAMUS.

Marshall's opinion, delivered 'for the unanimous Court,' vitally influenced the development of constitutional law in the U.S. It held that Madison had no right to withhold the commission, but maintained that section 13 of the Judiciary Act of 1789, empowering the Court to issue such a writ, was contrary to the Constitution and therefore invalid. Although in this instance the decision limited the power of the Supreme Court, by effecting review it made the American judiciary more powerful than any other in the world.

MARCOS de NIZA (*c.* 1495–1558), missionary explorer in Spanish North America, was a Franciscan friar. In 1539, at the head of an expedition sent by the viceroy of Mexico, Fray Marcos penetrated present New Mexico in search of the fabled 'Seven Cities of Cibola.' The expedition discovered the Zuñi pueblos, on which they reported, but Fray Marcos's honest (and significant) account was soon inflated by popular imagination. The viceroy thereupon outfitted the splendid expedition of CORONADO (1540–42).

MARCY, WILLIAM LEARNED (1786–1857), a graduate of Brown (1808), became a dominant figure in the powerful New York Democratic party machine known as the ALBANY REGENCY. As U.S. Senator (1831–32), he publicly defended 'the rule that to the victor belong the spoils of the enemy.' Thrice governor of New York (1833–39), he was Polk's Secretary of War (1845–49) during the Mexican War, and reached the peak of his career as Secretary of State under Pierce (1853–57). He was skillful in his handling of the negotiation of the Gadsden Purchase, as well as the troubles rising from the filibuster of WILLIAM WALKER and those of the OSTEND MANIFESTO.

MARIN, JOHN (1872–1953), New Jersey-born landscape painter, received training at the Pennsylvania Academy and abroad. He exhibited his expressionist water colors in New York first in 1909, and annually thereafter. He rejected the mode of reproducing exact physical appearances as static; for instance, he painted the *Woolworth Building* (1915) revolving in air. His later canvases, expressing the sea, boats, and shore as he saw them on the Maine coast, led artists and critics to judge him as the leading American painter of his day.

Marine Corps, U.S., originally the skilled riflemen aboard military vessels, was temporarily established (1775) by the Continental Congress and became a permanent Corps in 1798, when the Navy was separated from the Army. Often employed in amphibious duty, the Corps has been engaged in all major wars and played a cardinal role during World War II in the invasion of the Pacific Islands. It is a department of the U.S. Navy, but for all practical purposes it is an independent arm of the defense establishment, commanded by a four-star general. In 1965 it maintained an authorized active duty strength of some 190,000 officers and men.

MARION, FRANCIS (*c.* 1732–95), South Carolina planter, was serving in the state legislature at the outbreak of the War of Independence. He immediately took action in the field, and was most effective at the head of guerrilla or partisan bands. The British were unable to capture this 'Swamp Fox,' a singularly able leader of irregular troops, who after 1781 served as a brigadier general of militia. In that year he received the thanks of Congress for his harrying tactics, which became remarkably useful in the closing months of the war. A hero to his men, Marion became almost a legendary figure, and is so depicted in many of the romances of W. G. Simms.

MARLOWE, JULIA, see *Sothern.*

Marne, Second Battle of the (18 July–6 August 1918), marked the turning point of World War I. The German offensive of 15 July on both sides of Rheims had been virtually stopped, when, on 18 July, Foch launched a counterattack, supported by Pershing's gathering strength of 270,000 field troops, 85,000 of whom were engaged in this successful action. The way was then opened for the final MEUSE-ARGONNE OFFENSIVE of September, which ended the war.

MARQUETTE, JACQUES (1637–75), French Jesuit missionary and explorer, was sent to New France in 1666. He studied Indian languages and in 1668 began his labors among Ottawa tribes in the upper Great Lakes region. With LOUIS JOLLIET he descended the Mississippi (1673) by canoe to the mouth of the Arkansas, thereby giving assurance that the French might extend colonization from the St. Lawrence to the Gulf of Mexico. His journal (published in 1681) became the official account of the discovery. In 1674 Marquette set out to found a mission among the Illinois Indians, but he died near Lake Michigan before accomplishing his task.

MARRYAT, FREDERICK (1792–1848), British naval captain and author of sea thrillers, after traveling in the U.S. and Canada (1837–39) wrote his *Diary in America* (1839). Its caustic humor, coupled with his tactless behavior and remarks during his travels, brought sharp attacks from the U.S. press. An irascible Tory, Marryat resented every intrusion upon his privacy, and ascribed every inopportune occurrence to some sinister operation of democratic principles. At Detroit he was burned in effigy, along with hundreds of his books.

MARSH, GEORGE PERKINS (1801–82), Vermont-born diplomat, linguist, and ecologist, after graduation from Dartmouth (1820) returned to Burlington to practice law and enter state politics. One of the prodigious American scholars of his day (though an amateur philologist by European standards), he spoke twenty languages with ease and made pioneer contributions to the study of linguistics in the U.S. He was widely known as a Scandinavian scholar, and his library of Scandinavian books, which he began building in the 1830's, is reputed to have been the largest private collection in the world outside of Scandinavia. His *Lectures on the English Language* (1860) was much in advance of its time in advocating a national independence of American speech.

While in Congress (1843–49), Marsh helped organize the Smithsonian Institution. Under both Taylor and Fillmore he served as minister to Turkey (1849–53). At the age of sixty he was sent as the first U.S. minister to Italy (1861), a post he filled so ably that he retained it until his death.

These occupations never subordinated Marsh's consuming love for geography. His masterpiece, *Man and Nature* (1864), he revised as *The Earth as Modified by Human Action* (1874). It was one of the most influential American geographical works of the 19th century, and it contributed importantly to the crystallization of the CONSERVATION MOVEMENT in the 20th century.

MARSH, JAMES (1794–1842), a graduate of Dartmouth (1817), became a Congregationalist minister and a professor of languages at the University of Vermont, which he served as president for seven years (1826–33). Although he was a stern Calvinist, in his effort to find a religion that would 'satisfy the heart as well as the head,' he edited Coleridge's *Aids to Reflection* (1829), emphasizing its distinctions between reason and understanding. His analysis of the problem strongly influenced New England TRANSCENDENTALISM.

MARSH, OTHNIEL CHARLES (1831–99), after graduation from Yale (1860) and study abroad, returned to Yale to occupy (1866–99) the first chair of paleontology in the U.S., which had been established by his uncle, GEORGE PEABODY, the philanthropist. Marsh organized and led many field expeditions in the West, from Nebraska to California, and gathered a collection of fossil vertebrates at Yale. It was the most extensive collection in the world during his lifetime. He discovered 500 new species, 225 new genera, 64 new families, and 19 new orders. He originated the 'authentic skeletal restorations' of dinosaurs (a name he coined), which caught the public eye and gave him contemporary fame.

His revelation of fossilized 'missing links' of lost animal forms intermediate in the process of evolution raised the prestige of Darwinism. When he discovered the extinct toothed birds that link reptiles and modern birds, he received Darwin's warm praise. He was also congratulated by evolutionists here and abroad for his notable reconstruction of the evolution of the horse from its tiny ancestor to the modern type. Most of his writings are in the reports of the U.S. Geological Survey. The acrid controversies that Marsh carried on with his rival, E. D. COPE, who supported the theory of the inheritance of acquired characteristics, gave them notoriety as two of the best haters in the history of science.

MARSH, REGINALD (1898–1954), born in Paris, upon graduation from Yale (1920), studied painting, engraving, and etching at the Art Students League under John Sloan and K. H. Miller. His first one-man show (1930) increased a popularity already begun by lively representations of American life in such magazines as the *New Yorker*. His frescoes in the Custom House, New York City, and the Post Office, Washington, D.C., are distinguished for their luminous color.

MARSHALL, GEORGE CATLETT (1880–1959), after graduation from Virginia Military Institute (1901), served in the U.S. Army for 43 years, during World War II as chief of staff (1939–45), and after 1944 as a General of the Army. In December 1945 General Marshall was sent on a major mission as ambassador-envoy to end the Chinese civil war, but he succeeded only in bringing about a brief truce. Failing to unite the Kuomintang and the Reds, he withdrew, angrily denouncing both sides for bad faith. Even generous U.S. military aid could not thereafter save Chiang from defeat.

President Truman selected Marshall as his Secretary of State (1947–49), and, in his commencement address at Harvard in June 1947, Marshall proposed the European Recovery Program, or MARSHALL PLAN, to rebuild the economy of Western Europe, which had been ravaged by war. His direction of that program was recognized in 1953, when he was awarded the Nobel Peace prize. For a year he held office as Secretary of Defense (1950–51).

No military leader in U.S. history has more fully won the confidence of Congress or of the Presidents under whom he served. Although he never commanded troops in combat (in World War I he was a staff officer), Marshall was a soldier-statesman whose brilliant grasp of detail and flexibility in administrative decision were tremendous assets in peace as well as in war.

MARSHALL, JOHN (1755–1835), 3rd Chief Justice of the U.S. (1801–35), was born in a log cabin on the Virginia frontier. His mother was related to the Lees and the Randolphs, and to Jefferson, who was later Marshall's great antagonist. His father was prominent in state politics. Marshall served as an officer in the Revolution and briefly attended William and Mary College, where he received his only formal education. He became a lawyer and settled in Richmond, where his brilliance in argument gave him a statewide reputation. His effectiveness as a commissioner in the XYZ AFFAIR (1797–98) made him a popular figure, and as a Federalist he was elected to Congress (1799). President Adams brought Marshall into his cabinet as Secretary of State, and at the moment of retirement appointed Marshall to the Supreme Court.

Marshall, by the discernment of his legal interpretations, raised the Supreme Court to its position of dignity and power more than any other person in U.S. history. He viewed the Constitution as an instrument of national unity, a document that not only set forth specific powers but also created its own sanctions by its IMPLIED POWERS. His important decisions fall broadly into three categories. MARBURY *v.* MADISON (1803) affirmed the constitutional power of the Court to engage in JUDICIAL REVIEW of state and Federal legislation. FLETCHER *v.* PECK (1810) and the DARTMOUTH COLLEGE CASE (1819) erected judicial barriers against populistic attacks upon property rights. MC CULLOCH *v.* MARYLAND (1819) gave judicial sanction to the doctrine of centralization of powers at the expense of the states.

Marshall headed the Court during the long Democratic administrations of Jefferson, Madison, Monroe, and Jackson. Since his Federalist bias was pronounced, his quarrels with the executive branch sometimes became acrimonious, but so absolute was his integrity and so compelling his arguments that he almost always won the adherence of his colleagues. In fact, Marshall so completely dominated the Court that in his 34 years of service he dissented only eight times, and of the 1100 opinions handed down in that period, he wrote 519.

A man of personal charm, Marshall enjoyed the unbounded affection of his friends and the respect of his enemies. His style combines conciseness with precision. His *Life of George Washington* (5 vols., 1804–7), though adulatory and partly plagiarized, enjoyed high repute in his day.

See A. J. Beveridge, *The Life of John Marshall* (4 vols., 1916–19), and E. S. Corwin, *John Marshall and the Constitution* (1919). Carl B. Swisher and others, *Justice John Marshall: A Reappraisal* (1955) is a scholarly symposium.

Marshall Plan (European Recovery Program) was a project instituted at the Paris Economic Conference (July 1947) to foster postwar economic recovery in those European countries outside the Soviet orbit. It followed Secretary of State George Marshall's proposal that the nations outline their needs so that material and financial aid from the U.S. could be integrated on a broad scale. The program was administered (at an expenditure of $12,500,000,000) by the Economic Cooperation Administration (ECA) until 1951, then transferred to the Mutual Security Program. All activities ceased in 1956.

Martial law in U.S. procedure is the exercise of control over the civil population by state or Federal military authority in situations beyond the control of civil authority. The term does not apply to wartime situations nor to 'military aid to the civil power,' as in the PULLMAN STRIKE of 1894. It has been proclaimed in such instances as DORR'S REBELLION (1842), but it is usually invoked only in the wake of such natural disasters as floods and conflagrations, to prevent looting and help re-establish civic order.

Martin* v. *Hunter's Lessee (1816) was a case that resulted in a ruling asserting the right of the U.S. Supreme Court to review the decisions of state courts, a right that had been challenged by the Virginia court of appeals. Justice Story ruled that the jurisdiction of the Supreme Court depended upon the nature of the case rather than upon the court from which it was appealed. The decision thus upheld the constitutionality of section 25 of the JUDICIARY ACT OF 1789. The principle that this opinion affirmed was vigorously reasserted in COHENS *v.* VIRGINIA (1821).

Martin* v. *Mott (1827) was a case that resulted in an opinion delivered by U.S. Supreme Court Justice Story, who held that when the President, acting under congressional authority, calls out state militia, his decision 'is conclusive upon all persons,' since prompt obedience obviates the need to maintain a standing army. The Court was acting on a case incident to the War of 1812, when state authorities in New England had asserted the right to withhold such requisition.

MARTINEAU, HARRIET (1802–76), English writer, sprang into prominence after she published *Illustrations of Political Economy* (9 vols., 1832–34), a conglomeration of political science illustrated by fiction. For two years she traveled through the U.S. (1834–36), and she recorded her impressions in *Society in America* (1837), a moral assessment that was generally sympathetic, although her strictures on slavery aroused antagonism in the South. She followed it with *Retrospects of Western Travel* (1838), a personal narrative written with a lighter touch.

MARTYR, PETER [PIETRO MARTIRE D'ANGHIERA] (1455–1526), Italian humanist scholar, in 1487 went to Spain, where he received clerical preferment in the court of Isabella. There he became acquainted with Columbus, da Gama, Magellan, and other New World explorers. Through them he gathered material for his *De orbe novo* (1516, trans. by Richard Eden, 1555). These *Decades* (groups of ten letters) constitute the first formal history of the Americas, and make clear the generally circulated view of the discoveries. (It was edited by F. A. MacNutt, 2 vols., 1912.)

Marx Brothers, the most celebrated team of motion picture comedians, were Julius (Groucho), Arthur (Harpo), Leonard (Chico), Milton (Gummo), and Herbert (Zeppo). Beginning in vaudeville, they first starred during the 1920's. They specialized in a chaotic world of improvisation humor and zany situations wherein the dialogue has slight relevance to the action. Such films as their 'Animal Crackers,' 'Duck Soup,' and 'A Night at the Opera' were produced in the 1930's and remained popular for three decades. Retirement of Gummo and Zeppo reduced them (1935) to the 'Three Marx Brothers.' The eloquence in pantomime of Harpo Marx (1893–1964) gave him rank as a great comedian.

Maryland, probably visited by Verrazano (1524), was first charted by Captain JOHN SMITH. It was formally established as a colony when Charles I gave a charter (1632) to GEORGE CALVERT, who named the region in honor of Queen Henrietta Maria. Parceled out as MANORS in quasi-feudal holdings to Catholic and Protestant emigrés, the grants were subject to disputes rising from religious conflicts, but in 1654 the Puritans gained political control. After the English Revolution of 1688 Maryland became a royal province, the Church of England was officially recognized, and Annapolis became the capital (1694). Marylanders were stalwart patriots on the issues that led to the War of Independence. In 1776 Maryland adopted its own constitution, and in 1788 it entered the Union as the seventh of the Thirteen Colonies.

Split by the 200-mile-long Chesapeake Bay, with its numerous rivers and estuaries, Maryland developed a farm economy relying on water transportation. The tidewater (eastern shore) area had a southern plantation culture. The rolling piedmont of the north and west was tied economically to the North, with BALTIMORE as a flourishing metropolis of 30,000 by 1800. A true border state during the Civil War, Maryland remained within the Union and was the scene of the ANTIETAM campaign, but loyalties were bitterly divided, and Marylanders fought on both sides.

Diversified industries sprang up after the Reconstruction period, and they became the dominant factor in a prospering economy that linked business of both the North and the South. The state's institutions of higher learning include St. John's College (Annapolis, est. 1696), the University of Maryland (Baltimore, est. 1807), the U.S. Naval Academy (Annapolis, est. 1845), and the Johns Hopkins University (Baltimore, est. 1875).

MASON, GEORGE (1725–92), statesman and political philosopher, was a wealthy member of Virginia's tidewater gentry. His liberal views, incorporated as he drafted them in the Virginia declaration of rights (1776), were drawn on by Jefferson for the famous early paragraphs of the Declaration of Independence, served as a model for other states, and influenced the French Declaration of the Rights of Man. Throughout his career he steadily opposed slavery. He took a stand against the Stamp Act and similar tax measures, and was an important member of the Federal Constitutional Convention. He opposed ratification of the instrument and refused to sign it, chiefly because it lacked a bill of rights. (The long Bill of Rights that he drew up formed the basis for the first Ten Amendments to the Constitution.) To a large degree he was responsible for the cession of Virginia's western lands to the U.S., and the securing (through the work of George Rogers Clark) of the Northwest Territory. Mason was a leading Anti-Federalist and an outstanding example of the political philosopher moved by the rationalistic spirit of the Enlightenment.

MASON, JAMES MURRAY, see *Trent Affair.*

MASON, LOWELL (1792–1872), Massachusetts-born musician, after compiling a music collection for the Boston Handel and Haydn Society (1821), became director of music in three Boston churches. He founded the Boston Academy of Music (1832), and the New York Normal Institute (1853). He became a teacher of far-reaching influence through his lectures in the U.S. and England, in which he advocated musical training in the public schools on the learning-by-doing principles of Pestalozzi. He compiled some 50 books of music and composed more than 1200 hymns, including 'Nearer, My God, to Thee,' 'My Faith Looks Up to Thee,' and 'From Greenland's Icy Mountains.' The hymn 'America' first appeared in his collection, *The Choir* (1832). After his death his large music library and manuscript collection were presented to Yale.

Mason-Dixon line, the boundary between the present states of Pennsylvania (north), and Delaware, Maryland, and West Virginia (south), was surveyed (1763–67) by the English astronomers Charles Mason and Jeremiah Dixon, to settle a boundary dispute of long standing between the colonies of Pennsylvania and Maryland. The services of the surveyor DAVID RITTENHOUSE were also used.

Before the Civil War the term popularly designated the boundary dividing the slave and free states, and it still is used metaphorically to distinguish the North from the South.

Masons, see *Freemasons.*

Mass production, which should not be confused with large-scale production, is chiefly dependent upon standardization of process and continuity of operation. Pioneers in mass production were ELI WHITNEY, who in 1798 introduced the system of interchangeable parts (the most revolutionary invention in the history of MANUFACTURING), and OLIVER EVANS, who in the same period combined several operations in one machine and co-ordinated machines in a continuous process.

During the 1880's F. W. Taylor made important contributions to INDUSTRIAL MANAGEMENT, leading to the true mass production inaugurated by HENRY FORD. Ford's design of multiple assembly lines funneling into a final assembly line, and of specialized operations in which conveyor belts bring work to a stationary assembler, proved a marvel of timing and continuity. Mass production was the theme of Charlie Chaplin's movie *Modern Times* (1936), a commentary on the depersonalizing effect of speed-up and regimentation.

Massachuset Indians were an Algonquian stock inhabiting the New England coast in the early 17th century. When the first colonists arrived in the 1620's they were already declining in importance as a tribe. By mid-century they had been absorbed by the PRAYING INDIANS.

Massachusetts, most populous of the New England states, was named for the Indian tribe inhabiting its coast. It was explored by BARTHOLOMEW GOSNOLD (1602), and charted and described by JOHN SMITH (1614). It was first settled by the PILGRIMS, who landed at Plymouth on Cape Cod in 1620. SALEM (1626) became the nucleus of the earliest Puritan company, and when the patent of the

MASSACHUSETTS BAY COMPANY was confirmed by royal charter (1629), the great Puritan migration from England began. Massachusetts became the center of PURITANISM in America, with BOSTON as capital of the commonwealth since 1632.

Because only church members were eligible to sit in the General Court (still the official name of the state legislature), many prominent freemen moved elsewhere into the wilderness, thus founding other New England settlements. The franchise was limited to male property owners who were church members, but the democratic town meeting became an established feature, and local self-government still continues to be a deeply cherished institution. To provide education the Boston Latin School (1635) and Harvard College (1636) were founded, and in 1647 the legislature demanded the appointment of a teacher of reading and writing in towns with 50 householders. This was the first law in the English-speaking world that required communities to establish and maintain schools.

With the restoration of the monarchy (1660), troubles for the colony multiplied. The extension of its jurisdiction over Maine (1659) was not recognized, and the revocation of its charter in 1684 ended the authority of the 'Bible commonwealth.' (Meanwhile during the 1670's Indian issues were brought to a head in KING PHILIP'S WAR, which almost decimated the male population.) In 1691 a new charter united Massachusetts Bay, Plymouth, and Maine as one royal colony of Massachusetts. It also abolished church membership as a qualification for the franchise, although Congregationalism remained the established religion until 1833. When the long struggle for empire between France and England ended in 1763, the villages along the Massachusetts frontier were no longer subject to Indian attacks.

Meanwhile the colony had expanded its shipping interests, and the increasing British tendency to regulate colonial affairs without local consultation was most unwelcome. Mounting tensions led to the battle of LEXINGTON AND CONCORD (1775); thus began the War of Independence. Economic conditions following the war were especially severe in western Massachusetts and erupted in SHAYS'S REBELLION (1786), which frightened conservatives into strong support of the new Federal Constitution, adopted by the colony in 1788.

The EMBARGO ACT of 1807 was a severe blow to the lucrative China trade, but the Massachusetts economy quickly recovered by nursing its infant industries (textiles in particular), which were shielded by protective tariffs after 1816. The state then entered upon its golden age. Leading men of letters include EMERSON and LOWELL, HAWTHORNE and THOREAU. BULFINCH and AGASSIZ were pre-eminent, respectively, in architecture and science. Among historians PARKMAN, PRESCOTT, and BANCROFT won note. Such crusaders as HORACE MANN (public education), DOROTHEA DIX (hospital reform), W. E. CHANNING (religious liberalism), and W. L. GARRISON (abolition of slavery) aroused national interest in problems of social betterment. The state was the first to respond to Lincoln's call for troops in the Civil War, and vigorously supported the Union throughout the conflict.

During the latter half of the 19th century, Massachusetts became overwhelmingly industrial, as it adjusted to the decline of shipping from New England ports and the growth of rail centers elsewhere. Today its population is predominantly urban. Other than Greater Boston, there are such large cities as Worcester, Springfield, and Fall River. Massachusetts is one of the most thickly settled states in the U.S. Mass immigration of the Irish, who came to work in factories, altered the character of the Puritan commonwealth. Their religion (Roman Catholic) and political allegiance (Democratic) at first set them apart from the Yankee stock, but their contributions multiplied and in 1960 John F. Kennedy, a Roman Catholic of Irish extraction, was elected to the presidency of the U.S.

The state's textile industry, which has been moving to the South since the 1930's, has been replaced by a diversity of light industries, such as electronics. Massachusetts has extraordinary educational resources, and no other state has so many nationally known institutions of higher learning. Among the older foundations are HARVARD (est. 1636), WILLIAMS (est. 1791), AMHERST (est. 1821), and MASSACHUSETTS INSTITUTE OF TECHNOLOGY (est. 1861). The University of Massachusetts (Amherst, est. 1863) in

1965, with a faculty of 650, enrolled 10,500 students.

Massachusetts Bay Company (1628), an outgrowth of the DORCHESTER COMPANY, was formed by a leading group of English Puritans, including Sir RICHARD SALTONSTALL, THOMAS DUDLEY, and JOHN WINTHROP, who wished to migrate to New England. They obtained a charter from King Charles (1629), and in a fleet of seventeen ships some 1000 men and women with their families arrived at Salem (1630), founded Boston, and began other settlements. The group established itself between the Charles and Merrimac rivers, under a governor and legislative body. Only church members had the franchise. The original procedural rules had far-reaching consequences.

The transfer of both charter and company to America in effect gave the new colony a political structure that was incorporated into American institutions. The stockholders (freemen) were voters, and the company officers, eighteen ASSISTANTS, were legislators. Thus the system of TRADING COMPANIES was applied to the political organization of what ultimately became federated states, in fact, the United States.

By 1644 the deputies (executives) and assistants (advisers) had separated into two houses, and since there was no royal governor or parliamentary agent, the independence of the colony from formal government authority advanced radically. The company and the colony were synonymous until 1684, when the crown rescinded the charter and the company ceased to exist.

But the structure of two legislative bodies, with annual elections, took root elsewhere, and in time became an integral feature of Federal and state constitutions in the U.S. Such organizations gave a corporate precedent to the American system of government, distinct from the parliamentary establishment in England.

Massachusetts Body of Liberties (1641) was drawn up by NATHANIEL WARD and adopted by the General Court. Based largely upon English common law, it gave a perspective that prepared assemblies to think in terms later set forth in the BILL OF RIGHTS. In force for seven years, it was supplanted (because it gave too much authority to magistrates) by the MASSACHUSETTS GENERAL LAWES AND LIBERTYES (1648).

Massachusetts Circular Letter (1768) was the document drafted by Samuel Adams, and approved by the Massachusetts assembly, after the full import of the TOWNSHEND ACTS had been discerned. It informed the lower houses of the other twelve colonies that the Massachusetts General Court denounced the Acts as violating the principle of no taxation without representation. Its tone was as moderate as that of the twelve 'Farmer's Letters' that had been recently published by JOHN DICKINSON, but because it was an official action, the British government made an issue of it. Lord HILLSBOROUGH ordered that the respective assemblies be prevented from endorsing the letter, by dissolution if necessary. Massachusetts defied Governor Bernard's order to expunge its resolution of approval, and its assembly was dissolved. Virginia supported Massachusetts by a set of resolves, and its assembly was likewise dissolved. But so effective were the obstructionist tactics of the NONIMPORTATION AGREEMENTS, which were adopted throughout the colonies, that in 1769 the British government repealed all the Townshend duties except the tax on tea.

Massachusetts General Lawes and Libertyes (1648), built upon the earlier MASSACHUSETTS BODY OF LIBERTIES (1641), which it replaced, was the first modern legal code of the Western World, antedating by twenty years the project of Jean Baptiste Colbert in France. The Puritan commonwealth drew upon its past by keeping some elements of English legal procedure, rejecting others, and carrying out reforms that many Englishmen had long desired. For example, the colony parceled out land to individuals under FREEHOLD tenure only, thus avoiding feudal encumbrances, and it secured titles by requiring a public record of all deeds and mortgages, a requirement of many English boroughs but not of the British government.

The *Body of Liberties,* as reflected by the *General Lawes,* led the world in establishing, or extending beyond former limits, the freedom to offer dissenting opinions within judicial bodies, freedom of speech in town meetings, freedom of travel, equal protection of the laws for all, the right to bail, the right to appeal, the rule against double jeopardy, and the privilege against self-incrimination. It stripped the church of temporal authority, and in criminal cases removed much of the retributive element from punishment. This carefully planned legislative action pointed the way to democratic social and political institutions that were gradually incorporated in the legal structures of other colonies and of other nations.

Massachusetts Government Act (1774), the second of Parliament's COERCIVE ACTS, revoked the Massachusetts charter and abolished TOWN MEETINGS. It focused the colonists' attention upon the need for immediate action against Great Britain lest their political principles be sacrificed.

Massachusetts Historical Society (est. 1791), the oldest organization of its kind in the U.S., was founded by JEREMY BELKNAP and other historians and antiquarians who felt moved by a sense of patriotic devotion to preserve the materials that would record the story of their past. It specializes in the history of Massachusetts and early New England, and is the repository of the most important collection of American manuscripts outside the Library of Congress. Its publications include *Collections* (1792–current) and *Proceedings* (1859–current).

Massachusetts Indians, see *Massachuset.*

Massachusetts Institute of Technology (1865), at Cambridge, is a leading scientific and engineering school. It opened the first department of architecture in the U.S. (1866) and has pioneered in many fields of pure and applied science. Its four-year programs include schools of Engineering, Science (and science teaching), Industrial Management, and Humanities and Social Studies. In 1965, with an endowment of $170,000,000 and a faculty of 1377, it enrolled 7150 students.

MASSASOIT (*c.* 1580–1661), chief of the WAMPANOAG INDIANS, was one of the most powerful native rulers of New England. The treaty he signed with the Pilgrims at Plymouth (1621) he faithfully observed until his death. It was later broken by his son, Metacomet (KING PHILIP).

Materialism, in philosophy, is the system of thought that holds the nature of the world to be entirely dependent on matter and motion, beyond which there is no reality. It is thus related to DETERMINISM, but as expounded by GEORGE SANTAYANA it is 'the dominance of matter in every existing being, even when that being is spiritual.' Such materialism postulates that all moral and scientific beliefs are controlled by the dynamics of nature.

Mathematics as a systematic discipline was slighted by the English universities until late in the 17th century, and the example of Oxford and Cambridge adversely affected the cultivation of the mathematical sciences at Harvard. Before 1650 arithmetic and geometry were studies left to masons, surveyors, and mechanics; and although they later became a part of the Harvard curriculum, no algebra appears to have been taught there before 1721. The first college teacher of mathematics was HUGH JONES at William and Mary (1717). In 1727 ISAAC GREENWOOD of Harvard was called to the first endowed chair in the subject, and Greenwood's successor (1738), JOHN WINTHROP, introduced the study of calculus. Thereafter mathematics and physics were an important part of college curriculums.

The first considerable mathematical work to appear in America was the great edition of Laplace's *Mécanique céleste* (1829–39), translated by NATHANIEL BOWDITCH. When Johns Hopkins opened (1876), President Gilman called the English mathematician J. J. SYLVESTER to the chair of mathematics, and Sylvester founded (1878) the *American Journal of Mathematics.* The American pioneer in mathematical logic, C. S. PEIRCE, was a vital contributor to scientific methodology. In recent years pure and applied mathematics has been notably advanced by NORBERT WIENER in the field of cybernetics; by C. E. SHANNON in information theory; and especially by JOHN VON NEUMANN, who contributed greatly to the design of high speed computers.

For the early period, see D. E. Smith and Jekuthiel Ginsburg, *A History of*

Mathematics in America before 1900 (1934).

MATHER, Cotton (1663–1728), son of INCREASE MATHER, after graduation from Harvard (1678) became a colleague of his father as pastor of the North Church in Boston (1685), and successor to his father in 1723. Precocious and immensely learned, Mather was the author of nearly 500 books, tracts, and pamphlets on a great variety of subjects, and the most celebrated New England writer of his day. A leader in civic as well as church affairs, in *Political Fables* (1692) he defended the new Massachusetts charter, which his father had recently brought back from England. His laudatory biography (1697) of Governor Phips touched off investigations of the Salem WITCHCRAFT DELUSION of 1692, during which probe Mather's arrogance and aggressiveness made him unpopular. Frustrated in his ambition to succeed his father as president of Harvard in 1701, and in political disfavor in his own colony, he gave hearty support to the establishment of Yale as a bulwark of orthodoxy.

Mather's greatest work, and one of the monuments of 17th-century scholarship, was his *Magnalia Christi Americana* (1702), a church history of the pioneer development of New England, with vigorous and authentic portraits of its worthies. His most lasting contributions after the *Magnalia* were in the field of natural history, in which his observant and practical mind resembled that of Benjamin Franklin. In his youth Franklin was greatly influenced by Mather's *Essays to do Good* (1710). As a student of phenomena, Mather sent nearly 100 scientific papers to fellow-naturalists abroad, and he won an honorary degree from the University of Aberdeen (1710) and a coveted membership in the Royal Society (1713), to whose *Transactions* a very large number of his reports were communicated. One letter describing variety crossing in Indian corn (to James Petiver, 24 September 1716) is the earliest authenticated account of a plant hybrid, and since it is the first known statement of any kind of botanical hybridization, its importance in the history of botany is immense.

Mather was interested in medicine from his youth (he had once considered taking it up professionally), and early in the 1720's he wrote 'The Angel of Bethesda,' the first significant treatise on medicine in America, a small portion of which was published in 1722. Its important sections appeared in 1954. Mather's insistence that ZABDIEL BOYLSTON administer smallpox inoculations (1721), against the judgment of most Boston physicians and despite the violence of a Boston mob, demonstrated that inoculations were rarely deadly. In the next smallpox epidemic (1729) Boston doctors inoculated their own patients.

Mather's *Christian Philosopher* (1721), which drew upon Newtonian physics for its argument, is a summary of scientific knowledge. It is eclectic in temper, and it opened the way for all latter-day Puritans to reconcile religion and science. Mather was a scholar; he could read seven languages with ease, and by the time of his death he had assembled a library of nearly 4000 volumes in all branches of learning. (Only William Byrd's library in Virginia equaled Mather's in size and variety.) During the 19th century and later, Mather's name symbolized all the less attractive features of Puritanism. He emerges today as a notable scholar and scientist.

MATHER, Increase (1639–1723), son of RICHARD MATHER, after graduation from Harvard (1656) studied at Trinity college, Dublin (M.A. 1658). He returned to Boston, and after 1664 was pastor of the North Church for the rest of his life (later with his son COTTON MATHER as colleague). For a time he served as president of Harvard (1685–1701), but he devoted himself principally to his church and to the political welfare of the colony. A pioneer in American diplomacy, in 1688 he went to England to carry the grievances of Massachusetts in the matter of the abrogated charter, and his efforts were successful to the extent that Governor Andros was replaced by Sir William Phips, and the new charter he secured gave the colonies some of the powers they sought.

His *Discourse Concerning Comets* (1683) is a classic of early American science and places him in the front rank of astronomical investigators in his time. Although he has been charged with instigating the proceedings that resulted in court procedures during the Salem WITCHCRAFT DELUSION, actually his *Cases of Conscience Concerning Evil Spirits* (1693) condemned the court's emphasis on 'spectral evidence.' Never a bigot, Mather supported his convictions with the authority of his position as a leader in the commonwealth. He was author of some 130 books on almost every subject of interest to the colonists of his day, and he typifies the Puritan intellect during the sunset hour of clerical control in America.

MATHER, RICHARD (1596–1669), English-born Puritan clergyman, was the father of INCREASE MATHER. He migrated to New England (1635) after he was suspended from his ministry in Lancashire, and he was pastor of the church in Dorchester from 1636 until his death. He was one of the authors of the BAY PSALM BOOK (1640), and as a leader of Massachusetts Congregationalism he drafted the CAMBRIDGE PLATFORM (1648), a formal statement of church polity. Mather's advocacy of the HALF-WAY COVENANT (1662) as a means of extending church membership is evidence of his practical approach to ecclesiastical affairs.

MATHEW, THEOBALD (1790–1856), Irish Capuchin priest and 'apostle of temperance,' took a pledge of total abstinence in 1838 and during the 1840's came to America, where he gained an enormous following. In a period of large-scale temperance crusades, no exhorter appealed to the multitude more fervently than Father Mathew.

MATHEWSON, CHRISTY [CHRISTOPHER] (1880–1925), even before graduation from Bucknell University (1902) had become a professional baseball player. With the New York Giants (1902–16) he rose to greatness as a pitcher, winning 373 games. In 1905 he led his team to a world series victory by pitching three shutouts.

MATTHEWS, [JAMES] BRANDER (1852–1929), born in New Orleans, graduated from Columbia (1871) and was teaching literature there (1892–1900) when he was made the first professor of dramatic literature in the U.S. (1900–1924). During his 50 years as a critic and essayist he lectured widely and contributed regularly to British and American magazines, interpreting literature (particularly French drama) to the reading public. The paucity of critical commentary on Matthews, 'the last of the gentlemanly school of critics and essayists,' belies the extraordinary influence he had as a journeyman writer on both playwrights and the public taste. His numerous books including his interesting autobiography, *These Many Years* (1917), dealt with the craft of writing and with literary and dramatic criticism.

MAURY, MATTHEW FONTAINE (1806–73), Virginia-born hydrographer, entered the Navy in 1825. He served as superintendent of the Depot of Charts and Instruments (now the U.S. Naval Observatory) from 1842 until the outbreak of the Civil War, during which he became a commander in the Confederate navy and an agent in England, where he secured warships and presented the Confederate cause. He later became professor of meteorology at Virginia Military Institute (1868–73).

Maury was largely self-educated, but his systematic collection of meteorological and navigational data laid the foundation for hydrographic surveys. His excellent guides for trade winds and ocean currents, compiled from a study of ships' logs, led to the discovery of the strong and steady westerlies in the 'roaring forties' south latitude, and cut the sailing time on many ocean routes. The uniform system of recording oceanographic data that he advocated was adopted at the Brussels International Congress (1853) for worldwide use by naval vessels and merchant ships. His *The Physical Geography of the Sea and Its Meteorology* (1855) was the first text of modern oceanography. It was translated and published in numerous editions, most recently in 1963. As a scientist Maury sometimes expounded theories more imaginative than sound, but as a pioneer in his field his accomplishments were impressive, and he was widely honored in his day at home and abroad.

Maverick, an unbranded animal, is so called because the Texas lawyer Samuel Maverick (1803–70) failed to brand his calves, which then strayed or were stolen.

The term is applied to any unbranded animal in the cattle region. Such yearlings may be claimed by whoever first brands them. Since the occupation of 'mavericking' often led to thieving, in the western U.S. the term by extension came to mean anything dishonestly acquired, and as a verb it applies to an illegal appropriation: as, to maverick a saddle. It also in common usage designates a recalcitrant individual who bolts his party, or, as a 'loner,' acts independently.

Maxim Family became famous as inventors and munitions manufacturers. HIRAM STEVENS MAXIM (1840–1916), born in Maine, in 1881 went to England, where he invented the Maxim gun, an automatic firearm that uses the recoil of the gun to serve as the power for reloading. His other ordnance inventions include a smokeless powder and a delayed-action fuse. He became a consulting engineer for Vickers Armstrong, Ltd., and was knighted in 1901.

A brother, HUDSON MAXIM (1853–1927), took up the business of ordnance and explosives in 1888, and was the first to make smokeless powder in the U.S. at Maxim, New Jersey. Some of his inventions were sold to du Pont. His maximite was the first high explosive to pierce heavy armor plate, and his motorite was a self-combustive material used to propel torpedoes.

HIRAM PERCY MAXIM (1869–1936), a son of Hiram Stevens Maxim, graduated from Massachusetts Institute of Technology (1886) and became a mechanical engineer. He invented (1908) a silencer for mechanical explosions, and served as president of the Maxim Silencer Company at Hartford, Connecticut.

MAXIMILIAN (1832–67), Austrian archduke and brother of Emperor Francis Joseph, was persuaded by Napoleon III of France to become puppet emperor of Mexico (1864–67). U.S. protests went unheeded until after the Civil War. In February 1866 Secretary of State Seward issued a strong letter demanding French withdrawal from Mexico. In the spring of 1867 Napoleon (influenced by this as well as by pressures at home) withdrew his forces, and Maximilian, deprived of military aid, was captured by Mexican partisans and shot.

MAXIMILIAN, ALEXANDER PHILIP (1782–1867), German prince of Wied, in 1832 began his two-year natural science expedition into the hinterland of North America. He ascended the Missouri river to Fort Mackenzie, in what is now Montana. He stayed for some time at Fort Union, and wintered at Fort Clarke in the North Dakota region. He was accompanied by the Swiss artist CARL BODMER, whose 81 'elaborately colored plates' form the great attraction of Maximilian's *Travels in the Interior of North America* (2 vols., 1839–41; trans., 1843). In 1962 his diaries, detailed journals, maps, and correspondence were acquired from the archives of the Wied-Neuwied Rhineland palace and deposited in the Joslyn Art Museum of Omaha, Nebraska. The full accomplishment of Maximilian awaits analysis of these documents.

MAYER, LOUIS BURT (1885–1957), Russian-born motion picture producer, helped organize Metro Pictures Corporation. In 1924 the Metro and Mayer Corporations merged with that of SAMUEL GOLDWYN to become Metro-Goldwyn-Mayer, one of the giants of the industry. A talented organizer, Mayer was among those who helped turn the motion picture industry into big business.

Mayflower, 180 tons burden, was the ship that brought the PILGRIMS from England to New England in 1620. After interminable delays she set out from Plymouth (16 September) in the worst season of the year for an Atlantic crossing, and after a rough passage anchored (21 November) in the present Provincetown harbor. Before landing the company drew up the MAYFLOWER COMPACT.

Mayflower Compact, drafted on the day (21 November 1620) that the Pilgrims anchored off Cape Cod, was an agreement among the 41 male adults binding them together in a civil body politic to frame laws and to constitute offices for the general good of the proposed colony. The anonymous journal of the voyage, *Mourt's Relation* (1622), is the only record of this document, which, though it lacked legal status, had the strength of common consent.

MAYHEW, JONATHAN (1720–66), son of Experience Mayhew, the Massachusetts

Indian missionary (1673–1758), was a Boston minister and a leading exponent of ARMINIANISM. His liberalism involved him in theological controversies with Jonathan Edwards, but made him a congenial friend of such political spokesmen as James Otis and John Adams, whose theories of liberty he shared. His sermon on the repeal of the Stamp Act, *The Snare Broken* (1766), was widely influential as a religious sanction for civil disobedience to the point of rebellion.

MAYO, ELTON (1880–1949), Australian-born psychologist, was a professor of industrial research (1926–47) at Harvard Business School. Invited by the Western Electric Company in the mid-1920's to investigate morale and improve productivity at their Hawthorne Works in Chicago, Mayo performed the classic experiment of industrial (and social) psychology. Working with an experimental group, he found that shortened hours, improved working conditions, and added amenities increased productivity. But to double-check his conclusions he persuaded his group to revert to the original conditions, only to discover that production still soared. This stupefying result led Mayo to conclude that, since every change in conditions had been discussed in advance with the members of the group, they came to feel a sense of the dignity and importance of the work, regardless of conditions.

MAYO, WILLIAM JAMES (1861–1939), who specialized in abdominal surgery, and his brother, CHARLES HORACE MAYO (1865–1939), who specialized in goiter and cataract operations, developed the internationally famous Mayo Clinic, opened by their father in 1889 at Rochester, Minnesota. In 1919 they established the Mayo Foundation for Medical Education and Research, as part of the graduate school of the University of Minnesota. The first and largest organization of its kind, it offers training in clinical branches of medicine and laboratory research.

Maysville Road Veto (1830) was President Jackson's response to a bill authorizing Federal expenditures for INTERNAL IMPROVEMENTS, in this instance the construction of a turnpike in Kentucky. This veto was important, as it ended a struggle over the political and constitutional issue of Federal aid to inland transportation, first raised by Madison's BONUS BILL VETO (1817). The West therefore was opened up by private enterprise under state authority.

MEADE, GEORGE GORDON (1815–72), a graduate of the U.S. Military Academy (1835), served in the Mexican War and was given a brigade command of Union troops during the summer of 1861. Having fought at Second Bull Run and at Antietam, he was chosen to succeed Joseph Hooker as commander of the Army of the Potomac (June 1863), which he led to victory at Gettysburg, though his failure to pursue Lee after the battle is said to have prolonged the Civil War. After Grant was given supreme command of Union forces (March 1864), Meade continued to the war's end as a division commander, and from the Wilderness to Appomattox was Grant's right arm. He was a competent, routine, general officer.

Meat packing, one of the largest modern industries, was centered chiefly at Cincinnati in 1840. After the Civil War Chicago dominated the industry. Modern meat packing began with the introduction of refrigeration (1870). Refrigerated railroad cars and warehouses permitted such packers as GUSTAVUS SWIFT and PHILIP ARMOUR to build nation-wide distributing and marketing organizations, and thus to dominate the industry. After the MUCKRAKING movement had revealed the unsanitary conditions prevailing in the Chicago stockyards, Congress passed the Meat Inspection Act (1906). Today distribution centers include Chicago, Kansas City, Omaha, St. Louis, Indianapolis, Fort Worth, and Sioux City.

Mecklenburg Declaration of Independence, so called, is a set of resolutions purported to have been adopted (20 May 1775) by the citizens of Mecklenburg county, North Carolina, declaring themselves free and independent from Great Britain. Although the tale persists, no documentary evidence supports the claim, and it is now generally regarded as spurious. The Mecklenburg Resolves adopted by the citizens (31 May 1775) are strong in their patriot sympathies, but they do not mention independence.

Medal of Honor, for conspicuous valor in action, is the highest award conferred by the U.S. government on its own troops and officers. It was established by Congress (1861) at the outbreak of the Civil War, and it is always bestowed by the President. (Although it is officially designated The Medal of Honor, it is often called The Congressional Medal of Honor.)

Mediation, in international affairs, is a type of intervention in which the disputing states accept the offer of a third state to recommend a solution for their controversy. It differs from ARBITRATION in being a diplomatic rather than judicial procedure. The charter of the United Nations requires all members to submit disputes to mediation on recommendation of the Security Council, but parties are not bound to accept the mediator's decision. The U.S. was mediator between Bolivia and Chile (1882), and between Russia and Japan (1905).

Mediation in domestic affairs is the practice of counseling adversaries in a conflict, and as such it has been used often by the U.S. government in the settlement of labor-management disputes.

Medicine, at the time of the 17th-century migrations to America, was not a subject for study at the English universities. In the colonies for the first 100 years physicians customarily were trained by apprenticeship. Ministers often combined the practice of medicine in 'angelical conjunction' with their pastoral duties. Midwives attended women at childbirth, and a few published and time-tested herbals circulated among neighbors. By 1700 a small number of Edinburgh-trained physicians had settled in the colonies. Such were WILLIAM DOUGLASS of Boston, JOHN MITCHELL of Virginia, CADWALLADER COLDEN of New York, and ALEXANDER GARDEN of Charleston. During the 1721 smallpox epidemic in Boston the effective advocates of inoculation were the minister COTTON MATHER and the physician ZABDIEL BOYLSTON, who had no medical degree.

Treatment of the ill in a general hospital began in Philadelphia (1751), where THOMAS BOND established the Pennsylvania Hospital. The College of Philadelphia (1765), the first medical school, was founded by JOHN MORGAN, and such teachers as WILLIAM SHIPPEN and BENJAMIN RUSH made it the center of medical training in the colonies. SAMUEL BARD organized the medical school of King's College (Columbia) in 1767, JOHN WARREN that of Harvard in 1782, and NATHAN SMITH had established several others by 1813. Warren's son founded Massachusetts General Hospital (1811), where W. T. G. MORTON introduced anesthesia. In the West, a pioneer medical school was organized at Transylvania (1799), and the surgical skill of EPHRAIM MC DOWELL of Kentucky and the clinical observations of DANIEL DRAKE of Ohio were known abroad.

In 1800 BENJAMIN WATERHOUSE of Harvard introduced Jenner's discovery of vaccination. Institutional care of the insane had begun in New York and Boston by 1818, and a college of dental surgery was founded in Baltimore (1840) by C. A. HARRIS. By 1850 MARION SIMS was pioneering in gynecological surgery; WILLIAM BEAUMONT had published his classic study of gastric physiology; JACOB BIGELOW and J. W. DRAPER were contributing to medical advances; DOROTHEA DIX had successfully crusaded for special treatment of the insane; and ELIZABETH BLACKWELL, the first woman in the U.S. to be granted a medical degree, had established the New York Infirmary.

After the Civil War JOHN SHAW BILLINGS organized the notable Surgeon General's Library, S. WEIR MITCHELL made the Philadelphia Orthopaedic Hospital a center for treatment of nervous diseases, HENRY I. BOWDITCH created in Massachusetts the first state board of health (1869), a school of nursing was instituted at Bellevue Hospital in New York (1873), THEOBALD SMITH introduced the first department of bacteriology in the U.S. at George Washington University (1886), GREENE V. BLACK was making notable contributions to DENTISTRY, and WILLIAM H. PARK set up the first municipal laboratory for public health (1894) in New York City.

At the turn of the century no medical faculty matched that which DANIEL COIT GILMAN assembled at Johns Hopkins. Among those who taught there were

WILLIAM OSLER, W. H. WELCH, W. S. HALSTED, H. A. KELLY, F. P. MALL, H. W. CUSHING, J. J. ABEL, and R. G. HARRISON. At the same time American expansionism was reaching tropical lands (and diseases), where the cause of public health was advanced by the work of WALTER REED and W. C. GORGAS. The establishment in 1901 of the Rockefeller Institute for Medical Research, with which SIMON FLEXNER was long associated, added a new dimension to the study of medicine. The famous report (1910) of ABRAHAM FLEXNER gave impetus to a much needed reorganization of medical training. During these years ADOLF MEYER pushed forward work in the field of mental health.

Special American competence has been recognized in the fields of preventive medicine, dentistry, public health, clinical observation, and general practice. In recent years notable contributions have been made by W. B. CANNON (hormones), G. W. CORNER (embryology), P. D. WHITE (heart disease), ALFRED BLALOCK (surgery), and JONAS SALK (vaccine).

Americans who have been awarded the Nobel Prize in physiology and medicine are as follows.

1912 ALEXIS CARREL (Rockefeller Institute). Work on vascular suture and transplantation of blood vessels and organs.

1930 Karl Landsteiner (Rockefeller Institute). Discovery of human blood groups.

1933 Thomas H. Morgan (California Institute of Technology). Studies of heredity.

1934 George H. Whipple (Rochester), George R. Minot (Harvard), and William P. Murphy (Harvard). Researches on diabetes and diseases of the blood.

1943 Edward A. Doisy (St. Louis). Discovery of the chemical nature of vitamin K, by which normal functioning of the liver and of blood clotting is assisted. Shared with the Danish biochemist Henrik Dam.

1944 Joseph Erlanger (Washington University), and Herbert S. Gasser (Rockefeller Institute). Discoveries about the electrophysiology of nerves, making possible the detection and measurement of certain types of brain damage.

1946 Herman J. Muller (Indiana). Discovery of the production of mutations by means of X-ray irradiations.

1947 Carl F. and Gerty T. Cori (Washington University). Research on carbohydrate metabolism and enzymes. Shared with B. A. Houssay of Argentina.

1950 Edward C. Kendall and Philip S. Hench (both Mayo Clinic). Isolation and synthesis of the principal hormone of the adrenal cortex (cortisone), used in the treatment of rheumatoid arthritis.

1952 Selman A. Waksman (Rutgers). Discovery of streptomycin, an antibiotic effective against tuberculosis.

1953 Fritz A. Lipmann (Harvard). Discovery of coenzyme A, a factor in accelerating chemical transformations in plant and animal digestion. (Shared with the English biochemist H. A. Krebs.)

1954 John F. Enders (Harvard), Thomas H. Weller (Harvard), and Frederick C. Robbins (Western Reserve). Application of tissue culture methods to the study of virus diseases.

1956 André F. Cournand and Dickson W. Richards (both Columbia). Research on problems of pulmonary and cardiac physiology.

1958 George W. Beadle, Edward L. Tatum, and Joshua Lederberg (all Stanford at the time). Application of chemistry to the study of genetics.

1959 Severo Ochoa (New York University) and Arthur Kornberg (Stanford). Discoveries that opened the way for the deliberate changing by man of many of his biological processes.

1961 George Von Bekesy (Harvard). Discoveries about the mechanism of the inner ear.

1962 James D. Watson (Harvard). Determination of the structure of deoxyribosenucleic acid (DNA), the substance of heredity. (Shared with two British scientists, F. H. C. Crick and M. H. K. Wilkins.)

1964 Konrad E. Bloch (Harvard). Discoveries concerning the mechanics and regulation of fatty acid metabolism. (Shared with the German biochemist Feodor Lynen.)

Medicine show, a type of entertainment in rural America during the 19th century, was devised to advertise 'sovereign remedies' and cure-alls, hawked from traveling wagons. Such shows featured song-and-dance 'artists,' costumed as Indian medicine men, or as blackface comedians, or as freaks. The ballyhoo methods of the medicine show have survived in modern journalistic and broadcast advertising.

MEDILL, JOSEPH (1823–99), was admitted to the Ohio bar in 1846, but soon gave up the law (1849) to enter journalism. Having merged two papers to form the Cleveland *Leader,* in 1855 he bought an interest in the CHICAGO TRIBUNE, of which he assumed full control after 1874. Medill built his *Tribune* into a major influence in the Midwest. (He was also a founder of the Republican party, which he is said to have planned and named in the office of the *Leader.*) Although Medill attacked unions and carried on a bitter feud with the progressive governor, John Peter Altgeld, he also sponsored effective crusades against political corruption. His daughter Elinor married ROBERT W. PATTERSON; another daughter, Katherine, married ROBERT S. MC CORMICK. Medill thus founded a newspaper dynasty.

Meetinghouses, best known in America as Puritan and Quaker places of religious assembly, in New England towns were the Cities upon a Hill, which became the social centers that served for town meetings and other public gatherings. The early square meetinghouse, with a central tower, was later replaced by an oblong structure with an end-tower topped by a spire. Meetinghouses are usually white frame structures, with simple interiors, the Quaker meetinghouses consisting chiefly of pews, and the Congregational meetinghouses, derived directly from the Puritan, are dominated by a pulpit. The Puritans reserved *church* to designate a covenanted ecclesiastical society, although in larger towns the meetinghouse soon came to be called the 'church.' Today in Quaker communities, and in the smaller New England communities where 17th-century traditions obtain, the name and the architectural form are still used.

MELLON, ANDREW WILLIAM (1855–1937), Pittsburgh banker and capitalist, by helping to finance vast oil, steel, aluminum, and electrical enterprises became one of the wealthiest men in the U.S. He served as Secretary of the Treasury (1921–32) under Harding, Coolidge, and Hoover, identifying himself with a conservative policy of taxation which his critics said favored corporate industry and the amassing of large fortunes. He enforced substantial economies, reduced the postwar debt by one-third, and defended his tax cuts and refunds for high taxpayers as stimulating to the national economy. Mellon epitomized the Republican slogan of 1920, 'More business in government, less government in business.' He gave his great art collection to the U.S., together with funds to establish the National Gallery of Art (1937).

'Melting pot,' a phrase signifying the amalgamation of many ethnic and cultural groups, is suggested in Crèvecœur's essay, 'What Is an American' (1780). It is applied to the U.S. in a drama so titled (1914) by Israel Zangwill. The preferred term recently has become 'cultural blend.'

MELVILLE, HERMAN (1819–91), was born in New York City, a descendant of colonial families. His father's bankruptcy and death in 1831 left the large family virtually destitute, and Melville's schooling ended when he was fifteen. His eighteen-month voyage on the whaler *Acushnet* (1841–42) provided the factual basis for his greatest novel, *Moby-Dick* (1851), which he dedicated to his friend Hawthorne. He described the months that he spent in the South Seas in *Typee* (1846) and *Mardi* (1849), exotic romances, which, with others of the sort, gave him fame. His popularity abruptly waned with the publication of *Pierre* (1852), which was iconoclastic and deeply metaphysical. In 1856 he toured the Holy Land.

Melville continued writing, and his poetry in *Battle-Pieces* (1866) shows his concern for both his country and the nature of man. After 1866 he made a living as an inspector in the Customs Service at New York. His major work thereafter was the long poem *Clarel* (1876), documenting his quest for faith, which ended only in uncertainty. (He had gathered the material for the poem during his trip to Palestine.)

The last twenty years of Melville's life were spent in obscurity, and his death was virtually unnoticed. His memorable short novel, *Billy Budd,* written near the end of his life, was published in 1924, five years after Melville was rediscovered by literary scholars in 1919. He then became the subject of intense study. Today he ranks as a great stylist, a penetrating social critic, and a philosopher of profound tragic vision.

Memorial Day, or Decoration Day (30 May), was inaugurated in 1868 as a holiday on which the graves of Civil War veterans were decorated. It is now observed as a public holiday in the U.S., dedicated to the memory of the dead of all wars.

MENCKEN, H. L. [HENRY LOUIS] (1880–1956), Baltimore journalist, critic, and essayist, was associated with G. J. Nathan as co-editor of the *Smart Set* (1914–23). Together they launched the *American Mercury* (1924), which Mencken edited until 1933. His pungent iconoclasm, aimed at pretentiousness, complacencies, and the fatuousness of contemporary life, though it roused much popular antagonism, performed a useful function and enlivened many magazines besides his own. He collected much of the best of his writing in the celebrated series of *Prejudices* (6 vols., 1919–27). (His 'prejudices' included not only book-bannings, philistinism, and lynchings, but also social planners, feminists, and theories of racial equality.)

His monumental work of scholarship, *The American Language* (1919, 4th ed., 1936, with two later supplements), is a lively discussion of the development of English in the U.S. In later years his inconsistent and negative criticism was seldom enlightening, and after 1930 his influence had largely waned.

MENÉNDEZ de AVILÉS, PEDRO (1519–74), Spanish colonizer, left Cadiz in the summer of 1565 with a fleet of eleven ships and a large number of colonists. He entered the Florida harbor that he named St. Augustine, routed the French Huguenot settlement commanded by JEAN RIBAUT, and established a base (1566) to protect treasure fleets from French and English marauders. One of the ablest admirals of his day, within two years he had erected a string of forts from Tampa Bay to Port Royal, South Carolina, and established Spanish power in Florida.

MENKEN, ADAH ISAACS (1835–68), stage name of Dolores Adios Fuertes, was born near New Orleans, and began her hectic career as a dancer in that city. Her performance in the frantic circus-act adapted (1861) from Byron's *Mazeppa* made her a favorite in Virginia City, Nevada, and in San Francisco. Gaudy and extravagant, she later became a sensation in New York and London. Her husbands were said to be almost as numerous as her marital infidelities. She was the friend of such diverse literary personalities as Whitman, Twain, and Longfellow, Swinburne, Gautier, and Dumas *père,* and she dedicated her volume of poems, *Infelicia* (1868), to Dickens. She died in poverty at thirty-three.

Mennonites, a Protestant sect originating among European ANABAPTISTS, derive their name from the Dutch reformer Menno Simons (1496–1561). Mennonites first emigrated to America from the Palatinate, and their earliest permanent settlement (1683) was at Germantown, Pennsylvania. Mennonites have always been most numerous in the rural areas of Pennsylvania, Ohio, and the Middle West. Congregations are at liberty to establish their forms of worship, but all agree in baptism for believers only, dependence on the Bible as the rule of faith, refusal to bear arms or to take oaths, and avoidance of worldly concerns.

Such religious sanctions have held the Mennonites in tight communities and have regulated their habits of clothing and speech, as well as disciplines that they extend to the fine care of their fields and livestock. Mennonites still remain apart from the main currents of American life. One of the most conservative divisions is the Amish church (followers of Jacob Amman), which separated from the orthodox body in the 17th century. The Amish are principally located near Lancaster, Pennsylvania. In 1965 the Mennonite bodies in the U.S. totaled some 174,000 members.

Mercantilism, the economic doctrine defined as the pursuit of economic power through national self-sufficiency, was accepted by the ruling classes of every Western European state (except the Netherlands) by 1660. The doctrine was implicit in the founding of Virginia. Mercantilism was made explicit in the NAVIGATION ACTS (1650–1767), a succession of legislative measures adopted by Parliament to make the British Empire self-sustaining and to confine profits to English subjects. Such prosperity and power were to be secured by maintaining an adequate stock of metals, protecting home industries against foreign (and colonial) competition, and building sources of raw material in the colonies at low production cost through the use of subsistence labor. Products 'enumerated' in the laws could be exported only to England. As time passed the enumerated list expanded, until by the 1760's only salt fish could be freely marketed.

From the English mercantilist point of view the most valuable colonies in America were those in the South and in the West Indies. They produced raw material by subsistence labor and imported luxuries and manufactured necessities from England. New England and the Middle Colonies came to be provisioners of grain and other commodities to the South and the West Indies. New England with its growing industries, managed, by various circumventions, to become something of a competitor to English industry. In time, opposition to mercantilism came from free traders like Adam Smith, who admitted that the system worked but maintained that its principles were unenlightened. Americans did not object to it so long as its measures were purely regulatory and taxes were not levied upon the colonists. Besides, the mercantilist laws were largely unenforced during the 'period of salutary neglect' before 1763. Opinion is still divided on the degree to which the system benefited or harmed the American colonies.

Mercenaries in the War of Independence, see *Hessians.*

Merchant Marine, see *Shipping.*

Merchant Marine Act, see *Jones Act.*

Merchandising, retail, see *Chain stores, Department stores, Discount houses, Mail-order houses, Supermarkets.*

MERGENTHALER, OTTMAR (1854–99), German-born Baltimore machinist, came to the U.S. in 1872. In 1884 he invented the linotype, a keyboard-operated typesetting machine. This was the most important printing invention since Gutenberg's movable type; it made daily journalism possible by transforming typesetting into a rapid mechanical process. Mergenthaler later devised more than 50 patented improvements. The linotype has been cited as a classic example of a machine that, by increasing demand, creates more jobs, even though, when first used, it results in technological unemployment.

Mergers, as a form of BUSINESS CONSOLIDATION for the purpose of increasing profits or decreasing losses, in the U.S. have been made chiefly in the decades since World War I, though they began late in the 1890's. During the 1920's more than 3700 utility companies were absorbed by mergers, and in that and the following decade mergers spread rapidly in the automobile, aluminum, chemical, motion picture, and communications industries. In November 1951 the Federal Trade Commission declared that 'a great wave of mergers' had reached the highest level in twenty years. The trend has continued.

Merit System, see *Civil Service, Foreign Service, Pendleton Act.*

Merrimac, see *Hampton Roads.*

Merrimack river, 110 miles long, is formed by the confluence of two smaller streams in central New Hampshire. It flows southeast past Concord and Manchester into Massachusetts, then east through Lowell, Lawrence, and Haverhill to the Atlantic. The river was a main artery for early settlements in the interior of New England. Its power has long been used for textile and other mills.

Merryman Case (1861) involved suspension of the writ of HABEAS CORPUS in wartime, and the question then raised was whether under the Constitution (Art. I, sec. 9) Congress or the President has the right to suspend the writ in case of rebellion or invasion. John Merryman, a Baltimore secessionist, was imprisoned in Fort McHenry by presidential authority. Chief Justice Taney, sitting as a circuit judge, ruled that Merryman was illegally detained and issued a writ of habeas corpus. The commanding officer refused to comply, on the ground that he was carrying out an Executive order. Taney cited the commander for contempt and filed an opinion that Congress alone has the power to suspend the writ. Lincoln ignored the judgment, and in a message to Congress (July 1861) justified his action. Taney protested in vain against the presidential decision, to which Lincoln adhered throughout the Civil War.

Actually the Constitution does not specify who has the right of suspension, and the issue has never been officially resolved. Many constitutional lawyers, however, regard Taney's ruling as correct.

Merry Mount, see *Morton, Thomas.*

Mesabi, a range of low hills in northeast Minnesota, is rich in deposits of iron ore. The open-pit mines there first became economically important in 1890, and in 1893 large holdings in the range came under the control of John D. Rockefeller. He sold them to Andrew Carnegie, who also purchased large holdings from Henry W. Oliver of Pittsburgh. For half a century the Mesabi was the primary supply of iron ore for the iron-steel industry.

Mesa Verde is a national park (est. 1906) of 51,000 acres in southwestern Colorado. It is the best preserved prehistoric cliff dwelling area in the U.S. The cliff dwellers, predecessors of the PUEBLOS, flourished there from the 10th to the 13th century.

'Message to Garcia, A' (1899), was an essay written by ELBERT HUBBARD recounting the heroic journey of Lieutenant Andrew S. Rowan, who had been sent by President McKinley to meet the leader of the Cuban insurgents during the Spanish-American War. The essay was an exhortation to fidelity and enterprise, and it became enormously popular among businessmen, who distributed copies of it among their employees as 'inspiration.' Its total circulation is said to have been above 40,000,000.

METACOMET, see *King Philip.*

Meteorology, as a separate discipline of the physical sciences, is of recent origin, since theoretical meteorology is wholly dependent upon a knowledge of thermodynamics in working out mathematical formulas dealing with immensely complex atmospheric forces and motion. The collecting of weather data, however, has a long history. Official attention was given to the subject in the U.S. in the first decade of the 19th century, when President Jefferson commissioned WILLIAM DUNBAR to make weather observations in the Old Southwest, extending to the Mississippi. Systematic records, however limited in scope, were always made by official expeditions, beginning with that of Lewis and Clark (1804–6). The General Land Office (1817) was the first agency to make tri-daily observations. In 1841 the Patent Office instituted a recording system, and the appointment (1842) of J. P. ESPY as meteorologist to the War Department spurred the effort to chart weather forecasts. Before 1850 the Smithsonian Institution was publishing forecasts based on simultaneous telegraphic reports.

During these years the pioneer research of William C. Redfield (1789–1857), James H. Coffin (1806–73), and especially WILLIAM FERREL increased the knowledge of air motion and turbulence. In 1870 Congress created a Federal weather service in the Army Signal Corps, with CLEVELAND ABBE as director; in 1891 the service was transferred to the Department of Agriculture as the U.S. Weather Bureau. Academic chairs in meteorology were not established in the U.S. until the 20th century. The pioneer work in meteorological physics before 1925 of William J. Humphreys (1862–1949) was advanced by such specialists as C. G. A. ROSSBY and J. A. B. BJERKNES, and after World War II research suggested the possibility of artificial weather-making. But long-term weather prediction has remained so unreliable that current researchers are extending their investigations into outer space to discover relationships of weather with forces whose origins are as yet little understood.

Methodists are the adherents of the doctrine, polity, and worship of Protestant denominations organized under the evangelical teaching of John Wesley (1703–91) and his brother Charles (1707–88). (As students at Oxford the Wesleys conducted religious meetings according to a 'rule and method.') Methodist leaders were ordained in the Church of England, but since Methodism sought to awaken a sense of the immediacy of the Holy Spirit by stressing personal religion, most Anglican churches were closed to Methodist preachers. Thus they held services wherever an audience could assemble — in houses, barns, or in open fields. Methodism was introduced in America when the Wesleys visited Georgia in 1735, but its spread throughout the colonies followed the many visits (1738–70) of the Methodist revivalist GEORGE WHITEFIELD.

In 1771 John Wesley sent FRANCIS ASBURY as a missionary to America, where Asbury ordained many of the lay preachers, or CIRCUIT RIDERS, who carried the gospel along the frontier. During the War of Independence Methodism was associated with Toryism. (John Wesley was outspokenly hostile to the American cause.) Methodists were persecuted in Maryland and Virginia by Anglicans and fought the Baptists in Kentucky and Tennessee.

Asbury organized the Methodist Episcopal Church of America at a Baltimore conference in 1784, and designated himself as the Church's first bishop. Unlike the Congregationalists, Presbyterians, and Baptists, who early founded colleges to be assured of a trained ministry, the Methodists were glad to recruit itinerant preachers, who were selected for their zeal. The first college organized by Methodists was Wesleyan (est. 1831), at Middletown, Connecticut.

A schism first divided American Methodists on matters of church government in 1830, and later the main body split on issues raised by slavery. (In 1844 the church broke apart into the northern and southern divisions.) The three main branches of the church were finally reunited in 1939. In 1965 the Methodist bodies in the U.S. totaled 12,900,000 members.

Metropolitan Museum of Art, New York City, opened in 1880 on its present site in Central Park, facing Fifth Avenue. It is the largest and most important art museum in the U.S., and it displays collections of all types of art from all countries and periods. Of particular interest are its representations of Egyptian art, Near Eastern and Far Eastern art, and late 19th and early 20th century European prints and paintings. Its collections of American paintings and decorative arts are displayed in period rooms in the American wing. Its medieval art is located chiefly in the CLOISTERS, at Fort Tryon Park. It has a reference library approaching 150,000 volumes.

Metropolitan Opera Company, since its founding in New York City (1883), has been a shaping influence on operatic taste in the U.S. For more than 80 years, under directors and conductors of first rank, it has attracted notable artists. In recent years it has helped to develop promising American talent, in part through the Metropolitan Auditions of the Air, an annual contest for young singers. On occasion it has produced operas by American composers, but only three have been performed in the last twenty years.

Meuse-Argonne Offensive, the greatest battle in which American troops had ever been engaged, was stretched over a period of 40 days (26 September–11 November 1918). It was designed by Marshal Foch to destroy the German army and bring World War I to an end. The battle involved every available American division (1,200,000 U.S. troops) and inflicted 117,000 casualties. Supported by the French and British, the Americans, under the command of General Pershing, conducted a war of attrition until, in the final phase (after 1 November), they pursued the Germans to Sedan, and by cutting the German communications broke the famous Hindenburg line.

The armistice of 11 November ended the war.

Mexican Border Campaign (1916) occurred when repeated raids by the bandit Villa across the Texas border forced President Wilson's hand. After Venustiano Carranza, leader of the Mexican Constitutional party, took over the government (1914), the U.S. gave him *de facto* recognition. But conditions were so unstable in Mexico that the U.S. State Department advised all American citizens to withdraw from the country, and some 40,000 did so. After Villa killed eighteen American engineers who had been invited to operate some abandoned mines, congressional pressure compelled Wilson to give up his policy of 'watchful waiting,' and General J. J. Pershing headed a punitive expedition that pursued Villa into Mexico. The violation of Mexican soil antagonized Carranza, and Villa made good his escape. The prospect of imminent war with Germany led Wilson to withdraw the expeditionary force (January 1917). A new Mexican constitution was proclaimed in February, Carranza was elected president, the U.S. extended *de jure* recognition to the new government, and the affair was over.

Mexican Cession, see *Guadalupe Hidalgo.*

Mexican War (1846–48) stemmed in part from diplomatic ineptness during the 1830's in the handling of Mexican–U.S. relations, which were finally severed after the annexation of Texas (1845). In part it was brought on by American claims against Mexico, rising from injuries to persons and loss of American property in the Mexican revolutions. Buttressed by the philosophy of 'MANIFEST DESTINY,' the southern planters, strong in Congress and determined to acquire new land for their cotton culture, had precipitated the Texas crisis. President Polk himself was determined to have California and the large New Mexico territory, preferably by peaceful means, but when JOHN SLIDELL failed in his mission to purchase the territory from Mexico, Polk was prepared to go to war. By sending American troops into the disputed area between the Nueces and Rio Grande rivers, Polk brought about a skirmish that enabled him to say that Mexico had 'shed American blood upon the American soil.' On 13 May Congress declared war.

In the Mississippi valley the war was highly popular, and thousands of western volunteers, with vision of gold and glory, were eager to press on to the halls of Montezuma. But in the older states opposition was strong, and knowledgeable Southerners, such as Calhoun, believed that a conquest would increase sectional differences by adding new land over which disputes might arise on the issues of slavery and race.

An army under Zachary Taylor invaded Mexico, and though Taylor captured Monterrey (September 1846), Congress repudiated the resulting armistice and the fighting was renewed. Meanwhile, during the summer a naval squadron under Commander J. S. SLOAT had seized the California ports, and Sloat declared California a part of the U.S. S. W. KEARNEY, having captured Santa Fe and marched on to California, joined uneasy forces with J. C. FRÉMONT. By the end of 1846 the territory was completely in the hands of the Americans.

When Taylor defeated Santa Anna at BUENA VISTA in February 1847, he was clearly in line as the next Whig candidate for President. Polk had adopted General Winfield Scott's plan to end the war by marching on Mexico City from Vera Cruz, a campaign that proved to be a brilliant feat of arms, performed by 10,000 troops led by insubordinate volunteer officers, many of them political appointees. After the battle of CHAPULTEPEC, Mexico City surrendered (17 September 1847), Santa Anna abdicated, and the war was ended by the treaty of GUADALUPE HIDALGO (February 1848), which ceded all territories originally sought. Thus in a small way the U.S. had become an imperialist nation, the control of the South in national politics was reinforced, and the slavery issues were revived in deadly earnest.

The fullest account is Justin H. Smith, *The War with Mexico* (2 vols., 1919). See also R. S. Henry, *The Story of the Mexican War* (1950).

MEYER, ADOLF (1866–1950), Swiss-born professor of psychiatry at Cornell (1904–9) and Johns Hopkins (1910–41), began his association with various hospitals for the insane shortly after he came to the

U.S. in 1892. He was a founder of the mental hygiene movement in the U.S. (1908), and his system of psychobiology established the principle that the patient's problems must be viewed in the light of the patient's total personality. His selected papers are gathered in *Commonsense Psychiatry* (1948).

Miami Indians, of Algonquian stock, having been pushed from the Wisconsin region by other tribes, settled largely in the Miami valleys of southwestern Ohio. By various treaties (1795–1854) they ceded their Ohio-Indiana lands, and ultimately the small remaining group was given a reservation in Oklahoma. Their most famous chief, LITTLE TURTLE, signed the Treaty of GREENVILLE.

MICHELSON, ALBERT ABRAHAM (1852–1931), German-born physicist, after graduation from the U.S. Naval Academy (1873) and post-graduate studies in physics abroad, joined E. W. MORLEY in the famous Michelson-Morley experiment (1887), which measured the wave length of light. Their studies of ether drift proved compatible with Einstein's special theory of relativity. Michelson headed the department of physics at the newly established University of Chicago (1892), where he remained throughout his life, devoting his research chiefly to optics, a branch of physics to which he made lasting contributions. In 1907 he was awarded the Nobel Prize in physics. He was the first American scientist so honored.

Michigan was originally inhabited by Algonquian tribes, and its name presumably derives from Chippewa, 'large water' (*micigama*). It was first reached by the French explorer ÉTIENNE BRULÉ through the narrows of Sault Ste. Marie (1618). MARQUETTE (1668), LA SALLE (1679), and CADILLAC (1683) opened the Mackinac region to the fur trade. Cadillac founded Detroit (1701) as a part of the French policy to control the interior of North America, but the vast, thinly held region was lost to the British at the conclusion of the French and Indian Wars (1763). Although it was surrendered to the U.S. by the British in the TREATY OF PARIS of 1783, and incorporated in the NORTHWEST TERRITORY (1787), Michigan in fact remained under British control until the battle of Lake Erie (1813) restored American power in the Old Northwest. The opening of the Erie Canal (1825) speeded the flow of pioneers into Michigan, which was admitted to the Union as the 26th state in 1837. The capital, first at Detroit (1805), was transferred to Lansing in 1847.

Geographically Michigan is divided into two peninsulas. The Upper Peninsula, between Lake Michigan and Lake Superior, is the 'North Woods' country, a region of low forested mountains, which first attracted fur traders and lumbermen and has proved to be rich in iron ore. The Lower Peninsula, between Lake Michigan and Lake Huron, now supports farms and factories. The day of the lumber baron has long since passed. The enormous growth of the automobile industry has shaped the economy of the state, and DETROIT and neighboring cities have become industrial centers. With some 10,000 lakes, Michigan is a resort state. Isle Royale, a rugged wilderness in Lake Superior, has been a national park since 1940.

Michigan's twenty institutions of higher learning include the UNIVERSITY OF MICHIGAN and Michigan State University (East Lansing, est. 1855).

Michigan, Lake, third largest of the GREAT LAKES, is the only one that lies entirely within the U.S. It is 307 miles long and covers an area of 22,400 square miles. It was discovered by the explorer JEAN NICOLET (1634), and was further investigated by MARQUETTE and JOLLIET. The lake divides the state of Michigan in two, and also borders upon Wisconsin (Milwaukee, Racine), Illinois (Chicago), and Indiana (Gary). The Straits of Mackinac at the northeast end, where Lake Michigan joins the western tip of Lake Huron, is its only natural outlet. The Illinois Waterway gives passage to the Mississippi river.

Michigan, University of, opened as a school in Detroit (1817), and as a college at its present site in Ann Arbor (1841). One of the leading state universities in the U.S., it was the first established in the Middle West and the first to become co-educational (1872). Its William L. Clements Library (1923) has notable collections of Americana. In 1965, with an endowment of $41,000,000 and a faculty of 2968, the University enrolled 29,100 students.

Middle border, see *Prairie region.*

'Middle passage,' see *Slave trade.*

Middle West, the area stretching west from the Ohio river, falls roughly into two divisions: the PRAIRIE REGION (to the east) and PLAINS REGION (to the west). It does not include Colorado, Wyoming, and Montana, which are High Plains or Mountain States.

'Midnight judges,' so called, were the judges appointed in February 1801 by President John Adams, in accordance with the newly passed JUDICIARY ACT, which increased the number of Federal courts. Because Adams, on the very eve of his retirement, filled the new places with Federalists, and conferred the chief justiceship on John Marshall, an antagonist of President-elect Jefferson, the incoming Republicans derided the incumbents as 'midnight judges.' They asserted that the judiciary had become a hospital for decayed politicians, and replaced the Act a year later.

Midway, Battle of (3–6 June 1942), was an engagement in which almost every capital ship of the Japanese navy was deployed in an effort to capture the Midway Islands and thus obtain a staging-point for air raids that would render the Hawaiian naval base at Pearl Harbor unusable by the U.S. Pacific Fleet. Naval intelligence was able to inform Admiral Nimitz, with his numerically inferior force, of Admiral Yamamoto's complicated plan, the success of which depended upon complete surprise.

In a decisive battle, the first major defeat of Japanese naval forces in modern times, U.S. land and carrier planes repulsed the assault, sinking at least four enemy carriers and heavily damaging other warships and planes. The tactical decisions of Admiral RAYMOND A. SPRUANCE were a determining factor in the victory. Thereafter the ambitious plans of the Japanese navy to conquer Port Moresby, Fiji, New Caledonia, and Samoa were canceled, and they turned to defensive tactics, thus permitting the U.S. Pacific Fleet to initiate an aggressive strategy.

Midway Islands, two atolls 1200 miles northwest of Honolulu, form the outermost tip of the Hawaiian group. They were annexed to the U.S. in 1867 as part of Secretary of State Seward's expansionist policy. The Islands were of strategic importance during World War II. Today they supply a naval and air base, and are a stopover point for transpacific flights. They are administered by the Federal Aviation Agency.

MIES VAN DER ROHE, LUDWIG (1886–), German-born architect, after his arrival in the U.S. (1938) helped advance the 'International Style,' represented by the Seagram Building in New York City and the campus for the Illinois Institute of Technology, both of which he designed. He brought to the U.S. the traditions of the Bauhaus School (of which he had been director 1932–33), which combined the teaching of the pure arts with the study of crafts.

Migratory labor in the U.S. is the term chiefly applied to those transient workers hired to harvest crops. It is a phenomenon that has steadily increased since the 1930's and involves millions of workers. It extends to every state in the Union and goes on the year round, since there is always a harvest somewhere. Some workers may be city dwellers who get seasonal jobs and are transported from place to place by a contractor. But most are rootless migrants, so-called 'slaves for rent,' who are subject to exploitation and grinding poverty, and create health problems on a large scale.

During the 1940's the WETBACKS, Mexican farm workers who entered the U.S. illegally by swimming across the Rio Grande, created a strain on Mexican-American relations until labor adjustments were made. Since 1955 *braceros,* or temporary Mexican farm hands, have been legally admitted.

Farm lobbies have continued to press for more cheap labor, but unions protest, and critics charge employers with unfair labor practices generally. By 1964 some legislation had been enacted to help states improve migrant education, give day-care to children of migrants, and provide field sanitation. But no over-all solution to the problem has yet been found.

Milan Decree (1807), designed by Napoleon to strengthen his BERLIN DECREE in an attempt to enforce the CONTINENTAL SYSTEM, authorized French warships and privateers to capture neutral vessels sailing from any British port. The English government retaliated by ORDERS IN COUNCIL.

Military Academy, U.S., founded (1802) at West Point, New York, as a school of engineering, first took rank with similar military institutions abroad during the administration of SYLVANUS THAYER (1817–33). Control of the Academy formally passed to the War Department in 1866, and the present authorized corps of cadets (2500) is maintained by appointment. Eight are chosen from each state at large, four from each congressional district, 172 from the U.S. at large, and 180 from the regular army and the national guard. A few cadets are selected from foreign countries.

Military law, as distinguished from MARTIAL LAW, in the U.S. is the legal system adopted for the administration of law in military establishments. Since World War II it has been carried out by the Unified Code of Military Justice (UCMJ). Courts-martial are statute-fixed tribunals, set up by the first Congress to enforce the constitutional requirement of 'discipline necessary to the efficiency of the army and navy.' In general they cover criminal as well as military offenses.

Militia, now officially termed the National Guard in the U.S., is the body of armed forces within the states, formed by enlistments. State governors are the commanders in chief except in time of war, when militias are incorporated into the regular armed forces of the nation.

The militia idea has been present from the earliest colonial times, when war was an omnipresent danger to settlers impinging upon Indian tribal lands. Colonial assemblies required all able-bodied citizens (except ministers and magistrates) to own rifles, and each town had its company of militia, and held periodic trainings and inspection of arms. The system gained root in frontier America. Wars could be fought without a professional army, without generals, and even without 'soldiers' in the European sense. Indeed, a standing army came to be judged the instrument of tyrants. In the Declaration of Independence, George III was accused of permitting standing troops to be maintained without the consent of colonial legislatures. Thus was created the long-standing myth of a constantly prepared American citizenry, to be disbanded immediately at war's end, however precarious the resulting peace.

The free-and-easy life of a provincial militiaman, who preferred to stay close to home so that he might return to his family in case of need, created serious problems. Colonial assemblies were forced to grant concessions on the issue of where fighting men might be compelled to go. Discipline was haphazard, appallingly so in the judgment of British regulars. Enlistments were short-term — often only a few months — desertions were commonplace, and a commander never really knew how many men were at his disposal. The intense separatism of the colonies and their determination to keep local resources near at hand created the almost insuperable difficulties that afflicted the colonial armies during the War of Independence. Yet since local pride was not to be overcome, Washington made a virtue of necessity, and displayed genius in harnessing that pride in the common cause.

The Federal Constitution gave Congress the power to wage war, but the Second Amendment specifies that 'A well regulated Militia, being necessary to the security of a free State, the right of the people to keep and bear Arms, shall not be infringed.' Thus the spirit of local allegiance was fostered from the moment the nation was founded.

MILLER, ALFRED JACOB (1810–74), Baltimore-born artist, after study with Thomas Sully and further training in Europe, in 1837 accompanied Sir William Drummond Stewart to the Rocky Mountains, where he made sketches intended to be developed into paintings for Stewart's castle in Scotland. These unpublished drawings, which had been stored in the Peale Museum in Baltimore, were uncovered in 1935. They are important delineations of the life of the Indians and the MOUNTAIN MEN in the late 1830's. They were first published as illustrations in Bernard De Voto's *Across the Wide Missouri* (1947).

MILLER, Samuel Freeman (1816–90), Kentucky-born jurist, after graduation from the medical school of Transylvania University (1838), practiced for twelve years before turning to the law. In 1850 he moved to Keokuk, Iowa, and became a state leader in the Republican party. Lincoln elevated him to the U.S. Supreme Court, where for nearly 30 years (1862–90) he was a staunch supporter of the national authority. He wrote the majority opinion in the slaughterhouse cases (1873), arguing that the Fourteenth Amendment was intended primarily to protect the freedmen's rights, not to make the Court 'a perpetual censor upon all legislation of the States.' His concern with the welfare of society rather than the protection of vested property interests, at a time in the Court's history when the judges tended toward economic conservatism, made him a frequent dissenter.

Miller-Tydings Act, see *Fair trade laws.*

Millerites, see *Adventists.*

Milligan, Ex parte (1866), an important ruling of the U.S. Supreme Court on the issue of habeas corpus, was a decision involving the wartime trial and conviction of a civilian by a military commission functioning at Indianapolis by authority of the President. The Court denied the authority of the commission, holding that neither the Constitution nor any usage of war would sanction martial law in districts where the civil courts were open.

MILLIKAN, Robert Andrews (1868–1953), professor of physics at Chicago (1896–1921), and at the California Institute of Technology (1921–53), made basic contributions in the field of physics by proving experimentally Einstein's photoelectric equation and evaluating Planck's Constant. He gave the first accurate determination of the charge of the electron by his famous 'oil-drop' experiment, for which he was awarded the Nobel Prize in physics in 1923. In later years he advanced the frontier of knowledge about the nature and origin of cosmic rays. His writings include *The Electron* (1917), and *Cosmic Rays* (1939).

Milling, as a commercial enterprise, became especially important with the development of the grain export trade in the Middle Colonies prior to the Revolution. After the invention of the grain elevator and the conveyor belt by oliver evans in the 1790's, milling in the U.S. became a major industry, with Baltimore and Rochester as centers. After the Civil War the grain fields of the West, the development of spring wheat, steel rollers, and railroad and Great Lakes transportation created a large wheat industry with milling centers at Minneapolis and St. Paul. In more recent years Canadian wheat and proximity to eastern facilities has given Buffalo a lead in the industry.

'Millions for Defense, but not one cent for tribute,' see *XYZ Affair.*

MILLS, Clark (1810–83), New York–born sculptor, was entirely self-taught. He designed and cast the first bronze equestrian statue in the U.S., the figure of General Jackson, which is the central monument in Lafayette Square, Washington. Mills had never seen his subject or such a statue, but he was able to balance the horse on its hind legs without supporting mechanics. So grateful was Congress for this technical feat that it voted Mills $20,000 in addition to the contract price of $15,000. Mills later cast in his foundry Thomas Crawford's *Armed Freedom* (1860), which crowns the Capitol dome.

MILLS, Robert (1781–1855), South Carolina–born architect and one of the first native-born professionals, was influential in establishing the classic revival. His designs, notable for their proportion and unadorned, simple masses, include the Monumental Church, Richmond (1812); Washington Monument, Baltimore (1814); Treasury Building, Washington (1836); Washington Monument, Washington, D.C. (begun 1836); and Bunker Hill Monument, Boston (1843). In 1836 President Jackson appointed him Architect of Public Buildings in Washington. Mills's hospital designs embodied a humane concern for effective care. His State Hospital for the Insane at Columbia (S.C.) stressed cheerful lighting, an encompassing roof garden, and hospital services instead of the usual features of imprisonment.

Mills Bill (1888), see *Tariff*.

Minimum wage legislation, see *Fair Labor Standards Act* (1938).

Mining in the American colonies began when JOHN WINTHROP, JR. developed iron mines in New England during the 1640's, and despite the IRON ACT (1750), the colonies were ahead of England itself in IRON MANUFACTURE by 1775. COAL MINING, profitable on a small scale in the 18th century, became a major industry after the Civil War. The search for metal from the earliest period had been a motive for adventuring, and the lead and copper deposits uncovered in the Ohio and Mississippi valleys were among the most profitable reasons for frontier expansion westward in the early years of the young Republic. The discovery of gold in California (1848) led to prospecting for the vast ore deposits of the Rocky Mountain area.

Even before the Civil War, mining camps were making history in Colorado, Nevada, Arizona, Idaho, Montana, and Wyoming, and soon thereafter wagons were dotting hillsides with the slogan 'Pike's Peak or Bust' scrawled on their canvas. The Nevada silver of the famous COMSTOCK LODE (1859) made 'bonanza kings.' Panning and placer mining (where the metal is obtained by washing) gave way to quartz mining, in which expensive machinery and engineering are used to extract the ore. This proved to be an enormously lucrative business for those who could afford the initial outlay. Thus the ephemeral 'rush' frontier came to an end, and CALAMITY JANE and WILD BILL HICKOK entered American legend.

But this frontier had been important in the development of the West and of the nation. The miners paved the way for railroads and for the later permanent farming population, and they also roughed out codes of law suited to the West. The development of the great MESABI range during the 1890's was for several decades thereafter of chief importance to the American iron-steel industry.

The 'money question' created before 1900 by the mining of a billion-dollars' worth of SILVER (and an even greater quantity of GOLD) was for twenty years a political issue. COPPER MINING is an important industry; the U.S. furnished one-third of the world's supply. In 1960 the U.S. was producing a grand total of minerals valued at more than $16,500,000,000, nearly half of which derived from petroleum, the mineral that has created the vast OIL INDUSTRY.

See T. A. Rickard, *A History of American Mining* (1932).

Minnesota derives its name from a Siouan term describing the 'cloudy water' of the Minnesota river. It was first penetrated in the 17th century by French traders and missionaries, who established friendly relations with the Ojibwa and Sioux Indians, and made the region a western part of the fur-trading empire in New France. Headwater of three great river systems (the Mississippi to the Gulf of Mexico, Red river to Hudson Bay, and the Great Lakes to the Atlantic), it is an expanse of rolling prairies, boulder-strewn hills, and some 11,000 lakes, whose beds were scoured by ancient glaciers. Its eastern part was included in the NORTHWEST TERRITORY; the area west of the Mississippi was joined to the U.S. by the Louisiana Purchase (1803). Settlements, begun after the War of 1812, markedly increased during the 1840's. In 1849 Congress granted the region territorial status, and in 1858 Minnesota was admitted to the Union as the 32nd state, with St. Paul as its capital.

Opened up as a land of small holdings, tilled by farmers of British, Irish, and German extraction, Minnesota supplied much of the wheat for the Union during the Civil War. In the later decades of the 19th century it attracted Scandinavian immigrants, who helped create a boom in lumbering, and the important CO-OPERATIVE SOCIETIES among farmers. As the railroads were pushed west, the twin cities of Minneapolis and St. Paul developed great flour mills, and today they constitute a metropolitan area in which is concentrated one-half of the state's population. Duluth, at the head of Lake Superior and the largest inland harbor in the U.S., is the outlet for iron ore from such mines as those in the

MESABI range, which have yielded great profits. In 1960 the Minneapolis–St. Paul population totaled 800,000; that of Duluth, 107,000. Chief among its two-score institutions of higher learning is the University of Minnesota (Minneapolis, est. 1869). In 1965, with an endowment of $69,470,000 and a faculty of 2900, it enrolled 53,800 students. With it is affiliated the Mayo Foundation for Medical Education and Research.

Minority Presidents, see *Presidents, Minority.*

Minstrel show, entertainment by whites in Negro makeup, was first popularized by the comedian T. D. RICE in his solo 'Jim Crow' act, about 1828. DAN EMMETT was an early minstrel, but E. P. CHRISTY later crystallized the pattern, with semicircular arrangement of performers in blackface, an interlocutor in the center, and two end-men; he cracked jokes with 'Mr. Tambo' and 'Mr. Bones,' who played the tambourine and the bone castinets, while variety acts, accompanied by banjo, fiddle, and percussion instruments, filled in. Many minstrel organizations toured the U.S. and England, shaping the popular concept during the 19th century of Negro music and humor. With the rise of vaudeville, minstrel shows declined, and they disappeared with the advent of motion pictures and radio entertainment.

Carl Wittke, *Tambo and Bones* (1930), is a history of the American minstrel stage.

Mint, Federal, was established at Philadelphia (1793) for the minting of gold, silver, and copper coins, but not until 1807 did its coinage exceed $1,000,000. Three later branches, at New Orleans and in Georgia and North Carolina, were closed at the outset of the Civil War. By terms of the COINAGE ACT OF 1873 all mint and assay offices were organized in the Treasury Department under a newly created Bureau of the Mint, which now administers the gold bullion depository at FORT KNOX. The branch offices are located in Philadelphia, San Francisco, and Denver; the assay offices are in New York and Seattle.

MINUIT, PETER (1580–1638), was the first director-general of New Netherland (1626–31). It was Minuit who purchased Manhattan Island from the Indians for $24, presumably the most famous bargain in American history. Although he was courageous and shrewd, he lacked diplomacy, and he was recalled to Holland by the West India Company to answer charges of maladministration. To the discomfiture of New Netherland, he headed a group sent out by Sweden in 1638 to establish a colony on the Delaware, and on the present site of Wilmington he erected a fort and a fur trading post. He was lost in a hurricane while on a commercial trip to the West Indies.

Minutemen, colonial militia or armed citizens, were so called because they agreed to be ready for any emergency 'at a minute's notice.' The term is especially associated with the volunteer farmers who defended Lexington and Concord (1775).

MIRANDA, [SEBASTIÁN] FRANCISCO DE (1750–1816), Venezuelan patriot and member of an old Spanish family, was imbued with revolutionary zeal. Stirred by the American cause, in 1783–84 he traveled in the U.S., and his *Diary* (ed. by W. S. Robertson, 1928) is an invaluable picture of the new nation as seen by a cultivated foreign observer.

Mission Indians, so called, were those tribes (chiefly Yuma and Shoshone) christianized by the Spanish Franciscans in southern California (1776–1831). Driven out of the missions by the Mexicans and neglected by the Americans, they were placed on reservations during the 1880's, largely at the instigation of the poet and novelist Helen Hunt Jackson.

Missionaries, persons undertaking to propagate Christian faith, accompanied explorers of North America from its earliest penetration. The FRANCISCANS began their missionary work in Florida in 1528 and established Spanish missions in the Southwest after 1581. The JESUITS made their chief contribution as missionaries by accompanying the French explorers who opened up the Great Lakes region and the Mississippi valley in the 17th century.

The oldest Protestant foreign missionary society in the world, the Society for

Propagation of the Gospel in New England (1649), was founded in London by act of Parliament, largely through the efforts of the 'Apostle to the Indians,' JOHN ELIOT. William III chartered the Society for the Propagation of the Gospel in Foreign Parts (1701) to assist the spread of Anglican churches in the American colonies. Soon thereafter every important Protestant denomination was engaged in missionary labors.

In 1806, in rural Massachusetts, the meeting of a small group of Williams College students led to the formation (1810) of the first national foreign missionary society in the U.S., the American Board of Commissioners for Foreign Missions. Thus the groundwork was laid for missionary labors which were extended particularly to Africa, Asia, and the Pacific islands. Home missionaries focused attention on minority groups. Since 1921 an International Missionary Council has aided national and regional organizations in meeting the needs of mission schools, hospitals, orphanages, and churches.

Missionary Ridge, Battle of (25 November 1864), the final engagement in the CHATTANOOGA CAMPAIGN, was an extraordinarily gallant action of the Civil War. Having driven the Confederates from the rifle-pits at the foot of the Ridge, General Thomas's men refused to obey an order to halt and kept straight up the rocky slope, where they overran the second and third lines of defense. They rushed the Confederate guns from the crest, turned them on the enemy, and with General Sheridan in the lead put General Bragg and the fleeing graycoats to rout down the eastern slope.

Mississippi, named for the river that forms most of its western boundary, was the region of the Choctaw, Chickasaw, and Natchez Indians, explored by DE SOTO in 1540. First settled by IBERVILLE (1699), it was part of Louisiana until 1763, then ceded to England, captured by Spain in 1779, and made part of the U.S. by terms of the PINCKNEY TREATY (1795). Created the MISSISSIPPI TERRITORY in 1798, with Natchez as its capital, it was swept by a land boom, with settlers thronging the delta area, a region of cheap and fertile land between Vicksburg, Mississippi, and Memphis, Tennessee. In 1817 it was admitted to the Union as the 20th state, with Jackson (since 1821) as its capital.

Strongly expansionist during the early 19th century, the state gave eager support to the Mexican War. It was among the first to join the Confederacy in 1861, and was the scene of large-scale fighting during Grant's VICKSBURG CAMPAIGN. It was controlled by CARPETBAGGERS throughout Reconstruction, and was readmitted to the Union in 1870. Its shattered cotton plantation economy was later replaced by sharecropping.

With a subtropical climate and a predominantly rural economy, the state produces much of the nation's cotton. A small minority of planters are wealthy, but the 'rednecks' who live in the hills in the eastern part of the state eke out a living on poor soil. Long beset by a depressed economy, Mississippi in 1960 had an average annual per capita income of $1173, the lowest in the country. Its Negro population (43 per cent) is the highest percentage of any state. It is especially plagued by the issue of DESEGREGATION. The leading institution of higher learning is the University of Mississippi (Oxford, est. 1848). Its campus was the scene (1962) of the most violent opposition to Federal court rulings since the Civil War, after the governor of the state in person sought to block the registration of a Negro student.

The industrial development of the state (petroleum, cotton, lumber, textiles) centers chiefly on Jackson, whose population in the period 1920–60 steadily soared from 20,000 to 144,000.

Mississippi bubble is the term applied to the disastrous failure of the Mississippi Company, a trading monopoly launched in 1718 by the Scots financier John Law. Public confidence in Law inspired wild speculation in the company's shares, and despite drastic governmental decrees, the company failed (1720). A few speculators made piratical fortunes from the entire investment loss of most of the stockholders.

Mississippi river, 2348 miles long, is the principal waterway in the U.S., draining all or parts of 31 states in the heartland of the nation. It rises from lakes in northern Minnesota, is joined by the great Missouri river system above St. Louis, and discharges into the Gulf of Mexico through enormous deltas south of New Orleans. De Soto crossed it near Memphis in 1541, but it was not used as a means of colonization until Marquette and Jolliet descended it (1673). Soon thereafter (1682) La Salle in the name of France claimed the territory through which the river flows. Its name probably derives from Chippewa, 'large river' (*mici zibi*).

A chain of forts extended the French Empire along its reaches in the next few decades, but the possibility that separate nations might be carved from the area ended when the Louisiana Purchase (1803) joined its vast basin to the U.S., and initiated a thrust of American immigration. River ports rapidly became centers of frontier life. Families moved west by flatboats, rafts, keelboats, and (after 1830) by steamboats, which for 30 years were the most lucrative and colorful element of the new West.

In the period of growing sectionalism it witnessed brawls and severe fighting on issues leading to the Civil War. Northern victories on the river, from New Orleans to Vicksburg, cut the Confederacy in two. Steamboat traffic was resumed after the war, but east-west rail transport quickly surpassed river trade. Although descendants of the mythical Negro roustabout John Henry still load and unload cargoes, Mississippi traffic today is best remembered in the vivid pages of Mark Twain's *Life on the Mississippi* (1883). (See *Flood control.*)

Mississippi Territory was created by Congress in 1798 and comprised areas within the present states of Mississippi and Alabama. The limits were extended north to Tennessee in 1804, and to the south in 1813 by the elimination of West Florida. When Mississippi was admitted as a state in 1817, the Territory of Alabama was formed, and two years later (1819) Alabama became a state.

Mississippi Valley Historical Association, organized at Lincoln, Nebraska, in 1907 by a group of seven historians of the Middle West, rapidly expanded to include in its membership students and teachers of American history from all parts of the U.S. It is the most important society of scholars concerned with the whole of American history. Since 1914 it has issued the *Mississippi Valley Historical Review* (founded by C. W. ALVORD), a journal that is national in coverage. In 1964 the society became the Organization of American Historians, and the *Review* was renamed the *Journal of American History.* Several volumes of the society's *Proceedings* have been published.

Missouri, the 24th state in the Union, in the heart of the PRAIRIE REGION, was penetrated by DE SOTO (1541), and explored by French traders and missionaries in the 17th century. It became part of the vast French possession that was transferred to the U.S. in the Louisiana Purchase (1803). Two great rivers have determined the history of Missouri. The Mississippi, flowing south along its entire eastern border, tied the region to the South. The Missouri, which crosses the state from the west, joins the Mississippi at St. Louis; it was the great avenue of pioneer advance westward into the continent. Planters from the South introduced the system of slavery, and the question of admitting Missouri (a territory after 1812) as a state created a national issue, since it involved the right to extend slavery into the territories. The MISSOURI COMPROMISE (1820) seemed to settle the issue. In 1821 Missouri joined the Union as a slave state, with Jefferson City as its capital.

As settlements spread south of the Missouri river into the Ozark mountains, and north into the rich cornland prairies, the slave system proved uneconomical, and by mid-19th century the voice of Missouri, through its compelling statesman THOMAS HART BENTON, was of the West rather than of the South. The slavery problem became acute with the passage of the KANSAS-NEBRASKA ACT (1854), but the activities of such strong Unionists as FRANCIS P. BLAIR kept Missouri officially loyal to the federal government, although guerrilla fighting continued there throughout the Civil War.

Steamboating and the river life gradually dwindled, and are now chiefly remembered in tradition and in the works of Missouri's celebrated son Mark Twain. Railroads tied the state more closely to the North and East, and European immigrants, particularly from Germany, poured in, attracted by the two rapidly expanding industrial cities. KANSAS CITY, on the western border, became a meat packing center. ST. LOUIS, long the chief gateway to the West, soon became a great manufacturing and distributing center. Still important for its diversified agricultural commerce, Missouri also has important mining industries, especially in the production of lead. Its leading institutions of higher learning include St. Louis University (est. 1818), the University of Missouri (Columbia, est. 1839), and Washington University (St. Louis, est. 1853).

Missouri Compromise (1820) was the famous Act of Congress, submitted by Henry Clay, that put the question of slavery extension at rest for almost a generation. It admitted Missouri as a slave state and Maine as a free state (making twelve each), and forbade slavery in the Louisiana Territory north of latitude 36°30′. The solution seemed fair enough to moderates. The South had obtained its immediate object, and the prospects were that Arkansas and Florida would soon be admitted as slave states. The North had secured the greater expanse of unsettled territory and reaffirmed the principle, set forth in the Federal Convention of 1787, that Congress if it chose could prohibit slavery in the Territories.

Politics subsided into delusive tranquillity, but the aged Jefferson presaged the Compromise, which drew a geographic line between slavery and freedom, as 'a fire bell . . . the knell of the Union.' J. Q. Adams likewise believed it to be 'a mere preamble — a title-page to a great, tragic volume.' The issues were brought up again in the COMPROMISE OF 1850, and the explicit repeal of the 1820 Act by passage of the KANSAS-NEBRASKA ACT (1854), which led immediately to the formation of the Republican party and the events that culminated in the Civil War.

Missouri river, longest in the U.S. (approx. 2700 miles), is the principal tributary of the Mississippi, which it joins above St. Louis. It rises in Montana and flows across the Great Plains. It was the chief artery of commerce for the Plains Indians, and its lower reaches became useful to fur traders in the 1760's. Lewis and Clark followed the river to its source in 1804, thus opening the mountain country to overland expeditions into the Pacific Northwest. The MOUNTAIN MEN investigated its headstreams (1820–40), and the American Fur Company brought the first steamboat to the mouth of the Yellowstone (1832). In the next two decades the Missouri with its tributaries, especially the Platte, furnished the overland route to Oregon and northern California, and it gave the Mormons the approach to Utah. It helped pioneers to settle Kansas and Nebraska. Its later use in developing the PLAINS REGION has been especially important for the hydroelectric power created along its falls.

Missouri river basin is the region in which a program was undertaken in 1946 by the U.S. Bureau of Reclamation as a further step in the CONSERVATION MOVEMENT. Eight states are principally involved in the gigantic scheme (Colorado, Wyoming, Montana, North Dakota, South Dakota, Kansas, Nebraska, Missouri), which will effect FLOOD CONTROL, impound water for irrigation, and develop electric power. By 1962, 30 multipurpose dams had been completed and eleven others were under construction.

MITCHELL, JOHN (1680–1768), Virginia physician and naturalist, received his medical training at Edinburgh. He pioneered in applying the Linnaean system of plant classification, and he discovered 25 new genera of plants. His paper on the life cycle and reproductive mechanism of the opossum was one of several published in the *Transactions* of the Royal Society, to which body he was elected in 1748.

Mitchell also won respect as a cartographer. His *Map of the British and French Dominions in North America* (London, 1755) was used by negotiators of the peace in 1783. It was still standard at the end of the 18th century, but its inaccuracies later accounted for the Northwest boundary gap and the Maine boundary controversy. In 1755 such mapping errors were unavoidable.

MITCHELL, JOHN (1870–1919), a coal miner, born in Braidwood, Illinois, joined the UNITED MINE WORKERS when it was formed (1890), and eight years later became its national president (1898–1908). His leadership during the

ANTHRACITE STRIKE (1902) gained a signal victory for labor, substantially increased membership in the union, and brought him national recognition as a union organizer. He became a member of the National Civic Federation (1908–11) and chairman of its Trade Agreement Department, but he was forced to resign by his union. After 1915 he served as commissioner of labor for New York.

MITCHELL, MARIA (1818–89), Massachusetts-born astronomer, was teaching school in Nantucket when she began her studies of sunspots, nebulae, and satellites. For her discovery of a comet in 1847 she was awarded a gold medal by Christian VIII of Denmark and elected (1848) to the American Academy of Arts and Sciences, the first woman so honored. In 1861 she removed from Nantucket to Lynn, where she continued her observations with a large equatorial telescope that had been presented to her by the women of America. After 1865 she was professor of astronomy and director of the observatory at Vassar College.

MITCHELL, SILAS WEIR (1829–1914), Philadelphia physician and pioneer neurologist, gained prominence for his application of psychology to medicine and for his work on injuries of the nerves. During his long association with the Philadelphia Orthopaedic Hospital, the institution became a center for the treatment of mental disorders. As author of many volumes of poetry and prose fiction, he is best remembered for his historical novel, *Hugh Wynne, Free Quaker* (1897).

MITCHELL, WESLEY CLAIR (1874–1948), was professor of political economy at Chicago (1902–12) and Columbia (1914–19). An economic pragmatist, he based his conclusions of economic behavior on statistical findings. In demand as economic adviser to government agencies, he took a lead in founding the National Bureau of Economic Research. His study of *Business Cycles* (1913; 2nd ed., 1927) traced their historical patterns and stimulated ideas on the methods of stabilizing violent fluctuations. He always denied that economic depressions are inevitable.

MITCHELL, WILLIAM LENDRUM (1879–1936), a graduate of George Washington University (1899), pioneered in U.S. Army aviation, and as a brigadier general commanded U.S. air forces in France during World War I. His conviction that military air power as a striking force was of immense strategic importance led to his public criticism of commanders in the war plans division, whom he accused of gross neglect. After his demotion and court-martial in 1926 he resigned from the service. When subsequent events demonstrated that Billy Mitchell had accurately foretold the course of aviation history, he was posthumously elevated to the rank of major general (1942). Mitchell Air Force Base (New York) is named for him.

MITCHILL, SAMUEL LATHAM (1764–1831), born on Long Island, received his medical degree at Edinburgh (1786), and served as professor of medicine at Columbia (1792–1801) before the founding of the College of Physicians and Surgeons, where he thereafter taught (1807–26). Mitchell established himself as a foremost zoologist with his work on the fish of New York (1814). A pioneer researcher on botany and mineralogy, he founded (1797) and edited until 1820 the quarterly *Medical Repository,* the first American scientific journal to have an extended life.

Mobile Bay, Battle of, see *Farragut.*

Modernism (Religious), see *Humanism.*

MODJESKA, HELENA (1844–1909), Polish-born actress, came to the U.S. in 1876. Her dignity and charm in portraying such characters as Ophelia, Lady Macbeth, and Juliet gave her stature as one of the greatest actresses of the century. As Nora she gave the first presentation in the U.S. of Ibsen's *The Doll's House,* at Louisville, Kentucky, in 1883. Her farewell testimonial (1905) was given in New York at the Metropolitan Opera House.

Modoc Indians, kinsmen of the KLAMATH, early in the 19th century lived in southwestern Oregon and northern California. The attempt to bring back a rebellious band (led by chief Captain Jack) to the Klamath reservation brought on the Modoc War (1872–73), during which General E. R. G. Canby was treacherously killed while conducting mediation. Today the Modoc in Oregon number some 300.

Mohave Indians, of Yuman stock, in mid-18th century lived on both sides of the Colorado river in Arizona and California, where Spanish missionaries encountered them. Semisedentary farmers, they were hostile to white traders when Jedediah Smith and Kit Carson encountered them in the 1820's. The tribal remnant occupies a reservation set up in Arizona in 1865.

Mohawk Indians, chief tribe of the IROQUOIS CONFEDERACY, were located principally along the Mohawk river valley in central New York, but their territory extended north to the St. Lawrence and south to the Catskills. They were in touch with the Dutch early in the 17th century and were the first Indians to obtain firearms. The historical HIAWATHA was probably a Mohawk, and JOSEPH BRANT was a distinguished Mohawk chief. They were allies of the English in the French and Indian Wars and during the War of Independence. That allegiance was cemented by Sir WILLIAM JOHNSON, the colonial agent. Remnants of the tribe took refuge in Canada, and surviving groups now live in Ontario.

Mohegan (Mohican) Indians, of Algonquian stock, were the eastern branch of the MAHICAN tribe, with whom they were not politically associated. When white settlers came to southwestern Connecticut, the Mohegan and the Pequot were living under the rule of Sassacus, against whom UNCAS rebelled. Thenceforth the branch under Uncas constituted one of the powerful tribes of southern New England. They later were decimated by disease and warfare, and by 1800 had all but disappeared. A remnant continues to occupy a small reservation in Connecticut.

MOHOLY-NAGY, LASZLO (1895–1946), Hungarian-born designer, was a professor (1923–28) at the Bauhaus School in Germany. In 1939 he opened the Chicago Institute of Design, which he headed until his death. His interest in the new and experimental was tied to a grasp of the fundamental principles of practical art, and his work deeply influenced American commercial and industrial design. His writings include *The New Vision* (English trans., 1928), and *Vision in Motion* (1947).

Molasses Act (1733) put prohibitive duties on molasses imported from non-English Caribbean islands, and had it been enforced it would have destroyed the lucrative New England rum industry. Actually, with the connivance of underpaid customs officers, it developed smuggling into a profitable industry for 30 years, until Parliament, at the end of the Seven Years' War, put teeth into its mercantile legislation. The SUGAR ACT (1764), which repealed the Molasses Act, was enforced.

Molly Maguires, a secret organization of Irish miners in the eastern Pennsylvania coal fields, terrorized the industry for several years (1865–77) by strong-arm methods. Since all law enforcement was controlled by the mine owners, the Molly Maguires, who were relatively few in number and had limited union objectives, resorted to intimidation, arson, and murder to combat oppressive conditions. In 1875 when evidence of their criminal assaults had been gathered by Pinkerton detectives, they were brought to trial, several of them were hanged, and the power of the organization was broken. There is still a question whether they ever were organized as a formal union.

Monitor, see *Hampton Roads.*

Monmouth, Battle of (28 June 1778), was fought in New Jersey. British troops under Sir Henry Clinton, who was evacuating Philadelphia to make New York his seat of action, were attacked by Americans under Major General Charles Lee. Washington, then leaving Valley Forge, had seen an opportunity to pounce on Clinton's rear. In the midst of a confused engagement the incompetent (but more probably treacherous) Lee began a retreat on which Clinton capitalized. Washington arrived at that moment and barely averted disaster by sending Lee off the field and personally regrouping his forces. Clinton meanwhile was able to reach New York.

After a court-martial Lee was suspended from the service for disobedience and wilful neglect of duty.

Monopoly, meaning exclusive trading rights, was the means by which European governments encouraged ventures in the New World, but since the founding of the Republic it has been a relatively rare phenomenon in the U.S. Instead, the oligopoly, or domination of an industry by relatively few firms (the 'big three' or 'big five') has come to be the practice. A few large companies seek to 'administer' prices for a common benefit. Such combinations include POOLS, TRUSTS, HOLDING COMPANIES, and the INTERLOCKING DIRECTORATE. Beginning with the Sherman Antitrust Act of 1890 (and its amendments), ANTITRUST LAWS have sought to regulate big business, but the doctrine of RESTRAINT OF TRADE is so complex that issues affecting it are still unresolved.

Franchise monopolies are regulated by the states. They usually are grants for transport or communication facilities in which competition would be inefficient and costly — telephone companies, for example. Postal service has been a Federal monopoly by common consent from colonial times. Holders of patents are given a monopoly position by law for seventeen years.

MONROE, JAMES (1758–1831), 5th president of the U.S. (1817–25), born in Westmoreland county, Virginia, left William and Mary College (1776) to serve in the patriot ranks during the Revolution. He studied law with Thomas Jefferson (1780–83), and the association was the foundation of his political career, which began with his election to the Virginia legislature (1782–83) and to the Continental Congress (1783–86). He supported Patrick Henry in opposing adoption of the new Constitution on the ground that it encroached on states' rights, and as U.S. Senator (1790–94) he vigorously assailed the Federalists. Washington sent him as minister to France in 1794, but recalled him two years later because he failed to defend JAY'S TREATY.

Monroe's fortunes rose while he was serving as governor of Virginia (1799–1802), for the Republicans came into power. Jefferson sent him as special envoy to France (1803) to assist Robert R. Livingston in negotiating the Louisiana Purchase, and immediately thereafter appointed him minister to England (1803–7), where Monroe had no success in arriving at a commercial treaty satisfactory to Jefferson. As Madison's Secretary of State (1811–17), Monroe handled foreign affairs during the War of 1812, and after the dismissal of John Armstrong, he served for a time as Secretary of War (1814–15).

In 1816, as the legitimate heir of the 'Virginia dynasty,' he easily won the presidential election, and so firmly entrenched had the Republican party become during the ensuing 'era of good feelings' that in the 1820 election Monroe captured all but one electoral vote. Three years later, with the unanimous approval of Congress, he promulgated his momentous MONROE DOCTRINE.

The 'good feelings' in part stemmed from the fact that the MISSOURI COMPROMISE (1820) seemed to have composed the issue of slavery in the western territories, that major boundary disputes with Canada were settled, and that Jackson's campaigns in Florida had led to the signing of the ADAMS-ONÍS TREATY. Also, the welcome experiment of the AMERICAN COLONIZATION SOCIETY (1817) had created the Negro federation of Liberia, the capital of which was named Monrovia. Actually, however, during Monroe's tenure bitter political rivalries were engendering JACKSONIAN DEMOCRACY, as the country was being transformed by revolutionary forces bred by an expanding frontier. But these were the problems of Monroe's successors. At the end of his second term this capable and energetic statesman retired to his estate, Oakhill, near Leesburg, Virginia. He was then, and is now, considered to have been an able administrator.

See W. P. Cresson, *James Monroe* (1946).

Monroe Doctrine (1823) followed the rapid turn of events in the years after the fall (1815) of the Napoleonic Empire. During 1823 European chancelleries buzzed with the rumor that a Franco-Spanish entente would lead to the dispatch of an expeditionary force to South America. In August, Foreign Minister Canning asked Richard Rush, the American minister in London, whether the U.S. would be willing to join England in warning France to stay out of the Western Hemisphere. When the details were communicated to President Monroe, he consulted his old friends Jefferson and Madison, both of whom, in reversal of their former policies and prejudices, advised him to accept an Anglo-American alliance. But Secretary of State J. Q. Adams opposed any further colonization or interference by European states in the Americas. He was counting on the implied support of the British fleet to implement that purpose, and Monroe followed his judgment.

A complicating circumstance was the fact that during the same period Russia was pushing her trading posts from Alaska southward even to San Francisco Bay, and the Tsar had issued a ukase in 1821 forbidding navigation and fishing within certain limits as far south as Oregon. In his annual message to Congress (December 1823) Monroe incorporated Secretary Adams's concept, and reaffirmed Washington's policy of nonintervention by the U.S. in European affairs. The significance of this statement of policy was not immediately appreciated; Polk was the first President to appeal to Monroe's principles by name.

The Doctrine was at first invoked to eject the puppet regime and French troops of MAXIMILIAN in Mexico (1864–67) and to compel Britain to accept arbitration in the VENEZUELA BOUNDARY DISPUTE (1899). But after the Spanish-American War, as the proposed Isthmian Canal became central to U.S. seapower strategy, requiring marine interventions to prevent European occupation of unstable but strategic Caribbean nations, the Doctrine was interpreted by anti-imperialists and Latin Americans as meaning not only the exclusion of European powers from this hemisphere, but U.S. hegemony over it. This seemed explicit in the PLATT AMENDMENT (1901), which permitted U.S. intervention in Cuba to quell disorders, and in the ROOSEVELT COROLLARY to the Doctrine (1904), which made the U.S. the policeman of the hemisphere.

With the defeat of Germany in World War I, Caribbean intervention was curbed and President-elect Hoover announced (and practiced) a noninterventionist 'Good Neighbor' policy, although the phrase was popularized by the New Deal. President F. D. Roosevelt not only abrogated the Platt Amendment, but he also withdrew the marines from Haiti. He 'continentalized' the Monroe Doctrine to mean that its application would depend upon full consultation and joint measures with Latin American states. (See *Act of Havana;* also *Interventionist movements.*)

See Dexter Perkins, *Hands Off: A History of the Monroe Doctrine* (1955).

Montana, in the heart of the Rocky Mountains, on the Canadian border, was known to some degree to 18th-century French-Canadian explorers. It became part of the U.S. through the Louisiana Purchase (1803), and was described in the first report (1806) of the LEWIS AND CLARK EXPEDITION. It was opened soon after by Canadian and American fur traders, but remained for several decades a wilderness of lofty granite peaks, great forests, blue lakes, and (in its eastern half) high plateaus over which roamed herds of buffalo. The discovery of gold there in the 1860's created boisterous shanty towns, even more lawless perhaps than the earlier camps in California. In 1864 the federal government set it off as a Territory, partly to bring order to the region. Cattle brought in from Texas over the BOZEMAN TRAIL made ranching a potential industry. The Sioux wars gradually ended, but not before the Sioux had annihilated CUSTER and his force at Little Bighorn in 1876. With the extermination of the buffalo, great ranches eventually spread across the plains, and such cow towns as Billings and Missoula grew into cities when the railroads, completed in the 1880's, encouraged commerce.

The discovery of silver at Butte (1875) attracted many prospectors, and one, MARCUS DALY, uncovered fabulous copper deposits in the vicinity of Anaconda. Since then the economy of Montana has been bolstered by its mineral wealth, today chiefly petroleum and copper.

Montana was admitted to the Union as the 41st state in 1889, with Helena as its capital. Its agriculture is mainly based on cattle and sheep ranching, and wheat farming. With a mean elevation of 3400 feet, it is a region of great natural beauty, with many game preserves and national forests. Its chief centers of population in 1960 were Great Falls (55,000) and Billings (53,000). The leading institutions of higher learning are the University of Montana (Missoula, est. 1893), and Montana State University (Bozeman, est. 1893), with enrollments, respectively, (in 1965) of 5210 and 4560.

MONTCALM-GOZON, Louis-Joseph de, Marquis de Saint-Véran (1712–59), as a veteran commander in European campaigns, was sent (1756) to defend Canada in the French and Indian War. His capture of Fort Ontario (1756) restored control of Lake Ontario to France, and in the following year he captured Fort William Henry, the key stronghold on Lake George. By concentrating a force at Ticonderoga (1758) he withstood the British assault. But in 1759, defending Quebec against General James Wolfe, he was compelled to fight an open battle above the city on the PLAINS OF ABRAHAM, where he lost not only his life but an empire. The best account of this famous action still remains Francis Parkman's *Montcalm and Wolfe* (1884).

Montevideo Conference (1933) was called as one of the three PAN-AMERICAN CONVENTIONS held during the 1930's to meet the threat of fascist and totalitarian regimes in Europe by cementing hemispheric solidarity. In 1934 the U.S. Senate unanimously ratified the pact that 'no state has the right to intervene in the internal or external affairs of another.'

MONTEZ, Lola (1818–61), stage name of the Irish-born actress Marie Dolores Eliza Rosanna Gilbert, began her adventurous career by marriage to an army officer, a scandalous divorce, and a continental tour as dancer. Though she was a mediocre artist, she was extravagantly beautiful, and in 1847 she became the official mistress of Ludwig I of Bavaria. As the countess of Lansfeld she virtually ruled the country. Banished during the Revolution of 1848, she returned to England, again married, and in 1851 toured the U.S. as ballet dancer and actress in a sketch of her own life, *Lola Montez in Bavaria,* which was especially popular in California mining towns. After a third marriage and an Australian tour (1855–56), she returned to lecture in New York City, where she died in poverty.

MONTGOMERY, Richard (1736–1775), born in Ireland, served in the British army during the French and Indian Wars. He settled near New York City in 1772 and married a daughter of ROBERT R. LIVINGSTON. As a brigadier general in the Continental army, he led the invasion of Canada in 1775, captured Montreal, and was killed in the assault on Quebec. Congress later honored him with a memorial in St. Paul's Church, New York.

Montgomery Convention, assembled at Montgomery, Alabama (4 February 1861), organized the CONFEDERATE STATES OF AMERICA. After 20 July it met at Richmond, Virginia, and when the permanent Confederate government was inaugurated (22 February 1862), the Convention adjourned.

Monticello is the hilltop mansion designed and built by Thomas Jefferson as his home near Charlottesville, Virginia, in 1770. First modeled in the style of Andrea Palladio's Villa Rotonda, it was essentially a practical farmhouse, though it had a porticoed entrance, flanking wings, and a dome. The arrangements gave Jefferson so much pleasure as an architectural idea that he modified his concept to include increased window space and terraced roofs facing the Blue Ridge Mountains. Jefferson landscaped it with great attention to detail. In 1923 the estate became a public monument.

MOODY, Dwight Lyman (1837–99), was a Boston-born evangelist who became America's most internationally famous Protestant religious leader, though he was never ordained. He preached the 'old time religion' simply and forcefully in the missions of Boston and Chicago. As a leader in the Chicago YMCA and the U.S. Christian Commission, he spoke fervently to Civil War soldiers, to whom he distributed gospel tracts. His famous partnership with Ira David Sankey (1840–1908), gospel singer and organist, began after 1870, and in repeated campaigns the two won armies of converts in Great Britain as well as in America. Their collections of gospel hymns were extraordinarily popular.

Moody was self-educated and did not have the backing of any ecclesiastical organization, but he did more to increase participation in religious observances than any other preacher in 19th-century America. His interest in religious training led him to found educational institutions, of which the schools (one for boys and one for girls) at East Northfield, Mass., are best known.

MOODY, William Vaughan (1869–1910), after graduation from Harvard (1893) taught English at Chicago (1895–1907). Even before his early death he became known as a poet and dramatist concerned with the problems of evil and the mystery of man's doom. An intellectual nationalist, Moody was also an idealist, and his anti-imperialist verses, typified by 'An Ode in Time of Hesitation' (1900), were powerful indictments of jingoism and the chauvinistic spirit then rampant in the U.S.

MOONEY, Tom [Thomas J.] (1884–1945), labor leader, was sentenced to death for the bomb killings in the San Francisco Preparedness Day parade of 1916. The report of confused and evidently perjured testimony at the trial enlisted the sympathy of President Wilson, and Mooney's sentence was commuted to life imprisonment. The case continued to arouse international interest, and in 1938 Mooney was unconditionally pardoned by Governor Olson of California.

Moqui Indians, see *Hopi*.

Moravians, adherents of an evangelical Protestant communion, originated (1457) in Moravia among followers of the martyred John Huss. The missionary Moravian movement of the 18th century brought Count Nicolaus Ludwig Zinzendorf (1700–1760) to America (1741–43), where he founded the noted Moravian colony at Bethlehem, Pennsylvania, and other colonies nearby. Moravians emphasize Christian unity and personal service, and have long been distinguished for the quality of their church music. Moravian College (Bethlehem, est. 1742) maintains their tradition of learning. In 1965 Moravian bodies totaled 69,000 members.

MORE, Paul Elmer (1864–1937), a graduate of Washington University (1887), taught Sanscrit at Harvard (1894–95) and Sanscrit and classics at Bryn Mawr (1895–97). As literary editor of the New York *Evening Post* (1903–9), and editor of the *Nation* (1909–14), he built the literary sections of those journals into a position of authority that has probably not since been rivaled in the U.S. His broad classical training is apparent in his collected *Shelburne Essays* (14 vols., 1904–35), and in such critical studies as *Platonism* (1917). More was a leader in the new humanism movement.

MORGAN, Daniel (1736–1802), Revolutionary soldier, as a captain of Virginia riflemen accompanied Benedict Arnold on the unsuccessful invasion of Canada (1775–76). He was a colonel of militia during the saratoga campaign (1777), in which he took a prominent part. In 1780 Congress raised him to the rank of brigadier general, and Nathanael Greene sent him to South Carolina to harass British outposts. There Morgan inflicted disastrous defeat upon Tarleton in the battle of cowpens (1781), a military classic, and a model for Greene at guilford courthouse and eutaw springs. Morgan later served as a Federalist in Congress (1797–99).

MORGAN, Sir Henry (*c.* 1635–88), Welsh buccaneer, having made a reputation for his daring and ruthless raids on Spanish towns and garrisons in the Caribbean, captured Panama in 1671 by defeating a force much larger than his own. Morgan's exploits gave the English substantial booty, and in 1674 this former freelancing pirate was knighted and appointed lieutenant governor of Jamaica.

MORGAN, John (1735–89), Philadelphia physician, after study abroad in leading medical schools, established the first medical school in America (1765) at the College of Philadelphia. In the same year he was elected to fellowship in the Royal Society. His historic *Discourse upon the Institution of Medical Schools in America* (1765) attacked the informality of medical training and urged the adoption of the European method of separate practice of 'physic, surgery and pharmacy.' Congress appointed Morgan chief of the medical department of the Continental army

(1775), but antagonism to his exacting requirements led to curtailment of his authority, and in 1777 he was replaced by WILLIAM SHIPPEN, his colleague and rival.

MORGAN, JOHN PIERPONT (1837–1913), was son of the Massachusetts-born financier Junius Spencer Morgan (1813–90), whose London banking house was one of the notable financial institutions of its day. J. P. Morgan built the family fortunes into a colossal financial and industrial empire, which in 1895 became J. P. Morgan and Company. He had gained control of the Albany and Susquehanna Railroad from Jay Gould in 1869, and thereafter he gave his attention chiefly to railroad development.

Largely because of his conservative and successful railroad reorganizations, Morgan won the confidence of European investors, and thus had first call on surplus European capital for investment in the U.S. In the depression of the 1890's he came into control of the largest group of railroads in the country, including the Atlantic Coast Line, the Lehigh, and the Erie. He then invested in steel. By purchasing (1901) the interests of Andrew Carnegie (the largest private financial transaction in U.S. history) and merging them with other steel companies, he formed the U.S. Steel Corporation, the first billion-dollar corporation in the world.

During this decade his firm came into control of a vast financial structure of insurance companies, mines, banks, and shipping lines. In 1912 Congress set up the PUJO COMMITTEE to investigate the 'money trusts,' and Morgan in particular. It found that his company had 72 directorates in 47 large corporations. Although widely assailed for his financial domination, Morgan was largely deaf to public criticism. He was a man of culture, an art and book collector who could talk as intelligently of French tapestries and first editions as of Wall Street. He dispensed many philanthropies, built up a notable library, and gave much of his art collection to the Metropolitan Museum of Art.

Studies of his career include those by Lewis Corey (1930), H. L. Satterlee (1937), and F. L. Allen (1949).

MORGAN, JOHN PIERPONT (1867–1943), son of the elder J. P. Morgan, after graduation from Harvard (1889) entered the family banking firm, of which he became head after his father's death. By 1933, according to the estimate of the Senate Committee on Banking and Currency, his banking house controlled, directly or indirectly through interlocking directorates and investments, some $74,000,000,000 worth of corporate wealth, nearly one-fourth of the total of such assets in the U.S. He continued his father's philanthropies and gave the MORGAN LIBRARY to the public.

Morgan, Justin, see *Justin Morgan.*

MORGAN, LEWIS HENRY (1818–81), pioneer in American anthropology, after graduation from Union College (1840) practiced law at Rochester, New York, where he studied the customs of the Iroquois tribes. He lived briefly among them, was adopted by a Seneca tribe, and wrote the first (and still the best) study of the natives of America from firsthand acquaintance, *The League of the Iroquois* (1851). His *System of Consanguinity* (1870), a landmark in the history of anthropology, originated the study of kinship systems by showing that the terminology for kinship relationships differs widely among different peoples.

Morgan believed that all peoples pass through the same stages of social development, though not necessarily at the same time, and he set forth his theory in *Ancient History* (1877), the summary of a lifetime of research. Modern anthropologists reject his theory, but his teachings influenced Darwin, and their adoption by Karl Marx and Friedrich Engels became politically significant. Morgan's *Indian Journals* (ed. by L. A. White, 1960) are documents in frontier history.

Morgan Library (The Pierpont Morgan Library), in New York City, was originally the private library of the elder J. P. Morgan. It was augmented by the younger J. P. Morgan and presented to the public in 1924 as an endowed research institution. It is known for its collections of manuscripts, incunabula, and first editions of English and American literature and history.

MORGENTHAU, HENRY (1891–), son of the banker and diplomat Henry

Morgenthau (1856–1946), was appointed (1933) governor of the FARM CREDIT ADMINISTRATION. As President F. D. Roosevelt's Secretary of the Treasury (1934–45), he administered tax programs that raised unprecedented revenues, and supervised the sale of more than two hundred billion dollars' worth of government bonds to finance America's defense and war activities. His plan for reducing Germany to a pastoral economy after World War II was endorsed at the 1944 Quebec Conference, but was later abandoned.

MORISON, SAMUEL ELIOT (1887–), lifelong teacher of history at Harvard (1915–55), specialized in the American colonial period. His *Tercentennial History of Harvard College and University, 1636–1936* (5 vols., 1930–36) concentrates on the early growth of the nation's oldest institution of higher learning. To gather material for his definitive biography of Columbus, *Admiral of the Ocean Sea* (1942), he retraced Columbus's route by sail. He was appointed official historian of naval operations in 1942, and his *History of U.S. Naval Operations in World War II* (15 vols., 1947–62) won him rank as a rear admiral. A prolific author with a notable prose style, he is recently represented by *John Paul Jones* (1959), and *The Oxford History of the American People* (1965), a summation of more than 50 years of authoritative scholarship. He was the first recipient of the Balzan Foundation prize for history (1963).

MORLEY, EDWARD WILLIAMS (1838–1923), professor of natural history and chemistry at Western Reserve (1882–1906), was known especially for the precision instruments he designed for research on ether drift, expansion of gases, and the density of oxygen and hydrogen. With A. A. MICHELSON in 1887 he developed the interferometer to measure the wave length of light. Although Einstein made it clear that the Michelson-Morley experiment did not establish the theory of relativity, there is logical consonance in the two events. The experiment demanded a radical recasting of physical concepts of nature, which Einstein, starting from another source, put forward.

Mormons are members of the Church of Jesus Christ of Latter-Day Saints (unofficially but generally called the Mormon Church), founded (1830) in New York state by JOSEPH SMITH. After the golden tablets containing the *Book of Mormon* had been revealed to Smith (1827) by the angel Moroni, according to Smith, as prophet and seer he gathered his followers and set up a co-operative theocracy. The *Book* is an anthology of personal 'guidance,' religious concepts, and fanciful history, which describes the Indians as the lost tribes of Israel. It prophesies their restoration, the rebuilding of Zion, the reign of Christ upon earth, and an earthly paradise for Mormons.

This close-knit body of poor farmers and artisans was regarded with suspicious dislike by their 'Gentile' neighbors. From Palmyra, New York, they moved first to Kirtland, Ohio, then to Independence, Missouri, and soon again to Nauvoo, Illinois, which by 1842, with converts pouring in, was briefly the largest town in the state. Smith's announcement (1843) that a divine revelation sanctioned polygamy split the Mormon ranks and roused the antagonism of non-Mormons. Smith was lynched by a mob, and under the leadership of BRIGHAM YOUNG the main body trekked across the continent (1846–47) to the remote valley of the Great Salt Lake. (A smaller group, which rejected polygamy, broke away and constituted themselves into the Reorganized Church, since 1904 in Independence, Missouri.)

The extraordinary industry of the Mormons, and Young's genius for organization, within a decade had made the desert bloom and created a self-contained and prospering economy, integrated by a singular faith and directed by able men of action. But the issue of polygamy, luridly discussed in the nation's newspapers, had to be resolved before Utah could achieve statehood. The antagonism was so great that Congress passed antipolygamy laws, aimed solely at Utah. Finally by church manifesto the practice was prohibited (1890), and six years later statehood was granted.

Mormon social and religious government remains predominantly theocratic, and is administered by ingrained custom and a complex church hierarchy. Mormon belief is founded on the Bible and the *Book of Mormon*. Mormons do not consider themselves Protestants, since they had no part in the original Protestant movement. Because Mormonism stresses the interdependence of temporal and spiritual life, the history of Utah has in large part been the history of the Church. Its especially active missionary labors have spread the faith elsewhere in the U.S. and abroad. In 1965 membership in Mormon bodies had reached 2,020,000.

See Nels Anderson, *Desert Saints* (1942); and Ray B. West, *Kingdom of the Saints* (1957).

Morrill Land Grant Act (1862) gave to each state within the Union 30,000 acres of land per congressman, for the purpose of endowing at least one mechanical and agricultural college in each state. The states with insufficient land could obtain title to undeveloped frontier regions. The government thus handed over more than 17,000,000 acres of public domain to the states, which sold the holdings for some $8,000,000. Contrary to popular belief, land grant colleges do not own large tracts of property.

This Act was sponsored through the far-sighted wisdom of Senator Justin S. Morrill (1810–98) of Vermont, and it was the most important piece of educational legislation up to that time. There are now some 70 land grant institutions throughout the nation. The second Morrill Act (1890) helped found colleges in sixteen southern states by authorizing endowments to land-grant institutions.

Morrill Tariff Act (1861) inaugurated the policy of high protectionism, which, with the exception of the UNDERWOOD-SIMMONS TARIFF ACT of 1913, lasted until 1934. Later PROTECTIVE TARIFF amendments steadily raised tariff rates from an average in 1861 of 18.8 per cent to the 41.57 per cent average of the HAWLEY-SMOOT TARIFF ACT of 1930.

MORRIS, GOUVERNEUR (1752–1816), scion of a wealthy, landholding New York family, after graduation from King's College (1768) was admitted to the bar and allied himself with the patriot cause. (Members of this large and influential colonial family were divided in their sympathies, and several remained Loyalists.) In the state provincial congress (1775–77) he helped draft its constitution, and in the Continental Congress (1778–79) he was prominent in financial and diplomatic affairs. When he failed to be re-elected, he moved to Philadelphia, where his series of newspaper articles on fiscal matters led ROBERT MORRIS (no relative) to appoint him Assistant Superintendent of Finance (1781–85). In the Constitutional Convention (1787) he favored a strong centralized government controlled by an aristocracy, for he was frankly cynical about the political wisdom of the people. He went to France (1789) as business agent for Robert Morris, where he remained as minister (1792–94) until the French government requested his recall because of his mischievous royalist intrigues. In the Senate (1800–1803) he remained a staunch Federalist. He is remembered as a brilliant debater and keen observer of human weakness.

MORRIS, ROBERT (1734–1806), English-born 'financier of the American Revolution,' came in his youth to America, where he showed such business acumen that by his early twenties he had become a leading Philadelphia merchant and banker. As a member of the Continental Congress (1775–78), he signed the Declaration of Independence. He also gave financial aid to the patriot cause, while indulging in profitable speculations of his own. Congress appointed him Superintendent of Finance (1781–84), a post to which he brought extensive practical knowledge. In fact, he came to wield the powers of a financial dictator. He organized the BANK OF NORTH AMERICA (1781), borrowed from European countries, persuaded Congress to levy taxes, and personally financed banking obligations that helped make possible the defeat of Cornwallis at Yorktown. He served in the Constitutional Convention, and as a senator from Pennsylvania strongly supported the Federalists (1789–95).

By that time he was reputedly the wealthiest man in America, but his enormous speculations in western lands so complicated his personal affairs that Washington, who greatly admired him, did not offer him a portfolio in the cabinet as secretary of the treasury. In 1797 Morris accepted the fact that his credit was extinguished, and for three years (1798–1801) he served in debtor's prison, where he was occasionally visited by some of his earlier associates, among them Jefferson and Gallatin. After his release he retired into obscurity.

MORSE, JEDIDIAH (1761–1826), Connecticut-born clergyman, immediately after his graduation from Yale (1783) won recognition as the first American 'specialist' in descriptive geography when he published the widely used school text, *Geography Made Easy* (1784). Its successor, *The American Geography* (1789), likewise went through many editions and earned him the sobriquet 'father of American geography.' For 30 years he was pastor of the Congregational church in Charlestown, Massachusetts (1789–1819). A strict Calvinist, he edited the *Panoplist* (1805–10) to combat Unitarianism. His appointment in 1820 to visit Indian tribes stemmed from his interest in missionary work, and resulted in the important *Report to the Secretary of War* (1822). S. F. B. MORSE was his son.

MORSE, SAMUEL FINLEY BREESE (1791–1872), son of JEDIDIAH MORSE, after graduation from Yale (1810), became a pupil of the painter Washington Allston, whom he accompanied to England (1811). Both studied there under Benjamin West. Returning to New York in 1815, Morse became known as one of the best portrait painters of his day. His real interest, however, was in historical themes, for which there was no market. His large, detailed canvas of American democracy in action, *The Old House of Representatives* (1822, Corcoran Gallery), executed in the manner West taught, is an achievement in its handling of light, mass, and perspective. His fellow artists acknowledged his accomplishments by electing him first president of the National Academy of Design (1826–42), but Morse gradually abandoned painting, because he felt the public slighted the profession.

Meanwhile his interest in the study of electricity, first stimulated at Yale, had been quickened by James F. Dana of Columbia, from whom Morse had learned the elementary facts of electromagnetism. The idea of an electric telegraph occurred to him in 1832, and for the next twelve years, with the financial backing of the inventor Alfred Vail (1807–59) and the encouragement of the physicist JOSEPH HENRY, he labored to perfect his instrument. He demonstrated its practicality to Congress (May 1844) by transmitting messages by wire from Baltimore to Washington. The invention brought him world acclaim. He later experimented with submarine cable telegraphy, and with J. W. DRAPER introduced the daguerreotype into the U.S. His *Letters and Journals* (1914) are important source material.

See Carleton Mabee, *The American Leonardo* (1943).

MORTON, 'JELLY ROLL' [FERDINAND JOSEPH LAMENTHE] (1885–1941), began as a ragtime piano player in New Orleans. He is best known as a jazz composer of pieces such as 'King Porter Stomp' (1906) and as the leader of a famous small-band recording group in Chicago, the Red Hot Peppers (1926–30).

MORTON, THOMAS (*fl.* 1622–47), British trader and adventurer, having first come to New England in 1622, returned in 1625 with Captain Wallaston to help found Mount Wallaston (now Quincy), Massachusetts. When Wallaston went to Virginia, Morton took charge of the new venture, renaming it Ma-re-Mount (Merry Mount). Morton was no Puritan, and his uninhibited practices seemed deplorable to neighboring colonizers. When he violated the frontier code by conducting a rum-and-gun-running house to attract the Indian fur trade, they took action. Plymouth was the nearest settlement, so in 1628 Myles Standish assumed the community task of arresting Morton.

Following a comic-opera skirmish, Morton was packed off to England. He returned a year later and again was forced to go back to England, where he was jailed. Then he wrote his diverting *New English Canaan* (1637), telling his side of the story, and satirizing Myles Standish as 'Captain Shrimp.' (The book had to be published in Amsterdam.) In 1643 Morton was again in the colonies. For a time he was jailed locally. He remained a thorn in the flesh of the magistrates in Massachusetts and Rhode Island until in 1645 he went to Ferdinando Gorges's holdings in Maine, where two years later he died.

This picturesque rogue is the subject of Hawthorne's story 'The Maypole of Merry Mount,' of two novels by the historian J. L. Motley, and of a grand opera (*Merry Mount,* 1934) by Howard Hanson.

MORTON, WILLIAM THOMAS GREEN (1819–68), dentist and pioneer in surgical anesthesia, in 1842 set up his dental practice in Boston. At the invitation of Dr. J. C. WARREN he first publicly administered ether anesthesia at Massachusetts General Hospital (1846) during an operation performed by Warren for excision of a neck tumor. The prior use of ether anesthesia by C. W. LONG in 1842 was not made known until after Morton's demonstration, and major credit goes to Morton, who in the presence of physician spectators took full responsibility for the consequences. Morton was greatly aided by the experience gained in the earlier administration of nitrous oxide (laughing gas) for dental surgery performed by his former partner HORACE WELLS.

Mosaic Code, so called, was the earliest compilation of New England legislation (1636). It was prepared by JOHN COTTON at the request of the Massachusetts General Court, and was called by John Winthrop, 'Moses His Judicials.' Massachusetts never adopted this code, which outlines a frame of government in harmony with the Pentateuch, but many of its clauses were embedded in the Fundamentals of the NEW HAVEN COLONY.

MOSBY, JOHN SINGLETON (1833–1916), Confederate colonel, after graduation from the University of Virginia (1852) practiced law in Bristol, Virginia. In the Civil War he served in Stuart's cavalry until January 1863, when he formed 'Mosby's Rangers,' sometimes called 'Mosby's Confederacy.' These PARTISAN BANDS, a handful of undisciplined but audacious and resourceful guerrillas, harried the enemy, appropriated supplies, cut communications, and captured or put to flight detachments often far larger than their own. Their ubiquity kept the Union army in a state of anxious vigilance. So ruthless were their methods that General Grant gave the order, 'When any of Mosby's men are caught, hang them without trial.' After the war Mosby, a warm admirer of Grant, joined the Republican party and held minor government positions. His *War Reminiscences* (1887), based on a series of lectures, deals with his exploits.

Moscow Conference of Foreign Ministers (October 1943), following the QUEBEC CONFERENCE, was the first World War II meeting attended by representatives of the three powers, Great Britain, Russia, and the U.S. It set up a European Advisory Commission, which worked out the basic principles for the treatment of Germany: the destruction of German militarism and military potential, the dissolution of the Nazi party and the punishment of war criminals, the zones of control, and the machinery for payment of reparations.

'Most-favored-nation' clause is the provision in commercial treaties stating that the signatory will enjoy benefits equal to those accorded to any other state. It was the conditional feature inserted in the alliance with France (1778), and as a formula became a standard article of U.S. treaties of commerce whenever it could be secured. It is not commercially advantageous to nations that base their foreign policy on MERCANTILISM.

Mother lode specifically applies to the 110-mile belt in the gold mining region of California from Mariposa to Georgetown, first exploited in 1849. Within a generation it had yielded metal valued at $300 million, and from it gold is still profitably extracted.

Motion pictures (moving pictures, movies, or cinema) developed from experiments made in France (1860) by whirling a series of pictures on a drum. The improvements of celluloid film led Thomas A. Edison in 1893 to create his kinetoscope, an instrument which allowed a single viewer to witness a continuous photographic sequence. In the same year that Thomas Armat demonstrated the prototype of the modern projector (1896), George Melies in Paris created motion pictures as an art form by using professional actors. Advancing Melies's concept of theater, Edwin S. Porter, an Edison employee, established the pattern of movie techniques with *The Great Train Robbery* (1903), the first to be given an edited continuity of shots. When D. W. GRIFFITH produced *The Birth of a Nation* (1915) he brought the technique of motion pictures to full maturity by way of the flash back, long shot, close-up, fade-in, and fade-out.

Meanwhile what had begun as a diversion began to burgeon into a giant industry. Its economic foundations rested mainly on two developments. In 1903 the establishment of a film exchange enabled producers to sell to one big buyer, and thus thousands of movie theaters could operate with a daily change of programs. And the creation of the 'star' system (1907) by the producer Carl Laemmle attracted performers from the legitimate stage, and catered to a public already eager to become fans. Among other factors, not least were the resourceful entrepreneurs such as LOUIS MAYER, who turned entertainment into big business.

Names still remembered among the first generation of featured movie actors include CHARLIE CHAPLIN, DOUGLAS FAIRBANKS, MARY PICKFORD, and WILLIAM S. HART; among producers, CECIL B. DE MILLE and SAMUEL GOLDWYN, who pioneered in engaging the talent of eminent authors. In 1928 the silent screen was permanently taken over by 'talkies.'

By 1930 Hollywood (a suburb of Los Angeles) had become the industrial center of movie production in the U.S., and as a symbol Hollywood set the fashion in dress, speech, and décor for millions of wishful-thinking moviegoers, and in its gaudiest aspects challenged the sovereignty of home, school, and church. In 1934 Hollywood established an internal censorship to control the release of films intended merely to shock audiences by representation of violence or sex.

Memorable productions are the comedies of the Marx Brothers and of W. C. Fields, the musicals of Rogers and Astaire, and the animated cartoons of Walt Disney. Technicolor, introduced about 1932, was used effectively in *Gone With the Wind* (1939), one of the most patronized films ever shown. Competition with television after 1950 forced Hollywood to emphasize unusual subjects, and to develop the wide screen and stereophonic effects. Since the majority of film-theater patrons are those in their teens or early twenties, the 'spectacular' is still counted on to gross large sums. When *Cleopatra* (1963) was released, it had cost $44,000,000, and was the most expensive movie ever made. Even so, motion pictures continue to develop as an art form, observable in the work of such directors as George Stevens (*A Place in the Sun,* 1951), and Stanley Kubrick (*Lolita,* 1962).

MOTLEY, JOHN LOTHROP (1814–77), upon graduation from Harvard (1831) studied and traveled abroad. He returned to Boston in 1834 and began his lifelong historical studies of the history of Holland. The appearance of *The Rise of the Dutch Republic* (3 vols., 1856), was greeted enthusiastically and immediately translated into Dutch, French, German, and Russian. The *History of the United Netherlands* (4 vols., 1860–67) was followed by *The Life and Death of John of Barnevelt* (2 vols., 1874), carrying the story forward to the Thirty Years' War. Meanwhile Motley served as minister to Austria (1861–67) and to Great Britain (1869–70). The books have sweep and unified pattern, and are strict in their detailed accuracy, but their overdramatization and didacticism, combined with imperfect research, have cost them in staying power.

MOTON, ROBERT RUSSA (1867–1940), Negro educator, after graduation from Hampton Institute (1890), taught there until he succeeded BOOKER T. WASHINGTON as president of Tuskegee Institute (1915–35). Moton served as presidential adviser on Negro affairs, and was a member of the National Advisory Commission on Education. His books include *Racial Good Will* (1916), and *What the Negro Thinks* (1929).

MOTT, LUCRETIA [COFFIN] (1793–1880), Quaker feminist, with her husband James Mott (1788–1868) worked constantly in liberal causes, particularly for slavery abolition and woman suffrage. In 1827 she allied herself with the Hicksite (liberal) Quaker group, and her Philadelphia home became a station of the Negro UNDERGROUND RAILROAD. She lectured widely, and with ELIZABETH CADY STANTON organized (1848) the first woman's rights convention in the U.S., at Seneca Falls, New York.

Mound Builders, sedentary farmers living in permanent villages, inhabited the large area between the Appalachians, Wisconsin, and the Gulf of Mexico. They knew how to weave, and their pottery modeling and stone carvings are impressive. The mounds they built were used both as building sites and burial places. They varied in size from one to 100 acres. The remains date from 2000 to 400 years ago, and were conspicuous features of the trans-Appalachian landscape as viewed by early explorers. They seem to indicate a widespread trading culture. The custom of mound building ceased shortly before the arrival of white men, for reasons that are still undetermined. The Mound Builders' culture was once thought to rival that of the Aztecs, but modern archaeology has reduced its importance by demonstrating its complete continuity with the North American Indian cultures that preceded and followed.

MOUNT, WILLIAM SIDNEY (1807–68), Long Island painter, after a year of study at the National Academy of Design (1826) began as a portraitist. He was the first native-born artist to venture outside that profitable field. He soon devoted himself to landscape and flower paintings, and to the genre pictures for which he became known. *Bargaining for a Horse* (N.Y. Historical Society) is representative of his work. The anecdotal scenes of the comfortable rural life he portrays appealed to his contemporaries. Mount takes rank as a painter who handled line, light, and transparency of color with delicacy and sound craftsmanship.

Mount Holyoke College, at South Hadley, Massachusetts, was opened (1837) as Mount Holyoke Female Seminary. Founded by MARY LYON, it became the model for later liberal arts institutions of higher education for women. Its present name and charter were adopted in 1893. It offers graduate work in the arts and in education. In 1965, with an endowment of $13,000,000 and a faculty of 170, it enrolled 1700 students.

Mount McKinley National Park (1917), 1,939,000 acres in south central Alaska, is second in size to Yellowstone National Park. It abounds in wildlife and is a region of spectacular mountain scenery, including Mount McKinley (20,320 ft.), the highest point in North America.

Mount Rainier National Park (1899), 241,000 acres in the Cascade Range in central Washington, is dominated by the snow-crowned volcanic peak of Mount Rainier (14,408 ft.). In it lies the greatest single-peak glacial system in the U.S., with more than twenty ice fields.

Mount Vernon, overlooking the Potomac river near Alexandria, Virginia, was the estate of George Washington. The mansion is a wooden structure of Georgian design, built in 1743 by Washington's half-brother Lawrence, whose widow rented the estate to Washington (1752–61) until he inherited it. Washington is buried on the hillside of the landscaped grounds in a tomb that he designed. The estate became a public monument in 1860.

Mountain men, trappers and pioneers of the Rocky Mountain West, were first lured by the virgin streams that offered prize catches of beaver. Since they came to have unique knowledge of the vast and forbidding terrain in the period when overland transcontinental routes were being sought through the mountains, they were the trail blazers and earliest explorers of the Far West. Trapper life had irresistible appeal to a variety of men: it offered adventure to the restless and daring, an asylum to the lawless, and a chance of profit to the fortunate. This unique breed flourished very briefly — roughly from 1822 to 1845. Some were members of fur companies, such as those organized by the ASHLEY EXPEDITIONS (1822–25), but many were free trappers. Actually few among the thousand or so earned more than a subsistence, and most of them did not survive the rigors and dangers long enough to return to a settled existence.

Wedded to the wilds and usually to an Indian squaw, mountain men became a recognizable type by their dress and 'mountain talk.' The annual August rendezvous at appointed mountain valleys in present Wyoming, Utah, or Idaho, an occasion of prodigal celebration, was the opportunity to exchange furs for supplies, liquor, and other expensive items that were transported from the trading headquarters at St. Louis. (In a few days the trapper's annual earnings usually had been spent.) With the decline of beaverskin prices in the 1840's the trapper-traders became scouts and guides for government exploring and military expeditions, and mountain men ceased to exist. Celebrated among them were JAMES BECKWOURTH, JAMES BRIDGER, KIT CARSON, THOMAS FITZPATRICK, and JEDEDIAH SMITH.

See Stanley Vestal, *Mountain Men* (1937).

Mountains, see *Adirondack Mountains, Appalachian Mountains, Cascade Range, Coast Ranges, Continental Divide, Cumberland Plateau, Great Smoky Mountains, Green Mountains, Olympic Mountains, Ozark Mountains, Rocky Mountains, Sierra Nevada,* and *White Mountains.*

Mourt's Relation (1622) in its full title (so long that it was immediately abbreviated) is *A relation or journall of the beginning and proceedings of the English plantation settled at Plimoth in New England.* One George Morton, a sympathizer of the New England venture (who then was using the name Mourt), saw it through the press in London. His name is thus associated with a volume that derives its importance from memoranda sent to him by William Bradford and Edward Winslow in the returning *Mayflower.* It is the only contemporary account of the famous crossing of the Pilgrims to Plymouth, and narrates the events of the first months of settlement.

Muckraking, the term applied after 1906 to the literature of exposure and protest in the U.S., had been inaugurated as a movement in 1881 by HENRY DEMAREST LLOYD in his *Atlantic Monthly* broadside against trusts, 'The Story of a Great Monopoly,' portraying the methods of the Standard Oil Company. The movement gained momentum during the 1890's, in the period of AGRARIAN REVOLT and of mounting protest against MONOPOLIES, and it aroused public opinion to the point where the generation of 1910 was giving strong local and national support to such important reforms as consumer protection, the direct election of senators, municipal ownership of utilities, and the city-manager system.

The term was first used by President Theodore Roosevelt (1906) in an attack on sweeping charges of corruption in politics. (He was alluding to a character in Bunyan's *Pilgrim's Progress,* who was so intent upon raking muck that he could not look up to see a celestial crown held over him.) But the term soon became almost a title of distinction. Muckrakers set themselves the task of saving political and economic democracy, and they were able to enlist the support of many brilliant critics of American life, not only journalists and novelists, but historians, economists, sociologists, and philosophers. Indeed, part of the credit for the success of the PROGRESSIVE MOVEMENT in the period before World War I belongs to the muckrakers. The public became aware of the issues after 1900, when such popular magazines as *McClure's, Everybody's, Collier's, Cosmopolitan,* and the *Independent* opened their pages to exposé literature. Contributors included such shapers of opinion as LINCOLN STEFFENS (the greatest of the muckrakers), IDA TARBELL, T. W. LAWSON, and R. S. BAKER.

Although much of the literature of protest was ephemeral, some books had a quality that assured them of permanence. HENRY GEORGE and THORSTEIN VEBLEN made lasting contributions to economic thought. Criticism of social conditions and exposure of political corruption were impressively set forth in the writings of JACOB RIIS, JANE ADDAMS, JOHN SPARGO, and Judge BEN LINDSEY. By no means least important were the novelists whose fiction dealing with social problems received wide attention: EDWARD BELLAMY, DAVID GRAHAM PHILLIPS, STEPHEN CRANE, JACK LONDON, FRANK NORRIS, WILLIAM ALLEN WHITE, and UPTON SINCLAIR.

An important account of the movement is given by Steffens in his *Autobiography* (1931). See also Louis Filler, *Crusaders for American Liberalism* (1950).

Mugwumps were those Republicans who, refusing to support Blaine in the presidential campaign of 1884, bolted the party and voted for Cleveland. The word, from Algonquian *mugwomp,* was used in John Eliot's translation of the Bible to render the English term *captain.* It was later applied in U.S. political slang to any independent voter.

MÜHLENBERG, HENRY MELCHIOR (1711–87), German-born Lutheran clergyman, was educated at Göttingen. After arriving in Philadelphia (1742), he became pastor of several Pennsylvania congregations, and as virtual founder of the Lutheran church in America he soon became the leader of all Lutheran groups in the country. He was a man of erudition and charm, and the father of eleven children, several of whom became important men of affairs.

His eldest son, JOHN PETER GABRIEL MUHLENBERG (1746–1807), also a clergyman, raised and led a regiment during the War of Independence, retired with the rank of major general, and later served three times as a Republican in Congress.

His second son, FREDERICK AUGUSTUS CONRAD MUHLENBERG (1750–1801), likewise a Lutheran clergyman, served as a Federalist in Congress, where his deciding vote as the first Speaker of the House insured the ratification of Jay's Treaty (1794).

His third son, GOTTHILF HENRY ERNEST MÜHLENBERG (1753–1815), as a Lutheran pastor became the first president of Franklin College (1787). He was an accomplished botanist, recognized abroad by election to learned societies. His accurate description of flora in and about Lancaster, Pennsylvania, made him a forerunner of such professionals in the field as John Torrey and Asa Gray.

MUIR, JOHN (1838–1914), Scottish-born naturalist and explorer, after studying at the University of Wisconsin made extended journeys throughout the U.S., often on foot. He discovered Muir glacier in Alaska. Through his impassioned writings Muir became a leader in the forest-conservation movement. His books include *The Mountains of California* (1894), *Our National Parks* (1901), *The Yosemite* (1912), and *Travels in Alaska* (1915). On the strength of such works, which have become a part of American literature, Muir takes rank as the best of the nature writers in the tradition of Thoreau.

Muller* v. *Oregon (1908) was a case in which the U.S. Supreme Court upheld an Oregon law that limited the hours of employment for women. It was notable as an apparent change of attitude on the part of the Court (see LOCHNER *v.* NEW YORK, 1905), for it established the principle that the courts might recognize the special circumstances that justify the exercise of POLICE POWER rather than be bound by traditional legal arguments alone. It was also important because the Court admitted as evidence the mass of physiological, sociological, and economic data (the 'Brandeis Brief') introduced by the counsel for Oregon, Louis D. Brandeis.

Mulligan letters, see *Blaine, J. G.*

MUMFORD, LEWIS (1895–   ), was professor of city and regional planning at Pennsylvania (1951–59) when he became research professor. He is one of the authorities in his field, and has written extensively. His critical analyses have appeared in such trenchant studies as *Sticks and Stones* (1924), an interpretation of American life and thought in terms of its architecture; and *The Brown Decades* (1931), a study of arts in the U.S. from 1865 to 1890. In three volumes, *Technics and Civilization* (1934), *The Culture of Cities* (1938), and *The Condition of Man* (1944), he analyzes the physical and social organization of cities in the Western World since the 10th century. Both as writer and lecturer he has urged a reconstruction of the 20th-century 'megalopolis' by regional planning and communal ownership of land.

Municipal government, see *City government.*

Municipal reform in the U.S. had its beginning as a result of the exposure of large-scale waste and corruption in the larger city governments during the years following the Civil War. Effective progress was slow until the 20th century, when charters were simplified, and other measures were legally adopted to eliminate or control the machines of political bosses. Some of the developments to that end include the use of municipal home rule (a greater measure of political autonomy within the terms of a state charter), PROPORTIONAL REPRESENTATION, and the CITY-MANAGER PLAN.

Municipality, a local area of government, in the U.S. takes the form of village, town borough (an incorporated village or town), township (usually a local division of a county), city, and county (in Louisiana called *parish*). In the Federal system of the U.S. the municipality is a non-sovereign entity, its powers deriving wholly from state constitutions or statutes. It may be incorporated, with a state charter providing a degree of autonomy with respect to local functions; or 'unincorporated,' with the state legislature exercising control by means of a local government. Municipal governments operate through a council, a board of trustees or supervisors, or a board of SELECTMEN. Incorporated municipalities usually have a mayor as executive officer, a city court, police, sheriffs, clerks, and legal staffs. Although COUNTIES are the largest subdivisions of a state, the most varied and complex administrative unit is the CITY GOVERNMENT.

Munitions investigation, see *Nye Committee.*

Munn* v. *Illinois (1876), first and most important of the GRANGER CASES, was a case in which the U.S. Supreme Court upheld an Illinois law (1873) that fixed maximum rates for grain storage. Chief Justice Waite declared the law a legitimate expression of the state's police power to regulate a business that affected 'a public interest,' and denied that the law violated the DUE PROCESS clause of the Constitution or that the state regulation of interstate commerce impaired the control of Congress in that area. (In dissent Justice Field asserted that procedural due process was insufficient protection for property rights.) It was one of the most far-reaching decisions in American law: it inaugurated the period of public regulation of private utilities.

MUNSEY, FRANK ANDREW (1854–1925), Maine-born publisher, in 1889 launched *Munsey's Weekly,* which two years later he converted into *Munsey's Magazine* (1891–1929), a popular journal that reached a mass market. Munsey, an entrepreneur, was allegedly interested solely in making money. For a time he owned the most valuable newspaper properties in the country. At one time or another he owned the New York *Press, Sun, Mail, Globe, Herald,* and *Telegram,* as well as papers in Baltimore, Washington, Philadelphia, and Boston. Most of these he merged or killed. Though in his lifetime he never showed the slightest interest in art, at his death he left $20,000,000 to the Metropolitan Museum of Art.

MÜNSTERBERG, HUGO (1863–1916), German-born psychologist, at the instigation of William James came to Harvard as professor of psychology (1892–1916). After 1905 he was director of the psychology laboratory. Before coming to the U.S. he had written his important study in applied psychology, *Beiträge zur experimentellen Psychologie* (4 vols., 1889–92). His idealistic views of philosophy, morality, and aesthetics are set forth in *The Principles of Art Education* (1905), and *The Eternal Values* (1909). In his day he was the most well-known psychologist in the U.S. The eclipse of his reputation has been attributed to his failure to establish a personal bond with his students. As a firm believer in the part motor response plays in conscious action, he anticipated the behaviorists.

'Murchison letter,' on the eve of the presidential election of 1888, dealt the Democrats a severe blow. It was ostensibly written by one 'Charles F. Murchison,' an English-born naturalized American, to the British Ambassador, Lionel Sackville-West, seeking his counsel on how to vote in the approaching election. Actually it was written by a California Republican, George A. Osgoodby. The Ambassador's reply intimated that 'Murchison' should vote for Cleveland. Republicans published the correspondence, and public indignation at 'foreign intervention' in internal affairs cost the Democrats many Irish-American votes and ended Sackville-West's usefulness as a diplomat.

'Murder Act,' see *Administration of Justice Act.*

Murfreesboro, Battle of (31 December 1862–3 January 1863), was an engagement in which General Rosecrans forced General Bragg to relinquish his control of central Tennessee and retreat toward Chattanooga. Though it was a Union success, it was immensely costly; each side sustained more than 9000 casualties.

MURRAY, LINDLEY (1745–1826), Pennsylvania-born Quaker grammarian, called 'Father of English grammar,' retired from his New York law practice in 1784 to settle near York, England, where he devoted himself to the study of grammar. For the Quaker school at York he compiled his *English Grammar* (1795; rev. ed., 1818), which for two generations remained the standard textbook throughout the English-speaking world. By 1850 some 200 editions had appeared. Two million copies may have been sold. He also wrote an *English Reader,* a *French Reader,* and other popular schoolbooks intended to promote correctness and elegance. In his later years this Anglo-American purist was visited by numbers of grateful well-wishers.

MURRAY, PHILIP (1886–1952), Scottish-born labor leader, in 1920 became vice president of the United Mine Workers of America. Soon after the Congress of Industrial Organizations was formed (1938), he succeeded John L. Lewis as president (1940), and two years later Murray became the militant president of the newly formed United Steelworkers of America (1942–52).

MURRELL, JOHN A. (*fl.* 1804–44), bandit and folk hero of the Old Southwest, led a gang reputedly numbering a thousand members. He specialized in stealing Negro slaves from one owner and selling them to another. If they came to be recognized, he 'disposed' of them. He was captured (1834), and imprisoned for ten years, through information gathered by Virgil A. Steward, a member of his band, who wrote the story of his life. He figures in romances by W. G. Simms.

MURRIETA, JOAQUIN (*c.* 1830–53), California bandit, having been driven from his gold mine claims, became the leader of a band of desperadoes, and for two years terrorized the state by his robberies and murders. After the legislature authorized a company of mounted rangers to wipe out the gang, Murrieta was shot and most of his followers were killed or captured. Though he was simply a border ruffian, his legend later was built into the image of a Robin Hood.

Muscle Shoals, see *Tennessee Valley Authority.*

Museum of Modern Art, in New York City, was founded (1929) by Mrs. John D. Rockefeller, Jr., as an outgrowth of her interest in such painting and sculpture as had been exhibited at the ARMORY SHOW in 1913. In 1939 the Museum moved into its own building, designed to express the simple functionalism that the institution consistently championed. With the primary purpose of displaying the visual arts of the present, it has also gathered extensive collections in all areas, including American folk art, industrial and graphic design, architecture, photography, and a noted library of motion picture films. It helped inaugurate a method of exhibition that displays full critical and explanatory information. It publishes documented books and catalogues.

Museums in the U.S. began in the 18th century as private 'cabinets' or collections of botanical and geological specimens. The first public museum was established (1773) by the Charles Town Library Society at Charleston, South Carolina. The present Peabody Museum at Salem, Massachusetts, began (1799) as an exhibit of the East India Marine Society. In 1802 Peale's Museum, the first natural history display, was opened briefly at Philadelphia by the painter C. W. PEALE. It attracted national attention. Its painted backgrounds and arrangements of nests and mounted birds foreshadowed the modern habitat groups. Scudder's American Museum in New York exhibited natural curiosities for profit, and after P. T. Barnum purchased it in 1841 he made it so popular that myriads of dime museums flourished throughout the country for several decades.

The oldest society in its field in the U.S. to display collections is the Academy of Natural Science (1812) in Philadelphia. The internationally famous SMITHSONIAN INSTITUTION (1846) from the first has steadily augmented its accumulations gathered on various government exploring expeditions. In 1866 GEORGE PEABODY founded the museum of American archaeology and ethnology at Harvard and the museum of physical sciences at Yale. The AMERICAN MUSEUM OF

NATURAL HISTORY (1869) in New York City has a scope unmatched in the U.S. That of the Chicago Museum of Natural History, endowed in 1893 by MARSHALL FIELD, is rapidly expanding. During the 19th century states, municipalities, and colleges had begun building their own collections and offering public lectures; special types, such as aquariums and arboretums, came into being. Early in the 20th century museums had begun to display almost every aspect of social, commercial, and industrial development. Indeed, WORLD'S FAIRS have always functioned as 'museums' of contemporary developments.

Museums of art, which developed more slowly than those of science, began with the Pennsylvania Academy of Fine Arts (1805) and the Boston Athenaeum (1807). The Corcoran Gallery of Art began as a private collection, and was presented to the City of Washington (1869) and opened to the public in 1874. The opening of the great METROPOLITAN MUSEUM OF ART (1880) in New York was soon followed by the building up of art collections in almost every major city. The NATIONAL GALLERY OF ART, Washington, D.C., since its opening in 1941, has attracted great collections, and has become a center in its field. State and local HISTORICAL SOCIETIES exhibit collections to recall the past. Numerous historic buildings, residences, and churches have been endowed or publicly maintained as museums. Such are INDEPENDENCE HALL, MOUNT VERNON, and the OLD SOUTH CHURCH in Boston.

Music in America as an art form developed slowly and only after communities were large enough to supply patronage. German musical traditions took root when JOHANN CONRAD BEISSEL in 1730 founded Ephrata Cloister at Lancaster, Pennsylvania, the earliest center for musical education and publication. Before 1750 the most important musical events were taking place at Bethlehem, Pennsylvania, the center of Moravian immigration. There singing groups were organized, with a Collegium Musicum (1744–1820), which performed chamber music and symphonies by Haydn, Mozart, and other noted contemporaries. A group at Charleston founded the St. Cecilia Society (1761–1912, later revived), the first musical society in America. The music school that opened at Philadelphia in 1763 was attended by FRANCIS HOPKINSON, who became leader of the musical life of that city. Conditions by then enabled musicians like WILLIAM BILLINGS in Boston to make a profession of music as an art. By 1770 all large communities were attempting some form of musical expression.

French operas were regularly performed in New Orleans after 1801. At Boston GOTTLIEB GRAUPNER organized the Philharmonic Society (1810–24) of instrumentalists, and a choral group, The Handel and Haydn Society (1815), which is still flourishing. Musical Fund Societies were established in Philadelphia in 1820 and in New York soon after. Garcia's Opera Company was formed in New York in 1825 especially to promote Italian music, under the guidance of Mozart's famous librettist, LORENZO DA PONTE.

The MINSTREL SHOW took hold as a tradition after 1830. By 1850 STEPHEN FOSTER was creating popular songs deeply rooted in a folk heritage. The Negro rhythms and melodies, a unique characteristic of American music, were gradually absorbed into the English, Irish, Scottish, and Spanish traditions.

By the second quarter of the 19th century publishing houses were specializing solely in musical items. Best known were the firms of Carl Fischer (1827) in New York and Oliver Ditson (1835) in Boston. LOWELL MASON initiated music teaching (1838) in public schools in Boston, thus creating an interest which spread and made possible the orchestra tours 30 years later of THEODORE THOMAS. Oberlin College in Ohio established the first conservatory of music (1865). Music as a discipline began to attract Americans to Europe for training, and those who returned to teach include JOHN K. PAINE and HORATIO PARKER.

The oldest among the scores of symphony orchestras throughout the country are the New York Philharmonic–Symphony Orchestra, founded as the Philharmonic in 1842, and merged in 1928 with the New York Symphony Orchestra, which had been founded in 1878, the Boston (1881), Chicago (1886), Pittsburgh (1893), Cincinnati (1895), and Philadelphia (1900). Under LEOPOLD DAMROSCH and ANTON SEIDL the Metropolitan Opera Company (1883) introduced Wagnerian opera, and within the decade American artists were making successful appearances in European concert halls. The pioneer in American musical criticism, JOHN S. DWIGHT, established the *Journal of Music* (1852), the first such periodical in the U.S.

After World War I many of Europe's most eminent teachers came to America, and foreign training became unnecessary. The establishment of scholarships in endowed foundations multiplied, assuring opportunity in such schools as Eastman (1918), Juilliard (1926), and the Berkshire Music Center (1940). Yet until schools came into being, very few American-born artists of first rank appeared. The first American operatic singer to win international acclaim was LILLIAN NORDICA. Until mid-20th century all leading conductors were European, including TOSCANINI, STOKOWSKI, and KOUSSEVITZKY. Among American composers, WILLIAM SCHUMAN, AARON COPLAND, DOUGLAS MOORE, ROY HARRIS, and, particularly, CHARLES IVES have been interested in developing native themes.

Music production as an industry was recognized by the formation (1896) of the American Federation of Musicians, an affiliate of the American Federation of Labor, comprising some 800 local unions. In 1914 a group formed the American Society of Composers, Authors and Publishers (ASCAP), primarily to protect copyright material and collect fees. The phonograph record industry developed as a large-scale commercial enterprise after World War I. With the introduction of long-play microgroove recordings in the 1940's, excellent tone quality was achieved, and it was further refined a decade later by the application of stereophonic reproduction. Regular symphony and opera broadcasts were initiated in the late 1920's, and by 1950 television programs were bringing live recordings of major musical events into millions of American homes.

See *Ballet, Band music, Hymns, Jazz, Operetta.*

J. T. Howard, *Our American Music* (rev. ed., 1954), and Gilbert Chase, *America's Music* (1955) deal with the whole field of American music.

Musical comedy, see *Operetta.*

Muskhogean Family, now considered to be of the same language group as the SIOUAN and IROQUOIS families, inhabited the Deep South from Florida to Louisiana. They were the first Indians of North America with whom the Spaniards came in contact. Among its tribes were the CHICKASAW, CHOCTAW, CREEK, NATCHEZ, SEMINOLE, and YAMASSEE.

Mustang, the small, swift, half-wild horse of the Southwest, was of Arabian origin, brought to Mexico by the Spaniards. A number of them escaped, and as the region was suitable to their survival, small, wild herds developed. These became the foundation stock of the *mesteño* (the strayed animal), adopted by Indian buffalo hunters, whose lives they revolutionized. The mustang, which was very hardy, later became the choice of cowboys and cavalrymen, and thus was a factor in shaping the West. The Cayuse Indians of Washington and Oregon became famous breeders of mustangs, and the name 'cayuse' signified an Indian pony. With the development of ranching, mustangs became nuisances and many were killed off. A bronco is an untamed mustang.

Mutiny Act, see *Quartering Acts.*

Mutual Security Act (1951), a replacement of the Defense Production Act (1950), administered by the ECONOMIC STABILIZATION ADMINISTRATION, authorized $7,483,000,000 for foreign aid in the form of military and economic supplies. The program, first administered by W. Averell Harriman, then by Harold E. Stassen, doubled its financial base in 1952. The agency was abolished in 1955 and its functions were transferred to the Departments of State and of Defense.

Myers* v. *U.S. (1926) was a case that resulted in a ruling by the U.S. Supreme Court which held that the President could remove executive officers without the consent of the Senate, even though their appointment required the Senate's approval. It thus invalidated an 1876 Act of Congress which had required that the President obtain the Senate's consent to remove postmasters. The decision was somewhat narrowed by the Court's ruling in HUMPHREY'S EXECUTOR *v.* U.S. (1935).

N

Napoleonic Wars, see *Berlin Decree, Continental System, Embargo Act, Milan Decree, Nonimportation Act, Nonintercourse Act, Orders in Council.*

Narragansett Indians, of Algonquian stock, in the early 17th century were a powerful tribe principally occupying Rhode Island. In 1636 CANONICUS sold Roger Williams the land on which he settled, and through Williams's influence the Narragansetts assisted the colonists in the Pequot War (1637). Suspected of treachery 40 years later in KING PHILIP'S WAR (1675–76), the Narragansetts were virtually annihilated in the so-called Swamp Fight near Kingston, Rhode Island.

NARVÁEZ, PÁNFILO DE (*c.* 1470–1528), Spanish conquistador, having served with Velázquez in Cuba, was outfitted by Charles V with five vessels to explore and settle Florida. He landed near Tampa Bay (April 1528) with some 400 men and 80 horses. Though constantly harassed by Indians, he fought his way up to the site of Tallahassee, but he failed to discover the gold he sought and retreated to the coast. This most unfortunate explorer, after floating rudely constructed boats to replace those that adverse weather and Indian forays had cost him, set out for Mexico with his remaining men. In a severe storm off the coast of Texas he was lost with all his party, except for CABEZA DE VACA and three others.

Nashoba Community (1825–29), near Memphis, Tennessee, was a utopian community founded by FRANCES WRIGHT to educate slaves whose freedom had been purchased. Support for the project came from abolitionists and liberal Southerners, but haphazard management doomed it. The few Negroes gathered there were eventually transported to Haiti.

Nashville, Battle of (15–16 December 1864), was the dramatic conflict in which GEORGE H. THOMAS all but destroyed the Confederate army of JOHN B. HOOD, and brought Hood's Tennessee campaign to an end. It freed Tennessee from organized Confederate resistance. The battle is described by students of maneuver as perfect tactics. It was one of the most smashing defeats of the Civil War.

Nashville Convention (1850), which met in two sessions (June and November), was instigated by Calhoun and the Mississippi Convention of 1849. Called for the purpose of protecting the slave property of the South, it was attended by Whigs and Democrats from nine states. The first session called for extension of the MISSOURI COMPROMISE westward. In September the enactment of the COMPROMISE OF 1850 seemed to most Southerners a solution to the menace of national division. The second session was attended chiefly by extremists, who denounced the Compromise of 1850 and called for secession. The Convention led to no action.

NAST, THOMAS (1840–1902), German-born political caricaturist and illustrator, at the age of fifteen became a draftsman for *Leslie's Weekly*. In 1862 he joined the staff of *Harper's Weekly,* and his pen drawings not only marked the beginning of the modern political cartoon but were a great force in contemporary politics. His cartoons attacking northern defeatists during the Civil War led Lincoln to call him 'our best recruiting sergeant.' His damning caricatures of the corrupt TWEED RING during the 1870's were instrumental in smashing that organization. Nast created the symbolic Tammany tiger, Republican elephant, and Democratic donkey. Although his greatest work was completed by 1885, throughout his life he continued to mold public opinion through the satire of his incomparable political cartoons.

Natchez-Muskhogean Family of North American Indians were living in agricultural villages in the lower Mississippi valley in the 17th century. They were expert potters and weavers, and were regarded by colonial observers as a superior Indian family. Their caste system, ranging from 'Suns' to 'Stinkards,' forbade intermarriage. The CHOCTAW, CHICKASAW, CREEK, and SEMINOLE were linguistically allied to them. Remnants of the family were for the most part forceably resettled in Oklahoma before 1850.

NATION, CARRY AMELIA MOORE (1846–1911), Kansas-born temperance agitator, became convinced of her divine mission to destroy saloons during the 1890's. In 1900 she supplemented her public prayers and exhortations by the destruction (with a hatchet) of bottles, kegs, and other saloon property. Her exploits gave her nationwide notoriety, and her temperance lecture tours took her all over the U.S. and to Europe. She summed up her ideas in *The Use and Need of the Life of Carry Nation* (1904), published three years after her husband had divorced her.

National Academy of Design (1828), a society of painters, sculptors, and engravers, was founded in New York City by 30 artists, prominent among whom were S. F. B. MORSE (who was its president for twenty years) and A. B. DURAND. In 1906 the Academy absorbed the Society of American Artists. At present it has an enrollment of about 200 members and 160 associates. It is affiliated with the Metropolitan Museum of Art and Columbia University, operates a tuition-free school of design, holds annual exhibitions, and offers various prizes.

National Academy of Sciences (1863) was created by Congress to give scientific advice to government departments upon request. It is unique in its quasi-governmental function, as it is a private organization which elects its own members. The membership is limited to 350 American scientists and 50 foreign associates. Its headquarters are in Washington, D.C. In 1916, with the co-operation of major scientific and technical societies, the Academy organized the National Research Council to co-ordinate scientific research on a national scale.

National Aeronautics and Space Administration, see *Space Age.*

National Anthem, see *Star-Spangled Banner.*

National Archives before 1934 were dispersed, each Federal department acting as custodian of its own records. Congress created The National Archives in 1934, and gave it responsibility for assembling, appraising, and storing or displaying all records belonging to the federal government. The Federal Records Act of 1950 established the statutory basis for administering the records, which by that time occupied some 875,000 cubic feet and included documents, maps, photographs, recordings, and films. Its publications include the daily FEDERAL REGISTER, statutes-at-large, and the public papers of Presidents, whose libraries it administers upon their retirement. In its exhibition hall are enshrined the Declaration of Independence, the Constitution, and the Bill of Rights.

Interest in archival problems, stimulated by the establishment of the National Archives, led to the founding (1936) of a professional organization, the Society of American Archivists, which in 1938 began publication of its quarterly journal, the *American Archivist.*

National Army, see *Army, U.S.*

National Association for the Advancement of Colored People, organized (1910) as a private interracial group, seeks the political and civil equality of the Negro people. Its more than 300 branches engage in educational programs and lobbying activities. In recent years the NAACP has led attacks upon the economic and social barriers that discriminate against Negroes, mainly by court action. The organization has sought to implement the historic U.S. Supreme Court ruling (1954) that segregation in the schools was unconstitutional under the Fourteenth Amendment.

National Association of Manufacturers (1895), one of the most powerful lobbying organizations in the U.S., with 16,000 member firms, is the largest and most influential organization protecting manufacturing interests. Long opposed to the BOYCOTT, CLOSED SHOP, or 'any interference with employment,' the NAM favors high tariffs and operates a comprehensive labor and social research program.

National Bank Act (1863), as amended in 1864, swept away the Independent Treasury system of 1846 in favor of one more attractive to private finance. Primarily adopted to provide a market for government bonds necessary to finance the Civil War, it authorized the issuance of national bank notes by national banks, and though such notes were never a satisfactory currency (since the amount in currency fluctuated more closely with the price of government bonds than with the needs of business), they nevertheless remained the sole bank currency until the establishment of the FEDERAL RESERVE SYSTEM (1913). They remained in circulation until 1935, when the bonds bearing the circulation privilege were retired by the Treasury.

National banks, see *Banking.*

National Conservation Commission, see *Conservation movement.*

National Constitutional Union party, see *Constitutional Union party.*

National convention, in the U.S., is the quadrennial meeting of the political parties, called for the purpose of drawing up a platform, nominating candidates for the presidency and vice presidency, and electing a new national committee. Until 1831 parties selected their candidates by a congressional CAUCUS, but in that year the Anti-Masonic party inaugurated the custom of letting state delegates (selected by state conventions or state primaries) make the nominations. Voting procedure on the national ticket is by roll call of the states, in alphabetical order. A majority vote of the delegates present is sufficient to nominate a candidate.

The national convention is a peculiarly American institution, a 'big show' whose pageantry attracts thousands of spectators and can be seen on television by millions more. Bands play, delegations parade, party heroes receive ovations, and political organizers scurry around to line up votes. Proceedings begin with a 'keynote' address. On the second or third day the platform is prepared, which by custom extols the history of the party, states the party's policies, and enumerates the failures and denounces the policies of other parties. This collection of generalities seldom meets opposition in the convention. When the convention has chosen and notified its candidate, he makes an acceptance speech, which is often an important political document, for it interprets the platform. Thereafter it is the candidate's speeches, not the activities of the national convention, that sway the electorate.

National Council of the Churches of Christ in the U.S. (1950), formed by the merging of the Federal Council of the Churches with seven other interchurch agencies, is an interdenominational organization composed of some 30 Protestant and four Eastern Orthodox groups. The Council is not a governing body; it promotes interchurch co-operation especially in the fields of social action, religious education, and home and foreign missions. A general assembly of some 600 delegates meets biennially.

National debt, see *Public debt, U.S.*

National Defense Act (1916) enlarged the regular army to 175,000, strengthened the national guard, and provided for an officers' reserve corps. At the same time Congress created a COUNCIL OF NATIONAL DEFENSE. The Act reflected the national philosophy of depending on volunteer citizen soldiers, employing local energies, and avoiding the alternative of a huge standing army.

National Democratic party was formed (1896) by conservative 'Gold Democrats,' who repudiated Bryan's free-silver platform and nominated Senator J. M. Palmer (Ill.) and General S. B. Buckner (Ky.) on an anti-Bryan ticket. Since many 'Gold Democrats' either voted for McKinley or avoided the polls, Palmer attracted only 131,000 votes.

National Education Association, the largest professional education organization in the U.S., was chartered by Congress (1906) from an association that grew out of the National Teachers group (est. 1857), through whose activity a Federal department of education had been established (1867). It sponsors commissions, publishes yearbooks and research studies, and through its important journal keeps teachers abreast of significant publications and educational affairs. Its headquarters are in Washington, D.C. It has a current membership upward of 950,000.

National forests, principally vast areas in the mountainous sections of the West, are reservations set aside as part of the national CONSERVATION MOVEMENT. They are administered by the Forest Service (in the Department of Agriculture), which carries on research work in all aspects of forestry. In 1965, a total of 186,475,000 acres was so designated in 44 states and in Puerto Rico and the Virgin Islands. The most extensive acreages are in Alaska (20,741,000), Idaho (20,346,000), California (20,004,000), Montana (16,635,000), Oregon (15,464,000), Colorado (14,346,000), and Arizona (11,417,000). There are no national forests in Connecticut, Delaware, Hawaii, Maryland, New Jersey, or Rhode Island.

National Foundation, first established (1938) to fight poliomyelitis, derives its support from voluntary contributions to the 'March of Dimes.' Its program underlay the discovery of the Salk and Sabin vaccines. In recent years it has extended grants to aid in combating arthritis and birth defects. Its appeals annually gross several million dollars.

National Gallery of Art, the largest marble building in the world, was established by Act of Congress (1937), and was built (1941) with funds given by Andrew Mellon, who donated to it his great collection of paintings. The Gallery has also benefited from the gifts of other donors, including the notable collections of Samuel H. Kress, Joseph E. Widener, and Lessing Rosenwald. Contemporary works are not included.

National Geographic Society, established (1888) in Washington, D.C., to encourage and engage in geographical research, is the world's largest and best-known geographic society. It publishes the *National Geographic Magazine,* a monthly periodical with popular accounts and photographs of explorations conducted by the Society and others. Its cartographic division has been issuing superior maps since 1889. No maps have enjoyed such a continuing reputation for reliability and beauty as those issued by the Society in recent decades.

National Grange, see *Granger movement.*

National Guard, see *Militia.*

National Industrial Recovery Act (1933) was designed to revive industrial and trade activity during the period of a severe business depression. The Act created the National Recovery Administration (NRA), through which agency the President was empowered to prescribe codes for industries. The courts could issue injunctions against violators, and actions under codes were exempt from the operation of ANTITRUST LAWS.

The NRA was designed to stabilize prices, spread employment, raise wages, and to provide emergency relief through its pump-priming PUBLIC WORKS ADMINISTRATION. The task of framing the codes was so complex that inevitably business wrote its own codes and big business imposed its will on small business.

Three features of the NRA presented peculiar difficulties. The labor provisions roused conservative opposition, suspension of antitrust laws strengthened big business unilaterally, and doubts as to its constitutionality encouraged noncompliance with its provisions. NRA was breaking down under its own weight when the Supreme Court in 1935 destroyed it by undermining its legal foundations (*Schechter Poultry Corp.* v. *U.S.*) on the ground that 'Congress cannot delegate legislative power to the President to exercise an unfettered discretion' in matters of trade and commerce, and on the ground that the Act invaded states' rights. More effective labor provisions were soon legislated in the WAGNER-CONNERY ACT (1935), and in the FAIR LABOR STANDARDS ACT (1938). The tendency of NRA to reduce price competition was continued through lobbies, which succeeded in promoting Federal and state 'fair trade' laws.

National Institute of Arts and Letters, see *American Academy of Arts and Letters.*

National Labor Board (NLB) was an administrative agency created (1933) 'to settle by mediation, or arbitration all controversies between employers and employees.' It was without specific statutory foundation, but in the first year of its existence it mediated 3061 grievances and arbitrated 1023 strikes. In 1935 it was replaced by the NATIONAL LABOR RELATIONS BOARD.

National Labor Reform party, see *National Labor Union.*

National Labor Relations Act, see *Wagner-Connery Act.*

National Labor Relations Board was created to administer the WAGNER-CONNERY ACT (1935). In 1947 the board was increased from three to five members by the TAFT-HARTLEY ACT, which also gave it quasi-judicial powers to administer both Acts. It has two basic functions: the prevention and remedy of UNFAIR LABOR PRACTICES, and the holding of hearings to determine who will act as employees' representatives in COLLECTIVE BARGAINING.

National Labor Union, organized at Baltimore (1866) by iron-molders, though it lasted but six years, may have attained a membership of 500,000. It was a conglomeration of trades' assemblies, farmers' societies, and reform groups. In 1872 the federation was transformed into the National Labor Reform party, and nominated Judge David Davis (Ill.) for President, but Davis withdrew, and both the party and the federation collapsed. In its brief existence it helped push through two important pieces of Federal legislation: the eight-hour law for employees on government jobs, and the repeal of the Contract Labor Law of 1864, a wartime measure that had authorized the importation of contract labor during a period of labor shortage.

National League, see *Baseball.*

National Mediation Board, see *Railroad Acts.*

National Monetary Commission (1908), established by authority of the ALDRICH-VREELAND ACT, after studying banking procedures abroad, proposed legislation to remedy a number of existing defects. The FEDERAL RESERVE SYSTEM (1913) was developed in part from the Commission's recommendations.

National monuments include buildings, statues, homesteads, battlefields, cemeteries, and sites of historic, scenic, or political significance. NATIONAL PARKS may be established only by Congress, but the President has the authority to designate national monuments. Upward of 100 such monuments have been established. Among them are Fort Sumter (South Carolina), Glacier Bay (Alaska), Grand Canyon (Colorado), the Statue of Liberty (New York), the Adams House (Massachusetts), Gettysburg Cemetery (Pennsylvania), and the Lincoln Memorial (Washington, D.C.). The PAINTED DESERT, a brilliantly colored badlands, is not a national monument.

National Origins Act, see *Johnson-Reed Act.*

National parks, which may be established only by Congress, are managed by a separate bureau within the Department of the Interior (which also has charge of NATIONAL MONUMENTS). There are national historical parks, national military parks, national memorial parks, national battlefield parks, national battlefield sites, national memorials, and national historical sites: a total of some 180 areas. Some of the more important of these parks and the years of their establishment are as follows.

1872 Yellowstone (Wyoming)
1890 Yosemite (California)
1890 Sequoia (California)
1899 Mount Rainier (Washington)
1902 Crater Lake (Oregon)
1903 Wind Cave (South Dakota)
1906 Mesa Verde (Colorado)
1906 Platt (Oklahoma)
1910 Glacier (Montana)
1915 Rocky Mountain (Colorado)
1916 Hawaii Volcanoes (Hawaii)
1916 Lassen Volcanic (California)
1917 Mount McKinley (Alaska)
1919 Grand Canyon (Arizona)
1919 Acadia (Maine)
1919 Zion (Utah)
1921 Hot Springs (Arkansas)
1928 Bryce Canyon (Utah)
1929 Grand Teton (Wyoming)
1930 Great Smoky Mountains (North Carolina)
1930 Carlsbad Caverns (New Mexico)
1935 Shenandoah (Virginia)
1936 Mammoth Cave (Kentucky)
1938 Olympic (Washington)
1940 King's Canyon (California)
1940 Isle Royale (Michigan)

1944 Big Bend (Texas)
1947 Everglades (Florida)
1956 Virgin Islands
1962 Petrified Forest (Arizona)

National Prohibition Act, see *Volstead Act.*

National Recovery Act, see *National Industrial Recovery Act.*

National Republican party, which was short-lived, stemmed from the result of the presidential election of 1824, in which all the candidates (Adams, Jackson, Clay, and Crawford) were Republicans and nationalists of various stripes. Adams won the election. Thereafter conservative Republicans and all others who feared Jackson's radicalism formed a coalition, which as a party of National Republicans grew stronger after Jackson's triumph in 1828. In 1831, with a platform upholding the tariff and the Bank of the U.S., they met in national convention, and nominated Clay. The Republican-Democrats then split, and Jackson as the Democratic candidate badly defeated Clay. During Jackson's second term various anti-Jackson groups, including the National Republicans, combined into a loose alliance, from which emerged (1836) the WHIG PARTY.

National Research Council, see *National Academy of Science.*

National Road, see *Cumberland Road.*

National Science Foundation (1950), established by Congress as an independent agency, is the only general-purpose science agency in the government. It seeks to develop a national policy for basic research and scientific education. Funds available for its grants, steadily increasing, in 1965 totaled $420,400,000.

National Security Act, see *Defense, Department of.*

National Security Council is an executive agency created (1947) by the National Security Act. Its members are the President, the Vice President, the Secretary of State, the Secretary of Defense, and the Director of the Office of Emergency Planning (a separate executive agency created at the same time). The U.S. Ambassador to the United Nations serves as representative to the Council. This five-man 'supercabinet' administers the planning, development, and co-ordinating of all functions concerned with the defense of the U.S. It evaluates the aims and commitment of the U.S. in existing or potential war. It advises the President on immediate policy decisions, determines security actions, and defines long-term American policies.

Nationalism, as a political or social ideology, is loosely defined as devotion to national interests, welfare, and independence. In U.S. history the term has been variously applied. The attempt to create and support a FEDERAL GOVERNMENT gave one type of stimulus to nationalism. The War of 1812 cemented the structure being erected, and it was followed by the resurgent nationalist feeling reflected in the 'ERA OF GOOD FEELINGS.' Manifestations of nationalist trends in the early decades of the Republic include congressional appropriations for INTERNAL IMPROVEMENTS, the PROTECTIVE TARIFF, the renewal of the BANK OF THE U.S., Clay's AMERICAN SYSTEM, the MONROE DOCTRINE, and the Supreme Court decisions of John Marshall.

As the frontier moved westward, the continent's geography gave American nationalism a new context. The impact of a new world with its tremendous resources inspired artists and writers with a national fervor. In 1837 Emerson spoke for the nation when he declared: 'Our day of dependence, our long apprenticeship to the learning of other lands, draws to a close . . . Events, actions arise, that must be sung, that will sing themselves.' Nationalism took on a gusty incisiveness, often noisy, but boundless in its self-confidence, as the oratory of the period attests. During the 1840's nationalist sentiment gave rise to the concept of MANIFEST DESTINY, which culminated at the turn of the 19th century in a trend toward IMPERIALISM.

Nativism, the policy of favoring the native inhabitants of a country over immigrants, in the U.S. chiefly resulted in antagonism toward Roman Catholics rather than toward racial groups. It was first intimately associated with the serious labor dislocations brought about by the arrival of millions of European immigrants during the 19th century, many of whom came from Catholic countries. Thus 'Catholic' was superimposed on the image of 'foreigner.'

The earliest anti-Catholic sentiment had been brought to America by the English colonists, but during the colonial period it never created nativist issues except in areas contiguous to the French jurisdictions in Canada and Louisiana. The liberal spirit of the Declaration of Independence and the French alliance of 1778 further dispelled it, but mounting immigration after 1820 gave incentive to nativist demonstrations. Street fights between natives and foreigners were common, and Catholic convents and churches and German turnverein headquarters were sometimes attacked. (Many German immigrants were Catholics.)

Much of the rancor was economic in motive, since immigrants competed with artisans who were trying to protect their standard of living by labor organizations. At the outbreak of the Civil War a common sign on workshops read 'no Irish need apply,' although such signs were never displayed at recruiting offices. Several years earlier intolerance had fostered anti-Catholic societies and newspapers. The KNOW-NOTHING movement of the 1840's was a political exploitation of nativistic sentiment, which revived again during the 1880's, when a new wave of immigration created a state of mind similarly receptive to anti-alien propaganda. On the West Coast nativism was directed against Chinese immigrants.

During the 1920's the KU KLUX KLAN drew an enormous following and dedicated itself to a program of hostility to minority and non-Protestant groups, and bitter nativistic bias was an important factor in the defeat of Alfred E. Smith (a Catholic) in the presidential campaign of 1928. But by 1961, with the sharp decline in immigration, a realignment of labor issues, the admission of such multiracial regions as Alaska and Hawaii to statehood, and a Catholic as President, nativism as a policy attracted few adherents.

See R. A. Billington, *The Protestant Crusade* (1938).

NATO, see *North Atlantic Treaty Organization.*

Natural gas, see *Gas.*

Natural history, see *Zoology.*

Natural philosophy, see *Physics.*

Natural resources, see *Agriculture, Conservation movement, Federal Power Commission, Fisheries, Flood control, Forests, Geological Survey.*

Natural rights, according to some schools, are those that belong to the individual before the creation of government. The concept was brought to the American colonies through the writings of JOHN LOCKE, who added the right of property to those of life and liberty. Such a concept became part of the revolutionary philosophy, was embodied in the Declaration of Independence, and codified in the bills of rights of the Federal and state constitutions. Later, Calhoun rejected individualistic political theory on the ground that government is not a matter of choice but a fundamental necessity. Since the Civil War, political theory in the U.S. as elsewhere has not adhered to individuality before organization. Recently, theorists have held that natural rights have, at most, ethical significance. Nevertheless, the doctrine is still asserted in judicial decisions that protect the individual against the arbitrary action of government.

Naturalization, the process of granting citizenship to aliens, in the U.S. is a power delegated to Congress by the Constitution (Art. I, sec. 8). By congressional action citizenship status has been conferred six times upon entire populations: native-born Negroes by implication in the Fourteenth Amendment to the Constitution (1868); the American Indians, when their numbers were deemed no longer a threat to national security (1924); and the residents of Hawaii (1900), Alaska (1912), Puerto Rico (1917), and the Virgin Islands (1927). Individual naturalization requires a five-year residence in the U.S., but children under eighteen become citizens automatically when their parents are naturalized.

Naturalization Act, see *Alien and Sedition Acts.*

Navaho Indians (or Navajo), of Athapascan stock, at some time in prehistory migrated from the north to the Southwest, where they assimilated other groups, notably Pueblo, Shoshone, and Yuma. A nomadic, predatory tribe, they were constantly on the warpath until Kit Carson subdued them (1863–64) by killing their sheep. When they were placed on their 16,000,000-acre reservation in New Mexico (1868) and supplied with new flocks, they numbered some 9000. Since then, as a pastoral and industrious people, their population has increased tenfold. (They now far surpass all other North American tribes in numbers.) Their metal work, weaving, and sand painting, together with records of their vast mythology, have been gathered in the Museum of Navajo Ceremonial Art at Santa Fe.

Naval Academy, U.S., founded (1845) at Annapolis, Maryland, by Secretary of the Navy GEORGE BANCROFT, replaced the irregular training previously given to prospective naval officers with systematic instruction. During the Civil War the Academy was temporarily moved to Newport, Rhode Island. The authorized enrollment of midshipmen (now 3400) is maintained by appointment: 75 by the President, five each by the Vice President and members of Congress, and others selected from the sons of navy personnel. Some appointments are reserved for students from other countries.

'Naval holiday,' see *Washington Conference (1921–22)*.

Naval Observatory, U.S., the government astronomical observatory in Washington, D.C., began as the Depot of Charts and Instruments, which was created by the Navy Department in 1830. Its 26-inch equatorial refracting telescope (then the largest in the world) was installed in 1873. The Observatory is the official U.S. timekeeper. Its library has built up a notable collection of mathematical and astronomical works.

Navigation Acts (Acts of Trade and Navigation) (1650–96) were efforts to foster MERCANTILISM by making the British Empire self-sustaining. They had their origin in regulations for coastwise trade, and when colonies developed, the laws were extended overseas. To liberate British trade from Dutch control and to subordinate colonial interests to those of the mother country, Parliament first (1650) forbade foreign ships to trade in the colonies without special license. It next (1651) provided that all goods imported into England from Asia, Africa, and America be carried in English ships manned by English crews, with further regulations governing imports from Europe.

The Act of 1660, among its other provisions, specified 'enumerated articles' (including tobacco, sugar, and cotton) that could be exported from the colonies only to English ports. (By the 1760's almost all products exported from the American colonies were 'enumerated.') The Act of 1663 placed a heavy duty upon all European goods entering the colonies unless trans-shipped through England in British or colonial-built vessels. The last of the Navigation Acts (1696) required royal approval for the acts of colonial governors, and provided for the establishment of customs houses and admiralty courts directed from London.

The net effect of these basic laws was to give Englishmen (including Americans) a legal monopoly of all trade. The 'enumerated' clauses operated in such a way that they gave American shipowners a practical monopoly of the trade between the continental and West Indian colonies. Residents of Great Britain in turn had a general monopoly in carrying heavy goods to the British Isles.

The Navigation Acts and Trade Acts were interchangeable terms for the same legislation, but the Trade Acts were a complicated series of controls developed chiefly after 1700, intended to make the trade of the different parts of the Empire complementary. Colonists were largely restricted to buying British manufactures, but an elaborate system of export bounties made British goods actually cheaper in the colonies than similar foreign articles. In addition, a series of rebates of duties on European goods exported to the colonies cost the Government formidable sums. The payments from the Treasury in bounty rebates in 1764 had mounted to some £250,000. Colonial products were encouraged by favorable tariff duties, although, to prevent competition with home manufacturing, Parliament adopted such measures as the WOOLEN ACT (1699), the HAT ACT (1732), the MOLASSES ACT (1733), and the IRON ACT (1750). These Acts were very generally circumvented until they were more vigorously enforced during the 1760's.

On the whole, however, so long as such Acts were limited to the regulation of trade and the promotion of total commercial well-being within the Empire, they were not especially unpopular. Indeed, the shipping industry of New England rested directly upon the protection of the Navigation Acts. However, the attempt of Parliament to use them after 1763 as a tax on the colonies to bolster a sagging home economy was a different matter. The 'enumerated articles' came largely from the colonies that sought to remain loyal, and the bounties went chiefly to those that revolted. But the fact that Parliament went over the heads of the colonial assemblies, and levied taxes that were designed not to regulate commerce, but to tap a new source of revenue, united the colonies in opposition and helped precipitate the Revolution.

See L. A. Harper, *The English Navigation Laws* (1939).

Navy, U.S., came into being as an adjunct of the Continental army in October 1775, when the Continental Congress set up a naval committee and appropriated funds for the construction of small naval craft. During the Revolution three naval forces (Continental, state, and private) engaged chiefly in privateering, for the Americans had no resources to provide capital ships, and naval warfare had to pay for itself. Gallant naval combats were fought by single ships or small squadrons, and from the war emerged the two naval heroes, JOHN BARRY and JOHN PAUL JONES. The navy was gradually dismantled thereafter, and when the Republic was founded in 1789 the navy had ceased to exist.

The U.S. Navy had its beginning in 1798 at the outbreak of the undeclared war with France, when Congress created the Department of the Navy. By the end of the year fourteen American men-of-war were at sea, and under Jefferson the fleet was employed to protect American merchantmen during the TRIPOLITAN WAR (1801–5). In the War of 1812 the navy, though diminutive, served to stimulate national unity by such victories as those secured by Isaac Hull off Nova Scotia, by Oliver Hazard Perry on Lake Erie, and by Thomas MacDonough on Lake Champlain.

Training of naval officers continued to be haphazard until the NAVAL ACADEMY was founded (1845). But even at the outbreak of the Civil War the navy was small and ill-prepared for the demanding tasks of protecting shipping, blockading Confederate ports, and preventing foreign intervention. However, under the capable direction of Secretary of the Navy Gideon Welles, and the skillful handling of such a commander as David Farragut, the first American naval officer to be granted the rank of ADMIRAL, the Navy came of age.

The Navy was built up as a striking force during the last two decades of the 19th century, and performed so well in the Spanish-American War (1898) that it helped determine national policy soon thereafter, as the round-the-world cruise of the 'Great White Fleet,' consisting of sixteen new battleships (dispatched by Theodore Roosevelt in 1907) was intended to demonstrate.

During World War I the Navy helped transport 1,000,000 troops to Europe and co-operated in destroying the effectiveness of German submarine warfare. Its greatest hour came during World War II when, having acquired unprecedented strength, it became an irresistible force in the vast reaches of the Pacific, in the air, on the surface, and under the water. In 1965, the Navy had some 671,000 personnel and an annual budget of $14,000,000,000.

Studies include H. I. Chappelle, *The History of the American Sailing Navy* (1949); and D. W. Knox, *A History of the U.S. Navy* (rev. ed., 1948). See also S. E. Morison, *History of U.S. Naval Operations in World War II* (15 vols., 1947–62), which is the official history.

Navy, Department of the, was created as part of the Department of War in 1789. The unsatisfactory administration of naval affairs by the War Department led Congress to create the Department of the Navy in 1798. In 1815 a Board of Navy Commissioners (three senior officers) was created to assist the Secretary; it was superseded (1842) by the Board of Commis-

Navy, Department of the

sioners, an advisory body. The office of Assistant Secretary was established in 1890, and that of the important Chief of Naval Operations, headed by a fleet admiral, was created in 1915. The Department was merged in 1947 with the Departments of the ARMY and the AIR FORCE into the Department of DEFENSE. The consolidation gave cabinet rank to the Secretary of Defense, and thenceforth removed from the cabinet the Secretaries of the Navy and the Army. The present structure consists of an Under Secretary, a Deputy Secretary, and three Assistant Secretaries: for Installations and Logistics, Financial Management, and Research and Development. Secretaries of the Navy that held cabinet rank and the Presidents under whom they served are as follows.

J. ADAMS
Benjamin Stoddert (Md.) 1798

JEFFERSON
Benjamin Stoddert (Md.) 1801
Robert Smith (Md.) 1801
Jacob Crowninshield (Mass.) 1805

MADISON
Paul Hamilton (S.C.) 1809
William Jones (Pa.) 1813
B. W. Crowninshield (Mass.) 1814

MONROE
B. W. Crowninshield (Mass.) 1817
Smith Thompson (N.Y.) 1818
Samuel L. Southard (N.J.) 1823

J. Q. ADAMS
Samuel L. Southard (N.J.) 1825

JACKSON
John Branch (N.C.) 1829
Levi Woodbury (N.H.) 1831
Mahlon Dickerson (N.J.) 1834

VAN BUREN
Mahlon Dickerson (N.J.) 1837
James K. Paulding (N.Y.) 1838

W. H. HARRISON
George E. Badger (N.C.) 1841

TYLER
George E. Badger (N.C.) 1841
Abel P. Upshur (Va.) 1841
David Henshaw (Mass.) 1843
Thomas W. Gilmer (Va.) 1844
John Y. Mason (Va.) 1844

POLK
George Bancroft (Mass.) 1845
John Y. Mason (Va.) 1846

TAYLOR
William B. Preston (Va.) 1849

FILLMORE
William A. Graham (N.C.) 1850
John P. Kennedy (Md.) 1852

PIERCE
James C. Dobbin (N.C.) 1853

BUCHANAN
Isaac Toucey (Conn.) 1857

LINCOLN
Gideon Welles (Conn.) 1861

A. JOHNSON
Gideon Welles (Conn.) 1865

GRANT
Adolph E. Borie (Pa.) 1869
George M. Robeson (N.J.) 1869

HAYES
Richard W. Thompson (Ind.) 1877
Nathan Goff, Jr. (W. Va.) 1881

GARFIELD
William H. Hunt (La.) 1881

ARTHUR
William E. Chandler (N.H.) 1882

CLEVELAND
William C. Whitney (N.Y.) 1885

B. HARRISON
Benjamin F. Tracy (N.Y.) 1889

CLEVELAND
Hilary A. Herbert (Ala.) 1893

MCKINLEY
John D. Long (Mass.) 1897

T. ROOSEVELT
John D. Long (Mass.) 1901
William H. Moody (Mass.) 1902
Paul Morton (Ill.) 1904
Charles J. Bonaparte (Md.) 1905
Victor H. Metcalf (Calif.) 1906
Truman H. Newberry (Mich.) 1908

TAFT
George von L. Meyer (Mass.) 1909

WILSON
Josephus Daniels (N.C.) 1913

HARDING
Edwin Denby (Mich.) 1921

COOLIDGE
Edwin Denby (Mich.) 1923
Curtis D. Wilbur (Calif.) 1924

HOOVER
Charles Francis Adams (Mass.) 1929

F. D. ROOSEVELT
Claude A. Swanson (Va.) 1933
Charles Edison (N.J.) 1940
Frank Knox (Ill.) 1940
James V. Forrestal (N.Y.) 1944

TRUMAN
James V. Forrestal (N.Y.) 1945

Neagle, In re (1890), was a case that arose after a deputy U.S. marshal, David Neagle, in line of duty under presidential executive order, shot and killed a man attempting murderous assault upon Supreme Court Justice Stephen J. Field. Arrested and charged with murder by the California state authorities, Neagle was released by the Federal circuit court, and the circuit court's ruling was upheld by the Supreme Court, thus basically establishing the authority of the executive branch of the government in such matters.

Near* v. *Minnesota (1931) was a case that resulted in a ruling by the U.S. Supreme Court declaring an Act of the state of Minnesota unconstitutional. The Minnesota law had forbidden publication of 'malicious, scandalous and defamatory' newspaper articles. The Court declared that the right to criticize public officials is a fundamental principle of free democratic government, and thus applied the guarantee of personal liberties under the First Amendment to state as well as Federal laws.

Nebbia* v. *New York (1934) was a case that resulted in a ruling by the U.S. Supreme Court concerning a state law fixing retail milk prices. Nebbia's counsel claimed that price fixing by the state, except in business affecting a public interest, such as utilities, was a violation of the DUE PROCESS clause of the Fourteenth Amendment. The Court declared that there is 'no closed category of business affected with a public interest,' and thus extended the police power of states.

Nebraska, in the central PLAINS REGION, slopes gently eastward to the Missouri river, into which drains the Platte, whose navigable branches cross the entire length of the state. The Omaha Indian name of the Platte, meaning *flat,* was adopted as the state's name. (The name of the river is the Spanish translation of the Indian word.) The region was first visited by Coronado (1541), but was not developed commercially until French fur traders opened posts early in the 18th century along its waterways. It was transferred to the U.S. in the Louisiana Purchase (1803).

The Platte valley, a natural overland highway, gave access to the Far West, and was the route used by exploring expeditions and the wagon trains of emigrant settlers. By the KANSAS-NEBRASKA ACT (1854) Nebraska became a territory, and it was admitted to the Union (1867) as the 37th state, with Lincoln as its capital. Farming pioneers, many of them immigrants from Scandinavia and central Europe, at first built sod houses in the timberless land, and the rich soil gradually yielded a wealth of wheat, corn, and livestock forage. With a severe continental climate, Nebraska is subject to extreme weather changes, and thus demands, in a region almost wholly dependent on agricultural pursuits, an unflagging alertness to the whims of nature.

Nebraska contains some of the finest Tertiary fossil beds in the world. They have been carefully studied by museums for many years to provide information about the succession of fauna in the Age of Mammals.

Omaha is its chief city, with a population (in 1960) of 300,000. It is in the heart of the nation's farming region, a port of entry, and one of the world's great livestock markets.

The state's leading institution of higher learning is the University of Nebraska (Lincoln, est. 1869).

Negro insurrections did not seriously affect the attitude of southern slave owners until the Gabriel Insurrection of 1800 in Virginia and the VESEY INSURRECTION (1822) in South Carolina. These insurrections led to a tightening of the 'black codes' as the only possible means of subordinating Negroes. (Previously there had been many instances in which 'maroons' had occurred, that is, bands of slaves had taken refuge with Indians in the forests or marooned themselves in swamps.) The most serious slave revolt was the TURNER INSURRECTION (1831) in Virginia. These uprisings led to an even tighter control system, as the Southerners feared that incipient and widespread rebellion among the slaves could culminate in serious trouble. Southern states became more united in their support of the FUGITIVE SLAVE LAWS, and in their opposition to the ABOLITION MOVEMENT, which the southern press consistently charged was at the root of slave unrest. (Historians have been unable to find any evidence for such allegations.)

Negro minstrels, see *Minstrel show.*

Negroes were brought to Virginia in 1619, and at first their status was similar to that of white indentured servants. Some came thereafter from the West Indies, but with the success of tobacco planting assured and the need for labor mounting, most were part of the inexhaustible supply available in West Africa. Negro SLAVERY, sanctioned by law in Virginia (1661) and Maryland (1663), created an institution that became the foundation of the economy in all the Southern Colonies. It never took root in the North, where a growing industrialism required artisans rather than field hands.

Some 5000 Negroes fought for the patriot cause during the War of Independence alongside their white comrades. Only South Carolina and Georgia refused to permit recruiting of Negroes. The invention of the cotton gin (1793) radically affected the economy of the South. Increasing numbers of field laborers were required as new lands were opened westward to the Mississippi. Since most Negroes were chattel (except in the North), laws forbade them to receive formal education, and religious instruction emphasized obedience and subservience. Miscegenation (involving almost exclusively white males and Negro females) was widespread, and the attractive quadroons of New Orleans, often set up in luxurious establishments maintained by rich young bloods, were a race apart. The free Negroes in the South gravitated as artisans to the larger centers, where they were feared and hated by the poor whites as economic competitors. More than 186,000 Negroes served in the Union ranks during the Civil War, half of them from the Confederate states. As in later wars they fought in segregated units led by white officers, although a large proportion were assigned to menial tasks.

With the Union triumph in 1865 came the 'day of jubilee,' and during RECONSTRUCTION Negroes in the South allied themselves with the radical Republicans. Passage of the Fourteenth Amendment (1868), conferring citizenship upon the Negroes, then numbering some 4,440,000 persons, gave them a theoretical right to compete on equal terms with whites for a place in American culture. But the general lack of education of Negroes in an increasingly complex society, and prejudices against them, which made economic upgrading impossible for many, added enormously to the problem of their adjustment to freedom.

Through the FREEDMEN'S BUREAU, which opened HOWARD UNIVERSITY (Washington, 1867), and with the help of other agencies, Negroes sought to equip themselves for their new status. The efforts of Southerners to help them were genuine and sometimes courageous. Other early Negro institutions of higher learning include Atlanta University (1865); FISK UNIVERSITY (1867) in Tennessee; HAMPTON INSTITUTE (1868) in Virginia; and TUSKEGEE INSTITUTE (1881), established by the Alabama legislature, with BOOKER T. WASHINGTON as its first president.

Nevertheless, the South with its tremendous Negro population (in some states in excess of the white) faced a unique problem, which it attempted to meet by keeping Negroes from political, social, and economic equality by the activities of such organizations as the KU KLUX KLAN and through passage of JIM CROW laws. Such forms of pressure were intended to establish the color line firmly. Race prejudice has persisted in both North and South, resulting in discrimination and sometimes in outbreaks of violence.

The demand for industrial labor during World War I greatly stimulated the exodus of Negroes from the South to northern cities such as Chicago, Baltimore, Philadelphia, and New York. The Negro population of HARLEM (500,000 in 1960) constitutes a city within a city. In spite of the wretched physical conditions under which Negroes found themselves in such congested areas, in the North they had the vote. They could attend places of amusement, ride on unsegregated conveyances, and send their children to public schools not subjected to racial discrimination. Their scope of activities, steadily widening, has been firmly championed by the NATIONAL ASSOCIATION FOR THE ADVANCEMENT OF COLORED PEOPLE (1910), and the nation-wide attention focused on the SCOTTSBORO CASE (1932) and that of the FREEDOM RIDERS (1961) has further advanced the cause of the Negroes in their search for social justice.

In World War I some 387,000 Negroes served in the armed forces, and the number increased to 1,000,000 in World War II. The fact that during the Second World War Benjamin O. Davis (1877–) became the first Negro general officer in the U.S. Army, and that in 1959 his son, Benjamin O. Davis, Jr. (1912–), was commissioned a major general in the Air Force gave clear indication of a breakdown of racial barriers. Under President Truman the traditional segregation of the armed forces ended.

Yet the 'American dilemma' is posed by the fact that more than 10 per cent of the nation's population (19,000,000 in 1960) are generally regarded as 'second-class citizens.' By states Negro population is concentrated in New York (1,417,000), Texas (1,187,000), Georgia (1,122,000), North Carolina (1,116,000), Louisiana (1,039,000), and Illinois (1,037,000); by cities, in New York (1,087,000), Chicago (812,000), Philadelphia (529,000), Detroit (482,000), Washington (411,000), Los Angeles (334,000), and Baltimore (326,000). Segregation is making the heart of the old cities into Negro communities characterized by large slums.

The issue of status for the Negro is pointed up by the historic U.S. Supreme Court decision in 1954 (BROWN *v.* BOARD OF EDUCATION), which reversed the long-standing previous interpretation of the Fourteenth Amendment by repudiating the 'separate but equal' doctrine, and requiring all public schools to integrate Negroes and whites in the classroom. Implementation of the ruling has been slow.

However underprivileged the Negroes have been in the 350 years of American history, they have always been a major factor in American life, and are increasingly important as a political force and as contributors to the nation's literature, art, scholarship, and science. Their distinctive culture survives in their SPIRITUALS, their contribution to JAZZ, and their folklore. The achievements of MARIAN ANDERSON and LEONTYNE PRICE in music, of RALPH BUNCHE in diplomacy, of ROBERT C. WEAVER in economics, of WILLIAM HASTIE in law, of PAUL ROBESON on the stage, and of JACKIE ROBINSON in sports are gains likewise exemplified in the increasing number of Negroes in executive offices in government and industry.

See J. H. Franklin, *From Slavery to Freedom* (1947); E. F. Frazier, *The Negro in the U.S.* (1949); and C. V. Woodward, *The Strange Career of Jim Crow* (1955). A classic study of the Negro problem in America is Gunnar Myrdal, *An American Dilemma* (2 vols., 1944).

Nelly Bly, see *Seaman, E. C.*

Neutral rights are the claims of a nation to remain at peace with belligerents whose wars affect the economy of nonbelligerents. Such rights were specified in the Plan of 1776, a model set of articles for treaties to be negotiated with foreign powers by the newly independent American colonies, and a document that remains significant because it first defined 'freedom of the seas.' In principle it asserted that cargoes of neutral ships, excepting contraband, are not subject to seizure by belligerents, and that neutrals may trade in noncontraband between ports of belligerents. These principles were embodied in the treaty of the FRANCO-AMERICAN ALLIANCE (1778) and in Washington's NEUTRALITY PROCLAMATION (1793).

Subsequent difficulties rising from continuing wars in Europe led to an evolution of U.S. policy. Such are set forth in JAY'S TREATY (1794), are manifest in the attitude of Congress during the undeclared WAR WITH FRANCE (1798–1800), and are embodied in the NONIMPORTATION ACT of 1806, the EMBARGO ACT of 1807, and the NONINTERCOURSE ACT of 1809. The claim by Great Britain of the right to search American vessels for British subjects was a factor in the War of 1812.

The problem of neutrality has always involved the issue of the BLOCKADE, one which became especially troublesome in Anglo-American relations during the Civil War. American concepts of neutrality rights were not accepted at the two HAGUE CONFERENCES (1899, 1907), and the denial of freedom of the seas by

Germany in 1916 was a primary reason for the entry of the U.S. in World War I. (Wilson later failed in his attempt to include a definition of freedom of the seas in the Versailles Treaty.)

The passage of the NEUTRALITY ACTS of the 1930's constituted an abandonment of the traditional American concept of neutral rights and waived privileges under international law that the nation had thought sufficiently important to fight for in 1917. Exactly what neutral rights may mean in the future is an open question, since modern methods of warfare, involving the conscription of all the resources of belligerent nations, exacts heavy restrictions on their freedom of intercourse with neutrals, and even of neutrals with each other.

Neutrality Acts (1935–39), a series of laws growing out of the investigations of the NYE COMMITTEE and passed piecemeal by Congress, were designed to prevent the involvement of the U.S. in any non-American war, seemingly at any cost. They prohibited loans or credits to belligerents, placed a mandatory embargo on direct or indirect shipments of arms or munitions, gave the President discretion to require payment and transfer of title before export to belligerents of any articles whatsoever, forbade American citizens to travel on the ships of belligerents, and prohibited the arming of American merchant vessels. The limitations were enjoined whether wars were civil or international.

More significant than the fact that these actions abandoned the traditional American doctrine of NEUTRAL RIGHTS was the principle implicit in this legislation that the U.S. would take no stand on issues of international morality by distinguishing between aggressor and victim nations. Such was the degree to which national policy at that time was shaped by the spirit of ISOLATIONISM. In 1939, after the outbreak of World War II, Congress modified the previous legislation to the extent that if Britain and France had the cash and the shipping (which they indeed had), they were welcome to come to the U.S. for arms and munitions on a 'cash and carry' basis. The Roosevelt Administration fought for repeal of the Acts on the ground that they encouraged Axis aggression and ultimately endangered our own security. Gradually they were relaxed.

Neutrality Proclamation (April 1793) was issued by Washington after word had arrived in the U.S. that France and Great Britain were at war. Washington announced that it was the 'disposition of the U.S.' to 'pursue a conduct friendly and impartial toward the belligerent powers.' Congress reinforced the Proclamation in its next session (June 1794) by passing a Neutrality Act that prohibited any U.S. aid to either belligerent.

Nevada, the 36th state admitted to the Union, is in the GREAT BASIN area of the Far West. The region was claimed by Spain in 1776. It came into the possession of Mexico in 1820 and was ceded to the U.S. by the Treaty of Guadalupe Hidalgo (1848). A challenge to early explorers, this 'unknown land,' with a mean elevation of 5500 ft., is an extraordinarily rugged region, with extremes of temperature and altitude. JEDEDIAH SMITH penetrated it in 1825, but the first full report was that made by JOHN C. FRÉMONT in 1845. Thereafter wagon trains began to cross Nevada into California, but the formidable character of the region became evident in the tragic experience of the DONNER PARTY (1846–47).

Discovery of silver in the fabulous COMSTOCK LODE (1859) brought prospectors in a pell-mell rush, and led to the booming growth of such towns as Virginia City, whose early days are memorably described in Mark Twain's *Roughing It.* Congress made Nevada a Territory in 1861, and shortly thereafter it was admitted to statehood (1864), with Carson City as its capital.

Most of Nevada's rivers, chief among them the HUMBOLDT, do not reach the sea. Except when they are diverted for irrigation, they end in desolate alkali sinks. Typical landscapes are arid stretches clothed with sagebrush and creosote brush. Mountain chains segment the state, with the lofty SIERRA NEVADA (*'snow clad range'*), whence its name, on the California border.

Sparsely populated, with much of its foodstuffs imported, Nevada has been dominated politically and economically by the mining of its various minerals (chiefly copper), although large sheep and cattle ranches have helped to stabilize the insecure basis of its mining economy. Resorts have recently been developed on a large scale. Lenient divorce laws, which attract out-of-state persons to temporary residence, and the huge earnings of Nevada's legal gambling industry are also mainstays of the state's economy. In the decade 1950–60, the population of the state rose from 160,000 to 285,000; that of its largest city, Las Vegas, from 24,600 to 64,400, and of Reno from 32,500 to 51,400. The leading institution of higher learning, with an enrollment (1965) of 4630, is the University of Nevada (Reno, est. 1874), known especially for its Mackay School of Mines.

NEVINS, ALLAN (1890–), professor of American history at Columbia (1931–58), was a leader in the movement to reconsider business biographies in the light of evidence taken from corporate archives rather than mainly from the records of court prosecutions. Thus he greatly raised the general reputation of Rockefeller and Standard Oil in *Study in Power* (2 vols., 1941). Nevins, who is versatile and prolific, later wrote such period studies as *Ordeal of the Union, The Emergence of Lincoln,* and *The War for the Union* (6 vols., 1947–59).

New Amsterdam, see *New Netherland.*

Newburgh addresses (1783), written by Major JOHN ARMSTRONG, were anonymous petitions to Congress by restive Continental army officers for redress of such grievances as arrears in pay and unsettled food and clothing accounts. The addresses had the support of General Horatio Gates and of Gouverneur Morris, who hoped to coerce the states into yielding more power to Congress, but Washington's condemnation of the defiant tone of the petitions led to their withdrawal.

NEWCOMB, SIMON (1835–1909), Canadian-born astronomer, in 1858 graduated from Harvard, where he was computer for the *Nautical Almanac* for 1857. In 1861 he was appointed professor of mathematics in the U.S. Navy, and was assigned to duty at the Naval Observatory, where he supervised the erection of the 26-inch equatorial telescope (1873). In 1884 he also became nonresident professor of mathematics and astronomy at Johns Hopkins.

One of the notable astronomers of the 19th century, and more internationally honored than any American since Benjamin Franklin, Newcomb had a talent for observation of the highest order, best reflected in his research on lunar motion. His tables of the planetary system were distinguished for their originality and accuracy, and they were adopted throughout the world. In 1906 by Act of Congress he was elevated to the rank of rear admiral.

New Deal was the term applied to the program of F. D. Roosevelt after his inauguration in 1933. (In his speech accepting the nomination, Roosevelt had declared: 'I pledge myself . . . to a new deal for the American people.') Based on the slogan 'Relief, Recovery, Reform,' it set out to enact legislation for those purposes on the broadest possible scale. A special session of Congress was called (9 March–16 June 1933) to deal with the banking crisis. During the 'Hundred Days' it enacted a comprehensive body of legislation with unprecedented speed. Among the Acts passed were the EMERGENCY BANKING RELIEF ACT, the CIVILIAN CONSERVATION CORPS ACT, the AGRICULTURAL ADJUSTMENT ACT, the GLASS-STEAGALL BANKING ACT, and the NATIONAL INDUSTRIAL RECOVERY ACT. It also created the TENNESSEE VALLEY AUTHORITY, a vast undertaking judged at first as the most radical of the New Deal measures.

The First New Deal (1933–35), designed to alleviate the emergency created by the depression, chiefly worked through traditional means; the measures succeeded only to the extent that they won the wholehearted support of the public. Rebuffed by big business and blocked by the Supreme Court, Roosevelt was convinced that more drastic measures were needed if he were to retain his leadership. Therefore, in his so-called Second New Deal (1935–38), he took further action. The WORKS PROGRESS ADMINISTRATION was a frank espousal of the principles of pump-priming and deficit-financing. The SOCIAL SECURITY ACT and the WAGNER-CONNERY ACT put the government squarely behind the 'forgotten man.' The revival of antitrust prosecutions identified the second New Deal more closely with the ideal of unlimited competition.

Although neither phase of the New Deal can claim to have pulled America out of the depression, the New Deal as a whole was immensely important for its rehabilitation of the nation's natural resources and its contribution to the CONSERVATION MOVEMENT. It extended Federal authority in all fields, notably in banking, agriculture, social security, and public welfare. It gave immediate attention to LABOR PROBLEMS, many of which it handled by revolutionary legislation. Basically it supported labor, farmers, and small businessmen, and indirectly Negroes, who were beneficiaries of legislation setting up minimum standards for wages, hours, relief, and security. The most intensive opposition to the New Deal came from conservatives of both parties, who branded the idea of government planning as state interference with private business. But the old distrust of state action in general gave way to the realization that in major crises of national affairs only the state can act effectively.

New England, a region including the present states of Maine, New Hampshire, Vermont, Massachusetts, Rhode Island, and Connecticut, is the northern area of the NORTHEAST. It was presumably named by Captain John Smith (on his map of 1616), who discovered the rich cod fisheries off Maine. The harsh climate, rocky soil, and paucity of natural products for a time discouraged colonization. Permanent settlements began with those of the Pilgrims at Plymouth (1620), followed by the larger influx of Puritans into the Massachusetts Bay (1630), and the expansion soon thereafter into Connecticut (1631), Rhode Island (1636), New Hampshire (1638), and Maine (1640). The threat of Dutch expansion and Indian raids led to the NEW ENGLAND CONFEDERATION (1643–84), which proved vital in New England's most devastating Indian conflict, KING PHILIP'S WAR (1675–76).

Because New England had more extensive foreign commerce than other colonies, it was more adversely affected by passage of the NAVIGATION ACTS (1651–96). It was the center of the events leading to the Revolution, especially after 1765, and the scene of the opening engagements (1775) of that War. The reorganization of commerce after the return of peace led to trade with China and the American Northwest, and so great was the opposition to the EMBARGO ACT of 1807 and to the War of 1812 that New England radicals threatened secession. But the area survived its economic depression and in fact soon experienced an industrial expansion that made it a manufacturing center, especially of textiles.

From New England stemmed the great migration to the Northwest Territory, and prior to the Civil War the section furnished leaders for most of the social and humanitarian movements in America. Its Puritan origin has made it a stronghold of Congregationalism, and the influence of New England families who emigrated to Ohio after 1800, and later to Oregon, shaped the frontier of both the Northwest Territory and the Pacific Northwest. Long a leading literary and educational center of the nation, it established seven of its well-known institutions of higher learning before 1800: Harvard (1636), Yale (1701), Brown (1764), Dartmouth (1769), Williams (1791), Vermont (1791), and Bowdoin (1794).

New Englanders, who were originally of British stock, in the 19th century were traditionally characterized as 'Yankees,' independent, thrifty, resourceful, with a knack for town government. Immigration from Europe after the Civil War helped create a dozen populous cities, with Boston as the hub of a metropolitan area (in 1960) of 2,600,000. Numerous French-Canadians came from the province of Quebec. The New Immigration made Boston an Irish city by the 20th century. It gave Rhode Island an Italian governor and Connecticut a Jewish governor, and the U.S. an Irish-Catholic President. The immigrant families gave support to traditional Puritan centers of learning as well as to commerce and industry, thus enriching the land of Cabots and Lodges.

Industrially the 200-odd different kinds of manufacture in New England (about two-thirds of all those in the U.S.) make it a 'little nation' within the Northeast region. Sectional as it remains, it continues to exert an influence on the rest of the nation quite out of proportion to its size and population.

New England Anti-Slavery Society, see *Antislavery societies.*

New England Company (1628–29), successor of the DORCHESTER COMPANY, was formed in an effort to revive that moribund joint-stock venture. It received a patent of land between the Merrimac and Charles rivers along the Massachusetts coast, and a small group of colonists (largely Puritan) took charge of the tiny settlement of Naumkeag (Salem), and appointed JOHN ENDECOTT as governor. They were shortly reorganized as the MASSACHUSETTS BAY COMPANY.

New England Company of 1649, see *Society for Propagation of the Gospel in New England.*

New England Confederation (1643), the most significant development of the period, was formed largely for defense against the Dutch, the French, and the Indians. As a result of experience in the Pequot War, in which military action had been poorly co-ordinated, representatives from the Massachusetts, Plymouth, Connecticut, and New Haven colonies met at Boston and organized the 'United Colonies of New England.' Boundary controversies were ironed out and the territorial integrity of each colony was guaranteed. The federation functioned through a board of eight commissioners, two from each colony, chosen annually by their respective legislatures. The commissioners were empowered to declare both offensive and defensive war, and were given jurisdiction over Indian affairs and intercolonial disputes. The league held together long enough to direct operations during King Philip's War (1675–76), and was not formally dissolved until 1684, when the Massachusetts charter was revoked.

Its chief weaknesses lay in the inability of the commissioners generally to do more than advise, and in the bickering among the colonies. Puritan Massachusetts, for instance, prevented liberal Rhode Island from joining. Yet it was the first confederation in American history and pointed the way toward federal union; in several respects it anticipated the Confederation of 1777.

New England Council, see *Council for New England.*

New England Dominion, see *Dominion of New England.*

New England Primer, famous schoolbook, was compiled by the Boston bookseller Benjamin Harris (*c.* 1673–1728), and first published about 1689. Crude couplets ('In Adam's fall/We sinned all') introduced the beginner to the alphabet and events in the Bible, both illustrated by woodcut pictures. The prayer, 'Now I lay me down to sleep,' was first printed in this primer. In its various revisions it held a central place in children's education, and during the next 150 years it was sold in immense quantities. Some 6,000,000 copies are conservatively estimated to have been printed, but today the book is rare.

New France was first permanently settled (Quebec, 1608) by CHAMPLAIN on the site discovered by CARTIER, whose voyages to Canada nearly three-quarters of a century earlier (1534–42) had established French claims to the St. Lawrence region. For the next 50 years the government made trading grants, but colonial growth was slow until Louis XIV assumed direct control (1663). He envisioned Canada as a loyal and religious peasant society, such as that of Brittany and Normandy (which in fact it became under British rule), but the young men attracted to the fur trade had different views, and the more adventurous of these trappers had reached the Dakotas before the English crossed the Appalachians.

Concurrently, intrepid JESUITS began their explorations and missionary work, and helped initiate the period of expansion whereby the boundaries of New France were extended to the Great Lakes and the entire Mississippi valley. These feats were accomplished by such men as JOLLIET, MARQUETTE, HENNEPIN, DULUTH, and especially LA SALLE, whose explorations into the central area of the North American continent were one of the glories of French enterprise. But these achievements had so little effect on French policy that in 1696 the aging Louis issued an edict commanding the *coureurs de bois* to cease exploring the wilderness for fur, select wives from the picked group of damsels he was sending over, and settle down.

The Glorious Revolution of 1688, which placed William III on the English throne, precipitated war between France and England. FRONTENAC, vigorous governor of New France for most of the quarter century before 1700 and one of the great colonial administrators in America, developed a strategy that France continued to follow even after his death in 1698. Frontenac envisaged a chain of forts, stretching along the St. Lawrence, through the Great Lakes, and down the Mississippi to New Orleans. Firmly entrenched in this semicircle, by solid alliance with the Indians and control of fur trade the French could put pressure on the western reaches of the English frontier from New England to Virginia. The friendly Spanish would do the same in the south, attacking north from Florida. This strategy was followed during the long period of dynastic struggles in the Old World (with intermittent truces) that resulted in four world wars, the American phases of which were known as the FRENCH AND INDIAN WARS (1689–1763).

Plausible as the French strategy was, it failed to retard the spread of English settlement or halt the growth of population in the English colonies. Thus more than a half-century of conflict remained indecisive. The last and most significant of the wars (1755–63) ended in America with the defeat of Montcalm on the Plains of Abraham above Quebec, which brought New France to an end as a political entity. But the remnant of that empire has left an indelible influence on both Canada and the U.S. The French people and their culture remain an enduring element both in the valley of the St. Lawrence and in Louisiana.

New Freedom was the term applied by Woodrow Wilson during his presidential campaign (1912) to the reforms he would seek to effect if elected. He outlined plans for lowering tariffs and revising the monetary system. In his view the federal government should act as umpire to reconcile diverging elements in the nation's economy. The New Freedom differed from Theodore Roosevelt's NEW NATIONALISM chiefly on the issue of monopoly control. Wilson viewed trusts as positive evils, threats to the very existence of free competition.

New Frontier was the term popularly used to characterize the aims of the Kennedy Administration (1961). It specifically applied to programs proposed to lessen unemployment, solve the housing problem, handle issues in the field of education, and provide medical care for the aged.

New Hampshire, one of the Thirteen Colonies, was the ninth (and decisive) state to ratify the Federal Constitution. Champlain visited (1605) at the mouth of the Piscataqua (the present site of Portsmouth), and John Smith's description (1614) publicized the region. The COUNCIL FOR NEW ENGLAND (1620) received much of it under royal grant, and Captain John Mason (1586–1635), former governor of Newfoundland (1615–21), having obtained rights between the Merrimack and Piscataqua rivers, in 1629 named the territory in honor of his English home county.

In 1630 farmers and fishermen from the south coast of England settled Portsmouth, New Hampshire's only seaport. New Hampshire was made a royal province in 1679, and its Massachusetts boundary was established in 1741. The dispute with New York over the so-called New Hampshire Grants (ultimately the state of Vermont) was settled in 1764. When the U.S.–Canada line was determined by the WEBSTER-ASHBURTON TREATY (1842), the present boundaries were fixed.

New Hampshire was settled largely by families moving up from Connecticut and Massachusetts. It was distinctly rural, inhabited during the colonial period only in the southern half, chiefly along the Connecticut and Merrimack rivers. Portsmouth, the one town of size and wealth, remained the capital until the Revolution, when New Hampshire became the first of the colonies to drive out the royal governor (1776). Exeter thereafter was the seat of government until 1808, when Concord was made the permanent capital.

During the 19th century the state's economy emerged primarily as industrial, and it continues to remain so, although on a relatively small, diversified scale. In the decade 1950–60 its population increased from 533,000 to 607,000. Manchester is its largest city (88,000). The WHITE MOUNTAINS, long a popular resort area, are important in the state's economy. The two leading institutions of higher learning are Dartmouth (Hanover, est. 1769), and the University of New Hampshire (Durham, est. 1866).

New Hampshire Grants, see *Vermont.*

New Harmony, a venture in UTOPIAN SOCIALISM, was the community on the Wabash river in Indiana, founded (1825) by ROBERT OWEN on the site previously occupied by the HARMONY SOCIETY. During the two years of its existence Owen sought to put in practice his communal theories of absolute equality of property and opportunity. He managed to attract a heterogeneous population of some 1000 settlers, but lack of any real authority bred dissensions that could not be harmonized. Its weekly journal, the *New-Harmony Gazette,* after 1829 became the *Free Enquirer,* an organ for socialist and agnostic opinion, edited by ROBERT DALE OWEN and FRANCES WRIGHT.

New Haven Colony was founded (1638) on Long Island Sound, chiefly in Connecticut, by members of the Massachusetts Bay Company under the leadership of JOHN DAVENPORT and THEOPHILUS EATON. It was the smallest of the Puritan commonwealths, and had no royal charter. It comprised the settlements in New Haven, Milford, Guildford, Stamford, and (on Long Island) Southold. The plantations all acquired their land from New Haven, and they recognized its jurisdiction. It was in fact an Old Testament commonwealth, more strict in its theocratic organization than Massachusetts. Since the Scriptures make no mention of trial by jury, New Haven did not permit them: magistrates dispensed justice. In this respect New Haven differed from the other New England colonies.

Eaton served as governor until his death (1658). During his administration the colony became a member of the NEW ENGLAND CONFEDERATION (1643). It was balked in its desire to make headway in commerce (it had purchased land on the Delaware from the Indians), and was hemmed in by Connecticut to the east and the Dutch to the west. It therefore supported itself by farming.

After the Restoration (1660), when JOHN WINTHROP, JR., went to England to procure a royal charter for Connecticut, he took with him New Haven's request for one under which the two colonial governments might function. The charter he secured (1662) unquestionably included New Haven, over which Connecticut began to extend its authority. New Haven fought absorption, but the surrender of New Netherland to English royal commissioners led the colonists to the reluctant conclusion that they would fare better under Connecticut rule than they would if they became a part of the province of the Duke of York. In 1664 the New Haven colony ceased to exist.

New humanism, which flourished in the U.S. during the 1920's, was an attempt to establish a standard for measuring artistic achievement, particularly in literature. Although the term had diverse meanings, under the leadership of IRVING BABBITT and PAUL ELMER MORE it emphasized the ethical human values that find their ultimate principle in restraint and reason, as exemplified in the classics.

New Jersey, one of the Thirteen Colonies, was originally that portion of NEW NETHERLAND lying between the Hudson and Delaware rivers ceded to Carteret and Berkeley in 1664 as the 'Province of Nova Caesaria or New Jersey.' Its boundaries were fixed as at present. From 1674 until 1702 the colony was divided under proprietary rule in a manner significant in the development of the state. South of a line running from Little Egg harbor (in the southeast) to the Delaware Water Gap (in the northwest), West Jersey was inhabited by Quakers who became an influential landed aristocracy. North of the line East Jersey was settled largely by Calvinists from Scotland and New England. Though the sections were politically united after 1702, until Trenton became the capital in 1790 the legislature met in alternate years at Perth Amboy (East Jersey) and Burlington (West Jersey). Subsequent cultural and economic ties in the north have remained with New York City, in the south with Philadelphia. As the conflict with England approached, anti-British sentiment spread from East Jersey through the colony, though the strength of the Tory party is attested by its contribution of six battalions of Loyalists. The patriot cause prevailed and a provincial congress assumed authority, and in 1776 they declared the state independent. During the war the state was strategically important, for it lay in the path of armies contending for control of the Hudson and Delaware rivers. For some time it was Washington's major concern and the scene of many engagements, notably the battles of TRENTON, PRINCETON, and MONMOUTH. After the war was concluded, New Jersey became the third state to ratify the Constitution.

During the next 50 years an enormous expansion transformed New Jersey, which had been a predominantly agricultural area, into an industrial region. Lying athwart land routes connecting the North and South, next to New York City and Philadelphia, with a network of canals and important shipping facilities, New Jersey became a main artery of commerce. After the Civil War the expanding labor market attracted large numbers of European immigrants. Since 1900 the population of the state has quadrupled, concentrated (in 1960) in the industrial cities of Newark (405,000), Jersey City (276,000), Paterson (143,000), Camden (117,000), and Trenton (114,000).

New Jersey is still an area of farm produce, especially truck farming. It is favored among the Middle Atlantic states because it has an economy that is both rural and urban. The oldest of its two-score institutions of higher learning are PRINCETON and RUTGERS.

New Jersey, College of, see *Princeton University.*

New Jersey Plan, see *Paterson Plan.*

New Jerusalem, Church of the, see *Swedenborgianism.*

Newlands Act (1913), one of the RAILROAD MEDIATION ACTS, established a Board of Mediation and Conciliation to persuade parties in labor disputes to engage in mediation. By 1916 this agency had adjusted over 60 controversies and averted strikes on 42 railroads. It was amended by the ESCH-CUMMINS ACT (1920).

Newlands Reclamation Act (1902) created the Reclamation Service (now the Bureau of Reclamation) in the Department of the Interior. It provided that revenue from the sale of arid lands in sixteen western states be placed in a fund for irrigation work. Important projects thus created include Elephant Butte Dam (New Mexico), Shoshone Dam (Wyoming), Lake Truckee Reservoir (Nevada), and the Gunnison Tunnel (Colorado).

New Lights, see *Great Awakening.*

New Mexico, first explored by Coronado (1540), was in 1598 annexed to the Spanish Empire as a region chiefly comprising the present states of Arizona and New Mexico. It soon became a great mission field, with Santa Fe (1609) as center of Indian trade and government, and (still) the capital. Albuquerque was laid out in 1706, thus establishing the foundations of the Spanish culture that remains today. The three bases of the unique cultural pattern of New Mexico are Indian, Spanish-American, and Anglo-American. The Anglo-American culture did not enter the area until after the Louisiana Purchase (1803). By 1822 wagon trains of American traders were moving along the SANTA FE TRAIL. Although the province was governed from Mexico City after 1821 (when Spanish rule ended), Mexican authority was weak on this frontier, and trade with the U.S. largely shaped economic conditions in New Mexico.

By the treaty of GUADALUPE HIDALGO (1848) the whole area became part of the U.S., and it was given territorial status in 1850. Its present boundary line with Mexico was fixed by the GADSDEN PURCHASE (1853), and the Arizona border was established in 1863. Indian troubles became less serious after the capture of GERONIMO in 1886. New Mexico was admitted to the Union as the 47th state in 1912.

A Rocky Mountain state with a mean elevation of 5700 feet, New Mexico is a region with a dry, invigorating climate, with spacious grazing lands, rugged mesas, wide deserts, and forested mountains with high, bare peaks. (Wheeler Peak rises to 13,160 ft.) Although the region is semi-arid, much of the area along the Rio Grande, which bisects the state, is irrigated. Some 13,000 square miles are under Federal control as national forests, national monuments, and Indian reservations (Apache, Navaho, Ute, and Pueblo). The stupendous Carlsbad Caverns, discovered in 1901 and still not fully explored, have been a National Park since 1930.

The chief minerals include petroleum, potassium salts, and natural gas. Its uranium deposits, the nation's largest, are being rapidly exploited. High-value manufacturing industries are developing on such a scale that in the decade 1950–60 the population of the state rose from 680,000 to 950,000; that of Albuquerque, the largest city, from 96,000 to 201,000. Atomic and space research centers are at Los Alamos, White Sands, Holloman, Kirtland, and Sandia. Santa Fe and Taos have attracted large artist colonies. The leading institution of higher learning is the University of New Mexico (Albuquerque, est. 1889).

New Nationalism was the phrase used by ex-President Theodore Roosevelt in a speech (August 1910), attacking the Supreme Court's attitude toward social legislation. It was interpreted as an assault upon the conservatism of the Taft administration. (The phrase and its philosophy derived from Herbert Croly's book, *The Promise of American Life,* 1909.) Roosevelt declared that the New Nationalism 'maintains that every man holds his property subject to the general right of the community to regulate its use to whatever degree the public welfare may require it.' He reaffirmed this principle in an address early in 1912, and laid special emphasis on the recall of judicial decisions, thereby widening the gulf between himself and Republican conservatives. On the issue of trusts the New Nationalism chiefly differed from Wilson's NEW FREEDOM (1912) in that Roosevelt believed trusts were not harmful so long as they were subject to Federal regulation. On such issues Roosevelt was proffered, and accepted, the presidential nomination of the newly formed PROGRESSIVE PARTY.

New Netherland, a territory of indefinite extent roughly from the site of Albany, New York, to Gloucester, New Jersey, was a commercial grant made in 1621 by the government of Holland to a company of merchants organized as the Dutch West India Company. Colonizers arrived in 1624 and marked out the Hudson river region for settlement. In 1626 PETER MINUIT, the first director-general (1626–31), purchased Manhattan Island from the Indians, and there established New Amsterdam as the seat of government.

Control was vested in wealthy PATROONS, who under the leadership of Minuit's successors, Wouter Van Twiller (1633–37), William Kieft (1638–47), and PETER STUYVESANT (1647–64), governed in the manner of feudal lords. The colony was afflicted by Indian wars, administrative squabbles, and commercial rivalries with England. In 1664 New Netherland was seized by authority of the Duke of York (later James II) and divided into two colonies, New York and New Jersey.

New Orleans, situated 100 miles above the mouth of the Mississippi river, is a major U.S. port of entry and the largest city in Louisiana, with a population (1960) of 627,000. Founded by BIENVILLE in 1718 as a strategic trading post, in 1722 it became the capital of French Louisiana. It was ceded to Spain in 1762, and reverted to France shortly before coming into the possession of the U.S. by the Louisiana Purchase (1803). When it became the capital of the state in 1818 (until 1849), it was a city of 18,000 with a European culture, predominantly Latin in character.

After Jackson had won his victory at the battle of New Orleans (1815), the 'queen city of the Mississippi' rapidly became the financial and commercial metropolis of the entire Mississippi valley, with a rapidly expanding population (160,000 in 1860). Ante-bellum New Orleans was a fabled combination of elegance and wickedness, culture and dockside brawls. It was noted for its gay society, its French opera, American theater, quadroon balls, cafés, and gambling houses. The charm of America's most picturesque city is still reflected in the distinctive architecture of the French quarter (*Vieux Carré*), the annual Mardi Gras festivals, the heritage of Creole and Cajun customs, and the Negro music from which jazz arose.

The golden era ended when New Orleans was captured (1862) in the Civil

War. The penetration of the Mississippi valley by railroads, the decline of steamboat traffic, and the growth of competing Gulf ports somewhat reduced the city's relative commercial importance. The life of New Orleans, with its long Spanish-French history, has produced a whole literature, best known in the works of Gayarré, Cable, Hearn, and Grace King. Its leading institution of higher learning is Tulane University (est. 1834).

New Orleans, Battle of (8 January 1815), the most spectacular U.S. victory in the War of 1812, and one of the worst defeats in the history of British arms, was unique in that it had no military value, since it was fought two weeks after the TREATY OF GHENT had been signed, ending the war. But Andrew Jackson's decisive repulse of the British attempt to seize the city (involving heavy losses to the enemy and almost none to the Americans) made Jackson a national hero and started him on a career that led to the White House.

New Plymouth Colony, see *Plymouth Colony.*

NEWPORT, CHRISTOPHER (*c.* 1565–1617), English mariner, was employed by the London Company to command its expeditions to Virginia. He made five voyages (1607–11). On the fourth voyage (1609) his ship was wrecked on the Bermudas. The incident furnished material for Shakespeare's *Tempest* and procured for England the lovely islands that are now her oldest colony.

Newport, Rhode Island, founded by WILLIAM CODDINGTON (1639), soon became a prosperous village. By 1700 it was an important seaport town, thriving on shipbuilding and the 'triangular trade' in rum, slaves, and molasses. Before the Revolution it had become a summer resort, attracting a considerable number of visitors from the South and the West Indies. During the Revolution the town was one of the most strategic seaports on the New England coast, and for more than three years it was occupied by the British (1776–79). Its population sharply decreased, and it never recovered its commercial prosperity. By mid-19th century it had developed as a fashionable resort for the very wealthy, whose expensive marble 'cottages' are now on occasion open to the public. Historic sites include the NEWPORT TOWER, Trinity Church (1726), the Sabbatarian Church (1729), the Redwood Library (1747), and the Touro Synagogue (1763). The Library and the Synagogue were designed by PETER HARRISON.

Newport Tower (Old Stone Tower) in Newport, Rhode Island, is a two-story circular structure built of native stone. Its origin is unknown, and it has been variously identified as a church (built by Norsemen?), a beacon, and a mill. A mill is mentioned in the will of Governor Benedict Arnold, who died in 1678.

New Republic, see *Croly, Herbert.*

New School for Social Research (1919), in New York City, was founded by such leading educators as J. H. ROBINSON, C. A. BEARD, JOHN DEWEY, and THORSTEIN VEBLEN as an institute to provide adult training in the social sciences and other fields of learning in a spirit of free inquiry. In 1933 it added a graduate faculty drawn from scholars driven from their posts in totalitarian countries, and it was known at the time as the 'University in Exile.' In 1965, with a faculty of 330, it enrolled 8000 students.

New Side, see *Great Awakening.*

New South, see *Grady, H. W.*

New Spain, the Spanish viceroyalty in North America, was created (1535) under Antonio de Mendoza, with Mexico City as its capital, and from it the Republic of Mexico is politically descended. The term came to signify loosely almost all the Spanish possessions in the Northern Hemisphere. Florida, much of the Gulf region, and the Southwest were explored by the CONQUISTADORS, and a great part of this continental expanse, the Southwest in particular, developed under Spanish law and customs for nearly 300 years. The power of New Spain in later years extended into the Far West, and in 1776 ANZA, who had been sent to explore Alta (Upper) California, founded San Francisco.

In 1670 Spain recognized the Savannah river as the northern boundary between the English colony of Georgia and

Spanish Florida. In Texas the boundary line shifted as Spanish influence moved eastward. In the Pacific Northwest and southward, Spanish retrogression began with the loss of Nootka (1790) and continued until 1853, when the GADSDEN PURCHASE completed the disposition of former Spanish territory in the U.S.

New Sweden, or New South Company, was organized (1633) with capital supplied by Dutch and Swedish investors. Through the influence of PETER MINUIT and others, the Company was chartered for settlement on the Delaware river. A small group of Swedes and Finns arrived there in 1638, and purchased land from the Indians on the west shore, from the site of Trenton, New Jersey, to the mouth of the Delaware Bay. Reorganized in 1642 with an extension of control by the Swedish crown, the Company bought out the Dutch, with whom thereafter they were in conflict. Under PETER STUYVESANT the Dutch built forts near Philadelphia and New Castle (Delaware), and thus controlled the approaches to New Sweden. When Stuyvesant took Fort Casimir (New Castle) in September 1655, Swedish rule in North America was ended. Official Swedish influence had been brief, but the log houses introduced by this venture gave an enduring architectural pattern to the westward-moving American frontier.

News agencies are local, national, international, or technical agencies which gather and distribute news to newspapers and news magazines. The oldest in the U.S., the ASSOCIATED PRESS, was an outgrowth of a combination dating back to the 1820's. The two next in size were Hearst's INTERNATIONAL NEWS SERVICE (1906), and the Scripps-Howard UNITED PRESS, which merged in 1958 to form United Press International. For the gathering of news the agencies depend on exchange agreements and on their own reporters. Information is generally transmitted to member publishers by teletype. Most of the news agencies in Europe are either controlled or subsidized by their governments; in the U.S. no such links exist.

Newspapers in the U.S. had their beginning with publication of the single issue of *Publick Occurrences* (Boston, 1690), which was unlicensed and was therefore promptly suppressed by royal authority. The first sustained journal was the Boston *News-Letter* (1704–76), which published local news gathered from many sources. Benjamin Franklin contributed lively items to his brother's *New England Courant* (1721–26) and was long associated with the Pennsylvania *Gazette* (1728–1815), which he edited (1729–66) and through which he introduced weather reports into American journalism. William Bradford edited the New York *Gazette* (1725–44), that colony's first newspaper. The Pennsylvania *Evening Post* appeared just at the close of the Revolution (1783). It was the earliest daily.

With the growth of political parties editors became primarily political henchmen rather than job printers, which formerly they had been. PHILIP FRENEAU, the first effective crusading newspaperman in America, edited the Jefferson-sponsored *National Gazette* (1791–93). NOAH WEBSTER, while editing the *American Minerva* (1793–1803), ardently supported the Federalists. But as the population increased and moved westward, national interests broadened and a basis was laid for the PENNY PRESS, independent of party and greatly extended in circulation.

The era of great editors who helped shape political affairs then began. JAMES GORDON BENNETT launched his New York *Herald* (1835) with no patron but the public, who were attracted by his pungent editorials and his comprehensive news coverage. Before the Civil War such leaders of opinion also included WILLIAM CULLEN BRYANT, HORACE GREELEY, SAMUEL BOWLES, and HENRY J. RAYMOND; after the war, WHITELAW REID, CHARLES A. DANA, E. L. GODKIN, HENRY W. GRADY, HENRY WATTERSON, JOSEPH MEDILL, JOSEPH PULITZER, and WILLIAM A. WHITE.

The methods of these editorial giants in dealing with the news varied widely. Pulitzer, like Bennett before him, and WILLIAM R. HEARST, exploited the sensational in a manner which came to be termed YELLOW JOURNALISM. Godkin and Reid were conservative. But all hold their place in the history of American JOURNALISM primarily for the vigor and persuasiveness of their editorial pages.

This period of individuality ended for the most part with the turn of the 19th century, when ADOLPH OCHS and others began shaping newspapers into commercial enterprises, emphasizing news over opinion, avoiding editorial leadership, and aiming chiefly at business success. By the second quarter of the 20th century news collecting, writing, editing, printing, distributing (by way of syndicated NEWS AGENCIES), and financing had become a gigantic industry, supported chiefly by advertising. Consolidation, standardization, technological advances in communication systems and photography, and disciplines inculcated through the study of reporting as an art changed the nature of American journalism. At its worst the change is reflected in the growth of TABLOIDS, largely dependent for their immense circulation upon COMIC STRIPS and other features designed for mass appeal. Yet at the same time newspapers made effective use of the columnist, whose comments on social problems and world affairs (often widely syndicated) might be quite independent of the policy of the paper in which they appeared. Such have been the columns of HEYWOOD BROUN, DOROTHY THOMPSON, MARK SULLIVAN, and WALTER LIPPMANN.

By 1965 English-language daily newspapers in the U.S. numbered more than 1700, with a combined circulation of 59,000,000 (550 Sunday papers, with a circulation of 47,000,000). (See separate articles on the New York *Evening Post,* New York *Herald, New York Times,* and New York *Tribune.*) At this time the newspaper with the largest circulation in the country is the tabloid New York *News* (2,224,000 daily, 3,206,000 Sunday). Well known and frequently quoted newspapers include Atlanta *Constitution,* Baltimore *Sun,* Chicago *Tribune, Christian Science Monitor,* Cleveland *Plain Dealer,* Denver *Post,* Des Moines *Register,* Detroit *Free Press,* Kansas City *Star,* Los Angeles *Times,* Louisville *Courier-Journal,* Philadelphia *Inquirer,* St. Louis *Post-Dispatch,* San Francisco *Examiner,* and Washington *Post.*

Newtown, see *Cambridge.*

New York, bordering on Canada, extends from Lake Champlain on the east to lakes Ontario and Erie on the west, with the Finger Lakes and the ADIRONDACK MOUNTAINS between. VERRAZANO presumably entered New York Bay in 1524, but the history of the region begins in 1609, the year in which CHAMPLAIN extended French claims by sailing down the lake that bears his name, and HENRY HUDSON in the service of the Dutch sailed up the Hudson river to Albany. During the 17th century French traders and missionaries penetrated its northern and western borders, but the IROQUOIS CONFEDERACY prevented French interference with the Dutch and English settlements that spread up the Hudson in the 18th century. The Dutch planted NEW NETHERLAND (1623), and established the PATROON system of landholding, the hallmark of colonial New York aristocracy. After the English Restoration (1660) the Duke of Albany and of York (later James II) received from his brother Charles II a patent to New Netherland, based on claims dating back to the explorations of JOHN CABOT. In 1664 an English expedition forced the Dutch to surrender New Amsterdam (then renamed New York) and thenceforth, except for a brief interlude in 1673–74, the colony remained a British possession until the Revolution.

The English alliance with the Iroquois opened up central New York to settlement, though the FRENCH AND INDIAN WARS hindered development, and much of western New York remained wilderness into the 19th century. During the 18th century the New York Assembly (as the state legislature is still named), aware of the colony's growing commercial importance, exercised increasing independence of royal authority. (The libel case of the printer JOHN PETER ZENGER in 1735 illustrates the merchants' protest against an arbitrary governor.) When the issues leading to war with Great Britain came to a head, New Yorkers were divided. Many of the great landholders were Loyalists, although patriotic sentiment was not entirely a matter of class division. The British captured New York City in 1776 and held it throughout the war, but the colony had declared its independence and functioned as a state from Kingston, its first capital. In 1777 control of New York was pivotal in the British over-all plan to sever New England from the South. The many patriot forays from the Mohawk to the Genessee rivers in general checked British aims, and the battle of SARATOGA (1777) proved decisive in the patriot cause.

Under the leadership of such statesmen as ALEXANDER HAMILTON, JOHN JAY, and GOUVERNEUR MORRIS, New York became the 11th state to ratify the Constitution (1788). For a brief period (1789–90) New York City was the capital of the new nation, and it continued to be so for the state until Albany was permanently chosen in 1797. Development thereafter was rapid, and by 1810 New York had become, as it remained for over 150 years, the most populous state in the union. (In 1963 California outstripped New York in population.) The trans-state ERIE CANAL (1825) opened western commerce to both the east and to Europe, and made New York City the great shipping and financial center it still continues to be.

A new constitution in 1827 abolished slavery. The growing leadership in the state in finance, commerce, and industry was reflected in the immense power it came to exert in politics, and its governors continue to be potential presidential candidates. Solidly for the Union in the issues leading to the Civil War, it helped swing the 1860 election to Lincoln, and generously furnished troops and supplies. The war was a factor in enlarging the size and number of the state's industrial and commercial enterprises, which today embrace the whole range of manufacture. Several of its cities were pioneers in industry, notably Buffalo, Rochester, Syracuse, and Schenectady. The conservative 'upstate' farmers are an important element in the state's economy, and farm produce from dairies, orchards, vineyards, and (Long Island) potato fields make New York the leading agricultural state in the Northeast.

Among the three-score institutions of higher learning the best known include Columbia (New York City, est. 1754), Union (Schenectady, est. 1795), Hamilton (Clinton, est. 1812), Colgate (Hamilton, est. 1819), and Cornell (Ithaca, est. 1865). In 1784 the University of the State of New York was chartered as a unique administrative organization to supervise all educational activity. In 1894 the state created a board of regents to control professional and technical schools through examinations. The legislature in 1948 created the State University of New York, composed of units throughout the state and administered by a board of trustees.

New York Central Railroad, largest system in the eastern U.S., originated (1853) as a consolidation of many small railroads of the state, connecting Albany and Buffalo. Cornelius Vanderbilt as president (1867–77) built the system into an empire that connected New York with Chicago. By 1914, with trunk lines in several states, the Central linked many of the cities of the eastern seaboard with those of the Midwest. In 1965 the Interstate Commerce Commission approved plans for a merger with the PENNSYLVANIA RAILROAD.

New York City, with a population (in 1960) of 7,782,000, is the nation's largest city and the center of the most congested metropolitan area (14,000,000 inhabitants within a radius of twenty miles) in the Western Hemisphere. Situated at the mouth of the Hudson river, Greater New York (so chartered in 1898) comprises the five boroughs of MANHATTAN, THE BRONX, BROOKLYN, Richmond (STATEN ISLAND), and Queens (on LONG ISLAND). As New Amsterdam, on the tip of Manhattan, in 1626 it was the capital of NEW NETHERLAND, and it so remained until the British seized and renamed it in 1664. Though the city was smaller and less important than Philadelphia and Boston during most of the colonial period, it nevertheless developed as a major commercial and shipping center during the first half of the 18th century, and by the time King's College (Columbia) was founded in 1754, many of the city's churches, schools, newspapers, and theaters were well established. After passage of the STAMP ACT (1765) it vigorously supported the patriot cause, and its SONS OF LIBERTY forced Governor Tryon from the city in 1775. Washington made it his headquarters (April 1776) after the British captured Boston, but his defeat in the Battle of Long Island in August forced him to evacuate his forces, and New York thereafter remained in the hands of the British until they formally withdrew in November 1783. Washington then led contingents of the American army down Bowery Lane and Pearl Street to the waterfront amid scenes of tumultuous welcome, and he bade farewell to his officers at a dinner in FRAUNCES TAVERN.

The city was the capital of the colony and state until 1797. In 1785 it became the capital of the confederated states, and it was the first capital of the new nation (1789–90). The seat of government was then transferred to Philadelphia. The balcony of Federal Hall (site of the present Subtreasury Building) was the scene of Washington's inauguration.

Second in size to Philadelphia until 1810, in that year the census reported their populations as 96,373 and 91,874. The phenomenal growth of New York thereafter as the financial, commercial, and shipping center of the nation (with a population of 813,000 in 1860) stemmed in large part from the excellence of its harbor, and from the completion of the Erie Canal (1825), whereby New York became the world-wide distribution point for burgeoning western manufactures and produce. The financing of vast railroad networks increased the significance and power of WALL STREET. By 1850 TAMMANY HALL had made the city a Democratic stronghold. Before the Civil War immigrants began pouring into the city from various European countries, creating the slum areas of the lower EAST SIDE. After the Civil War migration from the South made the population of HARLEM predominantly Negro. (The influx of Puerto Ricans began after 1940.) By the turn of the 20th century an influx from all sections of the U.S. was under way; New York had become the mecca of aspirants to careers in trade, finance, and the arts. In 1900 the population was nearly 3,500,000.

So cosmopolitan is the city, and so magnetic are its attractions to students, artists, authors, and all ranks of professional experts, that any summary of its essential 'character' is impossible. Long a center of musical activity (with such organizations as the METROPOLITAN OPERA COMPANY), it has from colonial days been the headquarters of the American theater, symbolized in the name BROADWAY. The resources of such institutions as the NEW YORK PUBLIC LIBRARY, the METROPOLITAN MUSEUM OF ART, and the AMERICAN MUSEUM OF NATURAL HISTORY, vast as they are, represent but a fraction of New York's cultural and educational facilities. Architecturally New York is best known for the modern development of the SKYSCRAPER. The great diversity of its people, of all races and national origins, has created colorful neighborhoods, of which only Harlem can be considered a ghetto in any real sense.

Besides Columbia, among the oldest and best of its score of institutions of higher learning are New York University (est. 1831), Fordham (est. 1841), and the College of the City of New York (est. 1847).

New York, City University of (1961), is a system first organized (1929) as the College of the City of New York. Seven colleges comprise the University, of which the principal institutions are City College (1847), Hunter College (1870), Brooklyn College (1930), and Queens College (1937). (The Community Colleges in the Bronx, in Queens, and on Staten Island are Junior Colleges.) In 1962, when 84,000 students were enrolled, the city's Board of Higher Education adopted plans for an expansion which is expected to increase the enrollment to 160,000 by 1975.

New York *Daily News*, see *Patterson, J. M.*

New York *Evening Post* was founded as a Federalist organ in 1801. WILLIAM CULLEN BRYANT joined the staff in 1826, and he became its editor. For 52 years the paper expressed Bryant's views emphatically, at first Democratic, and after 1854 Republican. Under CARL SCHURZ (1881–84) and E. L. GODKIN (1884–1900) the paper became famous for its independence. From 1881 to 1918 it was controlled by the VILLARD family. Since 1934 it has been called the *Post*. In 1965 it maintained a circulation of 337,500 daily and 261,000 Sunday issues.

New York *Herald*, founded (1835) as a penny daily by JAMES GORDON BENNETT and carried on by his son, was long known for its sensationalism (notably for financing Stanley's trip to find Livingstone in Africa), its full news coverage, and for feature writing by such authors as Mark Twain and Richard Harding Davis. In 1924 it merged with the NEW YORK TRIBUNE to form the New York *Herald Tribune,* a Republican daily known especially for such columnists as WALTER LIPPMANN, and for *Books,* a Sunday supplement of reviews. The younger Bennett founded the Paris *Herald* (1887), which became the best English-language paper on the continent, and continued after 1924 as the Paris edition of the *Herald Tribune*. In 1965 the New York edition had a circulation of 306,870 daily and 380,000 Sunday. Hampered by strikes, it ceased publication in 1966.

New York Philharmonic-Symphony Orchestra, see *Music*.

New York Public Library (1895), second in size to the Library of Congress among U.S. libraries, was consolidated from the Astor Library (1848), the Lennox Library (1870), and the Tilden Trust, created (1886) by the bequest of SAMUEL J. TILDEN. This forms its present reference department, to which have been added other notable collections. (Its circulation department is maintained by the city.) Its resources of books, manuscripts, maps, illustrations, and related material total nearly 30,000,000 items. It publishes reports and bulletins, and its facilities make it one of the leading research centers in the world.

New York, State University of, established in 1948, comprises units throughout the state and is administered from Albany by a single board of fifteen trustees. It includes the ten teachers colleges of the state, two liberal arts colleges, a maritime academy, and numerous technical and professional schools. In 1965 it enrolled 66,000 students.

New York *Sun*, founded (1833) by Benjamin Henry Day (1810–89), was New York's first penny daily newspaper, flourishing at first on a sensational police column and scientific hoaxes. Under the editorship (1868–97) of C. A. DANA it became known as the 'newspaperman's newspaper.' It was notable for its readability and for its feature articles, written by such able reporters as R. H. DAVIS, JACOB RIIS, and ALBERT BRISBANE. After Dana's death the *Sun* was managed by a succession of editors. In 1950 it merged with the New York *World-Telegram*.

New York Times, daily newspaper, was founded (1851) by HENRY J. RAYMOND, under whose guidance it was instrumental in helping to create the Republican party (1854), which it strongly supported until Raymond's death (1869). During the 1870's it worked for political reforms, and it led the attack on the TWEED RING. Its circulation later declined until it came under the ownership (1896) of ADOLPH OCHS, who not only re-established its original standards of accuracy, but, with a large corps of correspondents, gave it a world-wide circulation and a reputation as the most eminent of all American newspapers. Since the death of Ochs (1935), the *Times* has remained under the management of his family, who have continued his policy of conservative journalism, thorough and careful reporting, and coverage of 'All the News That's Fit to Print.' In 1965 its daily circulation had increased to more than 729,000, and its Sunday issue to more than 1,400,000.

New-York Tribune, daily newpaper, was founded (1841) by HORACE GREELEY, who edited it until his death (1872). Greeley attracted such journalists as C. A. DANA, for some years its managing editor (1849–62); and GEORGE RIPLEY, its literary critic (1849–80). During Greeley's editorship the *Tribune* became the most widely quoted newspaper in the U.S. WHITELAW REID succeeded Greeley, and under Reid's editorship (1872–1912) the *Tribune* remained the most powerful Republican organ in the country. In 1924 it merged with the NEW YORK HERALD to form the New York *Herald Tribune,* which continued under the ownership of Whitelaw Reid's son, Ogden Mills Reid (1882–1947), and of his son, Ogden Rogers Reid (1925–). In 1957 the Reid family sold the newspaper to John Hay Whitney. Hampered by strikes, it ceased publication in 1966.

New York University (1831), a privately endowed co-educational institution, since 1891 has been situated on several widely distributed campuses in New York City. It has extensive facilities, and it offers graduate training in many fields. Its pioneering ventures include the establishment of the first university chair in fine arts (1835), university teacher-training school (1890), school of retailing (1919), and school of aeronautics (1925). Its medical center (1898) is Bellevue Hospital Medical College. In 1965, with an endowment of $59,500,000 and a faculty of 3900, it enrolled 39,500 students.

New York, University of the State of, chartered in 1784, is a unique organization which now oversees all educational activities in the state. Its board of regents (1894), which is responsible only to the state legislature, acts as a legislative body to determine policy, and grants educational charters, professional licenses, and honorary degrees.

New York *World*, see *Pulitzer, Joseph.*

Nez Percé Indians, a Pacific Northwest tribe of Shahaptin stock, were so named by the French presumably because some of them wore nose pendants. Lewis and Clark encountered them in 1805. They then numbered some 6000. The uprising under Chief JOSEPH (1877) brought on the last and most extensive Indian war in the area. Today some 1500 are located on a reservation in Idaho.

Niagara Falls, one of the scenic splendors of North America, some 190 ft. high and 2500 ft. wide, are on the international line between Canada and the U.S. at a point near Buffalo where the water from Lake Erie drops into Lake Ontario. During the colonial period the Falls were strategic to the control of the upper Great Lakes and were the site of a border fort. The cataract was first described by HENNEPIN, who viewed it in 1678. The erection of the Niagara Falls power plant (1894) inaugurated the era of hydroelectric power. Its present plant, which was completed in 1963, generates more electricity than any other in the world (2,190,000 kw.).

Nick Carter, see *Dime novels.*

NICOLET, JEAN (1598–1642), French explorer of the Old Northwest, came to New France with Champlain (1618), under whose direction he made a notable voyage (1634) exploring the coast of Lake Michigan (which he discovered) as far as Green Bay. The maps he made of the region guided the early fur traders.

NICOLLET, JOSEPH NICOLAS (1786–1843), eminent French mathematician, emigrated to the U.S. in 1832 to escape embarrassing debts. With assistance from the wealthy St. Louis CHOUTEAU family of fur traders he led an expedition (1836–37) that surveyed the sources of the Mississippi. Secretary of War Joel Poinsett then sent him on a government surveying expedition (1838–41), with John C. Frémont as his chief assistant, which mapped the region between the upper waters of the Mississippi and Missouri rivers. The map bound into Nicollet's *Report* (1843) has been called 'one of the greatest contributions ever made to American geography.' Nicollet was the first explorer in America to make careful barometrical observations of altitudes.

NIEBUHR, REINHOLD (1892–), professor of applied Christianity at Union Theological Seminary (1930–60), was a leading Protestant theologian. He developed the theme that mere reason is pretentious, since faith is a rock deep-based in nonrational reality, and that man can never embody the will of God, since God is 'absolutely other.' His brilliant studies, which maintain that man has within him a power that cannot be derived from the natural order, include *Nature and Destiny of Man* (2 vols., 1941–43), *Faith and History* (1949), and *The Self and the Drama of History* (1955).

NILES, HEZEKIAH (1777–1839), Baltimore journalist, founded *Niles' Weekly Register* (1811–49). (In later years the title varied.) At a time of partisan journalism, this generally unbiased record of events had a national and international circulation surpassing that of any other American paper of its day, and it remains a major source for the history of the period. It was reprinted in 1947.

NIMITZ, CHESTER WILLIAM (1885–1966), a graduate of the U.S. Naval Academy (1905), was serving as chief of the Bureau of Navigation in 1941. He was selected to head the naval fighting forces in the Pacific when the U.S. entered World War II (8 December). His strategy of 'island hopping' up from the South Pacific made possible the decisive victory in the naval battle of GUADALCANAL (November 1942). He pursued the offensive during 1943, until his ships and planes were within effective bombing distance of Japan. At the war's end he commanded the largest fighting fleet in history (6256 ships and 4847 combat aircraft). Nimitz was made a fleet admiral of the navy in 1944, and for two years after the Japanese surrender he served as chief of naval operations (1945–47).

Nine-Power Pact, see *Washington Conference.*

Nineteenth Amendment (1920) to the U.S. Constitution prohibits the federal or state governments from restricting the right to vote 'on account of sex.' It was the culmination of the FEMINISM movement, which had long agitated for WOMAN SUFFRAGE.

Ninth Amendment to the U.S. Constitution, see *Bill of Rights.*

NIZA, see *Marcos de Niza.*

NOAH, MORDECAI MANUEL (1785–1851), born in Philadelphia, was scion of a distinguished Portuguese-Jewish family. He became prominent as a politician, journalist, and playwright. After serving as consul in Tunis (1813–15), he returned to New York, where he held public office, founded and edited several newspapers, and wrote for the New York stage. He was acutely aware of the problems of the Jewish people and was an early supporter of a movement that preceded the Zionist movement.

Nobel Prizes, five in number, were provided by the bequest of the Swedish scientist Alfred Nobel (1833–96). Since 1901 a committee in Stockholm has made annual awards for the most significant contributions in the fields of chemistry, physics, medicine, and literature. Nobel preferred to have the Peace Prize selected by a committee of Norwegians, and it is made in Oslo. The prizes may be given to persons of any nationality, and each amounts to approximately $40,000. American recipients of prizes in the sciences are named under CHEMISTRY, PHYSICS, and MEDICINE.

American recipients of the Peace Prize have been THEODORE ROOSEVELT (1906), ELIHU ROOT (1912), WOODROW WILSON (1919), CHARLES G. DAWES (1925), FRANK B. KELLOGG (1929), NICHOLAS MURRAY BUTLER and JANE ADDAMS (1931), CORDELL HULL (1945), J. R. MOTT and EMILY BALCH (1946), RALPH BUNCHE (1950), GEORGE C. MARSHALL (1953), LINUS C. PAULING (1962), and MARTIN LUTHER KING (1964).

American recipients of the prize in literature have been SINCLAIR LEWIS (1930), EUGENE O'NEILL (1936), PEARL BUCK (1938), T. S. ELIOT (1948), WILLIAM FAULKNER (1949), ERNEST HEMINGWAY (1954), and JOHN STEINBECK (1962).

Nobility, Titles of, are forbidden by the Constitution of the U.S. (Art. 1, sec. 9). During the colonial period only three native-born Americans were honored by title, all below the peerage. WILLIAM PHIPS was knighted (1687), and baronetcies were conferred on WILLIAM PEPPERRELL (1746) and WILLIAM JOHNSON (1755).

Nominating convention, see *National convention.*

'Non-entangling alliances' is a phrase from Washington's Farewell Address. See *Isolationism.*

Nonimportation Act (1806), intended as an answer to Napoleon's CONTINENTAL SYSTEM and the British ORDERS IN COUNCIL, forbade the importation of specified British goods, in an effort to force Great Britain to relax her rigorous rulings on cargoes. It was supplemented by a diplomatic mission to England for negotiations on impressments and seizures. The failure of the mission and the repeated postponement of implementation of the Act led to passage in 1807 of the much bolder EMBARGO ACT.

Nonimportation Agreements, see *Stamp Act* (1765), *Townshend Acts* (1767).

Nonintercourse Acts, see *Berlin Decree* (1806), *Milan Decree* (1807), *Embargo Act* (1807), *Macon's Bill No. 2* (1810).

Nonpartisan League (1915–20) originated among the radical Scandinavian and Russian wheat farmers of North Dakota, who were led by an ex-Socialist, Arthur C. Townley. It spread into fifteen wheat and corn states of the upper Mississippi valley. The League particularly denounced the Minneapolis millers and the railroads, and urged state-owned grain elevators and mills (which they managed to obtain in North Dakota) and stricter railroad regulations. By 1920 they felt strong enough to organize the national FARMER-LABOR PARTY as a successor to the League. They elected two Minnesota U.S. senators, a governor of South Dakota, and many state and national legislators. Out of this movement came the powerful farm bloc of the 1920's.

Nootka Sound Controversy (1789) arose when an Anglo-Spanish dispute erupted over fur trading rights on the coast of Vancouver Island. When a Spanish contingent highjacked the British traders and sent them as prisoners to Mexico, war threatened. A Convention (1790) settled the dispute and opened the North Pacific coast to British colonization, but the affair alerted Secretary of State Jefferson to the problem of American neutrality in matters of European rivalry west of the Mississippi, and to the nation's interest in future development of that vast terrain. He thus arrived at convictions that, as President, he implemented by the Louisiana Purchase.

NORDICA, LILLIAN (1857–1914), born Lillian Norton at Farmington, Maine, was the first American opera singer to gain international fame. She studied in Milan, where she made her debut (1879) as a soprano. She returned to America in 1883, and sang at the Metropolitan (1890–1908), where she attracted audiences by her authoritative Wagnerian interpretations, particularly in the role of Isolde.

Normal schools, see *Teachers colleges.*

'Normalcy,' a term coined (1920) in an address by Senator Warren G. Harding ('America's present need is not heroics but healing, not nostrums but normalcy'), specifically signified a return to high tariff, no government interference with business enterprise, and a nationalistic foreign policy. The slogan 'back to normalcy,' used effectively in the Republican campaign that year, helped carry Harding into the White House.

Normandy Campaign (6 June–25 July 1944), which opened the western front in the final European phase of World War II, was 'Operation Overlord,' the invasion of the continent through the Normandy region of France. The spearhead assault by a force of 176,000 troops was made possible by 4000 transports and 600 warships, which ferried troops and armor across the Channel from England, under a protective cover of 11,000 airplanes. In the first week the Allies landed 326,000 men, 50,000 vehicles, and 100,000 tons of supplies on the Cotentin peninsula. By late June U.S. forces had captured Cherbourg and demolished its harbor works, and the Allied armies were multiplying in number and effectiveness. The British captured Caen on 9 July, and U.S. troops entered Saint Lô, gateway to the south, on 18 July. The breakout from Saint Lô a week later was a powerful armored thrust into Brittany, which by 10 August had been overrun and cut off by the U.S. Third Army under General George Patton. The action thus concluded the Allied offensive in Normandy and opened the battle of France.

NORRIS, FRANK [BENJAMIN FRANKLIN] (1870–1902), Chicago-born novelist, pioneered in naturalism in American fiction with *McTeague* (1899), a picture of slow degeneration. His 'Epic of Wheat,' a trilogy dealing with the problems of Western farmers, began with *The Octopus* (1901), the first important thesis-novel written in the U.S., and was followed by *The Pit* (1903), a study of stock market greed. The third section (*The Wolf*), on exports, was still in outline when he died at thirty-two. The completed portions of the 'Epic' are documents in the history of MUCKRAKING.

NORRIS, GEORGE WILLIAM (1861–1944), while serving as a district judge in Nebraska was sent to Congress (1903–13), where his fearless liberalism won a reform in the House rules by making the powerful Rules committee elective. He was in the Senate for 30 years (1913–43), where he devoted himself to administrative reform, and without regard to party affiliations fought for Federal power projects and farm-relief measures, all of which ultimately were adopted. In

1936 he was read out of the Republican party, and he became an independent. He was father of TVA, and Norris Dam in Tennessee is named for him.

Norris–La Guardia Anti-Injunction Act (1932) was the first attempt to erect strong safeguards against the misuse of the injunction in labor disputes. A major gain for labor, it forbade injunctions that would sustain anti-union employment ('yellow-dog') contracts, or prevent strikes, boycotts, or picketing.

NORTH, FREDERICK, 8th Baron (1732–92), known as Lord North, was the British Prime Minister (1770–82) during the American Revolution. Though wiser as a statesman than his sovereign, he nevertheless supported the policies of George III, and aided the passage of legislation that the colonists considered intolerable. After the battle of Saratoga (1777), North was eager to recognize a major change in colonial dealings, but the king even forbade North's repeated efforts to resign until the surrender of Cornwallis at Yorktown.

North African Invasion (Operation Torch), which began 8 November 1942, was the first U.S. offensive in the European theater of operations in World War II. Commanded by Eisenhower, a combined army of 150,000 American and 140,000 British troops landed on the French North African coast. After brief resistance at Oran, Algiers, and Casablanca, the French under Admiral Darlan capitulated, and at Darlan's urging, French North Africa went over to the Allies. On 15 November Allied troops advanced into Tunisia, and two weeks later the French fleet (at Toulon) was scuttled by its crew to prevent seizure by the Germans. With U.S. and British approval, Darlan became chief of state in French North Africa (1 December). When he was assassinated (24 December) General Henri Giraud was made chief of state. In January 1943 Tripoli fell to the British, and on 6 February Eisenhower was appointed commander in chief of all Allied forces in North Africa. In the spring, after fighting their way toward the coastal plain along the Gulf of Tunisia, General Montgomery's British forces captured Tunis and General Bradley's American troops smashed into Bizerte (both fell on 7 May). On 12 May the remnants of Rommel's Axis armies surrendered, and the Allies had won their first important victory.

North American Phalanx (1843–54), established by ALBERT BRISBANE at Red Bank, New Jersey, was the most scientifically planned of the many short-lived Fourierist communities. The colony occupied a considerable area of fertile land, maintained a three-story phalanstery, a grist mill, and a large orchard. Families, totaling some 1200 persons, ate in commons but had separate living quarters. They devoted themselves to a voluntary agrarian-handicraft economy, and the children were carefully educated. When the mill burned down the association was dissolved.

North American Review (1815–1939), founded in Boston as an outgrowth of the *Monthly Anthology* (1803–11), the organ of the literary Anthology Club, as first edited by William Tudor sought chiefly to raise the standards of American literature and criticism. It was an informed and scholarly journal. The *Review* later achieved distinction for its historical studies under the editorship of such historians and men of letters as Edward Everett, Jared Sparks, J. G. Palfrey, C. E. Norton, J. R. Lowell, Henry Adams, and H. C. Lodge. After it moved to New York (1878), it gave increasing attention to contemporary social and political movements.

North Atlantic Treaty Organization (NATO), headed by a Council of foreign ministers, was constituted by the twelve signatories of the North Atlantic Treaty (1949): Belgium, Canada, Denmark, France, Great Britain, Iceland, Italy, Luxembourg, the Netherlands, Norway, Portugal, and the U.S. Greece and Turkey joined in 1952, West Germany in 1955.

Inaugurated by the TRUMAN DOCTRINE (1947), the Treaty was a basic element in the 'stop communism' foreign policy of the U.S. The parties agreed that an attack upon any one member should be considered an attack upon all. NATO forces operate under an integrated command in Paris, Supreme Headquarters of Allied Powers in Europe (SHAPE), but all retain their national identities.

Generals who have served NATO as Supreme Allied Commanders are as follows.

Dwight D. Eisenhower (1950–52)
Matthew B. Ridgway (1952–53)
Alfred Gruenther (1953–56)
Lauris Norstad (1956–62)
Lyman L. Lemnitzer (1962–)

North Carolina, one of the Thirteen Colonies, was first touched on by VERRAZANO in 1524, and in the 1580's Sir Walter Raleigh made an unsuccessful attempt to colonize ROANOKE ISLAND. In about 1653 settlers from Virginia began to locate along Albemarle Sound. Charles I had given a large patent south of Virginia to Sir Robert Heath, who named the area Carolina in honor of the king but failed to settle it. In 1663 Charles II made over the territory to the *Carolina Proprietors,* who appointed a governor for the province of Albemarle, known after 1691 as North Carolina. In 1729 it became a royal colony. During the next 40 years Scotch-Irish and Germans moved from Pennsylvania into the piedmont plateau, and by 1775 settlements had reached the western mountains. Patriots openly resisted the Stamp Act, and their delegates to the Continental Congress were the first to vote for independence. North Carolina, with Raleigh as its capital, became the 12th state to ratify the Constitution (1789). Prior to 1835 the planter-controlled government, unwilling to allot funds for education or transport in undeveloped areas, delayed the state's growth. The state joined the Confederacy in May 1861, managed to keep the important harbor of Wilmington free from blockade during most of the war, and was the site of the final surrender of Confederate armies, Johnston's capitulation to Sherman. After readmission to the Union in 1868, the state, almost entirely agricultural in its economy, suffered debilitating readjustment. The ante-bellum plantation system was replaced by farm tenancy, and though tobacco manufacturing created wealth for such 'tobacco barons' as J. B. Duke and R. J. Reynolds, agriculture long remained in a critical condition.

After World War I economic and social changes resulted from the merging of three state educational institutions into a greater UNIVERSITY OF NORTH CAROLINA, which became the most important single cultural influence in the state. DUKE UNIVERSITY came into prominence in 1925, when it was heavily endowed by James B. Duke.

Topographically North Carolina begins as a coastal plain, rising through the central plateau to the Blue Ridge of the Appalachian highlands. Here is located the Great Smoky Mountains National Park (est. 1930). In the decade 1950–60 the population of the three largest cities noticeably increased: Charlotte (134,000 to 201,000), Greensboro (74,000 to 120,000), and Winston-Salem (87,000 to 111,000).

North Carolina, University of, state coeducational institution at Chapel Hill, was founded (1789) as a men's college. In 1795 it was rechartered, and it became the first state university in the U.S. It is one of the leading educational institutions in the South, and it offers graduate training in many fields. In 1965, with a faculty of 2510, it enrolled 20,500 students.

North Dakota in its eastern portion lies in the PRAIRIE REGION. Its western reaches lead into the PLAINS REGION. (The name derives from that of a powerful tribe of Sioux Indians.) First inhabited by the Mandan, Arikara, and Hidatsa tribes, it was explored in the 18th century by French fur traders. The northwest half became part of the U.S. with the Louisiana Purchase (1803), and the southeast was acquired from Great Britain in 1818, when the international boundary with Canada was fixed at the 49th parallel. When Lewis and Clark wintered with the Mandans in 1804–5, Canadian trading posts were already established in the Red river valley, and for another half century the fur industry dominated the region. Only one permanent farming community (at Pembina, 1851) had been located when Dakota Territory was organized in 1861. By division of the area (into North and South Dakota), North Dakota was formed, and it was admitted a state of the union in 1889, with Bismarck as its capital. (Fargo is the largest city, with a population of 46,000 in 1960.)

Immigrants from central Europe and Scandinavia first developed agriculture, today the state's principal industry. Petroleum is its chief mineral product.

Vast supplies of lignite coal, annually produced in millions of tons, underlie the western counties. Exposed to the extremes of continental temperature, and treeless except along the rivers, the region is subject to constant winds. The fertility of the soil has made the state a leading wheat producer. The principal institution of higher learning is the University of North Dakota (Grand Forks, est. 1883).

Northeast (The North), in which are situated nine of the original Thirteen States, includes New England (the northern group), New York, Pennsylvania, New Jersey (central), and Delaware, Maryland, and West Virginia (southern). Historically the region first became known to Europeans after Verrazano explored the Atlantic seaboard from North Carolina to Maine (1524), but detailed information waited upon the later voyages of Champlain (1604–8), Henry Hudson (1609–11), and John Smith (1607–14). The earliest settlements were those of the Plymouth Colony (1620, English Separatists), Massachusetts Bay Colony (1630, English Puritans), New Sweden (1638, Swedish on the Delaware), and New Netherland (1655, Dutch on the Hudson). The grant to William Penn (1681) opened up settlements in Pennsylvania to large numbers of German immigrants.

The first attempt at union was proposed in the Albany Congress (1754), called in an attempt to make common cause in facing the impending French and Indian War (1755–63) on the western frontier. A great part of the region was the theater of the War of Independence (1775–83), and its largest centers, Boston, New York, and Philadelphia, were focally involved, the two latter becoming the first and second capitals of the new nation. New York outstripped Boston as a shipping center after the Erie Canal (1825) opened the port of New York to western commerce. The Civil War briefly reached northern soil in Pennsylvania, where the battle of Gettysburg helped determine the fate of the Union.

The Northeast is a metropolitan region with upward of 40 cities of 100,000 and a total population of more than 50,000,000 (in 1960), yet it occupies but 7 per cent of the nation's area. Though much of it remains as rural today as it was a century ago, the main axis of the region, stretching from southern New Hampshire to northern Virginia, and from the Atlantic to the Appalachian foothills (an area 600 miles long and 30 to 100 miles wide), has become a megalopolis: a huge complex of city centers radiating out from Boston, New York, Philadelphia, Baltimore, and Washington. In general they are decentralized residential and manufacturing areas with an increasing number of parklands. Although this strip is less than a third of the total Northeast, in 1965 it supported an estimated population of 40,000,000, nearly four-fifths of the region's total. The French geographer Jean Gottman has termed it 'the cradle of a new order in the organization of inhabited space,' since within its boundaries the old distinctions between urban and rural no longer apply. It has become the hub of U.S. corporate direction and the center for international relations. Here is concentrated nearly 40 per cent of the nation's wealth, with half the foreign trade clearing its ports.

The Northeast, closest to Europe geographically and culturally, has the most sophisticated and highly educated population in the U.S. Within the region are established the oldest and best-known publishing, music, art, and theater centers; libraries; museums; learned societies; and universities.

Northern Securities Case (1904), see *Hill, J. J.*

Northwest, see *Pacific Northwest.*

North West Company, a fur-trading combination of Montreal merchants, was permanently formed in 1787. The actual traders were 'Northwesters' who broke new territory from Lake Superior to the Pacific. Leading explorers included ALEXANDER HENRY and ALEXANDER MACKENZIE. The geographer DAVID THOMPSON made surveys for the Company of such accuracy that parts of his cartography of western North America are still incorporated in maps of Canada.

By 1821 the rivalry with the older HUDSON'S BAY COMPANY became so intense that the British government forced a merger of the two companies. The name of the older company was kept, but the trailblazing exploits of the 'Northwesters' remained as distinct accomplishments in the annals of the American and Canadian fur trade.

Northwest Ordinances, see *Ordinances of 1784, 1785, 1787; Northwest Territory.*

Northwest Passage, envisioned as a water route from Europe to Asia through the North American continent, was first sought when JOHN CABOT explored in the vicinity of Newfoundland (1497), which Cabot thought to be the coast of China. JACQUES CARTIER reached the site of Montreal in 1535, and 40 years later MARTIN FROBISHER entered Hudson Strait (1576). JOHN DAVIS continued the explorations of Frobisher a decade later (1585–87). The discoveries of HENRY HUDSON in 1610–11 were followed shortly by those of WILLIAM BAFFIN (1615–16), who (mistakenly) pronounced the bay named for him to be landlocked. Thereafter arctic explorations were less vigorously pursued. The separate voyages of LUKE FOXE and THOMAS JAMES in 1631 likewise failed of their primary purpose, and thus ended the first great period of explorations into the frozen north.

Yet great benefits had accrued from the search, especially to the English. Their persistence had opened trade with Russia, and established the Newfoundland cod fishery, thus giving England new sources of wealth. Immense regions had been added to the royal domain, and the frontiers of geographic knowledge had been greatly expanded.

In the first half of the 18th century the HUDSON'S BAY COMPANY sent out several expeditions to search for a passage along the west coast of the Bay. Later explorations, such as those of ALEXANDER MACKENZIE, began to show the contours of the continental barrier, but hope for the discovery of a commercial route was generally abandoned, and 19th-century explorations were made chiefly in the interests of science. The actual existence of a Northwest Passage was proved by the English explorer Robert McClure in his expedition of 1850–54, although half a century passed before the transit was made by Roald Amundsen (1903–6), from Baffin Bay west through Lancaster Sound. Thus, after four centuries, the long search ended, though by this time it was essentially antiquarian.

See Ernest S. Dodge, *Northwest by Sea* (1961).

Northwest Territory, officially 'the Territory Northwest of the River Ohio,' was the first national territory of the U.S. It was that region generally known in the 18th century as the Old Northwest, some 248,000 square miles lying between the Ohio, the Mississippi, and the Great Lakes west of Lake Ontario. The French became interested in it as a trading link between the Mississippi and lake posts at Detroit and Mackinac. The territory was sharply disputed by the British, who had organized the OHIO COMPANY (1749–70), and who won control of the area at the conclusion of the French and Indian Wars by the TREATY OF PARIS of 1763. During the War of Independence the region was the scene of the bold exploits of GEORGE ROGERS CLARK, and by the TREATY OF PARIS of 1783 it was awarded to the U.S. Although various states by terms of their early charters put forth conflicting claims to these imperfectly mapped WESTERN LANDS, the region was finally ceded to the federal government by New York (1781), Virginia (1784), Massachusetts (1785), and Connecticut (1786).

The area was organized under the ORDINANCE OF 1787, but for several years it remained under the domination of British traders, who hampered American occupation and roused the Indians to active hostility until Anthony Wayne won the battle of FALLEN TIMBERS (1794), a first step leading to British withdrawal of border forts. By 1803 the eastern portion was thickly enough settled to meet the population qualification for statehood (60,000 inhabitants), and Ohio was admitted to the Union. The quarrel with Great Britain over the western portion still smouldered, and it was a potent issue in precipitating the War of 1812. The dispute was settled by the TREATY OF GHENT (1814), which determined (in general) the Great Lakes boundary between Canada and the U.S. By the terms of the Ordinance the remaining large areas were later admitted as states: Indiana (1816), Illinois (1818), Michigan (1837), and Wisconsin (1848).

Northwestern University (1851), at Evanston, Illinois, is a privately endowed, nonsectarian, co-educational institution. Its principal campus is on Lake Michigan, but it has graduate and professional schools in Chicago and elsewhere. Its significant program of African Studies (1951) was organized by the anthropologist, Melville J. Herskovits. In 1965, with an endowment of $118,400,000 and a faculty of 2000, it enrolled 16,470 students.

North Woods are the lumbering regions of Michigan, Wisconsin, Minnesota, and northern Maine. (The Northland is applied to northern Canada.) The legendary PAUL BUNYAN features in the tall tales of the North Woods lumberjacks.

NORTON, CHARLES ELIOT (1827–1908), was the son of the Unitarian Biblical scholar Andrews Norton (1786–1853), professor of sacred literature at Harvard. After graduation from that institution (1846), C. E. Norton traveled widely abroad before devoting himself to literature and art. With James Russell Lowell he edited (1864–68) the *North American Review.* Harvard appointed him to the first chair of fine arts in any American university (1874–98). He was an Italian scholar with wide-ranging taste. His *Letters* (2 vols., 1913), and later separate collections, reveal his genius for friendship, which, with his literary works, accounts for his great influence in his day. He was a gifted reactionary, strangely limited by his prejudices, and his lifelong hatred of Catholic institutions on occasion warped his aesthetic judgment.

NORTON, JOHN (1606–63), a graduate of Cambridge (1624), emigrated to New England in 1635, where his strong Puritan sympathies made him welcome. He became pastor of the First Church in Boston after the death of JOHN COTTON in 1652, served as overseer of Harvard, and won respect for his scholarship. He lost his commanding influence when he failed to aid the colony as an agent to the court of Charles II. By his vigorous persecution of Quakers and other heretics he came nearer to the popular notion of a 'grim puritan' than any other of this group. His *Life* of Cotton (1657) was the first separately published biography of an American.

NOYES, JOHN HUMPHREY (1811–86), born in Vermont, after graduation from Dartmouth (1830) studied theology at Yale. He lost his license to preach (1834) when he propounded his doctrine of PERFECTIONISM, stressing man's innate sinlessness. At Putney, Vermont, he formed (1839) a society of Bible communists (Perfectionists), but when the colony's system of complex marriages roused the ire of the neighbors, Noyes left town in haste (1846). Though Noyes was more successful with his ONEIDA COMMUNITY (1848–79), in due course he was again threatened with action, and he removed to Canada, where he died. He expounded his views in such works as *Bible Communism* (1848), and *Male Continence* (1848). His *History of American Socialisms* (1870) is still important as a study of early communistic experiments.

Nuclear energy is the term applied to energy derived from the atomic nucleus. In 1911 the British physicist Ernest Rutherford obtained the first clear evidence of the structure of the atom. Nuclear scientists were then led to theorize that splitting (fission) the nucleus of the atom would release vast energy (atomic energy). In 1930 ERNEST O. LAWRENCE devised a 'magnetic resonance accelerator' (cyclotron), which produced high energy particles by bombarding nuclei in a magnetic field. Thus high energy physics entered the experimental stage.

When the German physicist Otto Hahn discovered the possibility of causing a chain reaction by splitting the uranium atom (1938), the development of the atom bomb could be envisioned. In 1939 the Danish physicist Niels Bohr alerted his American colleagues to the nature of German advances in nuclear physics. ALBERT EINSTEIN laid the case before President Roosevelt, who in 1940 set up the National Defense Research Committee, headed by VANNEVAR BUSH and (later) JAMES B. CONANT. In 1941 the Committee was enlarged into the Office of Scientific Research and Development, which instituted the vital MANHATTAN PROJECT for constructing a nuclear bomb. The combined efforts of the leading scientists of the U.S., Canada, and Britain were concentrated upon the task, including, among the Americans, ARTHUR HOLLEY COMPTON, KARL T. COMP-

TON, J. ROBERT OPPENHEIMER, ISIDOR I. RABI, EDWARD TELLER, HAROLD C. UREY, and ENRICO FERMI. (Fermi was a refugee from Axis-dominated Italy.)

The problems were formidable. Sufficient quantities of uranium-bearing ore had to be found; methods had to be devised for controlling the chain reaction of a particular isotope (uranium 235); plants for obtaining heavy water (deuterium) had to be built, and delicate machinery had to be assembled within the instrument. The work was carried out in great secrecy in selected university laboratories, which were augmented by others. The secret was kept well, for very few knew or understood what the parts of the assemblage were designed for. After three years and the expenditure of $2,000,000,000 a bomb was ready for testing. The explosion of the first atomic bomb, in the desert near Alamagordo, New Mexico (16 July 1945), was an event of such magnitude that it introduced a new era, the atomic age. Secretary of War Stimson called the bomb 'the greatest achievement of the combined efforts of science, industry, labor, and the military in history.'

Ten days after the demonstration the Allies at the POTSDAM CONFERENCE presented Japan with an ultimatum: 'The alternative to surrender is prompt and utter destruction.' At that time no head of state knew surely how 'utter' the destruction might be. Japan ignored the warning, and on 6 August a B-29 superfortress dropped the first atomic bomb on the city of Hiroshima. Three days later a more powerful bomb was dropped on the naval base of Nagasaki. The overwhelming devastation led to the immediate capitulation of Japan.

While work was going forward on the atomic bomb, the development of the hydrogen bomb was in progress. This bomb, which is triggered by an atomic bomb, explodes by a process of fusion, releasing immensely more energy than the fission bomb. The first hydrogen bomb to be detonated (November 1952), a combination of deuterium and tritium, dug a crater a mile long and 175 feet deep in the floor of the Pacific Ocean, vaporizing the test island. The second, exploded in March 1954, used lithium and deuterium, and released still greater energy. The cataclysmic destruction made possible by atomic and hydrogen bombs has created grave moral issues, and has raised security problems of great international concern.

The ATOMIC ENERGY COMMISSION, established in 1946, has full charge of all nuclear resources and production in the U.S. In that year the BARUCH PLAN was submitted to the United Nations as a means of outlawing the use of atomic bombs, but Soviet objections stood in the way of its adoption. The NUCLEAR TEST-BAN TREATY (1963) was a step in the direction of international control.

The same nuclear energy that destroys can also be harnessed for useful ends. In 1956 the UN General Assembly created the International Atomic Energy Agency to further the peaceful uses of nuclear power. A way has been found to release energy of fissionable materials without explosion, by removing it as heat from the chain reacting system and thus providing a source of energy. Nuclear power drives ocean vessels, but the heavy shield required to absorb dangerous radiation excludes its use from relatively light devices such as airplanes. *Civil Nuclear Power* (1963), prepared by the AEC, is a booklet with recommendations on various aspects including central station power reactors. Nuclear physicists have learned how to transmute elements by rendering ordinary ones radioactive. Their radioactive isotopes are made to serve as tracers in medical diagnosis and treatment.

Nuclear Test-Ban Treaty (1963), signed in Moscow by the Soviet Union, Great Britain, and the U.S., committed the world's three major nuclear powers to halt all tests in the atmosphere, under water, and in outer space. Explosions underground are permitted. By a vote of 80 to 19 the Senate gave its constitutional advice and consent to the Treaty, which has significance far beyond its immediate terms. Although it was a limited agreement, it was the first treaty on a point of major East-West conflict that the West had been able to work out with the Soviet Union in nearly a decade. (More than 100 other nations have subscribed to the Treaty.)

Nullification in U.S. political history has been the attempt of states to prevent enforcement of Federal authority in instances when states have felt that the Constitution did not give the central government the right to encroach on STATES' RIGHTS. The KENTUCKY AND VIRGINIA RESOLVES (1798), drafted respectively by Madison and Jefferson, were protests from two state legislatures asserting that the Federal judiciary was not the sole arbiter of constitutionality, and maintaining that nullification is 'the rightful remedy' when the national government exercises powers not specifically delegated to it.

Calhoun justified nullification in his 'South Carolina Exposition,' which reflected southern bitterness over the protective Tariff of 1828. Even though Congress somewhat modified its demands in the Tariff of 1832, the South Carolina legislature adopted the ORDINANCE OF NULLIFICATION (1833), declaring both tariff acts 'null and void,' and threatening secession and armed resistance if the federal government attempted to collect the tariff. President Jackson then issued a proclamation, terming nullification an 'impractical absurdity,' and concluding that 'disunion by armed force is treason.' After Congress had passed the FORCE ACT of 1833 and adopted the COMPROMISE TARIFF (1833), South Carolina repealed its ordinance. For a time therefore a crisis was averted, but during the next two decades the states' rights issues came to dominate national politics. The election of Lincoln (1860) led to the secession of South Carolina. Then followed the formation of the Confederacy and the Civil War.

NÚÑEZ CABEZA de VACA, see *Cabeza.*

Nuremberg trials, see *War crimes trials.*

NUTTALL, THOMAS (1786–1859), English-born curator (1822–32) of the Harvard botanical garden, was a pioneer in American paleontology. He recorded his expeditions through the continent to the Pacific coast in *The Genera of North American Plants* (1818) and *A Journal of Travels into the Arkansa Territory* (1821). He made further observations in *A Manual of the Ornithology of the U.S. and of Canada* (1832).

Nye Committee (1934–36) was a Senate Committee, under the chairmanship of Gerald Nye of North Dakota, which undertook an elaborate investigation into the record of the munitions industry and bankers during World War I, in an effort to disentangle U.S. economic interests from foreign wars. The findings revealed scandalously high profits, outspoken sympathy for the Allies before 1917, and studied hostility to disarmament, but the revelations were more sensational than important, for there was no shred of evidence to support the allegation that Wilson was at any time influenced by the financial 'stake' in his relation with Germany, or that the decision to fight in April 1917 would have been retarded or reversed had financial relations been otherwise.

But at the time of the investigation a whole generation of Americans had persuaded themselves that participation in World War I had been an avoidable mistake, concluded that the Wall Street bankers and 'merchants of death' had cunningly sold the war to an unsuspecting nation, and naïvely dismissed unpleasant facts as propaganda. So strong and widespread was the spirit of ISOLATIONISM that early the next year the Senate again rejected membership in the World Court and, in an effort to remain aloof from global problems, in the years 1935–39 passed the series of NEUTRALITY ACTS.

O

Oak Ridge, see *Manhattan Project.*

OAKLEY, Annie (1860–1926), Ohio-born star of Buffalo Bill's Wild West Show (1885–1902), performed remarkable feats as a 'dead shot' with a rifle. Complimentary theater tickets came to be known as 'Annie Oakleys,' because their characteristic punch marks looked like well-placed bullet holes.

O.A.S., see *Organization of American States.*

Oberlin College was founded (1833) at Oberlin, Ohio, by New England Congregationalists. It inaugurated co-education at the college level, and gave its first degrees to women in 1841. Oberlin was an abolitionist bulwark; it was the first college to enroll Negroes (1835). Its music conservatory was the earliest to be established in the U.S. (1865). In 1965, with an endowment of $50,680,000 and a faculty of 244, it enrolled 2500 students.

OCCOM, Samson (1723–92), Mohegan Indian educated by ELEAZAR WHEELOCK, was ordained as a Presbyterian minister and preached to his tribesmen in Connecticut and Massachusetts, and on Long Island. In 1766 he went to England, where he preached to raise funds for Dartmouth College. He was the editor of a collection of hymns (1774), several of which he composed. He was the first Presbyterian hymn writer in America.

Oceanography, as a science, had its beginning in the 19th century, when the development of accurate instruments made ships' logs useful to researchers studying the phenomena of sea surfaces. MATTHEW F. MAURY, while head of the Hydrographic Office of the U.S. Navy Department, laid the foundations of systematic hydrographic work when his recommendations for recording oceanographic data were adopted at an international congress in Brussels in 1853. In the same decade ALEXANDER BACHE mapped the entire Atlantic coast and supervised ocean research on a worldwide scale. ALEXANDER AGASSIZ made pioneer contributions to the knowledge of coral atolls and reefs in the 1880's. The Oceanographic Institution (1930) at Woods Hole, Massachusetts, maintains a research ship and a marine biological laboratory. The Scripps Institution of Oceanography, on the Pacific shore, was established (1912) at the University of California, on the La Jolla campus. At present, especially since the International Geophysical Year (July 1957–December 1958), studies are rapidly advancing in marine geology, geophysics, and biology.

OCHS, Adolph Simon (1858–1935), while publishing the Chattanooga (Tennessee) *Times* (after 1878), acquired and edited *The New York Times* (1896–1935). He undertook to provide coverage of the 'neglected non-sensational' news in such fields as commerce, education, and government affairs, with complete and accurate reports on a worldwide scale. By emphasizing news over editorial opinion, he sought to create a 'newspaper of record,' and under his management the *Times* achieved eminence.

O'CONNOR, William Douglas (1832–89), journalist friend of Walt Whitman, wrote *Harrington* (1860), an antislavery novel which was effective ABOLITIONIST PROPAGANDA. The title of his defense of Whitman, *The Good Grey Poet* (1866), gave Whitman his sobriquet.

ODELL, Jonathan (1737–1818), a grandson of JONATHAN DICKINSON, after graduation from the College of New Jersey (1759) became a surgeon in the British army and later an Anglican clergyman. He was a prominent Loyalist during the Revolution, and served as secretary to Sir Guy Carleton. He aided the British cause by contributing essays and satirical poetry to journals. After 1784 he lived in Canada.

OGDEN, Peter Skene (1794–1854), Canadian fur trader, led expeditions during the 1820's into the areas that comprise present Idaho, Nevada, Utah, and California. He discovered the Humboldt river (1828), and was one of the first white men to penetrate the basin of

Great Salt Lake. He later served as chief factor at Fort Vancouver in Washington. Ogden, Utah, is named for him.

OGDEN, Rollo (1856–1937), a graduate of Williams College (1877) and Union Theological Seminary (1880), left the Presbyterian ministry in 1887 to engage in literary work. For three decades, as the editor of the New York *Evening Post* (1903–20), and of *The New York Times* (after 1922), he maintained his liberal position and established a reputation as a leader of opinion. He championed anti-imperialism, civil service reform, Negro rights, and throughout his career was a staunch internationalist.

OGLETHORPE, James Edward (1696–1785), English general and philanthropist, after army service held a seat in Parliament for 32 years (1722–54). 'Driven by strong benevolence of soul,' as Pope said of him, he took up the cause of debtors, and with other gentlemen of wealth and prominence he secured a charter to establish Georgia as an asylum for carefully selected poor debtors. Oglethorpe brought 116 of these debtors to Charleston, and in 1733 he founded Savannah. He then instituted a system of military training and set up defenses against the Spanish, whose defeat in the battle of Bloody Marsh (1742) assured Georgia's survival. He returned to England soon after.

Ohio, admitted to the Union (1803) as the 17th state, was the first of the areas forming the NORTHWEST TERRITORY to be organized as a separate territory. It took its name from the great river that forms its southern boundary. The Ohio Company had been formed in 1747 by Virginia planters interested in western land speculation and the fur trade. The consequent rivalry with the French brought on the last of the French and Indian Wars (1755–63). The region thereafter was under British control. After the Treaty of Paris of 1783, which ended the Revolution, it became part of the U.S.

The Ohio Company of Associates (1786) were the New England homesteaders who founded Marietta (1788). Together with the settlers who opened up the WESTERN RESERVE in the Cleveland area they shaped the cultural pattern of the territory. When the Western Reserve lands were incorporated into the Northwest Territory (1800), the boundaries of the present state were fixed, with Chillicothe as the capital. Columbus was made the permanent capital in 1816. Commercial development was speeded by the completion of numerous canals after 1825, with the consequent increase of traffic down the Ohio and Mississippi rivers to St. Louis and New Orleans.

After the Civil War, Ohio industries, which had been quickened by a united effort to support the Union cause, multiplied rapidly. Mills and factories began to create flourishing cities, which attracted heavy immigration from Europe. The state's center of influence shifted from Cincinnati on the Ohio river to Cleveland on Lake Erie. Railroads extended trade into the West, ore shipments from Lake Superior encouraged the steel industry, and oil refineries became the basis of enterprises that created huge fortunes. These factors gave Ohio great political importance in the period 1869–1923, when the nation was largely dominated by the Republican party. During those years seven Ohioans entered the White House: Grant, Hayes, Garfield, Benjamin Harrison, McKinley, Taft, and Harding.

The two chief cities are CLEVELAND and CINCINNATI. Other centers include Akron, Dayton, and Toledo. The oldest among several score of institutions of higher learning are Ohio University (Athens, est. 1804), Miami University (Oxford, est. 1809), WESTERN RESERVE, OBERLIN, and ANTIOCH. In 1965 Ohio State University (Columbus, est. 1870), the largest, with a faculty of 3410, enrolled 34,500 students.

Ohio Company, see *Ohio*.

'Ohio Gang,' so called, was a group of self-seeking politicians, close to President Harding, who followed him to Washington. Attorney General Harry M. Daugherty (1860–1941) was perhaps the most prominent member. Some of them were involved in the TEAPOT DOME SCANDAL.

'Ohio Idea' was a proposal sponsored (1867) by Senator George H. Pendleton (1825–89) of Ohio to redeem the Civil

War bonds in greenbacks instead of gold. It was an inflationary measure supported by western delegates to both major party conventions in 1868, but neither party adopted it.

Ohio river, 981 miles long, is formed at Pittsburgh's 'golden triangle' by the junction of the Allegheny and Monongahela rivers. It flows across the western boundary of Pennsylvania, then southwest, between Ohio and West Virginia, along the northern boundary of Kentucky where it borders Ohio, Indiana, and Illinois, and enters the Mississippi near Cairo, at the southern tip of Illinois. The river's name derives from the Iroquois word meaning 'great.' La Salle, who was awed by its virgin beauty, descended it in 1670, presumably to the Falls at Louisville. It was little used until the mid-18th century, when it became strategically important in the struggle of the French and British for control of the interior of the continent.

The Ohio was successfully navigated by steamboats after the War of 1812, and for the next two decades it was the highway used by pioneers to establish settlements in the Middle West. Canals joined it to Baltimore and Philadelphia after 1825. As a key U.S. waterway it determined the history of such industrial centers as Pittsburgh, Cincinnati, and Louisville. Although river traffic sharply declined after railroads were laid in the 1850's, the Ohio is still used for transportation, and its dams provide hydroelectric power.

Oil industry as a profitable commercial exploitation of petroleum, began when Edwin L. Drake (1819–80) in 1859 became the first man in the world to tap petroleum at its source by drilling a well at Titusville, in western Pennsylvania. Immediately a boom in oil started, and during the Civil War annual oil production increased from 21,000,000 gallons to 104,000,000, with oil companies (chiefly in Pennsylvania) capitalized at nearly $500,000,000. Although the existence of petroleum in America had been known from earliest times, only the development of industrial chemistry made possible the exploitation of its virtually inexhaustible uses.

The growth of the industry in the U.S. has been enormous, and it has created fabulous fortunes, none more spectacular than that of JOHN D. ROCKEFELLER and others associated with the STANDARD OIL COMPANY. In the 1870's oil was discovered in Kentucky, California, New York, Ohio, Tennessee, and West Virginia. Wyoming became a leading producer in 1894, and by 1900 huge deposits were uncovered in Kansas, Illinois, Louisiana, Oklahoma, Texas, and Alaska. Overproduction from these deposits would have brought a collapse in the market, since electric lighting was replacing kerosene, then the chief petroleum product, but just at that time the internal combustion engine provided a vast and constantly expanding demand. By mid-20th century some 400 products and thousands of commodities were being manufactured from petroleum, and both the demand and the supply seemed limitless.

In 1953 Congress gave the states title to submerged land (tidelands oil). The Act asserts U.S. jurisdiction over the resources of the outer continental shelf. States that lead in petroleum production in the U.S. are Texas, California, Louisiana, Oklahoma, and Kansas, where it is the principal mineral in order of value. It is also produced in Alaska, Arkansas, Colorado, Illinois, Mississippi, Montana, Nebraska, New Mexico, North Dakota, and Wyoming.

Ojibwa Indians (or Chippewa Indians), a sedentary farming people of Algonquian stock, in mid-17th century occupied the shores of Lake Superior, where Father ALLOUEZ visited them. They were enemies of the Sioux and the Fox, whom they drove from the region. Some of the Ojibwa later migrated into North Dakota, where they established their westernmost branch. By mid-18th century they were one of the largest tribes north of Mexico (some 25,000), and they controlled the region from central North Dakota to eastern Michigan. They were allies of the French in the Indian Wars, and of the British in the War of 1812. They later signed peace treaties with the U.S., and at present are located on reservations in the Dakota area, where they number some 33,000.

'Okies,' see *Migratory labor.*

Okinawa, Invasion of, took place on 1 April–21 June 1945. It was the last great amphibious engagement in the Pacific during World War II. (Okinawa is the largest of the Ryukyu Island group, between Formosa and Japan, and a vital base from which the U.S. planned to launch the final attack on the Japanese mainland.) The invasion followed preliminary attacks on Japanese shipping and airfields by U.S. carrier planes. The U.S. Navy suffered heavy damage from the attacks of Japanese *kamikaze* (suicide) planes, against whose deadly tactics there was little defense. After the Japanese garrison had lost 103,000 of its 120,000 men, organized resistance ceased and the U.S. was in possession. This costliest campaign in men and ships exacted a toll among Americans of 12,500 killed and 36,600 wounded, and the destruction or disabling damage of 88 naval craft.

Oklahoma, 46th state admitted to the Union (1907), is part of the Plains region crossed by Coronado in 1541 and explored by La Salle and Jolliet in the next century. After 1834 it was known as INDIAN TERRITORY, a region set aside for the Five Civilized Tribes. As settlers pressed westward, land was opened for homesteads by lotteries and 'runs.' Prospective settlers lined up on the territory border and at high noon were allowed to cross on a 'run' to stake their claims. The first run took place in 1889, and the portion thus opened (including the Panhandle strip, or CIMARRON region) was organized as Oklahoma Territory in 1890. The Indian and Oklahoma Territories were joined when Oklahoma became a state. The name in Choctaw means 'red man.'

Oklahoma City has been the capital since 1910; by 1960 it had become a metropolis, with a population of 324,000. Vast oil fields have shaped the economy of the state and have made Oklahoma City and Tulsa great oil centers. Oklahoma is subject to drought and blizzards, and in the 1930's, when it was overplanted and overgrazed, dust storms destroyed thousands of acres of farmland. Large numbers of tenant farmers left their stricken farms and went to California as migrant laborers ('Okies'). With increased attention to irrigation and soil conservation much of the Dust Bowl has been reclaimed. The leading institution of higher learning is the University of Oklahoma (Norman, est. 1890), with an enrollment in 1965 of 15,280.

Old-age pension laws are the Federal and state laws that provide for lump payments and annuities to retired workers, generally at age sixty-five. In the depression years of the 1930's the SOCIAL SECURITY ACT (1935) established a co-ordinated national program of old-age pensions and unemployment insurance. Soon thereafter corporations adopted similar plans. By 1960 the total assets of public and private pension funds were upward of $90,000,000,000, more than half of which were the assets of corporate pension plans.

Old Colony, see *Plymouth Colony.*

Old Dominion, see *Virginia.*

'Old Fuss and Feathers,' sobriquet of Winfield Scott, referred to the general's love of military pageantry, and was used affectionately by those who appreciated his talents.

'Old Glory,' popular name given to the flag of the U.S., is said to have originated with William Driver, a Salem skipper, who so christened a flag before setting sail (1831) on his brig *Charles Doggett.*

Old Guard, a term introduced (1804) to designate Napoleon's imperial guard, came to mean any older conservative group. In U.S. politics it specifically designated reactionary Republican protectionists, especially in the era 1890–1910.

'Old Hickory,' sobriquet of Andrew Jackson, was given to him by his soldiers in 1813 to symbolize his endurance. Thereafter it was the term by which he was affectionately known among his followers.

'Old Ironsides,' see *Constitution.*

Old Lights, see *Great Awakening.*

'Old Man Eloquent,' sobriquet of John Quincy Adams, was applied in his later years, when he served in the House of Representatives. The phrase derives from Milton's reference to the Greek orator Isocrates in his sonnet to Lady Margaret Ley.

Old Migration, see *Immigration.*

Old North Church (Christ Church), the oldest church edifice (1723) in Boston, was the second Anglican church in the town. (King's Chapel had opened in 1689.) In its tower the signal lanterns were displayed for Paul Revere (18 April 1775). The steeple has been replaced twice in 148 years; on the second occasion it had been blown over by a hurricane (1954).

Old Northwest, see *Northwest Territory.*

'Old Rough and Ready,' sobriquet of Zachary Taylor during the Seminole War (1841), applied to his physical prowess and his informal military dress. The nickname helped win him votes during his presidential campaign (1848).

Old South, see *Plantation system; Slavery.*

Old South Church (third church in Boston), erected in 1729, replaced the original structure, built in 1670. Notable among its early ministers were SAMUEL WILLARD and THOMAS PRINCE. On the eve of the War of Independence it was a meeting place of the patriots, and during the siege of Boston it served the British as a riding-school. It continued in use as a church until after 1870. In 1876 it was opened to the public as a historic landmark.

Old Southwest, as distinguished from the present SOUTHWEST, was a term applied to the region comprising Tennessee and Kentucky, and extended to include Alabama and MISSISSIPPI TERRITORY. When the Treaty of Paris of 1783 fixed the western limits of the U.S. at the Mississippi river, eastern states whose boundaries had been settled demanded that Congress cede disputed western lands to the federal government. In 1792 the state of Kentucky was created from the area west of Virginia. North Carolina ceded Tennessee, which was admitted as a state in 1796, and South Carolina relinquished a strip south of Tennessee. The whole region was a frontier during the first decades of the 19th century, and it created its own folklore, which is still distinctively recorded in the music and tales of the rural sections.

Old Spanish Trail, an overland route between Santa Fe and Los Angeles, dates from 1775, when two Franciscan monks first traversed most of it. It did not become a regular trading route until 1831. It led up the Chama river, passed through Durango, Colorado, crossed the Grand and Green rivers into Utah, thence southwest across the desert to the Mohave river and over the mountains to Los Angeles. In the 1850's it was an important emigrant route to southern California.

Oligopoly, see *Monopoly.*

OLMSTED, DENISON (1791–1859), after graduation from Yale (1813), as professor of geology at the University of North Carolina (1817–25) prepared his *Report on the Geology of North Carolina* (1824–25), which was the first official state geological survey in the U.S. After 1825 he taught mathematics, physics, and astronomy at Yale. He was chiefly known for his observations on hail (1830) and on meteors, and for his speculations about the aurora borealis.

OLMSTED, FREDERICK LAW (1822–1903), Connecticut-born landscape architect, first became known as the author of vivid travel accounts. His *Walks and Talks of an American Farmer in England* (1852) was followed by three volumes of sketches of southern slaveholding society, a massive indictment of the slave system as a perpetuation of frontier backwardness. These were condensed as *The Cotton Kingdom* (2 vols., 1861; new abridged ed., 1953).

He prepared the design for Central Park in New York City with Calvert Vaux. Olmsted himself executed it. His success was followed by many similar commissions elsewhere, including parks in Montreal, Boston, and Buffalo. He designed the campuses of the University of California at Berkeley and Stanford University. A notable achievement was his landscaping of the World's Columbian Exposition in Chicago (1893), now Jackson Park. His professional writings draw upon his wide experience as a city planner and as the creator of such national parks as Yosemite.

OLNEY, Jesse (1798–1872), Connecticut educator, compiled a *Practical System of Modern Geography* (1828), which was a standard school text for decades and revolutionized the teaching of geography. Olney's method was to familiarize the student with his own environment before progressing to a study of distant lands.

OLNEY, Richard (1835–1917), lawyer and statesman, after graduation from Brown (1856) practiced law in Boston. President Cleveland appointed him Attorney General (1893–95), in which post he attracted public attention by obtaining an injunction in the PULLMAN STRIKE. As Cleveland's Secretary of State (1895–97) he helped negotiate the VENEZUELA BOUNDARY DISPUTE between the British and Venezuelan governments. Again he made headlines, this time by his provocative statement that the U.S. was 'practically sovereign on this continent.' However, this deliberate act of disrespect to Canada and Latin America did not seriously affect Anglo-American friendship. Olney later defended his brash language on the ground that the U.S. was so negligible in British eyes that 'only words equivalent to blows would be really effective.' At the expiration of Cleveland's term, Olney resumed the practice of law.

Olympic Games, in modern times were first held at Athens, Greece, in 1896. Nine nations sent participants to the contests. Since then more than 80 countries have sent thousands of athletes to represent them in the Games. In 1924 the Winter Olympic Games were added. Through 1965, 16 meets have been held; twice in the U.S., at St. Louis in 1904 and at Los Angeles in 1932.

Olympic Mountains, part of the COAST RANGES in northwest Washington, comprise a rugged area with peaks rising to 8000 ft. Olympic National Park (1938), which abounds in wild life and has many glaciers, is the finest remnant of virgin forest in the Pacific Northwest. Recorded rainfall there is the heaviest in the U.S.

Omaha Indians, of Siouan stock, migrated from the Ohio valley to the region near the confluence of the Mississippi and Missouri rivers, and finally (after 1800) to Nebraska, where, since 1854, they have lived on a reservation. At present they number about 2000.

Omnibus Bill, see *Compromise of 1850.*

OÑATE, Juan de (*fl.* 1549–1624), Mexican-born explorer in the Southwest, in 1595 was appointed governor of the New Mexico region. He took formal possession in 1598, near El Paso. In the next few years he made extensive journeys east to Oklahoma and Kansas, and west to the Gulf of California, searching for precious metals, which he never found. His real achievements in exploration did not receive the recognition they deserved, for although he retraced regions previously seen by Coronado and others, he brought to light better trails and established Spanish rule on the Rio Grande.

O'NEALE, Margaret, see *Eaton, Peggy.*

Oneida Community (1848–79), a socio-religious group of PERFECTIONISTS, was established in central New York state by J. H. NOYES. Members held property in common, practiced 'complex marriage,' and reared their children under communal care. The 300 members governed themselves by a system of mutual criticism, which they felt served as a cure for moral delinquency and physical ailments. The community won respect for its excellent schools and the quality of its manufactures and handicraft, but the society was threatened with action for maintaining a system of polygamy and polyandry. After 1879 they adopted monogamy. The town they established has continued as a prosperous manufacturing community.

Oneida Indians, see *Iroquois Confederacy.*

O'NEILL, Eugene [Gladstone] (1888–1953), dramatist, was son of the actor James O'Neill (1847–1920). He studied dramatic technique at Harvard under

George P. Baker (1913–14), and in 1916 became associated with the Provincetown Players, who produced many of his early one-act plays. He won the Pulitzer Prize for drama three times (*Beyond the Horizon,* 1920; *Anna Christie,* 1921; *Strange Interlude,* 1927). O'Neill displayed a sense of theater learned from traveling with his father's troupe and sharpened by the forward-looking techniques of Baker's 47 Workshop. His dramas stem directly from the LITTLE THEATER MOVEMENT, and more than any other playwright he invigorated the American theater. In 1936 he received the Nobel Prize in literature.

Onondaga Indians, see *Iroquois Confederacy.*

Ontario, Lake, smallest and most easterly of the GREAT LAKES, is 193 miles long and covers an area of 7600 square miles. It lies between the province of Ontario and the state of New York, receives the waters of Lake Erie from the Niagara river, and empties into the St. Lawrence. Etienne Brulé discovered the lake in 1615, and Champlain visited it later that year. It was the scene of engagements in the French and Indian War during the 1750's, and again in the War of 1812. From earliest times the lake has been the key of entry into the North American continent. Its transportation facilities are available to New York City by way of the New York State Barge Canal and the Hudson river. The chief ports on the American side of the lake are Rochester and Oswego, New York.

'Open covenants,' see *Fourteen Points.*

Open Door Policy, as first announced (1899) by Secretary of State John Hay, was intended to protect American commercial interests in China. At the time that moribund empire was not recognized as a sovereign state, and several nations, including Great Britain, France, Italy, Russia, and Japan, had marked out for themselves SPHERES OF INFLUENCE and rights of EXTRATERRITORIALITY. The 'open door' would grant to all nations equal commercial, tariff, and railroad rights in China, and the great powers accepted the idea in principle.

Within a year the economic issues had become political. The BOXER REBELLION (1900), an effort to drive 'foreign devils' from China, might easily have precipitated a general war. Hay's circular note stating that the policy of the U.S. was to 'preserve Chinese territorial and administrative entity' likewise won acceptance in principle, although actually the policy was ignored. A chief reason for convening the WASHINGTON CONFERENCE (1921–22) was to reaffirm the principle, but the Japanese seizure of Manchuria ten years later overtly repudiated the Open Door agreement, which had never actually been based on other than trade and business considerations. After World War II China's *de facto* position as a sovereign state was recognized, and the Open Door Policy ceased to exist.

Open shop, unlike the CLOSED SHOP, is an industry which employs either union or nonunion workers. In practice, prior to the 1930's (except on a number of railroads) only nonunion labor was hired. After World War I 'open shop-pism' was a term applied to the anti-union policy of large corporations that attempted to weaken LABOR UNIONS by curtailing the unions' welfare operations, employing labor spies, and calling state troops to break strikes. During the 1920's such corporations freely used COMPANY UNIONS, BLACKLISTS, 'YELLOW-DOG' CONTRACTS, and the INJUNCTION to effect the so-called 'American Plan,' which for a time reduced union strength. With the passage of the WAGNER-CONNERY ACT (1935), the trend was reversed.

Opera, see *Music.*

Operationalism, a concept formulated in 1927 by the physicist PERCY W. BRIDGMAN, has profoundly influenced the philosophy of science in general, and experimental psychology in particular. Bridgman's view is closely allied to the relativity theory, which postulates that all time-space measurements are relative to a frame of reference. Operationalism assumes that all observations are relative to a context, and that all concepts must be explicitly defined by a set of critical standards in terms of the concrete operations by which their places in an event are determined. The concept of length, for example, can be reached only by a set of operations, subject to check and recheck, by which length is measured. Operational analysis seeks increased precision in the description of an actual happening, and has become an important economic and business tool.

Operetta, or light opera, is a type of musical drama written chiefly to entertain, and was first notably composed in the U.S. early in the 20th century by VICTOR HERBERT. The stars of such musicals included Blanche Ring (1874–1961), Eva Tanguay (1878–1947), and Nora Bayes (1880–1928). After World War I the operetta form gave way to musical comedy, works written successfully by such composers as JEROME KERN, IRVING BERLIN, GEORGE GERSHWIN, and most recently by OSCAR HAMMERSTEIN II, RICHARD RODGERS, and COLE PORTER.

OPPENHEIMER, J. ROBERT (1904–), physicist, was director of the Institute for Advanced Studies (Princeton, N.J.) for eighteen years (1947–65). While on leave from the California Institute of Technology, as head of the atomic energy research project at Los Alamos, New Mexico (1942–45), he made significant contributions to the development of the first atomic bomb. He served as chairman of the general advisory committee of the Atomic Energy Commission (1947–53), in which capacity he greatly influenced the policies of the U.S. government in matters of the use and control of NUCLEAR ENERGY, but his allegedly indiscreet conduct on policy matters led to his suspension by the AEC as a security risk in 1953. The AEC's decision was appealed, but the action was upheld. Ten years later, in 1963, President Johnson presented Oppenheimer the Enrico Fermi award, the highest honor given by the Atomic Energy Commission.

Oratory has always been an element of American culture. From the first, colleges required training in rhetoric, and disputations in college halls gave future ministers, lawyers, and statesmen an awareness of persuasive language. During the 18th century the preachers who induced the GREAT AWAKENING left a stamp on pulpit oratory. In the cause of independence such men as Samuel Adams, James Otis, and Patrick Henry stirred the emotions of their hearers.

The art of effective public speaking was most fully developed in the U.S. during the first half of the 19th century. Daniel Webster, who was unmatched in the history of ceremonial oratory, could attract vast audiences. John C. Calhoun was literally spokesman for the South. Henry Clay was likewise the voice of the New West. Lesser men emulated them in a way that led one observer to comment that the American Eagle was kept in such flight that his shadow wore a trail across the Mississippi valley.

On the platform the tradition was maintained at its best by such scholar-orators as Edward Everett. Foremost in the pulpit were Henry Ward Beecher, Theodore Parker, and Phillips Brooks; before the bar, Rufus Choate and William A. Evarts. Yet Abraham Lincoln, simple and straightforward in address, remains the one American orator whose words survive as literary art.

Toward the end of the 19th century no politician was more skillful in manipulating the masses than William Jennings Bryan, whose flamboyant technique was spellbinding. The public demand for Robert Ingersoll was so great that in the words of his lecture manager he attracted more money to the box office than anyone else 'since lecturing began.'

But admiration for the art of oratory had been declining, perhaps in proportion as it was being used too consciously for effect. College debating societies fell into low esteem. Woodrow Wilson revived the tradition of great statesmen-orators, as did F. D. Roosevelt and John F. Kennedy. Yet the fact remains that few Americans in the 20th century have commanded respect, created loyalties, or moved men to action as did the great speakers who directed the course of American history in the half century before 1865.

Orders in Council, executive edicts in Great Britain in the name of the king, have the force of law until superseded by acts of Parliament. Two such Orders are of interest for their influence upon the U.S. They are those issued on 7 January and 11 November 1807 as a reaction to Napoleon's effort to establish a CONTINENTAL SYSTEM for the economic blockade of England. These Orders forbade neutral traders to visit ports from which the British were excluded, unless the vessels first touched at British ports to take on consignments of British goods. Since the Orders hamstrung the neutral trade of the U.S., whose ships were seized on the high seas and whose seamen were sometimes impressed into British service, they aggravated the strained Anglo-American relations. Although the Orders were repealed in June 1812, the revocation came too late to avert the War of 1812.

Ordinance of Nullification (1832) was a resolution passed by a state convention in South Carolina, which had been convened for the purpose of resisting the customs collections under the TARIFF OF 1832. The Ordinance, which declared the tariff act 'null and void,' was met by President Jackson, who gained from Congress the power to collect the revenues forcibly under terms of the FORCE ACT (1833).

Ordinance of 1784, drafted by Thomas Jefferson, was the first of three laws dealing with the survey and sale of the PUBLIC DOMAIN, and with the establishment of a plan for the admission of new states into the Union. It divided the WESTERN LANDS, from the Appalachian mountains to the Mississippi river, into sixteen territories, and provided that each territory would qualify for statehood when its population reached 20,000. Adopted by Congress, it was repealed by passage of the Ordinance of 1787.

Ordinance of 1785, drafted by another Jefferson committee on land disposal, provided for systematic surveys and subdivisions of the public domain, with clear-cut boundaries and titles. The unit was the township, 6 miles square, divided into 36 lots of 640 acres each. Land was sold by minimum 640-acre sections at $1 an acre, and for many years private land companies did most of the land-office business. The Ordinance, with various changes in detail, remained the basis of American public land policy until passage of the HOMESTEAD ACT (1862).

Ordinance of 1787, largely the work of RUFUS KING and the Massachusetts jurist Nathan Dane (1752–1835), was based on the Ordinance of 1784, which it superseded. It was the most significant Act in the history of the Confederation: it organized the NORTHWEST TERRITORY and set the precedent, since followed, for admitting new states to the Union. It provided for a system of limited self-government, evolving into an equal partnership with the older states. Congress reserved the right to appoint a governor and judges for each district, which might become a territory when it was populated by 5000 free male inhabitants of voting age. It then might elect a territorial legislature and send a non-voting delegate to Congress. When such a territory had 60,000 free inhabitants, it would be eligible for statehood. Thus was inaugurated the federal principle that colonies are parts of the nation with coequal responsibilities. One important provision of the Ordinance forbade slavery in this first Territory.

Oregon, in the PACIFIC NORTHWEST, was originally part of the Oregon Territory (1848), an area extending from the crest of the Rocky Mountains to the Pacific coast, including principally the present states of Oregon, Washington, and Idaho. (*Wauregan* is an Algonquian term meaning 'beautiful water.')

Oregon has a mean elevation of 3300 ft., and it is a region of contrasts. It is bisected by the snow-capped CASCADE RANGE; forested mountains and lush valleys stretch west of the great escarpment, and treeless deserts extend east. Mount Hood, which rises 11,245 ft., and Crater Lake, a national park since 1902, are in the Cascade Range.

The LEWIS AND CLARK EXPEDITION had arrived at the lower Columbia in 1805, and soon after John Jacob Astor founded his Pacific fur-trading post at ASTORIA (1811). Missionaries began to arrive during the 1830's, harbingers of the westward trek over the OREGON TRAIL of farmers, many of whom founded settlements before 1860 in the fertile Willamette valley. Conflicting claims arising from British and American explorations in the 18th century were settled by a treaty (1846) following the OREGON BOUNDARY DISPUTE. In 1859 Oregon was admitted to the Union as the 33rd state, with Salem as the capital.

By 1900 the mythical logger Paul Bunyan had crossed the Shining Mountains, great forests had brought fortunes to lumber barons, and cities along the Willamette river were flourishing commercial centers. The tremendous industrial expansion that began in the 1930's was made possible by the hydroelectric power supplied by such dams on the Columbia river as Bonneville and McNary. A third of the state's population is in the metropolitan area of Portland, with a population in 1960 of 372,000. Institutions of higher learning include Willamette University (Salem, est. 1842), the oldest in the Far West; Oregon State University (Corvallis, est. 1868); and the University of Oregon (Eugene, est. 1872).

Oregon Boundary Dispute, the question of the national ownership of the Pacific Northwest, involved the vast territory west of the Rocky Mountains, north of 42° and south of 54°40′. Conflicting claims of ownership were made by Spain, Great Britain, Russia, and the U.S. Challenged by England, Spain relinquished her claims at the Convention (1790) that followed the NOOTKA SOUND SEIZURE. By the ADAMS-ONÍS TREATY (1819) Spain surrendered all claims north of 42° to the U.S. Russia, whose claims were weakest, withdrew her claims south of 54°40′ by separate treaties with the U.S. (1824) and England (1825). The Anglo-American convention of 1818 extended the Canadian boundary to the Rockies, and provided that the Oregon territory be left in joint occupation of the two claimants.

American public interest in Oregon began in the 1840's, when American settlers made unsuccessful efforts to establish land claims. In April 1846 President Polk gave notice that the joint occupation was due to expire in a year. The two governments again undertook negotiations, and Lord Aberdeen proposed that the boundary be extended along latitude 49° to Puget Sound, leaving Vancouver Island to Canada. Polk and the Senate approved the proposal, and the boundary as it is formed today was so fixed by treaty (1846).

Oregon Trail was the emigrant route through more than 2000 miles of country beyond the frontier. It extended from Independence, Missouri, to the mouth of the Columbia river. The main trail followed the North Platte to Fort Laramie (Wyoming), passed through the mountains by way of SOUTH PASS, ran along the Snake river, and crossed the Blue Mountains into the Willamette valley. Roughly traced in the 1830's by explorers and fur traders, by 1842 it was beaten into rutted roadways by WAGON TRAINS, which converged at river crossings and other natural constrictions. The exigencies of such a journey required semi-military organization, for the trains traversed dangerous terrain. They faced such obstacles as prairie fires, hostile Indians, stampeding buffalo, sand storms, deserts, quicksands, and almost impassable mountains. This ruthless test of human endurance nevertheless gave occasion for the greatest migration in recorded history.

In 1843 the 'great migration' began (some 1000 persons and 2000 animals), with JESSE APPLEGATE and MARCUS WHITMAN prominent among its leaders. Four trains made the journey in 1844, and in 1845 some 3000 emigrants used the trail. It continued in use through the 1850's. The diaries of emigrants note with grim monotony the new graves passed each day, a number that totaled some 34,000. Experience gave later emigrants the advantage of selecting equipment more wisely. Routes were better established and oxen largely replaced horses. But so long as the trail was used it remained the way of hardship and danger. (Francis Parkman's classic *Oregon Trail* is an account of his trip over the eastern part of the route.)

Oregon Treaty (1846), see *Oregon Boundary Dispute.*

Organization of American States was chartered in 1948 at Bogotá, Colombia, as a regional agency within the United Nations. It deals with matters of mutual welfare among the states of the Western Hemisphere. Its 21 member nations function through a Council with headquarters at the Pan-American Union in Washington, D.C. The Inter-American Treaty of Reciprocal Assistance (1947) allows the O.A.S. to assemble member nations to make decisions on foreign affairs.

Orleans, Territory of, see *Louisiana.*

Osage Indians, the most important southern Siouan tribe of the western division, were first encountered in Missouri by Marquette (1673). Irving describes them enthusiastically in *A Tour on the Prairies* (1835). In 1808 they ceded all their lands in Missouri and Arkansas to the U.S., and in 1870 they were established on their present reservation, comprising the present Osage county in Oklahoma. They now number some 5000. Oil production from their tribal holdings has made them wealthy.

OSBORNE, THOMAS MOTT (1859–1926), a graduate of Harvard (1884), as chairman of the New York state commission on prison reform (1913), became a voluntary prisoner in the Auburn penitentiary, where he gathered material for *Within Prison Walls* (1914). While warden of Sing Sing (1914–15), he instituted a system of self-government for inmates; it aroused such public hostility that he resigned. (He was later commandant of the U.S. naval prison at Portsmouth, New Hampshire.) In later books he expressed his belief that prisons should rehabilitate criminal offenders, and he pioneered in advocating individualized treatment of prisoners.

OSCEOLA (*c.* 1800–1839), immensely capable Seminole leader during the SEMINOLE WARS (1835–42), by skillful tactics for three years defied the U.S. Army, which had been sent by President Jackson to remove the Seminole to the West. The U.S. acknowledged its defeat in the Florida Everglades by promising safe conduct to Osceola at a peace conference. He was captured by treachery while bearing a flag of truce and was imprisoned in Fort Moultrie, South Carolina, where he died.

OSLER, SIR WILLIAM (1849–1919), Canadian-born physician, after graduation from McGill (1872) taught medicine at Pennsylvania (1884–89), Johns Hopkins (1889–1904), and Oxford (1905–19). (He was knighted in 1911.) Osler was one of the great medical figures of the century; he was renowned as a physician, teacher, and medical historian. He was a pioneer in enlisting the general public in an assault on tuberculosis. His classic treatise on *The Principles and Practice of Medicine* (1892) was translated into many languages, and went into its sixteenth edition in 1947.

See Harvey Cushing, *Life of Sir William Osler* (2 vols., 1925).

Ostend Manifesto was a comic anticlimax (1854) to the truculent effort of southern congressmen to annex Cuba (by purchase or seizure) for additional slave territory. The American ministers to Spain, France, and Great Britain (Pierre Soulé, John Y. Mason, and James Buchanan), all proslavery Democrats, held a conclave at Ostend, Belgium, and declared that unless Spain would sell Cuba, the U.S. would be 'justified in wresting it from Spain.' The declaration was immediately repudiated, but it had lowered the prestige of the U.S. abroad and that of President Pierce at home.

OTIS, ELISHA GRAVES (1811–61), Vermont-born inventor, by working on an automatic safety device to prevent the fall of hoisting machinery (1852), developed the first passenger elevator (1857), which was installed in New York City. His company grew into a large industrial enterprise, and his invention, by making the construction of skyscrapers practical, became significant in architectural history.

OTIS, HARRISON GRAY (1765–1848), a graduate of Harvard (1783), practiced law in Boston, but devoted himself chiefly to leading the Federalist party during the era of its waning power. He served Massachusetts in Congress (1797–1801). Otis was a moderate, and, as a member of the state legislature (1802–17), he was largely responsible for convening the HARTFORD CONVENTION (1814), in the hope of giving the extreme Federalists, who sought secession, a chance to let off steam. But the convention became the butt of ridicule, and Otis's defense of it cost him the chance of becoming a national figure, though he later served in the U.S. Senate (1817–22). A lifelong champion of northern interests, who wished to 'snatch the sceptre from Virginia forever,' Otis continued to be prominent in Boston society and affairs, and an exemplar of the city's aristocratic traditions.

OTIS, JAMES (1725–83), a brother of MERCY OTIS WARREN, after graduation from Harvard (1743) became the ablest lawyer in Boston. His famous plea (1761) against WRITS OF ASSISTANCE (arbitrary search warrants), even though he lost the case, brought him to the forefront among leaders opposing coercive Parliamentary measures. 'Then and there,' John Adams declared, 'the child Independence was born.' The significance of the argument was that it anticipated ideas later set forth in the Declaration of Independence: that the rights to life, liberty, and property derive from nature and imply the guarantee of privacy. ('For a man's house is his castle. . . .')

As a member of the Massachusetts committee of correspondence (1764) Otis vigorously resisted the Stamp Act and wrote such influential pamphlets as *The Rights of the British Colonies Asserted and Proved* (1764). Following his abusive newspaper attack on a commissioner of customs (1769), Otis was caned by the commissioner, and his subsequent erratic behavior was attributed to this severe beating. Yet during the 1760's he was a luminary in the patriot cause, and a political orator matched in his day only by Patrick Henry.

Ottawa Indians, of Algonquian stock, were located on the Ottawa river in Canada when Champlain met them (1615). They were allied with the French and Hurons, and enemies of the Iroquois, who forced them from the Great Lakes region. They were dispersed over a wide area (though principally in Michigan) during the Indian wars of the Old Northwest, when PONTIAC was their chief. Today they live on reservations in Michigan and Oklahoma.

Overland Mail was established (1850) as a government mail service from Independence, Missouri, to Santa Fe and to Salt Lake City. Thirty days were allowed for each one-way trip. In 1851 service was opened between Salt Lake City and Sacramento, California, but mail from New York to San Francisco traveled much faster by steamer. In 1858, with government subsidy, the Southern (Butterfield) Overland Mail, running from St. Louis by way of El Paso and Tucson to San Francisco, began its semiweekly service on a 25-day schedule, to compete with the ocean route. The line run by James Birch from San Antonio to El Paso and San Diego was known as 'the jackass mail,' because mules had to be used in the desert.

Within the next decade thousands of miles of overland routes were in use. The PONY EXPRESS was established (1860) on the central route, but it was abandoned after eighteen months, since the cost proved ruinous. At the outbreak of the Civil War the Southern Overland Mail was removed to the central route to secure Federal protection, and it gave daily service. When Ben Holladay purchased the reorganized line (1862), this 'Napoleon of the Plains' extended branches to Oregon and Montana. In 1866 he sold his properties to WELLS, FARGO AND COMPANY. Even after completion of the UNION PACIFIC RAILROAD (1869), the Overland Mail continued to serve localities not reached by rail for many years.

Overland trails are generally thought of as the central migration routes to the Pacific. They had many starting points (principally in Missouri), numerous cutoffs, and diverse terminals. The OREGON TRAIL, the most famous, later was called the Overland Trail, when other principal routes, such as the CALIFORNIA TRAIL, branched from it west of SOUTH PASS. The BOZEMAN TRAIL was chiefly a military route. In the Southwest important trading routes included the SANTA FE TRAIL and the OLD SPANISH TRAIL. The CHISHOLM TRAIL was the most famous route for cattle drives north from Texas, and the Bozeman Trail was so used after 1877.

OVIEDO, FERNÁNDEZ DE (1478–1557), official Spanish historian of the Indies under Charles V, during ten years' residence in San Domingo (1514–23), and in the course of five later visits, gathered material for his *Historia general y natural de las Indias* (1535 and later). The first part, soon translated into English and French, was widely read, and the whole remains important source material.

OWEN, ROBERT (1771–1858), was a British socialist and pioneer in the cooperative movement. Having made a commercial success of his cotton mills at New Lanark, Scotland, he reconstructed the community into a model industrial town, which became famous in England and abroad as a social experiment in economic, moral, and educational reform. He presented his theories on the shaping power of environment in *A New View of Society* (1813), and to test his philosophy in the New World he established the ill-fated co-operative venture of NEW HARMONY in Indiana (1825). Thereafter he went on to construct similar short-lived communities in Britain, while followers introduced brief Owenite utopias in Indiana, New York, Ohio, and elsewhere.

OWEN, ROBERT DALE (1801–77), son of ROBERT OWEN, accompanied his father to New Harmony, Indiana, where he met FRANCES WRIGHT. After the failure of that venture in co-operative socialism (1825–27), with Miss Wright he established in New York the *Free Enquirer* (1829–35), a journal which advocated free inquiry in religion, state provision for public schools, and (for the first time publicly in America) birth control. As a respected member of the Indiana legislature he helped persuade the public to establish free schools in Indiana. He also set up free traveling libraries. Elected to Congress (1843–47), Owen drafted the bill that created the Smithsonian Institution. He later served under Pierce and Buchanan as minister to Italy (1853–58). His letter to Lincoln (September 1862), published as *The Policy of Emancipation* (1863), was credited by Secretary Chase as having strongly influenced Lincoln's views.

Owenites, see *New Harmony*.

Oxen were used as draft animals from the time of early settlements in America. Their strength made them superior to horses for logging and plowing, and, later, for canal and railroad building. Teams of oxen drew many of the household wagons of pioneer settlers in all of the great westward migrations. Later in the 19th century oxen were used in enormous numbers for freighting in the West.

P

Pacific Northwest is the region comprising Washington, Oregon, Idaho, and western Montana. The overland exploration of Lewis and Clark (1805), and the fur-trading activities of John Jacob Astor (1810), established U.S. interests in the region, which became U.S. territory when the OREGON BOUNDARY DISPUTE was resolved in 1846. Intensive settlement began after the Northern Pacific railroad linked Chicago and Seattle (1883). Until recently the chief industries were salmon fishing and lumbering, for the high tablelands to the west block the rains from the Pacific. Today the irrigation supplied by the great dams erected since 1940 on the Columbia-Snake river system has altered the economic pattern by vastly increasing the yield of arable land. Cheap hydroelectric power is attracting large-scale industry to the area.

Pacific Ocean, discovered by Balboa (1513), was first navigated by Magellan in 1520. After the Spanish founded Manila (1571), the Pacific became the trade route linking the west coast of Mexico with Spain. It engaged the attention of American statesmen as soon as trading vessels had rounded Cape Horn to open a fur trade with China (before 1790), and the voyages of whalers soon stirred an ambition for American supremacy in this vast ocean area.

President Polk's desire to annex California was quickened by the fear that England or France might forestall him, since both nations were active in the Pacific. The acquisition of California and Oregon (1846–48) focused attention on Pacific commerce. President Tyler sent CALEB CUSHING as the first American commissioner to China, where Cushing obtained access to treaty ports (1844). President Fillmore entrusted MATTHEW PERRY with the mission of opening trade with Japan. Perry anchored his armed squadron in Tokyo Bay in 1853, the year in which the Gadsden Treaty with Mexico specified the U.S. right of transit across the Isthmus of Tehuantepec.

Alaska was purchased and the Midway Islands were annexed in 1867. The annexation of Hawaii in 1898 and the acquisition soon after of the Philippines, Guam, Samoa, and Wake Islands gave the U.S. vital interests in the whole Pacific region. The emergence of Japan as a great power led to various attempts at the reconciliation of rival claims, but since the U.S. and Japan were in direct opposition, negotiation was impossible. The rivalry of the two nations was one of the chief causes of their confrontation in World War II. Although the U.S. gave up some of her Pacific possessions after the war (the Philippines became a republic in 1946), the admission of Alaska and Hawaii to statehood (1959) tied the Pacific Ocean to the national destiny.

Pacific Railway Act (1862) authorized a central transcontinental railroad. It granted rights of way to the UNION PACIFIC to build westward from Omaha, and the CENTRAL PACIFIC to build eastward from Sacramento. A second Act (1864) increased the land grants. Thus before construction started the corporations were liberally subsidized by loans and by grants of the public domain which furnished an incentive to venture upon a very large undertaking.

Pacifism, the uncompromising opposition to all war as an ethical conviction, has been a force of some importance in American history. Its chief exemplars have been Quakers, Mennonites, and other nonresistant religious sects. In the 18th century the Pennsylvania Quakers demonstrated the efficacy of their principles in dealing with Indians, and during the 1870's Quaker agents won official praise for their success in applying the peace policy to Indian affairs. Although some leading Americans, notably William Lloyd Garrison, Charles Sumner, and William Jennings Bryan, were pacifists during portions of their careers, the influence of pacifism for the most part has been indirect, or has tended to favor rigid neutrality or ISOLATIONISM.

In both World Wars pacifists generally served in noncombat duty, but in 1917–18 the 3900 non-religious CONSCIENTIOUS OBJECTORS, especially those who refused non-combat war service, suffered gross abuses from their guards in federal prisons. The status of 'conshies' improved considerably during World War II. The fact that in 1916 EMILY BALCH shared the Nobel Peace prize for her humanitarian accomplishments and her steadfast adherence to pacifist principles is a measure of the vitality of ethical individualism.

Pack trains were the means of transport in frontier regions where road building was difficult. In the U.S. they were first used on the Allegheny frontier in fur trading and on early military expeditions. After the Revolution they became a highly organized business, connecting inland settlements with coastal cities by way of old Indian trails. Such units generally consisted of fewer than 30 horses traveling in single file behind the 'bell horse,' commanded by a master driver with two or three assistants. With the development of the trading and mining frontier in the Rocky Mountains, trains of 200 or 300 horses supplied whole towns with all their furnishings and machinery. As roads were laid, pack trains were replaced by WAGON TRAINS.

Packet ships were the vessels that conveyed dispatches, mails, passengers, and freight, with fixed sailing days. The first transatlantic packet lines were inaugurated (1818) by New York merchants. By 1845, 52 transatlantic packets (with weekly sailings) were in use. The average time from New York to Liverpool in 1822 was 39 days. By 1852 improved ship designs had cut the time to 33 days. In the late 1840's steamboats were becoming competitive with packets. Two decades later, losing even steerage trade, the packets became scheduled freighters. The last ocean packet sailing was made in 1881.

Pact of Paris, see *Kellogg-Briand Pact (1928)*.

PAGE, WALTER HINES (1855–1918), diplomat, journalist, and philanthropist, was born in Cary, North Carolina, and educated at Randolph-Macon (1872–76) and at Johns Hopkins (1876–78), where Woodrow Wilson was a fellow student. After crusading for the revival of North Carolina's public schools as editor of the *Raleigh State Chronicle,* he moved north to continue his battle for mass education and welfare as editor of the *Forum* (1890–95), the *Atlantic Monthly* (1896–99), and the *World's Work* (1900–1913), which last he founded.

To Page 'the forgotten man' (a phrase he coined long before the New Deal popularized the term) was the impoverished illiterate Southerner. He helped persuade Rockefeller to charter the GENERAL EDUCATION BOARD (1903), and used his position on the Board's executive committee to strengthen southern high schools, agricultural training classes, and other educational projects.

An 'original' Wilson man, he promoted the pre-convention presidential campaign for the New Jersey governor in 1912, and received the ambassadorship to Great Britain (1913–18). Page was outspoken in his sympathy for the Allied cause, even though his Anglophilism embarrassed the President during the neutrality era.

PAINE, JOHN KNOWLES (1839–1906), Maine-born organist and composer, after study in Berlin began teaching music at Harvard (1862), where he later (1875–1905) occupied the first chair of music in an American university. Despite his pedantry and rigid academism, Paine was by far the best equipped American composer of symphonic music before 1885. His enduring influence, however, worked through the many eminent pupils he trained (including F. S. CONVERSE and J. A. CARPENTER), and the emphasis he gave to the importance of music in the curriculum.

PAINE, THOMAS (1737–1809), born in England, at thirteen was removed from school to begin an apprenticeship with his father, a corsetmaker. For the next twenty years he lived an unsettled life, briefly engaged as a sailor, a teacher, a tobacconist, a grocer, and an exciseman. His two unhappy marriages were brief. He possessed a lively intellectual curiosity, and had learned a little about a great many subjects. Benjamin Franklin was so impressed by his potential ability that he helped Paine start life anew in America. Soon after his arrival in Philadelphia (1774), Paine became an editor (1775–76) of the *Pennsylvania Magazine* at the moment when the resistance movement was being given national focus by Congress, and in Pennsylvania was entering a proletarian phase. With such enlightened humanitarians as Franklin and Benjamin Rush as his patrons, Paine came into fulfillment as champion of the common man.

In January 1776 Paine published his electrifying pamphlet, *Common Sense,* a call to the American colonies to declare their independence from Great Britain, written at a time when others were only debating matters of home rule. Washington testified to the 'powerful change' it wrought in the minds of men. Within a few months thousands of copies had been circulated in the colonies and four editions had been published in Europe.

Now famous, Paine set about writing the series of sixteen pamphlets titled *The American Crisis* (1776–83). The first appeared shortly before the battle of Trenton (December 1776), when the American cause seemed darkest, and the essay so impressed Washington that he ordered it read to his troops. Then and later, its eloquent patriotism, couched in language which is urgent and almost crudely simple, resolved the hesitation of many, both in and out of the army. Paine was rewarded by appointment as secretary to the congressional committee on foreign affairs (1777–79), and later he was sent to Paris (1781) to assist John Laurens in negotiating aid from France. Soon thereafter he retired to his farm in New Rochelle, New York, where he perfected an iron bridge which he demonstrated in England (1787), while traveling between London and Paris in the cause of revolution.

The revolution in the U.S. was over, but that erupting in France again stirred Paine to action. His essay on *The Rights of Man* (1791–92), directed against Edmund Burke and the detractors of the French revolutionists, attacked English institutions in such a way as to compel his flight to Paris (1792). There he was toasted, made a citizen of the Republic, and elected to the Legislative Assembly, where he allied himself with the moderates, who lost power during the Terror (1793).

Paine's fortunes thereafter ebbed. He had been outlawed by England and now was arrested by France as an enemy Englishman. In jail he wrote *The Age of Reason* (1794–95), the deistic work that incurred the wrath of many of his former admirers, who saw the volume as a scurrilous arraignment of the Bible. (Actually Paine was attacking sectarianism.) Released from jail at the request of Minister James Monroe, Paine returned to the reconstituted Assembly (1795). But his foolhardy *Letter to Washington* (1796) alienated large segments of the public by accusing the President and Gouverneur Morris, Monroe's predecessor as minister, of plotting against him. The fact is that Morris had deliberately left Paine in jail lest his release reopen the case and result in a death sentence.

Paine continued to play a vicarious part in American politics. Jefferson's championship of *The Rights of Man* created a partisan dispute with J. Q. Adams, who attacked both Paine and Jefferson and identified Jeffersonianism with Jacobinism. In 1802 Paine returned to the U.S., where persons of all parties, fearing his radical freethinking, accused him of atheism, adultery, cowardice, and drunkenness. He lived his last years in ostracism and poverty, and his body was interred on his farm because consecrated ground was refused him. The British reformer William Cobbett took the remains to England in 1819, intending to erect a monument, but his plan was never carried out, and after Cobbett's death the bones of Paine were lost.

Tom Paine the man will always be a subject of controversy. He thrived on social turmoil and languished in times of peace. He stirred emotions and affronted sober judgment. The pamphleteer of revolutions, he belonged to no country. Yet in an age of revolutions he was a democratic reformer and the most quotable phrasemaker in American history. 'These are the times that try men's souls. The summer soldier and the sunshine patriot will, in this crisis, shrink from the service of their country.' 'The right of voting for representatives is the primary right by which other rights are protected. To take away this right is to reduce a man to slavery.' 'He that would make his own liberty secure must guard even his enemy from oppression.' Such texts are part of the American heritage of freedom, government by the consent of the governed, and an enlightened concept of social justice.

Biographies include those by M. D. Conway (2 vols., 1892), and Hesketh Pearson (1937).

Painted Desert, in northern Arizona, is the 30-mile plateau of highly colored, severely eroded terrain stretching south to the PETRIFIED FOREST.

Painting in America began when artists, accompanying 16th-century explorers, made sketches of scenes in the New World. The first of these were published (1590) by the German engraver THEODOR DE BRY. The earliest American artists were self-taught portrait painters, most of whose names are forgotten. In the late 17th century several found employment in the larger towns, and their primitives sometimes reveal a refreshing naïveté. After 1700 the elegance of costume reflects the desire of New England merchants and New York patroons to record their growing prosperity.

The Swedish-born HESSELIUS, who was better schooled than most, painted in and near Philadelphia. JOHN SMIBERT, trained abroad, shares honors with the native-born ROBERT FEKE for the best executed portraits before 1750. The great period of colonial portraiture began with J. S. COPLEY, and was continued by American artists trained in the London studio of the historical painter BENJAMIN WEST. Such were GILBERT STUART, RALPH EARL, C. W. PEALE, REMBRANDT PEALE, and THOMAS SULLY. Historical painting itself, exemplified in the works of WASHINGTON ALLSTON, JOHN TRUMBULL, S. F. B. MORSE and JOHN VANDERLYN, attracted scant patronage in America.

As a well-defined artistic movement, romanticism in painting began with the work of Allston. The discovery that America itself could be interpreted by artists gave rise after 1825 to a distinctive landscape genre, the HUDSON RIVER SCHOOL. The same interest was reflected in the ornithological paintings of J. J. AUDUBON, the river and frontier scenes of G. C. BINGHAM, and the Indian sketches made in the trans-Mississippi West by GEORGE CATLIN and A. J. MILLER. In the same period anecdotal genre painting was developed by W. S. MOUNT, and carried with originality into the designs of JOHN QUIDOR.

Still life as an independent art form was initiated in America about 1810 at Philadelphia by the remarkable Peale family. It was then executed in the objectivist 'botanic-decorative' style.

Self-taught 19th-century artists whose works continue to attract attention include WILLIAM HARNETT, EDWARD HICKS, and RALPH BLAKELOCK. The landscapes of GEORGE INNESS have distinction. Popular art includes the lithographs of CURRIER & IVES and the illustrations of CHARLES DANA GIBSON and FREDERIC REMINGTON. After 1870 French IMPRESSIONISM strongly influenced the style of many American painters, including JAMES MC NEILL WHISTLER and MARY CASSATT. Painting in America had now reached its maturity, best displayed in the works of such masters as WINSLOW HOMER, THOMAS EAKINS, and ALBERT RYDER.

By 1900 the most successful artists were such fashionable portraitists as JOHN SINGER SARGENT. At the same time revolutionary modes were taking form. The break with traditionalism was manifest in 1908 when ROBERT HENRI formed 'The Eight,' the group that organized the New York ARMORY SHOW (1913). There 'modern' art was introduced, and the way was opened for a variety of important original work. In 1929 the Museum of Modern Art was established to encourage fresh interpretations.

A regional 'socially conscious' movement during the 1930's was led by GRANT WOOD, THOMAS HART BENTON, and REGINALD MARSH. ALFRED STIEGLITZ developed photography as an art. Social protest themes became prominent in mural paintings, especially under the aegis of the FEDERAL ARTS PROJECT (1935). The commonplace was rediscovered as a fitting subject for treatment in the works of such painters as CHARLES BURCHFIELD and EDWARD HOPPER.

After World War II American painting took a socially conservative direction. WILLEM DE KOONING was a leader among abstract expressionists and ANDREW WYETH developed a trend toward sharp-focus realism.

There is now unprecedented interest in all branches of the visual arts, reflected not only in the sums of money spent by private collectors and by foundations, but also in the number of exhibitions and art magazines. New York now rivals Paris as the art center of the world.

See Virgil Barker, *American Painting* (1950); Samuel Isham, *History of American Painting* (new ed., with supplemental chapters by Royal Cortissoz, 1927); and E. P. Richardson, *Painting in America* (1956).

'Pairing' is a practice permitted in both houses of Congress. Two members of opposing parties agree to allow their names to be recorded in absentia (for a specified period) on opposite sides of questions brought to vote. Pairing was first used (1824) in the House of Representatives, but not officially recognized in the Rules until 1880. The practice is recognized in many state legislatures.

Paiute Indians, of Uto-Aztecan stock, during the 19th century inhabited the GREAT BASIN, and with the Shoshone and the Bannocks were often designated as the Snake Indians. The southern Paiutes, who subsisted to a great degree on edible roots, are called Digger Indians. During the 1870's the Paiutes instituted the ritual 'GHOST DANCE,' a ceremony accompanied by hypnotic trances that had their counterpart in the religious gatherings among whites at frontier CAMP MEETINGS.

Paleontology, see *Geology*.

PALFREY, John Gorham (1796–1881), after graduation from Harvard (1815) became a Unitarian minister. He later taught sacred literature at Harvard (1831–39) and edited the *North American Review* (1835–43). Assuming the role of chief spokesman for the New England conscience against 'Southern Slave Power,' he created for himself an identity idealized by New England traditionalists. His *History of New England* (5 vols., 1858–90), though partisan in its sympathies and pedestrian in style, is a work of careful scholarship which covers the colonial period in great detail, and presents much material on social history.

PALMER, Erastus Dow (1817–1904), self-taught sculptor, established himself in a studio in Albany, New York, where he engaged American apprentice workmen in the Italian fashion, though he was one of the few professional American sculptors of his time who did not study in Italy. Palmer was successful in making portrait busts, and became a leading figure in the American art world. The clergy were attracted by the religious cast of many of his statues, and the 'Palmer Marbles' were exhibited (1856) in the Church of the Divine Unity, New York, where they attracted nation-wide attention. He is best known for *The White Captive* (1859) in the Metropolitan Museum, New York.

Palmer raids, so called, were sensational attacks (1919–20) upon persons alleged to be alien radicals. President Wilson's Attorney General A. Mitchell Palmer (1872–1936) reacted to unsolved bombings and postwar radicalism by using private spies to conduct a series of raids on private homes and labor headquarters suspected of harboring communist agitators. (Palmer's political aspirations are thought by some to have been an element in these well-publicized raids.) He rounded up nearly 3000 persons, held them incommunicado, and subjected them to drumhead trials. Ultimately a few hundred were deported. Most of those arrested were found to be harmless.

Panama Canal, across the isthmus of Panama, was built by the U.S. (1904–14) on territory leased in perpetuity from the Republic of Panama immediately after the bloodless PANAMA REVOLUTION. A French company had previously failed in a similar attempt, and work was resumed following the U.S. purchase of that company's holdings and franchises. Colonel GEORGE W. GOETHALS was given the entire civil, military, and engineering authority. The revolutionary sanitary measures of Dr. WILLIAM C. GORGAS eradicated malaria and yellow fever. Built at a cost of $366,650,000, the Canal was formally opened (July 1915) after three years of planning and seven of actual construction.

The Panama Canal Zone extends five miles on either side of the axis of the waterway (exclusive of the cities of Panama and Colón), and is under the jurisdiction of the Department of the Army. Agitation for revision of the treaty that established the zone became so vigorous that in 1963 the Republic of Panama broke off diplomatic relations with the U.S. Eleven months later (April 1964) diplomatic relations were resumed, but the issue of revising the treaty was not settled.

Panama Congress (1826) was summoned by Simón Bolívar primarily to discuss commercial treaties, adopt a code of international law, and arrive at a common Latin American policy toward Spain. In a special message to the Senate, President J. Q. Adams nominated two delegates, believing that the dominant position of the U.S. in the Western Hemisphere required representation at the Congress. Opposition was chiefly political, although some southern senators feared dangerous commitments on the slavery question at a Congress where some republics under the control of Negroes would be represented. Although the delegates were sent, the U.S. was not represented, for one delegate died en route and the other had not gone farther than Mexico City when the Congress adjourned.

Panama, Declaration of (1939), issued after the outbreak of World War II by the Inter-American Conference, announced sea safety zones in the Western Hemisphere, south of Canada, within which areas belligerent powers were warned to refrain from naval action.

Panama Revolution (1903) was a bloodless affair following rejection by the Colombian government of the HAY-HERRÁN TREATY, which would have leased a strip of land across the isthmus of Panama to the U.S. It was accomplished principally by 300 section hands from the Panama Railroad and the fire brigade of the city of Panama. The Governor of Panama consented to his own arrest, the Colombian Admiral on station was bribed to steam away, and U.S. warships prevented Colombian troops from being landed to 'restore order.' On 4 November Panama declared her independence, two days later the U.S. recognized the Republic of Panama, and within two weeks the Canal Zone was granted to the U.S. by the HAY-BUNAU-VARILLA TREATY.

Pan-American conferences were initiated in 1826 when Simón Bolívar called the PANAMA CONGRESS to discuss inter-American problems, but no further assemblage was held until Secretary of State Blaine convened the first International Conference of American States (1889) in Washington, attended by representatives of eighteen nations. Its agenda included programs for creation of a Pan-American customs union and the arbitration of international disputes. Since both proposals seemed unilaterally to favor the U.S., they were politely rejected, but from the conference stemmed the PAN-AMERICAN UNION. Since then congresses have been frequent.

The rise of totalitarian regimes in Europe during the 1930's underscored the need for unity among the nations of the Western Hemisphere, and three conferences dealt with the peril: the MONTEVIDEO CONFERENCE (1933) denied the right of any state to interfere in the affairs of another; the Buenos Aires Conference (1936), opened by President Roosevelt, adopted a pact pledging consultation whenever war threatened; and the Lima Conference (1938) propounded the Declaration of Lima, further providing for hemispheric solidarity. At the ninth congress, which met at Bogotá (1949), the Conference adopted the Charter of the Organization of American States, a regional agency within the United Nations.

Pan-American Union (1890), founded at the first of the modern PAN-AMERICAN CONFERENCES, until 1910 was known as the International Bureau of American Republics. It serves as a permanent agency for exchanging and disseminating information regarding all the American republics. The governing board is composed of the U.S. Secretary of State and the chiefs of mission in the U.S. from other Western Hemisphere republics. It is expressly prohibited from discussing political questions. Its headquarters are in the Pan-American Union building at Washington. In 1948 it was made the general secretariat for the ORGANIZATION OF AMERICAN STATES, an agency within the United Nations.

Pan-Americanism, a new contribution to U.S. policy during the 1880's, was primarily economic in character. It was formulated by Secretary of State Blaine. Since 87 per cent of Latin American exports to the U.S. (largely raw materials) entered duty free, Blaine threatened to clamp a tariff on them unless the countries lowered their duties on U.S. products, and with a view to effecting a customs union he called the first of the PAN-AMERICAN CONFERENCES (1889), from which stemmed the PAN-AMERICAN UNION.

Relations between the U.S. and Latin America were not cordial under the 'Big Stick' and 'Dollar Diplomacy' policies of the Theodore Roosevelt and Taft administrations, typified by such formulations as the PLATT AMENDMENT (1901), which practically made Cuba a U.S. protectorate. (The amendment was abrogated in 1934.) Under the administration of F. D. Roosevelt the GOOD NEIGHBOR POLICY bore fruit, and hemispheric solidarity was further strengthened by the creation of the ORGANIZATION OF AMERICAN STATES (1948) within the framework of the United Nations.

Panay Incident (1937) was the deliberately planned sinking on the Yangtze river of the U.S. gunboat *Panay* by Japanese army aviators. It aroused only slight indignation, and when Tokyo apologized and paid reparations, Americans were relieved. So far-reaching was the spirit of ISOLATIONISM in America that some militarists in totalitarian countries concluded that nothing could make America fight.

Panic of 1785, ushering in a period of hard times after the Revolution, lasted for three years. It was the result of the deflation that accompanied the end of army contracts, the resumption of British imports (a blow to American manufacturing), and lack of adequate credit facilities. It was accentuated by lack of machinery for promoting interstate trade, by such disorders among debtor groups as that of SHAYS'S REBELLION, and by British refusal to conclude a commercial treaty. It gave clear evidence of the need for a stronger national union and led business and propertied groups to support the Federal Constitutional Convention (1787).

Panic of 1819 was the result of a sharp contraction of bank credits initiated by the Second Bank of the U.S. after overextended credits, particularly in western land investments, had started a commodity inflation. Agricultural and industrial prices had dropped after the War of 1812, British textiles were flooding the American market, and late in 1818 the operations of western branches of the Bank of the U.S. were sharply curtailed. State banks collapsed, and payments due to the government for public lands, in arrears by many millions, were largely uncollectible. Hard times lasted until 1824.

Panic of 1837 followed a period of unparalleled speculation, especially in western land and canal and railroad construction. States had piled up enormous debts to finance enterprises, banks extended credit, and the enthusiasm of British investors for American securities stimulated business. The panic began when President Jackson, seeking to discourage wildcat speculation, during his last year in office (1836) issued his SPECIE CIRCULAR, ordering the Treasury to receive no paper money for public lands. Deposit banks contracted their credit. European capital was then an essential factor in American enterprises, and the crisis was precipitated when three English banking houses failed, forcing British creditors to call in their loans. New York banks suspended specie payment and other banks followed. Bank failures mounted, public works were suspended, and unemployment mounted. The universal distress, felt until 1843, contributed to the defeat of President Van Buren in 1840. The return of the Whigs to power may have been partly due to the fact that Van Buren rejected the idea of Federal aid to weak business.

Panic of 1857 was a cyclical depression following a boom decade after the Mexican War. Speculation in land and the overbuilding of railroads between 1849 and 1856 coincided with the growth of poorly regulated banks. Failure of the Ohio Life Insurance Company in Cincinnati touched off the panic, which quickly spread and was most serious in the growing industrial cities of the East and in the wheat belt of the West. It exhibited the customary phenomena of unemployment, bank failures, decline in national income, and deflation. It devitalized the growing labor movement. Since the cotton economy of the South had been but slightly affected, leading Senator James H. Hammond of South

Carolina to conclude that 'Cotton is King,' it intensified sectional feeling on the eve of the Civil War.

Panic of 1873 was brought on chiefly by unrestrained speculation in railroad construction and wildcat investment schemes in a variety of ventures. Since business practices were largely unregulated by statutory law, the U.S. financial structure had become increasingly shaky after the Civil War. Currency inflation and a trade imbalance of imports over exports further endangered business solvency. The failure of the banking house of JAY COOKE (18 September), which had been presumed to be sound, precipitated the crisis. The ten-day closing of the New York Stock Exchange was followed by the worst depression the nation had yet experienced. More than 18,000 business failures occurred during 1876–77, most railroads went into bankruptcy, and unemployment far outstripped the ability of charity to relieve hunger and destitution. The RAILROAD STRIKE OF 1877, which was accompanied by appalling violence, left a heritage of distrust by labor of the federal government because it had used troops to quell the strike. The general welfare began to improve in 1878, but the rift between classes was slow to mend.

Panic of 1883, actually a depression, began as a minor recession, but was prolonged and intensified by the financial crisis resulting from the overbuilding of railroads. It continued for some three years and was marked by the collapse of the movement for the eight-hour day and the decline of the Knights of Labor, a reaction to the violent HAYMARKET RIOT (1886).

Panic of 1893, a spectacular financial crisis, followed the recall of European securities investments from the U.S. The collapse of the New York stock market was accompanied by increased gold exports, the decline of the Treasury's gold reserve, and the falling-off of the prices of gold, silver, and commodities. Then ensued the cycle of business failures, unemployment, strikes, and depression. Recovery by 1897 resulted in such a vast wave of consolidations in tobacco, oil, steel, sugar, and whisky production that the trust issue became paramount in politics.

Panic of 1907 was a minor depression brought about by the failure of two large corporations, the Knickerbocker Trust Company of New York (22 October) and the Westinghouse Electric Company (23 October). The resulting collapse of the stock market was followed by several bank suspensions or failures. After the U.S. Treasury and J. P. Morgan and Company had each loaned New York banks $25,000,000, recovery was rapid. As a result of the panic, the ALDRICH-VREELAND ACT (1908) was passed. It aimed at correcting a weakness in the credit structure, which had prevented national banks from issuing notes on securities other than Federal bonds.

Panic of 1920 was a severe depression chiefly brought on by farm overproduction and postwar loss of foreign markets. A flight of gold from the country caused a marked advance in money rates, and by the year's end industrial stocks had declined 30 per cent. The depression continued into 1922, characterized by business and farm failures, industrial inactivity, and a continued drop in foreign trade.

Panic of 1929, the worst stock market and financial crash in the nation's history, was the culmination of an amazingly rapid decline in securities' prices, traceable to an unusual overspeculation in stocks after 1924. Factors included not only an unregulated stock market but purchasing power weaknesses due to earlier crises in farming, the sick coal and textile industries, the collapse of the real estate boom, the inability to control the downward thrust of the business cycle, the steady disruption of the prewar European market, and the long-chronic bank failures. The market broke on 24 October, and never before or since have prices declined so fast or so far. Established banking practice, however, averted a money panic.

Every field of business suffered huge losses, and the Great Depression set in, which, with minor upswings, lasted for a decade. Exports and imports fell off sharply, and unemployment rose to an estimated 17,000,000 as commercial failures mounted. President F. D. Roosevelt, in response to the failure of 5000 banks by the spring of 1933, declared a nationwide bank moratorium immediately after his inauguration. Congress in special session on 9 March passed the EMERGENCY BANKING RELIEF ACT, which prevented a money panic. Thereafter various banking acts, spearheaded by the GLASS-STEAGALL BANKING ACT (1933), gradually restored solvency, although the Great Depression did not actually end before our involvement in World War II.

Panics, see *Business cycles.*

Paper industry in the U.S. began in 1690, when the pioneer paper manufacturer William Rittenhouse (1644–1708), in partnership with the Philadelphia printer WILLIAM BRADFORD, erected the first paper mill in the colonies in nearby Roxborough. After a pulp engine had been introduced from Holland (1756) the number of mills increased. By 1810, when the census reported 202 paper mills in the country, the bulk of paper was domestically manufactured, mostly from rags. With the introduction during the 1820's of the Fourdrinier process for making paper on an endless cloth web, machinery supplanted handwork. Although straw and grass were sometimes used as raw material for paper, after 1850 wood was chemically disintegrated for pulp, creating new industries in forest areas. The Parson Paper Company began large-scale operation at Holyoke, Massachusetts, in 1853. After 1890 the industry was highly organized. By mid-20th century some 4000 firms were annually turning out 20,000,000 tons of paper and allied products.

Paper money, see *Bills of Credit, Continental Currency, Greenbacks, Legal Tender Cases.*

Parcel Post, see *Postal System.*

Paris, Treaty of (1763), following the Seven Years' War, of which the French and Indian War was the American phase, was a settlement between Great Britain, France, and Spain. By its terms all of French Canada and the Spanish Floridas were ceded to Great Britain. France yielded to Spain all territory east of the Mississippi except the city of New Orleans. The British Empire now girdled the globe. India was hers, as were all North America to the Central basin and the best islands of the West Indies. She was also mistress of the seas. 'What God in his providence has united,' James Otis fervidly proclaimed at a peace celebration in Boston, 'let no man dare attempt to pull asunder.' Unfortunately, by acquiring these vast possessions, Great Britain was beset by IMPERIAL PROBLEMS that within two decades were to lose her more than she had gained.

Paris, Treaty of (1783), ending the War of Independence, was formally negotiated in its preliminary stage during the autumn of 1782. The definitive peace treaty was signed (3 September 1783) by the American commissioners, John Adams, Benjamin Franklin, and John Jay, and by the British plenipotentiary, David Hartley. Its important provisions were (1) British recognition of U.S. independence; (2) the setting of boundaries between the U.S. and Canada; (3) U.S. fishing privileges in the territorial waters of British North America; (4) an agreement that creditors on either side should 'meet with no lawful impediment' to the recovery of prewar debts; (5) the stipulation that Congress should 'earnestly recommend' to the several states restoration of Tory property; and finally (6) an agreement that hostilities would cease and British land and sea forces be evacuated 'with all convenient speed.' (The other powers fared less well. France got nothing, and Spain received Florida in return for surrendering its hopes for Gibraltar.)

Actually the treaty was satisfactory neither to the U.S. nor to England. The loose wording created boundary disputes that were not settled for many decades. Although Congress did 'earnestly recommend' restoration of confiscated estates, very few Loyalists recovered their property. The article requiring the American courts to hear cases of British subjects seeking to recover their prewar debts was violated both in spirit and in letter. The British on their side, unwilling to abandon the fur trade, retained their military posts in the Northwest until 1796, a convenient delay of twelve years. But American independence had been achieved.

Paris, Treaty of (1898), ended the Spanish-American War (10 December). Spain granted the independence of Cuba and assumed the liability for the Cuban debt of some $400,000,000. Spain also ceded Puerto Rico, Guam, and the Philippine Islands to the U.S. Spain received $20,000,000 for the Philippines. The Senate ratified the treaty by a close vote after a heated debate over the issue of imperialism. The U.S. then emerged as a power in international affairs.

Parity payments, incorporated in the AGRICULTURAL ADJUSTMENT ACT (1938), established the principle of the 'ever-normal granary.' The Commodity Credit Corporation was authorized to make loans to farmers on their surplus crops at a level slightly below 'parity': a price based on an average of the 1909–14 level. The crops were stored by the government, to be marketed at parity during periods of crop failure. The program proved workable and to a large extent gave farmers the relief it was intended to provide.

PARKER, CHARLIE ['YARDBIRD,' or 'BIRD'] (1920–), Negro jazz musician, was born in Kansas City. Called the giant among saxophonists, he was the major musician in the BOP movement, and the foremost influence on jazz after World War II. His wealth of invention and rhythmic sense were evident both in his 'hot' style and in his 'cool' style, which later mode founded a new school of jazz.

PARKER, FRANCIS WAYLAND (1837–1902), New Hampshire–born educator, after study of educational methods abroad originated the 'Quincy movement' when he was superintendent of the Quincy, Massachusetts, schools (1875–80). He stressed a curriculum and a methodology based on child development and interest, thereby pioneering in the U.S. in PROGRESSIVE EDUCATION. As superintendent of schools in Boston (1880–83) he extended his influence, and as principal of the Cook County Normal School in Chicago (1883–96) his work in school curriculums and teacher training assumed national importance.

PARKER, HORATIO WILLIAM (1863–1919), Massachusetts-born composer, studied music at Munich, and in 1893 became organist of Trinity Church, Boston. He was called to the newly created chair of music at Yale in 1894, and organized the New Haven Symphony Orchestra. Thereafter he began composing anthems and hymns, many of them the best of their day. Strongly influenced by German romanticism, he is represented by choruses, oratorios, and organ compositions. His two operas, *Mona* (1912) and *Fairyland* (1915), won substantial prizes. (*Mona* was produced by the Metropolitan Opera Company.) One of the few significant 19th-century American compositions is his oratorio, *Hora Novissima* (1893). He and JOHN KNOWLES PAINE occupy parallel positions as founders of a professional composing tradition in American music.

PARKER, THEODORE (1810–60), after graduation from Harvard Divinity School (1836) became pastor of the Unitarian Church at West Roxbury, Massachusetts (1837–46). His sermon 'On the Transient and Permanent in Christianity' (1841) established him as the leading transcendentalist of his day. He amplified his liberal position in his scholarly *Discourse of Matters Pertaining to Religion* (1842), which was so radical that the orthodox Unitarian clergy ostracized him. His fiery nature rebelled against their 'sterile rationalism.' After 1846 he was pastor of a Boston church with a congregation that grew to 7000. Deeply concerned with problems of social living, he lectured at lyceums throughout the country and was a spokesman for reforms of every kind. His strenuous public life at last ended through sheer exhaustion (1859) and he died in his fiftieth year while seeking to recover his health in Europe.

Parker came to be known as 'the keeper of the public conscience.' His unceasing advocation of social reform, such as abolition of slavery and the improvement of welfare for all underdogs, often put him in danger of physical violence, though the causes he fought for later became popular. No man of his day more effectively reached his listeners, and he represents that type of spirit strong in life as well as in thought, who never sacrificed 'any opinion to the popular judgments and modes of action.' Emerson recalled him as 'my brave brother,' whose place 'cannot be supplied.'

See H. S. Commager, *Theodore Parker* (1936).

Parker* v. *Davis, see *Legal Tender Cases.*

PARKMAN, FRANCIS (1823–93), scion of a long established Boston family, even before he graduated from Harvard (1844), often took vacation trips into nearby wilderness regions because, as he phrased it, he had 'Injuns on the brain.' After a European tour (1843–44), in part to aid his health, in 1846 he set out from St. Louis on a 1700-mile journey along the Oregon Trail on horseback. He studied and lived with Indians, and he mingled freely with frontier hunters and trappers. Out of his experience came *The California and Oregon Trail* (1849), still the best contemporary description of the eastern part of that migration route.

Afflicted by partial blindness, arthritis, and illnesses certainly real whatever their psychosomatic element, he began his labors on his 'history of the American forest.' With the aid of friends who read to him he began writing the first volume of his vast design. This he did on a special wire frame, often setting down but a few lines a day.

Now known as *France and England in North America,* the series begins with the *History of the Conspiracy of Pontiac* (1851). It continues with *Pioneers of France in the New World* (1865), the struggle in Florida and the history of Champlain in America. Then followed *The Jesuits in North America in the Seventeenth Century* (1867), and *LaSalle and the Discovery of the Great West* (1869). *The Old Regime in Canada* (1874) is a picture of French feudalism, missionary problems, and the dangers of autocratic rule. *Count Frontenac and New France under Louis XIV* (1877) analyzes a situation in which a great administrator sought to maintain an untenable position. *Montcalm and Wolfe* (1884) is the classic account of the final struggle of two world powers for a continent, and *A Half-Century of Conflict* (1892) deals with the years leading to Montcalm's defeat. (The series is in historical sequence, except that both the first and last volumes precede *Montcalm and Wolfe* in time.)

One measure of the homage paid to this accomplishment is the fact that no one since Parkman has attempted to write again the full story of that massive struggle, and the work still remains the classic account of the wars on the Northern border and the exploration of the South and West. During the recurrent periods when nervous debilitation prohibited concentration on historical research, Parkman relaxed by writing a novel, *Vassall Morton* (1856), and a scientific study, *The Book of Roses* (1866), which won him an appointment at Harvard (1871) as professor of horticulture.

As a literary craftsman Parkman combines vivid detail with the exact historical method of German scholarship. He imbued himself, as he said, 'with the life and spirit of the time' by the use of firsthand documents, and visits to the scenes of the incidents he describes. He thus 'resurrected' the past. He appears subjective in his view of England as an ordered Protestant democracy and France as a Catholic military despotism, but his historical reconstruction is judged to be permanently great, and he remains America's foremost historian.

See the biographies by Mason Wade (1942), and Howard Doughty (1962).

PARLEY, PETER, see *S. G. Goodrich.*

PARRINGTON, VERNON LOUIS (1871–1929), Illinois-born professor of English, taught at the University of Washington after 1908. His *Main Currents in American Thought* (3 vols., 1927–30) was a widely discussed excursion into the history of ideas. It postulates the doctrine that only populism (liberal agrarian and Jeffersonian political beliefs) and economic realism have been important in molding American literature. His thesis was strongly attacked, but it led to a reexamination of traditional interpretations and to a critical movement that reassessed the 'usable past' of American political, social, and economic ventures.

PARSONS, THEOPHILUS (1750–1813), a graduate of Harvard (1769), was one of the Federalist leaders in Massachusetts. A member of the ESSEX JUNTO, he probably wrote *The Essex Result* (1778), which helped to secure the rejection of the proposed state constitution. The instrument was then revised (as he suggested) and adopted. He was the foremost lawyer of Massachusetts, and as its chief justice (1806–13) set many precedents for later rulings.

Parsons' Cause, a Virginia issue, was precipitated when the colony passed laws (1755, 1758) changing salary payments to ministers from tobacco (the traditional medium) to money, at a discounted rate. The ministers obtained a royal veto of the laws (1760), which in turn was upset by young Patrick Henry on the ground that vetoes against the public good were improper. The clergy's appeal to the Privy Council was dismissed (1766), but a new law in 1769 ended their agitation.

Partisan bands are detached light troops that engage in harassing the enemy. They are somewhat like guerrillas (who conduct hit-and-run raids), and somewhat like commandos in that they are nominally under constituted command. They were first used in America during the intermittent French and Indian Wars (1689–1763), when both organized militia and irregular 'rangers,' such as those led by ROBERT ROGERS, took part in campaigns. During the Revolution the GREEN MOUNTAIN BOYS and the followers of FRANCIS MARION and ANDREW PICKENS were partisan bands. Notable during the Civil War were MOSBY'S RANGERS.

PARTON, JAMES (1822–91), English-born writer, in 1827 was brought to the U.S. He later joined the staff of N. P. Willis's *Home Journal,* and in 1856 married Willis's sister, Sara Payson Willis (1811–72), who wrote popular sketches under the pseudonym 'Fanny Fern.' Parton was the first professional biographer in America, and he wrote with vigor and judiciousness. Still useful as personal portraits are his lives of Horace Greeley (1855), Aaron Burr (1858), Andrew Jackson (3 vols., 1860), Benjamin Franklin (2 vols., 1864), and John Jacob Astor (1865).

Party government is the assumption by the victorious political party of the responsibility for the conduct of government. In the U.S. party responsibility, as the term is used in England, has never existed, since in the U.S. parties as such do not formulate policies. Nevertheless the winning party in the U.S. can dominate in a variety of ways. It coordinates the activities of administration through conferences, caucuses, committees, and legally appointed officers. It appoints its members to chairmanships and other key positions, and from its number are chosen the majority leader and the Speaker of the House. The national and state committees of the party exercise great influence by integrating the executive and legislative branches as a smoothly functioning organism, and elected officials are indebted to such committees for political and financial support. Appointed governmental officers are usually indebted to the party leadership for their offices.

Party machines are the political organizations, operative on local, municipal, and state levels, that seek to develop party discipline and to control party politics. In the U.S. such organizations have traditionally been loosely bound associations, lacking comprehensive platforms and explicit programs. Inasmuch as discipline was difficult to exert on the organization itself, and on the rank and file of its members, the person who could make the machine function became the political boss. He in turn evolved the system of PATRONAGE because he was able to deliver his promises to the party faithful.

The first party machine in the U.S. to function on a state-wide level was the New York ALBANY REGENCY, which developed after 1820 and flourished for 30 years. Based on the principle that 'to the victor belong the spoils,' the party machine became a potent administrative and organizational factor in disposing of public funds and resources. Thus by its nature the machine invited practices that often involve fraud and corruption. But as citizens became increasingly interested in public affairs, the crude and irresponsible machine system was brought under scrutiny and control, and a merit system was established.

The invidious meaning of the term 'political boss' dates from the exposure of the TWEED RING in New York City

(1872). Effective bosses have been frequent in municipal government, less common in state government, and rare on the national level. The public is mulcted if the boss is corrupt, and the opportunities for spoliation are in proportion to the wealth of the community and the efficiency of the machine, but even the most notorious machine politicians have seldom done more than measure up to their opportunities. Some have had peculation as their aim, but most have chiefly sought to wield power. The long history of TAMMANY HALL as a powerful Democratic machine in New York illustrates the vices and virtues of the party machine.

The names of several colorful, if not exemplary, machine politicians have become part of American folklore. Such among city bosses (besides Tweed) have been RICHARD CROKER (New York), WILLIAM S. VARE (Philadelphia), GEORGE B. COX (Cincinnati), ABE RUEF (San Francisco), T. J. PENDERGAST (Kansas City), and JAMES M. CURLEY (Boston); among state bosses, T. C. PLATT (New York), SIMON CAMERON, M. S. QUAY, BOIES PENROSE (Pennsylvania), and HUEY LONG (Louisiana).

See Harold Zink, *City Bosses in the U.S.* (1930), and Richard Hofstadter, *The American Political Tradition* (1948).

Party system, see *Political parties.*

Party whip in Congress is the party member designated in caucus to round up other members for important roll calls, during which members are expected to vote along party lines. Republican Representative James E. Watson (1863–1948) was the first to be so designated in the House (1899). James H. Lewis (*c.* 1865–1939) was elected the first (Democratic) whip of the Senate (1913). Party whips are now regularly chosen in both houses, and their effectiveness is increased by a number of assistant whips, some of whom are present on the floor at all times.

PASTORIUS, FRANCIS DANIEL (1651–*c.* 1720), German-born lawyer, as agent for the Frankfort Pietists and Rhine MENNONITES, purchased land in Pennsylvania (1683) and laid out the settlement of Germantown. As a leading citizen, he served as mayor, land agent, teacher, and writer, particularly of books dealing with Pennsylvania. In 1688 he initiated a Quaker protest against slavery, the earliest of its kind in the English colonies.

Patent medicine by legal interpretation designates a medicine whose recipe is patented. Popularly it is applied to any proprietary medicine. The patent medicine business developed rapidly in the U.S. after 1815, and by the end of the 19th century it had become highly competitive, annually grossing some $75,000,000. Although medical societies fought it from the start, no effective action against pretentious claims was taken until 1905. In that year Samuel H. Adams (1871–1958) aroused public indignation through a series of articles in *Collier's Magazine* on 'The Great American Fraud,' and Harvey W. Wiley (1844–1930), chief chemist in the Department of Agriculture, at the request of President Theodore Roosevelt made recommendations that resulted in the passage of the PURE FOOD AND DRUG ACT (1906). The New Deal greatly expanded and strengthened this law by the Food, Drug, and Cosmetic Act of 1938, which specifically forbade many types of deception and required a statement of ingredients upon the labels. Thus began an interdiction of fraudulent claims for cure-alls, but the law plugged relatively few holes. The Kefauver Committee's Senate investigation of the drug industry in 1961 resulted in the Kefauver-Harris Drug Amendment of 1962, requiring that drugs, previously tested only for safety, must be proved to be effective by the manufacturers, who were also required to issue annual reports on their experiences with each drug. In spite of these Federal regulations, the annual 'take' for the promoters of specious medication at present is said to exceed a billion dollars.

See J. H. Young, *The Toadstool Millionaires: A Social History of Patent Medicines in America* (1961).

Patents, in law, secure to the inventor of a product or process a monopoly right to its use for a specified period. In the American colonies they were established by legislatures to encourage new industries. The first to be issued (1641) was granted to Samuel Winslow of Massachusetts for a process of manufacturing salt, the term of the patent to extend ten years. Shortly before the adoption of the Federal Constitution several states had issued patents for mechanical inventions, notably those of OLIVER EVANS and JOHN FITCH.

The U.S. Patent Office began functioning in 1790 under constitutional authority (Art. I, sec. 8) within the Department of State, largely through the efforts of JOHN STEVENS, the New Jersey inventor and industrialist. In 1802 it became a bureau managed by a Superintendent, who was elevated to the rank of Commissioner in 1836. In 1849 the Patent Office was transferred from State to the newly created Department of the Interior, and finally (1925) to the Department of Commerce. (It also administers the Federal trademark laws.) Patents carry a monopoly right for seventeen years.

A distinctive feature of U.S. legislation has been the 'improvement patent,' whereby the orginator of a new idea may benefit from his contribution to bettering an already protected process or device. Various amendments to patent law have sought to stimulate industrial invention. By 1840, 1000 patents had been issued; by 1850, 6500; and by 1965 more than 3,000,000 patents had been granted.

PATERSON, WILLIAM (1745–1806), brought to Princeton, New Jersey, by his Irish father, graduated from the College of New Jersey (1763). He practiced law and served his state as attorney general (1776–83). He headed the New Jersey delegation to the Federal Constitutional Convention (1787) and submitted the PATERSON PLAN, rejected on the issue of popular representation in Congress. As U.S. senator (1789–90) he took a prominent part in drafting the JUDICIARY ACT of 1789. He served his state as governor before his appointment to the U.S. Supreme Court (1793–1806), in which post he supported Federalist principles. In his devotion to the judiciary, he declined Washington's offer (1795) of the portfolio of State, and later the office of Attorney General. Paterson, New Jersey, is named for him.

Paterson Plan, also called the New Jersey Plan, was submitted to the Federal Constitutional Convention by WILLIAM PATERSON. It sponsored the demands of the small states for equal representation in the new government, and proposed a unicameral legislature. It was rejected in favor of the CONNECTICUT COMPROMISE, which advocated two legislative branches, one to represent states equally and one to represent population differences. The Paterson Plan contained a clause which in modified form became a key clause in the Constitution: that treaties and acts of Congress should be supreme in the land.

Patronage, as a political term, in the U.S. includes all forms of emolument at the disposal of successful candidates for public office. Within legal limits, public jobs and contracts may be disposed at the whim of the chief of governmental units involved, and are expected to further the interests of the officer or the party he represents. This SPOILS SYSTEM was first used on a large scale during the administration of President Jackson. When patronage becomes the adjunct of corrupt PARTY MACHINES, the taxpayer is not being assessed for public services but for the support of a party. In 1883 the PENDLETON ACT made possible a merit system in the Civil Service. The report of the HOOVER COMMISSION (1949) increased the scope of the service to include postmasters, customs officers, and U.S. marshals. In fact, the only important group of Federal officers still subject to political appointment are the heads and subheads of executive departments, ambassadors, presidential assistants, and certain members of Federal commissions and agencies.

Patrons of Husbandry, see *Granger movement*.

Patroons were the wealthy landowners in colonial NEW NETHERLAND. The Dutch West India Company first encouraged them to emigrate (1629) by granting them large estates, principally along the Hudson river. With feudal rights of perpetual ownership, and control of local offices and civil and criminal courts, they could exact payment from their tenants in money, goods, or services. This anachronistic system continued largely unchanged until 1775, when patroons became proprietors of estates.

It was not abolished until 1846, when, following the ANTI-RENT WAR, the New York legislature revoked the old tenure laws.

PATTERSON, ROBERT WILSON (1850–1910), after graduation from Williams (1871) became a reporter on the CHICAGO TRIBUNE. He married Elinor Medill, daughter of the *Tribune* owner, JOSEPH MEDILL. After his father-in-law died, Patterson became editor in chief of the newspaper.

His son, JOSEPH MEDILL PATTERSON (1879–1946), a graduate of Yale (1901), worked on the *Tribune* staff, and after 1914 gained part control, helping to edit the paper until 1925 with his cousins JOSEPH MEDILL MC CORMICK and ROBERT R. MC CORMICK. In 1919 he founded the New York *Daily News* (later the New York *News*), the first successful tabloid in the U.S. By sensational handling of sex and crime, and by extensive use of photography, the *News* soon came to have the largest newspaper circulation in the country (estimated in 1965 at 2,000,000 daily and 3,160,000 Sunday). After 1940 Patterson, a fervent isolationist, withdrew his support of President Roosevelt.

Robert Patterson's daughter, ELEANOR ['CISSY'] MEDILL PATTERSON (1884–1948), was at first associated with her brother's *Daily News*. In 1930 she became editor of the Hearst syndicate's Washington *Herald*. She later (1937) leased the Washington *Times*, so that she might have an organ to express her disagreements with Hearst. In 1939 she bought the *Herald* and merged her papers into the Washington *Times-Herald*. She followed the family tradition of slanted news and mass circulation.

PATTIE, JAMES OHIO (1804–50?), Kentucky-born trapper and explorer, made several extensive, hazardous, and unprofitable trips into the Southwest. Late in the 1820's, there was a smallpox epidemic in California. Pattie, who had a modest supply of vaccine in his possession, at the urgent request of the Mexican authorities visited nearly every settlement from San Diego to San Francisco. He is estimated to have inoculated some 23,000 persons with a supply of live vaccine, which he replenished from inoculated patients. The dollar a patient he had expected for the service was finally made dependent on such complex conditions that Pattie sought redress from the government in Mexico City. The President of Mexico was sympathetic but the claims were disallowed, and Pattie returned to Kentucky, bitter and impoverished. Timothy Flint edited Pattie's *Personal Narrative* (1831), an important contribution to frontier annals, even though its details are frequently inaccurate. Pattie joined the gold rush in 1849, visited San Diego, and camped in the Sierra, where he is said to have perished during a severe winter storm.

PATTON, GEORGE SMITH (1885–1945), a graduate of the U.S. Military Academy (1909), commanded the U.S. 2nd Corps in North Africa (1942–43), and the 7th Army in Sicily (1943), during World War II. (The much-publicized incident of his slapping a soldier suffering from battle fatigue temporarily cost him his command.) He was a brilliant tactician; his 3rd Army spearheaded the spectacular sweep through Brittany and across the Rhine (1944–45). He was commanding the U.S. 5th Army when he was killed in an automobile accident.

PAULDING, HIRAM (1797–1878), born in Westchester county, New York, began his naval career as a midshipman in the War of 1812. He describes his pursuit of mutineers in the Pacific in *Journal of a Cruise of the U.S. Schooner Dolphin* (1831). His *Bolívar in His Camp* (1834) is an account of a 1500-mile horseback trip in the Andes (1824) to deliver messages to Simón Bolívar from Admiral ISAAC HULL. As commander (1855–58) of the home squadron off Nicaragua, he arrested the American freebooter, WILLIAM WALKER, an act which delighted the Nicaraguans and embarrassed President Buchanan, who had recognized Walker's regime. Buchanan relieved Paulding of command. Paulding was restored to duty with the rank of rear admiral in 1862, and he was active throughout the Civil War.

PAULDING, JAMES KIRKE (1778–1860), was a prolific New York writer and a leading member of the KNICKERBOCKER GROUP. Nationalistic in all things, he established himself as an enthusiastic defender of Jeffersonian agrarianism in a series of books employing both realistic descriptions of the U.S., and burlesque comments about the English. In his defense of homespun American qualities he typified the new nation coming to self-awareness. Although he never relied upon literature exclusively for his livelihood, it was his real vocation. Fielding was his model for realistic fiction, and in such stories as *The Dutchman's Fireside* (1831) and *Westward Ho!* (1832) Paulding gave a panoramic picture of the last days of the American colonies. His lifelong interest in naval affairs brought him an appointment as member of the Board of Naval Commissioners (1815–23), and culminated in his service as Van Buren's Secretary of the Navy (1838–41).

PAULING, LINUS CARL (1901–), professor of chemistry at California Institute of Technology after 1931, made notable contributions in the field of organic chemistry. His theory of resonance in the molecular structure of organic chemicals led to a better understanding of certain properties of the carbon compounds. His work on the nature of serological reactions and the molecular structure of antitoxins advanced the frontier of immunology. He studied the forces binding proteins and molecules, reported in *The Nature of the Chemical Bond* (1939), for which research he received the 1954 Nobel Prize in chemistry. For his work to establish a ban on test explosions of nuclear weapons he was awarded the Nobel Peace prize for 1962.

Pauperism, see *Social Work.*

Pawnee Indians (or Pani Indians), of Caddoan stock, were four bison-hunting Plains 'village' tribes, settled in the valley of the Platte river when the Spaniards encountered them in the 16th century. Fierce fighters and expert horsemen, they had highly developed ceremonial systems and a rich mythology. Reduced by wars and epidemics, they were settled on a reservation in Oklahoma in 1876 and now number some 1200.

Paxton Boys, so called, were the band of 'back inhabitants' from Paxton, Pennsylvania, who in 1763, as a result of the insecurity of the frontier against Indian attacks, fell on a little settlement of peaceable Christian Indians, massacred them, then marched on Philadelphia intent on wiping out Indian refugees who had fled to the capital for protection. The incident was symptomatic of sectional tensions. The easterners controlled the assembly and kept the frontier under-represented. Probably frontiersmen provoked Indian uprisings to give color to their demand for better defense. Benjamin Franklin's diplomacy averted open conflict between the Paxton Boys and the authorities, but the episode revealed the bitterness of sectional hatred, similarly expressed during the 1780's by SHAYS'S REBELLION in New England, and by the uprising of REGULATORS in North and South Carolina. Indeed, in the 1760's a civil war among the colonists seemed more likely than a war for independence from Britain.

Payne-Aldrich Tariff Act (1909), although intended as a tariff reform in accordance with the Republican party's platform pledge of 1908, actually became a protective measure, with an average duty of 40.73 per cent. The heated debates over the bill suggested to the country a close connection between tariffs and big business. The Act contributed to the defeat of the party in the congressional elections of 1910, and constituted a political issue during the next presidential campaign, which the Democrats won.

PEABODY, ELIZABETH PALMER (1804–94), sister-in-law of Hawthorne and of Horace Mann, made a career of education and social reform. In the family's Boston home, where her father practiced dentistry, Elizabeth opened a bookshop which, as the Transcendental Club, became the rendezvous for the younger intellectuals, and there Margaret Fuller gave her 'Conversations' (1839–44), stimulating talks on social and literary topics. For a time Miss Peabody assisted Bronson Alcott with his Temple School, a venture she describes in *Record of a School* (1835); and as a disciple of the German educator Friedrich Froebel she later opened the first English-speaking kindergarten (1860) in the U.S. (Mrs. CARL SCHURZ had already opened a German-speaking kindergarten at Watertown, Wisconsin.)

Reminiscences of her gentle but highly individualistic life are set forth in *A Last Evening with Allston* (1886), a gathering of essays recalling in the title her recollections of the Boston painter. She was then known and loved as the 'grandmother of Boston,' an inveterate lecture-goer, always so absorbed in her projects that the story is told that on one occasion she walked into a tree: 'I saw it,' she reflected, 'but I did not realize it.'

PEABODY, GEORGE (1795–1869), born in South Danvers (now Peabody), Massachusetts, having established prosperous drygoods firms in eastern seaboard cities, settled permanently in London (1837) where, as the leading international banker of the late 19th century (allied with the Morgans), he became immensely wealthy. His large philanthropies included the pioneer educational foundation in the U.S. (1867), the Peabody Education Fund, a grant of $3,500,000 to promote education in the South, recognized by Congress with a vote of thanks. He also founded and endowed a number of scientific museums in his name, of which the best known are those at Baltimore, Harvard, and Yale.

Peace Corps, U.S. (1962), is a volunteer organization created by executive order of President Kennedy as 'a pool of trained men and women sent overseas by the U.S. government or through private institutions and organizations to help foreign countries meet their urgent needs for skilled manpower.' Congress immediately enacted legislation to give the Peace Corps permanent standing. Congressional appropriations in 1965 reached $115,000,000, sufficient for 14,000 volunteers.

'Peace' Democrats, see *Copperheads.*

Peace movements, see *American Peace Society* (1828), *Arbitration, League of Nations, Disarmament Conferences,* and *United Nations.* See also *William Ladd* and *Elihu Burritt.* A historical survey is Merle E. Curti, *Peace or War: The American Struggle, 1636–1936* (1936).

PEALE, CHARLES WILLSON (1741–1827), starting life as a saddler's apprentice in Annapolis, soon became his own master in a variety of trades which he taught himself, including watchmaking, sign painting, silversmithing, and upholstery. In 1765, to avoid imprisonment for debt, he fled to Boston, where for a year he studied portraiture under Copley. Convinced of his talent, prominent Maryland gentlemen sent him to London, where he continued his art training under Benjamin West (1766–69). On his return he traveled the countryside, painting the gentry. At Mount Vernon in 1772 he painted the earliest portrait of Washington (Penn. Hist. Soc.), the first of his seven paintings for which Washington posed. Honest, if stiff and crude in color, it is judged, like his others, to be more faithful as a representation than the more elegant portraits by Gilbert Stuart.

After settling in Philadelphia (1776) Peale raised a company of soldiers and served under Washington in the campaigns around Trenton and Princeton, meanwhile painting miniatures of high officers as historical record. With Stuart and Copley he was recognized as a leading American portrait painter. He experimented in all branches of graphic arts: oils, water color, sculpture, etching, and mezzotint.

Thrice widowed, Peale was the father of seventeen children (several of them very talented), and he adopted three more. In naming his offspring he honored the arts and sciences: Raphaelle, Rembrandt, Rubens, Titian, Linnaeus, Franklin, and so on. The household, guided by Peale's bustling enthusiasms, was extraordinarily happy. Almost all sang, accompanied by a variety of home constructed musical instruments, and likewise painted. In addition to the family, the household was frequently enlarged by brothers, sisters, nieces, nephews, and various transients, black, white, and Indian. The unlimited number of pets included bears, snakes, and a five-legged two-tailed cow, which provided dairy products. In the kitchen Peale experimented with taxidermy and manufactured such items as gunpowder, shoes, porcelain, eyeglasses, and false teeth. Under his management all functioned creatively, and Jefferson so warmly admired this egalitarian that he sent his grandson to live for a time with the Peales.

In 1801, learning of the discovery of

a mastodon skeleton on a New York farm, Peale purchased the right to exhume the bones. With a loan from the American Philosophical Society, of which Jefferson was president, and with equipment furnished by the Army, Peale conducted the first scientific expedition in the U.S. In the following year he opened Peale's Museum, the first natural history museum in the country. In 1805 he was instrumental in founding America's earliest public art gallery, the Pennsylvania Academy of the Fine Arts, and for seventeen years contributed to its exhibitions. At eighty-six, during the winter of 1827, when he was courting a prospective fourth wife, Peale died, but a true child of the Enlightenment and curious to the end, he expired while studying his own failing pulse.

Peale believed that any intelligent person could paint, and he taught all members of his family, including his brother, JAMES PEALE (1749–1831), who became a successful painter of miniatures and landscapes. His son, REMBRANDT PEALE (1778–1860), was, like his father, a pupil of West, and on his return from Europe (1810) devoted himself chiefly to portraiture. An original member of the National Academy of Design, in 1825 he succeeded John Trumbull as president of the Academy of Fine Arts. His idealized likeness of Washington (1823) hangs in the National Capitol. The two other sons eminent as painters were RAPHAELLE PEALE (1774–1825), presumably the finest artist in the family, a wit and an alcoholic, best known for his still lifes, and TITIAN PEALE (1799–1885), whose interest in nature studies led him to become a painter of animals.

See Charles C. Sellers, *Charles Willson Peale* (2 vols., 1947).

Pearl Harbor, one of the key U.S. naval bases (on the south coast of Oahu, Hawaii), was attacked early on Sunday morning, 7 December 1941, by Japanese carrier planes, while negotiations were still in progress in Washington between Secretary of State Hull and the Japanese envoys. At one stroke the entire Pacific battle fleet and half the planes on the island were wiped out. The local commanders, the government, and the nation at large were taken completely by surprise. Nobody in authority had believed that the Japanese could or would strike Hawaii. The attack united a hesitant America, bringing her angry and determined into World War II.

Of the 94 naval vessels in Pearl Harbor, 19 were sunk or disabled, 150 airplanes destroyed, and 2335 soldiers and sailors killed. Casualties among civilians exceeded 1200. After an exhaustive investigation the Joint Congressional Committee found that the top commanders at Pearl Harbor, Rear Admiral Husband Kimmel and Lieutenant General Walter Short, had been guilty of negligence.

PEARY, ROBERT EDWIN (1856–1920), a graduate of Bowdoin (1877), entered the navy as civil engineer. His interest in arctic exploration led him to make a trip to the interior of Greenland in 1886. On subsequent expeditions there he recorded important ethnological and meteorological observations, explored the arctic peninsula later named Peary Land (1892), and in 1897 brought back his noted meteorites. On his first search for the North Pole (1898–1902) he reached latitude 84°17′, and in 1905–6 he came within 175 miles of his objective. On 6 April 1909 he achieved his goal. A bitter controversy ensued when Dr. FREDERICK A. COOK made claims of prior discovery, but Congress recognized Peary's achievement, which later investigations verified. In 1911 Peary received the thanks of Congress and was retired from the navy with the rank of rear admiral.

Pecos Bill, legendary giant cowboy of the Southwest, in his exploits resembles PAUL BUNYAN and TONY BEAVER, the lumberjack heroes. In the heyday of ranching in west Texas along the Pecos river, 'west of the Pecos' was the term identifying the wild and mountainous region of the western tip of the state.

PEIRCE, CHARLES SANDERS (1839–1914), son of the Harvard mathematician Benjamin Peirce (1809–80), graduated from Harvard in 1859. He was an original thinker and voluminous writer, but was relatively unknown in his own day since he published very little. He is now established, however, as the greatest American logician of his century. He rejected the regimen of academic life and held only brief lectureships, chiefly at Johns

Hopkins (1879–84). He therefore made philosophy an avocation, while he spent his active years (1861–91) as a member of the U.S. Coast and Geodetic Survey. Yet during that time he founded PRAGMATISM, gained the enduring respect of William James, and helped shape the idealism of Josiah Royce and the later views of John Dewey.

Peirce made basic contributions to logic, scientific methodology, probability theory, and induction. Believing that logic is rooted in ethics, he opposed DETERMINISM, substituting 'fallibilism,' the theory of an evolutionary universe in which the reality of chance and the principle of continuity are absolute. He first outlined his pragmatic concept in the *North American Review* (October 1871) and amplified it in later articles, but the bulk of his writing remained in manuscript during his lifetime. Morris R. Cohen edited a few major essays in *Chance, Love, and Logic* (1923). His *Collected Papers* have now been gathered (8 vols., 1931–58).

PENDERGAST, THOMAS JOSEPH (1873–1945), after holding minor political offices in Kansas City, Missouri (1899–1910), became the acknowledged Democratic boss of the city and state. His support assured the election of Harry S Truman to the U.S. Senate (1934). Convicted of income-tax evasions (1939), he served time in Leavenworth until paroled (1940) on condition that he abstain from political activity for five years. He did not meet the condition, and he was sentenced for criminal contempt of court, but the U.S. Supreme Court reversed the decision in 1943 under the statute of limitations. Few PARTY MACHINES of his day were run with greater efficiency.

Pendleton Act, see *Civil Service Commission.*

Peninsular Campaign (April–July 1862) was the first large-scale operation in the eastern theater of the Civil War. General George B. McClellan intended to capture Richmond by advancing up the peninsula between the James and York rivers with his well trained and equipped force, 110,000 strong, the most redoubtable ever assembled on the continent. The Confederate Army of Northern Virginia was commanded by General Joseph E. Johnston who, with fewer men, was prepared to meet McClellan's advance.

The battle of FAIR OAKS (31 May–1 June), fought less than ten miles from Richmond, ended the first phase but decided no issue. Johnston was wounded, and General Lee took over command. McClellan withdrew to the protection of Union gunboats on the James, and while he waited for good weather to advance under cover of his superior artillery, Lee took the offensive. Then ensued the SEVEN DAYS' BATTLES (26 June–2 July), a decisive Confederate victory. The Federal forces were withdrawn from the peninsula, and not until the close of the war did the Union army again approach so near to Richmond.

PENN, WILLIAM (1644–1718), son of Admiral Sir William Penn (1621–70), became interested in Quakerism before he quit Oxford (1662). His father had served the Stuarts loyally and, as an official of the navy office, in the manner of the times had enriched himself. In his early twenties young Penn was arrested for attending a Quaker meeting (1667), and as a consequence he developed a profound concern for the persecuted of all sects. While lodged in the Tower of London (1669) for publishing a tract attacking religious orthodoxy, he wrote his best-known work, *No Cross, No Crown,* emphasizing that an inner light (the Quaker spirituality) was essential to the correction of the sins and abuses of the day. Determined to establish a colony in America as a refuge for all persecuted sectarians, through the favor of Charles II in 1681 Penn was granted a princely domain on the Delaware and the Susquehanna rivers for his 'holy experiment.' He called it Pennsylvania, 'a name the king would have given it in honor of my father.' The charter gave him proprietary rights and some feudal powers, and his persuasive tracts soliciting immigrants attracted some 3000 new citizens within a year after his arrival (1682).

He framed a liberal government and established the friendly relations with the Indians that distinguished the early history of the colony. Penn's friendship with the deposed James II led to his recall, and for a time (1692–94) the crown held the colony. It was later restored and for a brief period Penn returned (1699–1701), but the fraudulent actions of his steward again called him to London, where he was imprisoned for a debt. It was finally paid and he was released. Penn's last years, spent at the court of Queen Anne, were devoted to the business of his colony until 1712, when a stroke of apoplexy removed him from active life.

Penn was a complex character. An honest Quaker preacher, he was at the same time a successful courtier. As a proprietor he adopted policies that gave the citizens of Pennsylvania a personal liberty unknown in other colonies, yet he had a phenomenal propensity for making mistakes in judging those to whom he gave administrative authority. He was no Quaker pacifist, for he was ready to use force to carry out the decisions of the proposed world court and league of nations that he outlined in his notable *Essay Toward the Present and Future Peace of Europe* (1693). As an enlightened city planner he adopted the new orderly checkerboard pattern of streets for Philadelphia that the architect Christopher Wren had introduced in London after the Great Fire of 1666. A prolific writer on theological, moral, and political subjects, Penn was also a statesman who organized the colonies of New Jersey, Pennsylvania, and Delaware on the basis of religious toleration and political democracy.

Recent studies include those by W. W. Comfort (1944), and C. O. Peare (1957).

Pennsylvania, second of the Thirteen Colonies to ratify the Constitution and enter the Union (12 December 1787), in the early 17th century was a region known only in the Delaware river vicinity, the right to which was disputed by the English, Dutch, and Swedes. Very little effective settlement took place before WILLIAM PENN secured proprietary rights (1681) to almost all of the present state. The last of the PROPRIETARY COLONIES, it remained in the hands of the Penn family throughout the colonial era. Penn was a devout Quaker who viewed his colony as a holy experiment. In 1682 he constructed a Frame of Government that guaranteed to colonists complete religious freedom, laid out his City of Brotherly Love (Philadelphia), signed his famous treaty of friendship with the Indians, and created an assembly with executive and legislative branches.

The growing colony was steadily enriched by immigration. The Quakers (mostly English and Welsh), concentrated in the eastern counties, were the dominant political and commercial element throughout the 18th century. The Germans (called PENNSYLVANIA DUTCH) settled in the prize farmland of southeastern Pennsylvania. After 1718 Scotch-Irish immigrants began colonizing in the Cumberland valley, gradually pushing the frontiers into western Pennsylvania. Resentful of encroachments on their lands, the Indians allied themselves with the French, who were fortifying positions in the Ohio valley. The first battle of the French and Indian War was fought (1754) at the present site of PITTSBURGH.

Although the loyalist groups were strengthened at the outbreak of the War of Independence by the pacifist stand of Quakers and noncombatant Germans, the patriot cause was supported by such leaders as BENJAMIN FRANKLIN, JOHN DICKINSON, and ROBERT MORRIS. Throughout the war PHILADELPHIA was the center of events, and notable engagements were fought at BRANDYWINE and GERMANTOWN.

The state moved into the postwar period as dynamic leader of the new nation, with Philadelphia the financial center and national capital (1790–1800). Angered by the new burden of national taxes, frontier farmers defied Federal authority in a WHISKY REBELLION (1794), which was soon quelled. Thereafter intensive programs of internal improvements were carried forward. The importance of the westward movement was reflected by the removal of the state capital first to Lancaster (1799), then permanently to Harrisburg (1812). Pittsburgh and Erie became gateways to the West, with new industries spreading throughout the state. The Lancaster Turnpike (1794) inaugurated the era of TURNPIKES. Adequate provisions for free public education were implemented in 1849 by legislation requiring compulsory school attendance into the secondary level.

Pennsylvania troops were the first to arrive in Washington at the outbreak of the Civil War. The position of the 'keystone state' exposed it to invasion through the Cumberland valley, and on its soil was fought the decisive battle of GETTYSBURG (1863). At the close of the war the state emerged as a mighty industrial commonwealth, with oil, steel, and coal making it influential in world finance.

A complex of many racial and economic groups today, with a diversity of pressures and interests, the state is a miniature nation, possessing a degree of self-sufficiency enjoyed by few countries in the world. Five of its more than 100 institutions of higher education were established during the colonial period: University of Pennsylvania (Philadelphia, est. 1751), Dickinson (Carlisle, est. 1773), Washington and Jefferson (Washington, est. 1781), University of Pittsburgh (est. 1787), and Franklin and Marshall (Lancaster, est. 1787).

Pennsylvania Academy of the Fine Arts (1805), founded at Philadelphia by Charles Willson Peale, is the oldest art institution in the U.S. Its art collection is a representative cross section of American painting from the Revolutionary period to the present. Its art school has been especially influential.

Pennsylvania Dutch is the common but erroneous name for the German-American people of Pennsylvania and for their language, principally the tongue of the immigrants from southwestern Germany and Switzerland. In 1683 FRANCIS DANIEL PASTORIUS and his followers settled Germantown. CONRAD BEISSEL and his monastic brothers and sisters came to Lancaster county in 1720, and thereafter during the 18th and 19th centuries large numbers migrated to these prosperous farming communities, where they established churches, schools, printing presses, and newspapers. Segregated until recent times, they retained their customs and their language, a Palatinate dialect with a mixture of High German and English. Family and religious ties have been strong, the best known sects being the MENNONITES and DUNKARDS. A substantial Pennsylvania-German literature, mostly religious, was written in literary German, and the art and architecture of the region reflect a racial consciousness. The Pennsylvania-German Society (1891) publishes material dealing with local history.

Pennsylvania Railroad, chartered as a local project (1846), by 1854 connected Philadelphia and Pittsburgh. Branches were added, and during the Civil War it was immensely important in transporting troops and supplies. The present system, a great part of which was acquired between 1868 and 1872 through the efforts of J. Edgar Thomson (1808–74) and THOMAS SCOTT, consists of almost 12,000 miles of track. It is the principal rail link between the Atlantic seaboard and the Mississippi, as well as the Great Lakes and Ohio, and serves thirteen states. In 1965 the Interstate Commerce Commission approved plans for a merger with the NEW YORK CENTRAL RAILROAD.

Pennsylvania, University of, planned as a charity school (1740), opened in 1751 as an academy, with Benjamin Franklin as the first president of trustees. In 1755 it became the College and Academy of Philadelphia with WILLIAM SMITH as provost. The General Assembly voided its charter in 1779, alleging that the institution violated the state's constitutional guarantee of equal privileges for all denominations, and instead created the University of the State of Pennsylvania. With charter restored (1789), the college was joined in 1791 with the University under its present name.

Pennsylvania was a pioneer in secular education, and the first institution in the U.S. to open a school of medicine (1765), a university teaching hospital (1874), business school (1881), and psychological clinic (1896). Its archaeological field studies, especially in the Near East, have been conducted for many decades. In 1965, with an endowment of $88,800,000 and a faculty of 3800, it enrolled 18,800 students.

Penny press, so called, came into existence when the New York *Sun* went on sale (1833) for a penny. The growing educational movement and increased literacy demanded a cheap press with broad popular appeal, and almost immediately other penny papers were established.

Penology, see *Prison reform.*

PENROSE, BOIES (1860–1921), after graduation from Harvard (1881) began the practice of law in Philadelphia, where he displayed such a talent for political organization that he became invaluable to the Pennsylvania state Republican machine. Elected to the U.S. Senate (1897–1921), he not only dominated Pennsylvania politics after the death of MATTHEW QUAY in 1904, but for many years greatly influenced Republican national politics as well. He became the Republican leader in the Senate upon the retirement (1911) of NELSON W. ALDRICH.

Pensions, as financial payments to veterans who have served under arms, were offered as inducements to enlistment in colonial wars and in the Revolution. They have been granted by the U.S. to participants in most of its wars, including Indian wars, and to the regular servicemen in peacetime. Congress passed the first service pension law in 1818, and the first pensions for widows of Revolutionary soldiers in 1836. (Service pensions for the War of 1812 were granted in 1871, and for the Mexican War in 1887.) The first general Civil War pension bill, passed in 1862, was based on the sound theory of all earlier pension legislation. The government assumed an obligation to pension veterans who suffered from disabilities contracted while in service, and to assist the widows and children of those veterans. Soon after the Civil War private pension bills were presented by pension attorneys, and pushed through Congress by congressmen eager to make political capital. These small grabs soon became a raid on the public treasury.

In 1887 the pension scandal became a national disgrace with passage of the Dependent Pension Bill, pushed through by powerful G.A.R. lobbies, granting pensions to all veterans suffering from any kind of disability, regardless of how contracted. President Cleveland's veto of the bill was an important factor in his failure to be re-elected in 1888. Almost yearly thereafter some form of amendment augmented veterans' allowances, until the Act of 1904 transformed all previous legislation into a straight service pension by allotting monthly payments.

After World War I the grant of a veterans' BONUS (over the veto of four successive Presidents) and generous hospitalization privileges were given partly in the hope of averting an outright pension system. Following World War II the problem of veterans' readjustment compensation was intelligently handled by passage of the so-called G.I. BILL OF RIGHTS. In 1959 the Veterans' Pension Act made major revisions in benefits to needy veterans for non-service-connected disabilities, or to their widows and children. The cost over a 40-year period is estimated at $9 billion.

Pensions, Old-Age, see *Old-Age Pension Laws.*

People's party, see *Populist party.*

PEPPERRELL, SIR WILLIAM (1696–1759), wealthy Maine fish and lumber merchant, first came into prominence in 1730 when he was appointed chief justice of the Massachusetts court of common pleas. At the outbreak of KING GEORGE'S WAR (1744) Governor William Shirley placed Pepperrell in charge of 4000 militiamen with instructions to lay siege to the fortress of Louisbourg, built by the French on Cape Breton Island, Nova Scotia, and judged to be impregnable. The siege took place in 1745. Before it began British naval forces blocked the all-important sea approaches. (There were no naval engagements.) Then Pepperrell organized a commando raid which was successful, largely through sheer luck and audacious bumptiousness. The exploit was described by one participant as something like a boisterous Harvard commencement. Lacking naval support, the fortress was in fact untenable, since it was landlocked. George II was so impressed by the feat that he made Pepperrell a baronet, the first native American so honored. Later, as president of the council, Pepperrell served briefly as governor of Massachusetts. He was made a lieutenant general shortly before his death.

Pequot War (1637), one of the earliest New England engagements, was the massacre of an Algonquian tribe that had dominated southern Connecticut in the region between Rhode Island and the Connecticut river. The expedition was organized in retaliation for the killing of traders and frontier settlers. The Pequot were attacked near New

Haven and their stronghold was burned, as were most of the 500 Indians, including women and children. The captured remnant were either absorbed into other tribes or sold into slavery.

Perfectionism, the religious utopian doctrine advanced in the mid-19th century by J. H. NOYES, held that man by freeing himself from selfishness may be perfect on earth, a state best achieved by community selection of sexual partners and by economic communism. For a time Noyes held his group together in the ONEIDA COMMUNITY, in central New York state. The socio-religious idealism of the Perfectionists, though different in form, was similar in spirit to all COMMUNAL SOCIETIES of the day.

Periodicals, see *Magazines.*

PERKINS, FRANCES (1882–1965), a graduate of Mount Holyoke (1902), became an authority on industrial hazards and hygiene, and began lobbying in Albany for more comprehensive factory laws and for maximum-hour laws for women. She served on various New York state industrial commissions (1923–33) until President Roosevelt appointed her Secretary of Labor (1933–45). She was the first U.S. woman cabinet member. Though the appointment was bitterly criticized by business, labor, and political leaders, she held her post for twelve years and gained respect for skillfully administering its vastly increased duties under the New Deal.

Permanent Court of Arbitration, popularly known as the Hague Tribunal, was established (1899) by the first HAGUE CONFERENCE. Member nations (about 50) appointed up to four jurists, who constituted a panel from which the nations agreeing to arbitrate made their selections. After the creation of the LEAGUE OF NATIONS the Tribunal lost most of its power (arbitral and diplomatic) to the League's Permanent Court of International Justice (judicial) which was known as the World Court. It also sat at The Hague. The U.S. never joined this court because the Senate refused to ratify its protocol. (An American jurist, however, was always a member of the Court.) The World Court came to an end (1945) when its functions were transferred to the newly created INTERNATIONAL COURT OF JUSTICE, a body within the United Nations.

PERROT, NICOLAS (1644–*c.* 1718), trained by Jesuit missionaries in New France, learned Indian languages and became an influential fur trader in the Green Bay region of Wisconsin. With DULUTH he helped extend the authority of France into the Old Northwest. One of the most picturesque of the *coureurs de bois,* he left a *Mémoire* of his life in the upper Mississippi region, which was published in 1864.

PERRY, MATTHEW CALBRAITH (1794–1858), served under his older brother OLIVER HAZARD PERRY in the U.S. Navy, and took part in the War of 1812. He later pioneered in the application of steam power to warships and commanded one of the first U.S. naval vessels powered by steam, the *Fulton,* on which he conducted (1839–40) the first American naval school of gun practice. Given the rank of commodore, Perry was entrusted by President Fillmore with the mission of opening trade with Japan. In 1853 his armed squadron anchored in Yedo (Tokyo) Bay, where he so impressed the Shogunate by his display of armor and technology that after the epoch-making Treaty of KANAGAWA (1854), Japanese ports were opened to American trade. Congress awarded him $20,000 for his accomplishment, and paid for the publication of his *Narrative* of the expedition (3 vols., 1856).

PERRY, OLIVER HAZARD (1785–1819), Rhode Island–born naval officer and older brother of MATTHEW CALBRAITH PERRY, during the War of 1812 was commissioned to build, equip, and man a fleet of ten ships at Erie, Pennsylvania. His decisive victory in the battle of LAKE ERIE (1813) gave him opportunity to send General William Henry Harrison the well-known message: 'We have met the enemy and they are ours.' For the accomplishment, Perry was acclaimed a national hero and received the thanks of Congress. After completing a diplomatic mission to the Venezuela government (1819), he contracted yellow fever and died in Trinidad. He was buried at Newport, Rhode Island, where a monument was erected to him.

PERRY, Ralph Barton (1876–1957), a pupil and colleague of William James, was a professor of philosophy at Harvard (1913–46). He was a philosophical realist who believed that the things of thought are as real as the things of sense, and that logical entities are as real as physical ones. No presentation of the realist position reached a larger scholarly audience than his *General Theory of Value* (1926). His chief work remains *The Thought and Character of William James* (2 vols., 1935), a notable biography.

Perryville, Battle of (October 1862), was an unexpected Civil War engagement near Danville, Kentucky, between the Confederates under Braxton Bragg (advancing on Louisville from Chattanooga, Tennessee) and Union forces led by D. C. Buell. Though the outcome was indecisive, Bragg continued to dominate central Tennessee until he was forced to withdraw three months later after the costly battle of MURFREESBORO.

PERSHING, John Joseph (1860–1948), Missouri-born soldier, after graduation from the U.S. Military Academy (1886) served as a cavalryman in Indian campaigns and took part in the Spanish-American War. He commanded the campaign in the Philippines against the Moro (1899–1903), and later led the much publicized but unsuccessful punitive expedition (1916) against Pancho Villa during the MEXICAN BORDER CAMPAIGN. President Wilson named him as head of the American Expeditionary Force in World War I, and Pershing's talent for organization was largely responsible for the molding of hastily trained American troops into well-integrated combat units in France. In 1919 he was given permanent rank as General of the Armies of the U.S. Before his retirement he served as army chief of staff (1921–24).

Personal liberty laws, so called, were enactments (1820–50) by which several northern states impeded enforcement of the Fugitive Slave Act of 1793. Southerners believed such laws were a gross infringement of a constitutional guarantee, and cited them among the grievances (1861) justifying SECESSION.

Pet banks, so called, were the banks chosen as depositories for government funds when President Jackson removed Federal deposits from the Bank of the U.S. (1833). By 1836 nearly 90 banks throughout the country were thus selected.

PETER, Hugh (1598–1660), Puritan divine, in 1635 came to New England, where as pastor of the church at Salem he reorganized that body, which had been shattered by the heresies of ROGER WILLIAMS. Peter was active in politics and industrial promotion, and he returned to England in 1641 as an agent for the colony. One of the best-known Puritan figures during Cromwell's protectorate, he took a leading part in the Civil War, and was executed in the early months of the Restoration.

Petersburg Campaign (1864–65) was the most bitterly fought engagement of the Civil War, which it concluded. Three general Union assaults on Lee's entrenchments outside Petersburg failed, and Grant laid siege to the city. After Lee decisively repulsed Grant's attempt to cut a highway to Richmond (October 1864), field operations virtually ceased for the winter. The Union, aware only of stupendous losses, did not know that Grant's tactics were bringing the war to an end by preventing Confederate reinforcements from stopping Sherman's march through Georgia. By spring Lee's attenuated line extended some 35 miles and his resistance was broken at FIVE FORKS. Petersburg fell on 1 April, Richmond was captured, and on 12 April Lee surrendered.

Petrified Forest, 94,000 acres of petrified flora in eastern Arizona, was designated a national park by Congress in 1962.

Petroleum industry, see *Oil industry.*

Phi Beta Kappa, founded at William and Mary (1776) as a secret social undergraduate club, was the first college fraternity in the U.S. (It derives its name from the initials of its Greek motto: 'Philosophy the guide of life.') Chapters were established in other colleges, secrecy was abandoned in 1831, and since 1875 women have been admitted. Membership is limited to honor students selected in their upper-class years. Commencement ceremonies customarily include a Phi Beta Kappa poem or address, and such was the occasion of Emerson's 'The American Scholar' (1837), delivered before the Harvard chapter.

Philadelphia, largest city in Pennsylvania and fourth largest in the nation (2,000,000 in 1960), is situated on the Delaware river 100 miles from the Atlantic. For 30 years it had been the site of Dutch and Swedish trading posts when WILLIAM PENN chose it as capital of his Quaker colony in 1682 and adopted the checkerboard pattern of city growth after the model of Wren's London. Migrations of German sectarians followed the settlement of PASTORIUS in nearby Germantown (1683), and in 1701 Philadelphia became a chartered city. When young Benjamin Franklin arrived there (1723), it was a flourishing center of 10,000 inhabitants. Its industrial and shipping prosperity made it the nucleus of colonial enterprises, and, by mid-18th century, next to London it had become the largest metropolis in the British Empire. Here was founded the earliest American learned society, the AMERICAN PHILOSOPHICAL SOCIETY (1743), and the academy (1751) that became the University of Pennsylvania. It was the center of events during the Revolution, and the first Continental Congress assembled in INDEPENDENCE HALL. The British occupied the city for several months (September–June 1777–78) after the battles of Brandywine and Germantown. In 1790 the capital of the new nation was moved from New York to Philadelphia, and it remained there until the city of Washington became the permanent seat of government in 1800. It continued to be the state capital until 1799.

In 1800 it was the largest city (70,000) in the U.S. and the nation's cultural center. Although New York had a larger population in 1810 (96,000 as against 90,000), Philadelphia continued for some time as the financial hub, with an economy controlled by such wealthy merchants as STEPHEN GIRARD. It prospered from its manufacturing during the Civil War, which was chiefly financed through the banking house of JAY COOKE. Thereafter the city witnessed the rise and fall of speculators like C. T. YERKES, and in 1876 launched the CENTENNIAL EXPOSITION, the first great international exhibition in America.

By the end of the 19th century Philadelphia was not only a great commercial city, whose financial and commercial leaders included A. J. DREXEL, JOHN WANAMAKER, and CYRUS H. K. CURTIS, but one of the most important cultural centers in the hemisphere. Chief among its educational institutions, in addition to the University of Pennsylvania, are the Philadelphia Academy of Fine Arts (est. 1805), Franklin Institute (est. 1824), and Curtis Institute of Music (est. 1924). Nearby are the colleges Haverford (est. 1833), Swarthmore (est. 1864), and Bryn Mawr (est. 1880). The city has been a publishing center since 1700 (thereby attracting Franklin). Many leaders in medicine, architecture, painting, music, literature, and the theater have given distinction to the city, whose character is still conservative and leisurely.

Philadelphia Gas Ring, although less notorious than the New York TWEED RING, actually exerted greater political influence, for it lasted much longer (1865–87) and was more businesslike in its fraudulent practices. The trustees of the city gas department ultimately controlled state as well as city offices, until the organization was successfully prosecuted and an aroused electorate secured reforms.

Philadelphia lawyer, a term designating a shrewd legal mind, though now used disparagingly, originated soon after the Revolution from the high reputation of the Philadelphia bar.

Philanthropy in the colonies was a local matter of dispensing charity to the needy, and by mid-18th century charity societies had been organized in the principal cities to offer relief and to support CHARITY SCHOOLS. The first endowed academy in America was that established by SAMUEL PHILLIPS at Andover, Massachusetts (1778). Early in the 19th century the largest gifts, principally for education (as they long remained), were those made by THOMAS EDDY and by STEPHEN GIRARD. The establishment in

1818 of the Society for the Prevention of Pauperism in New York City was the beginning of SOCIAL WORK in the U.S.

After the Civil War philanthropic behavior became a distinguishing aspect of the national character. Colleges and universities continued to be the greatest beneficiaries of gifts, notably first made by GEORGE PEABODY, whose pioneer educational foundation was established in 1867. In 1885 LELAND STANFORD endowed the West Coast institution bearing his name, and a year later JOHN D. ROCKEFELLER made a gift of $600,000 to resuscitate the defunct University of Chicago. In the same decade ANDREW CARNEGIE enunciated his 'gospel of wealth,' stating that the rich should act as trustees for the public benefit.

A series of notable gifts for philanthropic purposes soon began to attract attention. ANDREW J. DREXEL in 1891 founded Drexel Institute in Philadelphia as a technical school, and in 1901 the bequest of PHILIP ARMOUR inaugurated similar institutions in Chicago. The free public libraries endowed in Chicago by Walter L. Newberry (1804–68) and by John Crerar (1827–89) were forerunners of similar library philanthropies.

Since 1900 the number of endowed FOUNDATIONS has vastly increased. By mid-20th century some 5000 philanthropic organizations in the U.S. were disbursing grants in all areas of welfare, science, and the humanities from assets aggregating nearly $12 billion.

Philippine Independence Act, see *Tydings-McDuffie Act.*

Philippine Islands, northeastern part of the Malayan Archipelago, are a group of 7100 islands of volcanic origin discovered (1521) by FERDINAND MAGELLAN, Portuguese navigator in the employ of Spain. Some 400 of the islands support permanent inhabitants, but of the eleven that compose the bulk only Luzon and Mindanao are very large. The rest are less than one square mile in area, and some 4000 are unnamed rocks. Manila, on Luzon, with the finest harbor in the Far East, became a fortified colony in 1571 and later the capital and chief city, with a population in 1960 of 3,000,000.

Spanish occupation began in 1565, and the group was named 'las Islas Filipina' to honor Philip II. It ended at the close of the Spanish-American War, when the Islands were ceded to the U.S. in the TREATY OF PARIS of 1898. The Filipinos, who had been in revolt against Spain, continued insurrections until 1902, though meanwhile (1900) under William Howard Taft a civil Philippine Commission had been established, and by the Organic Act of 1902 the Islands were recognized as an unincorporated territory of the U.S.

At that time the population of 7,000,000 (85 per cent Christian, 4 per cent Mohammedan, and the rest fiercely pagan) was eager for self-government and under the wise administration of Taft and his successors the way was paved to grant independence as soon as a stable government could be established. The JONES ACT of 1916 inaugurated far-reaching political reform. General Leonard Wood as Governor General (1921–27) reversed the enlightened policy of his predecessors, but the TYDINGS-MC DUFFIE ACT (1934) allowed the Philippine legislature to frame a constitution, and set 1946 as the date when Philippine independence would be proclaimed. The Islands then elected Manuel Quezon (1877–1944) as their first President. Occupied by Japan during World War II (1942–45), the Islands were liberated at the close of the PHILIPPINES CAMPAIGN. On 4 July 1946 the new republic was established. During the 1960's the capital was transferred to Quezon City, a Manila enclave. Though industrially the nation is still in its infancy, the Islands have one of the world's great stands of commercial timber and they abound in mineral resources.

Philippines Campaign (June 1944–July 1945) was the phase of World War II that liberated the Philippine Islands from Japanese occupation. It began with the naval and air battle of the Philippine Sea (19–20 June 1944), fought largely by carrier-based planes. Although the major part of the Japanese fleet remained intact, its carrier air groups were wiped out. Meanwhile U.S. forces had invaded the central Pacific islands, and by 15 June were in command of the strategic air and naval base of Saipan in the Marianas. In July President Roosevelt, General MacArthur, and Admiral Nimitz met at Honolulu to decide on the final assault. The agreement was reached to invade Leyte in the central Philippines first, then to move north to Luzon, the chief island. Then followed (23–25 October) the last naval engagement of the war (and the greatest in history), the battle of LEYTE GULF, by which the U.S. wrested control of the Philippines from Japan. In February 1945 U.S. forces recaptured Manila, and though Japanese units continued to fight for months in the mountains of Mindanao and Luzon, in July General MacArthur announced that 'all the Philippines are now liberated.'

PHILLIPS, DAVID GRAHAM (1867–1911), Indiana-born journalist, served his apprenticeship during the 1890's on the New York *Sun* and *World*. He then associated himself with the MUCKRAKING movement, and his articles on 'The Treason of the Senate' in *Cosmopolitan* (1906) were eventually influential in the passage (1913) of the Seventeenth Amendment for the direct election of senators. He wrote some twenty novels dealing with contemporary social problems, and his study of slum life and political corruption, *Susan Lenox* (1917), written in 1908, takes high rank in the literature of exposure. His death came suddenly in 1911 when a demented assassin shot him, alleging insults to his family in Phillips's novels.

PHILLIPS, SAMUEL (1752–1802), a graduate of Harvard (1771), manufactured powder for the Continental army. While serving as a member of the Massachusetts provincial congress (1775–80) he founded Phillips Academy at Andover (1778), the first endowed academy in America, under the direction of a board of trustees. His uncle, John Phillips (1719–95), philanthropist and land speculator, similarly endowed Phillips Exeter Academy (1783) at nearby Exeter, New Hampshire.

PHILLIPS, WENDELL (1811–84), member of a wealthy and influential Boston family, after graduation from Harvard (1831) was admitted to the bar. A professional agitator at heart, as an associate of William Lloyd Garrison in the antislavery movement he won especial fame as an orator. His lecture on Toussaint L'Ouverture, delivered more than 1000 times during the Civil War, enthralled even those who did not sympathize with his plea for racial brotherhood. He was impervious to criticism, and after the war he continued to goad America's conscience by advocating unpopular reforms, particularly on behalf of labor.

Philosophy in America. See *Education, History, Law, Science, Religion*. See also *Behaviorism, Determinism, Empiricism, Humanism, Idealism, Instrumentalism, Materialism, Positivism, Pragmatism, Psychology, Rationalism, Romanticism, Sociology, Transcendentalism, Utilitarianism*.

Recent studies of the field include W. H. Werkmeister, *A History of Philosophical Ideas in America* (1949); Joseph L. Blau, *Men and Movements in American Philosophy* (1952); Morris R. Cohen, *American Thought* (1954); Stow Persons, *American Minds* (1958).

PHIPS, SIR WILLIAM (1651–95), Maine-born colonial official, after commanding an expedition that recovered some £300,000 worth of Spanish treasure off Haiti (1687), was knighted, the first American so honored. He supported Increase Mather in the fight against Sir Edmund Andros, and in KING WILLIAM'S WAR (1690) led the successful expedition against Port Royal. Despite his failure to capture Quebec, he was appointed the first royal governor of Massachusetts (1692–94). He took the post at the moment the Salem WITCHCRAFT DELUSION was agitating the colony and set up the special court that tried the accused. High-handed and opinionated, he was frequently involved in quarrels. He died while in London whither he had been summoned to answer charges.

Phonograph was a pioneer among the instruments developed after electrical impulses proved convertible to sound waves. In 1877 Thomas A. Edison invented a machine in which a needle followed a groove of unwavering direction but varying depth. Ten years later the German inventor Emile Berliner devised the 'gramaphone,' a disc with grooves of unvarying depth but varying direction. Electronic refinements since 1948 have given limitless use for sound recordings, now a part of all communication systems.

Photography as it is practiced today originated with the process of reproducing images on silver-plated copper invented and perfected (1839) by the French physicist Louis Daguerre (1789–1851). The process was immediately introduced into the U.S. The daguerreotype remained the sole method of photographic representation until the wet collodion process was made practicable in England (1851).

In the U.S. MATHEW B. BRADY made notable use of photography when he recorded thousands of scenes and events during the Civil War. When the photographer Eadweard Muybridge (1830–1904), experimenting with moving objects, projected pictures on a screen (1881), he anticipated the development of MOTION PICTURES. Soon thereafter the stereoscope, an instrument which allows paired prints to be viewed as superimposed (this giving the illusion of depth or a third dimension), became a popular diversion in the American home.

A tremendous interest in amateur photography followed the invention of a dry-plate process by GEORGE EASTMAN, whose Kodak camera (1888) and roll film were put into mass production. The color film came into ordinary use in 1935.

PHYFE, DUNCAN (1768–1854), Scottish-born cabinetmaker, in the early 1790's established a shop in New York City. In his most productive period (before 1820) he adapted styles associated with the Adam brothers, Hepplewhite, and Sheraton, and made chairs, sofas, and tables noted for their graceful proportions, with simple ornaments precisely carved. During the 1820's he turned to the Empire style, and thereafter created heavy and overelaborate designs (he called it 'butcher furniture'), reflecting the taste of the day. Throughout his life, however, he demanded the highest quality of workmanship.

Physics, in the 17th century, embraced all the physical, chemical, and biological sciences. As late as 1650 students almost universally were taught scholastic physics through digests of Aristotle, with commentaries. A profound change took place during the last quarter of the 17th century when the discoveries of Galileo, Copernicus, Tycho Brahe, and Kepler won acceptance, and while Isaac Newton was professor at Cambridge (1669–1701), where he wrote his *Principia* (1687) and *Opticks* (1704). JAMES LOGAN of Philadelphia purchased the first copy of the *Principia* brought to the colonies (1708), COTTON MATHER took notice of Newtonian physics in *The Christian Philosopher* (1721), and ISAAC GREENWOOD at Harvard occupied the first endowed chair of science in America (1727).

The demonstrational method of instruction was founded by Greenwood's successor Professor JOHN WINTHROP, in 1738, and thereafter mathematics and physics were an established part of college curriculums. The first important contributions to physics in America were those made by BENJAMIN FRANKLIN in his observations of electricity (1751), and by JOSEPH HENRY in his contributions in the field of electromagnetism (1830). The most impressive 19th-century studies in the U.S. were those conducted at Yale by JOSIAH W. GIBBS, whose pioneer work in thermodynamics and statistical mechanics has proved to be fundamental.

At the present time the increased knowledge of matter has closely interrelated physics, chemistry, and biology, and has created the entirely new science of high energy physics. (See NUCLEAR ENERGY.)

The Nobel Prize in physics has been awarded to the following Americans:

1907 ALBERT A. MICHELSON (Chicago). Experiments that determined the speed of light.

1921 ALBERT EINSTEIN (then at Kaiser Wilhelm Institute). Work on photoelectricity, basic to his relativity theory.

1923 ROBERT A. MILLIKAN (California Institute of Technology). Contributions in the field of electronics.

1927 ARTHUR H. COMPTON (Chicago). Discovery of the change in wave length of scattered X-rays. (Shared with the English physicist C. T. R. Wilson.)

1936 CARL D. ANDERSON (California Institute of Technology). Discovery of the positively charged electron (positron). (Shared with the Austrian physicist V. F. Hess.)

1937 Clinton J. Davisson (Bell Telephone). Demonstration that matter has wavelike as well as corpuscular properties. (Shared with the English physicist G. P. Thomson, who made the same discovery independently.)

1937 ENRICO FERMI (Columbia). Research in the field of radioactivity.

1939 ERNEST O. LAWRENCE (California, Berkeley). Creating and developing the cyclotron, the experimental foundation of high energy physics.

1943 Otto Stern (Carnegie Institute of Technology). Discovery of the magnetic movement of the proton, thereby giving further support to the wave theory of matter.

1944 ISIDOR I. RABI (Columbia). Establishing the radio relations with atomic particles.

1946 PERCY W. BRIDGMAN (Harvard). Discoveries in the field of high pressure physics.

1952 Felix Bloch (Stanford) and Edward M. Purcell (Harvard). Measurement of magnetic fields in atomic nuclei.

1955 Polykarp Kusch (Columbia) and Willis E. Lamb (Stanford). Research that extended knowledge about the electromagnetic properties of the electron.

1956 Walter H. Brattain, John Bardeen, and William B. Shockley (all Bell Telephone). Invention of the transistor.

1957 Chen Ning Yang and Tsung-Dao Lee (both Institute for Advanced Study). Establishing the absolute distinction in nature between right and left, thereby disproving the 'law' in quantum physics of conservation of parity.

1959 Emilio Segre and Owen Chamberlain (both California, Berkeley). For producing a negative proton (anti-proton), thereby proving that all particles in nature are mirrored by their opposite.

1960 Donald A. Glaser (California, Berkeley). Advancing techniques in the study of subatomic particles.

1961 Robert Hofstadter (Stanford). Shedding light on the shape and size of the proton and neutron. (Shared with the German physicist R. L. Moessbauer.)

1963 Maria G. Mayer (California, La Jolla) and EUGENE P. WIGNER (Princeton). Advancing knowledge of the laws governing the mechanics of nuclear particles. (Shared with the German physicist J. H. D. Jensen.)

1964 Charles H. Townes (Massachusetts Institute of Technology). For his part in creating the maser (microwave amplification of stimulated emission of radiation). (Shared with two Russian physicists, N. Basov and A. Prokhorov.)

1965 Julian S. Schwinger (Harvard) and Richard P. Feynman (California Institute of Technology). For research that solved the difficulties in carrying out quantitative calculations of the interplay between charged particles in quantum electrodynamics. (Shared with the Japanese physicist Shinichiro Tomonaga.)

PICKENS, ANDREW (1739–1817), throughout the CAROLINA CAMPAIGN of the War of Independence, as a brigadier general at the head of PARTISAN BANDS in South Carolina performed useful service in harassing the British. He later subdued the Cherokee Indians, was prominent in state politics, and served in Congress (1793–95).

His grandson, FRANCIS WILKINSON PICKENS (1805–69), was an ardent supporter of NULLIFICATION, also served in Congress (1834–43), and went as Buchanan's minister to Russia (1858–60). He was governor of South Carolina (1860–62) when that state seceded from the Union, and his demand that troops be removed from the Federal forts in Charleston harbor led to the firing on Fort Sumter and the outbreak of the Civil War.

PICKERING, JOHN (1777–1846), son of TIMOTHY PICKERING, after graduation from Harvard (1796) traveled widely and later practiced law in Boston. An eminent philologist (he turned down a Harvard professorship in Greek and Hebrew), he is now recognized (with PETER DU PONCEAU) as one of the two most important American general linguists of his day. A thorough scholar, familiar with a score of languages, he compiled his *Vocabulary . . . of Words . . . Peculiar to the U.S.* (1816), a pioneer study of Americanisms. Unhappily he yielded to the chidings of English reviewers, and later said that many of the words he recorded 'ought not to be used elsewhere by those who would speak correct English.' Not until 1848 did the *Dictionary* of JOHN BARTLETT adequately defend American speech habits, a linguistic issue for another 50 years.

PICKERING, TIMOTHY (1745–1829), born in Salem, Massachusetts, after graduation from Harvard (1763) was admitted to the bar. During the Revolution he served as a member of the Board of War (1777) and quartermaster general (1780–85). He was Washington's Postmaster General (1791–95), Secretary of War (1795), and Secretary of State (1795–1800). He continued as Secretary of State under Adams, but he embroiled himself in the XYZ AFFAIR, and Adams dismissed him. An ardent Federalist in the U.S. Senate (1803–11) and House (1813–17), he was a leading figure in the ESSEX JUNTO.

Picketing, the concerted patrolling of a business establishment by workers on strike, is as old as strikes themselves, and in the early decades of the 19th century was judged an unlawful conspiracy. The famous Massachusetts Supreme Court decision in COMMONWEALTH *v.* HUNT (1842) eliminated the conspiracy doctrine from labor relations, but the right to picket, however peaceably, was denied workers by that same court in 1896 (Justice O. W. Holmes dissenting). Although after 1921 some state courts ruled that picketing in itself was not unlawful, not until 1952 were the basic judicial doctrines laid down that peaceful picketing was legal.

Pickett's charge, on the afternoon of 3 July 1863, was Lee's assault upon the strongest point of the Union center, and the culminating event of the battle of Gettysburg. Lee selected the division of George E. Pickett (1825–75) to lead the charge, supported by the division of James J. Pettigrew and two brigades from William Pender's division led by Isaac R. Trimble. As the three Confederate battle lines, 15,000 strong, charged Cemetery Ridge, they came under the raking fire of Federal batteries on Round Top. Fewer than half a company reached the crest, where they were shot down or captured. Confederate losses in the charge totaled 6000. The Confederate failure, for which Lee took all the blame, determined the outcome of the battle, but the effort was one of the most gallant in the military history of the U.S.

Piedmont (any foothill plateau) in U.S. history designates the plateau extending from Trenton, New Jersey, to Alabama, east of the Appalachians and west of the Atlantic coastal plain. It is cut by numerous small rivers, whose FALL LINE is the eastern edge of the region. The political, economic, and social history of the democratic up-country was one of sectional disagreement with the TIDEWATER aristocracy from earliest colonial times until well into the 19th century.

PIERCE, FRANKLIN (1804–69), 14th President of the U.S. (1853–57), was born at Hillsboro, New Hampshire, and after graduation from Bowdoin (1824) was admitted to the New Hampshire bar. He entered politics in his state as a Jacksonian Democrat, like his father, Benjamin Pierce (1757–1839), who twice served the state as governor, in 1827 and 1829. Franklin Pierce went to Washington as congressman (1833–37) and senator (1837–42) before establishing a lucrative law practice in Concord, New Hampshire, where his continued interest in national politics was an asset to his party. He declined Polk's invitation (1846) to enter the cabinet as attorney general, but he vigorously supported the Mexican War, in which he served, commissioned near its close as a brigadier general.

At the Democratic convention of 1852 the split in the party made Pierce, whose record was colorless, the acceptable dark horse compromise candidate. He was nominated on the 49th ballot and was swept into office by 254 electoral votes against Winfield Scott's 42. Pierce was the youngest man till then so chosen. He selected his cabinet to reconcile sectional factions by including JEFFERSON DAVIS (Miss.), CALEB CUSHING (Mass.), and WILLIAM L. MARCY (N.Y.). As an avowed expansionist he supported the GADSDEN PURCHASE and condoned the questionable activities of WILLIAM WALKER in Nicaragua. But his conciliation of the South by his support of the Kansas-Nebraska bill cost him the backing of northern Democrats. He thus lost the party nomination in 1856, and retired to obscurity. Personable and well-intentioned, Pierce brought no leadership to his high office.

See Roy F. Nichols, *Franklin Pierce* (1931).

PIKE, ZEBULON MONTGOMERY (1779–1813), New Jersey–born army officer, was commissioned by General JAMES WILKINSON to explore in the region of the Louisiana Purchase. On his first expedition (1805–6) he led a small party into Minnesota, and mistakenly believed that he had discovered the source of the Mississippi river. His second enterprise (1806–7) into the Southwest took him beyond the peak in Colorado that bears his name (he did not climb it) to the headwaters of the Arkansas river. On his return he was arrested by Spanish soldiers, imprisoned in Santa Fe, and later deported to the U.S., deprived of all records of his journey. On his return he was accused of complicity in the plot of Aaron Burr and Wilkinson to seize Spanish territory. He was exonerated by the Secretary of War, for whom quite possibly he had been gathering secret information.

Pike's *Account of Expeditions to the Sources of the Mississippi and through the Western Parts of Louisiana* (1810; ed. by Elliott Coues, 3 vols., 1895) is the first description of the region between the Plains and the upper Rio Grande valley. (It also supported the myth of the 'Great American Desert.') Pike was serving as a brigadier general when he was killed during the War of 1812 in the assault on York (Toronto), Canada.

Pike, The, so called, was discovered by writers during the 1850's and defined by Bayard Taylor as 'the Anglo-Saxon relapsed into semi-barbarism.' Named for Pike county, Missouri, he became the prototype of the western 'common man.' For two decades, as blood brother to the Hoosier of Indiana, the 'Cracker' of Georgia, and the Yankee peddler from New England, the Pike dominated western literature as a stereotype and became known in the East through the stories of Bret Harte and the dialect poems of John Hay. Wagon trains rolled westward to the strains of 'Sweet Betsy from Pike.'

Pilgrims, in American history, were the small band of humble Puritans of East Anglia who sought to prevent interference with their religious meetings by removing (1609) to Leyden, where they formed an English Congregational Church. Ten years later, having decided to begin anew in a world free from corrupting influences, they procured through Sir EDWIN SANDYS a grant from the Virginia Company, and a group of London merchants financed their venture. In September 1620, with MYLES STANDISH as their military leader, some 100 passengers embarked from Plymouth on the *Mayflower*.

After a rough crossing (it was the worst season to sail) on 11 November they entered Provincetown harbor at the tip of Cape Cod, where on the same day they drew up the famous MAYFLOWER COMPACT. Soon thereafter they elected JOHN CARVER as governor. This part of New England lay outside the Virginia jurisdiction, but they deliberately abandoned their patent, determined to establish themselves somewhere on Massachusetts Bay. For several weeks small parties explored the coast, and on 21 December they selected Plymouth harbor, where the *Mayflower* anchored. The winter was mild, but for the Pilgrims (44 of whose number perished before April) the first few months were grim, almost desperate. Those who survived did so because in the ensuing months friendly Indians taught these inexperienced yeomen and city workers how to catch fish and plant corn.

After the death of Carver (April 1621) the group chose WILLIAM BRADFORD as governor and began their new life under the ministry of elder WILLIAM BREWSTER. Some time in November of that year the Pilgrims celebrated the first Thanksgiving (three days of feast and entertainment for themselves and the neighborly Indians) to mark the arrival of the *Fortune,* which brought provisions augmenting their own harvest, their venison, and the 'great store of wild Turkies.' The contingent of pilgrims that came on the *Fortune* also brought a charter (dated 11 June 1621) that gave legality to the PLYMOUTH COLONY, whose political interests thenceforth were placed in the care of its agent, EDWARD WINSLOW.

Lean years followed, and for several

seasons only faith in their venture and stout-hearted determination kept the colonists one step ahead of famine. The total population a decade after the landing was but 300. Yet their daring idealism, symbolized in Plymouth Rock, has given the Pilgrim Fathers stature far beyond their narrow limits, as an image of enduring fortitude.

See William Bradford, *Of Plymouth Plantation* (ed. by S. E. Morison, 1952).

PINCHOT, GIFFORD (1865–1946), after graduation from Yale (1889) undertook further study of forestry in Europe, and became the first American professional forester by initiating systematic forest work at Biltmore, North Carolina (1892), and heading the Bureau of Forestry (now the Forest Service) in the U.S. Department of Agriculture (1898–1910). For many years he was professor of forestry at Yale (1903–36). His far-sighted work in the CONSERVATION MOVEMENT was of great importance, and his accusations leading to the acrimonious BALLINGER-PINCHOT CONTROVERSY were later substantiated to some extent. He twice served as governor of Pennsylvania (1923–27, 1931–35).

PINCKNEY, CHARLES (1757–1824), a cousin of THOMAS and CHARLES COTESWORTH PINCKNEY, fought in the Revolution and represented South Carolina in the Federal Constitutional Convention (1787), where his 'Pinckney Draught' helped shape the final instrument. He served his state as governor (1789–92, 1796–98, 1806–8), and was in the U.S. Senate (1798–1801) when Jefferson sent him as minister to Spain (1801–5). Later he served in the House of Representatives (1819–21), where he made a notable speech opposing the Missouri Compromise.

PINCKNEY, CHARLES COTESWORTH (1746–1825), a cousin of CHARLES and brother of THOMAS PINCKNEY, was educated in England and France. On his return to Charleston, South Carolina, he practiced law and entered politics. He fought in the Revolution and served as a delegate to the Federal Constitutional Convention. Sent in 1796 as minister to France (where he was not officially received), in 1797 with Elbridge Gerry and John Marshall he took part in the unsuccessful diplomatic mission known as the XYZ AFFAIR. He was later the Federalist candidate for Vice President (1800) and for President (1804, 1808).

PINCKNEY, THOMAS (1750–1828), like his brother, CHARLES COTESWORTH PINCKNEY, received his education in England and France. He returned to Charleston, South Carolina, to practice law and enter politics, and fought with distinction as a militiaman in the Revolution, from its outbreak until he was wounded and captured during the battle of CAMDEN (1780). He was governor of his state (1787–89), and while serving as Washington's minister to England (1792–96) was sent as envoy extraordinary to Spain (1794–95) to negotiate what is known as PINCKNEY'S TREATY. He was later a Federalist member of Congress (1797–1801), and served as a major general in the War of 1812.

Pinckney's Treaty (1795), officially named the Treaty of San Lorenzo, was an agreement (conducted in Madrid by THOMAS PINCKNEY) between the U.S. and Spain. The struggle of the young republic to acquire new territory and establish boundaries involved negotiations with Spain, France, and Great Britain. The Spanish holdings in Florida were subject to dispute, and Spanish possession of New Orleans gave them control of the outlet of the Mississippi valley. Spain, then involved in European wars, feared that JAY'S TREATY (1794) might contain a secret Anglo-American treaty, and thus concessions were relatively easy to obtain. By terms of the treaty Spain conceded what Westerners were so eager to obtain, the RIGHT OF DEPOSIT, or the right of transit at New Orleans. Spain also accepted U.S. boundary claims east of the Mississippi and in East and West Florida. Thus by treaty the U.S. gained control of strategic areas.

Pine-tree shillings, see *Colonial currency.*

PINKERTON, ALLAN (1819–94), Scottish-born detective, was appointed the first city detective on the Chicago police force (1850), and in the same year opened a private agency. During the

Civil War he organized an espionage system behind the Confederate lines, and his work led to the establishment of the Federal secret service. (To unions, as in the Homestead Strike of 1890, the Pinkertons were strikebreakers and industrial police.) The organization continued to flourish, and remains today the best-known private agency in the U.S. Allan Pinkerton is best remembered for directing President-elect Lincoln's secret night trip to Washington to avert assassins.

PINKNEY, WILLIAM (1764–1822), prominent Maryland lawyer and political leader, was sent to England (1796–1804) as a commissioner to adjust claims under JAY'S TREATY. He served both Jefferson and Madison as minister to England (1807–11), before entering Madison's cabinet as Attorney General (1811–14). While serving in Congress (1815–16), he resigned his post to become Madison's minister to Russia (1816–18). At the time of his death he was a member of the U.S. Senate (1819–22), where he won distinction as an orator, but made enemies by his haughty demeanor.

Piracy along the American coast developed profitably in the colonial period. When Great Britain was at war with Spain and France, the government authorized royal governors to distribute 'letters of marque and reprisal' to privateers to capture all enemy ships. The risks were great but so were the rewards. In intervals between the FRENCH AND INDIAN WARS (1689–1763) the temptation of restless mariners to resume predatory seafaring was compounded by the fact that smuggled goods found a ready market. Customs officials were well paid to let the contraband through, and sometimes royal governors granted 'privateering' commissions to freebooters and winked at their irregularities. Almost legendary among the early pirates were CAPTAIN KIDD and BLACKBEARD.

During the period 1805–25 piracy was especially rampant, notably off the Louisiana coast, where the LAFITTE brothers operated large-scale 'business' ventures. After 1823 the government made piracy the direct concern of naval squadrons, and thus brought it to an end along the American coast.

PITCHER, MOLLY [MARY LUDWIG HEIS] (*c.* 1754–1832), earned her sobriquet by carrying water for the soldiers during the battle of MONMOUTH (1778). The legend that she commanded her dead husband's cannon is apocryphal, and rose from confusion with MARGARET CORBIN.

PITT, WILLIAM, 1st Earl of Chatham (1708–78), headed the English coalition ministry (1757–60) until he was forced to resign when George III acceded to the throne. During the time Pitt headed the ministry he committed the government to unlimited warfare with France and reinforcements in America. He joined the Whig opposition in attacking the harsh American policy of the 'king's friends,' again headed the ministry for fifteen months (1766–67), and during the administration of the Duke of Grafton (1767–70) served as Lord Privy Seal. On the eve of the War of Independence he urged conciliation, and after its outbreak he favored any peace settlement that would keep the American colonies within the Empire he had worked so tirelessly to create. The efforts of this 'Great Commoner' to advance England's progress toward political reform were carried on by his son, WILLIAM PITT (1759–1806), who was chosen Prime Minister in 1783, a post he held without intermission for eighteen years. After the TREATY OF PARIS of 1783, concluding the War of Independence, the younger Pitt, like Lord SHELBURNE, steadily sought to consolidate Anglo-American friendship.

Pittsburgh, in western Pennsylvania, at the confluence of the Allegheny and Monongahela rivers (which there form the Ohio), is a major U.S. inland port of entry. It is a city of 700,000 in a metropolitan area of 2,500,000. Founded as Fort Duquesne (1754) by the French, five years later it fell to the English, who renamed it Fort Pitt. It was a site of action during the French and Indian Wars and the War of Independence. In 1794 it became a borough, and it was incorporated as a city in 1816. The center of great coal and oil fields, it is the largest steel-producing district in the nation. Such financiers as ANDREW CARNEGIE, HENRY C. FRICK, and ANDREW MELLON made their fortunes there. Its leading institution of higher learning, the University of Pittsburgh, from 1819 to 1908 was the Western University of Pennsylvania. In 1965, with an endowment of $61,388,000 and a faculty of 2090, it enrolled 15,000 students.

Pittsburg Landing, see *Shiloh, Battle of.*

Plains Indians, see *Arapaho, Blackfoot, Cheyenne, Comanche, Crow, Dakota, Hidatsa, Mandan, Omaha, Osage, Pawnee,* and *Ute.*

Plains of Abraham, a plateau above the city of Quebec, was the scene of the famous battle (1759) that ended the FRENCH AND INDIAN WARS and determined the fate of Canada. The site is now a national park.

Plains region (Great Plains) is the high, extensive grassland of western North America, a gently sloping plateau between the Rocky Mountains on the west and the Mississippi valley on the east. From western Canada the region extends south to the Texas panhandle. It comprises almost a quarter of the continental U.S. Its western elevation of 6000 ft. slopes down to 2000 ft. to the east, where the region merges with the prairie section of the Middle West. Generally level, treeless, and semiarid, the region includes Nebraska, Kansas, Oklahoma; the western part of the Dakotas; the eastern parts of Montana, Wyoming, Colorado, and New Mexico; and northwestern Texas. Its principal rivers, the Platte, Republican, Canadian, Kansas, Arkansas, and Cimarron, flow eastward. Enormous herds of bison once roamed throughout the region, together with the PLAINS INDIANS who hunted them.

Although the region was the last part of the U.S. to be settled, after the Civil War it steadily attracted colonizers, for it is natural grazing land. Early in the 20th century the attempts to convert dry, unprotected stretches into wheat-farming country resulted in soil erosion, and created the 'Dust Bowl.' Today irrigation and other methods of control such as strip planting have created profitable agricultural areas that supply markets with the produce of diversified crops, though aridity is still a major concern.

Plantation system, as it developed in colonial America, was the particular kind of group economy of the original plantations (colonies) in the South. The demand for labor was supplied by slavery, the 'peculiar institution' of the South until the Civil War. As a system it created farm units much larger in scale than elsewhere in the colonies. Plantations were compounds of orchards and fields, slave quarters, barns, and work houses, surrounding the 'Big House.' Robert 'King' Carter of Corotoman, Virginia, accumulated more than 300,000 acres of land, and at his death in 1732 he owned 1000 slaves. But such holdings were rare.

As finally evolved, the ideal unit was a laboring force of 100 slaves working 1000 acres of productive land under the direction of a manager. The huge demand of the British textile industry after 1790 made cotton the chief commodity in the economy, and the plantation system created a COTTON KINGDOM. After the Civil War most plantations were broken up, and large numbers of freed Negroes became TENANT FARMERS and SHARECROPPERS.

Plantations, in the 17th century, were the 'plantings,' or new settlements, made by colonizers from Virginia to New England who sought to establish commercial enterprises financed by business ADVENTURERS. Such were the ventures promoted by the early JOINT-STOCK COMPANIES. The term was later applied to estates within the PLANTATION SYSTEM.

Planters, see *Adventurers.*

PLATT, THOMAS COLLIER (1833–1910), New York politician, as a protégé of the Republican state leader ROSCOE CONKLING served in the U.S. House of Representatives (1875–79) and Senate (1881). He resigned his Senate seat in protest to President Garfield's appointment of reform Republicans to Federal jobs that he considered the political perquisite of the New York organization. After Conkling's death (1888), Platt succeeded to power, and during the 1890's he became undisputed boss of the New York Republican machine. Again in the Senate (1897–1909), he was largely responsible for the election (1898) of Theodore Roosevelt as governor of New York. But Roosevelt struck at corruption with such vigor that in self-defense Boss Platt and his machine in 1900 'shelved' Roosevelt into the vice presidency. Thereafter Platt's power declined.

Platt Amendment, formulated by Roosevelt's Secretary of War Elihu Root, and drawn up by Senator Orville H. Platt of Connecticut, was added as an amendment to the Cuban constitution in 1902. It provided that Cuba would make no treaties impairing her independence, or grant concessions to foreign powers, without the consent of the U.S. These and similar provisions, such as that which permitted the U.S. to intervene to preserve Cuban independence, in effect gave the U.S. a quasi-protectorate over Cuba. The amendment was abrogated in 1934.

Platt National Park (1906), in southern Oklahoma, is an area of 912 acres comprising numerous cold mineral springs.

Plattsburg, Battle of (11 September 1814), the most important U.S. naval victory in the War of 1812, was fought on Lake Champlain near Plattsburg, New York. A British fleet of four ships and twelve gunboats under Captain George Downie engaged an American flotilla of four ships and ten gunboats commanded by Captain THOMAS MACDONOUGH. The close-range combat lasted 2 hours and 20 minutes, resulted in the destruction of the British ships, and gave the U.S. undisputed control of the lake. The invading British army, under General Sir George Prevost, then left without naval support, was decisively defeated in the attack on Plattsburg, and was forced to retreat to Canada. The battle thus improved the American position in the peace negotiations then under way.

Plessy* v. *Ferguson, see *Brown* v. *Board of Education.*

Plymouth Colony, sometimes called the New Plymouth Colony, was the first settlement in Massachusetts, and its patent was obtained (June 1621) from the newly organized COUNCIL FOR NEW ENGLAND. Its first governor, JOHN CARVER, was succeeded late in 1621 by WILLIAM BRADFORD, who continued in office for more than 30 years. During the first decade Plymouth was the only settlement, but gradually ten other villages were established nearby. In 1643 the colony became a member of the NEW ENGLAND CONFEDERATION, with a government patterned after that of the Massachusetts Bay Colony. Under the charter granted to Massachusetts in 1691 Plymouth (with Maine) was absorbed into the royal colony of Massachusetts.

Plymouth Company (1606) was one of the two Virginia Companies, formed by London and Plymouth merchants, that were authorized to colonize America. The LONDON COMPANY (South Virginia) had jurisdiction up to the region of New York. The Plymouth Company (North Virginia) made explorations along the Maine coast in 1607, but abandoned its venture soon after. The report by Captain JOHN SMITH in 1614 of rich cod fisheries off the Maine coast revived interest in the Plymouth Company, which obtained a new charter under grant from the COUNCIL FOR NEW ENGLAND (1620). Thus the PILGRIMS secured their patent to settle on Cape Cod.

Plymouth Rock is the boulder on which the PILGRIMS reputedly landed near Plymouth, Massachusetts, in December 1620. The tradition is part of the American heritage. The rock, now moved inland, is protected by a granite portico.

POCAHONTAS (*c.* 1595–1617), daughter of the powerful Indian chieftain POWHATAN, while being held as hostage (1613) at Jamestown, Virginia, for English prisoners, was converted to Christianity and baptized as Rebecca. In 1614 she was given in marriage by her father to JOHN ROLFE, whom she accompanied to England. There she was treated as royalty and presented at court. She died suddenly just as she was embarking for America.

The famous story that her intercession (1607) saved the life of JOHN SMITH, though resting only on the testimony of Smith (and omitted in his earlier history of Virginia), is thought by some recent historians to be true.

Pocket veto is exercised by the President to prevent the passage of legislation of which he disapproves. It is effected under the terms of the Constitution (Art. I, sec. 7) whereby any bill presented to but not signed by the President within ten days before Congress adjourns does not become law. First resorted to by Madison, the pocket veto has been used by all Presidents since Pierce, most frequently by F. D. Roosevelt (260 times).

POE, EDGAR ALLAN (1809–49), was living in Baltimore (1831–35) when he began his career in literature. Thereafter, supporting himself chiefly by free-lance writing, he was associated with various Philadelphia and New York journals. Before his death he had attracted attention both at home and abroad, but his fame came later and has steadily mounted. The most important American poet before Whitman, and one of the few authentic innovators in American literature, Poe was also a master of the tale of terror and creator of the modern detective story. As a critic he emphasized textual analysis and placed his aesthetic values on the created work of art. Europeans hailed him as a creative force, and his influence on French symbolism spread through Baudelaire's recognition of Poe's ability to enrich the life of the imagination by plumbing the darker side of man's nature. The influence of Poe's work was extended into English and American literature through the revival of interest in French symbolism, for which T. S. Eliot and Wallace Stevens were largely responsible.

Point Four Program, so called because it developed from the fourth point of a program set forth in President Truman's 1949 inaugural address, was undertaken to make 'the benefits of our scientific advances available for the improvement and growth of underdeveloped areas.' The program is administered by the State Department, and it operates in some two-score countries around the globe. Technical skills and equipment are in part provided by the recipient nations. Congress has annually appropriated several hundred million dollars to give aid to long-term development of foreign industries, agriculture, and health and education programs.

Polar expeditions were first undertaken in an attempt to find a trade route to Asia by way of a NORTHWEST PASSAGE. They have been continuous ever since HENRY HUDSON skirted the ice barrier between Greenland and Spitsbergen (1607), though explorers made little progress in finding passages until the 19th century. ALEXANDER MACKENZIE made a notable arctic crossing in 1793. The search for the party of the British explorer Sir John Franklin, lost in the Arctic in 1847, renewed interest in polar exploration, especially in Europe. In 1881 U.S. army lieutenant A. W. GREELY mapped unknown segments of Greenland. ROBERT E. PEARY was the first to reach the North Pole (1909). (The prior claims of Dr. F. A. COOK were never substantiated.) LINCOLN ELLSWORTH conducted a transpolar flying expedition in 1926 with the Norwegian explorer Roald Amundsen. Polar air flights were continued by RICHARD E. BYRD, DONALD B. MAC MILLAN, and FLOYD BENNETT. In 1958 the nuclear-powered submarine *Nautilus,* William R. Anderson commanding, crossed the North Pole beneath the arctic ice.

CHARLES WILKES first announced the existence of the continent of Antarctica (1840); and penetration of the region, sporadically undertaken by explorers from many nations, has been continual since Byrd established LITTLE AMERICA (1929) south of the Bay of Whales.

Police power, the right of a government to regulate in matters of health, morals, safety, and welfare, is inherent in every sovereign state. In the U.S. the regulatory power of federal and state governments requires the accommodation of one with the other. Chief Justice Marshall ruled in *Brown* v. *Maryland* (1827) that the power of Congress over goods imported from abroad ceased once they had been broken out of their 'original package,' and that the goods were therefore no longer subject to Federal regulation. Chief Justice Taney in the CHARLES RIVER BRIDGE case (1837) held that, although Congress alone had the power to regulate interstate commerce, the police power of a state entitled it to make reasonable regulatory laws even if they appeared to contravene the literal terms of the Constitution.

After passage of the Fourteenth

Amendment (1868) the issue of police power became especially delicate: states must of course observe due process of law in curbing liberties, but critics felt that they should not be made helpless in dealing with large social and economic issues. At present the practice of the Supreme Court is generally to uphold the economic regulations of the states.

Political boss, see *Party machines.*

Political parties. See *Anti-Masonic, Anti-Monopoly, Communist, Democratic, Democratic-Republican, Farmer-Labor, Federalist, Free-Soil, Greenback, Know-Nothing (American), Liberal Republican, Liberty, National Republican, Populist, Progressive, Prohibition, Republican, Social Democratic, Socialist, Social Labor, States' Rights, Union, Union Labor, Whig.* See also *Third party movements.*

Studies include W. E. Binkley, *American Political Parties* (1943); and Richard Hofstadter, *The American Political Tradition and the Men Who Made It* (1948).

Political platforms represent statements of purpose by a party, and are drafted as planks at the different NATIONAL CONVENTIONS during presidential election years. They incorporate broad policies to be followed on matters of public concern and usually involve a consensus on various issues by the party in its appeal to the voter. The platforms are generally acknowledged to be 'not something you stand on, but something you git in,' and consequently the fulfillment of pledges is regarded with a degree of indulgence.

POLK, JAMES KNOX (1795–1849), 11th President of the U.S. (1845–49), was born in North Carolina. His family moved to Tennessee, and after graduation from the University of North Carolina (1818) he returned to practice law in Tennessee and serve his state in the U.S. House of Representatives (1825–39) where, as Speaker (1835–39), he was recognized as leader of the Democratic forces. Having gained further political experience as governor of Tennessee (1839–41), at the Democratic national convention in 1844 Polk was trotted out as the first dark horse in a presidential race. His unequivocal stand in favor of the young nation's concern with MANIFEST DESTINY suited the expansionist mood of the country, and in the election, relatively close by popular ballot, he defeated his Whig opponent Henry Clay with an electoral vote of 170 to 105.

Polk's cabinet, headed by JAMES BUCHANAN (State), included ROBERT J. WALKER (Treasury), WILLIAM L. MARCY (War), and GEORGE BANCROFT (Navy), statesmen who stood ready to support Polk's Democratic principles but did not shape his executive course. That Polk did himself, announcing 'four great measures' which in fact he carried through: the re-establishment of the INDEPENDENT TREASURY (1846), reduction of tariffs by the WALKER TARIFF ACT (1846), adjustment of the OREGON BOUNDARY DISPUTE (1846), and acquisition of western territory (a determination that had sufficient national backing to win the MEXICAN WAR, 1846–48). Next to Jefferson, Polk added more territory to the U.S. than any other President. By that act the Whig sneer of 1844, 'Who is James K. Polk?,' received its answer.

Determined and tenacious, never relaxing and seldom smiling, Polk made the presidency a full-time job. (He was absent from Washington but six weeks in four years.) He renounced a second term, and, in pursuit of executive rather than political aims, he forbade his cabinet to campaign for him or for themselves. The Whigs won the election of 1848 with Zachary Taylor, as Polk had foretold, and Polk retired to his Nashville home, where he died a few months later. Polk never became a popular hero, but his achievements gave stature to the presidency.

Allan Nevins edited *Polk: The Diary of a President, 1845–1849* (1952).

Poll tax, or head tax, is one levied upon a person rather than upon property. Although it is usually small, it is not graduated in amount, and thus bears no relation to the ability to pay. During the colonial period poll taxes at one time or another were levied in all the British colonies. Such a tax today is collected in some 35 states for many purposes, but it is generally associated in the public mind with the right to vote, since five states of the South (Alabama, Arkansas, Mississippi, Texas, and Virginia) require payment of a poll tax as a prerequiste to voting in order to discourage the Negro franchise. California, Ohio, and Maryland forbid the imposition of such taxes by constitutional provision. In 1964 the Twenty-fourth Amendment to the U.S. Constitution was ratified, barring the poll tax in Federal elections.

Pollock* v. *Farmers' Loan and Trust Company (1895) was a case that resulted in a 5 to 4 decision by the U.S. Supreme Court, invalidating the provision in the WILSON-GORMAN TARIFF ACT (1894) that subjected personal incomes above $4000 to a 2 per cent tax. The Court held that Federal taxes on personal property were direct taxes and therefore under the Constitution subject to the apportionment rule. The decision inspired an attack on 'judicial usurpation,' and led to the Democratic party income tax plank of 1896. The decision led Congress to propose and the states to ratify the SIXTEENTH AMENDMENT (1913), giving Congress the power to levy taxes on incomes.

Polo, introduced in England (1869) from India, where it had become a popular sport among British army officers, was brought to the U.S. in 1876 by the younger James Gordon Bennett. The leading club, the Meadow Brook Club of Nassau county, Long Island, was incorporated in 1881. Since 1886 English and American teams have competed from time to time for the International Polo Challenge Cups. The most famous polo player of all time is generally considered to have been THOMAS HITCHCOCK.

Newell Bent, *American Polo* (1929), is a history of the sport in the U.S.

PONCE de LEÓN, JUAN (1460–1521), after accompanying Columbus on his second voyage to America (1493), became governor of Puerto Rico (1509–12), where he made a fortune during the boom period in the Caribbean. In 1514 he secured a patent from the king of Spain to colonize the 'isle of Florida,' which he had discovered and coasted along the year before during the Easter season (*Pascua Florida*). The story that he was seeking a 'fountain of youth' may have arisen out of amiable banter, since this energetic conquistador was then fifty-three.

His second expedition was delayed for seven years. In 1521 he attempted to land on the west coast near Charlotte Harbor with 200 settlers, but he was mortally wounded by Seminole Indians, and the effort to colonize was abandoned. It was Ponce de León, nevertheless, who added the mainland of North America to the Spanish domain.

PONTIAC (*c.* 1720–69), Ottawa Indian chief based near Detroit, had been a firm ally of the French at the outbreak of the French and Indian War (1755). He could not believe that New France had been conquered after Montcalm's defeat at Quebec (1759). The western Indians had not been consulted in the surrender, and they were goaded to action by the arrogance of English officials, the dishonesty of traders, and the fear of losing their hunting grounds to settlers. Under Pontiac, who was renowned as an orator and political leader, several tribes formed a grand confederacy, and in the spring of 1763, by concerted attacks over a thousand miles of wilderness, they wiped out every western fort except Detroit and Pittsburgh and ravaged frontier settlements from Niagara to Virginia in the most formidable Indian outbreak of the century. Pontiac directed the strategy of this war (called Pontiac's Rebellion, or Conspiracy), and his siege of Detroit (1763–64) is classic in the annals of Indian warfare. British regulars finally gained control and a peace treaty was signed. Pontiac was pardoned. He later was slain in Illinois, presumably by an Indian bribed by an English trader.

The classic study is Francis Parkman, *History of the Conspiracy of Pontiac* (1851; repr. in *Works,* 1922).

Pony Express was an enterprise of the noted Missouri freighting firm of Russell, Majors and Waddell, inaugurated to disprove the judgment of Postmaster General Aaron Brown that only a southern route into California was feasible for year-round transportation of the OVERLAND MAIL. It operated for eighteen months (April 1860–October 1861) between St. Joseph, Missouri, and Sacramento, California. The route passed through Cheyenne, Salt Lake City, and Carson City. Most trips were made between the termini of the telegraphs then being constructed. The routes longest in use connected Fort Kearny in Nebraska with Fort Churchill in Nevada.

The Express was a relay, with stations spaced at intervals of fifteen miles. Fleet ponies raced between the stations, and fresh riders and horses were kept ready at each station to pick up the mail and carry it on. The service continued weekly (later semi-weekly) night and day, summer and winter, with 75 ponies participating in both directions. It took nearly two weeks to cover the full distance. The ruinous cost ended the venture, but the Pony Express was a vivid episode in the pageantry of the frontier.

Pools, as combinations of U.S. business units, were 'gentlemen's agreements' entered into as a means of controlling prices by apportioning markets. These unregulated monopolies were forbidden by the Interstate Commerce Act of 1887, and they were superseded by TRUSTS and HOLDING COMPANIES.

'Poor Richard,' see *Franklin, Benjamin.*

'Poor whites,' see *'Crackers.'*

POORE, BENJAMIN PERLEY (1820–87), Massachusetts-born journalist, for some 30 years (after 1854) reported on Washington politics for various newspapers over the widely known signature, 'Perley.' His numerous popular biographies range from Bonaparte to General Burnside. *Perley's Reminiscences of Sixty Years in the National Metropolis* (1886) is source material extending back to the administration of President J. Q. Adams. (The first 30 of the 60 years' reminiscences are historical.)

Historians and librarians know Poore as the editor of a four-volume collection of manuscripts relative to New France, which he had found in the French archives, and as the indefatigable compiler of various catalogs of government publications that he prepared as a U.S. Senate clerk.

POPÉ (*fl.* 1655–90), Tewa medicine man, led the Pueblo revolt of 1680, which temporarily liberated New Mexico from the Spaniards. Several hundred Spanish settlers were massacred, and the rest were driven to the El Paso region. With Taos as headquarters, Popé sought to obliterate all traces of Spanish culture and restore the old order. Internal dissension for a time deposed him, but he regained power in 1688. He did not live to see his work destroyed by the Spanish reconquest of the province in 1692.

POPE, JOHN (1822–92), Kentucky-born graduate of the U.S. Military Academy (1842), served as a major general of Union forces during the Civil War. After some successes as commander of the Army of the Mississippi, he was summoned to lead the newly organized Army of Virginia (June 1862). His troops were badly mauled in the second battle of BULL RUN two months later, and he was removed from field command and replaced by George McClellan. He remained in the service and was later in charge of frontier military departments.

Popular sovereignty in U.S. history refers to the doctrine, first enunciated (1847) by Senator LEWIS CASS, that the people of a territory had the right to determine whether slavery would exist within their jurisdiction. The doctrine applied only to the territorial stage, during which period Congress, if it chose, could invalidate enactments of a territorial legislature. Stephen A. Douglas included the principle in drafting the COMPROMISE OF 1850, and coined the phrase itself in the KANSAS-NEBRASKA ACT (1854). The issue of popular sovereignty, or 'squatter sovereignty' as opponents contemptuously dubbed it, was the substance of the LINCOLN-DOUGLAS DEBATES (1858), and a basic cause of the North-South split in the decade preceding the Civil War.

Popular vote in the U.S. selects members of the ELECTORAL COLLEGE, which legally elects the President and Vice President. Constitutionally the popular vote is not significant, yet it is important in that the candidate who receives a plurality or majority of the popular vote in each state carries that state and receives its total electoral vote. Two candidates, SAMUEL TILDEN (1876) and GROVER CLEVELAND (1888), lost an election even though they had a popular majority. Similarly, candidates may win even though they have polled a minority of the total popular vote. There have been fourteen MINORITY PRESIDENTS.

Population of the U.S. has grown from fewer than 500 in 1610 (British colonies) to 183,000,000 in 1960. The population of 1700 is estimated at 275,000; of 1750, at 1,207,000; of 1780, at 2,780,000. The actual count of the first census (1790) was 3,929,000. From 1790 to 1910 the rate of growth was about 30 per cent per decade, thereafter falling off to about 15 per cent. A large factor in this increase (until 1920) was a virtually unlimited IMMIGRATION.

The shift of population has consistently been from rural to urban areas. The 1960 urban population of 125,300,000 was an increase of 29 per cent over the urban total of 96,800,000 in 1950. The six most urban states in 1960 were New Jersey (89%), California (86%), Rhode Island (86%), New York (85%), Massachusetts (84%), and Illinois (81%).

Caucasians constituted 88.6 per cent of the population in 1960, a decrease of nearly one per cent since 1950. Negroes constituted 10 per cent of the population. American Indians numbered 523,000, an increase of 46 per cent since 1950. Other races included Japanese (464,000), Chinese (237,000), and Filipinos (176,000). Assuming that natural increase for the next two decades remains at the 1960 rate (but this rate is slowing down), the population in 1970 will be 212,000,000.

Populist party (People's party) began in 1889 as a grouping of southern and western agrarian organizations seeking political action to remedy the lot of debtor farmers. In a number of southern states such protest groups gained control of the Democratic party machinery in the 1890 elections, and were able to send four senators and more than 50 congressmen to Washington. Western agrarians, however, favored a third party, and the People's Party, as it was first called, met in national convention at Omaha in 1892. Their platform was drawn up by the eloquent IGNATIUS DONNELLY. Chiefly it called for a flexible currency system under government control, a graduated income tax, postal savings banks, public ownership of railroads and communication systems, an eight-hour day for labor, direct election of senators, the secret ballot, and unlimited coinage of silver as a means of swelling the currency.

Its presidential candidate, the veteran reform leader JAMES B. WEAVER, polled over 1,000,000 popular votes, 22 electoral votes, and carried four states in the High Plains (free silver) region. The South, despite its grievances, supported the Democrats, who represented white supremacy. In 1896 Bryan, the Democratic standard bearer, hoped to create an agrarian-labor ticket, and the Populists joined forces with the Democrats to elect him. But Bryan was defeated, farm prices began to rise, and the trend to insurgency dwindled, in large part because almost all the planks of this significant third party within a few years had been incorporated into the platforms of one or other of the two major parties.

'Pork barrel' legislation is that which provides Federal funds for special local projects that benefit only the districts of those congressmen who sponsor the bills. Such legislation is usually enacted by LOGROLLING, or reciprocal political help, and constitutes a reward for party service. The term derives its descriptive origin from the old plantation custom of setting aside a portion of the pork for slaves, who at the appointed time assembled at the pork barrel.

Port Authorities are relatively new units of local government in the U.S. The Port of New York Authority, a self-supporting, public, tax-free organization, was created in 1921 as a joint agency of the states of New Jersey and New York to deal with terminal and transportation problems along their 50-mile water boundary. It is administered by a board of commissioners (appointed by the governors of the two states) who serve without pay. It derives its income from tolls and rentals, and has been the model for similar agencies established since World War II in other large port cities throughout the country.

PORTER, DAVID (1780–1843), born in Boston, entered the navy as a midshipman (1798) and served in the West Indies and in the Tripolitan War. As commander of the frigate *Essex* in the War of 1812, he first captured British troop ships off Halifax and then, accompanied by his adopted son, DAVID FARRAGUT, raided British commerce in the Pacific. Late in the war he was defeated by the British off Valparaiso (1814). While on an expedition to the West Indies to suppress piracy (1823–25), he employed such highhanded methods against the friendly Spanish that he was suspended from the navy. He then served as a rear admiral in the Mexican navy (1826–29) until his friend President Jackson appointed him U.S. consul general in Algiers (1830) and chargé d'affaires at Constantinople (1831), where he remained, serving as minister after 1841.

His son, DAVID DIXON PORTER (1813–91), left the Mexican navy in 1829 to enter the U.S. Navy. In the Civil War he supported Farragut in the capture of New Orleans (1862), and won the thanks of Congress for his part in the capture of Vicksburg (1863). While superintendent of the U.S. Naval Academy (1865–69), to which he brought new vigor, he succeeded to Farragut's rank of vice admiral when Farragut was named a full admiral, and succeeded to that rank after Farragut's death (1870).

PORTER, NOAH (1811–92), professor of moral philosophy and metaphysics at Yale (1846–71) and president of the college (1871–86), as a staunch Calvinist was known in his day as a leading opponent of Darwinism. The symposium on 'Law and Design in Nature' (1879), conducted in the *North American Review* by Porter, JAMES MC COSH, and others, illustrates Porter's hostility to materialism and positivism. Porter's *The Human Intellect* (1868) was an early work on psychology, praised by contemporaries.

Port Folio (1801–27), the leading American literary magazine of its day, was founded in Philadelphia by JOSEPH DENNIE, who edited it for eight years. About it gathered the fellowship known as the Tuesday Club, and during the early years Federalist writers who leaned to British literature and culture contributed to it. At first a weekly, after 1809 it became a monthly, with a succession of editors. By 1816 it had become less dependent upon British models, and during its final decade it made a point of soliciting material dealing with the West.

PORTOLÁ, GASPAR DE (*fl.* 1723–84), in 1769 led an expedition from Mexico into Alta (Upper) California, of which he became the first Spanish governor. He established a presidio at Monterey, and thereby opened the way for the chain of Indian missions founded along the California coast by JUNÍPERO SERRA, who accompanied him.

Portsmouth, Treaty of (1905), ending the Russo-Japanese War, was formulated as the result of President Theodore Roosevelt's mediation. The conference was held at the Portsmouth (New Hampshire) navy yard, and by the terms of the treaty Japan's interests in Korea and southern Manchuria were advanced. Japan resented the fact that Roosevelt did not support her claim for indemnity, but on the whole the nations regarded the settlement as equitable. For his offices in the matter Roosevelt received the 1906 Nobel Peace award.

Positivism, as a philosophical system, was developed and named by the French philosopher August Comte (1798–1857). It postulates that knowledge originates only in experience, a positive process in which the empiric sciences are used to verify the properties and relations of phenomena. Positivism implies the 'law of the three stages'— the 'theological' came first, then the 'metaphysical,' and finally these culminated into the 'positive,' or scientific, stage. SOCIOLOGY (a term Comte coined), since it is a study of collective behavior, becomes the ultimate concern of man in his search for well-being.

POST, WILEY (1899–1935), with Harold Gatty as his navigator, flew around the world (1931) in 8 days, 15 hours, and 51 minutes. In 1933 he became the first person to do so alone, this time in 7 days, 18 hours, 49 minutes, a new record. He was accompanying WILL ROGERS on a flight to the Orient when their plane crashed in Alaska. Both were killed.

Post Office Department was created by the Second Continental Congress (1775) with Benjamin Franklin as Postmaster General. When the federal government was established (1789), Congress placed the POSTAL SYSTEM within the Treasury Department, where it remained until

Congress gave the Post Office Department a more independent status (1829), and President Jackson raised the Postmaster General to cabinet rank. (Actually the reorganization was not officially designated as an executive department until 1872.)

The Department is the largest agency of Federal patronage, with more than 20,000 positions at its disposal, and it has a total personnel of more than half a million. It operates under restrictive laws and somewhat inflexible business methods, and in consequence it continues to build up annual deficits of nearly $500,000,000. In 1963 it inaugurated a Zone Improvement Plan (ZIP), a code system of mail sorting and distribution to speed delivery by reducing the handling of mail and to hold down postal costs. (The ZIP code is a set of digits used by the sender as part of the address.)

Post roads in the American colonies were the highways along which the government had a monopoly for carrying mail. Stations along these roads kept fresh horses and riders ready to continue on the route. The earliest, established in the late 17th century, were the Boston Post Road (between New York and Boston) and the Old Post Road (between New York and Albany). During the Revolution the Continental Congress extended such post roads into the interior, and when the Federal Constitution became operative (1788), some 2000 miles of post roads were in use, generally paralleling the Atlantic coast, from New Hampshire to Georgia. By 1830 the mileage had increased to 115,000.

Although STAGECOACHES after 1785 became the means of postal service wherever roads were passable for vehicles, even as late as 1825 Postmaster General John McLean reported that 'the intelligence of more than half the nation is conveyed on horseback,' a reflection on the lag in road construction. Post roads ceased to be used as the means of mail carrying as rapidly as railroads were constructed (after 1835).

Postage stamps were first officially issued in the U.S. in 1847, although by congressional authority many postmasters had issued their own stamps during the two years preceding, a practice that was discontinued when the official stamps were issued. The first were a 5-cent (Franklin) and a 10-cent (Washington) stamp. When rates were reduced in 1851, a second issue added 1-, 3-, and 12-cent values. After 1856 further denominations appeared.

Philately became a hobby during the 1850's, and the first printed catalog of stamps was issued in 1861. So extensive is the field that collectors today usually concentrate on restricted areas or particular issues.

Postal Savings, a division of the U.S. Post Office Department since 1911, was established to extend the banking facilities of the Money Order system (1864). It was first advocated in the platform of the Populist party in 1892 as a means of giving easy and safe banking for small accounts. It receives savings deposits from $5 to $2500 from any person ten years of age or over, and pays a 2 per cent interest. Total deposits, rapidly declining, in 1965 were less than $343,000,000. In March 1966 President Johnson signed a bill authorizing discontinuance of the Postal Savings system.

Postal System, as a proprietary operation, began (1691) when the crown deputized Governor Andrew Hamilton of New Jersey to organize a line of post riders. They traveled widely between Portsmouth, New Hampshire, and New Castle, Delaware. By 1732 this arrangement extended into Virginia. In 1775 the Continental Congress established a POST OFFICE DEPARTMENT. After 1789 the federal government rapidly expanded mail routes, and by 1830 some 115,000 miles of POST ROADS were in operation, with mail delivered by STAGECOACHES. After 1835 railroads became the carriers as rapidly as they were constructed. With the introduction of the adhesive postage stamp (1847), envelopes came into use. Later services came to include registry (1855), free city delivery (1863), special delivery (1885), rural free delivery (1896), POSTAL SAVINGS (1910), and air mail delivery (1918).

Postimpressionism, see *Impressionism.*

POSTL, KARL, see *Sealsfield, Charles.*

Postmasters General have been appointed in America ever since Benjamin Franklin became Deputy Postmaster for the colonies in 1737. A POST OFFICE DEPARTMENT was created in 1775, and the organization has functioned at cabinet level since 1829. Because the department is in a position to control immense patronage, its head has almost always been a political lieutenant of the party in power. (The portfolio of Postmaster General is the only one that expires every four years.) Postmasters General and the Presidents under whom they served are as follows.

WASHINGTON
Samuel Osgood (Mass.) 1789
Timothy Pickering (Mass.) 1791
Joseph Habersham (Ga.) 1795

J. ADAMS
Joseph Habersham (Ga.) 1797

JEFFERSON
Joseph Habersham (Ga.) 1801
Gideon Granger (Conn.) 1801

MADISON
Gideon Granger (Conn.) 1809
Return J. Meigs, Jr. (Ohio) 1814

MONROE
Return J. Meigs, Jr. (Ohio) 1817
John McLean (Ohio) 1823

J. Q. ADAMS
John McLean (Ohio) 1825

JACKSON
William T. Barry (Ky.) 1829
Amos Kendall (Ky.) 1835

VAN BUREN
Amos Kendall (Ky.) 1837
John M. Niles (Conn.) 1840

W. H. HARRISON
Francis Granger (N.Y.) 1841

TYLER
Francis Granger (N.Y.) 1841
Charles A. Wickliffe (Ky.) 1841

POLK
Cave Johnson (Tenn.) 1845

TAYLOR
Jacob Collamer (Vt.) 1849

FILLMORE
Nathan K. Hall (N.Y.) 1850
Samuel D. Hubbard (Conn.) 1852

PIERCE
James Campbell (Pa.) 1853

BUCHANAN
Aaron V. Brown (Tenn.) 1857
Joseph Holt (Ky.) 1859
Horatio King (Me.) 1861

LINCOLN
Montgomery Blair (D.C.) 1861
William Dennison (Ohio) 1864

A. JOHNSON
William Dennison (Ohio) 1865
Alexander W. Randall (Wis.) 1866

GRANT
John A. J. Creswell (Md.) 1869
James W. Marshall (Va.) 1874
Marshall Jewell (Conn.) 1874
James N. Tyner (Ind.) 1876

HAYES
David McK. Key (Tenn.) 1877
Horace Maynard (Tenn.) 1880

GARFIELD
Thomas L. James (N.Y.) 1881

ARTHUR
Timothy O. Howe (Wis.) 1881
Walter Q. Gresham (Ind.) 1883
Frank Hatton (Iowa) 1884

CLEVELAND
William F. Vilas (Wis.) 1885
Don M. Dickinson (Mich.) 1888

B. HARRISON
John Wanamaker (Pa.) 1889

CLEVELAND
Wilson S. Bissel (N.Y.) 1893
William L. Wilson (W. Va.) 1895

MCKINLEY
James A. Gary (Md.) 1897
Charles E. Smith (Pa.) 1898

T. ROOSEVELT
Charles E. Smith (Pa.) 1901
Henry C. Payne (Wis.) 1902
Robert J. Wynne (Pa.) 1904
George B. Cortelyou (N.Y.) 1905
George von L. Meyer (Mass.) 1907

TAFT
Frank H. Hitchcock (Mass.) 1907

WILSON
Albert S. Burleson (Tex.) 1913

HARDING
Will H. Hays (Ind.) 1921
Hubert Work (Colo.) 1922
Harry S. New (Ind.) 1923

COOLIDGE
Harry S. New (Ind.) 1923

HOOVER
Walter F. Brown (Ohio) 1929

F. D. ROOSEVELT
James A. Farley (N.Y.) 1933
Frank C. Walker (Pa.) 1940

TRUMAN
Robert E. Hannegan (Mo.) 1945
Jesse M. Donaldson (Mo.) 1947

EISENHOWER
Arthur E. Summerfield (Mich.) 1953

KENNEDY
J. Edward Day (Calif.) 1961
John A. Gronouski (Wis.) 1963

L. B. JOHNSON
John A. Gronouski (Wis.) 1963
Lawrence F. O'Brien (Mass.) 1965

Potawatomi Indians, of Algonquian stock, closely related to the OJIBWA and OTTAWA, in mid-18th century were a tribe of some 2000 located in Illinois and Indiana. They allied themselves with the British in the War of 1812. Today about 4500 are settled on reservations.

Potomac, Army of the (1861–65), was created to guard the national capital immediately after the disastrous Union defeat in the first battle of BULL RUN (July 1861). General George B. McClellan began the task of whipping raw recruits into an effective fighting unit, and by year's end it numbered 138,000 troops. Despite political intrigue and bungling military leadership, it became the best trained U.S. army yet assembled in the country. It participated in the PENINSULAR CAMPAIGN, the SEVEN DAYS' BATTLES, ANTIETAM, GETTYSBURG, and the surrender of Lee at APPOMATTOX. Its commanders after McClellan were successively BURNSIDE, HOOKER, MEADE, and GRANT.

Potomac river, 287 miles long, is formed by the junction of streams in northern West Virginia flowing eastward between that state and Maryland. Between Maryland and Virginia it widens into a 125-mile estuary below Washington, D.C., and empties into Chesapeake Bay. It was mapped by John Smith in 1608 and became the early passageway to Maryland. Falls in its upper reaches made its use as an approach to the West impossible until canals after 1825 gave access to the Shenandoah and Ohio valleys.

Potsdam Conference (July 1945), held near Berlin, was attended by President Truman, Prime Minister Churchill (replaced in later meetings by the newly chosen Prime Minister Attlee), Premier Stalin, and their top-ranking foreign advisers. These wartime allies presented an unconditional surrender ultimatum to Japan, created a Council of Foreign Ministers to draw up peace treaties with Italy and the Axis satellites, and set up an Allied Control Council for the military administration of Germany, where occupation authorities were to treat the country as an economic unit, notwithstanding its division into occupation zones. They outlawed the Nazi party and all its affiliates, and reached agreements regarding German finance, trade, and industries.

POUND, EZRA [LOOMIS] (1885–), Iowa-born poet and critic, soon after graduation from Hamilton (1905) left the U.S. to live abroad. His influence in the renaissance of a vigorous interest in poetry, by launching the Imagist movement in England and the U.S., and by creating an enthusiasm for aesthetic standards in experimentation, was of major importance. He was an innovator and a 'difficult' poet, who in his later years became the emigré writer opposed to U.S. society.

He began his *Cantos* in 1925, and continued them throughout his life, as evaluations of human society in terms of 'Jeffersonian' economics. After his World War II broadcasts of Fascist propaganda over the Rome radio he was returned to the U.S. (1945) to face trial for treason, but he was adjudged of unsound mind, committed to a hospital, and later allowed to return to Italy under guardianship. His *Pisan Cantos* (1948) won the 1949 Bollingen poetry award, then newly established, but sponsorship of the award by the Library of Congress occasioned such embarrassment to that national institution that the bestowal of the award was immediately turned over to the Yale University Library.

POUND, ROSCOE (1870–1964), Nebraska-born professor of law at Harvard (1910–

37), for twenty years was dean of its law faculty (1916–36), and thereafter served the institution as University Professor (1937–47). In his *Introduction to the Philosophy of Law* (1922) he viewed the 'science of law' in the light of philosophy, analyzing both the part of law that is substantive concept and the part that is the intuitive formulation of accomplished jurists. His monumental *Jurisprudence* (5 vols., 1959) summarizes an active career of 70 years of leadership in the growth and reform of law. His works include more than 1000 titles, nearly 300 of which are books or major papers.

Pound was endowed with an encyclopedic mind, and though he earned a graduate degree only in botany, he was given many honorary degrees. He was sometimes called 'the schoolmaster of the American bar,' and takes rank as one of the world's first scholars in modern jurisprudence.

POWDERLY, TERENCE VINCENT (1849–1924), Pennsylvania-born labor leader, as Grand Master Workman of the KNIGHTS OF LABOR (1879–93) was largely responsible for the first CHINESE EXCLUSION ACT (1882) and the CONTRACT LABOR ACT of 1885. An idealist, he urged a method of co-operative production rather than a wage system, usually refrained from the strike weapon, and resigned because he disliked the tactics of combative unionism. Meanwhile he had been instrumental in the establishment of labor bureaus and arbitration systems in many states. In later years (1907–21) he was an official in the Bureau of Immigration. His writings on labor subjects include *Thirty Years of Labor* (1889), and a posthumously issued autobiography, *The Path I Trod* (1940).

POWELL, JOHN WESLEY (1834–1902), was serving as Professor of Geology at Illinois Wesleyan College, Bloomington, when he first led geological expeditions into Colorado and Utah (1867–69). He described his hazardous boat trip through the Grand Canyon in *Explorations of the Colorado River of the West* (1875; rev. and enl. as *Canyons of the Colorado,* 1895), a pioneer study in the field of physiographic geology. His contributions to ethnology appear in the *Reports* of the Bureau of American Ethnology, of which he became director in 1879. For many years (1880–94) he served as director of the U.S. Geological Survey. His *Lands of the Arid Region* (1878), which pointed out the dangers of soil erosion, was an immensely important blueprint for the formation of the Reclamation Service. Powell was the first of the great regional planners. Had his program been followed it might have spared the West the disasters of the DUST BOWL, but it met with repeated opposition among those western congressmen who had no desire to see a revision in the system of disposing of PUBLIC LANDS.

Powell* v. *Alabama, see *Scottsboro Case.*

'Power of the purse' is the financial power of a legislative body to control the executive branch by retaining the exclusive right to authorize appropriations and revenues. This right originated in medieval England and was brought to the British colonies in America. The principle is embodied in the Federal Constitution in the provision (Art. I, sec. 7) that assigns the power to originate revenue legislation to the House of Representatives.

'Power to tax involves the power to destroy,' see *McCulloch* v. *Maryland.*

POWERS, HIRAM (1805–73), Vermont-born sculptor, in 1837 settled in Italy, where he became the first American to win a European reputation as sculptor. The technical dexterity of his marble *Greek Slave* (1843) made it the most celebrated statue of its day, and its idealized sentimentalism seemed to express human aspirations at a time when the cause of Greek independence was attracting wide attention. Though its nudity shocked American sensibilities, it whetted American taste for neoclassical sculptor. Powers gained fame and wealth from his portrait busts, and his home in Florence was a mecca for American notables traveling abroad. His renown declined soon after his death, when marble busts went out of fashion.

POWHATAN (d. 1618), when the first English colonizers arrived, was the powerful chief of an Indian confederation, some 30 Algonquian tribes south of the Potomac river. In 1614 he gave his daughter POCAHONTAS in marriage to John Rolfe (1585–1622), thereby assuring Indian co-operation with the English. After Powhatan's death Indian attacks became frequent; Rolfe himself was a victim in one massacre. After 1665 chiefs were appointed by the governor of Virginia, and the Powhatan Confederacy was dissolved.

POWNALL, THOMAS (1722–1805), a graduate of Cambridge University (1743), came to New York (1753) as secretary of the governor, and was himself appointed governor of Massachusetts (1757–59) before he returned to England. His famous *The Administration of the Colonies* (1764) urged a reorganization of colonial affairs along lines that would give the colonists a greater incentive to close union with Britain. In Parliament (1767–80) he was sympathetic to the colonists' pleas until their resistance to Parliament's authority reached the point of demanding separation. In 1780 he introduced a bill favoring a negotiated peace, but Parliament rejected it. Pownall consistently urged that colonial policy be directed toward strengthening the ties of a British commonwealth.

Powwow (Algonquin: *priest, magician*) in the 17th century was extended to mean a gathering of Indians for a feast or ceremony. The term was later applied to all Indian ritual gatherings.

Pragmatism, the most important philosophical concept of the late 19th century, was founded by CHARLES PEIRCE, and developed by WILLIAM JAMES. It was basic in the conclusions of the mathematician CHAUNCEY WRIGHT and in the later thinking of JOHN DEWEY. Using the method of EMPIRICISM, which holds that knowledge derives from experience (or sense impressions), it postulates an open and unfinished universe, conditioned by no fixed and eternal pattern. Values are inherent in the process of seeking truth, since the search is neverending. James summed up this novelty among philosophical systems by saying, 'The truth of an idea is not a stagnant property inherent in it. Truth *happens* to an idea . . . The ultimate test of what a truth means is the conduct it dictates or inspires.' To pragmatists truth is to be reached by active participation, by a constant becoming, not by assuming some absolute end. In recent years CLARENCE LEWIS has carried forward pragmatic theory and logic.

Prairie region is the eastern portion of the Middle West, and includes Missouri, Iowa, Nebraska, Kansas, Minnesota, and the eastern areas of North and South Dakota. (Its western reaches lead into the PLAINS REGION.) Favored by soil and climate, it is one of the world's greatest agricultural regions.

Prairie schooners, see *Covered wagons, Wagon trains.*

Praying Indians is the term designating Indian converts to Christianity in New England during the colonial period, such as those converted by JOHN ELIOT. During KING PHILIP'S WAR (1675–76) the Praying Indians were mercilessly hunted down by their unconverted tribesmen. Jonathan Edwards went as a missionary (1751–57) to the Stockbridge Indians, members of the MAHICAN Confederacy in western Massachusetts. Missionary funds from London helped such enterprises as that of ELEAZAR WHEELOCK, who conducted an Indian charity school in Connecticut (1754–67), where he educated SAMSON OCCOM, and from which stemmed Dartmouth College (1769). Actually, however, the Christianizing of Indians had begun long before, in the INDIAN MISSIONS established by the Spanish and French.

Pre-emption Acts were the series of temporary laws passed by Congress affecting the sale and distribution of PUBLIC LANDS. Pre-emption in U.S. history was the settling on public land before it had been purchased or surveyed, in the hope that it might later thus be more easily acquired. It was illegal and always a liability, since the squatter might be forceably removed and lose the value of his improvements. Even so, settlers moving into the western frontier, especially during the 1830's, brought pressure upon Congress to give them legal title to the land.

The Act of 1841, called the 'Log-Cabin Act,' made the principles of the Act of 1830 permanent in public land policy. It provided for the grant of 160 acres of surveyed public lands to qualified settlers, who had the right to purchase the tract at $1.25 an acre before it was offered at public auction. This was a clear-cut frontier victory and a landmark among the agrarian measures passed by Congress.

Presbyterians, adherents of one of the principal denominations of CALVINISM, observe a church government midway between that of Anglicans (in the U.S., members of the PROTESTANT EPISCOPAL CHURCH) and of CONGREGATIONALISTS. Presbyterianism functions under a system of representative church government administered by presbyters, courts composed of clerical and lay elders who are equal in status. It was introduced in America by French HUGUENOTS in the 17th century, but theologically it made no headway for several decades.

The Presbyterians were strong in Scotland and England under Cromwell, but the first Presbyterian missionary, FRANCIS MAKEMIE, did not arrive in America until 1683. He began his labors in Maryland, and took the lead in forming the Philadelphia Presbytery (1706). By mid-18th century American Presbyterians were sharply divided during the GREAT AWAKENING into 'Old Side' (those who rejected evangelism) and 'New Side' (those who espoused it). The College of New Jersey (Princeton) was established by JONATHAN DICKINSON and other New Siders in 1746 to assure a trained ministry. On the eve of the Revolution, next to Congregationalists, Presbyterians were the most numerous body in the colonies, and the two groups remained the dominant cultural influence before the Civil War.

The Presbyterian Church in the U.S. (est. 1861) is often called the Southern Church. The largest of the Presbyterian bodies, the United Presbyterian Church in the U.S.A., is a merger of some 9000 churches whose schisms were minor. The various bodies have a total of some 4,000,000 members.

See W. L. Lingle, *Presbyterians: Their History and Beliefs* (2nd ed., 1944), and G. J. Slosser (ed.), *They Seek a Country* (1955), a historical symposium.

PRESCOTT, WILLIAM HICKLING (1796–1859), son of a wealthy Salem lawyer, after graduation from Harvard (1814) abandoned his plan to enter his father's office. An eye injury had virtually blinded him, and while traveling in Europe seeking medical treatment (1815–17), he became interested in writing history based on Spanish subjects. He began his research with the aid of a visual-aid device and secretaries who read aloud to him. By setting himself a Spartan regime he produced with notable rapidity *A History of the Reign of Ferdinand and Isabella* (1837), *A History of the Conquest of Mexico* (1843), *A History of the Conquest of Peru* (1847), and *A History of the Reign of Philip the Second* (3 vols., 1855–58). The last, left incomplete, was begun in 1849 and rushed through because he realized that his failing sight might not allow him to cover the extensive materials.

So thorough was Prescott in his research that after a century historians pay homage to his scholarly use of the sources then available. Primarily a literary craftsman, he gave close attention to Sir Walter Scott, whom he called 'the master of the picturesque'; and to Voltaire, on whom he modeled his topical, rather than chronological, arrangement. The fact that the *Mexico* and *Peru* are as fresh and vivid today as when they first appeared is a measure of his talent in giving epic sweep to great events and in dramatizing the tragedy that inevitably followed in the wake of the conquistadors. With less philosophy of history than of literary technique, Prescott tended to neglect social and economic problems. He remains nonetheless one of the great American historians, whose power lies in the clear grasp of facts, in characterization and vivid narration of incident, and in selection and synthesis.

No adequate life of Prescott has appeared since that by George Ticknor (1864), but see C. H. Gardiner (ed.), *The Papers of William H. Prescott* (1964).

Presidency, The, is a unique and peculiarly American institution, created both by law and custom. As Chief Executive, the President of the U.S. is the one official directed to 'take care that the laws be faithfully executed,' and thus he exercises immense moral and legal influence over all Americans. As Commander in Chief, he is the supreme head of all armed forces and the embodiment of the American belief in the supremacy of civil over military authority. He is the leader of his party, and hence through a mammoth bureaucracy he controls party patronage. His veto power, an executive prerogative, is not subject to any committee council, and it not only keeps him intimately associated with every stage in the legislative process but gives him a hand in shaping legislation.

His power of nominating personnel is far-reaching; it even applies to the Supreme Court, the third independent branch of government. At all times he must be the spokesman for his nation, and in moments of crisis or disaster he is expected to marshal aid and comfort for the people. He is the economic overseer who must act decisively in managing the nation's prosperity. Ambassadors are *his* ambassadors, for he is the sole representative of the U.S. in foreign countries: as chief of state, he is the ceremonial head of government.

The Constitution was sufficiently vague to initiate a struggle between two concepts of executive power, and the personalities of Presidents therefore materially affect the development of the office and its powers. So-called 'strong' Presidents have made the office, within generous limits, self-directing. Some Presidents have been subordinate to the legislative branch, but generally speaking the history of the Presidency has been one of increasing strength.

For one thing, in an effort to promote the vast growth of the American economy, Congress has delegated power to the executive branch by increasing the number of 'administrative regulations,' and thus the President has been assigned unprecedented administrative authority. As the U.S. continues to assume a greater role in world politics, the power of the President grows proportionately. A series of emergencies during the 20th century — two World Wars and the Great Depression — have tended to enhance the leadership and prestige of the President; therefore Congress increasingly looks to him for continuous political leadership. And finally, American democracy itself has come to regard the President as its most fitting national symbol and instrument for action.

At the same time, evidence has rapidly accumulated during the second half of the 20th century that presidential power and the person of the President are no longer one and the same thing. Presidential power extends to an ever-increasing White House staff (the Office of the President). The great departments of the Executive (the Cabinet) have their own enclaves. Independent executive agencies with their quasi-legislative and quasi-judicial power have proliferated. The President must therefore continually be alert lest his own executive household absorb the Presidency. See *Ex-Presidents*.

President *pro tempore* is the presiding officer of the U.S. Senate, selected by the members themselves to officiate at meetings when sessions are not chaired by the Vice President.

Presidential campaigns, conducted quadrennially in the U.S. to select candidates for the offices of President and Vice President, are political activities that lie entirely outside any constitutional provision. In the early decades no 'campaigns' occurred, in the sense of national party conventions organized to make nominations. In 1789 and 1792 Washington was informally chosen for President, and both times he was unanimously elected. The 1796 election was the first to be contested by political parties. The turning point came in 1800, when the Kentucky and Virginia Resolves were proffered by Madison and Jefferson as a party platform and Aaron Burr made use of early PARTY MACHINES. From 1796 to 1824 presidential candidates were nominated by congressional CAUCUS. So strong had the Republican (Jeffersonian) party become after 1800 that its caucus nominations were practically nominations by Congress itself.

Such a system could not endure, for to many it seemed a violation of the spirit of the Constitution, and in 1824 it was denounced by mass meetings throughout the country. It was replaced in 1832 by the NATIONAL CONVENTION system. Thereafter highly organized national committees took command of party forces. In time they were able to raise huge sums for stump speakers, campaign literature, and other less advertised means of persuasion.

Before 1900 candidates held aloof from direct campaigning, or made sedate appearances, as did McKinley in the 'front-porch' campaign of 1896. Later they took 'swings around the country,' addressing audiences from the rear platforms of trains at 'whistle stops.' Most recently they have themselves become the chief campaigners by using radio discourses and television appearances to reach millions of voters. The striking feature of the 1960 campaign was the series of televised 'debates' in which the candidates submitted to questions asked by reporters. See *Campaign of 1789, et seq.*

Presidential primaries are the preliminary quadrennial contests for President. They use one or both of two systems that allow the voter to express a choice of party candidate. These are (1) the preferential poll, a choice among candidates, and (2) the election of delegates, often instructed how to vote in the NATIONAL CONVENTION. Historically they are a product of the political reform movement of the early 1900's, and have evolved in a hit-or-miss fashion. They are held in only seventeen states and the District of Columbia (as of 1964), and the rules differ in almost every instance. (The states in which they are held are Alabama, California, Florida, Illinois, Indiana, Maryland, Massachusetts, Nebraska, New Hampshire, New Jersey, New York, Ohio, Oregon, Pennsylvania, South Dakota, West Virginia, and Wisconsin.)

Even more than most political mechanisms, these primaries are perplexing, contradictory, and sometimes falsely influential. Relatively few citizens cast their votes in this random selection ballot, and only for such candidates as are registered (or written in) at the time. But those primaries that are held first have inescapable propaganda value, since on occasion they can eliminate a would-be contender by a single defeat, or enhance his nomination possibilities by showing landslide trends.

Presidential Succession Acts are those laws passed by Congress that provide for the order of succession to the presidency in the event of the removal, resignation, death, or disability of the President. Constitutionally the Vice President succeeds. The first of these Acts (1792) provided for the succession, after the Vice President, of the PRESIDENT PRO TEMPORE of the Senate and the Speaker of the House, in that order. The Act of 1886 devolved the succession upon the heads of the executive departments in the order of their establishment. The Act of 1947 amended the law to provide for the succession, after the Vice President, of the Speaker of the House, the President *pro tempore* of the Senate, and then the heads of the executive departments. This revision was made in the belief that a popularly chosen figure rather than an appointed officer should be first in the line of succession. Between the time of President Kennedy's assassination (22 November 1963) and the election of President Johnson in November 1964, when the vice presidency was vacant, several problems of succession were debated in the Congress. In 1965 Congress became seriously aware of the problem and began to search for a solution, with a constitutional amendment in mind.

Presidents of the U.S.

1. George Washington (Federalist, 1789–97)
2. John Adams (Federalist, 1797–1801)
3. Thomas Jefferson (Democratic-Republican, 1801–9)
4. James Madison (Democratic-Republican, 1809–17)
5. James Monroe (Democratic-Republican, 1817–25)
6. John Quincy Adams (Independent, 1825–29)
7. Andrew Jackson (Democrat, 1829–37)
8. Martin Van Buren (Democrat, 1837–41)
9. William H. Harrison (Whig, 1841)
10. John Tyler (Whig, then Democrat, 1841–45)
11. James K. Polk (Democrat, 1845–49)
12. Zachary Taylor (Whig, 1849–50)
13. Millard Fillmore (Whig, 1850–53)
14. Franklin Pierce (Democrat, 1853–57)
15. James Buchanan (Democrat, 1857–61)
16. Abraham Lincoln (Republican, 1861–65)

17. Andrew Johnson (Democrat, 1865–69)
18. Ulysses S. Grant (Republican, 1869–77)
19. Rutherford B. Hayes (Republican, 1877–81)
20. James A. Garfield (Republican, 1881)
21. Chester A. Arthur (Republican, 1881–85)
22. Grover Cleveland (Democrat, 1885–89)
23. Benjamin Harrison (Republican, 1889–93)
24. Grover Cleveland (Democrat, 1893–97)
25. William McKinley (Republican, 1897–1901)
26. Theodore Roosevelt (Republican, 1901–9)
27. William H. Taft (Republican, 1909–13)
28. Woodrow Wilson (Democrat, 1913–21)
29. Warren G. Harding (Republican, 1921–23)
30. Calvin Coolidge (Republican, 1923–29)
31. Herbert Hoover (Republican, 1929–33)
32. Franklin D. Roosevelt (Democrat, 1933–45)
33. Harry S Truman (Democrat, 1945–53)
34. Dwight D. Eisenhower (Republican, 1953–61)
35. John F. Kennedy (Democrat, 1961–63)
36. Lyndon B. Johnson (Democrat, 1963–)

Presidents, Minority, are those candidates elected to the presidency even though they have polled a minority of the POPULAR VOTE. The device of the ELECTORAL COLLEGE can bring minority Presidents into office because a majority of electoral votes is necessary for election. In elections where three or more strong candidates have campaigned, none has usually received a popular majority. Minority Presidents of the U.S. are as follows.

President	*year*	*percentage of popular vote*
J. Q. Adams	1824	32.0
Polk	1844	49.5
Taylor	1848	47.4
Buchanan	1856	45.3
Lincoln	1860	39.9
Hayes	1876	47.9
Garfield	1880	48.3
Cleveland	1884	48.9
B. Harrison	1888	47.8
Cleveland	1892	46.0
Wilson	1912	41.8
Wilson	1916	49.3
Truman	1948	49.5
Kennedy	1960	49.8

Presidios were Spanish forts or posts on the American frontier, where soldiers lived with their families and augmented their subsistence allowance by cultivating the soil. Presidios were chiefly located in the Southwest.

Press, see *Journalism, Newspapers, Civil liberties.*

Press conference, the gathering of news by reporters at a conference interview, in the U.S. significantly applies to the presidential press conference, a unique institution which changes radically as new Presidents take office. Theodore Roosevelt was the first President to use press interviews effectively, though he did not permit general conferences and rarely allowed quotation. Coolidge selected questions from cards written in advance.

The nature of today's press conference, in which as many as 300 newsmen and women may assemble to seek statements, was established by Franklin Roosevelt, who met the press twice a week. He enjoyed the conferences, and dominated them with great skill. Since the administration of President Eisenhower, the scope of communicating with the nation has been vastly broadened by the addition of a Press Secretary to the White House Staff. President Kennedy showed exceptional ability in making the press conference a vehicle of communication with the people.

Pressure groups, see *Lobbying.*

Price Administration, Office of, was established by Executive Order (1941) with authority to issue price schedules on critical wartime commodities. In 1942 Congress granted the O.P.A. the power to impose price ceilings on commodities, services, and rents: the first national effort at price control. The agency was dissolved in 1946.

PRIESTLEY, JOSEPH (1733–1804), English chemist and nonconformist minister, wrote voluminously on theological, philosophical, and scientific subjects. He isolated oxygen in 1774 and perceived its true character in 1775, though he stubbornly clung to the 'phlogiston' theory. However, it was he who gave Lavoisier knowledge by which that French chemist could disprove the theory. Priestley's liberal political views made him so stout a defender of the American colonies and the French Revolution that in 1791 his house was sacked and his scientific apparatus destroyed. He emigrated to Pennsylvania in 1794, shortly before his friend THOMAS COOPER did, and there Priestley continued his scientific investigations, especially in the chemistry of gases. Priestley was ingenious in devising apparatus, and his arrival in the U.S. stimulated experimentation in chemical analysis.

Prigg* v. *Pennsylvania (1842), an opinion of the U.S. Supreme Court written by Justice Story, stemmed from an incident in which a slave, escaping from Maryland to Pennsylvania, was captured and returned to her owner by a Federal agent. The agent was indicted for kidnapping under a Pennsylvania fugitive slave law, and the decision was affirmed by the Pennsylvania Supreme Court. The Supreme Court declared the Pennsylvania statute unconstitutional, but it divided sharply over Story's argument that the power of Congress rendered invalid all state statutes on the subject. As a result several northern states enacted PERSONAL LIBERTY LAWS.

Primary election, see *Direct primary.*

Primogeniture, the exclusive right of an eldest son to inherit property, was essential as an economic basis for the European feudal structure, as it insured the continuance of an undivided estate. All the American colonies followed the practice. It came to be modified in Pennsylvania and all of New England except Rhode Island. In those regions property was equally divided among the male heirs, and the eldest son inherited a double portion. The entire system was abolished before 1800, first in Georgia (1777), North Carolina (1784), and Virginia (1785), and finally in Rhode Island (1798).

PRINCE, THOMAS (1687–1758), Massachusetts-born clergyman and historian, after graduation from Harvard (1707) traveled abroad, preaching often in Congregational churches in England (1709–17), before returning (1718) to accept the invitation of the Old South Church in Boston to become its pastor, which post he filled throughout his life. Prince was a scholar. He gathered an impressive library, which he used in writing *A Chronological History of New England* (2 vols., 1736–55; repr., 5 vols., 1887–88). It follows the Puritan concept that the advent of Puritans in America was part of God's design in shaping events to culminate with the founding of the Bay Colony. He therefore begins his story with the creation and devotes relatively little attention to the period after 1633. Its major historical virtue, which gives Prince high rank among early historical scholars in America, is its careful verification of detail. He bequeathed his library to his church, and that part of it which was not dispersed by later 'borrowings' now forms the Prince collection of the Boston Public Library.

Princeton, Battle of (3 January 1777), occurred eight days after the battle of TRENTON, which General Howe sought to avenge by dispatching Cornwallis from New York with a large force to strengthen the British garrison at Princeton. Washington's army of 5200 had recrossed from Pennsylvania into Trenton on 30–31 December, and when the British vanguard made contact with it on 2 January, Cornwallis was approaching Princeton by way of New Brunswick. He concluded from reports that Washington was in a precarious position, and gave orders to wait until the following morning to 'bag the old fox.'

During the night, by a rapid and brilliant maneuver, Washington stole around the British flank and moved north. Meanwhile, near Princeton, a unit of Continentals led by General Hugh Mercer (1725–77) clashed with a British column marching to join Cornwallis. Mercer was killed and the American contingent routed. At that moment Washington appeared and drove the British back toward New Brunswick, with heavy losses. Cornwallis, with the main body, fell back, fearing his supply depot might be jeopardized. Washington then drew his tired troops off to the northeast and dug in at Morristown.

The combined victories at Trenton and Princeton were a turning point in the War of Independence. They opened transport for the American army between New York and Philadelphia, and they immensely heartened the patriot cause at home and abroad.

Princeton University was chartered (1746) as the College of New Jersey by Presbyterians who sought to provide an institution to train ministers for the Middle Colonies. It opened in Elizabethtown (1747), moved to Newark (1748), and permanently settled in Princeton (1756) after Nassau Hall had been erected. It sponsored the 'New Side' wing of Presbyterianism in the GREAT AWAKENING. During his presidency (1768–94) JOHN WITHERSPOON not only healed the church schism but created a college.

Always a bulwark of the humanities, during the administration of JAMES MC COSH (1868–88) the college opened a school of engineering (1873), began graduate instruction, and soon thereafter became Princeton University (1896). The first layman to become its president, WOODROW WILSON (1902–10) introduced the preceptorial (individualized) system of instruction. Especially well known are its schools of architecture (1919) and public and international affairs (1930). A few women are admitted to graduate instruction, but the institution remains primarily a university for men. In 1965, with an endowment of $99,000,000 and a faculty of 780, it enrolled 4296 students.

Printing was first introduced in North America when a press was set up in Mexico City (*c.* 1539) by Spanish missionaries. In 1639 STEPHEN DAY established the first press in the English colonies at Cambridge, Massachusetts. William Nuthead opened a printing office in Maryland (1685). The press that WILLIAM BRADFORD set up in Philadelphia (1685) he later moved to New York (1693); he was thus the earliest printer in two colonies. Demand for the printing of public documents was largely responsible for presses being set up in Connecticut (1709), Rhode Island (1727), and South Carolina (1731). Thereafter presses began to multiply, chiefly to print NEWSPAPERS.

Three inventions during the 19th century revolutionized printing and created what later became a large-scale industry. By inventing the rotary press (1847) RICHARD HOE opened the way to mass production. (He also devised a machine for folding sheets.) WILLIAM BULLOCK invented a method (1865) for printing continuous rolls on both sides. But the greatest advance was made when OTTMAR MERGENTHALER created the linotype (1884), called the most important printing device since the invention of movable type (*c.* 1440). By mid-20th century the printing and publishing industry had become a major factor in the national economy.

See L. C. Wroth, *The Colonial Printer* (1938), and Hellmut Lehmann-Haupt, *The Book in America* (rev. ed., 1951).

Prison reform in the U.S. had its modest beginning in Philadelphia (1790), based on the concept that solitary confinement would promote moral regeneration by means of enforced meditation. The mental breakdowns thus induced led to modifications. In 1816 the Auburn (N.Y.) system permitted the congregation of prisoners during the day. Although such efforts were aimed at eliminating the inhuman nature of prison life, overcrowding prevented any fundamental improvements until the 1820's, when the first houses of correction and reform schools were established. After the 1840's the U.S. was peculiarly 'the home of penitentiary science,' for considerable efforts were made to study prison management. In 1870 the American Prison Association was formed to carry out the ideas of such reform leaders as ENOCH WINES and ZEBULON BROCKWAY, pioneers in stressing the importance of rehabilitation, a point of view carried forward by THOMAS MOTT OS-

BORNE. The reforms instigated by Governor JOHN PETER ALTGELD of Illinois (1893–97) were adopted elsewhere.

Gradually youthful offenders were separated from hardened criminals, good conduct was rewarded by shorter prison terms, and parole and probation were introduced. In the 20th century emphasis increasingly has been given to the role of occupational therapy, psychiatric care, social work, classification of inmates, and compensated labor. The suspended sentence and post-release supervision also became part of legal enactments, through the influence of such criminologists as SANFORD BATES and SHELDON GLUECK, who with others have given a new turn to the thinking of legislators and jurists in the field of penology.

Private schools, see *Academies.*

Privateering was formerly the custom of fitting out privateers — that is, armed private ships under government commission — to prey upon enemy commerce in time of war. Government licenses, letters of marque and reprisal, distinguished it from PIRACY. Particularly during the 18th century privateers aided naval vessels, and since privateersmen were granted a large share of the booty, many of them became very wealthy. During the War of Independence some 1100 privateers captured about 600 British ships, including sixteen men-of-war. In the War of 1812 more than 500 letters of marque were issued, and such naval heroes as JOSHUA BARNEY and STEPHEN DECATUR were skillful privateersmen. Although the U.S. observed the Declaration of Paris (1856), which abolished privateering, it did not sign the instrument, and thus could not effectively protest against Confederate privateering during the Civil War.

Prize fighting, see *Boxing.*

Proclamation of 1763 was the first of a series of measures undertaken by the British government after the Treaty of Paris of 1763, in an effort to solve the immensely complex IMPERIAL PROBLEMS created by winning the French and Indian War. In an effort to eliminate zones of friction, the Proclamation organized the government of the provinces of Quebec, East Florida, and West Florida, and sought to establish a policy regarding the Indians and western lands. It placed Indian trade under royal control, and banned white settlements west of the Alleghenies, the 'Proclamation Line.' This restriction was motivated by good intentions, but it was unrealistic. The Indians knew little or nothing about London's authority to make a reservation for them. Land speculators and frontiersmen strongly opposed it. Veterans who had been promised western lands were incensed at the withdrawal from public sale of these territories (encroachments of settlers was one cause of the rebellion of PONTIAC). The Proclamation in effect provided one more grievance of the colonies against the home government.

Progressive education, as developed in the U.S. by FRANCIS WAYLAND PARKER and JOHN DEWEY, followed the pattern established in Europe by Froebel, Pestalozzi, and Montessori in the late 19th century. It postulates that children can be made to feel that under direction their training becomes self-direction, subject matter should be adjusted to their innate capacities, and that formalized teaching methods are stultifying. Dewey applied the practice at the University of Chicago in his laboratory school (1896–1904), where the government of the group centered on a project of common interest. Where the Dewey influence was misapplied, it inspired a revolt against 'soft education,' costly fads and frills, and the narrow methodology of 'educationalists.'

The Dalton plan (Dalton, Massachusetts, 1919) began by creating units of work within specified limits. The Winnetka plan (Winnetka, Illinois, 1919) in general followed the Dalton plan but applied the co-operative method to outside activities. This so-called 'learning by doing' method has been so pervasive both in cultural and vocational training that in varying degrees it has won pedagogical acceptance in the U.S. on a wide scale, especially in schools where instruction is given by skilled teachers.

See L. A. Cremin, *The Transformation of the School: Progressivism in American Education, 1876–1957* (1961).

Progressive movement (1890–1917) was essentially the ideological and political response to the transformation of the nation from a rural, commercial economy to an urban, industrial one, and it made a concerted effort to provide the basic political, social, and economic reforms necessary to the new economy. The enormous advances made during the 19th century in establishing a continental nation had been achieved at the cost of such dislocations, evils, and abuses as concentration of economic power, inequitable taxation, wasteful consumption of the nation's resources, corrupt PARTY MACHINES, SWEATSHOPS, CHILD LABOR, and crowded SLUMS.

The early attempts at remedy were the SHERMAN ANTITRUST ACT (1890) and an organized start of the CONSERVATION MOVEMENT (1891). Protests against the alliance of business and corrupt politics were effectively voiced by those who spearheaded the MUCKRAKING movement, and were largely responsible for such legislation during the administration of Theodore Roosevelt as the HEPBURN ACT (1906), the PURE FOOD AND DRUG ACT (1906), and the creation of a Federal Children's Bureau. Later reform legislation set up the FEDERAL RESERVE SYSTEM (1913) and the FEDERAL TRADE COMMISSION (1914). The Sixteenth Amendment (1913) widened the tax base, the LA FOLLETTE SEAMAN'S ACT (1916) was an important labor measure, and the FEDERAL FARM LOAN ACT (1916) attempted agricultural relief. In the same period state and municipal laws provided housing, labor, and welfare reforms. Representative leaders of the progressive movement include THEODORE ROOSEVELT, WOODROW WILSON, JOHN PETER ALTGELD, EUGENE V. DEBS, JACOB RIIS, JANE ADDAMS, ROBERT M. LA FOLLETTE, and GEORGE W. NORRIS.

Two useful studies are A. M. Schlesinger, *The American as Reformer* (1950), and Daniel Aaron, *Men of Good Hope: A Story of American Progressives* (1951).

Progressive party of 1912 was formed after the Republican National Convention met at Chicago (18 June). A three-cornered contest developed between La Follette, Taft, and Roosevelt, and the fight between Roosevelt and Taft became acrimonious. Roosevelt had the overwhelming support of the party rank and file, but the bosses were with Taft. Since the Old Guard controlled the convention machinery, when Roosevelt saw that contested seats were invariably awarded to Taft men, he instructed his delegates to take no further part in the proceedings. Taft received the Republican renomination easily.

Roosevelt's followers began organizing a new party, and on 5 August the progressive party convened in Chicago, where enthusiastic delegates, parading to the strains of 'Onward Christian Soldiers,' nominated their 'Bull Moose' leader by acclamation. Their platform specified tariff revision, stricter regulation of big business, woman suffrage, and minimum wage standards. The presidential election was a contest between Taft, Roosevelt, and the Democratic nominee Woodrow Wilson. Although Wilson polled only 42 per cent of the popular vote, he won 435 votes in the electoral college, to Roosevelt's 88 and Taft's 8. The Progressive party thereafter disintegrated, for it had little organic unity beyond the personality of Roosevelt.

Progressive party of 1924 succeeded the defunct FARMER-LABOR PARTY of 1920 and, allied with the Socialists, ran Senator ROBERT LA FOLLETTE (Wis.) as candidate for President with Senator Burton K. Wheeler (Mont.) as running mate. The militant platform pledged a complete housecleaning of the executive departments affected by the Harding scandals, the public ownership of railroads and water power, control of all the nation's resources, reduction of income taxes, farm relief, and abolition of the labor injunction. La Follette polled nearly 5,000,000 votes and won the 13 electoral votes of his own state. Coolidge was returned to office. In modified form some of the party's reform measures were incorporated in the early New Deal legislation.

Progressive party of 1948 was a Democratic splinter group, heavily infiltrated by communists, consisting largely of erstwhile Democrats who opposed the 'get-tough-with-Russia' policy of the Truman administration, radical urban labor groups, and miscellaneous intellectuals. They ran HENRY A. WALLACE as their presidential candidate, and demanded civil rights laws, negotiations with Russia (presumably in the hope of undermining the MARSHALL PLAN), and repeal of the TAFT-HARTLEY ACT. Wallace polled 1,137,000 popular votes, chiefly by defection of Democrats in New York, Maryland, and Michigan. He received no electoral votes.

Prohibition, see *Temperance movement.*

Prohibition Era (1920–33) in the U.S. began when the Eighteenth Amendment, enforced by the VOLSTEAD ACT (1919) went into effect. (It ended with the repeal of the Eighteenth Amendment by the Twenty-first.) Despite the enthusiasm that greeted the start of Prohibition, enforcement of a constitutional law forbidding the 'manufacture, sale, or transportation of intoxicating liquors' soon proved to be extraordinarily difficult. The federal government took its task seriously, made annual appropriations of more than $10,000,000 to circumvent rum-running, and in the decade 1920–30 made over 500,000 arrests and secured some 300,000 court convictions.

But drinking continued. SPEAKEASIES replaced the corner saloon, home-brewing and BOOTLEGGING became established practices, and NIGHT CLUBS made illegal liquor operations fashionable. Large urban populations, especially among middle-class citizens who could afford high liquor prices, sabotaged the laws to an extent not matched since the North had nullified the fugitive slave laws nearly a century earlier. Political parties could not avoid the troublesome issue. By 1928 the 'wets' were in control of the Democratic party. Its presidential candidate, Alfred E. Smith, lost the election to Herbert Hoover, who genuinely tried to encourage 'an experiment noble in motive and far-reaching in purpose.' But after the WICKERSHAM COMMISSION in 1931 reported in effect that prohibition laws were unenforceable, the country was in a mood to repeal an Amendment that tended to breed disrespect for law in general.

See Andrew Sinclair, *Prohibition: The Era of Excess* (1962).

Prohibition party, still in existence, is the oldest of the minor political parties. Organized in 1869 after 70 years of TEMPERANCE agitation, it entered national politics in 1872. It won its greatest success in 1892, when it polled 271,000 votes. It still retains some influence in American politics; it received more than 46,000 votes in the election of 1960.

Proportional representation, as a method of voting for municipal officers, has gained favor in many localities in the U.S. It is an electoral arrangement that gives minority parties a share of the legislative representation proportional to their voting power. By instituting voting-at-large to replace district voting, which usually returns a single candidate to the exclusion of all others, and giving the voter an opportunity to indicate preferences that can be numerically listed, it offers minority parties the chance to elect candidates. However, it can encourage a multitude of conflicting small parties.

Proprietary colonies were that form of CHARTER COLONIES created by royal grants after 1632. They were the predominant type throughout the 17th century, and included Maine, New York, New Jersey, Pennsylvania, Maryland, and the Carolinas. Their precedent was familiar in English history. Broad territorial and political powers were bestowed upon a single person or a small group (the lord proprietor or the lords proprietors), who exercised feudal or even (with specified exemptions) sovereign powers. Politically they were feudal in name only, since they were governed by representative bodies. But the proprietary land was a great private domain, sold off at the will of the owner, and settled according to the terms he specified. After the Restoration (1660) the crown shaped its policy of consolidating colonial possessions, and set about converting proprietary into ROYAL COLONIES. By 1776 only Maryland and Pennsylvania remained proprietary colonies.

Protectionism, see *Tariff.*

Protestant Episcopal Church, the American body of the Anglican (Church of England) Communion, set up its own church government and adopted its present name in 1789, with SAMUEL SEABURY as presiding bishop. The Anglican Church was established by law in Virginia

(1610), but outside of Virginia and Maryland there were relatively few Anglican clergymen in the colonies. The Bishop of London, placed in charge of colonial churches (1635), was represented by 'Commissaries,' but the influence of the Church for many decades was limited by the mediocre quality of its parish clergy, its neglect of discipline, and by consequent substitution of lay control.

The Puritans of New England were doctrinally at one with the Anglicans, but they proscribed Anglican church government since it was determined by bishops who upheld royal supremacy in church affairs. But when the Massachusetts charter was revoked in 1684, Anglican curates were appointed, and King's Chapel was opened in Boston (1689). The Bishop of London sent JAMES BLAIR to Virginia (1685) to invigorate the intellectual life (Blair founded William and Mary in 1693), and commissioned THOMAS BRAY in 1699 to do likewise in Maryland, where Bray founded notable libraries. Christ Church in Philadelphia (1694) and Trinity Church in New York (1697) were chartered by William III. SAMUEL JOHNSON established the first Anglican church in Connecticut (1724) before going to New York as president of the newly founded King's College (Columbia, est. 1754).

Agitation for an American episcopate met repeated opposition during the 18th century from government officials and dissenters, and from southern Anglican laymen, who insisted on choosing their own ministers. During the Revolution most of the Anglican clergy remained Loyalists and fled to England or Canada (SAMUEL PROVOOST of New York was a prominent exception), but the southern laity overwhelmingly adhered to the patriot cause. In the colonial period the Anglican church had been established by law in Virginia, Maryland, the Carolinas, and Georgia (and in New York City and three neighboring counties). Disestablishment came about as a matter of course after the formation of new state governments during the 1770's, except in Virginia, which delayed separation of CHURCH AND STATE until 1785.

The Anglican Communion in America differs from that in England chiefly in that its constitution gives far more power to the laity in matters of church government. References to English royalty are deleted from the Book of Common Prayer.

Episcopal-sponsored institutions of higher learning founded before the Civil War include (in addition to Columbia) Hobart (New York, est. 1822), Trinity (Connecticut, est. 1823), Kenyon (Ohio, est. 1824), and University of the South (Tennessee, est. 1857). In 1965 the church reported a membership of 3,329,000.

Protestantism is the name applied to the principles or religion of those who, during the Reformation (after 1529), 'protested' edicts banning continued reforms within the Christian church. Although the term has come to be used in many different senses, broadly speaking the name Protestant applies to all Christians who do not belong to the Roman Catholic Church or to the Eastern churches. It first became the official title of a church when the American branch of the Church of England adopted the name Protestant Episcopal Church (1789).

The four main types of Protestantism, today as in the early Reformation period, are Lutheran (Evangelical), Calvinist (Reformed), Episcopalian, and 'independent.' The fourth type, which has greatly proliferated since the 16th century, is most numerous in the U.S. because immigrants from European countries brought their own forms of communion. In general Protestants (and 'independents' in particular) are united in the concept that the individual Christian is responsible to God and not to the Church, that he has liberty in secular as well as religious matters, and is not bound by tradition and authority.

For discussions of Protestant denominations in the U.S., see *Adventists, Anabaptists, Baptists, Christian Science, Congregationalists, Disciples of Christ, Dunkards, Huguenots, Jehovah's Witnesses, Lutherans, Mennonites, Methodists, Moravians, Presbyterians, Protestant Episcopal Church, Quakers, Reformed Church, Separatists, Shakers, Swedenborgians, Unitarians, Universalists.* (MORMONS are evangelical, but they are not Protestants.)

Protestant tendencies are referred to under *Antinomian Controversy, Armin-*

ianism, Calvinism, Circuit Riders, Communal Societies, Covenant Theology, Deism, Fundamentalism, Great Awakening, Half-Way Covenant, Humanism, Modernism, Perfectionism, Puritanism, Revivals.

Providence Plantations were the original Rhode Island settlements. ROGER WILLIAMS established his colony at Seekonk (1636) on Narragansett Bay. He purchased the site from the Indians and renamed it Providence to memorialize 'God's providence to him in his distress.' Another Boston exile, WILLIAM CODDINGTON, with Williams's help, bought the island of Aquidneck from the Indians and established himself (1639) and a group including ANNE HUTCHINSON and her husband at Portsmouth. The group soon split, but in 1640, after Coddington had founded Newport, the two colonies were joined. SAMUEL GORTON established a fourth settlement at Warwick (1643). Through the influence of Williams these four Rhode Island communities obtained a charter from Parliament (1644), uniting them as 'The Incorporation of Providence Plantations in the Narragansett Bay in New England.' The term still remains a part of the official title of the state of Rhode Island.

Provincetown Players, see *Little Theater movement.*

Psychology in its modern sense is defined as the science that studies the mind in all of its aspects. Closely allied to biology, anthropology, chemistry, and physics, it retains its identity by using other sciences to explain human behavior. Until the principle of evolution had been applied by the laboratory experiments of the Leipzig physiologist Wilhelm Wundt in the 1870's, psychology was dominated by philosophical debate. The contributions made to it in the 1880's by the Austrian psychiatrist Sigmund Freud did not, in fact, become widely understood for another fifty years.

Scientific psychology thus originated in Europe during the late 19th century. It was introduced into the U.S. by WILLIAM JAMES, who set up the first laboratories in the country at Harvard (1875–80). Other pioneers in the field include HUGO MÜNSTERBERG (applied), G. STANLEY HALL (educational), EDWARD L. THORNDIKE (animal and genetic), JAMES M. BALDWIN (child and social), WILLIAM MC DOUGALL (physiological), JAMES M. CATTELL and LEWIS TERMAN (testing), ELTON MAYO (industrial), and ROBERT YERKES (psychobiology). JOHN B. WATSON introduced BEHAVIORISM and KARL LASHLEY advanced research in neuropsychology. Since 1927 the concept of OPERATIONALISM has been an important factor in behavioral psychology, which later was the special field of BURRHUS F. SKINNER.

See A. A. Roback, *History of American Psychology* (1952).

Public debt, U.S., is the debt incurred by the U.S. government through the sale of bonds. When the Constitution was ratified in 1786, the national obligation included foreign and domestic debts (ultimately paid), inherited from the government that had functioned under the Articles of Confederation. In 1816, as a result of the War of 1812, the public debt had increased from $45,000,000 to $127,000,000. By 1835 unprecedented prosperity had reduced it almost to a vanishing point.

The Civil War created a debt of $2,332,000,000, which after World War I climbed to $25,234,000,000. Though it was reduced a third by 1930, it mounted in the ensuing depression years, and after World War II reached the sum of $270 billion. In 1955 Congress placed the permanent debt ceiling at $285 billion, but since then the public debt has steadily soared. Rather than increase the limit, Congress has annually approved temporary extensions. The national debt in June 1965 totaled a record $329 billion.

Public domain, as it applies in the U.S. to public lands, pertains to land owned by the federal government, and is distinct from 'national domain,' a term implying political jurisdiction. When seven of the original states ceded their western lands to the federal government (1781–1802), public ownership extended westward to the Mississippi. By the LOUISIANA PURCHASE (1803), the U.S. acquired the vast region westward to the Rockies, an area that increased the national territory by 140 per cent. Later followed the purchase of Florida (1819), the acquisition of the Oregon region (1846), the Mexican cession (1848), the GADSDEN PURCHASE (1853), and the purchase of Alaska (1867). The continental boundaries were thus completed.

As soon as the federal government was formed, it set about disposing of its public lands by PUBLIC LAND SALES, and during the 1830's it sought to encourage settlements by a series of PRE-EMPTIVE ACTS, measures that preceded the important HOMESTEAD ACT (1862) and the MORRILL LAND GRANT ACT (1862). The seemingly limitless expanses of land led to abuses of natural resources that were tardily corrected by such legislation as the DESERT LAND ACT (1877), the FOREST RESERVE ACT (1891), the CAREY LAND ACT (1894), and other reclamation provisions urged by the CONSERVATION MOVEMENT. In the 20th century much of the public land was set aside as National Parks and National Forests. The creation of the Bureau of Land Management in 1946 marked the official closing of the old public domain.

See R. M. Robbins, *Our Landed Heritage* (1942), and E. L. Peffer, *The Closing of the Public Domain* (1951).

Public land sales began as soon as the federal government came into possession of a PUBLIC DOMAIN. The Land Act of 1796 provided that the land be sold at auction in relatively large parcels (640-acre tracts) at a minimum price of $2 an acre. Few buyers were attracted because the unit was too large and full payment was required within a year. The Land Act of 1800 (also known as the Harrison Land Act) was administered by William Henry Harrison. It authorized minimum purchases of 320 acres and a four-year credit, in an effort to discourage land speculators and attract settlers. The Act is significant in frontier history; it served as a model for similar legislation until passage of the Land Act of 1820, which abolished the credit system, reduced the minimum price to $1.25 an acre and the minimum purchase to 80 acres. Under its provisions some 300,000 square miles were sold, an area equivalent to three large states. Since no restrictions were placed on purchases, speculation ran riot. Although the PRE-EMPTIVE ACTS of the 1830's and 1840's were a step toward encouraging settlers, not until passage of the HOMESTEAD ACT (1862) was there a reasonably satisfactory means of selling public lands to homesteaders.

The U.S. has disposed of some 1,029,000,000 acres of the public domain: 418,000,000 acres in grants to states and railroad corporations, and the rest in cash sales.

Public lands, see *Public domain.*

Public utilities are corporations that perform services for the entire community. They include the facilities for transportation, communication, gas and electric power, water supply and related services. During the 20th century public utility corporate organizations took the form of HOLDING COMPANIES and thus gained MONOPOLY control. Many have been taken over by the municipal, state, and federal governments, especially where excessive rates, costs, or taxes impair the ability of privately owned utilities to earn a fair return on huge investments. All are subject to such regulatory agencies as the INTERSTATE COMMERCE COMMISSION and the POLICE POWER of the states.

Public Welfare, see *City planning, Education, Housing, Humane societies, Medicine, Philanthropy, Prison reform, Slums, Social settlements, Social work, Unemployment compensation.*

Public Works Administration (PWA), established under the NATIONAL INDUSTRIAL RECOVERY ACT (1933), was created as a 'pump-priming' method of increasing employment and business activity through the construction of roads, public buildings, and similar undertakings. Administered by Secretary of the Interior HAROLD L. ICKES during the period of the Great Depression (1933–39), PWA expended $4,250,000,000 on some 34,000 public projects.

Publishers and publishing, see *Book publishing, Journalism, Magazines, Newspapers.*

Pueblo Indians are the various agricultural tribes in the Southwest who live in stone or adobe terraced community houses. They inherited the culture and ritual of the BASKET MAKERS (*c.* 1500 B.C.), and the later CLIFF DWELLERS, and are skilled in silver and textile work and in polychrome pottery manufacture. They are without linguistic unity, and today number some 20,000. Best known among the Pueblo groups are the HOPI and ZUÑI. POPÉ was a famous Pueblo chief.

Puerto Rico, 105 miles long and 25 miles wide, is the easternmost island of the West Indies group known as the Greater Antilles. It was visited by Columbus in 1493, and Ponce de León made it a Spanish outpost in 1509. After its present capital, San Juan, had been established as an important port (1521), the island contributed to the Spanish economy by producing tropical crops, chiefly sugar.

Negro slaves were introduced after the native Indian tribes proved intractable, and they provided labor during the three centuries of relatively quiet plantation existence, until slavery was abolished in 1873. Early in 1898 Spain granted autonomy to Puerto Rico, which became a Territory (unorganized) of the U.S. after the Spanish-American War. Citizenship was conferred on Puerto Ricans in 1917.

In 1947 the islanders were permitted to choose their own governor. Since 1952 Puerto Rico has been unique in its status as a free commonwealth associated with the U.S., and at the same time fully self-governed at home. (What this association means in terms of American constitutional law has yet to be determined.) After World War II pressing problems of overpopulation and unemployment led to heavy emigration to the continental U.S., and the relocation of more than 500,000 Puerto Ricans in New York City, where they have established communities, chiefly in Harlem. Today Puerto Rico has a population of more than 2,350,000. It derives its largest income from manufacturing, with agriculture and the tourist industry ranking high.

Pujo Committee (1912) was set up by Congress, to investigate the 'money trusts.' Representative Arsène Pujo was chairman. The committee reported that by consolidation, particularly in the hands of such New York financiers as J. P. Morgan (who testified), banks and trust companies were gaining control of insurance companies, railroads, utilities, and industrial corporations. The revelation led the incoming Wilson Administration to undertake a program of currency and banking reform, especially through the FEDERAL RESERVE SYSTEM and the CLAYTON ACT.

PULASKI, CASIMIR (1748–79), while commanding Polish patriot forces, was driven into exile. He went to Paris, where Benjamin Franklin wrote a letter of introduction for him to Washington. Soon after his arrival in Boston (1777) on Washington's recommendation Congress commissioned him a brigadier general of cavalry in the Continental army. He served with distinction at Brandywine, Germantown, and Valley Forge. In 1779 he took part in the unsuccessful assault on Savannah, where he was fatally wounded. The city erected a monument to him in 1855.

PULITZER, JOSEPH (1847–1911), Hungarian-born journalist, after coming to the U.S. (1864), became a reporter for the St. Louis *Westliche Post* (1868), and later its managing editor and part owner. Having successfully launched the St. Louis *Post-Dispatch* (1878), he purchased the New York *World* (1883), which soon gained wide circulation through illustration, colored comics, feature articles, and flamboyant exploitation of events. The lurid sensationalism resulting from the contest between Pulitzer's *World* and Hearst's *Journal* for news coverage during the Spanish-American War gave rise to the term YELLOW JOURNALISM. The *World* later abandoned sensationalism and won wide respect for its independent views and its fearless attacks on political corruption. In 1903 Pulitzer declared his intention of endowing the Columbia School of Journalism, and his bequest to Columbia established the PULITZER PRIZES.

Pulitzer Prizes in journalism, letters, and music were endowed by JOSEPH PULITZER, and are annually awarded by the trustees of Columbia University on recommendation of an Advisory Board of the School of Journalism. The selections, begun in 1918, are for distinction in the following categories: Meritorious Public Service (of a U.S. newspaper), a gold medal; Local Reporting (under pressure of a deadline), $1000; National

Reporting (since 1943), $1000; International Reporting (since 1943), $1000; Correspondence (Washington or foreign), $500 (since 1930, but discontinued in 1948); Editorial Writing, $1000; Cartoon (since 1923), $1000; News Photography (since 1943), $1000; Fiction, $500; Drama (preferably dealing with American life), $500; History, $500; Biography, $500; Poetry, $500; and Music (since 1944), $500.

PULLMAN, GEORGE MORTIMER (1831–97), Chicago industrialist born in western New York, was trained as a cabinetmaker. In 1859 he opened a shop in Chicago, where he began converting railroad coaches into sleeping cars, the first to be manufactured. In 1867 he founded the Pullman Palace Car Company. By the time he had established the industrial town of Pullman (1880), he had gained great wealth from his invention. The paralyzing PULLMAN STRIKE took place in his company-owned community.

Pullman Strike (1894), one of the most far-reaching in its consequences in U.S. history, was directed against the Pullman Palace Car Company in the model company-owned town of Pullman, Illinois. When GEORGE M. PULLMAN arbitrarily refused to discuss grievances with representatives of his employees, who were protesting wage cuts, a situation arose which eventually involved much larger issues. The cause of the workers was taken up by the powerful American Railway Union under the leadership of EUGENE V. DEBS. The union voted a boycott against all Pullman cars, and transportation throughout the North was paralyzed. President Cleveland's sympathies were with the company, and the Federal circuit court at Chicago served on the officers of the union a 'blanket injunction' against obstructing the railroads and the U.S. mails. When hooligans ditched a mail train, Cleveland responded by ordering out a regiment of the regular army.

This gratuitous action roused the ire of Governor JOHN PETER ALTGELD, who, ready and able to restore order with state militia, saw that the real purpose of the Federal interference was to break the strike, not to preserve order. His demands for withdrawal were ignored. Debs defied the injunction and went to jail, the Supreme Court upheld the government, and the strike was broken.

The significance of the affair lay in its revelation of the degree to which business interests could be protected at the expense of labor. Workers saw that the Sherman Antitrust Act was being enforced not against trusts but against labor unions. Big business found a convenient weapon against strikes in the injunction, the misuse of which was not finally prevented until 1932, by the Norris-La Guardia Anti-Injunction Act.

PUMPELLY, RAPHAEL (1837–1923), born in New York, made official geographical surveys (1861–65) in Japan and China, and became the first professor of mining at Harvard (1866–73). As state geologist of Michigan and Missouri (1871–73), he explored the mineral resources of those states. His transcontinental survey (1881–84) inaugurated the development of the iron-ore industry in Michigan and western Ontario. He later directed an expedition to study physical geography and archaeology in Central Asia (1903–4). Pumpelly was one of the few trained experts who joined in the exploitation of the West; his fortunate investments brought him wealth. His *Reminiscences* (2 vols., 1918) furnish significant comments on the mineral reserves of the U.S.

PURCHAS, SAMUEL (*c.* 1575–1626), English clergyman and collector, compiled various gatherings of travel literature and carried on the work of RICHARD HAKLUYT, though without Hakluyt's scholarly acumen. The final revision of *Purchas his Pilgrimage* (1613) was *Hakluytus Posthumus* (4 vols., 1625), the second division of which is devoted to travels in the New World, especially the attempts to find the NORTHWEST PASSAGE and to explore the Caribbean. Its importance stems from the fact that scholars trust it as a record of manuscripts since lost.

Pure Food and Drug Act (1906) followed investigations by Dr. HARVEY W. WILEY and others, which revealed an almost universal use of preservatives and dyes in canned and prepared foods. President Roosevelt urged congressional action, but business lobbies fought it determinedly, declaring that such action would be 'socialistic' interference. But when UPTON SINCLAIR described the nauseous conditions of the Chicago stockyards in *The Jungle* (1906), public demand led Congress to enact a meat inspection law. It also undertook to protect the public against dangerous drugs and PATENT MEDICINES. The Food, Drug, and Cosmetic Act of 1938 enlarged and strengthened the law by forbidding various kinds of deception and requiring a statement of ingredients on the label.

Puritanism began as an effort within the Anglican Church during the early reign of Elizabeth I to 'purify' traditional usages. The dispute, which had begun merely over unscriptural images and vestments, by the 1570's erupted into a vigorous and often rancorous argument against the authority of the bishops to determine matters of church government. Both Elizabeth I and her successor, James I, believed that uniformity was essential to the strength of the state, and they supported an episcopacy in which the monarch, by appointing bishops, exercised authority over the Church as well. The issue therefore was political, and in 1604, the year after James came to the English throne, a political party that had sought relatively minor concessions gained strength when James summarily rejected their pleas.

The extremists, or SEPARATISTS, who wished an independent church autonomy, fled to Holland (1609) and eleven years later were the core of the group of PILGRIMS who came to America and inaugurated the Congregational system of church government. The moderates hoped for reforms, but the gulf became unbridgeable when William Laud, first as Bishop of London (1628), then as Archbishop of Canterbury (1633), not only made no concessions but decreed church rules that virtually closed appointments to Puritans in both church and university positions. By 1630 the great Puritan migration to Massachusetts Bay had begun.

The Puritans of the Bay Colony were not Separatists, but moderate nonconformists, who regarded the established Church of England as the 'true' church. But their Congregationalist principles gave autonomy to the churches and therefore were especially adaptable to frontier conditions. In the early years, citizenship, regardless of social position, depended upon church membership, a franchise requirement that the New England settlers regarded as basic. Since the Church never officially controlled the State, Massachusetts was not a THEOCRACY, but rather a 'Bible Commonwealth' in which the magistrates sought counsel of the ministers.

The death of such first-generation 'Visible Saints' as JOHN COTTON, THOMAS HOOKER, and THOMAS SHEPARD weakened the authoritarian hold of Puritanism because church membership began to decline. To check that trend in 1662 the churches adopted the HALF-WAY COVENANT, which extended partial membership without requiring a confession of religious experience. The founding in Boston of the Brattle Street Church (1699), which extended full membership to all who wished to join, was the beginning of a liberal Congregational movement that spelled the doom of Puritanism as the term had been used until then, and in effect ushered out the New England Way.

There were stultifying elements in Puritanism; Puritans banned the theater, religious music, sensuous poetry, and the observance of Christmas (then associated with pagan revelry). One factor that contributed to the decline of the Puritan oligarchy was the support it gave to the Salem WITCHCRAFT DELUSION of 1692, when the clergy disastrously lost their bout with rationalism. On the other hand, the MASSACHUSETTS GENERAL LAWES AND LIBERTYES (1648) was a carefully planned legislative action that led the world in many forms of freedom and protection for the individual. Puritan divorce laws were more liberal than those in England. By nourishing the classics New Englanders preserved far more of the humanist tradition than did any other colonists prior to 1700. Although the term *puritan* became synonymous with *bigot* in the 19th and early 20th centuries, Puritans were in fact a closely knit group striving to transmit the inheritance of great civilizations, and as a catalytic force they inspired moral and intellectual traits that have persisted distinctively in American culture to the present day.

See H. W. Schneider, *The Puritan*

Mind (1930); Perry Miller, *The New England Mind* (1939); and T. J. Wertenbaker, *The Puritan Oligarchy: The Founding of American Civilization* (1947).

Purple Heart, Order of the, is the military award for meritorious action established during the Revolution (1782) by George Washington. It was revived in 1932 as a mark of distinction for servicemen wounded in action. It is a heart-shaped medal, worn on a purple ribbon, with the bust of Washington on its enameled center.

PUTNAM, Israel (1718–90), Connecticut militiaman, first saw action as a soldier in the French and Indian War (1755–63), in which he became conspicuous for his skill as an Indian fighter. Tradition has it that he was so stirred by the patriot cause that when he learned of the fighting at Lexington he stopped plowing, unhitched the horse, and rode post haste to Boston. He did take command of troops in the battle of Bunker Hill (1775), and, as a major general, commanded the fortifications of New York City until the arrival of Washington in April 1776. He later fought in various engagements until a paralytic stroke (1779) disabled him. Although Putnam had no outstanding tactical ability and tended to be dilatory in carrying out orders, his bluff heartiness and dauntless bravery made him the idol of his troops and one of the popular heroes of American history.

PYNCHON, William (*c.* 1590–1662), helped organize the Massachusetts Bay Company, migrated to America in 1630, founded Roxbury, and served as treasurer of the colony (1632–34). In 1636 he settled Springfield. He made a considerable fortune as fur trader, and returned to England in 1652. His son, John Pynchon (1626–1703), extended trading posts up the Connecticut valley and became the most considerable merchant of inland New England of his day.

Q

Quakers, see *Friends, Society of.*

Quartering Act (1774) was a punitive measure, passed by Parliament after the BOSTON TEA PARTY, requiring that quarters be provided for British troops in the colonies wherever order needed to be restored. Patriot organizations at that time were doing whatever they could to thwart British authority, and they used this Act to increase the sentiment for revolt.

QUAY, MATTHEW STANLEY (1833–1904), a graduate of Jefferson College (1850), practiced law, entered politics, and during the 1880's, after the demise of the PHILADELPHIA GAS RING, he became boss of the powerful Republican party machine in Pennsylvania. He served in the U.S. Senate (1887–99), until serious charges of venality prevented his reelection. He was able to block the election of a successor, and the governor appointed him Senator *ad interim,* but the Senate refused to seat him until 1901, when he was re-elected.

Quebec Act (1774), passed by Parliament, was intended to correct certain flaws in the PROCLAMATION OF 1763. It placed the country north of the Ohio river under the jurisdiction of the Province of Quebec, and re-established French civil law to assure Roman Catholics of religious freedom. But it thwarted the plans of the American land companies, and thus colonial propagandists effectively used the Act to widen the breach between the mother country and the colonies by claiming that the British government intended to establish the doctrine of royal absolutism and to encourage the spread of Roman Catholicism. The concessions did in fact help keep Canada loyal to England during the Revolution.

Quebec, Assault on, see *Canada, Invasion of.*

Quebec, Capture of, see *Wolfe, James.*

Quebec Conference (August 1943) was a meeting held at Quebec, Canada, between President F. D. Roosevelt and Prime Minister Churchill, with their top ranking advisers. They elaborated details for the invasion of Europe in 1944, and established a high command for the war in Southeast Asia.

At a second Quebec Conference (August 1944) they outlined strategic plans for final victory over Germany and Japan.

Queen Anne's War (1702–13) was the American phase of the War of the Spanish Succession (1701–14), which pitted Great Britain against France and Spain. In New England, the conflict, like that of KING WILLIAM'S WAR (1689–97), consisted largely of indecisive frontier raids. In the South, Carolinians seized Spanish St. Augustine, and in the West Indies, privateers were active, but otherwise few military operations were carried out. An armistice in 1712 preceded the TREATY OF UTRECHT (1713), which ended the war.

Queen's College, see *Rutgers University.*

Queenston Heights, Battle of (October 1812), was an ignominious American defeat just north of Niagara Falls during the War of 1812. Major General STEPHEN VAN RENSSELAER vainly urged the main force of his New York militia to cross the Niagara river into Canada to support a small detachment of regulars who had made a successful attack on Queenston Heights. The New Yorkers refused to budge, on the ground that they had turned out to defend their homes, not to invade Canada. They then calmly watched their comrades on the other bank shot down and forced to surrender.

QUEZON, MANUEL LUIS (1878–1944), Filipino statesman, served with Aguinaldo during the Philippine revolution of 1898, was admitted to the bar (1903), and became a member of the Philippine assembly (1907–8). A resident commissioner to the U.S. during the trying years when the Philippines were preparing for self-government (1909–16), he was long president of the Philippine Senate (1916–35), and was the Commonwealth's first president (1935–44). Quezon was a strong leader of his people.

QUIDOR, JOHN (1801–81), New York artist, painted with an originality generally unpleasing to his contemporaries. (He had begun making his living by painting panels for fire engines.) His vitality, eccentric designs, and comic exaggeration, depending on line rather than color, are represented by *Money Diggers* and *Wolfert's Will* (both in the Brooklyn Museum). The latter was inspired by one of Washington Irving's tales. His techniques (though not his aims) were modeled on Daumier.

QUIMBY, PHINEAS PARKHURST, see *Christian Science.*

QUINCY, JOSIAH (1744–75), born in Boston, within a decade after his graduation from Harvard (1763) had established himself as a brilliant lawyer, and even though he was an ardent patriot, he defended (with John Adams) the British soldiers involved in the BOSTON MASSACRE. Quincy was sent to England in 1774 as an agent to plead the colonial cause, but he met with no success. He died on the return voyage.

His son, JOSIAH QUINCY (1772–1864), likewise graduated from Harvard (1790), and became the Federalist minority leader in the U.S. House of Representatives (1805–13), from which he resigned as a protest against the War of 1812. He associated himself with state politics and served as mayor of Boston (1823–27). While president of Harvard (1829–45), he defended its liberal traditions in the face of strong conservative opposition, and established the law school and observatory.

QUITMAN, JOHN ANTHONY (1798–1858), Mississippi lawyer, as a major general in the Mexican War served as governor of Mexico City during its occupation by the Americans (1847–48). A leading 'southern rightist,' he was governor of his state (1850–51), but resigned when the federal government indicted him for aiding a freebooting expedition to Cuba. Later in the House of Representatives (1855–58), he continued to champion slavery.

Quitrents were feudal dues that the lord of the manor collected from his tenants. In the American colonies they were nominal levies, generally established by colonial charters, collected in the royal colonies by the crown and in the proprietary colonies by the proprietor. The states abolished them after the Revolution on the ground that they were not levied as taxes but as a source of private income.

Quivira, see *Coronado.*

Quota Act (1921), an emergency law to limit immigration to the U.S., sought to cut off an anticipated 'horde' of postwar immigrants and particularly to discourage immigration from southern and eastern Europe. Since its secondary purpose failed, it was replaced by the JOHNSON-REED ACT (1924).

R

RABI, Isidor Isaac (1898–), Austrian-born professor of physics at Columbia (after 1937), did research in the field of nuclear physics on magnetism, quantum mechanics, and molecular beams. His refinement of experimental techniques enabled him to apply the resonance method to the measurement of the magnetic properties of atomic nuclei. In 1944 he was awarded the Nobel Prize in physics for this work, which established 'radio relations with the most subtle particles of matter, with the world of the electron and of the atomic nucleus.'

RACHMANINOFF, Sergei [Wassilievitch] (1873–1943), Russian pianist and conductor, made his American debut in 1909. Highly regarded as a musical interpreter, he was twice offered (and twice refused) the permanent conductorship of the Boston Symphony Orchestra. In later years he resided in the U.S., and though known for his symphonies, piano pieces, and songs, he is best remembered as one of the greatest pianists of his age.

Racing as a spectator sport in America originally meant horse racing, a diversion that was informally organized by the well-to-do, especially in New York and Virginia, in colonial times. Racing and trotting horses sired by JUSTIN MORGAN and HAMBLETONIAN during the 19th century brought harness racing into great popularity in the 1870's. Saratoga Springs, New York, was a popular racing resort before the Civil War. After Churchill Downs opened at Louisville, Kentucky (1875), racing tracks were developed in great numbers throughout the country, and because they often were controlled by unscrupulous gamblers, they were under constant attack by reform groups.

States began setting up racing commissions, and in 1893 horse owners and trainers founded a national Jockey Club to govern the sport. The most important annual racing events in the U.S. are the Kentucky Derby at Churchill Downs; the Preakness at the Pimlico track outside Baltimore, Maryland; and the Belmont at Belmont Park, New York. The most famous stallion in the history of thoroughbred racing was Man o' War. As a two-year-old in 1919 he finished first in 9 out of 10 races; in 1920 he won all his 11 races.

Other forms of racing that have gained popularity in the U.S. include AUTOMOBILE RACING (the most popular), bicycle, dog, and airplane racing, BOAT RACING, and TRACK AND FIELD events.

C. B. Parmer, *For Gold and Glory* (1939) is a history of thoroughbred racing in America. Dwight Akers, *Drivers Up* (2nd ed., 1947) is the story of American harness racing.

Racketeering, in the sense of extortion for the protection of such illegal, organized activities as prostitution, gambling, and the sale of narcotics, has been a growing 20th-century phenomenon in the U.S. (The word *racket* has long been in use as a term for swindles overlooked by lax law-enforcement agencies.) Racketeering became especially profitable during the PROHIBITION ERA of the 1920's, and spread to such rackets as the extortion of money from a business or industry to 'protect' it from sabotage or burglaries. The KEFAUVER INVESTIGATION (1950–51) exposed nation-wide crime syndicates, such as the MAFIA, that were reaping huge profits. Law-enforcement drives against racketeering continue, with limited success.

Radcliffe College for women, in Cambridge, Massachusetts, was opened (1879) by ELIZABETH AGASSIZ, who served as president (1879–1903) with a faculty of Harvard professors. In 1894 it was rechartered and named for the first woman donor to Harvard, Ann Radcliffe, Lady Mowlson (d. 1661). Its present standards were established under the presidency (1903–23) of LE BARON BRIGGS. Harvard's faculty is now shared by Radcliffe, with classes of the two institutions held jointly. In 1965, with an endowment of $18,000,000, it enrolled 1170 students.

Radical Republicans were those abolitionist reformers, and often political opportunists, who made common cause of the right of Congress, not the President, to determine the rules by which the secessionist states might be readmitted to the Union. They were resolved to constitute those state governments in such a way that neither politically nor economically would the representatives from the South in Congress be able to shape legislation. Many were committed to the ideal of racial equality which they wrote in the Thirteenth, Fourteenth, and Fifteenth Amendments.

Lincoln's proclamation (December 1863) that he would recognize state governments of the South as soon as one-tenth of the voters in a state took an oath to support the Constitution was denounced as intolerably lenient, and the radicals won congressional approval of the WADE-DAVIS BILL (1864), that if enacted into law would have made readmission contingent upon an oath, by a majority of state voters, of both past and present loyalty to the Union. Lincoln killed the bill by a pocket veto, and at the time of his death, shortly after war's end, the executive and legislative branches were at an impasse. In the House, which the radicals controlled, the radical Republicans were led by HENRY WINTER DAVIS, THADDEUS STEVENS, and GEORGE BOUTWELL; in the Senate, by CHARLES SUMNER and BENJAMIN WADE. For a decade they proved themselves to be among the shrewdest parliamentarians in American history. Had Lincoln lived, as a political insider he would certainly have been able to maneuver with greater skill than did his successor, Andrew Johnson, a political outsider, who futilely sought to gain support for Lincoln's program.

The radicals dominated the JOINT COMMITTEE OF FIFTEEN (1865–67), which wrote the Fourteenth Amendment with its equal rights clause. In 1867 they drafted the RECONSTRUCTION ACTS designed to punish the South. Whereas in Lincoln's lifetime the radicals had been merely aggressive, by 1867 they had become strong enough to thwart Johnson whenever they wished to take issue with him, except when they failed (by one vote) to impeach him. They remained in power through the Grant Administrations (until 1877). Certain historians, such as CHARLES BEARD, argue that their motives were economic as well as political and humanitarian, dictated in part by a desire to control a government that would favor the business and financial interests of the Northeast.

Radio was theoretically foreseen in 1865 by the Scottish physicist James Clerk Maxwell. His electromagnetic equations led to experiments by the German physicist Heinrich Hertz, who, by using an electrical discharge, produced the 'hertzian,' or radio, waves (1886). His work was in turn advanced before 1900 by the research of the Italian physicist Guglielmo Marconi, and by the electrical engineer John Fleming, who perceived that a specially constructed light bulb ('diode') could serve to detect radio signals. The related invention in 1906 of the three-electrode vacuum tube by LEE DE FOREST made radio practicable by its ability to amplify weak signals.

Radio remained in its experimental stage until improvements, especially those by E. F. W. ALEXANDERSON, opened the way for a primitive form of broadcasting in 1920. Soon thereafter notable advances made possible the growth of broadcasting chains and the development of international transmission. Congress enacted the first basic statute controlling radio in 1927, and supplemented it in 1934 by setting up the FEDERAL COMMUNICATIONS COMMISSION. The invention in 1939 of a new form of radio transmission and reception, frequency modulation (FM), by E. H. ARMSTRONG, eliminated static and improved fidelity. Although federally controlled, almost all U.S. networks are privately owned and operated, and they are chiefly financed by advertisers. Since 1950 TELEVISION has greatly extended radio communication.

RADISSON, PIERRE ESPRIT (1636–1710), French explorer and 'king of the fur traders,' with his brother-in-law, Médard Chouart, Sieur des Groseilliers (1618–90), discovered the possibility of fur trade in the Lake Superior region (1659). Because they traded without a license (that is, failed to share their profits with the French government), their immense cargo of furs was confiscated, and they transferred their allegiance to the English. Radisson established Fort Nelson in northern Manitoba, and he helped persuade the English to found the HUDSON'S BAY COMPANY (1670). Later he briefly returned to the French and plundered the English, whom he soon rejoined, and by whom he was finally pensioned. The exploits of Radisson and Groseilliers still remain among the most tangled problems in the history of early explorations in North America.

RAFINESQUE, CONSTANTINE SAMUEL (1783–1840), born in Turkey of French-German parentage, came to Philadelphia in 1802 and began making trips to collect botanical specimens. He settled for a time in Kentucky (1818), where he taught botany at Transylvania. He relinquished his post in 1826 to resume his travels, and wrote extensively, if not always accurately, on a variety of subjects. His *Ichthyologia Ohiensis* (1820) and *New Flora and Botany of North America* (1836) represent his best achievements. Eccentric and disorganized, he nevertheless had a keen instinct for classification, and he contributed to the pioneer natural science studies of America.

Ragtime, popular music which flourished from 1896 to 1917, was introduced to the public by itinerant pianists, notably SCOTT JOPLIN, from the Midwest (where it originated) and the South. It was first effectively performed on the midways of various World's Fairs, at Chicago, St. Louis, Buffalo, and elsewhere. Unlike the SPIRITUALS and the BLUES, it is unfailingly cheerful in mood. It is limited to the diatonic scale in the tradition of European composition. Its tunes developed from the pattern of the march, syncopated always in the right hand, with a steady 2/4 rhythm in the left. Such metrical splitting of beat is characteristic of African music, and this blend of Negro rhythm and European form created a unique style. By 1900 TIN PAN ALLEY had taken over, and ragtime was a national craze. Its popularity waned when more sophisticated styles of JAZZ were developed.

Railroad Labor Act of 1926, see *Watson-Parker Act.*

Railroad Labor Act of 1934, see *Crosser-Dill Act.*

Railroad Mediation Acts began with passage of the Act of 1880, which provided for voluntary arbitration. The Erdman Act (1898) offered further mediatory assistance, and between 1906 and 1913, 61 railroad labor controversies were settled (26 by mediation). The NEWLANDS ACT (1913) created a Board of Mediation and Conciliation, which in the next four years settled 58 out of 71 disputes brought before it. The ADAMSON ACT (1916) established an eight-hour day for railroad employees. The ESCH-CUMMINS ACT (1920) provided for a Railroad Labor Board. It was followed by the WATSON-PARKER ACT (1926), which compelled unions to accept the decisions of a newly created Board of Mediation. Under the CROSSER-DILL ACT (1934), which was the last of the important railroad mediation laws, the right of employees to organize and bargain collectively was upheld.

Railroad Strikes of 1877, resulting from the general economic depression after the PANIC OF 1873, were the first major strikes in U.S. history. They followed the last of a series of wage cuts on the Baltimore and Ohio Railroad. At the request of the governor of West Virginia, President Hayes dispatched Federal troops. The strikes spread to Baltimore, Philadelphia, Pittsburgh, and other centers. Although they were finally broken, they left a heritage of resentment against the government for its use of troops, and stimulated the first general congressional investigation of labor problems.

Railroad Transportation Act, see *Esch-Cummins Act* (1920).

Railroads in the U.S. had their start with the chartering (1827) of the BALTIMORE AND OHIO, first operated in 1830 when PETER COOPER, with his *Tom Thumb,* demonstrated the practicability of locomotive steam power. Rail construction became general after 1835, and railroads soon linked neighboring cities. When Philadelphia and Charleston were joined by rail in 1840, the 60-hour 680-mile trip, made with seven junction changes, was hailed as a triumph of speed and convenience.

During the 1850's train movements were regulated for the first time by telegraph, coal-burning locomotives replaced woodburners, and GEORGE PULLMAN inaugurated sleeping-car service. Some 30,000 miles of rails had been laid by 1860, mostly in the North. Railroads were immensely important during the Civil War for moving troops, munitions, and supplies.

The completion of a transcontinental rail system by the linking of the CENTRAL PACIFIC and the UNION PACIFIC (1869) was an event of national importance. Soon thereafter railroad empires were created by such builders as CORNELIUS VANDERBILT, COLLIS HUNTINGTON, LELAND STANFORD, J. J. HILL, and E. H. HARRIMAN.

The assistance to private enterprise by Federal and state aid in the form of loans, tax exemption, liberal charters, monopolies, and land grants was a tremendous spur to rail construction. It also was the cause of stockjobbing, chicanery, the cynical buying of legislatures, and such episodes as the CRÉDIT MOBILIER scandal. Nevertheless, by 1900, 193,000 miles of tracks joined the two oceans by way of five transcontinental routes, and a network of trunk lines linked the great cities. Many abuses had been corrected by the Interstate Commerce Commission (1887), and the passage of a series of RAILROAD MEDIATION ACTS (1880–1934) steadily improved working conditions.

During the 1930's, the railroads adopted diesel motors, streamlined cars, and improvements in safety and comfort to compete for traffic with automobiles, trucks, buses, and airplanes. But the period of rail monopoly had ended. Between 1940 and 1960 total railroad mileage declined by 17,000, and those railroads that did not abandon their lines were forced to merge, to depend upon freight rather than passengers for profit, and to appeal to the federal and state governments for subsidy.

T. W. Van Metre, *Transportation in the U.S.* (2nd ed., 1950), is a general survey, with the greatest space devoted to railroads.

RAIN-IN-THE-FACE (d. 1905) was one of the Teton Sioux commanders who, with Sitting Bull and others, annihilated the forces under George A. Custer at Little Bighorn in 1876.

RALEIGH, SIR WALTER (*c.* 1552–1618), English courtier, navigator, and historian, as a favorite of Queen Elizabeth was granted valuable estates and lucrative wine monopolies. He conceived and organized the colonizing expeditions to ROANOKE ISLAND in Virginia (1585–91), which ended tragically. He is popularly (and erroneously) thought to have introduced potatoes and tobacco to England. Although he founded Virginia, and sought El Dorado up the Orinoco in South America, he never realized his dream of colonization. But his attempts smoothed the way for others who followed shortly.

Rambouillet Decree, see *Macon's Bill No. 2.*

RAMSAY, DAVID (1749–1815), after graduation from the College of New Jersey (Princeton, 1765), studied medicine in Philadelphia under Benjamin Rush and after 1773 practiced in Charleston, South Carolina, where he also became active in politics. Although his *History of the American Revolution* (2 vols., 1789–91) was heavily plagiarized, it is an important contemporary account because his knowledge of medicine and the arts enabled him to enrich it with details on American literature, music, and education, as well as to present an expert view of battlefield gains in surgery. In that and in his *History of South Carolina* (2 vols., 1809) he writes as one who had served as a conservative South Carolina legislator, expressing Federalist interpretations hostile to debtor farmers and paper money.

RANDOLPH, ASA PHILIP (1889–), Negro labor leader, in 1925 organized the Brotherhood of Sleeping Car Porters, whose economic welfare he steadily advanced. His White House conference with President F. D. Roosevelt in 1941 and the threat of a march on Washington led to the creation of the FAIR EMPLOYMENT PRACTICES COMMITTEE, the forerunner of laws in many states barring race restrictions in employment. In 1948 his intervention led President Truman to issue an Executive Order ending segregation in military establishments. In 1957 he became a vice president of A.F. of L.–C.I.O.

RANDOLPH, EDMUND (1753–1813), nephew of PEYTON RANDOLPH, was born near Williamsburg, Virginia, attended William and Mary, and studied law under his father, John Randolph (1727–84), a Loyalist, who went to England on the outbreak of the Revolution. Edmund served briefly as aide-de-camp to Washington, went as a delegate to the Continental Congress (1779–82), and while governor of Virginia (1786–88) was a prominent delegate to the Federal Constitutional Convention (1787), to which he submitted the RANDOLPH PLAN of congressional representation. Though vacillating by nature, he was the most popular Virginian next to Patrick Henry, and at the ratifying convention (1788) his recommendation for adoption carried great weight. He entered Washington's cabinet as the first Attorney General (1789–93), and succeeded Jefferson as Secretary of State (1794–95). He was the only cabinet member to oppose JAY'S TREATY with England (1794), and he resigned when accused (falsely) of asking for money from France to influence the Administration against Great Britain. He retired to the practice of law, and in 1807 was chief counsel for Aaron Burr in Burr's trial for treason.

RANDOLPH, EDWARD (*c.* 1632–1703), British commercial agent, was sent in 1676 by the Lords of Trade to Boston to investigate the colony's conformity with established laws. His denunciatory reports, though biased by his disapproval of Puritans in general, were based on fact, and they pointed the way to the annulment of the Massachusetts charter in 1684. Meanwhile he was appointed collector of customs for New England, a task made especially galling by the local magistrates, who repeatedly acquitted the illegal traders he arrested. During the Andros regime, after the charter was annulled, he served as secretary for the DOMINION OF NEW ENGLAND (1686–89). When the Dominion collapsed he was imprisoned along with other Dominion officials before being returned to England. In 1691 he returned as surveyor general of customs for North America, a post in which his unbending zeal continued to exacerbate old irritations. The colonists simply refused to enforce the laws of trade.

RANDOLPH, JOHN (1773–1833), Virginia statesman known as John Randolph of Roanoke, after brief periods of study at the College of New Jersey (Princeton) and at Columbia, abandoned the study of law to enter the House of Representatives where, except in 1814 and 1818 (and two years in the Senate, 1825–27), he served continuously for nearly 30 years (1799–1829). Brilliant, wealthy, and with a distinguished family background, Randolph grossly misused his considerable talents by his arrogant and malicious attacks on friend and foe alike. He broke with Jefferson over the Embargo Act and the acquisition of Florida; he opposed Madison, whom he despised, on major issues; he supported Monroe until Monroe entered Madison's cabinet, then turned on him.

Randolph stubbornly fought all nationalistic measures such as the Bank of the U.S. and the tariff, and vigorously opposed the Missouri Compromise. His intemperate abuse of Henry Clay and John Quincy Adams led to a bloodless duel with Clay (1826). Jackson sent Randolph as minister to Russia (1830), a post he immediately resigned upon arrival, to return as an ally of those who opposed Jackson's protective tariff. In his later years Randolph's eccentricities verged on mental illness. Randolph-Macon College was named for him and the North Carolina statesman Nathaniel Macon (1758–1837).

RANDOLPH, PEYTON (*c.* 1721–75), born in Williamsburg, Virginia, after attending William and Mary, studied law in London. On his return he was appointed the king's attorney for Virginia (1744–66), and long served in the House of Burgesses (1748–49, 1752–75). Chosen the first president of the First Continental Congress (1774), he stood for moderation (liberty, not independence) along with his friend Washington and such other representatives as JOHN DICKINSON of Pennsylvania and JOHN RUTLEDGE of South Carolina.

Randolph Plan, or Virginia Plan, was presented to the Federal Constitutional Convention (1787) by Governor EDMUND RANDOLPH on behalf of the Virginia delegation. It provided for a lower house to be elected by the people (and based on free population or property ownership), and an upper house elected by the lower. This legislative body was to choose the executive and the judiciary. The plan was opposed by the smaller states, which submitted the PATERSON PLAN, demanding equal representation in the legislature. Both plans were rejected in favor of the CONNECTICUT COMPROMISE.

Rappists, see *Harmony Society.*

RASLE, SÉBASTIAN, see *Abnaki.*

Rasmussen* v. *U.S., see *Insular Cases.*

Rathbun* v. *U.S., see *Humphrey's Executor* v. *U.S.*

Rationalism, a philosophical system derived from the doctrine of logic set forth by the German mathematician Gottfried Leibniz (1646–1716), holds that human reason is the source of knowledge, and it thus rejects all doctrines which justify knowledge by faith. See DETERMINISM, with which it is most closely allied.

RAUSCHENBUSCH, WALTER (1861–1918), as professor of church history at Rochester Theological Seminary (after 1902) was an influential Baptist leader in the CHRISTIAN SOCIALISM movement, which sought to make Christianity an instrument for social reform. An entire generation of ministers enthusiastically adopted his theology of the 'social gospel' as a way to reconstruct the social order. He set forth his views in *Christianity and the Social Crisis* (1907), and *Christianizing the Social Order* (1912).

RAYBURN, SAM [SAMUEL TALIAFERRO] (1882–1961), born in Tennessee, practiced law at Bonham, Texas, and as a Democrat in 1913 entered the U.S. House of Representatives, where he served continuously until his death. Both as a Representative and as Speaker of the House (1940–46, 1949–61) he broke the records for length of tenure in Congress. During the seventeen years that he occupied the Speaker's chair, 'Mr. Sam' displayed great skill as a parliamentary tactician. Although conservative by nature, he supported progressive social and economic legislation and sponsored some of the most famous of the early New Deal regulatory laws.

RAYMOND, HENRY JARVIS (1820–69), editor and politician, was born in Lima, New York, and graduated from the University of Vermont (1840). After serving an apprenticeship on Greeley's New York *Tribune* (1841–43), he became a staff member on James Watson Webb's *Courier and Enquirer,* an organ of the Whig party. He made his influence felt in state politics during the 1840's, and aligned himself with the Free-Soilers. His break with Webb led him to found *The New York Times* (1851), which helped launch the Republican party (1854). He later served briefly in Congress (1865–67). As *Times* editor, he directed his correspondent FREDERICK LAW OLMSTED to undertake extensive journeys through the South during the 1850's, which resulted in articles and books that became the best firsthand accounts of antebellum slavery. Raymond's journalism was distinguished for accuracy and fairness.

Reapportionment, see *Baker* v. *Carr* (state legislature reapportionment, 1962), and *Wesberry* v. *Sanders* (congressional reapportionment, 1964).

Rebates were refunds granted by railroads to favored shippers during the rate wars after the Civil War. Often the result of secret agreements, they were a discriminatory practice bitterly resented by those who paid the published rate. They were outlawed by the ELKINS ACT (1903).

Recall is a procedure whereby an elected state or municipal official may be removed from his position before his term of office has expired. This is usually done by a public vote, taken after a petition bearing a specified number of signatures has been filed. The recall was adopted in Los Angeles in 1903 and in Oregon in 1908. It has since been put into effect in several states but is used sparingly.

Recessions, see *Business cycles.*

Reciprocity is the system of agreements in international commerce by which concessions in tariff rates are granted in return for special advantages from other nations. Such was the Canadian Reciprocity Treaty (1854–66), which opened the U.S. market to Canadian produce in return for certain fishing and navigation rights. Secretary of State Blaine inaugurated the first basic reciprocity policy by arrangements that led to the founding of the PAN-AMERICAN UNION (1890). Although the MC KINLEY TARIFF ACT (1890) included a reciprocity provision, reciprocal arrangements between the U.S. and other nations were not permanent until the TRADE AGREEMENTS ACT of 1934 was passed.

Reclamation, see *Conservation movement.*

Reclamation Act, see *Newlands Reclamation Act.*

Reconstruction, following the Civil War, created problems of enormous complexity. The Union victory brought the tension of combat to an end and the South was submissive, but no precedent existed for conquerors who had fought total war to preserve national unity. The months following Appomattox were critical because the political, social, and economic life of the South was shattered. Transportation systems were paralyzed, manufacturing had almost ceased, few banks or insurance companies were solvent, Confederate securities were worthless, labor was demoralized, and in some sections starvation was imminent. Few civilian administrations functioned, churches had been destroyed, and schools were closed.

The situation thus demanded that the President, as intermediary between victor and vanquished, make a clear interpretation of the rituals appropriate to peacemaking. The issues involved were beyond the ability of President Andrew Johnson to handle, despite his good intentions. Politically they had been raised two years before Johnson came to office. In his proclamation of December 1863, Lincoln had outlined a reconstruction plan whereby any southern state government would receive executive recognition as soon as one-tenth of the voters in the state took an oath to support the Constitution.

But the deadlock between the President and the RADICAL REPUBLICANS in Congress was clearly manifest in the WADE-DAVIS BILL (1864), a punitive measure demanding far more submission by the states before their governments would be recognized, and designed to show that Reconstruction was the prerogative of Congress rather than the President. Lincoln's pocket veto of the bill presaged the contest which Lincoln, a political insider, probably would have won. But the issue was inherited by Johnson, a political outsider, who stubbornly refused to permit Congress to modify his lenient policy of dealing with the South. By driving its dominant party into the hands of the radicals he lost what influence he had for moderation. In his effort to assert executive authority, Johnson misinterpreted the North's mood to the South, and by playing up the intent of vindictive radicals to subjugate 'the proud traitors,' he encouraged the South to assume a rigid posture of defiance that persuaded the North it had been cheated of its dearly won victory.

The central figure and most difficult problem in Reconstruction was the Negro, a freedman after passage of the Thirteenth Amendment (1865). The sudden release from bondage of some 4,000,000 persons, most of whom lacked even elementary training for the responsibilities of a free society, was without parallel in history, and the complexity of the problem was compounded in those regions where the ratio of blacks to whites was narrow. To assure the Negro of his rights, such northern organizations as the UNION LEAGUE moved into the South, and Congress created the FREEDMEN'S BUREAU (1865), an agency sometimes used by CARPETBAGGERS for financial and political profit. The southern states therefore enacted a series of laws, the so-called 'black codes' (1865–66), in an attempt to meet the problem, which was especially acute in the Deep South, where whites were outnumbered by Negroes and large numbers of Negroes chose no form of employment. In the Deep South the codes were severe, in North Carolina and Virginia they were mild, in Tennessee no codes were adopted. All of the codes gave certain limited civil rights, but not the right to vote. To such radical organs as the Chicago *Tribune* the codes virtually established a system of peonage for Negroes.

To the southern whites the codes were constructive measures enacted as stopgap legislation to prevent chaos at a moment when a whole economic system erected on slavery had been destroyed and no machinery existed for educating Negroes to civic responsibility. But many Northerners viewed them differently. Those radical Republicans who intended to make political capital of the defeated South wanted the Negro vote, and idealists saw the codes as a covert attempt to revive slavery. The RECONSTRUCTION ACTS (1866–68) were therefore pushed through Congress to give the radicals complete military control of the South. Southern whites responded by organizing vigilante patrols, such as the KU KLUX KLAN, to intimidate the Negroes. Enactment of the Fourteenth Amendment (1868), conferring citizenship on Negroes, was followed by the Fifteenth in 1870, granting suffrage, and by passage of a series of FORCE ACTS (1870–75), designed to compel recognition of these statutes. This period of 'Black Reconstruction' (1868–77), when southern state legislatures were controlled by the radicals and Negroes participated in politics under Republican protection, was sometimes characterized by corruption, extravagance, and vulgarity (as in the North during the same period), but these so-called 'carpetbag legislatures' introduced public schools for both races, welfare institutions, and essential postwar recovery measures, which were necessarily costly.

Self-rule gradually returned to the states, and when President Hayes withdrew the last Federal troops in 1877, state jurisdiction was completely restored and the crucial race problem was left to the southern whites. Although animosities between the sections were all but forgotten by 1890, the moral and racial scars of Reconstruction were visible well into the 20th century, to be seen (until late in the 1920's) in a persisting pattern of the SOLID SOUTH.

General studies include J. G. Randall and David Donald, *The Civil War and Reconstruction* (1961), John Hope Franklin, *Reconstruction After the Civil War* (1961); and Kenneth Stampp, *The Era of Reconstruction* (1965).

Reconstruction Acts (1867–68), so called, were those pushed through Congress over the veto of President Johnson. They gave the RADICAL REPUBLICANS complete military control of the South. The 'conquered provinces' were divided into five military districts, each under the command of a major general, with authorization for state governments based partly on the Negro suffrage conferred by the first of the CIVIL RIGHTS ACTS (1866). Supplementary acts gave military commanders unlimited right of appointment and removal of state officials, and made a simple majority vote sufficient for ratification of proposed state constitutions.

Reconstruction Finance Corporation (RFC) on President Hoover's recommendation was established by Congress (1932), with CHARLES G. DAWES as president, as a 'pump priming' agency to institute a recovery program during the depression. It lent money to a great variety of agricultural, commercial, and industrial enterprises. During the first Roosevelt Administration alone it sustained more than 7000 banks and trust companies, and its aggregate loans totaled upward of $11,000,000,000. The life of RFC was repeatedly extended and its scope enormously widened to finance the construction and operation of war plants and to make loans to foreign governments. After World War II its lending powers were sharply curtailed. Scandals involving improper loans were exposed in 1952 and brought about a reorganization of the agency. It ceased to function in 1956.

Recreation, see *Entertainment; Sports.*

RED CLOUD (1822–1909), chief of the Oglala Sioux (Teton Dakota), seeking to prevent the building of forts along the BOZEMAN TRAIL, engaged U.S. troops so successfully that the government abandoned the forts and the trail in 1868. He later signed a peace treaty and was feted in Washington and New York. After 1881 he lived quietly on a reservation in South Dakota.

Red Cross, see *American National Red Cross.*

Redemptioners, see *Indentured servants.*

RED JACKET (*c.* 1758–1830), chief of the Seneca Indians, having supported the British during the War of Independence, later made peace with the U.S. government. On a visit to President Washington (1792) he received a silver medal as a token of the nation's good will. He was a noted orator, and, as the 'old forest king,' he was a favorite subject of painters and writers in his time.

REDFIELD, WILLIAM C. (1789–1857), made a classic meteorological study of wind motion, published in *American Journal of Science and Art* (1833), which led to his discovery that hurricanes are revolving storms (1840). Author of many papers on earth sciences, he helped found and served as first president (1848) of the American Association for the Advancement of Science.

REDPATH, JAMES (1833–91), Scottish-born journalist and lecture agent, came to the U.S. during the 1850's. He was an ardent abolitionist, and he became the Kansas correspondent for the New York *Tribune* during the period when 'Bleeding Kansas' was racked by civil strife over the slavery issue. In 1868 he founded the Boston (later Redpath) Lyceum Bureau, a central booking office for speakers. He was the leading lecture promoter of his day and an important figure in the LYCEUM movement.

REED, JOHN (1887–1920), son of a wealthy Portland (Oregon) family, after graduation from Harvard (1910), became a contributor to various radical journals and magazines. While he was a staff writer for the *Masses* in 1913, he began moving toward the dialectical materialism of Karl Marx. As a reporter in Europe during World War I, he became a close friend of Lenin, and when the Bolsheviks seized power (1917), his story of the revolution, *Ten Days that Shook the World* (1919), soon established itself as the classic eyewitness account of that event. He helped organize the first communist party in the U.S. and returned to Russia to assist in furthering the Soviet cause. He died of typhus in Moscow and was accorded the honor of burial in the Kremlin.

REED, THOMAS BRACKETT (1839–1902), a graduate of Bowdoin (1860), practiced law and served as a Republican in the Maine legislature. He was elected to Congress (1877–99), where he became a party leader because of his skill as a parliamentarian. As Speaker of the House (1889–91), this autocratic 'czar' inaugurated 'Reed's Rules' (1890), which increased the Speaker's power by making the Speaker and committee chairmen 'a petty oligarchy.' This attempt to increase Republican power touched off an explosive battle, which the Democrats won in 1890. Reed lost the speakership and his rules were modified. He was again chosen Speaker (1895–99) when the Republicans regained power. He supported the sound-money policies of Cleveland and McKinley, but he was a bitter foe of imperialism. In 1899 he resigned the speakership (and his seat in Congress) rather than preside over a majority that favored an expansionist policy. Although the speakership was to lose the autocratic powers introduced by Czar Reed under another Republican autocrat, Speaker Joseph Cannon of Illinois, Reed is credited with establishing the principle of party responsibility in the House.

REED, WALTER (1851–1902), took his medical degree at Virginia (1869) and was appointed an army surgeon in 1875. After graduate study in bacteriology at Johns Hopkins, he became a professor of bacteriology at the Army Medical School (1893). In 1900 he headed a commission sent to study yellow fever in Havana, where his work proving that the disease is transmitted by a variety of mosquito made possible the virtual elimination of yellow fever in Cuba and the U.S. The Army hospital in Washington, D.C., is named for him.

Reed-Bulwinkle Act (1948), see *Interstate Commerce Commission.*

REEVE, TAPPING (1744–1823), one of the great law teachers of his day, was born in Brookhaven, New York, and graduated from the College of New Jersey (Princeton, 1763). He practiced law in Connecticut after 1772, but his notable achievement was the founding (1784) of the Litchfield Law School, the earliest and for many years the most important in the country. A department of law had been established at William and Mary College in 1779, and in succeeding decades a few other colleges were offering systematic legal instruction, but Reeve's school attracted some 1000 students from most of the states before it closed in 1833. After Reeve was appointed a judge of the superior court (1798), most of the teaching was done by the colleagues of his selection. The school numbered among its graduates some of the most eminent men in public life, including Aaron Burr, John C. Calhoun, and Horace Mann.

Referendum is a procedure used in states and municipalities in the U.S. whereby a bill or constitutional amendment is submitted to the voters for their approval after having been passed by the legislative body. The referendum was introduced in South Dakota in 1898, and has since been adopted by many other states.

Reforestation, see *Conservation movement.*

Reformed Church in America (Dutch Reformed Church), Calvinistic in doctrine with a Presbyterian form of organization, was brought to America by Dutch settlers (1628). It became the established church of New Netherland. In 1754 the American assembly became independent of its allegiance to the parent church in Amsterdam. It secured a charter (1766) for Queen's College (Rutgers) in New Jersey, where it established the New Brunswick Theological Seminary (1784). By mid-19th century Reformed congregations and seminaries had spread to the Middle West, although the stronghold of the church still remains in New York and New Jersey. In 1965 various Reformed bodies reported a total membership of some 518,000.

Regions, see *Deep South, Eastern states, Far West, Great Basin, Gulf states, Middle Colonies, Middle West, Mississippi Territory, New England, Northeast (The North), Northwest Territory, North Woods, Old Southwest, Pacific Northwest, Plains region, Prairie region, Rocky Mountains, Southeast (The South), Southwest.*

Regulating Act, see *Massachusetts Government Act.*

Regulators, so called, were the organized groups of frontier settlers in the Carolinas who in 1768 began to protest their lack of representation in the colonial assemblies, and the tyranny of the aristocratic Tidewater politicians. Increasing disorders led to passage (January 1771) in North Carolina of the Johnson Bill (the 'Bloody Act'), declaring rioters guilty of treason. Tensions mounted, and to suppress this radical threat Governor Tryon led a force of 1200 militiamen into the Regulator country, and in the battle of Alamance (May 1771) subdued 2000 Regulators, many of whom were unarmed. Some of the rebellious leaders were hanged, and hundreds of the up-country farmers were compelled to swear allegiance to the established government. This civil war of East against West revealed deep-seated sectional differences that were only temporarily obscured by the War of Independence.

REID, WHITELAW (1837–1912), Ohio-born journalist and diplomat, after graduation from Miami University (1856) became a newspaper reporter. His distinguished Civil War correspondence led Horace Greeley to make Reid the managing editor of the New York *Tribune* (1869), which after Greeley's death Reid controlled (1872–1905) and carried on as one of the leading journals of the nation. He served as Harrison's minister to France (1889–92), and he represented both Roosevelt and Taft as ambassador to England (1905–12). His numerous books, reflecting his journalistic and diplomatic activities, are best represented by *After the War: A Southern Tour* (1866), a description of economic and social disorganization.

His son, OGDEN MILLS REID (1882–1947), for many years (1908–47) edited the *Tribune,* which in 1924 became the *Herald Tribune.*

Religion, see *Protestantism* (which also refers to the large number of entries on Protestant sects), *Roman Catholic Church, Jews, Eastern Orthodox Churches, Mormons.*

Religious liberty, the unique contribution of the American colonies, was slow in taking root. All European countries assumed that the unity of religion was essential to the unity of the state, and each had its national church. In America religious liberty was first won by the small minority bodies, generally poor, which patterned themselves on the primitive Christian churches. Roger Williams in Rhode Island sought complete separation of CHURCH AND STATE as a cardinal principle, and by gaining a royal charter (1663) that guaranteed the colony and his Baptist followers absolute toleration (to the disgust of the Puritan oligarchies in Massachusetts and Connecticut), he made Rhode Island the first haven of Jews and Quakers, who were likewise seeking to build communities in which people could live harmoniously regardless of religious differences.

Most of the colonies began as proprietary grants, controlled by private venture, and thus William Penn, Lord Baltimore, and the proprietors of the Carolinas and Georgia were able to welcome persecuted sects who could buy and settle the land. Furthermore, by the end of the colonial period much of the population was without church affiliation, and thus there developed an atmosphere that was inhospitable to special privileges for any one religious body. The waves of the GREAT AWAKENING during the 18th century considerably weakened the hold of the Anglican church, established by law in the colonies south of Pennsylvania, as they did that of the Congregational bodies, so instituted in New England. Besides, the fact of sectarianism compelled dissident groups to adopt toleration as a practical necessity. No direct religious issues were involved in the War of Independence, for the leaven had been so long at work that religious liberty was incorporated as a matter of course in the new state and Federal constitutions.

'Remember the *Maine*,' see *Maine*.

REMINGTON, FREDERIC (1861–1909), painter, sculptor, and illustrator, after study at the Yale School of Fine Arts and at the Art Students League, lived in the West as a cowboy, scout, and sheep rancher. He painted the horses, soldiers, cowboys, and Indians of the western plains with sympathetic understanding and usually in spirited action. Remington was a popular illustrator of Spanish-American War episodes, and an indefatigable worker. He completed some 2700 paintings and sketches, many of which were extensively reproduced in color prints. He was author of such books as *Pony Tracks* (1895), and his sculptures in bronze are represented by *Cavalry Charge on the Southern Plains* (Metropolitan Museum).

Remonstrants, see *Arminianism*.

REMSEN, IRA (1846–1927), after graduation from Columbia (M.D. 1867), occupied the first chair of chemistry (1876–1901) at Johns Hopkins when it opened. There he founded the first U.S. graduate research program in chemistry, and established the *American Chemical Journal* (1879). Remsen gave impetus to scientific education during his presidency of the institution (1901–13), made notable contributions in organic chemistry, and was the discoverer of saccharin.

Rendition, see *Extradition*.

Rensselaer Polytechnic Institute, at Troy, New York, was founded (1824) by STEPHEN VAN RENSSELAER as a technical school to apply 'science to the common purposes of life.' Opened under the direction of AMOS EATON, it pioneered in the laboratory method of class instruction, and was the first engineering school in the U.S. to grant degrees (1835). In 1965, with an endowment of $48,000,000 and a faculty of 564, it enrolled 4600 students.

RENWICK, JAMES (1818–95), New York architect, was son of James Renwick, professor of science at Columbia, from which the son graduated in 1836. With RICHARD UPJOHN he inaugurated a new phase in the Gothic revival by his design of Grace Church (1843–46) and St. Patrick's Cathedral (1858–79) in New York. Other edifices that he designed include the Smithsonian Institution (1846–47) and the main buildings of Vassar College (1865). Following the fashion of his times, Renwick in his later designs modeled his buildings upon the neo-Renaissance style then current in France.

Reorganization Act of 1949, see *Hoover Commission*.

Reparations, to be paid by Germany to the victorious Allies after World War I, were provided for in the Treaty of VERSAILLES (1919). The original sum was tentatively fixed by the Reparations Commission at $56 billion, but in 1921 it was somewhat more realistically reduced to $32 billion, plus payments in commercial and industrial goods. Methods of collecting this huge amount proved unsatisfactory, and in 1924 the Commission accepted the DAWES PLAN, which set up a workable schedule of annual payments, based on capacity to pay, which were faithfully met until 1928, when Germany faced default. The YOUNG PLAN (1929) was then adopted, but a world-wide depression had set in, and after the HOOVER MORATORIUM (1931) for all practical purposes German reparations were at an end.

Repeal Amendment, see *Twenty-first Amendment.*

Report on Manufactures (1791), see *Hamilton, Alexander.*

Republican party, the present 'Grand Old Party' (G.O.P.), was the amalgamation (1854) of local party movements. It began as an expression of sentiment among certain Independent Democrats (by way of the FREE-SOIL PARTY) and those Whigs who strongly opposed the KANSAS-NEBRASKA ACT, which extended slavery into western territories. It chose its name to revive the memory of the defunct Democratic-Republican party founded by Jefferson, whose influence reputedly had steered passage of the Northwest Ordinance of 1787, which had banned slavery in northern territory.

The party's first candidate for President, John C. Frémont (1856), lost the election but carried eleven states. With Lincoln as nominee in 1860, and with a platform that combined free-soil principles with a protective tariff, the party attracted the agricultural and industrial voters of the North and West as well as the antislavery forces, and won the election. Its national political success from the period of the Civil War to 1932 was interrupted by two Democrats, Cleveland (1884, 1892) and Wilson (1912, 1916). In that period it especially attracted voters interested in 'sound money,' a protective tariff, and expanding industry. It won the election of 1920 with Harding in a campaign strongly opposed to U.S. entry into the League of Nations, and in 1928 with Hoover, who was highly respected in the business world. From 1920 until World War II it usually remained strongly isolationist.

After five successive defeats in presidential elections (1932–48), and some alteration of its traditional policies, the party won the elections of 1952 and 1956 with Eisenhower, whose personal popularity was such that public opinion polls indicated he could have won as the candidate of either party. In the election of 1960, Richard M. Nixon came within a fraction of 1 per cent of victory in his race against Kennedy. The party's retreat from even moderate liberalism in running Senator Barry Goldwater of Arizona as its candidate in 1964 proved near fatal; Goldwater lost the election to Johnson in the most overwhelming defeat since Landon's (1936).

Reserved powers, see *Police power, State government.*

Resettlement Administration, see *Farm Security Administration.*

Residual powers, see *Police power, State government.*

Resolution, Legislative, in the U.S. Congress and in many state legislatures may be of three kinds. Simple resolutions are those by which rules of procedure are adopted, or committees are appointed. Concurrent resolutions embody agreements between the two Houses, and deal chiefly with minor matters of concern to the Houses alone. Joint resolutions are a form of legislation of a special or unusual nature, and are subject to executive veto or approval. If approved they have the force of law.

Resorts in America date back to the colonial period. In mid-18th century Newport, Rhode Island, attracted summer visitors in considerable numbers from the South and the West Indies, and after the Civil War it developed as a resort center for socialites, chiefly from New York. During the second quarter of the 19th century the curative baths and the horse racing at Saratoga Springs, New York, were drawing the fashionable from all over the country. 'All the world is here,' wrote the New York social leader PHILIP HONE in 1839, 'politicians and dandies, cabinet ministers and ministers of the gospel, humbuggers and the humbugged.' Nahant, on a rocky peninsula near Boston, was popular, and in New Jersey there were Long Beach and Cape May. Bretton Woods in the White Mountains became the site of resort hotels. The leading southern resort before the Civil War was White Sulphur Springs, Virginia. By 1890 the New York *Tribune* was publishing eight columns of summer resort notices, advertising the attractions of seashore or mountains, and the luxuries of large hotels. New England especially made the most of its opportunities for summer recreation. In recent years the availability of summer and winter vacation spots, the great increase in travel made attractive by paid vacations, and the democratization of recreational life have greatly diminished the importance of the resort center.

Restraining Acts, see *Coercive Acts.*

Restraint of trade, though originally confined in its meaning to covenants whereby parties engaged not to compete with each other, by mid-18th century was a term applied to combinations entered into by workmen with a view to raising their wages. In America it represented simply a judicial extension of the common-law doctrine of CONSPIRACY. Since the decision of COMMONWEALTH *v.* HUNT (1842), U.S. courts have generally declined to treat as in 'restraint of trade' labor federations that confine their efforts to securing adherence to agreed terms upon which employment is or will be accepted. The complexities of the doctrine have never been fully resolved, and they have led to the passage of a variety of ANTITRUST LAWS in an effort to prevent price fixing agreements between competing companies.

Resumption Act (1875), following the PANIC OF 1873, provided that the Treasury would redeem GREENBACKS in gold. In 1878 Congress declared that all greenbacks then outstanding were on a par with gold, and people lost their desire for redemption. (Greenbacks still circulate as currency.)

'Return to normalcy,' see *Harding, W. G.*

REUTHER, WALTER PHILIP (1907–), was active in organizing the United Automobile Workers of America (1935), and engaged in its factional battles. In 1946 he became its president, and he led the 113-day strike that focused national attention on the issue of 'wage increases without price increases.' He pioneered in making the 'annual guaranteed wage' part of union agreements and persuaded General Motors and others to make hourly rates vary with the changing cost of living. Reuther was active in ridding the unions of racketeers and communists, and in 1952 he became president of the C.I.O. After the federation of the A.F. of L.–C.I.O. (1955), he headed the C.I.O. division.

REVERE, PAUL (1735–1818), Boston silversmith and engraver, was a fervent propagandist in the patriot cause on the eve of the War of Independence. A leader among the Sons of Liberty, he took part in the BOSTON TEA PARTY, and was an official courier for the Massachusetts Committee of Correspondence. He became a figure of legend when he rode from Charlestown to Lexington on the night of 18 April 1775 to warn the countryside that British troops were approaching. (William Dawes and Samuel Prescott also acted as couriers, but popularly are not remembered because Longfellow did not mention them in his famous but generally inaccurate poem, 'Paul Revere's Ride.') Revere designed and printed the first Continental currency, established a copper-rolling and brass-casting foundry (he pioneered in America in copper plating), and became a prosperous merchant. Today he is popularly remembered as the leading New England silversmith of his time, though many silversmiths of the period were as good or better. His work is best represented by his chastely designed Liberty Bowl (1769, Boston Museum of Fine Arts).

Revivals, religious awakenings marked by fervid spiritual expression, have been recurrent in the history of Christianity from earliest times, but the phrase 'religious revivals' is usually applied to those evangelical renewals of faith (followed by periods of apathy and sometimes by physical exhaustion) dating from the 18th century. In America the most notable revivals occurred intermittently during the GREAT AWAKENING (1726–80), which occasioned deep stirrings in all the colonies, built up intercolonial interest, and led to the founding of a very large number of denominational colleges in the century following the establishment of Princeton (1746).

A Second Awakening (1797–1805), most spectacular in the West, began with the frontier CAMP MEETINGS and the preaching of JAMES MC GREADY. In New

England the eastern phase was associated with the colleges and was sponsored by President TIMOTHY DWIGHT of Yale, who was strongly opposed at first by such rationalists as the DEISTS and later by UNITARIANS. But revivalism after 1800 had become the accepted method of Congregationalists (LYMAN BEECHER and his son HENRY WARD BEECHER), Presbyterians (CHARLES G. FINNEY), Methodists (PETER CARTWRIGHT), and Baptists (at first, in the South, farmer-preachers). So susceptible were Yankees in central New York to Pentecostal enthusiasm that the region along the Erie Canal was known as the 'Burnt-over District.'

The most influential post–Civil War revivalist was DWIGHT L. MOODY, who for 35 years conducted meetings throughout the U.S. and in Great Britain. The 20th century has been a period of professional evangelists, characterized by high-pressure organizations and carefully arranged settings in enormous tabernacles. During the early decades William Ashley [Billy] Sunday (1863–1935), professional baseball player turned evangelist, drew large crowds. In mid-century William Franklin [Billy] Graham (1918–) addressed enormous audiences through radio and television, and by tours abroad.

See W. W. Sweet, *Revivalism in America* (1944), and B. A. Weisberger, *They Gathered at the River* (1958).

'Revolution of 1800,' see *Democratic-Republican party*.

'Revolution of 1828,' see *Jacksonian Democracy*.

Revolutionary War, see *War of Independence*.

RHETT, ROBERT BARNWELL (1800–1876), South Carolina lawyer and owner of the Charleston *Mercury,* served as U.S. Representative (1837–49) and Senator (1850–52), during which period his 'fire-eating' sentiments led him to vehement advocacy of secession for the whole South and for restoration of the slave trade. (He was the owner of two plantations and master of 190 slaves.) A born incendiary and single-minded propagandist, for 30 years he campaigned against 'northern oppression' with such zeal that even his friends thought him a bore. He served in the Confederate congress until he lost the 1863 election.

Rhode Island, in New England, is the smallest and most densely populated of the states, and derives its name from the largest island in Narragansett Bay. It was the last of the Thirteen Colonies to ratify the Constitution (29 May 1790). Its official name is 'The State of Rhode Island and Providence Plantations.' ROGER WILLIAMS established the first settlement at Providence (1636) on land purchased from friendly Indians, and other Puritan exiles from Massachusetts soon followed, including WILLIAM CODDINGTON, ANNE HUTCHINSON, and SAMUEL GORTON. Williams secured a parliamentary patent (1644) to organize the PROVIDENCE PLANTATIONS, to which Charles II guaranteed religious liberty in 1663.

The individualism and contentiousness of Rhode Island settlers bore out the statement that 'in the beginning Massachusetts had law but not liberty and Rhode Island liberty but not law.' Yet it was in Rhode Island that Quakers and Jews found haven, and the colony became a beacon pointing to the religious freedom of later generations. To neighboring orthodox colonies the Rhode Island democracy was regarded as the 'sink of New England,' and it was excluded from the NEW ENGLAND CONFEDERATION, but its charter government remained generally in force until 1776. At that time NEWPORT virtually dominated foreign commerce, but its economic position was ruined by British occupation during the War of Independence.

The state's industrial importance began when SAMUEL SLATER established cotton textile mills there during the 1790's. With the backing of wealthy merchants and shipowners, manufacturing throve thereafter in several towns, especially in Providence. DORR'S REBELLION (1842), on the issue of voting privilege, led to a new state constitution. Paternal mill ownership gradually gave way to diversified responsibility, and the textile industry declined during the 1930's, when cheaper labor invited such enterprises into the South. Newport shared the state government with Providence until 1900, since when Providence has been the capital, with a population in 1960 of 207,000. First among the state's many institutions of higher learning is BROWN UNIVERSITY (Providence, est. 1764).

Rhode Island College, see *Brown University.*

RHODES, JAMES FORD (1848–1927), having amassed a fortune as an associate of the Cleveland industrialist MARK HANNA, retired from business in 1885 to devote himself to the writing of history. His *History of the U.S.* (7 vols., 1893–1906), covering the years 1850–77, was a venture in 'scientific' historical writing that in fact helped to professionalize the field. Although later research has invalidated many of his assumptions (particularly his abolitionist and racist bias), the work is respected as a vivid, detailed study. Two supplementary volumes (1919–22) continue the chronological account to 1909.

Rhodes scholarships, founded by the British empire builder Cecil Rhodes (1853–1902), provide stipends for 32 Americans for two or (by individual decisions) three years of study at Oxford. Selection is competitive, and, except in the periods of the two World Wars, scholarships have been awarded annually since 1903.

RIBAUT, JEAN (*c.* 1520–65), French Huguenot colonizer, was sent (1562) by Admiral Coligny to establish a settlement in Florida for Huguenot exiles. Having landed and explored the coast, he claimed the territory for France, left a contingent on Parris Island, South Carolina, to make his claim good, and sailed for home, planning an early return with more men and provisions. But the religious wars long delayed him, and the starving colonists abandoned the settlement. (A very few managed to find their way back to France.)

Meanwhile RENÉ DE LAUDONNIÈRE had been able to establish a Huguenot post, Fort Caroline, near the mouth of the St. Johns river (1564). In 1565 Ribaut returned with five vessels, intending to make a full-fledged colonizing effort. But a week after Ribaut arrived, the Spanish colonizer MENÉNDEZ DE AVILÉS appeared off the coast with six warships, and put into St. Augustine's harbor. Ribaut descended on the Spanish, but a hurricane struck, scattering the French fleet. Menéndez routed Laudonnière's small garrison, and Ribaut and most of the French colonizers were massacred. Thus ended French settlements in Florida.

RICE, DAN [DANIEL MCLAREN] (1823–1900), began as a wandering showman and acrobat in Barnum's circus and later became a wealthy circus manager. The most famous American clown of his day, he was noted in later years for his cracker-barrel humor, remarks delivered in a costume which accentuated his likeness to the traditional representation of Uncle Sam. Because he used Shakespearean themes, he was often called the Shakespeare Clown.

RICE, 'JIM CROW' [THOMAS DARTMOUTH] (1808–60), New York–born minstrel singer, first appeared about 1828 at Louisville, Kentucky, in the song-and-dance act that gave him popularity as 'Jim Crow,' the name he gave his Negro impersonations. Because the routine became America's first international song hit, it made him known as 'the father of American minstrelsy.' His black-face acts later were featured in New York and London theaters.

Rice industry became important after 1700 in the tidal region of South Carolina, and adjoining regions of North Carolina and Georgia, where it supplied the chief source of income down to the Revolution. After 1820 steam power for threshing made towns rather than plantations the center of the industry. For the next 40 years rice was the basis of a wealthy aristocracy, but the Civil War and competition with a growing rice industry in the Gulf states brought rice growing in the Carolinas virtually to an end. Rice today is cultivated in the U.S. principally in Louisiana, but as an industry it is a major source of income to relatively few.

Rice University (1912) (formerly The Rice Institute), at Houston, Texas, was established by the merchant philanthropist William Marsh Rice (1816–1900), whose large fortune enabled it to open with an immense scholarship budget. It is a nonsectarian co-educational institution offering courses in pure science, engineering, architecture, and the liberal arts. Graduate work is offered in almost all subjects. In 1965, with an endowment of $74,500,000 and a faculty of 225, it enrolled 2400 students.

RICHARDSON, HENRY HOBSON (1838–86), Louisiana-born architect, after graduation from Harvard (1859), studied in Paris at the Beaux-Arts. He began practice in New York (1866) before moving to Boston, where he designed Trinity Church (1877), his first monumental edifice and his finest work. It departed from the Gothic revival then in vogue by introducing French Romanesque, to which he gave a personal interpretation by his use of ornament and varied materials to give a sense of strength and simplicity. In his country houses, made of wood and constructed with the same feeling for simple mass, he produced a distinct American type. He also designed the Brattle Square Church in Boston, Sever Hall at Harvard, and the Hay-Adams house in Washington (now demolished). His mode was widely imitated in the Northeast and Middle West, but the designs of less imaginative craftsmen tend to stolidity and over-ornamentation. Richardson is ranked as the foremost American architect of his day. Certain of his later designs, such as the Marshall Field Warehouse Building, have earned for Richardson a pioneer role in the history of functionalism, or modernism.

Richmond, since 1779 the capital of Virginia and its largest city (with a population in 1960 of 220,000), is situated at the head of navigation on the James river. It was settled in 1637 as a trading post, laid out as a town in 1737, and incorporated as a city in 1782. During the Civil War it was the capital of the Confederacy and the constant objective of Union strategy. After the Confederate defeat at the battle of FIVE FORKS (April 1865), the city was evacuated and much of it burned. Richmond is a shipping, financial, and cultural center, and the site of the University of Richmond (1830).

Rickaree Indians, see *Arikara.*

Riders, Legislative, are usually controversial amendments to a bill, and need bear no relation to the substance of the bill itself. They generally are added to appropriations bills, which the President would be reluctant to veto, and thus the passage of the particular measure assures the success of the amendment, which presumably would not pass on its own merit. The device is chiefly used by Congress, since the President lacks authority to use the ITEM VETO.

Right of deposit was the privilege of western merchants and farmers during the 1790's to unload their goods at New Orleans free of duty while awaiting transshipment on ocean-going vessels. The right was recognized by Spain in PINCKNEY'S TREATY (1795), and suspended by that country in 1802, but the Louisiana Purchase a year later settled the problem permanently.

RIIS, JACOB [AUGUSTUS] (1849–1914), Danish-born journalist and reformer, emigrated in 1870 to the U.S., where during the next two decades he wrote for New York newspapers. His exposure of slum conditions in American cities, *How the Other Half Lives* (1890), shocked the public to an awareness of its own backyards and was a factor during the MUCKRAKING movement in slum clearance and new building codes. *The Making of an American* (1901) is an autobiography.

RIMMER, WILLIAM (1816–79), English-born sculptor brought as a youth to the U.S., at 30 undertook the study and practice of medicine. He was self-taught as an artist, but his knowledge of anatomy gave forcefulness to such works as *The Falling Gladiator* (1861), *The Dying Centaur* (1870), and *The Fighting Lions* (1870), all in the Metropolitan Museum, New York. He was director of the School of Design for Women at Cooper Union, New York (1866–70), and in 1876 became professor of anatomy and sculpture at the School of Fine Arts in Boston. He is regarded today as the most creative American sculptor of his period.

Rio Grande (Sp., *great river*), 1885 miles long, rises in southwest Colorado and flows south through the middle of New Mexico. At El Paso it becomes the border between Texas and Mexico, flows through the deep canyons of Big Bend in western Texas (a national park since 1944), and finally enters the Gulf of Mexico. Indians were using its water for irrigation when Coronado passed through New Mexico in 1540. When the Republic of Texas seceded from Mexico (1836), it claimed the river as a boundary. The annexation of Texas by the U.S. (1845) brought on the Mexican War, which was settled by the Treaty of Guadalupe Hidalgo (1848). That treaty established the river as an international boundary from its mouth to El Paso.

RIPLEY, GEORGE (1802–80), after graduation from Harvard (1823), entered the Unitarian ministry (1826–41), which he did not find congenial. With F. H. HEDGE he edited *Specimens of Foreign Standard Literature* (14 vols., 1838–42), translations of such idealistic philosophers as Cousin, Schleiermacher, and Jouffroy. It was highly regarded by the New England Transcendentalists. He was a founder and leading spirit in the famous BROOK FARM experiment in communal living (1841–47), and remained its president until the group dissolved. Horace Greeley then was able to attract 'Archon' Ripley to New York as the literary critic for the *Tribune* (1849–80).

RITTENHOUSE, DAVID (1732–96), self-educated Philadelphia clockmaker, developed great skill in devising mathematical instruments. The leading surveyor of his day, he made boundary surveys in more than half the original colonies and helped to settle the dispute over the MASON-DIXON LINE. In 1767 he constructed the most accurate orrery (a working model of the solar system) in the colonies, and two years later made notable observations of the transit of Venus. He succeeded Franklin as president of the American Philosophical Society (1791–96), was elected to membership in the Royal Society (1795), and was judged in America, in Jefferson's extravagant words, 'second to no astronomer living.' He also served in the convention that framed the Pennsylvania constitution, and was state treasurer (1777–89) and director of the U.S. mint (1792–95).

Rivers, see *Colorado, Columbia, Connecticut, Delaware, Hudson, James, Merrimack, Mississippi, Missouri, Ohio, Potomac, Rio Grande, Sacramento, Susquehanna, Yukon.*

Roads became a matter of public concern when the inauguration of STAGECOACH passenger and mail service in the 18th century provided an inducement for road improvements, which were so extensive that a network of roads linked the colonies during the Revolution. Toll roads, or TURNPIKES, were introduced in 1785. The TRANSYLVANIA COMPANY opened up Kentucky, and the OHIO COMPANY built roads into the Old Northwest. Under Federal auspices the CUMBERLAND ROAD became a chief artery for western settlements during the 1820's and 1830's, and the SANTA FE TRAIL, the OLD SPANISH TRAIL, and the OREGON TRAIL extended commerce and settlements to the Southwest and the Pacific.

During the first third of the 19th century the federal government advanced funds for the construction of roads as part of its broad program of INTERNAL IMPROVEMENTS, and though Federal interest later declined, it revived in the 20th century under the impact of the tremendous growth of the automobile industry. The completion of the transcontinental Lincoln Highway in 1930 was made possible by Federal and state aid for construction. Since 1950 the number of limited access highway systems has steadily increased. In 1958 Congress authorized $25 billion to supplement Federal road contributions, to build 41,000 miles of roads over a thirteen-year period. The federal government assured co-operation of the states by providing nine dollars for every dollar the states contributed. Thus in effect a vast Federal road plan was superimposed upon those of the states.

Roanoke Island, off the northeast coast of North Carolina, was selected by Walter Raleigh for his colonizing expedition (1584). These first English colonists fared badly and soon returned to England. After a second small group failed, Raleigh sent some 118 hopeful colonizers (1587) under JOHN WHITE. Returning in 1591 from a mission to England for supplies, White found that the colony had vanished without trace except for the unexplained word 'Croatoan,' carved on a tree. No satisfactory solution to the mystery of the 'lost colony' has ever been given. The word may mean that the surviving colonists or their children were adopted by the Croatan Indians.

Such, at any rate, is the tradition among the Croatans (now called Lumbee) of North Carolina.

ROBERTSON, James, see *Watauga Settlement.*

ROBIE, Thomas (1689–1729), after graduation from Harvard (1708), as tutor in the college entered into correspondence with English scientists, at whose request he made astronomical observations and kept careful meteorological records despite the fact that he lacked both a thermometer and a barometer. He compiled the almanacs for the years 1709–20, and several of his astronomical articles, as well as his observations on the effect of inoculation for smallpox and the venom of spiders, were published in the *Transactions* of the Royal Society, to which body he was elected (1725).

ROBINSON, Edwin Arlington (1869–1935), grew up in Gardiner, Maine, attended Harvard (1891–93), and after writing two volumes of poetry, *The Torrent and the Night Before* (privately printed, 1896), and *The Children of the Night* (1897), settled in New York City. To give Robinson opportunity to develop as a poet, President Theodore Roosevelt aided him financially by appointing him to the New York customhouse (1905–10). General recognition came with publication of *The Man against the Sky* (1916). Later he was given three Pulitzer Prizes (1921, 1924, 1927). Robinson had made poetry his profession, in effect the first writer in the U.S. to do so. He tried few experiments, yet his verses were free from traditional poetic vocabulary. The somber, introspective nature of his poetry bears the stamp of his Puritan New England ancestry.

ROBINSON, James Harvey (1863–1936), received his doctorate from the University of Freiburg (1890), taught European history at Columbia (1895–1919), and became the first director of the New School for Social Research (1919). He believed that history should be an instrument to achieve a just social order, a view developed in *The New History* (1912). In his best-seller, *The Mind in the Making* (1921), he elaborated the concept, pointing out that much historical thinking has been mere rationalization, and not relevant to social action. He influenced both college and secondary school history teaching, especially in persuading schoolteachers to devote more time to present-day problems and less to antiquarian subjects, to the extent that the 'New History' concept became conventional in textbook writing.

Robinson-Patman Act (1936), also called the Federal Anti-Price Discrimination Act, was an amendment to the clayton antitrust act of 1914, and was aimed primarily at chain stores engaged in interstate commerce. It outlawed the unreasonably low prices that tended to put small retailers out of business, and empowered the Federal Trade Commission to abolish monopolistic price fixing.

ROCHAMBEAU, Jean Baptiste Donatien de Vimeur, Comte de (1725–1807), with the rank of lieutenant general was sent (May 1780) by Louis XVI to head an expeditionary force of 6700 regulars under naval escort to aid Washington in the War of Independence. He landed at Newport, Rhode Island, where for a year he was forced to remain inactive, waiting for news of the arrival in the West Indies of Admiral de Grasse with his fleet, sent to give strong naval support to land action either off New York or the Virginia coast.

When news arrived in the summer of 1781 that de Grasse was on his way up to the Chesapeake, Rochambeau marched his army across Connecticut to join Washington at White Plains, New York, where they worked out plans for the yorktown campaign, which ended the war. Rochambeau placed the invaluable resources of the French engineering and artillery staffs at Washington's disposal, and did so in a manner that did not create an atmosphere of jealousy. He returned home with the thanks of a grateful Congress. Among those from abroad who served the American cause Rochambeau stands next to Lafayette.

Rochester, University of (1850), is a private, nonsectarian, co-educational institution established by Baptists at Rochester, New York. It is known especially for the Eastman School of Music (1918), and for schools of medicine and dentistry. In 1965, with an endowment of $87,000,000 and a faculty of 1400, it enrolled 7100 students.

ROCKEFELLER, JOHN DAVISON (1839–1937), industrialist and philanthropist, in 1853 moved with his family from Tioga county, New York, to a village near Cleveland, Ohio, where during his twenties he formed a partnership to establish an oil refinery, which in 1870 became the STANDARD OIL COMPANY. He combined meticulousness of detail in guiding the rapid expansion of a new industry with a broad vision regarding the problems of top-level management. He selected his associates astutely. Rockefeller was convinced that the company's success depended upon eliminating competition, and before 1890 he had created a petroleum empire, close to a monopoly, which dominated the oil market on a global scale. The trusts and interlocking directorates that he created led to antitrust suits and Supreme Court action in 1911, which dissolved them.

Although Rockefeller did not formally retire until 1911, after 1890 he devoted most of his time to planning how to distribute his vast fortune and he organized large charities as meticulously as he had organized his industries. They include establishment of the UNIVERSITY OF CHICAGO (1892), the ROCKEFELLER INSTITUTE FOR MEDICAL RESEARCH (1901), the GENERAL EDUCATION BOARD (1903), and the ROCKEFELLER FOUNDATION (1913).

His son, JOHN D. ROCKEFELLER, JR. (1874–1960), succeeded him in business and continued to augment the family philanthropies. A son of the younger Rockefeller, NELSON ALDRICH ROCKEFELLER (1908–), held various government posts before serving as Republican governor of New York after 1958.

Rockefeller Center, largest privately owned business and entertainment center in the U.S., is located in New York City. It extends from 48th to 52nd Street, and from Fifth Avenue to Sixth Avenue. Built in the decade 1931–40, its fifteen towering buildings house a daily population of 160,000 persons, in stores, offices, restaurants, exhibition rooms, and radio and television studios. Its lower plaza is a wide court with diversified summer and winter dining and sports uses. The buildings were designed as a unit by Harrison and Abramovitz, and the decorative sculptures were executed by such artists as Lachaise, Zorach, Noguchi, and Manship.

Rockefeller Foundation, established (1913) by John D. Rockefeller, annually supports large international programs in the fields of medicine, public health, science, and the humanities. The Foundation itself does no research. It grants funds to universities and other research institutions, and awards post-doctoral fellowships. In 1965, from assets of $862,000,000, it disbursed $32,568,000.

The Rockefeller Brothers Fund, established (1940) by the five sons of the elder John D. Rockefeller, makes similar grants. Its activities include support, and, in some instances, direct operation, of experimental or new undertakings. In 1965, from assets of $209,743,000, it disbursed $8,440,000.

Rockefeller University (1901) in New York City, was opened as Rockefeller Institute, under the direction of WILLIAM H. WELCH, as a medical research organization, with departments in animal and plant pathology, a laboratory, and a hospital limited to cases under study. Its unique facilities were broadened in 1953 by the establishment of a graduate school for scientific research in many areas. In 1965, with an endowment of $83,654,000 and a faculty of 220, it enrolled 108 research scholars.

Rockets, see *Space exploration.*

ROCKINGHAM, CHARLES WATSON-WENTWORTH, 2nd Marquess of (1730–82), having formed a coalition government after the fall of the government of GEORGE GRENVILLE (1765), attempted conciliation with the American colonies by a repeal of the STAMP ACT, but his ministry resigned a year later rather than admit some of the 'king's men' to office. He was succeeded by CHATHAM. After the dismissal of Lord NORTH (1782) he again became prime minister, but he died before the peace treaty had been signed. This time SHELBURNE followed him in office.

ROCKNE, KNUTE KENNETH (1888–1931), Norwegian-born football coach, graduated from Notre Dame (1914). There as head coach (after 1918) he revolutionized the sport by stressing offensive tactics, developing the backfield shift, and perfecting line play. He brought football fame to the university and is considered by many the greatest of football coaches.

Rocky Mountain Fur Company, see *Ashley Expeditions.*

Rocky Mountain National Park (est. 1915), in north central Colorado, is an area of some 253,000 acres in the heart of the ROCKY MOUNTAINS. Estes Park is its headquarters.

Rocky Mountains are the series of ranges that extend from Mexico into the Canadian Arctic. In the U.S. this massive system rises from the GREAT PLAINS on the east, and is separated from the west coast by the GREAT BASIN. It traverses Arizona, New Mexico, Colorado, Utah, Idaho, Wyoming, and Montana. (It is not a part of the SIERRA NEVADA or CASCADE systems.) Its ranges (within the U.S.) include the Bitterroot, Absaroka, Wind River, Teton, Wasatch, Park, and Front Ranges. Its glaciers are to the north. Its five highest peaks are all in Colorado: Mount Elbert (14,431), Mount Harvard (14,420), Mount Massive (14,418), La Plata Peak (14,340), and Blanco Peak (14,317). These vast uplifts, cut by deep canyons, are veined with metals that have made the region a mining center. From the Rockies rise the great river systems of the Mackenzie, Missouri, Columbia, Colorado, and Rio Grande.

The CONTINENTAL DIVIDE is the crest of the Rockies, which were a formidable barrier to transcontinental crossing. They were first breached by ALEXANDER MACKENZIE (1793), and later explored by LEWIS AND CLARK (1804–6), ZEBULON PIKE (1806–7), STEPHEN LONG (1820), and especially by the host of MOUNTAIN MEN (1822–45), whose detailed knowledge opened travel through them. Today the area includes some 90,000,000 acres of national forests and five national parks: YELLOWSTONE, MESA VERDE, GLACIER, ROCKY MOUNTAIN, and GRAND TETON.

Rodeos were first popularized as public spectacles in the 1880's by the Wild West shows of Buffalo Bill (WILLIAM CODY). The participants show their skill in riding broncos and steers, roping and tying steers and calves, and using the lasso. Originally an adjunct to the ROUNDUP, which is still an annual event in the West, the rodeo in the East is an exhibition by professional entertainers, and travels like the circus.

RODGERS, RICHARD (1902–), popular song composer, with the lyricist Lorenz Hart (1895–1943) collaborated on the enormously successful musical comedy *Garrick Gaieties* (1925), and other productions. His later collaborations with OSCAR HAMMERSTEIN II have been notable in that, contrary to tradition, their plots have a serious strain and at times employ tragic overtones. The song hits from *Oklahoma!* (1943), and *South Pacific* (1949) became American classics.

ROEBLING, JOHN AUGUSTUS (1806–69), German-born engineer, after coming to the U.S. (1831) established a plant at Trenton, New Jersey, for manufacturing steel cable, and pioneered in the building of suspension bridges. He erected the railroad span at Niagara Falls (1851–55) and designed the Brooklyn Bridge, begun in 1870 and opened in 1883. Following an accident at the bridge site, he contracted tetanus and died; the work was seen to completion by his son, who himself was crippled in the process. With JAMES B. EADS, Roebling ranks as the foremost American bridge builder of the 19th century.

ROGERS, JOHN (1829–1904), Massachusetts-born sculptor, began modeling in clay as a pastime. His early statuette group, *The Slave Auction,* was widely publicized by abolitionist orators. After the Civil War he achieved immense popularity with such plaster 'Rogers groups' as *Coming to the Parson* (considered an ideal wedding gift), and *Checkers up at the Farm.* He patented his groups, of which he sold thousands of copies, and he was the first artist to distribute sculpture by mail order. His subjects are uniformly sentimental, but they are accurate social records of the period.

ROGERS, RANDOLPH (1825–92), having attracted the attention of New York merchants by modeling their portraits, was enabled (1848) to go to Italy to study sculpture. In 1851 he settled permanently in Rome, where he became a leading figure in the art colony there. His work was in such demand that it was widely distributed in replica. He is chiefly known today for his 'Columbia doors' of the National Capitol, and for the heroic figure of 'Michigan' atop the Detroit monument.

ROGERS, Robert (1731–95), Massachusetts-born soldier, served in the last French and Indian War (1755–63) in which he led the famous Rogers' Rangers, a corps of 600 frontiersmen who won repute as the eyes of the British army. Each Ranger was a mobile and self-sufficient soldier, intrepid and daring. The contingent of 180 that fought the 'battle on snowshoes' at Rogers' Rock, Lake George, in 1758, lost 130 of its members. In 1760 Rogers was given command of the Detroit fort, and he participated in the French surrender. He was feted in England, where his drama *Ponteach* (1766) was produced. Rogers later returned to the post at Mackinac, and from there he sent JONATHAN CARVER to search for a NORTHWEST PASSAGE.

At the outbreak of the War of Independence Rogers seemed uncertain whether to cast his lot with patriots or Loyalists, and Washington had him arrested as a spy. On his escape he led Loyalist troops for a time, but his untrustworthiness led the British to dismiss him from the service. He fled to England in 1780, and died fifteen years later in obscurity. Yet no frontier leader during the Indian wars deserves greater credit for acumen in handling his men.

ROGERS, Will [William Penn Adair] (1879–1935), one of the leading humorists of his day, made a stage career of his experience as an Oklahoma cowboy. Starting as a rope-twirler (1915) in the Ziegfeld *Follies,* he became world-famous as the 'cowboy philosopher,' through his books and newspaper columns. He was an airplane enthusiast, and he died (with WILEY POST) in a plane crash in Alaska.

Rogers Groups, see *Rogers, John.*

ROLFE, John (1585–1622), English colonist in Virginia, perfected the process of curing tobacco (about 1613), and thus gave the colony its staple export. His marriage in 1614 to POCAHONTAS assured peace with the local Indians through the lifetime of her father POWHATAN, but after her death (1617) and that of Powhatan (1618) outbreaks occurred, and Rolfe presumably was killed in the Indian massacre of 1622.

Roman Catholic Church, as a hierarchy in the U.S., dates from the appointment of JOHN CARROLL of Baltimore as prefect-Apostolic of the American Church (1784). The only colony in America founded as a refuge for Catholics was Maryland (1632), and though the colony became officially Protestant in 1688, the Catholic Church was always strong there. In 1790 Father Carroll was consecrated Bishop of Baltimore, with spiritual jurisdiction over all the 40,000 Catholics then in the nation. Sees established (1808) at Boston, New York, Philadelphia, and Bardstown, Kentucky, helped Carroll divide his labors, and thereafter the growth of the church in the U.S. was without parallel in the history of any nation. Its membership in 1965, nearly double that of the next largest religious body (Baptists), totaled 45,640,000.

The peaks of growth coincided with the great waves of immigration from Catholic countries from 1840 to 1910, and the serious dislocations thus created fostered NATIVISM, an antagonism transferred from 'foreigners' to 'Catholics.'

Catholic leadership in the U.S. has been principally concerned with matters of administration and education. Much has been written by Catholic spokesmen to refute the charge that the political teachings of the church are inconsistent with democratic ideology, but not until 1928 did a Catholic candidate for President win a nomination (Alfred E. Smith), and not until 1960 did a Catholic (John F. Kennedy) win election to the office.

Outstanding Americans in the history of the Church in the U.S. include JOHN JOSEPH HUGHES, JOHN IRELAND, and JAMES GIBBONS, founder of CATHOLIC UNIVERSITY.

A recent history is J. T. Ellis, *American Catholicism* (1956).

Romanticism, as a movement in the arts (especially in literature), originated in Germany and France late in the 18th century and soon spread elsewhere in Europe and America. In its wider aspects it was the artists' response to the growing complexity of an increasingly mechanized and industrial society, and it took many forms, all of which envisioned a greater personal freedom for the individual. Indeed, so involved were the forces that impelled the movement and so varied its manifestations that any concise summary of it can only point out its trends and its leading characteristics.

Its individualism had an origin in the Renaissance images of man, explored in politics, psychology, and art. The Reformation allowed it ideas that conflicted with traditional theology. The empiricism of its social and political philosophy stems from the teachings of JOHN LOCKE, and its transcendental idealism traces immediately to Immanuel Kant (1724–1804). Its reliance was always placed upon emotion, not reason.

Immensely influential were the writings of Jean Jacques Rousseau (1712–78), who believed that man, by nature good, is corrupted by bad institutions. The optimistic humanitarianism of the movement was consonant with scientific DEISM, which stressed the benevolence of the Creator. It paid tribute to a love of nature and the common man, and it derived inspiration from wild grandeur, the picturesque, the mysterious, and vanished or alien cultures. As a movement in the U.S. it coincided with such indigenous factors as a predominantly agrarian society moving westward into untamed frontiers, a fixed image of America as a continent of boundless resources, and a faith in the democratic principle. One social aspect resulted in experimental COMMUNAL SOCIETIES. Its religious impulses were remarkably varied and never orthodox; its philosophical aspirations were unsystematic and flowered in TRANSCENDENTALISM; its humanitarian bent found outlet in the ABOLITION MOVEMENT and in a variety of reform organizations.

Romanticism predominated in American literature (notably in the writings of every major author from Jefferson to Emerson and Whitman) and in other arts as well. The Gothic romance was paralleled by the Gothic revival in architecture. It created the HUDSON RIVER SCHOOL of landscape painters, and extended into the 20th century in various forms, one of which was IMPRESSIONISM.

ROMBERG, SIGMUND (1887–1951), Hungarian-born composer, in 1910 came to the U.S., where he soon assembled his own café orchestra. His popularity as operetta composer began with *Maytime* (1917), and was continued by *The Student Prince* (1924), *Blossom Time* (1926), and *The Desert Song* (1926). He later wrote scores for motion pictures, and toured with his own orchestra.

ROOSEVELT, [ANNA] ELEANOR (1884–1962), niece of Theodore Roosevelt and wife of Franklin D. Roosevelt (a distant cousin), took an active and lifelong interest in social work, youth movements, political issues, and the rights of minority groups. As first lady, she held the first press conference assembled for a President's wife (1933), wrote a syndicated newspaper column, 'My Day' (1935–38), and traveled and lectured widely to further her causes. She was appointed U.S. delegate to the United Nations (1945), and became chairman of its Commission on Human Rights in 1946. A woman of charm and vigor, she raised six children while finding time to write several books and numberless magazine articles. She stamped her personality on many humanitarian endeavors.

ROOSEVELT, FRANKLIN DELANO (1882–1945), 32nd President of the U.S., was born on the family estate at Hyde Park, New York. A year after graduation from Harvard (1904), while studying law at Columbia, he married a distant cousin, ELEANOR ROOSEVELT. He began his political career as a member of the New York state senate (1910–13), where he became a leader of the insurgent (anti-Tammany) Democrats. He campaigned vigorously for Woodrow Wilson in the election of 1912, and Wilson appointed him Assistant Secretary of the Navy (1913–20), a post Roosevelt filled competently throughout World War I. He was candidate for Vice President on the unsuccessful Democratic ticket with James M. Cox in 1920. During the following summer he was paralyzed from the waist down by poliomyelitis, but his unremitting efforts restored to him the partial use of his legs. At the Democratic National Conventions of 1924 and 1928 he delivered the nominating speech for ALFRED E. SMITH.

Elected governor of New York (1929–33), Roosevelt furthered such reforms as regulation of public utilities and a broader base for public welfare, which had been initiated by Smith, his predecessor. When the Great Depression set in, following the stock market crash of 1929, Roosevelt carried forward bold relief measures and gained sufficient political stature to become the standard bearer for the Democratic party in the 1932 presidential race against Herbert Hoover. Roosevelt won the election with a decisive popular majority (and an electoral vote of 472 to 59), and entered the White House with a 'clear mandate' to take vigorous action in the nation's worst economic crisis.

Roosevelt's inaugural address, outlining his program for a NEW DEAL through progressive legislation, was delivered with confidence and forcefulness. On the following day he summoned Congress into special session and declared a four-day general bank holiday. Because Congress itself was in a mood for emergency regulatory measures and social legislation, Roosevelt was able to advance his domestic program with extraordinary speed. The almost revolutionary social and economic changes that followed were possible because Roosevelt, with political acumen, championed reform while working through established bureaucracies. He made a team out of such diverse cabinet members as CORDELL HULL and FRANCES PERKINS, HAROLD ICKES and JAMES FARLEY. In a matter of weeks Congress, following Roosevelt's guidance, had set up agencies to reorganize industry and agriculture, appropriated large sums for 'pump priming,' and enacted laws to regulate banking and finance. In 1934 the gold standard was adjusted to the advantage of debtor groups, and in 1935 SOCIAL SECURITY gave a new dimension to public welfare.

These changes were not accomplished without dissent, sometimes rancorous, among the groups of presidential advisers. The great confidence that Roosevelt placed in the ideas and opinions of HARRY L. HOPKINS was especially galling to the more conservative administrators. But the President steadily carried his programs forward, reassuring the nation in his intimate and persuasive radio 'fireside chats.' The degree of his appeal was evidenced by his re-election (1936) in the greatest landslide in American history. His Republican opponent, Alfred M. Landon of Kansas, picked up only the eight electoral votes of Maine and Vermont.

But the impetus of the reform had begun to slow, and the enormous expenditures and the inevitable waste in the vast emergency projects brought on a strong reaction. Conservatives were bitter in denouncing him as a 'traitor to his class,' and the so-called COURT-PACKING PLAN (1937), intended to alter the shape of a Supreme Court that had been ruling against much New Deal legislation, aroused more general public indignation. In foreign affairs, however, Roosevelt strengthened ties with Latin America and made 'hemispheric solidarity' a reality. Aware of the ominous turn of events in Europe, even before the outbreak of World War II (1939) the President envisioned a cataclysm that might send Americans to fight in the far corners of the globe. He therefore began to make the U.S. an 'arsenal of democracy,' and after war broke out, the program for building U.S. strength could be more easily speeded. When France fell (1940), aid to Great Britain was increased, and in the presidential campaign of that year the two major parties raised no issue on foreign policy.

Roosevelt's acceptance of the nomination for a third term broke tradition and strengthened the opposition of some of his former associates chiefly for that reason alone. Vice President John N. Garner disapproved, James A. Farley would no longer manage Roosevelt's campaign, and John L. Lewis tried (unsuccessfully) to draw his large labor following into party rebellion. Although Wendell Willkie, the Republican candidate, won 45 per cent of the popular vote, Roosevelt was swept into office with an electoral vote of 449 to Willkie's 82.

In August 1941 Roosevelt and Prime Minister Churchill met at sea and drafted the ATLANTIC CHARTER, essentially a restatement of Woodrow Wilson's FOURTEEN POINTS dealing with democratic freedom. The Japanese attack on PEARL HARBOR (7 December 1941) plunged the U.S. into World War II, and thereafter Roosevelt conducted his own foreign affairs. His conferences with allied leaders during the next years were steps in the plans to invade Europe and defeat Japan: CASABLANCA (January 1943), QUEBEC (August 1943), CAIRO (November 1943), and TEHERAN (December 1943). The last helped lay the bases of the postwar world.

In 1944 for the fourth time Roosevelt was his party's candidate, with Harry S Truman as his running mate. His Republican opponent, Thomas E. Dewey, polled a large popular vote, but again Roosevelt won the election. But his period in office during this term was brief. When he attended the YALTA CONFERENCE (February 1945) to discuss final defeat of the Axis powers, he was ailing, and on 12 April he died of a cerebral hemorrhage.

Like Wilson, Roosevelt was a political liberal and he spoke eloquently for human freedom. Born to privilege, with a lifelong regard for scholarly minds, he had a confidence in the common people akin to Jefferson's, yet not since Lincoln has a President in office been so fiercely denounced or so fervently defended. No other Chief Executive has left so vivid a mark on the presidency. He was a master of politics, which he used for great ends, thus proving that political skill is an important ingredient of presidential effectiveness. Today he is accorded rank as one of the few great Presidents.

The biography by Frank Freidel (3 vols., 1962–66) is written by a historian; that by James M. Burns (1956) is the work of a political scientist.

ROOSEVELT, THEODORE (1858–1919), 26th President of the U.S. (1901–9), was born in New York City. A member of a prosperous and well-connected family, upon graduation from Harvard (1880) he studied law and served (1881–84) as a Republican member of the New York assembly. For two years after the death (1884) of his first wife, Alice Hathaway (mother of his eldest daughter), he retired to his ranch in the Dakota Territory. On his return he married Edith Kermit, mother of his five other children. As he gained stature in Republican circles, he was successively a member of the Civil Service Commission (1889–95), Police Commissioner of New York (1895–97), and Assistant Secretary of the Navy (1897–98). At the outbreak of the Spanish-American War Roosevelt helped organize and lead the 'ROUGH RIDERS.' He returned from Cuba so evidently a popular hero that Boss T. C. PLATT picked him as Republican candidate for governor of New York, a post to which Roosevelt brought (1899–1900) the same reforming zeal that had marked all his previous labors. Indeed, the vigor with which he struck at corruption was embarrassing to Platt, who in self-defense pressed the election of Roosevelt to the usually dead-end office of Vice President of the U.S. The assassination of McKinley brought Roosevelt (then forty-two) into the presidency, to the dismay of the party conservatives.

Roosevelt had a national point of view and a universal range of friendships. An Easterner by birth, he was also identified with the West, both by personal association and as a historian who could write with authority, notably in *The Winning of the West* (4 vols., 1889–96). He was known in the South because two uncles had been prominent Confederates. He was the image of the 'typical American' because of his versatility; and his zest for the 'strenuous life' made his public and private associations more exciting than any before in the history of the presidency. At the same time, his impetuous nature and his unshakable conviction of his righteous wisdom annoyed many, including his Secretary of State Elihu Root, who commented that Roosevelt on occasion imagined he had discovered the Ten Commandments.

At heart Roosevelt was a Democrat and a sincere progressive, who advocated 'trust-busting,' denounced 'malefactors of great wealth,' and demanded a 'square deal' for labor. In his first message to Congress he called for a score of forward-looking measures, including regulation of railroads, corporations, and banks; the creation of a Department of Commerce; reforms in civil service; and, most emphatically, a large-scale national conservation program.

During his first term he gave support to successful antitrust suits, sponsored the NEWLANDS RECLAMATION ACT, strengthened the Interstate Commerce Commission, and by vigorously championing the rights of the 'little man' captured the imagination of the American people. Thus in 1904 he was elected President 'in his own right' by an overwhelming popular majority, a mandate that encouraged him to enhance U.S. prestige in world affairs to a degree that alarmed anti-imperialists. His interference in the Panama revolution (1903) had prepared the way for American 'dollar diplomacy' in the Caribbean and aroused Latin American indignation. At the same time, he continued the OPEN DOOR POLICY in China, and mediated the Russo-Japanese War by arranging negotiations for the Treaty of PORTSMOUTH, an intervention that won him the 1906 Nobel Peace award. The political prestige of 'Teddy' Roosevelt by 1908 was such that he virtually dictated the nomination of his presidential successor, William Howard Taft. He then went big-game hunting in Africa and returned home after making a triumphal tour of the major European cities.

Roosevelt re-entered politics in 1910. The congressional victories of Democrats that year had made clear to all but Old Guard Republicans that Taft could not succeed himself, and in 1912 the insurgent Republican Progressives, who at first used Senator Robert M. La Follette as a stalking-horse, went over to their old leader. When Taft publicly denounced 'political emotionalists,' a long-standing friendship was severed. 'My hat is in the ring,' Roosevelt announced, and he became the standard bearer of the Progressive party, with the political platform of NEW NATIONALISM. This move was fatal to both Roosevelt and the Republicans, for he had bolted his party and split its vote. In the election Taft captured 8 electoral votes, Roosevelt 88, and the Democrat, Woodrow Wilson, was swept into office by 435. The popular vote was less inflated but emphatic nonetheless.

In 1913 Roosevelt went on an exploring trip into the Amazon jungles and thereafter continued his writings on history and politics. He died shortly after the end of World War I, in which he had wished to participate actively. Not since Thomas Jefferson had a President been so versatile. Controversial and paradoxical, Roosevelt was a master politician with a high sense of honor and duty, and a man of magnificent courage.

His fine capacity as a letter-writer is revealed in E. E. Morison's eight-volume edition of *Letters* (1951–54). Biographies include those by H. F. Pringle (1931) and W. H. Harbaugh (1961).

Roosevelt Corollary, see *Caribbean policy*.

ROOT, ELIHU (1845–1937), a graduate of Hamilton (1864), practiced law in New York City and entered Republican politics. As Secretary of War (1898–1904) under McKinley and Theodore Roosevelt, he made drastic reforms in the organization of the army and established the Army War College. In Roosevelt's second Administration, as Secretary of State (1905–9), Root negotiated the ROOT-TAKAHIRA AGREEMENT with Japan, and his efforts to create an international organization were recognized in 1912 by the Nobel Peace prize, bestowed while he was serving as U.S. Senator from New York (1909–15).

ROOT, GEORGE FREDERICK (1820–95), teacher of music at Lowell Mason's Boston Academy of Music and in various schools in New York, wrote gospel songs and sentimental ballads. He is best known for his Civil War songs *The Battle Cry of Freedom; Tramp, Tramp, Tramp;* and *Just Before the Battle, Mother.*

ROOT, JOHN WELLBORN (1850–91), Georgia-born architect, studied at Oxford and graduated from New York University (1869). After working in New York with JAMES RENWICK he became a partner of D. H. BURNHAM in Chicago. The firm pioneered in the development of steel-frame office buildings, and won international recognition by their planning of the WORLD'S COLUMBIAN EXPOSITION (1893).

Root-Takahira Agreement (1908) was made through an exchange of notes at Washington between Secretary of State Root and Ambassador Takahira. It provided that the U.S. and Japan would respect the territorial possessions belonging to each other in the Pacific, and that they would uphold the OPEN DOOR POLICY in China. Implicit in the agreement was the U.S. recognition of Japan's paramount influence in Korea and southern Manchuria.

ROSECRANS, WILLIAM STARKE (1819–98), Ohio-born graduate of the U.S. Military Academy (1842), served in the Union army as a major general, and performed with distinction under Grant in the western theater during 1862. In the CHATTANOOGA CAMPAIGN his performance at MURFREESBORO was a significant strategic accomplishment, but his defeat at Chickamauga (September 1863) was an unmitigated disaster. On the advice of General Grant and Secretary of War Stanton, Lincoln relieved him of command. He later served as minister to Mexico (1868–69), and as a member of Congress (1881–85).

ROSS, BETSY (1752–1836), Philadelphia upholsterer and flagmaker, may have cut and sewed together the first Stars and Stripes, designed by FRANCIS HOPKINSON, but no direct evidence links her with the flag adopted (1777) by the Continental Congress as the national emblem.

Rotary International, founded (1905) in Chicago as a luncheon club primarily for businessmen, in 1965 reported 569,000 members in 10,530 clubs in 116 countries. The organization supports charities, world-wide civic activities, and is chiefly devoted to promoting standards of 'Service.'

Rotation in office is the method used to assure frequent changes of personnel in public office. President Jackson said in his first annual message (1829) that the duties of public office are sufficiently simple that they should be made available to the many, not to the few, and because he often filled vacancies on a partisan basis, he is sometimes alleged to have introduced the SPOILS SYSTEM. Actually, ever since the rise of the party system in Washington's second administration, Presidents have been prone to rotate office holders in an effort to reward party faithfulness.

Rough Riders, so called, were the men officially designated as the First Regiment of U.S. Cavalry Volunteers, led by Colonel Leonard Wood and Lieutenant Colonel Theodore Roosevelt in the Spanish-American War (1898). The flamboyant unit, comprising rangers, cowboys, Indians, and adventurous college students, was recruited largely by Roosevelt, and its successful charge up SAN JUAN HILL (on foot, for their horses had been abandoned in Florida) was headlined in newspapers throughout the country.

Roundup was the method by which western ranchers collected their livestock during the open range cattle period, roughly 1866–90. Cowboys, mounted on ponies trained for the work, gathered cattle in herds, in the spring to brand them and in the fall to select stock for market. RODEOS, the contests of skill among the cowhands, were originally an adjunct of the roundup.

ROWLAND, HENRY AUGUSTUS (1848–1901), the first professor of physics at Johns Hopkins (after 1875), discovered in 1878 that the amount of the deflection of a magnetic needle by a charged sphere revolving about it is entirely a function of the velocity with which the sphere is moving, a phenomenon for which classical physics made no allowance. The discovery, though it did not call forth Einstein's work, anticipated it. Rowland invented the device that makes grating lines in a dividing apparatus, devised a means for ruling diffraction gratings on concave surfaces (thus advancing spectroscopy), and conducted experiments that helped determine the value of the ohm.

ROWLANDSON, MARY WHITE (*c.* 1635–*c.* 1678), daughter of John White, a wealthy proprietor of Lancaster, Massachusetts, was the wife of Joseph Rowlandson, the local minister. During King Philip's War she and her three children were abducted (1676) by hostile Indians. The youngest child died, but after 83 days her husband finally ransomed his wife and two children. In 1682 a colorful *Narrative* of her bondage was published. The account is among the most vigorous and popular of INDIAN CAPTIVITIES; it went through more than 30 editions, the last appearing in 1937.

Royal colonies became the standard type of colonial government in America. With the exception of Connecticut and Rhode Island (which began as squatter colonies, and were later incorporated), all the original Thirteen Colonies began either as CHARTER COLONIES or PROPRIETARY COLONIES. Virginia became the first royal colony in English history (1624), and by 1776 all save Maryland, Pennsylvania, Connecticut, and Rhode Island were royal colonies. In the royal colonies the king was represented by a royal governor assisted by a council, and although elected assemblies represented the people, enacted laws, and controlled the purse, the king had the power of veto. The colonial governments dealt with Parliament through the BOARD OF TRADE AND PLANTATIONS in civil matters, with the Secretary of State for the Southern Department in important political affairs, with the Treasury Department in customs collections, and with the Admiralty in maritime business.

Royal Society (est. 1662), was chartered (1663, 1669) as the Royal Society of London for Improving Natural Knowledge. It remains foremost among British scientific academies. During the American colonial period, election to the Society was an especially coveted honor, and before 1800, seventeen Americans were elected.

John Winthrop, Jr. (Conn.) 1663
William Byrd (Va.) 1696
Cotton Mather (Mass.) 1713
William Brattle (Mass.) 1714
John Leverett (Mass.) 1714
Paul Dudley (Mass.) 1721
Thomas Robie (Mass.) 1725
Zabdiel Boylston (Mass.) 1726
John Winthrop (Conn.) 1734
John Mitchell (Va.) 1748
Benjamin Franklin (Pa.) 1756
John Morgan (Pa.) 1765
John Winthrop (Mass.) 1766
Alexander Garden (S.C.) 1773
Benjamin Thompson, Count Rumford (Mass.) 1779
James Bowdoin (Mass.) 1788
David Rittenhouse (Pa.) 1795

ROYALL, ANNA NEWPORT (1769–1854), born in Maryland of uncertain background, lost the property she inherited from her well-to-do Virginia husband and in 1824 began making a living by writing about her travels from Maine to the Mississippi valley. Though garrulous and rambling, her books are frank, racy, and picturesque. They were widely read for their 'pen-sketches' of famous people whom she came to know or know about. She published two gossipy Washington journals: *Paul Pry* (1831–36) and *The Huntress* (1836–54). To John Quincy Adams she was a 'virago errant' (she was once legally convicted of being a common scold), but her vigorous opinions on government and religion, and her exposure of corrupt officials, were honest attempts to describe the manners of her day as she saw them. Her *Sketches of History, Life, and Manners in the U.S.* (1826), *Mrs. Royall's Pennsylvania* (2 vols., 1829), and *Mrs. Royall's Southern Tour* (2 vols., 1830) are source studies.

ROYCE, JOSIAH (1866–1916), foremost American proponent of ethical IDEALISM, was a lifelong teacher of philosophy at Harvard (1882–1916). His thorough espousal of Hegelianism led him to affirm the essential oneness of things. *The World and the Individual* (2 vols., 1900–1901) makes the point that since man is endowed with a moral will and independence, his ethical obligation is to make his unique contribution to the moral order. Royce developed his concept in *The Philosophy of Loyalty* (1908), which contends that the individual makes his adjustment to life by choosing a social aim that expresses loyalty to a cause. Men are 'saved by the community.' His ethical views were influential at a time when many commentators were contending that America was predominantly materialistic.

Rubber industry became possible after CHARLES GOODYEAR discovered the process of vulcanization (1839), the chemical treatment that strengthens crude rubber. The product thereafter was used for various commercial purposes, but the industry became big business only after automobiles created a market of unprecedented size. When Japan's conquests in Malaya during World War II cut off the Western World's most important natural rubber source, the U.S. speeded up the development and manufacturing of synthetic rubber. By 1960 natural rubber production in the U.S. was some 500,000 tons annually. Synthetic rubber production was twice that, and it amounted to 85 per cent of the world's total.

RUEF, ABE [ABRAHAM] (1865–1936), a graduate of the University of California at Berkeley (1884), practiced law and for a brief time (1903–7) was undisputed political boss of San Francisco through his labor party. In 1909 the 'Curly Boss' was convicted of bribery and extortion, and he was sentenced to a fourteen-year prison term.

RUFFIN, EDMUND (1794–1865), Virginia pioneer in soil chemistry, against much opposition maintained that worn-out soil could be restored to fertility by the application of marl. He propounded this view in *An Essay on Calcareous Manures* (1832), and proved it by bringing fruitfulness to worn-out tobacco lands of the tidewater region. He founded (1833) the *Farmer's Register,* an excellent agricultural journal which he edited for ten years. A violent 'fire-eater,' he was so ardent a secessionist that he moved to South Carolina before the Civil War, and was given the 'honor' of firing the first shot on Fort Sumter. He committed suicide upon hearing the news of Lee's surrender at Appomattox.

'Rugged individualism' is a popular concept of the political, economic, and social libertarian principles considered intrinsic to the American way of life. During the Hoover administration the phrase was used as a justification for the LAISSEZ-FAIRE approach to government regulation of business.

Rule of reason, so called, in U.S. Supreme Court decisions was the application of a 'reasonable' interpretation of legislation, the intent of which was open to question. The phrase developed in an effort to explain the meaning of the SHERMAN ANTITRUST ACT (1890): the Court tried to resolve the issue whether 'all combinations in restraint of trade' meant 'all *unreasonable* combinations in restraint of trade.' Chief Justice White, a strict constructionist, wrote the rule of reason decisions in antitrust cases. Justices O. W. HOLMES and J. M. HARLAN opposed this expansion of the discretion of judges at the expense of Congress, arguing that such interpretations were an unwarrantable interference with the POLICE POWER of the states. Their view was adopted in later Court rulings.

Rule of 1756, see *Essex Case.*

'Rum, Romanism, and Rebellion,' see *Blaine, J. G.*

Rum trade, see *West India trade.*

RUMFORD, COUNT, see *Thompson, Benjamin.*

Rural Free Delivery (1896) was a system created by a congressional enactment that extended postal service to those outside urban areas. The pressure of farm groups largely helped establish it. The system made possible the tremendous growth of MAIL-ORDER HOUSES in the two decades that followed its inauguration.

RUSH, BENJAMIN (1745–1813), the most influential American medical scientist of his day, after graduation from the College of New Jersey (Princeton, 1760) took his medical degree at Edinburgh (1768). In 1769 he became the first professor of chemistry in America, at the College of Philadelphia, and the next year he published *A Syllabus of a Course of Lectures on Chemistry,* the earliest American text on the subject. As a member of the Continental Congress (1776–77) he signed the Declaration of Independence, and thereafter he served for a time as Surgeon General of the Continental army. In 1782 he established the Philadelphia Dispensary, the first free dispensary in the country.

As professor of medicine and clinical practice at the University of Pennsylvania after 1792, Rush created the best medical school in the U.S., but his persistent advocacy of bloodletting for most ills delayed for some years the discontinuance of a practice that many doctors opposed. His *Medical Inquiries and Observations upon the Diseases of the Mind* (1812), though doctrinaire, is the earliest clinical work on mental disorders. He looked upon crime as a disease of the mind, called for the abolition of capital punishment and whipping posts, and outlined a program for the rehabilitation of criminals and for transforming jails into normal communities.

RUSH, RICHARD (1780–1859), lawyer and statesman, was the son of BENJAMIN RUSH. He graduated from the College of New Jersey (Princeton, 1797) and while practicing law in Philadelphia he accepted a government assignment which led to posts of responsibility under several Presidents. While acting temporarily as Monroe's Secretary of State (1817), he helped negotiate the RUSH-BAGOT AGREEMENT, settling a U.S.–Canada dispute resulting from the War of 1812, then went as minister to England (1817–25), where he negotiated a treaty for the joint occupation of Oregon. He aided John Quincy Adams in formulating the Monroe Doctrine (1823), and entered Adams's cabinet as Secretary of the Treasury (1825–28). He was vice presidential candidate in Adams's unsuccessful 1828 bid for reelection, and twenty years later he went as Polk's minister to France (1847–49). His talent for effecting high-level accommodations was used there during the revolution of 1848, which established the Second French Republic.

Rush-Bagot Agreement (1817), a sequel to the Treaty of GHENT, which ended the War of 1812, was the arrangement for mutual disarmament on the Great Lakes. It was effected through an exchange of notes between the British minister to the U.S., Charles Bagot, and the acting Secretary of State, RICHARD RUSH. The U.S. Senate gave it unanimous approval. It forestalled a threatened naval armament race by strictly limiting the number and size of naval forces on those inland waters. This treaty inaugurated a policy of amity between the U.S. and Canada which has never been altered.

Russian Church, see *Eastern Orthodox Churches.*

Rutgers University, with its chief campus at New Brunswick, New Jersey, was chartered by George III and opened (1766) as Queen's College by leaders of the Dutch Reformed Church. In 1825 it took its present name to honor the benefactions of Colonel Henry Rutgers (1745–1830), a New York philanthropist. In 1864 the New Jersey legislature designated the Rutgers Scientific School as the land grant college for the state, and in 1917 named Rutgers the state university. The New Jersey College for Women (now Douglass College) was established as an affiliate in 1918. Other divisions are located throughout the state. In 1965, with an endowment of $21,000,000 and a faculty of 1800, Rutgers enrolled 23,480 students.

RUTH, BABE [GEORGE HERMAN] (1895–1948), one of baseball's greatest players, began his professional career in 1914. As an outfielder, he was long with the New York Yankees (1920–34), and in 1927 he set a record of 60 home runs in one season. A colorful hero to millions of fans, the 'Bambino' set many other records, and for two seasons (1930–31) commanded the highest salary ($80,000) ever paid to a ball player up to that time. Almost singlehandedly he transformed baseball from a defensive to an offensive contest, in which strategy was subordinated to the sheer power of hitting home runs.

RUTLEDGE, ANN (1816–35), was daughter of the innkeeper at New Salem, Illinois, when Abraham Lincoln lived there (1831–37). She was engaged to Lincoln's friend John McNamar at the time, and the fact that her sudden death from malarial fever grieved Lincoln deeply grew into the legend (now discredited) of Lincoln's romantic attachment to her.

RUTLEDGE, JOHN (1739–1800), born in Charleston, South Carolina, after studying law in London, soon rose to prominence at the bar of South Carolina. He resigned as member of the Continental Congress (1774–76) to serve his state as president of its general assembly (1776–82), and then returned to Congress (1782–83). Washington appointed him an associate justice of the U.S. Supreme Court (1789), a post he left in 1791 to become chief justice of the supreme court of South Carolina. Washington called him back (1795) to succeed John Jay as Chief Justice of the U.S. Supreme Court, but the Senate rejected the nomination because Rutledge had strongly opposed JAY'S TREATY, which at that time was a burning political issue. He presided only during the August term.

RUXTON, GEORGE FREDERICK (1820–48), English explorer, after traveling northward from Mexico City, spent the winter of 1846–47 near Pueblo, on the Arkansas river, and reported vividly on the MOUNTAIN MEN in *Adventures in Mexico and the Rocky Mountains*

(1847), and *Life in the Far West* (1849, repr. 1915).

RYDER, Albert Pinkham (1847–1917), Massachusetts-born painter, lived most of his life as a recluse in New York. Largely self-taught, and indifferent to material success or critical acclaim, he constantly experimented in oils, and his 150 canvases, chiefly pastoral landscapes, show him to be among the most imaginative of American painters. Representative of his power to symbolize the mystery and loneliness of ocean vistas are *Toilers of the Sea* and *Moonlight—Marine* (Metropolitan Museum). The latter is abstract in form.

RYNNING, Ole (1809–38), Norwegian-born immigrant leader, settled in Illinois, where he wrote one of the first so-called 'America Books,' handbooks for immigrants. His *True Account of America for the Information and Help of Peasant and Commoner* (Christiana, 1838) was one of the earliest and most influential guides, and it encouraged the great Norwegian emigration in the two decades that followed its publication.

Ryswick, Treaty of (1697), which ended king william's war, restored the *status quo ante* in the American colonies, and turned the Hudson Bay dispute over to commissioners, who reached no agreement. Queen Anne's War began in 1702.

Ryukyu Islands (numbering 64), between southern Japan and Taiwan (Formosa), were ceded by Japan to the U.S. in 1951. Naha, Okinawa, is the seat of government, administered by a High Commissioner responsible to the Secretary of Defense. The islands are an important military base. They had a population of 932,000 in 1964.

S

SAARINEN, Eero (1910–61), son of the architect ELIEL SAARINEN, after graduation from Yale (1934) worked with his father. He was phenomenally productive. His gusto and imagination appear in such structures as the Thomas J. Watson Research Center, I.B.M. (Yorktown, N.Y.), the Dulles Memorial jet airport (Washington, D.C.), the General Motors Technical Center (Dearborn, Mich.), and the stainless steel arch of the Jefferson National Exposition Memorial (St. Louis). His never-ending 'search for form' contributed to the diversity of his accomplishments, which have led many to regard him as the foremost American architect of his generation.

SAARINEN, Eliel (1873–1950), Finnish-born city planner and architect, came to the U.S. in 1923, after establishing an international reputation by his functional designs of public buildings. Although his design (1922) for the proposed 30-story Chicago Tribune Building was rejected (because it won second prize), it is regarded as the most influential scheme ever offered in the history of architectural competitions. It combined engineering skill with aesthetic sense of volume, not mass. In the U.S. he is best known for such large buildings as those of the Cranbrook Foundation (Michigan), where he headed the Academy of Art.

SABIN, Joseph (1821–81), English-born bibliographer, in 1848 established himself as a dealer in rare books in New York and Philadelphia. His *Bibliotheca Americana: A Dictionary of Books Relating to America, from Its Discovery to the Present Time* (29 vols., 1868–1936) is a monumental work, distinguished for its coverage, bibliographical notes, and high degree of accuracy. (It was continued by Wilberforce Eames and completed by R. W. G. Vail.)

SACAJAWEA (*fl.* 1803–6), or 'Bird Woman,' was the Shoshone Indian guide on the LEWIS AND CLARK EXPEDITION, and wife of the expedition's interpreter, Toussaint Charbonneau. Her patient and heroic attitude during the hardships of the journey greatly impressed the leaders of the expedition. During the return she and her husband were allowed to leave the party at one of the Mandan villages. Her subsequent history is unknown.

Sacco-Vanzetti Case (1920–27) was a *cause celèbre* which developed after two Italian-born philosophical anarchists (Nicola Sacco and Bartolomeo Vanzetti) were accused of murdering a paymaster and his guard at a shoe factory in South Braintree, Massachusetts. Although the evidence against them was insubstantial, they were convicted (1921) and sentenced to death. The public protest, here and abroad, stemmed from the belief that they had been tried for their radical views rather than for the crime. In 1927 Governor Fuller appointed a commission (President Lowell of Harvard, chairman) which sustained the verdict, and the defendants were executed. Uncertainty about their guilt still persists.

Sacramento river, 382 miles long, rises in northern California near Mount Shasta, flows southwest, is joined by the San Joaquin river, and enters San Francisco Bay. Navigable some 260 miles inland by small steamer, the river was the main artery by which the Sacramento valley was opened to the gold rush. Reclamation projects in recent years along its course have developed the central valley of California into a fertile agricultural region.

ST. CLAIR, Arthur (1734–1818), Scottish-born major general in the Continental army, was in command at Fort Ticonderoga when it was surrendered to the British (1777) without a shot. (A court-martial fully cleared him of blame.) He was a Pennsylvania delegate to the Continental Congress (1785–87), and was serving as its president (1787) when he was appointed the first governor of the Northwest Territory. After his humiliating defeat by inferior numbers of Ohio Indians he resigned his commission (1792), and when he later opposed the creation of the state of Ohio, President Jefferson removed him from office (1802). He had proved dilatory or blundering in erecting key defenses, providing supplies and payments to the militia, and in assessing the Indian problem. In 1812 he published a defense of his conduct, which is useful as source material. He spent his last days in poverty.

SAINT-GAUDENS, AUGUSTUS (1848–1907), Irish-born sculptor, was reared from infancy in New York City and trained as a cameo-cutter. After professional study of sculpture in Paris and Rome, in 1872 he returned to the U.S., where his early *Hiawatha* (Saratoga, N.Y.) led to a commission for the statue of Admiral Farragut (1881) in New York City. This statue, animated and realistic, introduced a new standard for public monuments. Some of his other achievements are the *Shaw Memorial* (Boston Common), done in high relief, the notable equestrian *Sherman* (New York City), the bronze tablet of *Stevenson* in Edinburgh, and the seated *Lincoln* in Chicago.

Saint-Gaudens took pains to study and reflect upon the life and background of his subjects, and his statues are eloquent expressions of their personalities. He was gifted with high imagination and his techniques were those of a master craftsman. The foremost American sculptor of his time, he could also create imaginative feeling, perhaps no better expressed than in his (Henry) Adams Memorial (Rock Creek Cemetery, Washington, D.C.), with its suggestion of limitless repose.

St. Lawrence river, one of the principal rivers of North America, is the 744-mile-long outlet of the Great Lakes, and with them it forms a 2350-mile waterway from Lake Superior to the Atlantic. In 1535 Jacques Cartier ascended the river to Montreal. The river system was long the main highway into the continent for explorers, fur traders, and missionaries. That part of the river that flows from Lake Ontario along northern New York forms the border between the U.S. and Canada. The completion of the St. Lawrence Seaway in 1959 opened ocean navigation into the heart of the continent.

St. Lawrence Seaway, see *Great Lakes.*

St. Louis, just below the confluence of the Missouri and Mississippi rivers, is the principal city in the state of Missouri, with a population (in 1960) of 750,000. Founded as a fur trading post in 1764, it later became the capital of the Louisiana Territory (1805), and the chief market and supply point for western trade and exploration. It was the headquarters of the Lewis and Clark Expedition (1804–6) and the gateway north to the OREGON TRAIL and south to the SANTA FE TRAIL. Incorporated as a town in 1808 (and as a city in 1823), it came to be one of the great U.S. river ports, helped by a large immigration from Germany added to the earlier French element.

St. Louis was a Union stronghold during the Civil War, and soon thereafter it became a manufacturing and railroad center. Its cultural development has always kept abreast of its industrial growth; in 1904 the Louisiana Purchase Exposition was held there. It is the seat of many institutions of higher learning, including St. Louis University (est. 1818), the oldest west of the Mississippi, and Washington University (est. 1853).

St. Louis *Post-Dispatch,* see *Pulitzer, Joseph.*

St. Mihiel, Battle of (12–16 September 1918), was one of the most important American actions in World War I. After the battle of the MARNE, the American army conducted operations between the Moselle river and the Argonne forest. Nine American divisions and four French divisions, under the command of General John J. Pershing, faced nine German divisions deeply entrenched at St. Mihiel, the rail center linking Verdun, Toul, and Nancy. By obliterating the salient under attack and establishing their line in a position to threaten Metz, the Allies were in a position to begin the MEUSE-ARGONNE OFFENSIVE, the final push that ended the war.

'Salary Grab' Act (1873) doubled the President's salary to $50,000 a year and increased that of other government officials, including congressmen (from $5000 to $7500). Public indignation forced Congress to repeal the Act, but the increases for the President and the Supreme Court justices were kept.

Salem, Massachusetts, founded in 1626, was briefly the capital of the Massachusetts Bay Colony before Boston was settled (1630). Called Naumkeag by the Indians, Salem was the earliest Puritan settlement to build a church (1629). In nearby Salem Village (Danvers) the WITCHCRAFT DELUSION erupted (1692). Salem was a port of entry, and by the end of the 18th century it was a leading seaport and the home of prosperous merchants. Its decline set in about 1850, but mansions designed by SAMUEL MC INTIRE still recall the days of commercial affluence. Its population, steadily declining in the 20th century, was 39,000 in 1960. It was the birthplace of Nathaniel Hawthorne and is the site of the House of the Seven Gables. The Essex Institute specializes in colonial records.

Sales taxes, paid by the consumer on retail purchases, in the U.S. are collected only by state and municipal governments. Kentucky enacted the first such state tax (1930), and other states and municipalities soon adopted similar legislation as emergency measures in the wake of the depression following the PANIC OF 1929. Most such laws now have become part of the permanent statutes, and at present about 40 states levy sales taxes, generally ranging from 2 to 4 per cent. In 1965 the highest (5 per cent) were levied in New York and Pennsylvania.

Salish Indians, see *Flathead Indians.*

SALK, JONAS EDWARD (1914–), professor of preventive medicine at the University of Pittsburgh, in 1954 developed a vaccine for use against poliomyelitis. Tests of the Salk vaccine, carried out in 1955 in 44 states, indicated its high degree of effectiveness against paralytic strains of the virus. That same year Dr. Albert Bruce Sabin (1906–) announced his development of a live oral polio vaccine, which quickly won wide application.

SALOMON, HAYM (1740–85), Polish-born financier, after coming to America (1772), established a successful brokerage house in New York. Twice imprisoned by the British as a spy (1776–78), he escaped to the American lines, founded a business in Philadelphia, and aided Robert Morris not only by securing loans from the Netherlands and France, but also by pledging his own banking fortune. But his heavy loans to the patriot cause led to his postwar bankruptcy, and his sacrifices in health during imprisonment led to an early death. His heirs were left penniless.

SALTONSTALL, SIR RICHARD (1586–1658), member of a prominent Yorkshire family, was an original patentee and assistant of the Massachusetts Bay Company. With THOMAS DUDLEY and JOHN WINTHROP he led the migration in 1630, and helped found Boston and nearby towns. He later returned to England, but his children remained, and his descendants have continued to be leaders in public affairs to the present.

Salvation Army, an international evangelistic movement, was founded in England (1865) by William Booth (1829–1912), and organized in the U.S. in 1880. Its greatest expansion in the U.S. occurred during the period that EVANGELINE BOOTH, the founder's daughter, served as commander (1904–34). It is patterned on the structure of military groups, and has as its objective social service and the spiritual rehabilitation of the underprivileged. Its membership in the U.S. in 1965 exceeded 264,000.

Samoa, see *American Samoa.*

SAMPSON, WILLIAM THOMAS (1840–1902), was a graduate of the U.S. Naval Academy (1861), which he later served as superintendent (1886–90). He commanded the North Atlantic squadron at the outbreak of the Spanish-American War (1898) and planned the attack that captured the Spanish fleet at SANTIAGO. A controversy ensued over credit for the victory, since Commodore Winfield S. Schley (1839–1911) actually directed the engagement, but the dispute was officially settled in Sampson's favor.

Sanctions, as punitive measures, include military intervention or economic embargo. In 1934 the U.S. applied sanctions during the CHACO WAR between Bolivia and Paraguay by placing an embargo on arms. The efforts of the League of Nations to apply sanctions against Italy for its invasion of Abyssinia in 1935 proved ineffective. The power of the United Nations to punish aggression includes the infliction of sanctions, but the method is sparingly used.

SANDBURG, Carl [August] (1878–), son of a Swedish immigrant blacksmith, was born in Galesburg, Illinois. As a young man he was an active socialist. He published his first volume of unconventional free verse and colloquialisms, *Chicago Poems,* in 1916. As a poet he is often compared to Whitman, whose knowledge of the nation was less surely grounded. Sandburg's six-volume biography of Lincoln (1926–39) is the most readable of longer studies, especially in the earlier volumes. Sandburg was an articulate champion of all classes, regions, and races of the U.S., and everything he wrote expressed his belief in the collective wisdom of the people.

Sandemanians, followers of the Scottish-born Robert Sandeman (1718–71), were a religious sect that protested against church establishments and contended that salvation depends solely upon each man's 'just notion of the person and work of Christ.' Sandeman emigrated to New England in 1764, and for a time his churches gained adherents despite vigorous opposition from the orthodox. Sandeman churches ceased to exist during the 19th century.

SANDYS, Sir Edwin (1561–1629), was an English parliamentary leader and a chief promoter of the London Company (1606), which body he served as treasurer for two years (1619–20). Ingenious and resourceful, Sandys infused fresh life into a venture that had been dogged by disaster, and he dominated the lesser shareholders who were interested in developing trade in Virginia. But his enthusiasm led the company to overexpand, and in 1624 it was forced into receivership.

His brother, George Sandys (1578–1644), in 1621 accompanied the new governor of the colony, Sir Francis Wyatt, to Virginia, where he remained until 1631, serving on the governor's council. While in Virginia he produced his famous translation of Ovid's *Metamorphosis* (1626), the first translation of a classic in America.

San Francisco, major Pacific coast port, with a population (1960) of 740,000, is the center of a metropolitan area of 2,780,000. Situated in central California on one of the world's best harbors, it was founded by Anza (1776), and called Yerba Buena until it was renamed San Francisco in 1847. The California Gold Rush (1849) transformed it from a small village into a bustling, lawless frontier town, and by 1850 it had a population of 25,000 and was conducting a flourishing trade with the Orient. The discovery of the Comstock Lode in Nevada (1859) opened a second boom period, and soon the pony express (1860) and the Union Pacific Railroad (1869) linked the city with the East.

San Francisco became accustomed to rapid transitions early, and the city passed quickly through its era of grandiose castles on Nob Hill and settled into a conservatism uniquely its own. By 1880, with a population of 233,000, it had become the financial and cultural metropolis of the Far West. In April 1906 a catastrophic earthquake, followed by a four-day fire, demolished much of the city, but rebuilding was rapid and substantial. The opening of the Panama Canal, which swelled the trade of the port, was celebrated by the Panama-Pacific Exposition of 1915. Completion of two great bridges, the San Francisco-Oakland Bay Bridge and the Golden Gate Bridge across the mouth of the harbor, gave occasion for a second exposition (1939–40). The fact that the conference that drafted the United Nations Charter (1945) met in San Francisco confirmed its world importance. The cosmopolitan character and individuality of the city is legendary. Five major institutions of higher learning are situated in the area, including the University of California at Berkeley (est. 1873), and Stanford (est. 1885).

San Francisco Conference (April–June 1945), officially the United Nations Conference on International Organization, implemented the Senate's adoption of the Connally Resolution by calling together 50 nations at San Francisco (chosen to emphasize the growing importance of the Pacific region) to draw up the charter of the United Nations. The American delegation, headed by Secretary of State Edward R. Stettinius (1900–1949), was filled out by two Republicans, Senator Arthur Vandenberg and Representative Charles Eaton; and two Democrats, Senator Tom Connally and Representative Sol Bloom. By October, 29 nations had ratified the document, and the charter of the UNITED NATIONS ORGANIZATION went into effect.

Sanitary Commission, U.S., was created (1861) on the model of the British Sanitary Commission, which had been organized by Florence Nightingale during the Crimean War. It was a privately supported volunteer auxiliary to the Army Medical Corps, and gave aid by fitting out and supplying hospital units, caring for the wounded at the front, and looking after the comforts of the soldiers. Its functions were later taken over by the AMERICAN NATIONAL RED CROSS.

San Jacinto, Battle of (1836), the last important battle of the war for Texas independence, was won by General Sam Houston and his 800 Texans, fighting Santa Anna's 1400 Mexicans. Houston dictated armistice terms that established *de facto* independence.

San Juan Hill, Battle of (1 July 1898), the one major land engagement during the Spanish-American War, was part of the American advance on Santiago, Cuba. A division, including the ROUGH RIDERS, under heavy fire, seized the heights above the city, and thus were in position to place the Spanish fleet under artillery bombardment. (American casualties totaled 1500.) The success precipitated the naval battle of SANTIAGO, which ended the war.

SANKEY, IRA D., see *Moody, D. L.*

San Lorenzo, Treaty of, see *Pinckney's Treaty.*

SANTA ANNA, ANTONIO LÓPEZ DE (1794–1876), Mexican general, was dictator of Mexico when he led the attack on the ALAMO (1836). Following his defeat by Sam Houston at SAN JACINTO he went into temporary eclipse. An opportunist with a measure of political skill, he was president of Mexico and commanding general of his nation's forces during the Mexican War (1846–48). He was exiled after his defeat. His subsequent history, which continued to be turbulent, is entirely associated with Mexican power politics.

Santa Fe Trail, leading from Independence, Missouri, to Santa Fe, New Mexico, was the principal trading route into the Southwest from 1822 (when Santa Fe was freed from Spanish rule) until it was superseded by the Atchison, Topeka, and Santa Fe Railroad in the 1880's. When wagons were able to replace horses and pack mules after 1825, commerce in the Southwest was greatly expanded. Commercial rivals organized themselves into semi-military units to cross the dangerous Plains country, and they disbanded and resumed their rivalry when the trek was finished. This important caravan trail, which assured the growth of such early Spanish trade centers as Taos, is vividly described by JOSIAH GREGG in his *Commerce of the Prairies* (1844).

SANTAYANA, GEORGE (1863–1952), Spanish-born philosopher and poet, after graduation from Harvard (1886), for many years taught philosophy there (1889–1912). He then returned to Europe, eventually settling in Italy. His study *The Sense of Beauty* (1896) was an important contribution to aesthetics, but his major philosophical works appeared in two remarkable series: *The Life of Reason* (5 vols., 1905–6), and *The Realms of Being* (4 vols., 1927–40). The latter stresses the role of faith but retains his earlier belief that scientific analysis should be the method of reasoning. 'Everything ideal has a natural basis and everything natural an ideal development.' All moral preferences as well as scientific beliefs, he contended, are determined inflexibly by distributions of matter within men's brains, which no science can fathom, and are controlled by the material dynamics of nature.

His impressively large body of writing includes a collection of *Poems* (1923). *Character and Opinion in the U.S.* (1920) is an analysis of materialism and idealism. His novel, *The Last Puritan* (1935), gives fictional form to his philosophy, and it achieved considerable popular success. *Persons and Places* (3 vols., 1944–53) is his autobiography. Whether or not his philosophical theories gained a following among professional critics, his style, emotional depth, and poetic sensitivity assure him a permanent place in literature.

Santiago, Battle of (3 July 1898), the major naval engagement in the Spanish-American War, ended Spanish domination in Cuba. It took place two days after the successful American storming of SAN JUAN HILL placed Admiral Cervera's fleet, blockaded in the harbor, in the hazard of destruction by bombardment. Cervera chose to leave the harbor and engage the American fleet blockading him. In a four-hour engagement with part of Admiral Sampson's North American squadron, which was headed by Commodore Schley, the Spanish fleet was destroyed. American casualties: one killed and one wounded.

Santo Domingo, see *Dominican Republic*.

SAPIR, EDWARD (1884–1939), German-born linguist and anthropologist, graduated from Columbia (1904), and was professor of anthropology and linguistics at Chicago (1925–31) and at Yale (1931–39). He was an influential pioneer in the development of descriptive linguistics, edited several texts of American Indian languages, and became internationally known for such studies as *Time Perspective in Aboriginal American Culture* (1916), and *Language: An Introduction to the Study of Speech* (1921).

Saratoga Campaign (June–October 1777) in the War of Independence originated with the British plan for a knockout blow. In February the War Office approved a strategy intended to separate New England from New York and the other colonies. General JOHN BURGOYNE was to move south from Canada through the Champlain valley to Albany, General Sir WILLIAM HOWE was to move north from New York up the Hudson to meet him, and a contingent of British and Indian troops in the Mohawk valley, under Barry St. Leger, was to complete the triangular assault.

Burgoyne left Montreal in early June, with an expeditionary force numbering far fewer than the 8000 he had requested, and ill equipped for frontier fighting. The problems of co-ordinating such a venture were great in themselves, and compounded by the fact that by gross negligence the War Office delayed sending orders to Howe until August, when Howe was outside Philadelphia preparing for his engagement against Washington at Brandywine, which he successfully fought in September. Howe never moved north at all.

Burgoyne had little trouble in taking Ticonderoga in July, but the disasters thereafter were inevitable. St. Leger's contingent, after an encounter with troops led by General NICHOLAS HERKIMER, returned to Canada. A force of Burgoyne's Hessians, dispatched to raid patriot stores, was overwhelmed in the battle of BENNINGTON, and on 19 September Burgoyne himself lost an engagement at FREEMAN'S FARM. Only a quick retreat could have saved him, but he dug in, vainly hoping that Sir HENRY CLINTON, commanding British forces at headquarters in New York, could effect a juncture. Clinton's forces at that moment were nominal. He did attempt an advance up the Hudson valley, but the resistance he met at Kingston blocked further progress, and early in October he turned back.

Meanwhile desertions (principally Indians) decimated Burgoyne's army, then fallen back to Saratoga, where Americans were on his front, rear, and flanks, commanded by HORATIO GATES and his competent lieutenants BENEDICT ARNOLD, BENJAMIN LINCOLN, and THADDEUS KOSCIUSKO. On 17 October Burgoyne surrendered his entire army of some 5700 to Gates under the terms of the 'Convention of Saratoga,' by which Burgoyne was able to return his force to England, under pledge not to fight again. The victory was decisive in the war, for it encouraged France to give official aid to the colonies.

SARGENT, JOHN SINGER (1856–1925), born in Italy of American parents, was trained as a painter at the Beaux-Arts in Paris (1874). His first exhibit (1877) attracted favorable notice, and by 1885, when he had established himself in London, his portraits were in demand. He was a productive artist and a master of 'bravura' brushwork. His *Madame X* (Metropolitan Museum), the full-length delineation of a professional beauty, Mme. Gautreau, shocked the public and made Sargent famous. It is his masterpiece precisely because in it he rendered the surface with unadorned frankness. His symbolic murals, *The History of Religion* (Boston Public Library), depict man's aspirations with a similar cold urbanity. In later years he produced a series of skillfully impressionistic landscapes in water color.

SARTON, George [Alfred Leon] (1884–1956), Belgian-born science historian, began teaching at Harvard in 1916. Shortly after completing his graduate studies at the University of Ghent he founded (1912) and edited *Isis,* an international review devoted to the history and philosophy of science. In 1936 he founded and edited *Osiris,* studies in the history of learning and culture. Sarton was a wide-ranging and deeply informed scholar, and he wrote voluminously. His studies include *Introduction to the History of Science* (from Homer to Roger Bacon) (2 vols., 1927–31), *The Life of Science* (1948), and *Science and Tradition* (1951).

Sauk and Fox Indians, of Algonquian stock, during the 17th century were encountered by French explorers in the upper Great Lakes region, and were thought to number some 6500. During the 1830's their famous chief black hawk, seeking to stem the advance of frontier settlements into western Illinois, precipitated the black hawk war. Today remnants of their tribe (some 1600) are settled on reservations, mainly in Iowa and Oklahoma.

Savo Island, Battle of (9 August 1942), took place during the solomon islands campaign in World War II, when a Japanese cruiser force surprised, outfought, and sank four out of five heavy cruisers (three U.S., one Australian) that were protecting transports unloading off Guadalcanal. This was one of the worst defeats in the history of the U.S. navy. It deprived the U.S. forces on Guadalcanal of air and naval support. A six-month fight for the island followed, during which period the decisive naval victory in the battle of guadalcanal (November 1942) tipped the balance to the Allies.

Saybrook Platform (1708) was drawn up by a synod of churches at the request of the Connecticut legislature, to revise the ecclesiastical government of the colony. Believing that the cambridge platform (1648) gave too much autonomy to individual churches, conservatives wished to organize county associations with disciplinary powers and supervision over the choice of pastors. The Platform was adopted, and thereafter the church polity in Connecticut was in effect Presbyterian.

SAYE AND SELE, William Fiennes, 1st Viscount (1582–1662), prominent English Puritan, with Baron Brooke and others entered into colonization schemes. They obtained a deed to Saybrook, Connecticut (named for them), and set up john winthrop the younger as governor (1635). In the same decade they bought land in New Hampshire, where they planned to settle and establish a hereditary aristocracy, but they lost interest in the project when they encountered the strong antagonism of New Englanders, and they sold their properties (1641).

Scalawags, see *Carpetbaggers.*

Scalping, a sign of victory, was practiced by some Indian tribes, and was supposed to be performed only on the dead. After a circular cut was made around the crown of the head, the skin was torn off. The whites also engaged in the practice, with the difference that, while the Indians scalped for honor, the settlers did so for the Indian scalp bounties offered by colonial authorities at so much a head, usually $25 or $50.

SCHAFF, Philip (1819–93), Swiss-born biblical scholar and church historian, came to the U.S. in 1844, where he first taught in the German Reformed Theological Seminary, Mercersburg, Pennsylvania, and later in Union Theological Seminary (1869–93). He was widely recognized in his day as an interpreter of the religious thought of Germany. He wrote prodigiously and is best known as editor of the great *Schaff-Herzog Encyclopedia of Religious Knowledge* (1884). His *America: A Sketch of the Political, Social, and Religious Character* (1855; repr., 1961) is the pre-eminent account by an early 19th-century immigrant of the civilization of the U.S.

SCHECHTER, Solomon (1847–1915), Romanian-born rabbi, came to New York City (1902) from Cambridge University to assume the presidency of the

Jewish Theological Seminary of America. He was one of the notable Talmudists of his day, and he was recognized as the leader of Jewish scholarship in America. His writings include *Studies in Judaism* (2 ser., 1896, 1908), and *Some Aspects of Rabbinic Theology* (1909).

Schechter Case (1935), see *National Industrial Recovery Act.*

Schenck* v. *U.S. (1919) was a case that resulted in a unanimous U.S. Supreme Court ruling, delivered by Justice Holmes, upholding the wartime ESPIONAGE ACT as not in violation of the First Amendment. It found that Schenck's pamphlets (issued to draftees by the Socialist party) had encouraged real resistance to the draft in wartime. Holmes argued that 'the most stringent protection of free speech would not protect a man in falsely shouting fire in a theater and causing a panic.' The decision is memorable because it established a 'clear and present danger' (in this instance, war) as the only justification for suspending the constitutional guarantee of freedom of speech.

SCHLESINGER, ARTHUR MEIER (1888–1965), professor of history at Harvard (1924–54), was best known for his interpretation of social history in such books as *The Colonial Merchants and the American Revolution* (1918), *The Rise of the City, 1878–1898* (1933), and *Political and Social Growth of the American People, 1865–1940* (1941).

His son, ARTHUR MEIER SCHLESINGER, JR. (1917–), likewise a professor of history at Harvard (after 1946), first became widely known for his *Age of Jackson* (1945), which focuses on the struggle of Jacksonian democracy against the traditional Jeffersonians. Other writings include *The Crisis of the Old Order* (1957), *The Coming of the New Deal* (1958) and *A Thousand Days* (1965), dealing with the Kennedy era. He served as special assistant to President Kennedy (1961–63).

SCHOENBERG, ARNOLD (1874–1951), Austrian-born composer, and one of the important 20th-century musical innovators, developed musical forms of such technical difficulty as at first to arouse hostile demonstrations. He originated his enormously influential 12-tone, or serial, technique in his piano piece, *Opus 23, No. 5* (1923). In 1933 he began teaching in the U.S., and he became a citizen eight years later. During his 'American period' he alternated between rigorous use of the 12-tone technique (*Violin Concerto, Op. 36*) and a more traditional tonal style (*Variations on a Recitative, Op. 40*). Such works as his cantata, *A Survivor from Warsaw,* and his remarkable (unfinished) opera, *Moses and Aaron* (1932–51), reflect his close identification with Jewish traditions. Schoenberg's serial technique decisively shaped the course of American music in the mid-20th century.

SCHOOLCRAFT, HENRY ROWE (1793–1864), born near Albany, New York, was a pioneer in the broad study of Indian cultures. As geologist for the upper Great Lakes expedition of Lewis Cass, Schoolcraft made topographical surveys, and he described the region in *A Narrative Journal* (1821). He began his ethnological studies following his appointment (1822) as government superintendent of Indian affairs on the northwest frontier with headquarters at Sault Ste. Marie. There he married an Ojibwa woman and made studies of Ojibwa language and lore. His *Algic Researches* (1839), describing the inner and spiritual existence of Algonquian tribes, was followed by other investigations, the most voluminous being *Historical and Statistical Information Respecting . . . the Indian Tribes of the U.S.* (6 vols., 1851–57). Through him in large part the lore of the Indians entered American literature.

Schools, see *Education.*

SCHOULER, JAMES (1839–1920), historian and lawyer, after graduation from Harvard (1859) served in the Union army before taking up law practice in Boston. He lectured on law at Boston University (1883–1902) and at the National University, Washington, D.C. (1888–1908), and on American history at Johns Hopkins (1891–1908). His *History of the U.S.* (7 vols., 1880–1913), covering the period 1783–1877, is narrative in style and primarily a political and constitutional interpretation, defining history as the record 'of consecutive public events.' His other legal and historical writings include *The Law of Domestic Relations* (1889), and *Constitutional Studies* (1897). Like most of his professional rivals, Schouler disliked radical Reconstruction and the coming of the Irish and other immigrants, though he glorified the 'common man.'

SCHUMPETER, Joseph Alois (1883–1950), Austrian-born economist, taught at Graz and at Bonn, and served as Austrian minister of finance (1919–20), before coming to the U.S., where he was professor of economics at Harvard after 1932. His studies of the entrepreneur as the dynamic factor in shifting business equilibrium include *Business Cycles* (1939), an analysis of the capitalist process; and *Capitalism, Socialism, and Democracy* (1942).

SCHURZ, Carl (1829–1906), German-born statesman and political reformer, while a student at the University of Bonn (which later honored him with a degree) became a leader in the revolutionary movement (1848–49) and was compelled to flee his country. He migrated to the U.S. (1852), and in 1856 settled on a farm in Watertown, Wisconsin, where his wife opened the first kindergarten in the U.S., and where he joined the newly formed Republican party. An able orator, he was in wide demand during the campaign of 1860, and was so effective in tipping the election in Lincoln's favor that Lincoln appointed him minister to Spain (1861–62). Wishing to participate in the war, Schurz resigned his post, returned home, and was commissioned a brigadier general of volunteers in the Union army. He later commanded a division at Second Bull Run and Chancellorsville, and a corps at Gettysburg.

In the months following the war Schurz traveled through the South, reporting conditions as he observed them for the New York *Tribune*. For a time he edited the Detroit *Post*. While serving as senator from Missouri (1869–75), in an attempt to defeat Grant (1872), he helped organize the LIBERAL REPUBLICAN PARTY. Four years later President Hayes brought Schurz into his cabinet as Secretary of the Interior (1877–81), where Schurz brought new standards of honesty into the government, and cleaned up the corruption in the Bureau of Indian Affairs.

As a leader of the liberal wing of his party, Schurz helped organize the MUGWUMPS in 1884 to oppose the nomination of Blaine for President, an act of 'bolting the party' which killed his political future. He edited the New York *Evening Post* (1881–84), served as president of the National Civil Service Reform League (1892–1901), and devoted his later years to writing. (His *Henry Clay,* 1887, is a classic.) Fearless and level-headed, Schurz exercised wide influence through his speeches and writings, and helped bring about reforms in a period when spoilsmen held high office.

See C. M. Fuess, *Carl Schurz, Reformer* (1932).

SCHUYLER, Philip John (1733–1804), member of one of the wealthiest New York families, lived as a country gentleman on his Albany estate. During the French and Indian War he served as deputy commissary under Lord Howe (1758–60). At the outbreak of the War of Independence Congress commissioned him a major general assigned to command in northern New York. When General Arthur St. Clair without a shot surrendered Ticonderoga during the SARATOGA CAMPAIGN (1777), Schuyler was accused of negligence and was replaced by Horatio Gates. Schuyler demanded a court-martial, which acquitted him with honor. (St. Clair was recalled by Congress from service in the field.) Schuyler resigned from active duty in 1779, but continued to advise Washington. He later gave strong support to Federal union and twice served in the U.S. Senate (1789–91, 1797–98). His daughter married Alexander Hamilton.

SCHWAB, Charles Michael (1862–1939), Pennsylvania-born industrialist, having begun as a laborer in the steelworks of Andrew Carnegie, rose to the presidency of the company (1897). After negotiating the sale of the Carnegie properties to J. P. Morgan, he became the first president of the U.S. STEEL CORPORATION (1901–3). Schwab then began building up a rival firm, the Bethlehem Steel Company. He left U.S. Steel and assumed presidency of the new company (1904). Under his management Bethlehem became the largest independent manufacturer of steel products. During World War I he directed shipbuilding for the U.S. Shipping Board Emergency Fleet Corporation. Unwise investments outside the steel industry in the depression years left Schwab insolvent, but in his heyday he typified the successful entrepreneur capitalist.

Science in the U.S. since World War II has developed as a culture within a culture. By mid-20th century students seeking the best training in mathematics, theoretical physics, chemistry, and biology were coming to the U.S., as 30 years before they would have gone to Europe. It is significant that during the years 1943–63 the international Nobel prizes in chemistry, physics, and medicine were awarded respectively to 10, 18, and 21 Americans.

See the individual disciplines of *Archaeology, Astronomy, Botany, Chemistry, Ethnology, Geography, Geology, Mathematics, Medicine, Meteorology, Oceanography, Paleontology, Physics, Psychology, Sociology,* and *Zoology*. Various areas of applied science are discussed under such entries as *Electricity, Engineering,* and *Industrial management.* Subjects include *Automobiles, Aviation, Exploration, Invention, Radio, Space exploration,* and *Television.*

Scientific management, see *Industrial management.*

Scientific Research and Development, Office of, was a government agency established by executive order (1941) to recruit leading scientists to work on military problems during World War II. The agency was first directed by VANNEVAR BUSH, and later by JAMES B. CONANT. The OSRD made vital contributions to the Allied victory. Scientists employed by the agency developed radar, rocket weapons, magnetic mines, proximity fuses, jet propulsion, guided missiles, new procedures in military medicine, and, most significantly, the ATOMIC BOMB. In 1946 the OSRD was absorbed into the U.S. ATOMIC ENERGY COMMISSION.

Scientific societies in the U.S., inaugurated with the founding of the AMERICAN PHILOSOPHICAL SOCIETY in 1743, began to flourish in the early years of the Republic. The second foundation, the AMERICAN ACADEMY OF ARTS AND SCIENCES (1780), was followed by such specialized organizations as the Chemical Society of Philadelphia (1792), and the American Mineralogical Society (1799). Associations established before 1800 that are still in existence include the Maryland Academy of Sciences (1797), and the Connecticut Academy of Arts and Sciences (1799). To stimulate improvement in agriculture, such groups as the New Jersey Society for the Promotion of Agriculture, Commerce, and Arts (1781) were organized. Washington and Franklin were members of the Philadelphia Society for Promoting Agriculture (1785). Similar groups soon were established in other states. After 1800 scientific societies multiplied rapidly. The SMITHSONIAN INSTITUTION (1846) is a national foundation. Two leading organizations are the American Association for the Advancement of Science (1848), and the NATIONAL ACADEMY OF SCIENCES (1863), the latter incorporated by Congress as a private association of limited membership to promote government investigations in all fields.

Scopes trial (July 1925) occurred in Dayton, Tennessee, in a dramatic test case following the passage of a Tennessee statute prohibiting the teaching in public schools of theories of creation contrary to the literal account in Genesis. John T. Scopes went on trial for teaching the Darwinian theory in a biology class. The state was represented by William Jennings Bryan and the defendant by Clarence Darrow and other distinguished attorneys. Though Scopes was convicted, he was released on a technicality. The law still remains on the Tennessee statute books, but the nationwide publicity of the case discouraged similar legislation elsewhere.

SCOTT, THOMAS ALEXANDER (1823–81), as vice president of the Pennsylvania Railroad at the outbreak of the Civil War, handled transportation so efficiently that Congress created the office of Assistant Secretary of War, to which Scott was appointed and placed in charge of all government rail transportation. He later was active in promoting the enormous expansion of the Pennsylvania system and served as its president (1874–80).

SCOTT, Winfield (1786–1866), soldier and statesman, was born near Petersburg, Virginia. He attended William and Mary and briefly studied law before he embarked upon his long military career. In 1808 he was commissioned an artillery captain, and during the War of 1812 as a brigade commander he bore the brunt of the fighting at LUNDY'S LANE. In the decade following, he studied European army practices and wrote *Infantry Tactics* (rev. ed., 1835), a standard manual for many years. He participated in the BLACK HAWK WAR, and in the same year (1832) served as President Jackson's personal emissary during the South Carolina nullification troubles. He supervised the removal of the Cherokee tribe to the Southwest, skillfully handled the CAROLINE AFFAIR (1837), and negotiated the truce after the AROOSTOOK WAR (1839). In 1841 he became supreme commander of the U.S. Army, a post he filled for twenty years. In the Mexican War (1846–48) he led the march from Vera Cruz to Mexico City, and he returned home a national hero, raised to the rank of lieutenant general. He accepted the Whig nomination for President in 1852 and won 44 per cent of the popular vote, but he lost the election to Franklin Pierce by an electoral margin of 42 to 254.

Scott was still general in chief at the outbreak of the Civil War, and though a Southerner by birth, he opposed secession and retained his lifelong allegiance to the Union; but failing health and burdens too great for his age (he was seventy-five) compelled him to retire in November 1861. He lived to see the Union victorious, and was buried at West Point. Though his pompous bearing won him the sobriquet 'Old Fuss and Feathers,' Scott had superior military ability, and he enjoyed the complete confidence of his officers and men. He is generally regarded as the foremost U.S. military figure between Washington and Robert E. Lee.

See A. D. H. Smith, *Old Fuss and Feathers* (1937).

SCRIPPS, Edward Wyllis (1854–1926), began his independent venture as a newspaper publisher in 1878 by starting the Cleveland *Press*. With his brother George Scripps and with Milton A. McRae he soon set up the powerful Scripps-McRae League, a newspaper chain that championed labor and adopted liberal political principles. In 1907 Scripps organized the UNITED PRESS Association, with Roy W. Howard (after 1908) as managing editor. During the 1920's a son, Robert P. Scripps, made Howard a partner, and they established the newspaper chain known as the Scripps-Howard papers.

Sculpture, of all the arts, was the least cultivated in the American colonial period. Prior to 1785 the two identifiable native sculptors were Patience Lovell Wright (1725–86), who modeled in wax, and William Rush (1756–1833), who worked chiefly in wood. Before the Civil War a few self-taught American artists made names for themselves. John Frazee (1790–1852) was the first American to carve marble busts, and CLARK MILLS cast the first equestrian statue. Today the most highly regarded American sculptor of the mid-19th century, despite his small output, is WILLIAM RIMMER. The first American to choose sculpture as a profession was HORATIO GREENOUGH, who led the way to Italy, where several artists established residence and became widely known, including THOMAS CRAWFORD, HIRAM POWERS, W. W. STORY, and HARRIET HOSMER.

After the Civil War the second generation of professional sculptors sought to rescue the art from the lifeless Italianate classicism that Powers had inflicted upon America in the 1840's. A new vigor, with a trend toward realism, was fostered by J. Q. A. WARD, DANIEL CHESTER FRENCH, and especially by AUGUSTUS SAINT-GAUDENS, the foremost American sculptor of his day. By the end of the 19th century the establishment of many schools of sculpture throughout the U.S. greatly increased the opportunities for study.

During the first decade of the 20th century, sculpture, like painting in the same period, developed in entirely new ways. Believing that sculpture has more than a decorative or representational function, younger artists placed emphasis on design, subordinating detail to the formal character of the work. Experiments with new metals, plastics, and colored ceramics followed the invention of those materials, and by mid-20th century sculptors, like painters, were concerned with expressionism and abstractions.

Sea Witch, see *Clipper ships.*

SEABORG, GLENN THEODORE (1912–), professor of chemistry at the University of California, Berkeley (after 1945), conducted researches in nuclear chemistry and physics. In the decade 1940–50 he and his associates discovered five elements that are heavier than uranium (94–98), for which contributions in 1951 he received the Nobel Prize in chemistry (shared with his colleague, E. M. McMillan). By 1958 Seaborg had added five more transuranic elements and his methods had created the new technique of ultramicrochemistry. In 1961 he was appointed chairman of the Atomic Energy Commission, the first scientist to head that body.

SEABURY, SAMUEL (1729–96), Connecticut-born clergyman, after graduation from Yale (1747) studied medicine at Edinburgh but turned to theology. He eventually became an Anglican missionary in New Jersey and New York. Before the Revolution he so effectively pleaded the Loyalist cause in pamphlets written by 'A Westchester Farmer' that he was briefly jailed (1775) for his attacks on Congress. During the war he served as chaplain to British troops. He reconciled himself to the new government, and was made bishop of Connecticut (1783). When the Protestant Episcopal Church in the U.S. was formed (1789) as a separate branch of the Anglican body, Seabury became its first presiding bishop.

SEALSFIELD, CHARLES [KARL ANTON POSTL] (1793–1864), runaway monk from a Bohemian monastery who preserved his anonymity until his death, landed in New Orleans as a German immigrant (1823), and after extensive travels through the Mississippi valley and into the Southwest wrote essays and novels based on American themes, depicting frontier life, and assailing political corruption and all forms of oppression. Sealsfield was not far wrong in assuming that he was 'America's most famous author,' for his European reputation was considerable and his books were widely translated, imitated, and plagiarized. Longfellow regarded his 'favorite Sealsfield' highly. Among Sealsfield's translated works are *The United States as They Are . . .* (1827), and his accepted masterpiece, *The Cabin Book: or, Sketches of Life in Texas* (1844). He retired to Switzerland, where he died in seclusion.

SEAMAN, ELIZABETH COCHRAN (1867–1922), a journalist who wrote under the pseudonym 'Nelly Bly' (a character in the 1882 Grundy and Solomon operetta, *The Vicar of Bray*), specialized in sensational exposures. As a staff member on Pulitzer's New York *World,* she got herself committed to Blackwell's Island by feigning insanity, and published the account of her experience in *Ten Days in a Mad House* (1887). Pulitzer then dispatched her on a round-the-world journey to make reality out of Jules Verne's fictional *Around the World in 80 Days.* Nelly Bly accomplished the feat in 72 days, 6 hours, and 11 minutes (1889–90).

SEATO (Southeast Asia Treaty Organization) began as the group of eight nations that met in Manila (1954) to enter into a Pacific area defense alliance, signed by the U.S., Great Britain, France, Australia, New Zealand, the Philippines, Pakistan, and Thailand. A subsequent protocol extended the treaty to Cambodia, South Vietnam, and Laos. SEATO affirms the rights of Asian and Pacific peoples to equality and self-determination.

Seattle, laid out on hills rising from Puget Sound, is the chief city in the Pacific Northwest, with a population which increased in the decade 1950–60 from 467,000 to 557,000. Settled in 1852, the year before the present state of Washington became a separate territory, it remained a small lumber town until it was joined by rail to the East (1884). The Alaska gold rush of 1897 made it a boom town, but its real expansion began with the opening of the Panama Canal (1914). Since then it has been a major link with Canada and Alaska and with the Far East. During World War II Seattle became the center of west coast shipbuilding and one of the major centers of the aircraft industry. Chief among its institutions of higher learning is the University of Washington (est. 1861), which, in 1965, with a faculty of 2140, enrolled 24,000 students.

Secession of the states of the South over the issues of slavery and states' rights had been narrowly averted by the COMPROMISE OF 1850, which made adjustments on those issues previously contested by the North and South. But passage of the KANSAS-NEBRASKA ACT (1854) repealed the Compromise by establishing the doctrine of 'popular sovereignty,' that is, of congressional nonintervention in the territories. The slavery issue was bitterly fought in the presidential campaign of 1860, in which the Republicans pledged nonextension of slavery. Thus when Lincoln was elected, those Southerners who wished to see slavery extended knew that only by secession could they realize their aim.

In December 1860 the South Carolina legislature summoned a state convention which unanimously adopted a resolution dissolving 'the union subsisting between South Carolina and other States,' alleging among other reasons for her action that Northerners had 'denounced as sinful the institution of Slavery.' The Southerners' dream of an empire based on slavery penetrated far more deeply than Northerners realized, even though a strong Unionist party existed throughout the South when Lincoln was elected. South Carolina's secession immediately triggered similar action by other states. Within two months six other states in the lower South had passed like ordinances: Mississippi, Florida, Alabama, Georgia, Louisiana, and Texas. In his final weeks in office President Buchanan seemed to deny his own authority to act in a crisis. He believed secession to be unconstitutional, but he saw no way to coerce the states, and rather than risk war or give the upper South cause for secession, he suspended protection of Federal property, including forts and arsenals. He did, however, refuse the demand of the South Carolina commissioners that FORT SUMTER be evacuated, thus leaving that garrison beleaguered.

During these weeks Congress considered various compromise proposals, of which the CRITTENDEN COMPROMISE seemed most hopeful. It proposed a constitutional amendment which in essence would accept slavery where it existed and recognize a degree of extension into the territories. The bill received the support of the BORDER STATES, but it was unalterably opposed by the Republicans and died in committee. Compromise thus being impossible, representatives from the seceded states assembled in Alabama (4 February 1861) at the MONTGOMERY CONVENTION to organize a new nation. Though Lincoln declared in his inaugural address that the government would hold its property, he promised that 'it will not assail you.' His crucial decision to relieve Fort Sumter touched off the Civil War. Following bombardment of the fort (12–14 April) and Lincoln's call for volunteers, the upper South was compelled to make a choice between the Confederacy and the Union. Virginia, first of the remaining states to adopt a secession ordinance (17 April), was followed by Arkansas (6 May), Tennessee (7 May), and North Carolina (20 May). The border slave states, Maryland, Delaware, Missouri, and Kentucky, did not secede, though all save Delaware furnished troops in some number to the Confederacy. Forty counties in western Virginia nullified the Virginia ordinance in midsummer, and while the war was in progress were admitted to the Union (1863) as the new state of West Virginia.

See D. L. Dumond, *The Secession Movement* (1931); and A. O. Craven, *The Coming of the Civil War* (1957).

Secession movements, repeatedly started in the U.S. by minority groups in the period between the War of Independence and the Civil War, were the last-resort methods used to emphasize STATES' RIGHTS within a newly formed federation of state governments. Politicians on the frontier intrigued for secession when John Jay, as secretary of the Confederation for Foreign Affairs, proposed in 1786 that farmers in the West waive their RIGHT OF DEPOSIT at New Orleans in return for Spanish concessions to American shipping elsewhere. During Washington's first administration a similar movement envisioned an East-West split along the crest of the Appalachians. John Taylor of Caroline enunciated the doctrine of constitutional secession in 1798, when the Democratic-Republican party was in process of formation, but the more moderate views of Jefferson prevailed. Disgruntled Federalists at the HARTFORD CONVENTION (1814–15) sought formation of a New England Confederation if their program of constitutional reform failed, but the threat never became an issue. President Jackson averted a crisis in 1833 when South Carolina proposed nullification of a tariff measure. But the North-South split became ominous during the 1850's, and after the election of Lincoln (1860) eleven slave states seceded.

Second Amendment to the U.S. Constitution, see *Bill of Rights.*

Secondary boycott, see *Boycott.*

Secret Service, U.S., a division of the Treasury Department, is chiefly concerned with the investigation of Federal crimes, such as counterfeiting and forgery. The Secret Service was organized in 1864, and after the death of President Lincoln the agency was entrusted with the protection of the persons of the President and his family. During the two World Wars it was active in protecting the manufacture and shipment of munitions. The report compiled by the commission headed by Chief Justice Earl Warren after the assassination of President Kennedy recommended a major revision in the organization and operation of the Secret Service to bring it into closer association with other Federal agencies.

Sectionalism is the term applied to the political, cultural, and economic clashes between geographical sections of the U.S. It is generally recognized to be the result of the unequal distribution of resources, and it is strongly conditioned by such elements as climate, soil, and race. Sectionalism preceded nationalism in the New World as in the Old, and even today alignments suggest that the U.S. is a confederation of sections rather than a union of states. Sections always have subsections within them, and each section's influence varies from one era to the next. The South, for instance, did not always present the unified front that seemed to dominate its feeling in 1861, and in 1964 a segregationist governor of Alabama won a presidential primary contest in Wisconsin.

Three great sections — the East, the South, and the West — have always existed. The predominant economy of the East had become commercial and industrial before the Civil War. That of the South and West remained agricultural until well into the 20th century, and many parts of those regions continue to be the nation's bread basket. Issues bearing on sectionalism have included TARIFF, SLAVERY, FREE SILVER, STATES' RIGHTS, and CIVIL LIBERTIES.

Securities and Exchange Commission (1934) is a bipartisan independent agency of five members with five-year terms, created by Congress to administer the Federal Securities Act of 1933 and the Securities Exchange Act of 1934. With strong quasi-judicial powers, it licenses stock exchanges and requires full details of their organization and trading practices. Over the years the SEC has earned a general reputation for remarkable success in protecting investors.

Security Council, the executive agency of the UNITED NATIONS, exercises the responsibility for maintaining international peace. It is an eleven-member body, five of which have permanent seats (China, France, Russia, Great Britain, and the U.S.). The General Assembly chooses the remaining six for two-year terms. The Council sits in continuous session, and each of the members presides for one month. The Military Staff Committee and the Disarmament Commission report to it. The United Nations Charter requires that the five permanent members agree on substantive matters, and thus a veto is effected when the 'big five' do not vote unanimously. In practice, abstention from voting has not been construed as an exercise of the veto.

Sedition Act of 1798, see *Alien and Sedition Acts.*

Sedition Act of 1918, see *Espionage Act of 1917.*

Seekers were those who, during the 17th century, claimed that the existing churches did not conform to the pattern of the New Testament. They believed that the Bible was the instrument of faith, and they claimed to be in search of the true church, ministry, and sacraments. In a general way, ROGER WILLIAMS was a Seeker, as were the early Quakers.

Segregation, see *Brown* v. *Board of Education, Civil Rights Acts, Freedom Riders.*

Selective Service, see *Conscription, Universal Military Training.*

Selective Service and Training Act (1940), the Burke-Wadsworth Act, was the first peacetime conscription in U.S. history. It provided for the registration of all men between the ages of twenty-one and thirty-five, and for the training of 1,200,000 troops and 800,000 reserves. The original law, amended to extend the age limits after the U.S. entered World War II, expired in 1947. At present military service is provided by UNIVERSAL MILITARY TRAINING.

Selective veto, see *Veto.*

Selectmen, in New England towns, are the officers annually chosen at TOWN MEETINGS to manage a variety of civic concerns. Usually from three to nine in number, they constitute an executive authority that functions under state law. The office derives from that of select vestrymen in rural England, and has existed from the earliest colonial period.

Seminole Indians, of Muskhogean stock, were Creeks who as 'seminole' (separatists or renegades) early in the 18th century moved east to Florida. During the SEMINOLE WARS of 1835–42 they were under the leadership of OSCEOLA. Those who moved to Oklahoma in the 1840's formed one of the FIVE CIVILIZED TRIBES. Descendants of the remnant that stayed in Florida now number some 1000, settled on reservations in the Everglades.

Seminole Wars (1816–18; 1835–42) began when U.S. troops, ordered to search out escaped slaves south of the Georgia border, blew up 'Negro Fort' on the Apalachicola river in Spanish Florida. The Seminole retaliated, and in 1818 General Andrew Jackson was sent on a 'punitive' expedition, which gave him national stature but stirred up an international issue in the ARBUTHNOT AND AMBRISTER AFFAIR. His occupation of Spanish towns led to the ADAMS-ONÍS TREATY of 1819, by which Spain ceded East Florida to the U.S.

In 1832 the Seminole were coerced into signing a treaty by which they agreed to move west across the Mississippi. A large portion of the tribe, under the leadership of OSCEOLA (1835), refused to go, and for several years in the fastnesses of the Everglades they eluded the U.S. army. The 'war' ended ten years later, after most of the tribe had been exterminated. The cost to the U.S. was 1500 lives and some $20,000,000.

SEMMES, RAPHAEL (1809–77), an Alabama lawyer with naval training, as commander of the *Sumter,* the first of the Confederate raiders, did considerable damage to Union commerce before he was blockaded at Gibraltar. Soon thereafter he was given command of the *Alabama,* and became a Confederate hero. For two years he continued to disrupt the sea lanes. (*Alabama* was finally sunk by *Kearsarge.*) After the war Semmes returned to his law practice in Mobile and wrote several books about his exploits.

Senate Crime Committee, see *Kefauver Investigation.*

Senate, U.S., the upper house of CONGRESS, has co-equal power with the House of Representatives in the field of legislative enactments. Each state elects two senators, who serve six-year terms. (There are now 100 Senators.) Election to the Senate is staggered so that the terms of one-third of its members expire once every two years. Until passage of the Seventeenth Amendment (1913) the Constitution stipulated that senators should be elected by state legislatures. Since then they have been chosen by popular vote.

The Vice President presides, but he may cast no vote except in case of a tie. The Senate, which has constitutional power to make its own rules of procedure, has consistently declined to limit debate. Thus the Senate (unlike the House) seldom invokes CLOSURE and therefore the FILIBUSTER is common. The Senate enjoys exclusive power in the choice of the Vice President if there is a tie or lack of majority in the ELECTORAL COLLEGE. It alone has the function of ratifying treaties (by a two-thirds vote of those present), of confirming presidential appointments (by a simple majority vote of those present), and of acting as a high court in the trial of IMPEACHMENT cases.

The problems of leadership in the Senate are less difficult than in the House, partly because it is a smaller body and partly because among its members there are always several men whose experience derives from long service. Especially important among its standing committees (whose chairmen wield great power) are Appropriations, Armed Services, Banking and Currency, Finance, Foreign Relations, Government Operations, Judiciary, and Rules and Administration. Floor leaders, whips and steering committees function to secure party harmony, but their methods are usually informal. Individual senators enjoy more weight in party councils and more independence of action on the floor than do representatives in the House.

Senatorial courtesy is the term applied to the tradition by which the President submits the name of a proposed nominee for Federal patronage to the senators of the state in which the nominee resides, for approval prior to the nomination. In the event of disapproval, the Senate customarily refuses confirmation of the presidential choice. Thus in effect the Senate controls the distribution of patronage in areas where its veto power can be used for that purpose.

Seneca Falls Convention, see *Woman suffrage movement.*

Seneca Indians, see *Iroquois Confederacy.*

Separation of powers is the system of allotting the various powers of government to separate branches in order to keep any one branch from concentrating power. It is one of the fundamental American constitutional principles. The doctrine, which was derived from Montesquieu's *De l'esprit des lois,* 1748, was clearly recognized in the DECLARATION OF RIGHTS (1774) adopted by the First Continental Congress, and applied in the drafts of the state constitutions established during the Revolution.

At the time of the Convention of 1787 the framers of the Federal Constitution incorporated the doctrine in the 'distributive clauses' of the first three Articles, and applied it conjointly with the principle of CHECKS AND BALANCES in an effort to prevent any one of the three branches of government — executive, legislative, and judicial — from becoming an overruling influence on the others. Actually the separation of powers principle is not firmly adhered to, since each branch of the government does share powers belonging to the others. The framers likewise divided power between federal and state governments.

Separatists, bodies that withdrew from the Established Church in England during the 16th and 17th centuries, do not include the PURITANS, who usually regarded the Established Church as the true church. See PILGRIMS, FRIENDS, and BAPTISTS.

SEQUOYA (*c.* 1770–1843), half-breed Cherokee (also named George Guess), became a silversmith and trader, first in Georgia and later in Oklahoma. He created a Cherokee alphabet (or syllabary), which other tribes adapted, thus enabling thousands of Indians to read and write. His name was given to the giant redwood tree, the *sequoia.*

Sequoia National Park (1890), in the SIERRA NEVADA of eastern California, is an area of some 385,000 acres in which are located great groves of giant sequoias, which are among the largest and oldest of living things. Mount Whitney (14,495 ft.) is at its eastern border.

SERRA, JUNÍPERO (1713–84), Spanish Franciscan missionary, was sent to North America in 1749, and for several years labored among the Indians in Mexico. He went with PORTOLÁ to California in 1769, where he founded a chain of 21 missions, from San Diego north to San Francisco. He made Carmel his headquarters. The Franciscans, following Serra's plans, by 1830 virtually possessed all settled land in California. There industrious farmers and herdsmen under Church guidance produced livestock and commodities under a system that made the vast area, in the words of a French traveler, 'one continuous pasture.' The mellow buildings, nearly half of which were erected in Serra's lifetime, still reflect the importance of his undertaking, and the statue of him (1931) in the nation's Capitol pays homage to one of the notable pioneer missionaries in America.

Servicemen's Readjustment Act, see *G.I. Bill of Rights.*

SETON, ELIZABETH ANN [BAYLEY] (1774–1821), was daughter of Richard Bayley, professor of anatomy at Columbia. Her husband, William Seton, was a substantial New York merchant, who at his death (1803) left her with five young children. Her conversion to Roman Catholicism (1805) severed her family ties. In Maryland, with the aid of Bishop John Carroll, she opened the first Catholic free school (the beginning of American parochial education), and founded St. Joseph's College for women (1809). As Mother Seton, she became the superior of the newly formed Sisters of Charity. Seton Hall University (est. 1856) is named for her. In 1963 she was beatified.

Settlement houses, see *Social settlements.*

Seven Days' Battles (26 June–2 July 1862) were the successive offensive moves by which Lee, with 75,000 Confederate troops, hoped to force McClellan, with 100,000 Federals, to abandon his threatening position during the PENINSULAR CAMPAIGN, either by retreat or surrender. It was Lee's all-out attempt to win the war with one blow. McClellan beat off the first attack at Mechanicsville (26 June), and there and at Gaines' Mill (27 June), Savage's Station (29 June), and Frayser's Farm (30 June) the Federals inflicted heavy losses on the Confederates while withdrawing across the Chickahominy. Lee delivered his last telling blows in a series of attacks at Malvern Hill (1 July), eight miles from Richmond, but the Union troops, supported by Union gunboats, were able to survive. On 2 July McClellan withdrew to Harrison's Landing and Lee retired to Richmond. Thus the first great bout in the eastern theater of the Civil War had been won by Lee. Confederate casualties (20,000) exceeded Union casualties (16,000).

Historians recognize that Lee's brilliant strategy could have succeeded had advantage been taken of the opportunities offered. (McClellan believed that simply by escaping destruction he had accomplished a feat.) But Lee had held full command of his army for less than a month and had not acquired deftness of maneuver. His staff was incompetent and division leaders were not up to their jobs. The Seven Days' marked the turning point of the war, since thereafter the mobilization of the contenders became total and, in Lincoln's words, 'a remorseless revolutionary struggle.'

Seventeenth Amendment (1913) to the Federal Constitution authorizes the direct popular election of U.S. senators, who were previously elected by state legislatures or state conventions. By the Amendment the state governors are authorized to make temporary appointments in the Senate when vacancies occur. Public opinion was prepared for this amendment by such muckrakers as David Graham Phillips, whose *Treason of the Senate* condemned the Senate as a rich man's club.

Seven Years' War, see *French and Indian War* (1755–63).

Seventh Amendment to the U.S. Constitution, see *Bill of Rights.*

Seventh Day Adventists, see *Adventists.*

Seventh Day Baptists, see *Dunkards.*

Seventh of March Speech, see *Webster, Daniel.*

SEVIER, JOHN (1745–1815), Virginia frontiersman, became a leading figure in the early history of Tennessee, which had its beginnings in the WATAUGA SETTLEMENT (1769), largely directed by Sevier. He excelled as an Indian fighter, and he led militiamen against the British and the Indians in that region during the War of Independence. He was elected the first governor of Tennessee (1796–1801), and was later re-elected for six years (1803–9). He served in Congress (1811–15) as a veteran western politician, where he gave his support to the young 'WAR HAWKS.'

SEWALL, SAMUEL (1652–1730), was born in England during his family's temporary residence there. He was brought back to Boston in 1661, and graduated from Harvard (1671), where he was chosen a Fellow soon after. By his marriage to the daughter of JOHN HULL in 1676 he gained substantial wealth. Thereafter he entered a public career, chiefly as deputy to the General Court and member of the governor's council throughout most of his life. Though without legal training, he served after 1692 as a judge of the superior court of the colony, and in later years as chief justice (1718–28) he won respect for his clear thinking and humane understanding.

Sewall sat on the bench commissioned in 1692 for the Salem trials during the WITCHCRAFT DELUSION, and his public confession of error five years later (the only one made by the nine judges) is a measure of his integrity. He published essays on a variety of subjects, including *The Selling of Joseph* (1700), the first antislavery tract in America. But his literary reputation is permanently based on his *Diary* (3 vols., 1878–92), covering the years 1674–1729, except for an intermission of items (perhaps lost) for eight years (1677–85). The diary is the fullest personal record in America prior to that made by members of the ADAMS FAMILY. A corrected edition was completed in 1966 by M. H. Thomas of Princeton.

SEWARD, WILLIAM HENRY (1801–72), born in Florida, New York, after graduation from Union College (1820) established a law practice at Auburn, which he made his lifelong home. He threw himself into the Anti-Masonic movement, but soon joined the Whig party and was elected governor of New York (1839–42). Later, in the U.S. Senate (1849–61), he vigorously opposed the Compromise of 1850. On the slavery issue he was guided by a 'higher law than the Constitution,' and in 1855 he joined the newly formed Republican party. In spite of his prominence he did not win the presidential nomination he coveted, either in 1856 or in 1860, when Lincoln gained the party's support and won the election.

Seward had declared in a notable address in 1858 that an 'irrepressible conflict' would exist until the nation became either all slave or all free, and Lincoln selected him, as the most experienced statesman in the Republican party, to be Secretary of State. At first Seward viewed his task as that of a Metternich brought into office to guide a small-town lawyer. But when Lincoln early in 1861 deftly rejected Seward's quixotic scheme of waging war against Louis Napoleon's France as a means of uniting the nation, Seward recovered from his delusion, and thereafter he handled foreign affairs with skill. His negotiations with Great Britain during the TRENT AFFAIR and with France during the Mexican venture of MAXIMILIAN distinguish him as a statesman.

When Lincoln was assassinated, Seward was also attacked, but he recovered and was retained in office throughout the administration of President Johnson, whose policies Seward supported in the face of powerful opposition from the RADICAL REPUBLICANS. A consistent expansionist, he purchased Alaska (1867), which was then regarded as 'Seward's folly,' negotiated a treaty for the purchase of the largest of the Danish West Indies (the Virgin Islands), which the Senate failed to ratify, and advocated cementing friendly relations with China and the annexation of Hawaii and other available coaling stations in the Pacific. He was the first American statesman to formulate a clear Pacific policy.

See Frederic Bancroft, *Life of W. H. Seward* (2 vols., 1900).

'Seward's icebox,' see *Alaska.*

Sewing machine, see *Howe, Elias.*

SHAEF (Supreme Headquarters of the Allied Expeditionary Forces) in World War II was commanded by General Dwight D. Eisenhower, and was originally established in London. After the successful invasion of France the headquarters were transferred to Versailles.

Shakers, a millennial group who called themselves 'The United Society of Believers in Christ's Second Appearing,' originated in England during the 18th century among the Society of FRIENDS. They assumed a dual nature of the Deity: a male principle manifest in Jesus, and a female principle in 'Mother' ANN LEE, the illiterate mystic who brought a small following to America in 1774.

The communal group of men and women settled at Lebanon, New York, and offshoots established themselves as far west as Indiana. They were excellent small farmers and woodwork craftsmen. Since they were celibates and recruited only by conversion, by now they have virtually ceased to exist.

SHALER, NATHANIEL SOUTHGATE (1841–1906), Kentucky-born geologist, after graduation from Harvard (1862) taught paleontology and geology there throughout his life. His writings, which include *Nature and Man in America* (1891), and *Man and the Earth* (1905), by focusing on physiographic factors, gave a new dimension to the interpretation of history.

SHAPE, see *North Atlantic Treaty Organization.*

SHAPLEY, HARLOW (1885–), professor of astronomy at Harvard and director of the Harvard observatories (1921–53), did notable research on photometry and spectroscopy, with special attention to the structure of the universe. His studies of Cepheid variables were based on the work of his colleague Henrietta Swan Leavitt (1868–1921), whose measurement of the distances of stars made possible Shapley's studies of globular clusters and his discovery (1917) of the extent of the Milky Way. His writings include *Flights from Chaos* (1930), and *Galaxies* (1943).

Sharecroppers are those TENANT FARMERS who, in return for family living quarters, working stock, tools, seed, and commissary staples, work the land and receive a share of the crop (usually a third after the debt is deducted). This form of tenancy, peculiar to the South after the Civil War, at one time is estimated to have included 750,000 sharecropping families (3,000,000 persons). Government programs first undertaken in the 1930's to assist tenant farmers have improved the lot of sharecroppers, who by the nature of the system were seldom able to extricate themselves from a state of perpetual bondage.

'Share-the-Wealth' movements sprang up in various parts of the U.S., particularly in the South and West, during the early 1930's. The publicity concerning TECHNOCRACY, with its formula for utopia, was followed by the organization of groups seeking ways to redistribute wealth. Such were National Union for Social Justice proposed by Father CHARLES COUGHLIN, the old age pension scheme of the TOWNSEND PLAN, the Share-Our-Wealth clubs sponsored by HUEY LONG, and the more moderate EPIC program of Upton Sinclair in California. These politico-economic panaceas ran the gamut of reform tactics and briefly attracted very large numbers of converts. After passage of the SOCIAL SECURITY ACT (1935) the movements soon died.

SHAW, ANNA HOWARD (1847–1919), English-born woman suffragist, graduated from the Theological School (1878) and the Medical School (1885) of Boston University. The first woman to be ordained in the Methodist Church (1880), she resigned from the pulpit in 1885 to devote herself to the WOMAN SUFFRAGE MOVEMENT. Famous as a speaker, she was known throughout the U.S. and in Europe, and for several years she served as president of the National American Woman Suffrage Association (1904–15).

SHAW, LEMUEL (1781–1861), chief justice of the Supreme Judicial Court of Massachusetts (1830–60), not only reshaped the state's common law in accordance with changing industrial and social conditions, but through his opinions greatly influenced the course of American law. In railway and public utility law he invariably construed public grants in favor of the community, not private interests. His memorable decision in COMMONWEALTH *v.* HUNT (1842), in which he abandoned the old common-law rule that trade unions were illegal conspiracies in restraint of trade, has become permanently established in American jurisprudence.

However, Justice Shaw, in *Roberts* v. *City of Boston* (1849), a school segregation case, may have originated the segregationist doctrine of 'separate but equal' facilities, in order to restrict a Negro child to a Negro school. This doctrine was established nationally in 1896 by the Supreme Court in *Plessy* v. *Ferguson.*

Shawnee Indians, of Algonquian stock, in mid-18th century were a nomadic tribe in the Ohio valley. Under TECUMSEH, their most noted chief, they were a formidable barrier to white settlements in the Northwest Territory. By the Treaty of GREENVILLE (1795) they moved farther west. Today they live on reservations in Oklahoma, where they number some 1000.

SHAWNEE PROPHET [TENSKWATAWA] (*c.* 1768–1837), twin brother of TECUMSEH, through his plan to confederate tribes against the whites helped bring on the Creek War of 1813. In the War of 1812 he was allied with the British. He retired on a pension to Canada, but later he returned to Ohio, and moved with his tribe to a reservation in Kansas.

Shays's Rebellion (August–February 1786–87) developed when the Massachusetts legislature adjourned in July without heeding the petitions of debt-ridden farmers for paper-money issue, or laws to stay the mounting number of farm and home foreclosures. Protest meetings were followed by armed threats. Some 500 insurgents gathered at Springfield in September under Daniel Shays (1747–1825), a destitute farmer and former army captain, and forced the Supreme Court to adjourn. The real trouble began in December, when Shays led 1200 men toward the Springfield arsenal. The rebel bands, armed mostly with staves and pitchforks, were soon compelled to scatter into the low hills of central Massachusetts, where they were hunted like game in the heavy snow. Ultimately all were pardoned, but the rebellion had the effect of inducing the legislature to avoid direct taxation, to lower court fees, and to exempt such items as household goods and workmen's tools from debt process. Shays's Rebellion made the state legislatures aware that the Confederation was powerless to protect itself from invasion or domestic violence, and was a factor in the adoption of the Federal Constitution.

SHEA, JOHN DAWSON GILMARY (1824–92), abandoned a novitiate in the Jesuit order to devote himself to writing a history of his church in America. He wrote a history of Catholic missions and edited many volumes of narratives of discovery and exploration, but his *magnum opus* is *A History of the Catholic Church in the U.S.* (4 vols., 1886–92). The fruit of a lifetime of research, it covers the entire period to 1866 and remains one of the chief monuments of Catholic scholarship in America.

Sheep industry in the colonial period was a part of the self-sufficient agriculture of the time. It supplied wool for homespun clothing, but not until the introduction of Merino sheep from France and Spain (after 1800) and passage of the EMBARGO ACT (1807) did the quantity and quality of native wool make the industry commercially profitable. Although woolen imports from Britain offered competition after 1815, the growth of the factory system increased the home market, and the TARIFF OF 1816 raised the price of wool and made New England and New York sheep-raising centers. By 1850 Ohio had become the chief sheep-raising state, and the annexation of the Spanish Southwest brought under U.S. jurisdiction vast grazing regions which became the source of 'territorial wools.' The Civil War again made sheep raising an industry in the North for a time.

The center of the sheep industry continued to move westward, and by 1935 some 60 per cent of all sheep in the U.S. grazed in the Rocky Mountain and Pacific coast states. The importance of the sheep industry in the national economy, either for wool or meat, has never approached that of the CATTLE INDUSTRY.

SHELBURNE, WILLIAM PETTY FITZMAURICE, 2nd Earl of (1737–1805), as president of the BOARD OF TRADE AND PLANTATIONS in Grenville's cabinet (1763) had immediate responsibility for dealing with the IMPERIAL PROBLEMS rising out of the acquisition of a vast frontier after the fall of New France. He alone of the British ministers understood the issues involved, but he was soon forced out of office and his place taken by HILLSBOROUGH. After WILLIAM PITT (then Earl of Chatham) returned to power (1766), Shelburne became secretary of state for foreign affairs, but during Chatham's illness Shelburne's policy of conciliation toward the American colonies was not supported by his colleagues or by the king, and in 1768 he was dismissed from office. Shelburne was later prime minister for a brief time, and he concluded the TREATY OF PARIS OF 1783, ending the War of Independence.

Shenandoah National Park (1935) in northern Virginia is an area of some 193,000 acres, and the principal scenic section of the Blue Ridge Mountains. The Shenandoah valley between the Blue Ridge (east) and the Alleghenies (west) was the scene of many Civil War battles and the invasion route which the Confederates used to move into Pennsylvania before the battle of GETTYSBURG.

SHEPARD, THOMAS (1605–49), after graduation from Emmanuel College, Cambridge (1624), was ordained in the Established Church, but his Congregational principles led to his suspension, and in 1635 he emigrated to Massachusetts, where he became pastor of the church in Cambridge and a founder and overseer of Harvard College (1636–49). Cotton Mather said that 'the character of his daily conversation was a trembling walk with God,' yet Shepard was the most noted evangelist in early New England, and a leading theologian. His influence on JONATHAN EDWARDS was immense. His *Sincere Convert* ran to twenty editions between 1641 and 1812, and his collected works were gathered in three volumes in 1853. His *Autobiography* (1832, repr. 1932) reveals a man of deep compassion whose God 'passes by the transgressions of the remnant of his heritage, even because he delighteth in mercy.'

SHERIDAN, PHILIP HENRY (1831–88), son of an Irish immigrant who settled in Ohio, graduated from the U.S. Military Academy (1853). After service on the frontier he entered the Civil War as a Union colonel of cavalry. He led a brigade at PERRYVILLE (1862), and as a major general he took a prominent part during the CHATTANOOGA CAMPAIGN (1863). After April 1864 he commanded the cavalry corps of the Army of the Potomac. (His decisive victory at Cedar Creek is memorialized in T. B. Read's dramatic poem, 'Sheridan's Ride.') Lee's surrender was made inevitable when Sheridan cut off Lee's retreat at Appomattox in April 1865. At the war's end Sheridan was placed in charge of military departments in the South, and in 1884 he succeeded W. T. Sherman as commander of the U.S. Army. Sheridan's personal magnetism and restless energy were combined with painstaking skill, and he is remembered as one of the great fighting generals.

SHERMAN, JOHN (1823–1900), younger brother of WILLIAM TECUMSEH SHERMAN, after taking up the practice of law in Cleveland, Ohio (1853), helped organize the Republican party and began a long career of public service, first in the U.S. House of Representatives (1855–61) and then in the Senate (1861–77). As chairman of the powerful Senate finance committee (after 1867), he was an avowed partisan with a philosophy of expediency, but his financial conservatism made him a moderating influence on fiscal legislation during the rule of the RADICAL REPUBLICANS in the Reconstruction period. As Hayes's Secretary of the Treasury (1877–81) he promoted passage of the deflationist RESUMPTION ACT. Again in the Senate (1881–97), he wrote the SHERMAN ANTITRUST ACT (1890) and the SHERMAN SILVER PURCHASE ACT (1890). Late in life he was briefly McKinley's Secretary of State (1897), but increasing infirmity compelled his resignation. *Recollections of Forty Years . . .* (2 vols., 1895) is the personal record of his crowded career.

SHERMAN, ROGER (1721–93), Connecticut jurist, helped draft the Declaration of Independence, sat as a delegate in the Continental Congress (1774–81, 1783–84), and as a member of the Federal Constitutional Convention was one of the strongest advocates of union. He and Oliver Ellsworth there introduced the so-called CONNECTICUT COMPROMISE, which solved the problem of state representation in Congress. He later served in both the House of Representatives (1789–90) and the Senate (1791–93).

SHERMAN, WILLIAM TECUMSEH (1820–91), elder brother of JOHN SHERMAN, after graduation from the U.S. Military Academy (1840), served in the army until 1853, when he resigned to enter business. At the outbreak of the Civil War he rejoined the U.S. army, and led a brigade at first BULL RUN and a division at SHILOH. He participated in the VICKSBURG CAMPAIGN, and in March 1864 he succeeded Grant as chief commander in the west. His ATLANTA CAMPAIGN ended in the evacuation and burning of that city (September 1864), after which, with 60,000 men, he began his 'march to the sea.' He ordered his troops to live off the land, and by deliberate and disciplined destruction he not only wiped out the South's sources of supply, but sought to break the war spirit of civilians as well as soldiers. After he captured Savannah (21 December), he began his march northward to join Grant, and on 26 April 1865 he received the surrender of J. E. Johnston at Durham, North Carolina. In 1869 Sherman was given the full rank of general and succeeded Grant as commander of the U.S. army, a post he filled until his retirement in 1884.

One of the great Civil War generals, Sherman endeared himself to the troops by living 'rough,' and his alertness inspired their confidence. 'There's Uncle Billy. All's right.' He was patient and skillful in maneuver, and concepts developed from study of his large grasp of strategy had considerable influence. 'War is cruel,' he replied to the protests of the mayor of Atlanta, 'and you cannot refine it.' His *Memoirs* (1886) reflect the quality of his logical ruthlessness of 'total war' coupled with compassion.

The biography of Sherman by B. H. Liddell Hart (1929) is a study written by a military strategist.

Sherman Antitrust Act (1890), first of the Federal ANTITRUST LAWS designed to regulate big business, authorized the government to proceed against any 'combination in the form of trusts or otherwise, or conspiracy, in restraint of trade.' Its critical weakness was its ambiguous phrasing and its failure to define a 'trust,' a 'combination,' and 'RESTRAINT OF TRADE.'

In a series of rulings the Federal courts decided that its provisions embraced labor unions and railroads. But the law as a weapon against trusts proved ineffective. It neither retarded the growth of combines nor stamped out the abuses that accompany such growth, because the Supreme Court did not feel that the Act brought many 'reasonable' manufacturing ventures within its jurisdiction. The failure of the Act was recognized by passage of the CLAYTON ANTITRUST ACT (1914).

Sherman Silver Purchase Act (1890), passed by Congress to supplant the BLAND-ALLISON SILVER ACT (1878), was a futile compromise between inflationist western Republicans voting for a tariff (which they disliked) and eastern Republicans voting for FREE SILVER (which they feared). By requiring the government to purchase twice as much silver as before, the Act threatened to undermine the Treasury's gold reserves. It satisfied no one, and after the PANIC OF 1893 Congress repealed it.

Shiloh, Battle of (6–7 April 1862), the first great bloody conflict of the Civil War, was fought at Pittsburg Landing in Tennessee. The Union army of 33,000, under Grant, was attacked by 40,000 Confederate troops under A. S. Johnston. Thrown back on the first day of the assault (during which Johnston was killed), the Union forces with reinforcements on the second day assumed the offensive, and a charge led by Grant himself began the rout which ended in an unpursued Confederate withdrawal. (Though the battle appeared to settle nothing, it later made possible successful Union campaigns in the West.) Casualties on each side exceeded 10,000, and no battle of the war except Gettysburg has been the subject of more controversy. The valiant resistance that Grant had encountered made him say later that after Shiloh he gave up all hope of saving the Union except by 'complete destruction,' that is, by waging 'total war.'

Shipbuilding, fostered by the NAVIGATION ACT of 1660, became one of the most important industries in colonial America, where excellent timber was abundant and shipbuilding labor was plentiful and highly skilled. Building costs were low, ready foreign markets stimulated large construction programs, and merchant traders often sold both their ships and cargoes in foreign ports. By 1760 one-third of the total British tonnage (378,000) was built in the colonies. So long as wooden vessels plied the seas, American shipbuilding yards flourished, but the substitution of the metal steamship gave British shipbuilders a construction advantage, partly because Americans relied upon the swift clipper ship even after the advantages of the steamship had been demonstrated, and partly because Americans, turning after the Civil War to the development of the West and other internal activities, put little pressure on Congress to follow other nations in supplying adequate shipping subsidies. The shipping requirements of the two World Wars gave U.S. SHIPPING, for a time, an unprecedented boost, but by the mid 1960's the industry was in a serious decline.

SHIPPEN, WILLIAM (1736–1808), after taking his medical degree at Edinburgh (1761), became a pioneer lecturer in anatomy and surgery at the College of Philadelphia (1765). He was a bitter rival of his colleague JOHN MORGAN, whom he succeeded as surgeon-in-chief in the army medical service. Shippen later returned to teaching. His courses, combined with clinical instruction, did much to shape the pattern of early medical education in the U.S.

Shipping in the American colonies was carried on by the merchant trader, who owned both the ship and the cargo, and commerce abroad was conducted on a barter basis, since markets for products to and from America were sporadic. Piracy was a chief risk, though the privateers of the European wars always created maritime shipping problems. American SHIPBUILDING in the era of wooden vessels was an important industry, which the first national Congress fostered by enacting lower duties on foreign goods carried in American bottoms, and by virtually excluding foreign tonnage from the coastwise trade.

After the War of 1812 the merchant trader was superseded by the common carrier. In 1818 the Black Ball Line (New York to Liverpool) opened a scheduled monthly service, and for the next twenty years sailing packets were the main link across the Atlantic. The famous CLIPPER SHIPS in the era 1830–60 were designed almost solely for the long hauls to California and the Orient. After the Civil War the tramp liner became important as a second type of common carrier for intercontinental freight. Steam propulsion and steel vessels brought to the British merchant marine a virtual monopoly of the transportation of American goods in foreign trade, a predominance which continued into the 20th century.

After World War I American vessels, immensely increased in number by Federal subsidies, were carrying nearly half the ocean tonnage that cleared American ports. Though American shipping again declined, it was stimulated by the Merchant Marine Act of 1936, which merged the needs of defense, commerce, mail transportation, and economic revival; and created the Maritime Commission as an over-all regulatory agency. In 1938 Congress established the U.S. Merchant Marine Academy, at King's Point on Long Island.

The U.S. emerged from World War II with the world's largest merchant fleet, but from 1950 to 1965 it declined from 1212 ships to 910, and its share of U.S. foreign trade fell from 23.5 per cent to 8.5 per cent, with none of the six U.S. passenger lines showing a profit. The basic problem was labor, which on the docks and at sea cost up to five times as much as labor abroad. Such disparity encouraged many American shipping firms to sail under foreign flags.

A substantial economic history of shipbuilding and the shipping industries in America for the period it covers is John G. Hutchins, *The American Maritime Industries and Public Policy, 1789–1914* (1941).

SHIRLEY, WILLIAM (1694–1771), born in Sussex, England, after graduation from Cambridge University emigrated to Boston (1731), where he identified himself with the judiciary and so well represented imperial interests that in 1741 he was appointed royal governor of Massachusetts. He carried through sound money measures in a time of financial depression, and conceived the famous expedition (1745) against the French fortress of Louisbourg in Nova Scotia, successfully conducted by WILLIAM PEPPERRELL. He was briefly commander of British forces in North America after the death of General Braddock (1755), and as one of the most popular colonial governors made Massachusetts a fighting spearhead of the conquering empire. The wartime shift in the British ministry from Newcastle to Pitt (1756) led to his recall. Thereafter for a decade

(1758–68) he served as governor of the Bahamas. Upon retirement he returned to his handsome house in Roxbury, Massachusetts, where he died just as the revolutionary turmoil (for which he had no stomach) was beginning. 'Where the devil this brace of Adamses came from,' he wrote testily, 'I know not.'

See the biography by John A. Schutz (1961).

SHOLES, Christopher Latham (1819–90), Milwaukee journalist, in collaboration with Samuel W. Soulé and Carlos Glidden received a patent (1868) for the first practical TYPEWRITER. After he made numerous improvements, he sold his rights (1873) to the manufacturing firm of E. Remington and Sons (Remington Arms Company).

Shoshone Indians, of Uto-Aztecan stock, early in the 19th century were a primitive tribe living principally in the Great Basin. With the Paiute and the Bannock they are sometimes called the Snake Indians. The eastern Shoshone ranged the Great Plains as buffalo hunters. Today, they are settled on reservations in the Rocky Mountain region, where they number some 4500.

Showboats, small floating theaters that performed at waterfront towns, were popular forms of entertainment on the Ohio and Mississippi after 1830. After the Civil War they were expanded into elegant canal boats, flatboats, and keelboats. They continued into the 20th century, presenting circuses, melodramas, and minstrel shows. Today showboat performances are chiefly antiquarian.

Shriners, or Nobles of the Mystic Shrine for North America, are members of the fraternal order founded (1872) by the American comedian W. J. Florence (1831–91), who had been initiated at Cairo into the Ancient Arabic Order, which is dated by the Shriners from A.D. 656. Their membership is drawn from the Knights Templar and from Scottish Rite Masons, and in 1965 totaled 837,000. They are easily distinguishable in parades by their resplendent costumes. Shriners are particularly active in charity.

Sicily Campaign (July–August 1943), which laid the groundwork for the invasion of Italy during World War II, was planned by the Allies at the CASABLANCA CONFERENCE. This 'Operation Husky' was entrusted to General Dwight D. Eisenhower and his deputy General Sir Harold Alexander. It began (10 July) as an air and sea invasion by Anglo-American forces, the British led by General Sir Bernard Montgomery, the Americans by General George Patton. The naval arm was supplied by Admiral of the Fleet Sir Andrew Cunningham. This invasion, one of the biggest and boldest amphibious operations of the war, involved a total of 450,000 troops.

After Palermo fell to the Americans (24 July), and Catania to the British (5 August), Patton entered Messina (17 August), and the conquest was complete. The Mediterranean thenceforth was more secure for Allied shipping, and Sicily became a springboard for attacks on Sardinia and Italy. U.S. casualties totaled 7400.

Sierra Nevada, mountain range in eastern California, is a 430-mile-long uplift, sheer and rugged on its eastern front, but sloping gradually on its western face into the Sacramento and San Joaquin valleys. Its snow-capped peaks feed the many streams used for water power and irrigation in the state, and its forests yield timber. There are three national parks in the area: YOSEMITE, SEQUOIA, and KING'S CANYON.

SILLIMAN, Benjamin (1779–1864), after graduation from Yale (1796) was called to the newly created chair of chemistry and natural history at Yale (1802–53). He was the first to institute public laboratory instruction in chemistry. Silliman was an inspiring lecturer on the public platform as well as in the classroom, but he is lastingly remembered as the founder and first editor (1818–46) of the *American Journal of Science,* the periodical that came to be known as 'Silliman's Journal.'

His son, Benjamin Silliman (1816–85), laid the foundation of Sheffield Scientific School at Yale, and he succeeded his father as professor of chemistry and editor of the *Journal.* His investigations of petroleum products laid the foundation on which great industries were later built.

SILVER, Abba Hillel (1893–1963), Lithuanian-born Zionist leader and Reform rabbi, made his pulpit at The Temple in Cleveland (1917–63) famous for efforts to create a Jewish homeland in Palestine and to hasten its recognition as a state. He was president of the Zionist Organization of America and head of many other Jewish welfare and educational agencies, becoming a founder of Israel and its eloquent interpreter in America. He wrote *World Crises and Jewish Survival* (1941) and *Where Judaism Differed* (1956).

Silver mining in North America first became commercially profitable in the 16th century, when Mexican mines, exploited by Spanish venturers, supplied Europe with both coinage and silverware. It was one of the main factors that made the New World attractive to explorers from rival nations. Silver mining in the U.S. on a large scale began with the opening (1859) of the COMSTOCK LODE in Nevada. Thereafter the prosperity of the silver miners was intimately tied to the government's policy on silver valuation, especially on the issue of FREE SILVER after the Panic of 1873. The huge quantities of silver produced by the mines in Colorado, Utah, Idaho, and Montana during the 1880's depressed the price, and repeal of the SHERMAN SILVER PURCHASE ACT in 1893 put many mines out of business. Today only in Idaho is silver the principal mineral in order of value.

Silver Purchase Act, see *Sherman Silver Purchase Act.*

SIMMS, William Gilmore (1806–70), born in Charleston, South Carolina, was a prolific writer of prose and poetry, but he is chiefly remembered for his romances based on South Carolina history and frontier life, which were written with gusto. They include *Guy Rivers* (1834), *The Partisan* (1835), and *The Yemassee* (1835), one of the great American historical novels. Simms is the most representative man of letters of the Old South, which in fact neglected him. In the North he was championed by his lifelong friend Bryant, and Harper and Brothers published many of his best books. His material sacrifices for the Confederate cause during the Civil War left him impoverished.

SIMS, James Marion (1813–83), gynecologist, was a graduate of Jefferson Medical College, Philadelphia (1835). He first practiced in Alabama, where his operative skill brought him wide recognition. In 1853 he removed to New York City, founded the Woman's Hospital (1855), and became internationally known as a pioneer in gynecological surgery. He described his introduction of new instruments and new operations in *Clinical Notes on Uterine Surgery* (1866). His posthumous *The Story of My Life* (1884) is the personal record of a 19th-century leader in operative techniques.

SINCLAIR, Upton (1878–), after graduation from the College of the City of New York (1897), associated himself with the MUCKRAKING movement and socialism. His exposure of industrial evils in the Chicago stockyards in *The Jungle* (1906) led to congressional investigations and passage of the Meat Inspection Act of 1906, a landmark in consumer protection. His later exposure novels include *King Coal* (1917), *The Brass Check* (1919), dealing with journalism, and *Boston* (1928), covering the Sacco-Vanzetti case. Especially successful and socially conscious without strong socialist overtones were his Lanny Budd series, concerning national and international events, Nazism particularly.

In 1934 Sinclair was narrowly defeated when he ran as Democratic candidate for governor of California on a platform called EPIC ('End Poverty in California'), part of the 'SHARE-THE-WEALTH' movement of that era.

Siouan Family of North American Indians were a powerful group of tribes first encountered by French explorers during the 17th century in the upper Great Lakes region. They dominated the west bank of the Mississippi south to Louisiana, and in the 18th century, having driven the Cheyenne and the Kiowa out of the Black Hills, they controlled much of the Plains region.

The most important members of the family were the DAKOTA tribes. The ASSINIBOIN were a northern branch, as likewise were the CROW, HIDATSA, and MAN-

DAN (in the upper Missouri), and the OMAHA and OSAGE (in the lower Missouri). The Siouan tribes were often at war with each other as well as with tribes of the Algonquian and Iroquois families and the whites. In the 19th century they were finally deprived of their hunting grounds by determined U.S. military action in a series of wars that lasted until 1890. Today remnants of this large family occupy reservations in Minnesota, Montana, Nebraska, North Dakota, and South Dakota.

SITTING BULL (*c.* 1834–90), leader of the Hunkpapa (Dakota) Sioux Indians in their resistance (after 1866) to removal onto reservations, defeated GEORGE A. CUSTER in the battle of Little Bighorn (1876). Sitting Bull escaped to Canada, was later pardoned, returned in 1883, and in 1885 appeared in Buffalo Bill's Wild West Show. He was killed near Fort Yates, North Dakota, while 'resisting arrest' during the GHOST DANCE uprising shortly before the massacre at Wounded Knee.

Six Nations, see *Iroquois Confederacy*.

Sixteenth Amendment (1913) to the U.S. Constitution gives Congress the power to levy taxes on incomes, without apportionment among the several states and without regard to enumeration of their population. The Amendment stemmed from opposition to the U.S. Supreme Court decision in POLLOCK *v.* FARMERS' LOAN AND TRUST COMPANY (1895), which had invalidated the tax provision of the WILSON-GORMAN TARIFF ACT (1894).

Sixth Amendment to the U.S. Constitution, see *Bill of Rights*.

Skating, besides being a skill in the game of ice HOCKEY, has developed as a spectator sport for both speed skating and figure skating. (It is one of the most popular of the Olympic Games.) Contests are held in North America notably at Montreal, Canada, Lake Placid, New York, and Sun Valley, Idaho. Indoor events on skating rinks began to attract wide notice after Sonja Henie, an Olympic champion, made the ice carnival a popular diversion in 1936. Roller skating gained a large following in the 20th century, and many roller-skating tournaments are now held annually.

Skiing became an organized sport in the U.S. in 1904, when the U.S. National Ski Association was formed. (It has been a major event in the Winter Olympic Games since 1924.) Interest in the sport greatly increased in the U.S. after the Winter Olympics were held at Lake Placid, New York, in 1932. The types of events usually included in ski meets are the jump, the downhill race, the cross-country run, and the slalom (zigzag downhill race). The two most notable skiing centers in the U.S. are Sun Valley, Idaho, and Steamboat Springs, Colorado.

'Skinners,' see *Cowboys*.

Skyscraper, a steel-frame building of great height, was first developed in the U.S. late in the 19th century as a means of using space economically in crowded urban areas. It was the product of a uniquely American building movement, the Chicago school, which demonstrated for the first time on a large scale the potential of a new technology: an iron skeleton frame with supporting walls, which permitted large glass openings and flexible interior planning. The first true skyscraper was the ten-story Home Life Insurance Building (Chicago, 1885), designed by W. L. JENNEY.

During the 1890's the steel frame, developed to its final skyscraper form, became a riveted skeleton bearing all the structural load; the walls served merely as enclosing screens. Cass Gilbert (1859–1934) introduced the 'super-skyscraper' with the Woolworth Building (New York, 60 stories, 1913), for many years the world's tallest. The famous New York zoning ordinance (1916), by requiring setbacks as buildings gained in height, created 'wedding cake' structures, regarded by most architects as aesthetically unpleasing. The ordinance was revised in 1961, and the new law may have as profound an influence on the future skyline of the city as did the old law upon its past. It will encourage architects to design simpler buildings and set them back on plazas, thereby creating new open space for the public.

A revolution in the aesthetics of the skyscraper was brought about by ELIEL

SAARINEN, whose design (1922) for the proposed Chicago Tribune Building envisioned the use of engineering skill to create a sense of volume, not mass. The Empire State Building in New York (Shreve, Lamb, and Harmon, 102 stories, 1930) still remains the world's tallest structure. Buildings of such great height and complexity do not present insuperable engineering problems, but unless they can be located in very desirable or highly congested areas they become economic liabilities.

An early example of an open, landscaped environment is Rockefeller Center in New York, a complex of fifteen buildings (Reinhard and Hofmeister; Hood, Godley and Fouilhoux; Corbett, Harrison and MacMurray, 1928–47). It is the largest privately owned business and entertainment center in the world. Following the same trend, and widely acclaimed as pace-setters of contemporary office architecture, are Lever House (Skidmore, Owings and Merrill, 1952) and the Seagram Building (Mies van der Rohe and Philip Johnson, 1958), both in New York.

Population growth is a determining factor in the erection of skyscrapers, and very tall buildings are currently being erected throughout the world on a greater scale than ever before.

See Carl W. Condit, *The Rise of the Skyscraper* (1952).

SLATER, SAMUEL (1768–1835), English-born pioneer in the cotton textile industry, gained thorough knowledge of cotton-manufacturing machinery as supervisor in the mill of Jedediah Strutt, a partner of the inventor Richard Arkwright. Slater was induced to come to Rhode Island by the bounties offered by the textile industries in America. He set up his first mill at Pawtucket (1793). Since both textile workers and machinery were controlled in England by stringent laws, Slater had to emigrate in disguise. By a feat of memory he reconstructed Arkwright's complicated machinery. He soon established other mills elsewhere in New England, became a prosperous manufacturer, and created an industry which in his lifetime became one of the most important in the U.S.

Slaughterhouse Cases (1873) are indispensable for understanding modern U.S. constitutional law in the light of the Civil War Amendments. These cases stemmed from the contention that a monopoly grant of the Louisiana legislature was a violation of the 'privileges or immunities' clause of the Fourteenth Amendment. The majority decision of the Supreme Court, rendered for the defendant by Justice Miller, held that the purpose of the Amendment was to guarantee the freedom of former Negro slaves, not to transfer control over the entire domain of civil rights from the states to the Federal government. The decision only temporarily reversed the strong postwar trend toward Federal centralization. Negro rights were soon eclipsed by the tendency of the courts to emphasize the protection of corporations from allegedly unfair state regulation given by the Fourteenth Amendment.

Slave trade in America began when Negroes were landed at Jamestown, Virginia (1619), and sold for life as INDENTURED SERVANTS. At first imported from the West Indies, slaves were not commercially important until tobacco culture became profitable. Enslavement of Indians had disadvantages. They could escape too easily, and authorities frowned on a practice which might make slaves of members of friendly tribes who were important allies in time of need. In 1662 Charles II gave his brother James the slave trading rights in the English colonies, and until 1697, when Parliament threw open the slave trade, the Royal African Company of London possessed a monopoly. Thereafter the WEST INDIA TRADE, the so-called 'triangular trade,' became highly profitable.

Contrary to popular belief, only some of the slaves were free Africans kidnapped by Europeans. A large proportion had been kidnapped by other African coastal tribes or states in order to sell them in exchange for rum, salt, codfish, and Spanish dollars. The slave ships bringing Negroes from the Guinea coast sailed under the flags of all nations, and as the New England colonies developed, their vessels (the Guinea ships) were notorious among those that plied the 'Middle Passage' (the second leg of the triangular trade) with human chattel packed so tightly that the horrors of the voyage were indescribable.

Although Jefferson condemned the slave trade in the original draft of the Declaration of Independence, New England traders joined with southern planters to strike out the clause, and the Constitution itself prohibited Congress from interdicting the trade before 1 January 1808. The profits from the slave trade were so great that merchants thereby gained capital, which they invested heavily in mills, factories, mines, and transportation facilities. The slave trade provided much of the capital for the Industrial Revolution, both in England and in the U.S.

Actually all the states had ended the legal importation of foreign slaves before 1803, although South Carolina removed restrictions in 1804. In 1807 Congress exercised its power, and prohibited the importation of slaves at the year's end. Thereafter smuggling became profitable. It was pursued for 50 years on a large scale; perhaps as many as 10,000 to 15,000 were smuggled in annually during the 1850's alone. The total number of slave importations from colonial times down to the abolition of slavery in 1865 is conjectural, but reliable estimates set the figure in the neighborhood of 3,000,000.

Local domestic trade developed early, and after 1800 became a well-organized, long-distance business, with trading company headquarters in the upper South, at such assembly points as Cincinnati and Louisville, for distribution 'down the river' into markets opening into the Southwest. Slaves were sold from the auction block like any livestock, with scant consideration for human ties. When John Randolph of Roanoke was asked whom he believed to be the greatest orator of the age, he replied: 'A slave. She was a mother, and her rostrum was the auction-block.' The price of 'prime field hands,' eighteen to twenty-five years old, rose from $500 in 1832 to $1800 in the late 1850's. The total volume and value of the domestic slave trade is conjectural, but a moderate estimate for all the states on the eve of the Civil War is an annual turnover of 80,000, valued at $60,000,000. The passage of the Thirteenth Amendment to the Constitution (1865) ended the institution of SLAVERY in the U.S.

See Elizabeth Donnan, ed., *Documents Illustrative of the History of the Slave Trade in America* (4 vols., 1965).

Slavery in America developed profitably under the PLANTATION SYSTEM, and during the 17th century spread from Virginia to other colonies under the impetus of the SLAVE TRADE, which was favored by Britain as a commercial venture. Not all colonizers sanctioned the institution. Farmers in New England and the Middle Colonies found slave ownership unprofitable, and white artisans resented Negro slave competition. Sentiment opposing slavery on humanitarian grounds was expressed by a vote of Pennsylvania Quakers as early as 1688, but slaves and INDENTURED SERVANTS for another century formed the nucleus of labor in all the colonies throughout the colonial period. The census of 1790 reveals that there were nearly 700,000 slaves in the U.S., 20 per cent of the total population, and more than 40 per cent in the South, where the institution flourished. The first of the ANTISLAVERY SOCIETIES was founded in Philadelphia (1775), and thereafter the ABOLITION MOVEMENT gained headway, except in the Deep South, where it was bitterly resented. There the invention of the cotton gin (1793) had increased the advantage of the use of slaves as pickers, since the gin could handle so much more cotton. The earliest states to abolish slavery were Rhode Island (1774), Vermont in its state constitution (1777), and Pennsylvania (1780). Other states in the North followed shortly, and by the Ordinance of 1787 slavery was excluded from the Northwest Territory, the region now extending from Ohio to Wisconsin.

Between the Revolution and the Mexican War (1846) the issue of slavery was not generally raised in political controversy. Although the petition of Missouri for admission to the Union brought the question up, it was temporarily solved by the MISSOURI COMPROMISE (1820). The decade of the 1850's, however, witnessed prolonged struggles over slavery. The COMPROMISE OF 1850 was followed by widespread establishment of an UNDERGROUND RAILROAD, the surreptitious smuggling of slaves into the North and to Canada. Passage of the KANSAS-NEBRASKA ACT (1854), which culminated in border warfare, headlined in the North as 'BLEEDING KANSAS,' was part of the slavery issue of the decade, in which the DRED SCOTT CASE (1857), the LINCOLN-DOUGLAS DEBATES (1858), and the capture and hanging of JOHN BROWN (1859) were prominently associated with events leading to secession and the Civil War.

In 1860 there were some 4,000,000 slaves in a southern population of 12,000,000, and by this time the slavery issue was as much ideological as economic; to many Southerners enslavement now seemed to be the only feasible racial policy in areas of Negro concentration. Lincoln's EMANCIPATION PROCLAMATION (1862) fused the cause of the Union with that of human liberty, and the Thirteenth Amendment to the Constitution (1865) abolished slavery in the U.S.

See U. B. Phillips, *American Negro Slavery* (1918), and K. M. Stampp, *The Peculiar Institution* (1956).

SLIDELL, JOHN (1793–1871), a graduate of Columbia (1810), became a prominent lawyer in New Orleans, and while serving as a Democrat in Congress (1843–45) was appointed minister to Mexico; but since that country had broken diplomatic relations after the annexation of Texas (1845), it declined to receive him. Slidell was influential as a Senator from his state (1853–61), and during the Civil War he went as Jefferson Davis's commissioner to France, though he was unable to gain aid or recognition for the Confederacy. Slidell, with James M. Mason, figured in the TRENT AFFAIR.

SLOAN, JOHN (1871–1951), after studying at the Pennsylvania Academy of the Fine Arts, worked for twelve years as a newspaper illustrator. Moving to New York, in 1908 he became a member of the rebellious group of realistic artists called THE EIGHT, and for many years was a greatly respected teacher at the Art Students League. He painted city scenes with the sympathetic understanding of one familiar with them. He also became an interpreter of the Southwest, and in 1931 he formed a national organization for the advancement of American Indian art. Representative of his restrained strength and imaginative application of mass is *Sixth Avenue and Third Street* (Whitney Museum), and *McSorley's Bar* (Detroit Institute of Art).

SLOAT, JOHN DRAKE (1781–1867), having seen action in the U.S. navy during the War of 1812, later served against pirates in the West Indies. As commander of the Pacific squadron (1844–46), he occupied Monterey, California, in 1846 on the ground that the British were about to do so, and during the Mexican War he took San Francisco. He retired in 1861, and five years later he was promoted to the rank of rear admiral.

SMIBERT, JOHN (1688–1751), Scottish-born portrait painter, was one of the first professional artists to come to America. Having studied in Italy and demonstrated his ability in London, he came with Bishop Berkeley (1728) to Rhode Island, expecting to teach art in Berkeley's proposed college. The plans failed, and Smibert settled in Boston, where he exhibited copies he had made of Old Masters. This was the first art show in America (1730). His paintings, though formalized, are competent. His group portrait, *Bishop Berkeley and His Entourage* (Yale), is the earliest such made in the colonies (1731).

SMITH, ALFRED EMANUEL (1873–1944), born on New York City's East Side, as a young man joined Tammany Hall, rose through local political offices, and sat in the state legislature for twelve years, during the last two of which (1913–15), as an influential Democrat, he served as Speaker of the Assembly. While president of the New York City board of aldermen, he ran for governor (1918), won the election, and made so brilliant a record in securing progressive welfare laws and beating down ultraconservative legislation that this 'happy warrior' (as F. D. Roosevelt called him in a 1924 address) was re-elected three times, serving until 1929. By that time he was a wealthy man and president of the corporation that erected the towering EMPIRE STATE BUILDING.

The Democratic nomination of Smith for President in 1928 made him the first Irish Catholic and lifetime city dweller to be the choice of a major party in U.S. history. Smith lost the election to Hoover by an electoral vote of 444 to 87, for the rural South and West felt no enthusiasm for Smith, who was a Catholic, an out-and-out 'wet' during the Prohibition era, and a Tammany politician. (Besides, Herbert Hoover was then a very strong candidate.) Thereafter Smith sought no political office, but in 1934 he became a leader in the newly formed American Liberty League, a group of conservative Democrats including John W. Davis, the du Ponts, and other heads of corporations who strongly opposed Roosevelt's New Deal measures aimed at regulating manufacturers, investment houses, and stock exchanges. His personal record, *Up to Now* (1929), deals with the politics of his era.

SMITH, JEDEDIAH STRONG (1799–1831), one of the most notable of the MOUNTAIN MEN, was born near Binghamton, New York. He first came into prominence on the third of the ASHLEY EXPEDITIONS, when, by taking an exploring party through South Pass in Wyoming (1824), he opened a gateway for immigration into the Far West. This extraordinary feat was matched by his two journeys to California. After the Salt Lake rendezvous of 1826 he took his men across the Mohave Desert up into the San Joaquin valley. He left them there while he crossed the Sierra (it was the first west-east crossing of the Sierra by a white man), and he returned to the rendezvous. He then set out for California over the Salt Lake–Los Angeles Trail, journeyed up the entire Pacific coast into the northernmost Oregon region, and then went back through the entire length of Idaho to Pierre's Hole, Wyoming. Smith was made a partner in Ashley's powerful Rocky Mountain Fur Company. He was killed by Comanches while en route west on the Sante Fe Trail. His qualities of leadership in mountain regions became legendary, and his travels opened up more territory and broke more trails to California and the Pacific Northwest than those of any other explorer of the Rocky Mountains.

SMITH, JOHN (1580–1631), English explorer and colonizer in America, was son of a Lincolnshire farmer. At sixteen he became a soldier of fortune on the Continent, and for eight years he remained away from England, participating in wars in the Low Countries, Transylvania, and Hungary. Although the veracity of his extravagant *True Travels* (1630) was long questioned, recent investigations tend to confirm the truth of his statements. After his return to England in 1604 he invested in the Virginia Company and energetically promoted its plans to plant a colony in America. In 1606 as one of a party of 144 colonists he sailed to Virginia, and, after disembarking at Jamestown (May 1607), he was named a member of the governing council and began exploring the region.

Smith's *True relation of . . . occurrences in Virginia* (1608) is the earliest first-hand account of the settlement. He fell into the hands of chief Powhatan while attempting to establish trade with the Indians, and the narrative of his rescue from death by Powhatan's daughter, Pocahontas (an episode by which Smith is known throughout the English-speaking world), is held by recent authoritative scholarship to be probable. On his return to Jamestown, Smith became 'Governour of Virginia,' and by his tact and resourcefulness carried the colony through its grim 'starving time.' Injured by a gunpowder explosion, in 1609 he returned to England and published *A Map of Virginia* (1612), a primary contribution to cartography. The remaining twenty years of his life he devoted largely to promoting the colonization of New England.

Smith's first voyage on behalf of Sir FERDINANDO GORGES and other members of the PLYMOUTH COMPANY in 1614 yielded a valuable cargo of fish and furs. On a second voyage in 1615 Smith was captured by pirates, then by the French. To employ his mind while at sea, he wrote *A Description of New England* (1616). The tract is significant because it coined the name of the region and was the first book to give the English public a favorable picture of the resources lying about the 'Countrie of the Massachusets, which is the Paradise of all those parts.' The *Description* was embellished with a portrait of the author by authority of the Council that had sent him as the 'Admirall of New England,' together with an engraved map, by far the most accurate yet made available. Smith was eventually released in France, and he returned to England.

The Pilgrims declined Smith's offer to

guide them in 1620, 'to save charges.' They felt that his books and maps would suffice. The modest success of the Plymouth venture made good 'sales talk' for Smith, who incorporated early narratives of the settlers in the second edition (1622) of his 1620 colonization tract, *New England trials* (that is, *attempts*), and in his *Generall historie of Virginia, New-England, and the Summer Isles* (1624), a magniloquent reworking of earlier versions of his narrow escapes, triumphs, bad luck, and unappreciated greatness, together with a glamorously detailed account of the Pocahontas story.

Such promotional literature did in fact encourage haphazard settlements along the coast, and Smith never wavered in his faith that God in his good time would plant New England with English seed. His last pamphlet, *Advertisements for the unexperienced Planters of New-England, or anywhere* (1631), he dedicated to the archbishops of Canterbury and York, and speaks warmly of the Puritan leaders, 'those noble Gentlemen' who had the year before established a colony on the shores of Massachusetts Bay. Smith himself profited little from his principal life work, promotion of New England colonization, but no one did more to open the way for the founding of a nation than this practical adventurer.

See the biographies by Bradford Smith (1953), and Philip L. Barbour (1964).

SMITH, Joseph (1805–44), founder of Mormonism, was born on a hard-scrabble farm in Sharon, Vermont. His family drifted westward, finally settling on an equally unproductive frontier acreage in Palmyra, New York, where, according to Smith's later account, by revelation (1827) he discovered the hiding place of the golden tablets inscribed with mystic utterances which (from behind a curtain and with the aid of magic spectacles) he translated and others transcribed from his dictation. These 'reformed Egyptian' characters were published as the Book of Mormon (1830). Smith, as prophet and seer, then organized at Fayette, New York, the religious sect of Latter Day Saints generally known as MORMONS. Hostility of neighbors and disaffection within the group were the chief reasons for Smith's removal first to Kirkland, Ohio (1831), then to Independence, Missouri (1838), and finally to Nauvoo, Illinois (1840), where by further 'revelation' he was alleged by many of his followers to have sanctioned polygamy.

A general uprising against the Mormons in June 1844 led Smith to put Nauvoo under martial law, but since many of his ardent supporters were absent at the time, campaigning for his presidency of the U.S., Smith was unable to maintain order. With his brother Hyram he was imprisoned at Carthage on charges of treason, and on the night of 27 June a mob broke into the jail and lynched the brothers.

A highly controversial figure, Smith was the object of bitter vilification by the 'Gentiles' of his day. His successor, BRIGHAM YOUNG, led his followers to Utah. Disaffected followers founded a Reorganized Church in Missouri.

SMITH, Nathan (1762–1829), Massachusetts-born physician, after study at Harvard Medical School (1789–90) began practice in Cornish, New Hampshire. He undertook further study in Europe (1796–97) before helping to found medical schools at Dartmouth (1797) and at Yale (1813), where he thereafter taught. In high repute as a surgeon and a teacher, he gave impetus to the establishment of medical schools at Bowdoin (1820) and Vermont (1822). His emphasis on the value of accurate observation gave high standing to his *Practical Essay on Typhus Fever* (1824).

SMITH, Sir Thomas (1558–1625), the leading English businessman of his time and one of the most active commercial promoters in the age of colonial settlements, was a working member of many of the most important trading companies of London. A parliamentary leader and a principal officer of the navy, Smith had served for more than twenty years as governor of the East India Company when he was chosen (1609) Treasurer (governor) of the newly established LONDON COMPANY for the colonization of Virginia. During the next decade he gave that venture much time and money, but the rifts that occurred among the promoters led to his resignation (or ejection) in 1619. He was replaced by Sir EDWIN SANDYS.

SMITH, William (1727–1803), Scottish-born Episcopal minister, after coming to America (1751), published *A General Idea of the College of Mirania* (1753), an outline of the aims and types of courses he thought an American college should have. The essay so impressed the trustees of the College of Philadelphia that they elected him provost (1755–79). He was a prominent figure in the intellectual life of the city, but after the outbreak of the Revolution he was suspected of Loyalist sympathies, and the Assembly voided the charter of his college, alleging violation of the charter rights. He then founded Washington College in Maryland, but was called back to Philadelphia as provost when the charter was restored (1789), and he remained in office until the college was absorbed into the University of Pennsylvania (1791).

SMITH, William (1728–93), born in New York City, graduated from Yale (1745), practiced law in New York, and with William Livingston compiled the first digest of New York statutes (for 1691–1756). He is best known for *The History of the Province of New York* (to 1732), with primary emphasis on the 18th century (reprinted in 1829, with his continuation to 1762). An able if partisan account, it comments astutely on contemporary New York society. Smith was a Loyalist, and in 1783 he went to England. He later became Chief Justice of Canada (1786–93). His massive unpublished diary is in the New York Public Library.

Smith Act (1940), see *Alien Registration Act.*

Smith College was founded through the bequest of Sophia Smith (1796–1870), a wealthy Hatfield, Massachusetts, spinster. It opened in 1875 at Northampton. It sought to give women an education equivalent to that offered by the best colleges for men, and instruction was first given by Amherst professors. It pioneered in music courses, has a school for social work, a school of architecture and landscape architecture (at Cambridge), and offers graduate courses, to which men are now admitted. In 1965, with an endowment of $38,000,000 and a faculty of 250, it enrolled 2400 students.

Smith-Connally Antistrike Act (1943), also called the War Labor Disputes Act, was passed over President Roosevelt's veto. It authorized the government to seize plants where interference with war production was threatened by a labor disturbance, and forbade strikes in plants that the government seized. This controversial legislation followed the coal strikes of J. L. Lewis's UNITED MINE WORKERS. Under its terms the government twice took over the coal mines and, briefly, the railroads.

Smithsonian Institution, the earliest American foundation for scientific research, was established by Congress (1838) and opened in 1846 at Washington, D.C. For ten years prior to its establishment Congress had debated its constitutional right to accept a £100,000 bequest for 'an establishment for the increase and diffusion of knowledge among men,' given in the will of James Smithson (1765–1829), an English chemist. John Quincy Adams was instrumental in winning acceptance of the gift. The endowment, which was greater than that of any American university at the time, made possible the financing of original research in all branches of science.

Today its libraries and collections have made it the national institution of learning that Washington had recommended in his Farewell Address (1796). Secretaries of the Institution have been as follows.

Joseph Henry, physicist (1846–78)
Spencer Fullerton Baird, biologist (1878–87)
Samuel Pierpont Langley, physicist (1887–1907)
Charles Doolittle Walcott, geologist (1907–27)
Charles Greeley Abbot, astrophysicist (1928–44)
Alexander Wetmore, biologist (1945–52)
Leonard Carmichael, psychologist (1952–64)
S. Dillon Ripley, 2nd, ornithologist (1964–)

Smoot-Hawley Tariff Act, see *Hawley-Smoot.*

Snake Indians, a name at first incorrectly applied to several Indian families in the Far West, today designates the SHOSHONE and the northern PAIUTES.

Snake river, 1038 miles long, rises in Yellowstone National Park (Wyoming), flows west in a tremendous canyon across Idaho, then north and west to join the Columbia near Pasco, Washington. It was discovered in 1805 by the Lewis and Clark expedition. Rival fur traders made use of it to penetrate the Pacific Northwest, and during the 1830's and 1840's it was followed by emigrants on the Oregon Trail. Several of the river's waterfalls are spectacular. Hells Canyon, ten miles from rim to rim at its widest point, averages 5500 ft. deep for over 40 miles, and at one point is 7900 ft., a depth exceeding that of Grand Canyon. Today the turbulent waters of the Snake are being harnessed to produce hydroelectric power and to reclaim vast areas of dry but fertile land.

Soccer, originally called association football, developed in England when the London Soccer Association (1863) was formed to further a type of football that emphasized only the kicking of the ball. It is a secondary game in the U.S., largely because of the tremendous popularity of football, but it is the most popular sport played internationally.

Social Democratic party was an organization of political theorists who, with a following from labor unions, fostered a plan in 1898 to introduce the socialist program in state and local elections. Eugene V. Debs ran as the party's presidential nominee in 1900. In 1901 the party united with the moderate wing of the SOCIALIST LABOR PARTY to create the SOCIALIST PARTY.

Social Gospel movement, see *Christian Socialism.*

Social reform, as part of the LABOR MOVEMENT, was especially significant during the period 1840–52, when labor turned to UTOPIAN SOCIALISM and other humanitarian panaceas in an effort to ameliorate the depressing conditions with which it struggled. Co-operative programs like FOURIERISM, an agrarian-handicraft economy, were vigorously supported by such writers as ALBERT BRISBANE, G. H. EVANS, and HORACE GREELEY. Experimenters like ROBERT OWEN, with his informed sense of the gulf between a mill owner and his employees, were pioneers in labor reform. (The 'anarchist' JOSIAH WARREN had the most individualistic approach.) The most successful among the co-operative groups was the NORTH AMERICAN PHALANX, and for a time BROOK FARM helped tie them into a national culture. None of them, except the MORMONS, became self-sustaining, and they soon declined.

CO-OPERATIVE SOCIETIES in the same period set up central agencies to buy for retail trade, and the protest against economic abuses was carried forward by the GRANGER MOVEMENT. The TEMPERANCE crusade, at the time aimed in some measure to help the workingman save his wages, won a victory when Maine passed the first statewide prohibition law in 1846. But none of these attempts gave organized labor the power to meet organized capital on the relatively equal terms later created by TRADE UNIONS and COLLECTIVE BARGAINING.

Social Security Act (1935) was an elaborate administration measure intended to provide the U.S. citizen, while he works, with assurance that in later years when facing reduced circumstances he can meet his basic needs. Amended six times (as late as 1958), it authorizes three programs: social insurance (unemployment, old age, disability); public assistance to the needy; and child welfare. Its favorable terms attracted all states into a Federal-state system of UNEMPLOYMENT COMPENSATION. In 1965, Medicare was added to the Social Security system to provide hospital care, nursing homes, and other medical services for those over 65.

Social settlements developed in the U.S. in response to social problems created by the labor unrest after the PANIC OF 1873 and the New Immigration of the 1880's, and the need for community services and recreational facilities in the congested tenement areas in large cities. They were modeled on London's Toynbee Hall of the 1880's, where the socially minded youth of Oxford and Cambridge came as 'residents' to furnish the leadership needed in slum areas.

The University Settlement in New York City, which began as the Neighborhood Guild (1886), was soon followed by others, notably Hull-House, Chicago (JANE ADDAMS); South End House, Boston (ROBERT A. WOODS); Henry Street Settlement, New York (LILLIAN WALD); and Chicago Commons (GRAHAM TAYLOR). A national federation, organized in 1911, helped co-ordinate the work in various cities where the greatest single service was to break down the isolation of immigrant 'colonies,' especially in the years preceding World War I, by encouraging newcomers to utilize their skills or to learn new ones as part of a program of Americanization.

Social work, as an organized service in the U.S., originated in the establishment of such agencies as the Society for Prevention of Pauperism (New York, 1818) and subsequent philanthropic ventures conducted by volunteers and financed by wealthy merchants and socialites. Charles Loring Brace (1826–90), the social reformer, pioneered in CHILD WELFARE when he established the Children's Aid Society of New York (1854). The National Conference of Charities and Correction (now the National Conference of Social Work) was founded in 1873. In the same decade JOSEPHINE LOWELL began her important work, and by 1900 the 'economic aspects of altruism' were receiving the attention of college sociology classes.

The trend to professionalism developed out of the advances in psychology and psychiatry, encouraged by such organizations as the Sage Foundation, which were interested in social diagnosis and the work of SOCIAL SETTLEMENTS. After the founding of the American Association of Social Workers (1922), local, state, and Federal aid became increasingly available for housing reforms, preventive programs, and rehabilitation.

Socialism, as a political and economic theory of social organization, advocates collective (governmental) ownership and management of the essential means for producing and distributing goods. It argues that production is based on use, not profit, and that in a socialist society class warfare and BUSINESS CYCLES will be eliminated, thus assuring a more equitable distribution of the products of society.

In the U.S. various groups have advocated democratic or coercive measures to achieve their aims. SOCIAL REFORM movements have included UTOPIAN SOCIALISM, COMMUNAL SOCIETIES, and such political associations as the SOCIAL DEMOCRATIC PARTY, SOCIALIST LABOR PARTY, SOCIALIST PARTY, and COMMUNIST PARTY, as well as many LABOR UNIONS.

Pioneers among Americans who have studied collectivist movements, and thus helped create the field of SOCIOLOGY, are L. F. WARD and THORSTEIN VEBLEN.

See D. D. Egbert and Stow Persons, *Socialism and American Life* (2 vols., 1952).

Socialist Labor party, formed in 1877 as an outgrowth of a New York City workingmen's party (1874), was the first American socialist party on a national scale. Its program was strongly Marxist during the 1890's under the militant leadership of DANIEL DE LEON. Many members opposed De Leon, and they withdrew (1899) to join the less militant SOCIAL DEMOCRATIC PARTY, after which the Socialist Labor party sharply declined. It has continued to draw some support, and from time to time it has run presidential candidates, most recently in 1960.

Socialist party in the U.S., an outgrowth of the SOCIAL DEMOCRATIC PARTY, was founded (1901) by a group led by EUGENE V. DEBS and VICTOR BERGER. Thereafter Debs ran as the party's candidate for President at each election through 1912. MORRIS HILLQUIT long remained the theoretical strategist of the party. During World War I the Socialists pronounced against U.S. participation, and under terms of the wartime Espionage Act, Debs was sent to prison, where in 1920 he was again the party's presidential nominee and received 920,000 votes.

After a radical element withdrew in 1919 to form the Communist party, the Socialists won support of moderate groups who advocated a system of socialism through evolutionary means. They supported programs of improved labor conditions, social security, and welfare legislation. Thereafter the party's outstanding leader was NORMAN THOMAS, who was a candidate for President in six successive campaigns, from 1928 to 1948. In 1936 the party lost much of its right-wing support to the New Deal, though in local and state elections it continued to win offices.

Society for Propagation of the Gospel in New England (1649), the oldest Protestant foreign missionary society in the world, was founded in London by Act of Parliament, largely through the efforts of JOHN ELIOT, who directed his labors toward converting the Indians. The Act established the New England Company of 1649, which raised funds and provided workers to assist Eliot, who set up some fourteen villages of PRAYING INDIANS on land granted for the purpose. Eliot's work was largely destroyed by King Philip's War (1675), but the Company continued its efforts elsewhere. It was reorganized in 1787 as the Society for Propagating the Gospel among the Indians of North America, and carried on its work for many years.

Society for the Propagation of the Gospel in Foreign Parts (1701), organized in the American colonies by THOMAS BRAY, was chartered by William III to assist Anglican churches. The S.P.G. engaged in missionary activities and founded churches (notably in the Carolinas) from Maine to Georgia before it withdrew after the Revolution. In many localities it established the first schools and libraries.

Society of Jesus, see *Jesuits.*

Socinianism, see *Unitarians.*

Sociology, the science of human groups and societies, has been the concern of philosophers throughout the centuries. The term itself was not coined until 1838, when the French philosopher Auguste Comte first treated the subject systematically. The founder of modern sociology in the U.S. was LESTER FRANK WARD, who initiated evolutionary sociology in 1883, and vigorously opposed the highly popular laissez-faire teaching of WILLIAM GRAHAM SUMNER.

The first department of sociology in any university was that founded (1892) at Chicago by ALBION W. SMALL, who made it a center of sociological research and founded (1895) the *American Journal of Sociology*. Although THORSTEIN VEBLEN roused hostility by his *Theory of the Leisure Class* (1899), he laid the foundation for the institutional school of economics and shaped social theory more profoundly during the 1920's and 1930's than any other American. Among the key by-products of sociology was sociological jurisprudence, which made law a flexible tool for social action by stressing social facts more than legal precedents.

Field investigators before 1920 undertook an examination of the conditions of life among minority groups and tenement dwellers in American cities, with the purpose of ameliorating social conditions. Common to all was a study of such problems as housing, intemperance, and the malfunction of such institutions as the family and the church. Under the influence of the pioneer sociologist F. H. GIDDINGS studies were directed into analysis of the American community, both rural and urban, in its ecological context. At first empirical in their approach to generalizations, both sociologists and social anthropologists have recently put community surveys to newer uses, accumulating significant data on attitudes and habits previously neglected.

During the 1920's R. S. LYND and H. M. LYND pioneered in analyzing the general divisions of the community into classes, a procedure carried much further by W. LLOYD WARNER. Such concepts stemmed from the widely accepted 'small group' analysis of collective behavior given impetus at the turn of the century by C. H. COOLEY. Since World War II the base of sociological theory has been broadened by such analyses of social structure and attitudes as those presented by Robert K. Merton, David Riesman, and Talcott Parsons.

A pioneer effort to present a systematic view of the total American social structure is R. M. Williams, *American Society: A Social Interpretation* (1951).

Sod houses (1830–1910), first used by the Indians, were habitations made of thick strips of turf. They were peculiar to the prairie and plains regions of the U.S., where timber was sparse. During the pioneer period, in the area beyond the Missouri river, some 90 per cent of the settlers lived in sod houses. When they could afford frame structures, they used the old sod houses to shelter their stock.

Solid South, so called, developed during RECONSTRUCTION after the Civil War. Northern Republicans not only controlled Congress, but also, through the era of the CARPETBAGGERS, they dominated the legislatures of the former Confederate states, where they sought to extend their influence through the aid of the newly enfranchised Negro. Conservative white Democrats, determined to secure home rule, used every means possible, including intimidation and force, to eliminate the Negro vote and to establish white supremacy. When President Hayes withdrew the troops from the South (1877), every southern state fell under Democratic rule. In the decades that followed, the Republican party in the South existed largely for Federal patronage and minor offices. Memories of vindictive rule during the Reconstruction years outlasted the scars of war, and not until 1928 did a widespread break occur, when the issues of Catholicism and Prohibition split the Solid South. The increasing industrialization of the South during and after World War II further altered the pattern, and today with the advance of Republicanism in the South the term Solid South has lost much of its original meaning.

Solomon Islands Campaign (August 1942–November 1943) during World War II was a series of air, land, and sea battles in the South Pacific fought to recover the islands, which had been captured by the Japanese in March 1942. Landings by U.S. troops on Guadalcanal (7 August) and Tulagi (9 August) were made with relative ease, but the crushing defeat of the U.S. naval force off SAVO ISLAND (9 August) cut almost all support from the troops already landed, and gave the Japanese command of major sea routes in the area. Then followed a six-month campaign to gain control of life-lines between Australia (and the southern tip of Asia) and the Philippines, as a means of moving north to fight an offensive war against Japan.

The decisive engagement was the massive battle of GUADALCANAL, won in November 1942. By February 1943 the Japanese had evacuated Guadalcanal and Tulagi. They still held a maze of islands, including the Gilbert-Marshalls, the Carolines, and Rabaul, their great launching stronghold in New Guinea. In the battle of BISMARCK SEA (2–3 March), a major air-sea engagement, an entire Japanese troop convoy was destroyed. Subsequent sharp naval actions, tough jungle encounters, and shore-to-shore amphibious operations opened passage from the Coral Sea into the western Pacific. When U.S. Marines landed at Bougainville (1 November), the northernmost and largest of the Solomons, the Allies were in a position to thrust toward Rabaul. On the following day they cut off the Japanese supply lines in the decisive battle of Empress Augusta Bay, thus isolating all enemy forces in the Solomons. The U.S. flank for an advance to the Philippines was thus secured, and the bitter campaign was ended.

SONNECK, OSCAR GEORGE THEODORE (1873–1928), born in New Jersey, after education in Germany became chief of the music division of the Library of Congress (1902–17), where he built one of the notable music collections of the world. He founded (1915) the *Musical Quarterly,* which he edited until his death. After 1921 he was vice president of the house of G. Schirmer. Sonneck was one of the pioneer American musicologists, especially in the field of early American music, and his scholarship in musical classification gave him rank in such writings as *A Bibliography of Early Secular American Music* (1905; rev. by W. T. Upton, 1945), *Early Concert-Life in America* (1907), and *Early Opera in America* (1915).

Sons of Liberty were members of secret organizations formed in the American colonies during the summer of 1765 to oppose the STAMP ACT. (They took their name from a phrase used by Colonel Isaac Barré in a speech against the act in the House of Commons.) Sometimes led by such men of standing as SAMUEL ADAMS and PAUL REVERE in Massachusetts, and JOHN LAMB and ALEXANDER MC DOUGALL in New York, these groups on occasion resorted to intimidation and violence to prevent collection of the tax. In Boston the Sons of Liberty burned the records of the vice-admiralty court, ransacked the home of the comptroller of the currency, and burned and looted the mansion of Governor THOMAS HUTCHINSON. These rough tactics secured the 'voluntary' resignation of all stamp agents in the colonies before the effective date of the Act in November. The members usually assembled at Liberty Poles or under Liberty Trees, symbols of their aspiration, and they continued to harry the crown officials until the outbreak of the Revolution.

Sons of the American Revolution (1889) is a national society whose members claim descent from those who fought in the War of Independence. It was incorporated in 1906, and in 1960 it reported a membership of 18,000.

SOTHERN, EDWARD HUGH (1859–1933), was son of the English-born actor Edward Askew Sothern (1826–81), who was long associated with Laura Keene's New York company. E. H. Sothern first appeared with his father in 1879, and for thirteen years he starred in Daniel Frohman's company (1886–99). After 1900 he co-starred with Julia Marlowe (1866–1950) in a long series of Shakespeare revivals. He married her in 1911. Sothern and Marlowe were the leading exponents of Shakespearean drama in the U.S. for more than 25 years. Sothern's autobiography, *The Melancholy Tale of 'Me'* (1916), is among the best of theatrical reminiscences.

SOUSA, JOHN PHILIP (1854–1932), bandmaster and composer, was leader of the famous U.S. Marine Band (1880–92) before he organized his own group, which toured the U.S. and Europe with notable success. He made signal improvements in the instrumentation and quality of BAND MUSIC. Well known among the more than 100 compositions of 'the march king' are *Semper Fidelis* (1888), *Washington Post March* (1889), and *Stars and Stripes Forever* (1897). He was musical director for the U.S. army in the Spanish-American War and in World War I. *Marching Along* (1928) is his autobiography.

South, The, see *Southeast*.

South Carolina had a separate development, under the rule of the CAROLINA PROPRIETORS, from the northern section of the region named for Charles I. CHARLESTON, the earliest settlement (1670), was populated largely by English Protestants and French Huguenots. The colony remained under proprietary rule until 1719, when the legislative body, by usurping control from the proprietors, gave the crown an opportunity to appoint a royal governor. During the period of royal control (1719–76) industry prospered by exporting hides, rice, and indigo. Desire for self-government brought resistance to the STAMP ACT (1765) and subsequent support of a provincial congress. In 1775 the royal governor fled, and in 1776 the colony adopted its own constitution. Throughout the War of Independence the sporadic attacks of such partisan leaders as THOMAS SUMTER, ANDREW PICKENS, and FRANCIS MARION served the patriot cause. Charleston was under British occupation from 1780 to 1782. South Carolina was the eighth of the Thirteen Colonies to ratify the Constitution (May 1788).

The Blue Ridge Mountains cross the northern section of the state, and the FALL LINE separates the coastal plain from the PIEDMONT plateau. The social and economic cleavage between the small-property, democratic piedmont upcountry, and the aristocratic, slaveholding TIDEWATER planters was reflected by removal of the capital to Columbia in 1790, though until 1865 dual state offices functioned in Charleston and Columbia. Although it was strongly nationalistic through the War of 1812, South Carolina began to exhibit states' rights leanings in the 1820's, and under the political domination of JOHN C. CALHOUN it became the acknowledged leader of the STATES' RIGHTS doctrine. The ORDINANCE OF NULLIFICATION (1832) proved abortive, but the gathering force of the ABOLITION MOVEMENT united both Unionists and Nullifiers. In 1852 a secession threat failed only because no other state was ready to co-operate. South Carolina was the first to adopt (unanimously) the ORDINANCE OF SECESSION (1860), and the Civil War began with the firing on Fort Sumter in Charleston harbor (April 1861). In the final months of the war Sherman's army burned Columbia (February 1865).

No member of the Confederacy suffered greater distress during Reconstruction. Though South Carolina was readmitted to the Union in 1868, for six years thereafter, conservatives charged, the CARPETBAGGERS subjected the state to 'the rule of the robbers.' Under Wade Hampton and the Red Shirts the conservatives captured the state for white supremacy. By this time farm tenancy had replaced the plantation system. Today agricultural diversification and the use of new farming methods have helped to improve the lot of the farmer, and hydroelectric plants have spurred manufacture. The subtropical climate along the seacoast has created in that area a number of winter resorts, which are a growing element in the state's economy. The University of South Carolina (Columbia, est. 1801) is the state's leading educational institution.

South Carolina Exposition, see *Tariff of 1828.*

South Carolina Railroad (1833), from Charleston to Augusta, Georgia, extended 136 miles, and at the time was the longest in the world. Various branches were later added. Since 1899 it has functioned as part of the Southern Railway system.

South Dakota was part of Dakota Territory (1861) prior to its admission to the Union in 1889 as the 40th state. Its history until then was shared with that of NORTH DAKOTA, as is its topography and geology, recorded in the rock formations of the BLACK HILLS and the BADLANDS. South Dakota has a continental climate; the summers are hot and dry, and the winters cold and snowy. Like its sister state, South Dakota has an agricultural economy, with great wheat fields in the north and diversified crops in the central and southeastern areas. Most of the population is centered in small towns, first settled by immigrants from northern Europe. Sioux Falls is its largest city, with a population (in 1960) of 65,000.

South Dakota's early history was violent and colorful. At Little Bighorn the cavalry force of GEORGE A. CUSTER was annihilated by the Sioux in 1874. Deadwood, which was a wide-open frontier town during the gold rush in the late 1870's, is now a tourist center for the Black Hills, particularly Mount Rushmore, with its gigantic carvings of American Presidents. South Dakota is now the principal gold-producing state, and the site of the important Missouri River Basin dam and reservoir improvements. Chief among its institutions of higher learning are the University of South Dakota (Vermillion, est. 1882), the State College of Agriculture (Brookings, est. 1884), and the School of Mines (Rapid City, est. 1885).

South Pass, the most celebrated of the passes in the Rocky Mountains, is a broad level valley (at an altitude of 7500 ft.) which cuts across southwestern Wyoming. It was first effectively discovered in 1824 by JEDEDIAH SMITH and TOM FITZPATRICK, and long served as a gateway for emigration to the Far West. BENJAMIN BONNEVILLE took the first wagons over the pass in 1832.

Southeast, generally called *The South,* is the region including the present states of Virginia, Kentucky, Tennessee, North and South Carolina, Georgia, Florida, Alabama, Mississippi, Louisiana, and Arkansas. During the 16th century France and Spain sent expeditions to explore and colonize the area. (For details, see entries on the states.) Texas also was penetrated at that time. Until the Civil War the region was predominantly agrarian with an economy based on slave labor, and, apprehensive of political and financial encroachment by the North, strongly emphasized states' rights. Its varied cultures were represented by its leading cities, RICHMOND, CHARLESTON, ATLANTA, and NEW ORLEANS; by the democratic rural society of the OLD SOUTHWEST; and by Spanish and French traditions in the Gulf region. All the states (together with Texas) joined the Confederacy during the Civil War, whose battles were mostly waged in that area. The scars left by that national upheaval are reflected in the fiction of such novelists as Ellen Glasgow, Thomas Wolfe, William Faulkner, and R. P. Warren, who convey the region's sense of failure and frustration, and depict its years of poverty and its memory of a past rich in tradition.

After World War I the South began effectively to tap its great industrial potential, and by mid-20th century the value of its commerce and manufactures (concentrated in Richmond, Atlanta,

Louisville, Birmingham, Memphis, and New Orleans) had become 10 per cent of the national total. It still contrasted sharply with the North, in that, with twice the area, it had but two-thirds the population (mostly native born, 70 per cent rural, 30 per cent Negro), and less than half the per capita income.

Forty per cent of U.S. forest land is in the South, and its resources in petroleum (Arkansas, Louisiana, Mississippi) are large. It has the best Negro colleges in the country.

Southern California, University of, at Los Angeles, is a private, nonsectarian, co-educational institution, opened by Methodists in 1880. It comprises 25 schools and offers graduate study in many disciplines, including Commerce, Dentistry, Education, Engineering, Law, Library Science, Music, Public Administration, Religion, and Social Work. In 1965, with a faculty of 1013, it enrolled 18,800 students.

Southern Pacific Railroad, completed in 1884, was a merger of local lines and provided through service from New Orleans to San Francisco. Railroad surveys made in the 1840's mapped a desirable southern route along the Gila river, and the GADSDEN PURCHASE (1853) guaranteed an all-American right of way. The final consolidation was chiefly the work of LELAND STANFORD and COLLIS HUNTINGTON.

Southwest, historically the oldest and politically the youngest of the regions in the U.S., includes Oklahoma, Texas, New Mexico, and Arizona. It became known to Europeans through the accounts of the earliest Spanish explorers, notably Cabeza de Vaca (1536), Fray Marcos de Niza (1539), and Coronado (1540–42). Thereafter for 300 years the history of the Southwest (Oklahoma excluded) was part of the geographical, social, and political history of Spanish colonization. The region abounds in Spanish names. Its legal systems, art, architecture, and folklore are steeped in Spanish origins, and Spanish missions shaped the lives of generations of Indians. Its ranching system produced that popular American idol, the cowboy.

Overland routes were first established by the Spanish Trail (1775), from Santa Fe to California. Trappers and hunters soon blazed others, for use as cattle drives to the north or as emigrant and commercial routes to the west, notably the Southern Trail (Galveston to El Paso), the Desert Trail (El Paso to Los Angeles), and most important, the Santa Fe Trail (Kansas City to Santa Fe).

Oklahoma was part of the Louisiana Purchase (1803), and for 50 years it was set aside as an Indian territory, forbidden to white settlement. Texas, largely developed by Anglo-Americans, won independence from Mexico (1836), and was annexed to the U.S. (1845) three years before the rest of the region became part of the nation by the Treaty of Guadalupe Hidalgo (1848). The Colorado river, with its present vast system of dams, supplies power and irrigation to the western section. The ruins of the Indian and Mexican civilizations, and their surviving customs, are also tourist attractions, and they provide a profitable source of income.

Southwest Territory, see *Tennessee*.

Space exploration was first seen to be feasible after the physicist ROBERT H. GODDARD successfully launched the world's first liquid-fuel rocket in 1926. Rockets and guided missiles were used in World War II and their development was studied in government-financed experiments, especially in Germany, England, Russia, and the U.S. In 1942 the physicist and aeronautical engineer THEODORE VON KARMAN formed the Aerojet-General Corporation, which worked on ideas that resulted in a complex of inventions and innovations in rockets, especially in the development of liquid and solid fuel propellants. After 1950 government appropriations in Russia and the U.S. for rocket experiments became huge.

The space age opened when (4 October 1957) Russia orbited the first artificial earth satellite (Sputnik I). The U.S. launched Explorer I, its first satellite, in January 1958, and in that year created the National Aeronautics and Space Administration (NASA) to conduct research on problems of nuclear propulsion systems, space probes, and manned flights in space. In 1964 Congress appropriated $5,227,000,000 for NASA for the fiscal year 1965.

In the first four years of the space age both Russia and the U.S. launched a variety of rockets, including shots to and around the moon. This new and vast undertaking pools the skill of hundreds of engineers and taps basic knowledge in all fields of science, especially in the kinetics of chemical reaction and the study of corpuscular radiation. Russia first manned a space ship (April 1961), recovered after one orbit of the earth, and in August their scientists were able to study the effects on man of a long orbital flight, recovered in the 18th orbit. The first orbital flight by an American (February 1962), John C. Glenn, Jr., was recovered in the 3rd orbit.

In 1963 President Kennedy proposed a joint U.S.–Russian expedition to the moon, an offer renewed a year later by President Johnson. By 1964 the development of multi-seat spacecraft with increasing numbers of circuits to refine knowledge about the effects of space phenomena on the human body gave expectation of a moon landing within a decade. In the same year some 500 man-made satellites, each equipped to return specific information, were circling the earth. The Communication Satellite Corporation (Comsat) has in orbit satellites that receive and transmit television and radio programs. These work on a global scale without intermediary hookups. In 1965 Mariner 4 flew past Mars and transmitted a store of information back to Earth. This was one of the most significant scientific achievements of the space age. New probes constantly alter and extend the data here possible to record.

The importance of space exploration goes far beyond the practical ends of establishing satellite communications, long-range weather prediction, or finding means to launch lethal weapons from sites in space. For the first time man has been able to penetrate the mysteries of the stellar universe.

SPALDING, ALBERT GOODWILL (1850–1915), Chicago merchant and sportsman, gained national fame as a baseball pitcher with the Boston Club (1871–75) and the Chicago Club (1876–91). In 1876 he established the sporting goods firm of A. G. Spalding & Brothers. He was especially able as a manager of baseball clubs and helped to enhance the popularity of the sport by publication (after 1878) of his baseball guides. His *America's National Game* (1911) helped baseball gain status.

SPALDING, JOHN LANCASTER (1840–1916), Bishop of Peoria, was a voluminous writer who made important contributions to educational theory by such books as *Means and Ends of Education* (1895) and *Thoughts and Theories of Life and Education* (1897). Believing that the Catholic Church must enter into the vital controversies of the times, he argued that the Christian character alone could preserve the dignity of man, not by denying the validity of scientific tenets, but by interpreting and directing their conclusions.

Spanish-American War (1898) was touched off by the Cuban insurrection of 1895, brought about by Spanish political oppression and the economic prostration caused by the operation of high tariffs on tobacco and (especially) on sugar. A similar Cuban revolution earlier (1868–78) had not stirred Americans to help liberate Cuba from 'Spanish tyranny,' because at that time the temper of the American people and the policy of the government were different.

During the 1890's three factors coincided to give Americans a new sense of world problems. At one level, American economic interest in Cuba had enormously increased, and the destruction of the sugar industry was a blow to investors and to shipping interests. At another, America's entry into world affairs was reshaping the nation's philosophy of nationalism, and the resurgence of the spirit of Manifest Destiny gained support at all levels of public utterance. Finally, not only was imperialism frankly supported by newspapers throughout the country, but the techniques of journalism had developed to a point where the circulation or syndication of newspapers made possible the creation of a wave of war hysteria by feeding the flames of chauvinism, spectacularly successful in Pulitzer's New York *World* and Hearst's *Journal.*

The U.S. was deeply involved in the Cuban insurrection from the start. Scores of filibustering expeditions set out from American ports, and a Cuban 'junta' with headquarters in New York sold bonds and disseminated propaganda. Even anti-imperialist Democrats and Populists urged freedom for Cuba, and the humanitarian Governor Altgeld of Illinois wrote interventionist articles and interviews for the Hearst press. Americans with property interests in Cuba demanded protection. (The business press, however, opposed war.) Various incidents strained relations between Spain and the U.S., and, when incidents were few, the yellow press fabricated them. President Cleveland did his best to enforce neutrality, and when Congress passed a concurrent resolution (April 1896) asking Spain to accept the offices of the U.S. in helping to establish an independent Cuba, Cleveland ignored the gesture and Spain rejected the offer. In the autumn of 1896 McKinley was elected on a platform which incorporated a demand for Cuban independence, but McKinley began his administration with utmost circumspection on that point. Reforms inaugurated by a new Spanish regime in 1897, looking to home rule for Cuba, came too late, and loyalists and insurrectionists continued their war of extermination.

The publication (9 February 1898) of the tactless DE LÔME LETTER, which exacerbated relations between Spain and the U.S., was followed within a week by the destruction of the battleship MAINE (15 February) in Havana harbor with the loss of 260 lives. Congress thereupon appropriated $50,000,000 for national defense without a dissenting vote. McKinley's suggestions of a Cuban armistice, revocation of the concentration camp policy that had been functioning under General 'Butcher' Weyler, and American mediation between Spain and Cuba were conceded by Spain on every point. This gave McKinley the opportunity for a peaceful settlement, but the clamor for war in Congress, the press, and the country seemed to obsess the President with the idea that unless he yielded to popular demand he would lose party leadership. On 11 April he sent a message to Congress asking for the 'forceful intervention' of the U.S. to establish peace in Cuba. On 20 April Congress adopted a war resolution, which McKinley signed. (Its Teller Amendment disclaimed any intention of exercising sovereignty over Cuba.) On the following day diplomatic ties with Spain were severed, and the U.S. proceeded to blockade Cuban ports. On 24 April Spain declared war on the U.S., and on the 25th the U.S. made its own war declaration retroactive to the 21st.

The U.S. had embarked on this 'splendid little war' in a lighthearted spirit, even though, at the time, Spain was still — seemingly — a power to be reckoned with. In fact, the Spanish Empire had been decaying for more than a century, and, as inept and badly trained as the Americans were, they could hardly have failed to defeat the even more incompetent Spanish forces. Spain had 200,000 troops in Cuba, while America had a regular army of only 30,000, dispersed across the continent, and very inadequately commanded. In a military sense the U.S. was entirely unprepared. The U.S. did have a modern 'steel navy' in an advanced state of readiness and efficiency, but the harbor defenses along the Atlantic coast were so inadequate for war that the North Atlantic fleet was split; half of the ships were sent to blockade Havana, and the rest, hopefully called 'the Flying Squadron,' were stationed at Hampton Roads. Such tactics might well have been fatal in another situation, but the Spanish fleet was incredibly outmoded in armament and manned by poorly trained crews. All decisive battles of the war were naval engagements.

In February, two months before the war began, Theodore Roosevelt, then Assistant Secretary of the Navy, had sent Commodore GEORGE DEWEY secret instructions to keep his Asiatic squadron intact, and, in the event of war, to attack the Spanish in the Philippines. After the battle of MANILA BAY (1 May) Spanish power in the Pacific was effectively destroyed though Manila was not invaded until 13 August, one day after the armistice was signed.

In the Atlantic theater, the army planned an invasion of Cuba, and in spite of badly managed transportation, the U.S. Fifth Army Corps landed unopposed near Santiago, even though the Captain-General of Cuba had been forewarned of the intended assault for weeks. The invasion culminated in the successful storming, by the 'Rough Riders,' of SAN JUAN HILL, and the capture of its batteries, which commanded Santiago harbor. The Spanish fleet had been bottled up in the harbor by the American ships led by Admiral SAMPSON and Commodore SCHLEY, and when the Spanish admiral found his ships threatened by the shore batteries, he took his fleet to sea to face the Americans. In the battle of SANTIAGO (3 July) the Spanish fleet was wiped out.

In ten weeks' fighting the U.S. had won an empire and had become a world power, with vital interests in the western Pacific and Asia. Spain soon sued for peace, and the TREATY OF PARIS of 1898 ended the war.

Of the 306,000 U.S. land forces, 5400 died in service, but fewer than 400 of these were battle casualties. Most died of diseases caused by improper sanitation and lack of medical services.

See F. E. Chadwick, *The Relations of the U.S. and Spain: The Spanish-American War* (2 vols., 1911); and J. W. Pratt, *Expansionists of 1898* (1951).

Spanish Main, mainland of Spanish America, was the northeast coast of South America between the Orinoco river and the isthmus of Panama. Spanish treasure ships passing through the Caribbean north of the Main were attacked by English buccaneers. Today the term refers to the coast, the Caribbean, and the West Indies, regions associated with pirate legends.

Spanish Trail, see *Old Spanish Trail.*

SPARGO, JOHN (1876–1966), English-born reformer, before World War I was closely associated with the Socialist party. Best known among his books dealing with social problems is *The Bitter Cry of the Children* (1906), an exposure of child labor conditions and a document in the history of the MUCKRAKING movement.

SPARKS, JARED (1789–1866), Connecticut-born historian, after graduation from Harvard (1815) served as pastor of a Unitarian church in Baltimore (1819–23), then returned to Boston to edit the *North American Review* (1824–30). Sparks's services in breaking ground for the professional study of history were very important. One of the first Americans to work from manuscript sources, he edited *The Diplomatic Correspondence of the American Revolution* (12 vols., 1829–30), *The Writings of George Washington* (12 vols., 1834–37), and *The Works of Benjamin Franklin* (10 vols., 1836–40). With others he edited the *Library of American Biography* (25 vols., 1834–47). In 1839 he was appointed to the professorship of history at Harvard (the first in any American institution), and he later served there as president (1849–53).

Although the scholarship of Sparks was inexact by modern standards, his bowdlerizations were influenced by methods of writing and editing which had not yet become 'scientific.' He did no essential damage by tailoring Washington's grammar, and his 'corrections' of Franklin's text have been unjustly abused. His notes are still useful, and the impetus he gave to the documentary movement was of major significance.

Speakeasies, so called, were the restaurants and cabarets where liquor was illegally sold in the U.S. during the PROHIBITION ERA of the 1920's. Though police surveillance of speakeasies became notoriously lax, admittance to them was always surrounded by an air of secrecy and adventure.

Speaker of the House, see *House of Representatives.*

Specie Circular, issued by President Jackson in 1836 for the purpose of inhibiting the decline in value of paper money, provided (with minor exceptions) that only gold and silver would be accepted by the government in payment for public lands. The Circular helped precipitate the PANIC OF 1837.

Specie Resumption, see *Resumption Act (1875).*

SPEICHER, EUGENE EDWARD (1883–), Buffalo-born portrait and landscape painter, studied at the Art Students League, and with Chase and Henri. His paintings are known for their vigor, effective color, and skillful technique which gives a feeling of space. They are represented by *The White Fichu, Girl with Green Hat,* and *The Mountaineer.*

SPERRY, Elmer Ambrose (1860–1930), electrical engineer, founded various companies for manufacturing electrical equipment before establishing the Sperry Gyroscope Company (1910). Among his 400 inventions are the gyrocompass, which eliminates variations caused by the earth's magnetism, and the intensity searchlight, which produces one and a half billion candlepower.

Sphere of influence is the term applied since the late 19th century to a territorial area in which the special interests of outside nations are held to be paramount to the claims of the actual sovereign state. World powers first began developing such spheres in Africa, and after 1900 they extended them in the Pacific area by parceling undeveloped regions. The open door policy of the U.S. did not actually challenge these spheres when it was formulated. By mid-20th century spheres of influence were under attack all over the world.

Spirituals, religious folk songs of the Negroes, have been a cherished part of American culture for 100 years. They were the means by which the world became conscious of Negro music, especially after the Fisk (University) Jubilee Singers began their tours (1871) at home and abroad. The origin of spirituals is unknown, but informed opinion holds that they developed early in the 19th century in the South, and are Negro adaptations of European folk hymns (transplanted first to New England from the British Isles) blended with African musical traditions.

They grew out of the ring-shout (chanting back and forth), and combined harmony with a lengthened melody. The blend also produced the cheerful and rhythmic jubilee, such as 'When the Saints Go Marching In.' Spirituals lend themselves to mass extemporization, and uniquely combine pathos with an unquestioning faith. Their appeal is felt especially in their bittersweet blue tonality, at once both sad and gay. Representative spirituals include 'Swing Low, Sweet Chariot,' 'Nobody Knows the Trouble I've Seen,' and 'Go Down, Moses.'

Spoils system was based upon a phrase popularized by Senator William Marcy of New York in 1832 — 'to the victor belong the spoils' — to justify the discharge of public officeholders of the defeated party and the employment of adherents of the winning party. This political stratagem marked the beginning of party machines. Although President Jackson was accused of furthering a spoils system by his views on rotation in office, he did not actually fill any more vacancies on a partisan basis than Jefferson. It was after the Whigs came into power in 1841 that officeholders were removed wholesale. The spoils system continued to operate with little hindrance until the Pendleton Act (1883) created the civil service commission. But so ingrained had the system become that neither that Act nor later reform legislation has eradicated the spoils system in American politics, still often controlled by party bosses.

Spooner Act (1902) authorized the President of the U.S. to acquire the French concession in Panama for $40,000,000, providing Colombia would cede a strip of land across the isthmus of Panama 'within a reasonable time' and upon reasonable terms; otherwise the President was to open negotiations with Nicaragua for a canal to join the Atlantic and Pacific oceans. Under its authority the President purchased the concession and negotiated the hay-herrán treaty.

Sports (organized) in the U.S., both participation and spectator, have enormously increased during the 20th century. In the 19th century such organizations as the New York Yacht Club (1844) and the Knickerbocker Baseball Club of New York (1845) furnished diversion for the leisured and wealthy members of society.

From Britain came the competitive sport tradition and from Germany and other continental nations emerged calisthenics and group athletics. Urbanization created a demand for spectator sports, of which baseball was the first to win (and hold) national attention. Croquet, roller skating, and archery began a trend toward sports in which both men and women participated. When tennis and bicycling were added in the 1880's, outdoor activities furnished diversion for hundreds of thousands.

FOOTBALL became a significant part of intercollegiate sports programs in the 1870's, BOAT RACING and horse RACING increased in popularity, SOCCER and LACROSSE were introduced, TRACK AND FIELD events were organized, and by the end of the decade the National Association of Amateur Athletics was founded (1879). The one distinctively American game, BASKETBALL, was invented in 1891, and GOLF soon became popular. The OLYMPIC GAMES were revived in 1896, giving competitions an international character.

The growth of sports has been fostered by agencies which have become national in scope. Often the athletic departments of schools and colleges, and the leagues of clubs and municipal groups, function through elaborate systems. Newspapers devote special sections to sports events, and sporting magazines in wide variety are featured on newsstands.

Whether played on an amateur or professional basis, such sports as baseball, football, basketball, and BOXING draw immense crowds. More recently organized sports include BOWLING, AUTOMOBILE RACING, HOCKEY, BOBSLEDDING, and SKIING. The advent of television has increased audience participation in all sports events.

See J. A. Krout, *Annals of American Sport* (1929), and F. R. Dulles, *America Learns to Play: A History of Popular Recreation, 1607–1940* (1940).

SPOTSWOOD, ALEXANDER (1676–1740), royal governor of Virginia (1710–22), was one of the first appointed executives to give attention to the needs of actual settlers rather than the interests of land speculators. He personally led explorations (1716) which opened up large tracts of the Shenandoah valley to frontiersmen, whom he encouraged by freeing them from taxes and quitrent. He introduced the writ of habeas corpus, established a flourishing trade with the Indians, and developed an iron industry. After 1730 he served as deputy postmaster general for the colonies.

Spotsylvania, Battle of (8–12 May 1864), one of the major engagements during the WILDERNESS CAMPAIGN in the Civil War, was Grant's unsuccessful effort to outflank Lee, who, discovering Grant's intent, entrenched his army twelve miles southeast of Fredericksburg, Virginia. At Spotsylvania Court House they fought a five-day battle, the first in modern trench warfare. On the last day Lee exacted a heavy toll when the Union forces assaulted the salient ('the Bloody Angle') forming his center. Though Grant had lost 13,000 men, he sent word to General Halleck: 'I propose to fight it out along this line if it takes all summer.'

Springfield Republican, see *Bowles, Samuel.*

SPRUANCE, RAYMOND AMES (1886–), a graduate of the U.S. Naval Academy (1906), commanded a task force in the battle of MIDWAY (June 1942), and led the Fifth Fleet (1944–45) in its invasion of the Gilbert and Marshall Islands. (At the war's end he served as commander in chief of the Pacific Fleet.) No admiral during World War II was more admired as a flag officer. Spruance was superbly capable of making correct decisions in tactical operations. His performance at Midway gives him rank as one of the greatest admirals in the history of the American navy.

'Square Deal,' a phrase given political significance by President Theodore Roosevelt, was especially popular in 1906, when Roosevelt demanded a 'square deal' for labor. In his speech of 29 August 1910 he asserted: 'I stand for the square deal . . . I stand for having those rules changed so as to work for a more substantial equality of opportunity and reward.' Human welfare, he argued, anteceded property rights.

Squatter sovereignty, see *Popular sovereignty.*

SQUIER, EPHRAIM GEORGE (1821–88), newspaperman, archaeologist, and diplomat, began his lifelong study of prehistoric remains with an examination of the Ohio and Mississippi valleys. His *Ancient Monuments of the Mississippi Valley* (1847), a pioneer study of the MOUND BUILDERS, was issued as the first of the Smithsonian 'Contributions to

Knowledge' series, and was followed by *Aboriginal Monuments of the State of New York* (1851). Later as a government envoy in Latin America Squier assembled first-hand material, and he excited the interest of archaeologists by writing such books as *Nicaragua* (1852), *The States of Central America* (1858), and *Peru* (1877).

Stagecoaches by 1756 made through-connections between New York and Philadelphia, a three-day journey. Lines soon led out of the principal northern cities, and after the Revolution, encouraged by government mail contracts, stagecoaches plied the POST ROADS into the South. Lines connected the East with Pittsburgh by 1804, and the service east of the Mississippi reached its peak 35 years later. (The government tolerated combines of large stagecoach companies in the interest of efficient mail delivery.) After the railroads had completed their trunk lines, the stagecoach was profitable only in isolated or mountainous regions. In the trans-Missouri West, where (by 1851) the stagecoach connected the East with Santa Fe, Salt Lake City, and Sacramento, it became an institution, with monthly (later daily) service of the OVERLAND MAIL.

STAGG, AMOS ALONZO (1862–1965), after graduation from Yale (1888) began his lifelong career as athletic director and football coach at Chicago (1892–1933). At the age of seventy-one the 'grand old man of football' became football coach at the University of the Pacific in Stockton, California (1933–46). Stagg was regarded as an authority; he served on the football rules committee (1904–32), and wrote several books about the sport.

'Stalwarts' was the name applied to themselves by such professional politicians and spoilsmen as ROSCOE CONKLING and SIMON CAMERON during the administration of President Hayes. In 1880 they sought a third term for Grant, and they dubbed the anti-Grant wing of the Republican party 'HALF-BREEDS.' The designation was dropped soon after the election (1880) of Garfield, who was fatally shot by Charles J. Guiteau, a disappointed office seeker, who was a Stalwart.

Stamp Act (1765), the first direct tax levied by Parliament upon the American colonies, was designed to increase crown revenues by requiring a stamp duty on a large variety of printed items, including newspapers, almanacs, pamphlets, diplomas, and all legal documents. By this Act the sporadic objection to the SUGAR ACT (1764) was suddenly mobilized into a surprisingly violent and nearly unanimous opposition. The colonists were concerned over these questions: Was this but the first of many direct taxes? Was the grant of jurisdiction to vice-admiralty courts an assault upon the right to trial by jury? Was the imposition a deliberate attempt to weaken the colonies economically?

Almost overnight the colonies entered into NONIMPORTATION AGREEMENTS that were so effective that London merchants petitioned Parliament for a repeal of the tax. The degree and nature of the opposition led Parliament to repeal the Act in a matter of months (March 1766), but while doing so it passed the DECLARATORY ACT, asserting its ultimate authority in the colonies, which at the moment were so busy celebrating the repeal of the Stamp Act that they at first but dimly perceived the implications of the new one. Thus the significance of the Stamp Act remained. It had created a constitutional issue centering upon the question of representation in Parliament.

Stamp Act Congress (October 1765), the first intercolonial meeting summoned by colonial initiative, met in New York at the instigation of the Massachusetts legislature, and may be regarded as the opening move in the American Revolution. Nine colonies were represented by 27 delegates, who convened to draw up a declaration of rights and grievances for presentation to the King and Parliament. The petition, chiefly drawn by JOHN DICKINSON of Pennsylvania, stated that 'no taxes ever have been or can be constitutionally imposed on them, except by their respective legislatures,' and asserted that the Stamp Act undermined the 'rights and liberties of the colonists.' Thus the constitutional issue of representation was raised, soon to be made more acute by passage of the TOWNSHEND ACTS (1767).

Standard Oil Company was founded (1870) as an Ohio corporation by JOHN D. ROCKEFELLER, HENRY M. FLAGLER, and four others. It replaced a partnership that managed one of the largest oil refineries in the world. By 1872 it had absorbed nearly all refineries in the Cleveland area and within a decade, through subsidiary and associated companies, controlled more than 90 per cent of the refining capacity of the U.S., including pipelines, storage tanks, and marketing organizations at home and abroad. (Almost from the start 75 per cent of its markets were in Europe.)

It was the first company in the world to organize the whole of a complex industry, and by 1880 it was the richest and most powerful. It then set up the first trust (in the sense of MONOPOLY) in American history, 40 component companies administered by nine able trustees, headed by Rockefeller. The trust was declared illegal by the Ohio courts in the 1890's but unity was maintained by informal agreements. In 1899 it was reorganized under the more lenient laws of New Jersey. The U.S. Supreme Court forced a more complete dissolution in 1911. The net income in 1965 of the Standard Oil Company of New Jersey ($1 billion) ranked third among U.S. industries.

Standing Order was the designation into the 19th century implying that the Congregational churches in New England constituted the established church, from which all others were regarded as dissenters. Each such church was the church of the town, supported by a tax levied proportionately upon all the inhabitants. The separation of CHURCH AND STATE was longer delayed in New England than anywhere else in the U.S. Nonconforming bodies at last brought about disestablishment, finally in Massachusetts (1833).

STANDISH, MILES (*c.* 1584–1656), accompanied the SEPARATISTS to America on the *Mayflower* (1620) as captain of the guard. He became an influential member of the community, and he was sent to England as agent for the Plymouth Colony to negotiate for loans and property rights. With John Alden he founded Duxbury (1637), and later was treasurer of the colony (1644–49). At his death Standish left a small library, quite impressive in quality. (Longfellow's poem, 'The Courtship of Miles Standish,' is without historical foundation.)

STANFORD, LELAND (1824–93), born in Watervliet, New York, during the gold rush went to California where he became a successful merchant, entered politics, and as Republican governor (1861–63) helped keep California in the Union. With Collis P. Huntington he was a principal founder of the CENTRAL PACIFIC RAILROAD, whose construction he personally superintended (during the 1860's) and of which he was lifelong president. He later headed the Southern Pacific Railroad (1885–90) and served as U.S. Senator (1885–93). In memory of his son he founded STANFORD UNIVERSITY. Stanford was a railroad builder in the era when those who had money and political power stressed rugged individualism and fought public control. As he told his stockholders in 1878: 'It is a question of might, and it is to your interest to have it determined where the power resides.'

Stanford University, founded by LELAND STANFORD, opened at Palo Alto, California, in 1891 as the Leland Stanford Junior University (still its legal name), under the presidency of DAVID STARR JORDAN. Supported by an initial gift of $20,000,000, it became at once the leading private institution of learning west of the Mississippi. It is known for its research and graduate work. Its library collections include the Hoover Library on War, Revolution and Peace (1914). In 1965, with an endowment of $145,480,000 and a faculty of 1125, it enrolled 10,000 students.

STANLEY, SIR HENRY MORTON (1841–1904), English explorer (born John Rowlands), emigrated to the U.S. (1857), took the name of the New Orleans merchant who adopted him, and in 1862 became an American citizen. In the Civil War he fought in the Confederate army until his capture at Shiloh, after which he briefly served with the Union navy. Before 1870 he had won journalistic fame as a reporter. Among his dramatic assignments for the New York *Herald,* the most spectacular was his search (1870

–71) in equatorial Africa for the Scottish missionary David Livingstone, whom he found and casually greeted: 'Dr. Livingstone, I presume.' Stanley's later African explorations (1874–77, 1879–84) traced the course of the Congo, clarified the geography of central Africa, and led to the creation of the Congo Free State under Belgian rule. In 1895 Stanley resumed his British citizenship, and four years later he was knighted.

STANTON, EDWIN MCMASTERS (1814–69), after attending Kenyon College, practiced law in Ohio, and as his reputation grew, moved to Pittsburgh (1847) and to Washington, D.C. (1856). A 'War Democrat,' he was invited into Buchanan's cabinet (December 1860) as Attorney General. After SIMON CAMERON resigned as Secretary of War (January 1862), Lincoln brought Stanton into his cabinet as Cameron's successor. Stanton was vituperative and ill-mannered, and made no secret of his frequent objection to Lincoln's policies. He was no expert on military matters, but he rarely interfered with actual operations, and Lincoln rightly trusted him as a highly efficient administrator, determined and thorough.

Although Stanton probably had intelligence of the plot on Lincoln's life, the intimation that he was involved in the conspiracy has no support from competent historians. He clashed savagely with President Andrew Johnson, who favored a mild treatment of the South after the Civil War. Johnson's dismissal of Stanton in defiance of the TENURE OF OFFICE ACT (1867), by which the RADICAL REPUBLICANS had kept Stanton in Johnson's cabinet, was a chief reason for impeachment proceedings against Johnson. When Johnson was acquitted, Stanton resigned (1868). President Grant named Stanton to the Supreme Court, but Stanton died before he could take his seat.

See the biography by B. P. Thomas and H. M. Hyman (1962).

STANTON, ELIZABETH CADY (1815–1902), a pioneer in the woman-suffrage movement, with LUCRETIA MOTT organized (1848) at Seneca Falls, New York, the first woman's rights convention in the U.S. She later assisted SUSAN B. ANTHONY in editing the militant feminist magazine *Revolution* (1868–70). An able writer and compelling lecturer, she devoted her life to liberal causes, and was one of the authors of the first three volumes (1881–86) of *History of Woman Suffrage*.

Staple crops, those grown in large quantities, in colonial times were principally TOBACCO (Virginia, Maryland, North Carolina), RICE (South Carolina, Georgia), and INDIGO (South Carolina). Sugar was the chief staple in the West Indies, and its important by-product, molasses, was the foundation of the New England rum distilling industry, which was part of its WEST INDIA TRADE. (Cotton growing was not an important industry until after the Revolution.) These crops depended entirely upon slave labor, and largely on foreign capital and foreign markets.

In the 19th century the WHEAT INDUSTRY and the COTTON INDUSTRY became immensely important in the American economy.

Star Route frauds were collusions in the granting of contracts by the Post Office Department for transportation of mail over those western roads (designated on guide maps by an asterisk), where mail was carried by horse and wagon. Certain departmental officials conspired with mail contractors to impose worthless securities on the government, and to demand large appropriations for opening new and useless routes. The trials (1882–83) revealed frauds by which the government had lost some $4,000,000, but no convictions were obtained.

STARK, JOHN (1728–1822), began his military service under ROBERT ROGERS in the French and Indian War (1755–63), and later as a colonel took part in engagements of the Revolution from Bunker Hill to the battle of Trenton (1775–76). In 1777 he commanded a brigade of New Hampshire militia, and during the Saratoga Campaign he won the battle of BENNINGTON. Thereafter, as a brigadier general in the Continental army, he commanded the Northern Department. In 1783 he was breveted major general.

'Stars and Stripes,' see *Flag of the U.S.*

'Star-Spangled Banner' (the U.S. National Anthem), was composed by FRANCIS SCOTT KEY during and after the bombardment of Fort McHenry (at Baltimore) by the British (13–14 September 1814). The poem was set to the tune of 'Anacreon in Heaven,' a popular drinking song. It was later printed on broadsides. (The flag that gave Key his inspiration survived the bombardment, and it is preserved in the Smithsonian Institution.) The song became the unofficial national anthem after the Spanish-American War. In 1916 President Wilson ordered that it be played by the military services, and in 1931 by Act of Congress it was officially designated the National Anthem.

State banks were private institutions, chartered by the states, in which much of the surplus capital in the U.S. was deposited during most of the 19th century. (They created credit even if there was no available surplus.) The most successful systems to regulate these banks were devised in New York, New England, and Louisiana, but no uniformity prevailed, and in the newer sections of an expanding nation inexperience and unregulated speculation led to repeated bank failures. The INDEPENDENT TREASURY ACT (1837) was prompted by the PANIC OF 1837, and it created the subtreasury system, the first step in effective Federal control of all banking.

State fairs, held in late summer, became popular in the U.S. during the latter half of the 19th century. Although less numerous than county fairs, they are organized on a far more elaborate scale. They are chiefly agricultural exhibits which seek to aid in improving livestock and farm commodities. In the Midwest these annual fairs are the social occasion of the year for thousands of families. For many who attend, the fair is the year's two-week vacation. Some offer lavish entertainment and pay large premiums to the winners of horse races and livestock shows. Tent cities rise on camp sites, adjacent to the fair grounds, provided by the states. State fairs are a wholly American institution. They attract rural and city folk alike to see who will be named Bean Queen and Dairy Princess. Science has become a feature in their exhibits. At the Minnesota fair grounds 80 acres on 'Machinery Hill' are devoted to farm equipment makers. In 1962 at the Iowa fair military missile exhibitions and Telstar models were outstanding attractions.

State government in the U.S. designates the executive and legislative structure in each of the 50 territorial units of the Union, and it closely resembles the national government in form, function, and organization. Within the Federal system each state is a separate legal entity, with powers limited by provisions of the Federal and state constitutions. Each has its own judicial hierarchy, bicameral system (except Nebraska, which has a one-chamber legislature), and standards for regulating its internal affairs. The Tenth Amendment reserves to the states the powers not delegated to the Federal government, and the 'sovereignty' of the states consists chiefly of powers exercised for the general welfare. In case of legal conflict with the federal government, the state must bow to the supremacy of the national authorities. The exercise by Congress of its IMPLIED POWERS has been upheld by the Supreme Court, and therefore the authority of the national government has tended to increase.

State, U.S. Department of, was the first executive branch of government, established by Congress in July 1789. (A Department of Foreign Affairs had functioned from 1781.) The Secretary of State conducts foreign affairs, heading a department that has vastly proliferated since World War II. (Its budget in 1965 exceeded $379,000,000.) In addition to the Secretary, the department is headed by two Under Secretaries, a Deputy Under Secretary, an Ambassador at Large, and 11 Assistant Secretaries.

S. F. Bemis edited *The American Secretaries of State and Their Diplomacy* (10 vols., 1927–29), each chapter written by an authority on the period or subject. The Department of State has issued a short study of *The Secretaries of State: Portraits and Biographical Sketches* (1956). Two administrative histories are Gaillard Hunt, *The Department of State of the U.S.* (1914), and G. H. Stuart, *The Department of State* (1949).

Secretaries of State and the Presidents under whom they served are as follows.

WASHINGTON
Thomas Jefferson (Va.) 1789
Edmund Randolph (Va.) 1794
Timothy Pickering (Pa.) 1795

J. ADAMS
Timothy Pickering (Pa.) 1795
John Marshall (Va.) 1800

JEFFERSON
James Madison (Va.) 1801

MADISON
Robert Smith (Md.) 1809
James Monroe (Va.) 1811

MONROE
John Quincy Adams (Mass.) 1817

J. Q. ADAMS
Henry Clay (Ky.) 1825

JACKSON
Martin Van Buren (N.Y.) 1829
Edward Livingston (La.) 1831
Louis McLane (Del.) 1833
John Forsyth (Ga.) 1834

VAN BUREN
John Forsyth (Ga.) 1837

W. H. HARRISON
Daniel Webster (Mass.) 1841

TYLER
Daniel Webster (Mass.) 1841
Abel P. Upshur (Va.) 1843
John C. Calhoun (S.C.) 1844

POLK
James Buchanan (Pa.) 1845

TAYLOR
John M. Clayton (Del.) 1849

FILLMORE
Daniel Webster (Mass.) 1850
Edward Everett (Mass.) 1852

PIERCE
William L. Marcy (N.Y.) 1853

BUCHANAN
Lewis Cass (Mich.) 1857
Jeremiah S. Black (Pa.) 1860

LINCOLN
William H. Seward (N.Y.) 1861

A. JOHNSON
William H. Seward (N.Y.) 1865

GRANT
Elihu B. Washburne (Ill.) 1869
Hamilton Fish (N.Y.) 1869

HAYES
William M. Evarts (N.Y.) 1877

GARFIELD
James G. Blaine (Me.) 1881

ARTHUR
F. T. Frelinghuysen (N.J.) 1881

CLEVELAND
Thomas F. Bayard (Del.) 1885

B. HARRISON
James G. Blaine (Me.) 1889
John W. Foster (Ind.) 1892

CLEVELAND
Walter Q. Gresham (Ill.) 1893
Richard Olney (Mass.) 1895

MCKINLEY
John Sherman (Ohio) 1897
William R. Day (Ohio) 1898
John Hay (D.C.) 1898

T. ROOSEVELT
John Hay (D.C.) 1901
Elihu Root (N.Y.) 1905
Robert Bacon (N.Y.) 1909

TAFT
Philander C. Knox (Pa.) 1909

WILSON
William J. Bryan (Neb.) 1913
Robert Lansing (N.Y.) 1915
Bainbridge Colby (N.Y.) 1920

HARDING
Charles E. Hughes (N.Y.) 1921

COOLIDGE
Charles E. Hughes (N.Y.) 1923
Frank B. Kellogg (Minn.) 1925

HOOVER
Henry L. Stimson (N.Y.) 1929

F. D. ROOSEVELT
Cordell Hull (Tenn.) 1933
Edward R. Stettinius, Jr. (Va.) 1944

TRUMAN
James F. Byrnes (S.C.) 1945
George C. Marshall (Pa.) 1947
Dean G. Acheson (Md.) 1949

EISENHOWER
John Foster Dulles (N.Y.) 1953
Christian A. Herter (Mass.) 1959

KENNEDY
Dean Rusk (N.Y.) 1961

L. B. JOHNSON
Dean Rusk (N.Y.) 1963

State universities in the U.S. have made a distinctively American contribution to education. Their existence at first was precarious. Their curriculums were those of academies and they were regarded as private rather than public corporations. The University of North Carolina (est. 1789) was the first to begin instruction (1795). The University of Tennessee (est. 1794) opened in 1795 as Blount College. Georgia, chartered in 1785, was established in 1801. In the same decade, Vermont (est. 1791) opened in 1800, and South Carolina (est. 1801) in 1805. Virginia (est. 1819), the project conceived by Jefferson, began instruction in 1825.

The expansion of state universities took place in the Midwest. The ORDINANCE OF 1787 granted two townships to each state to be created within the Northwest Territory 'for the purpose of a university.' The University of Ohio was the first to open (1809). The success of the University of Michigan (est. 1841) in developing rigorous standards led to general recognition of the principle of state education. The movement to establish state universities received its greatest stimulus from the MORRILL LAND GRANT ACT (1862), the most important piece of educational legislation up to that time. Thereafter state universities were established throughout the nation. These institutions have been infused with a liberal spirit and a readiness to experiment. Today the control of most state universities is vested in a board of trustees or regents, an appointive body subject to legislative control. They are tax supported, often with generous appropriations.

Staten Island, a 57-square-mile island in New York Bay, was consolidated with New York City in 1898 as the Borough of Richmond. It was visited by Henry Hudson in 1609, bought by the English governor from the Indians in 1670, and served as English general headquarters during the Revolution. Today Staten Island is chiefly an area of residential communities. Parts of it still remain semirural.

States, Admission of, was provided by the ORDINANCE OF 1784 (amended in 1785 and 1787), which was the basis upon which all public lands of the U.S. have been organized as TERRITORIES for prospective statehood. (Vermont, Kentucky, Maine, Texas, California, and West Virginia did not pass through a territorial stage.) Congress appointed a governor and three judges, and gave those officials the authority to adopt and promulgate such laws of the already existing states as were best suited to the needs of the territory. Bicameral legislatures, set up when the free male population numbered 5000, elected a delegate to Congress with the right to participate in debate but with no vote.

When an organized territory grows large enough to justify admission as a state, Congress passes an enabling act for a territorial convention. Upon adoption of such a constitution by the people, the prospective state applies to Congress for admission to statehood. The states of the Union, the dates and order of their admission, and their capitals are given in the table on the following page.

States' rights is the political doctrine expressing theories that uphold the power of states against Federal encroachment. After the Constitution was adopted, the doctrine evolved from a STRICT CONSTRUCTION of that instrument. As a political principle, states' rights is an outgrowth of colonial particularism, and at various times it has been implemented by legislative action extending to NULLIFICATION and SECESSION. It was expressed in the KENTUCKY AND VIRGINIA RESOLVES (1798), and was a major reason for assembling the HARTFORD CONVENTION (1814). It was the subject of the famous WEBSTER-HAYNE DEBATE (1830), and of the southern manifestoes leading to the Civil War. The balance between a federal union of states, and states that are constitutionally sovereign units within the federation (as in the U.S.), is constantly dependent upon court decisions and state and Federal legislative action.

Opponents of centralization have relied upon the Tenth Amendment for the reserved powers of the states, but that provision has been increasingly offset by Supreme Court rulings favorable to the IMPLIED POWERS given to Congress by the Constitution (Art. I, sec. 8) and by the expansion of Federal power to regulate interstate commerce. Controversial issues in recent years have been created especially in the areas of civil rights and welfare expenditures.

TABLE OF STATES

State	*Date of Admission*	*Order of Admission*	*Capital*
Alabama	14 December 1819	Twenty-second	Montgomery
Alaska	3 January 1959	Forty-ninth	Juneau
Arizona	14 February 1912	Forty-eighth	Phoenix
Arkansas	15 June 1836	Twenty-fifth	Little Rock
California	9 September 1850	Thirty-first	Sacramento
Colorado	1 August 1876	Thirty-eighth	Denver
Connecticut	9 January 1788	Fifth (Original)	Hartford
Delaware	7 December 1787	First (Original)	Dover
Florida	3 March 1845	Twenty-seventh	Tallahassee
Georgia	2 January 1788	Fourth (Original)	Atlanta
Hawaii	12 March 1959	Fiftieth	Honolulu
Idaho	3 July 1890	Forty-third	Boise
Illinois	3 December 1818	Twenty-first	Springfield
Indiana	11 December 1816	Nineteenth	Indianapolis
Iowa	28 December 1846	Twenty-ninth	Des Moines
Kansas	29 January 1861	Thirty-fourth	Topeka
Kentucky	1 June 1792	Fifteenth	Frankfort
Louisiana	30 April 1812	Eighteenth	Baton Rouge
Maine	15 March 1820	Twenty-third	Augusta
Maryland	28 April 1788	Seventh (Original)	Annapolis
Massachusetts	6 February 1788	Sixth (Original)	Boston
Michigan	26 January 1837	Twenty-sixth	Lansing
Minnesota	11 May 1858	Thirty-second	St. Paul
Mississippi	10 December 1817	Twentieth	Jackson
Missouri	10 August 1821	Twenty-fourth	Jefferson
Montana	8 November 1889	Forty-first	Helena
Nebraska	1 March 1867	Thirty-seventh	Lincoln
Nevada	31 October 1864	Thirty-sixth	Carson City
New Hampshire	21 June 1788	Ninth (Original)	Concord
New Jersey	18 December 1787	Third (Original)	Trenton
New Mexico	6 January 1912	Forty-seventh	Santa Fe
New York	26 July 1788	Eleventh (Original)	Albany
North Carolina	21 November 1789	Twelfth (Original)	Raleigh
North Dakota	2 November 1889	Thirty-ninth	Bismarck
Ohio	1 March 1803	Seventeenth	Columbus
Oklahoma	16 November 1907	Forty-sixth	Oklahoma City
Oregon	14 February 1859	Thirty-third	Salem
Pennsylvania	12 December 1787	Second (Original)	Harrisburg
Rhode Island	29 May 1790	Thirteenth (Original)	Providence
South Carolina	23 May 1788	Eighth (Original)	Columbia
South Dakota	2 November 1889	Fortieth	Pierre
Tennessee	1 June 1796	Sixteenth	Nashville
Texas	29 December 1845	Twenty-eighth	Austin
Utah	4 January 1896	Forty-fifth	Salt Lake City
Vermont	4 March 1791	Fourteenth	Montpelier
Virginia	25 June 1788	Tenth (Original)	Richmond
Washington	11 November 1889	Forty-second	Olympia
West Virginia	20 June 1863	Thirty-fifth	Charleston
Wisconsin	29 May 1848	Thirtieth	Madison
Wyoming	10 July 1890	Forty-fourth	Cheyenne

States' Rights party was organized (1948) when several southern delegates to the Democratic Convention walked out in protest against the civil rights plank of the Democratic platform. They wrote a states' rights platform and nominated J. Strom Thurmond of South Carolina for President. He received 1,169,000 popular and 39 electoral votes.

Steamboats were constructed experimentally in the 1780's, but JOHN FITCH is generally credited with the invention of the first American steamboat, launched (1787) on the Delaware. In the same year James Rumsey (1743–93) launched a steamboat on the Potomac. JOHN STEVENS and OLIVER EVANS after 1790 procured patents for various steam boilers and Stevens built (1806–8) and navigated (1809) the first successful seagoing steamship. Two years earlier ROBERT FULTON had demonstrated that steam navigation was practical by sailing his 150-ft. *Clermont* up the Hudson from New York to Albany in 1807. The application of the steam engine to water transportation was the first American invention of worldwide significance.

The 300-ton two-masted sidewheeler *New Orleans* (1811) for a time served as a model for river navigation, plying up the Mississippi to Natchez. When Henry M. Shreve (1785–1851) built the *Washington* (1816), a double-deck shallow-hulled sidewheeler, the practicability of steam navigation on western rivers was established. The *Savannah,* a sailing vessel with auxiliary steam sidepaddlewheels, voyaged (1819) from Savannah to Liverpool in 29 days. This was the first transatlantic crossing made with the aid of steam.

Regular steamship service was inaugurated between New York and New Orleans in 1820. Inland water traffic increased until the boats became the floating palaces of Mark Twain's boyhood. Before the Civil War they annually carried over 10,000,000 tons of freight and had given economic status to Pittsburgh, Cincinnati, and St. Louis. With the extension of railroad systems after 1865, river traffic sharply declined.

Steel industry, a development of early IRON MANUFACTURE, was made possible after the English inventor Henry Bessemer discovered the basic principle involved in manufacturing steel from pig iron. The Bessemer process was patented in the U.S. in 1857, but the priority rights were awarded to the Kentucky iron furnace master WILLIAM KELLY, who began operating his plant near Detroit in 1864. The Bessemer-Kelly interests were consolidated, and the process was put to significant commercial use by A. L. HOLLEY at Troy, New York, in 1865. In 1868 ABRAM S. HEWITT introduced the open-hearth process, thus greatly extending the possible use of U.S. ore reserves.

The immense growth of industry in the four decades after 1860 generated a demand for steel, supplied by great new plants. ANDREW CARNEGIE established iron mills at Pittsburgh, and five years later he erected the largest steel mill in the country there. By 1900 the U.S. was producing 10,000,000 tons a year and led the world.

The industry has now reached the Pacific coast, and in the South great iron and steel holdings have been established in the Birmingham area. But the center of the industry is still the Pittsburgh-Youngstown–Lake Erie region. Well-known companies include U.S. Steel, Bethlehem Steel, Republic Steel, and National Steel.

STEFFENS, [JOSEPH] LINCOLN (1866–1936), after graduation from the University of California (1889) and study abroad, was associated (1902–11) with *McClure's* and other magazines. His articles made him a leader of the MUCKRAKING movement. His analysis of political corruption and of the alliance between business and politics appears in such books as *The Shame of Cities* (1904), *The Struggle for Self-Government* (1906), and *Autobiography* (1931).

STEICHEN, EDWARD (1879–), Luxembourg-born artist, pioneered in the 'new photography' (photography as an art medium), and became known for his experiments in photographic effects. He commanded the Photographic Division of the Air Service in the U.S. Army during World War I, and directed the U.S. Navy Photographic Institute in World War II. After 1947 he directed the department of photography in the Museum of Modern Art, where his 'Family of Man' (1955) attracted wide attention.

STEIN, Gertrude (1874–1946), after graduation from Radcliffe (1897) and medical study at Johns Hopkins, went abroad (1902). Thereafter she lived chiefly in Paris. Her salon attracted persons prominent in literature and the arts, and her influence through her criticisms, especially of American letters, was considerable. Her interest in subjective realism led her to experiment with complex syntax, repetitions of phrase, and abstract grammar to find a new medium for speech rhythms. Thus her own writing became 'difficult,' and gained a limited audience. She was essentially a catalyzer. *Three Lives* (1909) is a representative collection of her stories. *Four Saints in Three Acts* (1934) is the libretto for an opera by Virgil Thomson. She is credited with having coined the term, 'The Lost Generation,' according to Ernest Hemingway's novel, *The Sun Also Rises* (flyleaf).

STEINBECK, John [Ernst] (1902–), after attending Stanford University for a year (1919) and working at odd jobs, late in the 1920's began to write. He had a strong compassion for underdogs. His best-known novel, *The Grapes of Wrath* (1939), deals with the problem of agricultural exploitation in the Plains region during the 1930's, and it was an important element in the reform measures for the migrant workers in California. *The Moon Is Down* (1942) was considered by Europeans to be the most powerful propaganda instrument in helping Norway to resist Hitler. Steinbeck's belief in the value of solidarity has thus had great political significance. The initiative and dignity of the individual in the face of grim hardships is a theme which Steinbeck treats with sympathetic humor, and it is the core of such later novels as *East of Eden* (1952), *Sweet Thursday* (1954), and *The Winter of Our Discontent* (1961). In 1962 he was awarded the Nobel Prize in literature.

STEINMETZ, Charles Proteus (1865–1923), German-born electrical engineer, was associated with General Electric Company after 1892, and professor of electrical engineering at Union (1902–23). He discovered the law of hysteresis (the lag in the values of magnetization when the magnetizing force is changed). He also made valuable contributions to the study of electrical phenomena, particularly of lightning.

STEPHENS, Alexander Hamilton (1812–83), born on a small farm in Georgia, after graduation from the University of Georgia (1832) was admitted to the bar, entered politics as a Whig, and for many years served in Congress (1843–59), where, unlike most Southerners, he opposed the Mexican War. He stood firmly with his colleagues HOWELL COBB and ROBERT TOOMBS for Union, and he swung Georgia's support for the Compromise of 1850. He opposed secession but accepted his state's decision, and he became the vice president of the Confederacy (1861–65). Stephens was the emissary sent to negotiate peace in the abortive HAMPTON ROADS CONFERENCE (1865). He was later returned to the House (1873–82). He amassed a fortune, and in his later years he devoted much of his time to philanthropy and to writing history.

STEPHENS, John Lloyd (1805–52), New Jersey-born traveler and one of the most distinguished of American travel-writers, after graduation from Columbia (1822) practiced law in New York City for eight years. In 1834 he began his two-year tour of Europe and the Near East, and on his return published *Incidents of Travel in Egypt, Arabia Petraea, and the Holy Land* (2 vols., 1837), and *Incidents of Travel in Greece, Turkey, Russia, and Poland* (2 vols., 1838). These books were admired for their majestic descriptions and freshness of manner. They passed through many editions and fired the imagination of other writers, including Poe and Melville.

His later extensive trips (beginning with a diplomatic mission for President Van Buren in 1839) took him into Central America. There as an amateur archaeologist he gathered material for *Incidents of Travel in Central America, Chiapas, and Yucatan* (2 vols., 1841), and *Incidents of Travel in Yucatan* (2 vols., 1843). Present-day authorities recognize Stephens as the pioneer among those who recovered the Mayan civilization. He lacked the scholarly background to understand its origin and development, but he revealed in part the visible past of an America which in the 1840's was largely unknown.

STEUBEN, Friedrich Wilhelm, Baron von (1730–94), Prussian military commander, in 1777 was persuaded by his friend St. Germain, the French minister of war, to volunteer his services to the American Congress, as drill master to an army sorely in need of instruction in military tactics. Congress accepted Steuben's offer, and as inspector general he began his work with Washington's troops at Valley Forge. He thereafter aided the patriot cause so effectively that Congress pensioned him, and the states in which he had directed troops made him grants of land. He became a U.S. citizen in 1783, and spent his last years at Steubenville, New York.

STEVENS, Henry (1819–86), Vermont-born bibliographer and book dealer, during the 1840's had a shop in London, where he purchased rare Americana for clients in the States. He spent the rest of his life in England. His *Recollections of James Lennox* (1886), an account of the New York merchant prince (1800–80) whose splendid collection became a nucleus of the New York Public Library, is largely autobiographical. Stevens's lasting place in history derives from his pioneer labors in shaping three great libraries: the Lennox, the John Carter Brown Library (at Brown University), and the British Museum, for which he acted as agent in procuring books dealing with America.

STEVENS, John (1749–1838), upon graduation from King's College (Columbia) in 1768, studied law (1768–71), served as treasurer of New Jersey during the War of Independence, and later (1782–83) was the state's surveyor general. Because he wished to protect inventions stemming from his development of a practical steamboat (1788–98), he was largely responsible for the first U.S. patent laws (1790). With Nicholas Roosevelt and Robert Livingston he experimented in steam transportation and designed a screw propeller (1802).

A man of some wealth, Stevens built the *Phoenix* (1806–8), which cruised from New York to Philadelphia in 1809. This was the first successful seagoing trip made by a steamboat. He devoted himself to railroad activities after 1810. He received from New Jersey the first railroad charter in the U.S. (1815), and in 1826 he built a track for a pioneer locomotive. His sons, Robert Livingston Stevens (1787–1856) and Edwin Augustus Stevens (1795–1868), were closely associated with their father's enterprises, which they continued to develop. E. A. Stevens initiated construction of a railroad from New York to Philadelphia, invented the Stevens plow, and founded Stevens Institute of Technology.

See A. D. Turnbull, *John Stevens, An American Record* (1928).

STEVENS, Thaddeus (1792–1868), born in Vermont, after graduation from Dartmouth (1814) practiced law for many years in Gettysburg, Pennsylvania (1816–42). He entered politics and served in the state legislature as an Anti-Mason before being seated as a Whig in the U.S. House of Representatives (1849–53), which his fiercely abolitionist sentiments led him to quit. He organized the Republican party in his state and was returned by the Republicans to Congress (1859–68). As chairman of the Ways and Means committee he wielded immense power throughout the Civil War.

But it was in the early post-war years that his authority prevailed. He was the dominant member of the joint committee of fifteen, which wrote the Fourteenth Amendment and expressed an intent to see that the defeated Confederate states would be treated as 'conquered provinces,' and that the 'proud traitors' would be stripped of their 'bloated estates.' He battled for the thirteenth amendment, the freedmen's bureau, the civil rights bill, and Negro suffrage, and he fathered the fourteenth amendment. His efforts to keep Republicans in power by use of his unique abilities as a political strategist were interpreted as conspiratorial. He chaired the committee that prepared the impeachment charges against President Andrew Johnson and was the baleful and impressive House manager in the subsequent Senate trial.

A champion of underdogs, Stevens has been described as 'a humanitarian lacking in humanity; a man of boundless charities and vindictive hates.' No man in American history has led evaluators of a personality into greater oversimplification. The contradictions in Stevens's character are baffling. Did his large investments in iron account for his zeal for protective tariffs? Do the trauma of his club foot and his devotion to his mulatto mistress explain his malice toward the South and his crusade for Negroes? Were his Reconstruction measures prompted by the ideal of emancipation or by cynical party interest and control? There is no doubt about the importance of his achievements, but his motives and methods are open to question.

Recent biographies include those by Richard N. Current (1942), and Ralph Korngold (1956).

STEVENSON, Adlai Ewing (1900–1965), grandson of Vice President Adlai E. Stevenson (1835–1914), after graduation from Princeton (1922) practiced law in Chicago. While serving as governor of Illinois (1949–53), he won national attention for welfare advances and exposés of corruption, and he was chosen as Democratic candidate for President in 1952. Stevenson's campaign speeches were notable for their trenchant wit and acute analysis of the New Deal–Fair Deal program, but he lost the election to Eisenhower by an electoral vote of 89 to 442. He was the party's candidate again in 1956, when he lost by a similar margin. In 1961 President Kennedy appointed Stevenson the U.S. representative to the United Nations, with cabinet rank.

STEWART, Alexander Turney (1803–76), born in northern Ireland of Scottish Protestant parents, opened a shop in New York (1823), where he sold imported Irish lace. In 1846 he engaged in a wholesale and retail dry-goods business, which within four years was the largest in the city. In 1862 he established the first department store in the U.S., the largest retail store in the world, employing 2000 persons. (It was sold in 1896 to john wanamaker.) Stewart's controlling interests in hotels, mills, and other businesses both here and abroad made him one of the wealthiest businessmen of his day, and his mansion on Fifth Avenue, with its large art collection, was regarded as one of the finest in America. Although he was a hard-driving employer, he was an open-handed philanthropist.

STIEGEL, Henry William (1729–85), German-born iron and glass manufacturer, after purchasing an ironworks near Philadelphia developed the ten-plate stove, which served as standard for many generations. In 1768 he built a glassmaking plant and imported artisans whose knowledge introduced a German tradition in glass manufacture. Stiegel glass is now a collector's item.

STIEGLITZ, Alfred (1864–1946), New Jersey–born photographer and art exhibitor, became one of 20th-century America's vital cultural forces. While studying engineering in Germany (1881), he discovered photography as an art. At a time when others were imitating the clichés of academic painting, he made photographs that conveyed a sense of reality heightened by poetic sensitivity. In 1905 he established his gallery '291' at 291 Fifth Avenue, New York, to display photography as a fine art. This he enlarged to introduce the work of such modern French painters as Cézanne, Picasso, and Braque to America, and to exhibit the paintings of young Americans, including john marin, max weber, and georgia o'keeffe (whom he married in 1924). No American of his time did more to win for photography recognition as a fine art, or more generously championed the modern painters and sculptors who were breaking new ground.

STILES, Ezra (1727–95), after graduation from Yale (1746) served there as a tutor (1749–55) before holding pastorates for 22 years successively at Newport, Rhode Island, and Portsmouth, New Hampshire. As president of Yale (1778–95), he sought to fuse Puritan piety with the new enlightenment of the 18th century. He liberalized the curriculum and speeded the growth of the college, and his boundless intellectual curiosity kept him engaged in a wide correspondence. His *Literary Diary* (3 vols., 1901) and *Extracts from the Itineraries . . . 1755–1794* (1916) are source material on the cultural development of America.

See Edmund S. Morgan, *The Gentle Puritan: A Life of Ezra Stiles* (1962).

STILWELL, Joseph W. (1883–1946), a graduate of the U.S. Military Academy (1904), served in China during the 1920's and 1930's, and after the entry of the U.S. into World War II was appointed commanding general of U.S. forces in the China-Burma-India theater of operations (1942–44). Friction with Chiang Kai-shek led to the recall of the gallant if tactless 'Vinegar Joe,' who then headed (1945) the Army Ground Forces. At the war's end Stilwell commanded the 10th Army, which distinguished itself on Okinawa.

STIMSON, Henry Lewis (1867–1950), after graduation from Yale (1888) practiced law in New York with ELIHU ROOT. He entered politics as a Republican and served in Taft's cabinet as Secretary of War (1911–13). While governor general of the Philippines (1927–29) he pursued an enlightened policy of conciliation. He entered Hoover's cabinet as Secretary of State (1929–33), in which post he promulgated the STIMSON DOCTRINE. Roosevelt selected him as Secretary of War (1940–45) to push forward measures Stimson had advocated to aid Great Britain and to provide compulsory military training. (Republicans thereupon read Stimson out of the party.) He served through World War II and resigned from Truman's cabinet. Stimson was the first American to serve in the cabinets of four Presidents.

Stimson Doctrine (1932), as set forth in identical notes addressed by Secretary of State Stimson to Japan and China, declared that the U.S. did not 'intend to recognize any treaty or agreement . . . which may impair . . . the sovereignty, the independence, or the territorial and administrative integrity of the Republic of China.' The League of Nations Assembly unanimously adopted a resolution incorporating Stimson's principles, and Japan briefly suspended the violation of its OPEN DOOR agreement on the sovereignty of China. According to former President Herbert Hoover, the Stimson Doctrine was a peaceful substitute for the Secretary's proposal to invoke economic sanctions against Japan — an idea that Hoover believed would provoke war.

STITH, William (1707–55), Virginia-born educator and historian, was a graduate of Queen's College, Oxford (1728). His *History of the First Discovery and Settlement of Virginia* (1747) is the most voluminous (if pedestrian) study of the Southern Colonies published up to its time. It covers events only to 1624, but it is still respected for its accuracy and attention to documentary evidence. Stith later served as president of William and Mary (1752–55).

Stockbridge Indians, see *Mahican Indians.*

Stock Exchange is an association with facilities for the purchase and sale of securities. The oldest and largest in the U.S. is the New York Stock Exchange (1792). Trading of considerable volume started there and in Philadelphia after the formation of the BANK OF THE U.S., and during the period of the refunding of the Federal debt and the assumption of the state debts. Early in the 19th century exchanges were likewise created for state and municipal securities and for the stock of INSURANCE COMPANIES. The financing of canals and railroads opened new exchanges after 1830. Mining and oil stocks were offered in the 1850's, and by 1880 industrials and utilities were expanding the exchanges.

There are stock exchanges in all the financially important cities of the U.S. (Only a member who has a 'seat' in the organization may buy or sell directly.) The great stock market crash during the PANIC OF 1929 led Congress to set up the SECURITIES AND EXCHANGE COMMISSION (1934) to enforce the regulation of exchange practices.

Stockmarket crash, see *Panic of 1929.*

STOCKTON, Robert Field (1795–1866), U.S. naval officer, commanded the Pacific squadron during the Mexican War. He occupied Santa Barbara and Los Angeles, and installed John C. Frémont as governor of the newly organized civil government of California. Conflicting instructions from Washington led Stephen W. Kearny to contest Frémont's authority. (The issue was resolved in Kearny's favor.) Stockton left the navy in 1850, and he served briefly in the U.S. Senate (1851–53).

Stockyards, first located in eastern cities, moved westward with the advent of railroads, and in 1865 Illinois chartered the Union Stockyards in Chicago to consolidate the operation of individual companies. As the CATTLE INDUSTRY grew, large stockyards were established in Kansas City, St. Louis, Omaha, and Denver. Packing houses made Chicago the largest livestock center in the world.

STODDARD, SOLOMON (1643–1729), son of a Boston linen-draper, graduated from Harvard (1662) and served as the first college librarian (1667–72) before accepting a call to the church at Northampton (1672), where he remained throughout his life, and as 'Pope' Stoddard for over half a century ruled the Connecticut valley as New England's greatest autocrat. He set forth his ecclesiastical polity in one of the monuments of 17th-century Puritan literature, *The Safety of Appearing at the Day of Judgment* (1687), asserting the naked sovereignty of God at a time when the Boston ministers by way of COVENANT THEOLOGY were striving to convince their hearers that God was inherently a rational being.

While Stoddard was still in college, the churches had adopted the HALF-WAY COVENANT (1662) as a way of offering church membership (though not communion) to all who desired it even though such members could not offer evidence of conversion. Stoddard reversed the practice by calling the Lord's Supper a 'converting ordinance,' and offered it to all who wished to join the church. He managed to extend this polity, called Stoddardianism, by creating regional associations, Presbyterian in form, throughout the Connecticut valley, from Deerfield to the Sound. By adopting the SAYBROOK PLATFORM (1705), Connecticut gave legal status to these church organizations, which Massachusetts never officially recognized. Stoddard's grandson, JONATHAN EDWARDS, joined Stoddard as a colleague (1726) and succeeded him in 1729. Edwards's rejection of the Stoddardian principle during the 1740's led to his dismissal in 1750, and the Connecticut valley churches continued the practice to which they had long been accustomed.

STOKOWSKI, LEOPOLD (1882–), born in London of Polish-Irish parentage, came to the U.S. in 1905 and became a citizen in 1915. As conductor of the Philadelphia Orchestra (1912–36) he introduced much unfamiliar music, and by his own transcriptions helped popularize the works of Bach. He was prominently associated with radio and film productions and a pioneer in stereophonic recording techniques. He was a militant supporter of new American music. He became the permanent conductor of the Houston (Texas) Symphony in 1955.

STONE, HARLAN FISKE (1872–1946), a graduate of Amherst (1894), was a professor of law at Columbia (1902–10) and dean of its law school (1910–23), when Coolidge appointed him Attorney General (1924–25), a post in which he took the lead in restoring faith in the Justice Department after the TEAPOT DOME scandal. As an Associate Justice of the Supreme Court (1925–41) he established a reputation for his vigorous minority opinions during the early years of the New Deal. As a jurist, Stone was held in great respect by lawyers, and President Roosevelt recognized his talents by elevating him (1941) to the chief justiceship.

STONE, LUCY (1818–93), after graduation from Oberlin (1847) began her active career as reformer. She was a persuasive lecturer in the antislavery movement and later founded (1870) the *Woman's Journal,* long the official organ of the National American Woman Suffrage Association. She retained her maiden name after marrying Henry Blackwell, and women who followed her example were often called 'Lucy Stoners.'

Stony Point, see *Wayne, Anthony.*

STORY, JOSEPH (1779–1845), after graduation from Harvard (1798) practiced law in Salem. So marked was his legal eminence by 1811 that Madison appointed him an Associate Justice of the U.S. Supreme Court. (At thirty-two Story was the youngest person ever to be elevated to that high bench.) He was a Federalist, and his views greatly influenced those of John Marshall. Two of his opinions were especially important. He upheld the constitutionality of section 25 of the Judiciary Act of 1789 in

MARTIN *v.* HUNTER'S LESSEE (1816), and he wrote the opinion sanctioning the court's right of judicial review (MARTIN *v.* MOTT, 1827).

Story became the first Dane Professor of Law at Harvard (1829), and thereafter, while serving as jurist and teacher, he wrote texts elucidating the legal and philosophical bases of law. All of them appeared in several editions, that on equity jurisprudence (1836) in a fourteenth edition (1918). His *Commentaries on the Constitution* (5th ed., 1891) is a legal classic of continuing importance. No other scholar, except JAMES KENT, had so formative an influence on American legal education. WILLIAM WETMORE STORY was his son.

STORY, WILLIAM WETMORE (1819–95), son of Supreme Court Justice Joseph Story, after graduation from Harvard (1838), and Harvard Law School (1840), briefly practiced law. In 1847 he began the study of sculpture in Rome, where he remained. His work was executed with the smooth, sentimental neoclassicism then fashionable, and his brilliant personal gifts drew to his studio the social and artistic elite, thus enhancing the fame of his works, considered the most admirable sculptures of their day. He is represented by *Cleopatra,* a sensation when it was exhibited in London (1862); *Salome* (Metropolitan Museum); and *Jerusalem in Her Desolation* (Pennsylvania Academy). He published two volumes of poems and several books on Italy. Henry James wrote his biography (2 vols., 1903).

Storyville, see *Jazz.*

STOUGHTON, WILLIAM (1631–1701), after graduation from Harvard (1650) and study at Oxford, returned to Massachusetts, where he held at various times most of the important offices in the commonwealth. He served as lieutenant governor from 1692 until his death. Stoughton was a man of wealth and learning, but he is chiefly remembered for the judicial brutality with which he presided as chief justice and prosecutor at the Salem trials during the WITCHCRAFT DELUSION.

STOWE, CALVIN ELLIS (1802–86), graduated from Bowdoin (1824) and Andover Theological Seminary. While teaching Greek at Dartmouth (1831–33), he was invited by LYMAN BEECHER to become professor of Biblical literature at Lane Theological Seminary, Cincinnati (1833–50), where he met and married Harriet Beecher (1836). He was appointed a state commissioner to study European public schools, and his *Report on Elementary Instruction in Europe* (1837, repr. 1930) became the basis for the free common school system of Ohio, which accepted his recommendation of the extension of state control over local school boards (a system later adopted throughout the U.S.). Stowe then returned East as professor of religion at Bowdoin (1850–52) and professor of sacred literature at Andover (1852–64).

STOWE, HARRIET BEECHER (1811–96), daughter of the Reverend LYMAN BEECHER, moved with her family from Litchfield, Connecticut, to Cincinnati when her father became president of Lane Theological Seminary (1832). There she taught in the school opened by her sister CATHARINE BEECHER, and married CALVIN STOWE (1836). She was deeply stirred by her memory of the slavery problem, and after her husband joined the faculty of Bowdoin College in Brunswick, Maine (1850), she wrote *Uncle Tom's Cabin; or, Life among the Lowly,* which was published in the abolitionist *National Era.* It ran serially for ten months (1851–52) before it appeared in book form (1852).

Within a year the book sprang into unexampled popularity, was translated into more than a score of tongues, and was dramatized. But the popular image of the book probably took form largely from the stage version, which in the following decades reached millions who never read the book, and gave emphasis to the weakness of southern society that the book took pains to avoid. The book has been called the greatest of American propaganda novels, but the dramatic version may have played the principal role. When Mrs. Stowe visited England in 1853, she was received with frenetic enthusiasm. The vogue of *Uncle Tom* in the North became an incalculable factor in events leading to the Civil War. Charles Sumner said of the book that, without it, Lincoln would not have been elected President, and Lincoln (according to one version) later greeted Mrs. Stowe with the words: 'So you're the little woman who made the book that made this great war.'

As a novelist Mrs. Stowe wrote best about New England village folk, in such books as *The Pearl of Orr's Island* (1862), and *Oldtown Folks* (1869). Though she was not a great artist, she was a worldwide celebrity. After the death of her husband (1886) she lived chiefly in the seclusion of her home in Hartford, Connecticut.

See the biographies by Catherine Gilbertson (1937) and Forrest Wilson (1941).

STRAUS, NATHAN (1848–1931), German-born merchant, with his brother, Isador Straus (1845–1912), became associated (1888) with R. H. Macy and Company in New York City, and by 1896 the brothers owned the firm. A generous philanthropist, Nathan Straus is remembered for important contributions to social reform. Another brother, Oscar Solomon Straus (1850–1926), served as ambassador under three Presidents, and as Secretary of Commerce and Labor (1906–9) under Theodore Roosevelt.

STRAVINSKY, IGOR [FEODOROVICH] (1882–), Russian-born composer, had established his reputation throughout Europe before he came to the U.S. (1939) and became a citizen (1945). After his first U.S. tour, on which he played his own *Piano Concerto,* he accepted commissions from several American sources for works including *Dumbarton Oaks* (1938) and *Ebony Concerto* (1946). The neoclassic idiom initiated with his *Octet* (1923) he later refined in such works as *Sonata for Two Pianos* (1944), *Symphony in Three Movements* (1945), and *Orpheus* (1948). In *Septet* (1952) he altered his craft by absorbing the serial technique of the Austrian composer Anton von Webern (1883–1945), progressively manifest from *Canticum Sacrum* (1956) to *Threni* (1958).

Stravinsky's works sometimes have appeared in successive forms, first as ballets, then as operas and as orchestral pieces. With the choreographer GEORGE BALANCHINE he produced *Apollo, Agon,* and *Movement for Piano and Orchestra,* some of the greatest ballets of the century. As a conductor he continued to perform and record his own music. His opera, *The Rake's Progress* (1951), based on the Hogarth drawings and written in collaboration with the poet W. H. Auden, is a work of distinction. He delivered the Norton lectures at Harvard in 1939. His *Poetics of Music* (1947) is representative of ideas that have had a wide influence on younger composers.

STRICKLAND, WILLIAM (*c.* 1787–1854), as a student of architecture under B. H. LATROBE, superintended the construction of the Bank of the United States in Philadelphia (1819–24), completed after Latrobe's death. Thus trained in the tradition of CLASSIC REVIVAL, Strickland designed the Merchants' Exchange in Philadelphia (1834), his most distinctive work in the Greek mode, and the state capitol at Nashville, Tennessee, completed after his death.

Strict construction of the Federal Constitution is the interpretation that attempts to limit the powers of the national government by holding those powers to specifically delegated or enumerated items (Art. I, sec. 8). Such an interpretation was first made a political issue by the DEMOCRATIC-REPUBLICAN PARTY in Jefferson's struggle with the Federalists, who in their turn supported a loose constitutional construction, based on the IMPLIED POWERS of Congress.

Strikes, the concerted stoppage of work by a group of employees, are the chief weapon of organized labor in industrial disputes. In America strikes have occurred since colonial times (at first usually for higher wages), but few were successful until the 20th century. Significant changes appeared in the 1870's when unions began to gain some power. The widespread and violent RAILROAD STRIKES of 1877, broken by the use of Federal troops, led to the organization of LABOR PARTIES on a class basis.

Employers often attempted to continue operations by bringing in strikebreakers ('scabs') to take over the strikers' jobs. If the strikers retaliated by picketing, the employer used armed guards (or state or Federal troops) to clear out the pickets. The HAYMARKET RIOT (1886) grew out of a conflict between strikers and police. The use of strikebreakers gave the HOMESTEAD STRIKE (1892) national notoriety. The INJUNCTION had been introduced in the 1880's as a weapon against strikes, and it drew widespread attention in the PULLMAN STRIKE (1894).

The technique of the sit-down strike (the passive seizure of a plant by striking employees) was briefly in vogue during the 1930's, but it was declared illegal by the Supreme Court in 1939. A retaliatory measure of the employer, which is legal under some circumstances, is the LOCKOUT.

Some of the most important strikes in the U.S. have been waged by coal miners, organized as the powerful UNITED MINE WORKERS, who have gradually bettered their condition by repeated strikes, first notably in the ANTHRACITE STRIKE (1902) by which they won an eight-hour day. The steel workers, who were unsuccessful in the bitter strike of 1919, won concessions in the paralyzing strikes of 1937, 1941, 1946, and 1959. Strikes of maritime workers in 1936 and 1959 crippled ports on both coasts. Automobile strikes have likewise gained concessions to the unions. The numerous strikes of 1946 led Congress to enact the Taft-Hartley law, which revived the use of federal injunctions. The purpose and method of strikes generally (but not always) determine their legality.

The basic issue of the unsuccessful Boston Police Strike (1919) was whether it was sound public policy to permit public employees to strike. In January, 1966, the Transport Workers Union paralyzed New York City for twelve days, by cutting off all subway and bus services, and thereby caused great financial losses and severe inconvenience. Although the strike was adjudged illegal under the anti-strike law for public utilities, and strike leaders were jailed, the mayor yielded to most of the demands, and that strike was successful. President Johnson denounced the inflationary potential of the wage settlement. Such strikes by public employees were later condemned by WALTER REUTHER and other labor leaders.

STROHEIM, ERIC VON (1885–1957), Austrian-born motion picture actor and director, came to the U.S. in 1914. Today he is regarded as one of the most important directors in American film history, but his professional career in Hollywood virtually ended in the 1920's since his uncompromising artistic integrity was not a box-office asset in that decade. Of his many productions, *Greed* (1923), adapted from Frank Norris's *McTeague,* is best remembered. It is an honest reproduction of the psychological intent of the author.

STRONG, JOSIAH (1847–1916), after graduation from Western Reserve (1869) occupied various Congregational pulpits, but he made his influence felt chiefly after publishing *Our Country* (1885), a pioneer document in the liberal movement known as CHRISTIAN SOCIALISM. After 1902 he was president of the American Institute for Social Service, and he continued to write in defense of a militant Protestant program that combined demands for social justice with imperialistic expansion by Anglo-Saxons.

STRUNSKY, SIMEON (1879–1948), Russian-born journalist, after graduation from Columbia (1900) for many years was an editorial writer for the New York *Evening Post* (1906–20), before becoming its editor (1920–24). Thereafter he was on the editorial staff of *The New York Times.* The vigor and terseness of his writing appears in such books as *Post-Impressions* (1914), which draws upon his editorials, and *The Living Tradition* (1939).

STUART, GILBERT (1755–1828), Rhode Island-born artist, was the most celebrated portrait painter of his day. For five years (1775–80) he studied in London under Benjamin West, whose star pupil he became. Overnight Stuart won fame with a smashing exhibit in 1782 at the Royal Academy. He was immensely successful in both London and Dublin (to which latter city he fled to escape seizure for debts incurred by his extravagant living). He returned to America in 1792.

In New York and Philadelphia (1792–96) Stuart made three portraits of Washington, painted from life. The first (1795), known as the Vaughan Washington (National Gallery), is distinguished for its realism. From this he made at least fifteen replicas, the most famous being the unfinished Athenaeum portrait (Boston Museum). Since he seldom signed his canvases, controversy periodically arises whether a facsimile was painted by Stuart or by a copyist.

Among Stuart's sitters were Jefferson, Madison, Monroe, and John Jay. In 1805 he settled in Boston, where his reputation allowed him to select his commissions. His power extends beyond that of his famous teacher, for he could penetrate below the surface. At their best his character studies are lifelike and luminous, and they have given him an unrivaled reputation in American portraiture. Such is that painted in 1793 of *Mrs. Richard Yates* (National Gallery). But his later years were anticlimactic. High living kept him in reduced circumstances, and to forestall penury he turned out hack portraits of Boston worthies.

Biographies include those by J. H. Morgan (4 vols., 1926), W. T. Whitley (1932), and Charles M. Mount (1964).

STUART, JAMES EWELL BROWN [JEB] (1833–64), a graduate of the U.S. Military Academy (1854), resigned from the U.S. Army to serve as a Confederate cavalry officer. He was placed in command of a brigade after the first battle of Bull Run (July 1861), and in June 1862 he conducted the earliest of his celebrated cavalry raids. He proved to be a gallant horseman, and he was soon given command of all cavalry of the Army of Northern Virginia. His absence on a raid at the moment before Gettysburg gave advantage to Union forces. Stuart was mortally wounded during the WILDERNESS CAMPAIGN, and the death of no other commander, save Stonewall Jackson, gave the South a greater sense of personal loss.

STUYVESANT, PETER (1592–1672), having served as director of the West India Company's colony at Curaçao (where he lost a leg storming a French port), in 1647 became governor of NEW NETHERLAND. Though he set up a board of nine elected officials to advise him, he sought to dissolve it when 'The Nine' sent a remonstrance (1651) to the Dutch government protesting his arbitrary rule. He was ordered to grant the settlement a city government, and in 1653 New Amsterdam was proclaimed a municipality. In 1655, by gaining control of forts on the Delaware, he eliminated NEW SWEDEN as a rival commercial enterprise. His own rule was ended when the English seized his colony (1664). Stuyvesant then retired to his farm or *bouwerie* (BOWERY). He is most remembered for his violent temper and his ornamented silver leg.

Submarines, now perhaps the most formidable strategic weapons in all the armory of warfare, did not become an established part of modern navies until the 20th century. The first practical submarine, a rowboat encased in leather and propelled by oarsmen, was built in England about 1620 but was never put in action. The American inventor David Bushnell (*c.* 1742–1824) tried — unsuccessfully — to blow up a British frigate in New York harbor (1776) by using an underwater boat. ROBERT FULTON built his *Nautilus* in France (1800–1801), and his later improvements pointed the way to the modern submarine. During the Civil War submerged boats were employed for torpedoing, but the modern submarine was not developed until the late 19th century, through the inventions of J. P. HOLLAND and SIMON LAKE. Submarines became important offensive weapons during World War I, when the Germans developed 2100-ton underwater torpedo craft which wrought havoc with shipping.

Improvements continued; the typical submarine of World War II was a 300-foot steel craft, displacing 1350 tons, with a crew of 55, and diesel engines capable of surface speeds of 17 knots and electric engines capable of submerged speeds of 8 knots. Undersea raiders cost the Allies and neutrals a total of 4770 ships and 21,000,000 gross tons of shipping, and led to the decisive BATTLE OF THE ATLANTIC.

The launching in January 1954, at Groton, Connecticut, of the nuclear-powered *Nautilus* opened a new era in submarine history. Now equipped with atomic missiles, submarines have become underwater firing platforms. They can circle the globe without surfacing, can travel 60,000 miles without fueling, and can cruise submerged at a speed nearly equaling that of the fastest surface vessels. The successful undersea launching (July 1960) of a 14-ton Polaris missile and its landing on target 1150 miles away has created a new technique of warfare.

Subsidies, see *Federal Aid.*

Subways, as a means of urban transportation, were considered in New York City as early as 1860, but the engineering and financial problems long postponed their development. For a brief period (1870–73) the Pneumatic Underground Railway, privately constructed by the New York inventor Alfred Ely Beach (1827–96), ran a single car, pushed by air along a track for a short distance under lower Broadway. In 1900 Boston completed the first motor-powered subway in the U.S. by placing nearly two miles of trolley tracks under ground (later welded into an extensive system). New York opened a similar line in 1904, now extended into some 240 miles of underground traffic, by far the most extensive in the U.S. Other subway systems in the U.S. are in Chicago, Philadelphia, Newark, Los Angeles, and St. Louis.

Suffolk Resolves (1774), adopted by delegates from Boston and other towns in Suffolk county, Massachusetts, were resolutions denouncing the COERCIVE ACTS as unconstitutional. Unanimously adopted, they recommended stringent economic sanctions against England, and were immediately transmitted (by Paul Revere on horseback) to the Continental Congress in Philadelphia.

Suffrage, as a voting privilege, in the American colonies was restricted to those in the upper economic levels, and was controlled by a medley of voting qualifications which limited the franchise to a small fraction of the population. Even after the Constitution was adopted, voting was confined to property owners and taxpayers, and even today franchise requirements are not uniform among the states. In general, however, before the Civil War property tests had been eliminated, and white male adults could vote if they could meet state standards. The Fifteenth Amendment (1870) gave Negroes the constitutional right to vote, although in the period 1877–1904 Negroes were in general disfranchised throughout the South by the nature of voting requirements and practices.

Adoption of the Nineteenth Amendment (1920) gave women the vote and thus brought an end to the WOMAN SUFFRAGE MOVEMENT. Resistance in the South to Negro suffrage still persists to a considerable degree and is enforced by many devices. Yet Negro franchise has gradually been broadened as a result of such Supreme Court decisions as *U.S.* v. *Classic* (1941) and *Smith* v. *Allwright* (1944), which upheld the constitutional right of the federal government to regulate state primaries. Denial or abridgement of the right to vote in Federal elections because of failure to pay any poll tax was barred by the Twenty-fourth Amendment (1964), and in 1966 the Supreme Court, citing the Fourteenth Amendment, declared that the use of a poll tax as a qualification for voting in local elections was unconstitutional. The Voting Rights Act of 1965 provided for the suspension of literacy tests as a qualification for voting if less than 50 per cent of the population of voting age were registered to vote or voted in the November election of 1964. The active federal government promotion of a 'referee' system in states that flagrantly violate constitutional rights is also helping to extend suffrage.

See K. H. Porter, *A History of Suffrage in the U.S.* (1918).

Suffragettes, see *Woman Suffrage Movement.*

Sugar Act (1764), or American Revenue Act, was among the first passed by Parliament for the specific purpose of raising moneys in the colonies for the crown. Pursuant to the British Empire's MERCANTILISM policy, it stiffened the earlier (and unenforced) regulations of the MOLASSES ACT (1733), and, by requiring new customs regulations, became an ominous threat to American distillers and business men. Most significantly, it opened the debate on whether Parliament had the right to tax commodities for revenue rather than for regulation of trade, and created an opposition which crystallized after passage of the fateful STAMP ACT (1765).

Sugar industry before the Louisiana Purchase (1803) was limited in the U.S. to maple syrup products sold locally, for cane sugar was imported from the West Indies. By 1830 New Orleans claimed to be the largest sugar refinery in the world, with an annual capacity of 6000 tons, and other refineries had been established in many large cities. 'Sugar trusts' became monopoly issues in the 1890's, and today the industry is concentrated in a few large corporations. New York City is the nation's principal refining center.

The beet sugar industry had become commercially profitable in California by 1880, and by 1910 more beet sugar than cane sugar was refined in the U.S., chiefly in Colorado, California, Michigan, and Nebraska. This industry was very active in promoting protective tariff legislation. In 1962 Hawaii produced 1,100,000 tons of raw cane sugar. In the continental U.S. cane sugar production exceeded 850,000 tons, and beet sugar, 2,500,000 tons.

Sugar Trust, so called, was the consolidation (1887) of sugar refineries. When the consolidation was invalidated in New York state, it reorganized (1891) as a corporation, the American Sugar Refining Company, under the laws of New Jersey. Within a year it had acquired a virtual monopoly of sugar refining in the U.S. Although the company was prosecuted under the Sherman Antitrust Act, it was held to be functioning as a legal body in the case of U.S. *v.* E. C. KNIGHT (1895).

SULLIVAN, JOHN (1740–95), New Hampshire lawyer, commanded a brigade throughout the siege of Boston (1775–76), and as a major general fought under Washington in New Jersey and Pennsylvania (1777–78). He conducted his most effective campaign in 1779 along the New York frontier, where he materially reduced the threat of the Iroquois and of BUTLER'S RANGERS. He was later chief executive of New Hampshire (1786–90).

SULLIVAN, JOHN LAWRENCE (1858–1918), Boston-born pugilist, in 1882 won the bare-knuckle heavyweight boxing championship by knocking out Paddy Ryan in nine rounds at Mississippi City. The 'Great John L.,' a colorful swashbuckler and the idol of American sports fans, won his final bare-knuckle bout (1889) when he defeated Jake Kilrain after 75 grueling rounds at Richburg, Mississippi. In 1892, boxing with gloves, Sullivan lost the heavyweight title to JAMES J. CORBETT at New Orleans, though he still retained his bare-knuckle crown.

SULLIVAN, LOUIS HENRI (1856–1924), Boston-born architect, after attending Massachusetts Institute of Technology (1872–73), served an apprenticeship in the office of W. L. JENNEY, creator of the first steel-frame skyscraper. After further study in France Sullivan entered into a partnership in the Chicago firm of Adler and Sullivan (1881–1900), where he pioneered in the development of an architecture reflecting the belief of the new age: that outward form should express the function beneath. Though Sullivan was a guide to those who established organic structure, he won few adherents in the period when the classical modes of C. F. MC KIM were in vogue. Sullivan's Wainwright Building in St. Louis (1890) freely reflected its structural skeleton; and his Transportation Building at the Chicago World's Columbian Exposition (1893), unlike any other building at the fair, was heralded as a new mode. Later creations, emphasizing vertical piers to stress loftiness, include the Guaranty Building, Buffalo (1895); the Gage Building, Chicago (1898); and the Bayard Building, New York (1898). Sullivan's principles, set forth in *Autobiography of an Idea* (1924), were carried forward by FRANK LLOYD WRIGHT.

See Hugh Morrison, *Louis Sullivan: Prophet of Modern Architecture* (1935).

SULLIVAN, MARK (1874–1952), after graduation from Harvard (1900) began his career as journalist by supporting the MUCKRAKERS. Later, as a spokesman for the conservative Republican tradition, Sullivan was one of the leading political columnists of his day. His social history, *Our Times, 1900–1925* (6 vols., 1926–35), analyzes events and trends. His autobiography, *The Education of an American* (1938), is chiefly important as a commentary on American journalism in the first quarter of the 20th century.

SULLY, THOMAS (1783–1872), English-born portrait painter, came to America in 1792. A student first of Gilbert Stuart and later (in London) of Benjamin West, Sully established himself in Philadelphia (1810), where he enjoyed considerable popularity. Unlike Stuart, who caught the emotional depth of his subjects, Sully could not penetrate below the surface, though his dashing brushwork, represented by *Fanny Kemble as Bianca* (Pennsylvania Academy), is always arresting. His sitters included four Presidents: Jefferson, Madison, Monroe, and Jackson. In her youth Queen Victoria sat for him.

Summit conferences, as the term has been used since World War II, applies to the meeting of heads of government of the leading powers in an effort to reach broad measures of agreement. The first such meeting took place (July 1955) at Geneva. There President Eisenhower met with Prime Minister Eden of Britain, Premier Faure of France, and Premier Bulganin of Russia to discuss European security, East-West differences, and disarmament. No agreements were reached. Although similar meetings have been proposed since then, none has taken place, since a fixed agenda prepared by lower-level conferences seems to be a necessary prerequisite.

SUMNER, CHARLES (1811–74), born in Boston, after graduation from Harvard (1830) practiced law, wrote law text books, and entered politics. In 1849 he acted as counsel in the famous Negro school segregation case, *Roberts* v. *City of Boston,* arguing unsuccessfully for 'equality before the law' against Justice LEMUEL SHAW's 'separate but equal' doctrine. Though Sumner was defeated as a Free-Soil candidate for Congress in 1848 (proper Bostonians had been shocked by his Fourth of July oration in 1845 decrying the very war he had been invited to celebrate), in 1851 he was sent to the Senate by a combination of Free-Soilers and Democrats, and he remained there for the rest of his life.

Sumner was highly educated, sometimes supercilious and arrogant, and aggressively idealistic. Though lacking in warmth, he lived by moral principles, and thus reformers turned to him for leadership. In 1856 on the Senate floor he delivered a two-day oration, intended, as he said, to be 'the most thorough philippic ever uttered in a legislative body.' He excoriated the South for its 'crime against Kansas,' and singled out for special abuse Senator Andrew Butler of South Carolina, who was not there to reply. Two days later Sumner was brutally caned in the Senate chamber by Butler's nephew, Congressman Preston Brooks, and became the first martyr of the new Republican party.

Sumner resumed his seat three years later, and, after 1861, as chairman of the Foreign Relations Committee, he was a key figure in diplomacy. He hailed Lincoln's Emancipation Proclamation, though he thought it had been too long in coming. Convinced that the South by seceding had 'committed suicide,' after the war he looked on the former Confederate states as territories that should function only through the will of Congress. As party leader in the Senate, he supported the RADICAL REPUBLICANS and actively worked to secure the conviction of President Johnson on the impeachment charges. Sumner's courage as a crusader was most eloquently expressed in his repeated proposals for civil service reform, his denunciation of Grant's scheme to annex Santo Domingo (which turned his party against him in 1871, and cost him his committee chairmanship), and his famous excoriation of the President (1872) for bribery, nepotism, and unlawful interference in government business. Thus the influence that Sumner wielded in national politics in his final years, though somewhat diminished, was used to better purpose than it had been when he was at the height of his power.

The *Memoir and Letters* (4 vols., 1877–93), an admiring biography by Sumner's friend E. L. Pierce, is supplemented by David Donald's critical *Charles Sumner* (1960).

SUMNER, WILLIAM GRAHAM (1840–1910), after graduation from Yale (1863) and study abroad entered the Episcopal ministry, but after 1872 taught political and social science at Yale, where his brilliant lectures attracted two generations of undergraduates. A vigorous believer in the doctrine of evolution and a militant advocate of LAISSEZ FAIRE, he opposed all measures that tended to socialize business or interfere with competitive individualism. His influential *Folkways* (1907) contends that the persistence of folk customs, lacking rational validity, render useless all attempts at social reform. Important among his works are *What Social Classes Owe Each Other* (1883), and *Science of Society* (4 vols., 1927), completed by his pupil, A. G. Keller.

Sumter, Fort (named for the Revolutionary partisan leader, General Thomas Sumter, 1734–1832), is located at the mouth of the harbor of Charleston, South Carolina. It was the scene of the opening engagement of the Civil War (12–14 April 1861). Upon passing the ordinance of secession (December 1860), South Carolina demanded all Federal property within the state. Major Robert Anderson, commanding the harbor fortifications, concentrated his units at Fort Sumter, and when President Buchanan refused to order Anderson's evacuation, General F. W. Pickens of South Carolina trained guns on the Fort. After President Lincoln took office, he sent notice to Pickens (8 April) that a naval expedition was en route to provision the beleaguered garrison. Anderson refused the surrender demands, the Confederates opened fire, and the Civil War began.

Sun dance, a ritual in honor of the sun, was a ceremony performed by many of the Plains Indians, but with the most meticulous detail by the ARAPAHO and the CHEYENNE. Among the Missouri river tribes it incorporated a self-inflicted torture rite. Acting on the principle that the gods can be moved to pity providing a man willingly suffers unbearable pain, the zealous supplicant attached thongs to strips of skin on his breast or back, fastened the thongs to the center pole in the Sun Dance, and by straining away from the pole danced until the thongs were torn out. Scars were badges of honor because they certified that the warrior had proved himself worthy of divine protection.

SUNDAY, BILLY [WILLIAM ASHLEY], see *Revivals*.

Sunday schools originated in England during the 1780's as gathering places for impoverished working children on their only holiday. In them the children were taught to read and instructed in the catechism. From the beginning in the U.S. they were closely associated with the church and were organized solely for religious instruction. FRANCIS ASBURY is credited with forming the first Sunday school in America, in Hanover county, Virginia (1786), and soon thereafter the Methodist church officially adopted the practice. Sunday schools were soon used by all denominations. Publication of the *Sunday School Magazine* (1824) initiated the issuance of a vast body of Sunday school literature. After the Methodist bishop John H. Vincent (1832–1920) launched the periodical *Sunday School Teacher* (1866) and spearheaded the CHAUTAUQUA MOVEMENT (1874), training became systematic. By 1890 Sunday school membership in the U.S. and Canada was some 11,000,000, a figure which had quadrupled by 1965.

Superior, Lake, westernmost of the GREAT LAKES, is the largest fresh-water lake in the world. It is 350 miles long and covers an area of 31,800 square miles. This deep lake was originally scooped out by glacial action. It is fed by numerous rivers and is dotted with islands. (The largest, ISLE ROYALE, is a national park.) The international boundary between the U.S. and Canada runs roughly through the center of the lake, and its southern shore forms the northern border of Wisconsin and the Michigan peninsula. It empties through Sault Ste. Marie into Lake Huron. Lake Superior was first visited in the mid-17th century by French explorers. It has become the major transport route for the grain harvested in the center of the continent and for the large ore deposits near by. The cities of Duluth (Minn.) and Superior (Wis.) are situated on its western reaches.

Supermarkets are giant, self-service CHAIN STORES, principally selling food and related items. They were first operated on the West Coast after World War I, and they were introduced in the East during the 1930's. To provide parking space for shoppers and to decrease rental costs, since 1950 supermarkets increasingly have become suburban shopping centers.

Supreme Court, the highest body in the judicial system of the U.S., was established by the Constitution as a third branch of the government, independent of the legislative and executive branches.

It consists of a Chief Justice and such number of Associate Justices as Congress may determine. (Its original six members were reduced to five in 1801, restored to six in 1802, increased to seven in 1807, to nine in 1837, and to ten in 1863. In 1866 Congress reduced the membership to seven to prevent President Andrew Johnson from making appointments. Since 1869 the number has remained fixed at nine.) Members are nominated by the President and confirmed by the Senate, and they can be removed only by impeachment, a proceeding which was brought only once against a member of this high court, and then unsuccessfully (SAMUEL CHASE in 1804). The judicial power of the Court extends to all cases arising under the Constitution of the U.S., statutes and treaties of the U.S., and to such cases as lie outside the jurisdiction of the states.

Six JUSTICES constitute a quorum, and decisions are rendered by majority vote. The Court interprets and expounds the Acts of Congress, and examines Federal and state laws and Executive actions to determine their constitutionality by JUDICIAL REVIEW. It thus can mold the shape of law with a power unmatched by the judiciary of any other nation. Under JOHN MARSHALL (1801–35) the Court gained great prestige and the power of the federal government was substantially increased, to the dismay of Jefferson and the defenders of STATES' RIGHTS. But Marshall's successor, ROGER B. TANEY (1836–64) initiated a reaction by advancing the concept of the POLICE POWER of the states. After passage of the Fourteenth Amendment (1868) the flood of litigation arising over civil rights issues seriously delayed the disposition of cases, and in 1891 Congress created the circuit courts of appeal to settle most such cases.

The determination of constitutional issues had been carried so far by 1900 that an increasingly conservative Court in general held to established precedents, and, in step with the times, the Court usually decided for laissez faire in business activities. Thus the liberal views in the early years of the 20th century of JOHN M. HARLAN, OLIVER WENDELL HOLMES, and LOUIS D. BRANDEIS were often minority opinions.

After the Court had struck down several major pieces of NEW DEAL legislation in the mid 1930's, President Roosevelt (who in his first term had not had the appointment of a single justice) in 1937 proposed a measure designed to infuse the bench with new blood. His so-called 'court-packing' plan, which could have increased the number of Justices to fifteen, stirred both the public and the Court to thought. Following strong public sentiment, Congress took no action, but thereafter the Court's interpretation of the power of Congress to tax and spend for the general welfare, and its expansion of the power to regulate interstate commerce, amounted to a near revolution in the jurisprudence of the Court, a transformation unprecedented in the annals of that body. Circumstances gave Roosevelt in his last two terms the opportunity to appoint nine jurists, the largest number appointed since Washington's Administration.

The Court has been criticized for its inherent ability to exert political as well as legal power, as it has done notably in its decisions on racial issues, labor rulings, loyalty programs, and state and congressional reapportionment (to the consternation of some of its members). But the checks upon it are ample. Congress may alter its size, the Senate may reject an appointment to the bench, and Congress has the right of impeachment. Finally the nation has the right to reverse the Court's decisions by amending the Constitution, a right exercised over the years only three times (by passage of the Eleventh, Fourteenth, and Sixteenth amendments). The history of the Court does in fact reflect the evolution of American concepts — sociological, economic, and political. It derives its power and prestige from its ability to shape and act as guardian for the whole American legal system.

Historic among Supreme Court decisions are those listed below. See separate entry for each case.

1794, *Chisholm* v. *Georgia* (limiting state action). This decision was reversed by the Eleventh Amendment.
1803, *Marbury* v. *Madison* (voiding acts of Congress).
1810, *Fletcher* v. *Peck* (invalidating state laws).

1816, *Martin* v. *Hunter's Lessee* (power of review of state courts).
1819, *Dartmouth College Case* (impairment of contract).
1819, *McCulloch* v. *Maryland* (implied powers, banks).
1821, *Cohens* v. *Virginia* (appeal from state courts sustained).
1824, *Gibbons* v. *Ogden* (implied powers, commerce).
1827, *Martin* v. *Mott* (implied powers, militia).
1830, *Craig* v. *Missouri* (borrowing power of states).
1833, *Barron* v. *Baltimore* ('just compensation').
1837, *Charles River Bridge Case* (reinterpretation of impairment of contract).
1847, *License Cases* (state police powers).
1857, *Dred Scott Case* ('due process of law'). This decision was reversed by the Fourteenth Amendment.
1866, *Ex Parte Milligan* (habeas corpus).
1873, *Slaughterhouse Cases* (states' rights).
1877, *Munn* v. *Illinois* (public utilities).
1895, *Pollock* v. *Farmers' Loan* (income tax). This decision was reversed by the Sixteenth Amendment.
1898, *U.S.* v. *Wong Kim Ark* (citizenship).
1908, *Muller* v. *Oregon* (police power of states).
1918, *Hammer* v. *Dagenhart* (child labor).
1922, *Bailey* v. *Drexel* (child labor).
1931, *Near* v. *Minnesota* (freedom of press).
1934, *Nebbia* v. *New York* (police power of states).
1951, *Dennis* v. *U.S.* (limit of free speech).
1954, *Brown* v. *Board of Education* (desegregation).
1962, *Baker* v. *Carr* (state legislature reapportionment).
1964, *Wesberry* v. *Sanders* (congressional reapportionment).

See Charles Warren, *The Supreme Court in U.S. History* (2 vols., rev. ed., 1937); and R. K. Carr, *The Supreme Court and Judicial Review* (1942).

Surrealism originated in France as a movement in literature and art. Limited for the most part to painting, it grew out of the humorous rendering of the sense of futility expressed by the Dadaists, after World War I, who chose forms of irrationality as their themes. Painters began to see that the strangeness of such exhibits as Marcel Duchamp's famous fur-lined teacup could be used seriously in works based on the dream world, and thus express subconscious mental activities.

Surrealism was practiced in a variety of forms, but it became best known abroad in the paintings of the Spaniard Joan Miró, the Russian Pavel Tchelitchew, SALVADOR DALI, and PETER BLUME. It has never been widely exploited in the U.S.

Susquehanna river, 444 miles long, rises in southeastern New York, flows south across central Pennsylvania, and enters Chesapeake Bay at Havre de Grace, Maryland. The river became a main artery for settlements in western Pennsylvania during the 18th century. It traverses the anthracite region, and on its banks are such industrial cities as Binghamton and Owego, New York, and Wilkes-Barre and Harrisburg, Pennsylvania.

***Sussex* Affair** was precipitated (March 1916) when a German submarine torpedoed the unarmed English channel steamer *Sussex,* injuring several Americans. The U.S. regarded the attack as a violation of the pledge that had been given by Germany in 1915 after the *Arabic* had been torpedoed with the loss of two American lives. President Wilson gave notice that if such warfare continued, the U.S. would sever diplomatic relations with Germany. German submarines were instructed to spare neutral merchant vessels, but in February 1917 conditions led Germany to resume unrestricted submarine warfare.

Sutro tunnel (1869–79), built by the German-born engineer Adolph Sutro (1830–98), was one of the greatest engineering enterprises of the 19th century. It penetrated three miles into Mount Davidson (Nevada) to the rich COMSTOCK LODE, and it provided ventilation, drainage, and transportation.

SUTTER, JOHN AUGUSTUS (1803–80), Swiss-born frontiersman, went from Pennsylvania to the Oregon country in the 1830's, opened a coastwise trade in the Northwest, and finally settled in the Sacramento valley. He built Fort Sutter, encouraged colonization, and was well on his way to becoming a wealthy empire builder when news spread of the discovery of gold on his land. Then the mad CALIFORNIA GOLD RUSH began; crowds swarmed over his property, appropriating whatever they chose, and left Sutter a ruined man. He moved back to Pennsylvania, but his hope that the U.S. Congress would help redress the wrong proved vain, and the U.S. Supreme Court disallowed his land claims.

Swarthmore College (1864), at Swarthmore, Pennsylvania, is a nonsectarian coeducational institution founded by Quakers. Under the presidency of Frank Aydelotte (1921–40), the college pioneered in the program of Honors study, which allows freedom from class work to concentrate in broad fields of study. In 1965, with an endowment of $23,487,000 and a faculty of 124, it enrolled 995 students.

Sweatshops, factories employing children and adults under oppressive labor conditions, in the U.S. began during the Civil War, when wives and children of soldiers were set to work making uniforms. The evils of the system, which soon spread, included long hours (15 to 18 a day); inadequate light and heat, unsanitary conditions, and substandard wages. Attacks on sweatshops were led by social workers, trade unions, and the Department of Labor; and by the 1930's they had been virtually eliminated.

Swedenborgianism, the philosophical system based on the writings of the Swedish theologian Emanuel Swedenborg (1688–1772), was incorporated in the Church of the New Jerusalem, which was introduced in the U.S. (1784) from England. Formally organized as a New Church society in Baltimore (1792), it won adherents throughout the 19th century chiefly among intellectuals, and was of special interest to the New England Transcendentalists. (It largely declined as a church and as a system of thought after 1900.) Swedenborg believed that if one lived wholly from within, heeding the voice of the 'collective psyche' (which Emerson called the Over-Soul), one would be acting in harmony with the laws of life to which every natural object is obliged to correspond. The doctrine of correspondence — that each natural object expresses a divine essence — postulates a mystical relationship and does not answer questions which the understanding asks. Emerson had the Swedenborgian principle in mind when he said: 'Ineffable is the union of man and God in every act of the soul,' an influx which 'inspires awe and astonishment.'

Swedish settlements, see *New Sweden.*

SWIFT, GUSTAVUS FRANKLIN (1839–1903), meat packer and merchant, pioneered during the 1870's in the development of refrigerated railroad cars as an important factor in commerce and industry. He began shipping dressed beef from Chicago to the East in railroad cars in which fresh air was forced over ice and then circulated through the storage compartments. He built up the Chicago packing firm of Swift and Company.

Swimming was organized as an amateur sport late in the 19th century in many countries, and swimming matches were part of the events in the first modern Olympic Games (1896). Water polo, a game that resembles soccer but is played in a swimming pool, became an Olympic event in 1900. Most of the world swimming records in recent years (until 1960) were held by Australians. The U.S. holds many now.

SWING, RAYMOND GRAM (1887–), radio news analyst, after study at Oberlin began newspaper work in Cleveland (1906). He served as foreign correspondent for many journals (1913–34) before becoming a news commentator in 1935. He is respected for his wide-ranging knowledge of current affairs.

Swing music, which created the swing era (1935–45), led to a revolution in jazz music. It was sold by every resource of high-pressure tactics, and the terms 'jitterbugs' and 'bobby-soxers' were coined for its converts. The word was derived from the belief of enthusiasts that good jazz should 'swing.' Though it was actually not a new form of jazz, it was jazz on an amplified basis: the bands and dance halls were bigger.

Such bands as Casa Loma, with flowing, driving rhythm, and the call-and-response pattern between the sections, became immensely popular as early as 1931, but they were soon outmatched by the bands of BENNY GOODMAN and COUNT BASIE. From the momentum thus created grew BOP and the 'cool' school of jazz.

SWOPE, GERARD (1872–1957), after graduation from Massachusetts Institute of Technology (1895), was associated with various electrical engineering enterprises before he became president of the GENERAL ELECTRIC COMPANY (1922–39), during which period that giant corporation mapped out its program of broad diversification. Swope was a member of numerous government commissions, and author of *Stabilization of Industry* (1931), a program for meeting the depression following the PANIC OF 1929, often referred to as the 'Swope Plan.' It was influential in shaping the NATIONAL INDUSTRIAL RECOVERY ACT (1933).

SYLVESTER, JAMES JOSEPH (1814–97), English mathematician, became the first professor of mathematics at Johns Hopkins (1877–82), and in 1878 founded the *American Journal of Mathematics.* Later he was Savilian professor of geometry at Oxford (1883–94). He is best known for his work on the theory of numbers and on invariant algebra.

SZELL, GEORGE (1897–), Hungarian-born pianist and conductor, made his first appearance as pianist with the Vienna Symphony at the age of ten. At seventeen he made his debut as a conductor with the Berlin Philharmonic, and before he was forty had served as guest conductor of all Europe's leading orchestras. He came to the U.S. during the 1930's and performed in major engagements as conductor. As director of the Cleveland orchestra (after 1946) he built that organization into one of the world's notable musical ensembles. He was both admired and resented for his cold-eyed demand for perfection. Szell has been especially acclaimed for his interpretation of Haydn, Mozart, Beethoven, Brahms, Dvořák, and Mahler.

SZILARD, LEO (1898–1964), Hungarian-born physicist, became professor of nuclear physics at the University of Chicago in 1942. While working on atomic energy at Columbia (1939–42), in cooperation with EUGENE WIGNER and EDWARD TELLER he persuaded Einstein in the summer of 1939 to write President Roosevelt the letter that ultimately led to the MANHATTAN PROJECT. With ENRICO FERMI he devised the chain reaction system, composed of uranium and graphite, called an atomic pile. The system was proved practical beneath the football stadium at Chicago (1942), and it was immediately put into use in the manufacture of plutonium at the great government plant built at Hanford, Washington. A month before Szilard's death he joined the Salk Institute for Biological Studies at La Jolla, California.

T

Tabloids, picture newspapers half the size of the usual newspaper, met unusual success in the U.S. when JOSEPH M. PATTERSON launched the New York *Daily News* (1919), which within two years had built up and still maintains the largest circulation of any newspaper in the country. The appeal of the tabloid is based upon its sensational handling of crime, scandal, and sex and its increased proportion of pictures over text. By the mid 1960's more than 50 tabloids were being published in the larger cities.

TAFT, LORADO (1860–1936), Chicago sculptor, after graduation from the University of Illinois (1879) and study at the Beaux Arts, became a teacher in the Art Institute of Chicago. There, by his lectures and writings on esthetics, he helped shape the taste and craftsmanship of the young sculptors of the West. His workmanlike sculptures, influenced by Saint-Gaudens, include portraiture, monuments, and fountains. His statue of BLACK HAWK, overlooking the Rock river in Illinois, is an impressive historical memorial. His study, *The History of American Sculpture* (1903; new ed., 1930), is one of the few general treatments of the subject.

TAFT, ROBERT ALONZO (1889–1953), eldest son of WILLIAM H. TAFT, after graduation from Yale (1910) practiced law in Cincinnati and entered politics. As U.S. Senator (after 1938), he was a conservative leader of the Republican party before World War II, opposed to the New Deal program, and a persistent isolationist on European questions. He was a leading but unsuccessful presidential aspirant three times (1940, 1948, 1952). As Republican floor leader during the Truman administration, he strongly opposed its Korean policy and postwar economic controls. He was coauthor of the TAFT-HARTLEY ACT (1947). Although he had both strength of mind and character, 'Mr. Republican,' as he was banteringly called, was fated to spend most of his public career as the 'loyal opposition.'

TAFT, WILLIAM HOWARD (1857–1930), 27th President of the U.S. (1909–13) and ninth Chief Justice of the U.S. Supreme Court (1921–30), was born in Cincinnati, Ohio, where he practiced law after graduation from Yale (1878). He became nationally prominent when Benjamin Harrison appointed him U.S. Solicitor General (1890–92), and he acquired stature by his enlightened policies as first civil governor of the Philippines (1901–4) and later, informally, as President Theodore Roosevelt's 'trouble shooter.' After serving Roosevelt as Secretary of War (1904–8), he accepted his chief's suggestion that he become the Republican candidate for the presidency, was duly nominated, defeated Bryan in the election, and attempted to carry forward his predecessor's policies.

Although Taft was sympathetic to Roosevelt's program, he was conservative by nature and a constitutional lawyer by training, with a judicial rather than a political temper. He was singularly unfit for the complicated art of politics. When he took office, both houses were controlled by his party; the initiative soon passed to Old Guard Republicans in Congress whom Taft did not wish to antagonize, and on whose counsel he increasingly came to depend. Passage of the Payne-Aldrich Tariff (1909), a distinctly protective measure which the President signed after painful deliberation, enraged progressive Republicans. His inept handling of his conservation program (especially his dismissal of Gifford Pinchot in the BALLINGER-PINCHOT CONTROVERSY) further alienated party support.

Insurgent hostility toward Taft worked to the advantage of the Democrats, who in the mid-term elections of 1910 gained an impressive majority in the House, and so narrowed the Senate Republican majority that any realistic assessment would have shown that Taft could not succeed himself. Worst of all, Theodore Roosevelt, back from game hunting in Africa and lionizing in Europe, made his NEW NATIONALISM speech, which Taft interpreted as an assault on his administration, and thus a breach developed between the two friends. A public letter to Roosevelt early in 1912 from governors of seven states, urging him to announce his candidacy, led Taft to declare that supporters of the New Nationalism were 'neurotics.' The breach was now a gulf. Roosevelt as Progressive candidate split the Republican party, led by Taft. The Democratic candidate, Woodrow Wilson, won the three-sided race, and Taft carried but two states.

Yet during the Taft Administration valuable legislation was enacted. The Interstate Commerce Commission was strengthened, a postal savings bank and a parcel post were established, the merit system was expanded, a corporate income tax was initiated, and antitrust suits were vigorously prosecuted. Nevertheless, Taft had failed to win public support for his measures or to popularize his accomplishments.

For eight years Taft taught law at Yale (1913–21) and lectured widely, and during World War I he served as co-chairman of the National War Labor Board (1918–19). President Harding appointed Taft (1921) to succeed Edward D. White as Chief Justice, a post he filled until his death. A gracious and genial person, on the bench Taft was generally conservative (though not reactionary) in his political and social views. His achievement as a jurist was his prolonged and tireless labor for judicial reform.

See the biography by Henry F. Pringle (2 vols., 1939).

Taft Commission (1900–1901), organized under the chairmanship of William Howard Taft, was authorized by President McKinley to provide civil government for the Philippines. Within eighteen months it had given fundamental organization to local government. Taft was then appointed the first civil governor of the Islands (1901–4).

Taft-Hartley Act (1947), passed by Congress over President Truman's veto, banned the CLOSED SHOP and the secondary BOYCOTT, permitted employers to sue unions for broken contracts and for damages inflicted during strikes, required unions to abide by a 60-day 'cooling-off' period before striking, ended the 'check-off' system whereby the employer collected union dues (lest the employer thereby invade private rights of the union), and required unions to make public their financial statements. It also required union leaders to take an oath stating that they were not communists.

This elaborate Act followed stoppages in the coal industry that had far-reaching repercussions in industry generally, and threatened a nationwide tie-up of transportation. It passed both houses of Congress with thumping majorities since evidence was mounting that labor unions had become susceptible to racketeering and were believed to be permeated with alien ideologies. The Act was a political issue in the 1950 campaign, but Federal courts have upheld its major provisions.

Tall tales in the U.S. have been the frontier folk legends and myths, anecdotal and humorous in character, combining realistic details with a grotesquely impossible narrative. Such legendary heroes as SAM BASS, PAUL BUNYAN, TONY BEAVER, JOHN HENRY, and MIKE FINK, as well as such real frontier heroes as DANIEL BOONE and DAVY CROCKETT, have been the subjects of tall tales. The oral narration of the frontier story-teller created the tradition, which was later preserved by journalists and amateur and professional writers. The genre greatly amused Mark Twain, who used it effectively in his writing.

TALLEYRAND, CHARLES MAURICE DE (1754–1838), French statesman, as representative of the clergy in the States-General of 1789 sided with the revolutionists, although he was a lifelong advocate of constitutional monarchy and peace. He fled to England (1793) after the fall of the monarchy, took refuge briefly in the U.S. (1794–95), and under the Directory in France was made foreign minister (1797), in which post he engineered the XYZ AFFAIR (1797–98). As Napoleon's chief minister he opposed the LOUISIANA PURCHASE (1803), but Napoleon overruled him. Thereafter for three decades he was a major architect in shaping the diplomatic history of Europe.

Tammany societies were patriotic organizations that sprang up during the American Revolution. They were named for the Delaware Indian chief who is said to have welcomed William Penn. Later they served to promote various political and economic interests, but only the Tammany Society, or Columbian Order, in New York City (incorporated in 1789) endured. This group, with headquarters at Tammany Hall, during the 1830's became a power in the Democratic party, and by 1850 it was the most powerful political organization in the city.

In 1870, under the 'boss' system refined by WILLIAM TWEED, Tammany controlled state politics. Thereafter the fangs of the Tammany tiger (the symbol created by Thomas Nast in his cartoon attacking Tammany) were blunted from time to time by reform movements. Since 1932 Tammany has functioned as a county organization.

Tampico Incident, see *Vera Cruz Incident.*

TANEY, ROGER BROOKE (1777–1864), born in Maryland, the son of a wealthy slave-owning tobacco planter, after graduation from Dickinson College (1795) built up a large law practice and became a Federalist leader in state politics. In 1824 he abandoned the Federalists to support Andrew Jackson, who brought Taney into his cabinet, first (1831) as Attorney General to plan the strategy in Jackson's war on the BANK OF THE U.S., and later (1833) as Secretary of the Treasury to effect a withdrawal of Federal funds from the Bank. The Senate, incensed, refused to confirm the second appointment. By late 1836 the Senate's membership had been somewhat altered, and it ratified Jackson's appointment of Taney to succeed John Marshall as Chief Justice of the Supreme Court, to which Taney gave the stamp of his personality for 28 years.

During Marshall's long tenure (34 years), the judiciary had followed the Federalist concept of the Constitution as an instrument of national unity and Federal power. When Jackson left office (1837), seven of the nine judges were his appointees, most of them Southerners imbued with states' rights principles. Conservatives therefore were outraged when Taney's opinion in the CHARLES RIVER BRIDGE CASE (1837) substantially modified Marshall's contract doctrines by upholding the POLICE POWER of a state and asserting the principle of the social responsibility of private property. Taney's support of the slavery laws in the famous DRED SCOTT CASE (1857) brought furious opposition from the Republicans, and his decision in the MERRIMAN CASE (1861), though probably right, so irritated Lincoln (who looked upon Taney as an archenemy) that he refused to carry out the court order. Though antipathy to Taney was strong at the time of his death, students of the American legal system came to realize that his contribution to constitutional law gives him rank as one of the nation's great jurists.

See the biography by the political scientist Carl B. Swisher (1935).

TAPPAN, ARTHUR (1786–1865), with his brother, Lewis Tappan (1788–1873), as partner, established a highly lucrative dry-goods business in New York City, and founded the New York *Journal of Commerce* (1827). (In 1841 Lewis Tappan set up the first agency in the U.S. for rating commercial credit.) After the business became sustaining both devoted their time and money to various liberal causes, especially to the antislavery movement. Arthur Tappan gave large financial backing to help found Oberlin in Ohio (1833), the first college in the U.S. to admit Negroes.

TARBELL, IDA MINERVA (1857–1944), daughter of an independent oil producer in the Pennsylvania oil region, after graduation from Allegheny College (1880), began her investigations of industrial relations, first published as articles in *McClure's.* Her classic document in exposure literature, *History of the Standard Oil Company* (2 vols., 1904), was an analysis of ruthless business ethics which were often condoned by politicians. She later wrote biographies of Lincoln, Elbert H. Gary, and Owen D. Young.

Tariff action has been a continual feature of U.S. government since 1789, although interest in the problem has occasionally lapsed, to be revived by new revenue requirements, a desire to protect industries from foreign competition, business depressions, or political infighting. Prior to the Civil War, Congress enacted some half-dozen major tariff bills. The purpose of the TARIFF OF 1789 was chiefly revenue. During the period of embargo and nonintercourse preceding the War of 1812 domestic enterprises grew, but their prosperity was threatened by the large importations from Europe after 1815. Congress therefore enacted the protective TARIFF OF 1816. The debates leading to the TARIFF

OF 1828 (amended by the TARIFF OF 1832) were complicated by political intrigue, and these tariffs provided the highest protective rates of any before the Civil War. The COMPROMISE TARIFF of 1833 provided biennial reduction of rates for the next decade, at the end of which protectionist sentiment won enactment of the TARIFF OF 1842. More moderate rates were adopted in the WALKER TARIFF ACT (1846), and the TARIFF OF 1857 virtually placed the U.S. among free-trading nations.

The MORRILL TARIFF ACT (1861) put the U.S. on the course of protectionism that it followed into the 1930's. Tariff legislation became an active political issue in the 1880's, and although Congress authorized (1882) the appointment of a Tariff Commission, it ignored the Commission's recommendations, and subsequently legislated the body out of existence. The Democratic party thereafter pledged itself to tariff reduction (as in the Mills bill of 1888), but every attempt to reduce tariffs met a Republican opposition which long carried the field. When President Cleveland sought to replace the highly protective MC KINLEY TARIFF ACT (1890), all he gained was the WILSON-GORMAN TARIFF ACT (1894).

The DINGLEY TARIFF ACT (1897), highest until its time, was succeeded by the intended reform of the PAYNE-ALDRICH TARIFF ACT (1909). President Wilson secured passage of the UNDERWOOD TARIFF ACT (1913), which reversed the protectionist trend for a brief interval, but war conditions made it ineffective. Protection was the principle of the FORDNEY-MC CUMBER TARIFF ACT (1922) and of the HAWLEY-SMOOT TARIFF ACT (1930), the highest in U.S. history. Such barriers were symptomatic of the nation's choice during the 1920's of ISOLATIONISM. Passage of the TRADE AGREEMENTS ACT (1934), allowing the President freedom from specific congressional action, was a wedge which reduced the political importance of tariffs in the mid-20th century.

See Edward Stanwood, *American Tariff Controversies* (2 vols., 1903), and F. W. Taussig, *The Tariff History of the U.S.* (7th ed., 1923).

Tariff of Abominations, see *Tariff of 1828*.

Tariff of 1789, designed chiefly for revenue, provided for specific duties on 30 commodities, ad valorem rates (averaging some 8 per cent) on listed articles, and a 5 per cent duty on all other goods. The rates were somewhat increased during the next five years. The levy produced 88 per cent of the total receipts of the federal government.

Tariff of 1816, the first protective tariff in U.S. history, was introduced by John C. Calhoun and William Lowndes of South Carolina, in the belief that the South could be made to prosper as an industrial area. As spokesman for New England, Daniel Webster vigorously opposed it, fearing that it would destroy the commercial supremacy of that section. It imposed duties averaging 20 per cent ad valorem, with specific protection for manufactures that had been stimulated by the War of 1812 (cotton, iron, and wool). Actually the rates did not afford much protection against British imports in those three categories, but the duties were high enough to whet the appetite of American manufacturers for further increases, which were adopted in 1818 and 1824, and which reached the high point with the TARIFF OF 1828.

Tariff of 1828 was a political scheme, concerned, John Randolph said, with 'the manufacture of a President.' Pro-Jackson Democrats sought to make their candidate appear to be a free-trader to the South and a protectionist to the North. The bill placed such high duties on raw materials that New England was expected to vote with the South for its defeat, and the Jackson forces would then rally the protectionists of the middle Atlantic states, whose votes, coupled with those of his southern supporters, would elect him. But enough New Englanders voted for the bill — after modifying it — to secure its passage, creating such a 'tariff of abominations' that the South Carolina legislature adopted Calhoun's 'Exposition of 1828,' a precursor to the states' rights theories that South Carolina ratified in its ORDINANCE OF NULLIFICATION four years later.

Tariff of 1832, though attempting to mollify the South by removing some of the 'abominations' of the TARIFF OF 1828, maintained high duties on textiles and iron, and so roused the states' rights party in South Carolina that its legislature summoned a state convention, which adopted an ORDINANCE OF NULLIFICATION (1832).

Tariff of 1842, a Whig measure, was an upward revision which returned the tariff to the level of 1832, with duties averaging about 30 per cent. The Democrats modified it by the WALKER TARIFF ACT (1846).

Tariff of 1857, the last downward revision before the Civil War, still further moderated the WALKER TARIFF ACT (1846), and virtually placed the U.S. among the free-trading nations. The secession of the South later gave the protectionists the opportunity of legislating the MORRILL TARIFF ACT (1861).

Tarrateens, see *Abnaki Indians.*

TAUSSIG, FRANK WILLIAM (1859–1940), was a lifelong teacher of economics at Harvard (1882–1935), where he helped found the school of business administration. Long editor of the *Quarterly Journal of Economics* (1896–1937), he was an authority on international trade, and served as chairman of the U.S. Tariff Commission (1917–19). He believed in applying economics to public policy, urged the goal of moderate free trade (except for infant industries), and was generally progressive in outlook. As Wilson's expert in Paris, he drafted some of the economic provisions of the Treaty of Versailles. His many studies include *Tariff History of the U.S.* (1888; 7th ed., 1923), *Silver Situation in the U.S.* (1892), and *Social Origins of American Business Leaders* (1932).

Taxation in the American colonies was limited and relatively simple, the bulk of tax income being derived from import and export duties, fees, direct services, a POLL TAX, and QUITRENTS. Under the Articles of Confederation, Congress did not have the right to levy taxes, and met expenses by assessments on the states, a method which proved so chaotic that the framers of the Constitution specified that Congress should have the right to levy and collect taxes. Special taxes helped finance the Civil War, but on the whole the federal government depended largely upon customs duties and liquor and tobacco taxes for its revenues until 1909, when Congress levied a tax on corporations. Other forms soon followed: the INCOME TAX (1913), estate tax (1916), and, during both World Wars, special war taxes.

After 1920 the number and variety of direct and indirect taxes steadily increased. In general, state and local taxation follow the pattern of Federal assessment. The Constitution limits the collection of duties to Federal authority, and thus local governing bodies depend heavily upon property taxes.

In recent years taxation has come to be used more and more as an instrument by which social and economic change may be effected. This utilitarian concept of the greatest good to the greatest number is broad and various in court interpretations. The view of Justice Oliver Wendell Holmes, that 'taxes are the price we pay for civilization,' is one that the American public seems willing to accept.

See Sidney Ratner, *American Taxation* (1942), and Randolph E. Paul, *Taxation in the U.S.* (1954).

'Taxation without representation is tyranny' was a slogan current in the American colonies in the years preceding the War of Independence. (In 1820 John Adams attributed it to James Otis.) Although American representation in Parliament was an impossibility, and fully understood as such by colonial leaders, the slogan was a sharp propaganda weapon raised against such levies as those imposed by the STAMP ACT (1765) and the TOWNSHEND ACTS (1767). The real issue lay in the colonists' insistence that only their local assemblies had the right to legislate in matters of taxation. Colonial statesmen held that Parliament did not have the authority to levy external taxes without the consent of the colonies.

TAYLOR, BAYARD (1825–78), in an effort to escape from his Pennsylvania Quaker background, traveled in Europe as a correspondent for the New York *Tribune* and other journals (1844–46). His exotic *Views Afoot* (1846) so enchanted the public that Taylor found himself a man of letters. His *El Dorado* (1850), written after the *Tribune* had sent him to report on the California gold rush, sold by the thousands, and gave Taylor his longed-for opportunity to circle the globe. He wrote a succession of travel books (1854–55) pursued a lucrative career as a lyceum lecturer, and was appointed secretary of the U.S. legation in St. Petersburg (1862). The 'laureate of the gilded age' wrote novels and poetry as well as travel impressions, and his translation of Goethe's *Faust* was recognized by a nonresident professorship at Cornell (1870–77), and his appointment (1878) as U.S. minister in Berlin, where he died.

TAYLOR, [JOSEPH] DEEMS (1885–), New York composer and music critic, after graduation from New York University (1906) held journalistic posts, and later became intermission commentator (1936–43) for New York Philharmonic broadcasts. The Metropolitan Opera Company performed two of his operas: *The King's Henchman* (1927), with libretto by Edna St. Vincent Millay; and *Peter Ibbetson* (1931), based on the novel by George Du Maurier.

TAYLOR, EDWARD THOMPSON (1793–1871), born in Richmond, Virginia, began a life at sea as an orphan of seven. Converted to Methodism in Boston, he was licensed to preach (1814), and in 1819 he was ordained in the Methodist ministry. As missionary in charge of the Seaman's Chapel established at Boston (1830), 'Father Taylor' later impressed Walt Whitman as the 'perfect orator,' and when Melville created Father Mapple's famous sermon in *Moby-Dick* he had in mind Taylor's power to combine biblical imagery with Yankee sailor-talk. Taylor was often mentioned by writers of the period; he was widely known and much beloved.

TAYLOR, FREDERICK WINSLOW (1856–1915), industrial engineer, after graduation from Stevens Institute of Technology (1883) became foreman in a steel mill, where he pioneered in time and motion studies in an effort to determine whether workers handled machines efficiently and to define a reasonable day's work. 'Taylorization,' designed to increase labor production, became a synonym for INDUSTRIAL MANAGEMENT, and was widely adopted after 1900 in shops, offices, and industrial plants to maintain records, analyze work, and insure the objective hiring of employees. Taylor's studies, set forth in technical papers and summarized in *The Principles of Scientific Management* (1911), gave impetus to MASS PRODUCTION.

TAYLOR, GRAHAM (1851–1938), a graduate of Rutgers (1870), served in pastorates of the Dutch Reformed Church until 1892, when he became professor of social economics at the Chicago Theological Seminary. His Chicago Commons (1894) was one of the earliest social settlements in the country. It is described in his *Pioneering on Social Frontiers* (1930).

TAYLOR, HENRY OSBORN (1856–1941), after graduation from Harvard (1878) practiced law in New York. Although not a professional historian, he was a scholar respected for his study of the mind of Europe from classical times to the 17th century. His writings include *Ancient Ideals* (2 vols., 2nd ed., 1913), *The Mediaeval Mind* (2 vols., 5th ed., 1938), and *Thought and Expression in the Sixteenth Century* (2 vols., 2nd ed., 1930).

TAYLOR, JOHN (1753–1824), political philosopher and scientific farmer, was known as John Taylor of Caroline (Caroline county, Virginia). After study at William and Mary he began a lucrative law practice and served many years both in the Virginia house of delegates (1779–85, 1796–1800) and in the U.S. Senate (1792–94, 1803, 1822–24). As the high priest of Virginia republicanism, he was among the first to enunciate the doctrine of STATES' RIGHTS. He defended Monroe against Madison in political infighting (1806), and had no sympathy for Federalists, including the decisions of Chief Justice John Marshall. His *Inquiry into the Principles and Policy of the Government of the U.S.* (1814) ranks as a historic contribution to American political science.

As an agricultural reformer Taylor was much concerned with the land. His series of newspaper articles were gathered in *The Arator* (1813), which was an early analytical assessment of the problems of American agriculture. (It advocated rotation of crops, deep plowing, the use of cover crops, and manuring.)

Taylor was the pioneer among scientific farmers in the Old South.

TAYLOR, Zachary (1784–1850), 12th President of the U.S. (1849–50), was born in western Virginia, reared in Kentucky, and began his 40-year service in the U.S. Army when he was commissioned in 1808. He fought in the Black Hawk War (1832–33), the Seminole Wars (1837), where he won the nickname 'Old Rough and Ready,' and commanded the department of Florida (1838–40). In 1845 he was given command of the Army of Occupation on the Texas border, where his forces engaged in hostilities that precipitated the Mexican War (1846–48). His victories gained him the rank of major general, and his decisive defeat of Santa Anna at BUENA VISTA (1847) made him a national hero and the Whig choice for President in 1848. He won election by a close popular margin over his Democratic opponent, Lewis Cass.

Taylor's cabinet was undistinguished, with the exception of John M. Clayton, a Delaware senator whom Taylor named Secretary of State. But guided by his close friend WILLIAM H. SEWARD, Taylor unexpectedly showed himself to have a national rather than a sectional point of view. He thus lost the support of southern Whigs, who thought they had elected one of themselves. (To Taylor, a slave owner who abhorred the idea of secession, the slavery question was an abstraction.) Debate on the issue of slavery in the territories was still in progress when Taylor was stricken by acute gastroenteritis. He died sixteen months after taking office, and was succeeded by Vice President Fillmore.

'Old Zack' was a soldier of the old school — plain, honest, and uncomplicated. He had had no political experience whatsoever, distrusted most politicians (he had never voted in a presidential election), and therefore was at a disadvantage in dealing with Congress. It was as a soldier, when making the Midwest safe for settlement, that he contributed most permanently to the nation's history.

Biographies include those by Brainerd Dyer (1946), and Holman Hamilton (2 vols., 1941–51).

Tea Act (1773) was passed by Parliament at the urgent appeal of the EAST INDIA COMPANY, which was in financial straits and had a vast surplus of tea — 17,000,000 pounds. Wishing to give relief to the company, which had valuable holdings in India, the government granted the company a monopoly on all tea exported to America, with full remission of export duties, and the right to sell directly through its agents. It was not the tax that stirred the colonies to violent reaction, for there had been a tax on tea since the passage of the TOWNSHEND ACTS (1767). This Parliamentary favor, in effect giving a monopoly the power to raise taxes, stung merchants by its implications. They therefore allied themselves with the radical patriots, who in Boston staged the BOSTON TEA PARTY.

TEACH, Edward, see *Blackbeard.*

Teachers colleges in the U.S. began as part of the common school movement encouraged during the 1830's and 1840's by such intellectual leaders as HENRY BARNARD and HORACE MANN. (They were preceded by such training schools as that first opened in 1823 by SAMUEL R. HALL, and made common in the ACADEMIES.) Pedagogical instruction was offered when the first 'normal school' (modeled on the French *école normale*) opened at Lexington, Massachusetts, in 1839. A similar school, founded at Albany, New York (1844), developed into the State College for Teachers.

Soon after the founding (1882) of the National Herbart Society for the scientific study of education (named for the German philosopher and educator Johann Friedrich Herbart, 1776–1841), schools of education were established at the major universities, including New York University, Columbia, Harvard, Stanford, and Chicago. JOHN DEWEY, who taught at Chicago, formulated a philosophy based on a democratic educational system. Certification requirements for teaching have steadily advanced (though still too often with emphasis on method rather than subject matter), and in many states graduate work is required of public-school teachers as a prerequisite for advancement. Training of teachers for private secondary schools still remains largely a function of the liberal arts colleges. After 1920 the name 'teachers college' had largely replaced the name 'normal school.'

TEAGARDEN, JACK [WELDON JOHN] (1905–64), Texas-born jazz trombonist, was the first white musician to absorb and project the Negro BLUES tradition. Though he was almost entirely self-taught, he was generally regarded as one of the masters of the idiom. Teagarden was first associated with the Ben Pollack Orchestra (1928–33) and the Paul Whiteman Orchestra (1934–38). During the 1940's he toured with his own big band and later with groups he himself headed. He was one of the few musicians who aroused enthusiasm for the jazz of his day among all splinter groups. In 1958–59 he was selected by the State Department to tour the Far East.

Teamsters, International Brotherhood of, is the largest independent labor union in the U.S. (with a membership in 1965 of 1,505,000). The power of the Teamsters may be gauged from the fact that by 1960 the union controlled all transportation in many major metropolitan areas. The union achieved notoriety in the late 1950's, when its president, David Beck, was indicted for harboring criminals and plundering union funds. (The Teamsters were expelled from the A. F. of L.–C.I.O. in 1957.)

Beck's successor, James R. Hoffa, in 1964 was sentenced to jail and heavily fined for attempting to influence a Federal jury when he was on trial in 1962 for misusing company funds. One consequence of the Beck-Hoffa revelations was a strong popular demand for union restrictions and the passage of the Labor-Management Reporting and Disclosure Act of 1959, which was legislated to protect union members from exploitation by their officers.

Teapot Dome Scandal, one of the major disgraces of the Harding Administration (1921–23), was brought to light when a Senate investigating committee disclosed that the President, acting with the approval of Secretary of the Navy Edwin Denby (1870–1929), had transferred to Secretary of the Interior Albert B. Fall (1861–1944) the administration of naval oil reserves at Teapot Dome, Wyoming, and Elk Hills, California. In 1922 Fall leased the Teapot Dome reserve to oil operator Harry F. Sinclair (1876–1956), and the California fields to petroleum producer Edward L. Doheny (1858–1935). Both transactions were made in secret and bribes were evident. In 1927 the government secured cancellation of the oil leases. In 1929 Fall was convicted of accepting bribes, was fined, and went to prison. Technicalities led to the acquittal of Doheny and Sinclair, although Sinclair was subsequently imprisoned for contempt of the Senate.

Technocracy was a movement that flourished briefly following the PANIC OF 1929. Technocrats, seeking to end the alleged control by speculative finance, proposed that industrial recovery and economic stability could best be effected by a government of engineering experts. The movement was influenced by the philosophy of THORSTEIN VEBLEN. It aroused some discussion but no concrete action.

Technology, see *Invention.*

TECUMSEH (1768–1813), noted chief of the SHAWNEE INDIANS, in an effort to confederate Indian tribes on a large scale, enunciated the principle that Indian land was the possession of all tribes and could not be ceded or sold by an individual tribe. With his brother, 'The Prophet,' he organized a league, which, through his eloquence and political skill, he welded into a formidable body. His program called for peaceful settlement of disputes with white settlers. (Intoxicating liquor was banned.) Governor William Henry Harrison of Indiana, alarmed at the growing potential of such an Indian alliance, forced hostilities, and destroyed the league in the battle of TIPPECANOE (1811). In the War of 1812 Tecumseh was commissioned a brigadier general in the British army, and he was killed in the battle of the THAMES. He was a remarkable warrior and statesman, and takes rank among the greatest Indians in American history.

See Glenn Tucker, *Tecumseh: Vision of Glory* (1956).

Teheran Conference (November 1943), held during World War II at the capital of Iran, was attended by President Roosevelt, Prime Minister Churchill, and Premier Stalin. These heads of state agreed on the scope and timing of the projected Anglo-American invasion of Western Europe and outlined a specific plan for an international security organization after the war.

Telegraph, as a system of modern communication, was made possible in 1844 by the invention of S. F. B. MORSE. For some years legal disputes and unsubstantial construction hampered the growth of the industry. During the 1850's the Western Union Company began to consolidate telegraph lines. Edison's invention of the 'quadruplex method' (1874), which allowed four messages to be sent simultaneously over one wire, was a major improvement. In the 20th century, developments in telegraphy have been chiefly aided by RADIO.

Telephone, made possible by the invention patented (1876) by ALEXANDER GRAHAM BELL, through subsequent improvements such as the filter (1911), the amplifier (1912), and the mechanical switchboard (1922) gradually took first rank among communication media. THEODORE N. VAIL, as president of the AMERICAN TELEPHONE AND TELEGRAPH COMPANY (1907–20), laid the foundation of what became (and still remains) the largest corporation in America. Commercial transatlantic telephone service was inaugurated in 1927. Wireless transmission of sounds over long distances and across bodies of water is accomplished by radio telephony. Transcontinental dial telephone service came into general use during the 1950's. More than half of the 171,000,000 telephones in the world (as reported in 1965) are in the U.S.

Television was made possible by the development of the iconoscope (1925) by VLADIMIR ZWORYKIN, and the orthicon (1927) by PHILO FARNSWORTH. General Electric first successfully demonstrated 'the device for seeing by radio' in 1928, when Station WGY, at Schenectady, New York, inaugurated scheduled broadcasts. Although there were twelve regularly operating TV stations in the U.S. by 1932 (reaching some 30,000 homes), it was not until 1948 that the new medium became firmly established, when the nominating conventions were televised for the first time. In that year there were 200,000 TV sets in American homes. (World War II had delayed work on refinements of TV transmission.) In 1951 transcontinental broadcasts began and color was introduced.

The television industry in the U.S. opened important fields in art, education, and science, although telecasts have remained chiefly a medium for advertisements, entertainment and news services. By 1960 some 70,000,000 TV sets were in use throughout the country, and television had become a serious rival of motion pictures as a form of entertainment.

'Live' shows decreased during the 1950's with the advent of taping. After 1955 the sale of pre-1948 movie films to TV contributed to the decline of 'live' TV shows and greatly increased the number of quality programs. The quiz show scandals of that period resulted in Federal laws designed to curb 'payola' and the rigging of popular entertainment.

Political campaign history was made in 1960 when the Democratic and Republican presidential candidates, John F. Kennedy and Richard M. Nixon, debated issues over TV. In the same year the four-hour presentation of Eugene O'Neill's *The Iceman Cometh* was a milestone in TV drama. Since then prime air-time has increasingly been given to good, relatively recent motion picture films.

TELLER, EDWARD (1908–), Hungarian-born physicist, professor of nuclear physics at the University of California, Berkeley, since 1952, was earlier associated with the physics departments of George Washington University (1935–41), and Chicago (1945–52). His work in nuclear physics led him, in co-operation with EUGENE WIGNER and LEO SZILARD, to persuade Einstein in the summer of 1939 to write the famous letter to President Roosevelt that resulted in the MANHATTAN PROJECT. Teller's theoretical work during the 1940's was largely responsible for the development of the HYDROGEN BOMB. In 1960 he advocated an end to atmospheric testing, but he later changed his mind, and in 1963 he offered testimony against abandoning tests in the Senate hearings on the nuclear test-ban treaty. (The rest of the scientific community was overwhelmingly opposed to his views.) His writings include (with F. O. Rice) *The Structure of Matter* (1948), and (with A. L. Latter) *Our Nuclear Future* (1958).

Teller Amendment, see *Spanish-American War.*

Temperance movement in the U.S., largely impelled by evangelical Protestants, began early in the 19th century, but it got under way on a national scale in 1826 with the founding of the American Temperance Society, which sent out missionaries to preach the gospel of total abstinence from intoxicating beverages. The huge literary output that followed included eleven journals devoted solely to temperance, countless sermons, and millions of tracts. During the 1840's reformed drunkards, through their 'experience meetings,' aroused an emotionalism which became contagious, and the lectures of FATHER MATHEW and of JOHN B. GOUGH were sensational. The literary spearhead of the movement was the novel *Ten Nights in a Barroom* (1854), by TIMOTHY SHAY ARTHUR.

Between 1846 and 1855, following the lead of Maine, thirteen states passed prohibition laws, though several were repealed or declared unconstitutional. The creation of the PROHIBITION PARTY (1869) marked the appearance of the movement in national politics. Later followed the organization of the Woman's Christian Temperance Union (1874), which flourished especially under the presidency of FRANCES WILLARD; the establishment of the Anti-Saloon League (1893), with its powerful political lobby; and the spectacular career of CARRY NATION. The movement reached its height in 1919 with the passage of the Eighteenth Amendment to the Constitution, forbidding the manufacture, sale, or transportation of intoxicating liquors.

National prohibition was an integral part of the PROGRESSIVE MOVEMENT (1890–1917), promoted by both urban and rural Protestants. Agitation had been persistent, and by 1900 outstanding progressives and reformers were enlisted in the cause, which was defended by religious, social, economic, scientific, and political arguments. However, the PROHIBITION ERA (1920–33) bred such disrespect for laws involving enforcement of the Eighteenth Amendment that fourteen years later the nation repealed it by the Twenty-first Amendment. Since 1933 the issue has been decided by state or local option, though the Prohibition party continues to nominate candidates for national election. After Oklahoma abolished prohibition in 1959, Mississippi remained the only 'dry' state.

TEMPLETON, FAY (1865–1939), as a child actress made her debut in the famous sentimental melodrama, *East Lynne* (1868). One of the earliest vaudeville stars, she joined Weber and Field in 1905, and later played with George M. Cohan.

Tenant farmers are those who rent farms from the owner, and though farm tenancy in some form has existed throughout American history, it has developed especially in the South since the Civil War. For many young farmers in the North, tenancy was actually a 'social ladder' on the way to ownership. Poverty-stricken Negroes and whites in the South, unable to purchase farm property, were at the mercy of landlords who loaned money at high interest in anticipation of harvest, and collected rents as well. In 1934 the Resettlement Administration, later absorbed by the FARM SECURITY ADMINISTRATION (1937), undertook programs which greatly aided tenant farmers and SHARECROPPERS.

Tenement laws, see *City planning, Housing, Slums.*

TENNENT, WILLIAM (1673–1745), Irish-born Presbyterian clergyman, after graduation from Edinburgh (1726) was ordained in the Church of Ireland. In 1726 he settled at Neshaminy, Pennsylvania, where he established his famous Log College, and roused such evangelical zeal among his pupils that many became influential preachers during the GREAT AWAKENING. The effect of his labors was impressive, and the Log College became the model for other frontier institutions, notably the College of New Jersey (Princeton, est. 1746).

His son, GILBERT TENNENT (1703–64), soon after arriving in America with his parents, was installed as pastor at New Brunswick, New Jersey (1726), and, like his father, he became a leader of the revival movement in the Middle Colonies.

With GEORGE WHITEFIELD he toured New England (1740–41), where with 'New Side' enthusiasm he preached 'like a Boatswain of a Ship, calling the Sailors to come to Prayers and be damned.' The schism he caused in Presbyterianism (1741–58) by his fervid pietism he later worked to heal. Tennent had no intellectual pretensions, but he had (as he said) the courage 'to thrust the nail of terror into sleeping souls,' and his contribution to a dynamic religion along the frontier was noteworthy.

Tennessee, originally part of the Carolina grant of Charles II, was the home of Cherokee tribes whose villages on the Little Tennessee river were named Tanasi. The first permanent settlers came from the back country of Virginia and the Carolinas about 1770. When North Carolina ceded western lands to the U.S. in 1784, settlers in the East Tennessee region organized the 'State of Franklin,' which maintained a precarious existence until 1789, when North Carolina reestablished its jurisdiction. In 1790 the whole Tennessee region was officially organized as the 'Territory of the U.S. South of the River Ohio' (the Southwest Territory), and it was admitted to the Union as a state in 1796, the first to be carved out of national territory.

The early history of Tennessee, which had a strongly egalitarian society, is closely associated with the career of ANDREW JACKSON, who as political organizer completely dominated affairs. By the time Jackson became President (1829), Tennessee was a prosperous state. Memphis had become the metropolis of a fast growing cotton industry, and canals were linking towns and creating cities. Jackson's protégé, JAMES K. POLK, occupied the White House (1845–49) during the period of militant nationalism, and his call for volunteers in the Mexican War met with such overwhelming response that Tennessee has since been called the 'volunteer state.'

Although secession had been voted down early in 1861, a second referendum approved withdrawal from the Union. Tennessee was bitterly divided in loyalty; it was the last of the eleven states to join the Confederacy. Until 1862 East Tennessee continued to be represented in the U.S. Congress by ANDREW JOHNSON, who established a loyal government in the state. He was elected Vice President in 1864.

The state's large rivers made ideal invasion routes for Union forces, and, next to Virginia, Tennessee was the bloodiest battleground of the Civil War. Here were fought the campaigns leading to the capture of Fort Henry on the Tennessee and Fort Donelson on the Cumberland, and the battles of SHILOH, MURFREESBORO, CHICKAMAUGA, CHATTANOOGA, and KNOXVILLE. Because Tennessee ratified the FOURTEENTH AMENDMENT prior to forceable establishment of the 'carpetbag' regimes in the South, it was spared congressional RECONSTRUCTION and was readmitted to the Union in July 1866. But the postwar years were bitter, and the issue of 'white supremacy' in the state led to the founding there of the KU KLUX KLAN (1865).

Although industry has long since outdistanced agriculture in value of products, most Tennesseeans still earn their livelihood from the soil. The state can be divided geographically into three regions. In East Tennessee, where the CUMBERLAND PLATEAU and the GREAT SMOKY MOUNTAINS are located, farming is generally at a subsistence level, though the region has the two most industrialized of the large cities in the state, Chattanooga and Knoxville (the earliest capital). Nashville, founded in 1780 (and the permanent capital since 1843), is in the fertile bluegrass country of the Central Basin, through which flow the Tennessee and Cumberland rivers. West Tennessee is a plateau sloping to the rich bottom lands of the Mississippi. In 1925 Tennessee attracted international attention during the SCOPES TRIAL, and the fact that the state still bans the teaching of evolution in the public schools indicates the strong hold there of Protestant fundamentalism.

Establishment in 1933 of the TENNESSEE VALLEY AUTHORITY was an event of major importance, since it provides abundant hydroelectric power for a vast region, as well as for the great nuclear energy laboratories and installations at Oak Ridge. Memphis, a rail center and port of entry on the Mississippi, is the largest city, with a population in 1960 of 498,000. The University of Tennessee (Knoxville, est. 1794) is the state's best known institution of higher learning.

Tennessee Valley Authority (TVA), an independent corporate agency created by Congress (1933), implemented a proposal urged by the Progressives in the Senate for more than a decade. It took over a project (begun in 1916) for extracting nitrate at Muscle Shoals, Alabama, but it vastly expanded the project by providing for the development of the whole Tennessee river basin. The undertaking proved remarkably successful (although at first it had been judged the most radical of New Deal measures), and it served as a model for similar river projects in the U.S. and in other countries.

The TVA's system of multipurpose dams, hydroelectric plants, and navigation channels has been immensely important in the economy of the seven states directly affected. It covers an area of 41,000 square miles, which supports a rapidly growing population (initially some 3,000,000). Although TVA was attacked on economic grounds as a threat to private utilities, on social grounds as a neglect of local interests, and on legal grounds as unconstitutional, the Supreme Court fully sustained its legality.

Tennis became an organized sport in 1877, when the first championship match was played at Wimbledon, England, still the headquarters of the game. In 1881 the U.S. Lawn Tennis Association was formed, and the first U.S. singles tournament was held. By 1900 the game had been adopted internationally, and in that year the young enthusiast Dwight F. Davis (1879–1945), later Coolidge's Secretary of War, donated a cup as an international tennis trophy, thus initiating the annual Davis Cup matches. Public courts were added to school, college, and private clubs for the increasing number of players. Forest Hills stadium in New York City became the U.S. counterpart of Wimbledon. In 1923 the Wightman Cup (the gift of Hazel Hotchkiss Wightman) was established as an international trophy for women. Most noted among U.S. tennis players was WILLIAM T. TILDEN.

Tennis Cabinet was the name applied to the group of friends and agency heads who met with President Theodore Roosevelt from time to time as his unofficial advisers; they were so called because they frequently played tennis together. The group was similar to the KITCHEN CABINET of President Jackson, and the BRAIN TRUST of President F. D. Roosevelt.

Tenth Amendment to the U.S. Constitution, see *Bill of Rights*.

Tenure of Office Act (1867), passed over President Andrew Johnson's veto, denied the President the right to remove Federal officials without the consent of the Senate. Johnson's dismissal of Secretary of War Stanton in defiance of the Act was made a chief reason for impeachment proceedings against Johnson (although Lincoln, not Johnson, had appointed Stanton, and by the terms of the Act Johnson clearly had the right to remove the Secretary). Congress repealed the Act in 1887, and in 1926 the Supreme Court vindicated Johnson's contention that the Act had been unconstitutional (MYERS *v.* U.S.).

Tepee (*tipi*) in the Dakota language means *home*. Tepees differed from the eastern Indians' WIGWAM in that they were pointed or conical, not dome-shaped. They were covered with bark, skins, or mats. They were used by many of the Plains Indians in the region between the Mississippi and the Rocky Mountains.

TERMAN, LEWIS MADISON (1877–1956), chairman of the department of psychology at Stanford (1922–42), during World War I helped create a psychological testing program, which he later developed for application to school children. A lifelong student of the gifted child and the young genius, Terman is chiefly known for the Stanford Revision of the Binet-Simon Intelligence Tests (1916; rev. ed., 1937).

Territorial waters are all waters within the jurisdiction of a state. By international agreement such jurisdiction extends over the unenclosed waters reaching three miles beyond the low water mark. (This distance, the marine league, was set in the 18th century; it was the extreme effective range of shore batteries of that time, and therefore the limit of *de facto* sovereignty.) During the Napoleonic wars the U.S. sought to keep belligerents twelve miles off the coastal areas, and throughout the PROHIBITION ERA (1919–33) revenue cutters exercised the right to pursue smugglers within a twelve-mile limit. Though nations seek to make exceptions in special circumstances, territorial waters customarily remain the marine league, six miles, or twelve miles. The U.S. still recognizes the three-mile limit, over which it extends complete sovereignty.

Territories of the U.S., formed by Act of Congress, are divisions of the country not fully admitted to the rights of statehood. The administration of territories and possessions not organized into states varies according to circumstances, and the variations have been complex. (For a discussion of territories recognized as incorporated or unincorporated, see *Insular Cases.*)

A territory may be unorganized or organized. Unorganized territories are governed directly by Federal officers without the intervention of a legislative assembly. The governments of organized territories are similar to those of the states in form but are dependent for their status and power upon Congress, to which they may send one delegate, with a voice in territorial matters but no vote. Their chief officers are appointed by the President.

Thirty-one of the states passed through the territorial stage. (The exceptions are the original thirteen, Vermont, Kentucky, Maine, Texas, California, and West Virginia.) Most of them were formed by the breaking up of such parent areas as Louisiana Territory, Northwest Territory, and Oregon Territory. The last territories to be admitted to statehood were Alaska and Hawaii (1959). Today GUAM alone remains a territory (unincorporated). In 1952 PUERTO RICO was elevated to the status of a free commonwealth.

Outlying regions still administered by the U.S. include the CANAL ZONE, VIRGIN ISLANDS, AMERICAN SAMOA, WAKE ISLAND, MIDWAY ISLANDS, and RYUKYU ISLANDS. Canton and Enderbury Islands (midway between Hawaii and Australia) are under joint British and U.S. control. The 96 atolls and islands that comprise the Carolines, Marianas (excluding Guam), and Marshalls are under United Nations trusteeship and are administered by the U.S. Department of the Interior.

TESLA, NIKOLA (1856–1943), Croatian-born inventor, made his first electrical device, a telephone repeater, in 1881. He came to the U.S. in 1884 and for a brief time was associated with Edison. A pioneer in the field of high-tension electricity, he developed (1897–1905) the system of transmitting electric power without wires that made the advances in radio possible. Thereafter he engaged chiefly in developing telegraphy and telephony.

Teton Sioux, see *Dakota Indians.*

Texas, part of the SOUTHWEST, was traversed in the 16th century by Cabeza de Vaca (1530), Coronado (1541), and other Spanish explorers. La Salle's attempt (1685) to place a settlement on the Gulf shore gave France some claim to the region. Spanish missions were established in east Texas; the first (1690) was named San Francisco de los Tejas (after the Tejas or Texas Indians). Occupation of the vast area was desultory until the 19th century, although San Antonio (1718) had long been a Spanish settlement. In 1821 the Mexican government granted STEPHEN AUSTIN the right to bring settlers into the region between the Brazos and Colorado rivers. The history of Texas as a social unit begins with this colony of farmers and plantation owners.

The colonizers were drawn from all parts of the U.S., but they were predominantly from the slaveholding South. They rapidly formed a compact cell which resisted Mexican control. Open revolt in 1836 led to the massacre at the ALAMO, the victory at SAN JACINTO, and the establishment that year of the Republic of Texas, which was recognized by the U.S. Texas remained under its Lone Star flag for nearly ten years, with SAM HOUSTON as its leading figure. A movement for annexation to the U.S. was strengthened by the intrigues of French and British diplomats. Texas was admitted to the Union in 1845 as the 28th state, with Austin as its capital. The annexation (a principal cause of the MEXICAN WAR) brought Texas under its fifth flag. It came under its sixth in 1861 when it joined the Confederacy, to which it supplied provisions and men.

Texas was readmitted to the Union in 1870, and like the other states of the

South it underwent conversion from slave plantations to tenant farms. But Texas was still largely unsettled and its western ties were strengthened when stock raising during the 1870's became the leading industry. From the open range and, later, from great fenced ranches cowboys drove the cattle north to the railheads in Kansas and to the grasslands of Montana.

Geographically Texas includes the high, wind-swept semiarid plateau of the Panhandle and west Texas, which have extremes of temperature; the prairies of the Red river area; and the luxuriant subtropical coastal plains of the Gulf region. The transformation of large parts of Texas into an urban and industrial domain was quickened by spectacular oil discoveries after 1900. Oil has brought great wealth to the state, which produces 23 per cent of the nation's mineral output and ranks first among the states in the production of petroleum. Fruit and truck farms, cotton plantations, and great cattle and sheep ranches are also important in the state's economy.

The principal cities include San Antonio, the most important of Texas settlements in Spanish and Mexican days; El Paso, with its blend of Mexico and the U.S. and an immense international traffic; Galveston, a key port of entry; Dallas, a financial and insurance center with a growing electronics industry; Fort Worth, with large oil and aircraft industries; and HOUSTON, the state's largest city and one of the great ports of the nation. First among several score institutions of higher learning is the University of Texas (Austin, est. 1881), with an enrollment in 1965 of 30,000 students. (Its endowment in that year of $442,000,000 was the second largest in the country.) The oldest is Baylor (Waco, est. 1845).

Texas Rangers, a semi-military police force, were first loosely organized before the Texas Revolution (1835–36) as minutemen to protect settlers against Indians. About 1840 General SAM HOUSTON built up their strength to a force of some 1600 men who soon became noted for their esprit de corps. During the 1870's, at the peak of their usefulness, the Rangers protected hundreds of miles of Texas frontier against rustlers and marauders. They were equipped only with six-shooters and saddle guns, never drilled, and operated without uniforms or standard procedures. They were authorized as roving commissions on special duties. The Rangers were always picked men; they exercised a moral influence in the state, and their exploits have been portrayed in drama and fiction.

Textile industry became one of the most important in the U.S. after SAMUEL SLATER set up his first cotton mill at Pawtucket, Rhode Island, in 1790. FRANCIS CABOT LOWELL introduced (1814) the 'Waltham system,' at Waltham, Massachusetts, whereby all operations were co-ordinated under a single management, and his woolen mills at Lowell became world famous for producing standardized cloth patterns. After William Crompton (1806–91) successfully demonstrated a loom for the manufacture of figured woolens (1840), hand weaving largely disappeared. At the same time the COTTON INDUSTRY was doubling in capacity, with the number of spindles exceeding 2,280,000, and when steam power was installed in textile mills at Salem and New Bedford (1847), the industry was freed from the limitations of water power. After the Civil War, textile production increased in the South, although in 1890 New England still accounted for 76 per cent of the total U.S. spindles.

The ready-made clothing industry was expanded during the 1880's by the introduction of cutting machines and mechanical presses, an organized (take-home) sub-contract sewing system, and the brutal SWEATSHOPS, which functioned into the 1930's. After 1900 hydroelectric power accelerated textile manufacturing everywhere, but especially in the piedmont region of the South. By 1960 the leading fabric manufacturers in the U.S. (cotton, wool, silk, and synthetics) were employing more than 1,000,000 workers in some 8000 establishments.

Thames, Battle of the (October 1813), during the War of 1812 followed the British evacuation of Detroit (against the advice of Tecumseh). The British and Indians, under General Henry A. Proctor and Tecumseh, retreated into Upper Canada, pursued by American forces under General WILLIAM HENRY

HARRISON. Harrison overtook the British and Indians in central Ontario, where the Americans won a sweeping victory, the results of which were far-reaching. Tecumseh's death in the encounter brought about a collapse of the Anglo-Indian confederacy, and the U.S. frontier in the Northwest was made secure. The victory made Harrison a national hero and was a potent factor in his subsequent elevation to the presidency.

Thanksgiving Day in the U.S. by tradition commemorates the first harvest reaped by the Plymouth Colony in 1621. Some time (date not known) in November of that year the Pilgrims celebrated their survival with a feast. Similar observances later were local and sporadic until President Lincoln in 1863 began the practice of proclaiming a day. The date fixed was usually the last Thursday in November. In 1941 Congress by joint resolution decreed that Thanksgiving should fall on the fourth Thursday of November.

THAYER, ABBOTT HENDERSON (1849–1921), Boston-born painter, was known for his portraiture and for his landscapes and still lifes, represented by *Monadnock* (Metropolitan Museum) and *Roses* (Worcester Art Museum). In the late 19th century he became the center of an artist colony at Dublin, New Hampshire. As a naturalist he advanced the study of protective coloration. The summary of his discoveries was published by his son, Gerald H. Thayer, as *Concealing Coloration in the Animal Kingdom* (1909). The development of camouflage in World War I was in large part a result of Thayer's studies.

THAYER, ELI, see *Emigrant Aid Movement.*

THAYER, SYLVANUS (1785–1872), a graduate of Dartmouth (1807) and of the U.S. Military Academy (1808), during the War of 1812 served as an engineer. His study of European military schools and fortifications was followed by his appointment as superintendent of the Academy (1817–33), which he so thoroughly reorganized that he became known as the 'father of the Military Academy.' He later endowed an academy in his native Braintree, Massachusetts, and established and endowed (1867) the Thayer School of Civil Engineering at Dartmouth.

Theater in America, outlawed in all the colonies as a potential breeder of immorality and disorder, afforded little encouragement to native talent until the end of the 18th century. Some form of play-acting had been practiced from the first, albeit primitive in form and presented privately. In 1665 three Virginia amateurs were prosecuted (though acquitted) for performing an English play, *The Bare and the Cubb*. New England's hostility toward the drama was not broken down during the 150 years of colonial experience.

Professional actors gave New York its first taste of the legitimate theater when Richard Hunter was (presumably) granted a license in 1700. By the 1730's actors (chiefly British professionals assisted by local amateurs) were touring where they could, performing in coffeehouses, barns, or structures set up on the outskirts of towns to avoid interference by the authorities. Actors performed Addison's *Cato* in a Philadelphia warehouse in 1749. They were forced to leave, and in the following year they gave the first notable performance (in New York) of Shakespeare's *Richard III*.

Theatrical activity in America was inaugurated by the Hallam family, with a repertoire of some 24 Shakespearean and Restoration plays, beginning with the *Merchant of Venice,* presented at Williamsburg, Virginia, in 1752. For the next twenty years their tours spurred many similar attempts at private performances, impossible to suppress, and stimulated colleges to like expression, despite official disapproval.

The first permanent theater was erected (1766) in Philadelphia, and lasted 55 years (The Southwark). There was presented in 1767 *The Prince of Parthia,* by Thomas Godfrey (1736–63), America's pioneer dramatist. Others were built soon after, in New York (1767), Annapolis (1770), and Charleston (1773). During the War of Independence regular performances were given by British troops in occupied towns, thus further awakening interest in drama. The theater was finally given social distinction and approval by the attendance of such national figures as Washington, who greatly enjoyed it.

The American stage lacked playwrights of distinction in the 19th century, and it had to depend on revivals and on the reputation of such actors as CHARLOTTE CUSHMAN and EDWIN BOOTH. In the 1850's LAURA KEENE established her own company in New York, and the elder JOHN DREW and his wife opened theirs in Philadelphia. This too was the period when MINSTREL SHOWS and SHOWBOATS flourished. During the 1880's VAUDEVILLE won popularity. By 1900 such impresarios as DAVID BELASCO and CHARLES FROHMAN were managing the most successful actors of the day.

The decade 1910–20 is most important in the history of the American theater, for during that brief span important playwrights were trained in the theater laboratory of GEORGE P. BAKER at Harvard, the LITTLE THEATER MOVEMENT began, and the THEATRE GUILD was established. Broadway thus was at its peak in the 1920's and 1930's. After 1950 the off-Broadway theater began its remarkable growth, stressing experimental plays and attracting performers of rank. In 1962 the Ford Foundation made grants totaling $6,100,000 to aid American theater companies in establishing new levels of artistic achievement and financial stability.

Theatre Guild, an outgrowth of the LITTLE THEATER MOVEMENT, was founded in 1919 by members of the Washington Square Players in New York. So skillful was the Guild's financial management that in 1925 it built its own $1,000,000 theater, and it soon began presenting plays outside the city. Guild productions continue to set the highest standards for both writers and producers.

Theocracy, government of the state by the church, never technically existed in the Massachusetts Bay and the New Haven colonies, since the church did not officially control the civil government. More exactly, they were 'Bible Commonwealths,' in which the political theory assumed that specific laws must show Biblical warrant. Yet ministers possessed great influence and in times of crisis their opinions were sought, though not always followed. However, MORMONS lived in a true theocracy under Brigham Young.

Theological schools arose in the U.S. when the demand for trained ministers exceeded the ability of (essentially denominational) colleges to supply them. After the War of Independence, the Lutheran, Anglican, and Reformed bodies in Europe no longer sent young ministers to America, and American colleges themselves were giving less stress to ministerial education. Yet the number of pulpits was increasing, especially in the West.

The Dutch Reformed group in New Brunswick, New Jersey, first met the need (1784). Congregationalists set up the Andover Theological Seminary (1808) in Massachusetts after the chair of divinity at Harvard was occupied by a Unitarian in 1805. Presbyterians formed Princeton Theological Seminary (1812) to meet western demands, and thereafter denominational seminaries proliferated. Such were General (Episcopal, New York, est. 1817), Harvard Divinity (Unitarian, est. 1819), Newton (Baptist, Massachusetts, est. 1824), Gettysburg (Lutheran, Pennsylvania, est. 1826), and Union (originally Presbyterian, New York, est. 1836). Methodists at that time opposed theological education, and they did not open a seminary until 1846.

By mid-20th century there were some 200 Protestant theological schools in the U.S., and about 160 Catholic seminaries. The three principal Jewish theological schools are Hebrew Union College (1875), Yeshiva University (1886), and Jewish Theological Seminary (1887).

Theosophic movement, see *Blavatsky.*

Third Amendment to the U.S. Constitution, see *Bill of Rights.*

Third party movements in U.S. national politics have usually been short-lived, and rarely has a third party succeeded in winning a large number of electoral votes. But third parties have occasionally influenced the outcome of elections, and often their programs have later been incorporated in the planks of one or the other of the two major parties. The earliest third party was the ANTI-MASONIC PARTY, which ran a candidate in 1832.

During the 1840's the LIBERTY PARTY and the FREE-SOIL PARTY sprang up, the latter insuring the election (1848) of the Whig candidate by drawing votes from the Democratic nominee. In 1856 Fillmore won eight electoral votes as the candidate of the KNOW-NOTHING PARTY, and in 1860 Lincoln won the election for the Republicans because the CONSTITUTIONAL UNION PARTY split the Democrats; its candidate polled 39 electoral votes.

Various LABOR PARTIES sprang up after 1870, with social welfare and business regulation programs. Most influential in the 20th century was the PROGRESSIVE PARTY of 1912, whose candidate, Theodore Roosevelt, drew enough votes from Taft to seat Wilson. The longest lived of third parties, the PROHIBITION PARTY, entered national politics in 1872 and has run a presidential candidate ever since.

Third-Term Doctrine, so called, developed after both Washington and Jefferson refused third terms as President, and Madison and Monroe served but two each. Thus by tacit consent the custom seemed established that the President was ineligible for a third term. Jackson refused to serve a third time and favored a constitutional amendment limiting the President to a single term. When Grant in 1875 showed an inclination to serve a third term, the House of Representatives registered disapproval by a vote of 234 to 18, declaring that the practice would be 'unwise, unpatriotic, and fraught with peril to our free institutions.' In 1928 the Senate adopted a similar resolution (56 to 26) after Coolidge had equivocally stated that he did not 'choose to run.' The tradition was broken when F. D. Roosevelt was elected four times. However, in the late 1940's mounting opposition led to the adoption of the TWENTY-SECOND AMENDMENT (1951), which prohibits a third term.

Thirteen Colonies were the British colonies in America that became the original states of the U.S. In the order of their ratification of the Constitution, they are: Delaware (1787), Pennsylvania (1787), New Jersey (1787), Georgia (1788), Connecticut (1788), Massachusetts (1788), Maryland (1788), South Carolina (1788), New Hampshire (1788), Virginia (1788), New York (1788), North Carolina (1789), and Rhode Island (1790).

Thirteenth Amendment (1865) to the U.S. Constitution, first of the CIVIL WAR AMENDMENTS, abolished slavery. Although slavery as an institution was virtually dead at war's end, its legal status had not been determined. President Johnson required ratification of the Amendment by former seceded states as part of his RECONSTRUCTION program. In December the necessary votes had been secured, and the Amendment was proclaimed 'valid as part of the Constitution of the U.S.'

THOMAS, GEORGE HENRY (1816–70), a Virginia-born graduate of the U.S. Military Academy (1840), at the outbreak of the Civil War put loyalty to the U.S. Army, in which he had served for twenty years, ahead of loyalty to his state. He took part in campaigns in the western theater as a brigade commander, and his stand as 'the Rock of Chickamauga' (September 1863) during the CHATTANOOGA CAMPAIGN saved the Union army from rout. Thomas succeeded Rosecrans as commander of the Army of the Cumberland in the following month, and he served first under Grant, then under Sherman, in the ATLANTA CAMPAIGN. After annihilating the army of J. B. Hood in the battle of NASHVILLE (December 1864), he received the permanent rank of major general.

Thomas was one of the most gifted and successful of Union commanders, but he never fully enjoyed the confidence that Grant placed in Sherman and Sheridan. Historians today give Thomas a rank which popular judgment never accorded him in his lifetime. At the time of his death he was commanding the Military Division of the Pacific.

See the biography by Freeman Cleaves, *Rock of Chickamauga* (1948).

THOMAS, ISAIAH (1749–1831), of Worcester, Massachusetts, was the foremost American printer and publisher of his day, and issued more books than any of his contemporaries or predecessors. His books were distinguished for their typography and format. The *Specimen* of his types (1785) is valued as evidence of the equipment of a leading colonial printer. His *History of Printing in*

America (2 vols., 1810; 2nd ed., 2 vols., 1874) still remains a standard survey of colonial American printing. He founded and incorporated the American Antiquarian Society (1812), and served as its first president.

THOMAS, NORMAN [MATTOON] (1884–) after graduation from Princeton (1905) and Union Theological Seminary (1911) served as pastor of Presbyterian churches in New York City until 1918. During World War I he was a pacifist, and he joined the Socialist party, of which he became the leader after the death of EUGENE V. DEBS in 1926. He was the party's candidate for President in six successive campaigns, from 1928 to 1948. A constant critic of the American economic system and of both major parties, he was equally outspoken against fascism and communism. His writings include *Human Exploitation* (1934), *A Socialist's Faith* (1951), and *The Test of Freedom* (1954).

THOMAS, THEODORE (1835–1905), German-born violinist and conductor, came to the U.S. in 1845, and six years later began his self-sponsored concert tours. With William Mason he organized (1855) the Mason-Thomas quintet, important for the interest it aroused among American concertgoers in chamber music. He founded his own orchestra in 1862, and he toured the U.S., thereby inspiring many cities to develop orchestras of their own. He later conducted the New York Philharmonic and other orchestras, and introduced the major works of Brahms, Bruckner, Wagner, and Richard Strauss to American audiences. In 1891 he became permanent conductor of the Chicago Orchestra.

Thomas Jefferson Memorial, in West Potomac Park, Washington, D.C., is a circular domed structure surrounded by Ionic columns. The central chamber is dominated by a heroic bronze statue of Jefferson, designed by the sculptor Rudulph Evans. Four panels bear inscriptions from Jefferson's writings. President F. D. Roosevelt dedicated the Memorial (13 April 1943) on the 200th anniversary of Jefferson's birth.

THOMPSON, BENJAMIN [COUNT RUMFORD] (1753–1814), born at Woburn, Massachusetts, began to work as a merchant's apprentice at thirteen. A year later, without advantage of special training, he was sufficiently advanced in mathematics to calculate a solar eclipse within four degrees of accuracy. Brilliant and strikingly handsome, at nineteen he married a wealthy thirty-two-year-old widow from Rumford (later Concord), New Hampshire. During the War of Independence he served as a Loyalist agent in London, where, in 1780, he was advanced to the post of undersecretary of state for the Northern Department. His scientific pursuits, especially in the chemistry of gunpowder and the construction of firearms, led to his election (1779) as fellow of the Royal Society. He was later knighted.

In 1783, with the permission of the British government, Sir Benjamin entered the service of the Elector of Bavaria. For more than a decade he was the Elector's most trusted adviser, as lieutenant general, minister of war, and minister of police. Created a count of the Holy Roman Empire (1791), Thompson chose his title of Rumford from the name of the home of his wife. (She died a year later.)

Returning to London in 1795, Rumford devoted himself to experiments on heat transmission and moisture absorption. Again in Munich (1796–98) at the urgent request of the Elector, he continued his scientific investigations, and during another sojourn in London (1798–1804) he completed his *Essays, Political, Economical, and Philosophical* (4 vols., 1796–1802). At this time he founded and endowed the Royal Institution (1800).

Rumford's most vital contribution to science was made in a paper (1798) to the Royal Society, establishing the kinetic theory of heat. He spent the last ten years of his life as a world celebrity in Paris, where he married the widow of the chemist Lavoisier and was elected one of the eight foreign members of the Institute of France. His wealth allowed him to give material assistance to scientific achievements. He endowed the Rumford medals of the Royal Society and of the American Academy of Arts and Sciences. His residuary estate endowed the Rumford professorship of physics (1816) in Harvard College.

Arrogant and contentious in all his

dealings, as a politician Rumford was an unscrupulous careerist, but as a scientist he was unswervingly honest. Although he was highly esteemed in his lifetime, not until 30 years after his death was he recognized as the first to have measured the mechanical equivalent of heat. In his day he was preeminent as an inventor (shadow photometer to test the intensity of different light sources, the drip coffee pot, and the Rumford stove) and as an all-round man of science.

See the biographies by J. A. Thompson (1935) and W. J. Sparrow (1964).

THOMPSON, DAVID (1770–1857), English-born Canadian fur trader and explorer, began his career at fourteen with the Hudson's Bay Company. Although he was largely self taught as a geographer, he developed remarkable skill in geodetic observations, and as a member of the NORTH WEST COMPANY after 1797 made surveys in western Canada of such accuracy that parts (between the latitudes of 45 and 60 degrees) are still incorporated in maps of the region. He was the first to explore the upper Columbia river and to survey fully the shore line of Lake Superior. He received little public recognition in his lifetime, died penniless, and was buried in an unmarked grave in Montreal. Today he is ranked among the dauntless explorers of the New World and is acknowledged as one of the greatest of American surveyors. His journals (with those of ALEXANDER HENRY) were edited by Elliott Coues (3 vols., 1897).

THOMPSON, DOROTHY (1894–1961), newspaper columnist, was foreign correspondent after 1920 for various news syndicates. (For fourteen years, 1928–42, she was the wife of Sinclair Lewis.) She was a prodigious worker at her profession, and she was also influential as a broadcaster and public speaker. Fellow journalists as well as the public held her in high regard as a reporter of politics and foreign affairs.

THOMPSON, OSCAR (1887–1945), born in Indiana, served as music critic for the New York *Evening Post* (1928–34), the New York *Sun* (1937–45), and as editor (1936–43) of *Musical America*. He was the first teacher of musical criticism (1928) at the Curtis Institute, and he was later associated with Columbia and the New York College of Music. His writings include *Practical Musical Criticism* (1934) and *Debussy, Man and Artist* (1937).

THOMSON, ELIHU (1853–1937), English-born electrical engineer, organized an electrical company (later absorbed by General Electric Company), and served briefly (1920–23) as acting president of Massachusetts Institute of Technology. His inventions, which include the resistance method of electric welding, a three-phase electric dynamo, and the centrifugal cream separator, gave him international standing.

THOMSON, VIRGIL (1896–), born in Missouri, after graduation from Harvard (1922), studied composition with Nadia Boulanger. He demonstrated his highly simplified style of utmost refinement in two operas, with librettos by Gertrude Stein, *Four Saints in Three Acts* (1928), and *The Mother of Us All* (1947). His scores for motion pictures include *Louisiana Story,* awarded the 1949 Pulitzer Prize in music. For many years he was music critic for the New York *Herald Tribune* (1940–54). His writings include *The Art of Judging Music* (1948) and *Music Right and Left* (1951).

THOREAU, HENRY DAVID (1817–62), born in Concord, Massachusetts, after graduation from Harvard (1837) and intermittent teaching (1837–41), for a time lived in Emerson's home (1841–43), where he became one of the circle of Transcendentalists. His individual venture at Walden Pond (1845–47) enabled him to push his doctrine of simplification to its limits, and gave him the enjoyment, in Emerson's words, of 'an original relation to the universe.'

Thoreau's residence at Walden was interrupted by a day's imprisonment; he had refused to pay the state's poll tax during the Mexican War on the ground that such a tax abetted the expansionist scheme of southern slave power. (His record of the experience was published as 'Civil Disobedience' in 1849, and it became a testament for advocates of passive resistance, notably for Mahatma Gandhi, nearly a century later.) Thoreau's intimate relation with nature gave him inspiration for his most sustained literary work, notably in *A Week on the Concord and Merrimack Rivers* (1849) and *Walden* (1854), and the posthumous *Excursions* (1863), *The Maine Woods* (1864), and *Cape Cod* (1865).

As a political thinker and social philosopher Thoreau believed that moral imperatives take precedence over institutions, and he became outspoken toward the end of his life on these issues on the lyceum platform, especially as an abolitionist. As a poet-naturalist, Thoreau sought to create (in his own words) 'a very private history, which unostentatiously lets us into the secret of a man's life.' His *Journals* (14 vols.) and his *Works* (20 vols.) were published in 1906. They not only constitute the autobiography of a great individual, but the record of literary thought in New England during mid-19th century. Thoreau has taken a place among world figures in literature.

Recent studies of Thoreau include those by H. S. Canby (1939), J. W. Krutch (1948), W. M. Condry (1954), and H. B. Hough (1956).

THORFINN KARLSEFNI (*fl.* A.D. 1002–10), Icelandic leader and kinsman of LEIF ERICSSON, according to the 'Saga of Eric the Red' (in the *Hauksbók*) and the 'Saga of Olaf Tryggvason' (in the *Flateyjarbók*) — both 14th century manuscripts — attempted to colonize the North American mainland west of Greenland. A site yielding Viking artifacts was identified in 1963 at L'Anse aux Meadows, on the northern tip of Newfoundland, and is now thought to be the community Thorfinn established. Radiocarbon datings of charcoal show that the site was occupied about A.D. 1000.

THORNDIKE, EDWARD LEE (1874–1949), professor of educational psychology at Columbia (1904–40), was a pioneer in animal psychology and in the psychology of learning. He formulated the 'trial and error' concept of learning, devised methods for measuring and testing intelligence, and introduced twin-studies as a method of control. He was a prolific writer; such books as *Educational Psychology* (1903), *Animal Intelligence* (1911), and *Human Nature and the Social Order* (1940) are representative of his work.

THORNTON, WILLIAM (1759–1828), English-born architect, after receiving his medical degree at Aberdeen (1784), traveled widely and made a career of architecture. His plans for the proposed Capitol at Washington (1793) were accepted, and he supervised construction until 1802, when some details were modified by B. H. Latrobe and Charles Bulfinch. He also designed a number of residences. After 1802 he served throughout his life as commissioner of patents.

THORPE, JIM [JAMES] (1888–1953), Oklahoma Indian, while playing football at the Carlisle Indian School (1911–12), under the coaching of 'POP' WARNER led his team to startling upsets. He performed in track and field events in the Olympic Games held at Stockholm (1912), where he won several awards, later surrendered because he had previously (1909–10) played semiprofessional baseball. Thereafter, proclaimed 'the world's greatest athlete,' he played professional football and became supervisor for the Chicago parks.

THWAITES, REUBEN GOLD (1853–1913), Massachusetts-born historian, wrote numerous monographs on the history of New France and the Middle West. In 1886 he succeeded L. C. DRAPER as librarian of the Wisconsin Historical Society, and until his death he continued Draper's pioneer work of making the Society an effective institution of scholarship. Chief among his critically edited accounts of early western history are the JESUIT RELATIONS (73 vols., 1896–1901), and *Early Western Travels, 1748–1846* (33 vols., 1904–7).

TICKNOR, GEORGE (1791–1871), after graduation from Dartmouth (1807) was admitted to the bar. He soon abandoned the law and in 1815 with Edward Everett he went to Göttingen to study. While abroad he was appointed the first professor of modern languages at Harvard (1816–35). He resigned his chair to devote himself to further study abroad, and in the following decade he brought out his monumental *History of Spanish Literature* (3 vols., 1849). A Boston patrician, Ticknor was a leader in the intellectual life of his city, and as the first American master of European literature he inspired an interest in the culture in which he was steeped. At his death he left his valuable Spanish collection to the Boston Public Library, of which he was a founder.

Ticonderoga, in northeastern New York, was a strategic command point between Lake George and Lake Champlain during the last of the French and Indian Wars (1755–63). There the French built Fort Carillon (1755), successfully defended by Montcalm in 1758 against James Abercrombie in one of the bloodiest operations of that imperial struggle. It fell to Jeffrey Amherst in 1759, and was renamed Fort Ticonderoga. Since the French in retreat had blown up the fort, it was in a dilapidated condition, and Colonel BENEDICT ARNOLD and Colonel ETHAN ALLEN easily subdued its token garrison at the outbreak of the Revolution (May 1775). HENRY KNOX then ingeniously transported most of its heavy artillery to Boston, where it was used by Washington to force the British to evacuate. ARTHUR ST. CLAIR abandoned the fort to the British without a fight in the SARATOGA CAMPAIGN (1777). (A court-martial later cleared St. Clair of blame.) At the close of the war the fort was allowed to fall into ruins. Today it has been restored, in harmony with the original French plans, as a museum.

Tidelands oil was first discovered off the Louisiana coast, where producing oil wells were completed in 1939. Other offshore wells were in production during the next decade. In 1947 and 1950 the Supreme Court ruled that these oil resources belonged to the federal government. (The issue was a major one because the off-shore oil reserves along the Louisiana-Texas coast are estimated to be nearly 50 per cent of known reserves for the entire U.S.) The Submerged Lands Act of 1953 nullified the earlier Supreme Court rulings and assigned ownership to the seaboard states — three miles from the shore in the Atlantic and Pacific oceans and ten and a half miles in the Gulf of Mexico. But in 1960 the Supreme Court ruled that Louisiana owned the right to submerged lands only for a distance of three and a half miles. The issue has yet to be decided.

Tidewater region, in U.S. history, is that part of the Atlantic coastal plain (principally from Pennsylvania to Georgia) extending inland to the points reached along rivers by ocean tides, or to the FALL LINE. It was the region first occupied by English settlers, and it became an area of comparative wealth. Merchants and shipowners in the towns, and planters growing tobacco, rice, indigo, and cotton dominated colonial affairs politically, socially, and economically. (They maintained their domination for many years by disproportional representation.)

The later small-farm population that settled the PIEDMONT frontier to the west came to resent the slaveholding tidewater aristocracy, and the ensuing sectional differences broke into armed conflicts in such contentions as BACON'S REBELLION (1675–76) in Virginia, the riots of the PAXTON BOYS (1765) in Pennsylvania, and the REGULATOR MOVEMENT (1768–71) in North Carolina. The political history of the region was shaped by the sectional differences well into the 19th century. (West Virginia used the Civil War as an opportunity to secede from Virginia and form a state.)

TILDEN, SAMUEL JONES (1814–86), an eminent lawyer in New York City, became a strong partisan of the BARNBURNERS in New York Democratic politics. As state Democratic chairman after 1866, he effected reforms, and largely on his evidence the TWEED RING was smashed (1871).

While Tilden was governor of New York (1875–76), his party determined to make reform a campaign issue and nominated him to run for the presidency against Rutherford B. Hayes. The bitterly contested election was settled by an ELECTORAL COMMISSION in favor of Hayes (although Tilden had a clear popular majority), and Tilden retired to private life. His endowment for a free public library in New York City was a trust; it was joined with the Astor and Lenox libraries to form (1895) the New York Public Library.

TILDEN, WILLIAM TATEM (1893–1953), generally adjudged the foremost tennis player of the first half of the 20th century, had already established a reputation as a brilliant and versatile player before he graduated from Pennsylvania (1922). He won his first amateur championship in 1920, and repeatedly won tournaments for fifteen years. He became a professional in 1931, and in 1945, at the age of fifty-two, he and Vincent Richards won the professional doubles championship. His numerous books on tennis include *Aces, Places, and Faults* (1938).

TILLICH, Paul [Johannes] (1886–1965), German-born theologian, was professor of philosophical theology at Union Theological Seminary (1933–55) before becoming a University Professor at Harvard in 1955. Tillich was a leading proponent of religious existentialism; he steadily deepened his view that religious meaning is gained from a sense that prophetic utterance is above reason (which cannot be divorced from faith). His influence has been both deep and wide. His writings include *Systematic Theology* (2 vols., 1951–57), *The New Being* (1955), and *Theology of Culture* (1959).

TILLMAN, Benjamin Ryan (1847–1918), farmer and politician, became a radical leader of the South Carolina upcountry white farmers, and won the governorship (1890–94) from 'Bourbon' Wade Hampton, the conservative leader who had 'redeemed' the state from the carpetbaggers. Tillman preached a class war of the masses against the classes, but his reforms were usually constructive, except where they affected the Negro. As governor, he increased educational expenditures, equalized taxes, and effected needed improvements in state railroad and power commissions.

He won a U.S. Senate seat (1895–1918) in an initial campaign that attacked President Cleveland's conservatism in colorful language: 'I'll stick my pitchfork into his old ribs!' Thereafter as 'Pitchfork Ben' he directed his machine in a crusade against Negroes so crude and vitriolic that Republicans left the chamber and his colleagues from the South were embarrassed. Despite a personal feud with Theodore Roosevelt, he gave aid to the Republican administration in conducting key antitrust bills to victory. He kept an iron control over South Carolina politics in the interest of his idea of white supremacy, which became the stock-in-trade of other Dixie demagogues.

Timber culture, see *Conservation movement.*

Tin Pan Alley, popular and journalistic phrase coined about 1900, was originally applied to the district in New York City around 14th Street, where popular song publishers were then located. It moved uptown with the theater and amusement district. Association with the motion-picture industry and radio gave the term general application to commercialized music. Early composers for Tin Pan Alley include w. c. handy, george m. cohan, sigmund romberg, jerome kern, irving berlin, george gershwin, and rudolph friml.

'Tippecanoe and Tyler Too,' see *Harrison, W. H.*

Tippecanoe, Battle of (1811), was a calculated engagement that Governor William Henry Harrison of Indiana had long planned as a means of ending the authority of tecumseh and his visionary brother, 'The Prophet,' over the Shawnee Indians. The Indians were driven to retreat, and the Indian 'capital' on Tippecanoe creek, 150 miles north of Vincennes, was destroyed. This relatively minor fray, though dearly bought and far from decisive, was treated in the East as a victory, and, with John Tyler as his running mate, Harrison entered the White House on the slogan 'Tippecanoe and Tyler Too.'

Titles of Nobility, see *Nobility.*

Tobacco industry was a chief crop to early Virginia settlers, who by 1627 were annually producing some 500,000 pounds. Tobacco remained the most important export commodity throughout the colonial period, and by 1775 Virginia, Maryland, and North Carolina were shipping 100,000,000 pounds. After the War of 1812 tobacco culture expanded into the Mississippi valley, and by 1860 New York and Philadelphia were centers of cigar manufacture. (About 1900 a shade-grown leaf was introduced in the Connecticut valley and in Florida.)

The great tobacco trust built up after

1890 by JAMES B. DUKE was created by close attention to marketing procedures and large-scale advertising. (It was dissolved by the U.S. Supreme Court in 1911.) By 1960 the Federal excise tax on tobacco (10 per cent) was annually grossing more than $1,800,000,000. The medical reports of 1963 that gave evidence that cigarette smoking was linked to lung cancer have altered the pattern of cigarette advertisements, but there has been no appreciable decline in the production of tobacco.

TOCH, ERNST (1887–), self-taught Austrian-born composer, after emigrating to the U.S. (1934) continued to compose in a variety of musical forms. His symphony *No. 3* (1955) won the Pulitzer Prize in music. He is a particularly successful writer of piano concertos, and he has composed film music and such poignant vocal works as *Poems to Martha* (1946). For a time he served as professor of composition at the University of Southern California (1940–47).

TOCQUEVILLE, ALEXIS, Comte de (1805–59), French liberal politician and writer, as a magistrate obtained a commission (1831) from the French government to study the penal system of the U.S. The chief purpose of his eighteen-month journey into all parts of the young nation was to study American democratic ideas and practices. He wrote *De la démocratie en Amérique* (1835), a work immediately translated into many languages, and for generations the handbook of liberals in most countries of the world. Though Tocqueville failed to give sufficient consideration to new economic forces and to the Industrial Revolution then taking place, the influence of *Democracy in America* is still felt. It is a dispassionate examination of the American political and social systems and their shaping effect on American manners and intellect. He constantly searched for the permanent beneath the surface of changing phenomena, and, though many of his predictions did not materialize, his analysis of the social problems created in a democracy of many races is still relevant.

TOM THUMB, General, was the name given to the American dwarf Charles S. Stratton (1838–83), one of the sideshow attractions in the shows of P. T. BARNUM. The General grew to be 40 inches tall.

Tom Thumb, built by PETER COOPER, was the first efficient steam locomotive constructed in America (1830). Though it was only about the size of a small handcar, it proved the practicability of using steam power on rails.

Tomb of The Unknowns. On 11 November 1921, in the presence of President Harding, the Unknown Soldier of World War I was entombed in Arlington National Cemetery. The bodies of two unidentified servicemen, one who died in World War II and the other in the Korean War, were placed in crypts beside the first on Memorial Day, 30 May 1958, in ceremonies led by President Eisenhower. All rest beneath an entablature bearing this inscription: 'Here rests in honored glory an American soldier known but to God.'

TONTI, HENRI DE (1650–1704), French explorer, in 1678 went to Canada as the principal lieutenant of LA SALLE. In the following year at Niagara he constructed *Griffon,* the first sailboat to ply the upper Great Lakes. After penetrating the Illinois country, he descended the Mississippi river with La Salle (1682), and in 1686 he established the earliest French settlement in the lower Mississippi valley, on the Arkansas river. There he founded a Catholic mission (1689) at the Arkansas Post, which by 1700 had developed an extensive trade with the English in Carolina. In 1702 he joined IBERVILLE in directing French settlements at the Mississippi delta.

TOOMBS, ROBERT (1810–85), after graduation from Union College (1828) returned to Georgia, where, as a member of the ruling planter class, he practiced law, entered politics, and served eight years as a Whig in the House (1845–53) and, first as a Constitutional Unionist, then as a Democrat, in the Senate (1853–61). With HOWELL COBB and A. H. STEPHENS he was largely responsible for securing Georgia's ratification of the Compromise of 1850, and with them he stood firmly for the cause of Union until Lincoln was elected. He resigned from the U.S. Senate (1861) to help organize the secessionists in Georgia. During the Civil

War he commanded a brigade. After the war he remained an 'unreconstructed' Southerner. He helped to overthrow radical rule and decided (1877) to support the Republican Rutherford B. Hayes as the solution of Reconstruction evils.

Topographical mapping of the interior of North America (north of Mexico) began with the earliest efforts of Europeans to find a NORTHWEST PASSAGE to the Orient. SAMUEL CHAMPLAIN penetrated the continent (1603–31) up the St. Lawrence to Lake Huron, and his voyages resulted in several important maps. In the interests of the fur trade such French explorers as ETIENNE BRULÉ and JEAN NICOLET extended topographical knowledge. By 1650 all five of the Great Lakes had been partially surveyed, and the scholarly records of Jesuit and Recollect missionaries were supplying information about the entire Mississippi valley. The maps of LOUIS JOLLIET, named hydrographer of New France, were supplemented by the score compiled (1678–1708) by Jean Baptiste Louis Franquelin, who alternated with Jolliet as hydrographer. These are the best early maps of the interior of North America. In the same decades detailed maps of the colonies were being used to resolve boundary disputes.

During the 18th century the mapping of the interior was advanced by several able cartographers, including Guillaume Delisle, whose *Carte de la Louisiane* (1718) was long the basis for maps of the Mississippi region. The map of North America (1755) prepared by JOHN MITCHELL was used to lay down the first U.S. boundaries. The North American maps of the great London cartographer AARON ARROWSMITH were first issued in 1795, and reissued repeatedly with additions and corrections. The maps of LEWIS EVANS were the best for details of post roads. The War of Independence stimulated survey expeditions into all parts of the theater of war, and in 1784 ABEL BUELL produced the first large-scale map of the U.S. In the Southwest and Far West such intrepid Spanish missionaries as ESCALANTE were mapping territory from New Mexico to Utah, and the traders PETER POND and DAVID THOMPSON were surveying the Northwest.

After the Louisiana Purchase (1803) surveying and mapping of the vast regions in the West were undertaken by such expeditions as those led by ZEBULON PIKE, STEPHEN LONG, JEDEDIAH SMITH, and BENJAMIN BONNEVILLE. The extensive surveys of JOHN C. FRÉMONT (1842–46) beyond the Rockies were incorporated on a map published in 1848; it helped determine the route of transcontinental railroads. Voluminous reports, accompanied by maps, followed the expeditions into the West during the 1870's of F. V. HAYDEN, CLARENCE KING, C. M. WHEELER, J. W. POWELL, and C. E. DUTTON. The establishment in 1879 of the U.S. GEOLOGICAL SURVEY assured detailed mapping and classifying of public lands.

Tories, see *Loyalists.*

Tornadoes, often called 'cyclones' or 'twisters,' are highly destructive rotating windstorms, narrow in width and usually brief in duration, which attain velocities of 300 miles an hour with an updraft of like intensity. They are more numerous and violent in the prairie region of the U.S. than anywhere else in the world. (The tornado that crossed Missouri, Illinois, and Indiana in March 1925 took a toll of 689 lives.) In rural areas cyclone cellars are often constructed apart from dwellings, which, if in the wake of a tornado, literally explode.

TORREY, JOHN (1796–1873), professor of chemistry at Columbia (1827–55) and at Princeton (1830–54), was widely known as a botanist. He wrote *A Flora of the State of New York* (1843) and, with Asa Gray, *A Flora of North America* (2 vols., 1838–43), taxonomic works that systematized botanical collections and influenced all who followed him. He prepared botanical catalogs for the U.S. exploring expeditions of Captain Wilkes, John Frémont, and others. In 1860 he presented his valuable herbarium to Columbia.

TOSCANINI, ARTURO (1867–1957), Italian conductor, was one of the world's most notable musical interpreters. The centers of his activity were the opera houses and concert platforms of Milan and New York. In the U.S. he conducted at the Metropolitan Opera House (1908–15), led the New York Philharmonic Symphony (1926–36), and the National Broadcasting Company Symphony (1937–

54), which was especially organized for him to conduct. He had breadth of understanding that gave mastery to his interpretations of widely different schools, a phenomenal memory of scores, and a commanding personality, which dominated both his players and his audiences.

Town meetings originated in colonial New England as assemblages for the election of SELECTMEN and other local officers. They legislated on any matter that directly concerned the town. As the only example of direct democracy in American history, they continue to be an open forum on local affairs for hundreds of communities.

Townsend Plan, so called, was proposed in 1933 by Francis Everett Townsend (1867–1960), a physician in Long Beach, California. It called for a $200-a-month pension to any retired person over sixty. It was to be paid in scrip, and to be spent within a month. The funds were to be raised by a sales tax. The simplicity of the plan for an OLD AGE PENSION, together with Townsend's messianic zeal and the organization of Townsendites into a formidable pressure group (estimated at 30,000,000), brought increasing support for the proposal, despite the fact that it was condemned by competent economists. Bills to establish the Plan were brought up and defeated in Congress many times. The movement lost headway after passage of the SOCIAL SECURITY ACT (1935).

TOWNSHEND, CHARLES (1725–67), English politician, as secretary-at-war (1761–62) and president of the BOARD OF TRADE AND PLANTATIONS (1763) was for a time directly responsible for Great Britain's imperial policies. While chancellor of the exchequer (1766–67) in the second administration of CHATHAM, he sought to offset the defeat of his proposed land tax with the ill-starred TOWNSHEND ACTS, American import duties that united the colonies in their protest against external taxation.

Townshend Acts (1767) were passed by Parliament after CHARLES TOWNSHEND had become chancellor of the exchequer, in effect the leader of the government at that time. A reduction in the land tax, in defiance of the ministry, made a tapping of new revenue sources imperative, and Townshend secured passage of a bill to collect duties from the American colonies for such imports as glass, lead, paint, and tea. This external levy, like the resented (and repealed) STAMP TAX of 1765, was made a constitutional issue. Once more the colonies entered into NONIMPORTATION AGREEMENTS, so effective that government revenues from the Acts were but a trickle.

But the Townshend Acts had been adroitly formulated as the home office saw the issues. The customs service was reorganized, and new vice-admiralty courts were established. Royal governors and judges were made independent of colonial assemblies. Thus the legal battle enjoined between Parliament and the colonial lawyers began in earnest. Sparks were raised by *Letters from a Farmer in Pennsylvania* (1768) by JOHN DICKINSON, the most effective pamphlet issued in the cause of colonial liberties. The tensions created led to the BOSTON MASSACRE (1770). The government shortly repealed all of the Townshend duties except that on tea, which was kept as a token reminder to the colonies that Parliamentary authority was supreme. The TEA ACT (1773), which seemed to the British to be a reasonable extension of the Townshend deliberations, led to further alienation of the Colonies.

Track and field athletic events include running, jumping, and throwing (as of a discus, hammer, or javelin). The decathlon, a contest of ten track and field events, has always been a feature in the modern Olympic Games. The first track and field events in the U.S. date from the 1860's, and championship meets have been held since 1888 by the Amateur Athletic Union. Outstanding track and field stars include JIM THORPE, JESSE OWENS, and BABE DIDRICKSON ZAHARIAS.

Trade Acts, see *Navigation Acts.*

Trade Agreements Act (1934), sponsored by Secretary of State Cordell Hull, was based on the 'MOST-FAVORED-NATION' principle, and authorized the President (within specified limits) to negotiate tariff agreements on his own authority. Some 30 such agreements had been signed by 1937, and they had proved so satisfactory that the Act was renewed. It has been renewed regularly ever since.

Trade, Foreign, see *Commerce.*

Trade unions, also known as craft (horizontal) unions, are labor organizations based on membership in a given trade or craft, usually skilled. In America they have flourished since the colonial period and bear a resemblance to medieval guilds. Their objectives were higher wages, shorter hours, union control of apprenticeships, and a CLOSED SHOP. The longest-lived of the early trade unions was the Federal Society of Journeymen Cordwainers, Philadelphia (1794–1806). A number of trade unions held national conventions during the 1830's, and, although the panics of 1837 and 1857 aborted their aims, they later became the backbone of the LABOR MOVEMENT in the U.S. The oldest trade union in the U.S. is the International Typographical Union (ITU), founded (1850) in New York as the National Typographical Union. The most important historically is the AMERICAN FEDERATION OF LABOR (1886), which in 1955 affiliated with the CONGRESS OF INDUSTRIAL ORGANIZATIONS to form the A.F. of L.–C.I.O.

Trading companies, corporate groups organized to colonize America, were the means by which capital was raised after the failure of WALTER RALEIGH (1591) demonstrated that no single individual could finance such ventures. The British companies included (for settlements within the present U.S.) the LONDON COMPANY (1606), the COUNCIL FOR NEW ENGLAND (1620), and the MASSACHUSETTS BAY COMPANY (1628). Companies were variously organized, but all were combinations of private enterprise under state control. They were the great factor in establishing England as a naval, maritime, and commercial empire. The best-known type were JOINT-STOCK COMPANIES.

'Tragic Era,' see *Reconstruction.*

'Trail of Tears,' see *Five Civilized Tribes.*

Trails, see *Overland trails.*

Transcendentalism, as a philosophic concept, stems from the idea set forth by the German metaphysician Immanuel Kant (1724–1804) that what is 'transcendent' goes beyond what is presented in experience. As developed in the philosophic idealism of G. W. F. Hegel (1770–1831), transcendentalism came to mean that whatever transcends sense experience is fundamental in reality.

In the U.S., W. E. CHANNING, as the leading spokesman for Unitarians, paved the way for transcendentalism during the 1820's by his insistence on the validity of intuitive thought, and JAMES MARSH focused attention upon the distinction between reason and understanding in his analysis (1829) of Coleridge's *Aids to Reflection.* The transcendental movement in New England (*c.* 1836–60) was the earliest and most indigenous expression of ROMANTICISM as an individualistic, unsystematic attitude toward the world of nature and man, and it was set forth by the way of the language of German romanticism and Oriental mysticism.

Eclectic and monistic, transcendentalism stressed the unity of the world and God, holding that the soul of each individual latently contains all that the world contains. Thus man is capable of discovering truth by insights, without reference to dogma and established authority. The immanence of God in nature and the reliance upon intuition were central in the thinking of R. W. EMERSON, and in the preaching of THEODORE PARKER, the leading transcendentalist of his day. By emphasizing self reliance and individualism, transcendentalism necessarily permitted contradictions and diverse concepts.

The Transcendental Club, which met at Boston or Concord to discuss ideas, included, besides Emerson and Parker, FREDERICK HEDGE, HENRY THOREAU, JAMES DWIGHT, GEORGE RIPLEY, ELIZABETH PEABODY, BRONSON ALCOTT, and MARGARET FULLER. The *Dial* (1840–44) was the quarterly journal of the transcendentalists, and BROOK FARM (1841–47) and FRUITLANDS (1843) were its experiments in communal living. The movement was relatively brief, but it helped start the CONCORD SCHOOL of philosophy, and its contribution to American literature has been incalculable.

Recent studies of the movement include those by H. A. Pochmann (1948), and S. M. Vogel (1955). An anthology of source material is Perry Miller, *The Transcendentalists* (1950).

Transportation, see *Automobiles, Aviation, Camels, Canals, Clipper Ships, Covered Wagons, Horses, Maps, Mules, Mustang, Oxen, Pack Trains, Packet Ships, Pony Express, Post Roads, Railroads, Shipping, Sledges, Stagecoaches, Steamboats, Subways, Travois, Turnpikes, Wagon Trains.*

Much detailed information is in Seymour Dunbar, *History of Travel in America* (4 vols., 1937).

Transylvania Company, an unincorporated group of influential North Carolina land speculators, was organized (1775) to invest in unpatented lands within the chartered limits of North Carolina and Virginia. The Company (which had no authority to make the purchase) negotiated with the Cherokee (who had no exclusive right to sell) for all lands lying between the Ohio and the Cumberland rivers — virtually the entire region of Kentucky. It encouraged pioneers to settle, called a meeting of delegates, drafted articles of government, passed laws, and employed Daniel Boone to hew out what later became the WILDERNESS ROAD. As the self-styled 'Transylvania Colony,' it petitioned the Continental Congress (1778) for sovereign recognition. Though its petition was rejected, the Company was granted 200,000 acres as recompense for its labors in opening up so much frontier. After fourteen years of agitation the issue was closed when Kentucky was admitted to the Union (1792).

Trapping, see *Fur trade.*

Travois, the device used by the Plains Indians for transporting household goods, consisted of two trailing poles attached as shafts on either side of a dog or horse. The load rested on a platform of crosspieces. The travois, like the SLEDGE, antedates the Indians' knowledge of the wheel, which they first saw used by Europeans.

Treason, as defined in the Federal Constitution (Art. III, sec. 3), can consist only in making war against the U.S. or assisting its enemies; and though Congress is authorized to punish the offense, 'no attainder of treason shall work corruption of blood, or forfeiture except during the life of the person attainted.' By removing from Congress the power of defining treason, the Founding Fathers sought to insure against the procedural abuses that had been all too common in the English state trials. Conviction of treason can be secured only upon testimony of two witnesses to the same overt act, or confession in a public court.

Treason cases in the U.S. have been few, and, except for the trial of Aaron Burr, relatively uninteresting. Indeed, Marshall's rulings in the Burr affair intentionally made successful prosecutions of treason difficult. After the Civil War disloyal activities were dealt with in the famous Supreme Court decision *Ex parte* MILLIGAN (1866), which returned rulings to civil courts. Though wholesale indictments of Confederates were handed down after the war, they were dropped and amnesty was extended.

While treason was made difficult to establish, Congress greatly expanded the definition of sedition in 1918, added the idea of 'guilt by association' in the Smith Act of 1940, and passed the sweeping Internal Security Act of 1950 (the McCarran Act) intended to restrict severely the activities of communists.

Treasury, U.S. Department of the (1789), was one of the first executive branches created by Congress. Although the Department is now vastly enlarged, its present functions were basically envisioned in 1789. It includes the Customs Service (1789), the Mint (transferred from State to Treasury in 1795), Internal Revenue (1798), and allied fiscal bureaus. Under its jurisdiction are the U.S. Coast Guard and the U.S. Secret Service. In 1965 the Department's budget exceeded $12,700,000,000. (The BUREAU OF THE BUDGET, originally within the Department, has been a separate executive agency since 1939.)

Secretaries of the Treasury and the Presidents under whom they served are as follows.

WASHINGTON

Alexander Hamilton (N.Y.) 1789
Oliver Wolcott (Conn.) 1795

J. ADAMS

Oliver Wolcott (Conn.) 1797
Samuel Dexter (Mass.) 1801

JEFFERSON
Samuel Dexter (Mass.) 1801
Albert Gallatin (Pa.) 1801

MADISON
Albert Gallatin (Pa.) 1809
George W. Campbell (Tenn.) 1814
Alexander J. Dallas (Pa.) 1814
William H. Crawford (Ga.) 1816

MONROE
William H. Crawford (Ga.) 1817

J. Q. ADAMS
Edward Rush (Pa.) 1825

JACKSON
Samuel D. Ingham (Pa.) 1829
Louis McLane (Del.) 1831
William J. Duane (Pa.) 1833
Roger B. Taney (Md.) 1833
Levi Woodbury (N.H.) 1834

VAN BUREN
Levi Woodbury (N.H.) 1837

W. H. HARRISON
Thomas Ewing (Ohio) 1841

TYLER
Thomas Ewing (Ohio) 1841
Walter Forward (Pa.) 1841
John C. Spencer (N.Y.) 1843
George M. Bibb (Ky.) 1844

POLK
Robert J. Walker (Miss.) 1845

TAYLOR
William M. Meredith (Pa.) 1849

FILLMORE
Thomas Corwin (Ohio) 1850

PIERCE
James Guthrie (Ky.) 1853

BUCHANAN
Howell Cobb (Ga.) 1857
Philip F. Thomas (Md.) 1860
John A. Dix (N.Y.) 1861

LINCOLN
Salmon P. Chase (Ohio) 1861
William P. Fessenden (Me.) 1864
Hugh McCulloch (Ind.) 1865

A. JOHNSON
Hugh McCulloch (Ind.) 1865

GRANT
George S. Boutwell (Mass.) 1869
William A. Richardson (Mass.) 1873
Benjamin H. Bristow (Ky.) 1874
Lot M. Morrill (Me.) 1876

HAYES
John Sherman (Ohio) 1877

GARFIELD
William Windom (Minn.) 1881

ARTHUR
Charles J. Folger (N.Y.) 1881
Walter Q. Gresham (Ind.) 1884
Hugh McCulloch (Ind.) 1884

CLEVELAND
Daniel Manning (N.Y.) 1885
Charles S. Fairchild (N.Y.) 1887

B. HARRISON
William Windom (Minn.) 1889
Charles Foster (Ohio) 1891

CLEVELAND
John G. Carlisle (Ky.) 1893

MCKINLEY
Lyman J. Gage (Ill.) 1897

T. ROOSEVELT
Lyman J. Gage (Ill.) 1901
Leslie M. Shaw (Iowa) 1902
George B. Cortelyou (N.Y.) 1907

TAFT
Franklin MacVeagh (Ill.) 1909

WILSON
William G. McAdoo (N.Y.) 1913
Carter Glass (Va.) 1919
David F. Houston (Mo.) 1920

HARDING
Andrew W. Mellon (Pa.) 1921

COOLIDGE
Andrew W. Mellon (Pa.) 1923

HOOVER
Andrew W. Mellon (Pa.) 1929
Ogden L. Mills (N.Y.) 1932

F. D. ROOSEVELT
William H. Woodin (N.Y.) 1933
Henry Morgenthau, Jr. (N.Y.) 1934

TRUMAN
Fred M. Vinson (Ky.) 1945
John W. Snyder (Mo.) 1946

EISENHOWER
George M. Humphrey (Ohio) 1953
Robert B. Anderson (Tex.) 1957

KENNEDY
C. Douglas Dillon (N.J.) 1961

L. B. JOHNSON
C. Douglas Dillon (N.J.) 1963
Henry H. Fowler (Va.) 1965

Treaties, under the U.S. Constitution (Art. II, sec. 2) may be made by the President 'with the advice and consent of the Senate,' two-thirds of whose members must concur. Treaties with foreign nations were made immediately after the founding of the Republic, and they increased in number as the nation established BOUNDARIES, expanded COMMERCE, and settled problems of IMMIGRATION, NATURALIZATION, and EXTRADITION. The long story of INDIAN TREATIES is a special chapter in American history. Treaties are the supreme law of the land, take precedence over the writ of state legislatures and constitutions, and must be upheld by the courts.

An EXECUTIVE AGREEMENT has the validity of a treaty, and such agreements are more numerous than treaties. The 'MOST-FAVORED-NATION' clause has been standard in commercial treaties ever since the alliance with France in 1778. RECIPROCITY agreements led to the founding of the Pan-American Union (1890). Secret treaties are not barred by the Constitution, and they have been negotiated on occasion, but none has been ratified since the FRANCO-AMERICAN ALLIANCE, terminated in 1800. The precedent against them is so strong as virtually to be decisive.

In requiring the Senate's advice and consent to treaties the Founding Fathers had no intention of setting up machinery to review the President's foreign policies. They gave the Senate a veto power to protect the interests of individual states, and they believed that the two-thirds required vote would serve to protect small states and minority groups. They did not envision that such a requirement might possibly be a paralyzing restraint to policies of state. More than 100 treaties have been denied Senate consent, and some fundamental policies have been defeated. The most dramatic defeat was the Senate's rejection of President Wilson's proposal in 1919 to take the U.S. into the League of Nations.

The Senate probably reflects the democratic and popular estimate of basic executive policies. Since World War II, in addition to various peace treaties, it has consented to ratify the United Nations Charter (1945), the North Atlantic Treaty Organization (1949), the International Atomic Energy Agency (1956), and the Nuclear Test-Ban Treaty (1963).

***Trent* Affair** (November–December 1861) was an incident that almost involved the Union in a war with Great Britain. Captain CHARLES WILKES, commanding the U.S.S. *San Jacinto,* stopped the British steamer *Trent* and seized two Confederate commissioners, James M. Mason and John Slidell, en route to England. Although Wilkes was thanked by Congress, he had committed a diplomatic blunder. The war fever engendered in England abated when Secretary Seward ordered the commissioners released on the legitimate ground that Wilkes had erred in not bringing the ship, as well as its 'personal contraband,' to port for adjudication.

Trenton, Battle of (26 December 1776), took place when Washington, moving north on Christmas night with 2400 troops, crossed the ice-choked Delaware some eight miles above the town during a sleet storm, and fell on the merrymaking Hessian garrison, who were completely surprised. In a 50-minute fray, with scarcely a casualty, the Patriots captured the entire cantonment of 1200 (an outpost of General Howe's army, then wintering in New York). Washington then recrossed into Pennsylvania with his prisoners. On the last two days of the month he reoccupied Trenton. The chief importance of the victory lay in the fact that it led to the re-enlistment of men whose enlistments would have expired New Year's Day. It thus made possible the victory at PRINCETON (3 January 1777), a turning point in the war.

'Triangular trade,' see *West Indies trade.*

Tripolitan War (1801–15), or Barbary Wars, was a series of naval engagements in the Mediterranean between the U.S. and the Barbary states (Morocco, Algiers, Tripoli, and Tunis). In the early years of its existence as a nation, the U.S. followed the example of European countries by paying annual tribute to the Barbary corsairs for unmolested transit of merchantmen past the Barbary coast. (For more than two centuries no European power had been able to wipe out these nests of pirates who preyed on the merchant ships of Christian nations and enslaved the men they captured.) When the Pasha of Tripoli increased his rate of tribute from the U.S. in 1801, Jefferson dispatched warships, but not until Commodore Edward

Preble (1761–1807) took a squadron into the Mediterranean in 1803 was the war vigorously prosecuted.

Lieutenant STEPHEN DECATUR performed the most notable exploit in 1804, when he destroyed the frigate *Philadelphia*, previously captured by the Tripolitans. An effective blockade ended the war with Tripoli (1805), to whom payments ceased. Tribute to other Barbary states continued until after the War of 1812, when Decatur and others were ordered to the Mediterranean with an overwhelming force, which effectively cleared the way for a treaty (1815) ending American payments to all the Barbary states. (European states continued to pay tribute until the French conquered Algeria in 1830.)

TRIPPE, JUAN TERRY (1899–), after graduation from Yale (1921) associated himself with the airplane industry, and became president of Pan American World Airways in 1927. In that year his company was granted exclusive overseas airmail government contracts, and for the next decade by this 'chosen instrument' policy Trippe was able to expand his world-covering network of commercial airlines without competition. In 1938 the Civil Aeronautics Act ended his monopoly.

TRIST, NICHOLAS PHILIP (1800–1874), who had married Jefferson's granddaughter and later served as private secretary to President Jackson, was chief clerk of the Department of State when he was sent to Mexico (1847) as special envoy to conduct negotiations to end the Mexican War. He muddled affairs, and President Polk recalled him. Trist ignored the order and in due course negotiated the Treaty of GUADALUPE HIDALGO in accordance with his original instructions. Though Polk supported the treaty, he repudiated Trist, who did not recover his unpaid salary and expenses until near the end of his life.

TROLLOPE, FRANCES (1780–1863), for three years lived with her husband in Cincinnati (1827–30) where, in an effort to recover from severe financial reverses, they operated a fancy-goods 'bazaar,' in a building they made easily distinguishable by a Turkish dome, Grecian pillars, Gothic windows, an Egyptian portico, and a Norman tower. The enterprise failed and the Trollopes returned to England, though they soon went elsewhere to escape their creditors. But Mrs. Trollope wrote *Domestic Manners of the Americans* (1832), a book that sold widely and started her on a writing career. It was a most unflattering account of slavery, sharp business practices, anti-intellectualism, and American crudity in general, and it succeeded in angering Americans more than any book written by a foreign observer before or since (although Mark Twain thought that Mrs. Trollope had merely told the truth). She wrote four later books about America, a subject that fascinated her. Her sons, the novelists Anthony Trollope and Thomas Adolphus Trollope, likewise found it a profitable theme.

TRUMAN, HARRY S (1884–), 33rd President of the U.S. (1945–53), born at Lamar, Missouri, was reared on the family farm, which as a young man he tended. After serving as a captain of field artillery in France during World War I, he ran a haberdashery, attended Kansas City School of Law (1923–25), and, with the backing of the Democratic boss T. J. PENDERGAST, entered Kansas politics. He was presiding judge of Jackson county (1926–34) when he was elected to the U.S. Senate (1935–44), where he achieved national prominence as head of the very effective Senate Committee investigating wartime government expenditures. In 1944 he was his party's candidate for Vice President and took office with President F. D. Roosevelt.

When Roosevelt died (April 1945) Truman succeeded to the presidency. It was a most critical period in the nation's history. Though Truman rapidly replaced Roosevelt's cabinet with one of his own choosing, he continued his predecessor's policies until the war's end, attended the POTSDAM CONFERENCE (July 1945) at which the Allies made postwar plans, and at the end of the war (August 1945) he gave his attention to the responsibilities that the U.S. had inherited as the richest and most powerful of nations. To curb the spread of Soviet influence, he enunciated the TRUMAN DOCTRINE (March 1947) and implemented the MARSHALL PLAN (July 1947) for economic recovery in Europe. Diplomatic relations with the Soviet Union became increasingly strained when the Russian blockade of Berlin was answered by the BERLIN AIRLIFT (1948–49).

Though Truman was unpopular with the Southerners in his party because of his civil-rights program, he nevertheless received the Democratic nomination in 1948, and surprisingly defeated the Republican candidate, Thomas E. Dewey, by winning 24,000,000 popular votes (304 electoral votes to Dewey's 189). Yet few of his 'FAIR DEAL' proposals outlining his domestic program for the ensuing four years were enacted. Congress overrode his veto of the TAFT-HARTLEY ACT of 1947 and the MC CARRAN-WALTER IMMIGRATION ACT of 1952. On the other hand, he put through the Housing Act of 1949, which expanded low cost housing during a great shortage, and by executive authority he desegregated the armed forces and federally supported schools.

In 1949 Truman supported NATO (the first U.S. peacetime military alliance), devised the POINT FOUR PROGRAM for backward nations, and, when the communists attacked Korea (June 1950), he secured armed intervention from the United Nations. These accomplishments were landmarks in the nation's assumption of global responsibility. He declined to seek renomination in 1952, and retired to private life.

Truman Doctrine (1947) was the name applied to the anticommunist principle of foreign policy enunciated by President Truman in a message to Congress at a time when Greece and Turkey were in danger of communist subversion. In that message he stated, 'I believe that it must be the policy of the United States to support free peoples who are resisting attempted subjugation by armed minorities or by outside pressures.' He requested (and received) an appropriation for military and economic aid to countries whose political stability was threatened by communism. The chief instruments of the Truman Doctrine were NATO, the Marshall Plan, and 'Point Four,' which offered to raise the economic level of underdeveloped countries. Communists attributed the COLD WAR to the Truman Doctrine and its adjuncts. Western spokesmen attributed the salvation of Greece, Turkey, and, in a sense, Yugoslavia, to the Doctrine.

TRUMBULL, JOHN (1756–1843), son of the Connecticut governor, JONATHAN TRUMBULL, after graduation from Harvard (1773) served in the Continental army as an aide to Washington, and, with the rank of colonel, as an adjutant to Gates. Intent on painting, and encouraged by Jefferson and Benjamin West, with whom he studied in London, in 1784 he began his famous series in 'the grand historical style' of his master. In 1793 as secretary to minister John Jay, he began a ten-year government service, remaining in London as a commissioner to carry out provisions of the Jay Treaty.

Although Trumbull was never quite certain that a patrician should make a profession of the arts, by 1786 he had already completed his small canvases depicting the *Battle of Bunker's Hill* and *The Death of General Montgomery at the Siege of Quebec* (both at Yale). The latter is ranked among the most moving battle scenes ever painted. Four of his large historical canvases, completed much later in life, are in the National Capitol. They include the *Signing of the Declaration of Independence,* a representation of the great event rendered with restraint and vitality. He painted upward of 250 portraits of the nation's worthies and is ranked as the chief visual recorder of the Founding Fathers. After 1815 he lived in New York, where he served as president of the American Academy (1816–25). In 1832 he founded the Trumbull Gallery at Yale.

TRUMBULL, JONATHAN (1710–85), after graduation from Harvard (1727) returned to Lebanon, Connecticut, where he became the leading meatpacker in the colony, and for a time the leading exporter and importer of goods. Prominent in politics, he served as chief justice of the Connecticut supreme court (1766–69), and as governor of the colony and state (1769–84). He was the only colonial governor to champion the patriot cause. Washington relied upon his advice, and is said (without substantiation) to have coined the term 'Brother Jonathan' in reference to the governor.

Trumbull's three sons were likewise Harvard graduates. The eldest, Joseph

Trumbull (1738–78), served as commissary-general of the Continental army (1775–77). Jonathan Trumbull (1740–1809) served on Washington's staff, entered Congress as a Federalist (1789–95), and was governor of Connecticut from 1797 until his death. The youngest son, JOHN TRUMBULL, was a noted painter.

TRUMBULL, LYMAN (1813–96), having served as a justice of the Illinois supreme court (1848–53), was sent as a Democrat to the U.S. Senate (1855–73). There he became a Republican leader and a staunch supporter of Abraham Lincoln. A man of integrity whose sense of responsibility transcended personal or party interest, he was one of the few Republican Senators who refused to vote for the impeachment of President Johnson. In 1872 he was a leader of the LIBERAL REPUBLICAN PARTY, and he later rejoined the Democratic party, through which he tried to carry out reforms. Although he was unsuccessful in his bid for the governorship of Illinois (1880), he continued to be a force working for clean government in a period when spoilsmen were in the saddle.

'Trust Buster,' sobriquet of *Theodore Roosevelt.*

Trust Territory of the Pacific Islands comprises the 96 atolls and islands of the Caroline, Marshall, and Mariana Islands (except Guam). They are chiefly volcanic in origin, and are scattered over 3,000,000 square miles of ocean. The total land area is 687 square miles, with an estimated population (1964) of 88,000. Before World War I they were German colonies. Japan took them over after that war under a mandate from the League of Nations. It was from these islands that Japan launched the attack on Pearl Harbor in December 1941. After World War II they were placed under the trusteeship system of the United Nations. They are administered by the U.S. Department of the Interior.

Trusts are business combinations in which stockholders deposit their stock under agreement with trustees. In the U.S. such deposits had relatively small legal control, and after the New Jersey general incorporation law for HOLDING COMPANIES was adopted (1889), the trust form was rarely used, though the term became standard to identify large-scale business combination and consolidation. Oil trusts (the Standard Oil Company in 1878), 'whisky trusts' and 'sugar trusts' used business practices which were outlawed after 1890 by ANTITRUST LAWS.

TUBMAN, HARRIET (1821–1913), born a slave in Maryland, worked as a field hand before her escape to Philadelphia in 1849. Thereafter, known as 'Moses,' she became one of the shrewdest 'conductors' on the UNDERGROUND RAILROAD, annually leading scores of fugitive slaves into the free states and to Canada. She worked as a cook to finance her operations. John Brown, who used her assistance, called her 'General Tubman.' Her illiteracy was no bar to her effectiveness as an antislavery speaker. During the Civil War she served as a nurse and a Union spy behind the Confederate lines. After the war, she worked in the cause of Negro education in North Carolina. Her philanthropic interests led to the establishment of the Harriet Tubman Home for Aged Negroes (as it was subsequently known). Auburn, New York, was her home for many years, and, after her death, the citizens of the town erected a tablet in her honor.

TUCKER, SOPHIE [SOPHIE ABUZA] (1884–1966), Russian-born entertainer, was brought to the U.S. as an infant and began her career in vaudeville at Tony Pastor's Theatre (1906). She joined the Ziegfeld *Follies* in 1909 and later was a star in the Schubert *Gaieties* and the Earl Carroll *Vanities.* She was an especial favorite in New York and London. Billed as 'last of the red-hot mammas' in the 1920's, she retained that title into the 1960's.

TUGWELL, REXFORD GUY (1891–), professor of economics at Columbia (1931–37) and of political science at Chicago (1946–57), as a member of President F. D. Roosevelt's BRAIN TRUST helped formulate the Agricultural Adjustment Act (1933), and served as Under Secretary of Agriculture (1934–37). He was later (1941) governor of Puerto Rico. His numerous books on economics and government include *Industry's*

Coming of Age (1927), *Battle for Democracy* (1935), and *Stricken Land: Puerto Rico* (1947).

Tulane University, see *New Orleans.*

TUNNEY, GENE [JAMES JOSEPH] (1898–), New York–born boxer, in 1926 won the world heavyweight boxing championship by defeating JACK DEMPSEY in a ten-round (decision) fight at Philadelphia. The contest attracted a record-breaking crowd of 120,750 and brought $1,895,000 in gate receipts, the largest up to that time. In 1927 he repeated this victory over Dempsey in the same number of rounds, attracting receipts of $2,658,000, though the attendance fell to 104,940. (Thereafter boxing fell off financially.) Tunney retired undefeated in 1928. During World War II he directed the physical fitness program in the U.S. Navy.

TURNER, FREDERICK JACKSON (1861–1932), professor of history at Wisconsin (1885–1910) and Harvard (1910–24), and later research associate at the Henry E. Huntington Library, delivered an address before the American Historical Society in 1893 on 'The Significance of the Frontier in American History.' It brilliantly outlined his thesis that the receding frontier and cheap lands were dominant factors in creating American democracy and national character, a concept that soon revolutionized American historiography. The essay proved to be the most influential piece of writing about the West yet produced. It emphasized neglected factors in the interpretation of American history, and made itself felt in economics, sociology, literary criticism, and even in politics. (He gathered the address, with other papers, in *The Frontier in American History,* 1920.)

Two later studies, *The Significance of Sections in American History* (1932), and *The United States, 1830–1850* (1935), reemphasized what had long been an orthodox approach to the national past: that regional differences in the form of 'sections' had been the most compelling fact about the shape given to events. Although Turner's intellectual constructions were applied mechanically by many of his followers, he himself was modest and tentative in his conclusions. Yet critics increasingly have come to feel that Turner neglected the basic issues of slavery and race. Nevertheless, he opened a new and important path of investigation and is regarded as a distinguished American historian.

Turner Insurrection (1831) followed repeated disclosures of slave plots in the South. This most serious of the NEGRO INSURRECTIONS was an outbreak at Southampton, Virginia, led by Nat Turner (1800–1831), who believed himself a divine instrument to guide his people out of bondage. He and some 60 followers had killed nearly that number of whites before the community could act. After a sensational manhunt, in the course of which perhaps 100 Negroes were killed, 20 Negroes (including Turner) were hanged. But Virginia and other slave states, fearing a repetition of this uprising, strengthened their police measures against the slaves and became more united in their support of FUGITIVE SLAVE LAWS.

Turnpikes, or toll roads, long familiar in England, were not introduced in America until 1785, when Virginia authorized the Little River Turnpike. In 1794 the first private corporation completed a toll road in Pennsylvania (the Philadelphia-Lancaster Turnpike), and in the same decade the WILDERNESS ROAD invited settlement of the lower Ohio valley, soon connected by other surfaced highways with the Cumberland valley and the interior of Tennessee. By 1810 some 300 turnpike corporations had been chartered in New England, New York, and Pennsylvania, and they took the lead in developing the American corporation system, a growth first nurtured by the early POST ROADS. The CUMBERLAND ROAD (or Old National Road), begun in 1811, became a chief artery of western colonization, finally connecting Maryland with Illinois. The turnpike boom came to an end in the 1820's. After 1840 the competition of CANALS and RAILROADS had rendered most turnpikes obsolete. In time they were generally abandoned to the states.

Tuscarora Indians, see *Iroquois Confederacy.*

Tuscarora War (1711–13) began when the Tuscarora Indians in eastern North

Carolina, alarmed by the encroachment of white settlers, fell upon an English colony and almost wiped it out. Punitive expeditions followed, and when the Tuscarora were finally subdued, the tribe moved northward to join its kindred and make the Six Nations of the IROQUOIS CONFEDERACY. Thereafter North Carolina's opportunity for westward expansion lay open.

Tuskegee Institute in Alabama was chartered and opened in 1881 as a normal and agricultural school for Negroes. A college department was added in 1927, and since then its educational facilities have been greatly expanded. Its task was assumed to provide (in a rigidly segregated society) competent Negro teachers and businessmen who could educate Negro communities in practical affairs. Its first principal, BOOKER T. WASHINGTON, was succeeded in 1915 by ROBERT MOTON. The work of G. W. CARVER as director of agricultural research helped point the way toward diversified farming in the South. In 1965, with a faculty of 309, it enrolled 2536 students.

TWACHTMAN, JOHN HENRY (1853–1902), Ohio-born landscape painter and etcher, after study abroad became a leading exponent of impressionism. His atmospheric renderings of scenes inspired by the Connecticut countryside near his home, and the oil and pastel series he made at Yellowstone Park and at Niagara Falls, notably influenced the painters who studied under him. He did not live to know the high rank his works have taken in their genre. Representative is his *Waterfall* (Metropolitan Museum).

TWAIN, MARK, see *Clemens, S. L.*

TWEED, WILLIAM MARCY (1823–78), New York City political boss, after 1857 became a power in the TAMMANY machine, through which, as grand sachem by 1860, 'Boss' Tweed gained absolute control of the city's Democratic party. His influence was extended when he became a state senator (1868). His gang thrived on fraudulent city contracts and extortion. Exposure of the TWEED RING in 1871 brought about his downfall. He served one year of a twelve-year sentence, was again arrested on various charges, and after being extradited from Spain (1876), died in prison.

Tweed Ring was the political organization operating in New York City principally from 1869 to 1871. Headed by 'Boss' TWEED, the ring included A. Oakley Hall (mayor), Peter Sweeny (city chamberlain), and Richard B. Connolly (comptroller). Through bribery, faked leases, padded accounts, vote buying, and kickbacks, the ring controlled the TAMMANY machine. As state senator, in 1870 Tweed forced through a new city charter, insuring members of the ring complete control of municipal finances. The efforts of the reform Democrat, SAMUEL J. TILDEN, aroused public opinion, as did the cartoons of THOMAS NAST. Publication of evidence of wholesale graft helped smash the ring, but not before the brigandage had cost the city some $100,000,000.

Twelfth Amendment (1804) to the U.S. Constitution provides that electors cast their ballots separately for the President and the Vice President of the U.S. In the event that the electoral college lacks a majority, the House of Representatives will choose the President from the three highest candidates in the electoral count, and the Senate will choose the Vice President. The Amendment was adopted after Jefferson and Burr tied in 1800, and it first came into effect when the House elected John Quincy Adams (1824). It has not since been invoked.

Twentieth Amendment (1933) to the U.S. Constitution abolished the so-called 'lame duck' session of Congress, the short session from December to March, during which period in election years congressmen who had failed to be reelected still continued to legislate. The Amendment moved all congressional sessions forward to 3 January, and advanced the date of the President's inauguration to 20 January.

Twenty-fifth Amendment to the U.S. Constitution was submitted to the legislatures of the states in July 1965. When ratified, it will establish in detail the order of presidential succession in the event of the President's death or disability, and will provide for the appointment of a

Vice President in the event that a vacancy occurs in that office.

Twenty-first Amendment (1933) to the U.S. Constitution repealed the EIGHTEENTH AMENDMENT (1919), and thus brought to an end the PROHIBITION ERA on a Federal level.

Twenty-fourth Amendment (1964) to the U.S. Constitution forbids the collection of poll taxes as a requirement for voting in primaries and elections for President, Vice President, and members of Congress. It thus outlawed the poll taxes for Federal officers in effect in five states of the South: Virginia, Alabama, Arkansas, Mississippi, and Texas.

Twenty-one Demands (1915) were presented by the Japanese government to China in the form of an ultimatum, by which Japan demanded a virtual protectorate over China. They were a gross violation of the ROOT-TAKAHIRA AGREEMENT (1908) and of the OPEN DOOR POLICY. The protests of Secretary of State Bryan were largely ignored, and Japan continued her move toward domination of the Far East. The WASHINGTON CONFERENCE of 1922 was called in part to negotiate the problems thus created.

Twenty-second Amendment (1951) to the U.S. Constitution provides that no person shall be elected President more than twice, and that no person who has served in office for more than two years of a term shall thereafter be a candidate more than once. (The provision did not apply to the incumbent, President Truman.)

Opponents of the Amendment feel that such arbitrary ruling might deprive the country of the services of a distinguished statesman, and that it weakens the President's power as party leader during his second term.

Twenty-third Amendment (1961) to the U.S. Constitution gives the citizens of the District of Columbia the privilege of voting for the President and the Vice President, and provides them three votes in the electoral college.

Two-party system has prevailed in the U.S. ever since the nation was founded. The first two parties were the FEDERALISTS and ANTI-FEDERALISTS, the latter evolving by the mid-1790's into the DEMOCRATIC-REPUBLICAN PARTY. The line of the Federalists, who ceased to exist as a party after the War of 1812, can be traced to the NATIONAL REPUBLICAN PARTY (1824), which emerged as the WHIG PARTY (1836), replaced in turn by the REPUBLICAN PARTY (1854). The present DEMOCRATIC PARTY evolved directly from the Democratic-Republicans.

The inability of THIRD PARTY MOVEMENTS to dominate political campaigns in the U.S. in part stems from the fact that the majority of voters are attached to one or other of the two parties by business, social, or political ties. Furthermore, the two major parties have gradually built up elaborate PARTY MACHINES and can command ample financial support. Finally, the presidential system, by electing one man rather than a slate of candidates, favors the balance of one party in power and one in opposition. Actually the two-party system is not as common in democratic societies as the multi-party system.

Tydings-McDuffie Act (1934), also known as the Philippine Independence Act, substantially re-enacted the defunct HAWES-CUTTING ACT of 1933 granting independence to the Philippines in 1946, but it provided for the removal of U.S. military posts and negotiation for the future status of U.S. naval bases in the Islands. This Act was accepted unanimously by the Philippine legislature, and it established an almost completely autonomous government, though during the commonwealth period a resident U.S. High Commissioner had certain veto powers.

TYLER, JOHN (1790–1862), 10th President of the U.S. (1841–45), was born near Williamsburg, Virginia, and after graduation from William and Mary (1807) studied law under his father, John Tyler (1747–1813), who soon became governor of Virginia (1808–11). An unswerving states' rights Democrat, Tyler entered the state legislature, was sent to Congress (1817–21), elected governor of his state (1825–27), and then chosen as U.S. Senator (1827–36). But he was alienated from the Democrats by President Jackson's handling of fiscal policies and of the South Carolina NULLIFICATION issue. Tyler was then drawn to the new Whig party, which selected him to run with William H. Harrison in the 'Tyler too' presidential campaign of 1840, victorious at a moment when slogans served better than principles.

When Harrison died one month after taking office, Tyler became the first Vice President to succeed to the presidency. His rift with Henry Clay, the Whig party leader and a strong nationalist, was widened when, after Tyler's second veto of Clay's effort to secure passage of national banking acts, their differences became open warfare. Clay read Tyler out of the Whig party, and all but one of Tyler's cabinet, taken over intact from Harrison, resigned (September 1841). Secretary of State Webster stayed on for a time, partly to complete negotiations of the WEBSTER-ASHBURTON TREATY (1842), but mostly to show his independence of Clay. For two years Tyler unsuccessfully tried to rally the Whigs to his states' rights formula, and finally when Calhoun entered the cabinet as Secretary of State to assist Tyler in carrying out a 'reform' of the Democrats in line with Tyler's concept, a revolution in American politics took place. The loss of Tyler by the Whigs was swinging the internal balance of that party to the North, Calhoun's influence tipped the Democratic balance to the South, and by the following decade the main party division had become definitely sectional.

Tyler was an obstinate man of narrow views, yet he did sign the PREEMPTION ACT of 1841, an important frontier victory, and he pushed through plans for the annexation of Texas, carried to completion by his Democratic successor, James K. Polk. Tyler's motives were apparently those of the propertied slaveholders who wished to extend their hegemony.

Until the eve of the Civil War, Tyler held no public office, but his political opinions were constantly sought, and in 1861 he became a member of the Confederate Congress. In one sense he was a minor President of the U.S., yet he probably elevated the status of that office by the influence he exerted on the political developments of his day.

TYLER, MOSES COIT (1835–1900), Connecticut-born historian, after graduation from Yale (1857) briefly entered the Congregational ministry, from which he withdrew in 1862. He was professor of English at Michigan (1867–81) and of American History at Cornell (1881–1900), where he continued his pioneer work in the scholarly study of American literature. The two books upon which his fame chiefly rests are *A History of American Literature, 1607–1765* (2 vols., 1878) and *The Literary History of the American Revolution, 1763–1783* (2 vols., 1897). Careful and detailed, they still constitute the fullest treatment of the periods covered. In 1884 Tyler helped organize the American Historical Association.

Typewriters became commercially practical in the late 1860's. A 'writing machine' had been patented in England in 1714, and variations of the typewriting principle thereafter were employed in contrivances useful for making embossed letters. In 1829 William A. Burt of Michigan patented a 'typographic machine,' but it proved unworkable. In the next two decades some progress was made in England and France, but the devices had only limited use. The Milwaukee journalist C. L. SHOLES constructed the first successful 'typewriter' in 1867. Six years later he sold his rights to the Remington Arms Company, which converted Sholes's invention into a marketable product, the 'Remington typewriter.' The invention promoted the social revolution in the status of women by aiding their economic independence. The electric typewriter first came into use about 1935.

U

UMT, see *Universal Military Training.*

UNCAS (*fl.* 1600–1683), chief sachem of the MOHEGAN Indians, who, after the PEQUOT WAR (1637) absorbed the remnants of the Pequot tribe. Constantly at war with the Narragansetts, in 1643 he maneuvered the death of Miantunomi, the protector of Roger Williams. Only his name bears resemblance to the titular character in Cooper's *The Last of the Mohicans.*

Uncle Sam is the popular nickname for the U.S. (as a people or as a government). It first came into prominent use during the War of 1812, when it was applied scornfully to troops by those who opposed the war. The term may well have derived from the letters U.S. on uniforms and government property. The cartoon representation is that of a tall man, dressed in striped trousers, a jacket with stars, and a top hat with stars and stripes — a costume made familiar by a popular fictional character, Major Jack Downing, a Yankee peddler, created by the Maine journalist Seba Smith (1792–1868). Before the Civil War the name had entered the dictionary without derisive connotation.

Uncle Tom's Cabin, see *Stowe, H. B.*

Unconditional surrender occurs when an enemy yields completely to the victor without negotiating any terms of surrender. It was first imposed in U.S. history when General Grant secured the surrender of Fort Donelson in 1861. It was applied in World War I, and notably in World War II, when President Roosevelt and Prime Minister Churchill at the Casablanca Conference (1943) restated their formula in reference to the Axis powers.

Underground Railroad was the term applied to the secret and shifting network by which escaped slaves, chiefly after 1840, were aided in their flight to the free states and to Canada. Abolitionists in the North and South established 'stations' where slaves were given sanctuary and financial help. Some 3000 'conductors' participated, notably the abolitionist JOHN BROWN, the Quaker LEVI COFFIN, and the escaped slave HARRIET TUBMAN. The loss of slaves by this method (chiefly from border states) was relatively small, perhaps 1000 a year after passage of the FUGITIVE SLAVE LAW of 1850. But the rage that the 'U.G.' kindled in the breasts of slave owners was enormous.

Underwood Tariff Act (1913), legislated at Wilson's insistence by a Democratic Congress, though far from a free-trade measure, reversed a tariff policy that had been almost unchallenged since 1861. It reduced tariffs by an average of 10 per cent (from 37 to 27), and it put iron, steel, raw wool, and (later) sugar on the free list. To meet revenue obligations it made provision for a small graduated tax on incomes. During the years preceding World War I it worked admirably. It was succeeded by the protectionist FORDNEY-MC CUMBER TARIFF ACT (1922).

Unemployment, as a problem in industrial organization, is generally defined as the inability (not the unwillingness) of workers to find employment. Mass unemployment in the U.S. was first officially recognized in the 1890 census statistics. It is characteristic of the downswing in BUSINESS CYCLES and reaches its peak in depression periods. During the first half of the 20th century it varied from 5 per cent in boom years to more than 20 per cent in periods of stagnation. Seasonal unemployment is characteristic of trades affected by weather conditions and similar periodic changes. The most important steps taken to meet the problem of unemployment were passage of the SOCIAL SECURITY ACT (1935), with its provisions for UNEMPLOYMENT COMPENSATION, and the Maximum Employment Act of 1946, which implied Federal aid to avert depressions.

Technological unemployment (the displacement of labor by improved machinery or methods), though causing severe dislocations, has not generally affected the total volume of employment unfavorably in the past. However, the speed-up of AUTOMATION during the 1950's created new problems because machines supplanted not only the operator but the boss as well. The Bureau of Labor Statistics reported in 1950 some 4,000,000 unemployed in a civilian labor force of 63,000,000; in 1963, some 4,500,000 in a force of 74,000,000.

Unemployment Compensation, as established by the SOCIAL SECURITY ACT (1935), is a co-operative Federal-state system based on a tax offset method, by which the federal government allows the taxpayer an offset of 2.7 per cent for taxes paid to a state for unemployment insurance. The insurance is collected by the states, each of which has its own account, and deposited in a Federal trust fund. It is withdrawn by the states to finance disbursements. During fiscal 1965 more than 6,000,000 unemployed received benefits, the payments totaling some $2,800,000,000.

UNESCO (United Nations Educational, Scientific, and Cultural Organization) is a specialized agency of the United Nations. It seeks to further world peace by removing social, religious, and racial tensions, to encourage free interchange of ideas and of scientific and cultural achievements, and to improve educational facilities in undeveloped areas. Its headquarters are in Paris.

Unfair labor practices, as defined in the WAGNER-CONNERY ACT (1935) and the TAFT-HARTLEY ACT (1947), include interference with or coercion of employees in collective bargaining, employers' domination of unions (through financial contributions), discrimination against union members in employment or tenure, and the secondary BOYCOTT. The laws are administered by the NATIONAL LABOR RELATIONS BOARD.

'Unfair methods of competition,' see *Federal Trade Commission* (1914), *Antitrust Act* (1914), *Robinson-Patman Act* (1936).

Unicameral legislature is a legislative body with one chamber. Most assemblies in colonial America originally were unicameral. By 1700 all except Delaware and Pennsylvania had adopted bicameral legislatures, as did all the states during the Revolution except Georgia and Pennsylvania. They both soon became bicameral. (Vermont, the first state admitted to the Union, remained unicameral until 1836.)

The unicameral idea did not again assume importance until the second decade of the 20th century, when several states considered the system as a means of gaining efficiency and lowering the cost of government, but only Nebraska adopted and retained it (1936). Municipal assemblies are generally unicameral.

Union College (1795), at Schenectady, New York, is a nonsectarian institution for men, with divisions of engineering, humanities, science, and social studies. In 1845 it became the first general college to institute a course in engineering. It is associated in Union University (partly co-educational, 1873) with Albany Law School (1851) and other units at Albany. In 1965, with a faculty of 131, it enrolled 2018 students.

Union Labor party, a short-lived third party, was organized at Cincinnati (1887) in an attempt to unite the remnants of the GREENBACK LABOR PARTY with wage earners who were involved in the industrial conflicts of the period. Their nominee for President, Alson J. Streeter, polled 147,000 votes.

Union League clubs (1863) were among the score of patriotic 'Loyal Leagues' established throughout the North during the Civil War. The Union League took part in state and local Republican politics, and during Reconstruction it was used in the South as a political machine by the RADICAL REPUBLICANS. Its headquarters were in Washington. The Union League clubs of New York, Philadelphia, and Chicago have survived as archconservative social organizations.

Union Pacific Railroad, on which construction was begun (1865) at Omaha, pushed westward through Nebraska and Wyoming territories into the Great Basin, where it joined the CENTRAL PACIFIC four years later. (The entry on the CP summarizes the dramatic story.) Financed by the notorious CRÉDIT MOBILIER, it was later badly managed, and it went into bankruptcy during the PANIC OF 1893, but under the control of E. H. HARRIMAN it regained solvency and became one of the nation's premier railroads.

Union party (1861), organized after the first Union defeat at Bull Run, sought to win political support by a 'save the North' coalition ticket, which won state elections in the autumn of that year. It was shorter lived than the preceding CONSTITUTIONAL UNION PARTY.

Unions, see *Labor Unions.*

Unitarians were originally followers of Michael Servetus (1511–53) in Geneva and of Faustus Socinus (1539–1604) in Poland, both of whom were anti-Trinitarian in their concept of God in one person. In America, Unitarianism was officially recognized when the earliest Episcopal church in New England, King's Chapel, Boston, removed Trinitarian doctrines from the liturgy (1785), and became a Unitarian church. JOSEPH PRIESTLEY established a Unitarian church in Philadelphia (1796), and a liberal Congregational wing in New England gradually formed into a new denomination. The separation was foreshadowed when HENRY WARE was appointed professor of divinity at Harvard (1805), and was complete after W. E. CHANNING delivered (at Baltimore, 1819) the memorable sermon that became the platform of the denomination. Unitarian leaders, closely associated with TRANSCENDENTALISM, included GEORGE RIPLEY and J. F. CLARKE. (The 'sterile rationalism' of Unitarianism came under the vigorous attack of THEODORE PARKER during the 1840's.) Unitarianism requires no doctrinal profession either of the clergy or laity, and its churches adopt no creed.

In 1961 Unitarians merged with UNIVERSALISTS to form the Unitarian Universalist Association, a body which in 1965 numbered more than 167,000.

United Church of Christ (1957) is the first joinder in the U.S. of churches with differing forms of church government. It is the union of the Congregational Christian Churches with the Evangelical and Reformed Church. Its constitution was declared in force in 1961. In 1965 its membership was reported to be more than 2,000,000.

United Mine Workers of America (UMW) is an industrial union organized (1890) as a merger of two coal mining unions, one a unit of the KNIGHTS OF LABOR. It shortly became an affiliate of the AMERICAN FEDERATION OF LABOR. It strengthened its position during the decade by successful strikes, and under the leadership (1898–1908) of JOHN MITCHELL it won its fight for an eight-hour day.

During the long and militant presidency of JOHN L. LEWIS (1920–60) it achieved many more objectives. It was one of the first affiliates of the CONGRESS OF INDUSTRIAL ORGANIZATIONS (1935), and in 1937 it was expelled from the A.F. of L. It withdrew from the C.I.O. in 1942, and rejoined the A.F. of L. (1946), from which it withdrew in 1947 after a dispute over means of combating the restrictive TAFT-HARTLEY ACT. The UMW strikes at the time were successful, although they cost both Lewis and the union heavy fines. In 1965 it reported a membership of 450,000.

United Nations is the international organization established at the SAN FRANCISCO CONFERENCE (1945) to replace the League of Nations. (The name was coined in 1941 by President F. D. Roosevelt to describe those countries fighting the Axis.) Foundations were laid at the DUMBARTON OAKS CONFERENCE (1944), where proposals for a charter were made and substantially incorporated into the charter of the UN, which was declared in force on 24 October 1945. The permanent headquarters of the UN were established (1952) in New York City. In 1965 member nations totaled 117.

All the members compose the General Assembly, before which any matter may be brought which is within the scope of the charter. The eleven-member SECURITY COUNCIL is the executive agency of the body, which in addition to its basic objective of maintaining international peace performs many other functions. Its Economic and Social Council has broad responsibilities in matters relating to HUMAN RIGHTS, education, health, welfare, and international trade. Autonomous agencies include those seeking to raise living standards, facilitate the investment of capital, and promote collaboration (UNESCO, for example). Its Trusteeship Council works in the interest of territories that are not self-governing. Its INTERNATIONAL COURT OF JUSTICE is its chief judicial branch. In addition there are scores of *ad hoc* committees and councils. The Secretariat executes the business of the Assembly, and is headed by the Secretary-General. Since the UN functions not only as an arbitrating body but also as a military establishment that can enforce its decisions (and has done so on several occasions), it has achieved notable success in settling international disputes.

Diplomats who have served as chief U.S. representative at the UN are as follows.

Warren R. Austin (Vt.) 1947–53
Henry Cabot Lodge, Jr. (Mass.) 1953–61
Adlai E. Stevenson (Ill.) 1961–65
Arthur J. Goldberg (Ill.) 1965–

United Press, an international news agency, was organized (1907) by EDWARD W. SCRIPPS and Milton A. McRae to provide member newspapers with news gathered by its correspondents. Unlike its rival, the ASSOCIATED PRESS, it accepted members merely upon application. Formerly the United Press Associations, after merging with the International News Service in 1958, it was renamed the United Press International.

U.S. Housing Authority (1937), see *Wagner-Steagall Act.*

U.S. Information Agency was established in 1953 as an independent branch of the U.S. government to disseminate information about American policies abroad. It uses all means of communication, but it is known best for its radio service, VOICE OF AMERICA. In 1965 the USIA, with branches in 99 countries, was annually attracting some 30,000,000 visitors through its libraries, lecture rooms, and linguistics centers.

United States of America (the name) was first used officially in the Declaration of Independence (1776), where it replaced the name 'United Colonies,' previously used. It was thereafter taken over into the Articles of Confederation (1777) and the Federal Constitution (1787). Although the phrase 'United States of North America,' which Congress used briefly, appears in the treaty with France (1778), Congress rescinded its action, and the word 'North' was dropped from the name.

U.S. Shipping Board (1916) was created by Congress, which appropriated $50,000,000 to give shipbuilders and owners the means to purchase or construct merchant ships. At that time the American merchant marine had insufficient tonnage to carry American exports, which had been greatly increased by war demands in Europe.

U.S. Steel Corporation, largest steel company in the U.S., produces one-fourth of the nation's output. It was organized as the first 'billion dollar' corporation in 1901 by J. P. MORGAN, who merged the steel interests of ANDREW CARNEGIE, HENRY FRICK, and ELBERT GARY under the presidency of CHARLES M. SCHWAB. The corporation for many years was the largest holding company in the U.S., controlling not only steel mills, but iron mines and steamship and railroad lines.

U.S.* v. *Cruikshank (1876) was a case that resulted in a ruling by the U.S. Supreme Court holding that the 'due process' and 'equal protection' clauses of the FOURTEENTH AMENDMENT guarantee citizens against encroachment by the states, but do not protect them from each other. It further stipulated that the Constitution does not grant the right of peaceable assembly and the right to bear arms: it merely forbids Congress to infringe such rights.

U.S.* v. *E. C. Knight (1895) was a case that resulted in the first decision rendered by the U.S. Supreme Court on issues raised by the Sherman Antitrust Act (1890). The government had charged that the American Sugar Refining Company was a monopoly, but the Court by an 8-1 decision held that the company was engaged in manufacturing, not commerce, and that the Act did not prohibit combinations of manufacturers. Thus the enforcement of antitrust laws was seriously impaired, and most monopolies were placed beyond the reach of Federal control.

U.S.* v. *Harris (1883) was a case that resulted in a decision of the U.S. Supreme Court, which held that neither the FOURTEENTH nor the FIFTEENTH AMENDMENT to the U.S. Constitution authorized Congress to legislate directly upon the acts of citizens.

U.S.* v. *Wong Kim Ark (1898) was a case that resulted in a basic decision of the U.S. Supreme Court, establishing a principle of citizenship. Wong, an American-born Chinese laborer and the son of parents ineligible for citizenship under naturalization laws, visited China. The attempt of the federal government to prevent his return, under the CHINESE EXCLUSION ACTS, was disallowed by the high court, which held that, regardless of the fact that Wong's parents were ineligible, Wong himself was a citizen.

Universal Military Training (UMT) is the method by which young men are trained to serve in the armed forces of the U.S. (The legislation providing for UMT has been in effect since 1948.) The system registers, classifies, and selects men, several hundred thousand of whom annually enter the service, usually for two years of active duty and six years of stand-by duty in the Ready Reserve. Local boards rule on deferments and exemptions.

Universalists believe that God intends to save every individual from sin through the divine intercession of Christ. The doctrine is old but it did not become the distinctive feature of an organized body of believers until the 18th century. It was established first in America (1779) at Gloucester, Massachusetts, by an English-born preacher, John Murray (1741–1815), a convert who had been excommunicated by the Methodists for his public avowal of Universalism. The most important forerunner of the doctrine in America was a Boston minister, CHARLES CHAUNCY.

Abner Kneeland (1774–1844) was a New England Universalist clergyman who edited a succession of liberal magazines. He served a brief term in jail (1838) for expressing his views as a free thinker. The HOPEDALE COMMUNITY (1842–56) was a Universalist society. In 1961 the Universalists merged with the UNITARIANS to form the Unitarian Universalist Association, a body which in 1965 numbered more than 167,000.

Universities, see *Education.*

Unknown Soldier, see *Tomb of the Unknowns.*

UNRRA (United Nations Relief and Rehabilitation Administration) was established by the agreement of 44 nations (signed in Washington, 1943) to aid liberated populations in war-devastated areas of Europe and Asia. It was later (1947) extended to include the defeated Axis countries. UNRRA was administered by HERBERT H. LEHMAN.

Unwritten Constitution, so called, is the body of political customs and traditions that have developed in the American system without constitutional direction. Such are SENATORIAL COURTESY, LOBBYING, POLITICAL PARTIES, the CABINET system, and the customs followed by the ELECTORAL COLLEGE.

UPJOHN, RICHARD (1802–78), English-born cabinetmaker and architect, in 1829 emigrated to New England. There he executed several commissions before moving to New York (1839), where he remodeled Trinity Church (1841–46). With JAMES RENWICK he inaugurated a new phase in the Gothic revival. (Trinity Church was a pacemaker of the style that dominated American architecture through its neo-Gothic period.) Upjohn was a founder and first president of the American Institute of Architects (1857–76).

URBAN, JOSEPH (1872–1933), Austrian-born architect and stage designer, was known for his colorful stage sets, especially for productions in the Metropolitan Opera House and for the ornate settings of the Ziegfeld Follies. He practiced architecture in New York in addition to interior and stage art.

Urbanization, see *Cities.*

UREY, HAROLD CLAYTON (1893–), professor of chemistry at Columbia (1934–45) and at Chicago (after 1945), specialized in the structure of atoms and molecules, thermodynamic properties of gases, and separation of isotopes. He received the 1934 Nobel Prize in chemistry for his discovery of the hydrogen atom of atomic weight two (deuterium, or heavy hydrogen), a discovery that immediately led to the industrial production of this isotope and its oxide, 'heavy water.' He was research director (1942–45) of the MANHATTAN PROJECT.

Utah, in the heart of the ROCKY MOUNTAINS, is a plateau with a mean elevation of 6000 ft. It is traversed by the Wasatch Range. To the east are the snow-capped Uinta mountains, the highest of which is Kings Peak (13,498 ft.). The western region is part of the GREAT BASIN. The history of Utah is unique among the states. It was settled and developed by the MORMONS, who during the 1840's chose to found their Zion in a region that would offer little attraction to outsiders. BRIGHAM YOUNG led his followers to the green valley of Great Salt Lake, where in 1847 he founded Salt Lake City, today the headquarters of the Mormon church. At the end of the Mexican War (1848) the region was ceded to the U.S., and in 1850 it was constituted Utah Territory. The name Deseret (honey bee), proposed by the Mormons, was rejected by Congress in favor of that derived from the Ute (or Utah) Indians. Numerous petitions for admission to the Union were delayed 44 years because the federal government would not countenance polygamy, a practice the Mormons had publicly avowed in 1852. Difficulties followed, but in 1890 the Mormon church disavowed the practice, and Utah entered the Union as the 45th state in 1896.

The climate of Utah is dry and stimulating. The rugged plateaus in the south are for the most part uninhabitable, but in the area there are two national parks: Zion (est. 1919), noted for precipitous gorges; and Bryce Canyon (est. 1928), a region of fantastic uplifts. Less than 4 per cent of the land in Utah can be effectively tilled. The economy of the state largely depends upon its extensive mining industries, especially copper. Although non-Mormons, or 'Gentiles,' are important in such urban centers as Ogden, Provo, and Salt Lake City (the capital and metropolis, with a population in 1960 of 190,000), Mormons predominate throughout the state. Leading institutions of higher learning are the University of Utah (Salt Lake City, est. 1850), and Brigham Young University (Provo, est. 1875).

Ute Indians, of Uto-Aztecan stock with a Plains and Mountain (Great Basin) culture, were nomadic warriors. In the early 19th century they ranged through the Southwest and were a menace to sedentary villagers like the Pueblos. Various U.S. campaigns against them reduced their numbers. Today remnants are settled on reservations in Colorado and Utah.

Utilitarianism is the ethical concept that the useful is the good, and that the greatest happiness of the greatest number should be the criterion of morality. It was systematically developed by the English jurist Jeremy Bentham in the late 18th century, applied to economics by John Stuart Mill, and used by Herbert Spencer to expound DARWINISM. Thus postulated in SOCIOLOGY, it relates morality to physiological and psychological health.

Uto-Aztecan Family of North American Indians were a widely distributed linguistic stock, including groups ranging from the Northwestern U.S. to Central America. In the U.S. the family comprised the COMANCHE, HOPI, KIOWA, MISSION, PAIUTE, PUEBLO, SHOSHONE, and UTE.

Utopian Socialism is that phase of the American LABOR MOVEMENT which, in its effort to find ways of bettering the lot of the worker, looked for help from earnest idealists rather than from radical doctrines. Its COMMUNAL SOCIETIES, highly paternalistic, were usually short-lived, for they were too individualistic to have effective leadership. Very few survived the decade of the 1850's.

Utrecht, Treaty of (1713), ended QUEEN ANNE'S WAR, and by its terms France ceded Newfoundland, Acadia, and Hudson Bay to Great Britain, but retained Cape Breton Island and the islands of the St. Lawrence. The failure to define boundaries, particularly in the Hudson Bay region, left the door open to later conflict.

V

VACA, see *Cabeza de Vaca.*

VAIL, Theodore Newton (1845–1920), associated himself with the telephone industry in its infancy (1878), and installed telephone systems in the principal cities of the U.S. As president of the AMERICAN TELEPHONE AND TELEGRAPH COMPANY after 1907, he laid the foundation of what became (and still remains) the largest corporation in the U.S. One of the leading capitalists of his day, he was a director of many corporations in the U.S. and England.

VALLANDIGHAM, Clement Laird (1820–71), Ohio lawyer and journalist, for a time served in Congress (1858–63). Most prominent of the COPPERHEADS, he was courtmartialed for treasonable statements and sentenced to close confinement, but Lincoln humorously commuted the sentence to banishment behind the Confederate lines, where Vallandigham proved an embarrassment to his hosts. For a time he lived in Canada (1863–64). While there, he received the Democratic nomination for governor of Ohio *in absentia,* and he nearly won the election. He later returned to the U.S. In 1864 he became Supreme Commander of the Sons of Liberty, a secret anti-draft Copperhead society. He never was again selected for public office.

Valley Forge was the encampment ground for Washington's army of 11,000 regulars for six months (19 December–19 June 1777–78). After the Americans were defeated at GERMANTOWN and the British had occupied Philadelphia, Washington took up winter quarters on the heights above the west bank of the Schuylkill river, 22 miles northwest of Philadelphia. The winter began unexpectedly early, with heavy snows and abnormally cold weather. The troops were desperately short of food and medical supplies, and so scantily clad and ill-shod that many officers feared mutiny or desertion. Some 1100 American soldiers slipped into the British lines before spring, but those who remained were not the kind to mutiny; they were veterans with *esprit de corps* and a personal devotion to Washington, who shared their hardships and never lost their unfaltering confidence. Morale was rapidly improved in the spring by reorganization, expert drilling under the new inspector general, von STEUBEN, and a reform of the transportation system instituted by NATHANAEL GREENE. The Franco-American alliance (May 1778) brought new supplies of money, arms, and clothing, and by late June the troops were ready to engage the British on equal terms at MONMOUTH. The Valley Forge encampment is now a national shrine.

Van Allen belts were named for James Alfred Van Allen (1914–), head of the department of physics at Iowa after 1951. In 1958 Van Allen conducted research with deep space probes, which revealed that the earth's magnetic field arc (the newly discovered magnetosphere) lies in two belts surrounding the earth, one inside the other. (The constant 'solar wind' flattens the sunlit area of the magnetosphere and extends the darkened area into an elongated teardrop.) The first belt is highly charged and begins a few hundred miles out from the earth. The other is less powerfully charged but extends some 50,000 miles into space. This is believed to be a region in which ionized particles become trapped, creating a pulsating band of radiation. The Van Allen belts had been predicted in 1956 by the University of Maryland physicist S. Fred Singer (1924–).

VAN BUREN, Martin (1782–1862), 8th President of the U.S. (1837–41), was reared on his father's farm at Kinderhook, New York, in the Hudson valley. Admitted to the bar (1803), he successfully practiced law, entered politics, and by 1820 had become a dominant figure in the powerful New York Democratic party machine known as the ALBANY REGENCY. He served in the U.S. Senate (1821–28), and was elected governor of New York (1828), a post he resigned in 1829 to enter President Jackson's cabinet as Secretary of State. An intimate adviser of the President, he sided with Jackson against Vice President Calhoun in the famous PEGGY EATON affair, and to strengthen the President's hand he resigned (1831). It was a political maneuver that gave Jackson the opportunity to demand the resignation of most of his other officers, who were Calhoun men. Jackson then sent Van Buren as minister to England. (Calhoun blocked confirmation in the Senate, and Van Buren soon returned from London.)

In 1832 Van Buren was selected as Jackson's running mate, the Democrats won the election, and for four years Van Buren presided over the Senate. As the party's presidential candidate in 1836, Van Buren, the 'little magician,' polled a large electoral majority, took over all but one of Jackson's cabinet, and set out to follow in the footsteps of his predecessor.

The PANIC OF 1837 split the Democratic party. The radical faction, or LOCOFOCOS, supported Van Buren's Independent Treasury Bill (1837), a statesmanlike measure to which the conservative HUNKERS were so opposed that after its passage in 1840 many of them left the Democratic fold. Van Buren was the party's candidate in 1840 but he lost the election to William Henry Harrison, the first defeat by a diffuse coalition of an organized party in power since 1800.

In 1844 Van Buren again wanted to be his party's candidate, but his opposition to the annexation of Texas as a slave state cost him the nomination, which went to James K. Polk. He nevertheless remained prominent in party politics, and helped lead the BARNBURNERS, the progressive wing, in their struggle against machine control. In 1848 he was the presidential candidate for the newly organized FREE-SOIL PARTY (with which the Barnburners aligned themselves), and by polling nearly 300,000 votes he robbed Lewis Cass, the Democratic nominee, of enough votes to swing New York to the Whigs. Thus the election went to Zachary Taylor. Van Buren is chiefly remembered as a party leader, for as a statesman his accomplishments were few.

See Holmes Alexander, *The American Talleyrand* (1935).

VANCOUVER, GEORGE (1758–98), English explorer, in 1791 left England by way of the Cape of Good Hope and ports in the Pacific Ocean to explore and map the north Pacific coast of North America. He was especially instructed to search for navigable rivers which might serve as routes to connect the sea with inland lakes. He sailed around the island (first discovered by the Spanish) now named for him, and returned home by way of Cape Horn. The report of his accomplishment, a task he completed in four years (1792–95), appeared posthumously as *A Voyage of Discovery to the North Pacific Ocean and Round the World* (3 vols., 1798), with remarkably accurate charts of the Puget Sound area. Many of his geographic names are established in permanent usage.

VANDENBERG, ARTHUR HENDRICK (1884–1951), while serving as editor (1906–28) of the Grand Rapids *Herald,* was appointed U.S. senator from Michigan to fill a vacancy. He was thereafter repeatedly re-elected until his death. An influential Republican, in 1939 he led the isolationists in their fight against revising the NEUTRALITY ACTS (1935–37), but by 1945 his views on foreign affairs had undergone a change. As chairman (after 1946) of the powerful Senate Committee on Foreign Affairs, he proved himself the most internationally minded of Republican leaders by helping to secure passage of the MARSHALL PLAN (1948).

VANDERBILT, CORNELIUS (1794–1877), born on Staten Island, New York, gained control of most of the ferry lines plying the New York–New Jersey coast. He expanded his holdings to Long Island Sound and the Hudson river, and opened a bi-monthly shipping line (1851–53) between New York and California by way of a connecting road across Nicaragua, the shortest route to San Francisco. For a time the 'Commodore' operated freight and passenger service to Europe (1855–61).

Vanderbilt turned his attention to railroads at the same time, and having acquired the NEW YORK CENTRAL, he built his system into an empire by the customary ruthless maneuvers of the day. (His fierce struggle with DANIEL DREW for the ERIE RAILROAD was one of the colorful financial battles of the post–Civil War period.) He left the bulk of his $100,000,000 estate to his son, William Henry Vanderbilt (1821–85), who doubled the fortune while managing the family railroad properties.

VANDERLYN, John (1775–1852), born in Kingston, New York, was the first American painter to study in Paris rather than in London or Rome. He began a brilliant career painting nudes so realistically that he shocked his compatriots. (His *Ariadne* is in the Pennsylvania Academy.) His historical compositions found no market, and he died embittered and impoverished. Most of his paintings are in the Senate House Museum, in Kingston.

VANE, Sir Henry (1613–62), having attended Oxford and served in diplomatic missions on the continent, in 1635 came to New England, where, in May 1636, on the day before his twenty-third birthday, he was elected governor of Massachusetts. His support of Anne Hutchinson in the bitter ANTINOMIAN CONTROVERSY embroiled him in political quarrels, especially with John Winthrop, and he returned to England (1637), where he was knighted (1640), and thereafter served in Parliament as one of the ablest Puritan statesmen. His subsequent career belongs to English history, but while he was in America he was presiding officer of the Massachusetts General Court when Harvard College was founded, and Winthrop later said of Vane (who, after the Restoration, was charged with high treason and executed) that he always showed himself 'a true friend to New England, and a man of noble and generous mind.' Milton's sonnet to him honors his memory.

VAN RENSSELAER, Stephen (1764–1839), after graduation from Harvard (1782) devoted himself to managing the extensive family properties, which included most of the present Albany and Rensselaer counties of New York. As a major general of militia (after 1801) he unhappily directed the battle of QUEENSTON HEIGHTS in the War of 1812. He served in Congress (1823–29), and took a prominent part in constructing the Erie Canal. The technical school that he founded (1824) at Troy was incorporated in 1826 as Rensselaer Polytechnic Institute.

Vassar College for women, at Poughkeepsie, New York, was founded (1861) by the English-born, public-spirited brewer, Matthew Vassar (1792–1868). It opened in 1865 as the first institution for women on a collegiate level. It pioneered in music instruction, physical education, and (more recently) in experimental drama. Its instruction in euthenics first applied scientific principles to the betterment of living conditions. In 1965, with an endowment of $38,000,000 and a faculty of 174, it enrolled 1580 students.

Vaudeville in the U.S. was modeled on the English variety theater and had its beginning when TONY PASTOR opened his New York show in 1881. Two years later in Boston B. F. Keith gave currency to the term by continuous performances of unrelated sketches, songs, dances, skits, acrobatics, and other featured acts. With E. F. Albee, Keith established a chain of vaudeville theaters, which for a time (1885–1930) provided the most widely attended popular entertainment in the country. With the advent of radio and sound movies, vaudeville disappeared from the stage.

VAUX, Calvert (1824–95), English-born architect and landscape gardener, came to the U.S. in 1850, and with A. J. DOWNING designed and constructed a number of country houses. With F. L. OLMSTED he developed parks in various cities, notably Central Park in New York. A member of many commissions, Vaux published works dealing with his profession.

V-E Day (Victory-in-Europe Day, 8 May 1945), following the unconditional surrender of the German armies (7 May), marked the formal end of World War II in Europe.

VEBLEN, Thorstein [Bunde] (1857–1929), economist and social theorist, was reared in a Minnesota farm community by Norwegian parents. He received his education at Carleton College, Johns Hopkins, and Yale, and taught at Chicago (1892–1906), Stanford (1906–9), Missouri (1911–18), and the New School for Social Research (after 1919). His attack on the predatory commercialism of the wealthy in *The Theory of the Leisure Class* (1899) aroused hostility in the academic world, but came to have a profound influence on economic thinking.

It was followed by *The Theory of Business Enterprise* (1904), a critical analysis of the price system and the business cycle, urging the ideal of production for use rather than profit.

In *The Instinct of Workmanship* (1914) Veblen laid the foundations for the institutional school of economics by dissecting social and economic institutions and their psychological bases. He sought to demonstrate that engineers and technologists were best fitted to give direction to industry, and elaborated his ideas in *The Engineers and the Price System* (1921), and *Absentee Ownership and Business Enterprise in Recent Times* (1923). Veblen weakened the classical theories and gave impetus to social control. No other American social and economic theorist has exerted greater influence.

VELÁSQUEZ, DIEGO DE (*c.* 1460–1524), Spanish conquistador, sailed with Columbus on his second voyage (1493). In 1511 he commanded an expedition sent to conquer Cuba, a task completed in 1514 with the aid of his lieutenant, NARVÁEZ. Velásquez was established as governor of Cuba, and under his authority the island began to serve as the base for Spanish exploration of the Americas.

Venezuela Boundary Dispute was a controversy between Venezuela and Great Britain over the boundary line of British Guiana dating back to 1814, when the British took over that possession from the Dutch. The dispute took on a new importance with the discovery of gold in the contested region, and became so acrid by 1887 that Venezuela broke off diplomatic relations with Great Britain and asked the U.S. to arbitrate the case. Great Britain refused the offer, and refused it again when it was renewed by Cleveland in 1894. In 1895 Cleveland's Secretary of State, Richard Olney, sent a belligerent dispatch to the British Foreign Office declaring that the U.S. was 'practically sovereign on this continent,' and that British pressure on Venezuela would be regarded as a violation of the Monroe Doctrine. The British government asserted that the Doctrine did not apply to the case, and a third time rejected the U.S. offer of arbitration.

Cleveland then laid the diplomatic correspondence before Congress, recommending the creation of an independent commission whose decision the U.S. would regard as binding upon Britain. Olney's earlier assertion had been insultingly arrogant, but to the British government the dispute with Venezuela was a relatively minor matter, and, as Britain and Germany were rivals at the time, the friendship of the U.S. was desirable. The British therefore aided the U.S. authorities, and a treaty (1897) signed by Venezuela and Great Britain provided for arbitration. A Paris tribunal conferred a verdict in 1899, substantially in favor of British claims. The significance of the affair was that it emphatically reaffirmed the Monroe Doctrine, and afforded a notable victory for the principle of arbitration.

Vera Cruz Incident (April 1914) occurred when the insurgent President of Mexico, Victoriano Huerta (whom the U.S. did not recognize) ordered the arrest in Tampico of several U.S. marines, who by error had entered a restricted area. Admiral Henry Mayo demanded both an apology and a salute to the American flag. Huerta sought consolidation of Mexican support by refusing the salute. President Wilson backed Mayo by dispatching a fleet to Vera Cruz, which American troops occupied to prevent German arms from reaching Huerta. The American President was rescued from an acute situation by a proposal from Argentina, Brazil, and Chile (thereafter known as the ABC POWERS) to mediate. Wilson seized the opportunity, and war was averted.

VÉRENDRYE, PIERRE, see *La Vérendrye.*

VERGENNES, CHARLES GRAVIER, Comte de (1717–87), French statesman, was made foreign minister by Louis XVI in 1774. Although he signed the Franco-American treaty of alliance (1778), by May 1781 he calculated that the indecisive struggle had stretched out long enough, and expressed a willingness to accept a settlement on the basis of the status quo. But Washington's success at Yorktown five months later decisively altered the diplomatic balance, and Vergennes could only acquiesce in the negotiations that followed. He was the chief French representative in the TREATY OF PARIS of 1783, which formally ended the American War of Independence. Vergennes, Vermont (est. 1788), set off from neighboring towns in the year after his death, was named for him.

Vermont, the only New England state without a seacoast, is a moderately rugged terrain, still heavily wooded, bordering on Lake Champlain. It was first penetrated in 1609 by CHAMPLAIN, whose expedition from Canada against the Iroquois gave France claim to the region, and whose phrase for 'green mountains' was later adopted as the name of the state. In 1665 the French built a fort (later abandoned) on Isle la Motte. An English settlement was made at Chimney Point in 1690 by a party from Albany, but the first permanent villages grew up along the Massachusetts border after a fort was erected near Brattleboro in 1724. Later settlements continued north along the Connecticut river and penetrated inland from Lake Champlain along the valley that was strategic during the last French and Indian War (1755–63).

The claim of New Hampshire that her territory extended as far to the west as the similar claims of Massachusetts and Connecticut was put forward by New Hampshire's Governor Benning Wentworth in 1749. He immediately chartered Bennington (on the New York border) as a New Hampshire town, and later extended his patents throughout most of the present state of Vermont. The territory thenceforth was called the New Hampshire Grants, and thus arose the long controversy between New Hampshire and New York on the issue of jurisdiction over the region.

Under its charter of 1664 New York claimed eastward to the Connecticut river, and in 1764 the crown rendered a judgment for New York. But settlers who in good faith had purchased their land from Wentworth's agents would not surrender their claims. In 1771, under the leadership of ETHAN ALLEN and his 'Green Mountain Boys,' they took up arms in defense of their homesteads. Troubles were compounded by the outbreak of the War of Independence. With help from Connecticut, Allen's 'Boys' captured Fort Ticonderoga (May 1775) and took part in the expedition against Canada. In January 1777 representatives of the towns assembled at Westminster to adopt a declaration of independence, which they presented to the Continental Congress. That body urged the people to adopt a state constitution, and in July a convention at Windsor did so. Its clauses providing for the abolition of slavery and for universal manhood suffrage made Vermont the first state to take such action. The battle of BENNINGTON (August 1777), leading to the decisive engagement at SARATOGA in October, assured Vermont its new status.

Meanwhile New Hampshire and New York had formed a secret agreement to divide the state between themselves, with the central mountain spine as the line of division. Difficulties with New Hampshire were resolved in 1782, when the west bank of the Connecticut was accepted as the boundary. New York abandoned claims in 1790. Thus during the period 1777–91 Vermont continued as a sovereignty of indefinite status with some national perquisites unofficially recognized. It was admitted to the Union in March 1791, the first state to join the original thirteen. In 1808 the capital was permanently situated at Montpelier.

Vermont troops participated in the War of 1812, and the state energetically supported the Union cause in the Civil War. From pioneer days Vermonters for the most part have been self-sufficient farmers with little cash income. During the 19th century large numbers from the unproductive uplands migrated to the West, and throughout the state abandoned farms became a common sight. Transition to dairy farming after 1870 gave the state a stable economy and income, virtually unchanged since then.

The leading industries include maple syrup and sugar, granite and marble quarrying, and asbestos mining. The rapid expansion of both summer and winter recreation facilities has become an important economic factor. Conservative in politics, the state was solidly Republican from 1854 to 1962. Burlington, above Lake Champlain, is the largest city, with a population in 1960 of 35,000. Oldest among the institutions of higher learning are the University of Vermont (Burlington, est. 1800), Middlebury (est. 1800), and Norwich (Northfield, est. 1819).

VERRAZANO, GIOVANNI DA (c. 1480–1528), Italian navigator in the service of France, in 1524 explored the North American coast from Maryland to Cape Cod, searching for a water route to China. He was presumably the first European to enter New York Bay (April 1524), 85 years before the arrival of Henry Hudson. His report to Francis I was the earliest description of the seaboard region his five-month voyage had uncovered. (The 'Sea of Verrazano,' which the map of his voyage showed, appears as a gulf of the Pacific extending across the continent almost to Chesapeake Bay. The myth, which probably derived from the efforts of Indians to describe the Great Lakes, persisted into the 18th century.) In 1528 Verrazano was murdered by Caribbean tribesmen.

New York City has honored the navigator by placing a statue of him in Battery Park (1909), and naming the world's longest suspension bridge for him, the Verrazano-Narrows Bridge (1964), which connects Brooklyn and Staten Island.

Versailles Peace Conference (January–June 1919), held at Versailles, France, was a meeting held by the victorious Allies and associated powers after World War I to draft a peace treaty. It was attended by 32 nations, but the 'Big Four' made the principal decisions. They were Great Britain (Lloyd George), France (Clemenceau), Italy (Orlando), and the U.S. (Wilson). Wilson shattered precedent by taking personal charge of the American delegation, which included Secretary of State ROBERT LANSING, General TASKER BLISS, Colonel EDWARD HOUSE, and career diplomat HENRY WHITE. The basis of Wilson's selection of a delegation was inept. It included no representative of the Senate or of the Republican party regulars, and, except for Wilson himself, no person of international standing. It was, however, accompanied by hundreds of authorities to advise on historical, ethnological, and economic matters, and thus had the benefit of more expert advice than any political settlement ever negotiated.

Wilson failed to win support for his FOURTEEN POINTS. The able and disillusioned Clemenceau said he was bored by them. 'Why, God Almighty has only ten.' But the fourteenth led to the founding of the LEAGUE OF NATIONS.

Versailles, Treaty of (1919), drawn up at the VERSAILLES PEACE CONFERENCE to end World War I, was signed in June by 32 nations and submitted for German signature, soon affixed. Important clauses among its 440 articles included a statement of German war guilt; the demilitarization of the Rhineland; loss of the Saar basin; limitation of size of the German army and abolition of the German general staff; prohibition of German naval and air forces; the repayment by Germany to the Allies, ton for ton, of all destroyed Allied shipping; the abandonment by Germany of her colonies and the loss of much territory in Europe; and the imposition of an indemnity of $5,000,000,000 and of a REPARATIONS bill to be determined later. The covenant of the LEAGUE OF NATIONS, which concluded the treaty, was written at the insistence of President Wilson.

The U.S. Senate had already begun heated debate on the issue of the League even before Wilson had returned from Paris and called Congress into special session to consider ratification of the Treaty and the League of Nations. The 'irreconcilables,' led by such isolationists as WILLIAM BORAH and ROBERT LA FOLLETTE, were adamant in their opposition. (Though HENRY CABOT LODGE had sponsored reservations, he intended to defeat ratification.) From the start three-fourths of the Senate favored some form of membership in the League, which was the issue at stake, but Wilson stubbornly rejected any but the mildest interpretive reservations. To plead his cause he therefore set out on a 9500-mile speaking tour into the Middle and Far West, where he delivered 37 speeches in 29 cities. Stalked relentlessly by irreconcilables, Wilson made little headway against isolationism despite his impassioned eloquence. Disillusioned, he collapsed while on tour, and thus ended all hopes for the world order he envisaged.

The Lodge resolution of ratification of the treaty, with 14 reservations, was offered in November. Wilson urged defeat of the treaty on the ground that the reservations provided for the nullification, not the ratification, of the treaty. The Senate then rejected the Lodge resolution. Brought up for reconsideration in the next session of Congress, the resolution was again defeated (49 to 35), and in March 1920 the Senate gave the President formal notice of inability to ratify the Treaty.

In the presidential campaign of 1920 the Democratic candidate, James M. Cox, pledged support of the League, but Warren G. Harding and the Republicans straddled the issue. When the Republicans won, Harding abandoned any attempt to bring the U.S. into the League. In July 1921, nearly three years after the armistice, Congress by joint resolution declared World War I at an end, and during the summer separate peace treaties were concluded with Germany, Austria, and Hungary. The official U.S. attitude toward the League was expressed by President Harding, who declared (February 1923) in a special message to Congress that the League 'is not for us. Nothing could be more decisively stamped with finality.'

Vertical unions, see *Industrial unions.*

Vesey Insurrection (1822) was a spectacular slave uprising led by the mulatto Télémaque ('Denmark') Vesey, a carpenter who had purchased his freedom in 1800 after winning a Charleston lottery. He was a respected member of the African Methodist church. He managed to inspire a group of slaves with the idea of seizing the city of Charleston, but one of the conspirators betrayed him, and 37 Negroes (including Vesey) were tried and hanged before the revolt had really started. This was one of the most serious NEGRO INSURRECTIONS in the U.S., and it led to a tightening of the 'black codes' as the only effective means of subordinating Negroes.

VESPUCCI, AMERIGO (1451–1512), for whom the Americas were named, still remains the most controversial character in the Age of Discovery. A Florentine, in 1492 he was the commercial representative of the Italian house of Medici in Spain, and manager of a ship-chandlery business in Seville which helped fit out Columbus's voyages. In 1499 he presumably accompanied the conquistador Alonzo de Hojeda on a coastal operation off South America, and, as a junior officer in the service of Portugal after 1501, allegedly took part in three later voyages exploring several thousand miles of the coast of Brazil. The letters he wrote, some of which are judged authentic and others held to be forgeries, include the statement: 'These regions we may rightly call *Mundus Novus,* a New World, because our ancestors had no knowledge of them.' The writer of the letters shared the belief held by Columbus that he was exploring a region adjacent to or an appendage of eastern Asia. The vastness of the Pacific was not known until Magellan's circumnavigation of the globe in 1521; indeed, even Balboa, who discovered it in 1513 from the shore of Panama, thought he was gazing at an extension of the Indian Ocean.

It was the German cosmographer Martin Waldseemüller who first used the term America, and he applied it only to the portion of the newly discovered areas that the published version of the Vespucci letters had described. In his *Cosmographiae Introductio* (1507) he joined the discoveries of Columbus and Cabot to those of the Portuguese explorers off the coast of Brazil. The accompanying map shows a continuous new found land not far from Japan. The southern part he calls *America:* 'Since Americus Vespucius has discovered a fourth part of the world, it should be called after him.' To Spain and Portugal the northern continent long remained 'The Indies,' but elsewhere America became the name of both continents.

Veterans' Administration, established by Congress in 1930, regulates all laws affecting veterans. It operates the largest chain of hospitals in the U.S., one of the largest life insurance projects in the nation, and vast educational and training programs. In 1965 these benefits were available for some 21,850,000 veterans.

Veterans' Day, formerly Armistice Day (11 November), is a public holiday in the U.S. inaugurated on the day in 1918 when Germany accepted the armistice terms of the Allied Powers. It now commemorates the ending of World War II and the Korean War as well.

Veto power applies especially to the authority invested in the chief executive to prevent the enactment of measures passed by the legislature. A congressional measure becomes law without the President's signature after ten days, providing Congress is in session. If Congress adjourns within that period, the President's refusal to sign constitutes a POCKET VETO. (The President's veto may be overridden by a two-thirds vote of both houses of Congress.) The item veto, or selective veto, is the power of an executive to veto portions of a bill, a power generally granted state governors but denied to the President of the U.S.

Opinions have differed on what grounds the President is justified in employing the veto. Hamilton thought it the means by which the President could defend his prerogatives. Jefferson contended that unless the President is tolerably certain that a bill was constitutionally unauthorized, he should respect the wisdom of Congress. Jackson was the first to make bold use of the veto, believing that the President was free to follow his own judgment. Later Presidents generally have followed Jackson's practice.

The veto is most likely to be used when the President is of one party and Congress of another. Sometimes party leaders know in advance that a specific bill is to be vetoed, and thus members of Congress may carry out unpalatable promises made to their constituents, assured that the scheme will be blocked. Sometimes the veto becomes an effective political gambit. By threatening to use it on certain measures, the President may secure passage of bills which he favors.

Presidential vetoes have been exercised (through 1965) as follows.

	Vetoes	*Pocket vetoes*	*Total*
Washington	2		2
Madison	5	2	7
Monroe	1		1
Jackson	5	7	12
Tyler	6	4	10
Polk	2	1	3
Pierce	9		9
Buchanan	4	3	7
Lincoln	2	4	6
A. Johnson	21	7	28
Grant	44	48	92
Hayes	12	1	13
Arthur	4	8	12
Cleveland (first term)	304	110	414
B. Harrison	19	25	44
Cleveland (second term)	42	128	170
McKinley	6	36	42
T. Roosevelt	42	40	82
Taft	30	9	39
Wilson	33	11	44
Harding	5	1	6
Coolidge	20	30	50
Hoover	21	16	37
F. D. Roosevelt	371	260	631
Truman	180	70	250
Eisenhower	73	108	181
Kennedy	1		1
L. B. Johnson			

Vice presidency, the second highest executive office in the federal government of the U.S., requires the same qualifications as the presidency. In the event of a tie or lack of majority in the ELECTORAL COLLEGE, the election is determined by the Senate. The sole official function of the Vice President is to preside over the Senate, with a vote only in case of a tie. He succeeds to the presidency in the event that office is vacated.

The vice presidency is a peculiarly anomalous office. In theory the Vice President is second only to the President as a political figure. In practice, since passage of the Twelfth Amendment (1804) which made the elections of the two executives separate affairs, the vice presidency has seldom been occupied by men of eminence. The problem is inherent in the nature of the executive structure. The vice presidency, as John Adams observed, is 'nothing *in esse*' but 'everything *in posse*.' To strengthen the party ticket the Vice President is usually chosen from a geographical region other than that of the President, and, if possible, from a different wing of the party. In recent years Vice Presidents have been assigned special executive or administrative tasks by the President, and encouraged to participate in cabinet sessions, but such assignments are merely discretionary.

The Vice Presidents and the party to which they belonged are as follows.

(Names starred identify those who succeeded to the presidency upon the death of the President.)

1. John Adams (Federalist, 1789–97)
2. Thomas Jefferson (Democratic-Republican, 1797–1801)
3. Aaron Burr (Democratic-Republican, 1801–5)
4. George Clinton (Democratic-Republican, 1805–12)
5. Elbridge Gerry (Democratic-Republican, 1813–14)
6. Daniel D. Tompkins (Democratic-Republican, 1817–25)
7. John C. Calhoun (Democratic-Republican, 1825–32)
8. Martin Van Buren (Democrat, 1833–37)
9. Richard M. Johnson (Democrat, 1837–41)
10. John Tyler* (Whig, 1841)
11. George M. Dallas (Democrat, 1845–49)
12. Millard Fillmore* (Whig, 1849–50)
13. William R. King (Democrat, 1853)
14. John C. Breckinridge (Democrat, 1857–61)
15. Hannibal Hamlin (Republican, 1861–65)
16. Andrew Johnson* (Union Republican, 1865)
17. Schuyler Colfax (Republican, 1869–73)
18. Henry Wilson (Republican, 1873–75)
19. William A. Wheeler (Republican, 1877–81)
20. Chester A. Arthur* (Republican, 1881)
21. Thomas A. Hendricks (Democrat, 1885)
22. Levi P. Morton (Republican, 1889–93)
23. Adlai E. Stevenson (Democrat, 1893–97)
24. Garret A. Hobart (Republican, 1897–99)
25. Theodore Roosevelt* (Republican, 1901)
26. Charles W. Fairbanks (Republican, 1905–9)
27. James S. Sherman (Republican, 1909–12)
28. Thomas R. Marshall (Democrat, 1913–21)
29. Calvin Coolidge* (Republican, 1921–23)
30. Charles G. Dawes (Republican, 1925–29)
31. Charles Curtis (Republican, 1929–33)
32. John N. Garner (Democrat, 1933–41)
33. Henry A. Wallace (Democrat, 1941–45)
34. Harry S Truman* (Democrat, 1945)
35. Alben W. Barkley (Democrat, 1949–53)
36. Richard M. Nixon (Republican, 1953–61)
37. Lyndon B. Johnson* (Democrat, 1961–63)
38. Hubert H. Humphrey (1965–)

Vicksburg, on the high eastern bank of the Mississippi at the mouth of the Yazoo, was first settled about 1812. As the city thrived during the expansion of the cotton industry, it began to rival Natchez as Mississippi's center of wealth and political power. The decline of steamboating reduced its commercial importance after the Civil War.

Vicksburg Campaign (November 1862–July 1863) was the hotly contested struggle for control of the Mississippi river during the Civil War. With the river in its control, the Union could sever the South from the Southwest and restore commerce to the Northwest. Grant's capture in February of FORT HENRY (on the Tennessee) and FORT DONELSON (on the Cumberland) were preliminaries to the campaign. New Orleans and Memphis fell during the late spring. But the South still held 200 miles of the river between Port Hudson, Louisiana, and Vicksburg, Mississippi, at the mouth of the Yazoo river. Attempts to take Vicksburg by water (May–June 1862) and by land (December–early 1863) had failed, for the river city was strongly fortified and protected by natural defenses.

General Grant audaciously cut loose from his Union base at Memphis, moved down the west bank of the Mississippi to a point below Vicksburg, crossed the river, and with 20,000 troops (later reinforced) began his siege of the city on 22 May. This was a calculated risk of great magnitude. For nearly seven weeks

General John C. Pemberton with 30,000 Confederates withstood the bombardment, but on 4 July he accepted Grant's demand for the unconditional surrender of the 'Confederate Gibraltar.' (Each side had sustained 10,000 casualties.) Five days later Port Hudson fell, the Mississippi was under Union control, and the Confederacy was split. Grant's achievement was overshadowed at the time by the Union success at Gettysburg on the previous day, but it was fully as much a turning point of the war, for it opened the way to the march eastward to the coast.

Vietnam, U.S. military involvement in, was motivated by the same intent to forestall the spread of communism in the Far East that had triggered the KOREAN WAR (1950–53). Following the GENEVA CONFERENCE of 1954, which divided Vietnam North and South, communist guerrillas tried to take over South Vietnam, which was supported by the United States. In October 1961 President Kennedy sent General Maxwell D. Taylor to Vietnam to discuss with President Ngo Dinh Diem the best means of helping the country to defend itself against attacks by communist Vietcong (North Vietnam) guerrillas. Thereafter deliveries of U.S. military equipment to Vietnam were accelerated. In February 1962 the Defense Department created the Military Assistance Command (MAC) to aid South Vietnam in preventing a communist take-over. In November 1963 Diem was a fatal victim of a revolution, and General Duong Van Minh came into power, with a government recognized by the U.S. and supported by units from the U.S. Seventh Fleet.

In a bloodless coup (January 1964) Major General Nguyen Khanh proclaimed himself Premier, but despite U.S. aid the Saigon regime failed to stem the accelerated Vietcong guerrilla drives. During the year U.S. military and economic aid to South Vietnam amounted to a half billion dollars, and some 21,000 U.S. troops and military advisers were stationed there. Defense Secretary McNamara arrived in Saigon in May on his fifth fact-finding mission and on his return predicted that what lay ahead was 'a long, hard war.'

During 1965 direct U.S. involvement progressively increased. American strength exceeded 300,000 by late summer 1966, when the toll of Americans killed in action passed 5000. The communist drive was checked, but the cost was now annually reckoned in billions of dollars. Sentiment against the large commitment both of men and money was expressed by 'peace parades' and by political pressures against involvement in a war that could not be won by either side. In August 1966 the Vietcong put prices on the heads of Vietnamese and American civilian and military leaders. The U.S. objective, however, continued, aimed at proving that U.S. troops could not be thrown out by the North Vietnamese, that South Vietnam could not be taken by force, and that North Vietnam should negotiate on those terms.

Vigilantes were the volunteer committees that flourished on the American frontier west of the Mississippi as organizations for suppressing lawlessness in regions where law and order were not synonymous. Such committees, which often resorted to LYNCH LAW, were especially effective in California during the gold rush of the 1850's, and later in the parts of the West that were plagued by horse, sheep, and cattle thefts. When led by responsible citizens, vigilantes meted out a rough justice; otherwise they were the resort of lawless malcontents.

VILLA, FRANCISCO [PANCHO VILLA] (1877–1923), Mexican revolutionist, joined Venustiano Carranza and the Constitutionalists in the fight against Victoriano Huerta in 1913. After the elimination of Huerta (1914) and U.S. recognition of Carranza (1915), with whom Villa was by then at odds, Villa made repeated raids across the New Mexican border (1916). This prompted President Wilson to dispatch General J. J. Pershing on a 'punitive expedition' into Mexico (March 1916–February 1917) to capture Villa, 'dead or alive.' The campaign (a failure) did not improve relations between the neighboring countries. Bold, impetuous, and daring, Villa was idolized by the masses, and after his assassination his exploits were perpetuated in folk tales and ballads.

VILLARD, HENRY (1835–1900), German-born journalist and financier, established a reputation as correspondent for New York newspapers during the Civil War. Thereafter he took a major part in organizing rail transportation in the Far West. He served as president (1881) of the Northern Pacific, and later (1890) helped found the General Electric Company, during which period he renewed his interest in journalism by purchasing control of the New York *Evening Post.*

VILLARD, OSWALD GARRISON (1872–1949), son of HENRY VILLARD and grandson of WILLIAM LLOYD GARRISON, soon after graduation from Harvard (1893) began his journalistic career in Philadelphia (1896). He took over control of the New York *Evening Post,* which he edited for twenty years (1897–1918). In 1918 he purchased the *Nation,* and during his editorship (until 1932), he transformed it into a vigorous weekly of opinion and social protest, covering politics and the arts.

Vinland, see *Leif Ericsson.*

VINSON, FREDERIC MOORE (1890–1953), 12th Chief Justice of the U.S. Supreme Court (1946–53), was born in Kentucky, where he practiced law. He served in Congress from 1923 to 1938 (except for two years), and there established a reputation as a fiscal expert. For a time he sat as a justice of the U.S. Court of Appeals for the District of Columbia. A director of various Federal agencies during World War II, he was briefly Roosevelt's Secretary of the Treasury (1945–46). Roosevelt appointed him to the high court as successor to Harlan F. Stone. Vinson's notable dissent in the Youngstown Sheet and Tube case (1952), in which the court struck down a presidential order as constituting executive lawmaking, won the support of many eminent legal scholars.

Virgin Islands, the most easterly outlying possession of the U.S., are a group of some 100 rocks and small islands, volcanic in origin, east of Puerto Rico, divided between the U.S. and Great Britain. They were discovered by Columbus (1493), were a center for slave trading in the 18th century, and have long been populated mainly by Negroes.

The Virgin Islands of the U.S. (with a population in 1962 of 33,000) are divided into two municipalities: St. Thomas and St. John, and St. Croix. Settlement of St. Thomas was begun by the Danish West India Company, and the Islands remained under Danish control until the U.S. bought them from Denmark (1917) for $25,000,000. The inhabitants have been U.S. citizens since 1927, but have no voice in U.S. elections. The government has its own local legislature, but is administered by the Department of the Interior. The governor is appointed by the President. Virgin Islands National Park (1956) is a scenic area of some 5000 acres.

Virginia, tenth of the Thirteen Colonies to ratify the Constitution and enter the Union (25 June 1788), was named by Sir Walter Raleigh, who fitted out the expedition in 1584 to stake claims in the New World for Elizabeth, the Virgin Queen of England. The fate of the colony on ROANOKE ISLAND is not precisely known. The commercial venture of the LONDON COMPANY in 1607 established the first permanent English settlement in America, at JAMESTOWN. During the earliest period the name Virginia embraced all North America not secured by Spain and France; and the term 'Old Dominion,' by which the state is known, evidently derives from early documents referring to the area as 'the colony and dominion of Virginia.'

First under the governorship of Baron DE LA WARR and later successively under that of Sir THOMAS GATES, GEORGE PERCY, and others, the colony survived the terrible 'starving time' of 1609–10. A more liberal charter in 1612 stimulated further settlements and attracted colonizers to the 'hundreds,' land divisions along the TIDEWATER. In 1619 the first representative government in the New World (the house of burgesses) met at Jamestown. When a shipload of maidens arrived in 1620 the colony began to thrive. In 1624 Virginia became a royal colony, the first in English history. By 1641, with Sir WILLIAM BERKELEY as governor, the colony had assumed recognized importance. It then had a population of some 7500, and it was a region of well established plantations and farms, growing tobacco for export and corn for subsistence.

Negroes, like white servants and apprentices, at first generally were indentured servants, not slaves. During the

English Commonwealth (1649–60), and especially after the arrival of an expedition sent by Cromwell in 1652, Virginia was practically independent, enjoying free trade with foreign nations. Newcomers invested in tobacco lands and engaged in the growing fur trade. The NAVIGATION ACTS halted this early prosperity. Wealthy planters were able to diversify their activities but frontier farmers faced ruin. Berkeley's refusal to offer them protection from Indian attacks led to BACON'S REBELLION (1676). The political control, administered from the capital of WILLIAMSBURG, for the next 100 years remained firmly in the hands of the wealthy tidewater planters. Negro slavery steadily increased as tobacco cultivation became the major industry. Many planters, like WILLIAM BYRD, made handsome profits from land speculation.

The Shenandoah valley was settled after 1730 by newcomers, especially from Pennsylvania. The OHIO COMPANY (1749) opened areas beyond the mountains and Virginians were prominent in the FRENCH AND INDIAN WARS. During the 1760's, Virginia, with Massachusetts, led the opposition to Parliament's colonial policies, and in 1773 the House of Burgesses organized one of the COMMITTEES OF CORRESPONDENCE, so effective in uniting the colonies in the patriot cause. The Virginia leaders proposed an intercolonial assembly and Virginia's PEYTON RANDOLPH was elected president of the First Continental Congress (1774). The last royal governor, the earl of DUNMORE, was forced to flee in 1775 and the colony declared its independence in 1776. The roster of Virginia notables in this and the succeeding decades is unmatched in U.S. history. It includes not only such public servants as GEORGE MASON, PATRICK HENRY, EDMUND RANDOLPH, and JOHN MARSHALL, but seven of the first twelve Presidents: WASHINGTON, JEFFERSON, MADISON, MONROE, W. H. HARRISON, TYLER, and TAYLOR.

The War of Independence was concluded with the surrender of Cornwallis at YORKTOWN (1781). In 1784 Virginia ceded to the U.S. that portion of its western lands north of the Ohio, soon incorporated into the NORTHWEST TERRITORY. It likewise ceded (1789) a portion of its Potomac lands to create the District of Columbia. In 1792 Kentucky, a Virginia county since 1776, was admitted to the Union as a state.

The ALIEN AND SEDITION ACTS (1798) prompted an early defense of states' rights in the KENTUCKY AND VIRGINIA RESOLVES and led to the downfall of the Federalists and the consequent rise of the so-called 'Virginia dynasty' in the federal government. Jefferson had been largely responsible for molding a new society within the state. Entail and primogeniture were abolished, and the Anglican church ceased to be the state church. Cotton replaced tobacco as the staple in the east. Western Virginia grew rapidly as small-scale planters, leaving their exhausted soil, carved out new settlements in the PIEDMONT region. But politics was dominated by the tidewater gentry, bitterly resented by the up-country farmers. Virginians west of the Appalachians were not tied into a slave economy, and they used the Civil War as an opportunity to form the state of West Virginia (1863). Meanwhile, in April 1861, Virginia had joined the Confederacy, of which RICHMOND became the capital.

Though such prominent Virginians as ROBERT E. LEE and JOSEPH E. JOHNSTON entered the military service of the new Confederate government, many, including WINFIELD SCOTT and GEORGE H. THOMAS, remained loyal to the Union. Since the two capitals, Richmond and Washington, were the constant objectives of opposing armies, Virginia was the chief battleground of the Civil War, which impoverished the land and the people. But Virginia managed to evade the 'carpetbagger' control of radical Republicans during the period of Reconstruction. The state was readmitted to the Union in January 1870, and with transportation facilities restored, industry grew, particularly coal mining and the manufacture of textiles and tobacco products. A large proportion of the nation's shipyards are concentrated on the shores of Hampton Roads. Norfolk, which has a superb natural harbor, is the huge operational base of the U.S. Atlantic Fleet.

Chief among the valleys of the state is the fertile Shenandoah, in which were fought many of the Civil War campaigns. (It has been a national park since 1935.) The leading institution of higher learning is the UNIVERSITY OF VIR-

GINIA (Charlottesville, est. 1825). Others are the College of WILLIAM AND MARY (Williamsburg, est. 1693), second oldest in the country, and WASHINGTON AND LEE (Lexington, est. 1749).

Virginia and Kentucky Resolves, see *Kentucky and Virginia Resolves.*

Virginia Company of London, see *London Company.*

Virginia Declaration of Rights, see *Mason, George.*

Virginia dynasty is the term applied to the succession of Presidents of the U.S., in the period 1801–25, who were Virginians: Jefferson, Madison, and Monroe.

Virginia Plan, see *Randolph Plan.*

Virginia, University of, at Charlottesville, was chartered in 1819 and opened in 1825 as a state university. Both its curriculum and its buildings (architecturally the best designed collegiate group in the U.S.) were planned by Thomas Jefferson, its first rector. Jefferson's hopes for high scholastic standards were at first thwarted by inadequate state support, but in time the institution became the South's chief contribution to American education. It is notable for its law school. In 1965, with an endowment of $85,000,000 and a faculty of 1080, it enrolled 17,000 students.

***Virginius* Incident** (1873) occurred during the Cuban rebellion (1868–78), when Spanish authorities captured the arms-running ship *Virginius,* illegally flying the American flag, and summarily shot 53 of the crew (among them Americans) as pirates. Spain recognized that the attack upon the *Virginius,* whatever her defects of registry, was an injury, and paid an indemnity of $80,000 for the families of the executed Americans.

V-J Day (Victory-in-Japan Day, 15 August 1945), following the unconditional surrender of Japanese armed forces (14 August), marked the formal end of World War II.

Voice of America, a daily international short-wave radio broadcast, was established (1948) by Congress within the Department of State. In 1953 it was transferred to the independent U.S. INFORMATION AGENCY. In 1965 it was transmitting regular broadcasts in 37 languages from stations located in some two score countries.

Volstead Act (1919), designed to provide the enforcement apparatus for the Eighteenth Amendment to the U.S. Constitution, ushered in the PROHIBITION ERA. It defined as 'intoxicating liquor' any beverage containing more than one-half of one per cent of alcohol.

VON. See some proper names.

VON KARMAN, THEODORE (1881–1963), Hungarian-born aeronautical engineer, after coming to the U.S. in 1930, occupied distinguished lectureships in several universities from time to time. He was director of the Guggenheim Aeronautical Laboratories (1930–49), and founded the Aerojet-General Corporation (1942). After 1951 he was chairman of the advisory group for Aeronautical Research and Development in NATO. As a trained theoretical physicist with engineering skill of the first order, he gave support to ideas that resulted in a complex of inventions and innovations in the development of ROCKETS. His latest studies opened the field of magneto-fluiddynamics. He summarized much of the work he accomplished during the earlier period in *Aerodynamics* (1954).

VON NEUMANN, JOHN (1903–57), Hungarian-born mathematician, after teaching mathematics at Princeton (1930–33), in 1933 became one of the first permanent members of the Institute for Advanced Study. One of the most creative and versatile scientists of the 20th century, Von Neumann directed the Institute's Electronic Computer Project, and designed high-speed computers, or 'electronic brains,' notably MANIAC (mathematical analyzer, numerical integrator, and computer). He speeded development of the hydrogen bomb by various ideas, and made fundamental contributions to the theory of automata, to quantum theory, and to operational research, notably in *Theory of Games and Economic Behavior*

(1944), written with the economist OSKAR MORGENSTERN. In 1954 Von Neumann became a member of the Atomic Energy Commission.

Voting, see *Ballot, Direct primary, Party machine, Suffrage*.

Voyageurs, or *engagés,* were a distinct class of young Frenchmen employed by the fur companies to handle canoes and perform other labors in transporting men and goods to and from trading posts in the interior of North America. Some 5000 are said to have been annually engaged in such work during the late 18th and early 19th century. They are not to be confused with the earlier *coureurs de bois*.

W

Wabash Case, see *Granger cases.*

WACS (Women's Army Corps), established (1948) as a permanent branch of the U.S. regular army, grew out of the Women's Army Auxiliary Corps (WAAC), created in 1942 to relieve soldiers for combat duty. With the exception of combat training, instruction for WACS parallels that for men.

WADE, BENJAMIN FRANKLIN (1800–1878), an uncompromising Ohio abolitionist, while law partner and political protégé of JOSHUA GIDDINGS, was sent as a Whig to the U.S. Senate (1851–69), where he became a leader among the RADICAL REPUBLICANS and sponsored the WADE-DAVIS BILL. Had Wade been able to secure the conviction of President Andrew Johnson in the trial of his impeachment, a proceeding in which Wade ardently engaged, as President *pro tempore* of the Senate he would have succeeded to the presidency. (So certain was he of success that he began selection of his cabinet while the trial was in progress.) Thwarted by the acquittal and failing to be re-elected, he returned to his law practice. Wade was a man of truculent vigor and political acumen, respected even by those who opposed his principles.

Wade-Davis Bill (1864), the blueprint for Reconstruction of the RADICAL REPUBLICANS (who controlled Congress), would have required a majority of the electorate in each state of the defeated Confederacy to take an oath of past as well as future loyalty to the federal government as a condition for readmission to the Union. Lincoln killed the bill by a pocket veto. The radicals in Congress, maneuvering to counter the wartime expansion of executive power, then supported the Wade-Davis Manifesto, which accused Lincoln of 'studied outrage on the legislative authority of the people,' from personal ambition. Horace Greeley published the manifesto in his powerful *Tribune* in August, but the success of Sherman's campaign in the autumn restored Lincoln's prestige. The executive-legislative friction did not create flame until after Lincoln's death, when Congress impeached Johnson.

Wages and Hours Law, see *Fair Labor Standards Act.*

WAGNER, HANS [HONUS] [JOHN PETER] (1874–1955), Pennsylvania-born baseball player, played shortstop with the Pittsburgh Pirates, and led the National League in batting eight times (1900, 1903–4, 1906–9, 1911). Squat and massively built, the 'Flying Dutchman' had a lifetime batting average of .329. (He batted over .300 in seventeen consecutive years.) He retired in 1917, but later returned to the Pirates as coach (1933–52).

Wagner-Connery Act (1935), also known as the National Labor Relations Act, created the NATIONAL LABOR RELATIONS BOARD and gave it power to administer all interstate commercial LABOR RELATIONS. The Act defines UNFAIR LABOR PRACTICES, and protects unions against such coercive measures as the BLACKLIST and COMPANY UNIONS. This legislation was soon complemented by state 'Wagner Acts.'

Wagner-Steagall Act (1937), designed to improve housing conditions of low-income groups, established the U.S. Housing Authority (USHA) within the Department of the Interior. It extends low-interest loans to local public agencies engaged in slum clearance and grants subsidies for low-rent housing projects.

Wagon trains, during the period of the U.S. westward movement, became the means of overland freight transport as soon as roads were built. They took over the function of the more primitive, outmoded PACK TRAINS. By late 18th century COVERED WAGONS, crossing the Allegheny barrier, were penetrating the Ohio valley. Settlers moving further into the continent crossed the Great Plains in canvas-topped 'prairie schooners,' usually drawn by two or four horses or oxen. Such trains were family groups banded together for protection, with elected leaders, who both on the trail and in camp regulated discipline with almost military precision. Wagon trains ceased with the advent of railroads: in the East during the 1840's, in the West after the completion of the Union Pacific (1869).

WAITE, MORRISON REMICK (1816–88), Connecticut-born jurist, after graduation from Yale (1837) practiced law in Ohio, where he soon became a leader of the state bar. He gained national prominence as a U.S. counsel in the settlement of the ALABAMA CLAIMS, and Grant appointed him to succeed Salmon P. Chase as Chief Justice of the U.S. Supreme Court (1874–88), in which post Waite sought to affix limits to the extension of the powers of the federal and state governments. His most notable opinions were rendered in the GRANGER CASES (1877). His interpretation of the Fourteenth Amendment in *Santa Clara Co.* v. *Southern Pacific Railroad* (1886) extended the protection of the due process clause to legal persons, a decision which long encouraged the substantive interpretation of the clause as a defense of corporate property rights. In *Stone* v. *Farmers' Loan* (1886) he laid the foundation for the modern interpretation of due process as a limitation of state power.

Wake Island, an atoll in the central Pacific between Hawaii and Guam, was claimed by the U.S. after the Spanish-American War and was made a naval reservation in 1934. Taken by the Japanese (1941) during World War II, it was formally surrendered in 1945. It is chiefly important as a stopping place for transpacific aircraft.

WALCOTT, CHARLES DOOLITTLE (1850–1927), while director of the U.S. Geological Survey (1894–1907), enlarged its field to include the Reclamation Service, the Forest Service, and the Bureau of Mines. His contributions to paleontology (Cambrian rocks and fauna of the U.S.) were extensive. For twenty years he served as Secretary of the Smithsonian Institution (1907–27).

WALD, LILLIAN D. (1867–1940), a pioneer in public health nursing, in 1893 organized a visiting nurse service, which soon became the notable Henry Street Settlement in New York City, where she originated the first public school nursing service in the world (1902). At her suggestion the U.S. Children's Bureau was founded (1912), as were other health services. She served on many welfare commissions, organized the Women's Trade Union League, and crusaded for woman suffrage. *The House on Henry Street* (1915) and *Windows on Henry Street* (1934) are autobiographical.

WALKER, JIMMY [JAMES JOHN] (1881–1946), with Tammany backing became the dapper, debonair mayor of New York City (1925–32). He was immensely popular with the electorate, but when extensive frauds were exposed in the municipal government, Walker hastily resigned. For a number of years he lived in Europe.

WALKER, ROBERT JOHN (1801–69), after graduation from the University of Pennsylvania (1819), practiced law briefly in Pittsburgh before moving to Natchez, Mississippi (1826), where he made a reputation in his profession and entered politics. He served in the U.S. Senate (1835–45) as an ardent (and lifelong) expansionist. As Secretary of the Treasury in Polk's cabinet, he sponsored the WALKER TARIFF ACT (1846). His *Report* (1845) on the state of finances took rank as a classic of free-trade literature, and his administration is judged one of the ablest in the history of the Treasury.

He served as governor of Kansas Territory during the 'Bleeding Kansas' era (1857–58) and supported the Union during the Civil War, serving in Europe as the government's fiscal agent. He took part in planning the transcontinental railroad and helped negotiate the purchase of Alaska.

WALKER, WILLIAM (1824–60), Tennessee-born filibuster, educated in medicine and law, in his restless search for democratic causes went first to New Orleans, then to San Francisco. In 1853 this 'grey-eyed man of destiny' sailed with an 'army' of a few dozen for Lower California, where he proclaimed a republic with himself as president and 'annexed' the neighboring state of Sonora. U.S. government interference ended this venture. Walker then took his army to Nicaragua, where he established enough of a government to be recognized by the U.S. in 1856. His regime soon roused the enmity of CORNELIUS VANDERBILT, whose trans-Nicaraguan transportation system was being disrupted, and Walker 'surrendered' to the U.S. Navy. Torn between the vague ideal of freeing Central America from native peonage and the idea of establishing an empire supported by Negro labor, which American slaveholders gave him money and arms to bring into being, Walker attempted the conquest of Honduras. The British navy captured him and turned him over to a Honduran firing squad.

Walker Tariff Act (1846), sponsored by Polk's Secretary of the Treasury, ROBERT J. WALKER, was a downward revision which adopted schedules more moderate than those of the principal European countries. It introduced the warehouse system (still in effect) of storing goods until the duty is paid.

Wall Street since the early 19th century has been synonymous with high finance in the U.S. and is in fact the financial center of the country. A narrow thoroughfare off lower Broadway in New York City, near the tip of Manhattan, it takes its name from the wall or stockade erected in the 17th century by the Dutch burghers as a protection against the Indians.

WALLACE, HENRY AGARD (1888–1965), was a grandson of Henry Wallace (1836–1916) and son of Henry Cantwell Wallace (1866–1924). In 1895 H. Wallace and H. C. Wallace founded *Wallace's Farmer,* soon recognized as the leading agricultural newspaper in the U.S. (H. C. Wallace entered President Harding's cabinet in 1921 as Secretary of Agriculture, and died in office.)

Henry Agard Wallace, upon graduation from Iowa State College (1910), became associate editor (1910–24) and editor (1924–29) of the family periodical. He developed several strains of hybrid corn that are extensively used by farmers in the corn belt, and his knowledge of agricultural subjects made him an authority on farm economics. As F. D. Roosevelt's Secretary of Agriculture (1933–40), he administered the Agricultural Adjustment Act. A leader of the New Deal program, Wallace was elected Vice President (1941–45) in Roosevelt's third term, and served President Truman briefly as Secretary of Commerce (1945), until his open opposition to Truman's foreign policy forced his resignation. As presidential candidate (1948) of the newly formed leftist Progressive party, Wallace polled over 1,000,000 votes. He wrote numerous books on agricultural problems and on politics.

WALLACE, LEW [LEWIS] (1825–1905), having served in the Mexican War and the Civil War, in which he attained the rank of major general, in 1865 returned to his law practice at Crawfordsville, Indiana. The success of his romance of Spanish conquest, *The Fair God* (1873), led him to write one of the most popular novels of the century, *Ben-Hur* (1880), also highly successful on the stage and screen. He served as territorial governor of New Mexico (1878–81) and minister to Turkey (1881–85). Thereafter he settled into a career of writing and lecturing.

Walsh-Healey Act (1936), administered by the Department of Labor, provides the same standards for work on Federal contracts as those which came generally to prevail under the FAIR LABOR STANDARDS ACT (1938). The purpose of the Act was to confine bidding on Federal projects to established concerns, and to prevent bids from employers whose labor policies were sub-standard.

WALTER, BRUNO (1876–1962), one of the world's foremost conductors, left Germany in 1939, and shortly thereafter became a U.S. citizen. He conducted music in every form, but he was pre-eminent in opera, symphony, and choral conducting. His readings were marked by their polish, carefully shaded nuances, and fidelity to the composer's intentions. For many years his Mozart interpretations were considered the criterion against which all others were measured. His supremacy as a conductor of Brahms, Mahler, and Bruckner was universally conceded.

WALTER, THOMAS USTICK (1804–87), Philadelphia architect, after training under WILLIAM STRICKLAND designed the main buildings of Girard College in Philadelphia (1833–47). It is the most complete example of Greek Revival style in the U.S., elaborate to the point that some historians of architecture believe that it helped end Greek Revival in the U.S. As government architect (1851–65), Walter added the wings and the cast iron dome to the national Capitol. His many other buildings, chiefly in the Greek Revival tradition, include the interior of the Library of Congress, the Patent Office, and the Treasury. In his day he was accorded rank at the head of his profession in the U.S.

'Waltham System,' see *Lowell, F. C.*

Wampanoag Indians, of Algonquian stock, in the early 17th century occupied villages along the Massachusetts coast. They were the first Indians encountered by the Pilgrims. Their great chief, MASSASOIT, was a friend of the English settlers, but the deadly conflict precipitated by his son, KING PHILIP (1675), not only decimated the New England settlements, but ruined the tribe, which by 1700 had virtually disappeared.

Wampum, beads made of small black or white shells, pierced and strung, was used by Indians as ceremonial pledges or as ornaments. In the early colonial period wampum served as a medium of barter between whites and Indians on the Atlantic and Pacific coasts, but rarely elsewhere.

WANAMAKER, JOHN (1838–1922), Philadelphia merchant and pioneer in the development of DEPARTMENT STORES, began his career as an errand boy. In 1868 he opened his own store, which grew rapidly and by 1876 had become spectacularly successful. Always an innovator, like his contemporary MARSHALL FIELD, Wanamaker strengthened the one-price system by guaranteeing refunds to dissatisfied customers, used publicity effectively, and gave his employees training and recreational facilities. In 1896 he acquired the New York City department store of ALEXANDER T. STEWART.

As an active Republican Wanamaker fought the Quay political machine and helped finance the presidential election of Benjamin Harrison. He was rewarded by appointment to the postmaster-generalship (1889–93) and applied to that office the same methods of efficiency that had proved successful in private business. He spearheaded the introduction of rural free delivery and campaigned for a parcel post and postal savings system, later adopted. In his private life he promoted Sunday School and temperance work.

War Between the States, see *Civil War.*

War crimes trials, following World War II, grew out of the determination of Allied leaders to bring German and Japanese war lords before the bar of justice on issues involving international law, humanity, and the laws of war. An International Military Tribunal (the U.S., Great Britain, France, and Russia) tried the principal Nazi offenders at Nuremberg, Germany (1945–46). The appointment of Supreme Court Justice ROBERT H. JACKSON as chief prosecutor for the U.S. was a measure of the importance attached to the trials. All the accused were tried individually on specific charges. Twenty-four Nazi leaders were condemned to death, 128 were given prison terms, and 35 were acquitted.

Comparable trials of Japanese leaders were held at Tokyo (1946–48). Seven Japanese war lords were hanged, including former premier Hideki Tojo, and sixteen were sent to prison.

The trials were criticized on the grounds that they were *ex post facto* proceedings and that their prosecutions were in no ordinary sense 'judicial.' Yet the attempt to brand aggressive warfare as a crime (as Jackson did, citing the KELLOGG-BRIAND PACT of 1928) was accepted by the United Nations, whose Declaration of Human Rights in effect endorsed the findings of the tribunals.

War Democrats were the Democrats in the North who supported the Union cause during the Civil War. Led by such statesmen as Stephen A. Douglas and Andrew Johnson, they opposed the 'Peace Democrats,' or COPPERHEADS, because they believed that the issue of maintaining the Union overshadowed all others in the war crisis.

War, Department of, was created by Congress (1789) as the Department of War and Navy, with a Secretary of cabinet rank. (The Department of the Navy was given separate status in 1798.) It was a continuation of the Board of War established by the Second Continental Congress (1776), but no permanent system of staff departments was created until 1816. Under Secretary Calhoun (1817–25) the system was carefully developed, and it underwent little basic change until a General Staff Corps to co-ordinate all branches of the service was instituted in 1903. The reorganization that took place after World War I gave the Department essentially the structure it has today, with an Under Secretary, a Director of Research, and three Assistant Secretaries: one for Financial Management; one for Logistics; and one for Man Power, Personnel, and Reserve Forces.

In 1947, as the DEPARTMENT OF THE ARMY, it was merged with the Departments of the Navy and the Air Force into the DEPARTMENT OF DEFENSE. The consolidation gave cabinet rank to the Secretary of Defense, and thenceforth removed from such rank the Secretaries of the Army and the Navy.

Secretaries of War and the Presidents under whom they served are as follows.

WASHINGTON

Henry Knox (Mass.) 1789
Timothy Pickering (Mass.) 1795
James McHenry (Md.) 1796

J. ADAMS

James McHenry (Md.) 1797
John Marshall (Va.) 1800
Samuel Dexter (Mass.) 1800
Roger Griswold (Conn.) 1801

JEFFERSON

Henry Dearborn (Conn.) 1801

MADISON

William Eustis (Mass.) 1809
John Armstrong (N.Y.) 1813
James Monroe (Va.) 1814
William H. Crawford (Ga.) 1815

MONROE

John C. Calhoun (S.C.) 1817

J. Q. ADAMS

James Barbour (Va.) 1825
Peter B. Porter (N.Y.) 1828

JACKSON

John H. Eaton (Tenn.) 1829
Lewis Cass (Ohio) 1831
Benjamin F. Butler (N.Y.) 1837

VAN BUREN

Joel R. Poinsett (S.C.) 1837

W. H. HARRISON

John Bell (Tenn.) 1841

TYLER

John Bell (Tenn.) 1841
John McLean (Ohio) 1841
John C. Spencer (N.Y.) 1841
James M. Porter (Pa.) 1843
William Wilkins (Pa.) 1844

POLK

William L. Marcy (N.Y.) 1845

TAYLOR

George W. Crawford (Ga.) 1849

FILLMORE

Charles M. Conrad (La.) 1850

PIERCE

Jefferson Davis (Miss.) 1853

BUCHANAN

John B. Floyd (Va.) 1857
Joseph Holt (Ky.) 1861

LINCOLN

Simon Cameron (Pa.) 1861
Edwin M. Stanton (Pa.) 1862

A. JOHNSON

Edwin M. Stanton (Pa.) 1865
Ulysses S. Grant (Ill.) 1867
Lorenzo Thomas (Del.) 1868 (interim)
John M. Schofield (Ill.) 1868

GRANT

John A. Rawlins (Ill.) 1869
William T. Sherman (Ohio) 1869
William W. Belknap (Iowa) 1869
Alphonso Taft (Ohio) 1876
J. Don Cameron (Pa.) 1876

HAYES

George W. McCrary (Iowa) 1877
Alexander Ramsey (Minn.) 1879

GARFIELD

Robert T. Lincoln (Ill.) 1881

ARTHUR

Robert T. Lincoln (Ill.) 1881

CLEVELAND

William C. Endicott (Mass.) 1885

B. HARRISON

Redfield Procter (Vt.) 1889
Stephen B. Elkins (W. Va.) 1891

CLEVELAND

Daniel S. Lamont (N.Y.) 1893

McKINLEY

Russel A. Alger (Mich.) 1897
Elihu Root (N.Y.) 1899

T. ROOSEVELT
Elihu Root (N.Y.) 1901
William H. Taft (Ohio) 1904
Luke E. Wright (Tenn.) 1908

TAFT
Jacob M. Dickinson (Tenn.) 1909
Henry L. Stimson (N.Y.) 1911

WILSON
Lindley M. Garrison (N.J.) 1913
Newton D. Baker (Ohio) 1916

HARDING
John W. Weeks (Mass.) 1921

COOLIDGE
John W. Weeks (Mass.) 1923
Dwight W. Davis (Mo.) 1925

HOOVER
James W. Good (Iowa) 1929
Patrick J. Hurley (Okla.) 1929

F. D. ROOSEVELT
George H. Dern (Utah) 1933
Harry H. Woodring (Kan.) 1936
Henry L. Stimson (N.Y.) 1940

TRUMAN
Robert P. Patterson (N.Y.) 1945
Kenneth C. Royall (N.C.) 1947

'War Hawks,' so called, were members of the Twelfth Congress (1811–13) from the West and South who campaigned for war with Great Britain. All were young and exuberant. The Westerners were eager to annex Canada; the Southerners, Florida and Texas. As spokesmen for their sections they expressed the expansionist tendencies of the day and sparked the drive that culminated in the War of 1812. Notable among their leaders were HENRY CLAY, JOHN C. CALHOUN, and THOMAS HART BENTON.

War Industries Board (1917) was established by Congress to co-ordinate the efforts of American production during World War I. Headed by BERNARD BARUCH, it mobilized resources, fixed prices, and allocated raw materials. It was abolished at the war's end.

War of 1812, allegedly fought for 'Free Trade and Sailors' Rights,' began when the U.S. declared war on Great Britain, 18 June 1812. It lasted two and a half years. It consisted of a series of engagements, waged chiefly along the American coastline and the Canadian border. It was never a popular war (until it was over), and when President Madison sent Congress a message recommending war with England because of its continued IMPRESSMENT of American seamen and its ORDERS IN COUNCIL, he found Congress, like the nation, sharply divided. The maritime states, knowing that their commerce would be ruined, were overwhelmingly for peace. But the inland and western states, with their expansionist sentiment, saw a chance to retaliate by a conquest of Canada and Florida. The vote favored war by close margins (79 to 49 in the House, 19 to 13 in the Senate), with one-quarter of the Republicans abstaining.

The issues stemmed from two sources. First were the maritime problems created by England and France who, in their life-and-death struggle (1803–15), paid scant heed to the rights of neutrals. Napoleon's decrees, which sought to exclude neutral ships from trade with Great Britain, had been answered by British countervailing prohibitions. The various NONINTERCOURSE ACTS, adopted by Congress as a means of pitting England and France against each other in a rivalry for America's commercial favors, proved diplomatically embarrassing and were ineffective as coercive instruments. The embroilment was clearly foreshadowed when the British foreign minister, George Canning, repudiated the ERSKINE AGREEMENT (1809), which would have postponed the issue of impressment. The second and equally important issue was the longstanding trouble over western lands, supposedly settled by the TREATY OF PARIS of 1783. This issue was made to appear a problem created by the British in Canada, who were allegedly instigating and equipping the hostile Indians. The frontier representatives in the Republican party, the WAR HAWKS, swung the vote for war.

Congress levied no war tax and made no provision to increase the navy. The regular army, less than 7000 men, in the course of time was augmented by some 400,000 state militia, few of whom were effectively deployed. The War Department, unprepared in both strategy and armament, was headed by William Eustis (1753–1825), an amiable politician whose inefficiency soon forced him from office. His successor, JOHN ARMSTRONG, resigned after the British burned the city of Washington. The senior army officer, Major General HENRY DEARBORN, was so unsound a strategist that within a year he was relieved of duty. The Canadians, on the other hand, fighting defensively against superior numbers, were led at the start by the 'hero of Upper Canada,' Isaac Brock (1769–1812), who was knighted for gallantry shortly before his death at Queenston Heights. Had England then been free to devote her main resources to war in America, her military superiority might easily have resulted in a national calamity.

The improvised plan of operations called for a three-pronged drive into Canada, but miscalculation and timidity thwarted success. General WILLIAM HULL, instead of advancing into Canada from Detroit, surrendered the fort with its large quantity of supplies to General Brock (16 August). On the Niagara front General STEPHEN VAN RENSSELAER could not persuade his troops to leave New York state, and thus he lost the battle of QUEENSTON HEIGHTS (13 October). General Dearborn, stationed at Plattsburg with the largest force of Americans under arms, headed north for Montreal (19 November), but before reaching the border his men completed the year's fiasco by compelling their leader to march them back to Plattsburg.

The military disasters were somewhat offset by the American seamen's skill and valor, never more brilliantly displayed than during this war. Before the year's end the frigate *Constitution,* Captain ISAAC HULL, had defeated *Guerrière* off Nova Scotia; *Wasp* had bested *Frolic* off the Virginia coast; and when the frigate *United States,* Captain STEPHEN DECATUR, subdued *Macedonian* off the Madeira Islands and brought her to New London as a prize, morale was raised. Actually the military value of these and later sea victories was slight, and the tightening British blockade of the American coastline forced American privateers to transfer their operation to European and Far Eastern waters.

In 1813 Detroit was recovered; Perry won the battle of LAKE ERIE, thereby forcing the British to fall back to a defensive line along the Niagara frontier; and General William Henry Harrison secured the Northwest frontier by his victory at the THAMES. But the year closed with the defeat of the Americans at CHRYSLER'S FARM, the signal failure of General JAMES WILKINSON to capitalize on Harrison's victory and move on Montreal, the defeat of Wade Hampton at CHATEAUGAY, and the capture by the British of Fort Niagara and the burning of Buffalo.

By the summer of 1814, under the competent leadership of Generals JACOB BROWN and WINFIELD SCOTT, the northern army developed a fighting spirit, demonstrated at CHIPPEWA and LUNDY'S LANE, where Americans showed their prowess but failed to win any territory. During that summer 16,000 British troops arrived in Canada to begin an invasion of the U.S. by way of Lake Champlain, but in September the American naval force under Thomas Macdonough won the battle of PLATTSBURG, forcing the British to abandon their campaign, a circumstance that improved the American position at the peace conference already under way.

Meanwhile the British blockade of the U.S. seaboard, begun in November 1812, had brought maritime trade to a virtual standstill, from Maine to Louisiana, both foreign and coastwise. The blockade was disastrous to private business. Government revenues were sharply curtailed, and economic ruin was averted only by the ending of the war. (In New England the Federalist loathing of 'Mr. Madison's war' led to the resolutions passed at the HARTFORD CONVENTION that doomed the Federalist party by attaching to it the stigma of unpatriotism.) Throughout the summer of 1814 the British navy moved at will, establishing one expeditionary force on the tip of Cape Cod and a second on the shores of Chesapeake Bay. After the Americans lost the battle of BLADENSBURG in Maryland, the British proceeded to Washington, where they burned most of the public buildings, including the Capitol and the White House, and then moved on to Baltimore. There the naval bombardment of Fort McHenry proved a failure (thus inspiring Francis Scott Key to write 'The Star Spangled Banner'), and the attacking forces withdrew to their transports. When a third British force reached New Orleans in December 1814, it was decisively repulsed by Andrew Jackson in the battle of NEW ORLEANS. This was the only major American land victory of the war, and, ironically, it was won (8 January 1815) two weeks after the peace terms had been signed.

Although the war was a failure, since it settled nothing and affairs returned to a *status quo ante bellum,* in a larger sense it might be considered both justified and necessary. The legal provocation had been beyond dispute. Psychologically, failure to assert the independence officially recognized after the Revolution would have bred contempt in European chancelleries, and the new nation could well have disintegrated into factions or have returned to a quasi-colonial status. The war in fact marked the end of two centuries of involvement in the affairs of the Old World. The TREATY OF GHENT (1814), superbly conducted by the American emissaries, ended the war and made the nation truly independent.

See F. F. Beirne, *The War of 1812* (1949) and Reginald Horsman, *The Causes of the War of 1812* (1962).

War of Independence (1775–83), by which the Thirteen Colonies in America broke their tie with Great Britain, was unlike later world-shaking revolutions, such as those in France and Russia, in that it was a movement for national independence. It was unique in world history in that it was led by conservative philosopher-statesmen who directed events from a working democracy already well established under a code of laws. It was a revolt of colonies against imperialism, but it bears only superficial resemblance to 20th-century movements in Asia and Africa against European rule. It was in fact a civil war within an empire bound together by common institutions and a common language, a transition from 'colonial subservience' that was more evolutionary than revolutionary.

Until George III ascended the throne (1760), political issues had not created friction between Britain and the American colonies in any major way. For decades the colonies had been allowed a degree of freedom unequaled anywhere, and thus they had created local political institutions with deep roots. The 'arbitrary domination' of the new king was only incidentally the 'tyranny' described in the Declaration of Independence. The struggle with the mother country began as an effort to *restore* old rights, liberties, and privileges, at a moment when a well-meaning though somewhat obtuse monarch was able to place his own party henchmen in office. Actually the king had neither the desire nor the power to be a tyrant.

The seeds of revolution were sown when the king sought to govern through a political party created at a moment when statesmanship was depreciated by confusion and apathy. Britain seemed to have solved her IMPERIAL PROBLEMS by the exclusion of France from the American continent by the TREATY OF PARIS of 1763. The well-intentioned but short-sighted ministry of GEORGE GRENVILLE (1763–65), by securing passage of the SUGAR ACT (1764) and the STAMP ACT (1765), mobilized a surprisingly violent opposition among American merchants, businessmen, journalists, clergymen, and, especially, lawyers, who kept the constitutional issue in the forefront. The coalition ministry of Rockingham (1765–66), and that of Chatham and Grafton (1766–70), attempted conciliatory measures, but the subservient Lord North, who succeeded to power in 1770 and held office for twelve years, by inviting the king's boroughmongers into the Cabinet gave George III a Pyrrhic victory — and lost the war.

The legislation that Parliament began to enact united the colonies in protest. The PROCLAMATION OF 1763 had placed Indian trade under royal control, and the consequent ban against settlements west of the Alleghenies, though motivated by good intentions, was both galling and unrealistic. Passage of the Sugar Act (1764) and the Stamp Act (1765) had seemed a highhanded method of coercion, although at the time the colonists had no thought of revolution.

The DECLARATORY ACT (1766) gave Parliament the authority to annul colonial legislation, but it was the TOWNSHEND ACTS (1767) that made the constitutional issues acute. The ominous QUARTERING ACT of 1765 touched off the so-called BOSTON MASSACRE (1770), and when, by 1772, the colonies found themselves unable to secure redress of grievances through petitions to the king, they began their patriot union through COMMITTEES OF CORRESPONDENCE. The BOSTON TEA PARTY (1774) evoked the punitive

COERCIVE ACTS and led to the assembly of the first Continental Congress, which framed a 'declaration of rights and grievances.' In the same year by the QUEBEC ACT Parliament gave Canada the whole western region, which would thus legally become French in law and language, and Roman Catholic in religion. For many colonists the trend was intolerable. Historians today point out that the king and his ministers were unable to perceive that a new society had been formed in the American colonies, which were fully capable of self-government and for decades had been given an unprecedented degree of liberty, now in serious jeopardy. At stake were constitutional rights. Americans by this time were convinced that their liberties were no longer safe within the British Empire. In February 1775 Parliament rejected Chatham's plan of conciliation, and in April the first blood in the War of Independence was shed in the battle of LEXINGTON AND CONCORD.

It is still a matter of wonder that the Americans, who seldom won a battle, won the war. At the start they had no navy. Washington had to recruit an army of raw militiamen, short-term Continentals, and farmers and tradesmen, who served as officers and enlisted men, often with slight distinction between them. This aggregation was pitted against larger contingents of disciplined regulars led by such experienced generals as CARLETON, HOWE, CLINTON, BURGOYNE, and CORNWALLIS. The rolls indicate that nearly 400,000 Americans served during the seven years of war, but Washington never had more than 21,000 men under his command at any one time, often much fewer. In retrospect he observed that his army was 'composed of Men sometimes half starved; always in Rags, without pay, and experiencing, at times, every species of distress which human nature is capable of undergoing.' And this conflict took place in a region where a third of the population remained LOYALISTS, of whom as many served in the British army as fought at any one time under Washington.

But on the other side of the ledger was the indomitable will of Washington, who at no moment wavered in his determination to resist, and who displayed genius in keeping his army from disintegration and destruction. The patriots were also greatly helped by such foreign officers as LAFAYETTE, STEUBEN, KOSCIUSZKO, and PULASKI. They were favored too by campaigning on native ground, by their lifelong acquaintance with firearms (and the American rifle was superior to the British smoothbore musket in range and accuracy), and by the number of fighters who had gained their experience in earlier frontier wars. They were further aided by the immense distance of the British command from its chief source of supply, and by the vast and varied terrain with which European soldiers were unfamiliar. The British delay in mobilizing the Loyalists as an effective force was a factor in their defeat, but chiefly their military and political leaders underestimated the American will to resist.

The Second Continental Congress assembled in May 1775 and established a government under authority of the people of the colonies. It made provision for raising an army and appointed Washington commander in chief. After the battle of BUNKER HILL (17 June) Washington arrived in Cambridge, where on 3 July he took formal command of an army of 14,500 and began the siege of Boston. That lasted until March 1776, when Sir William Howe evacuated the town and transferred the British headquarters to New York. The invasion of CANADA, attempted at that time, was a failure, but it diverted British troops and set the stage for the decisive SARATOGA CAMPAIGN in the following summer. Meanwhile, public opinion, inflamed by events and stirred by Thomas Paine's *Common Sense,* began to crystallize in favor of independence. In June Congress appointed a committee to draft the Declaration of Independence, adopted on 4 July 1776.

Financing the war was a most difficult problem. The CONTINENTAL CURRENCY that the Congress authorized was supplemented by direct requisitions upon the states for commodities, and by domestic loans, lotteries, and prize money received from the sale of captured enemy ships. (Throughout the war the states refused to levy taxes.) The foreign loans later procured from France, Spain, and Holland through the representations made by Franklin and John Adams proved invaluable. When Robert Morris was appointed to the new office of Superintendent of Finance (1781), he introduced proper fiscal administration.

Sea power, the decisive factor in winning the war, could not challenge British sea supremacy until the capital ships of the French navy came into service (after 1780). Until then the Americans improvised naval forces of single ships or small squadrons under the command of such men as ESEK HOPKINS, JOHN PAUL JONES, JOHN BARRY, and JOSHUA BARNEY. In 1777, 34 Continental vessels were in commission, and hundreds of privateers made the British sea routes hazardous, seizing ships as prizes, and obtaining valuable goods for the army and the people. The delaying action of Benedict Arnold on Lake Champlain in October 1776 had some strategic value, but until late in the war most of the action took place on land. Washington had followed Howe to New York, but after the disastrous battle of LONG ISLAND (August 1776) Washington was compelled to retreat, first to Harlem Heights, then across New Jersey into Pennsylvania. At the year's end he raised the patriot morale with his successes at TRENTON (26 December) and at PRINCETON (3 January 1777).

The British plan to divide the states along the line of the Hudson was put into operation when Burgoyne initiated the SARATOGA CAMPAIGN (June–October 1777), proceeding south from Canada. His defeat proved the turning point of the war, since it stirred France to action in support of the colonies. (In December Congress authorized Silas Deane to recruit FOREIGN OFFICERS in Paris, and their aid was important.) Meanwhile Howe attacked Philadelphia, and after defeating Washington at BRANDYWINE (11 September) the British occupied the city. Washington, again overwhelmed at GERMANTOWN (4 October), settled into winter quarters at VALLEY FORGE. Following adoption of the ARTICLES OF CONFEDERATION in November, Congress signed a treaty of alliance with France (February 1778).

Lord North then presented Parliament with his plan for conciliating the Americans, and sent a commission to negotiate with Congress, but with the French alliance an assured fact, only independence would satisfy a determined people. In June Sir Henry Clinton evacuated Philadelphia; he reached New York after his encounter at MONMOUTH with Washington, who took up a position north of Clinton. When the French fleet arrived in July, Washington planned a co-ordinated land and sea attack on the British at Newport, Rhode Island, but a storm prevented an engagement of the French and British fleets, and the siege of Newport was abandoned. But on the western frontier George Rogers Clark completed the conquest of the Old Northwest (February 1779), and by June Spain came in for the kill, hoping to recover Gibraltar and the Floridas.

At this late moment the British under Cornwallis began to draw effectively on Loyalist support. The Loyalists were strongest in the South, and they concentrated their efforts in Georgia and the Carolinas. Savannah had capitulated in 1778, and after the surrender of Charleston (May 1780) the British began the CAROLINA CAMPAIGN. Washington then saw his chance to launch the YORKTOWN CAMPAIGN, a brilliantly coordinated land and sea operation (with the French) that bottled up Cornwallis.

By that time Great Britain was sick of the war, which had proved to be the most expensive military undertaking in British history. Parliament repudiated the coercive policy of the North ministry, and the new Rockingham government (March 1782) was given a mandate to make peace. The definitive TREATY OF PARIS of 1783 officially recognized American independence.

See G. W. Allen, *A Naval History of the American Revolution* (1913); R. A. East, *Business Enterprise in the American Revolutionary Era* (1938); and S. F. Bemis, *The Diplomacy of the American Revolution* (1935).

War of the Rebellion, see *Civil War.*

WARD, ARTEMAS (1727–1800), Massachusetts politician and soldier, fought in the last French and Indian War (1755–63). Congress commissioned him a major general when the Continental army was formed, and he was chief commander at the siege of Boston (1775) until Washington arrived. After the British evacuation (1776) he resigned from the service. He later served in the Continental Congress (1780–81) and the U.S. Congress (1791–95).

WARD, John Quincy Adams (1830–1910), Ohio-born sculptor, trained in New York under H. K. Brown, introduced a vigorous realism into a tradition suffering from a vapid Italianate classicism. His virile craftsmanship, inspired by American themes, is reflected in his early *Indian Hunter* (1864) in Central Park. Ward gained a fluency in the handling of mass; he is best represented by such later characterizations as the equestrian statues of General Thomas and General Sherman in Washington, D.C.; *Lafayette,* in Burlington, Vermont; and *Washington,* on the steps of the New York Subtreasury building.

WARD, Lester Frank (1841–1913), a founder of modern sociology, served in the Union army, worked in the U.S. Treasury Department (1865–81), and took degrees in medicine and law (1869 and 1871) at Columbian College (now George Washington University). Though for some years he was a government geologist and paleontologist (1881–1906), his important work was done in the field of human relationships. His *Dynamic Sociology* (1883), which initiated evolutionary sociology, was followed by *Outlines in Sociology* (1898), *Pure Sociology* (1903), and *Glimpses of the Universe* (6 vols., 1913–18), a collection of his writings that he called his 'mental autobiography.'

After 1906 Ward occupied a chair in sociology at Brown. He was profoundly influenced by the doctrine of evolution, which he interpreted as a cosmic force by which the mind itself can be a determining power, not as a blind mechanistic process. Therefore he urged a systematic application of economic and social planning. The government agencies set up during the 1930's were precisely the democratic and humanitarian procedures that Ward envisioned, since they created a community responsibility for individual well being and reversed the trend toward laissez faire which had been the traditional American way, as advocated by such evolutionary determinists as WILLIAM GRAHAM SUMNER.

WARD, Nathaniel (1578–1652), after graduation from Emmanuel College, Cambridge (1600), studied and practiced law in London, and traveled on the Continent. A member of a distinguished Puritan family, he became a convert and preacher, and he was suspended and imprisoned for two years by Archbishop Laud (who always held him in respect). At the age of fifty-five he emigrated (1634) to Massachusetts, serving as minister of Ipswich (Agawam) until 1636, when he resigned his frontier pastorate.

He compiled the notable MASSACHUSETTS BODY OF LIBERTIES (1641), a check upon the arbitrary government of John Winthrop, and he led the struggle of democracy against theocracy in an effort to secure for the people a government of laws and not of men. His witty and urbane pamphlet *The Simple Cobler of Aggawam* (1647) championed political tolerance to the extent of defending Charles I. It was published a year after Ward returned to England, where he was invited to preach before the House of Commons. But the House disapproved the quips of a lawyer and preacher who saw virtues on both sides of burning issues, and thereafter Ward lived in quiet retirement.

WARE, Henry (1764–1845), a graduate of Harvard (1785), as pastor of the First Church, Hingham, Massachusetts (1787–1805), became known for his liberal (unitarian) inclinations, and when he was chosen as the first nonorthodox theologian to occupy the Hollis chair of divinity at Harvard (1805–40), he precipitated a crisis that hastened the separation of the Unitarians from the Congregationalists. He went on to establish the college's Divinity School (1819), and with W. E. CHANNING is recognized as the founder in the U.S. of Unitarianism as a denomination.

His son, Henry Ware (1794–1843), pastor of the second Unitarian Church, Boston (1817–30), was likewise a professor in the Harvard Divinity School (until 1842), and editor of the *Christian Disciple* (1819–22), the first organ of Unitarianism.

Another son, William Ware (1797–1862), became pastor of the first Unitarian Church in New York (1821–36), and wrote a popular fictional trilogy on the struggle of early Christian churches against the authoritarianism of their day.

Warehouse Act, see *Farm Legislation.*

WARFIELD, David (1866–1951), began his successful career as an actor under David Belasco in 1900, and achieved fame in his favorite role of the title part in *The Return of Peter Grimm* (1911). His last stage venture was as Shylock in *The Merchant of Venice* (1924).

WARNER, Olin Levi (1844–96), Connecticut-born sculptor, after study in Paris executed works in marble and bronze which have given him rank as a portrait and decorative artist. His *Garrison* (Boston) and *Diana* (Metropolitan Museum) convey his sensitivity to plastic form, as do his handsome bronze doors for the Library of Congress.

WARNER, 'Pop' [Glen Scobey] (1871–1954), a graduate of Cornell (1894), gained nationwide repute as a football coach. At Carlisle Indian School (1899–1903, 1907–14) he developed several outstanding players, including JIM THORPE. Three of the teams which he coached at Pittsburgh (1915–23) held undefeated records, and at Stanford (1924–32) he produced three Rose Bowl teams.

WARNER, Seth (1743–84), a leader of the GREEN MOUNTAIN BOYS at the outbreak of the American Revolution, after capturing Crown Point (May 1775) took part in the invasion of CANADA, and shared command with John Stark in the battle of BENNINGTON. Commissioned a brigadier general in 1778, he continued to serve as one of the popular local heroes of the war.

WARNER, W. Lloyd (1898–   ), professor of anthropology and sociology at Chicago (1935–59) and of social research at Michigan State (after 1959), was the principal scholarly investigator of class distinctions in 20th-century America. He enunciated the physiological doctrine of homeostasis, the tendency of an organism by means of its own regulatory mechanism to maintain within itself relatively stable conditions. His concepts of Yankee City (Newburyport, Massachusetts) and himself are thinly veiled in J. P. Marquand, *Point of No Return*. His writings include (with collaborators) *Color and Human Nature* (1941), 'Yankee City Series,' (4 vols., 1941–47), and *Social Class in America* (1949).

Warning out was a practice in colonial New England intended to protect the town from legal responsibility for the support of a newcomer in the event he proved unable to support himself. Selectmen gave the constable a warrant to be served, simply as a warning, in an attempt to keep relief rolls down.

WARREN, Charles (1868–1954), Boston lawyer, was a leading authority in the field of constitutional history. He lectured widely in law schools throughout the country, served on arbitral tribunals, and became assistant attorney general of the U.S. His writings include *History of the American Bar . . . to 1860* (1911), *The Supreme Court in U.S. History* (2 vols., rev. ed., 1937), and *Congress, the Constitution, and the Supreme Court* (1935).

WARREN, Earl (1891–   ), served as attorney general of California (1939–42), was Thomas Dewey's running mate in 1948, and thrice governor of California (1942–53), from which office President Eisenhower appointed him successor to Fred M. Vinson as Chief Justice of the U.S. Supreme Court. Warren was instrumental in securing the unanimous court ruling on *Brown* v. *Board of Education* (1954) that segregation in the schools was unconstitutional under the Fourteenth Amendment because 'separate and equal' schools were not equal. At the time of Kennedy's assassination, President L. B. Johnson appointed Warren to head a seven-man commission of investigation which established the sole responsibility of Lee Harvey Oswald for the killing. The Commission went far to refute rumors of plots by communist agents or right wing organizations.

WARREN, John (1753–1815), brother of JOSEPH WARREN, after graduation from Harvard (1771) became the leading medical practitioner in New England. He served as surgeon in the War of Independence, was appointed professor of anatomy and surgery at Harvard (1782), and founded the Harvard Medical School (1783).

His son, John Collins Warren (1778–1856), graduated from Harvard in 1797, and served as professor in the Medical School for nearly 40 years (1809–47). He was a founder of Massachusetts General Hospital (1811), and the first surgeon to operate on strangulated hernia. Upon his invitation in 1846 W. T. G. MORTON made the first public demonstration of ether used as anesthetic.

WARREN, JOSEPH (1741–75), elder brother of JOHN WARREN, after graduation from Harvard (1759) practiced medicine in Boston, where with Samuel Adams he took a prominent part in supporting the patriot cause on the eve of the War of Independence. Having drafted the SUFFOLK RESOLVES, he served as president *pro tempore* of the provincial Congress. He was commissioned a major general of militia at the outbreak of the war and was killed at Bunker Hill. Next to the Adamses, Warren was the most influential leader of the radical faction, and his death spurred zeal for the patriot cause.

WARREN, JOSIAH (1798–1874), early American anarchist, began as a follower of ROBERT OWEN, but soon rejected Owen's political socialism to advocate 'the sovereignty of the individual.' He devised a system of 'equity stores' and 'labor notes,' inspired by the Owenite labor bazaars, based on the idea of exchanging goods for labor and adhering to the principle that cost should be the limit of price. His *True Civilization* (1863) at the time of his death had gone into its fifth edition.

WARREN, MERCY OTIS (1728–1814), sister of James Otis, wife of James Warren, and herself in the center of Revolutionary politics, used her gift of satire to write propaganda poems and political dramas (probably never performed) for the American cause. Her *History of the . . . American Revolution* (3 vols., 1805), the earliest written by an American, is lively and astute, but it is colored by anti-Federalist personal criticism, particularly of her old friend John Adams, who for a time bitterly resented it. As history it typifies the patriotic spirit of the day.

WASHAKIE (*c.* 1804–1900), one of the notable Indian personalities in American history, for 60 years was chief of the Shoshone. In the Indian wars of the 1870's he was an ally of the U.S. in fighting the Blackfoot, Cheyenne, and Sioux, and was accorded high respect by the U.S. Army, in which he later held a commission. He was given a military funeral, and the inscription on his tomb at Fort Washakie bears the inscription: 'Always loyal to the Government and to his white brothers.'

WASHINGTON, BOOKER TALIAFERRO (1856–1915), son of a Negro slave and a white father, graduated from Hampton Institute (1875) and taught there until he was chosen to organize (1881) TUSKEGEE INSTITUTE, which he thereafter served as principal. In his controversial Atlanta Exposition address (1895) he formulated the ideas of racial conservatism, frankly accepting segregation. 'The opportunity to earn a dollar in a factory just now is worth infinitely more than the opportunity to spend a dollar in an opera house.' He felt that segregation was a temporary tactic and believed that if the Negro would make himself economically indispensable and concentrate upon learning the crafts, acquiring homeownership, and entering business whenever profitable, then social equality would follow.

His policies won him extraordinary gifts from philanthropists, and even southern legislative grants for Negro schools, and he became the spokesman for his race before Presidents as well as the great industrialists. Younger Negroes, especially the intellectuals like W. E. B. DU BOIS, while agreeing with Washington upon the need for vocational education for the Negro masses (for which Tuskegee was a symbolic center), attacked his neglect of higher education for the 'Talented Tenth,' and his unwillingness to embark upon any program of agitation for civil rights. His numerous books include a classic autobiography, *Up from Slavery* (1901), and *The Story of the Negro* (1909).

WASHINGTON, GEORGE (1732–99), 1st President of the U.S. (1789–97), was born on 22 February, the first son of Augustine Washington and his second wife, Mary Ball, on the family estate 'Wakefield,' in Westmoreland county, Virginia. The family of this moderately well-to-do planter was large; he had ten children, four by his first marriage, six by his second. George idolized his eldest half brother, Lawrence, whom he first came to know when Lawrence returned from his education in England (1738), and who acted as a second father to the boy when Augustine died in 1743. The marriage of Lawrence that year to a daughter of Colonel William Fairfax allied the Washingtons to one of the most powerful families of Virginia, a connection which shaped the career of George, who at seventeen was invited to help survey Fairfax property west of the Blue Ridge. The long journey gave the youth, six feet tall, sturdy, and immensely vital, a contact with the frontier and an enduring interest in western lands.

After Lawrence died (1752), George inherited a part of Lawrence's Mount Vernon estate, and as a young major in 1753 was sent by Virginia's governor, Robert Dinwiddie, in the interest of the OHIO COMPANY into the western frontier to warn the French not to encroach on English claims. The dispute continued, and as a lieutenant colonel Washington was sent (1754) with a detachment to protect the workmen building a fort at the forks of the Ohio, but Fort Duquesne had been captured before he arrived. At Great Meadows (near Pittsburgh) Washington built the entrenched camp, Fort Necessity, and ordered the first shots in a skirmish which killed ten Frenchmen and won him a colonelcy. The encounter also created an international incident, since, by touching off the French and Indian War (1755–63), it led to the great world war (the Seven Years' War) that ensued. The French avenged Washington's first military victory by capturing the fort. 'Soundly beaten,' as he reported, Washington returned to Virginia. In 1755 as an aide to General Edward Braddock he participated in the disastrous expedition against Fort Duquesne, after which debacle he was given command of the Virginia militia to defend the colony's western frontier. Three years later he led one of the three brigades which succeeded in reducing Duquesne (thereafter named Fort Pitt). Thus ended his pre-Revolutionary military career.

In 1759 Washington married a wealthy young widow, Martha Dandridge Custis (1732–1802), settled down with his bride and her children as a country squire on the Mount Vernon estate, and served in the House of Burgesses (1759–74). As a tobacco planter Washington experienced at first hand the damage that the British policy of the 1760's was doing to the economy of Virginia. Crops brought poor prices in England, and imports were becoming excessively expensive. Even worse, the Royal Proclamation of 1763 discouraged settlement in the trans-Appalachian West, a situation which Washington viewed with deep concern, for his large investments in western land had been made while he was acting as agent and adviser to veterans who had served under his command. This conservative aristocrat, amiable and prudent, was at the same time sensitive, deeply emotional, and obstinate, and he became one of the first to protest British colonial policy. He refused to buy British-taxed articles, and gave the boycott his wholehearted support. To him the Stamp Act (1765) was legal thievery.

As a leader in Virginia's opposition to British measures, Washington served (1774–75) as a delegate to the Continental Congress, and after the outbreak of hostilities at Lexington (April 1775) he attended sessions in the buff and blue outfit of the Fairfax militia, the only delegate in uniform. He thus announced his readiness for action, and neither he nor Congress doubted his ability for leadership. On 15 June 1775 he was named commander in chief of Continental forces.

On 3 July at Cambridge, Massachusetts, Washington assumed command, not of an army, but of raw, short-term militiamen, led by officers equally untrained, who had to face British regulars. Washington's soldiers gained their training during the long siege of Boston (July–March 1775–76), which General Howe finally evacuated, concentrating a large British land and sea force in New York. Washington followed, but his faulty planning of the near-fatal battle of LONG ISLAND (August 1776), which could have ended the war, was redeemed only by a masterly retreat, continued into New Jersey and Pennsylvania. Colonial morale, then at its lowest ebb, was somewhat raised when Washington crossed the Delaware on Christmas night, 1776, defeated a British garrison at Trenton, and pushed on to surround a second outpost at Princeton. Following the successive defeats in the autumn of 1777 at Brandywine and Germantown, after which Philadelphia was occupied by the British, the so-called CONWAY CABAL sought to replace Washington with Horatio Gates, but the public overwhelmingly supported Washington, and the incident passed.

Washington then went into winter quarters at VALLEY FORGE, where his moral fortitude surmounted problems of misery and want seldom equaled in military history. Late in the spring of 1778 he emerged with a striking force superbly trained and personally devoted to him. The battle of Monmouth (June 1778) closed Washington's active campaigning until the end of the war, which during 1779 was fought principally in the Old Northwest and in the South. Washington directed strategy elsewhere while devoting himself to watching Sir Henry Clinton in and about New York, and keeping open the channels to New England. The fortunes of war markedly favored the patriot cause with the arrival (1780) of French military and naval aid, and Washington's brilliant strategy during the YORKTOWN CAMPAIGN, which brought hostilities to an end (1781), concluded his active military career. He had carried immense burdens from the beginning, and by his patient tenacity, with flashes of impulsive daring, had already acquired a prestige greater than that of the U.S., for his canonization had begun. He was then the indispensable symbol of selfless patriotism and integrity, indeed, the father of his country. He resigned from the army (1783) and retired to Mount Vernon, but his position in American public life was unique to the point that any opinion of Washington on political issues took on the quality of incantation. Inevitably he presided at the Federal Constitutional Convention (1787), where his influence was probably decisive in the adoption of the Constitution. In 1789 the unanimous vote of the electors made him the first President.

To the end that his official family should represent different political factions he balanced Thomas Jefferson (State) and Edmund Randolph (Attorney General) against Alexander Hamilton (Treasury) and Henry Knox (War), and he himself gave official intercourse a degree of dignity and poise that amounted to aloofness. To fulfill his obligation as chosen representative of the new federation, he made two official tours through the country, once into the North, and once into the South. Since he himself tried to remain above partisanship, he sought to balance factions against each other and thus neutralize the effects of parties. He probably never fully understood the inevitable necessity of party government in democracies, and the conservative drift of his mind was toward the Federalists. Before the end of his first term he reluctantly accepted the cabinet resignation of Jefferson, who strongly opposed the economic policies of Hamilton. Washington consistently supported Hamilton. (Hamilton and the President were alike in their practical sagacity and aggressive courage.) Washington therefore roused the anger of lesser partisan Republicans, who hinted that his suppression of the Whisky Rebellion was the beginning of a military despotism; that Jay's Treaty, in which Washington acquiesced, was a stinging diplomatic victory for Britain; and that the President's firmness in thwarting the activities of the French minister, Citizen GÊNÊT, was insulting to France. With brutal virulence they attacked the 'stepfather of his country.' Indeed, unprincipled newspaper assaults drove this hot-blooded leader to impassioned comment at cabinet meetings, and embittered his second term as President.

By this time Washington had given his country more than 22 years of almost continuous service at the helm in war and peace. He was sixty-four years old, and tired, and though his election for a third term in 1796 would doubtless have been unanimous, he craved rest and retirement to his beloved Mount Vernon. There for the two remaining years of his life he enjoyed the society of his family (he adopted two of his wife's grandchildren), received the visitors who flocked to the broad acres above the Potomac, and kept up his wide-ranging correspondence. His sudden death from a pulmonary disorder followed exposure during a long ride in a snowstorm, and his illness was very brief.

The phrase 'essential greatness' applies to Washington. Under his firm leadership sister colonies had united to win independence after six years of war, and he inaugurated the traditions and powers of the presidential office. His apotheosis is the more remarkable in that it began during the so-called Age of Reason. England paid him honor. In France, Bonaparte ordered a week of mourning, and his 'Farewell Address' girdled the globe. Oratory, journalism, art, and fiction continue to create a marble figure of an extraordinarily human person, who had the unique opportunity to preside among other great statesmen to form a government of laws, not of men.

J. C. Fitzpatrick edited Washington's *Writings* (39 vols., 1931–44). Recent biographies include those by Bernhard Knollenberg (1940), N. W. Stephenson and W. H. Dunn (2 vols., 1940), and Douglas C. Freeman (6 vols., 1948–54). The first volume of a projected three-volume biography is that by James T. Flexner (1965).

Washington, northernmost state in the PACIFIC WEST, was originally part of Oregon Territory (1848) and shares with OREGON the early history of northwest explorations. During the 1840's several missions were established within its present boundaries, but the massacre of MARCUS WHITMAN and members of his post near Walla Walla in 1847 prefaced Indian wars that delayed settlement. In 1853 it was organized as a separate territory with Olympia as capital, and in 1889 it was admitted to the Union as the 42nd state. Thereafter, with rail communications established, population enormously increased, especially along Puget Sound, soon a great commercial center and gateway to Alaska and the Far East.

Lumbering, shipbuilding, and fisheries brought early prosperity to Olympia, Everett, Tacoma, and especially to SEATTLE, which by 1910 had become a major city. Spokane is the center of an 'Inland Empire,' a vast area on the Columbia Plateau, which with its irrigated lands and diversified farming is one of the great crop producing regions of the nation. During World War II the government built a plutonium plant at Hanford, on the banks of the COLUMBIA river, which with its system of hydroelectric installations has supplied limitless industrial power to the state.

The topography of Washington is boldly featured. The lofty CASCADE RANGE (with Mount Rainier rising 14,410 ft.) divides the state into a western and eastern section. The moisture of the warm ocean air from the Japanese Current is precipitated in the west. (The eastern area of the Columbia Plateau was semiarid before irrigation made it productive.) Two national parks abound in wildlife and preserve dense forests: Mount Rainier (1899) with its glaciers, and Olympic (1938), which has the greatest rainfall in the U.S. Chief among institutions of higher learning are the University of Washington (Seattle, est. 1861), and State College of Washington (Pullman, est. 1892).

Washington and Lee University, at Lexington, Virginia, is a liberal arts college for men. It was opened (1749) by Presbyterians as Augusta Academy, later called Liberty Hall Academy and (following a gift from George Washington) Washington Academy. It became Washington College in 1813. Robert E. Lee served as its president after the Civil War (1865–70), and since 1871 it has been Washington and Lee University. In 1965, with an endowment of $11,300,-000, and a faculty of 120, it enrolled 1300 students.

Washington Conference (1921–22), attended by representatives of Great Britain, France, Italy, Japan, the U.S., China, the Netherlands, Portugal, and Belgium, was designed both to reduce naval armaments and to avoid conflict in the Far East. Secretary of State Hughes, as chairman, outlined a program, accepted by the other naval powers, intended to prevent a naval race. The U.S. agreed to scrap fifteen new capital ships, Great Britain accepted parity, and both the U.S. and Great Britain agreed not to strengthen fortifications between Singapore and Hawaii to induce Japan to accept the formula. The proportion of capital ships was fixed at a ratio of 5 (U.S.), 5 (Britain), 3 (Japan), 1.6 (France), 1.6 (Italy). The treaties provided for a ten-year naval holiday, during which no capital ships would be built.

The Far East problem involved the territorial integrity and political sovereignty of China, impaired after World War I by Japanese aggression. The nine treaties, reiterating the OPEN DOOR principle in China, were signed by all participants. The U.S. Senate ratified all the treaties, and for a decade peace was preserved in the Pacific.

Washington, District of Columbia, is situated on the Potomac river 40 miles southwest of Baltimore. It has been the permanent seat of the U.S. government since 1800, and it was the first national capital in the world planned and built expressly for the purpose. The District, a tract of 70 square miles coterminous with the city, was established by acts of Congress (1790–91) on land selected by George Washington, and ceded by Maryland and Virginia. The present territorial government (given final shape in 1878) is an executive board of three commissioners appointed by the President and acting for Congress. The inhabitants have no voice in their local government, and no representation in Congress. Since the adoption of the Twenty-third Amendment (1961), they may vote for President and Vice President.

This 'Federal City' was designed by PIERRE L'ENFANT and laid out by the surveyor Andrew Ellicott (1754–1820). Construction of the WHITE HOUSE began in 1792, and of the CAPITOL a year later. Jefferson was the first President to be inaugurated in Washington. When it was captured by the British in 1814, it was sacked and most of the public buildings were burned, including the White House and the Capitol. Strongly manned during the Civil War, it was often threatened by Confederate forces but never captured. Something of a mudhole and largely an unkempt village before 1870, by the end of the 19th century the city was developed according to L'Enfant's plan (previously ignored). It is a gridiron arrangement of streets cut by diagonal avenues radiating from the Capitol and the White House, with systems of parks and open spaces at frequent intervals.

The seat of all departments of the federal government (and with a population in 1960 of 763,000), Washington has become the site of notable museums, monuments, and national memorials. It is the headquarters of many learned societies. Among its educational institutions are the Library of Congress, the Smithsonian Institution, the Folger Library, and five universities: Georgetown (est. 1791), George Washington (est. 1821), Howard (est. 1867), Catholic (est. 1887), and American (est. 1893).

Washington National Monument, designed by the architect ROBERT MILLS, is a hollow marble obelisk, 555 ft. high (55 ft. square at the base), situated in Washington, D.C. The cornerstone was laid in 1848, and after long delays the monument was completed in 1884 at a cost of $1,300,000, and dedicated in 1885. Set into the interior walls are 189 memorial stones from states, cities, organizations, and foreign countries.

Washington Square Players, see *Little Theater movement.*

Washington, Treaty of (1871), was a covenant between the U.S. and Great Britain providing for submission to arbitration of boundary disputes, the fisheries question, and the ALABAMA CLAIMS rising from the building and supplying of Confederate raiders by British subjects during the Civil War. Carried forward by Secretary of State HAMILTON FISH, it was one of the few notable achievements of the Grant administration, and liquidated all outstanding diplomatic controversies between the two countries. It was distinguished by two unprecedented features: an expression of regret by Great Britain for the escape of the *Alabama* from British waters, and an agreement upon rules of neutrality to govern the arbitral tribunal scheduled for the following year.

Watauga Settlement, the first permanent settlement in Tennessee (1769), developed from the westward migration of Virginia and North Carolina frontiersmen to the Watauga river. By 1772 the groups had become sufficiently numerous to prompt formation of a local government known as the Watauga Association, important as the nucleus of subsequent Tennessee and Kentucky settlements. At the outbreak of the Revolution these hardy pioneers formed a western bulwark against the British and their Indian allies.

'Watchful waiting' described the policy of President Jackson in refusing to take diplomatic action in 1836 on the question of Texan independence. In 1913 President Wilson used the phrase to describe his policy with respect to Mexico at the beginning of the Huerta regime.

WATERHOUSE, Benjamin (1754–1846), Boston physician, after study at Edinburgh and Leyden, in 1783 became the first professor of medical theory and practice at Harvard. In 1800 he introduced Jenner's method of vaccination into America, and by superseding the older and more hazardous method of inoculation used by Zabdiel Boylston, established vaccination as a general practice. Thus the most appalling health menace on the American continent was removed.

Water polo, see *Swimming*.

Water power was first importantly developed in the U.S. when the Blackstone river at Pawtucket, Rhode Island, was tapped (1790) with the view to the sale of such power for industry. In the next 30 years similar industrial centers powered by water were developed on the Passaic (New Jersey), and the Fall and the Merrimack (Massachusetts). Later many canals sold the power produced at their locks. In 1894 a hydroelectric station was opened at Niagara Falls. During the 20th century enormous hydroelectric plants, such as those constructed under the TENNESSEE VALLEY AUTHORITY, and built along such river systems as the COLORADO, the COLUMBIA, and the MISSOURI, have substantially advanced the nation's economy. The waterpower industry is regulated by the FEDERAL POWER COMMISSION.

WATKINS, Franklin Chenault (1894–), New York-born painter, studied at the Pennsylvania Academy of the Fine Arts. A noted colorist and adherent of POSTIMPRESSIONISM, he is known for his portraits and for his imaginative individuality of style. He creates moods by distorting forms and by wavering of lines. Characteristic paintings are *Springtime* (1935), *Death in the Orchard* (1938), and *The Sideboard* (1940).

WATSON, John Broadus (1878–1958), professor of experimental and comparative psychology at Johns Hopkins (1908–20), was an early exponent in the U.S. of BEHAVIORISM. He introduced the 'behavioristic' approach to the investigation of psychological issues in *Behavior* (1914). (After 1920 he pursued a successful career with large advertising firms.) Other writings include *Behaviorism* (1925, rev. ed., 1930), and *Psychological Care of Infant and Child* (1928).

Watson-Parker Act (1926), a railroad labor law, created a five-man Mediation Board, appointed by the President, which legally bound railroad labor to accept the Board's decisions, but it failed because it provided no penalty for violation by employers. It was superseded by the CROSSER-DILL ACT (1934).

WATTERSON, Henry (1840–1921), was born in Washington, D.C., where he early became a reporter and editor (1858–61). He served in the Confederate army, and in 1868 assumed management of the Louisville (Kentucky) *Journal,* which he consolidated with the *Courier* to establish the *Courier-Journal,* a newspaper that he controlled for 51 years. Called the 'last great personal editor,' Watterson wrote editorials which were considered news in his region, and gained national attention by the force of his opinion. During the Reconstruction period he became a major factor in reunifying the North and South, and at that time 'Marse Henry' was probably the most widely quoted editor in America.

WAVES (Women Appointed for Voluntary Emergency Service), the auxiliary service for women troops connected with the U.S. Navy during World War II, was abolished in 1948. Women now may join the regular navy and naval reserve.

WAYNE, Anthony (1745–96), a prosperous farmer-tanner of Chester county, Pennsylvania, at the outbreak of the War of Independence organized a battalion of Pennsylvania troops which he led in the invasion of CANADA. For some months he commanded at Fort Ticonderoga (1776), and as a brigadier general in 1777 he joined Washington's army in New Jersey. His successful raids on British supplies were paramount in sustaining morale at Valley Forge, and his skill and courage at Monmouth helped turn a near rout into a sustaining operation.

Wayne is chiefly famous for his gallant storming of Stony Point (1779), on the Hudson. The capture of that fort heightened the morale of the entire Continental army. Thereafter known as 'Mad Anthony,' this cool-headed disciplinarian served his country as a leading military figure. His effective generalship in the South was rewarded by the state of Georgia with a liberal grant of land. In 1792 Congress made him a major general and Washington appointed him to command the western armies, which won the affair at FALLEN TIMBERS (1794) and secured the Treaty of GREENVILLE, thus opening up the Northwest Territory. Flamboyant and gregarious, Wayne in action combined careful planning with vigorous execution.

See the biography of Wayne by H. E. Wildes (1941).

Ways and Means Committee, the powerful standing committee of the U.S. House of Representatives, was created in 1795 to supervise tariffs, taxation, and similar financial legislation. Few congressional committees wield so much political power, and the chairman of its 25-man membership has unique political prerogative in dispensing patronage.

'We have met the enemy and they are ours,' see *Perry, O. H.*

Weather Bureau, see *Meteorology.*

WEAVER, JAMES BAIRD (1833–1912), Iowa lawyer, served as a brigade commander in the Civil War. Sent to Congress (1879–81) by the GREENBACK PARTY, he was the party's presidential candidate in 1880. In 1892, as standard-bearer for the POPULIST PARTY, he polled over 1,000,000 popular votes and won 22 electoral votes. He threw his support to Bryan in the 1896 campaign, and, thereafter, with the decline of Populism, retired from national politics.

WEAVER, ROBERT CLIFTON (1907–), economist and public servant, after graduation from Harvard (1929) became an adviser on Negro affairs in the Department of the Interior (1933–37) and special assistant to the administrator of the U.S. Housing Authority (1937–40). He was serving as administrator of the Housing and Home Finance Agency (1961–65) when that Agency in effect was given cabinet status (1965) by the creation of the Department of HOUSING AND URBAN DEVELOPMENT. In 1966 President Johnson appointed Weaver Secretary of the Department. Weaver thus became the first Negro to enter the cabinet.

Webb-Pomerene Act (1918) authorized exporters to organize associations for export trade without becoming liable for violation of ANTITRUST LAWS. A stimulant to foreign exports, it was another step in restricting competition.

WEBER, MAX (1881–1961), Russian-born artist, was brought by his parents to New York in 1891. After studying painting with Laurens in Paris, where he came under the influence of Picasso, Matisse, and Rousseau, he returned (1908) to the U.S. to teach and paint. (He devoted himself solely to painting after 1927.) One of the pioneers of abstract art, Weber created personal, highly organized 'architectural' forms, with a subtle application of color. His distortions were denounced by early critics as 'grotesqueries,' but they later were judged as a deliberate effort to achieve a balance in space relations. Representative are *Interior Stairway* (1916), and *Seated Woman* (1956), both in the Downtown Gallery, New York.

WEBSTER, DANIEL (1782–1852), born in New Hampshire, graduated from Dartmouth (1801), practiced law in his state, and sat in the U.S. House of Representatives (1813–17). He first attracted national attention and won a reputation as a great constitutional lawyer by winning such notable cases before the Supreme Court as the DARTMOUTH COLLEGE CASE (1819), MC CULLOCH *v.* MARYLAND (1819), and GIBBONS *v.* OGDEN (1824). As U.S. Senator from Massachusetts (where he made his home in Marshfield), he remained in office for fourteen years (1827–41) and became a leading political figure in the nation. By 1830 he had won immense fame as an orator, not only before the bar and on the public platform but in the halls of Congress, where his Olympian presence gave his intellectual power an unsurpassed dramatic force. His addresses furnished declamations to generations of American schoolboys, and his Second Reply to Senator Hayne of South Carolina, delivered in 1830, is easily the most famous oration in the history of American parliamentary address, still impressive even in cold print.

Webster reflected the shift in the economic development of New England by supporting the TARIFF OF 1828, and he backed President Jackson on NULLIFICATION, though he took vehement issue with Jackson's fiscal policies. An ardent protectionist (he was financially ruined by the PANIC OF 1837), to many he seemed the tool of New England's vested interests, but he was a nationalist (by 1828) and, with Clay, the principal leader of the WHIG PARTY, the New England wing of which put him forward in 1836 as presidential nominee. In the election Webster won only the electoral vote of Massachusetts, and though he sought the Whig nomination in 1840, it went to W. H. Harrison, who, upon election, brought Webster into his cabinet as Secretary of State (1841–43). In that office (most of it served under Tyler following Harrison's death) Webster negotiated the WEBSTER-ASHBURTON TREATY (1842), settling the disputed northeastern U.S. boundary, but he resigned with other Whigs who believed that Tyler was deserting party principles by championing states' rights. Again in the Senate (1845–50), he made a paramount issue of nationalism, but his support of the WILMOT PROVISO (1846) and of the COMPROMISE OF 1850, the latter of which angered secessionists and abolitionists alike, ended his political future. The Seventh of March Speech (1850) on 'The Constitution and the Union' was wise and temperate, but because it defended the constitutional rights of slaveholders it brought down on Webster the wrath of his New England liberal friends.

Still guided by his principles, Webster served Fillmore, again as Secretary of State (1850–52). He continued to work for Clay's compromise measures and for republicanism everywhere, especially by trying to help LOUIS KOSSUTH establish the independence of Hungary.

Webster's death at Marshfield was an occasion for such universal expression of grief as had not been felt in the U.S. since the death of Washington. The 'god-like Daniel' had been the most commanding figure in the Senate, and the final and solemn sentence of the Second Reply to Hayne symbolizes Webster's contribution on a vast national scale. It became in fact the rallying cry of Union troops in 1861: 'Liberty *and* Union, now and forever, one and inseparable.'

Biographies of Webster include those by C. M. Fuess (2 vols., 1930); and R. N. Current (1955).

WEBSTER, NOAH (1758–1843), Connecticut-born lexicographer, after graduation from Yale (1778) served in the Revolution. While teaching at Goshen, New York, he prepared his famous 'Blue-Backed Speller,' grammar, and reader, *A Grammatical Institute of the English Language* (3 parts, 1783–85), which declared that 'America must be as independent in *literature* as she is in *politics,* as famous for *arts* as for *arms.*'

One of the best sellers of all time, the *Spelling Book* is still a serviceable manual. (It was reissued in 1963 by Teachers College of Columbia University.) It had an estimated printing of 15,000,000 copies by 1837, of more than 70,000,000 by 1890, and today is the only American book ever to sell 100,000,000 copies. It was prepared as a challenge to traditionalism, and it became enormously influential in standardizing spelling and pronunciation in the U.S. as distinguished from prevailing British forms. It was in fact a mighty tool for helping Americans pull themselves together as a nation, for Webster knew the binding power of a common language.

Webster became an ardent Federalist, possibly because he discovered that in order to protect his literary property he must copyright it in all thirteen states; his *Sketches of American Policy* (1785) was one of the earliest and best arguments for a more perfect union. After practicing law briefly at Hartford (1789–93), he actively supported the Federalists by founding in New York the daily *American Minerva* (1793), which he edited for ten years as a political organ, at the same time writing essays on banking, medicine, statistics, and American history.

In 1803 he abandoned journalism, moved to New Haven, and began his career as lexicographer. His *Compendi-*

ous Dictionary (1806) did not satisfy him. He therefore set himself the task of learning some twenty languages (seven of which were Asiatic) and in 1828 issued *An American Dictionary of the English Language,* the most ambitious publication yet undertaken in America and one which, by setting a new standard for etymological investigation and for accuracy of definition, assured his reputation in the U.S. and abroad as a pioneer in the science of lexicography. (It included 70,000 words, 12,000 more than in any previous English-language dictionary.) Soon after its publication JOSEPH E. WORCESTER brought out a rival compilation, and Webster's charge of plagiarism led to the 'war of the dictionaries,' which continued long after Webster's death. In 1864 Webster's dictionary was generally adopted as standard in schools and colleges throughout the country.

Biographies include those by H. R. Warfel (1936), and E. C. Shoemaker (1936).

Webster-Ashburton Treaty (1842), negotiated by Secretary of State Daniel Webster and the British minister, Alexander Baring, 1st Lord Ashburton, fixed the present northeastern Maine-Canada border, and settled a long-standing dispute. By its terms the U.S. received about 7000 of the 12,000 square miles under contest, and though the acceptance of the treaty was accompanied in both countries by a 'battle of the maps,' both governments assuaged domestic opposition by pointing to conflicting early maps and maintaining that concessions in both directions were more than fair.

Webster-Hayne Debate (January 1830), one of the most significant debates ever held in Congress, began when Senator Robert Y. Hayne of South Carolina attacked a proposal of Senator Foote of Connecticut for restricting the sale of public lands, denouncing the 'selfish and unprincipled' protectionist attitude of the East. Daniel Webster of Massachusetts led Hayne into an exposition of the South's policies of strict construction, states' rights, and nullification (the fullest analysis up to that time), and Foote's resolution was all but forgotten. Webster's Second Reply, the greatest recorded American oration, defended the supremacy of Congress, and attacked the nullification and compact doctrines of the South as impractical, absurd, and a violation of the Constitution. Though Hayne was correct to a considerable extent in his historical arguments, Webster's immortal peroration, concluding that 'Liberty and Union' are 'one and inseparable' was declaimed on thousands of school platforms in the North and West, and more than any other document established the image of Union in the hearts of people.

WEED, THURLOW (1797–1882), for a short time was, with his lifelong friend WILLIAM SEWARD, a leader of the new and shortlived ANTI-MASONIC PARTY. As editor of the Albany *Evening Journal* after 1830, and later as a New York City resident, he became a power in the Whig party, helped secure the election of William Henry Harrison (1840), and thereafter came to be regarded as the party boss. When the Whig party disintegrated, Weed joined the new Republican party (1854), and became a staunch supporter of Lincoln, whom he assisted on a special diplomatic mission to England during the Civil War. Weed thereafter built up the most formidable party machine that ever had functioned in the state of New York, and was recognized as one of the most distinguished (and sometimes unscrupulous) political leaders of his day.

WEEMS, MASON LOCKE (1759–1825), born in Maryland, studied theology in London. Though he served various Episcopal parishes after his return, in 1794 he became an itinerant bookseller, and for 30 years was thus the servant of God in a wider field. Author of a variety of improving tracts, Parson Weems established his fame by writing *The Life and Memorable Actions of George Washington* (1800), which in its fifth edition (1806) he rewrote as *The Life of Washington the Great,* 'enriched' with fiction to increase its appeal. Here he introduced the story of 'the little hatchet and the cherry-tree' and other 'curious anecdotes,' thus creating the most popular escape literature for the American boy prior to the tales of Peter Parley. The *Life* was immensely popular; it was reprinted as late as 1962, in a full scholarly edition by Marcus Cunliffe.

WEIR, Julian Alden (1852–1919), son of the painter and stained glass window designer, Robert Walter Weir (1803–89), studied with his father, long a teacher of drawing at West Point, and with Gérôme in Paris. One of the first Americans to come under the spell of impressionism, he is represented by *Portrait of a Young Girl* (Luxembourg Museum), a canvas subtle in the gradations of light and tone. A founder of the Society of American Artists (1886), he was a president of the National Academy (1915–17). His brother, John Ferguson Weir (1841–1926), was director of the School of Fine Arts at Yale (1896–1913).

WEISER, Conrad (1696–1760), German-born frontiersman, emigrated with his family to America, and four years later, as a youth of seventeen, spent a winter near Schoharie, New York, among the Mohawks, acquiring the foundation for his unrivaled knowledge of Indian language and customs. In 1729 he moved into the Pennsylvania frontier, where he became the official Indian interpreter, and for two decades the principal mediator between the whites and Indians. More than any other individual he kept the IROQUOIS CONFEDERACY faithful to the English during the last of the French and Indian Wars. A leader among Pennsylvania Germans, he helped establish a German-language press, and was prominent in German religious movements.

WELCH, William Henry (1850–1934), Connecticut-born son and grandson of physicians, after graduation from Yale (1870), studied medicine at Columbia and abroad. While teaching at Bellevue Hospital Medical College (1879–84), he pioneered in medical research by founding the first pathological laboratory in America. As professor of pathology at Johns Hopkins (1884–1916) he helped organize its hospital (1889) and medical school (1893) as great medical centers for teaching, research, and clinical medicine. He later served as director of its school of hygiene (1916–26) and professor of the history of medicine (1926–30). Often called the 'dean of American medicine,' he made notable contributions to bacteriology and immunology, set forth in such studies as *The Biology of Bacteria, Infection, and Immunity* (1894) and *Thrombosis and Embolism* (1899).

WELD, Theodore Dwight (1803–95), Massachusetts reformer, after 1830 devoted himself entirely to the abolition movement, notably converting to the cause the New York philanthropists ARTHUR and LEWIS TAPPAN, the southern patrician JAMES G. BIRNEY, and such public figures as EDWIN M. STANTON and LYMAN BEECHER. A tireless and effective organizer, Weld acted as adviser to the antislavery Whigs in Congress who broke with their party, and his anonymous tract *American Slavery as It Is* (1839) furnished inspiration for Harriet Beecher Stowe's *Uncle Tom's Cabin*. In 1838 he married Angelina Grimké (1805–79) of South Carolina, who, with her sister, Sarah Moore Grimké (1792–1873), wrote and lectured vigorously on reform causes, virtually repudiating their planter-family background. A dedicated and influential abolitionist, and certainly one of the most attractive, Weld remained long unknown in American history because he avoided personal publicity of any kind.

WELD, Thomas (1595–1661), a graduate of Trinity College, Cambridge, was ejected from his pulpit for nonconformity and emigrated to Massachusetts (1632), where he became pastor of the church at Roxbury. He is chiefly known as a joint author of the BAY PSALM BOOK. In 1641, as agent for the colony, he returned to England, where he remained.

'Welfare State' is the term applied to a government that gives wide extension of social services to the people. The inability of private charity, or state and municipal agencies, to cope with the host of serious problems created by the complex industrial systems in modern nations has led to the development of programs of Federal aid. To conservatives like Senator Robert A. Taft, the term seemed equivalent to socialism.

WELLES, [George] Orson (1915–), actor and director, founded the Mercury Theatre (1937) in New York, where he attracted attention by his production of *Julius Caesar* in modern dress. His radio version of H. G. Wells's *The War of Worlds* (1938), mistaken for the report of an actual Martian invasion, made news. He directed and acted in such notable films as *Citizen Kane* (1940) and *Jane Eyre* (1943). After 1955 he carried on his profession chiefly in Europe.

WELLES, GIDEON (1802–78), as a Connecticut journalist and convert from the Democratic party to the Republican, was chosen by Lincoln as Secretary of the Navy (1861–69) to represent New England factions in the cabinet. He held his post through Johnson's Administration. Painstaking and incorruptible, Welles built the powerful Union navy of the Civil War. As a spokesman for liberal Republicans he was deeply attached to Lincoln and his cause, and Welles's salty *Diary* (3 vols., 1911), though impaired by his later alterations, is a vivid and important sketch of persons and a chronicle of events during his years of public service.

Wellesley College, at Wellesley, Massachusetts, was chartered in 1870 and opened in 1875, the first woman's college to be equipped with a scientific laboratory. Its faculty traditionally has been a constructive influence in social movements. In 1965, with an endowment of $59,500,000 and a faculty of 175, it enrolled 1783 students.

WELLS, HORACE (1815–48), after studying dentistry in Boston, began practicing at Hartford, Connecticut, about 1836. The first to use nitrous oxide (laughing gas) as an anesthetic in dentistry (1844), he performed an unsuccessful demonstration (1845) before Boston authorities. He was nevertheless a vital link in the introduction of ether by his former partner, W. T. G. MORTON. His early death by suicide was brought about by discouragement, and occurred shortly after he had abandoned his practice.

Wells, Fargo and Company (1852), organized to transport express between New York and California, within a decade had obtained a monopoly of the express business west of the Mississippi, and in the two decades after the Civil War was virtually the only postal service in the mining and lumber camps of the Far West. As the agency for transporting bullion to markets in the East, it succeeded the PONY EXPRESS. In 1918, it merged with the Adams Express and other agencies to form the American Railway Express Company.

Wesberry* v. *Sanders (1964) was a case that resulted in a U.S. Supreme Court ruling which held that the Constitution requires the congressional districts within each state to be substantially equal in population. At the time, in some 37 states the most populous district contained 100,000 more persons than the least populous. (In several states the disparity was much greater.) In this redistricting rural areas were the losers, since population trends in much of the nation have created city or suburban enclaves.

The effects of this decision on political action extended the ruling in BAKER *v.* CARR (1962), which declared that state legislature apportionments are 'justiciable' by Federal courts. It is revolutionary in that it altered the shape of future elections to the House of Representatives (and to the Electoral College) by removing from the states a prerogative that they previously exercised. The case therefore was a landmark, as it opened the question whether the Supreme Court had asserted a legislative function, thereby breaching the separation of executive, legislative, and judicial powers.

Wesleyan University (1831) at Middletown, Connecticut, is a nonsectarian men's college, the first to be chartered and opened by Methodists. It maintains its liberal arts traditions and has one of the highest per capita endowments in the country. In 1965, with an endowment of $45,210,000 and a faculty of 190, it enrolled 1300 students.

WEST, BENJAMIN (1738–1820), born near Philadelphia of Quaker parents, exhibited astonishing talent as an artist, and became a professional portrait painter at eighteen. After three years of study in Italy (1760–63) he established himself permanently in London, where he immediately became a sensation. George III took him under special patronage, and in 1772 West was appointed historical painter to the king. He was a founder of the Royal Academy, and in 1792 he succeeded Joshua Reynolds as its president.

His 400 canvases on historical, mythological, and biblical themes are generally heroic in scale and skillfully patterned, but their lack of vigor and monotonous color deaden their effectiveness. West's contemporary reputation as the greatest painter of the age did not outlast the years of royal favor, although he was accorded burial in Westminster Abbey.

His influence on American painting was overwhelming. In his household were trained Earl, Stuart, Copley, Trumbull, Sully, Dunlap, C. W. Peale, Rembrandt Peale, Allston, and Samuel F. B. Morse. More correct than vital, more didactically intellectual than emotional, West could communicate only his style to his pupils, and thus in many instances he hindered the development of individual talent. Representative of his works are *The Death of General Wolfe* (Ottawa), *Christ Healing the Sick* (Pennsylvania Hospital), and *Colonel Guy Johnson* (National Gallery).

WEST, MAE (1893–), began her career as an actress in vaudeville. Later popular as a movie star, she became widely known for her large bosom, swaying hips, and uninhibited representation of sex in such films as the melodrama *Diamond Lil* (1933), a picture of life in the New York Tenderloin. During World War II, an inflatable life-belt for aviators was called a 'Mae West.'

West Coast Hotel Company* v. *Parish (1937) was a case that resulted in a U.S. Supreme Court ruling (5–4) that upheld a Washington minimum wage law. One of the important New Deal measures, it expressly overruled the decision rendered in ADKINS *v.* CHILDREN'S HOSPITAL (1923).

West Florida, established as a British province by the PROCLAMATION OF 1763, was the strip along the 31° parallel west from the Apalachicola river, across Mobile bay to the Mississippi river. Somewhat increased in size in 1764 along its northern boundary to include Mississippi settlements, its original boundaries were restored (1795) by PINCKNEY'S TREATY. In 1812 the western portion was absorbed into the new state of Louisiana, and the remainder was added to the Mississippi Territory (1813). By the terms of the ADAMS-ONÍS TREATY (1819), West Florida was eliminated, and the region east of the Perdido river was joined to EAST FLORIDA to form the Territory of Florida; the area west became the southern portions of Alabama and Mississippi.

West Indies trade, the backbone of New England prosperity until the 1760's, was the 'triangular trade' between the American colonies, Africa, and the West Indies. Ships from New England ports, laden with rum and a great variety of home manufactured articles, sailed to Africa, where the shipmaster bartered rum in exchange for slaves. Then in the West Indies ports the skippers traded the Negroes and most of the original cargo for sugar and molasses, later distilled into New England rum. Each leg of the course was expected to show a profit, but the base of the triangle, the fearful 'Middle Passage' from Africa to the New World, which carried the supply of labor for the SLAVE TRADE, was the most profitable part of the voyage, at the highest cost in human suffering.

This extensive commerce not only brought wealth to the merchants, but it also supported an extensive artisanship on land and on sea. Although Great Britain by the MOLASSES ACT (1733) hoped to impose duties that would make trading with the French and Dutch islands prohibitive, widespread smuggling nullified the Act, which had bred deep-seated resentment. When at length Parliament gave firm shape to its intention by passage of the SUGAR ACT (1764) and the STAMP ACT (1765), the diverging interests of the colonies and the mother country were brought into bold relief. 'It is no secret,' John Adams later asserted, 'that rum was an essential ingredient in the American Revolution.' This trade was abruptly halted after the War of Independence, since free ports were closed to American shipping. Merchants soon thereafter developed the CHINA TRADE.

West Point, see *Military Academy, U.S.*

West Virginia, originally 40 counties of Virginia, in 1861 at the outbreak of the Civil War voted against secession, adopted a state government, and chose its name. In June 1863 it was admitted to the Union, with Wheeling as capital (intermittently) until 1885. A mountainous terrain in the Appalachian range, the area was first explored in the 1670's by frontiersmen crossing the Alleghenies to the Ohio valley. Settlements made in the 1750's gradually increased, and the completion of the NATIONAL ROAD (1818) from Cumberland, Maryland, to Wheeling brought prosperity to the region.

This piedmont section of Virginia was never tied into the slave economy of the TIDEWATER. Farmers tilled their own soil and increasingly came to resent the political domination of the tidewater gentry. Under Virginia law slaves were taxed at a lower rate than cattle, yet slaves were numbered as persons in determining the apportionment of representation in the state assembly. In 1859 JOHN BROWN attempted to seize the arsenal at Harpers Ferry in an effort to free slaves. Although the raid in general united the South against abolition, it intensified abolitionist sentiment in western Virginia.

In 1885 Charleston became the capital. (It is in the center of the state; Wheeling is on the Ohio border.) Thereafter the state began to develop its huge mineral resources, chiefly coal and natural gas. Although it remains primarily rural, its economy is dependent on the profits of its mines, steel mills, and chemical industry. Charleston is a trading center and the largest city, with a population in 1960 of 85,000. Wheeling remains the commercial center. White Sulphur Springs, on its western slopes, had become a fashionable health resort even in the early years of the new Republic. The leading institution of higher learning is the University of West Virginia (Morgantown, est. 1867).

Western lands, so called, were the extensive areas beyond the Appalachians conflictingly claimed by Virginia, the Carolinas, Georgia, New York, Massachusetts, and Connecticut during the 'critical period' when the U.S. was governed under the ARTICLES OF CONFEDERATION (1781–89). Virginia's claim was largest and best founded, extending west to the Mississippi and north to Lake Superior, but it overlapped the claims of Massachusetts and Connecticut. The claims of the states south of Virginia did not overlap, but likewise extended to the great river.

Small states feared that the power of large ones would encroach unless limits could be effected, and Maryland declined to ratify the Articles until all claims were relinquished to the Federal government. In 1780 New York led the way, and Congress immediately passed a resolution guaranteeing that the relinquished lands would be organized as states. The other sovereignties soon followed New York's example (though Connecticut, piqued by a legal decision in connection with the issue, and for other reasons as well, withheld the WESTERN RESERVE until 1800), and Congress fulfilled its promise by the ORDINANCES OF 1784, 1785, and 1787.

Western Reserve, also known as the Connecticut Western Reserve, was a large section of land west of Pennsylvania reserved by Connecticut in 1786, when it ceded its other western lands to the federal government. Its objective in retaining the 3,000,000 acres on the south shore of Lake Erie (granted by royal charter in 1662) was an advantageous disposal of a potentially valuable estate. In 1792 Connecticut assigned 500,000 acres from the western end to such of its inhabitants as had suffered acutely by raids of the British during the Revolution. Three years later the Connecticut Land Company purchased the remaining tract, a heavily forested area unfavorable for profitable sale. In 1800 an agreement between Connecticut and the federal government provided for the transfer of the Western Reserve to the Ohio Territory. In the process of development, the Reserve became an extension of New England into the West. The term still survives in the name of the university, founded in 1826, and in that of the Western Reserve Historical Society.

Western Reserve University, founded (1826) at Hudson, Ohio, as a men's college, became an urban institution when it moved to Cleveland (1882). It soon became co-educational and was chartered as a university in 1884. (The coordinating units are Adelbert College for men and Mather College for women.) Its graduate schools include Arts and Science, Medicine, Dentistry, Nursing, Law, Social Work, Library Science, and Business. In 1965, with an endowment of $70,900,000 and a faculty of 1538, it enrolled 7627 students.

Western Union, a telegraph company organized in Rochester, New York (1851), by 1860 had absorbed most competing companies and had extended its service to the Mississippi valley. With the acquisition in 1928 of the Postal Telegraph Company by the International Telephone and Telegraph Corporation, Western Union became virtually the sole provider of telegraph service in the U.S.

Western University of Pennsylvania, see *Pittsburgh, University of.*

WESTINGHOUSE, GEORGE (1846–1914), by his invention of the air brake (1869) revolutionized railroad transportation by making high-speed rail travel safe. Many of his 400 patented inventions have contributed to the development of electrical engineering, especially to the introduction of high-tension systems using single-phase alternating currents. He organized the Westinghouse Electric and Manufacturing Company (1886) after his Westinghouse Airbrake Company had laid the foundations of a great industrial enterprise.

Westward movement, as the term is generally applied to the settlement of the U.S., began with the expansion from the Atlantic coast into the interior. Its character, volume, and rate of progress are unparalleled in world history, for within a period of 300 years small groups of individuals (not invading armies) had conquered a wilderness and welded geographically and politically a populous nation in the heartland of North America, spanning the continent.

The exodus of Thomas Hooker's congregation (1636) from Massachusetts Bay symbolizes the entire movement. They set out on foot, 100 strong, driving their cattle before them in search of the Promised Land, and from this and similar migrations the Connecticut river valley towns were founded, a frontier extending well into Vermont, New Hampshire, and Maine by mid-18th century. Such was the pattern all along the seaboard. Land-hungry PIONEERS simultaneously were staking agricultural outposts up the Mohawk in New York, and moving southward from Pennsylvania to the Shenandoah valley and the Appalachian barrier. In Virginia they were crossing the FALL LINE to the Blue Ridge. The occupation of the PIEDMONT and the mountain regions in the Carolinas followed shortly and in the same manner.

Before the Revolution settlements had been established in West Florida and central Tennessee, and the TRANSYLVANIA COMPANY had been organized to open up the region of Kentucky. Thereafter the dates of the admission of states to the Union indicate the volume and direction of the movement: Vermont (1791), Kentucky (1792), Tennessee (1796), Ohio (1803), Louisiana (1812). From the NORTHWEST TERRITORY (1787) were carved Indiana (1816), Illinois (1818), Michigan (1837), and Wisconsin (1848). Soon thereafter California (1850) and Oregon (1859) qualified for statehood.

During the decades of the 1870's and 1880's the region of the Great Plains began filling in: Colorado (1876), and the Dakotas and Montana (1889). By this time the pioneer phase of the occupation of land within the continental U.S. (excepting Alaska) had virtually ended, and though the population movement westward still continues, most of the physical FRONTIER had disappeared.

'Wetbacks,' so-called, are Mexican workers who enter the U.S. illegally by swimming the Rio Grande. During the 1940's more than 1,000,000 border-jumpers annually entered the country. They dispersed to the fruit and vegetable farms from Texas to California and became a major problem of MIGRATORY LABOR. The U.S. Immigration and Naturalization Service attempted to stem the flow, but it had an 1800-mile border to patrol.

Underpaid, exploited, and housed with few sanitary facilities, the wetbacks created a health menace and a labor situation which organized labor charged as unfair competition. In 1952 Congress proposed remedies, but the only major action was that taken to speed the 'voluntary' departure of more than 1,000,000 across the border in 1954. In 1955 Mexico and the U.S. by treaty legalized the entry of 144,000 Mexicans a year. In 1964 Congress allowed certain earlier (and permissive) legislation on migratory workers to lapse and thus curtailed such migration, but there are still many wetbacks in California and elsewhere in the Southwest.

Whaling, to provide spermaceti for candles and oil for lamps (and, for a short time, whalebone for corsets), was established as an industry in America by the middle of the 17th century. Starting in a small way on Long Island, Cape Cod, and Nantucket, after 1755 it centered at New Bedford, Massachusetts, which became the greatest whaling port in the world before petroleum products (after 1850) replaced whale oil as an illuminant. The capture of a sperm whale (1712) by a Nantucket whaler led the adventurous into more distant waters in search of the superior cachalot. In 1791 an American whaler rounded Cape Horn into the South Pacific, and for the next 60 years vessels plied the seven seas to fill their holds, a task which often required an absence of three or four years from the home port. Melville's *Moby-Dick* is the classic fictional account of whaling in the period when seamen in oar-propelled boats fought perilous battles with wounded whales.

The peril and romance of whaling disappeared after the invention of the explosive harpoon head in the 1850's. At present an international whaling commission restricts the period of whaling to a few months. The industry is now carried out on factory ships and has come virtually to an end.

See W. S. Tower, *A History of the American Whale Fishery* (1907), and E. P. Hohman, *The American Whaleman* (1928).

Wheat industry in the U.S. before 1820 was centered in the Mohawk and Hudson valleys. Soon thereafter it spread to the Genesee region of New York and to Pennsylvania. It developed into a business attracting investment after CYRUS MC CORMICK patented his reaping machine in 1834. By 1851 he was turning out a thousand reapers a year at his Chicago plant to meet the demand of great wheatfields spread across the land from northern Ohio to Wisconsin. (Wheat exports were greatly stimulated after 1846 when Britain repealed the Corn Laws which to a large extent had barred wheat imports.)

The rapid building of railroads into the prairie country during the 1850's was accompanied by a rising price of wheat on the New York market: from 93 cents a bushel in 1851 to $2.50 in 1855. The passage of the HOMESTEAD ACT (1862) attracted settlers to the Middle West. Indeed, during the Civil War some 15,000 homesteads were thereby pre-empted, and a succession of bumper crops assured England's neutrality (she could get wheat from the North, but cotton from the South was blockaded) and vastly aided the economy of the Union in the war period. With a growing world market, wheat production spread westward to the Great Plains, which by 1890 became and remained the center of wheat farming, and to the Columbia valley, a source of wheat for the Orient.

Although corn is the leading grain crop, no agricultural commodity has determined the shape of U.S. history more than wheat. It aligned the West politically with the East during the Civil War, and stimulated interstate and international migration into the West. It hastened large-scale commercial agriculture and was an important factor in the AGRICULTURAL REVOLUTION, which began to have effect in the late 1860's. The AGRICULTURAL ADJUSTMENT ACT of 1938 set up facilities to maintain an 'ever normal granary,' immensely important during and after World War II, when the U.S. became (as it still remains) the largest exporter of wheat in the world.

The status of two rival economies was revealed by President Kennedy's announcement in October 1963 that he had approved the sale of $250,000,000 worth of wheat to the Soviet Union, a step followed by further large wheat shipments to Soviet satellite nations. This policy was continued by President L. B. Johnson.

WHEATON, HENRY (1785–1848), jurist and diplomat, after graduation from Rhode Island College (Brown) in 1802, and study abroad, became a leader of the New York bar and a vigorous supporter of Jeffersonianism as editor of the *National Advocate* (1812–15). He prepared the *Reports* of the cases argued before the U.S. Supreme Court (12 vols., 1816–27), distinguished for the fullness of their notes. For the next two decades he served in diplomatic posts abroad: in Denmark (1827–35) and Prussia (1835–46), during which time he wrote his *History of the Northmen* (1831), defending the pre-Columbian discovery of America. His *Elements of International Law* (1836), and *History of the Law of Nations* (1845), companion studies, give him rank among the foremost American legal writers.

WHEELER, GEORGE MONTAGUE (1842–1905), Massachusetts-born army engineer, graduated from the U.S. Military Academy in 1866. Five years later he was placed in charge of the government topographical and geological survey west of the 100th meridian (from North Dakota south through Texas). Wheeler conducted this large-scale expedition (1872–79) with a staff of geologists, ethnologists, and zoologists. The definitive *Reports* (7 vols. and 2 atlases) have notable scientific value.

Wheeler-Howard Act (1934) amended the BURKE ACT (1906) by providing for return to tribal ownership of surplus Indian lands hitherto open to sale, and ended land allotments in severalty. This is sometimes referred to as the New Deal for Indians, since it halted the indiscriminate assimilation of Indians and encouraged traditional elements in tribal culture.

Wheeler-Rayburn Act (1935), which provided a more direct approach to the utilities problem than that set up under the TENNESSEE VALLEY AUTHORITY, authorized the Federal Power Commission to regulate the interstate transmission and sale of electric power, and gave the Federal Trade Commission similar authority over gas. By a 'death sentence' clause, any holding company that could not demonstrate its localized and efficient character after a term of five years would be dissolved. Though bitterly denounced by power companies, the Act was declared constitutional by the Supreme Court, and in due course holding companies divested themselves of some 700 affiliates, whose assets totaled $10,300,000,000.

WHEELOCK, ELEAZAR, see *Dartmouth College.*

Whig party, one of the dominant political groups in the U.S. during the second quarter of the 19th century, as a party came into existence in 1834, when an anti-Jackson coalition charged 'King Andrew' with executive tyranny, and adopted the name of the English political party which had grown up during the 17th- and 18th-century contests respecting royal prerogatives. Its nucleus was the NATIONAL REPUBLICAN PARTY, but all political elements opposed to Jackson adhered to it: the states' rights advocates in the South, proponents of Clay's 'AMERICAN SYSTEM' of internal improvements in the West, and those in the East who opposed Jackson's bank policies. By 1836 the group had formed a loose alliance, though it was unable to agree on a single presidential candidate. In fact four Whigs then ran for office, including Daniel Webster and William Henry Harrison, and the election went to Jackson's choice, Martin Van Buren.

The party won its first national election in 1840 with Harrison, and again in 1848 with Taylor. (The two great leaders of the party, Webster and Clay, were never able to achieve a victory, for sectionalism created factions stronger than party ties.) The party disintegrated following its refusal to take a stand on the free-soil and slavery issues, and a bitter struggle developed between 'Conscience Whigs' (antislavery elements in the North) and 'Cotton Whigs' (proslavery Southerners). In 1852 the party ran Winfield Scott, who polled only 42 electoral votes. Thereafter its remnants for the most part gravitated to the DEMOCRATIC PARTY and to the newly formed REPUBLICAN PARTY (1854).

Whip, see *Party whip.*

WHIPPLE, FRED LAWRENCE (1906–), professor of astronomy at Harvard (after 1950) and director of the Smithsonian Astrophysical Observatory (after 1955), was an active leader of the project on Upper-Atmosphere Research by way of Meteor Photography, sponsored by the U.S. Navy (1946–51). His research has contributed knowledge of meteors and of comets (he discovered six new comets).

His writings include *Earth, Moon, and Planets* (1942).

Whisky Rebellion (1794), a result of discontent over enforcement of a whisky tax, erupted in the Monongahela valley of western Pennsylvania among frontier farmers who viewed Hamilton's Excise Act of 1791 in the same light as the colonists had viewed the odious Stamp Act. Governor Mifflin of Pennsylvania at first refused to send in the state militia, and President Washington at the urgent request of Secretary of the Treasury Hamilton called for 15,000 militia from nearby states as a test case of Pennsylvania's defiance of Federal law. The rebellion was quelled (Washington pardoned two ringleaders convicted of treason), and the power of the federal government was vindicated. But the frontiersmen's anger at Hamilton and the Federalists had long-lasting political repercussions.

Whisky Ring was the group of distillers and revenue officials formed in St. Louis, who were revealed (1875) to have been systematically defrauding the government of millions of dollars in taxes on distilled whisky. Evidence was unmistakable that the Ring had operated with the collusion of Treasury officials and of President Grant's private secretary, General Orville Babcock. Though some 238 persons were indicted, most escaped conviction, including Babcock (with Grant's connivance), but the revelation of the scandal was a factor in the ensuing presidential election when the Republicans nominated the reform governor of Ohio, Rutherford B. Hayes, as their candidate.

WHISTLER, James Abbott McNeill (1834–1903), born in Lowell, Massachusetts, received his first art training in St. Petersburg, where his father was supervising the building of a Russian railroad. He returned with his family to the U.S. in 1849, and entered the U.S. Military Academy from which he was dismissed (1854) for failing chemistry. ('Had silicon been a gas, I would have been a major general.') In 1855 he went to Paris, where he associated himself with the French Impressionists. Having received some notice in 1863 for his *White Girl* (National Gallery), shown at the Salon des Refusés, he took up permanent residence in England, where his eccentricities and stinging wit made him conspicuous from the first.

Strongly imbued with the doctrine of 'art for art's sake,' by dint of lectures, polemics, audacity, and his very evident virtuosity, Whistler won a reluctant British public to his view. But he infuriated academicians, who demanded a story, and Pre-Raphaelites, who emphasized clarity and meticulousness. Long interested in the decorative quality of the Japanese print and the atmospheric values of Velásquez, Whistler replaced contrasts with a pervading gray tone, blended subtly with admirable draftsmanship.

In 1865 he began his series called nocturnes, harmonies, and symphonies, in one of which he expresses night over the Thames by spots of color on a dark background. John Ruskin, the arbiter of British taste, called them an imposture for which with 'Cockney impudence' a coxcomb was demanding 200 guineas 'for flinging a pot of paint in the public's face.' Whistler won a lawsuit for libel, but his caustic facetiousness on the witness stand got him the insulting damages of one farthing.

Whistler's 400 etchings, like his paintings, are brilliantly executed though never profound. Classified as *Little French Series, Thames Series,* and *Venice Series,* they give him rank among great artists in that genre. His most famous painting is the portrait of his mother, *Arrangement in Grey and Black* (Louvre). His writings include *The Gentle Art of Making Enemies* (1890), amusing essays scorning the taste of both critics and the public.

See the biography by E. R. and Joseph Pennell (rev. ed., 1911).

WHITE, Andrew Dickson (1832–1918), after graduation from Yale (1853) and study in Europe, taught history at Michigan (1857–63), and developed his concept of a university which, detached from sects and dogma, would foster free inquiry. Returning to New York, he was soon able to effect his ideas. He was elected to the New York state senate (1864–67), and, as chairman of the educational committee, with the financial aid of a fellow senator, Ezra Cornell, he secured a land grant for the institution that became CORNELL UNIVERSITY. As its first president (1867–85), White introduced free elective studies and emphasized the natural sciences.

He was a champion of Darwinism, which he defended in his famous Cooper Union speech, 'The Battlefields of Science,' embodied in *The Warfare of Science* (1876) and expanded into *A History of the Warfare of Science with Theology in Christendom* (2 vols., 1896). By his effective enrichment of the curriculum, he was able to attract to his young institution scholars of international repute. (He was the first president of the American Historical Society, 1884–85.)

White served as minister, and later as ambassador, to Germany (1879–81, 1897–99), and as minister to Russia (1892–94). Through his efforts Andrew Carnegie built the Palace of Justice at The Hague, and White headed the American delegation to the first Hague Conference (1899). White takes rank as a leader in shaping higher education in the U.S.

WHITE, EDWARD DOUGLASS (1845–1921), Louisiana-born jurist, fought in the Confederate ranks during the Civil War, took up law practice, and in 1879 became a member of the Louisiana supreme court. He was serving in the U.S. Senate (1891–94) when President Cleveland appointed him to the U.S. Supreme Court. When Chief Justice Melville Fuller died in 1910, the other Associate Justices petitioned President Taft to appoint White to head the court. In that post White wrote the 'RULE OF REASON' decisions in antitrust cases (differentiating between legal and illegal business combinations). Conservative in his judgments, White contributed most by the spirit of unity which he engendered among his colleagues. The reconciliation of the North and South which he fostered was exemplified when in 1915 he wrote the opinion declaring unconstitutional the so-called 'GRANDFATHER CLAUSES,' provisions in the constitutions of the former slave states that disfranchised Negroes.

WHITE, E. B. [ELWYN BROOKS] (1899–), after graduation from Cornell (1921) in the same decade began his long career as a chief contributor to the *New Yorker*. His essays collected in *One Man's Meat* (1946) first appeared in *Harper's*. They gave him rank as a master of sophisticated humor in the vein of his 'Talk of the Town' unsigned editorials in the *New Yorker,* collected in *The Wild Flag* (1946). His essays are light in style but incisive, ironic, and with serious undercurrents. White revived the art of the personal essay as a literary form. *Here Is New York* (1949), with its love of nature and simplicities, describes the metropolis in the manner that Thoreau presented the microcosm of Concord to his neighbors a century earlier. *The Points of My Compass* (1962) is a collection of letters written from his farm in Maine and from his office in New York.

WHITE, HENRY (1850–1927), the first 'career diplomat' in the U.S., was ambassador at Rome (1905–7), and at Paris (1907–9). He headed the U.S. delegation at the ALGECIRAS CONFERENCE (1906), and accompanied Wilson as a delegate to the VERSAILLES PEACE CONFERENCE.

WHITE, JOHN (*fl.* 1577–93), Virginia colonist and artist, having spent a year (1585) with the settlers on ROANOKE ISLAND, returned to England with his friend Sir Francis Drake. In 1587 he arrived at the Island again, this time as governor of the colony, but his stay was brief, for the colonists sent him back to England for supplies. When he finally was able to return (1591) after England's war with Spain, the colony had disappeared.

During his residence in 1585 he made three-score exquisite watercolors of Indians and of the fauna and flora of the country, the first authentic pictorial records of life in the New World. They became known in part when THEODOR DE BRY in 1590 set forth 23 as published engravings. All were later reproduced in one way or another, but not until recently were the watercolors reproduced in their original colors with a quality of performance that matched the fidelity of De Bry, in *The American Drawings of John White* (2 vols., 1964). The originals are in the British Museum.

WHITE, PAUL DUDLEY (1886–), long associated with Harvard as professor of clinical medicine, engaged in research, practice, and teaching, especially in the field of heart disease, a subject to which he has contributed many authoritative studies. His *Heart Diseases* (1931) has gone through several editions, and is the classic in its field. He won popular attention as Eisenhower's specialist at the time of the President's heart attack in 1955.

WHITE, PEARL (1889–1939), Missouri-born film star, appeared as heroine in such week-to-week movie serials during the World War I era as *The Exploits of Elaine* and *The Perils of Pauline.* Audiences were so enthralled by watching the heroine jump from flaming yachts or change planes in mid air, leap from trains or fall into live volcanoes, that when she left the country for Europe in 1922, she was reputed to have earned $2,000,000. The fad of such stunt pictures (often crudely faked but done at first without doubles) had brief popularity.

WHITE, STANFORD, see *McKim, Mead, and White.*

WHITE, WILLIAM ALLEN (1868–1944), a staunch but independent-minded Republican, in 1895 bought the *Emporia* (Kansas) *Gazette,* which he edited for the rest of his life, achieving a national reputation as a 'grass roots' spokesman for liberal movements both in and outside his party. Although his own newspaper sold but a few thousand copies, his editorials were widely reprinted or quoted elsewhere, and reached millions of readers.

White's fiction for reformist purposes includes *Stratagems and Spoils* (1901), *A Certain Rich Man* (1909), and *In the Heart of a Fool* (1918), exposures of corruption in politics. His charming autobiography (1916) is a valuable document in the MUCKRAKING movement.

WHITEFIELD, GEORGE (1714–70), English evangelist, was closely associated with John and Charles Wesley in the early days of Methodism. (He later broke with the Wesleys to become leader of the Calvinistic Methodists.) He was ordained a deacon in the Church of England in 1736, but his sensational preaching excluded him from most Anglican pulpits. In the course of seven trips to America (1738–70) he attracted huge crowds on his tours from Georgia to New England.

Although in print Whitefield's sermons repel by their sentimental bombast, by his histrionic improvisations before audiences he could throw his hearers, as David Garrick attested, into paroxysms by just pronouncing 'Mesopotamia.' (Even Benjamin Franklin, somewhat of a skeptic, felt moved by Whitefield's oratory.) Jonathan Edwards opened his pulpit to Whitefield, whose triumphal progress during the GREAT AWAKENING left a whole society 'sweetly melted.' His later tours in Great Britain and America continued to draw throngs. He delivered his last sermon in the open air at Andover, Massachusetts, the day before he died in Newburyport, where he is buried.

WHITEHEAD, ALFRED NORTH (1861–1947), British mathematician and philosopher, having established pre-eminence in England as a logician and philosopher of science, came permanently to the U.S. as professor of philosophy at Harvard (1924–36), where he began his remarkable career as metaphysician. In collaboration with Bertrand Russell he had already written one of the impressive achievements of modern thought, *Principia Mathematica* (3 vols., 1910–13), which seeks to mold a unified scientific religion. Whitehead's later thinking is set forth in his major work, *Process and Reality* (1929). Every event, he postulates, is essentially an endeavor to reach a greater fullness of being. Elective affinities are involved, and 'things' are settled ways in which one set of events feels other sets of events. This 'philosophy of organism' assumes that the world process is apparent in the adjustment of interrelated things to their environment, which they alter by their adjustment: 'the ultimate natures of things lie together in a harmony which excludes mere arbitrariness.' God is 'the poet of the world,' the universal pressure toward rationality within the world of events.

Thus religious experience and the concept of God as ultimate good are fundamental in Whitehead's later philosophy, which has achieved a wide influence on American thought, though the turbidity of his style and the introduction of coined words make his works difficult reading. His semi-popular books, also important, include *Science and the Modern World* (1925), *Religion in the Making* (1926), and *The Aims of Education* (1929). *Modes of Thought* (1938) is a summary introduction to his philosophy.

White House, the official home of the President of the U.S., was formally so designated by Congress in 1902. (Previously, though painted white, it had variously been termed the President's Palace, the President's House, or the Executive Mansion.) It has 18 acres of grounds. It was situated a mile and a half from the Capitol to provide a distance for ceremonial panorama. It was the first public building erected in Washington, from the designs of JAMES HOBAN. John and Abigail Adams were able to take residence in it in 1800. The British burned it during the War of 1812, and when Hoban completed rebuilding it in 1817, he retained the basic design originally approved by L'Enfant, who had planned the architecture of the city.

The interior was rebuilt and refurnished in 1902. When engineers discovered in 1948 that the White House was unsafe, the interior was completely removed and new foundations were laid. The rebuilding was completed in 1952.

WHITEMAN, PAUL (1891–), Denver-born concert band conductor, served as an army band leader in World War I. Believing that jazz in the New Orleans and Chicago styles was important but crude, in 1924 he inaugurated the period of 'symphonic jazz' by presenting in New York at Aeolian Hall a concert of jazz music. There he conducted the première of George Gershwin's *Rhapsody in Blue.* As 'king of jazz' Whiteman advanced the cause of jazz music by bringing it seriously to the attention of critics. By thus giving jazz bands easier access to jobs, he speeded up the evolution of jazz patterns.

White Mountains, a part of the Appalachian system in northern New Hampshire, comprise the Presidential Range (with Mount Washington rising 6288 ft.) and the Franconia Mountains, separated by Franconia Notch. Some 1200 square miles are set aside as a national forest. Mount Washington, though a relatively low mountain, is subject to fierce gales and extremely low temperatures.

WHITLOCK, BRAND (1869–1934), Ohio journalist and lawyer, while serving as reform mayor of Toledo (1905–13), wrote two of his realistic novels concerned with municipal politics, *The Turn of the Balance* (1907), and *The Gold Brick* (1910). As U.S. minister and ambassador to Belgium (1913–22), he won international repute for his care of refugees, and for his efforts in behalf of Edith Cavell, the British nurse. His autobiography, *Forty Years of It* (1914), is supplemented by his *Letters and Journals* (ed. by Allan Nevins, 2 vols., 1936).

WHITMAN, MARCUS (1802–47), left his medical practice in upper New York, and in 1836, as a 'missionary physician,' set out for the remote Oregon country with his bride, Narcissa Prentiss Whitman, the first woman over the Oregon Trail. That autumn Whitman established a Congregationalist mission near Walla Walla, Washington. In 1842 he returned East (for a large portion of the trip riding on horseback in winter) in an effort to further his missionary aims, and in 1843 he was an invaluable adjunct in guiding the 'great migration' to Oregon across the mountains. The Cayuse Indians, with their own religious traditions, grew hostile because Whitman was not always able to stem fatal outbreaks of such white men's diseases as amoebic dysentery and measles. They murdered Whitman, his wife, and twelve others. News of the massacre helped spur passage of the bill that made Oregon a U.S. territory (1848).

WHITMAN, WALT [WALTER] (1819–92), born in West Hills, Long Island, grew up in a family of nine children, supported by a carpenter father who struggled to make ends meet. After elementary schooling Walt became a printer's apprentice, taught school (at sixteen), and as a journeyman printer in the decade 1838–48 spent most of his time in and near New York as a hack writer for magazines and as editor for Democratic newspapers. (In 1842 he wrote a temperance novel, *Franklin Evans,* on commission.)

In the printing office Whitman learned the politics of America at first hand, received and reviewed the books of the day, and secured tickets for the theater and opera, sources of inspiration for his poetry. During that time, and later when he took up carpentering (1851–54), he was a serious reader in libraries and a frequent attendant at popular lectures. Significantly, he was fashioning poetry which he knew was expressing the American nativity that he had taken into himself: its people, landscape, and speech. *Leaves of Grass* (1855) in its first small edition, which Whitman published himself, struck a new and indigenous note in American poetry. It received scant public notice, with the exception of Whitman's own anonymous and enthusiastic reviews, but Whitman had sent a copy to Emerson, and Emerson's letter of recognition ('I greet you at the beginning of a great career') was a crucial factor in Whitman's growth as a poet. The book thereafter grew with him through its twelve editions (1855–92), each with additions, revisions, and rearrangements.

During the Civil War Whitman worked as a volunteer nurse in the army hospitals in Washington, and later (1865) became a clerk in the Department of the Interior, but he was soon dismissed by Secretary Harlan on the ground that *Leaves of Grass,* in its frank celebration of sex, was immoral. Following a paralytic stroke in 1873, Whitman moved to Camden, New Jersey, where he thenceforth resided. During these later years 'the Good Grey Poet' won recognition abroad.

As the bard of democracy, Whitman extols the average man and the uniqueness of the individual. He was one of the significant voices of the 19th century. His new rhythms came to have immense influence on poetic experimentation, and no American poet has received more critical study. Biographies include those by Bliss Perry (1906), H. S. Canby (1943), and Gay W. Allen (1955).

WHITNEY, Eli (1765–1825), Massachusetts-born inventor, soon after graduation from Yale (1792) produced a model of his cotton gin (1793) while sojourning as a guest at 'Mulberry Grove,' the Savannah plantation of Mrs. Nathanael Greene. Conspicuous from boyhood for his 'handiness,' Whitney was encouraged by Mrs. Greene to contrive a practical means of separating the short staple cotton from its seed. Almost overnight Whitney's labor-saving device revolutionized the cotton industry; an export business of 138,000 pounds in 1792 rose by 1794 to 1,600,000 pounds. In partnership with Phineas Miller, Mrs. Greene's plantation manager, Whitney patented an improved model, which was manufactured on a large scale at New Haven. After expensive litigation, infringement of the patent was settled (1807) in Whitney's favor, but Congress in 1812 denied a petition for its renewal. Thus an invention which brought great wealth to many, and created an immense upheaval in the social and economic life of the nation, gave Whitney scant return on his investment. Meanwhile he had built a firearms factory (1798) near New Haven, and devised a system of interchangeable parts for his muskets. The new technique was immediately adopted throughout the U.S. as a defense measure, and soon the 'AMERICAN SYSTEM,' successfully applied to hundreds of inventions, paved the way for mass production, thus proving itself to be the most revolutionary invention in American history.

WHITNEY, Josiah Dwight (1819–96), geologist, was the eldest son of the Northampton (Massachusetts) banker, Josiah Dwight Whitney, and a brother of WILLIAM DWIGHT WHITNEY. He was graduated from Yale (1839), studied abroad, and took part in geological surveys in the West, at first in the Lake Superior region (1847–49). Later as state geologist of California (1860–74) and after 1865 as professor of geology at Harvard, he specialized in economic geology. He directed many scientific explorations into the cordilleran ranges of the West which uncovered important ore deposits. Mt. Whitney, the highest peak in California, is named for him.

WHITNEY, William Collins (1841–1904), born in Conway, Massachusetts, after graduation from Yale (1863) became a successful corporation lawyer in New York City. As Cleveland's energetic Secretary of the Navy (1885–89), he laid the basis for a modern 'steel navy,' which by 1900 had made the U.S. a ranking naval power. His son, Harry Payne Whitney (1872–1930), was a New York banker whose wife, the sculptor Gertrude Vanderbilt Whitney, founded the WHITNEY MUSEUM.

WHITNEY, WILLIAM DWIGHT (1827–94), philologist, was a brother of JOSIAH DWIGHT WHITNEY. After graduation from Williams (1845) and study in Germany, he became professor of Sanskrit (1854) and of comparative philology (1870) at Yale. His *Sanskrit Grammar* (1879) was a landmark in the study of linguistics. As a lexicographer he served as editor in chief of the *Century Dictionary* (6 vols., 1889–91; later supplemented and enlarged to 12 vols.), a work with encyclopedic features, which has not yet been superseded in matters of definition.

WHITNEY, WILLIS RODNEY (1868–1958), nonresident professor of theoretical chemistry at Massachusetts Institute of Technology after 1908, was director (1900–1928) of the Research Laboratory of General Electric Company, Schenectady, New York, the first major undertaking of its kind. After 1928 Whitney served General Electric as vice president in charge of research.

Whitney Museum of American Art, in New York City, was founded (1930) by the sculptor Gertrude Vanderbilt Whitney (Mrs. Harry Payne Whitney) (1876–1942). It was the first museum in the U.S. devoted exclusively to native art. Its own collections are all works by artists of the 20th century, but it organizes exhibits of the work of early American artists.

WHITTIER, JOHN GREENLEAF (1807–92), born in Haverhill, Massachusetts, was largely self-educated. At first a writer of newspaper verse, from 1833 to 1860 he was an active abolitionist and a crusading antislavery editor (1847–59) for the Washington *National Era.* Because he was a Quaker, he felt horror-struck at the approaching fratricide of the Civil War, but his war poems are Union in sentiment, and fervent in 'Laus Deo,' which celebrates the freeing of slaves. A pioneer in regional literature, he is at his best in depicting New England life and legend, and *Snow-Bound* (1866), his finest idyl, is a memorable achievement. In the course of his long life he produced some 40 books, and as a poet won a household popularity in America second only to that of Longfellow. Many of his devotional lyrics are in hymnals, and include 'Dear Lord and Father of mankind,' one of the notable hymns of the 19th century.

A full-length study of Whittier is that by J. A. Pollard (1949).

Wickersham Commission was the Law Observation and Enforcement Commission appointed (1929) by President Hoover. It was headed by former Attorney General George W. Wickersham (1858–1936). The social and political problems created by the breakdown of the Eighteenth Amendment during the PROHIBITION ERA were becoming grave. The Commission was asked to conduct a survey that might serve as a basis for forming public policy to deal with complex issues. Its report (1931) said in effect that Federal liquor prohibition was unenforceable but should be enforced, that it was a failure but should not be abandoned. Two years later the Eighteenth Amendment was repealed.

WIENER, NORBERT (1894–1964), called the father of automation, was a lifelong professor of mathematics at Massachusetts Institute of Technology (1932–60). (A child prodigy, he received his Ph.D. from Harvard at nineteen.) He made fundamental contributions in the fields of mathematics, engineering, and logical science, especially to analysis and information theory. His *Cybernetics* (1948), which added a new word to the language, opened up a science concerned with finding common principles in the functions of automatic machines and of the human nervous system. Later books include *The Human Use of Human Beings* (1950), and *Nonlinear Problems in Random Theory* (1958).

WIGGLESWORTH, MICHAEL (1631–1705), after graduation from Harvard (1651) became lifelong minister of the church at Malden, Massachusetts. His theological poem, *The Day of Doom* (1662), versified standard Puritan doctrine in jog-trot ballad meter. The most popular single work in colonial New

England, it was issued in at least ten editions before 1760. The first edition, literally read to pieces, has entirely disappeared. Until the 19th century it remained the best known poem in America. Its stress upon the relentless torments that would be meted out to the unregenerate was a factor in producing the abnormal fears culminating in the hysteria of the Salem WITCHCRAFT DELUSION of 1692.

WIGMORE, JOHN HENRY (1863–1943), for many years dean of the law faculty at Northwestern (1901–29), compiled the monumental *Treatise of Evidence* (4 vols., 1904; 3rd ed., 10 vols., 1940), a critical survey and a manual of practice for lawyers. His studies in comparative law are set forth in *Panorama of the World's Legal Systems* (3 vols., 1928).

WIGNER, EUGENE PAUL (1902–), Hungarian-born mathematical physicist, became professor of theoretical physics at Princeton in 1938. During World War II he was associated with the Metallurgical Laboratory at Chicago (1942–47), serving as director in 1946–47. He formulated the laws governing the mechanics of the nuclear particles (proton and neutron) and established the symmetry principles underlying the interaction of nuclear particles in accordance with the direction of their spinning motion. For this work in 1963 he shared with two other nuclear scientists (MARIA MAYER and the German physicist J. H. D. Jensen) the Nobel Prize in physics.

Wigwam, the Abnaki word for *house,* was the dome-shaped Indian dwelling covered with bark or mats. The word was applied by early New Englanders to all Indian houses. Actually the wigwam differs markedly from the conical TEPEE of the Plains Indians.

Wilderness Campaign (May–June 1864), the first major Civil War engagement in the eastern theater after the battle of GETTYSBURG (July 1863), was Grant's attempt to clear the wild and almost impenetrable Wilderness region west of Fredericksburg, Virginia, before a final assault on Lee's Army of Northern Virginia. The Battle of the Wilderness (5–6 May) was bloody, disjointed, and indecisive, and led to the even more sanguinary battle of SPOTSYLVANIA (8–12 May), where Grant was repulsed. Fearing that Lee might withdraw to the defenses of Richmond, Grant engaged him at COLD HARBOR (1–3 June), in the most futile and costly slaughter of the war. Grant lost some 60,000 men in the campaign (Lee a proportionately larger 20,000), and withdrew across the James river, where, after renewing his strength, later in the summer he began the PETERSBURG CAMPAIGN, the final engagement of the war.

Wilderness Road was first created (1775) by DANIEL BOONE at the instigation of the TRANSYLVANIA COMPANY, as a trail to link Virginia with the trans-Allegheny west through the gap into the CUMBERLAND PLATEAU. It became a primitive road during the 1790's, and extended through Kentucky to Ohio, with a branch leading (through Louisville) to Indiana. It was some 300 miles long. After it became a TURNPIKE early in the 19th century it matched the Ohio river as a highway into the growing empire of the new nation.

Wildcat banks, so called, were the state banks chartered in great numbers in the West before the National Bank Act of 1863. They had scant capital, and they issued notes in excess of any capacity to redeem them.

WILKES, CHARLES (1798–1877), born in New York City, having received an appointment as midshipman, surveyed Narragansett Bay (1832–33), and served as head of the naval Depot of Charts and Instruments. Placed in charge of the first national marine exploration (1838), and accompanied by trained scientists, he took his squadron of six ships around South America, visited the Antarctic, much of the Pacific, and the Pacific Northwest, completing his globe-circling tour at New York in 1842. His *Narrative of the United States Exploring Expedition* (5 vols. and atlas, 1844) was followed by a series of scientific reports (20 vols., 11 atlases, 1844–74). Wilkes recognized in 1838 that Antarctica was another continent, a fact not generally accepted until the Shackleton expedition of 1908–9. Impetuous by nature (he was twice court-martialed),

Wilkes was responsible early in the Civil War for the TRENT AFFAIR, which nearly involved the Union in a war with England. He was promoted to the rank of commodore in 1862 and commanded a squadron in the West Indies. In 1866 he was retired with the rank of rear admiral.

WILKINSON, JAMES (1757–1825), Maryland-born soldier and adventurer, began his army service in 1776, took part in Arnold's Quebec campaign, and after the battle of Saratoga was given the honor of taking to Congress the news of Burgoyne's defeat. Although Congress censured him for delay in carrying the dispatch, it promoted him to brigadier general (1777) and made him secretary to the board of war (1778), a post he was forced to resign because of his involvement in the CONWAY CABAL. Charged with irregularities as clothier general of the army (1779–81), he resigned that post. During the 1780's Wilkinson moved to Kentucky, where he accepted bribes to make his state a 'bastion of Mexico,' and became notorious among the western conspirators intriguing for secession as the most effective way to gain Spanish ports for American shipping.

In 1791 Wilkinson re-entered the army and, on the death of Anthony Wayne (1796), became its ranking officer. He was still in Spanish pay when, as governor of Louisiana Territory (1805–6), he discussed with Aaron Burr aspects of Burr's western (and probably treasonable) schemes. Evidently deciding that Burr was worth more to betray than to befriend, Wilkinson revealed to President Jefferson Burr's 'deep, dark, wicked, and wide-spread conspiracy,' and was the prosecution's chief witness at Burr's trial. He had in fact betrayed every trust reposed in him. Though his reputation was tarnished, he retained his command, and was cleared by an army board of inquiry (1811).

In the War of 1812 Wilkinson signally failed in his Montreal campaign and was replaced. Again an official inquiry cleared him. For a time he lived on his Louisiana plantation but later appeared in Mexico City, where he died.

See T. R. Hay and M. R. Werner, *The Admirable Trumpeter . . . General James Wilkinson* (1941).

WILLARD, EMMA [HART] (1787–1870), pioneer in women's education, at Middlebury, Vermont, opened her small seminary (1814) to teach such subjects as mathematics, philosophy, and sciences, studies not then available to women. Largely self-educated, she wrote history and geography textbooks, and introduced modern teaching methods adapted for women, many of whom she trained for teaching posts. Her *Plan for Improving Female Education* (1819) was an appeal to the New York legislature, and it led Governor Clinton to invite her to move to that state. In 1821 she opened the Troy Female Seminary, which offered a curriculum considered unusually rigorous for women, but one which served as a model for similar schools both in Europe and America. (Her poetry includes the very popular 'Rocked in the Cradle of the Deep.') After she retired from active management (1838), the school was renamed in her honor.

WILLARD, FRANCES ELIZABETH (1839–98), having served as dean of women at Northwestern University, resigned her post to devote herself to reform causes, particularly the temperance movement. She helped organize the Woman's Christian Temperance Union (1874), and for the last twenty years of her life she served as its president (1879–98).

WILLARD, JESS (1883–), Kansas-born pugilist, in 1915 won the world heavyweight boxing championship by defeating JACK JOHNSON in a 23-round bout at Havana, Cuba. He lost the title in 1919 to JACK DEMPSEY when Dempsey scored a technical knockout after three rounds of a scheduled twelve-round match at Toledo, Ohio.

WILLARD, SAMUEL (1640–1707), son of Major Simon Willard, the stout planter of Concord, after graduation from Harvard (1659), occupied the frontier pulpit at Groton before becoming pastor of the Third (Old South) Church in Boston (1678–1707), where his influence in the Massachusetts Bay colony became very important. Though he lacked the brilliance of Increase Mather, he was a sound scholar and the leading New England exponent of COVENANT THEOLOGY, which he set forth in a series of expository lectures on the Assembly's Shorter Catechism, posthumously issued in a 1000-page folio volume (the largest ever issued in the colonies) as a *Compleat Body of Divinity* (1726). When Increase Mather's quarrel led the General Court to drop Mather as president of Harvard, Willard as vice president (1700–1707) took over the interim with quiet ability. Essentially a theologian, not a political leader, Willard avoided public utterances outside his competence.

William and Mary, College of, second oldest institution of higher learning in the U.S., was established at Williamsburg, Virginia, by JAMES BLAIR for the training of an Episcopal clergy, under a charter (1693) granted by the British sovereigns. PHI BETA KAPPA was founded (1776) there. In 1779 the college became a university by adding schools of modern languages, medicine, and law. Indeed, after the war the institution probably had the best liberal arts curriculum in the country, although the Episcopal Church had too great a control to allow it to become a state university.

The college was closed during the Civil War, and it was again closed (1881–88) for lack of funds. Since 1906 the college has been state supported, and, since 1918, co-educational. The main building, designed by Sir Christopher Wren (1695) was restored in 1929 as part of the restoration of WILLIAMSBURG. In 1965, with a faculty of 220, it enrolled 3300 students.

WILLIAMS, JOHN (1664–1729), after graduation from Harvard (1683) became the first minister at Deerfield, Massachusetts. During the great Indian massacre in that frontier settlement (1704), he and his family were taken captive, and his wife and two of his children died before he was transported to Canada. Ransomed in 1706, he returned to Deerfield where he wrote (at the urgent request of Cotton Mather) *The Redeemed Captive Returning to Zion* (1707), one of the most widely read INDIAN CAPTIVITIES. For a century it was a best-seller; it went through a score of reprintings and at least six editions.

WILLIAMS, ROGER (*c.* 1603–83), son of a London merchant tailor, became the protégé of Sir Edward Coke and was thus destined for the law when he entered Pembroke College, Cambridge, but after receiving his degree (1627) he took Anglican orders. A born inquirer and never a conformist, Williams soon became a Puritan. So strong did his Separatist convictions grow that on arriving in New England (1631) he refused the proffered post of teacher (in religious instruction) in the Boston church because it had not wholly broken with Anglicanism. The more liberal Salem body accepted his 'leveler' principles, but when he insisted that the Massachusetts charter was invalid because it was an expropriation of Indian rights, and that civil magistrates had no power over matters of conscience, the General Court decreed his banishment. His insistence that his *own* conscience made a law raised a dangerous ANTINOMIAN issue. In 1635 he took the path toward Narragansett, and on land purchased from the Indians he founded Providence as a refuge for all SEEKERS.

Williams's assertion of toleration came not from political scruples but from a conviction that man's spiritual life cannot be coerced. Gifted with imagination, the quick-witted, pugnacious Master Roger Williams was the embodiment of the Protestant individualist. His Plantation became the center for Baptists after he established his church (1639). He set forth his reflections clearly in *The Bloudy Tenent of Persecution for Causes of Conscience* (1644), a work that was anathema to JOHN COTTON, the spokesman of the Bay Colony. Furthermore he lived up to his principles when, as president of the Providence colony (1654–57), he defied both Massachusetts and New Netherland by giving asylum to the Quakers, even though he thought that their doctrine of 'Inward Light' was blasphemous.

Actually everything that Williams later acted upon is foreshadowed in his first book, *A Key into the Language of America* (1643). It was begun as a practical handbook through which the missionary-trader might communicate with the Narragansetts. It became not only a vivid picture of Indian life but a revealing self-portrait. In important ways the Indians enlarged his views of human nature and made him receptive to ideas alien to his own. It was as a Seeker that Williams twice went to England (1643–

44, 1651–54), where through the influence of such powerful friends as the younger Sir Henry Vane, Milton, and Cromwell, he obtained a patent (confirmed by royal charter in 1663) uniting Portsmouth and Newport with his own Providence Plantations under a grant of absolute liberty of conscience.

The social program that Williams outlined in *Experiments of Spiritual Life and Health* (1652) is animated by the spirit of Christian fellowship which regards men as brothers, irrespective of rank, caste, or race. It is in no sense 'mystic' (a term he would have applied to Quakerism), but a series of meditations which yearn after spiritual satisfactions as revealed through the Bible.

Williams wrote his principles into the law and customs of Rhode Island, where he never allowed toleration to depend upon political concessions. He outlived most of his generation and died in relative obscurity. He was buried near the site of a spring in Providence, which in 1721 was marked: 'Liberty is reserved for the inhabitants to fetch water at this spring forever.'

See O. E. Winslow, *Master Roger Williams* (1957).

WILLIAMS, TENNESSEE [THOMAS LANIER] (1914–), Mississippi-born author, achieved distinction as a playwright with *The Glass Menagerie* (1945). *A Streetcar Named Desire* (1947, Pulitzer Prize), likewise dealing with a dream world in a slum setting, is located in the Deep South, as is *Cat on a Hot Tin Roof* (1955), which depicts family tensions in an atmosphere of greed and mendacity. His dramas focus on lonely outsiders, the 'fugitive kind,' usually victims of weakness, guilt, or illusion. He has concerned himself with the power of dream and desire in which conflicts lie beyond the scope of reason or social order. His sensational treatment of deviates from the norm has brought him unusual popular success.

Williamsburg, in southeastern Virginia, was settled in 1633 as Middle Plantation, and given its present name in 1699 when it became the capital. In 1693 it was chosen for the site of William and Mary, the second oldest college in the colonies, and it was the first city incorporated in Virginia (1722). It was the scene of important conventions during the pre-Revolutionary period, but declined after 1779, when the capital was permanently moved to Richmond.

In 1928 the most extensive restoration in the U.S. (financed by John D. Rockefeller, Jr.) was undertaken to give the entire colonial area its original appearance. More than 500 buildings were restored or reconstructed, including the Capitol (1705) and the Governor's Palace (1720). Its population (1960) is some 6800.

Williams College (1793) is a nonsectarian liberal arts college for men. The meeting of a small group of students there in 1806 led to the formation (1810) of the first national foreign missionary society. The college became nationally prominent during the presidency of MARK HOPKINS (1836–72). Under the presidency of Harry A. Garfield (1908–34) it sponsored an Institute of Politics (1921), which became a model for similar forums. In 1965, with an endowment of $35,790,000 and a faculty of 162, it enrolled 1235 students.

WILLISTON, SAMUEL (1861–1963), Massachusetts-born lawyer and teacher, after graduation from Harvard (1882) and its law school (1888), briefly engaged in practice before becoming a lifelong professor of law at Harvard (1890–1938). His study of *Some Modern Tendencies in Law* (1929) reflects the intellectual life of the 1920's. But his chief contributions to legal scholarship are *The Law of Sales* (4 vols., 1909; 2nd ed., 1924), and *The Law of Contracts* (9 vols., 1920; 2nd ed., 1936–38). These writings helped create enduring legal mechanisms to encourage uniformity in commerce among the states.

WILLKIE, WENDELL LEWIS (1892–1944), after graduation from Indiana University (1913) practiced law in Indiana and Ohio (1916–29) before moving to New York, where he became a power in Wall Street and president (after 1933) of the Commonwealth and Southern Corporation. A quondam Democrat, without political affiliations and despite his wealth and business connections, in 1940 Willkie won the Republican presidential nomination. In his campaign against F. D. Roosevelt he attacked New Deal extravagance but supported the government's foreign commitments. A conservative with great charm, Willkie won a personal following matched by no Republican since Theodore Roosevelt. He polled some 22,000,000 popular votes (though F. D. Roosevelt's 27,000,000 carried 449 electoral votes to Willkie's 82). A foe of isolationism, Willkie later served as the President's personal emissary (1941–42) to England, Russia, and the Far East, and set forth his internationalist views in *One World* (1943).

WILLS, HELEN NEWINGTON (1906–), gained international attention by repeatedly winning women's tennis championships in the U.S. and in Europe during the period 1923–38. She is generally regarded as the foremost woman tennis player of her day, an era of brilliant women players.

Wilmot Proviso (1846), introduced in the U.S. House of Representatives by David Wilmot of Pennsylvania, was an amendment to a bill providing appropriation of $2,000,000 (later raised to $3,000,000) to facilitate negotiations with Mexico for territorial adjustment. The bill was under congressional consideration during the progress of the Mexican War. The amendment stipulated that none of the territory acquired should be open to slavery. The amended bill passed the House in two successive sessions (1846, 1847), but was defeated in the Senate. The terms of the Proviso gave a rallying principle to the FREE-SOIL forces, and crystallized the sectional split between the North and South.

WILSON, ALEXANDER (1766–1813), born at Paisley, Scotland, in 1794 came to the U.S., where he became a pioneer in ornithology. Instructed by his friend the naturalist William Bartram, Wilson toured (mostly on foot) the East, the Ohio and Mississippi valley frontier, and the Deep South in search of material for his *American Ornithology* (9 vols., 1808–14). It is a work of sound scholarship, and the bird biographies, often written in the presence of the birds that he describes, abound in picturesque detail and are accompanied by his attractive illustrations. He was living in Philadelphia at the time of his death.

His poetry, forgotten today, was as good as any being written in America during his twenty years of residence, although it does not begin to match his contributions as a naturalist. *The Foresters* (1805) is a long nature poem (typical of others), written during the year that he penetrated the wild Niagara country. *Poems, chiefly in the Scottish Dialect* (1816) were continuously in print throughout the 19th century in Scotland. A statue was erected to him at Paisley in 1876.

WILSON, JAMES (1742–98), Scottish-born jurist, came to Philadelphia (1765), where he successfully practiced law and supported the Revolutionary cause as a pamphleteer. He contended that Parliament lacked authority to deal with the colonies, which in fact were dominions under a common sovereign. As a conservative member of Congress (1782–83, 1785–87) he laid the foundation for the Bank of the U.S. One of the most influential delegates to the Federal Constitutional Convention, he worked to incorporate the principle that sovereignty resides in the people. Washington appointed him an Associate Justice of the Supreme Court (1789), and in 1790 Wilson became the first professor of law at the College of Philadelphia. In 1793 he wrote a notable opinion in CHISHOLM *v.* GEORGIA, upholding the Federal against the states' authority. He was a heavy land speculator, and to avoid arrest for debt he was compelled to move from state to state. Threatened with impeachment for attempting to influence legislation, he died in acute nervous collapse at fifty-six. Wilson's chief contributions to the founding of the Republic were his grasp of the Federal idea and his vision of a future expansion controlled by Congress.

WILSON, [THOMAS] WOODROW (1856–1924), 28th President of the U.S. (1913–21), was born at Staunton, Virginia, the son of an austere Presbyterian minister, who left an indelible stamp upon the son's character, as did the early years spent in Georgia and South Carolina during the Reconstruction period. Upon graduation from Princeton (1879) he studied law at the University of Virginia, opened a law office in Atlanta, but soon abandoned practice to study government and history at Johns Hopkins, where he took his Ph.D. (1886). As professor of jurisprudence and political economy at Princeton (after 1890), he established a reputation as a stimulating teacher, and in 1902 he was elected president, the first nonclerical head of the institution. Prompted by his strong democratic principles, he devoted himself to reforms, inaugurated the 'preceptorial system' by which student and teacher were brought into a more intimate relationship, and gave intellectual leadership of high order. But Wilson by temperament was unable to compromise on issues where he felt that his judgment was right, and in his bitter struggle with the group headed by Dean Andrew West of the Graduate School he lost out. Feeling that his position had become untenable, he resigned (1910).

With the backing of influential Democrats, including wealthy conservatives who believed he would stamp out radical Bryanism, Wilson won election as governor of New Jersey in 1910, and in 1911–13, as a forward-looking progressive, established a record which brought him to the forefront of national politics. He won the Democratic presidential nomination in 1912 and gained the election because the Taft-Roosevelt forces had split. (Electoral vote: Wilson 435, Roosevelt 88, Taft 8.)

Although a minority President, Wilson was in a remarkably strong political position when he assumed office. The Republicans were at loggerheads, a Democratic majority prevailed in both Houses, and Wilson's reforming zeal captured independent congressional support. Sensitive to the demands of public opinion, he secured passage of legislation that his collection of eloquent campaign speeches, *The New Freedom* (1913), had envisaged. The UNDERWOOD TARIFF ACT (1913) reversed a protectionist trend almost unchallenged in 60 years, and it was followed by the establishment of the FEDERAL RESERVE SYSTEM (1913), one of Wilson's great administrative achievements. His program for regulating trusts began with the creation of the FEDERAL TRADE COMMISSION (1914) and passage of the CLAYTON ANTITRUST ACT (1914). In 1916 the FEDERAL FARM LOAN ACT eased credit for farmers, and the ADAMSON ACT established an 8-hour day.

In foreign affairs the difficulties beginning to come to a head in Latin America stemmed in part from inherited commitments, and culminated in partial protectorates in Nicaragua, Haiti, and Santo Domingo (1915–16). Wilson was unwilling to recognize the *de facto* Huerta government in Mexico on moral grounds, and began a period of 'watchful waiting.' His 'punitive expedition' (1916) against the Mexican bandit Villa was likewise prompted in part by his missionary impulse. His naïveté in judging foreign relations in terms of Golden Rule Diplomacy had been evident from the moment he brought William Jennings Bryan into his cabinet as Secretary of State.

Meanwhile, upon the outbreak of World War I (1914), Wilson was determined to remain absolutely aloof, although by February 1915 he was warning Germany of her 'strict accountability.' When the *Lusitania* was sunk in May, the President was moved to bolder speech, and Bryan resigned. The election of 1916 was keyed to the phrase 'He kept us out of war,' and Wilson won the election by the close popular and electoral votes (over Charles Evans Hughes) of 9,100,000 to 8,500,000 and 277 to 254. But after Germany renewed unrestricted submarine warfare, the President called for war (April 1917), declaring that 'The world must be made safe for democracy.'

In January 1918 Wilson proposed his FOURTEEN POINTS as the basis for peace, and in September he stated that the League of Nations was the 'most essential part' of the peace settlement. With those thoughts in mind, Wilson broke the precedent of his office to head the American delegation when he sailed for Paris in December 1918 to attend the VERSAILLES PEACE CONFERENCE. (For his work he received the 1919 Nobel Peace prize.) He was feted to a degree resembling the reception accorded Franklin more than a century earlier. But lacking Franklin's genius for accommodation, on his return to Washington, Wilson sought unconditional approval for the League Covenant, and Senate ratification of it in the TREATY OF VERSAILLES. Meeting stubborn opposition, he made a nationwide tour to appeal to the people. Lesser statesmen followed in his wake to contest his principles and to capitalize on the isolationist mood of the Middle and Far West. Overworked and disillusioned, on his tour Wilson suffered a physical breakdown from which he never recovered.

Wilson's greatest contribution was his expansion of the powers of the presidency. He seized party leadership, and as spokesman of the people he used public opinion as a spur to Congress, where he exerted a decided influence on the drafting and passage of all great measures enacted before Republican majorities were elected in 1918 to both houses of Congress. His unswerving moral determination, characteristic of the prophet rather than of the statesman, cost him the realization of his hope for a new world order, but it helped to give renewed prestige to moral standards in international politics, and established for him a lasting place in world history.

A full-length study of Wilson's career is that by Arthur S. Link (4 vols., 1947–57). Herbert Hoover writes from personal experience in *The Ordeal of Woodrow Wilson* (1958).

Wilson-Gorman Tariff Act (1894), which erected a high protective barrier, followed the effort of President Cleveland to redeem the Democratic party pledge to reduce tariffs. The bill as introduced in the House by Representative W. L. Wilson was an honest effort to lower duties, but Democratic Senator A. P. Gorman of Maryland led a powerful tariff lobby (Democrats from the East were no more interested in reductions than their Republican colleagues), and when the bill emerged from joint committee it was unrecognizable: a total of 634 changes had been made, most of them upward, with protective rates advanced to an average level of 40 per cent. Cleveland denounced the bill as 'party perfidy and party dishonor,' but he allowed it to become law without his signature because he believed it to be some improvement on the MC KINLEY TARIFF ACT of 1890.

The tariff ruined many Cuban planters by greatly raising U.S. duties on tobacco and sugar, their chief exports, thus contributing to the tensions of civil war in the island. At the same time, a well-intentioned proviso in the Act for a tax of 2 per cent on incomes above $4000 was soon nullified by the Supreme Court in POLLOCK *v.* FARMERS' LOAN AND TRUST CO. (1895).

Wind Cave National Park (1903), in the Black Hills of southwestern South Dakota, is an area of some 25,000 acres, and is chiefly a region of limestone caverns.

WINES, ENOCH COBB (1806–79), while secretary of the Prison Association of New York (after 1861) wrote his *Report* (1867) on U.S. prisons and reformatories. His recommendation of the development of prisons as correctional institutions and the substitution of reformatories for time sentences, especially for youthful offenders, was a pioneer study of prison management, and many of his ideas were later incorporated into law. His son, FREDERICK HOWARD WINES (1838–1912), also labored for prison reforms and his *Punishment and Reformation* (1895) was influential.

WINSLOW, EDWARD (1595–1655), came to America on the *Mayflower* (1620). The account of the voyage and the early days of the Plymouth colony in MOURT'S RELATION is substantially based on Winslow's record. He served briefly as agent for the colony in England (1623–24), where he published his propaganda brochure, *Good News from New England* (1624), and returned to take a leading part in the colony's affairs, three times as governor (1633, 1636, 1644). Respected by Cromwell, he later journeyed to England twice to defend the Puritan regime in pamphlet warfare. He died while on a mission to the West Indies for the Protector.

WINSOR, JUSTIN (1831–97), while serving as librarian of Harvard (1877–97), edited the co-operative *Narrative and Critical History of America* (8 vols., 1884–89), the best 19th-century survey in its field. Its scholarly notes, map reproductions, and bibliographical essays still give it standing.

WINTHROP, JOHN (1588–1649), scion of a family of prominence in Suffolk, England, left Trinity College, Cambridge after two years, married at seventeen, was admitted to the Inner Temple (1628), and became a prosperous attorney. As an intense Puritan discouraged about the future of religion in England, he became interested in the Massachusetts Bay Company, of which he was governor (1629) when the decision was made to embark for Salem. He settled at Boston in 1631, and for most of his remaining years he was either governor or deputy governor of the colony, and at all times its leading citizen.

His influence on the history of Massachusetts was immense. He supported the banishment of Roger Williams, fought ARMINIANISM, and guided the community through several crises during the 1640's. He began his *Journal,* sometimes called *The History of New England,* when the Bay Company was about to sail from Southampton (1630), and kept it up intermittently throughout his life. It was not published until 1790, but early historians had access to it. It typifies the Puritan concept of history (the expression of the will of God) by recording the minute as well as the great happenings.

WINTHROP, John, Jr. (1606–76), eldest son of Governor JOHN WINTHROP, pursued studies at Trinity College, Dublin, and was admitted to the Inner Temple (1624). He traveled in Italy and the Near East before emigrating to New England in 1631. For a year (1634) he served as colonial representative in England before assuming leadership in settling towns in Connecticut, where he was annually elected governor (except for one year) from 1657 until his death. After the Restoration he obtained a charter (1662) which remained in force until Connecticut became a state.

By far the most scientifically inclined New Englander of his century, and a much loved practicing physician, Winthrop collected a large library especially related to astronomy, chemistry, medicine, mathematics, and occult lore. With knowledge that allowed him to assay ores and prospect for minerals, he initiated industrial chemistry in America by erecting (1644) an iron works at Saugus, Massachusetts.

He was a lifelong friend and correspondent of such Europeans as Robert Boyle, von Helmont, Christopher Wren, Kepler, and Kenelm Digby. It is now known that he was making astronomical observations as early as 1660 with a ten-foot telescope, an instrument comparable to those used by leading European scientists. While sojourning in London he was elected to the ROYAL SOCIETY (1663), the first American so honored. The three-foot refractor that he probably brought back with him he presented to Harvard in 1672. His energy as an industrial pioneer and his quality of aristocratic leadership give him rank among the architects of the American commonwealth.

WINTHROP, John (1681–1747), grandson of Governor JOHN WINTHROP of Connecticut, after graduation from Harvard (1700), married a daughter of Governor Dudley of Massachusetts and took residence on his large Connecticut estate. In 1724 an extensive property lawsuit took him to London, where he remained. He enjoyed the society of learned men, and though his contributions to science were negligible, in recognition of the many specimens he presented to the Royal Society he was honored in 1734 by membership in that body.

WINTHROP, John (1714–79), son of Judge Adam Winthrop of Boston, after graduation from Harvard (1732), was appointed in 1738 to the chair of mathematics vacated by ISAAC GREENWOOD. The first important scientist to teach in America, Professor Winthrop founded the experimental method here. In 1746 he gave the earliest laboratory demonstration of electricity and magnetism, and among his classroom instruments was an electric battery purchased and assembled in London by Franklin. In 1751 Winthrop introduced the study of Newtonian fluxions, later developed into differential and integral calculus. His study of the earthquake of 1755 gives him rank as a founder of seismology. Many of his papers were published in the *Transactions* of the Royal Society, to which body he was elected in 1766. In 1771 Edinburgh awarded him an LL.D., and two years later Harvard conferred the same honor, the first to be awarded in America.

Wireless, see *Radio.*

WIRT, William (1772–1834), Virginia lawyer, having anonymously published various sketches of the manners and customs of the South, under his own name wrote a *Life* of Patrick Henry (1817). He won fame as the prosecutor (1807) in the trial of Aaron Burr. As Attorney General under Monroe and J. Q. Adams (1817–29), he initiated the practice of having his opinions published as precedents. In 1832 he was nominated as presidential candidate by the ANTI-MASONIC PARTY, and polled 7 electoral votes.

Wisconsin is located between the two upper Great Lakes (Superior and Michigan) and the Mississippi river. The terrain is predominantly rolling and lowlying, with most of its 2500 lakes in the glaciated northern and eastern sections. Forest covers nearly half its land area. It was first explored by JEAN NICOLET in 1634, and formally annexed to France in 1671. Thereafter the region became a network of French fur-trading posts. It was surrendered to the British in 1763, and though nominally under U.S. jurisdiction after 1783 as part of the NORTHWEST TERRITORY, it actually continued under British sway until after the War of 1812.

Settlements rapidly increased after the defeat of BLACK HAWK in the last of the Indian wars east of the Mississippi (1832). In 1836, with a population of 12,000, the area was organized as a territory with its capital at Madison. The Chippewa name for its principal river gave the state its name. (It acquired its nickname, 'Badger State,' because in early lead-mining days miners often lived in dugouts like the hillside burrows of badgers.)

During the twelve years of territorial life the southern prairie region attracted thousands of settlers, principally from New England and New York. European immigrants, mostly Germans, soon came in accelerating numbers. In 1848, with a population of 300,000, Wisconsin was admitted to the Union as the 30th state. The Republican party was formed at Ripon (1854), and the state was carried by the Republicans during its early years. It supported the Union during the Civil War.

After 1865 lumbering and manufacturing rapidly increased. The northern section was settled, and wheat raising gave way to dairying. (Wisconsin is now the leading dairy state.) Milwaukee, with a population (1960) of 741,000, is the chief city and the shipping and industrial center in a metropolitan area of more than 1,000,000. The state's fourteen Great Lakes ports receive transatlantic shipping through the St. Lawrence Seaway.

The 'Wisconsin idea,' put forward under the leadership of the elder ROBERT LA FOLLETTE early in the 20th century, was a term given to the co-operation between the experts in the University of Wisconsin and the administration of the state under the Progressive party. The liberal political views resulted in many social reforms, particularly in labor-management relations, and at the time such forward-looking legislation gave Wisconsin the reputation of being radical. Liberalism has in fact been part of the Wisconsin tradition since the arrival of intellectual leaders in the state, men who had left Germany after the failure of the Revolution of 1848. The survival today of German customs and language is marked. The state has attained a national reputation in education under the leadership of the UNIVERSITY OF WISCONSIN.

Wisconsin, University of, opened at Madison (1849) a year after it was chartered. The second of the state institutions of the Middle West (after Michigan) to become widely known, today it is distinguished for its graduate and research facilities. In 1965, with a faculty of 3660, it enrolled 26,290 students on its Madison campus and 11,300 on its Milwaukee campus.

WISE, ISAAC MAYER (1819–1900), German-born rabbi and scholar, after emigrating to the U.S. (1846), became the acknowledged head of the large Jewish community in Cincinnati after settling there in 1854. He founded Reformed Judaism in the U.S., and established Hebrew Union College (1875), the first American institution for training rabbis, and for 25 years thereafter was its president. He organized important conferences and edited periodicals. He remains one of the pervasive influences in the religious cultures of America.

WISE, JOHN (1652–1725), son of an indentured servant in Roxbury, Massachusetts, graduated from Harvard (1673) and became the lifelong minister of the Second Church of Ipswich (1680–1725). His pamphlets, *The Churches' Quarrel Espoused* (1710) and *A Vindication of the Government of New England Churches* (1717), championed the cause of the independence and autonomy of separate congregations. Written with learning, logic, and wit, they were widely read at the time, and were reissued as political tracts before the Revolution and again before the Civil War. Wise insists upon the natural equality of all men and argues that the people are the only source of power. His argument for paper money, *A Word of Comfort to a Melancholy Country* (1721) is a racy, hard-hitting defense of agrarian causes.

WISE, STEPHEN SAMUEL (1874–1949), reform rabbi and son and grandson of Hungarian rabbis, graduated from the College of the City of New York (1891). He founded in New York (1907) the Free Synagogue, over which he presided until his death. Active in reform movements, he was a foremost leader of Zionism and among the first of his faith to preach to Jews and Christians alike. His work in interfaith movements helped spur a continuing endeavor.

WISSLER, CLARK (1870–1947), professor of anthropology at Yale (1924–40), was for many years curator of anthropology at the American Museum of Natural History (1906–41). He was preeminently an interpreter of the American Indian, to the study of whom he devoted his life. *The American Indian* (1917, 3rd ed., 1950) is a notable exposition of the anthropological approach. His archaeological and ethnological studies include *Indian Cavalcade* (1938), a description of the early Indian reservations, and *Indians of the U.S.* (1940).

WISTAR, CASPAR (1761–1818), Philadelphia physician, was a grandson of Caspar Wistar (1696–1752), an early American glass designer. He was a lifelong professor of anatomy at the University of Pennsylvania (after 1789), and wrote the first American textbook on the subject, *A System of Anatomy* (2 vols., 1811–14). He succeeded Jefferson as president of the American Philosophical Society (1815), and was a leader in the intellectual life of Philadelphia. The botanist Thomas Nuttall named the genus *wistaria* for him.

Witchcraft delusion, a universal superstition of the Western World since prehistory, became especially acute during the 16th and 17th centuries, when many thousands of victims were hanged or burned in Europe. The delusion was brought to America as a matter of course, since the most learned and stable opinion held that persons could confederate with evil apparitions and defy natural laws, the accepted penalty for which was death. Witchcraft was an unexplained phenomenon, and the evidence of its existence seemed so strong that leading scientists had no doubt of its reality.

Although executions for witchcraft had occurred between 1648 and 1690 in scattered points in the colonies, the provincial tragedy at Salem was the manifestation of a madness that still on occasion infects all ranks and classes. In the spring of 1692 a group of young girls, somewhat as a prank, feigned the symptoms of hysteria and accused a family slave, half-Negro and half-Indian, of having bewitched them. Flogged into a false confession, to save her skin she named two respectable goodwives as her confederates. The frenzy spread, prominent people were drawn into the net, and mass agitation began when inflammatory sermons denounced the machinations of the devil. In mid-May civil authorities entered the case to examine the charges growing out of those first made by the 'afflicted children.' Governor WILLIAM PHIPS arrived at Salem and set up a special court to try the accused, with WILLIAM STOUGHTON as presiding judge. The atmosphere of terror increased during the summer and the judges themselves became victims of the panic. Some 150 accused persons were in prison awaiting trial and the number of executions was mounting. By early autumn fourteen women and five men had been hanged, and one man pressed to death for refusing to plead either guilty or not guilty. Meanwhile the leading ministers gathered to debate the legal aspect of 'spectral evidence,' that is, the testimony of 'bewitched' persons. The admission of such uncorroborated evidence was questionable, although it had been cited almost exclusively in these judicial murders.

Not until INCREASE MATHER laid his defense of the victims before the governor did the fury subside. Mather was aided by such fearless and outspoken laymen as THOMAS BRATTLE, who substantially helped bring the mania under control. In October the special court was dissolved and the prisoners released. Later the General Court passed a resolution deprecating the action of the judges, the jurymen signed a statement of regret, and indemnities were granted to the bereaved families. Never in the long history of such delusion has more been done to make restitution for error. The Salem affair virtually ended witchcraft trials in America.

See George L. Kittredge, *Witchcraft in Old and New England* (1929).

WITHERSPOON, JOHN (1723–94), Scottish-born educator and statesman, having won distinction in his fight against the established church in Scotland, came to America as president of the College of New Jersey at Princeton (1768–94). There he invigorated the Presbyterian Church by healing the schism between the Old Side and the New Side (those who opposed and those who favored revivalism). Deeply stirred by the cause of independence in civil as well as religious affairs, he sat as a New Jersey delegate in the Continental Congress (1776–79, 1781–82). He took part in drawing up the Articles of Confederation and signed the Declaration of Independence.

As a member of the Scottish 'common sense' school of philosophy, he denounced Berkeley's idealism. His influence on the college was profound, for he changed its emphasis from preparing young men for the ministry to training them for civic leadership. Of those who studied under him, several score held high office during the early days of the Republic, including President Madison. His own services to the new nation were considerable. Year after year he labored on many important congressional committees. The deference shown him throughout his career by colleagues and students is a measure of the respect that he won in his lifetime.

See V. L. Collins, *President Witherspoon* (2 vols., 1925).

'Wobblies,' see *Industrial Workers of the World.*

WOLFE, JAMES (1727–59), served with distinction in the British army on the Continent, and at the age of thirty-two was made second in command (1758) under General Jeffrey Amherst in the French and Indian War. He trained his men in precision of fire and concentrated musketry, and his ability to tell instinctively what risks to take amounted to genius. For his handling of the siege operations that reduced the Cape Breton bastion at Louisbourg, he was rewarded with the command of an expedition against Quebec. He took his force up a cliff the French believed unscaleable, and, on the Plains of Abraham above Quebec, he forced an open battle with MONTCALM, by which the French lost an empire. Both leaders were mortally wounded. The classic account of the struggle still is Francis Parkman's *Montcalm and Wolfe* (1884).

WOLFE, THOMAS [CLAYTON] (1900–38), born in Asheville, North Carolina, after graduation from the University of North Carolina (1920), studied playwriting at Harvard and taught English at New York University (1924–30), where he began his career as a novelist. *Look Homeward, Angel* (1929) was the first of four moving and clearly autobiographical novels; the other three are *Of Time and the River* (1935), *The Web and the Rock* (1939), and *You Can't Go Home Again* (1940). Massive in length, they combine mystical rhapsody with naturalism, and in them Wolfe struggled with a whole cosmos of experience and ideas, attempting to work out his concept of a better America. The search was conducted with daemonic energy, and Wolfe died at thirty-eight.

Wolves have always inhabited the North American continent, from central Mexico to the Arctic. They created a problem in frontier regions where they preyed on game and livestock. In the trans-Mississippi West they constituted an economic hazard for sheep and cattle ranchers, and most states sought to eradicate them by bounty systems. Wolf skins were an item in the fur trade. The timber wolf still roams the Canadian wilds, and the prairie wolf, or COYOTE, is found principally in the Great Plains. They have some use as scavengers.

Woman suffrage movement had its organized beginning in the U.S. at the Seneca Falls (New York) Convention in 1848, sponsored by such pioneers as ELIZABETH CADY STANTON and LUCRETIA MOTT. By 1870 the American Woman Suffrage Association, led by LUCY STONE and JULIA WARD HOWE, was rivaling the National Woman Suffrage Association, championed by Mrs. Stanton and SUSAN B. ANTHONY. During the 1890's the groups united in a national organization and widened their influence through press and platform, legislative lobbies and congressional hearings.

Wyoming Territory had given the vote to women in 1869, and retained female suffrage after becoming a state (1889). Three other states in the West soon conferred the franchise: Colorado (1893), Utah (1896), and Idaho (1896). During the first two decades of the 20th century the effective campaigning for woman suffrage, notably by ANNA HOWARD SHAW and CARRIE CHAPMAN CATT, led to its extension in other states. Though the militant tactics of some organizations made 'suffragettes' the butt of stage comedians and cartoonists, the movement gained momentum during World War I. In January 1918 President Wilson endorsed the proposed Nineteenth Amendment, extending female franchise on a national scale, and the proposal was ratified in time for the 1920 elections.

Women's Army Corps, see *WACS.*

Women's clubs in the U.S. came into existence chiefly as a result of the women's rights movement in the late 19th century. Devoted to social reform, educational programs, and suffrage for women, many of them associated with the temperance and social settlement groups. The General Federation of Women's Clubs (1889) was an amalgamation of many organizations, of which the DAUGHTERS OF THE AMERICAN REVOLUTION is the largest.

Women's educational movement was significantly under way in the U.S. when EMMA WILLARD opened Troy Female Seminary (1821). MARY LYON established Mount Holyoke Female Seminary (1837) as the first permanent institution for the higher education of women. In the same year Oberlin College, by allowing women to matriculate, initiated co-education at the college level, a policy that gained popularity with the growth of state universities. After the founding of Elmira (1855), Vassar (1865), and Smith (1875), the number of independent women's colleges, as well as such affiliates with men's institutions as Barnard and Radcliffe, rapidly increased.

Professional training of women began in the same decades. CATHARINE BEECHER worked tirelessly in the domestic sphere. ELIZABETH BLACKWELL pioneered in the medical education of women. The opening of the Female Medical School of Philadelphia (1850) was followed by a similar institution in Boston (1852). The earliest law degree to be granted to a woman was conferred in Chicago by Union College of Law (1870). By the turn of the century educational facilities for women were available in all the arts and sciences.

See Thomas Woody, *A History of Women's Education in the U.S.* (2 vols., 1929).

WOOD, GRANT (1892–1942), born in Iowa, began work as a craftsman in metal and handmade jewelry. After studying painting in Chicago and Paris, he returned to Iowa, where he taught art at the State University, and painted pictures of life in the Midwest, which were inspired by the provincialism of 15th-century German primitives. Representative of his work is *American Gothic* (Chicago Art Institute), deliberately stylized and meticulously drawn. With T. H. BENTON of Missouri and J. S. CURRY of Kansas, Wood was one of the leaders of regionalism in painting, a movement which sought to interpret the everyday life of the countrymen they knew.

WOOD, LEONARD (1860–1927), a graduate of Harvard Medical School (1884), became an army surgeon. He led the ROUGH RIDERS in the Spanish-American War (1898) and served with distinction as military governor of Cuba (1899–1902). As a major general he commanded the American military forces in the Philippines (1906–8), and later served as chief of staff of the U.S. army

(1910–14), but he was passed over for high command during World War I. He was unsuccessful in his bid for the 1920 Republican presidential nomination, and was shortly thereafter appointed Governor-General of the Philippines (1921–27), where his unwillingness to grant measures of local autonomy reversed the enlightened policies of his predecessor, Francis B. Harrison, and in part destroyed the reputation he had made in Cuba.

WOOD, Robert Williams (1868–1955), professor of experimental physics at Johns Hopkins (1901–38), was internationally known for his research in optics, spectroscopy, resonance radiation, and in the use of absorption screens in astronomical photography. He devised important supersonics improvements in diffraction gratings. In addition to some 260 papers published in technical journals, he wrote *Physical Optics* (1905, and later revisions), and *Researches in Physical Optics* (2 vols., 1913–19).

WOODS, Robert Archey (1865–1925), pioneer social worker, graduated from Amherst (1886), learned about settlements in the slums as a Resident at London's Toynbee Hall (1890), and used these ideas in founding Boston's first settlement house, South End House (1891), making it a social science laboratory for the nation. He published pioneer studies of depressed urban areas, notably *The City Wilderness* (1898), and developed the concept of the unitary neighborhood. He advanced the idea of public recreation, organized and headed the National Federation of Settlements (1911), and wrote authoritatively on the settlement movement.

WOODWARD, Robert Burns (1917–), professor of chemistry at Harvard (after 1946), contributed notably to theoretical science by synthesizing quinine (1944), cholesterol (1951), cortisone (1951), strychnine (1954), and other substances. He deduced the structure of such antibacterial acids as penicillin (1945), and terramycin (1952). His writings have appeared in professional journals.

Wool industry, see *Sheep industry*.

Woolens Act (1699), designed to prevent competition of colonial manufactures with British goods, forbade the export of wool and woolens outside the colony where it was woven. Actually the Act produced no hardship in America, where most rural families carded, spun, and wove their own wool.

WOOLMAN, John (1720–72), was born near Mount Holly, New Jersey. After an apprenticeship as tailor and baker, he experienced a profound awareness 'that true Religion consisted in an inward life,' and in 1743 he began his career as an itinerant Quaker minister throughout the colonies. A humanitarian with a keen awareness of social injustice, he set forth his plea for racial equality in *Some Considerations on the Keeping of Negroes* (1754, 1762). Other essays dealing with social issues include *A Plea for the Poor* (1793), and *Conversations on the True Harmony of Mankind* (first published in 1837). Woolman is best known for his classic *Journal* (1774), informed with a poignant consciousness of God's infinite tenderness, and written (though Woolman had but little formal education) with a purity of style unmatched by that of any other 18th-century Quaker.

See the biographies by Janet Whitney (1942) and C. O. Peare (1954).

WOOLWORTH, Frank Winfield (1852–1919), a self-educated farm boy of northern New York, established his first five-and-ten-cent store in Lancaster, Pennsylvania, after the failure that year (1879) of his five-cent store in Utica, New York. By 1911, when the F. W. Woolworth Company was incorporated, Woolworth owned more than 1000 such stores throughout the world. He stressed his constant search for a variety of low-priced articles and often contracted for the entire annual output of factories. The Woolworth Building in New York City, 792 ft. high and the tallest building in the world at the time of its erection, was completed in 1913.

WORCESTER, Joseph Emerson (1784–1865), a graduate of Yale (1811), having published gazetteers and school texts (principally dictionaries), issued his own *Comprehensive . . . Dictionary* (1830), immediately a rival to the *American*

Dictionary of NOAH WEBSTER. The 'war of the dictionaries' thus precipitated lasted until 1864, when the uncompromising orthodoxy of Worcester in defending British purist standards of spelling and pronunciation gave way finally to Webster's broader concept that such elements of language undergo changes that are national in character. But so strong was the hold of Worcester's sense of traditionalism that Holmes could facetiously remark in one of his widely read essays that literary men of Boston are 'by special statute' allowed to be sworn on Worcester instead of the Bible.

Worcester* v. *Georgia, see *Cherokee Indians.*

Workers' party, see *Communist party.*

Workingmen's party (1829–30) was organized by unemployed New York City artisans, who sought an effective lien law and the abolition of imprisonment for debt. They were supported by ROBERT DALE OWEN, FRANCES WRIGHT, and the young agrarian reformer G. H. EVANS, who established the *Working Man's Advocate* (1829–37), the first important labor paper in the country. Elements of the party who objected to the leadership assumed by Owen and Miss Wright led a secession, and the party broke up.

Workmen's Compensation, or employers' liability for injuries suffered by employees, as part of the PROGRESSIVE MOVEMENT in the first decade of the 20th century received impetus when a Federal law (1908) covering certain Federal employees was upheld. Between 1910 and 1920 most of the states and territories had adopted such measures; in 1948 Mississippi became the final state to pass compensation laws. Some states have made employers' compensation insurance compulsory and a few have created state insurance funds to secure payments even when the employer is insolvent.

Works Projects Administration (WPA) was a relief measure established (1935) by Executive Order as Works Progress Administration, and redesigned in 1939 when it was transferred to the Federal Works Agency. Headed by HARRY L. HOPKINS and supplied with an initial congressional appropriation of $4,880,000,000, it offered work to the unemployed on an unprecedented scale by spending money on a wide variety of programs, including highway and building construction, slum clearance, reforestation, and rural rehabilitation. So gigantic an undertaking was inevitably attended by confusion, waste, and political favoritism, yet the 'pump-priming' effort stimulated private business during the depression years and inaugurated reforms that states had been unable to subsidize.

Particularly novel were the special programs. The Federal Writers' Project prepared state and regional guide books, organized archives, indexed newspapers, and conducted useful sociological and historical investigations. The Federal Arts Project gave unemployed artists the opportunity to decorate hundreds of post offices, schools, and other public buildings with murals, canvases, and sculptures; musicians organized symphony orchestras and community singing. The Federal Theatre Project experimented with untried modes, and scores of stock companies toured the country with repertories of old and new plays, thus bringing drama to communities where it had been known only through the radio. By 1939 the WPA had given employment to some 8,500,000 persons at a total cost of $11 billion. Its appropriation was then drastically cut, and in 1942 it officially expired.

World Bank (1945), officially the International Bank for Reconstruction and Development, was authorized by Congress following the BRETTON WOODS CONFERENCE. It functions as an agency related to the United Nations. It lends money in underdeveloped areas, and promotes international trade, especially where economic rehabilitation can be effected. In 1965 its capital, largely derived from paid-in subscriptions of 103 countries, exceeded $21,600,000,000. An affiliate, the International Finance Corporation (1956), promotes the flow of private capital internationally; in 1965 this establishment comprised 78 member nations.

World Court, see *Permanent Court of International Justice.*

World War I (1914–18) had threatened to erupt on several occasions during the first decade of the 20th century, when a precarious balance was maintained by two sets of alliances: the Triple Alliance, or Central Powers (Italy, Germany, Austria-Hungary), and the Triple Entente (Great Britain, France, Russia). Late in June 1914 a Serbian revolutionary assassinated the heir to the throne of the Dual Monarchy, Archduke Franz Ferdinand, and Austria sought to end the Slavic threat by making such demands on Serbia as virtually to end her independence, thereby making a general war inevitable.

Austria declared war on Serbia on 28 July 1914. Russia, with hegemony in the Slavic world, mobilized her army. Lest she be caught between two enemies, Germany declared war on Russia (1 August) and on France (3 August), and struck first at France through Belgium, whose neutrality she and the other powers were bound by treaty to respect. On 4 August Great Britain declared war on Germany, and the first global war had begun. (Turkey and Bulgaria later joined the Central Powers. Italy disregarded her alliance and in 1915 joined the Entente, as in the course of time did Romania, Portugal, Greece, Japan, and the U.S.)

The determination of Americans to stay out of Europe's embroilment was thoroughgoing, and it cut through political, sectional, racial and class lines. It was given official sanction early in September 1914 when President Wilson proclaimed the neutrality of the U.S., thus invoking the long-standing tradition of neutral rights.

Of primary significance among the reasons for the entry of the U.S. three years later is the fact that in general, from the start, American sympathies were predominantly with the allies, and ultimately German provocations tipped the balance. In scores of ways, both tangible and intangible, and especially in national origins, the ties with England and France were strong. Relations were not cordial with Germany, a nation regarded with suspicion as militaristic and unfriendly to democracy. Thus to enter the war on the side of the Allies, however agonizing the decision, was conceivable. To support Germany was contrary to reason. Allied publicists sedulously played up such provocations as Germany's violation of Belgium neutrality and the sinking of the LUSITANIA, and they created hatred by embroidering atrocity stories. By joining Canadian contingents or the French Foreign Legion thousands of young Americans gave psychological support to the Allied cause. The Allied blockade of Germany was so effective that within a year the U.S. economy began to depend on the success of the Allies, and neither Congress nor public opinion looked upon armed merchantmen, transporting commodities and munitions to France and England, as 'warships.' Bank credits were extended, and before the U.S. entered the war the American public had lent $1,500,000,000 to the Allies and $27,000,000 to the Central Powers. Yet it was not propaganda or trade or loans that tipped the balance and led the U.S. to declare war on Germany; indeed, the financial stake favored neutrality. America went to war in reaction to German submarine warfare.

The blockade that France and England enforced against Germany, although it violated neutral rights (and was constantly protested by the State Department), was an economic stranglehold which the Germans tried to break by the use of mines and submarines, with a resulting and steadily mounting toll of American lives. Wilson's 'strict accountability' note to Germany early in 1915 therefore forced the issue. With a presidential election approaching in 1916, Wilson sought to capture the vote of the militant element by outlining a program of military preparedness; at the same time his managers campaigned under the slogan 'He kept us out of war.' He was re-elected, but, rebuffed in his repeated appeals to the belligerents for a 'peace without victory,' he was faced with Germany's decision to embark on unrestricted U-boat warfare. The German high command now discounted any additional aid to the Allies, since they believed that by destruction of merchant tonnage they could starve Britain out and win the war in six months. Diplomatic relations between Germany and the U.S. were severed in February 1917.

The U.S. could have stayed out of the war if the American people had been willing to suffer the consequences of a disastrous shipping embargo and surrender to German demands. But by the spring of 1917 the preservation of peace and honor seemed to the American public what Wilson declared, an 'impossible and contradictory thing.' It accepted his crusading slogan that the U.S. should make 'the world safe for democracy,' and by joint resolution (6 April 1917) Congress declared war on Germany.

Then began the gigantic task of converting U.S. industry to a war footing at a time when the Allies were approaching exhaustion in munitions and commodities, and the effectiveness of German submarines was most complete. The Emergency Fleet Corporation immediately set out to build a 'bridge to France,' and was soon laying down two ships for every one sunk by U-boats. The government took over the railroads and the WAR INDUSTRIES BOARD regimented the national economy to a degree never before known. Food and fuel were rationed. The cost of financing both U.S. and Allied expenses was met by heavy taxation and by loans. (At war's end the total direct levy on U.S. citizens amounted to $36,000,000,000, a massive figure at the time.) Public opinion was mobilized by every means imaginable, for unless the nation as a whole believed that the war was both righteous and necessary, it would not have supported the curbs on personal liberties. Indeed, the degree to which 'disloyalty' was punished by the ESPIONAGE ACT of 1917 has never before or since been matched in American history.

The German high command had expected to win the war before American aid could adversely affect their military situation, but they misjudged the character of the American people and the organizational genius of such leaders as BERNARD BARUCH (War Industries), HERBERT HOOVER (Food Administration), and above all, Secretary of War NEWTON BAKER, who within eighteen months created an effective army of 4,000,000 men, half of whom were transported to France. The navy immediately set out to make war on U-boats, and in June General JOHN PERSHING arrived in France with the first contingent of the AMERICAN EXPEDITIONARY FORCE.

Yet the Allied fortunes grew worse as the year advanced. Unable to budge the German armies from the Hindenburg line, France was bogged down in a trench warfare of attrition. The Flanders offensive (June–November) by the British was indecisive. Following the Bolshevik Revolution in November, Russia was lost as a military ally, and masses of German troops were released for service on the western front. At the close of the year the Italians suffered disaster in the Caporetto campaign. The balance of strength on land clearly lay with the Germans.

But by the spring of 1918 effective U.S. resources of manpower, finances, raw materials, and munitions had altered the picture, and by May American troops were deployed in large numbers along the front. The initial American success at CANTIGNY (late May) was quickly followed by thrusts at CHÂTEAU-THIERRY and BELLEAU WOOD (June). The turning point of the war came in the second battle of the MARNE (July), in which some 275,000 American troops were engaged. The first distinctively American engagement at ST. MIHIEL in mid-September (involving 550,000 American troops) preceded the final push, the MEUSE-ARGONNE OFFENSIVE (26 September–11 November), the greatest battle in which U.S. troops (1,200,000) had ever been engaged. The fighting ended with the signing of the armistice on the last day of the Offensive. The TREATY OF VERSAILLES (1919) formally concluded World War I.

World War II (1939–45), the greatest and most terrible in history, followed the disintegration of collective security among the major nations. Its causes were those inherent in WORLD WAR I and stemmed in part from the political and economic rearrangements which the Treaty of Versailles had sought to effect. Although the U.S. had helped win that war and draw up the peace treaty, she assumed no responsibility for subsequent events in Europe, and increasingly built up a wall of isolationism. She never joined the League of Nations and was indifferent to the fate of the new nations she had helped to create. The WASHINGTON CONFERENCE (1921), the KELLOGG-BRIAND PACT (1928), and the HOOVER MORATORIUM (1931) were sincere efforts to stabilize the peace, but America's high tariff extended the economic barriers, and her isolationism, becoming official policy, took on the character of moral apathy. When the democracies began to allow international agreements to go by default, the totalitarian states filled the vacuum by extending their spheres of influence.

The devastating civil war in Spain after 1936 was the prelude to World War II, now inevitable because treaties and agreements under international law were being formally repudiated. France, Great Britain, and the U.S., unwilling to face the implications of this war, adopted a policy of non-intervention. Spain under Franco set up a dictatorship. Thus the totalitarian powers had gained both prestige and an ally.

Japan now advanced into China, and when the sinking of a U.S. gunboat in the PANAY INCIDENT (1937) aroused only mild indignation, the totalitarian countries had every reason to believe that nothing would stir America from her isolationist roost. Hitler's confidence in his growing military strength was shared by his general staff, and his anti-communist alliance (the Rome-Berlin Axis) soon included Japan. In spite of the fact that Ethiopia, Spain, China, and Austria had been sacrificed to appeasement, after the 1938 Czech crisis Prime Minister Chamberlain said: 'If we have to fight, it must be on larger issues than this.' He was expressing the sentiment of millions on both sides of the Atlantic, for the bankruptcy of the democracies was now appalling. The NEUTRALITY ACTS (1935–37) had played into the hands of aggressor nations by laying an embargo on American supplies for the Allies, but Congress and the people believed the Acts to be a bulwark against attack. (When the President declared after the *Panay* incident that unless lawlessness was stopped, the Western Hemisphere would indeed be attacked, he was denounced for 'war-mongering.')

On 1 September 1939 Great Britain formally supported Poland's refusal of Germany's demand for the 'Polish Corridor' to Danzig, which separated East Prussia from the rest of Germany. Germany invaded Poland and two days later Great Britain and France declared war on Germany. The U.S. immediately (5 September) proclaimed its neutrality, but World War II had begun.

The early stages of the war, the German 'blitzkrieg' through Poland, the 'phony' war along the Maginot Line in France, the battle of Britain (1940), and the widening theater were frightening events. Congress voted $37,000,000,000 (a sum larger than the total cost of World War I) for a two-ocean navy, a vast army, wholesale production of airplanes, and aid to the Allies. The ACT OF HAVANA (1940) looked to hemispheric solidarity, the SELECTIVE SERVICE AND TRAINING ACT (1940) provided military conscription, and the President's DESTROYER TRANSFER AGREEMENT (1940) with Prime Minister Churchill built up defenses along the entire North Atlantic seaboard. The BATTLE OF THE ATLANTIC was assuming grim proportions. The LEND-LEASE ACT (1941) helped offset the exhaustion of British credits and made the U.S., in Roosevelt's words, the 'arsenal of democracy.' By supplying the fighting democracies (including the governments in exile) with billions of dollars' worth of arms and services, it officially abandoned any pretense at neutrality.

A succession of astounding triumphs had brought all of Europe, from France to Albania and Greece, under the Nazi heel. Hitler now took an audacious gamble that could open the gates of India by means of the vast industrial resources of the Donets and the Volga basins. In June 1941 he hurled his legions upon the Russian armies massed on his eastern frontiers, and by so doing gave England a powerful ally. In August Roosevelt and Churchill aboard warships met off Newfoundland and formulated the ATLANTIC CHARTER, broad postwar aims soon endorsed by fifteen anti-Axis nations.

Meanwhile tensions mounted in the Pacific. Japan had joined the Axis and in July had occupied French Indo-China. President Roosevelt immediately took two momentous steps. He froze all Japanese credits in the U.S. and he nationalized the armed forces of the Philippines, giving command of the U.S. Army in the Far East to General Douglas MacArthur. Such an embargo on oil and credits gave the Japanese war lords the choice of withdrawal from the mainland or war with the U.S. Their plans had long been shaped and they were executed with masterly skill on 7 December

1941 when they launched a devastating attack on the U.S. Pacific Fleet at PEARL HARBOR and simultaneous blows in the Philippine Islands and Malaya.

The Pearl Harbor attack, by achieving its aim of practically wiping out the Pacific Fleet, abruptly altered the spirit of isolationism in the U.S. On 8 December Congress declared war on Japan and Admiral Chester Nimitz was given naval command in the Pacific. Three days later Germany and Italy declared war on the U.S.

The military situation of the Allies, already bleak, became desperate during 1942. Eastern Europe, the Mediterranean, and much of North Africa was under Axis control, and Hitler had pushed deep into the heart of Russia. German submarines were taking an appalling shipping toll in the Atlantic, and a determined thrust into the Caucasus would surely establish an Axis foothold in India. The Japanese were moving with astonishing speed toward conquest of the entire Pacific and Malaya. The balance could be tipped only if the immense Allied manpower reserves and industrial potential could be mobilized before the Axis powers had circled the globe and made themselves invulnerable.

Yet the military and political leaders of Britain and America never doubted their ability to achieve ultimate victory, for they possessed decisive advantages. They were internally united and they had merged their war effort into a unified alliance far more effective than anything of the sort in World War I. In contrast, Germany, Italy, and Japan were fighting with separate objectives and scant concerted operational planning. The Allied decision to concentrate upon Germany, the most formidable of the Axis partners, was dictated by the need to give all possible aid to Russia by opening a second front and thus blocking the German advance into Egypt and beyond.

In the Pacific theater during 1942 the Japanese enjoyed every advantage, and they outdid the Germans in rapid conquest. Before March they had occupied strategic islands, seized Malaya, Burma, and Indonesia, and, by destroying an Allied fleet in the Java Sea (27 February), they had opened the sea lanes to Australia. President Roosevelt then ordered General MacArthur to leave the Philippines and set up headquarters in Australia. The gallant resistance of General Jonathan Wainwright in the Philippines could only be a holding operation, and the islands were overrun. After the fall of BATAAN (8 April) and the surrender of CORREGIDOR (6 May), Japanese control reached from the Aleutian Islands to New Guinea.

Now began the slow and painful process of dislodging the Japanese from their farflung outposts. The first Allied naval successes were scored in the battles of the CORAL SEA (May 1942), which kept open the lifeline to Australia, and of MIDWAY (June), which foiled a Japanese attempt to render Pearl Harbor untenable. In August the Allies took the offensive on land in the bitter SOLOMON ISLANDS CAMPAIGN, which lasted for fifteen months but ultimately assured the return of the Allies to the Philippines.

The summer of 1942 was the darkest period of the war. The Axis forces under General Erwin Rommel were sweeping into Egypt, and General Friedrich von Paulus had launched an all-out attack on Stalingrad. Unless the Allies could win the battle of the Atlantic, they would lose the war. Yet by autumn the tide was beginning to turn. The vast U.S. industrial potential was mobilized for a total war effort. General Bernard Montgomery's victory at El Alamein (4 November) forced Rommel into full retreat. The NORTH AFRICAN INVASION (8 November), commanded by General Dwight Eisenhower, made headway, and by April 1943 some 250,000 Axis troops had surrendered, thus giving the Allies their first major victory. In the same months the heroic defense of Stalingrad stopped the German advance into the Caucasus. In February 1944 Paulus surrendered with the remnants of his army. The total loss to the Axis in that theater was 330,000 men. Meanwhile, at the CASABLANCA CONFERENCE in January, Roosevelt and Churchill had planned the SICILY CAMPAIGN, which Eisenhower began in July. By mid August this amphibious operation, the boldest yet undertaken, had opened the Mediterranean to Allied shipping and provided a springboard for attacks on Italy.

Five days after British and American forces crossed the Straits of Messina,

Italy had accepted (8 September 1943) the Allied terms of unconditional surrender, thereby draining off German offensive forces into armies of occupation, divisions which seized the leading cities, including Rome. The costly Allied landing at ANZIO (January 1944), in an attempt to outflank the German lines, was followed in March by the assault against Cassino, which fell in May. On 4 June Anglo-American troops entered Rome. Thenceforth the Italian front remained a tense but unprogressive field of action until the collapse of Germany at war's end. Two days after Rome fell the Allies began their massive assault on the coast of Normandy.

The date (1 May 1944) for the opening of a second front in Europe through Normandy had been set at the Anglo-American Conference (Trident) held in Washington in May 1943, and that date was reaffirmed three months later at the first QUEBEC CONFERENCE. Details were hammered out at the TEHERAN CONFERENCE (November 1943) and at the CAIRO CONFERENCE (December 1943), where Eisenhower was named supreme commander of the Allied Expeditionary Force and was called to England to organize the great undertaking. By this time Germany had lost the battle of the Atlantic, air warfare had turned overwhelmingly in favor of the Allies, and during the spring of 1944 the arrival of troops and supplies made the British Isles a vast staging area.

The NORMANDY CAMPAIGN (Operation Overlord, 6 June–25 July 1944) was the beginning of the end of the European phase of World War II, and the largest amphibious operation in all history. At the same time the Russian armies were breaking the German hold on the eastern front. The battle of France began late in July, and shortly after Paris had been liberated (25 August), the U.S. Third Army reached the Marne, and British and Canadian troops were pushing through Belgium and Luxembourg. By 5 September the Allies had landed 2,000,000 men and 3,400,000 tons of supplies in Western Europe, and the battle for Germany could begin. Aachen capitulated on 21 October, then Metz (22 November) and Strasbourg (23 November). The German armies never recovered offensive strength after their last desperate effort in the BATTLE OF THE BULGE (16–26 December). Germany collapsed when the Western and Russian armies met (25 April) at Torgau in Saxony. Hitler committed suicide in his Berlin bunker on the day before that city, in flames, surrendered (2 May). Thus ended the Reich that was to have endured for a thousand years. Field Marshal Jodl signed an unconditional surrender at Rheims (7 May) and V-E Day, proclaimed on 8 May, marked the formal end of the war in Europe.

Allied successes in the Pacific, following the decisive U.S. naval victory at GUADALCANAL (November 1943), continued 'up the ladder' of the Solomons, the Gilberts and Marshalls, the Marianas, and the Bonin Islands, until Japan was within effective bombing reach. Under Lord Louis Mountbatten, supreme commander in Southeast Asia, General Joseph Stilwell began the final offensive (March 1944) in the long BURMA CAMPAIGN (1942–45), described by U.S. Chief of Staff George Marshall, the principal architect of U.S. strategy throughout the war, as the most difficult of all operations. Political events soon limited China as a military ally, and in July 1944 General MacArthur met President Roosevelt and Admiral Nimitz at Pearl Harbor to plan the great PHILIPPINES CAMPAIGN (1944–45), which was climaxed by the battle of LEYTE GULF (October 1944), the engagement that mortally crippled Japanese sea power. The sea lanes to Tokyo were opened by bloody advances through IWO JIMA and OKINAWA (March and April 1945). At the YALTA CONFERENCE in February of that year and at the POTSDAM CONFERENCE in July the war's end was contemplated. The atomic bombing of HIROSHIMA (6 August), the declaration of war by Russia on Japan (8 August), and a second nuclear attack on the naval base of NAGASAKI (9 August) ended the fighting. V-J Day (15 August), following the Japanese surrender on 14 August, marked the conclusion of World War II.

Then began the many negotiations and conferences to protect the ends which the democracies had fought to achieve. The later WAR CRIMES TRIALS (1945–46) revealed a degree of suffering and degradation of the war's victims which exceeded the comprehension of those who had been spared. The political consequences of World War II made the U.S. and the Soviet Union immensely powerful rivals.

World's Columbian Exposition, authorized by Congress (1890) to celebrate the 400th anniversary of the discovery of America, was an international exhibition held at Chicago, May–November 1893. One of the notable artistic displays of modern times, the 'White City' on the shore of Lake Michigan was an assemblage of some 150 buildings, predominantly 'classical' in style, planned under the supervision of D. H. BURNHAM, who enlisted the talents of the ablest American artists of the day. F. L. OLMSTED designed the landscape. Among the architects were R. M. HUNT, C. F. MC KIM, STANFORD WHITE, LOUIS SULLIVAN, and Burnham himself. AUGUSTUS SAINT-GAUDENS, D. C. FRENCH, LORADO TAFT, and FREDERICK MAC MONNIES were associated as sculptors; EDWIN BLASHFORD, KENYON COX, and GARI MELCHERS as painters.

The Exposition attracted thousands of Americans, whose values were influenced by what they saw. Its imitative quality, particularly in its Classical and Renaissance architecture, did little to further the development of native art. Only Sullivan's Transportation Building aroused the unqualified admiration of foreign critics. The chief importance of the Exposition was its revelation of the improvement in the taste of American artists during the few years intervening since the Philadelphia CENTENNIAL EXPOSITION of 1876.

World's fairs in the U.S. began when the Crystal Palace was opened in New York City (July 1853), modeled on the London Exhibition of 1851. The CENTENNIAL EXPOSITION in Philadelphia (1876) was the first international exposition in the U.S., and it gave stimulus to the growing aesthetic, social, and industrial consciousness of the nation. The WORLD'S COLUMBIAN EXPOSITION in Chicago (1893) was one of the notable artistic displays of the 19th century. Later world's fairs in the U.S. that have attracted widespread attention include the Pan-American Exposition (Buffalo, 1901); the Louisiana Purchase Exposition (St. Louis, 1904); the Panama-Pacific International Exposition (San Francisco, 1915); the CENTURY OF PROGRESS INTERNATIONAL EXPOSITION (Chicago, 1933–34). The New York World's Fair of 1939–40 gave emphasis to new architectural trends. Plans for the 1964–65 New York World's Fair were laid in 1960. The Fair opened with a record-breaking advance sale of 28,000,000 tickets, but total attendance fell far short of the 40,000,000 expected in early 1964. Most impressive was the Hall of Science with its marvels of space engineering and the industrial and international exhibits.

WOVOKA, see *Ghost Dance*.

WRIGHT, CHAUNCEY (1830–75), immediately upon graduation from Harvard (1852) became computer for *American Ephemeris and Nautical Almanac.* He was trained in mathematics and physics and developed a strong interest in philosophy, to which he applied a scientific rather than a metaphysical method. Though he wrote little, he was esteemed as a pioneer positivist philosopher and a precursor of William James. He was appointed an instructor in mathematical physics at Harvard in 1874, but he died soon after the appointment. A brilliant talker, he was famous for his Socratic sessions with William James. C. E. Norton edited his *Philosophical Discussions* (1877).

WRIGHT, ELIZUR (1804–85), Connecticut-born insurance actuary, after graduation from Yale (1826) actively engaged in the abolitionist movement, serving (1833–39) as corresponding secretary of the American Anti-Slavery Society. After lobbying successfully in the Massachusetts legislature for a law to compel insurance companies to increase their reserves, he was appointed the state commissioner of insurance (1858–66), in which post he directed important reforms, chiefly by formulating reserve policies to give stability to insurance companies. His work to that end and his subsequent development of actuarial tabulations, while engaged as actuary for several companies, made him known in the U.S. as 'the father of life insurance.'

WRIGHT, FRANCES (1795–1852), Scottish-born freethinker, while touring the U.S. (1818–20), produced her play, *Altorf* (1819), dealing with the Swiss fight for independence, and published her enthusiastic *Views of Society and Manners in America* (1821). Again in the U.S. (1824), she accompanied Lafayette on his triumphal tour, and through him she met Jefferson and Madison, who encouraged her to found NASHOBA COMMUNITY (1825–28) for the purpose of emancipating slaves. When it came to an untimely end, this vigorous apostle of woman's rights took to the lecture platform, from which she advocated free inquiry in religion, free marital union, birth control, and a system of education free from the contaminating influence of parents. In New York she helped ROBERT DALE OWEN edit the *Free Enquirer* (1829) and with him joined the WORKINGMEN'S PARTY. She was denounced in the press as a 'bold blasphemer and voluptuous preacher of licentiousness,' and the ensuing infighting promptly broke up the party. After her brief marriage (1831–35) to William D'Arusmont had been dissolved, Fanny Wright spent her last days in Cincinnati, devoting herself to her many causes.

See W. R. Waterman, *Frances Wright* (1924).

WRIGHT, FRANK LLOYD (1869–1959), Wisconsin-born architect, after a seven-year apprenticeship in the Chicago office of LOUIS SULLIVAN, established himself at Oak Park, Illinois, where he practiced radical innovations and introduced methods of building that have become internationally current. He pioneered in the three-dimensional form, which uses walls and roof as mere enclosing planes. His 'prairie style' emphasizes low, horizontal exterior lines which are given interior treatment by way of a unified, flowing space. Wright used distinctively a kind of floating foundation (a reinforced slab) in constructing the Tokyo Imperial Hotel (1916–20), which firmly withstood the earthquake of 1923. In later years he was concerned with problems involving distribution of mass and with the use of modern materials to carry out decorative effects. He was the first to use the cantilever noncommercially. Wright gave expressive form to the American desire for both mobility and permanence. His great works after 1930 culminated in (during the 1950's) the continuous enclosing spirals of his Guggenheim Museum in New York City. More influential abroad than any other American architect, Wright expressed his philosophy in such books as *On Architecture* (1941), and *When Democracy Builds* (1945).

WRIGHT, PATIENCE LOVELL (1725–86), New Jersey-born sculptor, modeled in wax, and her likenesses, praised in their day, are the earliest known attempts at sculptural expression in the American colonies. After 1772 she lived in England, where, serving as a secret agent for the patriot cause, she modeled George III, Queen Charlotte, and other notables.

WRIGHT, WILBUR (1867–1912) and ORVILLE (1871–1948), brothers, pioneered in aviation. Excellent mechanics, they used the facilities of their Dayton, Ohio, bicycle shop to construct gliders, which they tested (1900–1901) at Kitty Hawk, North Carolina, to verify the operation of wing and biplane surfaces. In December 1903, using an engine of their own design and construction, Orville Wright made the first piloted flight in a power-driven airplane. They received their first public recognition in France (1908). The U.S. Army accepted their plane in 1909, and they organized the Wright Aeroplane Company, from which Orville resigned in 1915 to devote his time to research. Since 1948 the first Wright plane has been on exhibit at the Smithsonian Institution.

Writ of Mandamus, issued as a matter of sovereign right, legally directs the performance of a ministerial function (one which an official duty requires). It is an extraordinary remedy, similar to INJUNCTION, and is used in such instances as those in which a court has illegally refused to accept a suit.

Writs of Assistance, general search warrants issued to customs officers by colonial courts, were first handed down by Massachusetts judges in 1751. Though legally tested a decade later when James Otis contested their constitutionality, they seemed to have given no especial problem and were sustained by the British government, but their revival in the TOWNSHEND ACT of 1767 created a major issue. By 1772 the courts of most of the colonies refused to issue them, and the ensuing dispute was a contributing factor in the American Revolution. The Declaration of Independence specified writs of assistance as a grievance common to all the colonies.

Wyandot Indians, see *Huron Indians.*

WYATT, Sir Francis (1588–1644), succeeded Sir Edwin Sandys as treasurer of the LONDON COMPANY (1621) and as governor of Virginia (1621–26). He brought to Virginia the first written constitution for an English colony. Disasters forced the crown to annul the company's charter in 1624, but Wyatt by request stayed on as governor of the royal colony for two years. He was succeeded by Sir GEORGE YEARDLEY. Wyatt again served as governor of the colony (1639–41), this time with instructions to summon a popular assembly 'once a year or oftener.' Thus was established a precedent of consequence in the development of American political practice — that the people of a royal colony might share in the making of laws. Wyatt was followed in office by Sir WILLIAM BERKELEY.

WYETH, Andrew (1917–), artist, son of the illustrator and mural painter, Newell Converse Wyeth (1882–1945), had his first water color show in 1936. Acclaimed for his sharp-focus realism in tempera, he set three successive records for the highest price paid by a museum for a painting by a living American (1949, 1962, 1963). Exhibited by both conservative and modern museums, Wyeth has been the recipient of numerous official and popular awards. *Christina's World* (1948, Museum of Modern Art) combines emotional force with technical mastery. Similar disciplined reserve characterizes *Ground Hog Day* (1959, Philadelphia Museum), and *Her Room* (1963, Farnsworth Museum, Me.).

WYNN, Ed (1886–1966), actor and producer, enjoyed phenomenal box-office success as a comedian during the 1920's in such extravaganzas as *The Perfect Fool* and *Ed Wynn's Carnival.* He wrote the lyrics and tunes for many of his comedies, and was the first producer to broadcast an entire musical on the radio. After 1930 he appeared chiefly on the screen, radio, and television.

Wyoming, named for Wyoming valley in Pennsylvania, is in the heart of the ROCKY MOUNTAINS, and has a mean elevation of 6700 ft. Its eastern plateau stretches into the PLAINS REGION. The Lewis and Clark Expedition (1804–6) did not go through the area although trappers soon after began to cover portions of it. Bonneville crossed it with wagons (1832), and in 1834 Fort Laramie was established as a fur trading center near the junction of the Laramie and North Platte rivers. Frémont explored the country in 1842–43, and immediately thereafter the OREGON TRAIL became the historic highway across it. Such later trails as the OVERLAND and the BOZEMAN provided new courses for population flow, and in 1867 the Union Pacific Railroad reached westward to Cheyenne.

The discovery of gold at South Pass in 1867 within three years had created a population of 6000. In 1868 Wyoming was carved as a territory from portions of Dakota, Idaho, and Utah territories, and established its government with Cheyenne as capital. Its legislature was the first to grant woman suffrage (1869), and in 1870 women began serving on juries. In 1890, with a population of 62,000, the territory was admitted to the Union as the 44th state.

Most of the state's early history is associated with open-range cattle and sheep herding. Cattle rustling soon led to the organization of vigilante groups, but, after 1900, as vast acres were fenced and winter pastures established, the open range became a thing of the past. The economy of the state, largely dependent upon farms and ranches, is buttressed by an expanding oil industry, with hydroelectric power supplied by the Missouri River Project. Irrigation is reclaiming thousands of acres of semiarid land, and great mineral resources (especially uranium) are being tapped. The tourist trade is important, for here are located two national parks: Yellowstone and Grand Teton. Cheyenne is the largest city, with a population in 1960 of 43,000. The leading institution of higher learning is the University of Wyoming (Laramie, est. 1887).

Wyoming Massacre (July 1778), called the 'surpassing horror of the Revolution,' occurred in Wyoming valley of eastern Pennsylvania. Tory Rangers and their Mohawk allies descended on a frontier patriot garrison, which easily fell. But the Indians were out for blood, and the ensuing carnage led Washington to send a punitive expedition into the territory.

WYTHE, George (1726–1806), Virginia lawyer and delegate to the Continental Congress (1775–76), with Thomas Jefferson and Edmund Pendleton revised the laws of the state. Wythe was also a delegate to the Federal Constitutional Convention (1787). One of the greatest lawyers of his generation, he occupied the chair of law at William and Mary (1779–90), the first in an American college, and his concept of law helped shape the liberal opinions of Jefferson, Marshall, Monroe, and Clay. He later served as judge in the Virginia chancery (1778–88) and as its sole judge (1788–1801).

X-Y

XYZ Affair (1797–98) was a diplomatic incident which involved the U.S. in difficulties with France. The GENÊT AFFAIR and similar incidents had strained Franco-American relations to such a degree that President Adams sent C. C. Pinckney, Elbridge Gerry, and John Marshall to Paris as a commission to devise means of avoiding open hostilities. The French Directory, through its foreign minister, Talleyrand, chose to regard JAY'S TREATY with England as dangerously pro-British, and compelled the commissioners to bargain with political lackeys whom the commissioners in their dispatches home designated X, Y, and Z. As a condition for negotiation, the U.S. was expected to 'loan' France a large sum of money, and to make a substantial 'gift' to Talleyrand. Pinckney's alleged reply, 'No, not a sixpence,' became the toast of the day: 'Millions for defense, but not one cent for tribute.' This latest indignity led an enraged U.S. to enter upon the undeclared War with FRANCE (1798–1800).

Yachting as a competitive sport began in 1851, when the British Royal Yacht Squadron, Cowes, England, offered a silver cup as a trophy for a 60-mile race around the Isle of Wight. Members of the New York Yacht Club (founded 1844) crossed the Atlantic in *America,* which won the competition, thereby giving the name *America*'s Cup to the most coveted international yachting prize. Successive efforts of British yachtsmen have failed to recover the cup, which remains in the U.S.

After 1920 small yachts, especially of one-design classes, gained great popularity, and most racing is now done by yachts 30 to 50 ft. in length. The most important regattas in the U.S. take place at the three principal yachting centers on the Atlantic coast — Marblehead, Massachusetts; Long Island Sound; and Miami, Florida. Important distance races include Newport to Bermuda, Miami to Nassau, and Los Angeles to Honolulu.

Yale University was established (1701) by a group of Congregational ministers as a 'collegiate school' under a charter granted by the colony of Connecticut. (In a strictly legal sense the colonies probably had no right to issue such COLONIAL CHARTERS. The legality was never challenged, but the original designation presumably was selected to avert any issue.)

The college opened at Saybrook, but its classes were held for the most part at Killingworth and at Milford until the institution was permanently transferred to New Haven (1716). It was then renamed Yale College to honor the gifts received from Elihu Yale (1649–1721), a Boston-born merchant and the governor of Madras in British India. By a second charter (1745), still in force today, the college was incorporated. Its first professorship (1755) was a chair in divinity. By 1771 it had established faculties in mathematics, astronomy, and physics.

Yale was the first American college to equip an art gallery (1832), establish (1869) a school of fine arts, and award the degree of Doctor of Philosophy (1861). In 1887 it became a university. Today it offers courses of study in two undergraduate schools: Yale College (1701), and the School of Engineering (a reorganization, 1932, of the Sheffield Scientific School, 1861). Its nine other schools are Medicine (1813), Divinity (1822), Law (1824), Graduate (1847), Art and Architecture (1869), Music (1894), Forestry (1900), Nursing (1923), and Drama (1955), each with a dean and faculty. The University Library, which has special manuscript collections in American and English literature and more than 4,000,000 printed items, is one of the largest in the country. In 1965, with an endowment of $335,500,000 and a faculty of 2500, it enrolled 8600 students.

Yalta Conference (February 1945), the last and most important meeting of President Roosevelt, Prime Minister Churchill, and Premier Stalin, was held at Yalta in the Crimea. It reaffirmed the principles laid down in the MOSCOW CONFERENCE (1943), and addressed itself primarily to details for the final defeat of the Axis powers, the problems of postwar occupation, and the establishment of an organization to deal with matters of international concern. Of special importance was the Soviet consent to enter the war against Japan 'within two or three months' after the surrender of Germany.

Although Yalta was later regarded as a victory for Stalin, since Soviet influence was extended by it in the Far East, actually it neither advanced nor retarded the cause of peace. On the other hand, it did little if anything to justify the hope expressed by Roosevelt in his report to Congress that the conference 'was a turning point . . . in the history of the world.' Concessions in the Far East seemed to be justified in the months before the atom bomb had been fully tested, since the cost of conquering the Japanese homeland was then estimated at more than a million casualties. Thus a substantial price was paid for Russia's entrance into the Far Eastern theater. As for the controversial concessions in eastern Europe, it seemed impossible, with the Red Army controlling Poland, to insist on the holding of 'free and unfettered elections' promised by Stalin at Yalta.

Yamassee Indians, of Muskhogean stock, having revolted against the Spaniards in Florida, at the beginning of the 18th century were living in South Carolina on the lower Savannah river. They made slaving raids on the Creek and Cherokee, selling their captives in Charleston to brokers who profited by resale principally in the West Indies, but also in New England. In 1715 they became hostile to the English settlers, were defeated, and returned to Florida, where the Creek destroyed them as a tribe about 1733. They frequently appear in the writings of southern authors, notably in those of William G. Simms.

YANCEY, William Lowndes (1814–63), South Carolinian in ancestry, was born in Georgia. After his father died his mother remarried. The family was living in Troy, New York, when Yancey attended Williams College (1830–33). He settled in Alabama, where he won prominence as a lawyer and entered politics. He represented his state in Congress (1844–46) but resigned his seat, disgusted with the unaggressive attitude of Democrats from the North on slavery issues. For the next decade he devoted all his energies in support of slavery as an institution. A zealous 'fire-eater,' he drew up the Alabama Platform (or 'Yancey platform') as an answer to the WILMOT PROVISO (1848) and openly advocated secession.

He expressed the same demands in the Democratic convention of 1860. When the Northerners refused to accept his platform, most of the Southerners followed Yancey out of the convention. (The seceders held a separate convention and nominated Vice President John C. Breckinridge for President on a platform of slavery extension.) At the outbreak of the Civil War Yancey went to Europe as a Confederate agent. He died while serving as a member of the Confederate senate.

Yankee, a term of uncertain origin, first applied to the Dutch in the 17th century. Early in the 18th century it was used jocosely of New Englanders. The song YANKEE DOODLE gave the word currency during the Revolution, applied by Americans with humorous pride, and by the British with derision. During the Civil War, Confederates used the word as a term of contempt for Union soldiers ('damyankees'). On the stage the Yankee has been a quietly humorous, shrewd, homespun fellow, speaking with a New England twang. In later years, though applied to America as a whole by Europeans ('Yankee-land'), the word in general has designated a New Englander. In World War I it was used in a spirit of good fellowship ('The Yanks are coming').

Yankee Doodle, a popular song of uncertain origin, was known in England in the mid-18th century, and was perhaps introduced in America by British soldiers during the French and Indian War (1755–63) in derision of provincial troops. First published in the U.S. in 1794, it has steadily been used, in scores of versions, as a quasi-national marching song and air.

Yazoo Land Frauds (1795) was a notorious bribe by four land companies of the Georgia legislature, which granted the companies an enormous tract of land (extending into Alabama and Mississippi) for a nominal sum. The corrupt deal was soon exposed, and in the following year a newly elected legislature repudiated the Yazoo Act. This invalidation led to such confusion that Congress appointed a commission to investigate the various claims, and in 1802 Georgia sought to cut the Gordian knot by ceding its western lands to the U.S. The issue over claims was ultimately reviewed by the U.S. Supreme Court, and in 1810 Chief Justice Marshall in his famous ruling FLETCHER *v.* PECK declared that the state of Georgia could not revoke its first act, however corrupt, since to do so impaired an obligation of contract. Thus Congress was compelled to award speculators some $4,000,000.

YEARDLEY, SIR GEORGE (*c.* 1580–1627), colonial deputy-governor (1616–17) and governor (1618–21, 1626–27) of Virginia, in 1619 was instructed by the Virginia Company to introduce English common law and to call a general assembly of planters once every year, to allow each of the eleven districts to elect two burgesses. That small assembly, which met in the church at Jamestown, was the first representative body to meet in America.

'Yellow dog contracts,' so called, were agreements by which an employee contracted with his employer not to join a labor union; they were especially entered into during the 1920's, and were enforced in the courts. The NORRIS-LA GUARDIA ANTI-INJUNCTION ACT (1932) invalidated them.

Yellow journalism is the phrase applied to newspapers that play up sensationalism. Though the elder James Gordon Bennett had introduced the method in the U.S. when he established the New York *Herald* (1835), the term itself first came into use to describe the sensational battle of 1896 between Pulitzer's New York *World* and W. R. Hearst's *Journal,* over the use of R. F. Outcault's highly popular 'bad boy' comic strip character, *The Yellow Kid.*

Yellowstone National Park (est. 1872), partly in Idaho and Montana but mainly in Wyoming, is an area of some 3500 square miles. A plateau and mountain region, 7000–11,000 ft. above sea level, it comprises lakes, geysers, hot springs, canyons, living and petrified forests, and wild animal herds. It has long been one of the most widely known parks in the world.

YERKES, CHARLES TYSON (1837–1905), Philadelphia financier, after establishing his own banking house (1862), dominated the city's financial affairs until he failed in 1871, when he was jailed for embezzlement. He was later pardoned. He made a second fortune at the time of the failure of JAY COOKE (1873), and became prominent in street railway operations in Philadelphia and Chicago (1881–1900), and in London, whose subways he built. His endowment made possible the Yerkes Observatory (1897) of the University of Chicago. Two of Theodore Dreiser's novels, *The Financier* and *The Titan,* are based on Yerkes's career.

YERKES, ROBERT MEARNS (1876–1956), taught psychology at Harvard (1901–17) and at Yale (1924–44). He served (1919–44) on the National Research Council soon after that body was organized by the NATIONAL ACADEMY OF SCIENCE. He was a leading authority on comparative psychology and psychobiology and pioneered in the study of animal behavior. His writings include *The Mental Life of Monkeys and Apes* (1916) and *The Mind of a Gorilla* (2 vols., 1926–27).

Y.M.C.A. (Young Men's Christian Association) was organized in England (1844) to develop the spiritual and social welfare of its members. Introduced in the U.S. in 1851, by the end of the century the movement had become world-wide. Its 1700 associations now comprise some 2,000,000 members.

The Y.W.C.A. (Young Women's Christian Association), established at Boston in 1866, parallels the services and facilities (including resident accommodation) of the men's organization.

Yorktown Campaign (30 August–19 October 1781), which ended the War of Independence, began at the close of the CAROLINA CAMPAIGN. Cornwallis, in retreat, decided to move north into Virginia. In May he joined Benedict Arnold at Petersburg, where he commanded some 5000 troops. Unable to persuade Clinton to abandon New York and concentrate on Virginia, he then moved toward Richmond against Lafayette, who with his green militia of 3000 began a retreat. Cornwallis was able to augment his force to 8000, and to better his strategy by moving to the coast, through Williamsburg to Yorktown, where the protecting force of the Royal Navy under Admiral Thomas Graves could come far into the land mass of the Chesapeake Bay. His calculations were upset by the unexpected arrival of the entire French West Indies fleet (28 ships) under Admiral Comte de Grasse. On 5 September the two fleets engaged in sharp action which, though seemingly indecisive, in fact gave the French control over the Bay and coastal waters. The French squadron of Admiral Comte de Barras was coming down from Newport and by 13 September no fewer than 36 French ships of the line barred the entrance of the Bay to the British. (On the day of Cornwallis's surrender Washington wrote: 'The naval engagement appears to have been of much greater importance than was at first estimated.')

Meanwhile Washington, who with Rochambeau was pinning Clinton down in New York and knew of the impending naval movements, sensed the possibility of a *coup de grâce*. Leaving a decoy to distract Clinton's attention, on 19 August he and Rochambeau began their march south. He arrived at Lafayette's headquarters on 14 September. With the arrival of Rochambeau soon after, Washington had 16,000 troops under his command.

Thus was conducted one of the most superbly co-ordinated amphibious operations in military annals. The land sorties of Cornwallis were blocked in all directions. Yorktown was laid under siege, and the chances of Cornwallis's escape were exactly nil. On the day that Cornwallis surrendered (19 October), Clinton arrived nearby with a relief expedition, but sailed back to New York. The war was over. As Washington had predicted, but not fully seen at first, in the unnamed engagement of 5 September, the 'casting vote' had been delivered by the navy.

Yosemite National Park (1890), in the SIERRA NEVADA of eastern California, is an area of some 758,000 acres. It is characterized by plunging waterfalls, sequoia groves, and lofty peaks. Yosemite Falls has an over-all drop of 2500 ft.

YOUNG, BRIGHAM (1801–77), born in Whitingham, Vermont, worked as a carpenter and glazier in a frontier village near Rochester, New York. He was attracted to Mormonism, and after he was baptized (1832) he led a group of the new sect to Kirkland, Ohio, where in 1835 he became one of the Council of Twelve (the Apostles). He was sent to England, where his missionary work attracted many converts to America.

When the uprising against the Mormons at Nauvoo, Illinois (1844) led to the assassination of the founder, JOSEPH SMITH, the mantle of the Prophet fell on Young, who thenceforth remained the greatest molder of Mormonism in its history. He conducted the mass migration to Utah (1846–47). As head of the church and governor of 'Deseret' in the valley of the Great Salt Lake, he ruled his communal theocracy with autocratic power, directing the lives of his people in minutest detail. President Fillmore appointed him governor of Utah Territory (1850), but when Young proclaimed the doctrine of polygamy (1852), President Buchanan removed him from office, though Young continued to rule through his successors, and the indictment against him (1871) was never pressed. (His estimated 19 to 27 wives bore him 56 children, although some of the wives were only doctrinally allied — that is, wives in name only.)

Not a skilled theologian, often harsh and rigid, Young worked with single-minded devotion in the cause of the Latter-Day Saints, and the prosperity and phenomenal growth of the Mormon community stemmed from Young's extraordinary competence as a social and economic administrator. Out of the desert wastes the patriarch built one of the notable commonwealths of modern times.

See the biographies by M. R. Werner (1925); and S. Y. Gates and L. D. Widtsoe (1930).

YOUNG, MAHONRI [MACKINTOSH] (1877–1957), Utah-born grandson of Brigham Young, studied sculpture in New York and Paris. Especially known for his statuettes of laborers, cowboys, and prizefighters, he created with vigor, simplicity, and craftsmanship. Representative of his larger works are the bronzes *Stevedore* and *Man With the Pick* (Metropolitan Museum). He executed the habitat groups of Navahoes, Hopis, and Apaches in the American Museum of Natural History.

YOUNG, Owen D. (1874–1962), after graduation from St. Lawrence University (1894) practiced law first in Boston, then in New York, where he became general counsel for General Electric Company, then its president (1922–39). He was associated with many corporations and frequently served as adviser to the federal government on economic affairs, both domestic and international. He became most widely known as formulator of the YOUNG PLAN for settling German reparations after World War I.

Young Communist League, see *Communist party*.

Young Plan (1929) was a formula to liquidate German reparations following five years of operation of the DAWES PLAN, which had been limited to the payment of annuities without determining total reparations. The new plan was drawn up by a committee headed by the financier OWEN D. YOUNG. It fixed the reparations bill at $28.8 billion (including interest) payable over a 59-year period, and providing for reductions in annuities in proportion as the war debt itself was reduced. But the collapse of the stock market, the bank crisis in central Europe, and the onset of a worldwide depression led to the HOOVER MORATORIUM (1931), followed by the Lausanne Conference (1932), at which 90 per cent of the reparations due under the Young Plan was canceled. America's chief debtors insisted that their payment of war debts to the U.S. was linked to Germany's payment of reparations to them, but no American president or Congress conceded this, even though the U.S. had supported the Dawes and Young Plans and issued the Hoover Moratorium, which suspended interallied debt payments. The U.S. ignored the Lausanne agreement, but thereafter all German reparations payments ceased.

'Young Turks,' a term applied to zealous, insurgent party reformers in the U.S. around 1910, originated when the reform party in Turkey came into power through the Revolution of 1909.

Yukon river, 1800 miles long, is formed by the confluence of Lewes and Pelly rivers in Yukon territory, Canada, and traverses the breadth of central Alaska to enter Bering Sea. One of the longest rivers in North America, the Yukon was first explored in its lower reaches by Russians in 1836. Navigable for most of its length by large steamers, during the KLONDIKE rush (1897–98) it was the major route to the gold fields. On its banks today towns are being established, most easily reached by air.

Z

ZAHARIAS, Mildred Babe [Didrikson] (1912–50), Texas-born athlete, became internationally famous by winning many track and field events and breaking four records in the 1932 Olympic Games. After her marriage (1938) to the wrestler George Zaharias she devoted herself to golf and won many titles, including two championships, the U.S. National Women's Amateur (1946) and the British Women's Amateur (1947). Skilled also at basketball and baseball, she has been called 'the greatest woman athlete.'

ZENGER, John Peter (1697–1746), German-born printer, journalist, and publisher, on arriving in New York (1710) learned his trade and later established the New York *Weekly Journal* (1733) to oppose the New York *Gazette,* organ of the provincial administration. Arrested and tried for seditious libel (1735) after his paper had attacked Governor William Cosby, he was brilliantly defended by ANDREW HAMILTON, who offered the relatively new defense that Zenger had told the truth and that truth was a defense against libel.

The jury, swayed by Hamilton's declaration that the cause of English liberty was at stake, acquitted 'the morning star of liberty,' as Gouverneur Morris later called Zenger. Although the Zenger case did not immediately establish freedom of the press, as has been popularly (but erroneously) supposed, or put an end to prosecutions for seditious libel, its outcome was of great importance. In the near future liberty of discussion did become an issue, and Zenger's name became a symbol of the individual's right to criticize his government.

ZIEGFELD, Florenz (1869–1932), after 1907 annually produced the *Ziegfeld Follies,* elaborate theater revues featuring choruses of beautiful girls and a variety of star performers. His spectacular successes include *Sally* (1920) and *Show Boat* (1927). He married first Anna Held (1897), then Billy Burke (1914), both Broadway stars.

ZIMBALIST, Efrem (1889–   ), Russian-born concert violinist, made his American debut in 1911. A faculty member of the Curtis Institute of Music since 1928, he became its director in 1941. He has composed works for orchestra, as well as songs and minor pieces.

Zimmermann note (17 January 1917), written by the German foreign minister to the German minister to Mexico, proposed that, should the U.S. declare war on Germany, Mexico might become a German ally, with the expectation of winning back her 'lost territory' of Texas, Arizona, and New Mexico. It also proposed that Mexico make an offensive alliance with Japan in the same contingency. British secret service intercepted and decoded the note, which it turned over to President Wilson late in February, a few weeks after Germany announced that she was resuming unrestricted submarine warfare. Wilson delayed releasing the Zimmermann note in the hope that peace was still possible since Germany had not yet sunk U.S. vessels, but after the isolationists in Congress refused to give him authority to arm merchant vessels, he issued the note to the press (1 March). As a result of this news of a possible German-supported attack by Mexico, American public opinion was aroused to a war fever.

ZINZENDORF, see *Moravians.*

Zion National Park (est. 1919), in southwestern Utah, is an area of some 130,000 acres. The gorge of Zion Canyon, which has precipitous walls, reaches a depth of 2500 ft.

Zoar Society (1817–98), a communal group in east central Ohio, was founded by German Separatists who emigrated under the leadership of Joseph Michael Bimeler (1778–1853). Zoarites established small industries, communally owned, and flourished during Bimeler's lifetime, but thereafter declined. At the end of the century the Society was dissolved.

Zoning, see *City planning.*

Zoology, as a branch of 'natural science,' remained descriptive natural history in the U.S. until the 19th century. In the colonial period and later, college curriculums provided for the teaching of natural science, a term which signified the description of all objects of nature, whether organic or inorganic; and the term 'natural history,' used to describe animals, plants, and minerals, still survives in the names of museums and learned academies.

Colonial students of phenomena and of plants and animal life communicated their observations to fellow-naturalists abroad. Accounts written by PAUL DUDLEY and COTTON MATHER were published in the *Transactions* of the Royal Society. Still enjoyable are Mark Catesby's *Natural History of Carolina* (1731–43), Thomas Jefferson's *Notes on the State of Virginia* (1784–85), and the ornithological studies of WILLIAM BARTRAM and ALEXANDER WILSON. Other pioneer specialists were WILLIAM PECK of Harvard, the earliest teacher of entomology (1805); S. L. MITCHILL of Columbia (1807), and C. S. RAFINESQUE of Transylvania (1815), contributors, among other subjects, to ichthyology. THOMAS SAY accompanied the Rocky Mountain expedition (1820–23) of STEPHEN H. LONG. At that time the two students of American fauna best known abroad were J. J. AUDUBON and JOHN BACHMAN.

By mid-19th century systematic inquiries in morphology and embryology had been undertaken by JOSEPH LEIDY, a specialist on protozoans. Although the distinguished Harvard zoologist LOUIS AGASSIZ firmly rejected the Darwinian principle of natural selection, he trained a generation of students in scientific method, and his work was carried on by his son, ALEXANDER AGASSIZ. E. D. COPE at Pennsylvania strongly supported Lamarck's theory of inherited characteristics, and the discoveries of O. C. MARSH at Yale had an important bearing on the teaching of evolution.

Advances by Americans during the 20th century in experimental biology, and their contributions to the study of heredity, have been especially significant, recognized by many Nobel awards in the field of MEDICINE.

ZORACH, WILLIAM (1887–   ), Lithuanian-born sculptor and painter, was brought to the U.S. in early childhood. After study in New York and Paris, he exhibited in the show of Younger American Artists at Stieglitz's '291' gallery (1910), the first exhibition of 'moderns' in the U.S., and at the ARMORY SHOW, three years later. Increasingly popular as watercolorist, Zorach also takes rank as sculptor for his craftsmanship and highly original style, represented by his aluminum *Spirit of the Dance* (Radio City Music Hall, New York).

Zuñi, an agricultural Indian tribe in western New Mexico, are PUEBLO INDIANS who speak the Zuñi language. Early Spanish explorers were attracted by stories of the wealth of the 'Seven Cities of Cibola,' which Coronado found to be their seven pueblo villages. Culturally allied to the HOPI, today they are known for their distinguished silver work.

ZWORYKIN, VLADIMIR KOSMA (1889–   ), Russian-born physicist and electronics engineer, pioneered in the development of television. He was a research engineer (1920–29) with Westinghouse, and thereafter was director of electronic research and vice president (1947–54) of Radio Corporation of America. He developed the Iconoscope (the 'electric eye'), and the Kinescope, or cathode-ray tube, both used in television receivers. The first electron microscope was constructed (1940) under his direction. His writings include *Photocells and Their Applications* (1932), and *Television in Science and Industry* (1958).

The Constitution of the United States

We the people of the United States, in Order to form a more perfect Union, establish Justice, insure domestic Tranquility, provide for the common defence, promote the general Welfare, and secure the Blessings of Liberty to ourselves and our Posterity, do ordain and establish this Constitution for the United States of America.

ARTICLE I

SECTION 1. All legislative Powers herein granted shall be vested in a Congress of the United States, which shall consist of a Senate and House of Representatives.

SECTION 2. The House of Representatives shall be composed of Members chosen every second Year by the People of the several States, and the Electors in each State shall have the Qualifications requisite for Electors of the most numerous Branch of the State Legislature.

No Person shall be a Representative who shall not have attained to the Age of twenty-five Years, and been seven Years a Citizen of the United States, and who shall not, when elected, be an Inhabitant of that State in which he shall be chosen.

Representatives and direct Taxes shall be apportioned among the several States which may be included within this Union, according to their respective Numbers, *which shall be determined by adding to the whole Number of free Persons, including those bound to Service for a Term of Years,*[1] and excluding Indians not taxed, *three fifths of all other Persons.*[2] The actual Enumeration shall be made within three Years after the first Meeting of the Congress of the United States, and within every subsequent Term of ten Years, in such Manner as they shall by Law direct. The Number of Representatives shall not exceed one for every thirty Thousand, but each State shall have at Least one Representative; *and until such enumeration shall be made, the State of New Hampshire shall be entitled to chuse three, Massachusetts eight, Rhode-Island and Providence Plantations one, Connecticut five, New-York six, New Jersey four, Pennsylvania eight, Delaware one, Maryland six, Virginia ten, North Carolina five, South Carolina five, and Georgia three.*[3]

[1] Altered by the Fourteenth Amendment.
[2] Rescinded by the Fourteenth Amendment.
[3] Temporary provision.

When vacancies happen in the Representation from any State, the Executive Authority thereof shall issue Writs of Election to fill such Vacancies.

The House of Representatives shall chuse their Speaker and other Officers; and shall have the sole Power of Impeachment.

SECTION 3. The Senate of the United States shall be composed of two Senators from each State, *chosen by the Legislature thereof,*[4] for six Years; and each Senator shall have one Vote.

Immediately after they shall be assembled in Consequence of the first Election, they shall be divided as equally as may be into three Classes. The Seats of the Senators of the first Class shall be vacated at the Expiration of the second Year, of the second Class at the Expiration of the fourth Year, and of the third Class at the Expiration of the sixth Year, so that one third may be chosen every second Year; *and if Vacancies happen by Resignation, or otherwise, during the Recess of the Legislature of any State, the Executive thereof may make temporary Appointments until the next Meeting of the Legislature, which shall then fill such Vacancies.*[5]

No Person shall be a Senator who shall not have attained to the Age of thirty Years, and been nine Years a Citizen of the United States, and who shall not, when elected, be an Inhabitant of that State for which he shall be chosen.

The Vice President of the United States shall be President of the Senate, but shall have no Vote, unless they be equally divided.

The Senate shall chuse their other Officers, and also a President pro tempore, in the Absence of the Vice President, or when he shall exercise the Office of the President of the United States.

The Senate shall have the sole Power to try all Impeachments. When sitting for the Purpose, they shall be on Oath or Affirmation. When the President of the United States is tried, the Chief Justice shall preside: And no Person shall be convicted without the Concurrence of two thirds of the Members present.

Judgment in Cases of Impeachment shall not extend further than to removal from Office, and disqualification to hold and enjoy any Office or honor, Trust or Profit under the United States: but the Party convicted shall nevertheless be liable and subject to Indictment, Trial, Judgment and Punishment, according to Law.

SECTION 4. The Times, Places and Manner of holding Elections for Senators and Representatives, shall be prescribed in each State by the Legislature thereof, but the Congress may at any time by Law make or alter such Regulations, except as to the Places of chusing Senators.

The Congress shall assemble at least once in every year, and such Meeting shall be on the first Monday in December, unless they shall by Law appoint a different day.[6]

[4] Modified by the Seventeenth Amendment.
[5] Modified by the Seventeenth Amendment.
[6] Superseded by the Twentieth Amendment.

SECTION 5. Each House shall be the Judge of the Elections, Returns and Qualifications of its own Members, and a Majority of each shall constitute a Quorum to do Business; but a smaller Number may adjourn from day to day, and may be authorized to compel the Attendance of absent Members, in such manner, and under such Penalties as each House may provide.

Each House may determine the Rules of its Proceedings, punish its Members for disorderly Behaviour, and, with the Concurrence of two thirds, expel a Member.

Each House shall keep a Journal of its Proceedings, and from time to time publish the same, excepting such Parts as may in their Judgment require Secrecy; and the Yeas and Nays of the Members of either House on any question shall, at the Desire of one fifth of those Present, be entered on the Journal.

Neither House, during the Session of Congress, shall, without the Consent of the other, adjourn for more than three days, nor to any other Place than that in which the two Houses shall be sitting.

SECTION 6. The Senators and Representatives shall receive a Compensation for their Services, to be ascertained by Law, and paid out of the Treasury of the United States. They shall in all Cases, except Treason, Felony and Breach of the Peace, be privileged from Arrest during their Attendance at the Session of their respective Houses, and in going to and returning from the same; and for any Speech or Debate in either House, they shall not be questioned in any other Place.

No Senator or Representative shall, during the Time for which he was elected, be appointed to any civil Office under the Authority of the United States, which shall have been created, or the Emoluments whereof shall have been increased during such time; and no Person holding any Office under the United States, shall be a Member of either House during his Continuance in Office.

SECTION 7. All Bills for raising Revenue shall originate in the House of Representatives; but the Senate may propose or concur with Amendments as on other Bills.

Every Bill which shall have passed the House of Representatives and the Senate shall, before it becomes a Law, be presented to the President of the United States; If he approve he shall sign it, but if not he shall return it, with his Objections to that House in which it shall have originated, who shall enter the Objections at large on their Journal, and proceed to reconsider it. If after such Reconsideration two thirds of that House shall agree to pass the Bill, it shall be sent, together with the Objections, to the other House, by which it shall likewise be reconsidered, and if approved by two thirds of that House, it shall become a Law. But in all such Cases the Votes of both Houses shall be determined by yeas and Nays, and the Names of the Persons voting for and against the Bill shall be entered on the Journal of each House respectively. If any Bill shall not be returned by the President within ten Days (Sundays excepted) after it shall have been presented to him, the Same shall be a Law, in like Manner as if he had signed it, unless the Congress by their Adjournment prevent its Return, in which Case it shall not be a Law.

Every Order, Resolution or Vote to which the Concurrence of the Senate and House of Representatives may be necessary (except on a question of Adjournment) shall be presented to the President of the United States; and before the Same shall take Effect, shall be approved by him, or being disapproved by him, shall be repassed by two thirds of the Senate and House of Representatives, according to the Rules and Limitations prescribed in the Case of a Bill.

SECTION 8. The Congress shall have Power To lay and collect Taxes, Duties, Imposts and Excises, to pay the Debts and provide for the common Defence and general Welfare of the United States; but all Duties, Imposts and Excises shall be uniform throughout the United States;

To borrow Money on the credit of the United States;

To regulate Commerce with foreign Nations, and among the several States, and with the Indian Tribes;

To establish an uniform Rule of Naturalization, and uniform Laws on the subject of Bankruptcies throughout the United States;

To coin Money, regulate the Value thereof, and of foreign Coin, and fix the Standard of Weights and Measures;

To provide for the Punishment of counterfeiting the Securities and current Coin of the United States;

To establish Post Offices and post Roads;

To promote the Progress of Science and useful Arts, by securing for limited Times to Authors and Inventors the exclusive Right to their respective Writings and Discoveries;

To constitute Tribunals inferior to the supreme Court;

To define and punish Piracies and Felonies committed on the high Seas, and Offences against the Law of Nations;

To declare War, grant Letters of Marque and Reprisal, and make Rules concerning Captures on Land and Water;

To raise and support Armies, but no Appropriation of Money to that Use shall be for a longer Term than two Years;

To provide and maintain a Navy;

To make Rules for the Government and Regulation of the land and naval Forces;

To provide for calling forth the Militia to execute the Laws of the Union, suppress Insurrection and repel Invasions;

To provide for organizing, arming, and disciplining, the Militia, and for governing such Part of them as may be employed in the Service of the United States, reserving to the States respectively, the Appointment of the Officers, and the Authority of training the Militia according to the discipline prescribed by Congress;

To exercise exclusive Legislation in all Cases whatsoever, over such District (not exceeding ten Miles square) as may, by Cession of particular States, and the Acceptance of Congress, become the Seat of the Government of the United States, and to exercise like Authority over all Places purchased by the Consent of the Legislature of the State in which the Same shall be, for the Erection of Forts, Magazines, Arsenals, dock-Yards, and other needful Buildings; — And

To make all Laws which shall be necessary and proper for carrying into Execution the foregoing Powers, and all other Powers vested by this Constitution in the Government of the United States, or in any Department or Office thereof.

SECTION 9. *The Migration or Importation of such Persons as any of the States now existing shall think proper to admit, shall be prohibited by the Congress prior to the Year one thousand eight hundred and eight, but a Tax or duty may be imposed on such Importation, not exceeding ten dollars for each person.*[7]

The Privilege of the Writ of Habeas Corpus shall not be suspended, unless when in Cases of Rebellion or Invasion the public Safety may require it.

No Bill of Attainder or ex post facto Law shall be passed.

No Capitation, or other direct, Tax shall be laid, unless in Proportion to the Census or Enumeration herein before directed to be taken.

No tax or Duty shall be laid on Articles exported from any State.

No Preference shall be given by any Regulation of Commerce or Revenue to the Ports of one State over those of another; nor shall Vessels bound to, or from, one State, be obliged to enter, clear, or pay Duties in another.

No Money shall be drawn from the Treasury, but in Consequence of Appropriations made by Law, and a regular Statement and Account of the Receipts and Expenditures of all public Money shall be published from time to time.

No Title of Nobility shall be granted by the United States: And no Person holding any Office of Profit or Trust under them, shall, without the Consent of the Congress, accept of any present, Emolument, Office, or Title, of any kind whatever, from any King, Prince, or foreign State.

SECTION 10. No State shall enter into any Treaty, Alliance, or Confederation; grant Letters of Marque and Reprisal; coin Money; emit Bills of Credit; make any Thing but gold and silver Coin a Tender in Payment of Debts; pass any Bill of Attainder, ex post facto Law, or Law impairing the Obligation of Contracts, or grant any Title of Nobility.

No State shall, without the Consent of the Congress, lay any Imposts or Duties on Imports or Exports, except what may be absolutely necessary for executing its inspection Laws: and the net Produce of all Duties and Imposts, laid by any State on Imports or Exports, shall be for the Use of the

[7] Temporary provision.

Treasury of the United States; and all such Laws shall be subject to the Revision and Controul of the Congress.

No State shall, without the Consent of Congress, lay any Duty of Tonnage, keep troops, or Ships of War in time of Peace, enter into any Agreement or Compact with another State, or with a foreign Power, or engage in War, unless actually invaded, or in such imminent Danger as will not admit of delay.

ARTICLE II

SECTION 1. The Executive Power shall be vested in a President of the United States of America. *He shall hold his Office during the Term of four Years,*[8] and, together with the Vice President, chosen for the same Term, be elected, as follows:

Each State shall appoint, in such Manner as the Legislature thereof may direct, a Number of Electors, equal to the whole Number of Senators and Representatives to which the State may be entitled in the Congress: but no Senator or Representative, or Person holding an Office of Trust or Profit under the United States, shall be appointed an Elector.

The Electors shall meet in their respective States, and vote by Ballot for two persons, of whom one at least shall not be an Inhabitant of the same State with themselves. And they shall make a List of all the Persons voted for, and of the Number of Votes for each; which List they shall sign and certify, and transmit sealed to the Seat of the Government of the United States, directed to the President of the Senate. The President of the Senate shall, in the Presence of the Senate and House of Representatives, open all the Certificates, and the Votes shall then be counted. The Person having the greatest Number of Votes shall be the President, if such Number be a Majority of the whole Number of Electors appointed; and if there be more than one who have such Majority, and have an equal Number of Votes, then the House of Representatives shall immediately chuse by Ballot one of them for President; and if no Person have a Majority, then from the five highest on the List the said House shall in like Manner chuse the President. But in chusing the President, the Votes shall be taken by States, the Representation from each State having one Vote; A quorum for this Purpose shall consist of a Member or Members from two thirds of the States, and a Majority of all the States shall be necessary to a Choice. In every Case, after the Choice of the President, the Person having the greatest Number of Votes of the Electors shall be the Vice President. But if there should remain two or more who have equal Votes, the Senate shall chuse from them by Ballot the Vice President.[9]

The Congress may determine the Time of chusing the Electors, and the Day on which they shall give their Votes; which Day shall be the same throughout the United States.

No Person except a natural born Citizen, or a Citizen of the United States, at the time of the Adoption of the Constitution, shall be eligible to the Of-

[8] Modified by the Twenty-second Amendment.
[9] Superseded by the Twelfth Amendment.

fice of President, neither shall any Person be eligible to that Office who shall not have attained to the Age of thirty-five Years, and been fourteen Years a Resident within the United States.

In Case of the Removal of the President from Office, or of his Death, Resignation, or Inability to discharge the Powers and Duties of the said Office, the Same shall devolve on the Vice President, and the Congress may by Law provide for the Case of Removal, Death, Resignation or Inability, both of the President and Vice President, declaring what Officer shall then act as President, and such Officer shall act accordingly, until the Disability be removed, or a President shall be elected.

The President shall, at stated Times, receive for his Services, a Compensation, which shall neither be encreased nor diminished during the Period for which he shall have been elected, and he shall not receive within that Period any other Emolument from the United States, or any of them.

Before he enter on the Execution of his Office, he shall take the following Oath or Affirmation: — "I do solemnly swear (or affirm) that I will faithfully execute the Office of President of the United States, and will to the best of my Ability, preserve, protect and defend the Constitution of the United States."

SECTION 2. The President shall be Commander in Chief of the Army and Navy of the United States, and of the Militia of the several states, when called into the actual Service of the United States; he may require the Opinion, in writing, of the principal Officer in each of the executive Departments, upon any Subject relating to the Duties of their respective Offices, and he shall have Power to grant Reprieves and Pardons for Offences against the United States, except in Cases of Impeachment.

He shall have Power, by and with the Advice and Consent of the Senate, to make Treaties, provided two thirds of the Senators present concur; and he shall nominate, and by and with the Advice and Consent of the Senate, shall appoint Ambassadors, other public Ministers and Consuls, Judges of the supreme Court, and all other Officers of the United States, whose Appointments are not herein otherwise provided for, and which shall be established by Law; but the Congress may by Law vest the Appointment of such inferior Officers, as they think proper, in the President alone, in the Courts of Law, or in the Heads of Departments.

The President shall have Power to fill up all Vacancies that may happen during the Recess of the Senate, by granting Commissions which shall expire at the End of their next Session.

SECTION 3. He shall from time to time give to the Congress Information of the State of the Union, and recommend to their Consideration such Measures as he shall judge necessary and expedient; he may, on extraordinary Occasions, convene both Houses, or either of them, and in Case of Disagreement between them, with Respect to the Time of Adjournment, he may adjourn them to such Time as he shall think proper; he shall receive Ambassadors and other public Ministers; he shall take Care that the Laws be faithfully executed, and shall Commission all the Officers of the United States.

SECTION 4. The President, Vice President and all civil Officers of the United States, shall be removed from Office on Impeachment for, and Conviction of, Treason, Bribery, or other high Crimes and Misdemeanors.

ARTICLE III

SECTION 1. The judicial Power of the United States, shall be vested in one Supreme Court, and in such inferior Courts as the Congress may from time to time ordain and establish. The Judges, both of the supreme and inferior courts, shall hold their Offices during good Behaviour, and shall, at stated Times, receive for their Services, a Compensation, which shall not be diminished during their Continuance in Office.

SECTION 2. The judicial Power shall extend to all Cases, in Law and Equity, arising under this Constitution, the Laws of the United States, and Treaties made, or which shall be made, under their Authority; — to all Cases affecting Ambassadors, other public Ministers and Consuls; — to all Cases of admiralty and maritime Jurisdiction: — to Controversies to which the United States shall be a Party; — to Controversies between two or more States; — *between a State and Citizens of another State;* [10] — between Citizens of different States, — between Citizens of the same State claiming Lands under Grants of different States, and *between a State, or the Citizens thereof, and foreign States, Citizens or Subjects.*[10]

In all Cases affecting Ambassadors, other public Ministers and Consuls, and those in which a State shall be Party, the supreme Court shall have original Jurisdiction. In all the other Cases before mentioned, the supreme Court shall have appellate Jurisdiction, both as to Law and Fact, with such Exceptions, and under such Regulations, as the Congress shall make.

The Trial of all Crimes, except in Cases of Impeachment, shall be by Jury; and such Trial shall be held in the State where the said Crimes shall have been committed; but when not committed within any State, the Trial shall be at such Place or Places as the Congress may by Law have directed.

SECTION 3. Treason against the United States, shall consist only in levying War against them, or in adhering to their Enemies, giving them Aid and Comfort. No Person shall be convicted of Treason unless on the Testimony of two Witnesses to the same overt Act, or on Confession in open Court.

The Congress shall have Power to declare the Punishment of Treason, but no Attainder of Treason shall work Corruption of Blood, or Forfeiture except during the Life of the Person attainted.

[10] Restricted by the Eleventh Amendment.

ARTICLE IV

SECTION 1. Full Faith and Credit shall be given in each State to the public Acts, Records, and judicial Proceedings of every other State. And the Congress may by general Laws prescribe the Manner in which such Acts, Records and Proceedings shall be proved, and the Effect thereof.

SECTION 2. *The Citizens of each State shall be entitled to all Privileges and Immunities of Citizens in the several States.*[11]

A Person charged in any State with Treason, Felony, or other Crime, who shall flee from Justice, and be found in another State, shall on Demand of the executive Authority of the State from which he fled, be delivered up, to be removed to the State having jurisdiction of the Crime.

No Person held to Service or Labour in one State, under the Laws thereof, escaping into another, shall, in Consequence of any Law or Regulation therein, be discharged from such Service or Labour, but shall be delivered up on Claim of the Party to whom such Service or Labour may be due.[12]

SECTION 3. New States may be admitted by the Congress into this Union; but no new State shall be formed or erected within the Jurisdiction of any other State; nor any State be formed by the Junction of two or more States, or Parts of States, without the Consent of the Legislatures of the States concerned as well as of the Congress.

The Congress shall have Power to dispose of and make all needful Rules and Regulations respecting the Territory or other Property belonging to the United States; and nothing in this Constitution shall be so construed as to Prejudice any Claims of the United States, or of any particular State.

SECTION 4. The United States shall guarantee to every State in this Union a Republican Form of Government, and shall protect each of them against Invasion; and on Application of the Legislature, or of the Executive (when the Legislature cannot be convened) against domestic Violence.

ARTICLE V

The Congress, whenever two thirds of both Houses shall deem it necessary, shall propose Amendments to this Constitution, or, on the Application of the Legislatures of two thirds of the several States, shall call a Convention for proposing Amendments, which, in either Case, shall be valid to all Intents and Purposes, as Part of this Constitution, when ratified by the Legislatures of three fourths of the several States, or by Conventions in three fourths thereof, as the one or the other Mode of Ratification may be proposed by the Congress; *Provided that no Amendment which may be made prior to the Year One thousand eight hundred and eight shall in any Manner affect the first and fourth Clauses in the Ninth Section of the first Article;* [13] and that no State, without its Consent, shall be deprived of its equal Suffrage in the Senate.

[11] Made more explicit by the Fourteenth Amendment.
[12] Superseded by the Thirteenth Amendment in so far as pertaining to slaves.
[13] Temporary clause.

ARTICLE VI

All Debts contracted and Engagements entered into, before the Adoption of this Constitution, shall be as valid against the United States under this Constitution, as under the Confederation.[14]

This Constitution, and the Laws of the United States which shall be made in Pursuance thereof; and all Treaties made, or which shall be made, under the Authority of the United States, shall be the supreme Law of the Land; and the Judges in every State shall be bound thereby, any Thing in the Constitution or Laws of any State to the Contrary notwithstanding.

The Senators and Representatives before mentioned, and the Members of the several State Legislatures, and all executive and judicial Officers, both of the United States and of the several States, shall be bound by Oath or Affirmation, to support this Constitution; but no religious Test shall ever be required as a Qualification to any Office or public Trust under the United States.

ARTICLE VII

The Ratification of the Conventions of nine States, shall be sufficient for the Establishment of this Constitution between the States so ratifying the Same.

Done in Convention by the Unanimous Consent of the States present the Seventeenth Day of September in the Year of our Lord one thousand seven hundred and Eighty seven and of the Independence of the United States of America the Twelfth. In witness whereof We have hereunto subscribed our Names,

G^{o} WASHINGTON —Pres^{t}
and deputy from Virginia

New Hampshire	John Langdon Nicholas Gilman
Massachusetts	Nathaniel Gorham Rufus King
Connecticut	Wm Saml Johnson Roger Sherman
New York	Alexander Hamilton
New Jersey	Wil: Livingston David A. Brearley. Wm Paterson. Jona: Dayton
Pennsylvania	B Franklin Thomas Mifflin Robt Morris Geo. Clymer Thos FitzSimons Jared Ingersoll James Wilson Gouv Morris
Delaware	Geo: Read Gunning Bedford jun John Dickinson Richard Bassett Jaco: Broom
Maryland	James McHenry Dan of St Thos Jenifer Danl Carroll
Virginia	John Blair — James Madison Jr.
North Carolina	Wm Blount Richd Dobbs Spaight. Hu Williamson
South Carolina	J. Rutledge Charles Cotesworth Pinckney Charles Pinckney Pierce Butler.
Georgia	William Few Abr Baldwin

[14] Extended by the Fourteenth Amendment.

AMENDMENTS TO THE CONSTITUTION

Articles in addition to, and Amendment of the Constitution of the United States of America, proposed by Congress, and ratified by the Legislatures of the several States, pursuant to the fifth Article of the original Constitution.

ARTICLE I

[The First Ten Articles Proposed 25 September 1789; Declared in Force 15 December 1791]

Congress shall make no law respecting an establishment of religion, or prohibiting the free exercise thereof; or abridging the freedom of speech, or of the press; or the right of the people peaceably to assemble, and to petition the Government for a redress of grievances.

ARTICLE II

A well regulated Militia, being necessary to the security of a free State, the right of the people to keep and bear Arms, shall not be infringed.

ARTICLE III

No Soldier shall, in time of peace be quartered in any house, without the consent of the Owner, nor in time of war, but in a manner to be prescribed by law.

ARTICLE IV

The right of the people to be secure in their persons, houses, papers, and effects, against unreasonable searches and seizures, shall not be violated, and no Warrants shall issue, but upon probable cause, supported by Oath or affirmation, and particularly describing the place to be searched, and the persons or things to be seized.

ARTICLE V

No person shall be held to answer for a capital, or otherwise infamous crime, unless on a presentment or indictment of a Grand Jury, except in cases arising in the land or naval forces, or in the Militia, when in actual service in time of War or public danger; nor shall any person be subject for the same offence to be twice put in jeopardy of life or limb; nor shall be compelled in any criminal case to be a witness against himself, nor be deprived of life, liberty, or property, without due process of law; nor shall private property be taken for public use, without just compensation.

ARTICLE VI

In all criminal prosecutions, the accused shall enjoy the right to a speedy and public trial, by an impartial jury of the State and district wherein the crime shall have been committed, which district shall have been previously ascertained by law, and to be informed of the nature and cause of the accusation; to be confronted with the witnesses against him; to have compulsory process for obtaining witnesses in his favor, and to have the Assistance of Counsel for his defence.

ARTICLE VII

In Suits at common law, where the value in controversy shall exceed twenty dollars, the right of trial by jury shall be preserved, and no fact tried by a jury, shall be otherwise re-examined in any Court of the United States, than according to the rules of the common law.

ARTICLE VIII

Excessive bail shall not be required, nor excessive fines imposed, nor cruel and unusual punishments inflicted.

ARTICLE IX

The enumeration in the Constitution, of certain rights, shall not be construed to deny or disparage others retained by the people.

ARTICLE X

The powers not delegated to the United States by the Constitution, nor prohibited by it to the States, are reserved to the States respectively, or to the people. [The first ten amendments went into effect November 3, 1791.]

ARTICLE XI

[Proposed 5 September 1794; Declared Ratified 8 January 1798]

The Judicial power of the United States shall not be construed to extend to any suit in law or equity, commenced or prosecuted against one of the United States by Citizens of another State, or by Citizens or Subjects of any Foreign State.

ARTICLE XII

[Proposed 12 December 1803; Declared Ratified 25 September 1804]

The Electors shall meet in their respective states and vote by ballot for President and Vice-President, one of whom, at least, shall not be an inhabitant of the same state with themselves; they shall name in their ballots the person voted for as President, and in distinct ballots the person voted for as Vice-President, and they shall make distinct lists of all persons voted for as President, and of all persons voted for as Vice-President, and of the number of votes for each, which lists they shall sign and certify, and transmit sealed to the seat of the government of the United States, directed to the President of the Senate; — The President of the Senate shall, in presence of the Senate and House of Representatives, open all the certificates and the votes shall then be counted; — The person having the greatest number of votes for the President, shall be the President, if such number be a majority of the whole number of Electors appointed; and if no person have such majority, then from the persons having the highest numbers not exceeding three on the list of those voted for as President, the House of Representatives shall choose immediately, by ballot, the President. But in choosing the President, the votes shall be taken by states, the representation from each state having one vote, a quorum for this purpose shall consist of a member or members from two-thirds of the states, and a majority of all the states shall be necessary to a choice. And if the House of Representatives shall not choose a President whenever the right of choice shall devolve upon them, before the *fourth day of March* [15] next following, then the Vice-President shall act as President, as in the case of the death or other constitutional disability of the President.—The Person having the greatest number of votes as Vice-President, shall be the Vice-President, if such number be a majority of the whole number of Electors appointed, and if no person have a majority, then from the two highest numbers on the list, the Senate shall choose the Vice-President; a quorum for the purpose shall consist of two-thirds of the whole number of Senators, and a majority of the whole number shall be necessary to a choice. But no person constitutionally ineligible to the office of President shall be eligible to that of Vice-President of the United States.

ARTICLE XIII

[Proposed 1 February 1865; Declared Ratified 18 December 1865]

SECTION 1. Neither slavery nor involuntary servitude, except as a punishment for crime whereof the party shall have been duly convicted, shall exist within the United States, or any place subject to their jurisdiction.

SECTION 2. Congress shall have power to enforce this article by appropriate legislation.

ARTICLE XIV

[Proposed 16 June 1866; Declared Ratified 28 July 1868]

SECTION 1. All persons born or naturalized in the United States, and subject to the jurisdiction thereof, are citizens of the United States and of the State wherein they reside. No State shall make or enforce any law which shall abridge the privileges or immunities of citizens of the United States; nor shall any State deprive any person of life, liberty, or property, without due process of law; nor deny to any person within its jurisdiction the equal protection of the laws.

SECTION 2. Representatives shall be apportioned among the several States according to their respective numbers, counting the whole number of persons in each State, excluding Indians not taxed. But when the right to vote at any election for the choice of electors for President and Vice-President of the United States, Representatives in Congress, the Executive and Judicial

[15] Superseded by the Twentieth Amendment.

officers of a State, or the members of the Legislature thereof, is denied to any of the male inhabitants of such State, being twenty-one years of age, and citizens of the United States, or in any way abridged, except for participation in rebellion, or other crime, the basis of representation therein shall be reduced in the proportion which the number of such male citizens shall bear to the whole number of male citizens twenty-one years of age in such State.

SECTION 3. No person shall be a Senator or Representative in Congress, or elector of President and Vice-President, or hold any office, civil or military, under the United States, or under any State, who, having previously taken an oath, as a member of Congress, or as an officer of the United States, or as a member of any State legislature, or as an executive or judicial officer of any State, to support the Constitution of the United States, shall have engaged in insurrection or rebellion against the same, or given aid or comfort to the enemies thereof. But Congress may by a vote of two-thirds of each House, remove such disability.

SECTION 4. The validity of the public debt of the United States, authorized by law, including debts incurred for payment of pensions and bounties for services in suppressing insurrection or rebellion, shall not be questioned. But neither the United States nor any State shall assume or pay any debt or obligation incurred in aid of insurrection or rebellion against the United States, or any claim for the loss or emancipation of any slave; but all such debts, obligations and claims shall be held illegal and void.

SECTION 5. The Congress shall have power to enforce, by appropriate legislation, the provisions of this article.

ARTICLE XV

[Proposed 27 February 1869; Declared Ratified 30 March 1870]

SECTION 1. The right of citizens of the United States to vote shall not be denied or abridged by the United States or by any State on account of race, color, or previous condition of servitude.

SECTION 2. The Congress shall have power to enforce this article by appropriate legislation.

ARTICLE XVI

[Proposed 12 July 1909; Declared Ratified 25 February 1913]

The Congress shall have power to lay and collect taxes on incomes, from whatever source derived, without apportionment among the several States, and without regard to any census or enumeration.

ARTICLE XVII

[Proposed 16 May 1912; Declared Ratified 31 May 1913]

The Senate of the United States shall be composed of two Senators from each State, elected by the people thereof, for six years; and each Senator shall have one vote. The electors in each State shall have the qualifications requisite for electors of the most numerous branch of the State legislatures.

When vacancies happen in the representation of any State in the Senate, the executive authority of such State shall issue writs of election to fill such vacancies: *Provided,* That the legislature of any State may empower the executive thereof to make temporary appointments until the people fill the vacancies by election as the legislature may direct.

This amendment shall not be so construed as to affect the election or term of any Senator chosen before it becomes valid as part of the Constitution.

ARTICLE XVIII

[Proposed 3 December 1917; Declared Ratified 29 January 1919]

SECTION 1. *After one year from the ratification of this article the manufacture, sale, or transportation of intoxicating liquors within, the importation thereof into, or the exportation thereof from the United States and all territory subject to the jurisdiction thereof for beverage purposes is hereby prohibited.*

SECTION 2. *The Congress and the several States shall have concurrent power to enforce this article by appropriate legislation.*

SECTION 3. *This article shall be inoperative unless it shall have been ratified as an amendment to the Constitution by the legislatures of the several States, as provided in the Constitution, within seven years from the date of the submission thereof to the States by the Congress.*[16]

ARTICLE XIX

[Proposed 19 May 1919; Declared Ratified 26 August 1920]

The right of citizens of the United States to vote shall not be denied or abridged by the United States or by any State on account of sex.

The Congress shall have power by appropriate legislation to enforce the Provisions of this article.

ARTICLE XX

[Proposed 3 March 1932; Declared Ratified 6 February 1933]

SECTION 1. The terms of the President and Vice-President shall end at noon on the twentieth day of January, and the terms of Senators and Representatives at noon on the third day of January, of the years in which such terms would have ended if this article had not been ratified; and the terms of their successors shall then begin.

SECTION 2. The Congress shall assemble at least once in every year, and such meeting shall begin at noon on the third day of January, unless they shall by law appoint a different day.

[16] Rescinded by the Twenty-first Amendment.

SECTION 3. If, at the time fixed for the beginning of the term of the President, the President-elect shall have died, the Vice-President-elect shall become President. If a President shall not have been chosen before the time fixed for the beginning of his term, or if the President-elect shall have failed to qualify, then the Vice-President-elect shall act as President until a President shall have qualified; and the Congress may by law provide for the case wherein neither a President-elect nor a Vice-President-elect shall have qualified, declaring who shall then act as President, or the manner in which one who is to act shall be selected, and such person shall act accordingly until a President or Vice-President shall have qualified.

SECTION 4. The Congress may by law provide for the case of the death of any of the persons from whom the House of Representatives may choose a President whenever the right of choice shall have devolved upon them, and for the case of the death of any of the persons from whom the Senate may choose a Vice-President whenever the right of choice shall have devolved upon them.

SECTION 5. SECTIONS 1 and 2 shall take effect on the 15th day of October following the ratification of this article.

SECTION 6. This article shall be inoperative unless it shall have been ratified as an amendment to the Constitution by the legislatures of three-fourths of the several States within seven years from the date of its submission.

ARTICLE XXI

[Proposed 20 February 1933; Declared Ratified 5 December 1933]

SECTION 1. The eighteenth article of amendment to the Constitution of the United States is hereby repealed.

SECTION 2. The transportation or importation into any State, Territory, or possession of the United States for delivery or use therein of intoxicating liquors, in violation of the laws thereof, is hereby prohibited.

SECTION 3. This article shall be inoperative unless it shall have been ratified as an amendment to the Constitution by conventions in the several States, as provided in the Constitution, within seven years from the date of the submission thereof to the States by the Congress.

ARTICLE XXII

[Proposed 24 March 1947; Declared Ratified 1 March 1951]

SECTION 1. No person shall be elected to the office of the President more than twice, and no person who has held the office of President, or acted as President, for more than two years of a term to which some other person was elected President shall be elected to the office of the President more than once. But this Article shall not apply to any person holding the office of

President when this Article was proposed by Congress, and shall not prevent any person who may be holding the office of President, or acting as President, during the term within which this Article becomes operative from holding the office of President or acting as President during the remainder of such term.

SECTION 2. The article shall be inoperative unless it shall have been ratified as an amendment to the Constitution by the legislatures of three-fourths of the several States within seven years from the date of its submission to the States by the Congress.

ARTICLE XXIII

[Proposed 16 June 1960; Declared Ratified 3 April 1961]

SECTION 1. The District constituting the seat of Government of the United States shall appoint in such manner as the Congress may direct:

A number of electors of President and Vice-President equal to the whole number of Senators and Representatives in Congress to which the District would be entitled if it were a State, but in no event more than the least populous State; they shall be in addition to those appointed by the States, but they shall be considered, for the purposes of the election of President and Vice President, to be electors appointed by a State; and they shall meet in the District and perform such duties as provided by the twelfth article of amendment.

SECTION 2. The Congress shall have power to enforce this article by appropriate legislation.

ARTICLE XXIV

[Proposed 27 August 1962; Declared Ratified 23 January 1964]

SECTION 1. The right of citizens of the United States to vote in any primary or other election for President or Vice President, for electors for President or Vice President, or for Senator or Representative in Congress, shall not be denied or abridged by the United States or any State by reason of failure to pay any poll tax or other tax.

SECTION 2. The Congress shall have power to enforce this article by appropriate legislation.

ARTICLE XXV

[Proposed 6 July 1965; Declared Ratified]

SECTION 1. In case of the removal of the President from office or his death or resignation, the Vice President shall become President.

SECTION 2. Whenever there is a vacancy in the office of the Vice President, the President shall nominate a Vice President who shall take the office upon confirmation by a majority vote of both houses of Congress.

SECTION 3. Whenever the President transmits to the President pro tempore of the Senate and the Speaker of the House of Representatives his written declaration that he is unable to discharge the powers and duties of his office, and until he transmits to them a written declaration to the contrary, such powers and duties shall be discharged by the Vice President as Acting President.

SECTION 4. Whenever the Vice President and a majority of either the principal officers of the executive departments or of such other body as Congress may by law provide, transmit to the President pro tempore of the Senate and the Speaker of the House of Representatives their written declaration that the President is unable to discharge the powers and duties of his office, the Vice President shall immediately assume the powers and duties of the office as Acting President.

Thereafter, when the President transmits to the President pro tempore of the Senate and the Speaker of the House of Representatives his written declaration that no disability exists, he shall resume the powers and duties of his office unless the Vice President and a majority of either the principal officers of the executive department or of any such body as Congress may by law provide, transmit within four days to the President pro tempore of the Senate and the Speaker of the House of Representatives their written declaration that the President is unable to discharge the powers and duties of his office. Thereupon Congress shall decide the issue, assembling within 48 hours for that purpose if not in session. If the Congress, within 21 days after receipt of the latter written declaration, or, if Congress is not in session, within 21 days after Congress is required to assemble, determines by two-thirds vote of both houses that the President is unable to discharge the powers and duties of his office, the Vice President shall continue to discharge the same as Acting President; otherwise, the President shall resume the powers and duties of his office.